P9-CDK-215

Real World Approach

Profiles of Success *offer short sketches of successful students who use the principles of psychology in their professional lives.* »

profiles of **SUCCESS**

Courtesy of William Jess Greiner

NAME:	**William Jess Greiner**
SCHOOL:	**Pima Medical Institute**
DEGREE PROGRAMS:	**AAS Fire Science, Central Community College of New Mexico; BS Emergency Management, University of New Mexico; AAS, Physical Therapy Assisting, Pima Medical Institute**

All of us face transitions in life, but for William Jess Greiner, the transition he faced couldn't have been greater, or more challenging.

As a firefighter, which included activities such as parachuting from planes to reach fires, Greiner led a very active life. However, it all came to an abrupt end one day as the result of a serious accident. Although it left him wheelchair-bound for almost four years, it also led to a new future.

"Following my accident, I decided I wanted to start a new career," he explained. "I narrowed my choices down to the two occupations that had saved my life—nursing and physical therapy."

depression. While in counseling, he realized he felt challenged by those who felt his physical disabilities would impede his ability to be a physical therapist assistant. This realization only made him work harder to prove he could. And, at the same time, he drew on what he had learned from his past psychology courses.

"Studying psychology helped me understand depression," he explained. "Working with patients, I can understand the depressive side of having an injury and how the little things like not being able to pick up a glass, or button a shirt, can take an emotional toll."

Even while studying full time, Greiner endured lengthy physical therapy sessions and long commutes to

Pain is a response to a great variety of different kinds of stimuli. A light that is too bright can produce pain, and sound that is too loud can be painful. One explanation is that pain is an outcome of cell injury; when a cell is damaged, regardless of the source of damage, it releases a chemical called *substance P* that transmits pain messages to the brain.

Some people are more susceptible to pain than others. For example, women experience painful stimuli more intensely than men. These gender differences are associated with the production of hormones related to menstrual cycles. In addition, certain genes are linked to the experience of pain, so that we may inherit our sensitivity to pain (Nielsen, Staud, & Price, 2009; Fillingim, 2011).

© Comstock/Getty Images RF

From the perspective of . . .
A Medical or Dental Assistant How would you handle a patient who is anxiously awaiting treatment and complaining that her pain is getting worse?

From the Perspective of . . . *helps connect concepts with career realities by highlighting how psychology impacts a* « *variety of professions.*

Promoting Critical Thinking

Becoming an Informed Consumer of Psychology *discusses concepts in the context of the student as a consumer. Real-life scenarios enable students to consider and implement psychological concepts within the world around them and apply critical thinking skills to their personal and professional lives.* »

However, there is one more safeguard that a careful researcher must apply in an experiment such as this one. To overcome the possibility that experimenter expectations will affect the participant, the person who administers the drug shouldn't know whether it is actually the true drug or the placebo. By keeping both the participant and the experimenter who interacts with the participant "blind" to the nature of the drug that is being administered, researchers can more accurately assess the effects of the drug. This method is known as the *double-blind procedure*.

becoming an informed consumer of psychology

Thinking Critically about Research

If you were about to purchase an automobile, it is unlikely that you would stop at the nearest car dealership and drive off with the first car a salesperson recommended. Instead, you would probably mull over the purchase, read about automobiles, consider the alternatives, talk to others about their experiences, and ultimately put in a fair amount of thought before you made such a major purchase.

EXPLORING diversity

Human Diversity and the Brain

The interplay of biology and environment in behavior is particularly clear when we consider evidence suggesting that even in brain structure and function there are both sex and cultural differences. Let's consider sex first. Accumulating evidence seems to show intriguing differences in males' and females' brain lateralization and weight (Boles, 2005; Clements, Rimrodt, & Abel, 2006).

Exploring Diversity *features address how diversity and perspective relate to the study* « *of psychology.*

PSYCHOLOGY AND YOUR LIFE WITH P.O.W.E.R. LEARNING, THIRD EDITION

Published by McGraw-Hill Education, 2 Penn Plaza, New York, NY 10121. Copyright © 2018 by McGraw-Hill Education. All rights reserved. Printed in the United States of America. Previous editions © 2013, 2010. No part of this publication may be reproduced or distributed in any form or by any means, or stored in a database or retrieval system, without the prior written consent of McGraw-Hill Education, including, but not limited to, in any network or other electronic storage or transmission, or broadcast for distance learning.

Some ancillaries, including electronic and print components, may not be available to customers outside the United States.

This book is printed on acid-free paper.

1 2 3 4 5 6 7 8 9 LMN 21 20 19 18 17

ISBN 978-1-259-61039-4
MHID 1-259-61039-X

Chief Product Officer, SVP Products & Markets: *G. Scott Virkler*
Vice President, General Manager, Products & Markets: *Michael Ryan*
Vice President, Content Design & Delivery: *Betsy Whalen*
Managing Director: *William Glass*
Executive Director: *Krista Bettino*
Senior Brand Manager: *Nancy Welcher*
Director, Product Development: *Meghan Campbell*
Lead Product Developer: *Dawn Groundwater*
Senior Product Developer: *Cara Labell*
Senior Marketing Manager: *Ann Helgerson*
Senior Digital Product Analyst: *Neil Kahn*
Editorial Coordinator: *Elisa Odoardi*
Director, Content Design & Delivery: *Terri Schiesl*
Program Manager: *Debra Hash*
Content Project Managers: *Sandy Wille; Jodi Banowetz*
Buyer: *Sandy Ludovissy*
Designer: *Tara McDermott*
Content Licensing Specialists: (photo) *Shawntel Schmitt;* (text) *Melisa Seegmiller*
Cover Image: © Peopleimages.com/Getty Images
Design icon: (Becoming an Informed Consumer of Psychology) © *Hill Street Studios/Getty Images RF*
Compositor: *SPi Global*
Printer: *LSC Communications*

All credits appearing on page or at the end of the book are considered to be an extension of the copyright page.

Library of Congress Cataloging-in-Publication Data

Names: Feldman, Robert S. (Robert Stephen), 1947- author.
Title: Psychology and your life with P.O.W.E.R. learning / Robert S. Feldman, University of Massachusetts, Amherst.
Other titles: Psychology and your life
Description: Third edition. | New York, NY: McGraw-Hill Education, [2017] |
Earlier editions published as: Psychology and your life.
Identifiers: LCCN 2016032132 | ISBN 9781259610394 (alk. paper)
Subjects: LCSH: Psychology.
Classification: LCC BF121 .F35 2017 | DDC 150—dc23 LC record available at
https://lccn.loc.gov/2016032132

The Internet addresses listed in the text were accurate at the time of publication. The inclusion of a website does not indicate an endorsement by the authors or McGraw-Hill Education, and McGraw-Hill Education does not guarantee the accuracy of the information presented at these sites.

mheducation.com/highered

Psychology
and Your Life
with P O W E R Learning

Psychology
and Your Life

with P O W E R Learning

3e

Robert S. Feldma
University of Massachusetts Amhe

dedication

To Alex, Miles, Naomi, and Lilia, the best of the best.

about the author

ROBERT S. FELDMAN is Professor of Psychological and Brain Sciences and Deputy Chancellor of the University of Massachusetts Amherst. A recipient of the College Distinguished Teacher Award, he teaches psychology classes ranging in size from 15 to nearly 500 students. During the course of more than three decades as a college instructor, he has taught undergraduate and graduate courses at Mount Holyoke College, Wesleyan University, and Virginia Commonwealth University in addition to the University of Massachusetts.

Professor Feldman, who initiated the Minority Mentoring Program at the University of Massachusetts, also has served as a Hewlett Teaching Fellow and Senior Online Teaching Fellow. He initiated distance-learning courses in psychology at the University of Massachusetts.

A Fellow of the American Psychological Association, the Association for Psychological Science, and the American Association for the Advancement of Science, Professor Feldman received a BA with High Honors from Wesleyan University and an MS and PhD from the University of Wisconsin-Madison. He is a winner of a Fulbright Senior Research Scholar and Lecturer Award and the Distinguished Alumnus Award from Wesleyan. He is past President of the Federation of Associations in Behavioral and Brain Sciences (FABBS) Foundation, which advocates for the field of psychology, and is on the board of the Social Psychology Network (SPN).

He has written and edited more than 250 books, book chapters, and scientific articles. He has edited *Development of Nonverbal Behavior in Children, Applications of Nonverbal Behavioral Theory and Research, Improving the First Year of College: Research and Practice,* and co-edited *Fundamentals of Nonverbal Behavior.* He is also author of *P.O.W.E.R. Learning: Strategies for Success in College and Life.* His textbooks, which have been used by more than two million students around the world, have been translated into Spanish, French, Portuguese, Dutch, German, Italian, Chinese, Korean, and Japanese. His research interests include deception and honesty in everyday life, work that he described in *The Liar in Your Life,* a trade book published in 2009. His research has been supported by grants from the National Institute of Mental Health and the National Institute on Disabilities and Rehabilitation Research.

Professor Feldman loves music, is an enthusiastic pianist, and enjoys cooking and traveling. He serves on the Executive Committee and Board of New England Public Radio. He has three children, two granddaughters, and two grandsons. He and his wife, a psychologist, live in western Massachusetts in a home overlooking the Holyoke mountain range.

brief
TABLE OF CONTENTS

 McGraw-Hill Education Psychology's APA Documentation Style Guide

table of
CONTENTS

module 4   Research Challenges: Exploring the Process   36

chapter

2 Neuroscience and Behavior   46

module 5   Neurons: The Basic Elements of Behavior   48

module 6   The Nervous System and the Endocrine System: Communicating within the Body   56

module 7   The Brain   64

Mc Graw Hill Education **connect** McGraw-Hill Education Psychology's APA Documentation Style Guide

Preface

Students first.

If I were to use only a few words to summarize my goal for *Psychology and Your Life with P.O.W.E.R. Learning,* 3/e, as well as my teaching philosophy, that's what I would say. I believe that an effective textbook must be oriented to students—informing them, engaging them, exciting them about the field, and helping them to learn.

Luckily, psychology is a science that is naturally interesting to students. It is a discipline that speaks with many voices, offering a personal message to each student. Some students see the discipline as a way to better understand themselves, their family members, their co-workers, and people in general. For others, psychology offers information that can help prepare for a future career. Some students are drawn to the field simply because of their interest in psychological topics and how an understanding of psychology can improve their lives.

No matter what brings students into the introductory course and regardless of their initial motivation, *Psychology and Your Life with P.O.W.E.R. Learning,* 3/e is designed to draw students into the field by illustrating how psychology will affect them in their career—whether they are studying to become a medical assistant, a graphic designer, or a police officer, or enter any other program. The text integrates a variety of elements that foster students' understanding of psychology and its impact on their everyday lives.

Psychology and Your Life with P.O.W.E.R. Learning, 3/e was written to accomplish the following goals:

- To provide broad coverage of the field of psychology, introducing the basic concepts, theories, and applications that constitute the discipline.

- To build an appreciation of the relevance of psychology to everyday life, including learning to apply psychology to students' chosen areas of study.

- To maximize student learning of the material, helping students to think critically about psychological phenomena, particularly those that have an impact on their everyday lives.

The content and its ancillary materials include coverage of the traditional areas of psychology while also emphasizing applied topics. The flexibility of the content's organizational structure is considerable. Each chapter is divided into three or four manageable, self-contained modules, aiding students' reading and studying of the content and allowing instructors to choose and omit sections in accordance with their syllabus.

To further help students learn and think critically about the material in the text, *Psychology and Your Life with P.O.W.E.R. Learning,* 3/e uses the **P.O.W.E.R.** learning and critical thinking system to organize the material. **P.O.W.E.R.**

is a five-stage framework that systematically presents material in five steps: **P**repare, **O**rganize, **W**ork, **E**valuate, and **R**ethink. Each of the steps—which are described in detail later in the "To the Student" section—are indicated by a graphical icon, providing students with a clear, logical framework that will help them read, study, learn, and ultimately master the material in the book.

In addition, *Psychology and Your Life with P.O.W.E.R. Learning*, 3/e provides a complete framework for learning and assessment. Clear in-text learning outcomes, tied to each major section of the material, allow students to know exactly what it is they are supposed to learn. These learning outcomes also permit instructors to create assessments based on those outcomes. All the ancillary materials that accompany the student material, including every test item in the Test Bank, are keyed to these learning outcomes.

Furthermore, *Psychology and Your Life with P.O.W.E.R. Learning*, 3/e specifically takes into account the diverse population of students who are enrolled in college today. The content particularly is designed to address the needs of today's students who may work full- or part-time; who may be juggling their education, their families, and their jobs; who may be returning to school in search of a career change; or who are in a specific career-oriented program. I have taken great care to ensure students have an opportunity to explore why psychology is relevant to everyone—no matter what their background is and no matter what their area of study may be.

Psychology and Your Life with P.O.W.E.R. Learning, 3/e Promotes Student Success

Psychology and Your Life with P.O.W.E.R. Learning, 3/e includes many features designed to maximize students' success in their introductory course. Every chapter follows the same format, allowing students to be better able to master its content. The examples are drawn from across the spectrum of life, including the worlds of work, family, and community. The vocabulary has received particular focus in order to ensure clarity and ease of learning. The glossary includes expanded definitions, where appropriate, to ensure that students of all reading levels can gain their fullest understanding of the key terms and their definitions.

Furthermore, *Psychology and Your Life with P.O.W.E.R. Learning*, 3/e is divided into 43 short modules grouped into 12 chapters covering the major areas of psychology. An advantage of the modular structure is it allows students to study material in smaller chunks, which psychological research has long found to be the optimal way to learn. The modular approach, therefore, makes already manageable chapters even easier to absorb. Moreover, instructors can customize assignments for their students by asking them to read only those modules that fit their course outline and in the sequence that matches their syllabus.

At the beginning of each module, **Learning Outcomes** introduce the key concepts covered in the module. These key concepts are also the focus of activities available in McGraw-Hill Education's Connect Psychology.

To further help students learn the material, dozens of **Study Alerts** are included by key concepts. *Study Alerts* offer advice and hints for students, signaling them when critical concepts are presented and offering suggestions for learning those concepts effectively.

Another great feature that helps connect concepts with career realities is the **From the Perspective of** . . . feature. *From the Perspective of* . . . highlights how psychology impacts a variety of professions. Created to show the correlation between psychology and different professions, the feature helps students learn to comprehend what psychology means to their chosen program of study and answers the "why does psychology matter to me?" question. Whether students are in an allied health, nursing, criminal justice, technology, business, legal studies track, or any other program of study, they will have the chance to make connections between their area of study and their lives after completing their program.

From the perspective of . . .

A Medical or Dental Assistant How would you handle a patient who is anxiously awaiting treatment and complaining that her pain is getting worse?

In addition, the features are designed to engage and excite students. **Try It!** exercises are experiential self-assessment quizzes that reinforce chapter concepts in a nonthreatening (even fun!) manner and enable students to consider, compare, and contrast their preferences, behaviors, and attitudes. Similar to quizzes in popular magazines, students can readily apply their own answers directly to the concepts they are learning—active learning at its best!

Try It!

Psychological Truths?

To test your knowledge of psychology, try answering the following questions:

1. Infants love their mothers primarily because their mothers fulfill their basic biological needs, such as providing food. True or false?
2. Geniuses generally have poor social adjustment. True or false?
3. The best way to ensure that a desired behavior will continue after training is completed is to reward that behavior every single time it occurs during training rather than rewarding it only periodically. True or false?
4. People with schizophrenia have at least two distinct personalities. True or false?
5. Parents should do everything they can to ensure children have high self-esteem and a strong sense that they are highly competent. True or false?
6. Children's IQ scores have little to do with how well they do in school. True or false?
7. Frequent masturbation can lead to mental illness. True or false?
8. Once people reach old age, their leisure activities change radically. True or false?
9. Most people would refuse to give painful electric shocks to other people. True or false?

In the feature **Becoming an Informed Consumer of Psychology,** psychology concepts are discussed in the context of the student as a consumer. These real-life scenarios enable students to consider and even implement psychological concepts within the world around them and apply critical thinking skills to their personal and professional lives. This feature includes scenarios such as how to evaluate advertising, and how to determine if one should seek counseling.

becoming an informed consumer
of psychology

Improving Your Memory

Apart from the advantages of forgetting, say, a bad date, most of us would like to find ways to improve our memories. Among the effective strategies for studying and remembering course material:

■ *The keyword technique.* If you are studying a foreign language, try the keyword technique. In the *keyword technique,* you pair a foreign word with a common English word that has a similar sound. This English word is known as the *keyword.* For example, to learn the Spanish word for duck (*pato,* pronounced *pot-o*), you might choose the keyword pot. Once you have thought of a keyword, imagine the Spanish word "interacting" with the English

EXPLORING **diversity**

Teaching with Linguistic Variety: Bilingual Education

In New York City, one in six of the city's 1.1 million students is enrolled in some form of bilingual or English as a Second Language instruction. And New York City is far from the only school district with a significant population of nonnative English speakers. From the biggest cities to the most rural areas, the face—and voice—of education in the United States is changing. More and more schoolchildren today have last names like Kim, Valdez, and Karachnicoff. In seven states,

Exploring Diversity features, strategically placed within the modules, address how diversity and perspective relate to the study of psychology. *Exploring Diversity* promotes critical thinking about psychology concepts through the discussion and assessment of cultural and ethnic differences in direct correlation to research, study, and our lives.

Key terms and their definitions are easily identifiable (bolded and called out in the margins with definitions) within each module and are listed with page references at the end of every module. The glossary includes enhanced definitions—additional explanations of difficult or confusing terms using synonyms or expanded parenthetical definitions—allowing students to expand their knowledge of the terminology associated with psychology. Providing the most clear, accessible definitions helps students recognize, identify, define, and describe the terminology and definitions.

Recap/Evaluate/Rethink end-of-module activities are tied directly to the module's learning outcomes boosting students' opportunities to apply and analyze their knowledge beyond the definitions or simple explanations. These activities allow instructors to move students from memorization to application and analysis in a cohesive, logical manner through a variety of activities and exercises tied to the learning outcomes of the module. Instructors who are familiar with Bloom's Taxonomy or who want to provide activities for students with different learning styles will find a variety of exercises for homework or class discussion. The need to connect the modules with overarching chapter content is addressed in the **Looking Ahead/Looking Back** feature. *Looking Ahead* introduces the key concepts of every chapter; *Looking Back* summarizes content from the chapter as a whole to reinforce the learning outcomes of each module.

Psychology on the Web consists of various web-based activities found at the end of every chapter to promote Internet research of key chapter concepts. This feature is great for active learning and increasing students' abilities to conduct Internet research and critique Internet resources within the context of their psychology class.

Found at the end of each chapter, **Case Studies** allow students to apply and analyze the chapter content and discuss what they have learned in the context of a story or situation. Students will analyze a situation through critical thinking, discussion, and interaction with other students whose perspectives may differ from their own. In addition, **Profiles of Success** offer short sketches of successful students and how they may use the principles of psychology in their professional lives.

The **Visual Summaries** identify the correlation of the overarching chapter key concepts. Visual learners will benefit from these summaries that "tie everything together" by revisiting and reinforcing the key concepts for every module within each chapter.

connect Connect is a digital assignment and assessment platform that strengthens the link between faculty, students, and course work, helping everyone accomplish more in less time. Connect Psychology includes assignable and assessable videos, quizzes, exercises, and interactivities, all associated with the text's learning outcomes.

SMARTBOOK®

SmartBook creates a personalized reading experience by highlighting the most impactful concepts a student needs to learn at that moment in time. This ensures that every moment spent with SmartBook is returned to the student as the most value-added minute possible.

tegrity

With Tegrity, you can capture lessons and lectures in a searchable format and use them in traditional, hybrid, "flipped classes," and online courses. With Tegrity's personalized learning features, you can make study time efficient. Patented search technology and real-time learning management system (LMS) integrations make Tegrity the market-leading solution and service.

create

Easily rearrange chapters, combine material from other content sources, and quickly upload content you have written, such as your course syllabus or teaching notes, using McGraw-Hill Education's Create. Find the content you need by searching through thousands of leading McGraw-Hill Education textbooks. Arrange your book to fit your teaching style. Create even allows you to personalize your book's appearance by selecting the cover and adding your name, school, and course information. Order a Create book, and you will receive a complimentary print review copy in three to five business days or a complimentary electronic review copy via e-mail in about an hour. Experience how McGraw-Hill Education empowers you to teach *your* students *your* way at http://create.mheducation.com.

What's New in the Third Edition

Psychology and Your Life with P.O.W.E.R. Learning, 3/e contains a significant amount of new and updated content and features reflecting the advances in the field and the suggestions of reviewers. Hundreds of new citations have been added, and most of them refer to articles and books published in the last few years.

In addition, this edition incorporates a wide range of new topics. The following sample of new and revised topics provides a good indication of the material's currency.

Chapter 1
- Added psychological information about white supremacy and South Carolina church murders
- Updated the number of active psychologists
- Refined description of nature vs. nurture description
- Refined goal of case studies

Chapter 2
- Included new prologue on Stiff Person Syndrome

- Included volume of gray matter in cortex differs according to income level
- Revised thalamus presentation
- Clarified somatic division and autonomic division
- Refined association areas
- Added information on X chromosome
- Reworded transcranial magnetic stimulation (TMS)

Chapter 3

- Included new prologue on "face-blindness"
- Updated statistics on incidence and cost of chronic pain
- Clarified visual spectrum
- Explained mirror therapy for pain relief
- Included new definition of linear perspective
- Clarified biodfeedback with additional examples

Chapter 4

- Included new prologue on mindfulness meditation
- Refined definition of addictive drugs
- Clarified the uses of hypnosis
- Refined description of the reasons why people use drugs
- Updated latest marijuana use statistics
- Updated research findings on consequences of marijuana use
- Included use of Suboxone and Vivatrol in treatment of heroin addiction
- Added material about increased heroin use in the United States

Chapter 5

- Included new prologue on social media addiction
- Removed reference to autism and punishment
- Clarified positive and negative punishment
- Revised Little Albert conclusion
- Expanded conclusion regarding the impact of violent video games
- Explained Facebook addiction

Chapter 6

- Included new prologue on hyperthymestic syndrome
- Clarified role of hippocampus in memory

- Refined material on MRI scans of hippocampus
- Clarified role of amygdala in memory
- Refined discussion of nativist approach to language
- Clarified survival vs. dying frame study

Chapter 7

- Included new prologue on motivation for weight loss
- Clarified drawbacks to instinct approaches to motivation
- Redefined arousal approaches to motivation
- Redefined cognitive approaches to motivation
- Updated obesity statistics
- Updated statistics on premarital sex
- Updated section on transsexualism, now referred to as transgenderism

Chapter 8

- Included new prologue on aging
- Clarified zone of proximal development and scaffolding
- Changed description and prevalence figures for fetal alcohol syndrome
- Added additional information on nicotine use while pregnant
- Included more on emerging adulthood
- Revised Alzheimer's statistics
- Clarified discussion of conservation
- Updated statistics on working women

Chapter 9

- Included new prologue on personality
- Redefined id
- Redefined ego

- Redefined superego

- Revised the discussion of relationship between id, ego, and superego

- Revised discussion of penis envy

- Clarified discussion of defense mechanisms

- Redefined trait

- Revised statistics on use of personality testing in business and industry

Chapter 10

- Included new prologue on coping with schizophrenia

- Updated dissociative identity disorder

- Included new terminology to reflect *DSM-5*

- Clarified positive and negative symptoms of schizophrenia

- Clarified discussion of criticisms of cognitive perspective

- Refined discussion of sociocultural explanations of psychological disorders

- Clarified panic disorder vs. phobic disorder

- Revised discussion of causes of anxiety disorders

Chapter 11

- Included new prologue on treatment for depression

- Included discussion of deep brain stimulation (DBS)

- Refined presentation of behavioral approaches

- Updated discussion of rational-emotive therapy

- Redefined interpersonal therapy (IPT)

- Revised goals of family therapy

- Clarified overview of biological approaches to treatment

- Revised definition of drug therapy

Chapter 12

- Included new prologue on social attitudes

- Refined explanation of cognitive dissonance

- Updated discussion of the foot-in-the-door technique

- Refined discussion of the not-so-free-sample technique

- Clarified Darley & Latane helping model

- Added discussion of social networks and Facebook

- Included cumulative effects of cataclysmic events

- Updated statistics on amount spent on veterans with PTSD

The Instructor Resources have been updated to reflect changes to the new edition: These can be accessed by faculty through Connect Psychology.

Students First: The Bottom Line

Based on extensive feedback from reviewers in a variety of schools, I am confident that *Psychology and Your Life with P.O.W.E.R. Learning,* 3/e reflects what instructors want: material that motivates students to understand, learn, and apply psychology in the context of their present and future careers. The book and online content are designed to expose readers to the content—and promise—of psychology, and to do so in a way that will nurture students' excitement about psychology and keep their enthusiasm alive for a lifetime.

Acknowledgments

Psychology and Your Life with P.O.W.E.R. Learning benefited from the involvement of a wide array of professionals in the review process of the initial editions on which this 3rd edition is based. Hands-on involvement included evaluating the table of contents and design, and providing insights on instructor and student support features. This program is the best it can be because of the candid feedback and suggestions from everyone who was part of the development process.

I am extraordinarily grateful to the following reviewers who provided their time and expertise over the years to help ensure that *Psychology and Your Life with P.O.W.E.R. Learning,* 3e reflects the best that psychology has to offer:

Richard Ackley, *The Chicago School*

Mary Alexander, *Ashford University*

Kerri Augusto, *Becker College*

Laura Bailey, *San Joaquin Valley College*

Timothy Bauer, *Brown Mackie College*

Dr. Rhonda Baughman, *Brown Mackie College*

Elizabeth Beardmore, *Colorado Technical University Online*

Karen Bedell, *Baker College*

William Bell, *Coyne American Institute*

Phil Black, *Brown Mackie College*

Michael Bowers, *Art Institute of Colorado*

Allison Brown, *Miller-Motte Technical College*

Donice Brown, *Keiser University*

Dr. Raymond Brown, *Keiser University*

Jonathan Carrier, *National College*

Ketsia Chapman, *Centura College*

David Cooper, *Northwestern College*

Jay Cooper, *National College*

Lindsay Davis, *Stuatzenberger College*

Karen Durand, *Miller-Motte Technical College*

Al Elbert, *Brown Mackie College*

Patricia Evans, *Harrison College*

Jean Fennema, *Pima Medical Institute*

Mominka Fileva, *Davenport University*

Rupert Francis, *Art Institute of California, San Bernadino*

Dennis Gaynor, *Globe University*

Janell Gibson, *Keiser University*

David Gillespie, *Davenport University*

Katie Goike-Perry, *Bryant and Stratton*

Andrea Goldstein, *Keiser University*

Kathleen Hipp, *Brown Mackie College*

Kerri Holloway, *American Intercontinental University Online*

Jan Hoover, *Northwestern College*

Kristy Huntley, *Briarwood*

Barbara Ireland, *Laureate Education, Inc.*

Penny Janson, *Bryant and Stratton*

Bert Jerred, *Bryant and Stratton*

Ray Jones, *Art Institute of California, San Bernadino*

Robert Karney, *Tri-State Business Institute*

Kristie Kellis, *Globe University/ Minnesota School of Business*

Kevin Kelly, *Andover College*

Shannon Koh, *San Joaquin Valley College*

Deborah Koysdar, *McCann School of Business & Technology*

Dr. Pam Law, *Colorado Technical University*

Cathy Lawson, *Bryant and Stratton, Online*

Doreen Lewis, *Rasmussen College*

Mark Liverman, *National College*

Eric Lance Martin, *ECPI*

Julie Marty-Pearson, *San Joaquin Valley College*

Bernadette McCallister, *Baker College*

Susan Meindel, *National College*

Chris Menges, *Bryant and Stratton*

Katrina Neckuty-Fodness, *Globe University*

William Neiheisel, *Gwinnett College*

Regina Pierce, *Davenport University*

Dr. William Premo, *Globe University*

Donna Reavis, *Delta Colleges*

Leslie Rewald, *Trinity College*

Lori Ritter, *The Salter School*

Jesus Rivera, *Keiser University*

Larry Schankin, *National College*

Jan Sebestyen, *Brown Mackie College*

Dr. Mine Seniye, *Brown Mackie College*

Erin Shaffer, *Brown Mackie College*

Judy Shangraw, *Centura College*

Shelly Shields, *Indiana Business College*

Debra Silverman, *Keiser University*

Pamela Simon, *Baker College*

Michelle Slattery, *The Bradford School*

Matthew Smith, *San Joaquin Valley College*

Elizabeth Tice, *Ashford University*

Paula Tripp, *San Joaquin Valley College*

Sharon Vriend-Robinson, *Davenport University*

Shannon Warman, *University of Northwest Ohio*

Donald Webb, *Gibbs College*

Lois Weber, *Globe University/ Minnesota School of Business*

Christie West, *Harrison College*

David Weyand, *National College*

Jim Williams, *Med Tech College*

Marc Wilson, *Hesser College*

Joseph Yasain, *McIntosh College*

Many teachers along my educational path have shaped my thinking. I was introduced to psychology at Wesleyan University, where several committed and inspiring teachers—and in particular Karl Scheibe—conveyed their sense of excitement about the field and made its relevance clear to me.

Although the nature of the University of Wisconsin, where I did my graduate work, could not have been more different from the much smaller Wesleyan, the excitement and inspiration were similar. Once again, many excellent teachers molded my thinking and taught me to appreciate the beauty and science of the discipline of psychology.

I'm also grateful to the many students in my classes at the variety of schools at which I've had the privilege of teaching. They include students at career colleges, state colleges, and universities.

My colleagues and students at the University of Massachusetts Amherst provide ongoing intellectual stimulation, and I thank them for making the university such a fine place to work. Several people also provided extraordinary research and editorial help. In particular, I am grateful to my superb students, past and present, including Erik Coats, Sara Levine, Jim Tyler, Chris Poirier, and Matt Zimbler. John Bickford, in particular, provided invaluable editorial input that has enhanced the content considerably. Finally, I am grateful to John Graiff, whose hard work and dedication helped immeasurably on just about everything involving this content.

I also offer great thanks to the McGraw-Hill Education editorial and marketing team that participated in this new edition. Vice President and General Manager Mike Ryan, Executive Director Krista Bettino, Senior Brand Manager Nancy Welcher, and Senior Marketing Manager Ann Helgerson created a creative, energetic, and supportive environment, and I am in awe of their enthusiasm, commitment, and never-ending good ideas. I'm also happy that the indefatigable Cory Reeves provided input about all sorts of things. I thank them not only for their superb professionalism, but also for their friendship.

I also am grateful to Sue Ewing, developmental editor on this edition. Sue did a superb job of managing a myriad of details (as well as me). She brought motivation, intelligence, and good ideas to the project. Finally, every reader of this book owes a debt to Rhona Robbin and Judith Kromm, developmental editors on earlier editions of my intro psych books. Their relentless pursuit of excellence helped form the core of this book, and they taught me a great deal about the craft and art of writing.

Central to the design, production, and marketing process were Content Project Manager Sandy Wille, Text Content Licensing Specialist Melisa Seegmiller, Image Content Licensing Specialist Shawntel Schmitt, and Designer Tara McDermott. I would also like to thank my award-winning Marketing Manager Ann Helgerson for her enthusiasm and commitment to this project. I am proud to be a part of this world-class McGraw-Hill Education team.

Finally, I remain completely indebted to my family. My parents, Leah Brochstein and the late Saul D. Feldman, provided a lifetime foundation of love and support, and I continue to see their influence in every corner of my life. I am grateful, too, to the late Harry Brochstein, who enriched my life and thinking in many ways.

My extended family also plays a central role in my life. They include, more or less in order of age, my nieces and nephews, my terrific brother, and my brothers- and sisters-in-law, and the late Ethel Radler. Finally, my mother-in-law, the late Mary Evans Vorwerk, had an important influence on this book, and I remain ever grateful to her.

Ultimately, my children, Jonathan, Joshua, and Sarah; my daughters-in-law Leigh and Julie; my son-in-law Jeffrey; my grandsons Alex and Miles; my granddaughters Naomi and Lilia; and my wife, Katherine, remain the focal points of my life. I thank them, with immense love, and thank my lucky stars that they are in my life.

Robert S. Feldman
Amherst, Massachusetts

To the Student

Making the Grade: A Practical Guide to Studying Effectively

If you're reading this page, you're probably taking an introductory psychology course. Maybe you're studying psychology because you've always been interested in what makes people tick. Or perhaps you've had a friend or family member who has sought assistance for a psychological disorder. Or maybe you have no idea what psychology is all about, but are taking introductory psychology because it is a required course.

Whatever your reason for taking the course, it's a safe bet you're interested in maximizing your understanding of the material and getting a good grade. And you want to do it as quickly and efficiently as possible.

Good news: You're taking the right course, and you're learning the right material. Several subfields of psychology have identified a variety of guidelines and techniques that will help you learn and remember material not only related to psychology, but also relevant to every other discipline that you will study.

We'll consider a variety of guidelines relating to doing well in your psychology class—and every other class you'll take in your college career. Here's my guarantee to you: If you learn and follow the guidelines in each of these areas, you'll become a better student and get better grades—not only in your introductory psychology classes, but in your other classes as well. Always remember that *good students are made, not born,* and these suggestions will help you become an all-around better student.

Adopt a General Study Strategy: Using P.O.W.E.R.

Let's begin with a brief consideration of a general study strategy, applicable to all of your courses, including introductory psychology. Psychologists have created several excellent (and proven) techniques for improving study skills, one of the best of which is built into this content: P.O.W.E.R, or *P*repare, *O*rganize, *W*ork, *E*valuate, and *R*ethink. By employing this strategy, you can increase your ability to learn and retain information and to think critically, not just in psychology classes but also in all academic subjects.

P.O.W.E.R. The *P.O.W.E.R.* learning strategy systematizes the acquisition of new material by providing a learning framework. It stresses the importance of learning outcomes and appropriate preparation before you begin to study, as well as the significance of self-evaluation and the incorporation of critical thinking into the learning process. Specifically, use of the P.O.W.E.R. learning system entails the following steps:

- *Prepare.* Before starting any journey, we need to know where we are headed. Academic journeys are no different; we need to know what our goals are. The *Prepare* stage consists of thinking about what we hope to gain from reading a specific section of text by identifying specific goals that we seek to accomplish. In *Psychology and Your Life with P.O.W.E.R. Learning,* 3/e, these goals are listed as Learning Outcomes at the beginning of every module.

O Organize

- *Organize.* Once we know what our goals are, we can develop a route to accomplish those goals. The *Organize* stage involves developing a mental road map of where we are headed. *Psychology and Your Life with P.O.W.E.R. Learning,* 3/e highlights the organization of each upcoming chapter. Read the outline at the beginning of each chapter and module, indicated by an Organize icon (see margin), to get an idea of what topics are covered and how they are organized.

W Work

- *Work.* The key to the P.O.W.E.R. learning system is actually reading and studying the material presented in the content. Completing the *Work* will be easier because, if you have carried out the steps in the preparation and organization stage, you'll know where you're headed and how you'll get there. Remember, the main text isn't the only material that you need to read and think about. It's also important to read the boxes and the glossary terms in order to gain a full understanding of the material. *Work* is indicated by a Work icon (see margin).

E Evaluate

- *Evaluate.* The fourth step, *Evaluate,* provides the opportunity to determine how effectively you have mastered the material. In *Psychology and Your Life with P.O.W.E.R. Learning,* 3/e, a series of questions at the end of each module permits a rapid check of your understanding of the material and they are indicated by an Evaluate icon (see margin). Your instructor may choose to offer additional opportunities to test yourself through McGraw-Hill Education's Connect Psychology. Evaluating your progress is essential to assessing your degree of mastery of the material.

R Rethink

- *Rethink.* The final step in the *P.O.W.E.R.* learning system requires that you think critically about the content. Critical thinking entails reanalyzing, reviewing, questioning, and challenging assumptions. It affords you the opportunity to consider how the material fits with other information you have already learned. Every major section of *Psychology and Your Life with P.O.W.E.R. Learning,* 3/e ends with a *Rethink* section, indicated by a Rethink icon (see margin). Answering its thought-provoking questions will help you understand the material more fully and at a deeper level.

Making use of the P.O.W.E.R. system embedded in this text will help you study, learn, and master the material more effectively. Moreover, it is a system that will be helpful in your other courses as well.

Manage Your Time

Without looking up from the page, answer this question: What time is it?

Most people are pretty accurate in their answer. And if you don't know for sure, it's very likely that you can find out. There may be a cell phone in your pocket; there may be a clock on the wall, desk, or computer screen; or maybe you're riding in a car that has a clock in the dashboard. Even if you don't have a timepiece of some sort nearby, your body keeps its own beat. Humans have an internal clock that regulates the beating of our heart, the pace of our breathing, the discharge of chemicals within our bloodstream, and myriad other bodily functions.

Managing your time as you study is a central aspect of a successful plan. But remember: The goal of time management is not to schedule every moment so we become pawns of a timetable that governs every waking moment of the day. Instead, the goal is to permit us to make informed choices as to how we use our time. Rather than letting the day slip by, largely without our awareness, the time management procedures we'll discuss can make us better able to harness time for our own ends.

We'll consider a number of steps to help you improve your time management skills.

Create a Time Log. A *time log* is simply a record of how you actually have spent your time—including interruptions—and is the most essential tool for improving your use of time. It doesn't have to be a second-by-second record of every waking moment. But it should account for blocks of time in increments as short as 15 minutes.

By looking at how much time you spend doing various activities, you now know where your time goes. How does it match with your perceptions of how you spend your time? Be prepared to be surprised, because most people find that they're spending time on a lot of activities that just don't matter very much.

You should also identify the "vacuums" that suck up your time. We all waste time on unimportant activities that keep us from doing the things we should be doing or want to do. Suppose you're studying and your cell phone rings. Instead of speaking with a friend for a half hour, you might (a) let the phone ring but not answer it; (b) answer it, but tell your friend you are studying and will call her back; or (c) speak with her for only a short while. If you do any of these three things, you will have taken control of your time.

Set Your Priorities. By this point you should have a good idea of what's taking up your time. But you may not know what you *should* be doing.

To figure out the best use of your time, you need to determine your priorities. *Priorities* are the tasks and activities you need and want to do, rank-ordered from most important to least important. There are no right or wrong priorities; maybe spending time on your studies is most important to you, or maybe your top priority is spending time with your family. Only you can decide. Furthermore, what's important to you now may be less of a priority to you next month, next year, or in five years.

The best procedure is to start off by identifying priorities for an entire term. What do you need to accomplish? Don't just choose obvious, general goals, such as "passing all my classes." Instead, think in terms of specific, measurable activities, such as "spend one hour each day reading the textbook to prepare for upcoming psychology classes."

Identify Your Prime Time. Do you enthusiastically bound out of bed in the morning, ready to start the day and take on the world? Or is the alarm clock a hated and unwelcome sound that jars you out of pleasant slumber? Are you zombielike by 10:00 at night, or a person who is just beginning to rev up at midnight? Each of us has our own style based on some inborn body clock. Being aware of the time or times of day when you can do your best work will help you plan and schedule your time most effectively. If you're at your worst in the morning, try to schedule easier, less-involving activities for those earlier hours. On the other hand, if morning is the best time for you, schedule activities that require the greatest concentration at that time.

Master the Moment. You now know where you've lost time in the past, and your priority list is telling you where you need to head in the future. You've reached the point where you can organize yourself to take control of your time. Here's what you'll need:

- *A master calendar* that shows all the weeks of the term on one page. It should include every week of the term and seven days per week. Using your class syllabi, write on the master calendar every assignment and test you will have, noting the date that it is due. Pencil in tentative assignments on the appropriate date. Also include on the master calendar important activities from your personal life, drawn from your list of priorities. And don't forget to schedule some free time for yourself.

- *A weekly timetable*, a master grid with the days of the week across the top and the hours, from 6:00 a.m. to midnight, along the side. Fill in the times of all your fixed, prescheduled activities—the times that your classes meet, when you have to be at work, the times you have to pick up your child at day care, and any other recurring appointments. Add assignment due dates, tests, and any other activities on the appropriate days of the week. Then pencil in blocks of time necessary to prepare for those events.

- *A daily to-do list.* Your daily to-do list can be written on a small, portable calendar that includes a separate page for each day of the week, or you can maintain a calendar electronically, if that is your preference. List all the things that you intend to do during the next day, and their priority. Start with the things you know you must do and that have fixed times, such as classes, work schedules, and appointments. Then add in the other things that you should accomplish, such as an hour of study for an upcoming test; work on research for an upcoming paper; or finish up a lab report. Finally, list things that are a low priority but enjoyable, like a run or a walk.

Controlling Time. If you've followed the schedules that you've prepared and organized, you've taken the most important steps in time management. However, our lives are filled with surprises: Things always seem to take longer than we've planned. A crisis occurs; buses are late; computers break down; kids get sick.

The difference between effective time management and time management that doesn't work lies in how well you deal with the inevitable surprises. You can take control of your days and permit yourself to follow your intended schedule in several ways:

- **Just say no.** You don't have to agree to every request and every favor that others ask of you.

- **Get away from it all.** Lock yourself into your bedroom. Find an out-of-the-way unused classroom. Adopt a specific spot as your own, such as a corner desk in a secluded nook in the library. If you use it enough, your body and mind will automatically get into study mode as soon as you seat yourself at it.

- **Enjoy the sounds of silence.** Although many students insist they accomplish most while a television, radio, or CD is playing, scientific studies suggest otherwise—we are able to concentrate most when our environment is silent. Even experiment and work in silence for a few days. You may find that you get more done in less time than you would in a more distracting environment

- **Take an e-break.** We may not control when communications arrive, but we can make the message wait until we are ready to receive it. Take an e-break and shut down your communication sources for a period of time. Phone calls can be stored on voicemail systems, and text messages, IMs, and e-mail can be saved on a phone or computer. They'll wait.

- **Expect the unexpected.** You'll never be able to escape from unexpected interruptions and surprises that require your attention. But by trying to anticipate them in advance, and thinking about how you'll react to them, you'll be positioning yourself to react more effectively when they do occur.

- **Combat procrastination.** Even when no one else is throwing interruptions at us, we make up our own. *Procrastination,* the habit of putting off and delaying tasks that are to be accomplished, is a problem that many of us face. If you find yourself procrastinating, several steps can help you:

    1. Break large tasks into small ones.

    2. Start with the easiest and simplest part of a task, and then do the harder parts.

    3. Work with others—for example, a study session with several of your classmates.

    4. Keep the costs of procrastination in mind.

Reading Your Textbook Effectively

Reading a textbook is different from reading for pleasure. With textbooks, you have specific goals: understanding, learning, and ultimately recalling the information. You can take several steps to achieve these goals:

- **Read the front matter.** If you'll be using a text extensively throughout the term, start by reading the preface and/or introduction and scanning the table of contents—what publishers call the *front matter.* It is there that the author has a chance to explain, often more personally than elsewhere in the text, what he or she considers important. Knowing this will give you a sense of what to expect as you read. (Note: You're reading part of the front matter at this very moment!)

- **Identify your personal objectives.** Before you begin an assignment, think about what your specific objectives are. Will you be reading a textbook on which you'll be thoroughly tested? Or will your reading provide background information for future learning but it won't itself be tested? Is the material going to be useful to you personally? In your program? Your objectives for reading will help you determine which reading strategy to adopt and how much time you can devote to the reading assignment. You aren't expected to read everything with the same degree of intensity. Some material you may feel comfortable skimming; for other material you'll want to put in the maximum effort.

- **Identify and use the advance organizers.** The next step in reading a textbook is to become familiar with the *advance organizers*—outlines, overviews, section objectives, or other clues to the meaning and organization of new material—provided in the material you are reading. For example, *Psychology and Your Life with P.O.W.E.R. Learning,* 3/e includes Learning Outcomes in every module. These learning outcomes direct you to the key points of every section in this textbook. If you can work through the concepts presented in the learning outcomes, you have gained an understanding of exactly what each module is designed to do!

- **Stay focused as you read.** There are a million and one possible distractions that can invade your thoughts as you read. Your job is to keep distracting thoughts at bay and focus on the material you are supposed to be reading. Here are some things you can do to help yourself stay focused:

    - **Read in small bites.** If you think it is going to take you four hours to read an entire chapter, break up the four hours into more manageable time periods. Promise yourself that you'll read for one hour in the afternoon, another hour in the evening, and the next two hours spaced out during the following day.

- **Take a break.** Actually, plan to take several short breaks to reward yourself while you're reading. During your break, do something enjoyable—eat a snack, watch a bit of a ball game on television, play a video game, or the like. Just try not to get drawn into your break activity to the point that it takes over your reading time.

- **Highlight and take notes as you read.** Highlighting and taking notes as you read a textbook are essential activities. Good annotations can help you learn and review the information prior to tests, as well as helping you to stay focused as you read. You can do several things to maximize the effectiveness of your notes:

  - **Rephrase key points.** Make notes to yourself, in your own words, about what the author is trying to get across. Don't just copy what's been said. Think about the material, and rewrite it in words that are your own. The very act of writing engages an additional type of perception—involving the physical sense of moving a pen or pressing a keyboard.

  - **Highlight or underline key points.** Often the first or last sentence in a paragraph, or the first or last paragraph in a section, will present a key point. Before you highlight anything, though, read the whole paragraph through. Then you'll be sure that what you highlight is, in fact, the key information. You should find yourself highlighting only one or two sentences or phrases per page. In *highlighting and under-lining, less is more.* One guideline: No more than 10 percent of the material should be highlighted or underlined. You may find it helpful to highlight only the information that helps you work through the concepts presented in the Learning Outcomes.

  - **Use arrows, diagrams, outlines, tables, timelines, charts, and other visuals to help you understand and later recall what you are reading.** If three examples are given for a specific point, number them. If a sequence of steps is presented, number each step. If a paragraph discusses a situation in which an earlier point does not hold, link the original point to the exception by an arrow. Representing the material graphically will get you thinking about it in new and different ways. The act of creating visual annotations will not only help you to understand the material better but will also ease its later recall.

  - **Look up unfamiliar words.** Even though you may be able to figure out the meaning of an unfamiliar word from its context, look up unfamiliar words in a dictionary or online. You'll also find out what the word sounds like, which will be important if your instructor uses the word in class. *Psychology and Your Life with P.O.W.E.R. Learning, 3/e* includes a glossary with definitions designed to help you gain a clear understanding of all the key terms in the text. Be sure to check it out if you need further clarification on any of the key terms within the modules.

Taking Good Notes in Class

Perhaps you know students who manage to write down nearly everything their instructors say in class. And perhaps you have thought to yourself: "If only I took such painstaking notes, I'd do much better in my classes." Contrary to what many students think, however, good note taking does not mean writing down every word that an instructor utters. With note taking, less is often more. Let's consider some of the basic principles of note taking:

- **Identify the instructor's—and your—goals for the course.** On the first day of class, most instructors talk about their objectives for the course. Most review the information on the class syllabus, the written document that explains the assignments for the semester. The information you get during that first session and through the syllabus is critical. In addition to the instructor's goals, you should have your own. What is it you want to learn from the course? How will the information from the course help you to enhance your knowledge, improve yourself as a person, achieve your goals?

- **Complete assignments before coming to class.** Your instructor enthusiastically describes the structure of the neuron, recounting excitedly how electrons flow across neurons, changing their electrical charge. One problem: You have only the vaguest idea what a neuron is. And the reason you don't know is that you haven't read the assignment.

  Chances are you have found yourself in this situation at least a few times, so you know firsthand that sinking feeling as you become more and more confused. The moral: Always go to class prepared. Instructors assume that their students have done what they've assigned, and their lectures are based upon that assumption. Don't forget to bring your textbook to class—during those times when you aren't as prepared, you will at least be able to use your text to follow along with your class discussions!

- **Use a notebook that assists in note taking.** Loose-leaf notebooks are especially good for taking notes because they permit you to go back later and change the order of the pages or add additional material. Whatever kind of notebook you use, *use only one side of the page for writing; keep one side free of notes.* There may be times that you'll want to spread out your notes in front of you, and it's much easier if no material is written on the back of the pages.

- **Listen for the key ideas.** Not every sentence in a lecture is equally important. One of the most useful skills you can develop is separating the key ideas from supporting information. Good lecturers strive to make just a few main points. The rest of what they say consists of explanation, examples, and other supportive material that expand upon the key ideas. To distinguish the key ideas from their support, you need to be alert and always searching for the *meta-message* of your instructor's words—that is, the underlying main ideas that a speaker is seeking to convey.

  How can you discern the meta-message? One way is to *listen for keywords.* Phrases like "you need to know . . . ," "the most important thing that must be considered . . . ," "there are four problems with this approach . . . ," and—a big one—"this will be on the test . . ." should cause you to sit up and take notice. Also, if an instructor says the same thing in several ways, it's a clear sign that the material being discussed is important.

- **Use short, abbreviated phrases—not full sentences—when taking notes.** Forget everything you've ever heard about always writing in full sentences. In fact, it's often useful to take notes in the form of an outline. An outline summarizes ideas in short phrases and indicates the relationship among concepts through the use of indentations.

- **Pay attention to what is written on the board or projected from overheads and PowerPoint slides.**

  - **Listening is more important than seeing.** The information that your instructor projects on-screen, although important, ultimately is less critical than what he or she is saying. Pay primary attention to the spoken word and secondary attention to the screen.

  - **Don't copy everything that is on every slide.** Instructors can present far more information on their slides than they would if they were writing on a blackboard. Oftentimes there is so much information that it's impossible to copy it all down. Don't even try. Instead, concentrate on taking down the key points.

  - **Remember that key points on slides are . . . key points.** The key points (often indicated by bullets) often relate to central concepts. Use these points to help organize your studying for tests, and don't be surprised if test questions directly assess the bulleted items on slides.

  - **Check to see if the presentation slides are available online.** Some instructors make their class presentations available on the Web to their students, either before or after class time. If they do this before class, print them out and bring them to class. Then you can make notes on your copy, clarifying important points. If they are not available until after a class is over, you can still make good use of them when it comes time to study the material for tests.

  - **Remember that presentation slides are not the same as good notes for a class.** If you miss a class, don't assume that getting a copy of the slides is sufficient. Studying the notes of a classmate who is a good note taker will be far more beneficial than studying only the slides.

Memorizing Efficiently: Using Proven Strategies to Memorize New Material

Here's a key principle of effective memorization: Memorize what you need to memorize. *Forget about the rest.*

The average textbook chapter has something like 20,000 words. But, within those 20,000 words, there may be only 30 to 40 specific concepts that you need to learn. And perhaps there are only 25 keywords. *Those* are the pieces of information on which you should focus in your efforts to memorize. By extracting what is important from what is less crucial, you'll be able to limit the amount of the material that you need to recall. You'll be able to focus on what you need to remember.

You have your choice of dozens of techniques of memorization. As we discuss the options, keep in mind that no one strategy works by itself. Also, feel free to devise your own strategies or add those that have worked for you in the past.

Rehearsal. Say it aloud: rehearsal. Think of this word in terms of its three syllables: re–hear–sal. If you're scratching your head as to why you should do this, it's to illustrate the point of *rehearsal:* to transfer material that you encounter into long-term memory.

To test if you've succeeded in transferring the word *rehearsal* into your memory, put down this book and go off for a few minutes. Do something entirely unrelated to reading this book. Have a snack, catch up on the latest sports scores on ESPN, or read the front page of a newspaper. If the word *rehearsal* popped into your head when you picked up this book again, you've passed your first memory test—the word *rehearsal* has been transferred into your memory.

Rehearsal is the key strategy in remembering information. If you don't rehearse material, it will never make it into your memory. Repeating the information, summarizing it, associating it with other memories, and above all thinking about it when you first come across it will ensure that rehearsal will be effective in placing the material into your memory.

Mnemonics. This odd word (pronounced with the "m" silent—neh MON ix) describes formal techniques used to make material more readily remembered. *Mnemonics* are the tricks of the trade that professional memory experts use, and you too can use them to nail down the information you will need to recall for tests.

Among the most common mnemonics are the following:

- **Acronyms.** *Acronyms* are words or phrases formed by the first letters of a series of terms. The word *laser* is an acronym for "light amplification by stimulated emissions of radiation," and *radar* is an acronym for "radio detection and ranging."

  Acronyms can be a big help in remembering things. For example, Roy G. Biv is a favorite of physics students who must remember the colors of the spectrum (red, orange, yellow, green, blue, indigo, and violet). The benefit of acronyms is that they help us to recall a complete list of steps or items.

- **Rhymes and jingles.** "Thirty days hath September, April, June, and November." If you know the rest of the rhyme, you're familiar with one of the most commonly used mnemonic jingles in the English language.

Involve Multiple Senses. The more senses you can involve when you're trying to learn new material, the better you'll be able to remember. Here's why: Every time we encounter new information, all of our senses are potentially at work. Each piece of sensory information is stored in a separate location in the brain, and yet all the pieces are linked together in extraordinarily intricate ways.

What this means is that when we seek to remember the details of a specific event, recalling a memory of one of the sensory experiences can trigger recall of the other types of memories. You can make use of the fact that memories are stored in multiple ways by applying the following techniques:

- **When you learn something, use your body.** Don't sit passively at your desk. Instead, move around. Stand up; sit down. Touch the page. Trace figures with your fingers. Talk to yourself. Think out loud. By involving every part of your body, you've increased the number of potential ways to trigger a relevant memory later, when you need to recall it. And when one memory is triggered, other related memories may come tumbling back.

- **Draw and diagram the material.** It's often useful to structure written material by graphically grouping and connecting key ideas and themes. In contrast to an outline, such drawings help visually show related ideas fit together. (The *Visual Summary* features at the end of each chapter in this book are an example of this.) Creating drawings, sketches, and even cartoons can help us remember better.

- **Visualize.** You already know that memory requires three basic steps: the initial recording of information, the storage of that information, and, ultimately, the retrieval of the stored information. Visualization is a technique by which images are formed to ensure that material is recalled. Don't stop at visualizing images just in your mind's eye. Actually drawing what you visualize will help you to remember the material even better. Visualization is effective because it serves several purposes. It helps make abstract ideas concrete; it engages multiple senses; it permits us to link different bits of information together; and it provides us with a context for storing information.

Overlearning. Lasting learning doesn't come until you have overlearned the material. *Overlearning* consists of studying and rehearsing material past the point of initial mastery. Through overlearning, recall becomes automatic. Rather than searching for a fact, going through mental contortions until perhaps the information surfaces, overlearning permits us to recall the information without even thinking about it.

Test-Taking Strategies

Preparing for tests is a long-term proposition. It's not a matter of "giving your all" the night before the test. Instead, it's a matter of giving your all to every aspect of the course.

Here are some guidelines that can help you do your best on tests.

Know What You Are Preparing For. Determine as much as you can about the test *before* you begin to study for it. The more you know about a test beforehand, the more efficient your studying will be.

To find out about an upcoming test, first ask this question:

- Is the test called a test, exam, quiz, or something else? The names imply different things:
  - *Essay:* Requires a fairly extended, on-the-spot composition about some topic. Examples include questions that call on you to describe a person, process, or event, or those that ask you to compare or contrast two separate sets of material.
  - *Multiple-choice:* Usually contains a question or statement, followed by a number of possible answers (usually four or five of them). You are supposed to choose the best response from the choices offered.
  - *True–false:* Presents statements about a topic that are either accurate or inaccurate. You are to indicate whether each statement is accurate (true) or inaccurate (false).
  - *Matching:* Presents two lists of related information, arranged in column form. Typically, you are asked to pair up the items that go together (e.g., a scientific term and its definition, or a writer and the title of a book he wrote).
  - *Short-answer:* Requires brief responses (usually a few sentences at most) in a kind of mini-essay.
  - *Fill-in:* Requires you to add one or more missing words to a sentence or series of sentences.

Match Test Preparation to Question Types. Each kind of test question requires a somewhat different style of preparation.

- **Essay questions.** Essay tests focus on the big picture—ways in which the various pieces of information being tested fit together. You'll need to know not just a series of facts, but also the connections between them, and you will have to be able to discuss these ideas in an organized and logical way.

The best approach to studying for an essay test involves four steps:

1. Carefully reread your class notes and any notes you've made on assigned readings that will be covered on the upcoming exam. Also go through the readings themselves, reviewing underlined or highlighted material and marginal notes.

2. Think of likely exam questions. For example, use the key words, phrases, concepts, and questions that come up in your class notes or in your text. Some instructors give out lists of possible essay topics; if yours does, focus on this list, but don't ignore other possibilities.

3. Without looking at your notes or your readings, answer each potential essay question—aloud. Don't feel embarrassed about doing this. Talking aloud is often more useful than answering the question in your head. You can also write down the main points that any answer should cover. (Don't write out *complete* answers to the questions unless your instructor tells you in advance exactly what is going to be on the test. Your time is probably better spent learning the material than rehearsing precisely formulated responses.)

4. After you've answered the questions, check yourself by looking at the notes and readings once again. If you feel confident that you've answered specific questions adequately, check them off. You can go back later for a quick review. But if there are questions that you had trouble with, review that material immediately. Then repeat the third step above, answering the questions again.

- **Multiple-choice, true–false, and matching questions.** Whereas the focus of review for essay questions should be on major issues and controversies, studying for multiple-choice, true–false, and matching questions requires more attention to the details. Almost anything is fair game for multiple-choice, true–false, and matching questions, so you can't afford to overlook anything when studying. It's a good idea to write down important facts on index cards: They're portable and available all the time, and the act of creating them helps drive the material into your memory. Furthermore, you can shuffle them and test yourself repeatedly until you've mastered the material.

- **Short-answer and fill-in questions.** Short-answer and fill-in questions are similar to essays in that they require you to recall key pieces of information rather than—as is the case with multiple-choice, true–false, and matching questions—finding it on the page in front of you. However, short-answer and fill-in questions typically don't demand that you integrate or compare different types of information. Consequently, the focus of your study should be on the recall of specific, detailed information.

Test Yourself. Once you feel you've mastered the material, test yourself on it. There are several ways to do this. Often textbooks are accompanied by websites that offer automatically scored practice tests and quizzes. You can also create a test for yourself, in writing, making its form as close as possible to what you expect the actual test to be. For instance, if your instructor has told you the classroom test will be primarily made up of short-answer questions, your test should reflect that. Again, use the learning outcomes within each module to guide you.

You might also construct a test and administer it to a classmate or a member of your study group. In turn, you could take a test that someone else has constructed. Constructing and taking practice tests are excellent ways of studying the material and cementing it into memory.

Deal with Test Anxiety. What does the anticipation of a test do to you? Do you feel shaky? Is there a knot in your stomach? Do you grit your teeth? *Test anxiety* is a temporary condition characterized by fears and concerns about test taking. Almost everyone experiences it to some degree, although for some people it's more of a problem than for others. You'll never eliminate test anxiety completely, nor do you want to. A little bit of nervousness can energize us, making us more attentive and vigilant. Like any competitive event, testing can motivate us to do our best.

On the other hand, for some students, anxiety can spiral into the kind of paralyzing fear that makes their mind go blank. There are several ways to keep this from happening to you:

1. **Prepare thoroughly.** The more you prepare, the less test anxiety you'll feel. Good preparation can give you a sense of control and mastery, and it will prevent test anxiety from overwhelming you.

2. **Take a realistic view of the test.** Remember that your future success does not hinge on your performance on any single exam. Think of the big picture: Put the task ahead in context, and remind yourself of all the hurdles you've passed so far.

3. **Visualize success.** Think of an image of your instructor handing back your test marked with a big "A." Or imagine your instructor congratulating you on your fine performance the day after the test. Positive visualizations that highlight your potential success can help replace images of failure that may fuel test anxiety.

What if these strategies don't work? If your test anxiety is so great that it's getting in the way of your success, make use of your college's resources. Most provide a learning resource center or a counseling center that can provide you with personalized help.

Form a Study Group. *Study groups* are small, informal groups of students who work together to learn course material and study for a test. Forming such a group can be an excellent way to prepare for any kind of test. Some study groups are formed for particular tests, whereas others meet consistently throughout the term. The typical study group meets a week or two before a test and plans a strategy for studying. Members share their understanding of what will be on the test, based on what an instructor has said in class and on their review of notes and text material. Together, they develop a list of review questions to guide their individual study. The group then breaks up, and the members study on their own. If your class meets online, use online discussion tools as appropriate for your course. Ask your instructor if there is a way for you to hold these online discussions through your school.

A few days before the test, members of the study group meet again. They discuss answers to the review questions, go over the material, and share any new insights they may have about the upcoming test. They may also quiz one another about the material to identify any weaknesses or gaps in their knowledge.

Study groups can be extremely powerful tools because they help accomplish several things:

- They help members organize and structure the material to approach their studying in a systematic and logical way.

- They allow students to share different perspectives on the material.

- They make it more likely that students will not overlook any potentially important information.

- They force members to rethink the course material, explaining it in words that other group members will understand. This helps both understanding and recall of the information when it is needed on the test.

- Finally, they help motivate members to do their best. When you're part of a study group, you're no longer working just for yourself; your studying also benefits the other study group members. Not wanting to let down your classmates in a study group may encourage you to put in your best effort.

Some Final Comments

We have discussed numerous techniques for increasing your study, classroom, and test effectiveness. But you need not feel tied to a specific strategy. You might want to combine other elements to create your own study system. Additional learning tips and strategies for critical thinking are presented throughout *Psychology and Your Life with P.O.W.E.R. Learning, 3/e.*

Whatever learning strategies you use, you will maximize your understanding of the material in this book and master techniques that will help you learn and think critically in all of your academic endeavors. More important, you will optimize your understanding of the field of psychology. It is worth the effort: The excitement, challenges, and promise that psychology holds for you are significant.

Robert S. Feldman

CHAPTER

1

© paffy/Shutterstock.com

CHAPTER OUTLINE

A Man-Made Catastrophe

At first the loud popping noises seemed like they were a part of the show at Pulse, a well-known gay nightclub in Orlando, Florida. But as people began to drop to the floor, injured and dying, panicky clubgoers rushed to escape what turned out to be a barrage of bullets. Until he himself was killed by the police, the shooter, Omar Mateen, murdered and injured scores of people over the next three hours.

It was the worst act of domestic terrorism in the United States other than the 9/11 attack on the World Trade Center, showing the darkest side of human behavior. But at the same time the carnage was occurring, the best of humanity was also on display. Some people rushed to help the wounded, and survivors comforted those who were near death. Strangers risked their own lives to help those in desperate need. There was an outpouring of grief around the world.

INTRODUCTION TO PSYCHOLOGY

Looking Ahead

The Orlando massacre gives rise to a host of important psychological issues. For example, consider these questions asked by psychologists following the catastrophe:

- What motivated the shooter's rampage? Was he driven by political, social, or religious beliefs, or was he psychologically disturbed?
- What internal, biologically based changes occurred in those fleeing for their lives from the shooter?
- What memories did people have of the massacre afterward? Why were there contradictory eyewitness reports?
- What would be the long-term effects of the massacre on the psychological and physical health of the survivors and witnesses?
- What are the most effective ways to help people cope with the sudden and unexpected loss of loved ones, many of whom were in the prime of their lives?
- Could this tragedy have been prevented if the shooter had earlier received psychological therapy?

As you'll soon see, the field of psychology addresses questions like these—and many, many more. In this chapter, we begin our examination of psychology, the different types of psychologists, and the various roles that psychologists play.

Psychologists at Work

Learning Outcomes

>> **LO1.1** Define the science of psychology.

>> **LO1.2** Describe the subfields of psychology.

>> **LO1.3** List the major specialties for working in the field of psychology.

MODULE OUTLINE

What Is Psychology?

The Subfields of Psychology: Psychology's Family Tree

Try It! Psychological Truths?

Working at Psychology

W | Work

psychology The scientific study of behavior and mental processes

>> LO1.1 What Is Psychology?

Psychology is the scientific study of behavior and mental processes. The phrase *behavior and mental processes* means many things: it encompasses not just what people do but also their thoughts, emotions, perceptions, reasoning processes, memories, and even the biological activities that maintain bodily functioning.

Psychologists try to describe, predict, and explain human behavior and mental processes, as well as helping to change and improve the lives of people and the world in which they live. They use scientific methods to find answers that are far more valid and legitimate than those resulting from intuition and speculation, which are often inaccurate. Test your own knowledge of psychology by completing the accompanying Try It! feature.

The questions in the Try It! provide just a hint of the topics that we will encounter in the study of psychology. Our discussions will take us through the range of what is known about behavior and mental processes.

>> LO1.2 The Subfields of Psychology: Psychology's Family Tree

As the study of psychology has grown, it has given rise to a number of subfields (described in Figure 1). One way to identify the key subfields is to look at some of the basic questions about behavior that they address.

What Are the Biological Foundations of Behavior?

In the most fundamental sense, people are biological organisms. *Behavioral neuroscience* is the subfield of psychology that mainly examines how the brain and the nervous system—but other biological processes as well—determine

Try It!

Psychological Truths?

To test your knowledge of psychology, try answering the following questions:

1. Infants love their mothers primarily because their mothers fulfill their basic biological needs, such as providing food. True or false?
2. Geniuses generally have poor social adjustment. True or false?
3. The best way to ensure that a desired behavior will continue after training is completed is to reward that behavior every single time it occurs during training rather than rewarding it only periodically. True or false?
4. People with schizophrenia have at least two distinct personalities. True or false?
5. Parents should do everything they can to ensure children have high self-esteem and a strong sense that they are highly competent. True or false?
6. Children's IQ scores have little to do with how well they do in school. True or false?
7. Frequent masturbation can lead to mental illness. True or false?
8. Once people reach old age, their leisure activities change radically. True or false?
9. Most people would refuse to give painful electric shocks to other people. True or false?
10. People who talk about suicide are unlikely to actually try to kill themselves. True or false?

Scoring

The truth about each of these items is that they are all false. Based on psychological research, each of these "facts" have been proven untrue. You will learn the reasons why as we explore what psychologists have discovered about human behavior.

Source: Adapted from Lamal, 1979.

behavior. Thus, neuroscientists consider how our bodies influence our behavior. For example, they may examine the link between specific sites in the brain and the muscular tremors of people affected by Parkinson's disease or attempt to determine how our emotions are related to physical sensations (Willis, 2008; Paulmann & Pell, 2010; Albuquerque et al., 2016).

How Do People Sense, Perceive, Learn, and Think about the World?

If you have ever wondered why you are susceptible to optical illusions, how your body registers pain, or how to make the most of your study time, an experimental psychologist can answer your questions. *Experimental psychology* is the branch of psychology that studies the processes of sensing, perceiving, learning, and thinking about the world. (The term *experimental psychologist* is somewhat misleading: psychologists in every specialty area use experimental techniques.)

Several subspecialties of experimental psychology have become specialties in their own right. One is *cognitive psychology,* which focuses on higher mental processes, including thinking, memory, reasoning, problem solving, judging, decision making, and language.

> **STUDY ALERT**
>
> It is important to know the different subfields of psychology in part because we can look at the same behavior in multiple ways.

Subfield	Description
Behavioral genetics	*Behavioral genetics* studies the inheritance of traits related to behavior
Behavioral neuroscience	*Behavioral neuroscience* examines the biological basis of behavior
Clinical psychology	*Clinical psychology* deals with the study, diagnosis, and treatment of psychological disorders
Clinical neuropsychology	*Clinical neuropsychology* unites the areas of biopsychology and clinical psychology, focusing on the relationship between biological factors and psychological disorders
Cognitive psychology	*Cognitive psychology* focuses on the study of higher mental processes
Counseling psychology	*Counseling psychology* focuses primarily on educational, social, and career adjustment problems
Cross-cultural psychology	*Cross-cultural psychology* investigates the similarities and differences in psychological functioning in and across various cultures and ethnic groups
Developmental psychology	*Developmental psychology* examines how people grow and change from the moment of conception through death
Educational psychology	*Educational psychology* is concerned with teaching and learning processes, such as the relationship between motivation and school performance
Environmental psychology	*Environmental psychology* considers the relationship between people and their physical environment
Evolutionary psychology	*Evolutionary psychology* considers how behavior is influenced by our genetic inheritance from our ancestors
Experimental psychology	*Experimental psychology* studies the processes of sensing, perceiving, learning, and thinking about the world
Forensic psychology	*Forensic psychology* focuses on legal issues, such as determining the accuracy of witness memories
Health psychology	*Health psychology* explores the relationship between psychological factors and physical ailments or disease
Industrial/ organizational psychology	*Industrial/organizational psychology* is concerned with the psychology of the workplace
Personality psychology	*Personality psychology* focuses on the consistency in people's behavior over time and the traits that differentiate one person from another
Program evaluation	*Program evaluation* focuses on assessing large-scale programs, such as the Head Start preschool program, to determine whether they are effective in meeting their goals
Psychology of women	*Psychology of women* focuses on issues such as discrimination against women and the causes of violence against women
School psychology	*School psychology* is devoted to counseling children in elementary and secondary schools who have academic or emotional problems
Social psychology	*Social psychology* is the study of how people's thoughts, feelings, and actions are affected by others
Sport psychology	*Sport psychology* applies psychology to athletic activity and exercise

Figure 1   The major subfields of psychology. Photos: (top) © Alina Solovyova-Vincent/ Getty Images RF; (middle) © Design Pics/Don Hammond RF; (bottom) © Exactostock-1527/ Superstock RF; (DNA strand) © Lawrence Lawry/Getty Images RF

What Are the Sources of Change and Stability in Behavior across the Life Span?

A baby producing her first smile . . . taking her first step . . . saying her first word. These universal milestones in development are also singularly special and unique for each person. *Developmental psychology* studies how people grow and change from the moment of conception through death. *Personality psychology* focuses on the consistency in people's behavior over time and the traits that differentiate one person from another.

How Do Psychological Factors Affect Physical and Mental Health?

Frequent depression, stress, and fears that prevent people from carrying out their normal activities are topics that would interest a health psychologist, a clinical psychologist, and a counseling psychologist. *Health psychology* explores the relationship between psychological factors and physical ailments or disease. For example, health psychologists are interested in assessing how long-term stress (a psychological factor) can affect physical health and in identifying ways to promote behavior that brings about good health (Yardley & Moss-Morris, 2009; Kendall-Tackett, 2010; Proyer et al., 2013; Boyraz et al., 2016).

© George Doyle/Getty Images RF

Clinical psychology deals with the study, diagnosis, and treatment of psychological disorders. Clinical psychologists are trained to diagnose and treat problems that range from the crises of everyday life, such as unhappiness over the breakup of a relationship, to more extreme conditions, such as profound, lingering depression.

Like clinical psychologists, counseling psychologists deal with people's psychological problems, but the problems they deal with are more specific. *Counseling psychology* focuses primarily on educational, social, and career adjustment problems. Many large business organizations employ counseling psychologists to help employees with work-related problems.

Some clinical and counseling psychologists specialize in *forensic psychology,* which applies psychology to the criminal justice system and legal issues. For example, forensic psychologists may be asked to examine people accused of crimes to determine if they are competent to stand trial or have psychological disorders.

How Do Our Social Networks Affect Behavior?

Our complex networks of social interrelationships are the focus for a number of subfields of psychology. For example, *social psychology* is the study of how people's thoughts, feelings, and actions are affected by others. Social psychologists concentrate on such diverse topics as human aggression, liking and loving, persuasion, and conformity.

Cross-cultural psychology investigates the similarities and differences in psychological functioning in and across various cultures and ethnic groups. For example, cross-cultural psychologists examine how cultures differ in their use of punishment during child rearing.

Expanding Psychology's Frontiers

The boundaries of the science of psychology are constantly growing. Three newer members of the field's family tree—evolutionary psychology, behavioral genetics, and clinical neuropsychology—have sparked particular excitement, and debate, within psychology.

Evolutionary Psychology. *Evolutionary psychology* considers how behavior is influenced by our genetic inheritance from our ancestors. The evolutionary approach suggests that the chemical coding of information in our cells not only determines traits such as hair color and race but also holds the key to understanding a broad variety of behaviors that helped our ancestors survive and reproduce.

For example, evolutionary psychologists suggest that behavior such as shyness, jealousy, and cross-cultural similarities in qualities desired in potential mates are at least partially determined by genetics, presumably because such behavior helped increase the survival rate of humans' ancient relatives (Sefcek, Brumbach, & Vasquez, 2007; Blasi & Causey, 2010; Fost, 2015).

Behavioral Genetics. Another rapidly growing area in psychology focuses on the biological mechanisms, such as genes and chromosomes, that enable inherited behavior to unfold. *Behavioral genetics* seeks to understand how we might inherit certain behavioral traits and how the environment influences whether we actually display such traits (Loehlin, 2010; Kremen & Lyons, 2011; Maxson, 2013; Vukasović & Bratko, 2015).

Clinical Neuropsychology. *Clinical neuropsychology* unites the areas of neuroscience and clinical psychology: it focuses on the origin of psychological disorders in biological factors. Building on advances in our understanding of the structure and chemistry of the brain, this specialty has already led to promising new treatments for psychological disorders as well as debates over the use of medication to control behavior (Boake, 2008; Chelune, 2010).

» LO1.3 Working at Psychology

Help Wanted: Instructor at a growing career college. Teach courses in introductory psychology and courses in specialty areas of cognitive psychology, perception, and learning. Strong commitment to quality teaching necessary.

• • •

Help Wanted: Industrial-organizational consulting psychologist. International firm seeks psychologists for full-time career positions as consultants to management. Candidates must have the ability to establish a rapport with senior business executives and help them find innovative and practical solutions to problems concerning people and organizations.

• • •

Help Wanted: Clinical psychologist. PhD, internship experience, and license required. Comprehensive clinic seeks psychologist to work with children and adults providing individual and group therapy, psychological evaluations, crisis intervention, and development of behavior treatment plans on multidisciplinary team.

As these job ads suggest, psychologists are employed in a variety of settings. Many doctoral-level psychologists are employed by universities and colleges or are self-employed, usually working as private practitioners treating clients (see Figure 2). Other work sites include businesses, hospitals, clinics, mental health centers, counseling centers, government human-services organizations, and even prisons. Psychologists are employed in the military, working with soldiers,

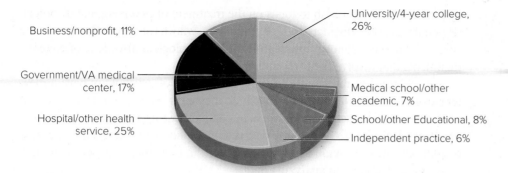

Figure 2 The breakdown of where U.S. psychologists (who have a PhD or PsyD degree) work. Why do you think so many psychologists work in college and university settings? Source: Adapted from Michalski et al., 2011.

veterans, and their families, and they work for the federal government Department of Homeland Security, fighting terrorism (DeAngelis & Monahan, 2008; American Psychological Association, 2009; Moscoso, Chaves, & Argilaga, 2013).

Psychologists: A Portrait

Although there is no "average" psychologist in terms of personal characteristics, we can draw a statistical portrait of the field. There are nearly 200,000 active psychologists working today in the United States, but they are outnumbered by psychologists in other countries. Europe has more than 290,000 psychologists, and there are 140,000 licensed psychologists in Brazil alone (Stevens & Gielen, 2007; Rees & Seaton, 2011; American Psychological Association, 2015).

In the United States, women outnumber men in the field, a big change from earlier years when women faced bias and were actively discouraged from becoming psychologists. Today, women far outnumber male psychologists: for every one male, there are 2.1 female psychologists. There is an active debate about whether, and how, to seek balance in the percentage of men and women in the field (Willyard, 2011; American Psychological Association, 2015; Gregor & O'Brien, 2015).

The vast majority of psychologists in the United States are white, thus limiting the field. Only around 16 percent of all professionally active psychologists are members of racial minority groups. The underrepresentation of racial and ethnic minorities among psychologists is troubling for several reasons. First, the field of psychology is diminished by a lack of the diverse perspectives and talents that minority-group members can provide. Furthermore, minority-group psychologists serve as role models for members of minority communities, and their underrepresentation in the profession might deter other minority-group members from entering the field. Finally, because members of minority groups often prefer to receive psychological therapy from treatment providers of their own race or ethnic group, the rarity of minority psychologists can discourage some members of minority groups from seeking treatment (Chandler, 2011; American Psychological Association, 2015; Stevens, 2015).

The Education of a Psychologist

How do people become psychologists? The most common route is a long one. Most psychologists have a doctorate, either a *PhD* (doctor of philosophy) or, less frequently, a *PsyD* (doctor of psychology). The PhD is a research degree that requires a dissertation based on an original investigation. The PsyD is obtained

STUDY ALERT

It is important to be able to differentiate the difference between a PhD (doctor of philosophy) and PsyD (doctor of psychology), as well as the difference between psychologists and psychiatrists.

by psychologists who wish to focus on the treatment of psychological disorders. (Psychologists are distinct from psychiatrists, who have medical degrees and specialize in the diagnosis and treatment of psychological disorders, often using treatments that involve the prescription of drugs.)

About a third of the people working in the field of psychology have a master's degree as their highest degree, which they earn after two or three years of graduate work. These individuals teach, conduct research, work in specialized programs dealing with drug abuse or crisis intervention, or—depending on state regulations—may provide therapy. Some work in universities, government, and business, collecting and analyzing data.

RECAP

Define the science of psychology.

- Psychology is the scientific study of behavior and mental processes, encompassing not just what people do but their biological activities, feelings, perceptions, memory, reasoning, and thoughts.

Describe the subfields of psychology.

- Behavioral neuroscientists focus on the biological basis of behavior, and experimental psychologists study the processes of sensing, perceiving, learning, and thinking about the world.
- Cognitive psychology, an outgrowth of experimental psychology, studies higher mental processes, including memory, knowing, thinking, reasoning, problem solving, judging, decision making, and language.
- Developmental psychologists study how people grow and change throughout the life span.
- Personality psychologists consider the consistency and change in an individual's behavior, as well as the individual differences that distinguish one person's behavior from another's.

- Health psychologists study psychological factors that affect physical disease, while clinical psychologists consider the study, diagnosis, and treatment of abnormal behavior. Counseling psychologists focus on educational, social, and career adjustment problems. Forensic psychologists apply psychology to the criminal justice system and legal issues.
- Social psychology is the study of how people's thoughts, feelings, and actions are affected by others.
- Cross-cultural psychology examines the similarities and differences in psychological functioning among various cultures.
- Other increasingly important fields are evolutionary psychology, behavioral genetics, and clinical neuropsychology.

List the major specialties for working in the field of psychology.

- Psychologists are employed in a variety of settings. Although the primary sites of employment are private practice and colleges, many psychologists are found in hospitals, clinics, community mental health centers, and counseling centers.

EVALUATE

1. Match each subfield of psychology with the issues or questions posed.

a. Behavioral neuroscience

b. Experimental psychology

c. Cognitive psychology

d. Developmental psychology

e. Personality psychology

f. Health psychology

g. Clinical psychology

h. Counseling psychology

i. Social psychology

j. Industrial psychology

1. Joan, an older student returning to college, is overwhelmed by the demands of studying while working at a full-time job. She needs to learn better organizational skills and work habits.
2. At what age do children generally begin to acquire an emotional attachment to their fathers?
3. During an election campaign, a politician devises strategies to change people's attitudes and persuade them to vote for her.
4. What chemicals are released in the human body as a result of a stressful event? What are their effects on behavior?
5. Luis is unique in his manner of responding to crisis situations, with an even temperament and a positive outlook.
6. Janetta's job is demanding and stressful. She wonders if her lifestyle is making her more prone to certain illnesses, such as cancer and heart disease.
7. A psychologist is intrigued by the fact that some people are much more sensitive to painful stimuli than others are.
8. A strong fear of crowds leads a young woman to seek treatment for her problem.
9. What mental strategies are involved in solving complex word problems?
10. Jessica is asked to develop a management strategy that will encourage safer work practices in an assembly plant.

RETHINK

Do you think intuition and common sense are sufficient for understanding why people act the way they do? In what ways is a scientific approach appropriate for studying human behavior?

Answer to Evaluate Question 1. a-4, b-7, c-9, d-2, e-5, f-6, g-8, h-1, i-3, j-10

KEY TERM

Psychology LO1.1

module 2

A Science Evolves
The Past, the Present, and the Future

Seven thousand years ago, people assumed that psychological problems were caused by evil spirits. To allow those spirits to escape from a person's body, ancient healers chipped a hole in a patient's skull with crude instruments—a procedure called *trephining.*

• • •

According to the seventeenth-century philosopher Descartes, nerves were hollow tubes through which "animal spirits" conducted impulses in the same way that water is transmitted through a pipe. When a person put a finger too close to a fire, heat was transmitted to the brain through the tubes.

• • •

Franz Josef Gall, an eighteenth-century physician, argued that a trained observer could discern intelligence, moral character, and other basic personality characteristics from the shape and number of bumps on a person's skull. His theory gave rise to the field of *phrenology,* employed by hundreds of practitioners in the nineteenth century.

Although these explanations might sound far-fetched, in their own times they represented the most advanced thinking about what might be called the psychology of the era. Our understanding of behavior has progressed tremendously since the eighteenth century, but most of the advances have been recent. As sciences go, psychology is one of the new kids on the block. (For highlights in the development of the field, see Figure 1.)

» LO2.1 The Roots of Psychology

The formal beginning of psychology as a scientific discipline is generally considered to be in the late nineteenth century, when, in Leipzig, Germany, Wilhelm Wundt established the first experimental laboratory devoted to psychological phenomena. At about the same time, William James was setting up his laboratory in Cambridge, Massachusetts.

When Wundt set up his laboratory in 1879, his aim was to study the building blocks of the mind. He considered psychology to be the study of conscious experience. His perspective, which came to be known as **structuralism,** focused on uncovering the fundamental mental components of perception, consciousness, thinking, emotions, and other kinds of mental states and activities.

To determine how basic sensory processes shape our understanding of the world, Wundt and other structuralists used a procedure called **introspection,** in which they presented people with a stimulus—such as a bright green object or a sentence printed on a card—and asked them to describe, in their own words and in as much detail as they could, what they were experiencing. Wundt argued that by analyzing their reports, psychologists could come to a better understanding of the structure of the mind.

Over time, psychologists challenged Wundt's approach. They became increasingly dissatisfied with the assumption that introspection could reveal the structure of the mind. Introspection was not a truly scientific technique, because there were few ways an outside observer could confirm the accuracy of others' introspections. Moreover, people had difficulty describing some kinds of inner experiences, such as emotional responses. Those drawbacks led to the development of new approaches, which largely replaced structuralism.

The perspective that replaced structuralism is known as functionalism. Rather than focusing on the mind's structure, **functionalism** concentrated on what the mind does and how behavior functions. Functionalists, whose perspective became prominent in the early 1900s, asked what role behavior plays in allowing people to adapt to their environments. For example, a functionalist might examine the function of the emotion of fear in preparing us to deal with emergency situations. Led by the American psychologist William James, the functionalists examined how behavior allows people to satisfy their needs and how our "stream of consciousness" permits us to adapt to our environment.

Another important reaction to structuralism was the development of gestalt psychology in the early 1900s. **Gestalt (geh SHTALLT) psychology** emphasizes how perception is organized. Instead of considering the individual parts

structuralism Wilhelm Wundt's approach, which focuses on uncovering the fundamental mental components (parts) of consciousness, thinking, and other kinds of mental states and activities

introspection A procedure used to study the structure of the mind in which subjects are asked to describe in detail what they are experiencing when they are exposed to a stimulus

functionalism An early approach to psychology that concentrated on what the mind does—the functions of mental activity— and the role of behavior in allowing people to adapt to their environments

Gestalt psychology An approach that focuses on the organization of perception through a series of principles describing how we organize bits and pieces of information into meaningful wholes

> Over time, psychologists challenged Wundt's approach. They became increasingly dissatisfied with the assumption that introspection could reveal the structure of the mind.

I ♥ Structuralism

Wilhelm Wundt

© McGraw-Hill Education

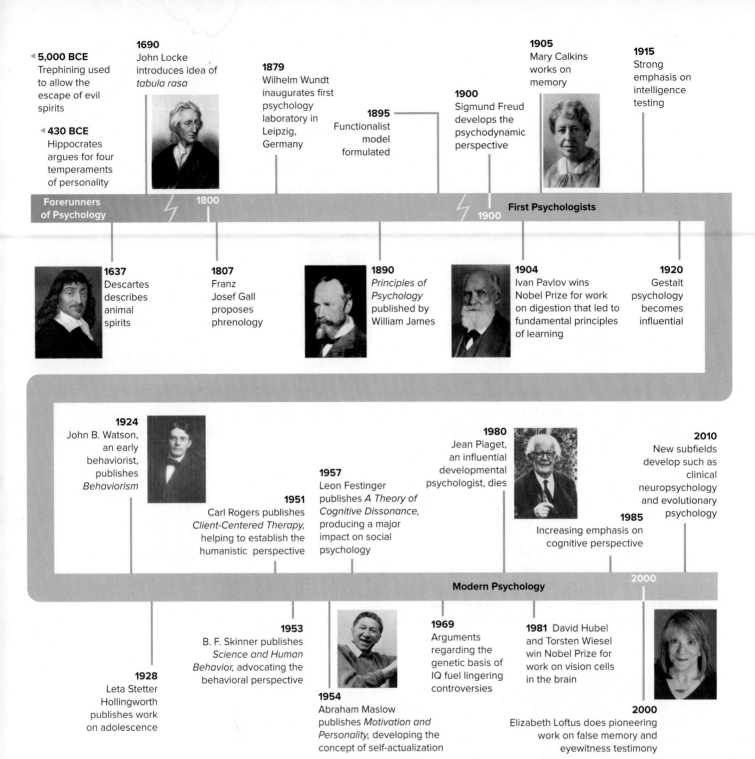

Figure 1 This timeline illustrates the major milestones in the development of psychology. Photos: (John Locke) © Bettmann/Getty Images; (Mary Calkins) Courtesy of the Wellesley College Archives; (Rene Descartes) © Sheila Terry/Science Source; (William James) © Sarin Images/The Granger Collection, NYC; (Ivan Pavlov) © Pictorial Press Ltd/Alamy Stock Photo; (John B. Watson) Courtesy of The Johns Hopkins University; (Jean Piaget) © The Granger Collection, NYC; (Abraham Maslow) © Bettmann/Getty Images; (Dr. Elizabeth Loftus) © Elizabeth Loftus

that make up thinking, Gestalt psychologists took the opposite tack, studying how people consider individual elements together as units or wholes. Gestalt psychologists proposed that "the whole is different from the sum of its parts," meaning that our perception, or understanding, of objects is greater and more meaningful than the individual elements that make up our perceptions. Gestalt psychologists have made substantial contributions to our understanding of perception.

Women in Psychology: Founding Mothers

As in many scientific fields, social prejudices hindered women's participation in the early development of psychology. For example, many universities would not even admit women to their graduate psychology programs in the early 1900s.

Despite the hurdles they faced, women made notable contributions to psychology, although their impact on the field was largely overlooked until recently. For example, Margaret Floy Washburn (1871–1939) was the first woman to receive a doctorate in psychology, and she did important work on animal behavior. Leta Stetter Hollingworth (1886–1939) was one of the first psychologists to focus on child development and on women's issues. She collected data to refute the view, popular in the early 1900s, that women's abilities periodically declined during parts of the menstrual cycle (Hollingworth, 1943/1990; Furumoto & Scarborough, 2002; Goodwin, 2010).

Mary Calkins (1863–1930), who studied memory in the early part of the twentieth century, became the first female president of the American Psychological Association. Karen Horney (pronounced "HORN-eye") (1885–1952) focused on the social and cultural factors behind personality as well as being the founder of the *American Journal of Psychoanalysis,* and June Etta Downey (1875–1932) spearheaded the study of personality traits and became the first woman to head a psychology department at a state university. Anna Freud (1895–1982), the daughter of Sigmund Freud, also made notable contributions to the treatment of abnormal behavior, and Mamie Phipps Clark (1917–1983) carried out pioneering work on how children of color grew to recognize racial differences (Horney, 1937; Stevens & Gardner, 1982; Lal, 2002; Galdi, 2015).

Anna Freud made important contributions to the treatment of psychological disorders.
© Imagno/Getty Images

STUDY ALERT

Knowing the basic outlines of the history of the field will help you understand how today's major perspectives have evolved.

» LO2.2 Today's Five Major Perspectives

The men and women who laid the foundations of psychology shared a common goal: to explain and understand behavior using scientific methods. Seeking to achieve the same goal, the tens of thousands of psychologists who followed those early pioneers embraced—and often rejected—a variety of broad perspectives.

The perspectives of psychology offer distinct outlooks and emphasize different factors. Just as we can use more than one map to find our way around a particular region—for instance, a map that shows roads and highways and another map that shows major landmarks—psychologists developed a variety of approaches to understanding behavior. When considered jointly, the different perspectives provide the means to explain behavior in its amazing variety.

Today, the field of psychology includes five major perspectives (summarized in Figure 2). These broad perspectives emphasize different aspects of behavior and mental processes, and each takes our understanding of behavior in a somewhat different direction.

The Neuroscience Perspective: Blood, Sweat, and Fears

When we get down to the basics, humans are animals made of skin and bones. The **neuroscience perspective** considers how people and nonhumans function biologically: how individual nerve cells are joined together, how the inheritance of certain characteristics from parents and other ancestors influences behavior,

neuroscience perspective The approach that views behavior from the perspective of the brain, the nervous system, and other biological functions

Neuroscience
Views behavior from the perspective of biological functioning

Behavioral
Focuses on observable behavior

Psychodynamic
Believes behavior is motivated by inner, unconscious forces over which a person has little control

Cognitive
Examines how people understand and think about the world

Humanistic
Contends that people can control their behavior and that they naturally try to reach their full potential

Figure 2 The major perspectives of psychology. Photos: (neuroscience) © McGraw-Hill Education; (cognitive) © David Sanger/Getty Images; (behavioral) © Camille Tokerud/Getty Images; (humanistic) © White Packert/Getty Images; (psychodynamic) © McGraw-Hill Education

how the functioning of the body affects hopes and fears, which behaviors are instinctual, and so forth. Even more complex kinds of behaviors, such as a baby's response to strangers, are viewed as having critical biological components by psychologists who embrace the neuroscience perspective. This perspective includes the study of heredity and evolution, which considers how heredity may influence behavior; and behavioral neuroscience, which examines how the brain and the nervous system affect behavior.

Because every behavior ultimately can be broken down into its biological components, the neuroscience perspective has broad appeal. Psychologists who subscribe to this perspective have made major contributions to the understanding and betterment of human life, ranging from cures for certain types of deafness to drug treatments for people with severe mental disorders. Furthermore, advances in methods for examining the anatomy and functioning of the brain have permitted the neuroscientific perspective to extend its influence across a broad range of subfields in psychology.

The Psychodynamic Perspective: Understanding the Inner Person

To many people who have never taken a psychology course, psychology begins and ends with the **psychodynamic perspective.** Proponents of the psychodynamic perspective argue that behavior is motivated by inner forces and conflicts about which we have little awareness or control. They view dreams and slips of the tongue as indications of what a person is truly feeling within a seething cauldron of unconscious psychic activity.

The origins of the psychodynamic view are linked to one person: Sigmund Freud. Freud was a Viennese physician in the early 1900s whose ideas about unconscious determinants of behavior had a revolutionary effect on twentieth-century thinking, not just in psychology but in related fields as well. Although some of the original Freudian principles have been roundly criticized, the contemporary psychodynamic perspective has provided a means not only to understand and treat some kinds of psychological disorders but also to understand everyday phenomena such as prejudice and aggression.

psychodynamic perspective
The approach based on the view that behavior is motivated by unconscious inner forces over which the individual has little control

The Behavioral Perspective: Observing the Outer Person

Whereas the neuroscience and psychodynamic approaches look inside the organism to determine the causes of its behavior, the behavioral perspective takes a very different approach. The **behavioral perspective** grew out of a rejection of psychology's early emphasis on the internal workings of the mind. Instead, behaviorists suggested that the field should focus on external behavior that can be observed and measured objectively.

John B. Watson was the first major American psychologist to use a behavioral approach. Working in the 1920s, Watson believed that one could gain a complete understanding of behavior by studying the environment in which a people operated. In fact, Watson thought that it was possible to produce any desired type of behavior by controlling a person's environment.

The behavioral perspective was championed by B. F. Skinner, a pioneer in the field. Much of our understanding of how people learn new behaviors is based on the behavioral perspective. As we will see, the behavioral perspective crops up along every byway of psychology. Along with its influence in the area of learning processes, this perspective has made contributions in such diverse areas as treating mental disorders, curbing aggression, resolving sexual problems, and ending drug addiction (Helfand, 2011; Schlinger, 2011; Ruiz, 2015).

behavioral perspective The perspective that looks at the behavior itself as the problem

cognitive perspective The perspective that suggests that people's thoughts and beliefs are a central component of abnormal behavior

humanistic perspective The approach that suggests that all individuals naturally strive to grow, develop, and be in control of their lives and behavior; The perspective that emphasizes the responsibility people have for their own behavior, even when such behavior is abnormal

The Cognitive Perspective: Identifying the Roots of Understanding

Efforts to understand behavior lead some psychologists straight into the mind. Evolving in part from structuralism and in part as a reaction to behaviorism, which focused so heavily on observable behavior and the environment, the **cognitive perspective** focuses on how people think, understand, and know about the world. The emphasis is on learning how people comprehend and represent the outside world within themselves and how our ways of thinking about the world influence our behavior.

Many psychologists who adhere to the cognitive perspective compare human thinking to the workings of a computer, which takes in information and transforms, stores, and retrieves it. In their view, thinking is *information processing*.

Psychologists who rely on the cognitive perspective ask questions ranging from how people make decisions to whether a person can watch television and study at the same time. The common elements that link cognitive approaches are an emphasis on how people understand and think about the world and an interest in describing the patterns and irregularities in the operation of our minds.

© Digital Vision/Getty Images RF

The Humanistic Perspective: The Unique Qualities of the Human Species

The humanistic perspective rejects the view that behavior is determined largely by automatically unfolding biological forces, unconscious processes, or the environment. Instead, the **humanistic perspective** suggests that all individuals naturally strive to grow, develop, and be in control of their lives and behavior. Humanistic psychologists maintain that each of us has the capacity to seek and reach fulfillment.

According to Carl Rogers and Abraham Maslow, who were central figures in the development of the humanistic perspective, people will strive to reach their full potential if they are given the opportunity. The emphasis of the humanistic perspective is on *free will,* the ability to freely make decisions about one's own behavior and life. The notion of free will stands in contrast to *determinism,* which sees behavior as caused, or determined, by things beyond a person's control.

The humanistic perspective assumes that people have the ability to make their own choices about their behavior rather than relying on societal standards. More than any other approach, it stresses the role of psychology in enriching people's lives and helping them achieve self-fulfillment. By reminding psychologists of their commitment to the individual person in society, the humanistic perspective has been an important influence (Nichols, 2011; Linley, 2013; Hayes, 2015).

» LO2.3 Psychology and Your Life

It is important not to let the abstract qualities of the broad approaches we have discussed lull you into thinking that they are purely theoretical: these perspectives underlie ongoing work of a practical nature, as we will discuss throughout this content. For example, these are a sampling of some of the real-world problems that psychology is addressing:

- **What are the causes of terrorism?** What motivates suicide bombers? Are they psychologically disordered, or can their behavior be seen as a rational response to a particular system of beliefs? Psychologists are gaining an understanding of the factors that lead people to embrace suicide and to engage in terrorism to further a cause in which they deeply believe (Mintz & Brule, 2009; Post et al., 2009; Post, 2015).

© Photodisc/Getty Images RF

From the perspective of . . .

A Health Care Worker   How can a basic understanding of psychology improve your job performance in the health care industry? In criminal justice? In your chosen career path?

- **How are social media changing the way we live?** Social networking media such as Facebook and Twitter have changed the way people communicate and the way news spreads around the world. How do social media affect the way people relate to each other? How do they affect our perceptions of world events? Psychologists are examining the motivations behind social networking, its influence on individuals and social institutions, and possible beneficial applications of the technology (Rice, Milburn, & Monro, 2011; Kosinski et al., 2015; Toma & Choi, 2015).

- **Why do eyewitnesses to crimes often remember the events inaccurately, and how can we increase the precision of eyewitness accounts?** Psychologists' research has come to an important conclusion: eyewitness testimony in criminal cases is often inaccurate and biased. Memories of crimes are often clouded by emotion, and the questions asked by police investigators often elicit inaccurate responses. Work by psychologists has been used to provide national guidelines for obtaining more accurate memories during criminal investigations (Busey & Loftus, 2007; Beaudry et al., 2015; Wixted et al., 2015).

What is it that leads suicide bombers to seek to injure others? Case studies can help us to understand the motivation behind such actions. © Stringer/EPA/Newscom

■ **Does texting while driving impair people's driving ability?** Several states have enacted controversial laws banning cell phone usage while driving. Although many people feel that they are perfectly able to talk and drive at the same time, psychological research on attention tells a different story: merely talking on a cell phone—whether hands-free or not—impairs people's driving about as much as if they were legally drunk. The problem, of course, is that drivers' attention is taken away from the road and focused instead on the conversation (Strayer et al., 2005; Taggi et al., 2007; Drews, Pasupathi, & Strayer, 2008; Charlton, 2009).

■ **What are the roots of obesity, and how can healthier eating and better physical fitness be encouraged?** Why are some people more predisposed to obesity than others are? What might be some social factors at play in the rising rate of obesity in childhood? As is becoming increasingly clear, obesity is a complex problem with biological, psychological, and social underpinnings. Approaches to treating obesity therefore must take many factors into account in order to be successful. There is no magic bullet providing a quick fix, but psychologists recommend a number of strategies that help make weight-loss goals more achievable (MacLean et al., 2009; Neumark-Sztainer, 2009; Puhl & Liu, 2015).

These topics represent just a few of the issues that psychologists address on a daily basis. To further explore the many ways that psychology has an impact on everyday life, check out the websites of the American Psychological Association (www.apa.org) and the Association for Psychological Science (www.psychologicalscience.org), which include psychological applications in everyday life.

» LO2.4 Psychology's Key Issues and Controversies

As you consider the many topics and perspectives that make up psychology, ranging from a narrow focus on minute biochemical influences on behavior to a broad focus on social behaviors, you might find yourself thinking that the discipline lacks cohesion. However, the field is more unified than a first glimpse might suggest. For one thing, no matter what topical area a psychologist specializes in, he or she will rely primarily on one of the five major perspectives. For

Issue	Neuroscience	Cognitive	Behavioral	Humanistic	Psychodynamic
Nature (heredity) vs. nurture (environment)	Nature (heredity)	Both	Nurture (environment)	Nurture (environment)	Nature (heredity)
Conscious vs. unconscious determinants of behavior	Unconscious	Both	Conscious	Conscious	Unconscious
Observable behavior vs. internal mental processes	Internal emphasis	Internal emphasis	Observable emphasis	Internal emphasis	Internal emphasis
Free will vs. determinism	Determinism	Free will	Determinism	Free will	Determinism
Individual differences vs. universal principles	Universal emphasis	Individual emphasis	Both	Individual emphasis	Universal emphasis

Figure 3   Key issues in psychology and the positions taken by psychologists subscribing to the five major perspectives of psychology. Photos: (neuroscience) © McGraw-Hill Education; (cognitive) © David Sanger/Getty Images; (behavioral) © Camille Tokerud/ Getty Images; (humanistic) © White Packert/Getty Images; (psychodynamic) © McGraw-Hill Education

example, a developmental psychologist who specializes in the study of children could make use of the cognitive perspective or the psychodynamic perspective or any of the other major perspectives.

Psychologists also agree on what the key issues of the field are (see Figure 3). Although there are major arguments regarding how best to address and resolve the key issues, psychology is a unified science because psychologists of all per-spectives agree that the issues must be addressed if the field is going to advance. As you contemplate these key issues, try not to think of them in "either/or" terms. Instead, consider the opposing viewpoints on each issue as the opposite ends of a continuum, with the positions of individual psychologists typically falling somewhere between the two ends.

Issue 1: Nature (heredity) versus nurture (environment) is one of the major issues that psychologists address. How much of people's behavior is due to their genetically determined nature (heredity), and how much is due to nurture, the influences of the physical and social environment in which a child is raised? Furthermore, what is the interplay between heredity and environment? These questions have deep philosophical and historical roots, and they are involved in many topics in psychology. Psy-chologists agree that neither nature nor nurture alone is the sole determi-nant of behavior; rather, it is a combination of the two. In a sense, then, the real controversy involves how much of our behavior is caused by heredity and how much is caused by environmental influences.

Issue 2: Conscious versus unconscious causes of behavior. How much of our behavior is produced by forces of which we are fully aware, and how much is due to unconscious activity—mental processes that are not accessible to the conscious mind? This question represents one of the great controversies in the field of psychology. For example, clini-cal psychologists adopting a psychodynamic perspective argue that psychological disorders are brought about by unconscious factors, whereas psychologists employing the cognitive perspective suggest that psychological disorders largely are the result of faulty thinking processes.

Issue 3: Observable behavior versus internal mental processes. Should psychology concentrate solely on behavior that can be seen by outside observers, or should it focus on unseen thinking processes? Some psychologists, particularly those relying on the behavioral perspective, contend that the only legitimate source of information for psychologists is behavior that can be observed directly. Other psychologists, building on the cognitive perspective, argue that what goes on inside a person's mind is critical to understanding behavior, and so we must concern ourselves with mental processes.

Issue 4: Free will versus determinism. How much of our behavior is a matter of **free will** (choices made freely by an individual), and how much is subject to **determinism,** the notion that behavior is largely produced by factors beyond people's willful control? An issue long debated by philosophers, the free-will/determinism argument is also central to the field of psychology (Vonasch & Baumeister, 2013; Goto et al., 2015).

free will The idea that behavior is caused primarily by choices that are made freely by the individual

determinism The idea that people's behavior is produced primarily by factors outside of their willful control

For example, some psychologists who specialize in psychological disorders argue that people make intentional choices and that those who display so-called abnormal behavior should be considered responsible for their actions. Other psychologists disagree and contend that such individuals are the victims of forces beyond their control. The position psychologists take on this issue has important implications for the way they treat psychological disorders, especially in deciding whether treatment should be forced on people who don't want it.

Issue 5: Individual differences versus universal principles. How much of our behavior is a consequence of our unique and special qualities, and how much reflects the culture and society in which we live? How much of our behavior is universally human? Psychologists who rely on the neuroscience perspective tend to look for universal principles of behavior, such as how the nervous system operates or the way certain hormones automatically prime us for sexual activity. Such psychologists concentrate on the similarities in our behavioral destinies despite vast differences in our upbringing. In contrast, psychologists who employ the humanistic perspective focus more on the uniqueness of every individual. They consider every person's behavior a reflection of distinct and special individual qualities.

Are thieves exercising free will by stealing? Or are their actions due to determinism, in which their behavior is caused by being raised in an impoverished, nonsupportive environment?
© Hill Street Studios/Blend Images LLC RF

The question of the degree to which psychologists can identify universal principles that apply to all people has taken on new significance in light of the tremendous demographic changes now occurring in the United States and around the world. These changes raise new and critical issues for the discipline of psychology in the twenty-first century.

RECAP

Explain the roots of psychology.

- Wilhelm Wundt laid the foundation of psychology in 1879, when he opened his laboratory in Germany.
- Early perspectives that guided the work of psychologists were structuralism, functionalism, and gestalt theory.

Discuss today's perspectives on psychology.

- The neuroscience approach focuses on the biological components of the behavior of people and animals.
- The psychodynamic perspective suggests that powerful, unconscious inner forces and conflicts about which people have little or no awareness are the primary determinants of behavior.
- The behavioral perspective de-emphasizes internal processes and concentrates instead on observable, measurable behavior, suggesting that understanding and control of a person's environment are sufficient to fully explain and modify behavior.

- Cognitive approaches to behavior consider how people know, understand, and think about the world.
- The humanistic perspective emphasizes that people are uniquely inclined toward psychological growth and higher levels of functioning and that they will strive to reach their full potential.

Apply psychology to your life.

- Psychologists study a variety of topics related to the real world and everyday life, including ways to reduce aggression, eyewitness testimony in trials, and the way that cell phone use impairs driving.

Summarize psychology's key issues and controversies.

- Psychologists study a variety of topics related to the real world and everyday life, including ways to reduce aggression, eyewitness testimony in trials, and the way that cell phone use impairs driving.

[EVALUATE E Evaluate]

1. Wundt described psychology as the study of conscious experience, a perspective he called _____.
2. Early psychologists studied the mind by asking people to describe what they were experiencing when exposed to various stimuli. This procedure was known as _____.
3. The statement "In order to study human behavior, we must consider the whole of perception rather than its component parts" might be made by a person subscribing to which perspective of psychology?
4. Jeanne's therapist asks her to recount a violent dream she recently experienced in order to gain insight into the unconscious forces affecting her behavior. Jeanne's therapist is working from a _____ perspective.
5. "It is behavior that can be observed that should be studied, not the suspected inner workings of the mind." This statement was most likely made by someone with which perspective?
   a. Cognitive perspective
   b. Neuroscience perspective
   c. Humanistic perspective
   d. Behavioral perspective

6. "My therapist is wonderful! She always points out my positive traits. She dwells on my uniqueness and strength as an individual. I feel much more confident about myself—as if I'm really growing and reaching my potential." The therapist being described most likely follows a _____ perspective.

7. In the nature-nurture issue, nature refers to heredity, and nurture refers to the _____.

[RETHINK R Rethink]

Focusing on one of the five major perspectives in use today (i.e., neuroscience, psychodynamic, behavioral, cognitive, and humanistic), can you describe the kinds of research questions and studies that researchers using that perspective might pursue?

Answers to Evaluate Questions 1. structuralism; 2. introspection; 3. Gestalt; 4. psychodynamic; 5. d; 6. humanistic; 7. environment

KEY TERMS

Structuralism   LO2.1

Introspection   LO2.1

Functionalism   LO2.1

Gestalt psychology   LO2.1

Neuroscience perspective   LO2.2

Psychodynamic perspective   LO2.2

Behavioral perspective   LO2.2

Cognitive perspective   LO2.2

Humanistic perspective   LO2.2

Free will   LO2.4

Determinism   LO2.4

Research in Psychology

Learning Outcomes [P] Prepare

>> **LO3.1** Define the scientific method, and list the steps involved.

>> **LO3.2** Describe how psychologists use research to answer questions of interest.

>> **LO3.3** Summarize the descriptive research method used by psychologists.

>> **LO3.4** Summarize the experimental research method used by psychologists.

[W] Work

>> LO3.1 The Scientific Method

"Birds of a feather flock together" . . . or "opposites attract"? "Two heads are better than one" . . . or "if you want a thing done well, do it yourself"? "The more the merrier" . . . or "two's company, three's a crowd"?

If we were to rely on common sense to understand behavior, we'd have considerable difficulty—especially because commonsense views are often contradictory. In fact, one of the major undertakings for the field of psychology is to develop suppositions about behavior and to determine which of those suppositions are accurate. Psychologists—as well as scientists in other disciplines—meet the challenge of posing appropriate questions and properly answering them by relying on the scientific method. The **scientific method** is the approach used by psychologists to systematically acquire knowledge and understanding about behavior and other phenomena of interest. As illustrated in Figure 1, it consists of four main steps: (1) identifying questions of interest, (2) formulating an explanation, (3) carrying out research designed to support or refute the explanation, and (4) communicating the findings.

Theories: Specifying Broad Explanations

Psychologists ask questions about the nature and causes of behavior. They may wish to explore explanations for everyday behaviors or for various phenomena. They may also pose questions that build on findings from their previous research or from research carried out by other psychologists. Or they may produce new questions that are based on curiosity, creativity, or insight.

Once a question has been identified, the next step in the scientific method is to develop a theory to explain the observed phenomenon. **Theories** are broad

scientific method The approach through which psychologists systematically acquire knowledge and understanding about behavior and other phenomena of interest

theories Broad explanations and predictions concerning phenomena of interest

hypothesis A prediction, stemming from a theory, stated in way that allows it to be tested

operational definition The translation of a hypothesis into specific, testable procedures that can be measured and observed

explanations and predictions concerning phenomena of interest. They provide a framework for understanding the relationships among a set of otherwise unorganized facts or principles.

All of us have developed our own informal theories of human behavior, such as "People are basically good" or "People's behavior is usually motivated by self-interest." However, psychologists' theories are more formal and focused. They are established on the basis of a careful study of the psychological literature to identify earlier relevant research and previously formulated theories, as well as psychologists' general knowledge of the field (Tateo & Valsiner, 2015; Devonport, 2016).

Hypotheses: Crafting Testable Predictions

Once a theory is formed, the next step is to test it. To do this, psychologists need to create a hypothesis. A **hypothesis** is a prediction stated in a way that allows it to be tested. Hypotheses stem from theories; they help test the underlying soundness of theories.

In the same way that we develop our own broad theories about the world, we also construct hypotheses about events and behavior. Those hypotheses can range from trivialities (such as why a supervisor wears those weird shirts) to more meaningful matters (such as what is the best way to save money for retirement). Although we rarely test these hypotheses systematically, we do try to determine whether they are right. Perhaps we try comparing two strategies: putting our retirement savings in a 401(k) plan or managing how it is invested ourselves. By assessing which approach yields better returns, we have created a way to compare the two strategies.

A hypothesis must be restated in a way that will allow it to be tested, which involves creating an operational definition. An **operational definition** is the translation of a hypothesis into specific, testable procedures that can be measured and observed in an experiment.

There is no single way to go about devising an operational definition for a hypothesis; it depends on logic, the equipment and facilities available, the psychological perspective being employed, and ultimately the creativity of the researcher. For example, one researcher might develop a hypothesis in which she uses as an operational definition of "fear" an increase in heart rate. In contrast, another psychologist might use as an operational definition of "fear" a written response to the question "How much fear are you experiencing at this moment?"

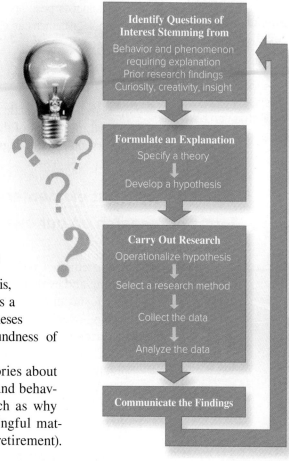

Figure 1 The scientific method, which encompasses the process of identifying, asking, and answering questions, is used by psychologists, and by researchers from every other scientific discipline, to come to an understanding about the world. What do you think are the advantages of this method? Photo: © Royalty Free/Visualphotos RF

Roz Chast/The New Yorker Collection/The Cartoon Bank

In short, the scientific method, with its emphasis on theories and hypotheses, helps psychologists pose appropriate questions. With properly stated questions in hand, psychologists then can choose from a variety of research methods to find answers.

» LO3.2 Psychological Research

Research—systematic inquiry aimed at the discovery of new knowledge—is a central ingredient of the scientific method in psychology. It provides the key to understanding the degree to which hypotheses (and the theories behind them) are accurate.

All of us carry out elementary forms of research on our own.

Just as we can apply different theories and hypotheses to explain the same phenomena, we can use a number of alternative methods to conduct research.

As we consider the major tools psychologists use to conduct research, keep in mind that their relevance extends beyond testing and evaluating hypotheses in psychology. All of us carry out elementary forms of research on our own. For instance, a supervisor might evaluate an employee's performance; a physician might systematically test the effects of different doses of a drug on a patient; a salesperson might compare different persuasive strategies. Each of these situations draws on the research practices we are about to discuss.

» LO3.3 Descriptive Research

descriptive research An approach to research designed to systematically investigate a person, group, or patterns of behavior

archival research Research in which existing data, such as census documents, college records, and newspaper clippings, are examined to test a hypothesis

naturalistic observation Research in which an investigator simply observes some naturally occurring behavior and does not make a change in the situation

Let's begin by considering several types of **descriptive research** designed to systematically investigate a person, group, or patterns of behavior. These methods include archival research, naturalistic observation, survey research, and case studies.

Archival Research

In **archival research,** existing data, such as census documents, college records, online databases, and newspaper articles, are examined to test a hypothesis. For example, college transcripts may be used to determine if there are gender differences in academic performance. Similarly, Facebook provides a huge pool of data from millions of users that can be used to collect data (Fisher & Barnes-Farrell, 2013; Kosinski et al., 2015).

Archival research is a relatively inexpensive means of testing a hypothesis because someone else has already collected the basic data; however, records with the necessary information often do not exist. In these instances, researchers often turn to another research method: naturalistic observation.

Naturalistic Observation

In **naturalistic observation,** the investigator observes some naturally occurring behavior and does not make a change in the situation. For example, a researcher investigating helping behavior might observe the kind of help given to victims in a high-crime area of a city. The important point to remember about naturalistic observation is that the researcher simply records what occurs, making no modification in the situation that is being observed (Kennison & Bowers, 2011; Haas et al., 2015).

Although the advantage of naturalistic observation is obvious—we get a sample of what people do in their "natural habitat"—there is also an important drawback: the inability to control any of the factors of interest. For example, we might find so few naturally occurring instances of helping behavior that we would be unable to draw any conclusions. Because naturalistic observation prevents researchers from making changes in a situation, they must wait until the appropriate conditions occur. Furthermore, if people know they are being watched, they may alter their reactions and produce behavior that is not truly representative.

Andrea Turkalo, a pioneer in the study of forest elephants in their native habitat, relies on naturalistic observation for her research. What are the advantages and disadvantages of this approach? © MICHAEL NICHOLS/National Geographic Creative

Survey Research

There is no more straightforward way of finding out what people think, feel, and do than asking them directly. For this reason, surveys are an important research method. In **survey research,** a *sample* of people chosen to represent a larger group of interest (a *population*) is asked a series of questions about their behavior, thoughts, or attitudes. Survey methods have become so sophisticated that even with a very small sample researchers are able to infer with great accuracy how a larger group would respond. For instance, a sample of just a few thousand voters is sufficient to predict within one or two percentage points who will win a presidential election—if the representative sample is chosen with care (Igo, 2006; Holbrook & Krosnick, 2010).

However, survey research has several potential pitfalls. For one thing, if the sample of people who are surveyed is not representative of the broader population of interest, the results of the survey will have little meaning. For instance, if a sample of voters in a town only includes Republicans, it would hardly be useful for predicting the results of an election in which both Republicans and Democrats are voting. Consequently, researchers using surveys strive to obtain a *random sample* of the population in question, in which every voter in the town has an equal chance of being included in the sample receiving the survey (Davern, 2013; Engel et al., 2015).

survey research Research in which people chosen to represent a larger population are asked a series of questions about their behavior, thoughts, or attitudes

case study An in-depth, intensive investigation of an individual or small group of people

The Case Study

When they read of a suicide bomber in the Middle East, many people wonder what it is about the terrorist's personality or background that leads to such behavior. To answer this question, psychologists might conduct a case study. In contrast to a survey, in which many people are studied, a **case study** is an in-depth, intensive investigation of a single individual or a small group. Case studies often include *psychological testing,* a procedure in which a carefully designed set of questions is used to gain some insight into the personality of the individual or group (Addus, Chen, & Khan, 2007; Baker & Mason, 2010).

© Mark MacEwen/Alamy Stock Photo

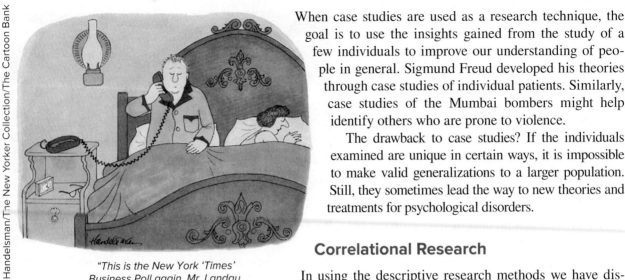

"This is the New York 'Times' Business Poll again, Mr. Landau. Do you feel better or worse about the economy than you did twenty minutes ago?"

When case studies are used as a research technique, the goal is to use the insights gained from the study of a few individuals to improve our understanding of people in general. Sigmund Freud developed his theories through case studies of individual patients. Similarly, case studies of the Mumbai bombers might help identify others who are prone to violence.

The drawback to case studies? If the individuals examined are unique in certain ways, it is impossible to make valid generalizations to a larger population. Still, they sometimes lead the way to new theories and treatments for psychological disorders.

Correlational Research

In using the descriptive research methods we have discussed, researchers often wish to determine the relationship between two **variables.** Variables are behaviors, events, or other characteristics that can change, or vary, in some way. For example, in a study to determine whether the amount of studying makes a difference in test scores, the variables would be study time and test scores.

variables Behaviors, events, or other characteristics that can change, or vary, in some way

correlational research Research in which the relationship between two sets of variables is examined to determine whether they are associated, or "correlated"

In **correlational research,** two sets of variables are examined to determine whether they are associated, or "correlated." The strength and direction of the relationship between the two variables are represented by a mathematical statistic known as a *correlation.*

A *positive correlation* indicates that as the value of one variable increases, we can predict that the value of the other variable will also increase. For example, if we predict that the more years of education that employees have, the higher their income will be and that the fewer years of education they have, the lower their income will be, we are expecting to find a positive correlation. (Higher values of the variable "years of education" would be associated with higher values of the variable "income," and lower values of "years of education" would be associated with lower values of "income.")

In contrast, a *negative correlation* tells us that as the value of one variable increases, the value of the other decreases. For instance, we might predict that as the years of education increases, the number of work-related injuries decreases. Here we are expecting a negative correlation. More education is associated with less work injury, and less work injury is associated with more education. Of course, it's quite possible that little or no relationship exists between two variables. For instance, we would probably not expect to find a relationship between number of years of education and height; knowing how educated someone is does not tell us anything about how tall he or she is.

When two variables are strongly correlated with each other, it is tempting to assume that one variable causes the other. For example, if we find that more education is associated with higher income, we might guess that more studying *causes* higher income. Although this is not a bad guess, it remains just a guess—because finding that two variables are correlated does not mean that there is a causal relationship between them. The strong correlation

Many studies show that the observation of violence in the media is associated with aggression in viewers. The *Grand Theft Auto* series of video games has become a lightning rod for controversy due to its highly violent content. Can we conclude that the observation of violence causes aggression? David J. Green-Lifestyle/ Alamy Stock Photo

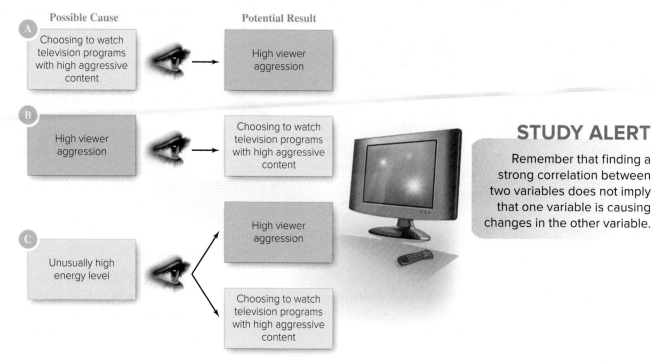

Possible Cause   Potential Result

A Choosing to watch television programs with high aggressive content → High viewer aggression

B High viewer aggression → Choosing to watch television programs with high aggressive content

C Unusually high energy level → High viewer aggression / Choosing to watch television programs with high aggressive content

Figure 2   If we find that frequent viewing of television programs with aggressive content is associated with high levels of aggressive behavior, we might cite several plausible causes, as suggested in this figure. For example, choosing to watch shows with aggressive content could produce aggression (A); or being a highly aggressive person might cause one to choose to watch televised aggression (B); or having a high energy level might cause a person to both choose to watch aggressive shows and act aggressively (C). Correlational findings, then, do not permit us to determine causality. Can you think of a way to study the effects of televised aggression on aggressive behavior that is not correlational?

suggests that knowing how many years of education a person has can help us predict how much money that person earns, but it does not mean that education causes the income. It might be, for instance, that people who are from affluent families can better afford to go to college, and that affluence, not education, predicts income. The mere fact that two variables occur together does not mean that one causes the other (see Figure 2).

The inability of correlational research to demonstrate cause-and-effect relationships is a crucial drawback to its use. There is, however, an alternative technique that does establish causality: the experiment.

» LO3.4 Experimental Research

Carrying out experiments is the *only* way psychologists can establish cause-and-effect relationships. In a formal **experiment,** the researcher investigates the relationship between two (or more) variables by deliberately changing one variable in a controlled situation and observing the effects of that change on other aspects of the situation. In an experiment, then, the conditions are created and controlled by the researcher, who deliberately makes a change in those conditions in order to observe the effects of that change.

The change that the researcher deliberately makes in an experiment is called the **experimental manipulation.** Experimental manipulations are used to detect relationships between different variables. Experimenters must

experiment The investigation of the relationship between two (or more) variables by deliberately producing a change in one variable in a situation and observing the effects of that change on other aspects of the situation

experimental manipulation The change that an experimenter deliberately produces in a situation

"What if these guys in white coats who bring us food are, like, studying us and we're part of some kind of big experiment?"

manipulate at least one variable in order to observe the effects of the manipulation on another variable while keeping other factors in the situation constant. However, the manipulation cannot be viewed by itself, in isolation; if a cause-and-effect relationship is to be established, the effects of the manipulation must be compared with the effects of no manipulation or a different kind of manipulation (Staub, 2011; Salazar, Crosby, & DiClemente, 2015).

Experimental Groups and Control Groups

Experimental research requires, then, that the responses of at least two groups be compared. One group will receive some special **treatment**—the manipulation implemented by the experimenter—and another group will receive either no treatment or a different treatment. Any group that receives a treatment is called an **experimental group;** a group that receives no treatment is called a **control group.** (In some experiments there are multiple experimental and control groups, each of which is compared with another group.)

> **By employing both experimental and control groups in an experiment, researchers are able to rule out the possibility that something other than the experimental manipulation produced the results observed in the experiment.**

By employing both experimental and control groups in an experiment, researchers are able to rule out the possibility that something other than the experimental manipulation produced the results observed in the experiment. Without a control group, we couldn't be sure that some other variable, such as the temperature at the time we were running the experiment, the color of the experimenter's hair, or even the mere passage of time, wasn't causing the changes observed.

For example, consider a medical researcher who thinks she has invented a medicine that cures the common cold. To test her claim, she gives the medicine one day to a group of 20 people who have colds and finds that 10 days later all of them are cured.

Eureka? Not so fast. An observer viewing this flawed study might reasonably argue that the people would have gotten better even without the medicine. What the researcher obviously needed was a control group consisting of people with colds who don't get the medicine and whose health is also checked 10 days later. Only if there is a significant difference between experimental and control groups can the effectiveness of the medicine be assessed. Through the use of control groups, then, researchers can isolate specific causes for their findings—and draw cause-and-effect inferences.

Independent and Dependent Variables

The **independent variable** is the condition that is manipulated by an experimenter. (You can think of the independent variable as being independent of the actions of those taking part in an experiment; it is controlled by the

treatment The manipulation implemented by the experimenter

experimental group Any group participating in an experiment that receives a treatment

control group A group participating in an experiment that receives no treatment

independent variable The variable that is manipulated by an experimenter

experimenter.) The **dependent variable** is the variable that is measured and is expected to change as a result of changes caused by the experimenter's manipulation of the independent variable. The dependent variable is dependent on the actions of the *participants* or *subjects*—the people taking part in the experiment. For example, whether people with colds are given medicine or not would be an independent variable, and whether they remained sick or got better 10 days later would be a dependent variable. *All* true experiments in psychology have an independent variable and a dependent variable.

In this experiment, preschoolers' reaction to the puppet are monitored. Can you think of a hypothesis that might be tested in this way? © J. Wilson/Woodfin Camp and Associates

Random Assignment of Participants

To make an experiment a valid test of the hypothesis, a final step must be added to the design: properly assigning participants to a particular experimental group.

The significance of this step becomes clear when we examine various alternative procedures. For example, the experimenters might assign just males to the experimental group and just females to the control group. If they had done this, however, any differences they found in the dependent variable could not be attributed with any certainty solely to the independent variable, because the differences might just as well have been due to gender. A more reasonable procedure would be to ensure that each group had roughly equal numbers of men and women; then the researchers would be able to make comparisons between groups with considerably more accuracy.

The problem becomes a bit more tricky, though, when we consider other participant characteristics besides gender. How can we ensure that participants in each experimental group will be equally intelligent, extroverted, cooperative, and so forth, when the list of characteristics—any one of which could be important—is potentially endless?

The solution is a simple but elegant procedure called **random assignment to condition:** participants are assigned to different experimental groups or "conditions" on the basis of chance and chance alone. The experimenter might, for instance, flip a coin for each participant and assign a participant to one group when heads came up, and to the other group when tails came up. The advantage of this technique is that there is an equal chance that participant characteristics will be distributed across the various groups. When a researcher uses random assignment—which in practice is usually carried out using computer-generated random numbers—chances are that each of the groups will have approximately the same proportion of intelligent people, cooperative people, extroverted people, males and females, and so on.

Figure 3 provides another example of an experiment. Like all experiments, it includes the following set of key elements, which are important to keep in mind as you consider whether a research study is truly an experiment:

- An independent variable, the variable that is manipulated by the experimenter.
- A dependent variable, the variable that is measured by the experimenter and that is expected to change as a result of the manipulation of the independent variable.

dependent variable The variable that is measured and is expected to change as a result of changes caused by the experimenter's manipulation (handling) of the independent variable

random assignment to condition A procedure in which participants are assigned to different experimental groups or "conditions" on the basis of chance and chance alone

STUDY ALERT

To remember the difference between dependent and independent variables, recall that a hypothesis predicts how a dependent variable *depends* on the manipulation of the independent variable.

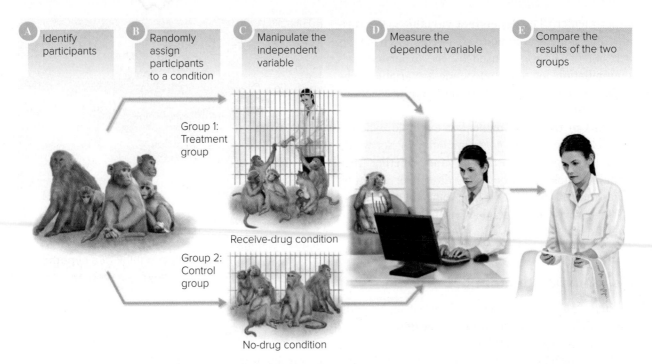

Group 1: Treatment group

Receive-drug condition

Group 2: Control group

No-drug condition

Figure 3 In this depiction of a study investigating the effects of the drug propranolol on stress, we can see the basic elements of all true experiments. The participants in the experiment were monkeys, who were randomly assigned to one of two groups. Monkeys assigned to the treatment group were given propranolol, hypothesized to prevent heart disease, whereas those in the control group were not given the drug. Administration of the drugs, then, was the independent variable.

- A procedure that randomly assigns participants to different experimental groups or "conditions" of the independent variable.
- A hypothesis that predicts the effect the independent variable will have on the dependent variable.

All the monkeys were given a high-fat diet that was the human equivalent of two eggs with bacon every morning, and they occasionally were reassigned to different cages to provide a source of stress. To determine the effects of the drug, the monkeys' heart rates and other measures of heart disease were assessed after 26 months. These measures constituted the dependent variable. The results? As hypothesized, monkeys that received the drug showed lower heart rates and fewer symptoms of heart disease than those who did not (Kaplan & Manuck, 1989).

Only if each of these elements is present can a research study be considered a true experiment in which cause-and-effect relationships can be determined. (For a summary of the different types of research that we've discussed, see Figure 4.)

Of course, one experiment alone does not forever resolve a question about human behavior. Psychologists require that findings undergo **replication,** in which research is repeated, sometimes using other procedures, in other settings, and with other groups of participants. Replication increases confidence in the validity of the results of any single experiment (Peterson & Brown, 2005; Tenenbaum & Ruck, 2007; Huang, 2010).

replication Research that is repeated, sometimes using other procedures, settings, and groups of participants, to increase confidence in prior findings

Research Method	Description	Advantages	Shortcomings
Descriptive and correlational research	Researcher observes a previously existing situation but does not make a change in the situation	Offers insight into relationships between variables	Cannot determine causality
Archival research	Examines existing data to confirm hypothesis	Ease of data collection because data already exist	Dependent on availability of data
Naturalistic observation	Observation of naturally occurring behavior, without making a change in the situation	Provides a sample of people in their natural environment	Cannot control the "natural habitat" being observed
Survey research	A sample is chosen to represent a larger population and asked a series of questions	A small sample can be used to infer attitudes and behavior of a larger population	Sample may not be representative of the larger population; participants may not provide accurate responses to survey questions
Case study	Intensive investigation of an individual or small group	Provides a thorough, in-depth understanding of participants	Results may not be generalizable beyond the sample
Experimental research	Investigator produces a change in one variable to observe the effects of that change on other variables	Experiments offer the only way to determine cause-and-effect relationship	To be valid, experiments require random assignment of participants to conditions, well-conceptualized independent and dependent variables, and other careful controls

Figure 4   Research strategies. Photos: (top) © Asia Images Group/Getty Images RF; (middle) © Jeff Greenberg/AGE Fotostock; (bottom) © fotografixx/E+/Getty Images RF

RECAP

Define the scientific method, and list the steps involved.

- The scientific method is the approach psychologists use to understand behavior. It consists of four steps: identifying questions of interest, formulating an explanation, carrying out research that is designed to support or refute the explanation, and communicating the findings.

- To test a hypothesis, researchers must formulate an operational definition, which translates the abstract concepts of the hypothesis into the actual procedures used in the study.

Describe how psychologists use research to answer questions of interest.

- Research in psychology is guided by theories (broad explanations and predictions regarding phenomena of interest) and hypotheses (theory-based predictions stated in a way that allows them to be tested).

Summarize the descriptive research method used by psychologists.

- Archival research uses existing records, such as old newspapers or other documents, to test a hypothesis. In naturalistic observation, the investigator acts mainly as an observer, making no change in a naturally occurring situation. In survey research, people are asked a series of questions about their behavior, thoughts, or attitudes. The case study is an in-depth interview and examination of one person or group.

- These descriptive research methods rely on correlational techniques, which describe associations between variables but cannot determine cause-and-effect relationships.

Summarize the experimental research method used by psychologists.

- In a formal experiment, the relationship between variables is investigated by deliberately producing a change—called the experimental manipulation—in one variable and observing changes in the other variable.

- In an experiment, at least two groups must be compared to assess cause-and-effect relationships. The group receiving the treatment (the special procedure devised by the experimenter) is the experimental group; the second group (which receives no treatment) is the control group. There also may be multiple experimental groups, each of which is subjected to a different procedure and then compared with the others.

- The variable that experimenters manipulate is the independent variable. The variable that they measure and expect to change as a result of manipulation of the independent variable is called the dependent variable.

- In a formal experiment, participants must be assigned randomly to treatment conditions, so that participant characteristics are distributed evenly across the different conditions.

[EVALUATE   E   Evaluate]

1. An explanation for a phenomenon of interest is known as a _____.

2. To test this explanation, a researcher must state it in terms of a testable question known as a _____.

3. An experimenter is interested in studying the relationship between hunger and aggression. She decides that she will measure aggression by counting the number of times a participant will hit a punching bag. In this case, her _____ definition of aggression is the number of times the participant hits the bag.

4. Match the following forms of research to their definition.

   1. Archival research
   2. Naturalistic observation
   3. Survey research
   4. Case study

   a. Directly asking a sample of people questions about their behavior.

   b. Examining existing records to test a hypothesis.

   c. Looking at behavior in its true setting without intervening in the setting.

   d. Doing an in-depth investigation of a person or small group.

5. Match each of the following research methods with its primary disadvantage.

   1. Archival research
   2. Naturalistic observation
   3. Survey research
   4. Case study

   a. The researcher may not be able to generalize to the population at large.

   b. People's behavior can change if they know they are being watched.

   c. The data may not exist or may be unusable.

   d. People may lie in order to present a good image.

6. A psychologist wants to study the effect of attractiveness on willingness to help a person with a math problem. Attractiveness would be the _____ variable, and the amount of helping would be the _____ variable.

7. The group in an experiment that receives no treatment is called the _____ group.

[RETHINK R Rethink]

Can you describe how a researcher might use naturalistic observation, case studies, and survey research to investigate gender differences in aggressive behavior at the workplace? First state a hypothesis and then describe your research approaches. What positive and negative features does each method have?

Answers to Evaluate Questions 1. theory; 2. hypothesis; 3. operational; 4. 1-b, 2-c, 3-a, 4-d; 5. 1-c, 2-b, 3-d, 4-a; 6. independent, dependent; 7. control

KEY TERMS

Scientific method LO3.1

Theories LO3.1

Hypothesis LO3.1

Operational definition LO3.1

Descriptive research LO3.3

Archival research LO3.3

Naturalistic observation LO3.3

Survey research LO3.3

Case study LO3.3

Variables LO3.3

Correlational research LO3.3

Experiment LO3.4

Experimental manipulation LO3.4

Treatment LO3.4

Experimental group LO3.4

Control group LO3.4

Independent variable LO3.4

Dependent variable LO3.4

Random assignment to condition LO3.4

Replication LO3.4

module 4

Research Challenges
Exploring the Process

Learning Outcomes

>> **LO4.1** Explain the major ethical issues that confront psychologists conducting research.

>> **LO4.2** Discuss the issues related to testing on animals.

>> **LO4.3** Identify threats to experimental validity.

MODULE OUTLINE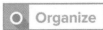

The Ethics of Research

Exploring Diversity: Choosing Participants Who Represent the Scope of Human Behavior

Should Animals Be Used in Research?

Threats to Experimental Validity: Avoiding Experimental Bias

Becoming an Informed Consumer of Psychology: Thinking Critically about Research

You probably realize by now that there are few simple formulas for psychological research. Psychologists must make choices about the type of study to conduct, the measures to take, and the most effective way to analyze the results. Even after they have made these essential decisions, they must still consider several critical issues. We turn first to the most fundamental of these issues: ethics.

>> LO4.1 The Ethics of Research

Because research has the potential to violate the rights of participants, psychologists are expected to adhere to a strict set of ethical guidelines aimed at protecting participants (American Psychological Association, 2002). Those guidelines involve the following safeguards:

informed consent A document signed by participants affirming that they have been told the basic outlines of the study and are aware of what their participation will involve

- Protection of participants from physical and mental harm
- The right of participants to privacy regarding their behavior
- The assurance that participation in research is completely voluntary
- The necessity of informing participants about the nature of procedures before their participation in the experiment

All experiments must be reviewed by an independent panel before being conducted, including the minority of studies that involve deception (Fisher, 2003; Smith, 2003; Nagy, 2011; Crano, Brewer & Lac, 2015).

One of psychologists' key ethical principles is **informed consent.** Before participating in an experiment, the participants must sign a document affirming that they have been told the basic outlines of the study and are aware of what their participation will involve, what risks the experiment may hold, and the fact that their participation is purely voluntary and they may terminate it at any time. Furthermore, after participation in a study, they must be given a debriefing in

STUDY ALERT

Because protection of participants is so essential, it is important to understand the key ethical guidelines that underlie research.

which they receive an explanation of the study and the procedures that were involved. The only time informed consent and a debriefing can be eliminated is in experiments in which the risks are minimal, as in a purely observational study in a public place (Fallon, 2006; Barnett, Wise, & Johnson-Greene, 2007; Albala, Doyle, & Appelbaum, 2010).

EXPLORING diversity

Choosing Participants Who Represent the Scope of Human Behavior

College students are used so frequently in experiments that psychology has been called—somewhat contemptuously—the "science of the behavior of the college sophomore." Using college students as participants has both advantages and drawbacks. The big benefit is that because most research occurs in university settings, college students are readily available. Typically, they cost the researcher very little: they participate for either extra course credit or a relatively small payment.

The problem is that college students may not represent the general population adequately. In fact, undergraduate research participants are typically a special group of people: relative to the general population, college students tend to be from **W**estern, **e**ducated, **i**ndustrialized, **r**ich, and **d**emocratic cultures. That description forms the acronym WEIRD, which led one researcher to apply the nickname to research participants (Jones, 2010; Lancy, 2015).

It's not that there's anything particularly wrong with WEIRD participants. It's just that they may be different from most other people—those who don't go to college or who didn't grow up in a democratic Western culture, who are less affluent, and so forth. All these characteristics could be psychologically relevant. Yet one review found that most research participants do come from the United States, and about the same proportion of those are psychology majors (Arnett, 2008; Henrich, Heine, & Norenzayan, 2010).

Because psychology is a science that purports to explain human behavior in general, something is therefore amiss. Consequently, psychological researchers have become increasingly sensitive to the importance of using participants who are fully representative of the general population. Furthermore, the National Institute of Mental Health and the National Science Foundation—the primary U.S. funding sources for psychological research—now require that experiments address issues of diverse populations (Carpenter, 2002; Lindley, 2006).

Although readily available and widely used as research participants, college students may not represent the population at large. What are some advantages and drawbacks of using college students as subjects? © Thomas Pflaum/Visum/The Image Works

» LO4.2 Should Animals Be Used in Research?

Like those who work with humans, researchers who use nonhuman animals in experiments have their own set of exacting guidelines to ensure that the animals do not suffer. Specifically, researchers must make every effort to minimize discomfort, illness, and pain. Procedures that subject animals to distress are permitted only when an alternative procedure is unavailable and when the research is justified by its prospective value. Moreover, researchers strive to

Research involving animals is controversial, but when conducted within ethical guidelines, yields significant benefits to humans. © Douglas Faulkner/Science Source

avoid causing physical discomfort, but they are also required to promote the psychological well-being of some species of research animals, such as primates (Lutz & Novak, 2005; Auer et al., 2007; Pagani, Robustelli, & Ascione, 2010).

But why should animals be used for research in the first place? Is it really possible to learn about human behavior from the results of research employing rats, gerbils, and pigeons?

The answer is that psychological research that does employ nonhumans is designed to answer questions different from those posed in research with humans. For example, the shorter life span of animals (rats live an average of two years) allows researchers to learn about the effects of aging in a relatively short time frame. It is also possible to provide greater experimental control over nonhumans and to carry out procedures that might not be possible with people. For example, some studies require large numbers of participants that share similar backgrounds or have been exposed to particular environments—conditions that could not practically be met with human beings.

Research with animals has provided psychologists with information that has benefited humans in important ways. For instance, it furnished the keys to detecting eye disorders in children early enough to prevent permanent damage; to communicating more effectively with children with severe intellectual disabilities; and to reducing chronic pain in people. Still, the use of research using nonhumans is controversial, involving complex moral and philosophical concerns. Consequently, all research involving nonhumans must be carefully reviewed beforehand to ensure that it is conducted ethically (Shankar & Simmons, 2009; Baker & Serdikoff, 2013; Grundy, 2015).

» LO4.3 Threats to Experimental Validity: Avoiding Experimental Bias

experimental bias Factors that distort how the independent variable affects the dependent variable in an experiment

Even the best-laid experimental plans are susceptible to **experimental bias**—factors that distort the way the independent variable affects the dependent variable in an experiment. One of the most common forms of experimental bias is *experimenter expectations:* an experimenter unintentionally transmits cues to participants about the way the experimenter expects them to behave. The danger is that those expectations actually cause the expected result to happen—results that otherwise might not have occurred (Rosenthal, 2002, 2003).

A related problem is *participant expectations.* If you have ever been a participant in an experiment, you know that you quickly develop guesses about what is expected of you. In fact, it is typical for people to develop their own hypotheses about what the experimenter hopes to learn from the study. If participants form their own hypotheses, it may be the participant's expectations, rather than the experimental manipulation, that produce an effect (Rutherford et al., 2009). To guard against participant expectations biasing the results of an experiment, the experimenter may try to disguise the true purpose of the experiment. Participants who do not know that helping behavior is being studied, for example, are more apt to act in a "natural" way than they would if they knew.

Sometimes it is impossible to hide the actual purpose of research; when that is the case, other techniques are available to prevent bias. Suppose you were interested in testing the ability of a new drug to alleviate the symptoms of severe depression. If you simply gave the drug to half your participants and not to the other half, the participants who were given the drug might report feeling less depressed merely because they knew they were getting a drug. Similarly, the participants who got nothing might report feeling no better because they knew that they were in a no-treatment control group.

To solve this problem, psychologists typically use a procedure in which all the participants receive a treatment, but those in the control group receive only a **placebo,** a false treatment, such as a pill, "drug," or other substance, that has no significant chemical properties or active ingredient. Because members of both groups are kept in the dark about whether they are getting a real or a false treatment, any differences in outcome can be attributed to the quality of the drug and not to the possible psychological effects of being administered a pill or other substance (Rajagopal, 2006; Crum & Langer, 2007; Bensing & Verheul, 2010; Porto, 2011).

However, there is one more safeguard that a careful researcher must apply in an experiment such as this one. To overcome the possibility that experimenter expectations will affect the participant, the person who administers the drug shouldn't know whether it is actually the true drug or the placebo. By keeping both the participant and the experimenter who interacts with the participant "blind" to the nature of the drug that is being administered, researchers can more accurately assess the effects of the drug. This method is known as the *double-blind procedure.*

STUDY ALERT

It's important to know the main types of potential bias in experiments: experimenter expectations and placebo effects.

placebo A false treatment, such as a pill, "drug," or other substance, without any significant chemical properties or active ingredient

becoming an informed consumer
of psychology

Thinking Critically about Research

If you were about to purchase an automobile, it is unlikely that you would stop at the nearest car dealership and drive off with the first car a salesperson recommended. Instead, you would probably mull over the purchase, read about automobiles, consider the alternatives, talk to others about their experiences, and ultimately put in a fair amount of thought before you made such a major purchase.

In contrast, many of us are considerably less conscientious when we hear about research findings. People often jump to conclusions on the basis of incomplete and inaccurate information, and only rarely do they take the time to critically evaluate the research and data to which they are exposed.

Because the field of psychology is based on an accumulated body of research, it is crucial to scrutinize thoroughly the methods, results, and claims of researchers. Several basic questions can help us sort through what is valid and what is not. Among the most important questions to ask are the following:

- What was the purpose of the research? Research studies should evolve from a clearly specified theory. Furthermore, we must take into account the specific hypothesis that is being tested. Unless we know what hypothesis is being examined, it is not possible to judge how successful a study has been.

- How well was the study conducted? Consider who the participants were, how many were involved, what methods were employed, and what problems the researcher encountered in collecting the data. There are important differences, for example, between a case study that reports the anecdotes of a handful of respondents and a survey that collects data from several thousand people.

- Are the results presented fairly? It is necessary to assess statements on the basis of the actual data they reflect and their logic. For instance, when the manufacturer of car X boasts that "no other car has a better safety record than car X," this does not mean that car X is safer than every other car. It just means that no other car has been proved safer, though many other cars could be just as safe as car X. Expressed in the latter fashion, the finding doesn't seem worth bragging about.

These three basic questions can help you assess the validity of research findings you come across—both within and outside the field of psychology. The more you know how to evaluate research, the better you will be able to assess what the field of psychology has to offer.

RECAP

Explain the major ethical issues that confront psychologists conducting research.

- One of the key ethical principles followed by psychologists is that of informed consent. Participants must be informed, before participation, about the basic outline of the experiment and the risks and potential benefits of their participation.

Discuss the issues related to testing on animals.

- Although the use of college students as participants has the advantage of easy availability, there are drawbacks, too. For instance, students do not necessarily represent the population as a whole. The use of nonhuman animals as participants may also have costs in terms of the ability to generalize to humans, although the benefits of using animals in research have been profound.

Identify threats to experimental validity.

- Experiments are subject to a number of biases, or threats. Experimenter expectations can produce bias when an experimenter unintentionally transmits cues to participants about her or his expectations regarding their behavior in a given experimental condition. Participant expectations can also bias an experiment. Among the tools experimenters use to help eliminate bias are placebos and double-blind procedures.

[EVALUATE E Evaluate]

1. Ethical research begins with the concept of informed consent. Before signing up to participate in an experiment, participants should be informed of which of the following?

    a. The procedure of the study, stated generally.

    b. The risks that may be involved.

    c. Their right to withdraw at any time.

    d. All of the above.

2. List three benefits of using animals in psychological research.

3. Deception is one means experimenters can use to try to eliminate participants' expectations. True or false?

4. A false treatment, such as a pill, that has no significant chemical properties or active ingredient, is known as a _____.

5. According to a report, a study has shown that men differ from women in their preference for ice cream flavors. This study was based on a sample of two men and three women. What might be wrong with this study?

[RETHINK R Rethink]

A researcher strongly believes that physicians tend to show female nurses less attention and respect than they show male nurses. She sets up an experimental study involving observations of health clinics in different conditions. In explaining the study to the physicians and nurses who will participate, what steps should the researcher take to eliminate experimental bias based on both experimenter expectations and participant expectations?

Answers to Evaluate Questions 1. d; 2. (1) We can study some phenomena in animals more easily than we can in people, because with animal subjects we have greater control over environmental and genetic factors. (2) Large numbers of similar participants can be easily obtained. (3) We can look at generational effects much more easily in animals, because of their shorter life span, than we can with people; 3. true; 4. placebo; 5. There are far too few participants. Without a larger sample, no valid conclusions can be drawn about ice cream preferences based on gender.

KEY TERMS

Informed consent   LO4.1

Experimental bias   LO4.3

Placebo   LO4.3

Looking Back

Psychology on the Web

1. Practice using several search strategies to find information on the Web about one of the key issues in psychology (e.g., free will versus determinism, nature versus nurture, or conscious versus unconscious determinants of behavior), using (a) a general-purpose search engine (such as Google at www.google.com) and (b) a more specialized search engine (such as Yahoo!'s Psychology section, under the "Social Science" heading, at www.yahoo.com). Summarize and then compare the kinds of information you have found through each strategy.

2. Search the Web for discussions of youth violence and try to find (a) an article in the general news media, (b) information from a psychological point of view (e.g., experimental information or recommendations for parents from a professional organization), and (c) political opinion or debate about how to address the issue of youth violence.

the case of . . .

CONFUSION

Alexis Dempsey had often wished that she could understand herself better. But the fight with her boyfriend the previous night really made her wonder what was driving her behavior. For no real reason at all, she had gotten annoyed with him at a party and had begun to criticize him. When he responded by asking her what her problem was, she had gotten really angry. She shouted at him that he was a total loser and that she didn't want to see him again. She stormed out of the party and had gone home.

By the time she reached home, though, she was miserable. She really did like her boyfriend, and she didn't want to end the relationship. She wondered why she'd gotten into the fight and why, in general, she was acting more and more aggressively with others. She wished she could find a way to reduce her combativeness and strengthen her relationships with important people in her life. She has gotten some random insights from browsing the Web and looking at some of the self-help books at her local bookstore, but mostly she ended up being confused.

1. What subfields of psychology might be of greatest relevance to Alexis's problem, and why?

2. If Alexis were to seek practical advice about making changes in her own life, which perspectives on psychology do you think would be most helpful, and why?

3. What do you think about Alexis's strategy of surfing the Web and looking at self-help books at the bookstore to better understand herself? What are the dangers of this approach?

4. What advice would you give Alexis to help her solve her problem?

profiles of SUCCESS

Courtesy of Mishica A. Stephans

NAME: **Mishica A. Stephans**

SCHOOL: **Miller-Motte Technical College (MMTC)**

DEGREE PROGRAMS: **AAS, Medical Assisting; BS, Allied Health Management**

When you are a single parent with six children, life can be a challenge. But when you then make the decision to pursue higher education, you need to quickly learn to adapt and meet those challenges head on.

"It is difficult, and I wouldn't dare say there is one method or way that works," said Mishica Stephans, who chose Miller-Motte Technical School for its flexibility and small classes.

"You have to schedule school time as a job, and unless there is an extreme emergency, stick to that schedule," she noted. "I had to sacrifice my personal time for school time in order to achieve the goals that I set for myself and my family."

Currently pursuing a BS degree, Stephans recalls her earlier years managing school and family.

"I found early that incorporating my children into my studying plan was a great idea. For example, I would go to the bookstore with the children, and they would entertain themselves with books while I would study or do research for an assignment," she said. "I would even review notes in the grocery line. Waiting anywhere would become review time for studying materials for my classes."

Making use of spare time anywhere and anytime became part of Stephans's dedication to pursuing a college degree and led to her personal motto: "My success is determined by my dedication"

"If you are struggling academically don't be afraid to ask for help, and utilize the resources that are available. People are always willing to help, however they don't know what you need if you don't say anything. When I needed help, I asked and found the resources to get an assignment accomplished," Stephans added.

For Stephans, school provided more than an education; it provided an insight into what she herself is capable of doing.

"I learned that my parents were right: I can do and be anything I set my mind to," she said. "I also learned that there is an inner strength that refuses to give up. As a result of the things I have learned, I pay it forward by helping and encouraging others that want to succeed in continuing their education."

[RETHINK R Rethink]

Do you think that psychologists would agree that people can do anything they set their minds to? Why or why not?

What kind of psychologist might study questions relating to persistence at academic tasks?

visual summary 1
INTRODUCTION TO PSYCHOLOGY

MODULE 1 Psychologists at Work

Subfields of Psychology

- Biological foundations
  - Behavioral neuroscience
- Sensing, perceiving, learning, and thinking
  - Experimental and cognitive psychology
- Sources of change and stability
  - Development and personality psychology
- Physical and mental health
  - Health, clinical, and counseling psychology
- Social networks
  - Social and cross-cultural psychology
- Expanding frontiers
  - Evolutionary psychology
  - Behavioral genetics
  - Clinical neuropsychology

Working at Psychology

- Where U.S. psychologists work

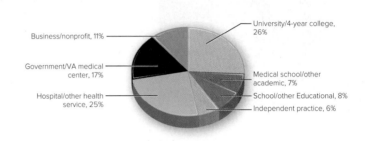

University/4-year college, 26%
Business/nonprofit, 11%
Government/VA medical center, 17%
Medical school/other academic, 7%
Hospital/other health service, 25%
School/other Educational, 8%
Independent practice, 6%

MODULE 2 A Science Evolves

Roots

- Structuralism
- Functionalism

Today's Five Major Perspectives

Neuroscience
Views behavior from the perspective of biological functioning

Behavioral
Focuses on observable behavior

Psychodynamic
Believes behavior is motivated by inner, unconscious forces over which a person has little control

Cognitive
Examines how people understand and think about the world

Humanistic
Contends that people can control their behavior and that they naturally try to reach their full potential

MODULE 3 Research in Psychology

Scientific Method

- Theories: Broad explanations
- Hypotheses: Testable predictions

Descriptive Research: Describes variables and does not explain causality

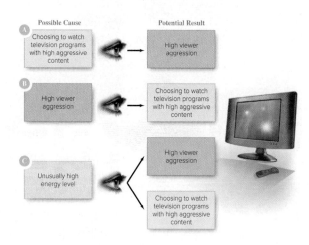

Experimental Research: Assesses cause-and-effect relationships between variables

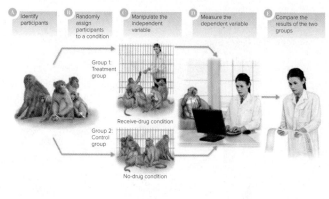

MODULE 4 Research Challenges

Ethics of Research: Informed consent

Animal Research: Has significantly benefited humans

Threats to Validity

- Experimental bias
- Participant and experimenter expectations

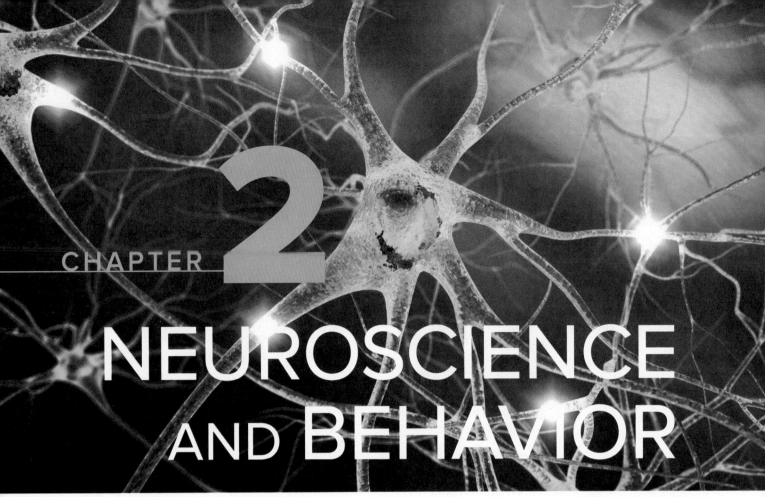

© SCIEPRO/Getty Images RF

CHAPTER **2**

NEUROSCIENCE AND BEHAVIOR

CHAPTER OUTLINE

Rebooting Her System

Jaime Russell-Polhemus, mother of three and manager of a small business, began to experience back pain, stiffness, and fatigue. Soon, she was suffering from abnormal heart rate, low blood pressure, and tremors. Two years later, any sound, touch, or emotional stress triggered painful, intense muscle spasms. Jaime was diagnosed with Stiff Person Syndrome, a rare neurological disorder. To treat this progressive and deadly autoimmune disease, she was given a course of strong drugs, which was only partially effective. She then entered trials for a new autoimmune disease treatment—a stem cell transplant—at Northwestern University. Her stem cells were harvested, then re-implanted after her diseased immune system was treated with chemo. The hope? The stem cells will reprogram her "cleaned up" immune system to function properly again (Renken, 2015).

Jaime's mysterious and devastating disorder appears to be the result of one particular antibody improperly interfering with an important neurotransmitter in the brain. Although it is too early to know if her revolutionary treatment has been able to "reboot" Jaime's immune system and return a normal life to her, her medical team is optimistic.

Looking
Ahead

Rapid advances in research on the brain are making what once were mere dreams a reality, and it is increasingly difficult to rule out anything when it comes to the workings of the human brain. The brain, an organ roughly half the size of a loaf of bread, controls our physical, emotional, and intellectual behavior through every waking and sleeping moment. Our movements, thoughts, hopes, aspirations, dreams—our very awareness that we are human—all depend on the brain and the nerves that extend throughout the body, constituting the nervous system.

Because of the importance of the nervous system in controlling behavior, and because humans at their most basic level are biological beings, many researchers in psychology and other fields as diverse as computer science, zoology, and medicine have made the biological underpinnings of behavior their specialty. These experts collectively are called neuroscientists (Gazzaniga, Ivry, & Mangun, 2002; Cartwright, 2006; Pickersgill, 2011).

Psychologists who specialize in considering the ways in which the biological structures and functions of the body affect behavior are known as **behavioral neuroscientists (or biopsychologists).** They seek to answer several key questions: How does the brain control the voluntary and involuntary functioning of the body? How does the brain communicate with other parts of the body? What is the physical structure of the brain, and how does this structure affect behavior? Are psychological disorders caused by biological factors, and how can such disorders be treated?

> **behavioral neuroscientists (or biopsychologists)** Psychologists who specialize in considering the ways in which the biological structures and functions of the body affect behavior

As you consider the biological processes that we'll discuss in this chapter, it is important to keep in mind why behavioral neuroscience is an essential part of psychology: our understanding of human behavior requires knowledge of the brain and other parts of the nervous system. Biological factors are central to our sensory experiences, states of consciousness, motivation and emotion, development throughout the life span, and physical and psychological health. Furthermore, advances in behavioral neuroscience have led to the creation of drugs and other treatments for psychological and physical disorders. In short, we cannot understand behavior without understanding our biological makeup (Gangestad, 2010; Everitt, 2014; Schlinger, 2015).

module 5

Neurons
The Basic Elements of Behavior

Learning Outcomes

» **LO5.1** Explain the structure of a neuron.

» **LO5.2** Describe how neurons fire.

» **LO5.3** Summarize how messages travel from one neuron to another.

» **LO5.4** Identify neurotransmitters.

MODULE OUTLINE

The Structure of the Neuron

How Neurons Fire

Where Neurons Connect to One Another: Bridging the Gap

Neurotransmitters: Multitalented Chemical Couriers

The nervous system is the pathway for the instructions that permit our bodies to carry out everyday activities such as scratching an itch as well as more remarkable skills like climbing to the top of Mount Everest. Here we will look at the structure and function of neurons, the cells that make up the nervous system, including the brain.

» LO5.1 The Structure of the Neuron

Playing the piano, driving a car, or hitting a tennis ball depend, at one level, on exact muscle coordination. But if we consider *how* the muscles can be activated so precisely, we see that there are more fundamental processes involved. For the muscles to produce the complex movements that make up any meaningful physical activity, the brain has to provide the right messages to them and coordinate those messages.

Such messages—as well as those which enable us to think, remember, and experience emotion—are passed through specialized cells called neurons. **Neurons,** or nerve cells, are the basic elements of the nervous system. Their quantity is staggering—perhaps as many as 1 *trillion* neurons throughout the body are involved in the control of behavior (Boahen, 2005).

Although there are several types of neurons, they all have a similar structure, as illustrated in Figure 1. In contrast to most other cells, however, neurons have a distinctive feature: the ability to communicate with other cells and transmit information across relatively long distances. Many of the body's neurons receive signals from the environment or relay the nervous system's messages to muscles and other target cells, but the vast majority of neurons communicate only with other neurons in the elaborate information system that regulates behavior.

As you can see in Figure 1, there's a cluster of fibers at the end of every neuron called dendrites. **Dendrites,** which look like the twisted branches of a tree, are

neurons Nerve cells, the basic elements of the nervous system

dendrite A cluster of fibers at one end of a neuron that receive messages from other neurons

STUDY ALERT

Remember that *dendrites detect* messages from other neurons; *axons* carry signals *away* from the cell body.

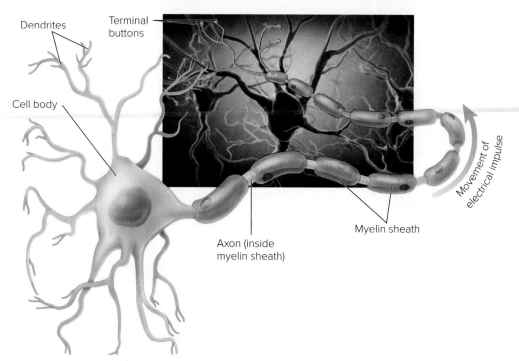

Dendrites

Terminal buttons

Cell body

Axon (inside myelin sheath)

Myelin sheath

Movement of electrical impulse

Figure 1 The primary components of the specialized cell called the neuron, the basic element of the nervous system. A neuron, like most types of cells in the body, has a cell body and a nucleus, but it also contains structures that carry messages: the dendrites, which receive messages from other neurons, and the axon, which carries messages to other neurons or body cells. In this neuron, as in most neurons, the axon is protected by the sausagelike myelin sheath. What advantages does the treelike structure of the neuron provide? Source: Van De Graaff, 2000; © Science Picture Co/Science Source

the part of the neuron that receives messages from other neurons. On the opposite side of every neuron is a long, slim, tubelike extension called an **axon.** The axon carries messages received by the dendrites to other neurons. The axon is considerably longer than the rest of the neuron. Although most axons are several millimeters in length, some are as long as three feet. Axons end in small bulges called **terminal buttons,** which send messages to other neurons.

The messages that travel through a neuron are electrical in nature. Although there are exceptions, those electrical messages, or *impulses,* generally move across neurons in one direction only, as if they were traveling on a one-way street. Impulses follow a route that begins with the dendrites, continues into the cell body, and leads ultimately along the tubelike extension, the axon, to adjacent neurons.

To prevent messages from short-circuiting one another, axons must be insulated in some fashion (just as electrical wires must be insulated). Most axons are insulated by a **myelin sheath,** a protective coating of fat and protein that wraps around the axon like links of sausage.

axon The part of the neuron that carries messages destined for other neurons

terminal buttons Small bulges at the end of axons that send messages to other neurons

myelin sheath A protective coat of fat and protein that wraps around the neuron

all-or-none law The rule that neurons are either on or off

resting state The state in which there is a negative electrical charge of about −70 millivolts within a neuron

≫ LO5.2 How Neurons Fire

Like a gun, neurons either fire—that is, transmit an electrical impulse along the axon—or don't fire. There is no in-between stage, just as pulling harder on a gun trigger doesn't make the bullet travel faster. Similarly, neurons follow an **all-or-none law:** they are either on or off, with nothing in between the on state and the off state. Once there is enough force to pull the trigger, a neuron fires.

Before a neuron is triggered—that is, when it is in a **resting state**—it has a negative electrical charge of about −70 millivolts. When a message arrives at a neuron, gates along the cell membrane open briefly to allow positively charged ions to rush in at rates as high as 100 million ions per second. The sudden arrival of these positive ions causes the charge within the nearby part of the cell to change momentarily from negative to positive. When the positive charge

STUDY ALERT

Think of a neuron as a sausage, and the myelin sheath as the case around it.

Figure 2 Movement of the action potential across the axon. Just before Time 1, positively charged ions enter the cell membrane, changing the charge in the nearby part of the neuron from negative to positive and triggering an action potential. The action potential travels along the axon, as illustrated in the changes occurring from Time 1 to Time 3 (from top to bottom in this drawing). Immediately after the action potential has passed through a section of the axon, positive ions are pumped out, restoring the charge in that section to negative.

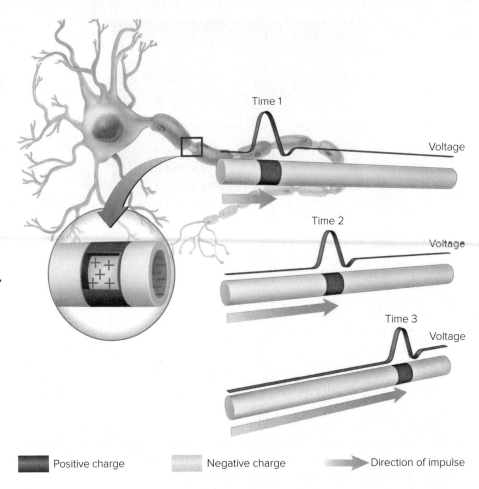

Time 1   Voltage

Time 2   Voltage

Time 3   Voltage

■ Positive charge   ■ Negative charge   ➡ Direction of impulse

action potential An electric nerve impulse that travels through a neuron when it is set off by a "trigger," changing the neuron's charge from negative to positive

mirror neurons Specialized neurons that fire not only when a person enacts a particular behavior, but also when a person simply observes *another* individual carrying out the same behavior

reaches a critical level, the "trigger" is pulled, and an electrical impulse, known as an action potential, travels along the axon of the neuron (see Figure 2).

The **action potential** moves from one end of the axon to the other like a flame moving along a fuse. Just after an action potential has occurred, a neuron cannot fire again immediately no matter how much stimulation it receives. It is as if the gun has to be reloaded after each shot. Eventually, though, the neuron is ready to fire once again.

Neurons differ not only in terms of how quickly an impulse moves along the axon but also in their potential rate of firing. Some neurons are capable of firing as many as a thousand times per second; others fire at much slower rates. The intensity of a stimulus determines how much of a neuron's potential firing rate is reached. A strong stimulus, such as a bright light or a loud sound, leads to a higher rate of firing than a less intense stimulus does. Thus, even though all impulses move at the same strength or speed through a particular axon—because of the all-or-none law—there is variation in the frequency of impulses, providing a mechanism by which we can distinguish the tickle of a feather from the weight of someone standing on our toes.

Although all neurons operate through the firing of action potentials, there is significant specialization among different types of neurons. For example, in the last decade, neuroscientists have discovered the existence of **mirror neurons,** neurons that fire not only when a person enacts a particular behavior, but also when a person simply observes *another* individual carrying out the same behavior (Schermer, 2010; Khalil, 2011; Spaulding, 2013; Brucker et al., 2015).

Mirror neurons may help explain how (and why) humans have the capacity to understand others' intentions. Specifically, mirror neurons may fire when we view others' behavior, helping us to predict what their goals are and what they may do next (Hickok, 2010; Avenanti & Urgesi, 2011).

» LO5.3 Where Neurons Connect to One Another: Bridging the Gap

If you have looked inside a computer, you've seen that each part is physically connected to another part. In contrast, evolution has produced a neural transmission system that at some points has no need for a structural connection between its components. Instead, a chemical connection bridges the gap, known as a synapse, between two neurons (see Figure 3). The **synapse** is the space between two neurons where the axon of a sending neuron communicates with the dendrites of a receiving neuron by using chemical messages.

When a nerve impulse comes to the end of the axon and reaches a terminal button, the terminal button releases a chemical courier called a neurotransmitter. **Neurotransmitters** are chemicals that carry messages across the synapse

synapse The space between two neurons where the axon of a sending neuron communicates with the dendrites of a receiving neuron by using chemical messages

neurotransmitters Chemicals that carry messages across the synapse to the dendrite (and sometimes the cell body) of a receiver neuron

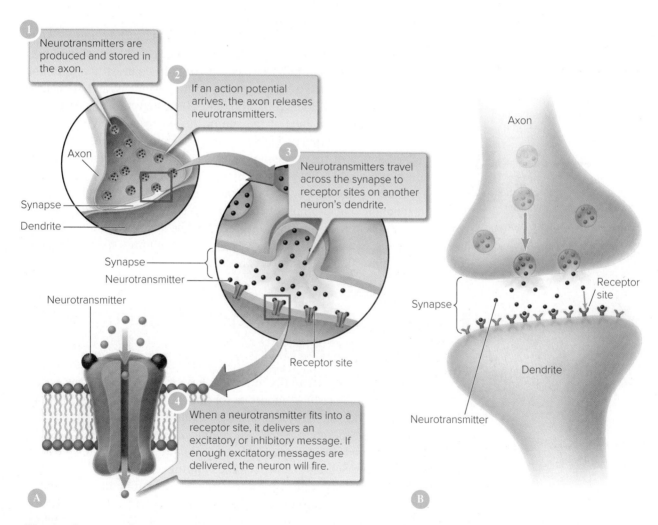

1 Neurotransmitters are produced and stored in the axon.

2 If an action potential arrives, the axon releases neurotransmitters.

3 Neurotransmitters travel across the synapse to receptor sites on another neuron's dendrite.

4 When a neurotransmitter fits into a receptor site, it delivers an excitatory or inhibitory message. If enough excitatory messages are delivered, the neuron will fire.

Axon
Synapse
Dendrite
Synapse
Neurotransmitter
Neurotransmitter
Receptor site

Axon
Synapse
Receptor site
Dendrite
Neurotransmitter

A   B

Figure 3   (A) A synapse is the junction between an axon and a dendrite. The gap between the axon and the dendrite is bridged by chemicals called neurotransmitters (Mader, 2000). (B) Just as the pieces of a jigsaw puzzle can fit in only one specific location in a puzzle, each kind of neurotransmitter has a distinctive configuration that allows it to fit into a specific type of receptor cell (Johnson, 2000). Why is it advantageous for axons and dendrites to be linked by temporary chemical bridges rather than by the hard wiring typical of a radio connection or telephone landline?

© David Muir/Getty Images

to a dendrite (and sometimes the cell body) of a receiving neuron. The chemical mode of message transmission that occurs between neurons is strikingly different from the means by which communication occurs inside neurons: although messages travel in electrical form *within* a neuron, they move *between* neurons through a chemical transmission system.

There are several types of neurotransmitters, and not all neurons are capable of receiving the chemical message carried by a particular neurotransmitter. In the same way that a jigsaw puzzle piece can fit in only one specific location in a puzzle, each kind of neurotransmitter has a distinctive configuration that allows it to fit into a specific type of receptor site on the receiving neuron (see Figure 3B). It is only when a neurotransmitter fits precisely into a receptor site that successful chemical communication is possible.

If a neurotransmitter does fit into a site on the receiving neuron, the chemical message it delivers is basically one of two types: excitatory or inhibitory. **Excitatory messages** are chemical messages that make it more likely that a receiving neuron will fire and an action potential will travel down its axon. In contrast, **inhibitory messages** do just the opposite; they provide chemical information that prevents or decreases the likelihood that the receiving neuron will fire.

Because the dendrites of a neuron receive both excitatory and inhibitory messages simultaneously, the neuron must integrate the messages by using a kind of chemical calculator. Put simply, if the excitatory messages ("fire!") outnumber the inhibitory ones ("don't fire!"), the neuron fires. In contrast, if the inhibitory messages outnumber the excitatory ones, nothing happens, and the neuron remains in its resting state (Mel, 2002; Rapport, 2005; Flavell et al., 2006;).

If neurotransmitters remained at the site of the synapse, receiving neurons would be a wash in a continual chemical bath, producing constant stimulation or constant inhibition of the receiving neurons—and effective communication across the synapse would no longer be possible. To solve this problem, neurotransmitters are either deactivated by enzymes or—more commonly—reabsorbed by the terminal button in an example of chemical recycling called **reuptake.** Like a vacuum cleaner sucking up dust, neurons reabsorb the neurotransmitters that are now clogging the synapse. All this activity occurs at lightning speed (Helmuth, 2000; Holt & Jahn, 2004; Cupertino et al., 2016).

excitatory messages Chemical messages that make it more likely that a receiving neuron will fire and an action potential will travel down its axon

inhibitory messages Chemical messages that prevent or decrease the likelihood that a receiving neuron will fire

reuptake The reabsorption of neurotransmitters by a terminal button

》LO5.4 Neurotransmitters: Multitalented Chemical Couriers

Neurotransmitters are a particularly important link between the nervous system and behavior. Not only are they important for maintaining vital brain and body functions, a deficiency or an excess of a neurotransmitter can produce severe behavior disorders. More than a hundred chemicals have been found to act as neurotransmitters, and neuroscientists believe that more may ultimately be identified (Penney, 2000; Schmidt, 2006; Alix & Domingues, 2011).

Neurotransmitters vary significantly in terms of how strong their concentration must be to trigger a neuron to fire. Furthermore, the effects of a particular neurotransmitter vary, depending on the area of the nervous system in which it is produced. The same neurotransmitter, then, can act as an excitatory message to a neuron located in one part of the brain and can inhibit firing in neurons located in another part. (The major neurotransmitters and their effects are described in Figure 4.)

Dopamine Pathways	Name	Location	Effect	Function
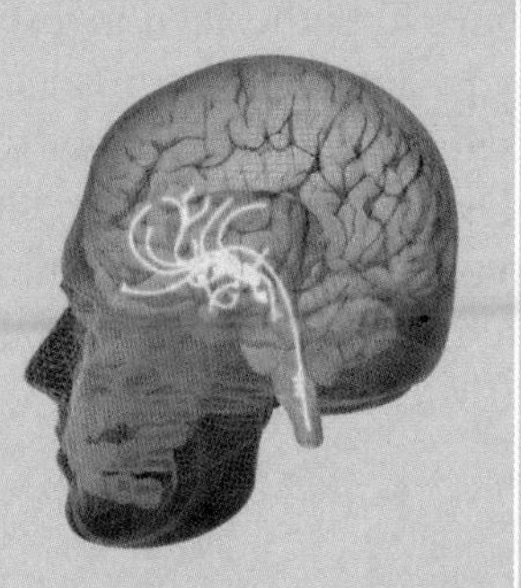	Acetylcholine (ACh)	Brain, spinal cord, peripheral nervous system, especially some organs of the parasympathetic nervous system	Excitatory in brain and autonomic nervous system; inhibitory elsewhere	Muscle movement, cognitive functioning
	Glutamate	Brain, spinal cord	Excitatory	Memory
	Gamma-amino-butyric acid (GABA)	Brain, spinal cord	Main inhibitory neurotransmitter	Eating, aggression, sleeping
Serotonin Pathways	Dopamine (DA)	Brain	Inhibitory or excitatory	Movement, attention, and learning
	Serotonin	Brain, spinal cord	Inhibitory	Sleeping, eating, mood, pain, depression
	Endorphins	Brain, spinal cord	Primarily inhibitory, except in hippocampus	Pain suppression, pleasurable feelings, appetites, placebos

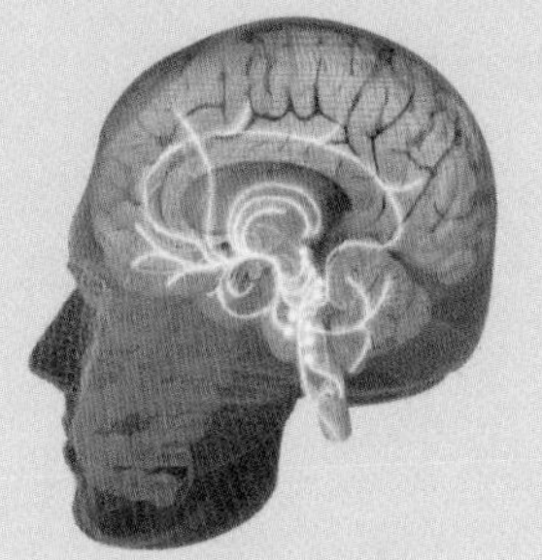

Figure 4   Some major neurotransmitters.

One of the most common neurotransmitters is *acetylcholine* (or *ACh,* its chemical symbol), which is found throughout the nervous system. ACh is involved in our every move, because—among other things—it transmits messages relating to our skeletal muscles. ACh is also involved in memory capabilities, and diminished production of ACh may be related to Alzheimer's disease (Bazalakova et al., 2007; Del Arco et al., 2010; Van der Zee, Platt, & Riedel, 2011).

Another major neurotransmitter is *dopamine (DA),* which is involved in movement, attention, and learning. The discovery that certain drugs can have a significant effect on dopamine release has led to the development of effective treatments for a wide variety of physical and mental ailments. For instance, Parkinson's disease, from which actor Michael J. Fox suffers, is caused by a deficiency of dopamine in the brain. Techniques for increasing the production of dopamine in Parkinson's patients are proving effective (Iversen & Iversen, 2007; Antonini & Barone, 2008; Schmitt et al., 2016).

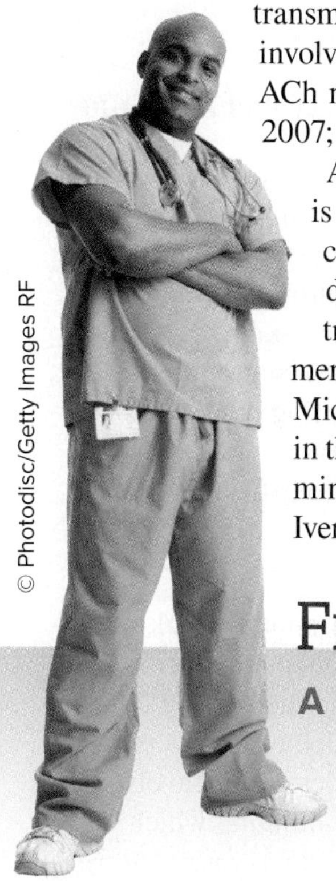

From the perspective of . . .

A Health Care Provider   How might your understanding of the nervous system help you explain the symptoms of Parkinson's disease to a patient with the disorder?

Actor Michael J. Fox, who suffers from Parkinson's disease, and his wife have become a strong advocates for research into the disorder. © Laura Cavanaugh/FilmMagic/Getty Images

In other instances, overproduction of dopamine is harmful. For example, researchers have hypothesized that schizophrenia and some other severe mental disturbances are affected or perhaps even caused by the presence of unusually high levels of dopamine. Drugs that block the reception of dopamine reduce the symptoms displayed by some people diagnosed with schizophrenia (Howes & Kapur, 2009; Seeman, 2011; Liddle et al., 2016).

RECAP

Explain the structure of a neuron.

- A neuron has a cell body (which contains a nucleus) with a cluster of fibers called dendrites, which receive messages from other neurons. On the opposite end of the cell body is a tubelike extension, an axon, which ends in a small bulge called a terminal button. Terminal buttons send messages to other neurons.

Describe how neurons fire.

- Most axons are insulated by a coating called the myelin sheath. When a neuron receives a message to fire, it releases an action potential, an electrical charge that travels through the axon. Neurons operate according to an all-or-none law: either they are at rest, or an action potential is moving through them. There is no in-between state.

Summarize how messages travel from one neuron to another.

- Once a neuron fires, nerve impulses are carried to other neurons through the production of chemical substances, neurotransmitters, that actually bridge the gaps—known as synapses—between neurons. Neurotransmitters may be either excitatory, telling other neurons to fire, or inhibitory, preventing or decreasing the likelihood of other neurons firing.

Identify neurotransmitters.

- Neurotransmitters are an important link between the nervous system and behavior. Common neurotransmitters include the following: *acetylcholine,* which transmits messages relating to our muscles and is involved in memory capabilities; *glutamate,* which plays a role in memory; *gamma-aminobutyric acid (GABA),* which moderates behaviors from eating to aggression; *dopamine,* which is involved in movement, attention, and learning; *serotonin,* which is associated with the regulation of sleep, eating, mood, and pain; and endorphins, which seem to be involved in the brain's effort to deal with pain and elevate mood.

[EVALUATE E Evaluate]

1. The _____ is the fundamental element of the nervous system.
2. Neurons receive information through their _____ and send messages through their _____.
3. Just as electrical wires have an outer coating, axons are insulated by a coating called the _____.
4. The gap between two neurons is bridged by a chemical connection called a _____.
5. Endorphins are one kind of _____, the chemical "messengers" between neurons.

[RETHINK R Rethink]

How might psychologists use drugs that mimic the effects of neurotransmitters to treat psychological disorders?

Answers to Evaluate Questions 1. neuron; 2. dendrites, axons; 3. myelin sheath; 4. synapse; 5. neurotransmitter

KEY TERMS

Behavioral neuroscientists (or biopsychologists) LO5.1

Neurons LO5.1

Dendrites LO5.1

Axon LO5.1

Terminal buttons LO5.1

Myelin sheath LO5.1

All-or-none law LO5.2

Resting state LO5.2

Action potential LO5.2

Mirror neurons LO5.2

Synapse LO5.3

Neurotransmitters LO5.3

Excitatory messages LO5.3

Inhibitory messages LO5.3

Reuptake LO5.3

The Nervous System and the Endocrine System
Communicating within the Body

W Work

**central nervous system
(CNS)** The part of the nervous
system that includes the brain
and spinal cord

spinal cord A bundle of
neurons that leaves the
brain and runs down the
length of the back and is the
main means for transmitting
messages between the brain
and the body

The complexity of the nervous system is astounding. Estimates of the number of connections between neurons within the brain fall in the neighborhood of 10 quadrillion—a 1 followed by 16 zeros. Furthermore, connections among neurons are not the only means of communication within the body; as we'll see, the endocrine system, which secretes chemical messages that circulate through the blood, also communicates messages that influence behavior and many aspects of biological functioning (Kandel, Schwartz, & Jessell, 2000; Boahen, 2005; Lynn et al., 2010).

>> LO6.1 The Nervous System

Whatever the actual number of neural connections, the human nervous system has both logic and elegance. We turn now to a discussion of its basic structures.

Central and Peripheral Nervous Systems

As you can see from the schematic representation in Figure 1, the nervous system is divided into two main parts: the central nervous system and the peripheral nervous system. The **central nervous system (CNS)** is composed of the brain and spinal cord. The **spinal cord,** which is about the thickness of a pencil, contains a bundle of neurons that leaves the brain and runs down the length of the back (see Figure 2). As you can see in Figure 1, the spinal cord is the primary means for transmitting messages between the brain and the rest of the body.

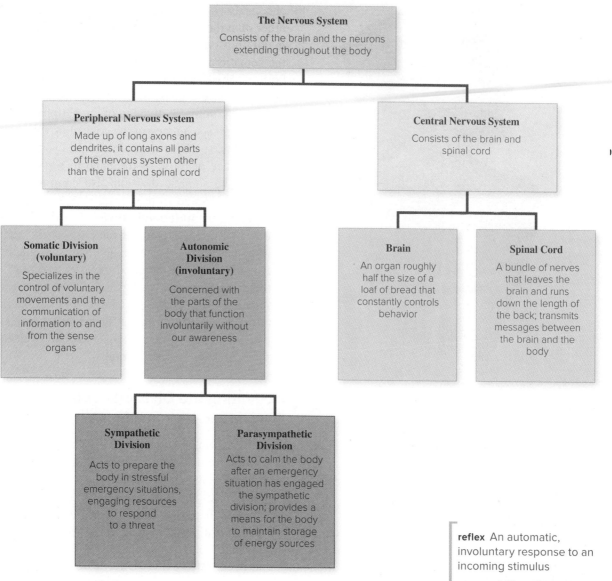

Figure 1 A schematic diagram of the relationship of the parts of the nervous system.

However, the spinal cord is not just a communication channel. It also controls some simple behaviors on its own, without any help from the brain. An example is the way the knee jerks forward when it is tapped with a rubber hammer. This behavior is a type of **reflex,** an automatic, involuntary response to an incoming stimulus. A reflex is also at work when you touch a hot stove and immediately withdraw your hand. Although the brain eventually analyzes and reacts to the situation ("Ouch—hot stove—pull away!"), the initial withdrawal is directed only by neurons in the spinal cord.

Three kinds of neurons are involved in reflexes. **Sensory (afferent) neurons** transmit information from the perimeter of the body to the central nervous system. **Motor (efferent) neurons** communicate information from the nervous system to muscles and glands. **Interneurons** connect sensory and motor neurons, carrying messages between the two.

As suggested by its name, the **peripheral nervous system** branches out from the spinal cord and brain and reaches the extremities of the body. Made up of neurons with long axons and dendrites, the peripheral nervous system

reflex An automatic, involuntary response to an incoming stimulus

sensory (afferent) neurons Neurons that transmit information from the perimeter of the body to the central nervous system

motor (efferent) neurons Neurons that communicate information from the nervous system to muscles and glands

interneurons Neurons that connect sensory and motor neurons, carrying messages between the two

peripheral nervous system The part of the nervous system that includes the autonomic and somatic subdivisions; made up of neurons with long axons and dendrites, it branches out from the spinal cord and brain and reaches the extremities of the body

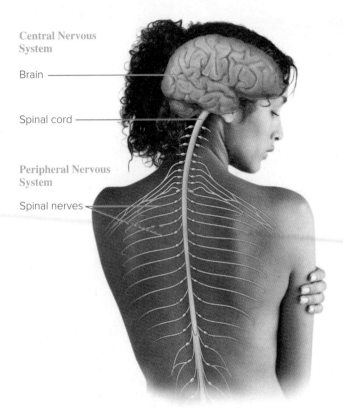

Central Nervous System

Brain

Spinal cord

Peripheral Nervous System

Spinal nerves

Figure 2 The central nervous system, consisting of the brain and spinal cord, and the peripheral nervous system.
© Larry Williams/Blend/Corbis RF

encompasses all the parts of the nervous system other than the brain and spinal cord. There are two major divisions of the peripheral nervous system—the somatic division and the autonomic division—both of which connect the central nervous system with the sense organs, muscles, glands, and other organs. The **somatic division** of the peripheral nervous system specializes in the control of voluntary movements, such as the motion of the eyes to read this sentence or those of the hand to scroll down a page. The somatic division also communicates information to and from the sense organs. On the other hand, the **autonomic division** of the peripheral nervous system controls the parts of the body that keep us alive—the heart, blood vessels, glands, lungs, and other organs that function involuntarily without our awareness. As you are reading at this moment, the autonomic division of the peripheral nervous system is pumping blood through your body, pushing your lungs in and out, and overseeing the digestion of your last meal.

Activating the Divisions of the Autonomic Nervous System

The autonomic division plays a particularly crucial role during emergencies. Suppose that as you are reading in bed you suddenly sense that someone is outside your bedroom window. As you look up, you see the glint of an object that might be a knife. As confusion and fear overcome you, what happens to your body? If you are like most people, you react immediately on a physiological level. Your heart rate increases, you begin to sweat, and you develop goose bumps all over your body.

The physiological changes that occur during a crisis result from the activation of one of the two parts of the autonomic nervous system: the **sympathetic division.** The sympathetic division acts to prepare the body for action in stressful situations by engaging all of the organism's resources to run away or confront the threat. This response is often called the "fight-or-flight" response.

In contrast, the **parasympathetic division** acts to calm the body after the emergency has ended. When you find, for instance, that the stranger at the window is actually your boyfriend who has lost his keys and is climbing in the window to avoid waking you, your parasympathetic division begins to predominate, lowering your heart rate, stopping your sweating, and returning your body to the state it was in before you became alarmed. The parasympathetic division also directs the body to store energy for use in emergencies. The sympathetic and parasympathetic divisions work together to regulate many functions of the body (see Figure 3).

Behavioral Genetics

Our personality and behavioral habits are affected in part by our genetic and evolutionary heritage. **Behavioral genetics** studies the effects of heredity on behavior. Behavioral genetics researchers are finding increasing evidence that cognitive abilities, personality traits, sexual orientation, and psychological

somatic division The part of the peripheral nervous system that specializes in the control of voluntary movements and the communication of information to and from the sense organs

autonomic division The part of the peripheral nervous system that controls involuntary movement of the heart, glands, lungs, and other organs

sympathetic division The part of the autonomic division of the nervous system that acts to prepare the body for action in stressful situations, engaging all the organism's resources to respond to a threat

parasympathetic division The part of the autonomic division of the nervous system that acts to calm the body after an emergency or a stressful situation has ended

behavioral genetics The study of the effects of heredity on behavior

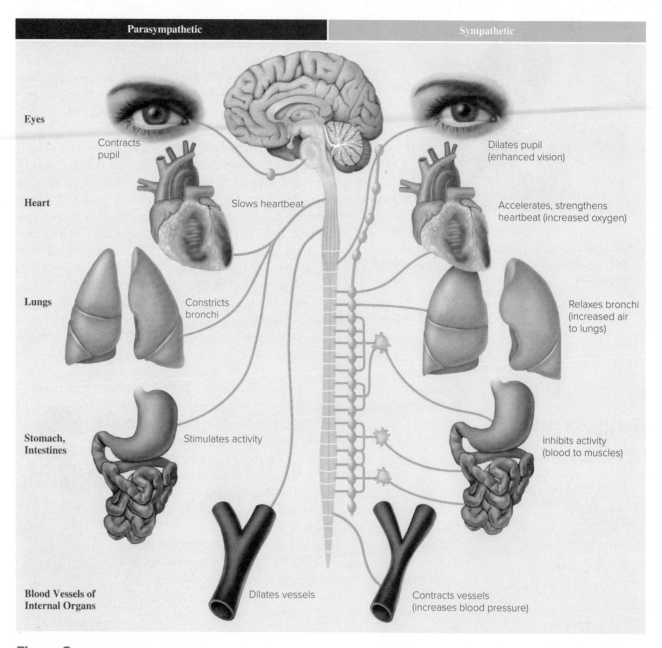

| Parasympathetic | Sympathetic |

Eyes
Contracts pupil — Dilates pupil (enhanced vision)

Heart
Slows heartbeat — Accelerates, strengthens heartbeat (increased oxygen)

Lungs
Constricts bronchi — Relaxes bronchi (increased air to lungs)

Stomach, Intestines
Stimulates activity — Inhibits activity (blood to muscles)

Blood Vessels of Internal Organs
Dilates vessels — Contracts vessels (increases blood pressure)

Figure 3 The major functions of the autonomic nervous system. The sympathetic division acts to prepare certain organs of the body for stressful situations, and the parasympathetic division acts to calm the body after the emergency has passed. Can you explain why each response of the sympathetic division might be useful in an emergency?
Source: Adapted from Passer & Smith, 2001.

disorders are determined to some extent by genetic factors (Vernon et al., 2008; O'Neill et al., 2010).

Behavioral genetics lies at the heart of the nature-nurture question, one of the key issues in the study of psychology. Although no one would argue that our behavior is determined *solely* by inherited factors, evidence collected by behavioral geneticists does suggest that our genetic inheritance predisposes us to respond in particular ways to our environment, and even to seek out particular kinds of environments. For instance, research indicates that genetic factors may be related to such diverse behaviors as level of family conflict, schizophrenia, learning disabilities, and general sociability (Davis, Haworth, & Plomin, 2009; Lakhan & Vieira, 2009; Gejman, Sanders & Duan, 2010).

Genetic testing can be done to determine potential risks to an unborn child based on family history of illness. © Gabriela Medina/Getty Images RF

Furthermore, important human characteristics and behaviors are related to the presence (or absence) of particular *genes,* the inherited material that controls the transmission of traits. For example, researchers have found evidence that novelty-seeking behavior is determined, at least in part, by a certain gene (Golimbet et al., 2007; Stedenfeld et al., 2011).

As we will consider later when we discuss human development, researchers have identified some 25,000 individual genes, each of which appears in a specific sequence on a particular *chromosome,* a rod-shaped structure that transmits genetic information across generations. In 2003, after a decade of effort, researchers identified the sequence of the 3 billion chemical pairs that make up human *DNA,* the basic component of genes. Understanding the basic structure of the human *genome*—the "map" of humans' total genetic makeup— brings scientists a giant step closer to understanding the contributions of individual genes to specific human structures and functioning (Dale & von Schantz, 2007; Plomin & Davis, 2009).

Behavioral Genetics, Gene Therapy, and Genetic Counseling. Behavioral genetics also holds the promise of developing new diagnostic and treatment techniques for genetic deficiencies that can lead to physical and psychological difficulties. In *gene therapy,* scientists inject genes meant to cure a particular disease into a patient's bloodstream. When the genes arrive at the site of defective genes that are producing the illness, they trigger the production of chemicals that can treat the disease (Isacson & Kordower, 2008; Odom et al., 2010).

The number of diseases that can be treated through gene therapy is growing, as we will see when we discuss human development. For example, gene therapy is now being used in experimental trials involving people with certain forms of cancer, leukemia, and blindness (Wagner et al., 2004; Hirschler, 2007).

© Comstock/Getty Images RF

STUDY ALERT

The endocrine system produces hormones, chemicals that circulate through the blood via the bloodstream.

From the perspective of . . .

A Physician's Assistant   How valuable would an understanding of the brain and neurosystem be in your job as a physician's assistant?

Advances in behavioral genetics also have led to the development of a profession that did not exist several decades ago: genetic counseling. Genetic counselors help people deal with issues related to inherited disorders. For example, genetic counselors provide advice to prospective parents about the potential risks in a future pregnancy, based on their family history of birth defects and hereditary illnesses. In addition, the counselor will consider the parents' age and problems with children they already have. They also can take blood, skin, and urine samples to examine specific chromosomes.

» LO6.2 The Endocrine System: Of Chemicals and Glands

Another of the body's communication systems, the **endocrine system** is a chemical communication network that sends messages throughout the body via the bloodstream. Its job is to secrete **hormones,** chemicals that circulate through the blood and regulate the functioning or growth of the body. It also influences—and is influenced by—the functioning of the nervous system.

As chemical messengers, hormones are like neurotransmitters, although their speed and mode of transmission are quite different. Whereas neural messages are measured in thousandths of a second, hormonal communications may take minutes to reach their destination. Furthermore, neural messages move through neurons in specific lines (like a signal carried by wires strung along telephone poles), whereas hormones travel throughout the body, similar to the way radio waves are transmitted across the entire landscape. Just as radio waves evoke a response only when a radio is tuned to the correct station, hormones flowing through the bloodstream activate only those cells which are receptive and "tuned" to the appropriate hormonal message.

A key component of the endocrine system is the tiny **pituitary gland.** The pituitary gland has sometimes been called the "master gland" because it controls the functioning of the rest of the endocrine system. But the pituitary gland is more than just the taskmaster of other glands; it has important functions in its own right. For instance, hormones secreted by the pituitary gland control growth. Extremely short people and unusually tall ones usually have pituitary gland abnormalities. Other endocrine glands, shown in Figure 4, affect emotional reactions, sexual urges, and energy levels.

Although hormones are produced naturally by the endocrine system, there are a variety of artificial hormones that people may choose to take. For example, physicians sometimes prescribe hormone replacement therapy (HRT) to treat symptoms of menopause in older women. However, because recent research suggests that the treatment has potentially dangerous side effects, health experts now warn that the dangers outweigh the benefits (Herrington & Howard, 2003; Lagro-Janssen et al., 2010).

Other artificial hormones can be harmful. For example, some athletes use testosterone, a male hormone, and drugs known as *steroids,* which act like testosterone. For athletes and others who want to bulk up their appearance, steroids provide a way to add muscle weight and increase strength. However, these drugs can lead to heart attacks, strokes, cancer, and even violent behavior, making them extremely dangerous. For example, in one infamous case, professional wrestler Chris Benoit strangled his wife, suffocated his son, and later hanged himself—acts that were attributed to his use of steroids (Sandomir, 2007; Teitelbaum, 2010).

endocrine system A chemical communication network that sends messages throughout the body via the bloodstream

hormones Chemicals that circulate through the blood and regulate the functioning or growth of the body

pituitary gland The major component of the endocrine system, or "master gland," which secretes hormones that control growth and other parts of the endocrine system

Steroids, and other drugs that can enhance performance, can provide added muscle strength. A number of well-known athletes, such as tennis star Maria Sharapova, have admitted the use of banned, performance-enhancing drugs. © Kevork Djansezian/Getty Images

Figure 4 Location and function of the major endocrine glands. The pituitary gland controls the functioning of the other endocrine glands and in turn is regulated by the brain. Steroids can provide added muscle and strength, but they have dangerous side effects. Source: Adapted from Brooker et al., 2008, p. 1062. Photo: © Laurence Mouton/Getty Images RF

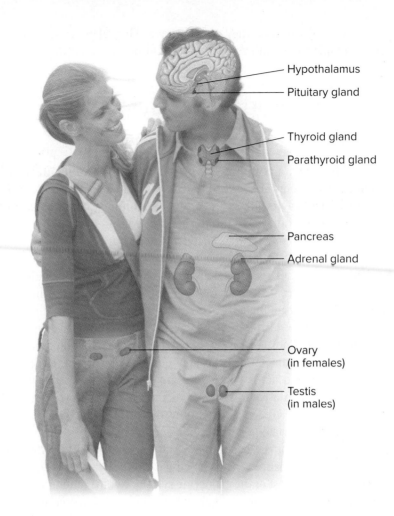

Hypothalamus
Pituitary gland
Thyroid gland
Parathyroid gland
Pancreas
Adrenal gland
Ovary (in females)
Testis (in males)

RECAP

Explain how the structures of the nervous system are linked together.

- The nervous system is made up of the central nervous system (the brain and spinal cord) and the peripheral nervous system. The peripheral nervous system is made up of the somatic division, which controls voluntary movements and the communication of information to and from the sense organs, and the autonomic division, which controls involuntary functions such as those of the heart, blood vessels, and lungs.

- The autonomic division of the peripheral nervous system is further subdivided into the sympathetic and parasympathetic divisions. The sympathetic division prepares the body in emergency situations, and the parasympathetic division helps the body return to its typical resting state.

- Behavioral genetics examines the hereditary basis of human personality traits and behavior.

Describe the operation of the endocrine system and how it affects behavior.

- The endocrine system secretes hormones, chemicals that regulate the functioning of the body, via the bloodstream. The pituitary gland secretes growth hormones and influences the release of hormones by other endocrine glands, and in turn is regulated by the hypothalamus.

1. If you put your hand on a red-hot piece of metal, the immediate response of pulling it away would be an example of a(n) _____.

2. The central nervous system is composed of the _____ and _____.

3. In the peripheral nervous system, the _____ division controls voluntary movements, whereas the _____ division controls organs that keep us alive and function without our awareness.

4. Maria saw a young boy run into the street and get hit by a car. When she got to the fallen child, she was in a state of panic. She was sweating, and her heart was racing. Her biological state resulted from the activation of what division of the nervous system?

   a. Parasympathetic

   b. Central

   c. Sympathetic

[RETHINK R Rethink]

In what ways is the "fight-or-flight" response helpful to humans in emergency situations?

Answers to Evaluate Questions 1. reflex; 2. brain, spinal cord; 3. somatic, autonomic; 4. sympathetic

KEY TERMS

Central nervous system (CNS)   LO6.1

Spinal cord   LO6.1

Reflex   LO6.1

Sensory (afferent) neurons   LO6.1

Motor (efferent) neurons   LO6.1

Interneurons   LO6.1

Peripheral nervous system   LO6.1

Somatic division   LO6.1

Autonomic division   LO6.1

Sympathetic division   LO6.1

Parasympathetic division   LO6.1

Behavioral genetics   LO6.1

Endocrine system   LO6.2

Hormones   LO6.2

Pituitary gland   LO6.2

The Brain

W Work

It is not much to look at. Soft, spongy, mottled, and pinkish-gray in color, it hardly can be said to possess much in the way of physical beauty. Despite its physical appearance, however, it ranks as the greatest natural marvel that we know and has a beauty and sophistication all its own.

The object to which this description applies: the brain. The brain is responsible for our loftiest thoughts—and our most primitive urges. It is the overseer of the intricate workings of the human body. Many billions of neurons make up a structure weighing just three pounds in the average adult. However, it is not the number of cells that is the most astounding thing about the brain but its ability to allow the human intellect to flourish by guiding our behavior and thoughts.

We turn now to a consideration of the particular structures of the brain and the primary functions to which they are related. However, a caution is in order. Although we'll discuss specific areas of the brain in relation to specific behaviors, this approach is an oversimplification. No simple one-to-one correspondence exists between a distinct part of the brain and a particular behavior. Instead, behavior is produced by complex interconnections among sets of neurons in many areas of the brain: our behavior, emotions, thoughts, hopes, and dreams are produced by a variety of neurons throughout the nervous system working in concert.

>> LO7.1 Studying the Brain's Structure and Functions: Spying on the Brain

Modern brain-scanning techniques provide a window into the living brain. Using these techniques, investigators can take a "snapshot" of the internal workings of

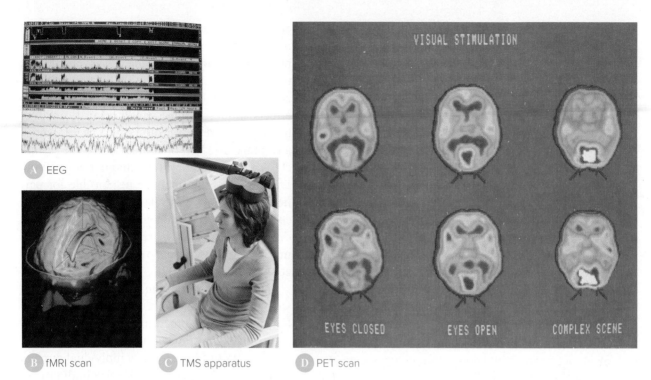

A EEG

B fMRI scan   **C** TMS apparatus   **D** PET scan

Figure 1 Brain scans produced by different techniques. (A) A computer-produced EEG image. (B) The fMRI scan uses a magnetic field to provide a detailed view of brain activity on a moment-by-moment basis. (C) Transcranial magnetic stimulation (TMS), the newest type of scan, produces a momentary disruption in an area of the brain, allowing researchers to see what activities are controlled by that area. TMS also has the potential to treat some psychological disorders. (D) The PET scan displays the functioning of the brain at a given moment. (a) © HANK MORGAN/Getty Images; (b) © Stegerphoto/Getty Images; (c) © Garo/Phanie/Science Source; (d) © Dr. M. Phelps & Dr. J. Mazziotta et al./Neurology/ Science Source

the brain without having to cut open a person's skull. The most important scanning techniques, illustrated in Figure 1, are the electroencephalogram (EEG), positron emission tomography (PET), functional magnetic resonance imaging (fMRI), and transcranial magnetic stimulation imaging (TMS).

The *electroencephalogram (EEG)* records electrical activity in the brain through electrodes placed on the outside of the skull. Although traditionally the EEG could produce only a graph of electrical wave patterns, new techniques are now used to transform the brain's electrical activity into a pictorial representation of the brain that allows more precise diagnosis of disorders such as epilepsy and learning disabilities.

Positron emission tomography (PET) scans show biochemical activity within the brain at a given moment. PET scans begin with the injection of a radioactive (but safe) liquid into the bloodstream, which makes its way to the brain. By locating radiation within the brain, a computer can determine which are the more active regions, providing a striking picture of the brain at work. For example, PET scans may be used in cases of memory problems, seeking to identify the presence of brain tumors (Gronholm et al., 2005; McMurtray et al., 2007; Spadoni et al., 2015).

Functional magnetic resonance imaging (fMRI) scans provide a detailed, three-dimensional computer-generated image of brain structures and activity by aiming a powerful magnetic field at the body. With fMRI scanning, it is possible to produce vivid, detailed images of the functioning of the brain.

Transcranial magnetic stimulation (TMS) exposes a tiny region of the brain to a strong magnetic field, thereby causing a momentary interruption of

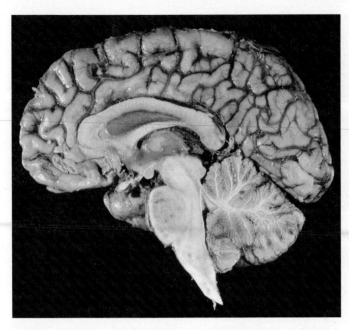

The brain (shown here in cross section) may not be much to look at, but it represents one of the great marvels of human development. Why do most scientists believe that it will be difficult, if not impossible, to duplicate the brain's abilities? © Martin M. Rotker/Science Source

electrical activity. Researchers then are able to note the effects of this interruption on normal brain functioning. One of the newest procedures used to study the brain, TMS is sometimes called a "virtual lesion" because it produces effects similar to what would occur if areas of the brain were physically cut. The enormous advantage of TMS, of course, is that the virtual cut is only temporary. In addition to identifying areas of the brain that are responsible for particular functions, TMS has the potential to treat certain kinds of psychological disorders, such as depression and schizophrenia, by shooting brief magnetic pulses through the brain (Holtzheimer et al., 2010; Prasser et al., 2015).

Future discoveries may yield even more sophisticated methods of examining the brain. For example, the emerging field of *optogenetics* involves genetic engineering and the use of special types of light to view individual circuits of neurons (Miesenbock, 2008; Gradinaru et al., 2009; LaLumiere, 2010; Rueckemann et al., 2016).

» LO7.2 The Central Core: Our "Old Brain"

central core The "old brain," which controls basic functions such as eating and sleeping and is common to all vertebrates

cerebellum The part of the brain that controls bodily balance

Although the capabilities of the human brain far exceed those of the brain of any other species, humans share some basic functions, such as breathing, eating, and sleeping, with more primitive animals. Not surprisingly, those activities are directed by a relatively primitive part of the brain. A portion of the brain known as the **central core** (see Figure 2) is quite similar in all vertebrates (species with backbones). The central core is sometimes referred to as the "old brain" because its evolution can be traced back some 500 million years to primitive structures found in nonhuman species.

If we were to move up the spinal cord from the base of the skull to locate the structures of the central core of the brain, the first part we would come to would be the *hindbrain,* which contains the medulla, pons, and cerebellum (see Figure 3). The *medulla* controls a number of critical body functions, the most important of which are breathing and heartbeat. The *pons* comes next, joining the two halves of the cerebellum, which lies adjacent to it. Containing large bundles of nerves, the pons acts as a transmitter of motor information, coordinating muscles and integrating movement between the right and left halves of the body. It is also involved in regulating sleep.

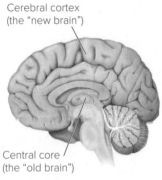

Cerebral cortex
(the "new brain")

Central core
(the "old brain")

Figure 2 The major divisions of the brain: the cerebral cortex and the central core. Source: Adapted from Seeley, Stephens, & Tate, 2000.

The **cerebellum** is found just above the medulla and behind the pons. Without the help of the cerebellum we would be unable to walk a straight line without staggering and lurching forward, for it is the job of the cerebellum to control bodily balance. It constantly monitors feedback from the muscles to coordinate their placement, movement, and tension. In fact, drinking too much alcohol seems to depress the activity of the cerebellum, leading to the unsteady gait and movement characteristic of drunkenness. The cerebellum is also involved

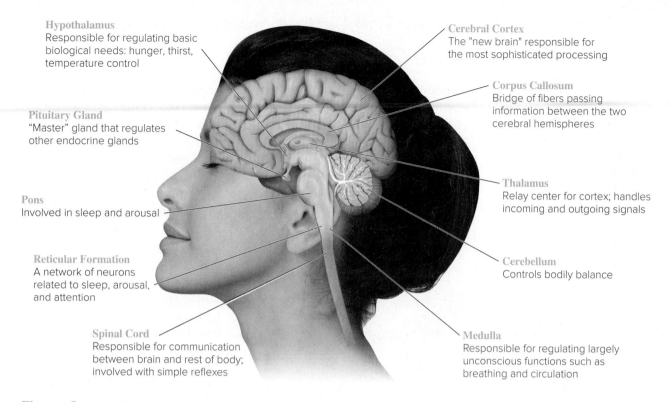

Hypothalamus
Responsible for regulating basic biological needs: hunger, thirst, temperature control

Pituitary Gland
"Master" gland that regulates other endocrine glands

Pons
Involved in sleep and arousal

Reticular Formation
A network of neurons related to sleep, arousal, and attention

Spinal Cord
Responsible for communication between brain and rest of body; involved with simple reflexes

Cerebral Cortex
The "new brain" responsible for the most sophisticated processing

Corpus Callosum
Bridge of fibers passing information between the two cerebral hemispheres

Thalamus
Relay center for cortex; handles incoming and outgoing signals

Cerebellum
Controls bodily balance

Medulla
Responsible for regulating largely unconscious functions such as breathing and circulation

Figure 3 The major structures in the brain. Source: Adapted from Johnson, 2000. Photo: © Fotosearch/Getty Images RF

in several intellectual functions, ranging from the analysis and coordination of sensory information to problem solving (Vandervert, Schimpf, & Liu, 2007; Tian et al., 2010, 2011).

The **reticular formation** extends from the medulla through the pons, passing through the middle section of the brain—or *midbrain*—and into the front-most part of the brain, called the *forebrain*. Like an ever-vigilant guard, the reticular formation is made up of groups of nerve cells that can activate other parts of the brain immediately to produce general bodily arousal. If, for example, we are startled by a loud noise, the reticular formation can prompt a heightened state of awareness to determine whether a response is necessary. The reticular formation serves a different function when we are sleeping, seeming to filter out background stimuli to allow us to sleep undisturbed.

The **thalamus,** which is hidden within the forebrain, acts primarily as a relay station for information about the senses. Messages from the eyes, ears, and skin travel to the thalamus to be communicated upward to higher parts of the brain. The thalamus also integrates information from higher parts of the brain, sorting it out so that it can be sent to the cerebellum and medulla.

The **hypothalamus** is located just below the thalamus. Although tiny—about the size of a fingertip—the hypothalamus plays an extremely important role. One of its major functions is to maintain *homeostasis,* a steady internal environment for the body. The hypothalamus helps provide a constant body temperature and monitors the amount of nutrients stored in the cells. A second major function is equally important: the hypothalamus produces and regulates behavior that is critical to the basic survival of the species, such as eating, self-protection, and sex.

> Like an ever-vigilant guard, the reticular formation is made up of groups of nerve cells that can activate other parts of the brain immediately to produce general bodily arousal.

reticular formation The part of the brain extending from the medulla through the pons and made up of groups of nerve cells that can immediately activate other parts of the brain to produce general bodily arousal

thalamus The part of the brain located in the middle of the central core that acts primarily to relay information about the senses

hypothalamus A tiny part of the brain, located below the thalamus, that maintains homeostasis and produces and regulates vital behavior, such as eating, drinking, and sexual behavior

» LO7.3 The Limbic System: Beyond the Central Core

The **limbic system** of the brain consists of a series of doughnut-shaped structures that include the *amygdala* and *hippocampus,* and borders the top of the central core and has connections with the cerebral cortex (see Figure 4). The structures of the limbic system jointly control a variety of basic functions relating to emotions and self-preservation, such as eating, aggression, and reproduction. Injury to the limbic system can produce striking changes in behavior. For example, injury to the amygdala, which is involved in fear and aggression, can turn animals that were meek and tame into hostile beasts. Conversely, animals that are usually wild and uncontrollable may become submissive and obedient following injury to the amygdala (León-Carrión & Chacartegui-Ramos, 2010; Smith et al., 2013; Reznikova et al., 2015).

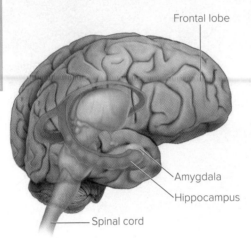

Figure 4 The limbic system consists of a series of doughnut-shaped structures that are involved in self-preservation, learning, memory, and the experience of pleasure.

The limbic system is involved in several important functions, including self-preservation, learning, memory, and the experience of pleasure. These functions are hardly unique to humans; in fact, the limbic system is sometimes referred to as the "animal brain" because its structures and functions are so similar to those of other mammals. To identify the part of the brain that provides the complex and subtle capabilities that are uniquely human, we need to turn to another structure—the cerebral cortex.

» LO7.4 The Cerebral Cortex: Our "New Brain"

As we have proceeded up the spinal cord and into the brain, our discussion has centered on areas of the brain that control functions similar to those found in less sophisticated organisms. But where, you may be asking, are the portions of the brain that enable humans to do what they do best and that distinguish humans from all other animals? Those unique features of the human brain—indeed, the very capabilities that allow you to come up with such a question in the first place—are embodied in the ability to think, evaluate, and make complex judgments. The principal location of these abilities, along with many others, is the **cerebral cortex.**

The cerebral cortex is referred to as the "new brain" because of its relatively recent evolution. It consists of a mass of deeply folded, rippled, convoluted tissue. Although only about one-twelfth of an inch thick, it would, if flattened out, cover an area more than two feet square. This configuration allows the surface area of the cortex to be considerably greater than it would be if it were smoother and more uniformly packed into the skull. The uneven shape also permits a high level of integration of neurons, allowing sophisticated information processing.

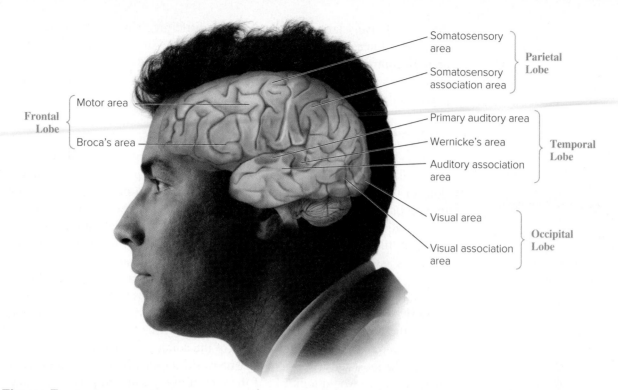

Figure 5 The cerebral cortex of the brain. The major physical structures of the cerebral cortex are called lobes. This figure also illustrates the functions associated with particular areas of the cerebral cortex. Are any areas of the cerebral cortex present in nonhuman animals? Photo: © Ron Krisel/Getty Images RF

The cortex has four major sections called **lobes.** If we take a side view of the brain, the *frontal lobes* lie at the front center of the cortex and the *parietal lobes* lie behind them. The *temporal lobes* are found in the lower center portion of the cortex, with the *occipital lobes* lying behind them. These four sets of lobes are physically separated by deep grooves called *sulci.* Figure 5 shows the four areas.

Another way to describe the brain is in terms of the functions associated with a particular area. Figure 5 also shows the specialized regions within the lobes related to specific functions and areas of the body. Three major areas are known: the motor areas, the sensory areas, and the association areas. Although we will discuss these areas as though they were separate and independent, keep in mind that this is an oversimplification. In most instances, behavior is influenced simultaneously by several structures and areas within the brain, operating interdependently.

lobes The four major sections of the cerebral cortex: frontal, parietal, temporal, and occipital

motor area The part of the cortex that is largely responsible for the body's voluntary movement

The Motor Area of the Cortex

If you look at the frontal lobe in Figure 5, you will see a shaded portion labeled **motor area.** This part of the cortex is largely responsible for the body's voluntary movement. Every portion of the motor area corresponds to a specific locale within the body. If we were to insert an electrode into a particular part of the motor area of the cortex and apply mild electrical stimulation, there would be involuntary movement in the corresponding part of the body. If we moved to another part of the motor area and stimulated it, a different part of the body would move.

The motor area is so well mapped that researchers have identified the amount and relative location of cortical tissue used to produce movement in specific parts of the human body. For example, the control of movements that are relatively large scale and require little precision, such as the movement of a knee or a hip, is centered in a very small space in the motor area. In contrast, movements that must be precise and delicate, such as facial expressions and finger movements, are controlled by a considerably larger portion of the motor area (Schwenkreis et al., 2007).

The Sensory Area of the Cortex

Given the one-to-one correspondence between the motor area and body location, it is not surprising to find a similar relationship between specific portions of the cortex and the senses. The **sensory area** of the cortex includes three regions: one that corresponds primarily to body sensations (including touch and pressure), one relating to sight, and a third relating to sound. For instance, the somatosensory area in the parietal lobe encompasses specific locations associated with the ability to perceive touch and pressure in a particular area of the body. As with the motor area, the amount of brain tissue related to a particular location on the body determines the degree of sensitivity of that location: the greater the area devoted to a specific area of the body within the cortex, the more sensitive that area of the body. For example, our fingers are related to a larger portion of the somatosensory area in the brain and are the most sensitive to touch. The weird-looking individual in Figure 6, shows what we would look like if the size of every external part of our body corresponded to the amount of brain tissue related to touch sensitivity.

The senses of sound and sight are also represented in specific areas of the cerebral cortex. An *auditory area* located in the temporal lobe is responsible for the sense of hearing. If the auditory area is stimulated electrically, a person will hear sounds such as clicks or hums. It also appears that particular locations within the auditory area respond to specific pitches (Hyde, Peretz, & Zatorre, 2008; Bizley et al., 2009; Tsuchida, Ueno, & Shimada, 2015).

The visual area in the cortex, located in the occipital lobe, responds in the same way to electrical stimulation. Stimulation by electrodes produces the experience of flashes of light or colors, suggesting that the raw sensory input of images from the eyes is received in this area of the brain and transformed into meaningful stimuli. The visual area provides another example of how areas of the brain are intimately related to specific areas of the body: specific structures in the eye are related to a particular part of the cortex—with, as you might guess, more area of the brain given to the most sensitive portions of the retina (Wurtz & Kandel, 2000; Stenbacka & Vanni, 2007; Fergenbaum et al., 2010).

The Association Areas of the Cortex

In a freak accident in 1848, an explosion drove a three-foot-long iron bar completely through the skull of railroad worker Phineas Gage, where it remained after the accident. Amazingly, Gage survived, and, despite the rod lodged through his head, a few minutes later seemed to be fine.

But he wasn't. Before the accident, Gage was hardworking and cautious. Afterward, he became irresponsible, drank heavily, and drifted from one

sensory area The site in the brain of the tissue that corresponds to each of the senses, with the degree of sensitivity related to the amount of the tissue allocated to that sense

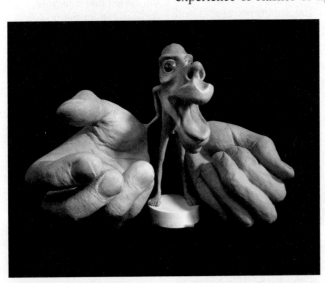

Figure 6 The greater the amount of tissue in the somatosensory area of the brain that is related to a specific body part, the more sensitive is that body part. If the size of our body parts reflected the corresponding amount of brain tissue, we would look like this strange creature. © Natural History Museum, London/Science Source

wild scheme to another. In the words of one of his physicians, he was "no longer Gage" (Harlow, 1869, p. 14; Della Sala, 2011).

What had happened to the old Gage? Although there is no way of knowing for sure, we can speculate that the accident may have injured the region of Gage's cerebral cortex known as the **association areas,** which are the site of higher mental processes such as thinking, language, memory, and speech (Rowe et al., 2000).

The association areas make up a large portion of the cerebral cortex and consist of the sections that are not directly involved in either sensory processing or directing movement. The association areas control *executive functions,* which are abilities relating to planning, goal setting, judgment, and impulse control.

Much of our understanding of the association areas comes from patients who, like Phineas Gage, have suffered some type of brain injury. For example, when parts of the association areas are damaged, people undergo personality changes that affect their ability to make moral judgments and process emotions. At the same time, people with damage in those areas can still be capable of reasoning logically, performing calculations, and recalling information (Damasio, 1999).

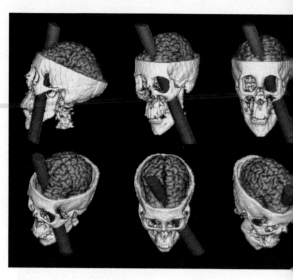

A model of the injury sustained by Phineas Gage. © Patrick Landmann/Science Source

» L07.5 Neuroplasticity and the Brain

"Shortly after he was born, Jacob Stark's arms and legs started jerking every 20 minutes. Weeks later he could not focus his eyes on his mother's face. The diagnosis: uncontrollable epileptic seizures involving his entire brain.

His mother, Sally Stark, recalled: "When Jacob was two and a half months old, they said he would never learn to sit up, would never be able to feed himself. . . . They told us to take him home, love him and find an institution." (Blakeslee, 1992, p. C3)

Instead, Jacob had brain surgery when he was five months old in which physicians removed 20 percent of his brain. The operation was a complete success. Three years later Jacob seemed normal in every way, with no sign of seizures.

The surgery that helped Jacob was based on the premise that the diseased part of his brain was producing seizures throughout the brain. Surgeons reasoned that if they removed the misfiring portion, the remaining parts of the brain, which appeared intact in PET scans, would take over. They correctly bet that Jacob could still lead a normal life after surgery, particularly because the surgery was being done at so young an age.

The success of Jacob's surgery illustrates that the brain has the ability to shift functions to different locations after injury to a specific area or in cases of surgery. But equally encouraging are some new findings about the regenerative powers of the brain and nervous system. Scientists have learned in recent years that the brain continually reorganizes itself in a process termed **neuroplasticity.** Although for many years conventional wisdom held that no new brain cells are created after childhood, new research finds otherwise. Not only do the interconnections between neurons become more complex throughout life, but it now appears that new neurons are also created in certain areas of the brain during adulthood—a process called *neurogenesis.* Each day, thousands of new neurons

association areas One of the major regions of the cerebral cortex; the site of the higher mental processes, such as thought, language, memory, and speech

neuroplasticity Changes in the brain that occur throughout the life span relating to the addition of new neurons, new interconnections between neurons, and the reorganization of information-processing areas

STUDY ALERT

Remember that neuroplasticity is the reorganization of existing neuronal connections, while neurogenesis is the creation of new neurons.

are created, especially in areas of the brain related to learning and memory (Poo & Isaacson, 2007; Shors, 2009; Kempermann, 2011).

The ability of neurons to renew themselves during adulthood has significant implications for the potential treatment of disorders of the nervous system. For example, drugs that trigger the development of new neurons might be used to counter diseases like Alzheimer's that are produced when neurons die (Waddell & Shors, 2008; Hamilton et al., 2013; Ekonomou et al., 2015).

» LO7.6 The Specialization of the Hemispheres: Two Brains or One?

The most recent development, at least in evolutionary terms, in the organization and operation of the human brain probably occurred in the last million years: a specialization of the functions controlled by the left and right sides of the brain (Hopkins & Cantalupo, 2008; MacNeilage, Rogers, & Vallortigara, 2009; Tommasi, 2009).

The brain is divided into two roughly mirror-image halves. Just as we have two arms, two legs, and two lungs, we have a left brain and a right brain. Because of the way nerves in the brain are connected to the rest of the body, these symmetrical left and right halves, called **hemispheres,** control motion in—and receive sensation from—the side of the body opposite their location. The left hemisphere of the brain, then, generally controls the right side of the body, and the right hemisphere controls the left side of the body. Thus, damage to the right side of the brain is typically indicated by functional difficulties in the left side of the body.

Despite the appearance of similarity between the two hemispheres of the brain, they are somewhat different in the functions they control and in the ways they control them. Certain behaviors are more likely to reflect activity in one hemisphere than in the other, that is, the brain experiences **lateralization.**

For example, for most people, language processing occurs more in the left side of the brain. In general, the left hemisphere concentrates more on tasks that require verbal competence, such as speaking, reading, thinking, and reasoning. In addition, the left hemisphere tends to process information sequentially, one bit at a time (Hines, 2004; Rogers, 2011).

The right hemisphere has its own strengths, particularly in nonverbal areas such as the understanding of spatial relationships, recognition of patterns and drawings, music, and emotional expression. The right hemisphere tends to process information globally, considering it as a whole (Gotts et al., 2013; Longo et al., 2015; Critchley & Nagai, 2016).

On the other hand, the differences in specialization between the hemispheres are not great, and the degree and nature of lateralization vary from one person to another. (To get a rough sense of your own degree of lateralization, complete the questionnaire in the Try It! box.) If, like most people, you are right-handed, the control of language is probably concentrated more in your left hemisphere. By contrast, if you are among the 10 percent of people who are left-handed or are ambidextrous

hemispheres Symmetrical left and right halves of the brain that control the side of the body opposite to their location

lateralization The dominance of one hemisphere of the brain in specific functions, such as language

It's likely that Vincent Van Gogh created *Wheat Fields with Cypresses* by relying primarily on the right hemisphere brain processing. What are some functions that might involve both hemispheres? © Heritage Images/Getty Images

Try It!

Assessing Brain Lateralization

To get a rough sense of your own preferences in terms of brain lateralization, complete the following questionnaire.

1. I often talk about my and others' feelings of emotion. True _____ False _____
2. I am an analytical person. True _____ False _____
3. I methodically solve problems. True _____ False _____
4. I'm usually more interested in people and feelings than objects and things. True _____ False _____
5. I see the big picture, rather than thinking about projects in terms of their individual parts. True _____ False _____
6. When planning a trip, I like every detail in my itinerary worked out in advance. True _____ False _____
7. I tend to be independent and work things out in my head. True _____ False _____
8. When buying a new car, I prefer style over safety. True _____ False _____
9. I would rather hear a lecture than read a textbook. True _____ False _____
10. I remember names better than faces. True _____ False _____

Scoring

Give yourself 1 point for each of the following responses: 1. False; 2. True; 3. True; 4. False; 5. False; 6. True; 7. True; 8. False; 9. False; 10. True. Maximum score is 10, and minimum score is 0.

The higher your score, the more your responses are consistent with people who are left-brain oriented, meaning that you have particular strength in tasks that require verbal competence, analytic thinking, and processing of information sequentially, one bit of information at a time.

The lower your score, the more your responses are consistent with a right-brain orientation, meaning that you have particular strengths in nonverbal areas, recognition of patterns, music, and emotional expression, and process information globally.

Remember, though, that this is only a rough estimate of your processing preferences, and that all of us have strengths in both hemispheres of the brain.

Source: Adapted in part from Morton, 2003.

(you use both hands interchangeably), it is much more likely that the language centers of your brain are located more in the right hemisphere or are divided equally between the left and right hemispheres.

Furthermore, the two hemispheres of the brain function in tandem. It is a mistake to think of particular kinds of information as being processed solely in the right or the left hemisphere. The hemispheres work interdependently in deciphering, interpreting, and reacting to the world.

Researchers also have unearthed evidence that there may be subtle differences in brain lateralization patterns between males and females and members of different cultures, as we see next.

EXPLORING diversity

Human Diversity and the Brain

The interplay of biology and environment in behavior is particularly clear when we consider evidence suggesting that even in brain structure and function there are both sex and cultural differences. Let's consider sex first. Accumulating evidence seems to show intriguing differences in males' and females' brain lateralization and weight (Boles, 2005; Clements, Rimrodt, & Abel, 2006).

> **The interplay of biology and environment in behavior is particularly clear when we consider evidence suggesting that even in brain structure and function there are both sex and cultural differences.**

For instance, most males tend to show greater lateralization of language in the left hemisphere. For them, language is clearly relegated largely to the left side of the brain. In contrast, women display less lateralization, with language abilities apt to be more evenly divided between the two hemispheres. Such differences in brain lateralization may account, in part, for the superiority often displayed by females on certain measures of verbal skills, such as the onset and fluency of speech (Frings et al., 2006; Petersson et al., 2007).

Other research suggests that men's brains are somewhat bigger than women's brains even after taking differences in body size into account. In contrast, part of the *corpus callosum*, a bundle of fibers that connects the hemispheres of the brain, is proportionally larger in women than in men (Luders et al., 2006; Smith et al., 2007; Taki et al., 2013).

Men and women also may process information differently. For example, in one study, fMRI brain scans of men making judgments discriminating real from false words showed activation of the left hemisphere of the brain, whereas women used areas on both sides of the brain (Rossell et al., 2002; Dulebohn et al., 2016).

From the perspective of . . .

An Office Worker   Could personal differences in people's specialization of right and left hemispheres be related to occupational success? For example, might a designer who relies on spatial skills have a different pattern of hemispheric specialization than a paralegal?

The meaning of such sex differences is far from clear. Consider one possibility related to differences in the proportional size of the corpus callosum. Its greater size in women may permit stronger connections to develop between the parts of the brain that control speech. In turn, this would explain why speech tends to emerge slightly earlier in girls than in boys.

Before we rush to such a conclusion, though, it is important to consider an alternative hypothesis: the reason verbal abilities emerge earlier in girls may be that infant girls receive greater encouragement to talk than do infant boys. In turn, this greater early experience may foster the growth of certain parts of the brain. Hence, physical brain differences may be a *reflection* of social and environmental influences rather than a *cause* of the differences in men's and women's behavior. At this point, it is impossible to know which of these alternative hypotheses is correct.

Culture also gives rise to differences in brain size and lateralization. For example, the volume of gray-matter material in the cortex is greater in higher-income adolescents than in low-income adolescents (Mackey et al., 2015).

Furthermore, native speakers of Japanese seem to process information regarding vowel sounds primarily in the brain's left hemisphere. In contrast, North and South Americans, Europeans, and individuals of Japanese ancestry who learn Japanese later in life handle vowel sounds principally in the right hemisphere.

The Split Brain: Exploring the Two Hemispheres

The patient, V.J., had suffered severe seizures. By cutting her corpus callosum, the fibrous portion of the brain that carries messages between the hemispheres, surgeons hoped to create a firebreak to prevent the seizures from spreading. The operation did decrease the frequency and severity of V.J.'s attacks. But V.J. developed an unexpected side effect: she lost the ability to write at will, although she could read and spell words aloud. (Strauss, 1998, p. 287)

People like V.J., whose corpus callosum has been surgically cut to stop seizures and who are called *split-brain patients,* offer a rare opportunity for researchers investigating the independent functioning of the two hemispheres of the brain. For example, psychologist Roger Sperry—who won the Nobel Prize for his work—developed a number of ingenious techniques for studying how each hemisphere operates (Sperry, 1982; Savazzi et al., 2007; Kingstone, 2010; Bagattini et al., 2015).

In one experimental procedure, blindfolded patients touched an object with their right hand and were asked to name it (see Figure 7). Because the right side of the body corresponds to the language-oriented left side of the brain, split-brain patients were able to name it. However, if blindfolded patients touched the object with their left hand, they were unable to name it aloud, even though the information had registered in their brains: when the blindfold was removed, patients could identify the object they had touched. Information can be learned and remembered, then, using only the right side of the brain. (By the way,

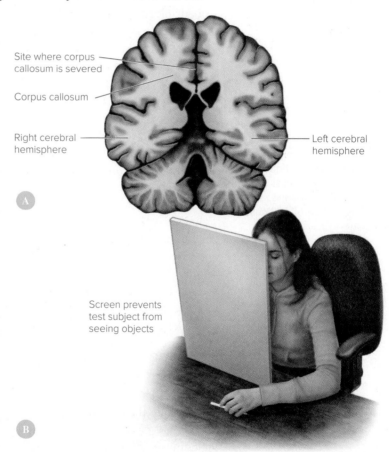

Figure 7 The hemispheres of the brain. (A) The corpus callosum connects the cerebral hemispheres of the brain. (B) A split-brain patient is tested by touching objects behind a screen. Patients could name objects when they touched it with their right hand, but couldn't if they touched with their left hand. If a split-brain patient with her eyes closed was given a pencil to hold and called it a pencil, what hand was the pencil in? Source: Adapted from Brooker, Widmaier, Graham, & Stilling, 2008, p. 943.

unless you've had a split-brain operation, this experiment won't work with you, because the bundle of fibers connecting the two hemispheres of a normal brain immediately transfers the information from one hemisphere to the other.)

It is clear from experiments like this one that the right and left hemispheres of the brain specialize in handling different sorts of information. At the same time, it is important to realize that both hemispheres are capable of understanding, knowing, and being aware of the world, in somewhat different ways. The two hemispheres, then, should be regarded as different in terms of the efficiency with which they process certain kinds of information, rather than as two entirely separate brains. The hemispheres work interdependently to allow the full range and richness of thought of which humans are capable.

becoming an informed consumer
of psychology

Learning to Control Your Heart—and Mind—through Biofeedback

When Tammy DeMichael was involved in a horrific car accident that broke her neck and crushed her spinal cord, experts told her that she was doomed to be a quadriplegic for the rest of her life, unable to move from the neck down. But they were wrong. Not only did she regain the use of her arms, but she was able to walk 60 feet with a cane (Morrow & Wolff, 1991; Hess, Houg, & Tammaro, 2007; Lofthouse et al., 2011).

The key to DeMichael's astounding recovery: biofeedback. **Biofeedback** is a procedure in which a person learns to control through conscious thought internal physiological processes such as blood pressure, heart and respiration rate, skin temperature, sweating, and the constriction of particular muscles. Although it traditionally had been thought that the heart rate, respiration rate, blood pressure, and other bodily functions are under the control of parts of the brain over which we have no influence, psychologists have discovered that these responses are actually susceptible to voluntary control (Nagai et al., 2004; Cho et al., 2007).

In biofeedback, a person is hooked up to electronic devices that provide continuous feedback relating to the physiological response in question. For instance, someone interested in controlling headaches through biofeedback might have electronic sensors placed on certain muscles on her head and learn to control the constriction and relaxation of those muscles. Later, when she felt a headache starting, she could relax the relevant muscles and abort the pain (Andrasik, 2007; Nestoriuc et al., 2008).

In DeMichael's case, biofeedback was effective because not all of the nervous system's connections between the brain and her legs were severed. Through biofeedback, she learned how to send messages to specific muscles, "ordering" them to move. Although it took more than a year, DeMichael was successful in restoring a large degree of her mobility.

Although the control of physiological processes through the use of biofeedback is not easy, it has been employed with success in a variety of ailments, including emotional problems (such as anxiety, depression, phobias, tension headaches, insomnia, and hyperactivity), physical illnesses with a psychological component (such as asthma, high blood pressure, ulcers, muscle spasms, and migraine headaches), and physical problems (such as DeMichael's injuries, strokes, cerebral palsy, and curvature of the spine) (Morone & Greco, 2007; Reiner, 2008; Ugbolue & Nicol, 2010).

You can get a sense of how biofeedback works in the accompanying Try It!

biofeedback A procedure in which a person learns to control through conscious thought internal physiological processes such as blood pressure, heart and respiration rate, skin temperature, sweating, and the constriction of particular muscles

Try It!

Biofeedback on Your Own

You can demonstrate to yourself how biofeedback works by trying this procedure for raising the temperature of your finger (Brown, 1982; Schwartz & Andrasik, 2005).

First purchase or borrow an ordinary thermometer, about 6 to 8 inches long and filled with red mercury. Tape the bulb end of the thermometer to the pad of your middle finger with masking tape, making sure that it is not so tight that circulation is blocked.

After about five minutes of sitting quietly with your eyes closed, see what the temperature reading is. Then, while still sitting quietly, say these phrases to yourself:

"I feel relaxed and warm."

"My hand feels heavy."

"My arm feels heavy."

"My hand feels warm."

"My hands feel warm and relaxed."

"I feel calm and relaxed."

Say each of these phrases slowly, and then go through the series again. Every 5 to 10 minutes check your finger temperature.

After 10 or 20 minutes, most people begin to show a rise in finger temperature—some just a few degrees, and some as many as 10 degrees. Do you?

RECAP

Illustrate how researchers identify the major parts and functions of the brain.

- Brain scans take a "snapshot" of the internal workings of the brain without having to cut surgically into a person's skull. Major brain-scanning techniques include the electroencephalogram (EEG), positron emission tomography (PET), functional magnetic resonance imaging (fMRI), and transcranial magnetic stimulation imaging (TMS).

Describe the central core of the brain.

- The central core of the brain is made up of the medulla (which controls functions such as breathing and heartbeat), the pons (which coordinates the muscles and the two sides of the body), the cerebellum (which controls balance), the reticular formation (which acts to heighten awareness in emergencies), the thalamus (which communicates sensory messages to and from the brain), and the hypothalamus (which maintains homeostasis, or body equilibrium, and regulates behavior related to basic survival). The functions of the central core structures are similar to those found in other vertebrates. This central core is sometimes referred to as the "old brain." Increasing evidence also suggests that male and female brains may differ in structure in minor ways.

Describe the limbic system of the brain.

- The limbic system, found on the border of the "old" and "new" brains, is associated with eating, aggression, reproduction, and the experiences of pleasure and pain.

Describe the cerebral cortex of the brain.

- The cerebral cortex—the "new brain"—has areas that control voluntary movement (the motor area); the senses (the sensory area); and thinking, reasoning, speech, and memory (the association areas).

Recognize neuroplasticity and its implications.

- Neuroplasticity refers to changes in the brain relating to the addition of new neurons, new interconnections between neurons, and the reorganization of information-processing areas.

Explain how the two hemispheres of the brain operate interdependently and the implications for human behavior.

- The brain is divided into left and right halves, or hemispheres, each of which generally controls the opposite side of the body.
- The left hemisphere specializes in verbal tasks, such as logical reasoning, speaking, and reading.
- The right side of the brain specializes in nonverbal tasks, such as spatial perception, pattern recognition, and emotional expression.

[EVALUATE **E** Evaluate]

1. Match the name of each brain scan with the appropriate description.
   - a. EEG
   - b. fMRI
   - c. PET

   1. By locating radiation within the brain, a computer can provide a striking picture of brain activity.
   2. Electrodes placed around the skull record the electrical signals transmitted through the brain.
   3. Provides a three-dimensional view of the brain by aiming a magnetic field at the body.

2. Match the portion of the brain with its function.
   - a. Medulla
   - b. Pons
   - c. Cerebellum
   - d. Reticular formation

   1. Maintains breathing and heartbeat.
   2. Controls bodily balance.
   3. Coordinates and integrates muscle movements.
   4. Activates other parts of the brain to produce general bodily arousal.

3. A surgeon places an electrode on a portion of your brain and stimulates it. Immediately, your right wrist involuntarily twitches. The doctor has most likely stimulated a portion of the _____ area of your brain.

4. Each hemisphere controls the _____ side of the body.

5. Nonverbal realms, such as emotions and music, are controlled primarily by the _____ hemisphere of the brain, whereas the _____ hemisphere is more responsible for speaking and reading.

Before sophisticated brain-scanning techniques were developed, behavioral neuroscientists' understanding of the brain was based largely on the brains of people who had died. What limitations would this pose, and in what areas would you expect the most significant advances once brain-scanning techniques became possible?

Answers to Evaluate Questions 1. a-2, b-3, c-1; 2. a-1, b-3, c-2, d-4; 3. motor; 4. opposite; 5. right, left

KEY TERMS

Central core   LO7.2

Cerebellum   LO7.2

Reticular formation   LO7.2

Thalamus   LO7.2

Hypothalamus   LO7.2

Limbic system   LO7.3

Cerebral cortex   LO7.4

Lobes   LO7.4

Motor area   LO7.4

Sensory area   LO7.4

Association areas   LO7.4

Neuroplasticity   LO7.5

Hemispheres   LO7.6

Lateralization   LO7.6

Biofeedback   LO7.6

Psychology on the Web

1. Biofeedback research is continuously changing and being applied to new areas of human functioning. Find at least two websites that discuss recent research on biofeedback and summarize the research and any findings it has produced. Include in your summary your best estimate of future applications of this technique.

2. Find one or more websites on Parkinson's disease and learn more about this topic. Specifically, find reports of new treatments for Parkinson's disease that do not involve the use of fetal tissue. Write a summary of your findings.

the case of . . .

THE FALLEN ATHLETE

Since he was a boy, Tim Levesque has always loved sports. From football and basketball in high school through rugby in college, Tim enjoyed the hours of training, the satisfaction of mastering complex plays, and especially the thrill of facing challenging competitors. He remained physically active in the years that followed and spent many evenings and weekends coaching his son Adam's Little League baseball team. He continued to challenge himself to learn new skills, as when he took up bowling and practiced regularly until he was good enough to join a league.

Six months ago, Tim suffered a stroke while he was taking his morning jog. Immediately afterward, much of the right side of Tim's body was paralyzed and he was having great difficulty trying to talk. When Adam saw him in the hospital, he barely recognized his strong, active father now lying weak and incapacitated in a hospital bed. Although his physicians could not give him a clear prognosis, Tim was determined to regain his strength and mobility and fully resume his active lifestyle.

Today Tim has not quite reached his goal, but he has made a remarkable recovery. He is out of the hospital and receiving regular physical therapy. His speech has returned with only occasional difficulty, and he is able to walk and move well enough to return to work. He can't quite manage to roll a 12-pound bowling ball with the ease and accuracy as he previously could, but that doesn't bother him much. What really excites Tim is the ever increasing likelihood that he'll be back to coach Adam's team next season.

1. Is there any evidence to suggest which hemisphere of Tim's brain suffered damage during his stroke?

2. What imaging technology would best reveal the location and extent of damage to Tim's brain produced by his stroke, and why?

3. If physicians did not have any means of viewing the damage to Tim's brain directly, what other clues might they have to the location of the damage? Where might the damage be if Tim had lost his vision after the stroke? Where might it be if he lost sensation on the left side of his body? Where might it be if his personality suddenly changed?

4. Explain how the endocrine system played a role in keeping Tim's body performing optimally whether he was exercising strenuously or relaxing. How might Tim have been able to manipulate his endocrine system function to enhance his athletic performance, if he so chose? What might be some risks of doing so?

5. Describe the brain phenomena that are chiefly responsible for Tim's recovery of lost speech and motor functions. How likely do you think Tim is to completely return to his prestroke level of functioning, and why?

profiles of **SUCCESS**

Courtesy of Marie-Lyn Rouchanian

NAME:	**Marie-Lyn Rouchanian**
SCHOOLS:	**University of California, Santa Cruz; Gurnick Academy of Medical Arts**
DEGREE PROGRAMS:	**BS, Neuroscience, University of California Santa Cruz; Medical Assisting at Gurnick Academy of Medical Arts**

Motivation for pursuing a college education varies considerably for each individual, but for Marie-Lyn Rouchanian, it was a deeply emotional and personal experience that led her to the field of medicine.

Having seen family members struggle with Alzheimer's and dementia, as well as serious effects from automobile accidents, Rouchanian wanted to understand the causes behind their physical and mental changes.

"I would constantly ask myself questions like, 'What is happening in his brain that is making him act like a completely different person?' and 'Why does she think that her grown son is still a child?'

"Rather than simply accepting their situations, I became curious and decided to pursue neuroscience in hopes of unraveling answers on a biological, molecular, and psychological level," she added. "Personal challenges, when applied constructively, can reveal invaluable truths."

Going to school offered another set of challenges, but Rouchanian was determined to achieve her goal of helping others while honing her study skills.

"Throughout my college courses, I retained information more efficiently by reading, writing, and using a hands-on approach rather than auditory or visual means," Roucharian explained. "This meant I would make stronger and newer connections in my brain each time I reread and rewrote the information, and applied it to physical objects.

"Some habits I developed were reviewing materials before class, actively participating during class, and then integrating the information afterward. Discussing information was always critical to my studying, and if I could accurately teach another person using simple words and terms, it meant that I understood the material," she added.

According to Rouchanian, managing her time also was important, especially considering her involvement in school and volunteer work.

"Early in my college career, I had to learn how to manage time effectively. Seldom did I feel overwhelmed," she said. "What encouraged me most in managing my obligations was using a planner to schedule, communicating clearly about expectations, asking for help when necessary, and surrounding myself with supportive people."

[RETHINK R Rethink]

When Rouchanian works with patients, what aspects of her understanding of neuroscience and behavior can help her advise them about the healing process?

Working in the health care field, Rouchanian will most likely encounter patients in stressful situations every day. How might she use her knowledge of the nervous system and the brain to help them relax and control their feelings of stress?

visual summary 2
NEUROSCIENCE AND BEHAVIOR

MODULE 5 Neurons

Neuron Structure

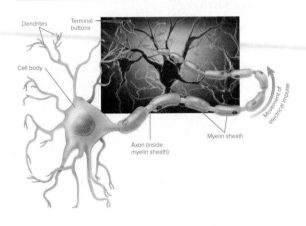

- Dendrites
- Terminal buttons
- Cell body
- Axon (inside myelin sheath)
- Myelin sheath
- Movement of electrical impulse

Neuron Function

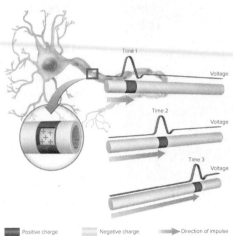

- Time 1
- Time 2
- Time 3
- Voltage

■ Positive charge ▨ Negative charge ➡ Direction of impulse

Synapse
- Neurotransmitters
  - Acetylcholine
  - Serotonin
  - Dopamine
  - Endorphins

MODULE 6 Nervous System and the Endocrine System

Central Nervous System

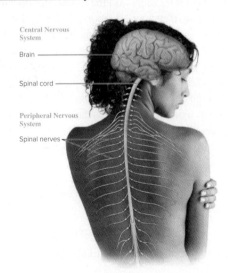

- Central Nervous System
- Brain
- Spinal cord
- Peripheral Nervous System
- Spinal nerves

Peripheral Nervous System
- Somatic division
- Autonomic division
  - Sympathetic division: Fight-or-flight response
  - Parasympathetic division: Calming response

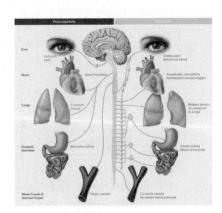

Endocrine System

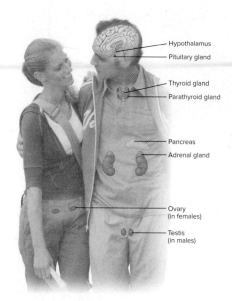

Hypothalamus
Pituitary gland
Thyroid gland
Parathyroid gland
Pancreas
Adrenal gland
Ovary (in females)
Testis (in males)

MODULE 7 The Brain

Areas of the Brain

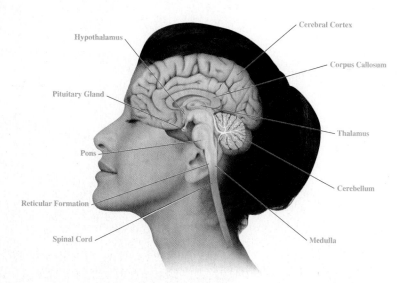

Hypothalamus
Pituitary Gland
Pons
Reticular Formation
Spinal Cord
Cerebral Cortex
Corpus Callosum
Thalamus
Cerebellum
Medulla

The Central Core: "Old brain"
- Cerebellum
- Reticular formation
- Thalamus
- Hypothalamus

The Cerebral Cortex: "New brain"
- Motor area
  - Voluntary movement
- Sensory area
  - Somatosensory area
  - Auditory area
  - Visual area
- Association areas
  - Executive functions
  - Personality

Brain Features
- Neuroplasticity
- Lateralization: Two hemispheres with specialized functions
- The Split Brain: Corpus callosum with independent hemispheric functions

The Limbic System
- Emotion
- Self-preservation
- Amygdala
- Hippocampus

CHAPTER 3

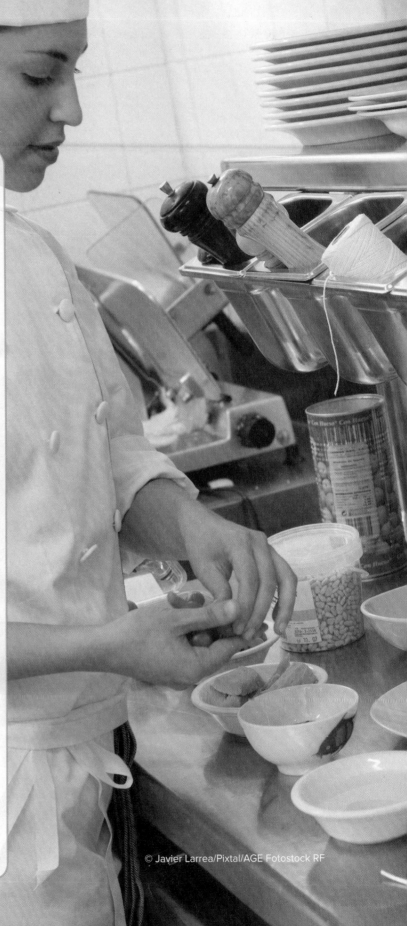

© Javier Larrea/Pixtal/AGE Fotostock RF

Do I Know You?

For neurologist and author Oliver Sacks and painter Chuck Close, everyone they encountered had the face of a stranger, even their close friends and family. Both men suffered from prosopagnosia, a neurological disorder commonly known as "face blindness," in which the brain sees the face in parts (eyes, mouth, nose) instead of as a whole that it can file away in memory. It was frustrating and socially awkward, but Sacks and Close, who were good friends, developed coping techniques. They used other characteristics, such as hair, voice, or gait, to identify people. Sacks joked that when he encountered a big man with a beard and enormous ears, he knew he was seeing himself in a mirror (McDougle, 2010; Freeman, 2012).

SENSATION AND PERCEPTION

Looking Ahead

Researchers aren't certain what caused the *face blindness* that Sacks and Close experienced, but they think it may involve abnormal functioning in the fusiform gyrus, a region of the brain's temporal lobe believed to be important in facial recognition. Though face blindness prevents the brain from taking in other people's faces as a single entity that can be filed away in memory, the rich complexity of the brain allows people like Sacks and Close to call on other sensory and perceptual abilities—the timbre of a person's voice, for instance—to aid in recognition.

Conditions such as super-recognition and face blindness illustrate how much we depend on our senses and our perceptual abilities to function normally. Our senses offer a window to the world, providing us with not only an awareness, understanding, and appreciation of the world's beauty, but alerting us to its dangers. Our senses enable us to feel the gentlest of breezes, see flickering lights miles away, and hear the soft murmuring of distant songbirds.

In this set of modules, we focus on the field of psychology that is concerned with the ways our bodies take in information through the senses and the ways we interpret that information. We will explore both sensation and perception. Sensation encompasses the processes by which our sense organs receive information from the environment. Perception is the brain's and the sense organs' sorting out, interpretation, analysis, and integration of stimuli.

Although perception clearly represents a step beyond sensation, in practice it is sometimes difficult to find the precise boundary between the two. The primary difference is that sensation can be thought of as an organism's first encounter with a raw sensory stimulus, whereas perception is the process by which that stimulus is interpreted, analyzed, and integrated with other sensory information. For example, if we were considering sensation, we might ask about the loudness of a ringing fire alarm. If we were considering perception, we might ask whether someone recognizes the ringing sound as an alarm and identifies its meaning.

To a psychologist interested in understanding the causes of behavior, sensation and perception are fundamental topics because so much of our behavior is a reflection of how we react to and interpret stimuli from the world around us. The areas of sensation and perception deal with a wide range of questions—among them, how we respond to the characteristics of physical stimuli; what processes enable us to see, hear, and experience pain; why visual illusions fool us; and how we distinguish one person from another.

Sensing the World Around Us

Learning Outcomes

>> **LO8.1** Define absolute thresholds.

>> **LO8.2** Explain the difference threshold and Weber's law.

>> **LO8.3** Discuss sensory adaptation.

MODULE OUTLINE

Absolute Thresholds: Detecting What's Out There

TryIt! How Sensitive Are You?

Difference Thresholds: Noticing Distinctions between Stimuli

Sensory Adaptation: Turning Down Our Responses

As Isabel sat down to Thanksgiving dinner, her husband carried the turkey in on a tray and placed it squarely in the center of the table. The noise level, already high from the talking and laughter of family members, grew louder still. As Isabel picked up her fork, the smell of the turkey reached her and she felt her stomach growl hungrily. The sight and sound of her family around the table, along with the smells and tastes of the holiday meal, triggered happy childhood memories and put Isabel in a relaxed, contented mood.

Put yourself in this setting and consider how different it might be if any one of your senses was not functioning. What if you were blind and unable to see the faces of your family members or the welcome shape of the golden-brown turkey? What if you had no sense of hearing and could not listen to the conversations of family members or were unable to feel your stomach growl, smell the dinner, or taste the food? Clearly, you would experience the dinner very differently than would someone whose sensory apparatus was intact.

Moreover, the sensations mentioned barely scratch the surface of sensory experience. Although perhaps you were taught that there are just five senses—sight, sound, taste, smell, and touch—that enumeration is too modest. Human sensory capabilities go well beyond the basic five senses. For example, we are sensitive not merely to touch but to a considerably wider set of stimuli—pain, pressure, temperature, and vibration, to name a few.

To consider how psychologists understand the senses and, more broadly, sensation and perception, we first need a basic working vocabulary. In formal terms, **sensation** is the activation of the sense organs by a source of physical energy. **Perception** is the sorting out, interpretation, analysis, and integration of stimuli carried out by the sense organs and brain. A **stimulus** is any passing source of physical energy that produces a response in a sense organ.

Stimuli vary in both type and intensity. Different types of stimuli activate different sense organs. For instance, we can differentiate light stimuli (which activate the sense of sight and allow us to see the colors of a tree in autumn) from sound stimuli (which, through the sense of hearing, permit us to hear the sounds of an orchestra).

STUDY ALERT

Remember that sensation refers to the activation of the sense organs (a physical response), while perception refers to how stimuli are interpreted (a psychological response).

sensation The activation of the sense organs by a source of physical energy

perception The sorting out, interpretation, analysis, and integration of stimuli by the sense organs and brain

stimulus Physical energy that produces a response in a sense organ

How intense a light stimulus needs to be before it can be detected and how much perfume a person must wear before it is noticed by others are questions related to stimulus intensity.

The issue of how the intensity of a stimulus influences our sensory responses is considered in a branch of psychology known as psychophysics. **Psychophysics** is the study of the relationship between the physical aspects of stimuli and our psychological experience of them. Psychophysics played a central role in the development of the field of psychology, and many of the first psychologists studied issues related to psychophysics (Bonezzi, Brendl, & De Angelis, 2011; Acuna et al., 2015).

Crowded conditions, sounds, and sights can all be considered noise that interferes with sensation. Can you think of other examples of noise that is not auditory in nature? © Comstock/ Stockbyte/Getty Images RF

» LO8.1 Absolute Thresholds: Detecting What's Out There

Just when does a stimulus become strong enough to be detected by our sense organs? The answer to this question requires an understanding of the concept of absolute threshold. An **absolute threshold** is the smallest intensity of a stimulus that must be present for it to be detected (Aazh & Moore, 2007).

Our senses are extremely responsive to stimuli. For example, the sense of touch is so sensitive that we can feel a bee's wing falling on our cheeks when it is dropped from a distance of one centimeter. Test your knowledge of the absolute thresholds of other senses by completing the questionnaire in the Try It! box.

> **psychophysics** The study of the relationship between the physical aspects of stimuli and our psychological experience of them
>
> **absolute threshold** The smallest intensity of a stimulus that must be present for the stimulus to be detected

Try It!

How Sensitive Are You?

To test your awareness of the capabilities of your senses, answer the following questions.

1. How far can a candle flame be seen on a clear, dark night?
   a. From a distance of 10 miles
   b. From a distance of 30 miles
2. How far can the ticking of a watch be heard under quiet conditions?
   a. From 5 feet away
   b. From 20 feet away
3. How much sugar is needed to allow it to be detected when dissolved in 2 gallons of water?
   a. 2 tablespoons
   b. 1 teaspoon
4. Over what area can a drop of perfume be detected?
   a. A 5-foot by 5-foot area
   b. A 3-room apartment

Scoring

In each case, the answer is b, illustrating the tremendous sensitivity of our senses.

Source: Based on Galanter, 1962.

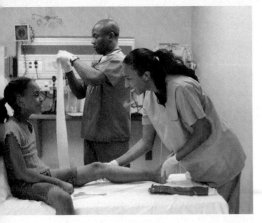

Of course, the absolute thresholds we have been discussing are measured under ideal conditions. Normally our senses cannot detect stimulation quite as well because of the presence of noise. *Noise,* as defined by psychophysicists, is background stimulation that interferes with the perception of other stimuli. Hence, noise refers not just to auditory stimuli, as the word suggests, but also to unwanted stimuli that interfere with other senses.

LO8.2 Difference Thresholds: Noticing Distinctions between Stimuli

When Liz began working as a medical assistant, she was overwhelmed by the smells in the clinic. Now that she has been in her job for a few months, she no longer notices.
© ERproductions Ltd/Getty Images RF

Suppose you wanted to choose the six best apples from a supermarket display—the biggest, reddest, and sweetest apples. One approach would be to compare one apple with another systematically until you were left with a few so similar that you could not tell the difference between them. At that point, it wouldn't matter which ones you chose.

Psychologists have discussed this comparison problem in terms of the **difference threshold,** the smallest level of added (or reduced) stimulation required to sense that a *change* in stimulation has occurred. Thus, the difference threshold is the minimum change in stimulation required to detect the difference between two stimuli, and so it also is called a just noticeable difference (Nittrouer & Lowenstein, 2007; Qin et al., 2010; Namdar, Ganel & Algom, 2016).

The stimulus value that constitutes a just noticeable difference depends on the initial intensity of the stimulus. The relationship between changes in the original value of a stimulus and the degree to which a change will be noticed forms one of the basic laws of psychophysics: Weber's law. **Weber's law** (with *Weber* pronounced "vay-ber") states that a just noticeable difference is a *constant proportion* of the intensity of an initial stimulus.

For example, Weber found that the just noticeable difference for weight is 1:50. Consequently, it takes a 1-ounce increase in a 50-ounce weight to produce a noticeable difference, and it would take a 10-ounce increase to produce a noticeable difference if the initial weight were 500 ounces. In both cases, the same proportional increase is necessary to produce a just noticeable difference—1:50 = 10:500. Similarly, the just noticeable difference distinguishing changes in loudness between sounds is larger for sounds that are initially loud than it is for sounds that are initially soft, but the proportional increase remains the same.

Weber's law helps explain why a person in a quiet room is more startled by the ringing of a cell phone

difference threshold (just noticeable difference) The smallest level of added or reduced stimulation required to sense that a change in stimulation has occurred

Weber's law A basic law of psychophysics stating that a just noticeable difference is in constant proportion to the intensity of an initial stimulus

© Tetra Images/Getty Images RF

From the perspective of . . .

A Software Designer How might you use principles of psychophysics to direct the software user's attention?

than is a person in an already noisy room. To produce the same amount of reaction in a noisy room, a cell phone ring would have to be set to a much higher level. Similarly, when the moon is visible during the late afternoon, it appears relatively dim—yet against a dark night sky, it seems quite bright.

» LO8.3 Sensory Adaptation: Turning Down Our Responses

You enter a movie theater, and the smell of popcorn is everywhere. A few minutes later, though, you barely notice the smell. The reason you acclimate to the odor is sensory adaptation. **Adaptation** is an adjustment in sensory capacity after prolonged exposure to unchanging stimuli. Adaptation occurs as people become accustomed to a stimulus and change their frame of reference. In a sense, our brain mentally turns down the volume of the stimulation it's experiencing (Willert & Eggert, 2011; Erb et al., 2013; Nourouzpour et al., 2015).

One example of adaptation is the decrease in sensitivity that occurs after repeated exposure to a strong stimulus. If you were to hear a loud tone over and over again, eventually it would begin to sound softer. Similarly, although jumping into a cold lake may be temporarily unpleasant, eventually we probably would get used to the temperature.

This apparent decline in sensitivity to sensory stimuli is due to the inability of the sensory nerve receptors to fire off messages to the brain indefinitely. Because these receptor cells are most responsive to *changes* in stimulation, constant stimulation is not effective in producing a sustained reaction (Wark, Lundstrom, & Fairhall, 2007; Zhuang & Shevell, 2015).

adaptation An adjustment in sensory capacity after prolonged exposure to unchanging stimuli

RECAP

Define absolute thresholds.

■ Sensation is the activation of the sense organs by any source of physical energy. In contrast, perception is the process by which we sort out, interpret, analyze, and integrate stimuli to which our senses are exposed.

■ Psychophysics studies the relationship between the physical nature of stimuli and the sensory responses they evoke.

■ The absolute threshold is the smallest amount of physical intensity at which a stimulus can be detected. Under ideal conditions absolute thresholds are extraordinarily sensitive, but the presence of noise (background stimuli that interfere with other stimuli) reduces detection capabilities.

Explain the difference threshold and Weber's law.

■ The difference threshold, or just noticeable difference, is the smallest change in the level of stimulation required to sense that a change has occurred. According to Weber's law, a just noticeable difference is a constant proportion of the intensity of an initial stimulus.

Discuss sensory adaptation.

■ Sensory adaptation occurs when we become accustomed to a constant stimulus and change our evaluation of it. Repeated exposure to a stimulus results in an apparent decline in sensitivity to it.

[EVALUATE

1. _____ is the stimulation of the sense organs; _____ is the sorting out, interpretation, analysis, and integration of stimuli by the sense organs and the brain.

2. The term *absolute threshold* refers to the _____ intensity of a stimulus that must be present for the stimulus to be detected.

3. Weber discovered that for a difference between two stimuli to be perceptible, the stimuli must differ by at least a _____ proportion.

4. After completing a very difficult rock climb in the morning, Carmella found the afternoon climb unexpectedly easy. This case illustrates the phenomenon of _____.

[RETHINK ☐R Rethink]

Do you think it is possible to have sensation without perception? Is it possible to have perception without sensation?

Answers to Evaluate Questions 1. sensation; perception; 2. smallest; 3. constant; 4. adaptation

KEY TERMS

Sensation LO8.1

Perception LO8.1

Stimulus LO8.1

Psychophysics LO8.1

Absolute threshold LO8.1

Difference threshold
(just noticeable difference) LO8.2

Weber's law LO8.2

Adaptation LO8.3

module 9

Vision
Shedding Light on the Eye

Learning Outcomes

»LO9.1 Explain the basic structure of the eye.

»LO9.2 Compare and contrast color vision with color blindness.

MODULE OUTLINE

Illuminating the Structure of the Eye

Try It! Find Your Blind Spot

Color Vision and Color Blindness: The Seven-Million-Color Spectrum

If, as poets say, the eyes provide a window to the soul, they also provide us with a window to the world. Our visual capabilities permit us to admire and react to scenes ranging from the beauty of a sunset, to the configuration of a lover's face, to the words written on the pages of a website.

Vision starts with light, the physical energy that stimulates the eye. Light is a form of electromagnetic radiation waves, which, as shown in Figure 1, are measured in wavelengths. The sizes of wavelengths correspond to different types of energy. The range of wavelengths that humans are sensitive to—called the *visual spectrum*—is relatively small.

Light waves coming from some object outside the body (such as the butterfly in Figure 2) are sensed by the only organ that is capable of responding to the visible spectrum: the eye. Our eyes convert light to a form that can be used by the neurons that serve as messengers to the brain. The neurons themselves take up a relatively small percentage of the total eye. Most of the eye is a mechanical device that is similar in many respects to a traditional, nondigital electronic camera that uses film, as you can see in Figure 2.

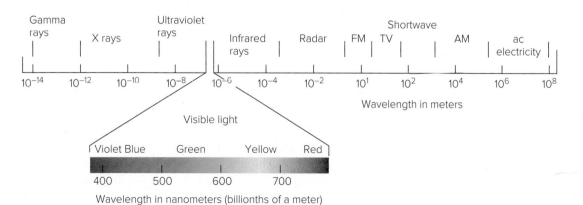

Figure 1 The visible spectrum—the range of wavelengths to which people are sensitive—is only a small part of the kinds of wavelengths present in our environment. Is it a benefit or disadvantage to our everyday lives that we aren't more sensitive to a broader range of visual stimuli? Why?

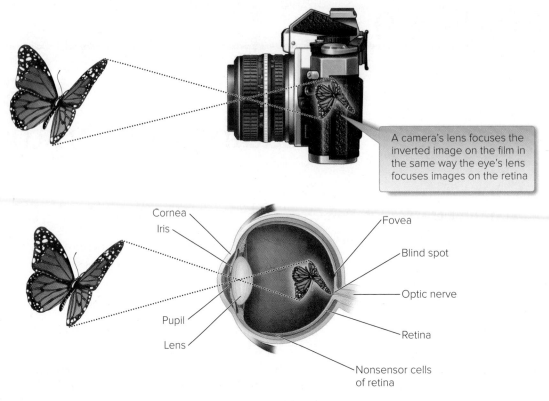

A camera's lens focuses the inverted image on the film in the same way the eye's lens focuses images on the retina

Cornea
Iris
Fovea
Blind spot
Optic nerve
Pupil
Lens
Retina
Nonsensor cells of retina

Figure 2   Although human vision is far more complicated than the most sophisticated camera, in some ways basic visual processes are analogous to those used in traditional, nondigital photography.

> **Despite the similarities between the eye and a traditional camera, vision involves processes that are far more complex and sophisticated than those of any camera.**

Despite the similarities between the eye and a traditional camera, vision involves processes that are far more complex and sophisticated than those of any camera. Furthermore, once an image reaches the neuronal receptors of the eye, the eye/camera analogy ends, for the processing of the visual image in the brain is more reflective of a computer than it is of a camera.

» LO9.1 Illuminating the Structure of the Eye

The ray of light being reflected off the butterfly in Figure 2 first travels through the *cornea,* a transparent, protective window. The cornea, because of its curvature, bends (or *refracts*) light as it passes through to focus it more sharply. After moving through the cornea, the light traverses the pupil. The *pupil* is a dark hole in the center of the *iris,* the colored part of the eye, which in humans ranges from a light blue to a dark brown. The size of the pupil opening depends on the amount of light in the environment. The dimmer the surroundings are, the more the pupil opens to allow more light to enter.

Once light passes through the pupil, it enters the *lens,* which is directly behind the pupil. The lens acts to bend the rays of light so that they are properly focused on the rear of the eye. The lens focuses light by changing its own thickness, a

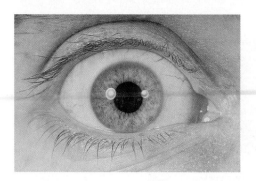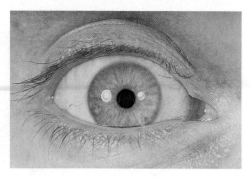

Like the automatic lighting system of a camera, the pupil in the human eye expands to let in more light (first) and contracts to block out light (second). Can humans adjust their ears to let in more or less sound in a similar manner? (first) © Biophoto Associates/Getty Images; (second) © Biophoto Associates/Science Source

process called *accommodation:* it becomes flatter when viewing distant objects and rounder when looking at closer objects.

Reaching the Retina

Having traveled through the pupil and lens, our image of the butterfly finally reaches its ultimate destination in the eye: the retina. The **retina** is within the part of the eye that converts the electromagnetic energy of light to electrical impulses for transmission to the brain. Interestingly, as the image travels through the lens, it has reversed itself. Consequently, the image reaches the retina upside down (relative to its original position). Although it might seem that this reversal would cause difficulties in understanding and moving about the world, this is not the case. The brain automatically interprets the image in terms of its original position.

The retina consists of a thin layer of nerve cells at the back of the eyeball (see Figure 3). There are two kinds of light-sensitive receptor cells in the retina. The names they have been given describe their shapes: rods and cones. **Rods** are thin, cylindrical receptor cells that are highly sensitive to light. **Cones** are cone-shaped, light-sensitive receptor cells that are responsible for sharp focus and color perception, particularly in bright light. The rods and cones are distributed unevenly throughout the retina. Cones are concentrated on the part of the retina called the *fovea.* The fovea is a particularly sensitive region of the retina. If you want to focus on something of particular interest, you will automatically try to center the image on the fovea to see it more sharply.

The rods and cones are not only structurally dissimilar but they also play distinctly different roles in vision. Cones are primarily responsible for the sharply focused perception of color, particularly in brightly lit situations; rods are related to vision in dimly lit situations and are largely insensitive to color and to details as sharp as those the cones are capable of recognizing. The rods play a key role in *peripheral vision*—seeing objects that are outside the main center of focus—and in night vision.

Sending the Message from the Eye to the Brain

When light energy strikes the rods and cones, it triggers a neural response that moves out of the back of the eyeball and into the brain through a bundle of ganglion axons called the **optic nerve.**

Because the opening for the optic nerve passes through the retina, there are no rods or cones in the area, and that creates a blind spot. Normally, however, this absence of nerve cells does not interfere with vision because you automatically

retina The part of the eye that converts the electromagnetic energy of light to electrical impulses for transmission to the brain

rods Thin, cylindrical receptor cells in the retina that are highly sensitive to light

cones Cone-shaped, light-sensitive receptor cells in the retina that are responsible for sharp focus and color perception, particularly in bright light

optic nerve A bundle of ganglion axons that carry visual information to the brain

STUDY ALERT

Cones relate to **c**olor vision.

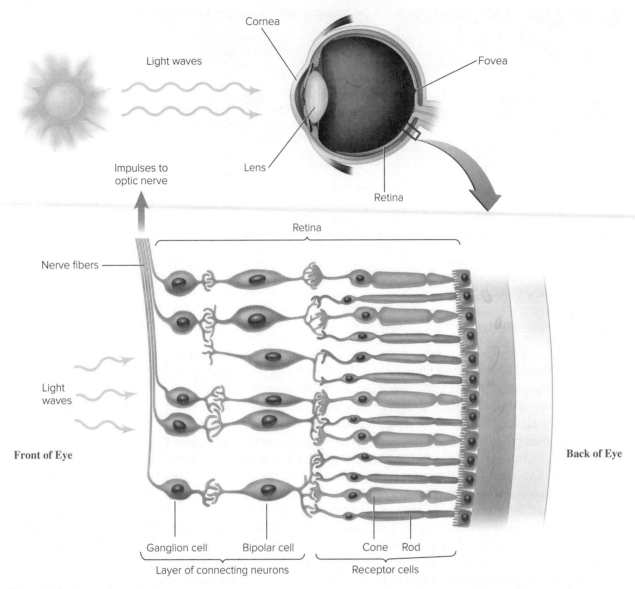

Cornea

Light waves

Fovea

Impulses to
optic nerve

Lens

Retina

Retina

Nerve fibers

Light
waves

Front of Eye

Back of Eye

Ganglion cell   Bipolar cell   Cone   Rod

Layer of connecting neurons   Receptor cells

Figure 3   The basic cells of the eye. Light entering the eye travels through the ganglion and bipolar cells and strikes the light-sensitive rods and cones located at the back of the eye. The rods and cones then transmit nerve impulses to the brain via the bipolar and ganglion cells. Source: Adapted from Shier, Butler, & Lewis, 2000.

compensate for the missing part of your field of vision. (To find your blind spot, see the Try It! box.)

Once beyond the eye itself, the neural impulses relating to the image move through the *optic nerve*. As the optic nerve leaves the eyeball, its path does not take the most direct route to the part of the brain right behind the eye. Instead, the optic nerves from each eye meet at a point roughly between the two eyes—called the *optic chiasm* (pronounced ki-asm)—where each optic nerve then splits.

When the optic nerves split, the nerve impulses coming from the right half of each retina are sent to the right side of the brain, and the impulses arriving from the left half of each retina are sent to the left side of the brain. Because the image on the retinas is reversed and upside down, however, those images coming from the right half of each retina actually originated in the field of

Try It!

Find Your Blind Spot

Close your right eye and look at the haunted house with your left eye. You will see the ghost on the periphery, or edge, of what you can see. Now, while staring at the house, move the page toward you. When the page is about a foot from your eye, the ghost will disappear. At this moment, the image of the ghost is falling on your blind spot. But also notice how, when the page is at that distance, not only does the ghost seem to disappear, but the line seems to run continuously through the area where the ghost used to be. This shows how we automatically compensate for missing information by using nearby material to complete what is unseen. That's the reason you never notice the blind spot. What is missing is replaced by what is seen next to the blind spot. Can you think of any advantages that this tendency to provide missing information gives humans as a species?

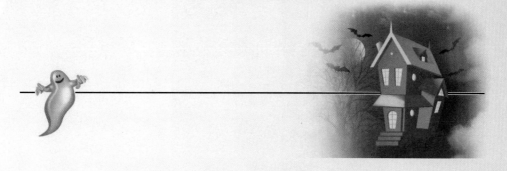

vision to the person's left, and the images coming from the left half of each retina originated in the field of vision to the person's right (see Figure 4).

> **feature detection** The activation of neurons in the cortex by visual stimuli of specific shapes or patterns

Processing the Visual Message

Most processing of visual images takes place in the visual cortex of the brain, and it is here that the most complex kinds of processing occur. Many neurons in the cortex are extraordinarily specialized, being activated only by visual stimuli of a particular shape or pattern—a process known as **feature detection.** Researchers have found that some cells are activated only by lines of a particular width, shape, or orientation. Other cells are activated only by moving, as opposed to stationary, stimuli (Fox, Fairhall & Daniel, 2010; Grünert et al., 2011; Sanes & Masland, 2015).

More recent work has added to our knowledge of the complex ways in which visual information coming from

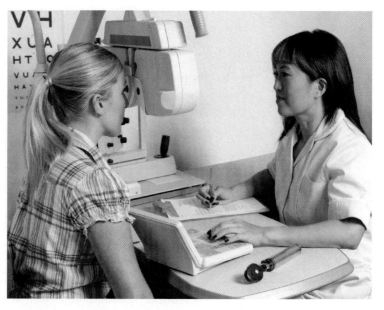

Most of us rarely think of our own vision, but optometrists and their assistants focus on it daily. What are some other careers that involve the senses? © Peter Dazeley/Getty Images RF

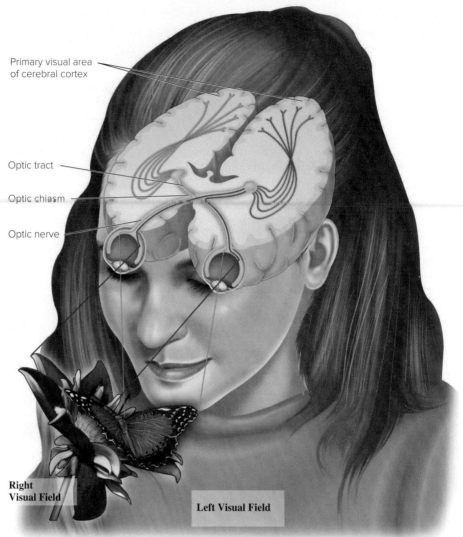

Figure 4 Because the optic nerve coming from each eye splits at the optic chiasm, the image to a person's right is sent to the left side of the brain and the image to the person's left is transmitted to the right side of the brain. Source: Based on Mader, 2000.

Primary visual area of cerebral cortex

Optic tract

Optic chiasm

Optic nerve

Right Visual Field

Left Visual Field

individual neurons is combined and processed. Different parts of the brain process nerve impulses simultaneously according to the attributes of the image. For instance, one brain system processes shapes, one processes colors, and others process movement, location, and depth. Furthermore, different parts of the brain are involved in the perception of specific *kinds* of stimuli, showing distinctions, for example, between the perception of human faces, animals, and inanimate stimuli. The brain's integration of visual information does not occur in any single step or location in the brain but instead is a process that occurs on several levels simultaneously (Platek & Kemp, 2009; Mullen, Beaudot, & Ivanov, 2011; Schindler & Bartels, 2016).

» LO9.2 Color Vision and Color Blindness: The Seven-Million-Color Spectrum

Although the range of wavelengths to which humans are sensitive is relatively narrow, at least in comparison with the entire electromagnetic spectrum, the portion to which we are capable of responding allows us great flexibility in sensing the world. Nowhere is this clearer than in terms of the number of colors we can discern (Rabin, 2004; Palmer & Schloss, 2010).

Although the variety of colors that people are generally able to distinguish is vast, there are certain individuals whose ability to perceive color is quite limited—the color-blind. Interestingly, the condition of these individuals has provided some of the most important clues to understanding how color vision operates (Bonnardel, 2006; Jordan et al., 2010; Alfaro et al., 2015).

A person with normal color vision is capable of distinguishing no less than 7 million different colors, but approximately 50 men or 1 in 5,000 women are color-blind. For most people with color blindness, the world looks quite dull. Red fire engines appear yellow, green grass seems yellow, and the three colors of a traffic light all look yellow. In fact, in the most common form of color blindness, all red and green objects are seen as yellow. There are other forms of color blindness as well, but they are quite rare. In yellow-blue blindness, people are unable to tell the difference between yellow and blue, and in the most extreme case an individual perceives no color at all. To such a person the world looks something like the picture on a black-and-white television set.

© Fuse/Getty Images RF

From the perspective of …

A Graphic Designer How might you market your products similarly or differently to those who are color-blind versus those who have normal color vision?

Explaining Color Vision

To understand why some people are color-blind, we need to consider the basics of color vision. There are two processes involved. The first process is explained by the **trichromatic theory of color vision.** This theory suggests that there are three kinds of cones in the retina, each of which responds primarily to a specific range of wavelengths. One is most responsive to blue-violet colors, one to green, and the third to yellow-red (Brown & Wald, 1964). According to trichromatic theory, perception of color is influenced by the relative strength with which each of the three kinds of cones is activated. If we see a blue sky, the blue-violet cones are primarily triggered, and the others show less activity.

However, there are aspects of color vision that the trichromatic theory is less successful at explaining. For example, the theory does not explain what happens after you stare at something like the flag shown in Figure 5 for about a minute. Try this yourself and then look at a blank white page: you'll see an image of the traditional red, white, and blue U.S. flag. Where there was yellow, you'll see blue, and where there were green and black, you'll see red and white.

The phenomenon you have just experienced is called an *afterimage*. It occurs because activity in the retina continues even when you are no longer staring at the original picture. The fact that the colors in the afterimage are different from those in the original calls into question the trichromatic theory, which has led scientists to develop alternative explanations for color vision. According to the **opponent-process theory of color vision,** receptor cells are linked in pairs, working in opposition to each other. Specifically, there is a blue-yellow

trichromatic theory of color vision The theory that there are three kinds of cones in the retina, each of which responds primarily to a specific range of wavelengths

opponent-process theory of color vision The theory that receptor cells for color are linked in pairs, working in opposition to each other

Figure 5 Stare at the dot in this flag for about a minute and then look at a piece of plain white paper. What do you see? Most people see an afterimage that converts the colors in the figure into the traditional red, white, and blue U.S. flag. If you have trouble seeing it the first time, blink once and try again.

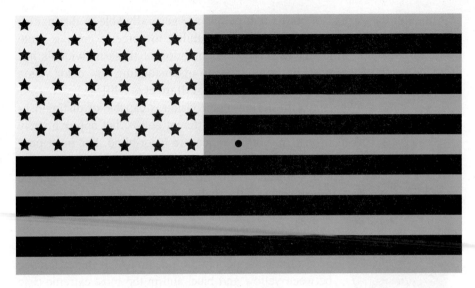

pairing, a red-green pairing, and a black-white pairing. If an object reflects light that contains more blue than yellow, it will stimulate the firing of the cells sensitive to blue, simultaneously discouraging or inhibiting the firing of receptor cells sensitive to yellow—and the object will appear blue. If, in contrast, a light contains more yellow than blue, the cells that respond to yellow will be stimulated to fire while the blue ones are inhibited, and the object will appear yellow (D. N. Robinson, 2007).

The opponent-process theory provides a good explanation for afterimages. When we stare at the yellow in the figure, for instance, our receptor cells for the yellow component of the yellow-blue pairing become fatigued and are less able to respond to yellow stimuli. In contrast, the receptor cells for the blue part of the pair are not tired, because they are not being stimulated. When we look at a white surface, the light reflected off it would normally stimulate both the yellow and the blue receptors equally. But the fatigue of the yellow receptors prevents this from happening. They temporarily do not respond to the yellow, which makes the white light appear to be blue. Because the other colors in the figure do the same thing relative to their specific opponents, the afterimage produces the opponent colors—for a while. The afterimage lasts only a short time, because the fatigue of the yellow receptors is soon overcome, and the white light begins to be perceived more accurately.

Both opponent processes and trichromatic mechanisms are at work in allowing us to see color. However, they operate in different parts of the visual sensing system. Trichromatic processes work within the retina itself, whereas opponent mechanisms operate both in the retina and at later stages of neuronal processing (Puller & Haverkamp, 2011; Horiguchi et al., 2013; Bunce, 2015).

RECAP

Explain the basic structure of the eye.

- Vision depends on sensitivity to light that is either reflected off objects or produced by an energy source. The eye shapes the light into an image that is transformed into nerve impulses and interpreted by the brain.

- As light enters the eye, it passes through the cornea, pupil, and lens and ultimately reaches the retina, where the electromagnetic energy of light is converted to nerve impulses for transmission to the brain. These impulses leave the eye via the optic nerve.

- The visual information gathered by the rods and cones is transferred through the optic nerve, which leads to the optic chiasm—the point where the optic nerve splits.

Compare and contrast color vision with color blindness.

- Color vision seems to be based on two processes described by the trichromatic theory and the opponent-process theory.

- The trichromatic theory suggests that there are three kinds of cones in the retina, each of which is responsive to a certain range of colors. The opponent-process theory presumes pairs of different types of cells in the eye that work in opposition to each other.

[EVALUATE E Evaluate]

1. Light entering the eye first passes through the _____, a protective window.
2. The structure that converts light into usable neural messages is called the _____.
3. A woman with blue eyes could be described as having blue pigment in her _____.
4. What is the process by which the thickness of the lens is changed in order to focus light properly?
5. The proper sequence of structures that light passes through in the eye is the _____, _____, _____, and _____.
6. Match each type of visual receptor with its function.
   a. Rods
   b. Cones
   1. Used for dim light, largely insensitive to color.
   2. Detect color, good in bright light.
7. _____ theory states that there are three types of cones in the retina, each of which responds primarily to a different color.

[RETHINK R Rethink]

If the eye had a second lens that "unreversed" the image hitting the retina, do you think there would be changes in the way people perceive the world?

Answers to Evaluate Questions 1. cornea; 2. retina; 3. iris; 4. accommodation; 5. cornea, pupil, lens, retina; 6. a-1, b-2; 7. trichromatic

KEY TERMS

Retina LO9.1

Rods LO9.1

Cones LO9.1

Optic nerve LO9.1

Feature detection LO9.1

Trichromatic theory of color vision LO9.2

Opponent-process theory of color vision LO9.2

Hearing and the Other Senses

 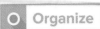

The blastoff was easy compared with what the astronaut was experiencing now: space sickness. The constant nausea and vomiting were enough to make him wonder why he had worked so hard to become an astronaut. Even though he had been warned that there was a two-thirds chance that his first experience in space would cause these symptoms, he wasn't prepared for how terribly sick he really felt.

Whether or not the astronaut wishes he could head right back to Earth, his experience, a major problem for space travelers, is related to a basic sensory process: the sense of motion and balance. This sense allows people to navigate their bodies through the world and keep themselves upright without falling. Along with hearing—the process by which sound waves are translated into understandable and meaningful forms—the sense of motion and balance resides in the ear.

>> LO10.1 Sensing Sound

Although many of us think primarily of the outer ear when we speak of the ear, that structure is only one simple part of the whole. The outer ear acts as a reverse megaphone, designed to collect and bring sounds into the internal portions of the ear (see Figure 1). The location of the outer ears on different sides of the head helps with *sound localization,* the process by which we identify the direction from which a sound is coming. Wave patterns in the air enter each ear at a slightly different time, and the brain uses the discrepancy as a clue to the sound's point of origin. In addition, the two outer ears delay or amplify sounds of particular frequencies to different degrees.

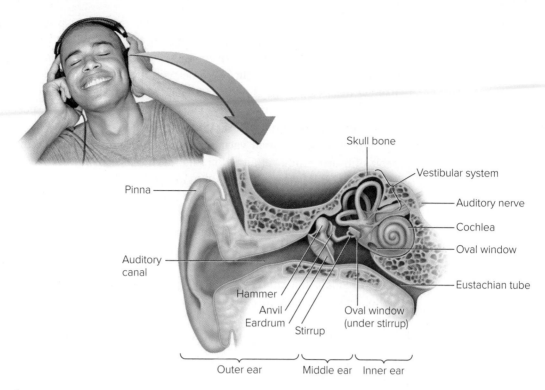

Figure 1 The major parts of the ear. Source: Adapted from Brooker et al., 2008, p. 956.
Photo: © Tyler Edwards/Getty Images RF

Sound is the movement of air molecules brought about by a source of vibration. Sounds, arriving at the outer ear in the form of wavelike vibrations, are funneled into the *auditory canal,* a tubelike passage that leads to the eardrum. The **eardrum** is aptly named because it operates like a miniature drum, vibrating when sound waves hit it. The more intense the sound, the more the eardrum vibrates. These vibrations are then transferred into the *middle ear,* a tiny chamber containing three bones that transmit vibrations to the oval window, a thin membrane leading to the inner ear.

The *inner ear* is the portion of the ear that changes the sound vibrations into a form in which they can be transmitted to the brain. (As you will see, it also contains the organs that allow us to locate our position and determine how we are moving through space.) When sound enters the inner ear through the oval window, it moves into the *cochlea,* a coiled tube that looks something like a snail and is filled with fluid that vibrates in response to sound. Inside the cochlea is the *basilar membrane,* a structure that runs through the center of the cochlea, dividing it into an upper chamber and a lower chamber. The basilar membrane is covered with *hair cells.* When the hair cells are bent by the vibrations entering the cochlea, the cells send a neural message to the brain (Tritsch & Bergles, 2010; Imtiaz et al., 2016).

When an auditory message leaves the ear, it is transmitted to the auditory cortex of the brain through a complex series of neural interconnections. As the message is transmitted, it is communicated through neurons that respond to specific types of sounds. Within the auditory cortex itself, there are neurons that respond selectively to very specific sorts of sound features, such as clicks and whistles. Some neurons respond only to a specific pattern of sounds, such as a steady tone but not an intermittent one. Furthermore, specific neurons transfer information about a sound's location through their particular pattern of firing (De Lucia, Clarke & Murray, 2010; Romero-Guevara et al., 2015).

sound The movement of air molecules brought about by a source of vibration

eardrum The part of the ear that vibrates when sound hits it

© Rubberball/Erik Isakson/Getty Images RF

Neighboring cells in the auditory cortex of the brain are responsive to similar sound frequencies. The auditory cortex, then, provides us with a "map" of sound frequencies, just as the visual cortex furnishes a representation of the visual field. In addition, because of the asymmetry in the two hemispheres of the brain (which we discussed in the chapter about neuroscience and behavior), the left and right ears process sound differently. The right ear reacts more to speech, while the left ear responds more to music (Sininger & Cone-Wesson, 2004, 2006).

We are sensitive to broad variations in sound. The strongest sounds we are capable of hearing are over a trillion times as intense as the very weakest sound we can hear. This range is measured in *decibels*. When sounds get higher than 120 decibels, they become painful to the human ear.

Our sensitivity to different sounds of different pitches changes as we age. For instance, as we get older, the range of pitches we can detect declines, particularly for high-pitched sounds. This is why high school students sometimes choose high-pitched ring tones for their cell phones in settings where cell phone use is forbidden: the ringing sound goes undetected by their aging teachers (Vitello, 2006; Fitzgibbons & Gordon-Salant, 2010).

Balance: The Ups and Downs of Life

semicircular canals Three tubelike structures of the inner ear containing fluid that sloshes through them when the head moves, signaling rotational or angular movement to the brain

Several structures of the ear are related more to our sense of balance than to our hearing. The **semicircular canals** of the inner ear (refer to Figure 1) consist of three tubes containing fluid that sloshes through them when the head moves, signaling rotational or angular movement to the brain. The pull on our bodies caused by the acceleration of forward, backward, or up-and-down motion, as well as the constant pull of gravity, is sensed by the *otoliths,* tiny, motion-sensitive crystals in the semicircular canals. When we move, these crystals shift like sands on a windy beach. The brain's inexperience in interpreting messages from the weightless otoliths is the cause of the space sickness commonly experienced by two-thirds of all space travelers (Mallery et al., 2010; Yoder et al., 2015).

» LO10.2 Smell and Taste

Until he bit into a piece of raw cabbage on that February evening . . . Raymond Fowler had not thought much about the sense of taste. The cabbage, part of a pasta dish he was preparing for his family's dinner, had an odd, burning taste, but he did not pay it much attention. Then a few minutes later, his daughter handed him a glass of cola, and he took a swallow. "It was like sulfuric acid," he said. "It was like the hottest thing you could imagine boring into your mouth." (Goode, 1999, pp. D1–D2)

It was evident that something was very wrong with Fowler's sense of taste. After extensive testing, it became clear that he had damaged the nerves involved in his sense of taste, probably because of a viral infection or a medicine he was taking. (Luckily for him, a few months later his sense of taste returned to normal.)

Even without disruptions in our ability to perceive the world such as those experienced by Fowler, we all know the important roles that taste and smell play. We'll consider these two senses next.

Smell

Although many animals have keener abilities to detect odors than we do, the human sense of smell (*olfaction*) permits us to detect more than 10,000 separate smells. We also have a good memory for smells, and long-forgotten events and memories can be brought back with the mere whiff of an odor associated with a memory (Herz, 2010; Arshamian et al., 2013).

Results of "sniff tests" have shown that women generally have a better sense of smell than men do. People also have the ability to distinguish males from females on the basis of smell alone. In one experiment, blindfolded students who were asked to sniff the breath of a female or male volunteer who was hidden from view were able to distinguish the sex of the donor at better than chance levels. People can also distinguish happy from sad emotions by sniffing underarm smells, and women are able to identify their babies solely on the basis of smell just a few hours after birth (Doty et al., 1982; Haviland-Jones & Chen, 1999; Fusari & Ballesteros, 2008).

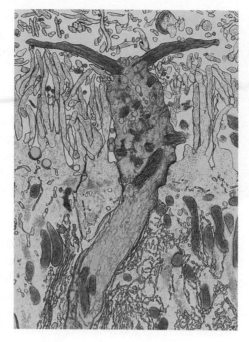

More than 1,000 types of receptor cells, known as olfactory cells, are spread across the nasal cavity. The cells are specialized to react to particular odors. Do you think it is possible to "train" the nose to pick up a greater number of odors? © Professor Pietro M. Motta/Science Source

The sense of smell is sparked when the molecules of a substance enter the nasal passages and meet *olfactory cells,* the receptor neurons of the nose, which are spread across the nasal cavity. More than 1,000 separate types of receptors have been identified on those cells so far. Each of these receptors is so specialized that it responds only to a small band of different odors. The responses of the separate olfactory cells are then transmitted to the brain, where they are combined into recognition of a particular smell (Zou & Buck, 2006; Jia & Hegg, 2015; Yu et al., 2015).

Smell may also act as a hidden means of communication for humans. It has long been known that nonhumans release *pheromones,* chemicals they secrete into the environment that produce a reaction in other members of the same species, permitting the transmission of messages such as sexual availability. Some psychologists believe that human pheromones affect emotional responses, although the evidence is inconclusive (Hawkes & Doty, 2009; Hummer & McClintock, 2009; Doty, 2010).

Taste

The sense of taste (*gustation*) involves receptor cells that respond to four basic stimulus qualities: sweet, sour, salty, and bitter. A fifth category also exists, a flavor called *umami,* although there is controversy about whether it qualifies as a fundamental taste. Umami is a hard-to-translate Japanese word, although the English "meaty" or "savory" comes close. Chemically, umami involves food stimuli that contain amino acids (the substances that make up proteins).

> The sense of taste (gustation) involves receptor cells that respond to four basic stimulus qualities: sweet, sour, salty, and bitter.

Although the specialization of the receptor cells leads them to respond most strongly to a particular type of taste, they also are capable of responding to other tastes as well. Ultimately, every taste is simply a combination of the basic flavor

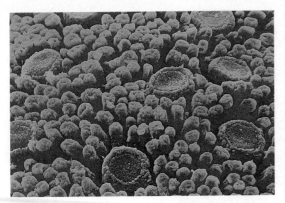

There are 10,000 taste buds on the tongue and other parts of the mouth. Taste buds wear out and are replaced every 10 days. What would happen if taste buds were not generated? © Omikron Omikron/Getty Images

qualities, in the same way that the primary colors blend into a vast variety of shades and hues (Yeomans, Tepper, & Reitzschel, 2007; Spence, Auvray, & Smith, 2015).

The receptor cells for taste are located in roughly 10,000 *taste buds,* which are distributed across the tongue and other parts of the mouth and throat. The taste buds wear out and are replaced every 10 days or so. That's a good thing, because if our taste buds weren't constantly reproducing, we'd lose the ability to taste after we'd accidentally burned our tongues.

The sense of taste differs significantly from one person to another, largely as a result of genetic factors. Some people, dubbed "supertasters," are highly sensitive to taste; they have twice as many taste receptors as "nontasters," who are relatively insensitive to taste. Supertasters (who, for unknown reasons, are more likely to be female than male) find sweets sweeter, cream creamier, and spicy dishes spicier, and weaker concentrations of flavor are enough to satisfy any cravings they may have. In contrast, because they aren't so sensitive to taste, nontasters may seek out relatively sweeter and fattier foods in order to maximize the taste. As a consequence, they may be prone to obesity (Snyder, Fast, & Bartoshuk, 2004; Pickering & Gordon, 2006).

Are you a supertaster? To find out, complete the accompanying Try It! questionnaire.

» LO10.3 The Skin Senses: Touch, Pressure, Temperature, and Pain

It started innocently when Jennifer Darling hurt her right wrist during gym class. At first it seemed like a simple sprain. But even though the initial injury healed, the excruciating, burning pain accompanying it did not go away.

Even administration of the most powerful drugs may be insufficient to alleviate pain. © Flirt Collection/Masterfile

Instead, it spread to her other arm and then to her legs. The pain, which Jennifer described as similar to "a hot iron on your arm," was unbearable—and never stopped.

The source of Darling's pain turned out to be a rare condition known as reflex sympathetic dystrophy syndrome, or RSDS for short. For a victim of RSDS, a stimulus as mild as a gentle breeze or the touch of a feather can produce agony. Even bright sunlight or a loud noise can trigger intense pain.

Pain such as Darling's can be devastating, yet a lack of pain can be equally bad. If you never experienced pain, for instance, you might not notice that your arm had brushed against a hot pan, and you would suffer a severe burn. Similarly, without the warning sign of abdominal pain that typically accompanies an inflamed appendix, your appendix might eventually rupture, spreading a fatal infection throughout your body.

Pain has other benefits, as well. Pain helps us better appreciate pleasurable experiences. It also may lead us to affiliate more closely with others, by arousing their empathy. And pain may lead us to be more vigilant about our surroundings as we seek to avoid or moderate pain we are experiencing (Bastian et al., 2014).

skin senses The senses of touch, pressure, temperature, and pain

In fact, all our **skin senses**—touch, pressure, temperature, and pain—play a critical role in survival, making us aware of potential danger to our bodies. Most of these senses operate through nerve receptor cells located at various depths

Try It!

Take a Taste Test

1. **Taste Bud Count**

   Punch a hole with a standard hole punch in a square of wax paper. Paint the front of your tongue with a cotton swab dipped in blue food coloring. Put wax paper on the tip of your tongue, just to the right of center. With a flashlight and magnifying glass, count the number of pink, unstained circles. They contain taste buds.

2. **Sweet Taste**

   Rinse your mouth with water before tasting each sample. Put 1/2 cup sugar in a measuring cup, and then add enough water to make 1 cup. Mix. Coat front half of your tongue, including the tip, with a cotton swab dipped in the solution. Wait a few moments. Rate the sweetness according to the scale shown below.

3. **Salt Taste**

   Put 2 teaspoons of salt in a measuring cup and add enough water to make 1 cup. Repeat the previous steps listed, rating how salty the solution is.

Taste Scale

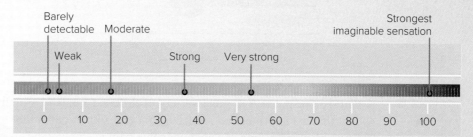

4. **Spicy Taste**

   Add 1 teaspoon of Tabasco sauce to 1 cup of water. Apply with a cotton swab to first half inch of the tongue, including the tip. Keep your tongue out of your mouth until the burn reaches a peak, then rate the burn according to the scale.

	Supertasters	**Nontasters**
No. of taste buds	25 on average	10
Sweet rating	56 on average	32
Tabasco	64 on average	31

Average tasters lie in between supertasters and nontasters. Bartoshuk and Lucchina lack the data at this time to rate salt reliably, but you can compare your results with others taking the test.

Source: Based on Bartoshuk & Lucchina, 1997.

throughout the skin, distributed unevenly throughout the body. For example, some areas, such as the fingertips, have many more receptor cells sensitive to touch and as a consequence are notably more sensitive than other areas of the body (Gardner & Kandel, 2000; see Figure 2).

Probably the most extensively researched skin sense is pain, and with good reason: people consult physicians and take medication for pain more than for any other symptom or condition. Chronic pain afflicts more than 116 million American adults and costs around $600 billion a year in the United States alone (Park, 2011; Jensen & Turk, 2014; Robinson-Papp et al., 2015).

STUDY ALERT

Remember that there are multiple skin senses, including touch, pressure, temperature, and pain.

Figure 2 Skin sensitivity in various areas of the body. The lower the average threshold is, the more sensitive a body part is. The fingers and thumb, lips, nose, cheeks, and big toe are the most sensitive. Why do you think certain areas are more sensitive than others? Source: Adapted from D. R. Kenshalo, 1968, p. 200. Photo: © Chase Jarvis/Getty Images

Pain is a response to a great variety of different kinds of stimuli. A light that is too bright can produce pain, and sound that is too loud can be painful. One explanation is that pain is an outcome of cell injury; when a cell is damaged, regardless of the source of damage, it releases a chemical called *substance P* that transmits pain messages to the brain.

Some people are more susceptible to pain than others. For example, women experience painful stimuli more intensely than men. These gender differences are associated with the production of hormones related to menstrual cycles. In addition, certain genes are linked to the experience of pain, so that we may inherit our sensitivity to pain (Nielsen, Staud, & Price, 2009; Fillingim, 2011).

© Comstock/Getty Images RF

From the perspective of . . .

A Medical or Dental Assistant How would you handle a patient who is anxiously awaiting treatment and complaining that her pain is getting worse?

But the experience of pain is not determined by biological factors alone. For example, women report that the pain experienced in childbirth is moderated to some degree by the joyful nature of the situation. In contrast, even a minor stimulus can produce the perception of strong pain if it is accompanied by anxiety (like a visit to the dentist). Clearly, then, pain is a perceptual response that depends heavily on our emotions and thoughts (Kennedy et al., 2011; Jensen & Turk, 2014).

According to the **gate-control theory of pain,** particular nerve receptors in the spinal cord lead to specific areas of the brain related to pain. When these receptors are activated because of an injury or problem with a part of the body, a "gate" to the brain is opened, allowing us to experience the sensation of pain (Melzack & Katz, 2004; Vasudeva et al., 2015).

However, another set of neural receptors can, when stimulated, close the "gate" to the brain, thereby reducing the experience of pain. The gate can be shut in two different ways. First, other impulses can overwhelm the nerve pathways relating to pain, which are spread throughout the brain. In this case, non-painful stimuli compete with and sometimes displace the neural message of pain, thereby shutting off the painful stimulus.

Psychological factors account for the second way a gate can be shut. Depending on an individual's current emotions, interpretation of events, and previous experience, the brain can close a gate by sending a message down the spinal cord to an injured area, producing a reduction in or relief from pain. Thus, soldiers who are injured in battle may experience no pain. The lack of pain probably occurs because a soldier experiences such relief at still being alive that the brain sends a signal to the injury site to shut down the pain gate (Turk, 1994; Gatchel & Weisberg, 2000; Pincus & Morley, 2001).

> **gate-control theory of pain** The theory that particular nerve receptors lead to specific areas of the brain related to pain

becoming an informed consumer
of psychology

Managing Pain

Are you one of the 50 million people in the United States who suffer from chronic pain? Psychologists and medical specialists have devised several strategies to fight pain. Among the most important approaches are the following.

- *Medication.* Painkilling drugs are the most popular treatment in fighting pain. Drugs range from those which directly treat the source of the pain—such as reducing swelling in painful joints—to those which work on the symptoms. Medication can be in the form of pills, patches, injections, or liquids. In a recent innovation, drugs are pumped directly into the spinal cord (Kalb, 2003; Pesmen, 2006; Bagnall, 2010).

- *Nerve and brain stimulation.* Pain can sometimes be relieved when a low-voltage electric current is passed through the specific part of the body that is in pain. In even more severe cases, electrodes can be implanted surgically directly into the brain, or a handheld battery pack can stimulate nerve cells to provide direct relief. This process is known as transcutaneous electrical nerve stimulation, or TENS (Tugay et al., 2007; Claydon et al., 2008; Binder & Baron, 2010).

- *Light therapy.* One of the newest forms of pain reduction involves exposure to specific wavelengths of red or infrared light. Certain kinds of light increase the production of enzymes that may promote healing (Evcik et al., 2007; Rastad, Ulfberg, & Lindberg, 2008).

- *Hypnosis.* For people who can be hypnotized—not everyone is susceptible—hypnosis can greatly relieve pain. In fact, it can affect the brain and spinal-cord functioning in injured people, actually improving their physical functioning (Accardi & Milling, 2009; Lee & Raja, 2011; Jensen & Patterson, 2014).

- *Biofeedback and relaxation techniques.* Using biofeedback, people learn to control what are usually involuntary functions such as heartbeat, respiration, and muscle tension. For instance, people with tension headaches or back pain can be trained to relax their bodies to bring themselves relief (Vitiello, Bonello, & Pollard, 2007).

- *Surgery.* In one of the most extreme methods, nerve fibers that carry pain messages to the brain can be cut surgically. Still, because of the danger that other bodily functions will be affected, surgery is a treatment of last resort, used most frequently with dying patients (Cullinane, Chu, & Mamelak, 2002; Lai, Chen, & Chien, 2007).

- *Cognitive restructuring.* Cognitive treatments are effective for people who continually say to themselves, "This pain will never stop," "The pain is ruining my life," or "I can't take it anymore," and are thereby likely to make their pain even worse. By substituting more positive ways of thinking, people can increase their sense of control—and actually reduce the pain they experience (Liedl et al., 2011; Ehde, Dillworth, & Turner, 2015).

- *Mirror pain therapy.* One surprising treatment for people who suffer from phantom-limb pain (where a person with an amputated limb experiences pain where the missing limb used to be) employs mirrors. By using a mirror to make it appear that both limbs are intact, the brain of the amputee stops sending messages perceived as pain (Foell et al., 2014).

RECAP

Describe how we sense sound.

- Sound, motion, and balance are centered in the ear. Sounds, in the form of vibrating airwaves, enter through the outer ear and travel through the auditory canal until they reach the eardrum.

- The vibrations of the eardrum are transmitted into the middle ear, which consists of three bones: the hammer, the anvil, and the stirrup. These bones transmit vibrations to the oval window.

- In the inner ear, vibrations move into the cochlea, which encloses the basilar membrane. Hair cells on the basilar membrane change the mechanical energy of sound waves into nerve impulses that are transmitted to the brain. The ear is also involved in the sense of balance and motion.

Discuss smell and taste.

- Smell depends on olfactory cells (the receptor cells of the nose), and taste is centered in the tongue's taste buds.

Distinguish the skin senses.

- The skin senses are responsible for the experiences of touch, pressure, temperature, and pain. Gate-control theory suggests that particular nerve receptors, when activated, open a "gate" to specific areas of the brain related to pain, and that another set of receptors closes the gate when stimulated.

- Among the techniques used frequently to alleviate pain are medication, hypnosis, biofeedback, relaxation techniques, surgery, nerve and brain stimulation, and cognitive therapy.

[EVALUATE

1. The tubelike passage leading from the outer ear to the eardrum is known as the _____.
2. The purpose of the eardrum is to protect the sensitive nerves underneath it. It serves no purpose in actual hearing. True or false?
3. The three middle ear bones transmit their sound to the _____.
4. The three fluid-filled tubes in the inner ear that are responsible for our sense of balance are known as the _____.
5. Touch, pressure, temperature, and pain are collectively known as our _____.

[RETHINK R Rethink]

Much research is being conducted on repairing faulty sensory organs through devices such as personal guidance systems and eyeglasses, among others. Do you think that researchers should attempt to improve normal sensory capabilities beyond their "natural" range (for example, make human visual or audio capabilities more sensitive than normal)? What benefits might this ability bring? What problems might it cause?

KEY TERMS

Sound   LO10.1

Eardrum   LO10.1

Semicircular canals   LO10.1

Skin senses   LO10.3

Gate-control theory of pain   LO10.3

Perceptual Organization
Constructing Our View of the World

 W Work

Consider the vase shown in Figure 1A for a moment. Or is it a vase? Take another look, and instead you may see the profiles of two people.

Now that an alternative interpretation has been pointed out, you will probably shift back and forth between the two interpretations. Similarly, if you

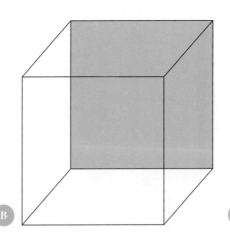

Figure 1 When the usual cues we use to distinguish figure from ground are absent, we may shift back and forth between different views of the same figure. If you look at each of these objects long enough, you'll probably experience a shift in what you're seeing. In (A), you can see either a vase or the profiles of two people. In (B), the shaded portion of the figure, called a Necker cube, can appear to be either the front or the back of the cube. Finally, in (C), you'll be able to see a face of a woman if you look at the drawing long enough.

examine the shapes in Figure 1B long enough, you will probably experience a shift in what you're seeing. The reason for these reversals is this: because each figure is two-dimensional, the usual means we employ for distinguishing the *figure* (the object being perceived) from the *ground* (the background or spaces within the object) do not work.

The fact that we can look at the same figure in more than one way illustrates an important point. We do not just passively respond to visual stimuli that happen to fall on our retinas. Instead, we actively try to organize and make sense of what we see.

We turn now from a focus on the initial response to a stimulus (sensation) to what our minds make of that stimulus—perception. Perception is a constructive process by which we go beyond the stimuli that are presented to us and attempt to construct a meaningful situation.

"I'm turning into my mother."

Paul Noth/The New Yorker Collection/The Cartoon Bank

» LO11.1 The Gestalt Laws of Organization

Some of the most basic perceptual processes can be described by a series of principles that focus on the ways we organize bits and pieces of information into meaningful wholes. Known as **Gestalt laws of organization,** these principles were set forth in the early 1900s by a group of German psychologists who studied patterns, or gestalts (Wertheimer, 1923). Those psychologists discovered a number of important principles that are valid for visual (as well as auditory) stimuli, illustrated in Figure 2: closure, proximity, similarity, and simplicity.

Gestalt laws of organization The principles of organization of perception

Figure 2A illustrates *closure*. We usually group elements to form enclosed or complete figures rather than open ones. We tend to ignore the breaks in Figure 2A and concentrate on the overall form. Figure 2B demonstrates the principle of *proximity:* We perceive elements that are closer together as grouped together. As a result, we tend to see pairs of dots rather than a row of single dots in Figure 2B.

A Closure	B Proximity	C Similarity	D Simplicity

Figure 2   Organizing these various bits and pieces of information into meaningful wholes constitutes some of the most basic processes of perception, which are summed up in the gestalt laws of organization. Do you think any other species share this organizational tendency? How might we find out?

STUDY ALERT

The gestalt laws of organization are classic principles in the field of psychology. Figure 2 can help you remember them.

Elements that are *similar* in appearance we perceive as grouped together. We see, then, horizontal rows of circles and squares in Figure 2C instead of vertical mixed columns. Finally, in a general sense, the overriding gestalt principle is *simplicity:* when we observe a pattern, we perceive it in the most basic, straightforward manner that we can. For example, most of us see Figure 2D as a square with lines on two sides, rather than as the block letter *W* on top of the letter *M.* If we have a choice of interpretations, we generally opt for the simpler one.

Although gestalt psychology no longer plays a prominent role in contemporary psychology, its legacy endures. One fundamental gestalt principle that remains influential is that two objects considered together form a whole that is different from the simple combination of the objects. Gestalt psychologists argued that the perception of stimuli in our environment goes well beyond the individual elements that we sense. Instead, it represents an active, constructive process carried out within the brain (Richards, 2010; Wagemans et al., 2012; see Figure 3).

» LO11.2 Top-Down and Bottom-Up Processing

Ca- yo- re-d t-is -en-en-e, w-ic- ha- ev-ry -hi-d l-tt-r m-ss-ng? It probably won't take you too long to figure out that it says, "Can you read this sentence, which has every third letter missing?"

If perception were based primarily on breaking down a stimulus into its most basic elements, understanding the sentence, as well as other ambiguous stimuli, would not be possible. The fact that you were probably able to recognize such an imprecise stimulus illustrates that perception proceeds along two different avenues, called top-down processing and bottom-up processing.

top-down processing Perception that is guided by higher-level knowledge, experience, expectations, and motivations

In **top-down processing,** perception is guided by higher-level knowledge, experience, expectations, and motivations. You were able to figure out the meaning of the sentence with the missing letters because of your prior reading experience, and because written English contains redundancies. Not every letter of each word is necessary to decode its meaning. Moreover, your expectations played a role in your being able to read the sentence. You were probably expecting a statement that had *something to do with psychology,* not a recipe for meatloaf.

Top-down processing is illustrated by the importance of context in determining how we perceive objects. Look, for example, at Figure 4. Most of us perceive that the first row consists of the letters *A* through *F,* while the second contains the numbers 10 through 14. But take a

Figure 3 Although at first it is difficult to distinguish anything in this drawing, keep looking, and eventually you'll probably be able to see the figure of a dog (James, 1966). The dog represents a gestalt, or perceptual whole, which is something greater than the sum of the individual elements.

more careful look and you'll see that the "B" and the "13" are identical. Clearly, our perception is affected by our expectations about the two sequences—even though the two stimuli are exactly the same.

However, top-down processing cannot occur on its own. Even though top-down processing allows us to fill in the gaps in ambiguous and out-of-context stimuli, we would be unable to perceive the meaning of such stimuli without bottom-up processing. **Bottom-up processing** consists of the progression of recognizing and processing information from individual components of a stimulus and moving to the perception of the whole. We would make no headway in our recognition of the sentence without being able to perceive the individual shapes that make up the letters. Some perception, then, occurs at the level of the patterns and features of each of the separate letters.

Top-down and bottom-up processing occur simultaneously, and interact with each other, in our perception of the world around us. Bottom-up processing permits us to process the fundamental characteristics of stimuli, whereas top-down processing allows us to bring our experience to bear on perception. As we learn more about the complex processes involved in perception, we are developing a better understanding of how the brain continually interprets information from the senses and permits us to make responses appropriate to the environment (Westerhausen et al., 2009; Baluch & Itti, 2011; Falasca et al., 2015).

Figure 4   The power of context is shown in this figure. Note how the B and the 13 are identical. Source: Adapted from Coren and Ward, 1989.

> **bottom-up processing**
> Perception that consists of the progression of recognizing and processing information from individual components of a stimuli and moving to the perception of the whole

» LO11.3 Perceptual Constancy

Consider what happens as you finish a conversation with a friend and she begins to walk away from you. As you watch her walk down the street, the image on your retina becomes smaller and smaller. Do you wonder why she is shrinking?

Of course not. Despite the very real change in the size of the retinal image, you factor into your thinking the knowledge that your friend is moving farther away from you because of perceptual constancy. *Perceptual constancy* is a

When the moon is near the horizon, we do not see it by itself, and perceptual constancy leads us to take into account a misleading sense of distance.
© imageBROKER/Alamy Stock Photo RF

phenomenon in which physical objects are perceived as unvarying and consistent despite changes in their appearance or in the physical environment.

In some cases, though, our application of perceptual constancy can mislead us. One good example of this involves the rising moon. When the moon first appears at night, close to the horizon, it seems to be huge—much larger than when it is high in the sky later in the evening. You may have thought that the apparent change in the size of the moon was caused by the moon's being physically closer to the earth when it first appears. In fact, though, this is not the case at all: the actual image of the moon on our retina is the same, whether it is low or high in the sky.

Instead, the moon appears to be larger when it is close to the horizon primarily because of the phenomenon of perceptual constancy. When the moon is near the horizon, the perceptual cues of intervening terrain and objects such as trees on the horizon produce a misleading sense of distance. The phenomenon of perceptual constancy leads us to take that assumed distance into account when we view the moon, and it leads us to misperceive the moon as relatively large.

In contrast, when the moon is high in the sky, we see it by itself, and we don't try to compensate for its distance from us. In this case, then, perceptual constancy leads us to perceive it as relatively small. To demonstrate perceptual constancy for yourself, try looking at the moon when it is relatively low on the horizon through a paper-towel tube; the moon suddenly will appear to "shrink" back to normal size (Kaufman, Johnson, & Liu, 2008; Rogers & Naumenko, 2015).

Perceptual constancy is not the only explanation for the moon illusion, and it remains a puzzle to psychologists. It may be that several different perceptual processes are involved in the illusion (Gregory, 2008; Kim, 2008; Matthen, 2010).

» LO11.4 Depth Perception: Translating 2-D to 3-D

As sophisticated as the retina is, the images projected onto it are flat and two-dimensional. Yet the world around us is three-dimensional, and we perceive it that way. How do we make the transformation from 2-D to 3-D?

The ability to view the world in three dimensions and to perceive distance—a skill known as **depth perception**—is due largely to the fact that we have two eyes. Because there is a certain distance between the eyes, a slightly different image reaches each retina. The brain integrates the two images into one composite view, but it also recognizes the difference in images and uses it to estimate the distance of an object from us. The difference in the images seen by the left eye and the right eye is known as *binocular disparity* (Kara & Boyd, 2009; Foster et al., 2011; Valsecchi et al., 2013).

depth perception The ability to view the world in three dimensions and to perceive distance

To get a sense of binocular disparity for yourself, hold a pencil at arm's length and look at it first with one eye and then with the other. There is little difference between the two views relative to the background. Now bring the pencil just six inches away from your face, and try the same thing. This time you will perceive a greater difference between the two views.

The difference between the images in the two eyes varies provides us with a way of determining distance. If we view two objects, and one is considerably closer to us than the other is, the retinal disparity will be relatively large. That disparity leads us to have a greater sense of depth between the two. However, if two objects are a

Our perception makes the dog biscuits appear huge. How would we function if we were not able to make that distinction? © MIKE CLARKE/AFP/Getty Images

similar distance from us, the retinal disparity will be minor. Therefore, we will perceive them as being a similar distance from us.

In some cases, certain cues permit us to obtain a sense of depth and distance with just one eye. These cues are known as *monocular cues*. One monocular cue—*motion parallax*—is the change in position of an object on the retina caused by movement of your body relative to the object. For example, suppose you are a passenger in a moving car, and you focus your eye on a stable object such as a tree. Objects that are closer than the tree will appear to move backward, and the nearer the object is, the more quickly it will appear to move. In contrast, objects beyond the tree will seem to move at a slower speed, but in the same direction as you are. Your brain is able to use these cues to calculate the relative distances of the tree and other objects.

From the perspective of . . .

A Computer Game Designer   What are some techniques you might use to produce the appearance of three-dimensional terrain on a two-dimensional computer screen? What are some techniques you might use to suggest motion?

Similarly, experience has taught us that if two objects are the same size, the one that makes a smaller image on the retina is farther away than is the one that provides a larger image—an example of the monocular cue of *relative size*. The quality of the image on the retina also helps us judge distance. The monocular cue of *texture gradient* provides information about distance because the details of things that are far away are less distinct (Proffitt, 2006).

Finally, anyone who has ever seen railroad tracks that seem to join together in the distance knows that distant objects appear to be closer together than are nearer ones, a phenomenon called linear perspective. *Linear perspective* is a type of perspective in which objects in the distance appear to converge. We use it as a monocular cue in estimating distance, allowing the two-dimensional image on the retina to record the three-dimensional world (Shimono & Wade, 2002; Bruggeman, Yonas, & Konczak, 2007).

» LO11.5 Motion Perception: As the World Turns

When a batter tries to hit a pitched ball, the most important factor is the motion of the ball. How is a batter able to judge the speed and location of a target that is moving at some 90 miles per hour?

The answer rests in part on several cues that provide us with relevant information about the perception of motion. For one thing, the movement of an object across the retina is typically perceived relative to some stable, unmoving background. Moreover, if the stimulus is heading toward us, the image on the retina will expand in size, filling more and more of the visual field. In such cases, we assume that the stimulus is approaching—not that it is an expanding stimulus viewed at a constant distance.

It is not, however, just the movement of images across the retina that brings about the perception of motion. If it were, we would perceive the world as moving every time we moved our heads. Instead, one of the critical things we learn about perception is to factor information about our own head and eye movements along with information about changes in the retinal image.

Sometimes we perceive motion when it doesn't occur. Have you ever been on a stationary train that feels as if it is moving, because a train on an adjacent track begins to slowly move past? Or have you been in an IMAX movie theater, in which you feel as if you were falling as a huge image of a plane moves across the screen? In both cases, the experience of motion is convincing. *Apparent movement* is the perception that a stationary object is moving. It occurs when different areas of the retina are quickly stimulated, leading us to interpret motion (Lindemann & Bekkering, 2009; Brandon & Saffran, 2011).

» LO11.6 Perceptual Illusions: The Deceptions of Perceptions

If you look carefully at the Parthenon, one of the most famous buildings of ancient Greece, still standing at the top of an Athens hill, you'll see that it was built with a bulge on one side. If it didn't have that bulge—and quite a few other "tricks" like it, such as columns that incline inward—it would look as if it were crooked and about to fall down. Instead, it appears to stand completely straight, at right angles to the ground.

The fact that the Parthenon appears to be completely upright is the result of a series of visual illusions. **Visual illusions** are physical stimuli that consistently produce errors in perception. In the case of the Parthenon, the building appears to be completely square, as illustrated in Figure 5A. However, if it had been built that way, it would look to us as it does in Figure 5B. The reason for this is an illusion that makes right angles placed above a line appear as if they were

visual illusions Physical stimuli that consistently produce errors in perception

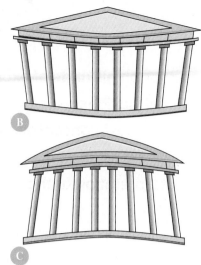

Figure 5 In building the Parthenon, the Greeks constructed an architectural wonder that looks perfectly straight, with right angles at every corner, as in (A). However, if it had been built with completely true right angles, it would have looked as it does in (B). To compensate for this illusion, the Parthenon was designed to have a slight upward curvature, as shown in (C). Source: Adapted from Luckeish, 1921. Photo: © G Ross John/Getty Images

bent. To offset the illusion, the Parthenon was constructed as in Figure 5C, with a slight upward curvature.

The *Müller-Lyer illusion* (illustrated in Figure 6) has fascinated psychologists for decades. Although the two lines are the same length, the one with the arrow tips pointing inward (Figure 6A, right) appears to be longer than the one with the arrow tips pointing outward (Figure 6A, left).

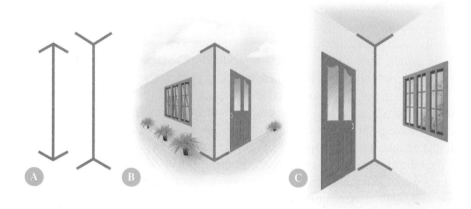

Figure 6 In the Müller-Lyer illusion (A), the vertical line on the right appears longer than the one on the left. One explanation for the Müller-Lyer illusion suggests that the line with arrow points directed inward is to be interpreted as the inside corner of a rectangular room extending away from us (C), and the line with arrow points directed outward is viewed as the relatively close corner of a rectangular object, such as the building corner in (B). Our previous experience with distance cues leads us to assume that the outside corner is closer than the inside corner and that the inside corner must therefore be longer.

Although all kinds of explanations for visual illusions have been suggested, most concentrate either on the physical operation of the eye or on our misinterpretation of the visual stimulus. For example, one explanation for the Müller-Lyer illusion is that eye movements are greater when the arrow tips point inward, making us perceive the line as longer than it is when the arrow tips face outward. In contrast, a different explanation for the illusion suggests that we unconsciously attribute particular significance to each of the lines (Gregory, 1978). When we see the line on the right in Figure 6A, we tend to perceive it as if it were the inside corner of a room extending away from us, as illustrated in Figure 6C. In contrast, when we view the line on the left in Figure 6A, we perceive it as the relatively close outside corner of a rectangular object such as the building corner in Figure 6B. Because previous experience leads us to assume that the outside corner is closer than the inside corner, we make the further assumption that the inside corner must therefore be larger.

> Although all kinds of explanations for visual illusions have been suggested, most concentrate either on the physical operation of the eye or on our misinterpretation of the visual stimulus.

Despite the complexity of the latter explanation, a good deal of evidence supports it. For instance, cross-cultural studies show that people raised in areas where there are few right angles—such as the Zulu in Africa—are much less susceptible to the illusion than are people who grow up where most structures are built using right angles and rectangles (Segall, Campbell, & Herskovits, 1966).

EXPLORING diversity

Culture and Perception

As the example of the Zulu indicates, the culture in which we are raised has clear consequences for how we perceive the world. Consider the drawing in Figure 7. Sometimes called the "devil's tuning fork," it is likely to produce a mind-boggling effect, as the center tine of the fork alternates between appearing and disappearing.

Now try to reproduce the drawing on a piece of paper. Chances are that the task is nearly impossible for you—unless you are a member of an African tribe with little exposure to Western cultures. For such individuals, the task is simple; they have no trouble reproducing the figure. The reason is that Westerners automatically interpret the drawing as something that cannot exist in three dimensions, and they therefore are inhibited from reproducing it. The African tribal members, in contrast, do not make the assumption that the figure is "impossible" and instead view it in two dimensions, a perception that enables them to copy the figure with ease (Deregowski, 1973).

Cultural differences are also reflected in depth perception. A Western viewer of Figure 8 would interpret the hunter in the drawing as aiming for the antelope in the foreground, while an elephant stands under the tree in the background. A member of an isolated African tribe, however, interprets the scene very differently by assuming that the hunter is aiming at the elephant. Westerners use the difference in sizes between the two animals as a cue that the elephant is farther away than the antelope (Hudson, 1960).

The misinterpretations created by visual illusions are ultimately due, then, to errors in both fundamental visual processing and the way the brain interprets the information it receives. But visual illusions, by illustrating something fundamental about perception, become more than mere psychological curiosities. There is a basic connection between our prior knowledge, needs, motivations, and expectations about how the world is put together and the way we perceive it.

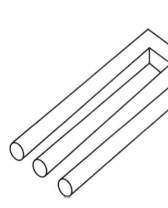

Figure 7 The "devil's tuning fork" has three prongs. . . . or does it have two?

Figure 8 Is the man aiming for the elephant or the antelope? Westerners assume that the differences in size between the two animals indicate that the elephant is farther away, and therefore the man is aiming for the antelope. In contrast, members of some African tribes, not used to depth cues in two-dimensional drawings, assume that the man is aiming for the elephant. (The drawing is based on Deregowski, 1973.) Do you think Westerners, who view the picture in three dimensions, could explain what they see to someone who views the scene in two dimensions and eventually get that person to view it in three dimensions?

Our view of the world is very much an outcome, then, of fundamental psychological factors. Furthermore, each person perceives the environment in a way that is unique and special (Knoblich & Sebanz, 2006; Repp & Knoblich, 2007).

RECAP

Explain the gestalt laws of organization.

- Perception is a constructive process in which people go beyond the stimuli that are physically present and try to construct a meaningful interpretation.

- The gestalt laws of organization are used to describe the way in which we organize bits and pieces of information into meaningful wholes, known as gestalts, through closure, proximity, similarity, and simplicity.

Identify top-down and bottom-up processing.

- In top-down processing, perception is guided by higher-level knowledge, experience, expectations, and motivations. In bottom-up

processing, perception consists of the progression of recognizing and processing information from individual components of a stimuli and moving to the perception of the whole.

Define perceptual constancy.

- Perceptual constancy permits us to perceive stimuli as unvarying in size, shape, and color despite changes in the environment or the appearance of the objects being perceived.

Explain depth perception.

- Depth perception is the ability to perceive distance and view the world in three dimensions even though the images projected on our retinas are two-dimensional. We are able to judge depth and distance as a result of binocular disparity and monocular cues, such as motion parallax, the relative size of images on the retina, and linear perspective.

Relate motion perception to daily life.

- Motion perception depends on cues such as the perceived movement of an object across the retina and information about how the head and eyes are moving.

Determine the importance of perceptual illusions.

- Visual illusions are physical stimuli that consistently produce errors in perception, causing judgments that do not reflect the physical reality of a stimulus accurately. One of the best-known illusions is the Müller-Lyer illusion.
- Visual illusions are usually the result of errors in the brain's interpretation of visual stimuli. Furthermore, culture clearly affects how we perceive the world.

[EVALUATE E Evaluate]

1. Match each of the following organizational laws with its meaning.

   a. Closure
   b. Proximity
   c. Similarity
   d. Simplicity

   1. Elements close together are grouped together.
   2. Patterns are perceived in the most basic, direct manner possible.
   3. Groupings are made in terms of complete figures.
   4. Elements similar in appearance are grouped together.

2. Processing that involves higher functions such as expectations and motivations is known as _____, whereas processing that recognizes the individual components of a stimulus is known as _____.

3. When a car passes you on the road and appears to shrink as it gets farther away, the phenomenon of _____ permits you to realize that the car is not in fact getting smaller.

4. _____ is the ability to view the world in three dimensions instead of two.

5. The brain makes use of a phenomenon known as _____, or the difference in the images the two eyes see, to give three dimensions to sight.

6. Match the monocular cues with their definitions.

   a. Relative size
   b. Linear perspective
   c. Motion parallax

   1. Straight lines seem to join together as they become more distant.
   2. An object changes position on the retina as the head moves.
   3. If two objects are the same size, the one producing the smaller retinal image is farther away.

[RETHINK R Rethink]

In what ways do painters represent three-dimensional scenes in two dimensions on a canvas? Do you think artists in non-Western cultures use the same or different principles to represent three-dimensionality? Why?

Answers to Evaluate Questions 1. a-3, b-1, c-4, d-2; 2. top-down, bottom-up; 3. perceptual constancy; 4. depth perception; 5. binocular disparity; 6. a-3, b-1, c-2

KEY TERMS

Gestalt laws of organization   LO11.1

Top-down processing   LO11.2

Bottom-up processing   LO11.2

Depth perception   LO11.4

Visual illusions   LO11.6

Psychology on the Web

1. Select one topic of personal interest to you that was mentioned in this set of modules (for instance, absolute thresholds, visual illusions). Find one "serious" or scientific website and one "popular" or commercial website with information about the chosen topic. Compare the type, level, and reliability of the information that you find on each site. Write a summary of your findings.

2. Are there more gestalt laws of organization than the four we've considered (closure, proximity, similarity, and simplicity)? Find the answer to this question on the Web and write a summary of any additional gestalt laws you find.

the case of . . .

THE CAUTIOUS PILOT

Captain Kevin Mueller has been flying private and commercial aircraft for almost 30 years. His flight from Boston to Dallas on the night of November 4 was as routine as any other; Mueller and his copilot had run through their preflight routine in the darkness of the cockpit and, after a 20-minute delay, were cleared for takeoff. Halfway through the flight, Captain Mueller noticed something unusual out of the corner of his eye: a point of light that was initially very faint but growing brighter. It stood out against the backdrop of terrestrial light sources because it appeared to be much closer, and possibly moving. Knowing that no other aircraft were operating in the area, Mueller focused his attention on the mysterious light source, concerned only with whether it might pose a threat to the safety of his passengers and crew.

When at last Mueller still couldn't make out what the mysterious object was after observing it for several minutes, he decided to take no chances. He rapidly increased altitude to put more distance between his aircraft and the object, which eventually faded from view and did not return. A later investigation could make no determination of what Mueller saw, but concluded that he acted appropriately to protect his passengers.

1. Why would Captain Mueller and his copilot sit in darkness before taking off on a night flight?

2. Why would the mysterious object have first appeared to Mueller in his peripheral vision?

3. What cues might Captain Mueller have used to determine that the mysterious object was much closer to his aircraft than any light source on the ground? Why might it have been difficult to determine whether the object was actually moving?

4. Even though many of the passengers were awake and looking out their windows, only Captain Mueller and his copilot noticed anything amiss. Why might the passengers have failed to notice the object when it was so obvious to the pilots?

5. Several of the passengers did, however, notice when Captain Mueller changed altitude despite having no visual cues as a reference. Describe the sense that allowed these passengers to detect the aircraft's motion.

profiles of **SUCCESS**

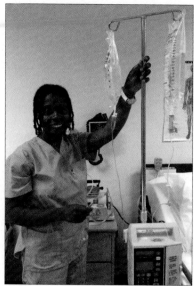

Courtesy of Nykeama Robinson

NAME:	**Nykeama Robinson**
SCHOOL:	**Lincoln Technical Institute**
DEGREE PROGRAM:	**Practical Nursing**

Nurses often confront complex situations, and according to Nykeama Robinson the profession requires a knowledge of a variety of approaches to health care, including the use of the principles of psychology.

"I think a class in psychology will allow you to get a better picture of human behavior," she said. "You can apply what you've learned to be better equipped to handle different obstacles that come your way."

"Because we are nurses, and constantly in the public's eye dealing with people regularly, I've had to deal with many challenges and difficulties in my professional endeavors," she explained. "I am now able to handle them very differently than I would have before, and I am very proud of myself for how I've grown as a result."

Pursuing the degree, however, was not without its challenges.

"It was difficult working full time and going to school," said Robinson, who would bring books to work to complete assignments, as well as setting aside vacation time for her studies. However, the challenges that Robinson faced in school proved to be the catalyst she needed to achieve her goal.

"I learned that I will make mistakes, and I learned that I had to develop a persevering attitude," she said. "All in all, I think it has allowed me to become a more unique individual."

Her advice to other students is straightforward:

"Hang in there! You can definitely do it! It may seem tough and the road is a little rocky, but don't give up," she stressed. "If you do step back, get right back in there and try again!"

[RETHINK R Rethink]

How might Robinson's knowledge of the senses and the biological basis of pain acquired in her psychology class help her to better understand and treat patient pain?

What are some of the biases and illusions in sensation and perception that would affect a nurse's ability to accurately understand a patient's symptoms?

visual summary 3
SENSATION AND PERCEPTION

MODULE 8 Sensing the World Around Us

Absolute Thresholds

Difference Thresholds
- Just noticeable difference
- Weber's law

Sensory Adaptation

MODULE 9 Vision

Eye Structure
- Retina
  - Rods
  - Cones

Visual Processing
- Color vision
  - Trichromatic theory
  - Opponent process theory
- Feature detection

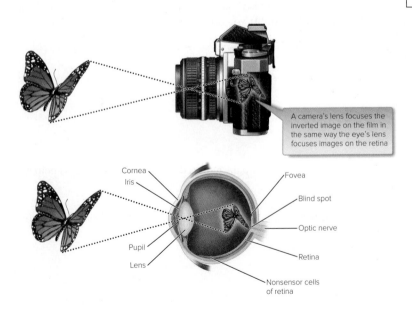

A camera's lens focuses the inverted image on the film in the same way the eye's lens focuses images on the retina

Cornea
Iris
Pupil
Lens
Fovea
Blind spot
Optic nerve
Retina
Nonsensor cells of retina

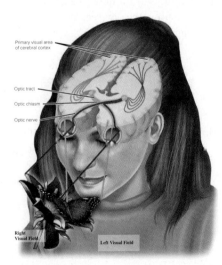

Primary visual area of cerebral cortex
Optic tract
Optic chiasm
Optic nerve
Right Visual Field
Left Visual Field

MODULE 10 Hearing and Other Senses

Ear Structure

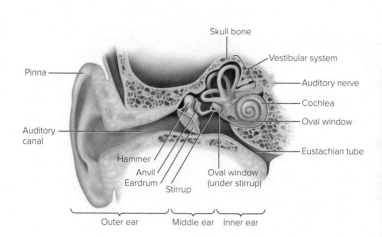

Skull bone

Vestibular system

Pinna

Auditory nerve

Cochlea

Oval window

Auditory canal

Eustachian tube

Hammer

Anvil

Oval window (under stirrup)

Eardrum

Stirrup

Outer ear Middle ear Inner ear

Other Senses

- Smell
- Taste
- Skin senses

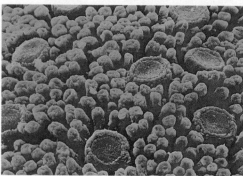

MODULE 11 Perceptual Organization

Gestalt Laws of Organization

| A | Closure | B | Proximity | C | Similarity | D | Simplicity |

Top-Down and Bottom-Up Processing

A B C D E F

9 10 11 12 13 14

Perceptual Constancy

Depth Perception

Motion Perception

Perceptual Illusions

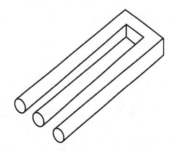

STATES OF
CONSCIOUSNESS

CHAPTER OUTLINE

The Power of Meditation

Renata Tebaldi, in her early 30s, has had three bouts of depression, but she says meditation helped prevent a relapse.

She first suffered depression following the death of her mother. Although she was prescribed antidepressants, she didn't want to rely on drugs. So she turned to mindfulness meditation.

Tebaldi learned to use meditation to relax. She was taught how to focus on her breathing and to spend time thinking about everyday things such as the sound of birds. It soon became second nature, and it helped her relieve her daily life stress enough to prevent a relapse of her depression.

Looking Ahead

Meditation is one of a number of methods people can use to alter their state of consciousness. It is an experience that many people find relaxing and pleasurable. Why this is so, what conscious experience is, and how and why we can alter it are some of the questions we address as we turn our attention to the study of consciousness.

Consciousness is the awareness of the sensations, thoughts, and feelings being experienced at a given moment. Unobservable to outsiders, consciousness is our subjective understanding of both the environment around us and our private internal world.

> **consciousness** The awareness of sensations, thoughts, and feelings being experienced at a given moment

In *waking consciousness,* we are awake and aware of our thoughts, emotions, and perceptions. All other states of consciousness are considered *altered states of consciousness.* Among these, sleeping and dreaming occur naturally; drug use and hypnosis, in contrast, are methods of deliberately altering one's state of consciousness.

Because consciousness is so personal a phenomenon, psychologists were sometimes reluctant to study it. After all, who can say that your consciousness is similar to or, for that matter, different from anyone else's? Contemporary psychologists reject the view that the study of consciousness is unsuitable for the field of psychology. Instead, they argue that several approaches permit the scientific study of consciousness. For example, behavioral neuroscientists can measure brain-wave patterns under conditions of consciousness ranging from sleep to waking to hypnotic trances. And new understanding of the chemistry of drugs such as marijuana and alcohol has provided insights into the way they produce their pleasurable—as well as adverse—effects (Baars & Seth, 2009; Wells, Phillips, & McCarthy, 2011; Malouff & Rooke, 2013).

Whatever state of consciousness we are in—be it waking, sleeping, hypnotic, or drug induced—the complexities of consciousness are profound.

module 12

Sleep and Dreams

Learning Outcomes Prepare

》 **LO12.1** Summarize the stages of sleep.

》 **LO12.2** Explain REM sleep.

》 **LO12.3** Explain why we sleep and how much sleep is necessary.

》 **LO12.4** Differentiate the explanations of dreaming.

》 **LO12.5** State the impact of sleep disturbances.

》 **LO12.6** Explain circadian rhythms.

MODULE OUTLINE Organize

The Stages of Sleep

REM Sleep: The Paradox of Sleep

Why Do We Sleep, and How Much Sleep Is Necessary?

The Function and Meaning of Dreaming

Sleep Disturbances: Slumbering Problems

Try It! Are You Getting Enough Sleep?

Circadian Rhythms: Life Cycles

Becoming an Informed Consumer of Psychology: Sleeping Better

W Work

During a 9-day cross-country bike race, 29-year-old Mike Trevino averaged one hour of sleep per day. The first three days he didn't sleep at all, and over the next six he took completely dream-free naps of at most 90 minutes. His waking thoughts became fuzzy, depicting movie-like plots starring himself and his crew. The whole experience was like a serial dream in which he remained conscious, if only barely. He finished in second place. (Source: Adapted from Springen, 2004, p. 47)

Trevino's case is unusual—in part because he was able to function with so little sleep for so long—and it raises a host of questions about sleep and dreams. Can we live without sleep? What is the meaning of dreams? More generally, what is sleep?

Although sleeping is a state that we all experience, there are still many unanswered questions about sleep that remain, along with a considerable number of myths. Test your knowledge of sleep and dreams by answering the questionnaire in Figure 1.

》 LO12.1 The Stages of Sleep

Most of us consider sleep a time of tranquility when we set aside the tensions of the day and spend the night in uneventful slumber. However, a closer look at sleep shows that a good deal of activity occurs throughout the night, and that what at first appears to be a unitary state is, in fact, quite diverse.

Measures of electrical activity in the brain show that the brain is active throughout the night. It produces electrical discharges with systematic, wavelike patterns that change in height (or amplitude) and speed (or frequency) in regular sequences. There is also significant physical activity in muscle and eye movements.

© Stockbyte/Getty Images RF

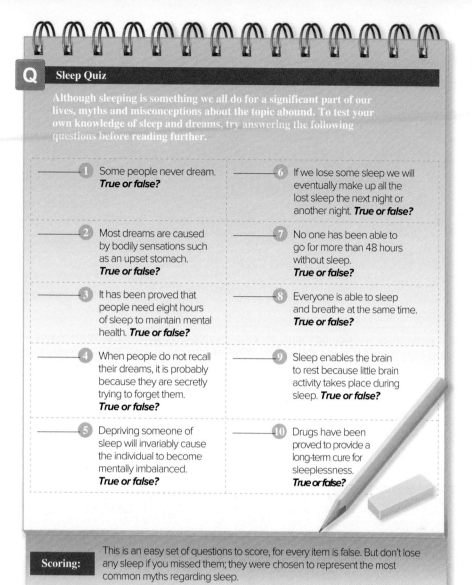

Q Sleep Quiz

Although sleeping is something we all do for a significant part of our lives, myths and misconceptions about the topic abound. To test your own knowledge of sleep and dreams, try answering the following questions before reading further.

1 Some people never dream. *True or false?*

2 Most dreams are caused by bodily sensations such as an upset stomach. *True or false?*

3 It has been proved that people need eight hours of sleep to maintain mental health. *True or false?*

4 When people do not recall their dreams, it is probably because they are secretly trying to forget them. *True or false?*

5 Depriving someone of sleep will invariably cause the individual to become mentally imbalanced. *True or false?*

6 If we lose some sleep we will eventually make up all the lost sleep the next night or another night. *True or false?*

7 No one has been able to go for more than 48 hours without sleep. *True or false?*

8 Everyone is able to sleep and breathe at the same time. *True or false?*

9 Sleep enables the brain to rest because little brain activity takes place during sleep. *True or false?*

10 Drugs have been proved to provide a long-term cure for sleeplessness. *True or false?*

Scoring: This is an easy set of questions to score, for every item is false. But don't lose any sleep if you missed them; they were chosen to represent the most common myths regarding sleep.

People progress through a series of distinct stages of sleep during a night's rest—known as *stage 1* through *stage 4* and *REM sleep*—moving through the stages in cycles lasting about 90 minutes. Each of these sleep stages is associated with a unique pattern of brain waves, which you can see in Figure 2. (In a newer version of the sleep stages proposed by the American Academy of Sleep Medicine, stage 3 and stage 4 sleep have been combined, but it is not yet used as frequently as the traditional four-stage description of sleep.)

When people first go to sleep, they move from a waking state in which they are relaxed with their eyes closed into **stage 1 sleep,** which is characterized by relatively rapid, low-amplitude brain waves. This is actually a stage of transition between wakefulness and sleep and lasts only a few minutes. During stage 1, images sometimes appear, as if we were viewing still photos, although this is not true dreaming, which occurs later in the night (see Figure 2).

As sleep becomes deeper, people enter **stage 2 sleep,** which is characterized by a slower, more regular wave pattern. However, there are also momentary interruptions of sharply pointed, spiky waves that are called *sleep spindles*. It becomes increasingly difficult to awaken a person from sleep as stage 2 progresses.

As people drift into **stage 3 sleep,** the brain waves become slower, with higher peaks and lower valleys. By the time sleepers arrive at **stage 4 sleep,** the pattern is even slower and more regular, and people are least responsive to outside stimulation.

stage 1 sleep The state of transition between wakefulness and sleep, characterized by relatively rapid, low-amplitude waves

stage 2 sleep A sleep deeper than that of stage 1, characterized by a slower, more regular wave pattern, along with momentary interruptions of sleep spindles

stage 3 sleep A sleep characterized by slow brain waves, with greater peaks and valleys in the wave pattern than in stage 2 sleep

stage 4 sleep The deepest stage of sleep, during which we are least responsive to outside stimulation

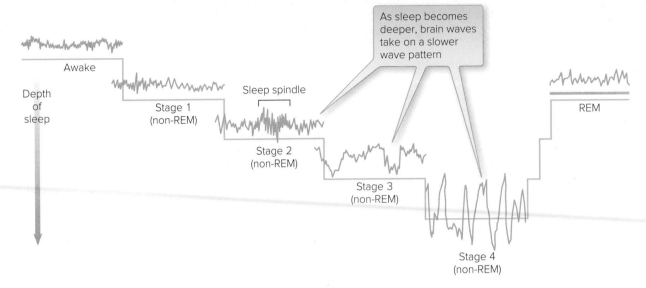

Awake

Depth of sleep

Stage 1 (non-REM)

Sleep spindle

As sleep becomes deeper, brain waves take on a slower wave pattern

REM

Stage 2 (non-REM)

Stage 3 (non-REM)

Stage 4 (non-REM)

Figure 2 Brain-wave patterns (measured by an EEG apparatus) vary significantly during the different stages of sleep (Hobson, 2007). As sleep moves from stage 1 through stage 4, brain waves become slower. Source: Adapted from Hobson, 1989.

As you can see in Figure 3, stage 4 sleep is most likely to occur during the early part of the night. In the first half of the night, sleep is dominated by stages 3 and 4. The second half is characterized by stages 1 and 2—as well as a fifth stage during which dreams occur.

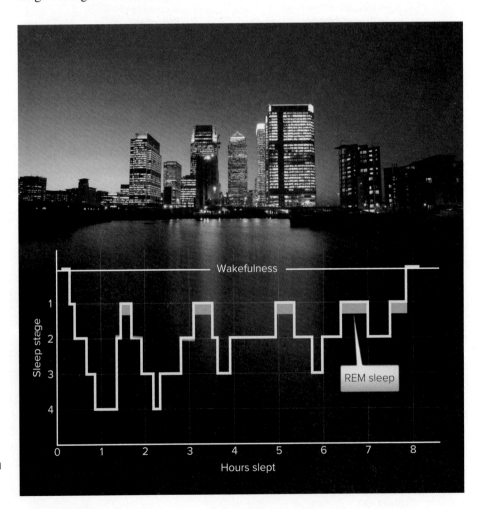

Figure 3 During the night, the typical sleeper passes through all four stages of sleep and several REM periods. Source: Adapted from Hartmann, 1967. Photo: © Dominic Burke/Getty Images

» LO12.2 REM Sleep: The Paradox of Sleep

Several times a night, when sleepers have cycled back to a shallower state of sleep, something curious happens. Their heart rate increases and becomes irregular, their blood pressure rises, and their breathing rate increases. Most characteristic of this period is the back-and-forth movement of their eyes, as if they were watching an action-filled movie. This period of sleep is called **rapid eye movement, or REM, sleep** and contrasts with stages 1 through 4, which are collectively labeled *non-REM* (or *NREM)* sleep. REM sleep occupies a little over 20 percent of adults' total sleeping time.

Paradoxically, while all this activity is occurring, the major muscles of the body appear to be paralyzed. In addition, and most important, REM sleep is usually accompanied by dreams, which—whether or not people remember them—are experienced by *everyone* during some part of the night. Although some dreaming occurs in non-REM stages of sleep, dreams are most likely to occur in the REM period, where they are the most vivid and easily remembered (Leclair-Visonneau et al., 2010; Manni & Terzaghi, 2013; Herlin et al., 2015).

There is good reason to believe that REM sleep plays a critical role in everyday human functioning. People deprived of REM sleep—by being awakened every time they begin to display the physiological signs of that stage—show a *rebound effect* when allowed to rest undisturbed. With this rebound effect, REM-deprived sleepers spend significantly more time in REM sleep than they normally would. In addition, REM sleep may play a role in learning and memory, allowing us to rethink and restore information and emotional experiences that we've had during the day (Kookoolis, Pace-Schott, & McNamara, 2010; Rivera-Garcia et al., 2011; Nielsen et al., 2015).

rapid eye movement (REM) sleep Sleep occupying 20 percent of an adult's sleeping time, characterized by increased heart rate, blood pressure, and breathing rate; erections (in males); eye movements; and the experience of dreaming

STUDY ALERT

It is important to differentiate the five stages of sleep (stage 1, stage 2, stage 3, stage 4, and REM sleep), which produce different brain-wave patterns.

People progress through four distinct stages of sleep during a night's rest spread over cycles lasting about 90 minutes. REM sleep, which occupies only 20 percent of adults' sleeping time, occurs in stage 1 sleep. These photos, taken at different times of night, show the synchronized patterns of a couple accustomed to sleeping in the same bed. (all) © Ted Spagna/Science Source

>> LO12.3 Why Do We Sleep, and How Much Sleep Is Necessary?

> Sleep is a requirement for normal human functioning, although, surprisingly, we don't know exactly why.

Sleep is a requirement for normal human functioning, although, surprisingly, we don't know exactly why. It is reasonable to expect that our bodies would require a tranquil "rest and relaxation" period to revitalize themselves, and experiments with rats show that total sleep deprivation results in death. But why?

Some researchers, using an evolutionary perspective, suggest that sleep permitted our ancestors to conserve energy at night, a time when food was relatively hard to come by. Others suggest that the reduced activity of the brain during non-REM sleep may give neurons in the brain a chance to repair themselves. Another hypothesis suggests that the onset of REM sleep stops the release of neurotransmitters called *monoamines,* and so permits receptor cells to get some necessary rest and to increase their sensitivity during periods of wakefulness. Still, these explanations remain speculative (McNamara, 2004; Steiger, 2007; Tononi & Cirelli, 2013).

Scientists have also been unable to establish just how much sleep is absolutely required. Most people today sleep between seven and eight hours each night, which is three hours a night less than people slept a hundred years ago. In addition, there is wide variability among individuals, with some people needing as little as three hours of sleep (see Figure 4). Sleep requirements also vary over the course of a lifetime: as they age, people generally need less and less sleep.

People who participate in sleep deprivation experiments, in which they are kept awake for stretches as long as 200 hours, show no lasting effects. It's no fun—they feel weary and irritable, can't concentrate, and show a loss of creativity, even after only minor deprivation. They also show a decline in logical reasoning ability. However, after being allowed to sleep normally, they bounce back quickly and are able to perform at predeprivation levels after just a few days (Mograss et al., 2009; Jackson et al., 2013; Maturana et al., 2015).

In short, as far as we know, most people suffer no permanent consequences of such temporary sleep deprivation. But—and this is an important but—a lack of sleep can make us feel edgy, slow our reaction time, and lower our performance on academic and physical tasks. In addition, we put ourselves, and others, at risk when we carry out routine activities, such as driving, when we're very sleepy (Anderson & Home, 2006; Morad et al., 2009; Kong, Soon, & Chee, 2011).

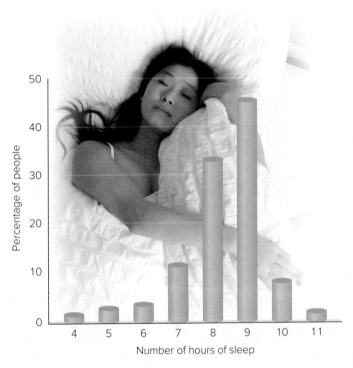

Figure 4 Although most people report sleeping between eight and nine hours per night, the amount varies a great deal. Where would you place yourself on this graph, and why do you think you need more or less sleep than others? Source: Adapted from Borbély, 1986, p. 43. Photo: © B2M Productions/Getty Images RF

» LO12.4 The Function and Meaning of Dreaming

The average person experiences 150,000 dreams by the age of 70. They typically encompass everyday events such as going to the supermarket, working at the office, and preparing a meal. Students dream about going to class; professors dream about lecturing. Dental patients dream of getting their teeth drilled; dentists dream of drilling the wrong tooth. The English have tea with the queen in their dreams; in the United States, people go to a bar with the president (Schredl & Piel, 2005; Taylor & Bryant, 2007; Nosek et al., 2015). Figure 5 shows the most common themes found in people's dreams.

But what, if anything, do all these dreams mean? Whether dreams have a specific significance and function is a question that scientists have considered for many years, and they have developed the three alternative theories discussed next (and summarized in Figure 6).

Do Dreams Represent Unconscious Wish Fulfillment?

Sigmund Freud viewed dreams as a guide to the unconscious (Freud, 1900). In his **unconscious wish fulfillment theory,** he proposed that dreams represent unconscious wishes that dreamers desire to see fulfilled. However, because these wishes are threatening to the dreamer's conscious awareness, the actual wishes—called the **latent content of dreams**—are disguised. The true subject and meaning of a dream, then, may have little to do with its apparent story line, which Freud called the **manifest content of dreams.**

unconscious wish fulfillment theory Sigmund Freud's theory that dreams represent unconscious wishes that dreamers desire to see fulfilled

latent content of dreams According to Sigmund Freud, the "disguised" meaning of dreams, hidden by more obvious subjects

manifest content of dreams According to Sigmund Freud, the apparent story line of dreams

STUDY ALERT

Use Figure 6 to learn the differences between the three main explanations of dreaming.

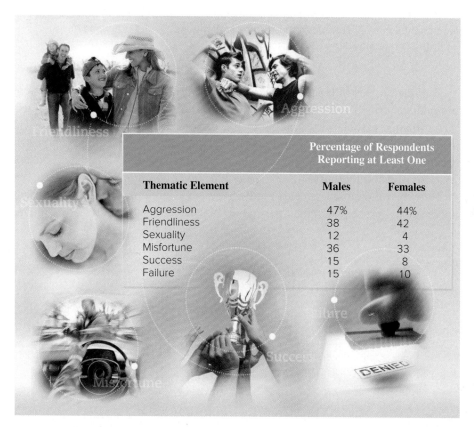

Thematic Element	Percentage of Respondents Reporting at Least One	
	Males	**Females**
Aggression	47%	44%
Friendliness	38	42
Sexuality	12	4
Misfortune	36	33
Success	15	8
Failure	15	10

Figure 5 Although dreams tend to be subjective to the person having them, there are common elements that frequently occur in everyone's dreams. Why do you think so many common dreams are unpleasant and so few are pleasant? Do you think this tells us anything about the function of dreams? Source: Domhoff & Schneider, 1999. Photos: (family) © Image Source/PunchStock RF; (boys fighting) © BananaStock/PunchStock RF; (couple) © George Doyle/Getty Images RF; (car driving) © Dimitri Otis/Getty Images RF; (trophy) © Digital Vision/Getty Images RF; (denied stamp) © John Knill/Getty Images RF

Theory	Basic Explanation	Meaning of Dreams	Is Meaning of Dream Disguised?
Unconscious wish fulfillment theory (Freud)	Dreams represent unconscious wishes the dreamer wants to fulfill	Latent content reveals unconscious wishes	Yes, by manifest content of dreams
Dreams-for-survival theory	Information relevant to daily survival is reconsidered and reprocessed	Clues to everyday concerns about survival	Not necessarily
Activation-synthesis theory	Dreams are the result of random activation of various memories, which are tied together in a logical story line	Dream scenario that is constructed is related to dreamer's concerns	Not necessarily

Figure 6 Three theories of dreams. Researchers have yet to agree on the fundamental meaning of dreams, and so several theories about dreaming have emerged. © gosphotodesign/Shutterstock.com

To Freud, it was important to pierce the armor of a dream's manifest content to understand its true meaning. To do this, Freud tried to get people to discuss their dreams, associating symbols in the dreams with events in the past. He also suggested that certain common symbols with universal meanings appear in dreams. For example, to Freud, dreams in which a person is flying symbolize a wish for sexual intercourse. (See Figure 7 for other common symbols.)

Many psychologists reject Freud's view that dreams typically represent unconscious wishes and that particular objects and events in a dream are

Figure 7 According to Freud, dreams contain common symbols with universal meanings.

Symbol (Manifest Content of Dream)	Interpretation (Latent Content)
Climbing up a stairway, crossing a bridge, riding in an elevator, flying in an airplane, walking down a long hallway, entering a room, train traveling through a tunnel	Sexual intercourse
Apples, peaches, grapefruits	Breasts
Bullets, fire, snakes, sticks, umbrellas, guns, hoses, knives	Male sex organs
Ovens, boxes, tunnels, closets, caves, bottles, ships	Female sex organs

symbolic. Instead, they believe that the direct, overt action of a dream is the focal point of its meaning. For example, a dream in which we are walking down a long hallway to take an exam for which we haven't studied does not relate to unconscious, unacceptable wishes. Instead, it simply may mean that we are concerned about an impending test. Even more complex dreams can often be interpreted in terms of everyday concerns and stress (Siegel, 2010; Duesbury, 2011; Fischmann, 2016).

Dreams-for-Survival Theory

According to the **dreams-for-survival theory,** dreams permit information that is critical for our daily survival to be reconsidered and reprocessed during sleep. Dreaming is seen as an inheritance from our animal ancestors, whose small brains were unable to sift sufficient information during waking hours. Consequently, dreaming provided a mechanism that permitted the processing of information 24 hours a day.

According to this theory, dreams represent concerns about our daily lives, illustrating our uncertainties, indecisions, ideas, and desires. Dreams are seen, then, as consistent with everyday living. Rather than being disguised wishes, as Freud suggested, they represent key concerns growing out of our daily experiences (Ross, 2006; Horton, 2011).

Research supports the dreams-for-survival theory, suggesting that certain dreams permit people to focus on and consolidate memories, particularly dreams that pertain to "how-to-do-it" memories related to motor skills. For example, rats seem to dream about mazes that they learned to run through during the day, at least according to the patterns of brain activity that appear while they are sleeping (Stickgold et al., 2001; Kuriyama, Stickgold, & Walker, 2004; C. Smith, 2006).

dreams-for-survival theory The theory suggesting that dreams permit information that is critical for our daily survival to be reconsidered and reprocessed during sleep

activation-synthesis theory J. Allan Hobson's theory that the brain produces random electrical energy during REM (rapid eye movement) sleep that stimulates memories stored in the brain

Activation-Synthesis Theory

According to psychiatrist J. Allan Hobson, who proposed **activation-synthesis theory,** the brain produces random electrical energy during REM sleep, possibly as a result of changes in the production of particular neurotransmitters. This electrical energy randomly stimulates memories lodged in various portions of the brain. Because we have a need to make sense of our world even while asleep, the brain takes these chaotic memories and weaves them into a logical story line, filling in the gaps to produce a rational scenario (Hobson, 2005; Hangya et al., 2011).

Activation-synthesis theory has been refined by the *activation information modulation (AIM) theory.* According to AIM, dreams begin in the brain's pons, which sends random signals to the brain's cortex. Areas of the cortex that are related to particular waking behaviors are related to the content of dreams. For example, areas of the brain related to vision are involved in the visual aspects of the dream, while areas of the brain related to movement are involved in aspects of the dream related to motion (Hobson, 2007; Dang-Vu et al., 2010).

Activation-synthesis and AIM theories do not entirely reject the view that dreams reflect unconscious wishes. He suggests that the particular scenario a dreamer produces

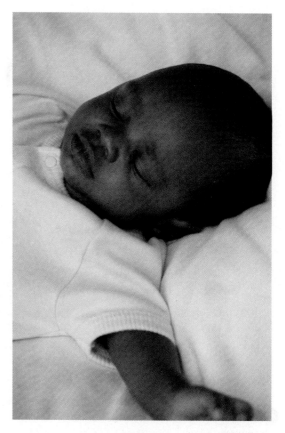

Sleep is important to general well-being at any age. Do you feel you get enough sleep? © Fuse/Getty Images RF

is not random but instead is a clue to the dreamer's fears, emotions, and concerns. Hence, what starts out as a random process culminates in something meaningful.

» LO12.5 Sleep Disturbances: Slumbering Problems

At one time or another, almost all of us have difficulty sleeping—a condition known as *insomnia*. It could be due to a particular situation, such as the breakup of a relationship, concern about a test score, or the loss of a job. Some cases of insomnia, however, have no obvious cause. Some people are simply unable to fall asleep easily, or they go to sleep readily but wake up frequently during the night. Insomnia is a problem that afflicts as many as one-third of all people (Henry et al., 2008; Karlson et al., 2013; Eidelman et al., 2016). To get a sense of your own issues with sleep, complete the Try It!

> **Some people are simply unable to fall asleep easily, or they go to sleep readily but wake up frequently during the night.**

Try It!

Are You Getting Enough Sleep?

How likely are you to doze off in the following situations? Rate the chance that you would fall asleep in the following circumstances during the day, using this scale:

1 = Highly unlikely I would fall asleep
2 = Moderate chance I would fall asleep
3 = Very high chance I would asleep

1. Reading a book ____
2. Watching television or a movie ____
3. Participating in a meeting ____
4. Taking a nap in the afternoon ____
5. Chatting with someone ____
6. Studying after lunch ____
7. Riding as a passenger in a car ____

Interpretation

Add up the numbers that you marked above. If your score is 7 to 13, you are probably getting enough sleep. If you score 14 or higher, you may not be getting enough sleep, and you should consider trying to spend more time sleeping.

Other sleep problems are less common than insomnia, although they are still widespread. For instance, some 20 million people suffer from sleep apnea. *Sleep apnea* is a condition in which a person has difficulty breathing while sleeping. The result is disturbed, fitful sleep, as the person is constantly reawakened when the lack of oxygen becomes great enough to trigger a waking response. Some people with apnea wake as many as 500 times during the course of a night, although they may not even be aware that they have wakened. Not surprisingly, such disturbed sleep results in extreme fatigue the next day. Sleep apnea also may play a role in *sudden infant death syndrome (SIDS)*, a mysterious killer of seemingly normal infants who die while sleeping (Tippin, Sparks, & Rizzo, 2009; Arimoto et al., 2011; Bjornsdottir et al., 2015).

Night terrors are sudden awakenings from non-REM sleep that are accompanied by extreme fear, panic, and strong physiological arousal. Usually occurring in stage 4 sleep, night terrors may be so frightening that a sleeper awakens with a shriek. Although night terrors initially produce great agitation, victims usually can get back to sleep fairly quickly. They are much less frequent than nightmares and occur most frequently in children between the ages of 3 and 8 (Lowe, Humphreys, & Williams, 2007; Carter, 2010).

From the perspective of . . .

A Law Enforcement Officer What impact would an irregular sleep schedule have on your job performance? What would you do to ensure you were getting enough rest?

Narcolepsy is uncontrollable sleeping that occurs for short periods while a person is awake. No matter what the activity—holding a heated conversation, exercising, or driving—a narcoleptic will suddenly fall asleep. People with narcolepsy go directly from wakefulness to REM sleep, skipping the other stages. The causes of narcolepsy are not known, although there could be a genetic component because narcolepsy runs in families (Ervik, Abdelnoor, & Heier, 2006; Vignatelli et al., 2011; Zamarian et al., 2015).

We know relatively little about sleeptalking and sleepwalking, two sleep disturbances that are usually harmless. Both occur during stage 4 sleep and are more common in children than in adults. Sleeptalkers and sleepwalkers usually have a vague consciousness of the world around them, and a sleepwalker may be able to walk with agility around obstructions in a crowded room. Unless a sleepwalker wanders into a dangerous environment, sleepwalking typically poses little risk. And the common idea that it's dangerous to wake a sleepwalker? It's just superstition (Guilleminault et al., 2005; Lee-Chiong, 2006).

» LO12.6 Circadian Rhythms: Life Cycles

The fact that we cycle back and forth between wakefulness and sleep is one example of the body's circadian rhythms. **Circadian rhythms** (from the Latin *circa diem,* or "around the day") are biological processes that occur regularly on approximately a 24-hour cycle. Sleeping and waking, for instance, occur naturally to the beat of an internal pacemaker that works on a cycle of about

circadian rhythms Biological processes that occur regularly on approximately a 24-hour cycle

7:00 A.M.
• Hay fever symptoms are worst

8:00 A.M.
• Risk for heart attack and stroke is highest
• Symptoms of rheumatoid arthritis are worst
• Helper T lymphocytes are at their lowest daytime level

Noon
• Level of hemoglobin in the blood is at its peak

6:00 A.M.
• Onset of menstruation is most likely
• Insulin levels in the bloodstream are lowest
• Blood pressure and heart rate begin to rise
• Levels of the stress hormone cortisol increase
• Melatonin levels begin to fall

3:00 P.M.
• Grip strength, respiratory rate, and reflex sensitivity are highest

4:00 P.M.
• Body temperature, pulse rate, and blood pressure peak

4:00 A.M.
• Asthma attacks are most likely to occur

6:00 P.M.
• Urinary flow is highest

2:00 A.M.
• Levels of growth hormone are highest

9:00 P.M.
• Pain threshold is lowest

1:00 A.M.
• Pregnant women are most likely to go into labor
• Immune cells called helper T lymphocytes are at their peak

11:00 P.M.
• Allergic responses are most likely

Figure 8 Day times, night times: regular body changes over every 24-hour period. Over the course of the day, our circadian rhythms produce a wide variety of effects. Source: Adapted from Young, 2000. Photo: © Medioimages/Photodisc/Getty Images RF

24 hours. Several other bodily functions, such as body temperature, hormone production, and blood pressure, also follow circadian rhythms (Blatter & Cajochen, 2007; Karatsoreos et al., 2011; Labrecque & Cermakian, 2015). Circadian cycles are complex, and they involve a variety of behaviors (see Figure 8).

Circadian rhythms explain the phenomenon of *jet lag,* caused by flying through multiple time zones. Pilots, as well as others who must work on constantly changing time shifts (police officers and medical personnel), must fight their internal clocks. The result can be fatigue, irritability, and, even worse, outright error. In fact, many major disasters caused by human error occurred late at night (Refinetti, 2005; Kyriacou & Hastings, 2010).

becoming an informed consumer of psychology

Sleeping Better

Do you have trouble sleeping? You're not alone—70 million people in the United States have sleep problems. For those of us who spend hours tossing and turning in bed, psychologists studying sleep disturbances have a number of suggestions for overcoming insomnia (Benca, 2005; Finley & Cowley, 2005; Reddy, 2013). Here are some ideas.

■ *Exercise during the day (at least six hours before bedtime) and avoid naps.* Not surprisingly, it helps to be tired before going to sleep! Moreover, learning systematic relaxation techniques and biofeedback can help you unwind from the day's stresses and tensions.

- *Choose a regular bedtime and stick to it.* Adhering to a habitual schedule helps your internal timing mechanisms regulate your body more effectively.

- *Avoid long naps—but consider taking short ones.* If you have trouble sleeping at night, it's best to avoid long naps. On the other hand, a short nap lasting 10 to 20 minutes may be ideal to boost energy and increase alertness. In fact, research shows that, at least in preschool children, midday naps improve recall of material learned earlier in the day—although we don't yet know if that applies to older individuals (Kurdziel, Duclos, & Spencer, 2013).

- *Avoid drinks with caffeine after lunch.* The effects of beverages such as coffee, tea, and some soft drinks can linger for as long as 8 to 12 hours after they are consumed.

- *Drink a glass of warm milk at bedtime.* Your grandparents were right when they dispensed this advice: milk contains the chemical tryptophan, which helps people fall asleep.

- *Avoid sleeping pills.* Even though 25 percent of U.S. adults report having taken medication for sleep in the previous year, in the long run sleep medications can do more harm than good because they disrupt the normal sleep cycle.

- *Try not to sleep.* This approach works because people often have difficulty falling asleep because they are trying so hard. A better strategy is to go to bed only when you feel tired. If you don't get to sleep within 10 minutes, leave the bedroom and do something else, returning to bed only when you feel sleepy. Continue this process all night if necessary. But get up at your usual hour in the morning, and don't take any naps during the day. After three or four weeks, most people become conditioned to associate their beds with sleep—and fall asleep rapidly at night (Ubell, 1993; Smith, 2001).

© Stockbyte/Getty Images RF

© Sabine Scheckel/Getty Images RF

For long-term problems with sleep, you might consider visiting a sleep disorders center. For information on accredited clinics, consult the American Academy of Sleep Medicine at www.aasmnet.org.

RECAP

- Consciousness is a person's awareness of the sensations, thoughts, and feelings at a given moment. Waking consciousness can vary from more active to more passive states.

- Altered states of consciousness include naturally occurring sleep and dreaming, as well as hypnotic and drug-induced states.

Summarize the stages of sleep.

- Using the electroencephalogram, or EEG, to study sleep, scientists have found that the brain is active throughout the night, and that sleep proceeds through a series of stages identified by unique patterns of brain waves.

Explain REM sleep.

- REM (rapid eye movement) sleep is characterized by an increase in heart rate, a rise in blood pressure, an increase in the rate of breathing, and, in males, erections. Dreams occur during this stage.

Explain why we sleep and how much sleep is necessary.

- Sleep is a requirement for normal functioning, although it is not yet known why it is necessary.

- There is great variability regarding how much people sleep.

Differentiate the explanations of dreaming.

- Freud suggests dreams have both a manifest content (the story line) and a latent content (the true meaning).
- The dreams-for-survival theory suggests that information relevant to daily survival is reconsidered and reprocessed in dreams.
- The activation-synthesis theory proposes that dreams are a result of random electrical energy that stimulates different memories, which then are woven into a coherent story line.

State the impact of sleep disturbances.

- Insomnia is a sleep disorder characterized by difficulty sleeping. Sleep apnea is a condition in which people have difficulty sleeping and breathing at the same time. People with narcolepsy have an uncontrollable urge to sleep. Sleepwalking and sleeptalking are relatively harmless.
- Psychologists and sleep researchers advise people with insomnia to increase exercise during the day, avoid caffeine and sleeping pills, drink a glass of warm milk before bedtime, and try to avoid going to sleep.

Explain circadian rhythms.

- Circadian rhythms are biological processes that occur regularly on approximately a 24-hour cycle.
- Sleep, wakefulness, body temperature, and other bodily functions follow circadian rhythms.

[EVALUATE E Evaluate]

1. _____ is the term used to describe our understanding of the world external to us, as well as our own internal world.
2. A great deal of neural activity goes on during sleep. True or false?
3. Dreams occur in _____ sleep.
4. _____ are internal bodily processes that occur on a daily cycle.
5. Freud's theory of unconscious _____ states that the actual wishes an individual expresses in dreams are disguised because they are threatening to the person's conscious awareness.
6. Match the theory of dreaming with its definition.

   1. Activation-synthesis theory
   2. Dreams-for-survival theory
   3. Unconscious theory wish fulfillment

   a. Dreams permit important information to be reprocessed during sleep.
   b. The manifest content of dreams disguises the latent content of the dreams.
   c. Electrical energy stimulates random memories, which are woven together to produce dreams.

[RETHINK R Rethink]

Suppose that a new "miracle pill" will allow a person to function with only one hour of sleep per night. However, because a night's sleep is so short, a person who takes the pill will never dream again. Knowing what you do about the functions of sleep and dreaming, what would be some advantages and drawbacks of such a pill from a personal standpoint? Would you take such a pill?

Answers to Evaluate Questions 1. consciousness; 2. true; 3. REM; 4. circadian rhythms; 5. wish fulfillment; 6. 1-c, 2-a, 3-b

KEY TERMS

Consciousness   LO12.1

Stage 1 sleep   LO12.1

Stage 2 sleep   LO12.1

Stage 3 sleep   LO12.1

Stage 4 sleep   LO12.1

Rapid eye movement (REM) sleep   LO12.2

Unconscious wish fulfillment theory   LO12.4

Latent content of dreams   LO12.4

Manifest content of dreams   LO12.4

Dreams-for-survival theory   LO12.4

Activation-synthesis theory   LO12.4

Circadian rhythms   LO12.6

Hypnosis and Meditation

Learning Outcomes  **Prepare**

» **LO13.1** Define hypnosis.

» **LO13.2** Describe the effects of meditation.

MODULE OUTLINE ⊙ Organize

Hypnosis: A Trance-Forming Experience?

Meditation: Regulating Our Own State of Consciousness

Exploring Diversity: Cross-Cultural Routes to Altered States of Consciousness

You are feeling relaxed and drowsy. You are getting sleepier. Your body is becoming limp. Your eyelids are feeling heavier. Your eyes are closing; you can't keep them open anymore. You are totally relaxed. Now, place your hands above your head. But you will find they are getting heavier and heavier—so heavy you can barely keep them up. In fact, although you are straining as hard as you can, you will be unable to hold them up any longer.

An observer watching this scene would notice a curious phenomenon occurring. Many of the people listening to the voice are dropping their arms to their sides. The reason for this strange behavior? Those people have been hypnotized.

» LO13.1 Hypnosis: A Trance-Forming Experience?

hypnosis A trancelike state of heightened susceptibility to the suggestions of others

People under **hypnosis** are in a trancelike state of heightened susceptibility to the suggestions of others. In some respects, it appears that they are asleep. Yet other aspects of their behavior contradict this notion, for people are attentive to the hypnotist's suggestions and may carry out bizarre or silly suggestions.

Despite their compliance when hypnotized, people do not lose all will of their own. They will not perform antisocial behaviors, and they will not carry out self-destructive acts. People will not reveal hidden truths about themselves, and they are capable of lying. Moreover, people cannot be hypnotized against their will—despite popular misconceptions (Raz, 2007; Lynn, Laurence, & Kirsch, 2015).

There are wide variations in people's susceptibility to hypnosis. About 5 to 20 percent of the population cannot be hypnotized at all, and some 15 percent are very easily hypnotized. Most people fall somewhere in between. Moreover, the ease with which a person is hypnotized is related to a number of other characteristics. People who are hypnotized readily are also easily absorbed while reading books or listening to music, becoming unaware of what is happening around them, and they often spend an unusual amount of time daydreaming. In sum, then, they show a high ability to concentrate and to become completely absorbed in what they are doing (Rubichi et al., 2005; Benham, Woody, & Wilson, 2006).

A Different State of Consciousness?

The question of whether hypnosis is a state of consciousness that is qualitatively different from normal waking consciousness is controversial. Some psychologists believe that hypnosis represents a state of consciousness that differs significantly from other states. In this view, the high suggestibility, increased ability to recall and construct images, and acceptance of suggestions that clearly contradict reality suggest it is a different state. Moreover, there are specific changes in electrical activity in the brain that are associated with hypnosis. Such changes support the position that hypnosis is a state of consciousness different from normal waking (Capafons, et al., 2008; Hinterberger, Schöner, & Halsband, 2011).

> The question of whether hypnosis is a state of consciousness that is qualitatively different from normal waking consciousness is controversial.

On the other side of the controversy are psychologists who reject the notion that hypnosis is a state significantly different from normal waking consciousness. They argue that altered brain-wave patterns are not sufficient to demonstrate a qualitative difference because no other specific physiological changes occur when people are in trances. Furthermore, little support exists for the contention that adults can recall memories of childhood events accurately while hypnotized. That lack of evidence suggests that there is nothing qualitatively special about the hypnotic trance (Hongchun & Ming, 2006; Wagstaff, 2009; Hunter, 2011).

Despite common misconceptions, people cannot be hypnotized against their will, nor do they lose all will of their own. Why, then, do people sometimes behave so unusually when asked to by a hypnotist? © AP Images/Midland Daily News, Erin Painter

There is increasing agreement that the controversy over the nature of hypnosis has led to extreme positions on both sides of the issue. More recent approaches suggest that the hypnotic state may best be viewed as lying along a continuum. In this view, hypnosis is neither a totally different state of consciousness nor totally similar to normal waking consciousness (Lynn et al., 2000; Kihlstrom, 2005b; Jamieson, 2007).

From the perspective of . . .

A Retail or Restaurant Supervisor Would you allow (or even encourage) employees to engage in meditation during the workday? Why or why not?

≫ LO13.2 Meditation: Regulating Our Own State of Consciousness

meditation A learned technique for refocusing attention that brings about an altered state of consciousness

When traditional practitioners of the ancient Eastern religion of Zen Buddhism want to achieve greater spiritual insight, they turn to a technique that has been used for centuries to alter their state of consciousness. This technique is called meditation.

Meditation is a learned technique for refocusing attention that brings about an altered state of consciousness. Meditation typically consists of the repetition of a mantra—a sound, word, or syllable—over and over. In other forms of meditation, the focus is on a picture, flame, or specific part of the body. Regardless of the nature of the particular initial stimulus, the key to the procedure is concentrating on it so thoroughly that the meditator becomes unaware of any outside stimulation and reaches a different state of consciousness.

After meditation, people report feeling thoroughly relaxed. They sometimes relate that they have gained new insights into themselves and the problems they are facing. The long-term practice of meditation may even improve health because of the biological changes it produces. For example, during meditation, oxygen usage decreases, heart rate and blood pressure decline, and brain-wave patterns change (Lee, Kleinman, & Kleinman, 2007; Travis et al., 2009; Steinhubl et al., 2015; see Figure 1).

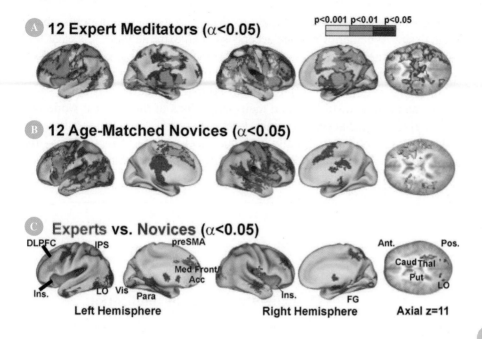

Figure 1 These fMRI brain scans show the regions of brain activation in (A) expert meditators who had between 10,000 and 54,000 hours of practice in meditating, (B) novice meditators who had no experience meditating, and (C) the comparison between the two. In (C), red hues show greater activation in the experts, and blue hues show greater activation for the novices.

Anyone can meditate by following a few simple procedures. The fundamentals include sitting in a quiet room with the eyes closed, breathing deeply and rhythmically, and repeating a word or sound—such as the word one—over and over. Practiced twice a day for 20 minutes, the technique is effective in bringing about relaxation (Aftanas & Golosheykin, 2005; Bærentsen et al., 2010).

Meditation is a means of altering consciousness that is practiced in many different cultures, though it can take different forms and serve different purposes across cultures. In fact, one impetus for the study of consciousness is the realization that people in many different cultures routinely seek ways to alter their states of consciousness (Walsh & Shapiro, 2006).

STUDY ALERT

Remember that although there are several alternate techniques used in meditation, they are all designed to bring about an altered state of consciousness in which attention is refocused.

EXPLORING diversity

Cross-Cultural Routes to Altered States of Consciousness

A group of Native American Sioux men sit naked in a steaming sweat lodge as a medicine man throws water on sizzling rocks to send billows of scalding steam into the air.

Aztec priests smear themselves with a mixture of crushed poisonous herbs, hairy black worms, scorpions, and lizards. Sometimes they drink the potion.

During the sixteenth century, a devout Hasidic Jew lies across the tombstone of a celebrated scholar. As he murmurs the name of God repeatedly, he seeks to be possessed by the soul of the dead wise man's spirit. If successful, he will attain a mystical state, and the deceased's words will flow out of his mouth.

Each of these rituals has a common goal: suspension from the bonds of everyday awareness and access to an altered state of consciousness. Although they may seem exotic from the vantage point of many Western cultures, these rituals represent an apparently universal effort to alter consciousness (Bartocci, 2004; Irwin, 2006).

Some scholars suggest that the quest to alter consciousness represents a basic human desire. Whether or not one accepts such an extreme view, it is clear that variations in states of consciousness share some basic characteristics across a variety of cultures. One is an alteration in thinking, which may become shallow, illogical, or otherwise different from normal. In addition, people's sense of time can become disturbed, and their perceptions of the physical world and of themselves may change. They may lose self-control, doing things that they would never otherwise do. Finally, they may feel a sense of ineffability—the inability to understand an experience rationally or describe it in words (Finkler, 2004; Travis, 2006).

RECAP

Define hypnosis.

- Hypnosis produces a state of heightened susceptibility to the suggestions of the hypnotist. Under hypnosis, significant behavioral changes occur, including increased concentration and suggestibility, heightened ability to recall and construct images, lack of initiative, and acceptance of suggestions that clearly contradict reality.

Describe the effects of meditation.

- Meditation is a learned technique for refocusing attention that brings about an altered state of consciousness.
- Different cultures have developed their own unique ways to alter states of consciousness.

[EVALUATE E Evaluate]

1. _____ is a state of heightened susceptibility to the suggestions of others.
2. A friend tells you, "I once heard of a person who was murdered by being hypnotized and then told to jump from the Golden Gate Bridge!" Could such a thing have happened? Why or why not?
3. _____ is a learned technique for refocusing attention to bring about an altered state of consciousness.
4. Leslie repeats a unique sound, known as a _____, when she engages in meditation.

[RETHINK R Rethink]

Why do you think people in almost every culture use psychoactive drugs and search for altered states of consciousness?

KEY TERMS

Hypnosis LO13.1   **Meditation** LO13.2

module 14

Drug Use
The Highs and Lows of Consciousness

Learning Outcomes  Prepare

>> **LO14.1** Explain the effects of stimulants.

>> **LO14.2** Explain the effects of depressants.

>> **LO14.3** Explain the effects of narcotics.

>> **LO14.4** Explain the effects of hallucinogens.

MODULE OUTLINE  Organize

Stimulants: Drug Highs

Depressants: Drug Lows

Try It! Consider Your Drinking Style

Narcotics: Relieving Pain and Anxiety

Hallucinogens: Psychedelic Drugs

Becoming an Informed Consumer of Psychology: Identifying Drug and Alcohol Problems

Drugs of one sort or another are a part of almost everyone's life. From infancy on, most people take vitamins, aspirin, cold-relief medicine, and the like, and surveys find that 80 percent of adults in the United States have taken an over-the-counter pain reliever in the last six months. However, these drugs rarely produce an altered state of consciousness (Dortch, 1996).

In contrast, some substances, known as psychoactive drugs, lead to an altered state of consciousness. **Psychoactive drugs** influence a person's emotions, perceptions, and behavior. Yet even this category of drugs is common in most of our lives. If you have ever had a cup of coffee or sipped a beer, you have taken a psychoactive drug. A large number of individuals have used more potent—and dangerous—psychoactive drugs than coffee and beer (see Figure 1); for

W Work

psychoactive drugs Drugs that influence a person's emotions, perceptions, and behavior

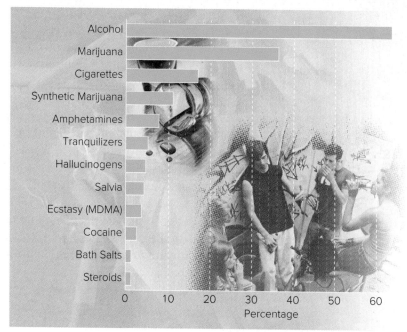

Figure 1 How many teenagers use drugs? The results of the most recent comprehensive survey of 14,000 high school seniors across the United States show the percentage of respondents who have used various substances for nonmedical purposes at least once (Johnston et al., 2014). Can you think of any reasons why teenagers—as opposed to older people—might be particularly likely to use drugs? Photos: (top) © Ingram Publishing/AGE Fotostock RF; (bottom) © BananaStock/PunchStock RF

Figure 2 Different drugs affect different parts of the nervous system and brain and each drug functions in one of these specific ways.

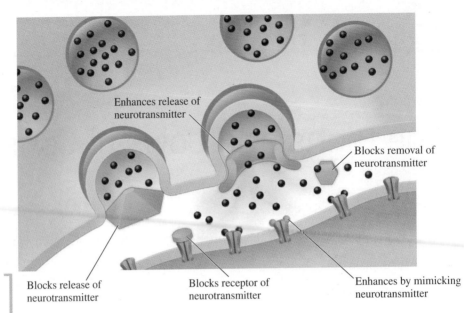

Enhances release of neurotransmitter

Blocks removal of neurotransmitter

Blocks release of neurotransmitter

Blocks receptor of neurotransmitter

Enhances by mimicking neurotransmitter

addictive drugs Drugs that produce a biological or psychological dependence in the user so that withdrawal from them leads to a craving for the drug that, in some cases, may be nearly irresistible

STUDY ALERT

Use Figure 2 to learn the different ways that drugs produce their effects on a biological level.

Researchers disagree as to whether e-cigarettes serve as a gateway to other kinds of tobacco use. With nicotine being an addictive drug and the use of e-cigarettes on the rise among teens, what are some preventative measures parents can use? © VOISIN/ Phanie/Alamy Stock Photo

instance, surveys find that 41 percent of high school seniors have used an illegal drug in the last year. In addition, 30 percent report having been drunk on alcohol. The figures for the adult population are even higher (Johnston et al., 2014).

Of course, drugs vary widely in the effects they have on users, in part because they affect the nervous system in very different ways. Some drugs alter the limbic system, and others affect the operation of specific neurotransmitters across the synapses of neurons. For example, some drugs block or enhance the release of neurotransmitters, others block the receipt or the removal of a neurotransmitter, and still others mimic the effects of a particular neurotransmitter (see Figure 2).

The most dangerous drugs are addictive. **Addictive drugs** produce a biological or psychological dependence in the user. When a drug is addictive, withdrawal from the drug leads to a craving for it that, in some cases, may be nearly irresistible. In *physiological drug dependence,* the body becomes so accustomed to functioning in the presence of a drug that it cannot function without it. In *psychological drug dependence,* people believe that they need the drug to respond to the stresses of daily living. Although we generally associate addiction with drugs such as heroin, everyday sorts of drugs, such as caffeine (found in coffee) and nicotine (found in cigarettes), have addictive aspects as well (Li, Volkow, & Baler, 2007).

Why do people take drugs in the first place? There are many reasons, including the perceived pleasure of the experience itself, the escape that a drug-induced high affords from the everyday pressures of life, or an attempt to achieve a religious or spiritual state. In some cases, the motive is simply the thrill of trying something new. Finally, the sense of helplessness experienced by unemployed individuals trapped in lives of poverty may lead them to

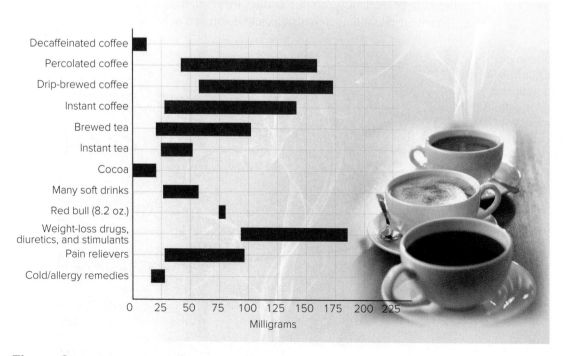

try drugs as a way of escaping from the bleakness of their lives. Regardless of the forces that lead a person to begin using drugs, drug addiction is among the most difficult of all behaviors to modify, even with extensive treatment. Most experts believe that the best hope for dealing with the overall societal problem of substance abuse is to prevent people from becoming involved with addictive drugs in the first place (Kouimtsidis & Drummond, 2010; Thompson, Goldsmith, & Tran, 2011; Chapman & Wu, 2015).

From the perspective of . . .

A Co-worker How could you determine whether your co-worker was addicted to drugs or alcohol? What steps would you take to help him or her? As an employee, what are the limits to which you could get involved?

≫ LO14.1 Stimulants: Drug Highs

Does your day not start until you've had your morning cup of coffee? *Caffeine* is one of a number of **stimulants**, drugs whose effect on the central nervous system causes a rise in heart rate, blood pressure, and muscular tension. Caffeine is present in tea, soft drinks, and chocolate as well as coffee (see Figure 3).

> **stimulants** Drugs that have an arousal effect on the central nervous system, causing a rise in heart rate, blood pressure, and muscular tension

Decaffeinated coffee
Percolated coffee
Drip-brewed coffee
Instant coffee
Brewed tea
Instant tea
Cocoa
Many soft drinks
Red bull (8.2 oz.)
Weight-loss drugs, diuretics, and stimulants
Pain relievers
Cold/allergy remedies

0   25   50   75   100   125   150   175   200   225
Milligrams

Figure 3   How much caffeine do you consume? This chart shows the range of caffeine found in common foods, drinks, and legal drugs.   Source: Adapted from Center for Science in the Public Interest, 2007. Photo: © Media Bakery

> **Regular users who suddenly stop drinking coffee may experience headaches or depression.**

Caffeine produces several reactions. The major behavioral effects are an increase in attentiveness and a decrease in reaction time. Caffeine can also bring about an improvement in mood, most likely by mimicking the effects of a natural brain chemical, adenosine. Too much caffeine, however, can result in nervousness and insomnia. People can build up a biological dependence on the drug. Regular users who suddenly stop drinking coffee may experience headaches or depression. Many people who drink large amounts of coffee on weekdays have headaches on weekends because of the sudden drop in the amount of caffeine they are consuming (Ganio et al., 2011; Kennedy & Haskell, 2011; Kamimori et al., 2015).

Nicotine, found in cigarettes, is another common stimulant. The soothing effects of nicotine help explain why cigarette smoking is addictive. Smokers develop a dependence on nicotine, and those who suddenly stop smoking develop strong cravings for the drug. This is not surprising: nicotine activates neural mechanisms similar to those activated by cocaine, which, as we see next, is also highly addictive (Haberstick, Timberlake, & Ehringer, 2007; Ray et al., 2008).

Amphetamines

Amphetamines are strong stimulants, such as Dexedrine and Benzedrine, popularly known as speed. In small quantities, amphetamines—which stimulate the central nervous system—bring about a sense of energy and alertness, talkativeness, heightened confidence, and a mood "high." They increase concentration and reduce fatigue. Amphetamines also cause a loss of appetite, increased anxiety, and irritability. When taken over long periods of time, amphetamines can cause feelings of being persecuted by others, as well as a general sense of suspiciousness. People taking amphetamines may lose interest in sex. If taken in too large a quantity, amphetamines overstimulate the central nervous system to such an extent that convulsions and death can occur (Carhart-Harris, 2007).

We are not alone in our consumption of coffee. This Starbucks indicates that the desire for caffeine may be universal. Why do you think a company like Starbucks can be successful in so many countries and cultures?
© Nic Cleave Photography/Alamy Stock Photo

Methamphetamine is a white, crystalline drug that U.S. police now say is the most dangerous street drug. "Meth" is highly addictive and relatively cheap, and it produces a strong, lingering high. It has made addicts of people across the social spectrum, ranging from soccer moms to urban professionals to poverty-stricken inner-city residents. After becoming addicted, users take it more and more frequently and in increasing doses. Long-term use of the drug can lead to brain damage (Kish et al., 2009; Seger, 2010; Rindone, 2015).

More than 1.5 million people in the United States are regular methamphetamine users. Because it can be made from nonprescription cold pills, retailers such as Walmart and Target have removed these medications from their shelves. Illicit labs devoted to the manufacture of methamphetamine have sprung up in many locations around the United States (Jefferson, 2005; Hauer, 2010).

Bath salts are an amphetamine-like stimulant containing chemicals related to cathinone. They can produce euphoria and a rise in sociability and sex drive, but the side effects can be severe, including paranoia and agitation (Cottencin, Rolland, & Karila, 2013; Airuehia, Walker, & Nittler, 2015).

Cocaine

Although its use has declined over the last decade, the stimulant cocaine and its derivative, *crack,* still represent a serious concern. Cocaine is inhaled or "snorted" through the nose, smoked, or injected directly into the bloodstream. It is rapidly absorbed into the body and takes effect almost immediately.

When used in relatively small quantities, cocaine produces feelings of profound psychological well-being, increased confidence, and alertness. Cocaine produces this "high" through the neurotransmitter dopamine. Dopamine is one of the chemicals that transmit between neurons messages that are related to ordinary feelings of pleasure. Normally when dopamine is released, excess amounts of the neurotransmitter are reabsorbed by the releasing neuron. However, when cocaine enters the brain, it blocks reabsorption of leftover dopamine. As a result, the brain is flooded with dopamine-produced pleasurable sensations (Redish, 2004; Jarlais, Arasteh, & Perlis, 2007; Suto et al., 2010). Figure 4 provides a summary of the effects of cocaine and other illegal drugs.

However, there is a steep price for the pleasurable effects of cocaine. The brain may become permanently rewired, triggering a psychological and physical addiction in which users grow obsessed with obtaining the drug. Over time, users deteriorate mentally and physically. In extreme cases, cocaine can cause hallucinations—a common one is of insects crawling over one's body. Ultimately, an overdose of cocaine can lead to death (George & Moselhy, 2005; Paulozzi, 2006; Little et al., 2009).

STUDY ALERT

Figure 4, which summarizes the different categories of drugs (stimulants, depressants, narcotics, and hallucinogens), will help you learn the effects of particular drugs.

≫ LO14.2 Depressants: Drug Lows

In contrast to the initial effect of stimulants, which is an increase in arousal of the central nervous system, the effect of **depressants** is to impede the nervous system by causing neurons to fire more slowly. Small doses result in at least temporary feelings of *intoxication*—drunkenness—along with a sense of euphoria and joy. When large amounts are taken, however, speech becomes slurred and muscle control becomes disjointed, making motion difficult. Ultimately, heavy users may lose consciousness entirely.

depressants Drugs that slow down the nervous system

Alcohol

The most common depressant is alcohol, which is used by more people than is any other drug. Based on liquor sales, the average person over the age of

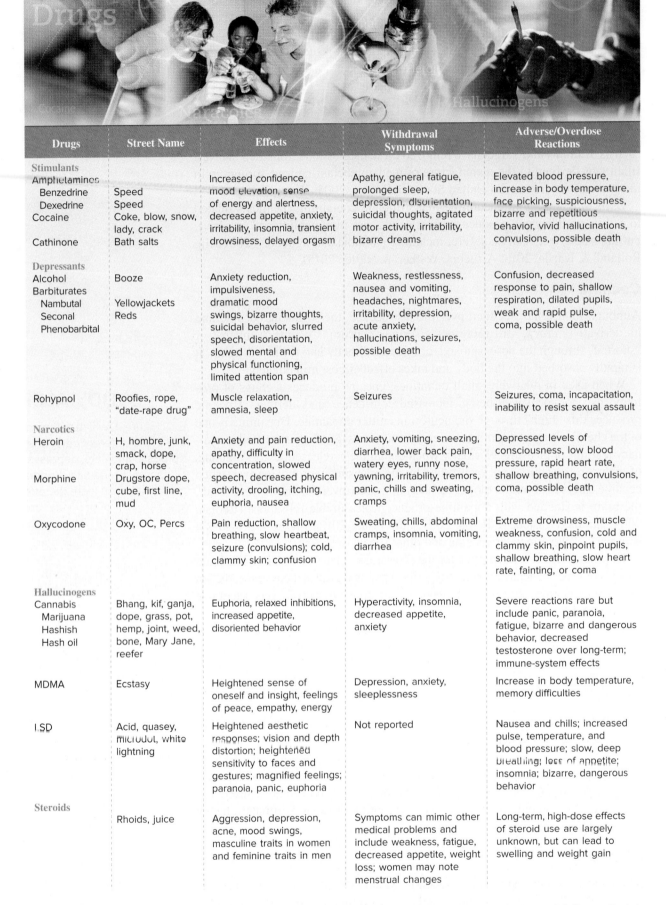

Drugs	Street Name	Effects	Withdrawal Symptoms	Adverse/Overdose Reactions
Stimulants				
Amphetamines		Increased confidence, mood elevation, sense of energy and alertness, decreased appetite, anxiety, irritability, insomnia, transient drowsiness, delayed orgasm	Apathy, general fatigue, prolonged sleep, depression, disorientation, suicidal thoughts, agitated motor activity, irritability, bizarre dreams	Elevated blood pressure, increase in body temperature, face picking, suspiciousness, bizarre and repetitious behavior, vivid hallucinations, convulsions, possible death
Benzedrine	Speed			
Dexedrine	Speed			
Cocaine	Coke, blow, snow, lady, crack			
Cathinone	Bath salts			
Depressants				
Alcohol	Booze	Anxiety reduction, impulsiveness, dramatic mood swings, bizarre thoughts, suicidal behavior, slurred speech, disorientation, slowed mental and physical functioning, limited attention span	Weakness, restlessness, nausea and vomiting, headaches, nightmares, irritability, depression, acute anxiety, hallucinations, seizures, possible death	Confusion, decreased response to pain, shallow respiration, dilated pupils, weak and rapid pulse, coma, possible death
Barbiturates				
Nambutal	Yellowjackets			
Seconal	Reds			
Phenobarbital				
Rohypnol	Roofies, rope, "date-rape drug"	Muscle relaxation, amnesia, sleep	Seizures	Seizures, coma, incapacitation, inability to resist sexual assault
Narcotics				
Heroin	H, hombre, junk, smack, dope, crap, horse	Anxiety and pain reduction, apathy, difficulty in concentration, slowed speech, decreased physical activity, drooling, itching, euphoria, nausea	Anxiety, vomiting, sneezing, diarrhea, lower back pain, watery eyes, runny nose, yawning, irritability, tremors, panic, chills and sweating, cramps	Depressed levels of consciousness, low blood pressure, rapid heart rate, shallow breathing, convulsions, coma, possible death
Morphine	Drugstore dope, cube, first line, mud			
Oxycodone	Oxy, OC, Percs	Pain reduction, shallow breathing, slow heartbeat, seizure (convulsions); cold, clammy skin; confusion	Sweating, chills, abdominal cramps, insomnia, vomiting, diarrhea	Extreme drowsiness, muscle weakness, confusion, cold and clammy skin, pinpoint pupils, shallow breathing, slow heart rate, fainting, or coma
Hallucinogens				
Cannabis	Bhang, kif, ganja, dope, grass, pot, hemp, joint, weed, bone, Mary Jane, reefer	Euphoria, relaxed inhibitions, increased appetite, disoriented behavior	Hyperactivity, insomnia, decreased appetite, anxiety	Severe reactions rare but include panic, paranoia, fatigue, bizarre and dangerous behavior, decreased testosterone over long-term; immune-system effects
Marijuana				
Hashish				
Hash oil				
MDMA	Ecstasy	Heightened sense of oneself and insight, feelings of peace, empathy, energy	Depression, anxiety, sleeplessness	Increase in body temperature, memory difficulties
LSD	Acid, quasey, microdot, white lightning	Heightened aesthetic responses; vision and depth distortion; heightened sensitivity to faces and gestures; magnified feelings; paranoia, panic, euphoria	Not reported	Nausea and chills; increased pulse, temperature, and blood pressure; slow, deep breathing; loss of appetite; insomnia; bizarre, dangerous behavior
Steroids				
	Rhoids, juice	Aggression, depression, acne, mood swings, masculine traits in women and feminine traits in men	Symptoms can mimic other medical problems and include weakness, fatigue, decreased appetite, weight loss; women may note menstrual changes	Long-term, high-dose effects of steroid use are largely unknown, but can lead to swelling and weight gain

Figure 4 The most commonly used drugs and their effects. (first) © Seth Resnick/Getty Images; (second) © George Doyle/ Getty Images RF; (third) © Jonnie Miles/Getty Images RF; (fourth) © PhotoAlto/Sanna Lindberg/Getty Images RF

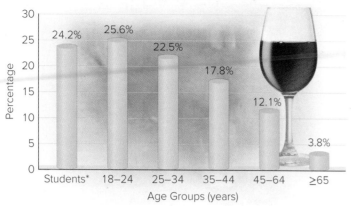

Percentage of People Who Reported Binge Drinking in the Past 30 Days

Age Groups (years)

*high school students

Students* 24.2%
18–24 25.6%
25–34 22.5%
35–44 17.8%
45–64 12.1%
≥65 3.8%

Figure 5 Self-reported binge drinking at different ages. For men, binge drinking was defined as consuming five or more drinks in one sitting; for women, the total was four or more. Adapted from Centers for Disease Control and Prevention. (2010). Youth risk behavior surveillance system--2009. Surveillance Summaries. MMWR 2010; 59 (No. SS-#). Photo:© Plainview/Getty Images RF

14 drinks 2½ gallons of pure alcohol over the course of a year. This works out to more than 200 drinks per person. Although alcohol consumption has declined steadily over the last decade, surveys show that more than three-fourths of college students indicate that they have had a drink with the last 30 days. In addition, the frequency of binge drinking is significant; see Figure 5 (Jung, 2002; Midanik, Tam, & Weisner, 2007; Norman, 2011).

Generally, women are typically somewhat lighter drinkers than men—although the gap between the sexes is narrowing for older women and has closed completely for teenagers. Women are more susceptible to the effects of alcohol, and alcohol abuse may harm the brains of women more than those of men (Mann et al., 2005; Mancinelli, Binetti, & Ceccanti, 2007; Naimi, Nelson, & Brewer, 2010).

Although alcohol is a depressant, most people believe that it increases their sense of sociability and well-being. This belief is caused because initially alcohol may lead to a reduction in tension and stress, feelings of happiness, and loss of inhibitions (Steele & Josephs, 1990; Sayette, 1993).

However, as the dose of alcohol increases, the depressive effects become more pronounced (see Figure 6). People may feel emotionally and physically unstable. They also show poor judgment and may act aggressively. Moreover, memory is impaired, brain processing of spatial information is diminished, and speech becomes slurred and incoherent. Eventually they may fall into a stupor and pass out. If they drink enough alcohol in a short time, they may die of alcohol poisoning (Zeigler et al., 2005; Thatcher & Clark, 2006).

Although most people fall into the category of casual users, 14 million people in the United States—1 in every 13 adults—have a drinking problem. *Alcoholics,* people with alcohol-abuse problems, come to rely on alcohol and continue to drink even though it causes serious difficulties. In addition, they become increasingly immune to the effects of alcohol. Consequently, alcoholics must drink progressively more to experience the initial positive feelings that alcohol produces.

In some cases of alcoholism, people must drink constantly in order to feel well enough to function in their daily lives. In other cases, though, people drink inconsistently, but occasionally go on binges in which they consume large quantities of alcohol.

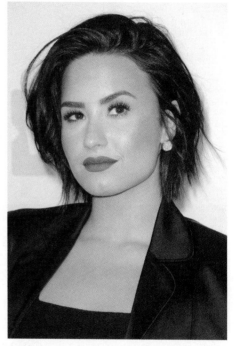

After entering a rehab program while still a teen, Demi Lovato, who was born in 1992, has worked hard to fight addictions, even living in a sober facility to help her not drink. Her success story is unlike that for some other celebrities. Why are some people able to get and stay sober and others are not? © Tinseltown/Shutterstock.com

Number of Drinks Consumed in Two Hours	Alcohol in Blood (Percentage)	Typical Effects
2	0.05	Judgment, thought, and restraint weakened; tension released, giving carefree sensation
3	0.08	Tensions and inhibitions of everyday life lessened; cheerfulness
4	0.10	Voluntary motor action affected, making hand and arm movements, walk, and speech clumsy
7	0.20	Severe impairment—staggering, loud, incoherent, emotionally unstable, 100 times greater traffic risk; exuberance and aggressive inclinations magnified
9	0.30	Deeper areas of brain affected, with stimulus-response and understanding confused; stuporous; blurred vision
12	0.40	Incapable of voluntary action; sleepy, difficult to arouse; equivalent of surgical anesthesia
15	0.50	Comatose; centers controlling breathing and heartbeat anesthetized; death increasingly probable

Note: A drink refers to a typical 12-ounce bottle of beer, a 1.5-ounce shot of hard liquor, or a 5-ounce glass of wine

Figure 6 The effects of alcohol. The quantities represent only rough benchmarks; the effects vary significantly depending on an individual's weight, height, recent food intake, genetic factors, and even psychological state.

It is not clear why certain people become alcoholics and develop a tolerance for alcohol, whereas others do not. There may be a genetic cause, although the question whether there is a specific inherited gene that produces alcoholism is controversial. What is clear is that the chances of becoming an alcoholic are considerably higher if alcoholics are present in earlier generations of a person's family. However, not all alcoholics have close relatives who are alcoholics. In these cases, environmental stressors are suspected of playing a larger role (Nurnberger & Bierut, 2007; Gizer et al., 2011; Buckner & Shah, 2015).

To determine your own drinking style, complete the Try It!.

Barbiturates

Barbiturates, which include drugs such as Nembutal, Seconal, and phenobarbital, are another form of depressant. Barbiturates produce a sense of relaxation and are frequently prescribed by physicians to induce sleep or reduce stress. They are psychologically and physically addictive and, when combined with alcohol, can be deadly, since such a combination relaxes the muscles of the diaphragm to such an extent that the user stops breathing.

Try It!
Consider Your Drinking Style

If you drink alcohol, do you have a style of use that is safe and responsible? Read the statements below and rate the extent to which you agree with them, using the following scale.

1 = Strongly disagree
2 = Disagree
3 = Neutral
4 = Agree
5 = Strongly agree

	1	2	3	4	5
1. I usually drink alcohol a few times a week.	___	___	___	___	___
2. I sometimes go to class after I've been drinking alcohol.	___	___	___	___	___
3. I frequently drink when I'm alone.	___	___	___	___	___
4. I have driven while under the influence of alcohol.	___	___	___	___	___
5. I've used a fake ID card to purchase alcohol.	___	___	___	___	___
6. I'm a totally different person when I'm drinking alcohol.	___	___	___	___	___
7. I often drink so much that I feel drunk.	___	___	___	___	___
8. I wouldn't want to go to party where alcohol wasn't being served.	___	___	___	___	___
9. I avoid people who don't like to drink alcohol.	___	___	___	___	___
10. I sometimes urge others to drink more alcohol.	___	___	___	___	___

Scoring

The lower your score (i.e., the more 1s and 2s), the better able you are to control your alcohol consumption and the more likely it is that your alcohol use is responsible. The higher your score (i.e., the more 4s and 5s), the greater is your use and reliance on alcohol, and the more likely it is that your alcohol consumption may be reckless. If your score is over 40, you may have an alcohol problem and should seek professional help to control your alcohol usage.

Rohypnol

Rohypnol is sometimes called the "date rape drug," because when it is mixed with alcohol, it can prevent victims from resisting sexual assault. Sometimes people who are unknowingly given the drug are so incapacitated that they have no memory of the assault.

» LO14.3 Narcotics: Relieving Pain and Anxiety

narcotics Drugs that increase relaxation and relieve pain and anxiety

Narcotics are drugs that increase relaxation and relieve pain and anxiety. Two of the most powerful narcotics, *morphine* and *heroin,* are derived from the poppy seed pod. Although morphine is used medically to control severe pain, heroin is illegal in the United States. This has not prevented its widespread abuse.

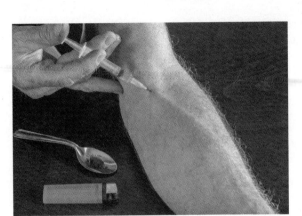

The use of heroin creates a cycle of biological and physical dependence. Combined with the strong positive feelings produced by the drug, this makes heroin addiction especially difficult to cure. © thodonal88/Shutterstock.com

Heroin users usually inject the drug directly into their veins with a hypodermic needle. The immediate effect has been described as a "rush" of positive feeling, similar in some respects to a sexual orgasm—and just as difficult to describe. After the rush, a heroin user experiences a sense of well-being and peacefulness that lasts three to five hours. However, when the effects of heroin wear off, users feel extreme anxiety and a desperate desire to repeat the experience. Moreover, larger amounts of heroin are needed each time to produce the same pleasurable effect. These last two properties are all the ingredients necessary for biological and psychological addiction: the user is constantly either shooting up or attempting to obtain ever-increasing amounts of the drug. Eventually, the life of the addict revolves around heroin.

Heroin abuse has reached epidemic proportions recently. Heroin use has more than doubled among young adults 18 to 25 years old from 2002–2004 to 2011–2013. Furthermore, the rate of overdose deaths related to heroin increased 286 percent between 2002 and 2013. Although it's not totally clear why use of the drug has increased so rapidly, one reason is that the cost of heroin has plummeted at the same time the supply has increased substantially (Cook, 2015).

Because of the powerful positive feelings the drug produces, heroin addiction is particularly difficult to cure. One treatment that has shown some success is the use of alternative drugs that reduce heroin (and other addictive opiates) users' dependence on drugs.

For example, *methadone* is a synthetic chemical that satisfies a heroin user's physiological cravings for the drug without providing the "high" that accompanies heroin. Similarly, *Suboxone* is a painkiller that reduces the withdrawal symptoms from heroin. Suboxone comes in tablet form as well as small film strips, both of which are put under the tongue to dissolve quickly. Finally, *Vivitrol* is injected into heroin users, and each shot lasts about a month. It prevents withdrawal symptoms, and it also prevents heroin from producing the positive effects that users crave if heroin is used (Shah, Young, & Vieira, 2014).

Methadone, Suboxone, and Vivitrol allow heroin users to function relatively normally and without the drug cravings. However, although such drugs remove the psychological dependence on heroin, they replace the physiological dependence on heroin with a physiological dependence on the alternative drugs. Consequently, researchers are attempting to identify nonaddictive chemical substitutes that do not produce a physiological craving (Verdejo, Toribio, & Orozco, 2005; Joe, Flynn, & Broome, 2007; Oviedo-Joekes et al., 2009).

Oxycodone (sold as the prescription drug *OxyContin*) is a type of pain-reliever that has led to a significant amount of abuse. Many well-known people (including Courtney Love and Rush Limbaugh) have become dependent on it.

≫ LO14.4 Hallucinogens: Psychedelic Drugs

What do mushrooms, jimsonweed, and morning glories have in common? Besides being fairly common plants, each can be a source of a powerful **hallucinogen,** a drug that is capable of producing hallucinations, or changes in the perceptual process.

Marijuana

The most common hallucinogen in widespread use today is *marijuana,* whose active ingredient—tetrahydrocannabinol (THC)—is found in a common weed, cannabis. Marijuana is typically smoked in cigarettes or pipes, although it can be cooked and eaten. Close to 40 percent of high school seniors and around 15 percent of eighth-graders report having used marijuana in the last year (Johnston et al., 2014; see Figure 7).

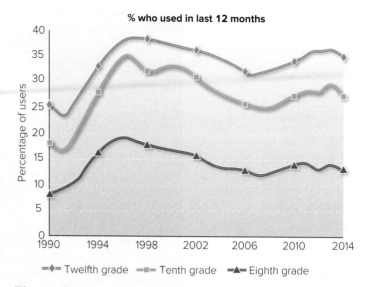

% who used in last 12 months

=◆= Twelfth grade   =■= Tenth grade   =▲= Eighth grade

Figure 7 Although the level of marijuana use has declined slightly in recent years, overall the absolute number of teenagers who have used the drug in the last year remains relatively high. Source: Johnston et al., 2014.

> **hallucinogen** A drug that is capable of producing hallucinations, or changes in the perceptual process

The effects of marijuana vary from person to person, but they typically consist of feelings of euphoria and general well-being. Sensory experiences seem more vivid and intense, and a person's sense of self-importance seems to grow. Memory may be impaired, causing the user to feel pleasantly "spaced out."

Marijuana does not seem to produce addiction except for a small number of heavy users. Overall, most research suggests its use is less harmful than the use of tobacco and alcohol. On the other hand, some research suggests that there are similarities in the way marijuana and drugs such as cocaine and heroin affect the brain as well as evidence that heavy use may impact negatively on cognitive ability in the long run. Furthermore, heavy use may at least temporarily decrease the production of the male sex hormone testosterone, potentially affecting sexual activity and sperm count (Rossato, Pagano, & Vettor, 2008; Barcott & Scherer, 2015; Pardini et al., 2015).

In addition, marijuana smoked during pregnancy may have lasting effects on children who are exposed prenatally, although the research results are inconsistent. Heavy use also affects the ability of the immune system to fight off germs and increases stress on the heart, although it is unclear how strong these effects are. Finally, there is one unquestionably negative consequence of smoking marijuana: the smoke damages the lungs much the way cigarette smoke does, producing an increased likelihood of developing cancer and other lung diseases (Julien, 2001; Reid, MacLeod, & Robertson, 2010).

Despite the possible dangers of marijuana use, there is little scientific evidence for the popular belief that users "graduate" from marijuana to more dangerous drugs. Furthermore, the use of marijuana is routine in certain cultures. For instance, some people in Jamaica habitually drink a marijuana-based tea related to religious practices. In

> **Although marijuana does not seem to produce addiction by itself, some evidence suggests that there are similarities in the way marijuana and drugs such as cocaine and heroin affect the brain.**

In recent years the use of Ecstasy has been romanticized in connection with club hopping and raves. What are the potential consequences of idealizing such a harmful drug? © Carey Russell Photography/Getty Images RF

addition, marijuana has several medical uses; it can be used to prevent nausea from chemotherapy, treat some AIDS symptoms, and relieve muscle spasms for people with spinal cord injuries (Iversen, 2000; Seamon et al., 2007; Chapkis & Webb, 2008; Cohen, 2009).

Many states have made use of the drug legal if it is prescribed by a health care provider—although it remains illegal under U.S. federal law. And a handful of states, including Alaska, Colorado, Oregon, and Washington, have made its use and sale legal, even for recreational use, with no prescription required (Krishman, Cairns, & Howard, 2009; Baumrucker et al., 2011; Roffman, 2013).

MDMA (Ecstasy) and LSD

MDMA ("Ecstasy") and *lysergic acid diethylamide (LSD, or "acid")* fall into the category of hallucinogens. Both drugs affect the operation of the neurotransmitter serotonin in the brain, causing an alteration in brain-cell activity and perception (Buchert et al., 2004; Aleksander, 2013).

Ecstasy users report a sense of peacefulness and calm. People on the drug report experiencing increased empathy and connection with others, as well as feeling more relaxed, yet energetic. Although the data are not conclusive, some researchers have found declines in memory and performance on intellectual tasks, and such findings suggest that there may be long-term changes in serotonin receptors in the brain (Montgomery et al., 2005; El-Mallakh & Abraham, 2007; Jones et al., 2008).

LSD, which is structurally similar to serotonin, produces vivid hallucinations. Perceptions of colors, sounds, and shapes are altered so much that even the most mundane experience—such as looking at the knots in a wooden table—can seem moving and exciting. Time perception is distorted, and objects and people may be viewed in a new way, with some users reporting that LSD increases their understanding of the world. For others, however, the experience brought on by LSD can be terrifying, particularly if users have had emotional difficulties in the past. Furthermore, people occasionally experience flashbacks, in which they hallucinate long after they initially used the drug (Baruss, 2003; Wu, Schlenger, & Galvin, 2006; Iaria et al., 2010).

becoming an informed consumer
of psychology

psych 101

Identifying Drug and Alcohol Problems

In a society bombarded with commercials for drugs that are guaranteed to do everything from curing the common cold to giving new life to "tired blood," it is no wonder that drug-related problems are a major social issue. Yet many people with drug and alcohol problems deny they have them, and even close friends and family members may fail to realize when occasional social use of drugs or alcohol has turned into abuse.

© Hill Street Studios/Getty Images RF

Certain signs, however, indicate when use becomes abuse (National Institute on Drug Abuse, 2000). Among them are the following:

- Always getting high to have a good time
- Being high more often than not
- Getting high to get oneself going
- Going to work while high
- Missing or being unprepared for work because you were high
- Feeling bad later about something you said or did while high
- Driving a car while high
- Coming in conflict with the law because of drugs
- Doing something while high that you wouldn't do otherwise
- Being high in nonsocial, solitary situations
- Being unable to stop getting high
- Feeling a need for a drink or a drug to get through the day
- Becoming physically unhealthy
- Failing on the job
- Thinking about liquor or drugs all the time
- Avoiding family or friends while using liquor or drugs

Any combination of these symptoms should be sufficient to alert you to the potential of a serious drug problem. Because drug and alcohol dependence are almost impossible to cure on one's own, people who suspect that they have a problem should seek immediate attention from a psychologist, physician, or counselor.

You can also get help from national hotlines. For alcohol difficulties, call the National Council on Alcoholism at (800) 622-2255. For drug problems, call the National Institute on Drug Abuse at (800) 662-4357. You can also check websites for a local listing of Alcoholics Anonymous or Narcotics Anonymous. Finally, check out the websites of the National Institute on Alcohol Abuse and Alcoholism (www.niaaa.nih.gov) and the National Institute on Drug Abuse (www.nida.nih.gov).

> **Because drug and alcohol dependence are almost impossible to cure on one's own, people who suspect that they have a problem should seek immediate attention from a psychologist, physician, or counselor.**

RECAP

Explain the effects of stimulants.

- Drugs can produce an altered state of consciousness. However, they vary in how dangerous they are and in whether they are addictive.

- Stimulants cause arousal in the central nervous system. Two common stimulants are caffeine and nicotine. More dangerous are cocaine and amphetamines, which in large quantities can lead to convulsions and death.

Explain the effects of depressants.

- Depressants decrease arousal in the central nervous system. They can cause intoxication along with feelings of euphoria. The most common depressants are alcohol and barbiturates.

- Alcohol is the most frequently used depressant. Its initial effects of released tension and positive feelings yield to depressive effects as the dose of alcohol increases. Both heredity and environmental stressors can lead to alcoholism.

Explain the effects of narcotics.

- Morphine and heroin are narcotics, drugs that produce relaxation and relieve pain and anxiety. Because of their addictive qualities, morphine and heroin are particularly dangerous.

Explain the effects of hallucinogens.

- Hallucinogens are drugs that produce hallucinations or other changes in perception. The most frequently used hallucinogen is marijuana, which has several long-term risks. Two other hallucinogens are LSD and Ecstasy.

- A number of signals indicate when drug use becomes drug abuse. A person who suspects that he or she has a drug problem should get professional help. People are almost never capable of solving drug problems on their own.

[EVALUATE E Evaluate]

1. Drugs that affect a person's consciousness are referred to as_____.
2. Match the type of drug to an example of that type.

   1. Narcotic—a pain reliever   a. LSD
   2. Amphetamine—a strong stimulant   b. Heroin
   3. Hallucinogen—capable of producing hallucinations   c. Dexedrine or speed

3. Classify each drug listed as a stimulant (S), depressant (D), hallucinogen (H), or narcotic (N).

   1. Nicotine
   2. Cocaine
   3. Alcohol
   4. Morphine
   5. Marijuana

4. The effects of LSD can recur long after the drug has been taken. True or false?

5. _____ is a drug that has been used to cure people of heroin addiction.

[RETHINK R Rethink]

Why have drug education campaigns largely been ineffective in stemming the use of illegal drugs? Should the use of certain now-illegal drugs be made legal? Would it be more effective to stress reduction of drug use rather than a complete prohibition of drug use?

Answers to Evaluate Questions 1. psychoactive; 2. 1-b, 2-c, 3-a; 3. 1-S, 2-S, 3-D, 4-N, 5-H; 4. true; 5. methadone

KEY TERMS

Psychoactive drugs   LO14.1

Addictive drugs   LO14.1

Stimulants   LO14.1

Depressants   LO14.2

Narcotics   LO14.3

Hallucinogen   LO14.4

«« Looking Back

Psychology on the Web

1. Find a resource on the Web that interprets dreams and another that reports the results of scientific dream research. Compare the nature and content of the two sites in terms of the topics covered, the reliability of information provided, and the promises made about the use of the site and its information. Write a summary of what you found.

2. There is considerable debate about the effectiveness of D.A.R.E., the Drug Abuse Resistance Education program. Find a discussion of both sides of the issue on the Web and summarize the arguments on each side. State your own preliminary conclusions about the D.A.R.E. program.

the case of . . .
THE WOMAN WHO DREAMS OF STRESS

Arlene Amarosi, a working mother, has been under a lot of stress this year. She has been having difficulty getting to sleep and often lies in bed staring at the ceiling while worrying about her problems. As a result, she's often tired throughout her workday and relies on coffee and caffeinated energy drinks to keep her going.

Lately Arlene's sleep has been disturbed even more often than usual. Several times over the past week she has been awakened by disturbing dreams. In these dreams she is always at work, struggling to keep up with an impossible workload. She is struggling with the new software that her company recently trained her to use, but no matter how fast she goes, she can't keep up with the workflow. The dream ends when Arlene wakes up in a panic. It often takes Arlene hours to get back to sleep, and she has been feeling even more tired than usual during work.

1. Arlene is worried that her recent dream experiences indicate that something is wrong with her. If you were Arlene's friend and wanted to reassure her, how would you help her to understand the normal experience of sleep and dreams?

2. Which theory of dreaming seems to best explain Arlene's disturbing dreams, and why?

3. How might meditation help Arlene?

4. If you were Arlene's health care provider, how would you advise her to overcome her insomnia?

5. What are some effects on Arlene of her high caffeine intake? What would happen if she just suddenly stopped drinking coffee and energy drinks? How would you advise her to modify her caffeine use?

profiles of SUCCESS

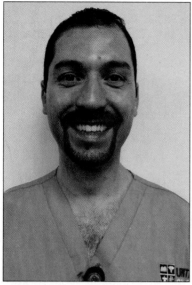

Courtesy of Luciano Virgilio

NAME: **Luciano Virgilio**

SCHOOL: **Unitek College, Fremont, CA**

DEGREE PROGRAM: **AD in Vocational Nursing**

Sometimes the path to achieving your vocational goals takes a longer and more twisted route than you ever imagined. This was certainly true in the case of Luciano Virgilio.

From a young age, Virgilio had a keen interest in biology and medicine. But a serious car accident left him with an even greater appreciation of the role nurses play in the process of healing.

"There, I was touched by the dedication and professionalism of the nurses who caringly watched after me," he recalled. "It was then I knew I wanted to become a nurse."

But rather than follow his dream, he followed the guidance of academic and family advisers and pursued careers ranging from land surveying to financial services.

"After years of working in jobs that left me feeling unfulfilled, and with the support of my spouse, I finally began the journey to achieving my dream of a nursing degree," said Virgilio.

Returning to school at a later point in life proved to be a challenge for Virgilio.

"Going back to school after so many years was challenging from a psychological standpoint, wondering, as I did, if I would be able to learn as I used to," he said. "But I was able to plan ahead financially, making sure that I could be a full-time student. Additionally, I had the moral and financial support of my wonderful partner who facilitated my complete transition to the role of a student."

Following his graduation from Unitek College's Vocational Nursing program, Virgilio was offered a job as a lab technician assistant at the college. This gave him the opportunity to practice his new skills and continue his studies by enrolling in the Registered Nursing program.

"It's hard to say exactly which area of specialization I most prefer, at this point in my journey," he explains. "But I know for certain that I want to provide high quality patient care and that I want to be part of a team that is likewise dedicated to excellence in the profession."

[RETHINK   R Rethink]

What are some of the reasons it is so challenging to return to school later in life?

Given the importance of sleep as discussed in this chapter, what advice would you give Virgilio in terms of juggling the multiple demands on his time?

visual summary 4
STATES OF CONSCIOUSNESS

MODULE 12 Sleep and Dreams

Stages of Sleep: Four stages of sleep, plus REM sleep

- Stage 1
  - Transition from wakefulness to sleep
  - Rapid brain waves
- Stage 2
  - Slower, more regular brain waves
  - Sleep spindles
- Stages 3 & 4
  - Slow, high-peaked waves
  - Least responsive to stimulation
- REM sleep
  - Rebound effect
  - Dreaming

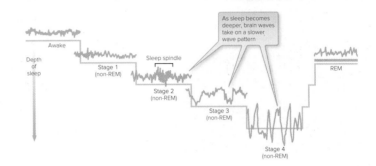

Function and Meaning of Dreams: Dreams typically encompass everyday events

- Unconscious wish fulfillment theory
- Dreams-for-survival theory
- Activation-synthesis theory

Sleep Disturbances

- Insomnia
- Sleep apnea
- SIDS
- Night terrors
- Narcolepsy

Circadian Rhythms: 24-hour cycle

MODULE 13 Hypnosis and Meditation

Hypnosis: A trancelike state of heightened suggestibility

Meditation: Learned technique for refocusing attention

Stimulants: Increase arousal in the nervous system
- Caffeine
- Cocaine
- Amphetamines

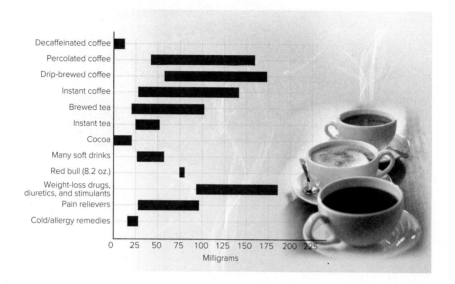

Depressants: Impede the nervous system
- Alcohol
- Barbiturates
- Rohypnol: "Date-rape" drug

Percentage of People Who Reported Binge Drinking in the Past 30 Days

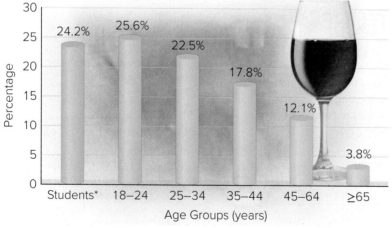

*high school students

Narcotics: Reduce pain and anxiety
- Heroin
- Morphine

Hallucinogens: Produce changes in perceptual processes
- Marijuana
- MDMA
- LSD

(MODULE 12) Source: Adapted from Hobson, 1989; (MODULE 13) © AP Images/Midland Daily News, Erin Painter; © Liquidlibrary/PictureQuest RF; (MODULE 14) Source: Adapted from Center for Science in the Public Interest, 2007; © Media Bakery; © Pixtal/SuperStock RF

LEARNING

© Dick Luria/Getty Images RF

Facebook Junkie?

Can you be addicted to social media? Citing research findings (e.g., the average teen checks social media 11 times a day; two-thirds of teens report they couldn't survive a month without texting), some researchers are labeling frequent social media use a compulsion, and likening it to addictions such as gambling and alcoholism. They cite the characteristics that frequent social media users share with addicts: constant need for stimulation, desire for peer approval, need for instant gratification, and narcissistic impulses. Less convinced researchers point to brain studies showing that, while the brains of both social media "junkies" and drug addicts show increased activity in the amygdala and striatum (brain regions linked to impulsive behavior), the brain systems that inhibit these behaviors remain stable in social media users, in contrast with those of substance addicts (Sass, 2015; Ghose, 2015).

Looking
Ahead

Theories that paint high-frequency social media users as addicts—or refute the notion—make headlines. But let's consider for a moment what may actually be taking place when a teen, hungry for friendship and feeling the need to belong, logs on to Facebook. She sees pictures of her friends. Maybe she's in some of them. She gets the latest gossip. She can "like" what she sees. Add a comment. Write a post. Suddenly, she's in the swing of things, part of a global group of peers. She feels good about herself. She goes back for more. Each log-in adds to her feelings of belonging to something important. She begins to get nervous if she's gone too long—a few hours, a whole day—without connecting to the group. She fears she may be missing out. Losing status. How are these experiences shaping her behavior? Can it be said that she is learning something from her social media experiences that influences or directs her future behavior?

Learning is a fundamental topic for psychologists and plays a central role in almost every specialty area of psychology. For example, a psychologist studying perception might ask, "How do we learn that people who look small from a distance are far away and not simply tiny?" A developmental psychologist might inquire, "How do babies learn to distinguish their mothers from other people?" A clinical psychologist might wonder, "Why do some people learn to be afraid when they see a spider?" A social psychologist might ask, "How do we learn to believe that we've fallen in love?"

Each of these questions, although drawn from very different branches of psychology, can be answered only through an understanding of basic learning processes. In each case, a skill or a behavior is acquired, altered, or refined through experience.

Psychologists have approached the study of learning from several angles. Among the most fundamental are studies of the type of learning that is illustrated in responses ranging from a dog salivating when it hears its owner opening a can of dog food to the emotions we feel when our national anthem is played. Other theories consider how learning is a consequence of rewarding circumstances. Finally, several other approaches focus on the cognitive aspects of learning, or the thought processes that underlie learning.

Classical Conditioning

Learning Outcomes  Prepare

LO15.1 Describe the basics of classical conditioning and how they relate to learning.

LO15.2 Give examples of applying conditioning principles to human behavior.

LO15.3 Explain extinction.

LO15.4 Discuss stimulus generalization and discrimination.

MODULE OUTLINE  Organize

The Basics of Classical Conditioning

Applying Conditioning Principles to Human Behavior

Try It! What's Your Test-Taking Style?

Extinction

Generalization and Discrimination

 Work

learning A relatively permanent change in behavior brought about by experience

Does the mere sight of the golden arches in front of McDonald's make you feel pangs of hunger and think about hamburgers? If it does, you are displaying an elementary form of learning called classical conditioning. *Classical conditioning* helps explain such diverse phenomena as crying at the sight of a bride walking down the aisle, fearing the dark, and falling in love.

Classical conditioning is one of a number of different types of learning that psychologists have identified, but a general definition encompasses them all: **learning** is a relatively permanent change in behavior that is brought about by experience.

We are primed for learning from the beginning of life. Infants exhibit a primitive type of learning called habituation. *Habituation* is the decrease in response to a stimulus that occurs after repeated presentations of the same stimulus. For example, young infants may initially show interest in a novel stimulus, such as a brightly colored toy, but they will soon lose interest if they see the same toy over and over. (Adults exhibit habituation, too: newlyweds soon stop noticing that they are wearing a wedding ring.) Habituation permits us to ignore things that have stopped providing new information.

Most learning is considerably more complex than habituation, and the study of learning has been at the core of the field of psychology. Although philosophers since the time of Aristotle have speculated on the foundations of learning, the first systematic research on learning was done at the beginning of the twentieth century, when Ivan Pavlov (does the name ring a bell?) developed the framework for learning called classical conditioning.

›› LO15.1 The Basics of Classical Conditioning

Ivan Pavlov, a Russian physiologist, never intended to do psychological research. In 1904 he won the Nobel Prize for his work on digestion, testimony to his contribution to that field. Yet Pavlov is remembered not for his physiological research

but for his experiments on basic learning processes—work that he began quite accidentally (Samoilov & Zayas, 2007; Goodwin, C. J. (2010). *Annotated readings in the history of modern psychology.* Hoboken, NJ: John Wiley & Sons Inc. Grant & Wingate, 2011).

Pavlov had been studying the secretion of stomach acids and salivation in dogs in response to eating varying amounts and kinds of food. While doing his research, he observed a curious phenomenon: sometimes salivation would begin in the dogs when they had not yet eaten any food. Just the sight of the experimenter who normally brought the food, or even the sound of the experimenter's footsteps, was enough to produce salivation in the dogs. Pavlov's genius lay in his ability to recognize the implications of this discovery. He saw that the dogs were responding not only on the basis of a biological need (hunger) but also as a result of learning—or, as it came to be called, classical conditioning. **Classical conditioning** is a type of learning in which a neutral stimulus (such as the experimenter's footsteps) comes to elicit a response after being paired with a stimulus (such as food) that naturally brings about that response.

To demonstrate classical conditioning, Pavlov (1927) attached a tube to the salivary gland of a dog, allowing him to measure precisely the dog's salivation. He then rang a bell and, just a few seconds later, presented the dog with meat. This pairing occurred repeatedly and was carefully planned so that, each time, exactly the same amount of time elapsed between the presentation of the bell and the meat. At first the dog would salivate only when the meat was presented, but soon it began to salivate at the sound of the bell. In fact, even when Pavlov stopped presenting the meat, the dog still salivated after hearing the sound. The dog had been classically conditioned to salivate to the bell.

As you can see in Figure 1, the basic processes of classical conditioning that underlie Pavlov's discovery are straightforward. However the terminology he chose is not simple. Consider first the diagram in Figure 1A. Before conditioning, there are two unrelated stimuli: the ringing of a bell and meat. We know that normally the ringing of a bell does not lead to salivation but to some irrelevant response, such as pricking up the ears or perhaps a startle reaction. The bell is therefore called the **neutral stimulus** because it is a stimulus that, before conditioning, does not naturally bring about the response in which we are interested. We also have meat, which naturally causes a dog to salivate—the response we are interested in conditioning. The meat is called an **unconditioned stimulus (UCS),** because food placed in a dog's mouth automatically causes salivation to occur. The response that the meat elicits (salivation) is called an unconditioned response. An **unconditioned response (UCR)** is a natural, innate, reflexive response that is not associated with previous learning. Unconditioned responses are always brought about by the presence of unconditioned stimuli.

classical conditioning A type of learning in which a neutral stimulus comes to bring about a response after it is paired with a stimulus that naturally brings about that response

neutral stimulus A stimulus that, before conditioning, does not naturally bring about the response of interest

unconditioned stimulus (UCS) A stimulus that naturally brings about a particular response without having been learned

unconditioned response (UCR) A response that is natural and needs no training (e.g., salivation at the smell of food)

STUDY ALERT

Figure 1 can help you learn and understand the process (and terminology) of classical conditioning, which can be confusing.

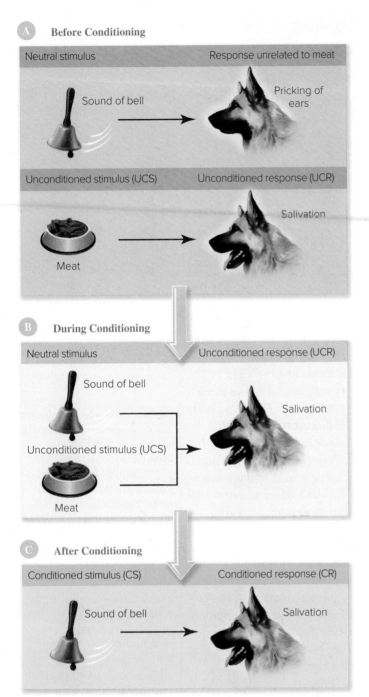

A Before Conditioning

Neutral stimulus | Response unrelated to meat

Sound of bell → Pricking of ears

Unconditioned stimulus (UCS) | Unconditioned response (UCR)

Meat → Salivation

B During Conditioning

Neutral stimulus | Unconditioned response (UCR)

Sound of bell → Salivation

Unconditioned stimulus (UCS)

Meat

C After Conditioning

Conditioned stimulus (CS) | Conditioned response (CR)

Sound of bell → Salivation

Figure 1 The basic process of classical conditioning. (A) Before conditioning, the ringing of a bell does not bring about salivation—making the bell a neutral stimulus. In contrast, meat naturally brings about salivation, making the meat an unconditioned stimulus and salivation an unconditioned response. (B) During conditioning, the bell is rung just before the presentation of the meat. (C) Eventually, the ringing of the bell alone brings about salivation. We now can say that conditioning has been accomplished: the previously neutral stimulus of the bell now is a conditioned stimulus that brings about the conditioned response of salivation.

Figure 1B illustrates what happens during conditioning. The bell is rung just before each presentation of the meat. The goal of conditioning is for the dog to associate the bell with the unconditioned stimulus (meat) and therefore to bring about the same sort of response as the unconditioned stimulus. After a number of pairings of the bell and meat, the bell alone causes the dog to salivate.

When conditioning is complete, the bell has evolved from a neutral stimulus to what is now called a **conditioned stimulus (CS).** At this time, salivation that occurs as a response to the conditioned stimulus (bell) is considered a **conditioned response (CR).** This situation is depicted in Figure 1C. After conditioning, then, the conditioned stimulus evokes the conditioned response.

The sequence and timing of the presentation of the unconditioned stimulus and the conditioned stimulus are particularly important. Like a malfunctioning warning light at a railroad crossing that goes on after the train has passed by, a neutral stimulus that *follows* an unconditioned stimulus has little chance of becoming a conditioned stimulus. However, just as a warning light works best if it goes on right before a train passes, a neutral stimulus that is presented *just before* the unconditioned stimulus is most apt to result in successful conditioning (Bitterman, 2006; Jennings et al., 2013).

Although the terminology Pavlov used to describe classical conditioning may seem confusing, the following summary can help make the relationships between stimuli and responses easier to understand and remember:

- Conditioned = learned.

- Unconditioned = not learned.

- An *un*conditioned stimulus leads to an *un*conditioned response.

- *Un*conditioned stimulus–*un*conditioned response pairings are *un*learned and *un*trained.

- During conditioning, a previously neutral stimulus is transformed into the conditioned stimulus.

- A conditioned stimulus leads to a conditioned response, and a conditioned stimulus–conditioned response pairing is a consequence of learning and training.

- An unconditioned response and a conditioned response are similar (such as salivation in Pavlov's experiment), but the unconditioned response occurs naturally, whereas the conditioned response is learned.

» LO15.2 Applying Conditioning Principles to Human Behavior

Although the initial conditioning experiments were carried out with animals, classical conditioning principles were soon found to explain many aspects of everyday human behavior. Recall, for instance, the earlier illustration of how people may experience hunger pangs at the sight of McDonald's golden arches. The cause of this reaction is classical conditioning: the previously neutral arches have become associated with the food inside the restaurant (the unconditioned stimulus), causing the arches to become a conditioned stimulus that brings about the conditioned response of hunger.

Emotional responses are especially likely to be learned through classical conditioning processes. For instance, how do some of us develop fears of mice, spiders, and other creatures that are typically harmless? In a now infamous case study, psychologist John B. Watson and colleague Rosalie Rayner (1920) showed that classical conditioning was at the root of such fears by conditioning an 11-month-old infant named Albert to be afraid of rats. "Little Albert," like most infants, initially was frightened by loud noises but had no fear of rats.

In the study, the experimenters sounded a loud noise whenever Little Albert touched a white, furry rat. The noise (the unconditioned stimulus) evoked fear (the unconditioned response). After just a few pairings of noise and rat, Albert began to show fear of the rat by itself, bursting into tears when he saw it. The rat, then, had become a CS that brought about the CR, fear. Furthermore, the effects of the conditioning lingered: five days later, Albert reacted with fear not only when shown a rat, but when shown objects that looked similar to the white, furry rat, including a white rabbit, a white seal-skin coat, and even a white Santa Claus mask. By the way, we don't know for certain what happened to Little Albert, and his fate remains a source of considerable speculation. In any case, Watson, the experimenter, has been condemned for using ethically questionable procedures that could never be conducted today (Beck, Levinson, & Irons, 2009; Powell et al., 2014; Griggs, 2015.)

Learning by means of classical conditioning also occurs during adulthood. For example, you may not go to a dentist as often as you should because of previous associations of dentists with pain. Similarly, some students associate academic tests with negative emotions and anxiety, which can hinder their performance. (For a sense of your own test-taking reactions, complete the Try It!.)

In more extreme cases, classical conditioning can lead to the development of *phobias,* which are intense, irrational fears that we will consider later in the book. For example, an insect phobia might develop in someone who is stung by a bee. The insect phobia might be so severe that the person refrains from leaving home. In addition, *posttraumatic stress disorder (PTSD),* suffered by some war veterans and others who have had traumatic experiences, can also be produced by classical conditioning. Even years after their battlefield experiences, veterans may feel a rush of fear and anxiety at a stimulus such as a loud noise (Schreurs, Smith-Bell, & Burhans, 2011; Rosellini et al., 2015; Böttche et al., 2016).

What's Your Test-Taking Style?

Do you feel anxious at the very thought of a test, or are you cool and calm in the face of testing situations? Get a sense of your test-taking style by checking off every statement below that applies to you.

☐ 1. The closer a test date approaches, the more nervous I get.

☐ 2. I am sometimes unable to sleep on the night before a test.

☐ 3. I have "frozen up" during a test, finding myself unable to think or respond.

☐ 4. I can feel my hands shaking as I pick up my pencil to begin a test.

☐ 5. The minute I read a tough test question, all the facts I ever knew about the subject abandon me and I can't get them back no matter how hard I try.

☐ 6. I have become physically ill before or during a test.

☐ 7. Nervousness prevents me from studying immediately before a test.

☐ 8. I often dream about an upcoming test.

☐ 9. Even if I successfully answer a number of questions, my anxiety stays with me throughout the test.

☐ 10. I'm reluctant to turn in my test paper for fear that I can do better if I continue to work on it.

If you checked off more than four statements, you have experienced fairly serious test anxiety. If you checked off more than six statements, your anxiety is probably interfering with your test performance. In particular, statements 3, 5, 6, 7, and 10 may indicate serious test anxiety.

However, classical conditioning also accounts for pleasant experiences. For instance, you may have a particular fondness for the smell of a certain perfume or aftershave lotion because thoughts of an early love come rushing back whenever you encounter it. Or hearing a certain song can bring back happy or bittersweet emotions due to associations that you have developed in the past. Classical conditioning, then, explains many of the reactions we have to stimuli in the world around us.

≫ LO15.3 Extinction

What do you think would happen if a dog that had become classically conditioned to salivate at the ringing of a bell never again received food when the bell was rung? The answer lies in one of the basic phenomena of learning: extinction. **Extinction** occurs when a previously conditioned response decreases in frequency and eventually disappears.

To produce extinction, one needs to end the association between conditioned stimuli and unconditioned stimuli. For instance, if we had trained a dog to salivate (the conditioned response) at the ringing of a bell (the conditioned stimulus), we could produce extinction by repeatedly ringing the bell but *not* providing meat. At first the dog would continue to salivate when it heard the bell, but after a few such instances, the amount of salivation would probably decline, and the dog would eventually stop responding to the bell altogether. At that point, we could say that the response had been extinguished. In sum, extinction occurs when the conditioned stimulus is presented repeatedly without the unconditioned stimulus (see Figure 2).

extinction A basic phenomenon of learning that occurs when a previously conditioned response decreases in frequency and eventually disappears

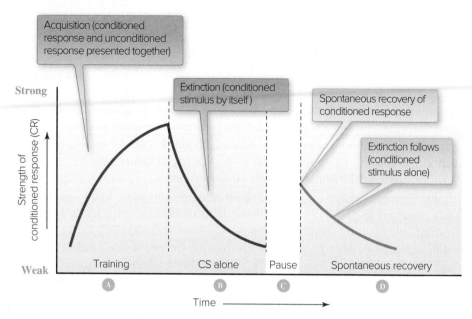

Figure 2 Acquisition, extinction, and spontaneous recovery of a classically conditioned response. A conditioned response (CR) gradually increases in strength during training (A). However, if the conditioned stimulus is presented by itself enough times, the conditioned response gradually fades, and extinction occurs (B). After a pause (C) in which the conditioned stimulus is not presented, spontaneous recovery can occur (D). However, extinction typically recurs soon after.

Once a conditioned response has been extinguished, has it vanished forever? Not necessarily. Pavlov discovered this phenomenon when he returned to his dog a few days after the conditioned behavior had seemingly been extinguished. If he rang a bell, the dog once again salivated—an effect known as **spontaneous recovery,** or the reemergence of an extinguished conditioned response after a period of time and with no further conditioning.

Spontaneous recovery helps explain why it is so hard to overcome drug addictions. For example, cocaine addicts who are thought to be "cured" can experience an irresistible impulse to use the drug again if they are subsequently confronted by a stimulus with strong connections to the drug, such as a white powder (Díaz & De la Casa, 2011; Tunstall, Verendeev, & Kearns, 2013).

> **spontaneous recovery** The reemergence of an extinguished conditioned response after a period of rest and with no further conditioning

» LO15.4 Generalization and Discrimination

Despite differences in color and shape, to most of us a rose is a rose is a rose. The pleasure we experience at the beauty, smell, and grace of the flower is similar

STUDY ALERT

Remember that stimulus generalization relates to stimuli that are *similar* to one another, while stimulus discrimination relates to stimuli that are *different* from one another.

From the perspective of . . .

A Veterinary Assistant How might knowledge of classical conditioning be useful in your career?

© Fuse/Getty Images RF

for different types of roses. Pavlov noticed a similar phenomenon. His dogs often salivated not only at the ringing of the bell that was used during their original conditioning but at the sound of a buzzer as well.

Such behavior is the result of stimulus generalization. **Stimulus generalization** is a process in which, after a stimulus has been conditioned to produce a particular response, stimuli that are similar to the original stimulus produce the same response. The greater the similarity between two stimuli, the greater the likelihood of stimulus generalization. Little Albert, who, as we mentioned earlier, was conditioned to be fearful of white rats, grew afraid of other furry white things as well. However, according to the principle of stimulus generalization, it is unlikely that he would have been afraid of a black dog, because its color would have differentiated it sufficiently from the original fear-evoking stimulus.

On the other hand, **stimulus discrimination** occurs if two stimuli are sufficiently distinct from each other that one evokes a conditioned response but the other does not. Stimulus discrimination provides the ability to differentiate between stimuli. For example, my dog, Cleo, comes running into the kitchen when she hears the sound of the electric can opener, which she has learned is used to open her dog food when her dinner is about to be served. She does not bound into the kitchen at the sound of the food processor, although it sounds similar. In other words, she discriminates between the stimuli of can opener and food processor. Similarly, our ability to discriminate between the behavior of a growling dog and that of one whose tail is wagging can lead to adaptive behavior—avoiding the growling dog and petting the friendly one.

stimulus generalization A process in which, after a stimulus has been conditioned to produce a particular response, stimuli that are similar to the original stimulus produce the same response

stimulus discrimination The process that occurs if two stimuli are sufficiently distinct from each other that one evokes a conditioned response but the other does not; the ability to differentiate between stimuli

Because of a previous unpleasant experience, a person may expect a similar occurrence when faced with a comparable situation in the future, a process known as stimulus generalization. Can you think of ways this process is used in everyday life? © Dave Nagel/Getty Images

RECAP

Describe the basics of classical conditioning and how they relate to learning.

- One major form of learning is classical conditioning, which occurs when a neutral stimulus—one that normally brings about no relevant response—is repeatedly paired with a stimulus (called an unconditioned stimulus) that brings about a natural, untrained response.

- After repeated pairings, the neutral stimulus elicits the same response that the unconditioned stimulus brings about. When this occurs, the neutral stimulus has become a conditioned stimulus, and the response a conditioned response.

Give examples of applying conditioning principles to human behavior.

- Examples of classical conditioning include the development of emotions and fears.

Explain extinction.

- Learning is not always permanent. Extinction occurs when a previously learned response decreases in frequency and eventually disappears.

Discuss stimulus generalization and discrimination.

- Stimulus generalization is the tendency for a conditioned response to follow a stimulus that is similar to, but not the same as, the original conditioned stimulus. The converse phenomenon, stimulus discrimination, occurs when an organism learns to distinguish between stimuli.

[EVALUATE E Evaluate]

1. _____ involves changes brought about by experience.
2. _____ is the name of the scientist responsible for discovering the learning phenomenon known as _____ conditioning, in which an organism learns a response to a stimulus to which it normally would not respond.

Refer to the passage below to answer questions 3 through 5:

The last three times little Theresa visited Dr. Lopez for checkups, he administered a painful preventive immunization shot that left her in tears. Today, when her mother takes her for another checkup, Theresa begins to sob as soon as she comes face-to-face with Dr. Lopez, even before he has a chance to say hello.

3. The painful shot that Theresa received during each visit was a(n) _____ that elicited the _____, her tears.
4. Dr. Lopez is upset because his presence has become a _____ for Theresa's crying.
5. Fortunately, Dr. Lopez gave Theresa no more shots for quite some time. Over that period she gradually stopped crying and even came to like him. _____ had occurred.

[RETHINK R Rethink]

How likely is it that Little Albert, Watson's experimental subject, went through life afraid of Santa Claus? Describe what could have happened to prevent his continual dread of Santa.

Answers to Evaluate Questions 1. Learning; 2. Pavlov, classical; 3. unconditioned stimulus, unconditioned response; 4. conditioned stimulus; 5. Extinction

KEY TERMS

Learning LO15.1

Classical conditioning LO15.1

Neutral stimulus LO15.1

Unconditioned stimulus (UCS) LO15.1

Unconditioned response (UCR) LO15.1

Conditioned stimulus (CS) LO15.1

Conditioned response (CR) LO15.1

Extinction LO15.3

Spontaneous recovery LO15.3

Stimulus generalization LO15.4

Stimulus discrimination LO15.4

Operant Conditioning

 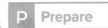

Very good . . . What a clever idea . . . Fantastic . . . I agree . . . Thank you . . . Excellent . . . Super . . . Right on . . . This is the best paper you've ever written; you get an A . . . You are really getting the hang of it . . . I'm impressed . . . You're getting a raise . . . Have a cookie . . . You look great . . . I love you . . .

Few of us mind being the recipient of any of these. But what is especially noteworthy about them is that each of these simple statements can be used, through a process known as operant conditioning, to bring about powerful changes in behavior and to teach the most complex tasks. Operant conditioning is the basis for many of the most important kinds of human, and animal, learning.

Operant conditioning is learning in which a voluntary response is strengthened or weakened, depending on its favorable or unfavorable consequences. When we say that a response has been strengthened or weakened, we mean that it has been made more or less likely to recur regularly.

Unlike classical conditioning, in which the original behaviors are the natural, biological responses to the presence of a stimulus such as food, water, or pain, operant conditioning applies to voluntary responses, which an organism performs deliberately to produce a desirable outcome. The term *operant* emphasizes this point: the organism *operates* on its environment to produce a desirable result. Operant conditioning is at work when we learn that toiling industriously can bring about a raise or that studying hard results in good grades.

operant conditioning Learning in which a voluntary response is strengthened or weakened, depending on its favorable or unfavorable consequences

» LO16.1 The Basics of Operant Conditioning

The inspiration for a whole generation of psychologists studying operant conditioning was one of the twentieth century's most influential psychologists, B. F. Skinner (1904–1990). Skinner was interested in specifying how behavior varies as a result of alterations in the environment.

Skinner conducted his research using an apparatus called the Skinner box (shown in Figure 1), a chamber with a highly controlled environment that was used to study operant conditioning processes with laboratory animals. Let's consider what happens to a rat in the typical Skinner box (Moore, 2010; Huston et al., 2013; Lins & Howland, 2016).

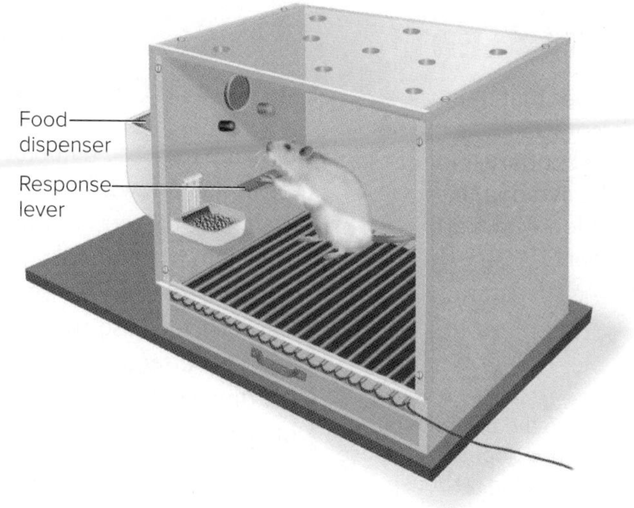

Suppose you want to teach a hungry rat to press a lever that is in its box. At first the rat will wander around the box, exploring the environment in a relatively random fashion. At some point, however, it will probably press the lever by chance, and when it does, it will receive a food pellet. The first time this happens, the rat will not learn the connection between pressing a lever and receiving food and will continue to explore the box. Sooner or later the rat will press the lever again and receive a pellet, and in time the frequency of the pressing response will increase. Eventually, the rat will press the lever continually until it satisfies its hunger, thereby demonstrating that it has learned that the receipt of food is contingent on pressing the lever.

Figure 1 A Skinner box used to study operant conditioning. Laboratory rats learn to press the lever in order to obtain food, which is delivered in the tray.

Reinforcement: The Central Concept of Operant Conditioning

Skinner called the process that leads the rat to continue pressing the key "reinforcement." **Reinforcement** is the process by which a stimulus increases the probability that a preceding behavior will be repeated. In other words, pressing the lever is more likely to occur again because of the stimulus of food.

In a situation such as this one, the food is called a reinforcer. A **reinforcer** is any stimulus that increases the probability that a preceding behavior will occur again. Hence, food is a reinforcer because it increases the probability that the behavior of pressing (formally referred to as the *response* of pressing) will take place.

What kind of stimuli can act as reinforcers? Bonuses, toys, and good grades can serve as reinforcers—if they strengthen the probability of the response that occurred before their introduction.

There are two major types of reinforcers. A *primary reinforcer* satisfies some biological need and works naturally, regardless of a person's previous experience. Food for a hungry person, warmth for a cold person, and relief for a person in pain all would be classified as primary reinforcers. A *secondary reinforcer*, in contrast, is a stimulus that becomes reinforcing because of its association with a primary reinforcer. For instance, we know that money is valuable because we have learned that it allows us to obtain other desirable objects, including primary reinforcers such as food and shelter. Money thus becomes a secondary reinforcer (Moher et al., 2008; Shahan, 2010; Qu, Zhang, & Chen, 2013).

reinforcement The process by which a stimulus increases the probability that a preceding behavior will be repeated

reinforcer Any stimulus that increases the probability that a preceding behavior will occur again

STUDY ALERT

Remember that primary reinforcers satisfy a biological need; secondary reinforcers are effective due to previous association with a primary reinforcer.

positive reinforcer A stimulus added to the environment that brings about an increase in a preceding response

negative reinforcer An unpleasant stimulus whose removal leads to an increase in the probability that a preceding response will be repeated in the future

punishment A stimulus that decreases the probability that a previous behavior will occur again

» LO16.2 Positive Reinforcers, Negative Reinforcers, and Punishment

In many respects, reinforcers can be thought of in terms of rewards; both a reinforcer and a reward increase the probability that a preceding response will occur again. But the term *reward* is limited to *positive* occurrences, and this is where it differs from a reinforcer—for it turns out that reinforcers can be positive or negative.

A **positive reinforcer** is a stimulus *added* to the environment that brings about an increase in a preceding response. If food, water, money, or praise is provided after a response, it is more likely that that response will occur again in the future. The paychecks that workers get at the end of the week, for example, increase the likelihood that they will return to their jobs the following week.

In contrast, a **negative reinforcer** refers to an unpleasant stimulus whose *removal* leads to an increase in the probability that a preceding response will be repeated in the future. For example, if you have an itchy rash (an unpleasant stimulus) that is relieved when you apply a certain brand of ointment, you are more likely to use that ointment the next time you have an itchy rash. Using the ointment, then, is negatively reinforcing, because it removes the unpleasant itch. Negative reinforcement, then, teaches the individual that taking an action removes a negative condition that exists in the environment. Like positive reinforcers, negative reinforcers increase the likelihood that preceding behaviors will be repeated (Magoon & Critchfield, 2008; McCarthy et al., 2010).

Note that negative reinforcement is not the same as punishment. **Punishment** refers to a stimulus that *decreases* the probability that a prior behavior will occur again. Unlike negative reinforcement, which produces an *increase* in behavior, punishment reduces the likelihood of a prior response. If we receive a shock that is meant to decrease a certain behavior, we then are receiving punishment, but if we are already receiving a shock and do something to stop that shock, the behavior that stops the shock is considered to be negatively reinforced. In the first case, the specific behavior is apt to decrease because of the punishment; in the second, it is likely to increase because of the negative reinforcement.

There are two types of punishment: positive punishment and negative punishment, just as there are positive reinforcement and negative reinforcement. (In both cases, "positive" means adding something, and "negative" means removing something.) *Positive punishment* weakens a response by applying an unpleasant stimulus. For instance, spanking a child for misbehaving or sending someone to jail for 10 years for committing a crime are examples of positive punishment. (In both cases, an unpleasant stimulus has been applied.)

In contrast, *negative punishment* consists of the removal of something pleasant. For instance, when a teenager is told she can no longer use her cell phone because she stayed out past her curfew, or when an employee is informed that he will have a cut in pay because of a poor job evaluation, negative punishment is being administered. (In both cases, something pleasant—cell phone use or more pay—is being removed.)

Both positive and negative punishment result in a decrease in the likelihood that a prior behavior will be repeated. So a jail term is meant to lead to a reduction in criminal behavior, and loss of a teenager's cell phone is meant to reduce the likelihood of staying out past curfew.

The following rules (and the summary in Figure 2) can help you distinguish these concepts from one another:

- Reinforcement *increases* the frequency of the behavior preceding it; punishment *decreases* the frequency of the behavior preceding it.

Intended Result	When Stimulus is Added, the Result is . . .	When Stimulus is Removed or Terminated, the Result is . . .
Increase in behavior (reinforcement)	**Positive Reinforcement** Example: Giving a raise for good performance Result: *Increase* in response of good performance 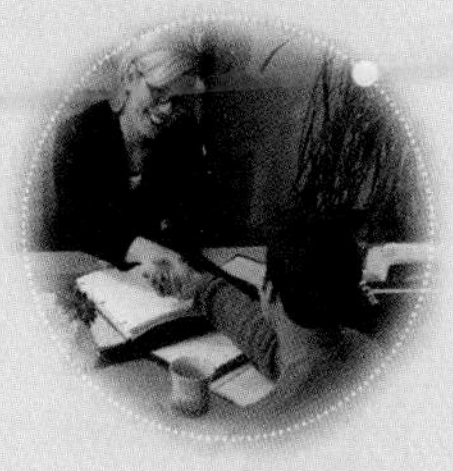	**Negative Reinforcement** Example: Applying ointment to relieve an itchy rash leads to a higher future likelihood of applying the ointment Result: *Increase* in response of using ointment 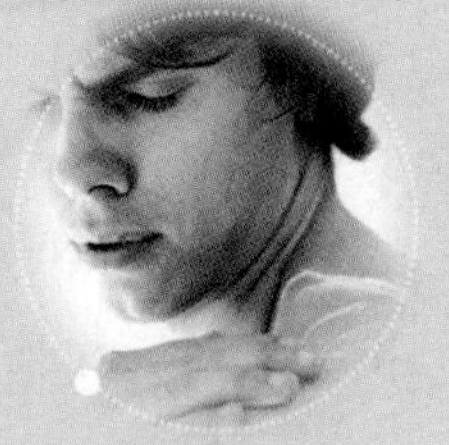
Decrease in behavior (punishment)	**Positive Punishment** Example: Yelling at a teenager when she steals a bracelet Result: *Decrease* in frequency of response of stealing 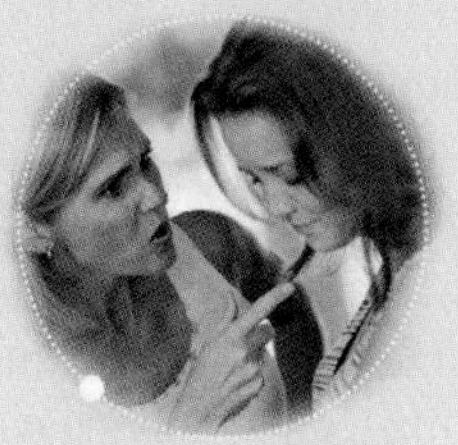	**Negative Punishment** Example: Teenager's access to car restricted by parents due to teenager's breaking curfew Result: *Decrease* in response of breaking curfew 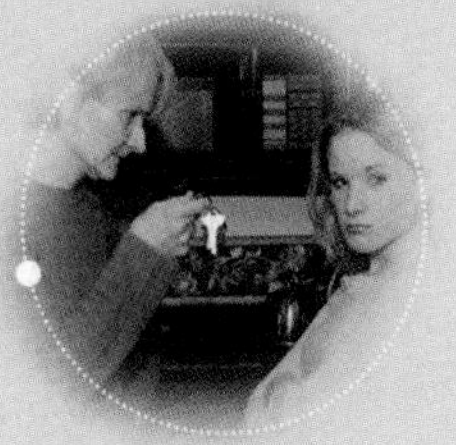

Figure 2 Types of reinforcement and punishment. Photos: (first) © Ryan McVay/Getty Images RF; (second) © Stockbyte/Getty Images RF; (third) © BananaStock/PunchStock RF; (fourth) © Amy Etra/PhotoEdit

- The *application* of a *positive* stimulus brings about an increase in the frequency of behavior and is referred to as positive reinforcement; the *application* of a *negative* stimulus decreases or reduces the frequency of behavior and is called punishment.
- The *removal* of a *negative* stimulus that results in an increase in the frequency of behavior is negative reinforcement; the *removal* of a *positive* stimulus that decreases the frequency of behavior is negative punishment.

STUDY ALERT

The differences between positive reinforcement, negative reinforcement, positive punishment, and negative punishment are tricky, so pay special attention to Figure 2 and the rules in the text.

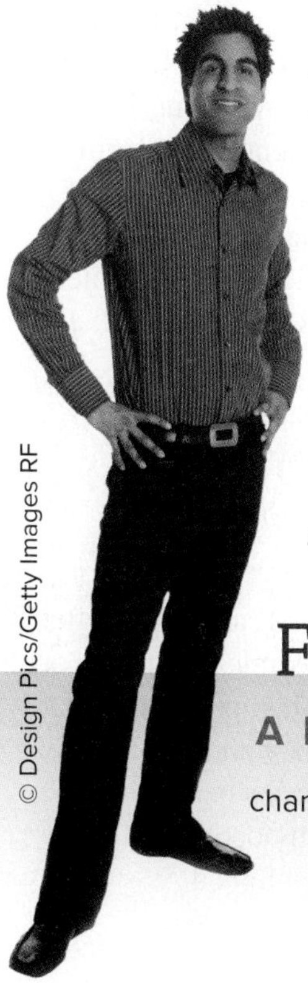

© Design Pics/Getty Images RF

» LO16.3 The Pros and Cons of Punishment: Why Reinforcement Beats Punishment

Is punishment an effective way to modify behavior? Punishment often presents the quickest route to changing behavior that, if allowed to continue, might be dangerous to an individual. For instance, a parent may not have a second

From the perspective of . . .

A Retail Supervisor How might you use the principles of operant conditioning to change employee behavior involving tardiness, customer service, or store cleanliness?

chance to warn a child not to run into a busy street, and so punishing the first incidence of this behavior may prove to be wise. Moreover, the use of punishment to suppress behavior, even temporarily, provides an opportunity to reinforce a person for subsequently behaving in a more desirable way.

> **Punishment has several disadvantages that make its routine use questionable.**

However, punishment has several disadvantages that make its routine use questionable. For one thing, punishment is frequently ineffective, particularly if it is not delivered shortly after the undesired behavior or if the individual is able to leave the setting in which the punishment is being given. An employee who is reprimanded by the boss may quit; a teenager who loses the use of the family car may borrow a friend's car instead. In such instances, the initial behavior that is being punished may be replaced by one that is even less desirable.

Even worse, physical punishment can convey to the recipient the idea that physical aggression is permissible and perhaps even desirable. A father who yells at and hits his son for misbehaving teaches the son that aggression is an appropriate, adult response. The son soon may copy his father's behavior by acting aggressively toward others. In addition, physical punishment is often administered by people who are themselves angry or enraged. It is unlikely that individuals in such an emotional state will be able to think through what they are doing or control carefully the degree of punishment they are inflicting. Ultimately, those who resort to physical punishment run the risk that they will grow to be feared. Punishment can also reduce the self-esteem of recipients unless they can understand the reasons for it (Miller-Perrin, Perrin, & Kocur, 2009; Smith, Springer, & Barrett, 2011; Gómez-Ortiz, Romera & Ortega-Ruiz, 2015).

Finally, punishment does not convey any information about what an alternative, more appropriate behavior might be. To be useful in bringing about more desirable behavior in the future, punishment must be accompanied by specific information about the behavior that is being punished, along with specific suggestions concerning a more desirable behavior. Punishing a child for staring out the window in school could merely lead her to stare at the floor instead. Unless we teach her appropriate ways to respond, we have merely managed to substitute one undesirable behavior for another. If punishment is not followed up with reinforcement for subsequent behavior that is more appropriate, little will be accomplished. That's why the scientific research is clear: spanking is both ineffective and ultimately harmful to children. Even punishment in the form of yelling is damaging (Wang & Kenny, 2013; Kubanek, Snyder, & Abrams, 2015).

In short, the research findings are clear: reinforcing desired behavior is a more appropriate technique for modifying behavior than using punishment (Hiby, Rooney, & Bradshaw, 2004; Sidman, 2006; Erdle & Rushton, 2010).

» LO16.4 Schedules of Reinforcement: Timing Life's Rewards

The world would be a different place if poker players never played cards again after the first losing hand, fishermen returned to shore as soon as they missed a catch, or telemarketers never made another phone call after their first hang-up. The fact that such unreinforced behaviors continue, often with great frequency and persistence, illustrates that reinforcement need not be received continually for behavior to be learned and maintained. In fact, behavior that is reinforced only occasionally can ultimately be learned better than can behavior that is always reinforced.

When we refer to the frequency and timing of reinforcement that follows desired behavior, we are talking about **schedules of reinforcement.** Behavior that is reinforced every time it occurs is said to be on a **continuous reinforcement schedule;** if it is reinforced some but not all of the time, it is on a **partial (or intermittent) reinforcement schedule.** Although learning occurs more rapidly under a continuous reinforcement schedule, behavior lasts longer after reinforcement stops when it is learned under a partial reinforcement schedule (Casey, Cooper-Brown, & Wacher, 2006; Reed, 2007; Holtyn & Lattal, 2013).

Why should intermittent reinforcement result in stronger, longer-lasting learning than continuous reinforcement? We can answer the question by examining how we might behave when using a candy vending machine compared with a Las Vegas slot machine. When we use a vending machine, prior experience has taught us that every time we put in the appropriate amount of money, the reinforcement, a candy bar, ought to be delivered. In other words, the schedule of reinforcement is continuous. In comparison, a slot machine offers intermittent reinforcement. We have learned that after putting in our cash, most of the time we will not receive anything in return. At the same time, though, we know that we will occasionally win something.

Now suppose that, unknown to us, both the candy vending machine and the slot machine are broken, and so neither one is able to dispense anything. It would not be very long before we stopped depositing coins into the broken candy machine. Probably at most we would try only two or three times before leaving the machine in disgust. But the story would be quite different with the broken slot machine. Here, we would drop in money for a considerably longer time, even though there would be no payoff.

In formal terms, we can see the difference between the two reinforcement schedules: partial reinforcement schedules (such as those provided by slot machines) maintain performance longer than do continuous reinforcement schedules (such as those established in candy vending machines) before *extinction*—the disappearance of the conditioned response—occurs (Bouton et al., 2011).

Certain kinds of partial reinforcement schedules produce stronger and lengthier responding before extinction than do others. Some schedules are related to the *number of responses* made before reinforcement is given, and others are related to the *amount of time* that elapses before reinforcement is provided (Reed & Morgan, 2008; Okouchi, 2010; Manzo et al., 2015).

Fixed- and Variable-Ratio Schedules

In a **fixed-ratio schedule,** reinforcement is given only after a specific number of responses. For instance, a rat might receive a food pellet every 10th time it pressed a lever; here, the ratio would be 1:10. Similarly, garment workers are generally paid on fixed-ratio schedules: they receive a specific number of dollars for every blouse they sew. Because a greater rate of production means more reinforcement, people on fixed-ratio schedules are apt to work as quickly as possible (see Figure 3).

In a **variable-ratio schedule,** reinforcement occurs after a varying number of responses rather than after a fixed number. Although the specific number of

schedules of reinforcement Different patterns of frequency and timing of reinforcement following desired behavior

continuous reinforcement schedule Reinforcement of a behavior every time it occurs

partial (or intermittent) reinforcement schedule Reinforcing of a behavior some but not all of the time

fixed-ratio schedule A schedule by which reinforcement is given only after a specific number of responses are made

variable-ratio schedule A schedule by which reinforcement occurs after a varying number of responses rather than a fixed number

STUDY ALERT

Remember that the different schedules of reinforcement affect the rapidity with which a response is learned and how long it lasts after reinforcement is no longer provided.

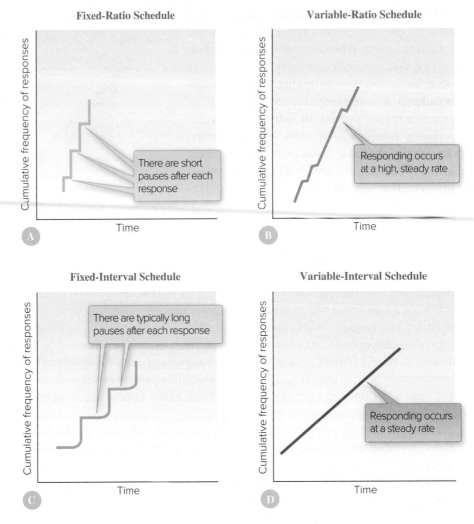

Figure 3 Typical outcomes of different reinforcement schedules. (A) In a fixed-ratio schedule, short pauses occur after each response. Because the more responses, the more reinforcement, fixed-ratio schedules produce a high rate of responding. (B) In a variable-ratio schedule, responding also occurs at a high rate. (C) A fixed-interval schedule produces lower rates of responding, especially just after reinforcement has been presented, because the organism learns that a specified time period must elapse between reinforcements. (D) A variable-interval schedule produces a fairly steady stream of responses.

responses necessary to receive reinforcement varies, the number of responses usually hovers around a specific average. A good example of a variable-ratio schedule is a telephone salesperson's job. She might make a sale during the third, eighth, ninth, and twentieth calls without being successful during any call in between. Although the number of responses that must be made before making a sale varies, it averages out to a 20 percent success rate. Under these circumstances, you might expect that the salesperson would try to make as many calls as possible in as short a time as possible. This is the case with all variable-ratio schedules, which lead to a high rate of response and resistance to extinction.

Fixed- and Variable-Interval Schedules: The Passage of Time

In contrast to fixed- and variable-ratio schedules, in which the crucial factor is the number of responses, fixed-*interval* and variable-*interval* schedules focus on the amount of time that has elapsed since a person or animal was rewarded. One example of a fixed-interval schedule is a weekly paycheck. For people who receive regular, weekly paychecks, it typically makes relatively little difference exactly how much they produce in a given week.

Because a **fixed-interval schedule** provides reinforcement for a response only if a fixed time period has elapsed, overall rates of response are relatively low. This is especially true in the period just after reinforcement, when the time before another reinforcement is relatively great. Students' study habits often exemplify this reality. If the periods between exams are relatively long (meaning that the opportunity for reinforcement for good performance is given fairly infrequently), students often study minimally or not at all until the day of the exam draws near. Just before the exam, however, students begin to cram for it, signaling a rapid increase in the rate of their studying response. As you might expect, immediately after the exam there is a rapid decline in the rate of responding, with few people opening a book the day after a test. Fixed-interval schedules produce the kind of "scalloping effect" shown in Figure 3 (Saville, 2009).

One way to decrease the delay in responding that occurs just after reinforcement, and to maintain the desired behavior more consistently throughout an interval, is to use a variable-interval schedule. In a **variable-interval schedule,** the time between reinforcements varies around some average rather than being fixed. For example, a professor who gives surprise quizzes that vary from one every three days to one every three weeks, averaging one every two weeks, is using a variable-interval schedule. Compared to the study habits we observed with a fixed-interval schedule, students' study habits under such a variable-interval schedule would most likely be very different. Students would be apt to study more regularly because they would never know when the next surprise quiz was coming. Variable-interval schedules, in general, are more likely to produce relatively steady rates of responding than are fixed-interval schedules, with responses that take longer to extinguish after reinforcement ends.

fixed-interval schedule A schedule that provides reinforcement for a response only if a fixed time period has elapsed, making overall rates of response relatively low

variable-interval schedule A schedule by which the time between reinforcements varies around some average rather than being fixed

shaping The process of teaching a complex behavior by rewarding closer and closer approximations of the desired behavior

» LO16.5 Shaping: Reinforcing What Doesn't Come Naturally

Consider the difficulty of using operant conditioning to teach people to repair an automobile transmission. If you had to wait until they chanced to fix a transmission perfectly before you provided them with reinforcement, the Model T Ford might be back in style long before they mastered the repair process.

There are many complex behaviors, ranging from auto repair to zoo management, that we would not expect to occur naturally as part of anyone's spontaneous behavior. For such behaviors, for which there might otherwise be no opportunity to provide reinforcement (because the behavior would never occur in the first place), a procedure known as shaping is used. **Shaping** is the process of teaching a complex behavior by rewarding closer and closer approximations of the desired behavior. In shaping, you start by reinforcing any behavior that is at all similar to the behavior you want the person to learn. Later, you reinforce only responses that are closer to the behavior you ultimately want to teach. Finally, you reinforce only the desired response. Each step in shaping, then, moves only slightly beyond the previously learned behavior, permitting the person to link the new step to the behavior learned earlier (Krueger & Dayan, 2009; Gadzichowski, Kapalka, & Pasnak, 2016). Shaping allows even

Concept	Classical Conditioning	Operant Conditioning
Basic principle	Building associations between a conditioned stimulus and conditioned response.	Reinforcement increases the frequency of the behavior preceding it; punishment decreases the frequency of the behavior preceding it.
Nature of behavior	Based on involuntary, natural, innate behavior. Behavior is elicited by the unconditioned or conditioned stimulus.	Organism voluntarily operates on its environment to produce particular consequences. After behavior occurs, the likelihood of the behavior occurring again is increased or decreased by the behavior's consequences.
Order of events	Before conditioning, an unconditioned stimulus leads to an unconditioned response. After conditioning, a conditioned stimulus leads to a conditioned response.	Reinforcement leads to an increase in behavior; punishment leads to a decrease in behavior.
Example	After a physician gives a child a series of painful injections (an unconditioned stimulus) that produce an emotional reaction (an unconditioned response), the child develops an emotional reaction (a conditioned response) whenever he sees the physician (the conditioned stimulus).	A student who, after studying hard for a test, earns an A (the positive reinforcer) is more likely to study hard in the future. A student who, after going out drinking the night before a test, fails the test (punishment) is less likely to go out drinking the night before the next test.

Figure 4   Comparing key concepts in classical conditioning and operant conditioning. Photos: (first) © Bruce Ayres/ Getty Images; (second) © Fancy/Veer/Corbis/Glow Images RF

lower animals to learn complex responses that would never occur naturally, ranging from lions jumping through hoops, dolphins rescuing divers lost at sea, or rodents finding hidden land mines.

Comparing Classical and Operant Conditioning

We've considered classical conditioning and operant conditioning as two completely different processes. And, as summarized in Figure 4, there are a number of key distinctions between the two forms of learning. For example, the key concept in classical conditioning is the association between stimuli, whereas in operant conditioning it is reinforcement. Furthermore, classical conditioning involves an involuntary, natural, innate behavior, but operant conditioning is based on voluntary responses made by an organism.

becoming an informed consumer of psychology

Using Behavior Analysis and Behavior Modification

A couple who had been living together for three years began to fight frequently. The issues of disagreement ranged from who was going to do the dishes to the quality of their love life.

Disturbed, the couple went to a *behavior analyst,* a psychologist who specialized in behavior-modification techniques. He asked them to keep a detailed written record of their interactions over the next two weeks.

When they returned with the data, he carefully reviewed the records with them. In doing so, he noticed a pattern: each of their arguments had occurred just after one or the other had left a household chore undone, such as leaving dirty dishes in the sink or draping clothes on the only chair in the bedroom.

Using the data the couple had collected, the behavior analyst asked them to list all the chores that could possibly arise and assign each one a point value depending on how long it took to complete. Then he had them divide the chores equally and agree in a written contract to fulfill the ones assigned to them. If either failed to carry out one of the assigned chores, he or she would have to place $1 per point in a fund for the other to spend. They also agreed to a program of verbal praise, promising to reward each other verbally for completing a chore.

The couple agreed to try it for a month and to keep careful records of the number of arguments they had during that period. To their surprise, the number declined rapidly.

This case provides an illustration of **behavior modification,** a formalized technique for promoting the frequency of desirable behaviors and decreasing the incidence of unwanted ones. Using the basic principles of learning theory, behavior-modification techniques have proved to be helpful in a variety of situations. People with severe intellectual disability have, for the first time in their lives, started dressing and feeding themselves. Behavior modification has also helped people lose weight, give up smoking, and behave more safely (Kalarchian et al., 2011; Etienne, 2013; Zale, Maisto & Ditre, 2016).

> **behavior modification** A formalized technique for promoting the frequency of desirable behaviors and decreasing the incidence of unwanted ones

The techniques used by behavior analysts are as varied as the list of processes that modify behavior. They include reinforcement scheduling, shaping, generalization training, discrimination training, and extinction. Participants in a behavior-change program do, however, typically follow a series of similar basic steps that include the following:

- *Identifying goals and target behaviors.* The first step is to define *desired behavior.* Is it an increase in time spent studying? A decrease in weight? A reduction in the amount of aggression displayed by a child? The goals must be stated in observable terms and must lead to specific targets. For instance, a goal might be "to increase study time," whereas the target behavior would be "to study at least two hours per day on weekdays and an hour on Saturdays."

- *Designing a data-recording system and recording preliminary data.* To determine whether behavior has changed, it is necessary to collect data before any changes are made in the situation. This information provides a baseline against which future changes can be measured.

- *Selecting a behavior-change strategy.* The most crucial step is to select an appropriate strategy. Because all the principles of learning can be employed to bring about behavior change, a "package" of treatments is normally used. This might include the systematic use of positive reinforcement for desired behavior (verbal praise or something more tangible, such as food), as well as a program of extinction for undesirable behavior (ignoring a child who throws a tantrum). Selecting the right reinforcers is critical, and it may be necessary to experiment a bit to find out what is important to a particular individual.

- *Implementing the program.* Probably the most important aspect of program implementation is consistency. It is also important to reinforce the intended behavior. For example, suppose a mother wants her daughter to spend more time on her homework, but as soon as the child sits down to study, she asks for a snack. If the mother gets a snack for her, she is likely to be reinforcing her daughter's delaying tactic, not her studying.

- *Keeping careful records after the program is implemented.* Another crucial task is recordkeeping. If the target behaviors are not monitored, there is no way of knowing whether the program has actually been successful.

- *Evaluating and altering the ongoing program.* Finally, the results of the program should be compared with baseline, preimplementation data to determine its effectiveness. If the program has been successful, the procedures employed can be phased out gradually. For instance, if the program called for reinforcing every instance of picking up one's clothes from the bedroom floor, the reinforcement schedule could be modified to a fixed-ratio schedule in which every third instance was reinforced. However, if the program has not been successful in bringing about the desired behavior change, consideration of other approaches might be advisable.

Behavior-change techniques based on these general principles have enjoyed wide success and have proved to be one of the most powerful means of modifying behavior. Clearly, it is possible to employ the basic notions of learning theory to improve our lives.

RECAP

Define the basics of operant conditioning.

- Operant conditioning is a form of learning in which a voluntary behavior is strengthened or weakened. According to B. F. Skinner, the major mechanism underlying learning is reinforcement, the process by which a stimulus increases the probability that a preceding behavior will be repeated.

- Primary reinforcers are rewards that are naturally effective without prior experience because they satisfy a biological need. Secondary reinforcers begin to act as if they were primary reinforcers through association with a primary reinforcer

Explain reinforcers and punishment.

- Positive reinforcers are stimuli that are added to the environment and lead to an increase in a preceding response. Negative reinforcers are stimuli that remove something unpleasant from the environment, also leading to an increase in the preceding response.

- Punishment decreases the probability that a prior behavior will occur. Positive punishment weakens a response through the application of an unpleasant stimulus, whereas negative punishment weakens a response by the removal of something positive. In contrast to reinforcement, in which the goal is to increase the incidence of behavior, punishment is meant to decrease or suppress behavior.

Present the pros and cons of punishment.

- Although punishment often presents the quickest route to changing behavior that, if allowed to continue, might be dangerous to an individual, it has disadvantages that make its routine use questionable. For example, punishment is frequently ineffective, particularly if it is not delivered shortly after the undesired behavior. Worse, physical punishment can convey to the recipient the idea that physical aggression is permissible and perhaps even desirable.

- The research findings are clear: reinforcing desired behavior is a more appropriate technique for modifying behavior than using punishment.

Discuss schedules of reinforcement.

- Schedules and patterns of reinforcement affect the strength and duration of learning. Generally, partial reinforcement schedules—in which reinforcers are not delivered on every trial—produce stronger and longer-lasting learning than do continuous reinforcement schedules.

- Among the major categories of reinforcement schedules are fixed- and variable-ratio schedules, which are based on the number of responses made; and fixed- and variable-interval schedules, which are based on the time interval that elapses before reinforcement is provided.

Explain the concept of shaping.

- Shaping is a process for teaching complex behaviors by rewarding closer and closer approximations of the desired final behavior.

[EVALUATE E Evaluate]

1. _____ conditioning describes learning that occurs as a result of reinforcement.

2. Match the type of operant learning with its definition:

   a. Positive reinforcement
   b. Negative reinforcement
   c. Positive punishment
   d. Negative punishment

   1. An unpleasant stimulus is presented to decrease behavior.
   2. An unpleasant stimulus is removed to increase behavior.
   3. A pleasant stimulus is presented to increase behavior.
   4. A pleasant stimulus is removed to decrease behavior.

3. Sandy had a rough day, and his son's noisemaking was not helping him relax. Not wanting to resort to scolding, Sandy told his son in a serious manner that he was very tired and would like the boy to play quietly for an hour. This approach worked. For Sandy, the change in his son's behavior was

   a. Positively reinforcing
   b. Negatively reinforcing

4. In a _____ reinforcement schedule, behavior is reinforced some of the time, whereas in a reinforcement schedule, behavior is reinforced all the time.

5. Match the type of reinforcement schedule with its definition:

   a. Fixed-ratio
   b. Variable-interval
   c. Fixed-interval
   d. Variable-ratio

   1. Reinforcement occurs after a set time period.
   2. Reinforcement occurs after a set number of responses.
   3. Reinforcement occurs after a varying time period.
   4. Reinforcement occurs after a varying number of responses.

[RETHINK R Rethink]

Using scientific literature as a guide, what would you tell parents who wish to know if the routine use of physical punishment is a necessary and acceptable form of child rearing?

KEY TERMS

Operant conditioning   LO16.1

Reinforcement   LO16.1

Reinforcer   LO16.1

Positive reinforcer   LO16.2

Negative reinforcer   LO16.2

Punishment   LO16.2

Schedules of reinforcement   LO16.4

Continuous reinforcement schedule   LO16.4

Partial (or intermittent) reinforcement schedule   LO16.4

Fixed-ratio schedule   LO16.4

Variable-ratio schedule   LO16.4

Fixed-interval schedule   LO16.4

Variable-interval schedule   LO16.4

Shaping   LO16.5

Behavior modification   LO16.5

module 17

Cognitive Approaches to Learning

Consider what happens when people learn to drive a car. They don't just get behind the wheel and stumble around until they randomly put the key into the ignition, and later, after many false starts, accidentally manage to get the car to move forward, thereby receiving positive reinforcement. Instead, they already know the basic elements of driving from prior experience as passengers, when they more than likely noticed how the key was inserted into the ignition, the car was put in drive, and the gas pedal was pressed to make the car go forward.

Clearly, not all learning is due to operant and classical conditioning. In fact, such activities as learning to drive a car imply that some kinds of learning must involve higher-order processes in which people's thoughts and memories and the way they process information account for their responses. Such situations argue against regarding learning as the unthinking, mechanical, and automatic acquisition of associations between stimuli and responses, as in classical conditioning, or the presentation of reinforcement, as in operant conditioning.

Some psychologists view learning in terms of the thought processes, or cognitions, that underlie it—an approach known as **cognitive learning theory.** Although psychologists working from the cognitive learning perspective do not deny the importance of classical and operant conditioning, they have developed approaches that focus on the unseen mental processes that occur during learning, rather than concentrating solely on external stimuli, responses, and reinforcements.

In its most basic formulation, cognitive learning theory suggests that it is not enough to say that people make responses because there is an assumed link between a stimulus and a response—a link that is the result of a past history of

 Work

cognitive learning theory An approach to the study of learning that focuses on the thought processes that underlie learning

STUDY ALERT

Remember that the cognitive learning approach focuses on the internal thoughts and expectations of learners, whereas classical and operant conditioning approaches focus on external stimuli, responses, and reinforcement.

reinforcement for a response. Instead, according to this point of view, people, and even lower animals, develop an *expectation* that they will receive a reinforcer after making a response.

Two types of learning in which no obvious prior reinforcement is present are latent learning and observational learning.

» LO17.1 Latent Learning

Evidence for the importance of cognitive processes comes from a series of animal experiments that revealed a type of cognitive learning called latent learning. In **latent learning,** a new behavior is learned but not demonstrated until some incentive is provided for displaying it (Tolman & Honzik, 1930). In short, latent learning occurs without reinforcement.

In the studies demonstrating latent learning, psychologists examined the behavior of rats in a maze such as the one shown in Figure 1A. In one experiment, a group of rats was allowed to wander around the maze once a day for 17 days without ever receiving a reward. Understandably, those rats made many errors and spent a relatively long time reaching the end of the maze. A second group, however, was always given food at the end of the maze. Not surprisingly, those rats learned to run quickly and directly to the food box, making few errors.

A third group of rats started out in the same situation as the unrewarded rats, but only for the first 10 days. On the 11th day, a critical experimental manipulation was introduced: from that point on, the rats in this group were given food for completing the maze. The results of this manipulation were dramatic, as you can see from the graph in Figure 1B. The previously unrewarded rats, which had earlier seemed to wander about aimlessly, showed such reductions in running time and declines in error rates that their performance almost immediately matched that of the group that had received rewards from the start.

To cognitive theorists, it seemed clear that the unrewarded rats had learned the layout of the maze early in their explorations; they just never displayed their latent learning until the reinforcement was offered. Instead, those rats seemed to develop a *cognitive map* of the maze—a mental representation of spatial locations and directions.

People, too, develop cognitive maps of their surroundings. For example, latent learning may permit you to know the location of a kitchenware store at a local mall you've frequently visited, even though you've never entered the store and don't even like to cook.

The possibility that we develop our cognitive maps through latent learning presents something of a problem for strict operant conditioning theorists. If we consider the results of the maze-learning experiment, for instance, it is unclear what reinforcement permitted the rats that initially received no reward to learn the layout of the maze, because there was no obvious reinforcer present. Instead, the results support a cognitive view of learning, in which changes occurred in unobservable mental processes (Iaria et al., 2009; Lin et al., 2011; Malin et al., 2015).

latent learning Learning in which a new behavior is acquired but is not demonstrated until some incentive is provided for displaying it

Gahan Wilson/The New Yorker Collection/The Cartoon Bank

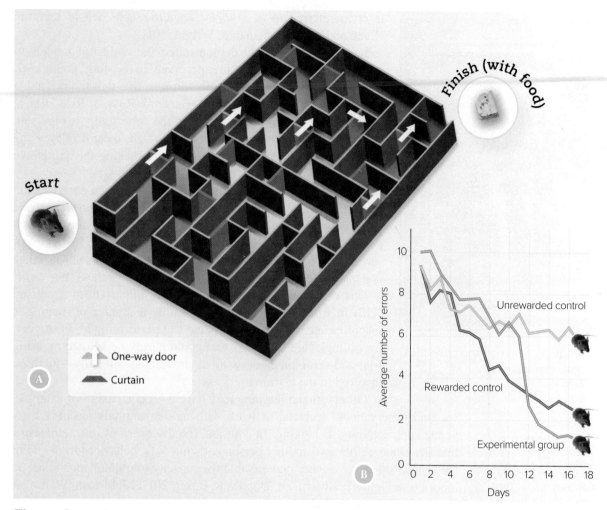

Figure 1 (A) In an attempt to demonstrate latent learning, rats were allowed to roam through a maze of this sort once a day for 17 days. (B) The rats that were never rewarded (the nonrewarded control condition) consistently made the most errors, whereas those that received food at the finish every day (the rewarded control condition) consistently made far fewer errors. But the results also showed latent learning: rats that were initially unrewarded but began to be rewarded only after the 10th day (the experimental group) showed an immediate reduction in errors and soon became similar in error rate to the rats that had been rewarded consistently. According to cognitive learning theorists, the reduction in errors indicates that the rats had developed a cognitive map—a mental representation—of the maze. Can you think of other examples of latent learning?

≫ LO17.2 Observational Learning: Learning Through Imitation

Let's return for a moment to the case of a person learning to drive. How can we account for instances in which an individual with no direct experience in carrying out a particular behavior learns the behavior and then performs it? To answer this question, psychologists have focused on another aspect of cognitive learning: observational learning.

According to psychologist Albert Bandura and colleagues, a major part of human learning consists of **observational learning,** which is learning by watching the behavior of another person, or *model.* Because of its reliance on observation of others—a social phenomenon—the perspective taken by Bandura

> **observational learning** Learning by observing the behavior of another person, or model

Albert Bandura examined the principles of observational learning.
© Albert Bandura

This girl is displaying observational learning based on prior observation of her mother. How does observational learning contribute to defining gender roles? © Henrik Sorensen/Getty Images

is often referred to as a *social cognitive* approach to learning (Bandura, 2004; Buchanan & Wright, 2011).

Bandura dramatically demonstrated the ability of models to stimulate learning in a classic experiment. In the study, young children saw a film of an adult wildly hitting a five-foot-tall inflatable punching toy called a Bobo doll (Bandura, Ross, & Ross, 1963a, 1963b). Later the children were given the opportunity to play with the Bobo doll themselves, and, sure enough, most displayed the same kind of behavior, in some cases mimicking the aggressive behavior almost identically.

Not only negative behaviors are acquired through observational learning. In one experiment, for example, children who were afraid of dogs were exposed to a model—dubbed the Fearless Peer—playing with a dog (Bandura, Grusec, & Menlove, 1967). After exposure, observers were considerably more likely to approach a strange dog than were children who had not viewed the Fearless Peer.

Observational learning is particularly important in acquiring skills in which the operant conditioning technique of shaping is inappropriate. Piloting an airplane and performing brain surgery, for example, are behaviors that could hardly be learned by using trial-and-error methods without grave cost—literally—to those involved in the learning process.

Observational learning may have a genetic basis. For example, we find observational learning at work with mother animals teaching their young such activities as hunting. In addition, the discovery of *mirror neurons* that fire when we observe another person carrying out a behavior (discussed in the chapter on neuroscience) suggests that the capacity to imitate others may be inborn (see Figure 2; Huesmann, Dubow, & Boxer, 2011; McElreath, Wallin, & Fasolo, 2013; Fernald, 2015).

Not all behavior that we witness is learned or carried out, of course. One crucial factor that determines whether we later imitate a model is whether the model is rewarded for his or her behavior. If we observe a friend being rewarded for putting more time into her studies by receiving higher grades, we are more likely to imitate her behavior than we would if her behavior resulted only in being stressed and tired.

Models who are rewarded for behaving in a particular way are more apt to be mimicked than are models who receive punishment. Observing the punishment of a model, however, does not necessarily stop observers from learning the behavior. Observers can still describe the model's behavior—they are just less apt to perform it (Bandura, 1977, 1986, 1994).

Observational learning is central to a number of important issues relating to the extent to which people learn simply by watching the behavior of others. For instance, the degree to which observation of media aggression produces subsequent aggression on the part of viewers is a crucial—and controversial—question, as we discuss next.

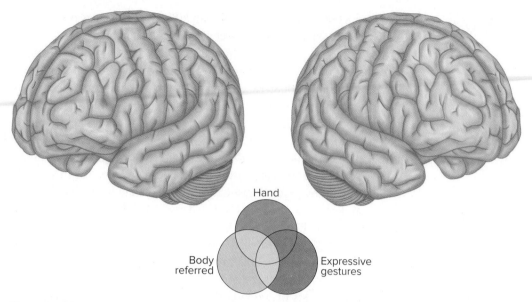

Figure 2 This fMRI scan shows the activation of specific regions of the brain related to mirror neuron systems when participants in an experiment observed three different kinds of behavior: hand movements (such as twisting a lid), shown in blue; body-referred movements (such as brushing teeth), shown in green; and expressive gestures (such as threatening gestures), shown in red. The brain activation occurred in perception-related areas in the occipital and temporal lobes of the brain as well as the mirror neuron system in the lateral frontal and superior parietal lobes. Source: Adapted from Lotze et al., 2006, p. 1790.

» LO17.3 Violence in Television and Video Games: Does the Media's Message Matter?

In an episode of *The Sopranos,* the famous television series, fictional mobster Tony Soprano murdered one of his associates. To make identification of the victim's body difficult, Soprano and one of his henchmen dismembered the body and dumped the body parts.

A few months later, two real-life half brothers in Riverside, California, strangled their mother and then cut her head and hands from her body. Victor Bautista, 20, and Matthew Montejo, 15, were caught by police after a security guard noticed that the bundle they were attempting to throw in a Dumpster had a foot sticking out of it. They told police that the plan to dismember their mother was inspired by this episode of *The Sopranos* (Martelle, Hanley, & Yoshino, 2003).

Like other "media copycat" killings, the brothers' cold-blooded brutality raises a critical issue: does observing violent and antisocial acts in the media lead viewers to behave in similar ways? Because research on modeling shows that people frequently learn and imitate the aggression that they observe, this question is among the most important issues being addressed by psychologists.

Certainly, the amount of violence in the mass media is enormous. By the time of elementary school graduation, the average child in the United States will have viewed

Game of Thrones is often cited as being ultraviolent. Despite the nature of the show and the medieval age in which it is set, is observation at all to blame for violence in viewers? © Photos 12/ Alamy Stock Photo

more than 8,000 murders and more than 800,000 violent acts on network television (Adachi & Willoughby, 2011; Lee et al., 2011; Valkenburg, Peter & Walther, 2016).

Most experts agree that watching high levels of media violence makes viewers more susceptible to acting aggressively, and recent research supports this claim (Savage & Yancy, 2008; Boxer et al., 2009; Anderson et al., 2010; Ferguson, 2015). For example, one survey of serious and violent young male offenders incarcerated in Florida showed that one-fourth of them had attempted to commit a media-inspired copycat crime (Surette, 2002). A significant proportion of those teenage offenders noted that they paid close attention to the media.

Violent video games have also been linked with actual aggression. In one of a series of studies by psychologist Craig Anderson and his colleagues, for example, college students who frequently played violent video games, such as *Postal* or *Doom,* were more likely to have been involved in delinquent behavior and aggression. Frequent players also had lower academic achievement (Anderson et al., 2004; Swing & Anderson, 2007; Anderson & Carnagey, 2009).

On the other hand, there are contrary research findings. For example, a recent meta-analysis of video game influences finds the effects of video games on aggression are not substantial. Furthermore, some researchers argue that violent video games may produce certain positive results—such as a rise in social networking (Ferguson, 2010, 2011, 2015).

From the perspective of ...

A Video Game Designer What responsibility would you have regarding how much violence was projected in your design?

Several aspects of media violence may contribute to real-life aggressive behavior (Bushman & Anderson, 2001; Johnson et al., 2002; Bushman, Chandler, & Huesmann, 2010). For one thing, experiencing violent media content seems to lower inhibitions against carrying out aggression—watching television portrayals of violence makes aggression seem a legitimate response to particular situations. Exposure to media violence also may distort our understanding of the meaning of others' behavior, predisposing us to view even nonaggressive acts by others as aggressive. Finally, a continuous diet of aggression may leave us desensitized to violence, and what previously would have repelled us now produces little emotional response. Our sense of the pain and suffering brought about by aggression may be diminished (Bartholow, Bushman, & Sestir, 2006; Weber, Ritterfeld, & Kostygina, 2006; Carnagey, Anderson, & Bushman, 2007).

EXPLORING diversity

Does Culture Influence How We Learn?

When a member of the Chilcotin Indian tribe teaches her daughter to prepare salmon, at first she only allows the daughter to observe the entire process. A little later, she permits her child to try out some basic parts of the task. Her response to questions is noteworthy. For example, when the daughter asks about how to do "the backbone part," the mother's response is to repeat the entire process with another salmon. The reason? The mother feels that one cannot learn the individual parts of the task apart from the context of preparing the whole fish. (Tharp, 1989)

It should not be surprising that children raised in the Chilcotin tradition, which stresses instruction that starts by communicating the entire task, may have difficulty with traditional Western schooling. In the approach to teaching most characteristic of Western culture, tasks are broken down into their component parts. Only after each small step is learned is it thought possible to master the complete task.

Do the differences in teaching approaches between cultures affect how people learn? Some psychologists, taking a cognitive perspective on learning, suggest that people develop particular *learning styles,* characteristic ways of approaching material, based on their cultural background and unique pattern of abilities (Anderson & Adams, 1992; Wilkinson & Olliver-Gray, 2006; Li, 2011). Learning styles differ along several dimensions. For example, one central dimension relates to our receptive learning style, or the way in which we initially receive information from our sense organs and then process that information. As you can see for yourself in the following Try It!, you probably have a receptive learning style in which you prefer to have material presented in a particular manner. For example, you may prefer to learn from visual/graphic material, rather than through reading written material.

Another important learning style is relational versus analytical approaches to learning. As illustrated in Figure 3, people with a *relational learning style* master material best through understanding the "big picture" about something. They need to understand the complete picture of what they're studying before they understand its component parts.

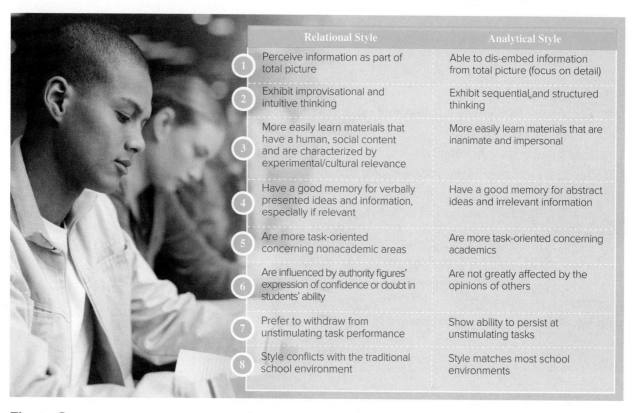

Relational Style	Analytical Style
1 Perceive information as part of total picture	Able to dis-embed information from total picture (focus on detail)
2 Exhibit improvisational and intuitive thinking	Exhibit sequential and structured thinking
3 More easily learn materials that have a human, social content and are characterized by experimental/cultural relevance	More easily learn materials that are inanimate and impersonal
4 Have a good memory for verbally presented ideas and information, especially if relevant	Have a good memory for abstract ideas and irrelevant information
5 Are more task-oriented concerning nonacademic areas	Are more task-oriented concerning academics
6 Are influenced by authority figures' expression of confidence or doubt in students' ability	Are not greatly affected by the opinions of others
7 Prefer to withdraw from unstimulating task performance	Show ability to persist at unstimulating tasks
8 Style conflicts with the traditional school environment	Style matches most school environments

Figure 3 A comparison of analytical versus relational approaches to learning offers one example of how learning styles differ along several dimensions. Photo: © Stockbyte/Getty Images RF

What's Your Receptive Learning Style?

Read each of the following statements and rank them in terms of their usefulness to you as learning approaches. Base your ratings on your personal experiences and preferences, using the following scale:

1 = Not at all useful
2 = Not very useful
3 = Neutral
4 = Somewhat useful
5 = Very useful

	1	2	3	4	5
1. Studying alone	___	___	___	___	___
2. Studying pictures and diagrams to understand complex ideas	___	___	___	___	___
3. Listening to class lectures	___	___	___	___	___
4. Performing a process myself rather than reading or hearing about it	___	___	___	___	___
5. Learning a complex procedure by reading written directions	___	___	___	___	___
6. Watching and listening to film, computer, or video presentations	___	___	___	___	___
7. Listening to a book or lecture on tape	___	___	___	___	___
8. Doing lab work	___	___	___	___	___
9. Studying teachers' handouts and lecture notes	___	___	___	___	___
10. Studying in a quiet room	___	___	___	___	___
11. Taking part in group discussions	___	___	___	___	___
12. Taking part in hands-on classroom demonstrations	___	___	___	___	___
13. Taking notes and studying them later	___	___	___	___	___
14. Creating flash cards and using them as a study and review tool	___	___	___	___	___
15. Memorizing and recalling how words are spelled by spelling them "out loud" in my head	___	___	___	___	___
16. Writing key facts and important points down as a tool for remembering them	___	___	___	___	___
17. Recalling how to spell a word by seeing it in my head	___	___	___	___	___

(continued)

18. Underlining or highlighting important facts or passages in my reading

19. Saying things out loud when I'm studying

20. Recalling how to spell a word by "writing" it invisibly in the air or on a surface

21. Learning new information by reading about it in a textbook

22. Using a map to find an unknown place

23. Working in a study group

24. Finding a place I've been to once by just going there without directions

Scoring

The statements cycle through four receptive learning styles:

- **Read/write:** If you have a read/write learning style, you prefer information that is presented visually in a written format. You feel most comfortable reading, and you may recall the spelling of a word by thinking of how the word looks. You probably learn best when you have the opportunity to read about a concept rather than listening to a teacher explain it.

- **Visual/graphic:** Students with a visual/graphic learning style learn most effectively when material is presented visually in a diagram or picture. You might recall the structure of a chemical compound by reviewing a picture in your mind, and you benefit from instructors who make frequent use of visual aids such as videos, maps, and models. Students with visual learning styles find it easier to see things in their mind's eye—to visualize a task or concept—than to be lectured about them.

- **Auditory/verbal:** Have you ever asked a friend to help you put something together by having her read the directions to you while you worked? If you did, you may have an auditory/verbal learning style. People with auditory/verbal learning styles prefer listening to explanations rather than reading them. They love class lectures and discussions, because they can easily take in the information that is being talked about.

- **Tactile/kinesthetic:** Students with a tactile/kinesthetic learning style prefer to learn by doing—touching, manipulating objects, and doing things. For instance, some people enjoy the act of writing because of the feel of a pencil or a computer keyboard—the tactile equivalent of thinking out loud. Or they may find that it helps them to make a three-dimensional model to understand a new idea.

To find your primary learning style, disregard your 1, 2, and 3 ratings. Add up your 4 and 5 ratings for each learning style (i.e., a "4" equals 4 points and a "5" equals 5 points). Use the following chart to link the statements to the learning styles and to write down your summed ratings:

Learning Style	Statements	Total (Sum) of Rating Points
Read/write	1, 5, 9, 13, 17, and 21	____
Visual/graphic	2, 6, 10, 14, 18, and 22	____
Auditory/verbal	3, 7, 11, 15, 19, and 23	____
Tactile/kinesthetic	4, 8, 12, 16, 20, and 24	____

The total of your rating points for any given style will range from a low of 0 to a high of 30. The highest total indicates your main receptive learning style. Don't be surprised if you have a mixed style, in which two or more styles receive similar ratings.

Even though these friends have grown up next door to one another and are similar in many ways, they have very different learning styles. What might account for this? © Clarissa Leahy/Getty Images

In contrast, those with an *analytical learning style* do best when they analyze the various components underlying a phenomenon or situation. By developing an understanding of the individual parts, they are best able to understand the full picture.

According to educators James Anderson and Maurianne Adams, particular minority groups in Western societies display characteristic learning styles. For instance, they argue that Caucasian females and African American, Native American, and Hispanic American males and females are more apt to use a relational style of learning than Caucasian and Asian American males, who are more likely to employ an analytical style (Anderson & Adams, 1992; Adams et al., 2000; Richardson, 2011).

The conclusion that members of particular ethnic and gender groups have similar learning styles is controversial. Because there is so much diversity within each particular racial and ethnic group, critics argue that generalizations about learning styles cannot be used to predict the style of any single individual, regardless of group membership.

Still, it is clear that values about learning, which are communicated through a person's family and cultural background, have an impact on how successful students are in school. One theory suggests that members of minority groups who were voluntary immigrants are more apt to be successful in school than those who were brought into a majority culture against their will. For example, Korean children in the United States—the sons and daughters of voluntary immigrants—perform quite well, as a group, in school. In contrast, Korean children in Japan, who were often the sons and daughters of people who were forced to immigrate during World War II, essentially as forced laborers, tend to do poorly in school. Presumably, children in the forced immigration group are less motivated to succeed than those in the voluntary immigration group (Ogbu, 1992, 2003; Foster, 2005).

RECAP

Explain latent learning and how it works in humans.

- Cognitive approaches to learning consider learning in terms of thought processes, or cognition. Phenomena such as latent learning—in which a new behavior is learned but not performed until some incentive is provided for its performance—and the apparent development of cognitive maps support cognitive approaches.

Discuss the influence of observational learning in acquiring skills.

- Learning also occurs from observing the behavior of others. The major factor that determines whether an observed behavior will actually be performed is the nature of

the reinforcement or punishment a model receives.

- Observational learning, which may have a genetic basis, is particularly important in acquiring skills in which the operant conditioning technique of shaping is inappropriate.

Describe research findings about observational learning and media violence.

- Observation of violence is linked to a greater likelihood of subsequently acting aggressively.

- Experiencing violent media content seems to lower inhibitions against carrying out aggression; may distort our understanding of the meaning of others' behavior, predisposing us to view even nonaggressive acts by others as aggressive; and desensitizes us to violence.

[EVALUATE E Evaluate]

1. Cognitive learning theorists are concerned only with overt behavior, not with its internal causes. True or false?

2. In cognitive learning theory, it is assumed that people develop a(n) _____ about receiving a reinforcer when they behave a certain way.

3. In _____ learning, a new behavior is learned but is not shown until appropriate reinforcement is presented.

4. Bandura's theory of _____ learning states that people learn through watching a(n) _____ another person displaying the behavior of interest.

[RETHINK R Rethink]

The relational style of learning sometimes conflicts with the traditional school environment. Could a school be created that takes advantage of the characteristics of the relational style? How? Are there types of learning for which the analytical style is clearly superior?

Answers to Evaluate Questions 1. false; cognitive learning theorists are primarily concerned with mental processes. 2. expectation; 3. latent; 4. observational, model

KEY TERMS

Cognitive learning theory   LO17.1

Latent learning   LO17.1

Observational learning   LO17.2

«« Looking Back

Psychology on the Web

1. B. F. Skinner had an impact on society and on thought that is only hinted at in our discussion of learning. Find additional information on the Web about Skinner's life and influence. See what you can find out about his ideas for an ideal, utopian society based on the principles of conditioning and behaviorism. Write a summary of your findings.

2. Select a topic discussed in this set of modules that is of interest to you—for example, reinforcement versus punishment, teaching complex behaviors by shaping, violence in video games, relational versus analytical learning styles, behavior modification, and so on. Find at least two sources of information on the Web about your topic and summarize the results of your quest. It may be most helpful to find two different approaches to your topic and compare them.

the case of . . .
THE MANAGER WHO DOUBLED PRODUCTIVITY

When Cliff Richards took over as the new department manager, he discovered that the existing staff was unusually inefficient and unproductive. Cliff learned that the previous manager often criticized and chided staff members for every little mistake until many of the best people had left, and the rest felt demoralized.

Cliff resolved not to criticize or punish staff members unless it was absolutely necessary. Instead, he frequently complimented them whenever they did a good job. He set daily production goals for them, and every Friday afternoon he bought lunch for all staff members who met their goals every day that week. Moreover, Cliff randomly conducted spot checks on what staff members were doing, and if he found them hard at work, he gave them small rewards such as extra break time.

Within just three months, productivity in Cliff's department nearly doubled. It became the most efficient department in the company.

1. How did Cliff take advantage of principles of operant conditioning to modify his staff's behavior?

2. Why did Cliff's predecessor's strategy of punishing undesirable behavior not work very well? Even if punishment and reinforcement strategies were equally effective at controlling behavior, why would reinforcement remain preferable?

3. How did Cliff make use of partial reinforcement schedules? What kinds of schedules did he use?

4. How could Cliff use his technique to train his staff to complete a complex new task that they had never done before?

5. How might Cliff make use of principles of cognitive learning theory to improve his staff's productivity even further?

profiles of **SUCCESS**

Courtesy of Elizabeth Reyes-Fournier

NAME: Elizabeth Reyes-Fournier, PhD

SCHOOLS: Loyola Marymount University and Keiser University

DEGREE PROGRAMS: BA, Psychology; MA, Counseling; PhD, Psychology

By her own admission, Elizabeth Reyes-Fournier was probably not as academically disciplined as she should have been as an undergraduate student. But in the course of pursing advanced degrees, she was able to find her stride.

"When I was an undergrad, my study habits were nothing to write home about. I waited until the last minute, crammed, panicked," she explained. "Doing my graduate studies, I changed. When I was working on my doctorate, I had to consider my family and how that would affect them, and had to schedule myself to the minute.

"I always was ahead of the class in case something happened with my family. This meant that I had my reading, assignments, and papers completed at least two weeks before they were due."

Her experience with graduate school resulted in Reyes-Fournier refining the art of scheduling to organize her busy life.

"I managed my school time with scheduling," she noted. "Since I worked at home as a writer, I would start my days at the same time, work a certain amount of time, and then shift to school work. By the time my kids came home from school, I was almost done with schoolwork. I did my schoolwork six days a week with Saturdays off for 'good behavior'."

While being organized with a solid schedule served her well with school it also played an important part during a personal setback while pursuing her degree.

"The hardest thing I had to overcome while working on my doctorate was my mother's passing," said Reyes-Fournier. "I was in the middle of classes when she went into hospice. Part of me wanted to leave school, and I don't think anyone would have faulted me for that.

"But I knew that my mother would have been so angry if I did, so I pushed on. This is one of those places where being ahead of schedule saved me. I was able to finish my courses without missing even one deadline. The loss of my biggest cheerleader was devastating but also pushed me to finish for her," she added.

[RETHINK R Rethink]

After doing schoolwork for six days a week, Reyes-Fournier treated herself to a day off. How do the principles of learning and reinforcement explain the importance of rewarding oneself in this way?

Reyes-Fournier's scheduling skills served her well through a personal crisis. How can being organized and having a schedule help in other areas outside of school?

visual summary 5
LEARNING

MODULE 15 Classical Conditioning

Ivan Pavlov: Basic principles of classical conditioning

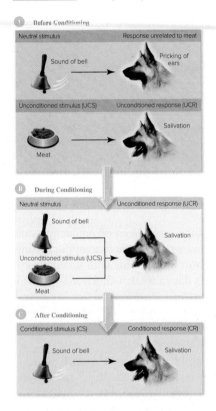

Additional key principles of classical conditioning

- Extinction:
  Conditioned response disappears over time

- Stimulus generalization:
  Stimuli that are similar to the conditioned stimulus also elicit the conditioned response

- Stimulus discrimination:
  Stimuli that are different from the conditioned stimulus do not elicit the conditioned response

MODULE 16 Operant Conditioning

Basic Principle: Behavior changes in frequency according to its consequences

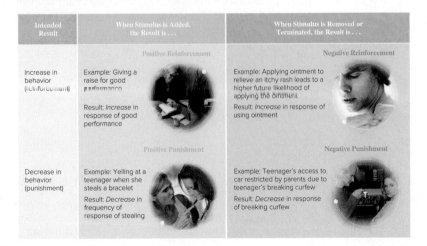

Intended Result	When Stimulus is Added, the Result is . . .	When Stimulus is Removed or Terminated, the Result is . . .
	Positive Reinforcement	**Negative Reinforcement**
Increase in behavior (reinforcement)	Example: Giving a raise for good performance Result: *Increase* in response of good performance	Example: Applying ointment to relieve an itchy rash leads to a higher future likelihood of applying the ointment Result: *Increase* in response of using ointment
	Positive Punishment	**Negative Punishment**
Decrease in behavior (punishment)	Example: Yelling at a teenager when she steals a bracelet Result: *Decrease* in frequency of response of stealing	Example: Teenager's access to car restricted by parents due to teenager's breaking curfew Result: *Decrease* in response of breaking curfew

Basic Principle: Behavior changes in frequency according to its consequences *(continued)*

- Schedules of reinforcement

- Shaping: Reinforcing successive approximations of behavior

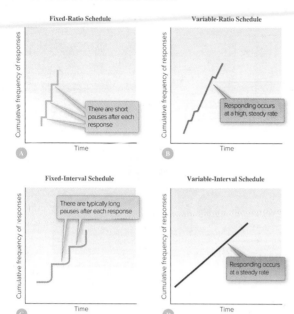

MODULE 17 Cognitive Approaches to Learning

Cognitive Learning Theory: Focuses on the internal thoughts and expectations

- Latent learning: A new behavior is learned but is not demonstrated until it is reinforced

- Observational learning: We learn by watching the behavior of others

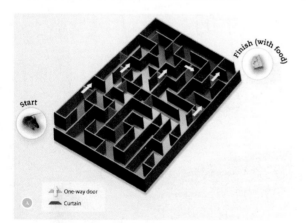

(MODULE 16) © Ryan McVay/Getty Images; © Stockbyte/Getty Images; © BananaStock/PunchStock; © Amy Etra / PhotoEdit
(MODULE 17) © Henrik Sorensen/Getty Images

6 THINKING: MEMORY, COGNITION, AND LANGUAGE

CHAPTER OUTLINE

Stuck in the Past

What do Jill Price, Brad Williams, and Rick Baron have in common? They are among the handful of people diagnosed with *hyperthymestic syndrome,* a condition in which a person can recall the events of their own past in extraordinary detail. Ask any one of them what they were doing on a specific date and they will be able to tell you where they were, who else was there, what was happening, and even how they felt. For Jill and Rick, this ability dates from their early adolescence, but Brad can remember everything back to age five.

While most of us would like to improve our memory, people with hyperthymesia often feel overwhelmed because the memories continually flood their thoughts. It's like reliving your past every moment of the present (Internetwriter62, 2011; Price, 2013; Waleed, 2014).

 **Looking** Ahead

Researchers take a keen interest in people like Jill, Brad, and Rick. By studying those who have been diagnosed with hyperthymesia, they hope to find solutions to diseases involving memory loss such as Alzheimer's. In Jill's case, an MRI brain scan revealed two abnormally large areas of her brain: the caudate nuclei and a section of the temporal lobe, both involved in memory (Elias, 2009; Ally, Hussey, & Donahue, 2013; McGaugh & LePort, 2014).

Hyperthymesia illustrates the complexity and the mystery of the phenomenon we call memory. Memory allows us to retrieve a vast amount of information. We are able to remember the name of a friend we haven't talked with for years and recall the details of a picture that hung in our bedroom as a child. At the same time, though, memory failures are common. We forget where we left the keys to the car and fail to answer an exam question about material we studied only a few hours earlier. Why?

Answers to this and other questions come from **cognitive psychology,** the branch of psychology that focuses on the study of higher mental processes, including thinking, language, memory, problem solving, knowing, reasoning, judging, and decision making. Clearly, the realm of cognitive psychology is broad.

Cognitive psychology centers on three major topics: memory, thinking and reasoning, and language. We start this chapter by considering memory and forgetting. Then we examine how people think and reason as well as different strategies for approaching problems. Finally, we discuss how language is developed and acquired, its basic characteristics, and the relationship between language and thought.

The Foundations of Memory

Learning Outcomes   P Prepare

>> **LO18.1** Define sensory memory.

>> **LO18.2** Define short-term memory.

>> **LO18.3** Define long-term memory.

MODULE OUTLINE   O Organize

Sensory Memory

Short-Term Memory

Long-Term Memory

W Work

© AGE fotostock/Alamy Stock Photo RF

You are playing a game of *Trivial Pursuit,* and winning the game comes down to one question: on what body of water is Mumbai located? As you rack your brain for the answer, several fundamental processes relating to memory come into play. You may never, for instance, have been exposed to information regarding Mumbai's location. Or if you have been exposed to it, it simply may not have registered in a meaningful way. In other words, the information might not have been recorded properly in your memory. The initial process of recording information in a form usable to memory, a process called *encoding,* is the first stage in remembering something.

Even if you had been exposed to the information and originally knew the name of the body of water, you may still be unable to recall it during the game because of a failure to retain it. Memory specialists speak of *storage,* the maintenance of material saved in memory. If the material is not stored adequately, it cannot be recalled later.

Memory also depends on one last process—*retrieval:* material in memory storage has to be located and brought into awareness to be useful. Your failure to recall Mumbai's location, then, may rest on your inability to retrieve information that you learned earlier.

cognitive psychology The branch of psychology that focuses on the study of higher mental processes, including thinking, language, memory, problem solving, knowing, reasoning, judging, and decision making

memory The process by which we encode, store, and retrieve information

In sum, psychologists consider **memory** to be the process by which we encode, store, and retrieve information (see Figure 1). Each of the three parts of this definition—encoding, storage, and retrieval—represents a different process. You can think of these processes as being analogous to a computer's keyboard (encoding), hard drive (storage), and software that accesses the information for display on the screen (retrieval). Only if all three processes have operated will you experience success and be able to recall the body of water on which Mumbai is located: the Arabian Sea.

Recognizing that memory involves encoding, storage, and retrieval gives us a start in understanding the concept. But how does memory actually function? How do we explain what information is initially encoded, what gets stored, and how it is retrieved?

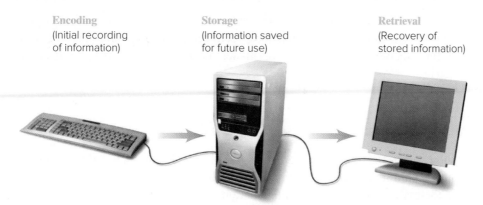

Encoding
(Initial recording
of information)

Storage
(Information saved
for future use)

Retrieval
(Recovery of
stored information)

Figure 1 Memory is built on three basic processes—encoding, storage, and retrieval—that are analogous to a computer's keyboard, hard drive, and software to access the information for display on the screen. The analogy is not perfect, however, because human memory is less precise than a computer. How might you modify the analogy to make it more accurate?

According to the *three-system approach* to memory that dominated memory research for several decades, there are different memory storage systems or stages through which information must travel if it is to be remembered (Atkinson & Shiffrin, 1968, 1971). Historically, the approach has been extremely influential in the development of our understanding of memory, and—although new theories have augmented it—it still provides a useful framework for understanding how information is recalled.

The three-system memory theory proposes the existence of the three separate memory stores shown in Figure 2. **Sensory memory** refers to the initial, momentary storage of information that lasts only an instant. Here an exact replica of the stimulus recorded by a person's sensory system is stored very briefly. In a second stage, **short-term memory** holds information for 15 to 25 seconds

sensory memory The initial, momentary storage of information, lasting only an instant

short-term memory Memory that holds information for 15 to 25 seconds

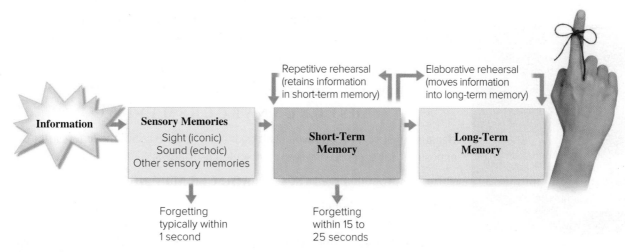

Figure 2 In this three-stage model of memory, information initially recorded by the person's sensory system enters sensory memory, which momentarily holds the information. The information then moves to short-term memory, which stores it for 15 to 25 seconds. Finally, the information can move into long-term memory, which is relatively permanent. Whether the information moves from short-term to long-term memory depends on the kind and amount of rehearsal of the material that is carried out. Source: Atkinson & Shiffrin, 1968. Photo: © C Squared Studios/Getty Images RF

and stores it according to its meaning rather than as mere sensory stimulation. The third type of storage system is **long-term memory.** Information is stored in long-term memory on a relatively permanent basis, although it may be difficult to retrieve.

» LO18.1 Sensory Memory

A momentary flash of lightning, the sound of a twig snapping, and the sting of a pinprick all represent stimulation of exceedingly brief duration, but they may nonetheless provide important information that can require a response. Such stimuli are initially   and fleetingly—stored in sensory memory, the first repository of the information the world presents to us.

Sensory memory can store information for only a very short time. If information does not pass into short-term memory, it is lost for good. However, despite the brief duration of sensory memory, its precision is high: sensory memory can store an almost exact replica of each stimulus to which it is exposed (Vlassova & Pearson, 2013; Rimmele, Sussman, & Poeppel, 2015; Pastukhov, 2016).

» LO18.2 Short-Term Memory

long-term memory Memory that stores information on a relatively permanent basis, although it may be difficult to retrieve

chunk A meaningful grouping of stimuli that can be stored as a unit in short-term memory

rehearsal The repetition of information that has entered short-term memory

Because the information that is stored briefly in sensory memory consists of representations of raw sensory stimuli, it is not meaningful to us. If we are to make sense of it and possibly retain it, the information must be transferred to the next stage of memory: short-term memory. Short-term memory is the memory store in which information first has meaning, although the maximum length of retention there is relatively short (Hamilton & Martin, 2007; Prime & Jolicoeur, 2010).

Short-term memory has incomplete representational capabilities: the specific amount of information that can be held in short-term memory has been identified as seven items, or "chunks," of information, with variations up to plus or minus two chunks. A **chunk** is a meaningful grouping of stimuli that can be stored as a unit in short-term memory. A chunk can be individual letters or numbers, permitting us to hold a seven-digit phone number (like 226–4610) in short-term memory.

But a chunk also may consist of larger categories, such as words or other meaningful units. For example, consider the following list of 21 letters:

P B S F O X C N N A B C C B S M T V N B C

Because the list exceeds seven chunks, it is difficult to recall the letters after one exposure. But suppose they were presented as follows:

PBS FOX CNN ABC CBS MTV NBC

In this case, even though there are still 21 letters, you'd be able to store them in short-term memory, since they represent only seven chunks.

Although it is possible to remember seven or so relatively complicated sets of information entering short-term memory, the information cannot be held there very long. Most psychologists believe that information in short-term memory is lost after 15 to 25 seconds—unless it is transferred to long-term memory.

The transfer of material from short- to long-term memory proceeds largely on the basis of **rehearsal,** the repetition of information that has entered short-term

A momentary flash of lightning leaves a sensory visual memory, a fleeting but exact replica of the stimulus that fades rapidly. © Paul Avis/Getty Images

memory. Rehearsal accomplishes two things. First, as long as the information is repeated, it is maintained in short-term memory. More important, however, rehearsal allows us to transfer the information into long-term memory (Jarrold & Tam, 2011; Grenfell-Essam, Ward, & Tan, 2013; Lucidi et al., 2016).

Whether the transfer is made from short- to long-term memory seems to depend largely on the kind of rehearsal that is carried out. If the information is simply repeated over and over again—as we might do with a telephone number someone tells us as we rush to store it in our phone—it is kept current in short-term memory, but it will not necessarily be placed in long-term memory. Instead, as soon as we stop punching in the phone numbers, the number is likely to be replaced by other information and will be completely forgotten.

From the perspective of . . .

A Marketing Specialist How might ways of enhancing memory be used by advertisers and others to promote their products?

In contrast, if the information in short-term memory is rehearsed using a process called elaborative rehearsal, it is much more likely to be transferred into long-term memory. *Elaborative rehearsal* occurs when the information is considered and organized in some fashion. The organization might include expanding the information to make it fit into a logical framework, linking it to another memory, turning it into an image, or transforming it in some other way.

> **declarative memory** Memory for factual information: names, faces, dates, and the like

» LO18.3 Long-Term Memory

Material that makes its way from short-term memory to long-term memory enters a storehouse of almost unlimited capacity. Like a new file we save on a hard drive, the information in long-term memory is filed and coded so that we can retrieve it when we need it.

Long-Term Memory Modules

Many contemporary researchers now regard long-term memory as having several different components, or *memory modules*. Each of these modules represents a separate memory system in the brain.

One major distinction within long-term memory is that between declarative memory and procedural memory. **Declarative memory** is memory for factual information: names, faces, dates, and facts, such as "a bike has two wheels." In contrast,

HOW NOT TO REMEMBER NAMES

The ability to remember specific skills in the order in which they are used is is related to procedural memory. Assuming that driving involves procedural memory, why it is not safe to use a cell phone while driving? © antoniodiaz/Shutterstock.com

procedural memory Memory for skills and habits, such as riding a bike or hitting a baseball, sometimes referred to as *nondeclarative memory*

semantic memory Memory for general knowledge and facts about the world, as well as memory for the rules of logic that are used to deduce other facts

episodic memory Memory for events that occur in a particular time, place, or context

procedural memory (or *nondeclarative memory*) refers to memory for skills and habits, such as how to ride a bike or hit a baseball. Information about *things* is stored in declarative memory; information about *how to do things* is stored in procedural memory (Oberauer, 2010; Fosshage, 2011; Sundqvist et al., 2016).

Declarative memory can be subdivided into semantic memory and episodic memory. **Semantic memory** is memory for general knowledge and facts about the world, as well as memory for the rules of logic that are used to deduce other facts. Because of semantic memory, we remember that the zip code for Beverly Hills is 90210, that Mumbai is on the Arabian Sea, and that memoree is the incorrect spelling of memory. Thus, semantic memory is somewhat like a mental almanac of facts (Tulving, 2002; McNamara, 2013; Grady, St-Laurent, & Burianová, 2015).

In contrast, **episodic memory** is memory for events that occur in a particular time, place, or context. For example, recall of learning to ride a bike, our first kiss, or arranging a surprise 21st birthday party for our brother is based on episodic memories. Episodic memories relate to particular contexts. For example, remembering when and how we learned that $2 \times 2 = 4$ would be an episodic memory; the fact itself (that $2 \times 2 = 4$) is a semantic memory. (Also see Figure 3.)

Ed Fisher/The New Yorker Collection/The Cartoon Bank

"The matters about which I'm being questioned, Your Honor, are all things I should have included in my long-term memory but which I mistakenly inserted in my short-term memory."

STUDY ALERT

Use Figure 3 to help clarify the distinctions between the different types of memory.

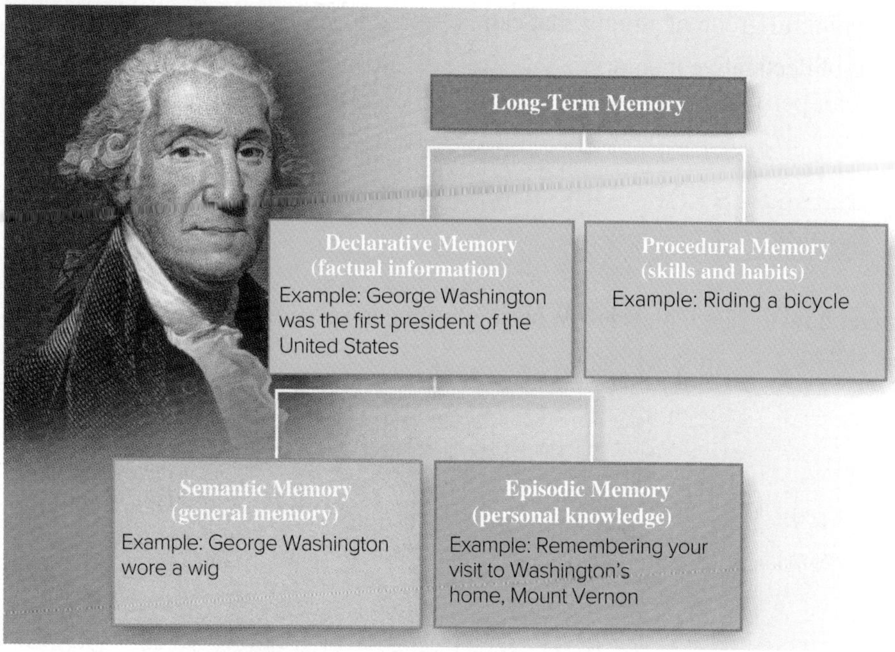

Long-Term Memory
Declarative Memory
(factual information)
Example: George Washington was the first president of the United States
Procedural Memory
(skills and habits)
Example: Riding a bicycle
Semantic Memory
(general memory)
Example: George Washington wore a wig
Episodic Memory
(personal knowledge)
Example: Remembering your visit to Washington's home, Mount Vernon

Figure 3 Long-term memory can be subdivided into several different types. What type of long-term memory is involved in your recollection of the moment you first arrived on your campus at the start of college? What type of long-term memory is involved in remembering the lyrics to a song, compared with the tune of a song?
Photo: © Popperfoto/Getty Images

RECAP

Define sensory memory.

- Sensory memory, corresponding to each of the sensory systems, is the first place where information is saved. Sensory memories are very brief, but they are precise, storing a nearly exact replica of a stimulus.

Define short-term memory.

- Roughly seven (plus or minus two) chunks of information can be transferred and held in short-term memory. Information in short-term memory is held from 15 to 25 seconds and, if not transferred to long-term memory, is lost.

Define long-term memory.

- Memories are transferred into long-term storage through rehearsal. If memories are transferred into long-term memory, they become relatively permanent.
- Long-term memory can be viewed in terms of memory modules, each of which is related to separate memory systems in the brain. For instance, we can distinguish between declarative memory and procedural memory. Declarative memory is further divided into semantic memory and episodic memory.

[EVALUATE E Evaluate]

1. Match the type of memory with its definition:
   1. Long-term memory
   2. Short-term memory
   3. Sensory memory

   a. Holds information 15 to 25 seconds.
   b. Stores information on a relatively permanent basis.
   c. Direct representation of a stimulus.

2. A(n) _____ is a meaningful group of stimuli that can be stored together in short-term memory.

3. There appear to be two types of declarative memory: _____ memory, for knowledge and facts, and _____ memory, for personal experiences.

[RETHINK **R** Rethink]

It is a truism that "you never forget how to ride a bicycle." Why might this be so? In what type of memory is information about bicycle riding stored?

KEY TERMS

Cognitive psychology   LO18.1

Memory   LO18.1

Sensory memory   LO18.1

Short-term memory   LO18.1

Long-term memory   LO18.1

Chunk   LO18.2

Rehearsal   LO18.2

Declarative memory   LO18.3

Procedural memory   LO18.3

Semantic memory   LO18.3

Episodic memory   LO18.3

module 19

Recall and Forgetting

》 LO19.1 Retrieval Cues

 Work

Have you ever tried to remember someone's name, convinced that you knew it but unable to recall it no matter how hard you tried? This common occurrence—known as the **tip-of-the-tongue phenomenon**—exemplifies how difficult it can be to retrieve information stored in long-term memory (Schwartz, 2002, 2008; Lindín & Díaz, 2010; Navarrete et al., 2015).

Perhaps recall of names and other memories is not perfect because there is so much information stored in long-term memory. How do we sort through this vast array of material and retrieve specific information at the appropriate time? One way is through retrieval cues. A *retrieval cue* is a stimulus that allows us to recall more easily information that is in long-term memory. It may be a word, an emotion, or a sound; whatever the specific cue, a memory will suddenly come to mind when the retrieval cue is present. For example, the smell of roasting turkey may evoke memories of Thanksgiving or family gatherings.

Retrieval cues are particularly important when we are making an effort to *recall* information, as opposed to being asked to *recognize* material stored in memory. In **recall**, a specific piece of information must be retrieved—such as that needed to answer a fill-in-the-blank question or to write an essay on a test. In contrast, **recognition** occurs when people are presented with a stimulus and

tip-of-the-tongue phenomenon The inability to recall information that one realizes one knows—a result of the difficulty of retrieving information from long-term memory

recall Memory task in which specific information must be retrieved

recognition Memory task in which individuals are presented with a stimulus and asked whether they have been exposed to it in the past or to identify it from a list of alternatives

Figure 1 Try to recall the names of these characters. Because this is a recall task, it is relatively difficult. © AF archive/Alamy Stock Photo

asked whether they have been exposed to it previously, or they are asked to identify it from a list of alternatives. As you might guess, recognition is generally a much easier task than recall (see Figures 1 and 2).

» LO19.2 Levels of Processing

One determinant of how well memories are recalled is the way in which material is first perceived, processed, and understood. The **levels-of-processing theory** emphasizes the degree to which new material is mentally analyzed. It suggests that the amount of information processing that occurs when material is initially encountered is central in determining how much of the information is ultimately remembered. According to this approach, the depth of information processing during exposure to material—meaning the degree to which it is analyzed and considered—is critical; the greater the intensity of its initial processing is, the more likely we are to remember it (Craik & Lockhart, 2008; Mungan, Peynircioğlu, & Halpern, 2011).

Because we do not pay close attention to much of the information to which we are exposed, very little mental processing typically takes place, and we forget new material almost immediately. However, information to which we pay greater attention is processed more thoroughly. Therefore, it enters memory at a deeper level—and is less apt to be forgotten than is information processed at shallower levels.

There are considerable practical implications to the notion that recall depends on the degree to which information is initially processed. For example, the depth of information processing is critical when learning and studying

levels-of-processing theory The theory of memory that emphasizes the degree to which new material is mentally analyzed

Figure 2 Naming the characters in Figure 1 (a recall task) is more difficult than solving the recognition problem posed in this list.

Answer this recognition question: Which of the following are the names of the seven dwarfs in the Disney movie *Snow White and the Seven Dwarfs?*	
Goofy	Bashful
Sleepy	Meanie
Smarty	Doc
Scaredy	Happy
Dopey	Angry
Grumpy	Sneezy
Wheezy	Crazy

(The correct answers are Bashful, Doc, Dopey, Grumpy, Happy, Sleepy, and Sneezy.)

course material. Rote memorization of a list of key terms for a test is unlikely to produce long-term recollection of information, because processing occurs at a shallow level. In contrast, thinking about the meaning of the terms and reflecting on how they relate to information that one currently knows results in far more effective long-term retention (Conway, 2002; Wenzel, Zetocha, & Ferraro, 2007; Albanese & Case, 2015).

≫ LO19.3 Explicit and Implicit Memory

Careful studies have found that people who are anesthetized during surgery can sometimes recall snippets of conversations they heard during surgery—even though they have no conscious recollection of the information (Sebel, Bonke, & Winograd, 1993). The discovery that people have memories about which they are unaware has been an important one. It has led to speculation that two forms of memory, explicit and implicit, may exist side by side.

Explicit memory refers to intentional or conscious recollection of information. When we try to remember a name or date we have encountered or learned about previously, we are searching our explicit memory.

In contrast, **implicit memory** refers to memories of which people are not consciously aware, but which can affect subsequent performance and behavior. Skills that operate automatically and without thinking, such as jumping out of the path of an automobile coming toward us as we walk down the side of a road, are stored in implicit memory. Similarly, a feeling of vague dislike for an acquaintance, without knowing why we have that feeling, may be a reflection of implicit memories. Perhaps the person reminds us of someone else in our past whom we didn't like, even though we are not aware of the memory of that other individual (Voss & Paller, 2008; Lozito & Mulligan, 2010; Wu, Y., 2013).

Implicit memory is closely related to the prejudice and discrimination people exhibit toward members of minority groups. Even though people may say and even believe they harbor no prejudice, assessment of their implicit memories may reveal that they have negative associations about members of minority groups. Such associations can influence people's behavior without their being aware of their underlying beliefs (Hofmann et al., 2008; Spataro, Mulligan, & Rossi-Arnaud, 2011; Enge, Lupo, & Zárate, 2015).

explicit memory Intentional or conscious recollection of information

implicit memory Memories of which people are not consciously aware, but which can affect subsequent performance and behavior

flashbulb memories Memories centered on a specific, important, or surprising event that are so vivid it is as if they represented a snapshot of the event

> Skills that operate automatically and without thinking, such as jumping out of the path of an automobile coming toward us as we walk down the side of a road, are stored in implicit memory.

≫ LO19.4 Flashbulb Memories

For anyone old enough to recall the day of the terrorist attacks that brought down the Twin Towers in New York City on September 11, 2001, they probably have little trouble recalling their exact location when they heard the news about the terrorist attack, even though the incident happened years ago.

Their ability to remember details about this fatal event illustrates a phenomenon known as flashbulb memory. **Flashbulb memories** are memories related to a specific, important, or surprising event that are so vivid they represent a virtual snapshot of the event.

In spite of passing away more than 40 years apart, both John F. Kennedy and Osama Bin Laden deaths can be cited as examples of flashbulb memories. Depending on your age and cultural point of view, you are likely to remember where you were when you discovered one (or both) of these individuals had died. What is an event in your own life that inspires a flashbulb memory? (first) © GL Archive/Alamy Stock Photo; (second) © Steve Skjold/Alamy Stock Photo

Several types of flashbulb memories are common among college students. For example, involvement in a car accident, meeting one's roommate for the first time, and the night of high school graduation are all typical flashbulb memories (Bohn & Berntsen, 2007; Talarico, 2009; Roehm, 2016; see Figure 3).

» LO19.5 Constructive Processes in Memory: Rebuilding the Past

As we have seen, although it is clear that we can have detailed recollections of significant and distinctive events, it is difficult to gauge the accuracy of such memories. In fact, it is apparent that our memories reflect, at least in part, **constructive processes,** processes in which memories are influenced by the meaning we give to events. When we retrieve information, then, the memory that is produced is affected not just by the direct prior experience we have had with the stimulus, but also by our guesses and inferences about its meaning.

The notion that memory is based on constructive processes was first put forward by Frederic Bartlett, a British psychologist. He suggested that people tend to remember information in terms of **schemas,** organized bodies of information stored in memory that bias the way new information is interpreted, stored, and recalled (Bartlett, 1932). Our reliance on schemas means that memories often consist of a general reconstruction of previous experience. Bartlett argued that schemas are based not only on the specific material to which people are exposed, but also on their understanding of the situation, their expectations

constructive processes Processes in which memories are influenced by the meaning we give to events

schemas Organized bodies of information stored in memory that bias the way new information is interpreted, stored, and recalled; sets of cognitions about people and social experiences

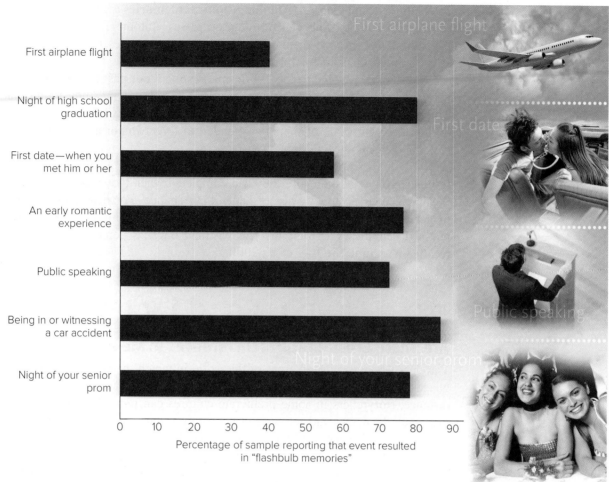

Figure 3 These are the most common flashbulb memory events, based on a survey of college students (Rubin, 1985). What are some of your flashbulb memories? Photos: (first) © Micha Krakowiak/Getty Images RF; (second) © Ryuichi Sato/Getty Images; (third) © Nick Daly/Getty Images; (fourth) © Tony Anderson/Getty Images

about the situation, and their awareness of the motivations underlying the behavior of others. In short, our expectations and knowledge affect the reliability of our memories (McDonald & Hirt, 1997; Newby-Clark & Ross, 2003; Thimm, 2010).

Autobiographical Memory: Where Past Meets Present

Your memory of experiences in your own past may well be a fiction—or at least a distortion of what actually occurred. The same constructive processes that make us inaccurately recall the behavior of others also reduce the accuracy of

© Photodisc/Getty Images RF

From the perspective of ...

A Criminal Justice Professional Given what you know about the constructive nature of memory, why might multiple eyewitnesses to the same event tell different stories about what happened?

autobiographical memories
Our recollections of circumstances and episodes from our own lives

autobiographical memories. **Autobiographical memories** are our recollections of circumstances and episodes from our own lives. Autobiographical memories encompass the episodic memories we hold about ourselves (Sutin & Robins, 2007; Sumner, Griffith & Mineka, 2011).

For example, we tend to forget information about our past that is incompatible with the way in which we currently see ourselves. One study found that adults who were well adjusted but who had been treated for emotional problems during the early years of their lives tended to forget important but troubling childhood events, such as being in foster care.

Similarly, when a group of 48-year-olds were asked to recall how they had responded on a questionnaire they had completed when they were high school freshmen, their accuracy was no better than chance. For example, although 61 percent of the questionnaire respondents said that playing sports and other physical activities was their favorite pastime, only 23 percent of the adults recalled it accurately (Offer et al., 2000).

EXPLORING diversity

Are There Cross-Cultural Differences in Memory?

Travelers who have visited areas of the world in which there is no written language often have returned with tales of people with phenomenal memories. For instance, storytellers in some preliterate cultures can recount long chronicles that recall the names and activities of people over many generations.

Such feats of memory initially led experts to believe that people in preliterate societies develop a different, and perhaps better, type of memory than do those in cultures that employ a written language. They suggested that in a society that lacks writing, people are motivated to recall information with accuracy, especially information relating to tribal histories and traditions that would be lost if they were not passed down orally from one generation to another (Daftary & Meri, 2002; Berntsen & Rubin, 2004).

Today, memory researchers dismiss that view. For one thing, preliterate peoples don't have an exclusive claim to amazing memory feats. Some Hebrew scholars memorize thousands of pages of text and can recall the locations of particular words on the page. Similarly, poetry singers in the Balkans can recall thousands of lines of poetry. Even in cultures in which written language exists, then, astounding feats of memory are possible (Strathern & Stewart, 2003; Rubin et al., 2007).

Memory researchers now believe that there are both similarities and differences in memory across cultures. Basic memory processes such as short-term memory capacity and the structure of long-term memory—the "hardware" of memory—are universal and operate similarly in people in all cultures.

> **Basic memory processes such as short-term memory capacity and the structure of long-term memory—the "hardware" of memory—are universal and operate similarly in people in all cultures.**

In contrast, cultural differences can be seen in the way information is acquired and rehearsed—the "software" of memory. Culture determines how people frame information initially, how much they practice learning it, and determines the strategies they use to try to recall it (Mack, 2003; Wang & Conway, 2006; Rubin et al., 2007). (To get a sense of how you remember information, complete the accompanying Try It!)

Try It!
Determine Your Memory Style

What's your dominant memory style? Do you most easily remember sounds, sights, or the way things feel? Read the statements below and circle the response choice that most closely describes your habits.

To help recall lectures, I...
- V. Read the notes I took during class.
- A. Close my eyes and try to hear what the instructor said.
- K. Try to place myself back in the lecture room and feel what was going on at the time.

To remember a complex procedure, I...
- V. Write down the steps I have to follow.
- A. Listen carefully and repeatedly to the instructions.
- K. Do it over and over again.

To learn sentences in a foreign language, I do best if I...
- V. Read them on paper to see how they're written.
- A. Hear them in my head until I can say them aloud.
- K. See someone speaking them and then practice moving my mouth and hands the way the speaker did.

If I have to learn a dance move, I like...
- V. To see a diagram of the steps before trying it.
- A. Someone to coach me through it while I try it.
- K. To watch it once and then give it a try.

When I recall a very happy moment, I tend to...
- V. Visualize it in my head.
- A. Hear the sounds that I heard when experiencing it.
- K. Feel with my hands and body what I felt at the time.

When I have to remember driving directions, I usually...
- V. See a map of the route in my mind.
- A. Repeat the directions aloud to myself.
- K. Feel my hands steering and the car driving along the correct route.

Answer Key

If you chose mostly V's, your main memory style is visual; your preference is to remember things in terms of the way they appear.

If you chose mostly A's, your main memory style is auditory; your preference is to recall material in terms of sound.

If you chose mostly K's, your main memory style is kinesthetic; your preference is to remember using your sense of touch.

Keep in mind that this questionnaire only gives a rough idea of how we usually use our memories. Remember: all of us use all of the memory styles during the course of each day.

Consider these questions: How do you think your memory style affects the way you recall academic information? How does your memory style relate to your learning style? How does it affect the way you learn things initially? How could you make greater use of your less-preferred styles?

» LO19.6 Forgetting

All of us who have experienced even routine instances of forgetting—such as not remembering an acquaintance's name or a fact on a test—understand the very real consequences of memory failure. Of course, memory failure is also essential to remembering important information. The ability to forget inconsequential details about experiences, people, and objects helps us avoid being burdened and distracted by trivial stores of meaningless data. Forgetting permits us to form general impressions and recollections. For example, the reason our friends consistently look familiar to us is because we're able to forget their clothing, facial blemishes, and other transient features that change from one occasion to the next. Instead, our memories are based on a summary of various critical features—a far more economical use of our memory capabilities.

The first attempts to study forgetting were made by German psychologist Hermann Ebbinghaus about a hundred years ago. Using himself as the only participant in his study, Ebbinghaus memorized lists of three-letter nonsense syllables—meaningless sets of two consonants with a vowel in between, such as FIW and BOZ. By measuring how easy it was to relearn a given list of words after varying periods of time had passed since the initial learning, he found that forgetting occurred systematically, as shown in Figure 4. As the figure indicates, the most rapid forgetting occurs in the first nine hours, particularly in the first hour. After nine hours, the rate of forgetting slows and declines little, even after the passage of many days.

Despite his primitive methods, Ebbinghaus's study had an important influence on subsequent research, and his basic conclusions have been upheld. There is almost always a strong initial decline in memory, followed by a more gradual

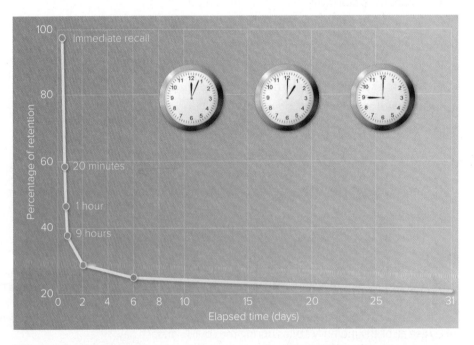

Figure 4 In his classic work, Ebbinghaus found that the most rapid forgetting occurs in the first nine hours after exposure to new material. However, the rate of forgetting then slows down and declines very little even after many days have passed (Ebbinghaus, 1885/1913). Check your own memory: What were you doing exactly two hours ago? What were you doing last Tuesday at 5 p.m.? Which information is easier to retrieve?

drop over time. Furthermore, relearning of previously mastered material is almost always faster than starting from scratch, whether the material is academic information or a motor skill such as serving a tennis ball (Wixted & Carpenter, 2007; Radvansky, Pettijohn, & Kim, 2015).

» LO19.7 Why We Forget

Why do we forget? One reason is that we may not have paid attention to the material in the first place—a failure of *encoding*. For example, if you live in the United States, you probably have been exposed to thousands of pennies during your life. Despite this experience, you probably don't have a clear sense of the details of the coin. (See this for yourself by looking at Figure 5.) Consequently, the reason for your memory failure is that you probably never encoded the information into long-term memory initially. Obviously, if information was not placed in memory to start with, there is no way the information can be recalled.

But what about material that has been encoded into memory and that can't later be remembered? Several processes account for memory failures, including decay, interference, and cue-dependent forgetting.

Decay is the loss of information through nonuse. This explanation for forgetting assumes that *memory traces,* the physical changes that take place in the brain when new material is learned, simply fade away over time (Grann, 2007).

Although there is evidence that decay does occur, this does not seem to be the complete explanation for forgetting. Often there is no relationship between how long ago a person was exposed to information and how well that information is recalled. Because decay does not fully account for forgetting, memory specialists have proposed an additional mechanism: **interference.** In interference, information in memory disrupts the recall of other information (Solesio-Jofre et al., 2011; Ecker, Tay, & Brown, 2015).

To distinguish between decay and interference, think of the two processes in terms of a row of books on a library shelf. In decay, the old books are constantly crumbling and rotting away, leaving room for new arrivals. Interference processes suggest that new books knock the old ones off the shelf, where they become inaccessible. Finally, forgetting may occur because of **cue-dependent forgetting,** forgetting that occurs when there are insufficient retrieval cues to rekindle information that is in memory. For example, you may not be able to remember where you lost a set of keys until you mentally walk through your day, thinking of each place you visited. When you think of the place where you lost the keys—say, the library—the retrieval cue of the

decay The loss of information in memory through its nonuse

interference The phenomenon by which information in memory disrupts the recall of other information

cue-dependent forgetting Forgetting that occurs when there are insufficient retrieval cues to rekindle information that is in memory

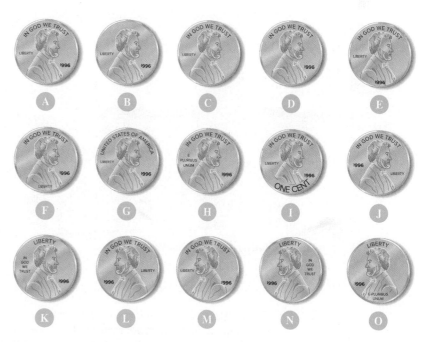

Figure 5 One of these pennies is the real thing. Can you find it? Why is this task harder than it seems at first? Source: Adapted from Nickerson & Adams, 1979.

If you don't have a penny handy, the correct answer is "A."

library may be sufficient to help you recall that you left them on the desk in the library. Without that retrieval cue, you may be unable to recall the location of the keys (Weller et al., 2013).

Most research suggests that interference and cue-dependent forgetting are key processes in forgetting. We forget things mainly because new memories interfere with the retrieval of old ones or because appropriate retrieval cues are unavailable, not because the memory trace has decayed (Radvansky, 2010).

» LO19.8 Proactive and Retroactive Interference: The Before and After of Forgetting

proactive interference
Interference in which information learned earlier disrupts the recall of newer information

retroactive interference
Interference in which there is difficulty in the recall of information learned earlier because of later exposure to different material

There are actually two sorts of interference that influence forgetting: proactive and retroactive. In **proactive interference,** information learned earlier disrupts the recall of newer material. For example, suppose you move and get a new telephone number. For the first several months afterward, whenever anyone asks for your telephone number, you can only think of your old number—not your new one (Bunting, 2006).

In contrast, **retroactive interference** refers to difficulty in the recall of information because of later exposure to different material. If, for example, you eventually become unable to recall your old telephone number anymore, retroactive interference is the culprit (see Figure 6). One way to remember the difference between *pro*active and *retro*active interference is to keep in mind that proactive interference progresses in time—the past interferes with the present—whereas retroactive interference retrogresses in time, working backward as the present interferes with the past (Jacoby, Bishara, Hessels, 2007).

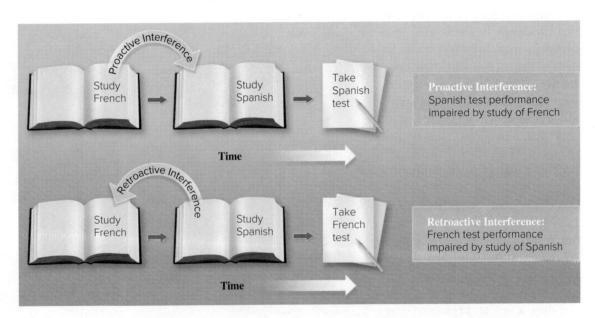

Figure 6 Proactive interference occurs when material learned earlier interferes with the recall of newer material. In this example, studying French before studying Spanish interferes with performance on a Spanish test. In contrast, retroactive interference exists when material learned after initial exposure to other material interferes with the recall of the first material. In this case, retroactive interference occurs when recall of French is impaired because of later exposure to Spanish.

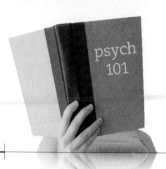

becoming an informed consumer of psychology

Improving Your Memory

Apart from the advantages of forgetting, say, a bad date, most of us would like to find ways to improve our memories. Among the effective strategies for studying and remembering course material:

- *The keyword technique.* If you are studying a foreign language, try the keyword technique. In the *keyword technique,* you pair a foreign word with a common English word that has a similar sound. This English word is known as the *keyword.* For example, to learn the Spanish word for duck (*pato,* pronounced *pot-o*), you might choose the keyword *pot.* Once you have thought of a keyword, imagine the Spanish word "interacting" with the English keyword. For example, you might envision a duck being cooked in a pot to remember the word *pato* (Wyra, Lawson, & Hungi, 2007).

- *Rely on organization cues.* Recall material you read in textbooks by organizing the material in memory the first time you read it. Organize your reading on the basis of any advance information you have about the content and about its arrangement. You will then be able to make connections and see relationships among the various facts and process the material at a deeper level, which in turn will later aid recall.

- *Take effective notes.* "Less is more" is perhaps the best advice for taking lecture notes that facilitate recall. Rather than trying to jot down every detail of a lecture, it is better to listen and think about the material, and take down the main points. In effective note taking, thinking about the material when you first hear it is more important than writing it down. This is one reason that borrowing someone else's notes is a bad idea; you will have no framework in memory that you can use to understand them (Feldman, 2016).

- *Talk to yourself.* If you have trouble remembering names of people who you have recently met, one way to help yourself is to say their names out loud when you are first introduced. It will make it easier to retrieve the information later because the information is stored in additional ways in your brain.

- *Practice, practice, practice.* Although practice may not necessarily make perfect, it helps. By studying and rehearsing material well beyond initial mastery—a process called overlearning—people are able to show better long-term recall than they show if they stop practicing after their initial learning of the material.

- *Don't believe claims about drugs that improve memory.* Advertisements for One-a-Day vitamins with ginkgo biloba or Quanterra Mental Sharpness Product would have you believe that taking a drug can improve your memory. Not so, according to the results of numerous studies. No research has shown that commercial memory enhancers are effective (McDaniel, Maier, & Einstein, 2002; Burns, Bryan, & Nettelbeck, 2006).

RECAP

Explain retrieval cues.

■ The tip-of-the-tongue phenomenon is the temporary inability to remember information that one is certain one knows. Retrieval cues are a major strategy for recalling information successfully.

Discuss levels of processing.

■ The levels-of-processing approach to memory suggests that the way in which information is initially perceived and analyzed determines the success with which it is recalled. The deeper the initial processing, the greater the recall.

Compare and contrast implicit and explicit memory.

■ Explicit memory refers to intentional or conscious recollection of information. In contrast, implicit memory refers to memories of which people are not consciously aware, but which can affect subsequent performance and behavior.

Define flashbulb memories.

■ Flashbulb memories are memories centered on a specific, important event. The more distinctive a memory is, the more easily it can be retrieved.

Describe the constructive processes of memory.

■ Memory is a constructive process: we relate memories to the meaning, guesses, and expectations we give to events. Specific information is recalled in terms of schemas, organized bodies of information stored in memory that bias the way new information is interpreted, stored, and recalled.

■ Autobiographical memory is influenced by constructive processes.

Explain the importance of forgetting.

■ Forgetting, or memory failure, plays several important roles.

Explain why we forget information.

■ Several processes account for memory failure, including decay, interference (both proactive and retroactive), and cue-dependent forgetting.

■ Among the techniques for improving memory are the keyword technique to memorize foreign language vocabulary; using the encoding specificity phenomenon; organizing text material and lecture notes; and practice and rehearsal, leading to overlearning.

Compare and contrast proactive and retroactive interference.

■ Proactive interference is interference in which information learned earlier disrupts the recall of newer material.

■ Retroactive interference is interference in which there is difficulty in the recall of information learned earlier because of later exposure to different material.

[EVALUATE E Evaluate]

1. While with a group of friends at a dance, Eva bumps into a man she dated last month, but when she tries to introduce him to her friends, she cannot remember his name. What is the term for this occurrence?

2. _____ is the process of retrieving a specific item from memory.

3. A friend of your mother tells you, "I know exactly where I was and what I was doing when I heard that John Lennon was killed." What is this type of memory phenomenon called?

4. _____ _____ _____ theory states that the more a person analyzes a statement, the more likely he or she is to remember it later.

5. _____ interference occurs when material is difficult to retrieve because of subsequent exposure to other material; _____ interference refers to difficulty in retrieving material as a result of the interference of previously learned material.

[RETHINK R Rethink]

What study strategies can you think of that would make effective use of the levels-of-processing approach to memory?

KEY TERMS

Tip-of-the-tongue phenomenon   LO19.1

Recall   LO19.1

Recognition   LO19.1

Levels-of-processing theory   LO19.2

Explicit memory   LO19.3

Implicit memory   LO19.3

Flashbulb memories   LO19.4

Constructive processes   LO19.5

Schemas   LO19.5

Autobiographical memories   LO19.5

Decay   LO19.7

Interference   LO19.7

Cue-dependent forgetting   LO19.7

Proactive interference   LO19.8

Retroactive interference   LO19.8

Thinking, Reasoning, and Problem Solving

Learning Outcomes Prepare

>> **LO20.1** Explain the concept of mental images.

>> **LO20.2** Discuss the process of categorizing the world.

>> **LO20.3** Describe the processes that underlie reasoning and decision making.

>> **LO20.4** Explain how people approach and solve problems.

MODULE OUTLINE  Organize

Mental Images: Examining the Mind's Eye

Concepts: Categorizing the World

Reasoning: Making Up Your Mind

Problem Solving

Try It! Find the Solution

W Work

thinking Brain activity in which people mentally manipulate information, including words, visual images, sounds, or other data.

Psychologists define **thinking** as brain activity in which people mentally manipulate information, including words, visual images, sounds, or other data. Thinking transforms information into new and different forms, allowing us to answer questions, make decisions, solve problems, and make plans.

Although a clear sense of what specifically occurs when we think remains elusive, our understanding of the nature of the fundamental elements involved in thinking is growing. We begin by considering our use of mental images and concepts, the building blocks of thought.

"What do you think I think about what you think I think you've been thinking about?"

» LO20.1 Mental Images: Examining the Mind's Eye

Think of your best friend. Chances are that you "see" some kind of visual image when asked to think of her or him, or any other person or object, for that matter. To some cognitive psychologists, such mental images constitute a major part of thinking.

Mental images are representations in the mind of an object or event. They are not just visual representations; our ability to "hear" a tune in our heads also relies on a mental image. In fact, every sensory modality may produce corresponding mental images (De Beni, Pazzaglia, & Gardini, 2007; Gardini et al., 2009; Koçak et al., 2011).

Some experts see the production of mental images as a way to improve various skills. For instance, many athletes use mental imagery in their training. Basketball players may try to produce vivid and detailed images of the court, the basket, the ball, and the noisy crowd. They may visualize themselves taking a foul shot, watching the ball, and hearing the swish as it goes through the net. And it works: the use of mental imagery can lead to improved performance in sports (Moran, 2009; Thompson, Hsiao, & Kosslyn, 2011; Velentzas, Heinen, & Schack, 2011).

Many athletes, such as Steph Curry, use mental imagery to focus on a task, a process they call "getting in the zone." What are some other occupations that require the use of strong mental imagery? © John G. Mabanglo/EPA/Newscom

© Andresr/Getty Images RF

From the perspective of …

A New Supervisor How might you use the research on mental imagery to improve employees' performance?

» LO20.2 Concepts: Categorizing the World

If someone asks you what is in your kitchen cabinet, you might answer with a detailed list of items ("a jar of peanut butter, three boxes of pasta, six novelty coffee mugs," etc.). More likely, though, you would respond by naming some broader categories, such as "food" and "dishes."

Using such categories reflects the operation of concepts. **Concepts** are mental groupings of similar objects, events, or people. Concepts enable us to organize complex phenomena into simpler, and therefore more easily usable, cognitive categories (Murphy, 2005; Connolly, 2007; Kreppner et al., 2011).

Concepts help us classify newly encountered objects on the basis of our past experience. For example, we can surmise that someone tapping a handheld screen is probably using some kind of computer or tablet, even if we have never encountered that specific model before. Ultimately, concepts influence behavior; we would assume, for instance, that it might be appropriate to pet an animal

mental images
Representations in the mind that resemble the object or event being represented

concepts Mental groupings of similar objects, events, or people

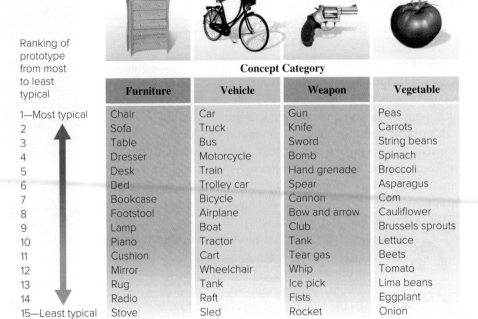

Ranking of prototype from most to least typical	Concept Category			
	Furniture	**Vehicle**	**Weapon**	**Vegetable**
1—Most typical	Chair	Car	Gun	Peas
2	Sofa	Truck	Knife	Carrots
3	Table	Bus	Sword	String beans
4	Dresser	Motorcycle	Bomb	Spinach
5	Desk	Train	Hand grenade	Broccoli
6	Bed	Trolley car	Spear	Asparagus
7	Bookcase	Bicycle	Cannon	Corn
8	Footstool	Airplane	Bow and arrow	Cauliflower
9	Lamp	Boat	Club	Brussels sprouts
10	Piano	Tractor	Tank	Lettuce
11	Cushion	Cart	Tear gas	Beets
12	Mirror	Wheelchair	Whip	Tomato
13	Rug	Tank	Ice pick	Lima beans
14	Radio	Raft	Fists	Eggplant
15—Least typical	Stove	Sled	Rocket	Onion

Figure 1 Prototypes are typical, highly representative examples of a concept. For instance, a highly typical prototype of the concept "furniture" is a chair, whereas a stove is not a good prototype. High agreement exists within a culture about which examples of a concept are prototypes. Source: Adapted from Rosch & Mervis, 1975.

after determining that it is a dog, whereas we would behave differently after classifying the animal as a wolf.

Many real-world concepts are ambiguous and difficult to define. For instance, concepts such as "table" and "bird" have a set of general, relatively loose characteristic features, rather than unique, clearly defined properties that distinguish an example of the concept from a nonexample. When we consider these more ambiguous concepts, we usually think in terms of examples called **prototypes.** Prototypes are typical, highly representative examples of a concept that correspond to our mental image or best example of the concept. For instance, for most people, the prototype of a dog is something like the common beagle, rather than the relatively rare shih tzu, Finnish spitz, otterhound, or mudi (breeds you've probably never heard of). Similarly, although a robin and an ostrich are both examples of birds, the robin is an example that comes to most people's minds far more readily. Consequently, robin is a prototype of the concept "bird."

Relatively high agreement exists among people in a particular culture about which examples of a concept are prototypes, as well as which examples are not. For instance, most people in Western cultures consider cars and trucks good examples of vehicles, whereas elevators and wheelbarrows are not considered very good examples. Consequently, cars and trucks are prototypes of the concept of a vehicle (see Figure 1).

prototypes Typical, highly representative samples of a concept

STUDY ALERT

Figure 1 will help you remember that prototypes represent "best" or most common examples of a particular concept. For example, a Prius might be a prototype of the concept of "hybrid car."

≫ LO20.3 Reasoning: Making Up Your Mind

Instructors deciding when students' assignments are due.
An employer determining who to hire out of a pool of job applicants.
The president concluding that it is necessary to send troops to a foreign nation.

What do these three situations have in common? Each of them requires *reasoning,* the process by which information is used to draw conclusions and make decisions.

Algorithms and Heuristics

When faced with making a decision, we often turn to various kinds of cognitive shortcuts, known as algorithms and heuristics, to help us. An **algorithm** is a rule that, if applied appropriately, guarantees a solution to a problem. We can use an algorithm even if we cannot understand why it works. For example, you may know that you can find the length of the third side of a right triangle by using the formula $a^2 + b^2 = c^2$, although you may not have the foggiest notion of the mathematical principles behind the formula.

For many problems and decisions, however, no algorithm is available. In those instances, we may be able to use heuristics to help us. A **heuristic** is a thinking strategy that may lead us to a solution to a problem or decision, but—unlike algorithms—may sometimes lead to errors. For example, when I play tic-tac-toe, I follow the heuristic of placing an X in the center square when I start the game. This tactic doesn't guarantee that I will win, but experience has taught me that it will increase my chances of success. Similarly, some students follow the heuristic of preparing for a test by ignoring the assigned textbook reading and only studying their lecture notes—a strategy that may or may not pay off.

algorithm A rule that, if applied appropriately, guarantees a solution to a problem

heuristic A thinking strategy that may lead us to a solution to a problem or decision, but—unlike algorithms—may sometimes lead to errors

STUDY ALERT

Remember that algorithms are rules that *always* provide a solution, while heuristics are shortcuts that *may* provide a solution.

» LO20.4 Problem Solving

In the Tower of Hanoi puzzle, three disks are placed on the first of three posts in the order shown in Figure 2. The goal of the puzzle is to move all three disks to the third post, arranged in the same order, by using as few moves as possible. There are two restrictions: only one disk can be moved at a time, and no disk can ever cover a smaller one during a move.

Why are cognitive psychologists interested in the Tower of Hanoi problem? Because the way people go about solving such puzzles helps illuminate how people solve complex, real-life problems. Psychologists have found that problem solving typically involves the three steps illustrated in Figure 3: preparing to create solutions, producing solutions, and evaluating the solutions that have been generated.

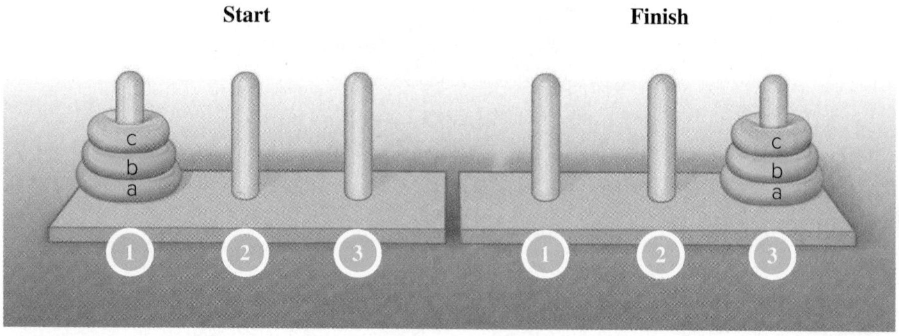

Figure 2 The goal of the Tower of Hanoi puzzle is to move all three disks from the first post to the third and still preserve the original order of the disks, using the fewest number of moves possible while following the rules that only one disk at a time can be moved and no disk can cover a smaller one during a move. Try it yourself before you look at the solution, which is listed according to the sequence of moves.

(Solution: Move C to 3, B to 2, C to 2, A to 3, C to 1, B to 3, and C to 3.)

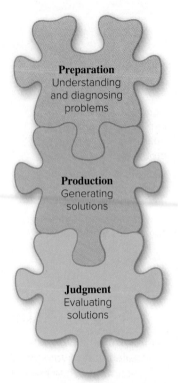

Preparation
Understanding
and diagnosing
problems

Production
Generating
solutions

Judgment
Evaluating
solutions

Figure 3   Steps in
problem solving.

STUDY ALERT

Use the three steps of
problem solving to organize
your studying: preparation,
production, and judgment
(PPJ).

Preparation: Understanding and Diagnosing Problems

When approaching a problem like the Tower of Hanoi, most people begin by trying to understand the problem thoroughly. If the problem is a novel one, they probably will pay particular attention to any restrictions placed on coming up with a solution—such as the rule for moving only one disk at a time in the Tower of Hanoi problem. If, by contrast, the problem is a familiar one, they are apt to spend considerably less time in this preparation stage.

Problems vary from well defined to ill defined. In *a well-defined problem*—such as a mathematical equation or the solution to a jigsaw puzzle—both the nature of the problem itself and the information needed to solve it are available and clear. Thus, we can make straightforward judgments about whether a potential solution is appropriate. With an *ill-defined problem*, such as how to increase morale on an assembly line or to bring peace to the Middle East, not only may the specific nature of the problem be unclear, the information required to solve the problem may be even less obvious (Kim & Grunig, 2011; Newman, Willoughby, & Pruce, 2011; Mayer, 2013).

The preparation stage of understanding and diagnosing is critical in problem solving because it allows us to develop our own cognitive representation of the problem and to place it within a personal framework. We may divide the problem into subparts or ignore some information as we try to simplify the task. Winnowing out nonessential information is often a critical step in the preparation stage of problem solving.

The way in which we represent a problem—and the solution we eventually come to—depends on the way a problem is initially framed for us. Imagine that you were a cancer patient having to choose between either the option of surgery or of radiation, as shown in Figure 4, and you were given some statistical information about the options. What would you choose?

Michael Maslin/The New Yorker Collection/The Cartoon Bank

*"I don't know about hair care, Rapunzel, but I'm thinking a good cream
rinse plus protein conditioner might just solve both our problems."*

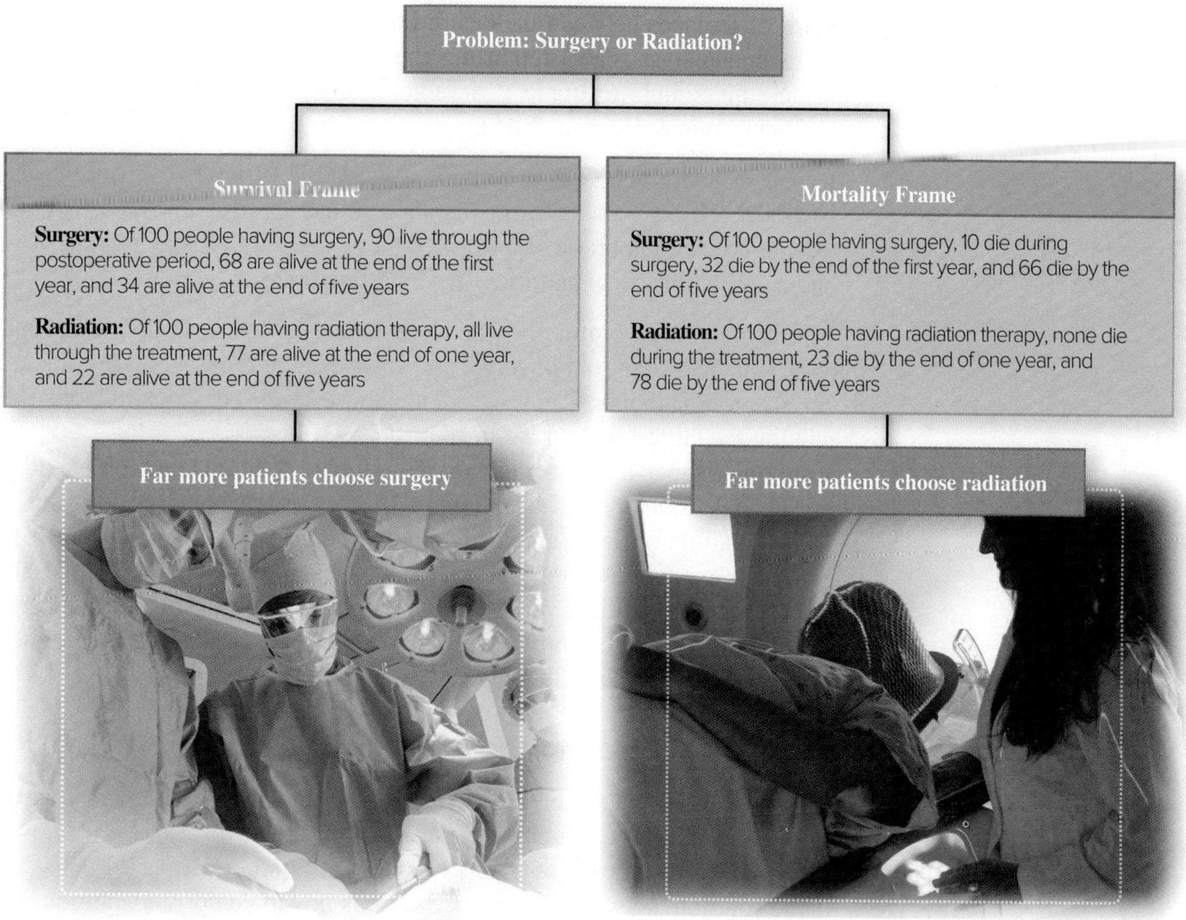

Problem: Surgery or Radiation?

Survival Frame

Surgery: Of 100 people having surgery, 90 live through the postoperative period, 68 are alive at the end of the first year, and 34 are alive at the end of five years

Radiation: Of 100 people having radiation therapy, all live through the treatment, 77 are alive at the end of one year, and 22 are alive at the end of five years

Far more patients choose surgery

Mortality Frame

Surgery: Of 100 people having surgery, 10 die during surgery, 32 die by the end of the first year, and 66 die by the end of five years

Radiation: Of 100 people having radiation therapy, none die during the treatment, 23 die by the end of one year, and 78 die by the end of five years

Far more patients choose radiation

Figure 4 A decision often is affected by the way a problem is framed. In this case, when mortality is the framework, most would choose radiation over surgery, despite similar results. Photos (first): © David Joel/Getty Images; (second) © Mark Kostich/Getty Images RF

It turns out that participants in a study made very different choices depending on how the problem was framed. When their choices were framed in terms of the likelihood of *survival,* only 18 percent of participants chose radiation over surgery. However, when the choice was framed in terms of the likelihood of *dying,* 44 percent chose radiation over surgery—even though the outcomes are similar with either treatment option (Tversky & Kahneman, 1987; Chandran & Menon, 2004).

Production: Generating Solutions

After preparation, the next stage in problem solving is the production of possible solutions. If a problem is relatively simple, we may already have a direct solution stored in long-term memory, and all we need to do is retrieve the appropriate information. If we cannot retrieve or do not know the solution, we must generate possible solutions and compare them with information in long- and short-term memory.

At the most basic level, we can solve problems through trial and error. The difficulty with this approach, of course, is that some problems are so complicated that it would take a lifetime to try out every possibility. In place of trial and error, complex problem solving often involves the use of heuristics, cognitive shortcuts that can generate solutions. Probably the most frequently applied heuristic in problem solving is a **means-ends analysis,** which involves repeated

means-ends analysis Problem solving which involves repeated tests for differences between the desired outcome and what currently exists

tests for differences between the desired outcome and what currently exists. In a means-end analysis, each step brings the problem solver closer to a resolution. Consider this simple example (Chrysikou, 2006; Bosse, Gerritsen, & Treur, 2011; Bieberstein & Roosen, 2015):

> I want to take my son to preschool. What's the difference between what I have and what I want? One of distance. What changes distance? My automobile. My automobile won't work. What is needed to make it work? A new battery. What has new batteries? An auto repair shop . . .

Another heuristic commonly used to generate solutions is to divide a problem into intermediate steps, or *subgoals,* and solve each of those steps. For instance, in our Tower of Hanoi problem, we could choose several obvious subgoals, such as moving the largest disk to the third post.

If solving a subgoal is a step toward the ultimate solution to a problem, identifying subgoals is an appropriate strategy. In some cases, however, forming subgoals is not all that helpful and may actually increase the time needed to find a solution. For example, some problems cannot be subdivided. Others—like some complicated mathematical problems—are so complex that it takes longer to identify the appropriate subdivisions than to solve the problem by other means (Kaller et al., 2004; Fishbach, Dhar, & Zhang, 2006).

Judgment: Evaluating the Solutions

The final stage in problem solving is judging the adequacy of a solution. Often this is a simple matter: if the solution is clear—as in the Tower of Hanoi problem—we will know immediately whether we have been successful (Varma, 2007).

If the solution is less concrete or if there is no single correct solution, evaluating solutions becomes more difficult. In such instances, we must decide which alternative solution is best. Unfortunately, we often quite inaccurately estimate the quality of our own ideas. For instance, a team of drug researchers working for a particular company may consider their remedy for an illness to be superior to all others, overestimating the likelihood of their success and downplaying the approaches of competing drug companies (Eizenberg & Zaslavsky, 2004).

If the solution is less concrete or if there is no single correct solution, evaluating solutions becomes more difficult.

Theoretically, if we rely on appropriate heuristics and valid information to make decisions, we can make accurate choices among alternative solutions. However, as we see next, several kinds of obstacles to and biases in problem solving affect the quality of the decisions and judgments we make.

Impediments to Solutions: Why Is Problem Solving Such a Problem?

Consider the following problem-solving test (Duncker, 1945).

> You are given a set of tacks, candles, and matches, each in a small box, and told your goal is to place three candles at eye level on a nearby door, so that wax will not drip on the floor as the candles burn [see Figure 5]. How would you approach this challenge?

If you have difficulty solving the problem, you are not alone. Most people cannot solve it when it is presented in the manner illustrated in the figure, in which the objects are *inside* the boxes. However, if the objects were presented *beside* the boxes, just resting on the table, chances are that you would solve the problem much more readily—which, in case you are wondering, requires tacking the boxes to the door and then placing the candles inside them (see Figure 6).

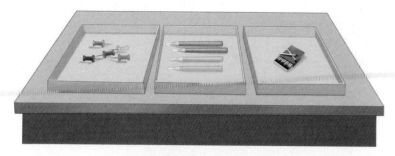

Figure 5   The problem here is to place three candles at eye level on a nearby door so that the wax will not drip on the floor as the candles burn—using only materials in the figure. For a solution see Figure 6.

The difficulty you probably encountered in solving this problem stems from its presentation, which misled you at the initial preparation stage. Actually, significant obstacles to problem solving can exist at each of the three major stages. Although cognitive approaches to problem solving suggest that thinking proceeds along fairly rational, logical lines as a person confronts a problem and considers various solutions, several factors can hinder the development of creative, appropriate, and accurate solutions.

The difficulty most people experience with the candle problem is caused by **functional fixedness,** the tendency to think of an object only in terms of its typical use. For instance, in the candle problem, because the objects are first presented inside the boxes, functional fixedness leads most people to see the boxes simply as containers for the objects they hold rather than as a potential part of the solution. They cannot envision another function for the boxes.

functional fixedness The tendency to think of an object only in terms of its typical use

mental set A framework for thinking about a problem based on our prior experience with similar problems.

Functional fixedness is an example of a broader phenomenon known as mental set. **Mental set,** is a framework for thinking about a problem based on our prior experience with similar problems. We employ mental sets because that original way of thinking about the problem worked for us previously.

Mental set can affect perceptions, as well as patterns of problem solving. It can prevent you from seeing beyond the apparent constraints of a problem. For example, try to draw four straight lines so that they pass through all nine dots in the grid below—without lifting your pencil.

● ● ●

● ● ●

● ● ●

If you had difficulty with the problem, it was probably because you felt compelled to keep your lines within the grid. If you had gone outside the boundaries, however, you would have succeeded by using the solution shown in Figure 7. (The phrase "thinking outside the box"—a term commonly used in business today to encourage creativity—stems from research on overcoming the constraining effects of mental set.)

Use your own problem-solving skills to find the solutions to the problems in the accompanying Try It!

Figure 6 A solution to the problem in Figure 5 involves tacking the boxes to the door and placing the candles in the boxes.

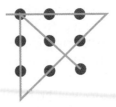

Figure 7 A solution to the nine-dot problem requires the use of lines drawn beyond the boundaries of the figure—something that our mental set may prevent us from seeing easily.

Try It!

Find the Solution

Try solving the following problems:

1. Anagrams: Can you rearrange the letters in each set to make an English word?

   EFCTA   BODUT   IKCTH   IAENV   LIVAN

2. What number comes next in the series?

   1 4 2 4 3 4 4 4 5 4 6 4

3. Water Jars: A person has three jars with the following capacities:

   Jar A = 28 ounces   Jar B = 7 ounces   Jar C = 5 ounces

   How can the person measure exactly 11 ounces of water?

RECAP

Explain the concept of mental images.

- Thinking is the manipulation of mental representations of information. Thinking transforms such representations into novel and different forms, permitting people to answer questions, solve problems, and reach goals.

- Mental images are representations in the mind of an object or event.

Discuss the process of categorizing the world.

- Concepts are categorizations of objects, events, or people that share common properties. Prototypes are representative examples of concepts.

Describe the processes that underlie reasoning and decision making.

- Decisions sometimes (but not always) may be improved through the use of algorithms and heuristics. An algorithm is a rule that, if applied appropriately, guarantees a solution; a heuristic is a cognitive shortcut that may lead to a solution but is not guaranteed to do so.

Explain how people approach and solve problems.

- Problem solving typically involves three major stages: preparation, production of solutions, and evaluation of solutions that have been generated.

- A crucial aspect of the preparation stage is the representation and organization of the problem.

- In the production stage, people try to generate solutions. They may find solutions to some problems in long-term memory. Alternatively, they may solve some problems through simple trial and error and use algorithms and heuristics to solve more complex problems.

- Using the heuristic of a means-ends analysis, a person will repeatedly test for differences between the desired outcome and what currently exists, trying each time to come closer to the goal.

- Several factors hinder effective problem solving. Mental set, of which functional fixedness is an example, is the tendency for old patterns of problem solving to persist. Inappropriate use of algorithms and heuristics can also act as an obstacle to the production of solutions.

[EVALUATE E Evaluate]

1. _____ _____ are representations in the mind of an object or event.

2. _____ are categorizations of objects that share common properties.

3. When you think of the concept "chair," you immediately think of a comfortable easy chair. A chair of this type could be thought of as a _____ of the category "chair."

4. When you ask your friend how best to study for your psychology final, he tells you, "I've always found it best to skim over the notes once, then read the content, then go over the notes again." What decision-making tool might this be an example of?

5. Thinking of an object only in terms of its typical use is known as _____ _____. In addition, _____ _____ is a framework for thinking about a problem based on our prior experience with similar problems.

[RETHINK **R** Rethink]

Why might people use heuristics, given that they do not assure a solution?

KEY TERMS

Thinking   LO20.1

Mental images   LO20.1

Concepts   LO20.2

Prototypes   LO20.2

Algorithm   LO20.3

Heuristic   LO20.3

Means-ends analysis   LO20.4

Functional fixedness   LO20.4

Mental set   LO20.4

module 21

Language

Learning Outcomes  Prepare

» **LO21.1** Describe how people use language.

» **LO21.2** Explain how language develops.

MODULE OUTLINE  Organize

Language Development: Developing a Way with Words

The Influence of Language on Thinking: Do Eskimos Have More Words for Snow Than Texans?

Exploring Diversity: Teaching with Linguistic Variety: Bilingual Education

The use of **language**—the communication of information through symbols arranged according to systematic rules—is an important cognitive ability, one that is indispensable for us to communicate with one another. Not only is language central to communication, it is also closely tied to the way in which we think about and understand the world (Hoff, 2008; Reisberg, 2009; LaPointe, 2013).

 Work

» **LO21.1** Language Development: Developing a Way with Words

To parents, the sounds of their infant babbling and cooing are music to their ears. These sounds also serve an important function. They mark the first step on the road to the development of language.

Babbling

Children **babble**—make speechlike but meaningless sounds—from around the age of 3 months through 1 year. While babbling, they may produce, at one time or another, any of the sounds found in all languages, not just the one to which they are exposed. Even deaf children display their own form of babbling, for infants who are unable to hear yet who are exposed to sign language from birth "babble" with their hands (Pettito, 1993; Majorano & D'Odorico, 2011; Shehata-Dieler et al., 2013).

An infant's babbling increasingly reflects the specific language being spoken in the infant's environment, initially in terms of pitch and tone and eventually in terms of specific sounds. Young infants can distinguish among all the basic units of speech that have been identified across the world's languages. However, after the age of 6 to 8 months, that ability begins to decline. Infants begin to "specialize" in the language to which they are exposed as neurons in their brains reorganize to respond to the particular phonemes infants routinely hear.

Some theorists argue that a *critical period* exists for language development early in life, in which a child is particularly sensitive to language cues and most

language The communication of information through symbols arranged according to systematic rules

babble Meaningless speechlike sounds made by children from around the age of 3 months through 1 year

easily acquires language. In fact, if children are not exposed to language during this critical period, later they will have great difficulty overcoming this deficit (Bates, 2005; Shafer & Garrido-Nag, 2007).

Production of Language

By the time children are approximately 1 year old, they stop producing sounds that are not in the language to which they have been exposed. It is then a short step to the production of actual words. In English, these are typically short words that start with a consonant sound such as *b, d, m, p,* and *t*—this helps explain why *mama* and *dada* are so often among babies' first words. Of course, even before they produce their first words, children can understand a fair amount of the language they hear. Language comprehension precedes language production.

After the age of 1 year, children begin to learn more complicated forms of language. They produce two-word combinations, the building blocks of sentences, and sharply increase the number of different words they are able to use. By age 2, the average child has a vocabulary of more than 50 words. Just six months later, that vocabulary has grown to several hundred words. At that time, children can produce short sentences, although they use **telegraphic speech**— sentences that sound as if they were part of a telegram, in which words not critical to the message are left out. Rather than saying, "I showed you the book," a child using telegraphic speech may say, "I show book," and "I am drawing a dog" may become "Drawing dog." As children get older, of course, they use less telegraphic speech and produce increasingly complex sentences (Volterra et al., 2003; Pérez-Leroux, Pirvulescu, & Roberge, 2011).

By age 3, children learn to make plurals by adding *s* to nouns and to form the past tense by adding *-ed* to verbs. This skill also leads to errors, since children tend to apply rules inflexibly. In such **overgeneralization,** children employ rules even when doing so results in an error. Thus, although it is correct to say "he walked" for the past tense of *walk,* the *-ed* rule doesn't work quite so well when

telegraphic speech Sentences in which words not critical to the message are left out

overgeneralization The phenomenon by which children apply language rules even when the application results in an error

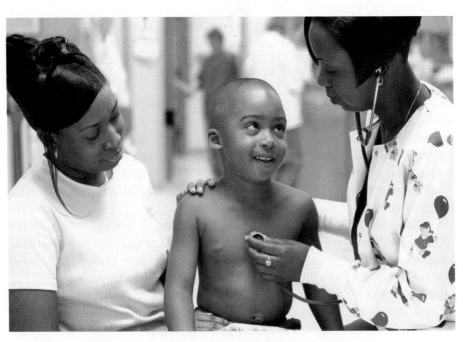

How might a working knowledge of how language develops help this nurse's aide communicate with her young patient? © Arthur Tilley/Getty Images RF

children say "he runned" for the past tense of *run*. By age 5, children have acquired the basic rules of language. However, they do not attain a full vocabulary and the ability to comprehend and use subtle grammatical rules until later (Howe, 2002; Rice et al., 2004; Gershkoff-Stowe, Connell, & Smith, 2006; Kidd & Lum, 2008).

Understanding Language Acquisition: Identifying the Roots of Language

Anyone who spends even a little time with children will notice the enormous strides that they make in language development throughout childhood. However, the reasons for this rapid growth are far from obvious. Psychologists have offered two major explanations, one based on learning theory and the other based on innate processes. A third approach also has been adopted to reconcile the differing views of the preceding two approaches.

How might these three sisters use language differently? © Steve Hix/Somos Image/AGE Fotostock RF

Learning-Theory Approach: Language as a Learned Skill. The **learning-theory approach to language development** suggests that language acquisition follows the principles of reinforcement and conditioning discovered by psychologists who study learning. For example, a child who says "mama" receives hugs and praise from her mother, which reinforce the behavior of saying "mama" and make its repetition more likely. This view suggests that children first learn to speak by being rewarded for making sounds that approximate speech. Ultimately, through a process of shaping, language becomes more and more like adult speech (Skinner, 1957; Ornat & Gallo, 2004).

In support of the learning-theory approach to language acquisition, the more that parents speak to their young children, the more proficient the children become in language use. The learning-theory approach is less successful in explaining how children acquire language rules. Children are reinforced not only when they use language correctly, but also when they use it incorrectly. For example, parents answer a child's "Why the dog won't eat?" as readily as they do the correctly phrased question, "Why won't the dog eat?" Listeners understand both sentences equally well. Learning theory, then, has difficulty fully explaining language acquisition.

Nativist Approach: Language as an Innate Skill. Pointing to such problems with learning-theory approaches to language acquisition, linguist Noam Chomsky (1978, 1991) provided a groundbreaking alternative. Chomsky argued that humans are born with an innate linguistic capability that emerges primarily as a function of maturation. According to his **nativist approach to language development,** all the world's languages share a common underlying structure called a **universal grammar.** Chomsky suggested that the human brain has a neural system, the **language-acquisition device,** that not only lets us understand the structure language provides but also gives us strategies and techniques for learning the unique characteristics of our native language (Lidz & Gleitman, 2004; McGilvray, 2004; White, 2007).

In support of the nativist approach, scientists have discovered a gene related to the development of language abilities that may have emerged as recently—in evolutionary terms—as 100,000 years ago. Furthermore, it is clear that specific sites exist within the brain that are closely tied to language, and that the shapes of the human mouth and throat are tailored to the production of speech. And there is

learning-theory approach to language development The theory suggesting that language acquisition (gaining) follows the principles of reinforcement and conditioning

nativist approach to language development The theory that a genetically determined, innate mechanism directs language development

universal grammar Noam Chomsky's theory that all the world's languages share a common underlying structure

language-acquisition device A neural system of the brain hypothesized by Noam Chomsky to permit understanding of language

evidence that features of specific types of languages are tied to particular genes, such as in "tonal" languages in which pitch is used to convey meaning (Gontier, 2008; Grigorenko, 2009; Perovic & Radenovic, 2011; Lieberman, 2015).

Interactionist Approach: A Combination. To reconcile the differing views, many theorists take an interactionist approach to language development. The **interactionist approach to language development** suggests that language development is both biological and social, produced through a combination of genetically determined predispositions and circumstances in one's social environment growing up that help teach language.

Specifically, proponents of the interactionist approach suggest that the brain's hardwired language-acquisition device that Chomsky and geneticists point to provides the hardware for our acquisition of language, whereas the exposure to language in our environment that learning theorists observe allows us to develop the appropriate software. But the issue of how language is acquired remains hotly contested (Pinker & Jackendoff, 2005; Hoff, 2008; Waxman, 2009).

© Cade Martin/Getty Images RF

From the perspective of ...

A Child-Care Provider   How would you encourage children's language abilities at the different stages of development?

interactionist approach to language development
The view that language development is produced through a combination of genetically determined predispositions and environmental circumstances that help teach language

linguistic-relativity hypothesis
The notion that language shapes and may determine the way people in a particular culture perceive and understand the world

» LO21.2 The Influence of Language on Thinking: Do Eskimos Have More Words for Snow Than Texans?

Do Eskimos living in the frigid Arctic have a more expansive vocabulary for discussing snow than people living in warmer climates?

It makes sense, and arguments that the Eskimo language has many more words for snow than does English have been made since the early 1900s. At that time, linguist Benjamin Lee Whorf contended that because snow is so relevant to Eskimos' lives, their language provides a particularly rich vocabulary to describe it—considerably larger than what we find in other languages, such as English (Martin & Pullum, 1991; Pinker, 1994).

The contention that the Eskimo language is especially abundant in snow-related terms led to the **linguistic-relativity hypothesis,** the notion that language shapes and, in fact, may determine the way people in a specific culture perceive and understand the world. According to this view, language provides us with categories that we use to construct our view of people and events in the world around us. Consequently, language shapes and produces thought (Whorf, 1956; Casasanto, 2008; Tan et al., 2008).

Let's consider another possibility, however. Suppose that instead of language's being the *cause* of certain ways of thinking, thought *produces* language. The only reason to expect that Eskimo language might have more words for snow than English does is that snow is considerably more relevant to Eskimos than it is to people in other cultures.

Which view is correct? Most recent research refutes the linguistic-relativity hypothesis and suggests, instead, that thinking produces language. In fact, new analyses of the Eskimo language suggest that Eskimos have no more words for snow than English speakers, for if one examines the English language closely, one sees that it is hardly impoverished when it comes to describing snow (consider, e.g., *sleet, slush, blizzard, dusting,* and *avalanche*).

Although research does not support the linguistic-relativity hypothesis that language *causes* thought, there is evidence that language *influences* how we think. And, of course, it certainly is the case that thought influences language, suggesting that language and thinking interact in complex ways (Thorkildsen, 2006; Proudfoot, 2009; Cardini, 2010).

Noam Chomsky argues that all languages share a universal grammar. © Haley/SIPA/ Newscom

EXPLORING diversity

Teaching with Linguistic Variety: Bilingual Education

In New York City, one in six of the city's 1.1 million students is enrolled in some form of bilingual or English as a Second Language instruction. And New York City is far from the only school district with a significant population of nonnative English speakers. From the biggest cities to the most rural areas, the face—and voice—of education in the United States is changing. More and more schoolchildren today have last names like Kim, Valdez, and Karachnicoff. In seven states, including Texas and Colorado, more than one-quarter of the students are not native English speakers. For some 55 million Americans, English is their second language (Holloway, 2000; Shin & Kominski, 2010; see Figure 1).

How to appropriately and effectively teach the increasing number of children who do not speak English is not always clear. Many educators maintain that *bilingual education* is best. With a bilingual approach, students learn some subjects in their native language while simultaneously learning English. Proponents of bilingualism believe that students must develop a sound footing in basic subject areas and that, initially at least, teaching those subjects in their native language is the only way to provide them with that foundation. During the same period, they learn English, with the eventual goal of shifting all instruction into English.

> **How to appropriately and effectively teach the increasing number of children who do not speak English is not always clear.**

In contrast, other educators insist that all instruction ought to be in English from the moment students, including those who speak no English at all, enroll in school. In *immersion programs,* students are immediately plunged into English instruction in all subjects. The reasoning—endorsed by voters in California in a referendum designed to end bilingual education—is that teaching students in a language other than English simply hinders nonnative English speakers' integration into society and ultimately does them a disservice. Proponents of English immersion programs point as evidence to improvements

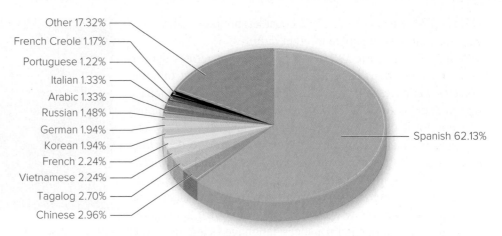

Figure 1 The language of diversity. One-fifth of the people in the United States speak a language other than English at home. Spanish is most prevalent; the rest of non-English speakers use an astounding variety of different languages. Source: Adapted from MLA, 2010.

in standardized test scores that followed the end of bilingual education programs (Wildavsky, 2000).

Although the controversial issue of bilingual education versus immersion has strong political undercurrents, evidence shows that the ability to speak two languages provides significant cognitive benefits over speaking only one language. For example, bilingual speakers show more cognitive flexibility and may understand concepts more easily than those who speak only one language. They have more linguistic tools for thinking because of their multiple-language abilities. In turn, this makes them more creative and flexible in solving problems (Kuo, 2007; Yim & Rudoy, 2013; Christoffels et al., 2015).

Furthermore, speaking several languages changes the organization of the brain. For example, bilingual speakers who learn their second language as adults show different areas of brain activation compared with those who learn their second language in childhood. In addition, brain scans show that people who speak multiple languages have distinct patterns of brain activity according to the language that they are using (see Figure 2; Kovacs & Mehler, 2009; Bialystok et al., 2010; Kluger, 2013).

Related to questions about bilingual education is the matter of *biculturalism,* that is, being a member of two cultures and its psychological impact. Some psychologists argue that society should promote an *alternation model* of bicultural competence. Such a model supports members of a culture in their efforts to maintain their original cultural identity, as well as in their integration into the adopted culture. In this view, a person can belong to two cultures and have two cultural identities without having to choose between them. Whether society will adopt the alternation model remains to be seen (Carter, 2003; Benet-Martínez, Lee, & Leu, 2006; Tadmor, 2007).

BILINGUALS > MONOLINGUALS · MONOLINGUALS > BILINGUALS

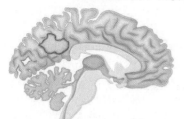  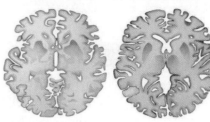

Figure 2   Researchers have found that people who speak two languages (bilinguals), compared to those who speak one language (monolinguals), process the second language in a slightly different area of the brain if they learned the second language as an adult. On the other hand, those who are bilingual from early childhood process both languages in the same area. Interestingly, bilinguals not only may use different areas of the brain to process language-related material, they may also differ in how they process other, non-linguistic material. For example, when naming pictures, the representational images indicate that bilinguals rely more heavily on different brain areas (shown on the left) than monolinguals (on the right). Source: Adapted from Palomar-García et al., 2015.

RECAP

Describe how people use language.

- Language is the communication of information through symbols arranged according to systematic rules.

Explain how language develops.

- Language production develops out of babbling, which then leads to the production of actual words. After 1 year of age, children use two-word combinations, increase their vocabulary, and use telegraphic speech, which drops words not critical to the message. By age 5, acquisition of language rules is relatively complete.

- Learning theorists suggest that language is acquired through reinforcement and conditioning. In contrast, the nativist approach suggests that an innate language-acquisition device guides the development of language. The interactionist approach argues that language development is produced through a combination of genetically determined predispositions and environmental circumstances that help teach language.

- The linguistic-relativity hypothesis suggests that language shapes and may determine the way people think about the world. Most evidence suggests that although language does not determine thought, it does affect the way people store information in memory and how well they can retrieve it.

- People who speak more than one language may have a cognitive advantage over those who speak only one.

[EVALUATE

1. _____ _____ refers to the phenomenon in which young children omit nonessential portions of sentences.

2. A child knows that adding *-ed* to certain words puts them in the past tense. As a result, instead of saying "He came," the child says "He comed." This is an example of _____.

3. _____ theory assumes that language acquisition is based on principles of operant conditioning and shaping.

4. In his theory of language acquisition, Chomsky argues that language acquisition is an innate ability tied to the structure of the brain. True or false?

[RETHINK R Rethink]

Do people who use two languages, one at home and one at school, automatically have two cultures? Why might people who speak two languages have cognitive advantages over those who speak only one?

Answers to Evaluate Questions 1. telegraphic speech; 2. overgeneralization; 3. learning; 4. true

KEY TERMS

Language LO21.1

Babble LO21.1

Telegraphic speech LO21.1

Overgeneralization LO21.1

Learning-theory approach to language development LO21.1

Nativist approach to language development LO21.1

Universal grammar LO21.1

Language-acquisition device LO21.1

Interactionist approach to language development LO21.1

Linguistic-relativity hypothesis LO21.2

« « Looking Back

Psychology on the Web

1. Memory is a topic of serious interest to psychologists, but it is also a source of amusement. Find a website that focuses on the amusing side of memory (such as memory games, tests of recall, or lists of mnemonics; hint: there's even a mnemonics generator out there!). Write down the addresses of any interesting sites that you encounter and summarize what you find.

2. Do animals think? What evidence is there on either side of this question? Search the Web for at least one example of research and/or argument on each side of this question. Summarize your findings and use your knowledge of cognitive psychology to state your own position on this question.

ROB STEERE, THE MAN WHO KNEW TOO MUCH

Rob Steere worked as a document archivist for a large university for almost a decade. His job entailed filing away books, documents, artifacts, multimedia, and other records in a large warehouse—and Rob was very good at it. Despite the complex filing system, Rob saw the logic behind it; and he knew where he could find just about any archived record that was called for.

Realizing that computer tracking eliminated the need to organize the archives topically, the university administrators last year instituted a new computerized filing system that would reorder the archives according to how densely the records could be filed together, thereby saving a great deal of expensive storage space. Since that time, though, Rob has gone from being one of the most efficient archive specialists working at this warehouse to one of the least efficient. He often gets lost and confused when trying to locate records, and he has repeatedly stored materials in the wrong place. Rob just cannot seem to make sense of the new filing system, and he has been looking for a new position elsewhere.

1. Is it reasonable to expect that anyone would be able to make good sense of a filing system such as this new one? Why or why not?

2. How would Rob's knowledge of the earlier filing system and the location of various archived records be organized in his memory?

3. Would the levels-of-processing theory predict that Rob (and other archivists) would have much more trouble with this new filing system than with the old one? Explain.

4. Why might Rob be having so much difficulty finding archived records under the new system? Why might he have developed his problem of filing records in the wrong place?

5. What advice would you give Rob for making the adjustment to this new filing system?

profiles of **SUCCESS**

Courtesy of Nicholas R. Beaudoin

NAME: **Nicholas R. Beaudoin**

SCHOOL: **Lincoln Technical Institute**

DEGREE PROGRAM: **Medical Assisting**

As someone who served in the U.S. Army, Nicholas Beaudoin was certainly aware of the importance of giving his all to a task. But he found that returning to school presented him with an entirely new and unexpected set of challenges.

"I learned that I can push myself farther than I previously thought possible. From my service in the U.S. Army, I knew that I could push myself physically to do better. But it was intellectual obstacles that I was afraid to tackle," he explained.

"However, while attending school, I learned that I could challenge myself intellectually," Beaudoin added. "I also learned that even when I felt as though the odds were stacked against me, and the outlook was gloomy, I could maintain a positive outlook."

His advice for other students who may feel that they have no place to turn when faced with personal or academic obstacles? Beaudoin urges them to reach out and ask for help.

"I would tell those students to keep their heads up and not feel ashamed or discouraged if they have to ask for help," he advised. "There have been many instances where I was in class and couldn't figure something out and I was in a rut. I found the best approach was to simply ask an instructor or fellow classmate for help.

"I would also tell those students to ensure they stay motivated and keep a goal in sight. Without that, all the hard work can seem frustrating and not worth the trouble. But rest assured in the end it will be."

Drawing on his courses in psychology and being able to relate to others' situations has helped him to be a better medical assistant.

"I can take what I've learned and use it to help me better empathize with others," Beaudoin said. "Being in the medical field I will meet people with a wide variety of ailments and injuries. Using what I've learned about psychology I think I'll be better equipped to try and understand what others are thinking, or what could be going on in their mind."

[RETHINK R Rethink]

Based on what psychologists know about problem solving, why would having a goal in mind lead to better academic outcomes?

What strategies might Beaudoin have used to better recall information he was studying?

visual summary 6
THINKING: MEMORY, COGNITION, AND LANGUAGE

MODULE 18 The Foundations of Memory

Memory: Encoding, storing, and retrieving information

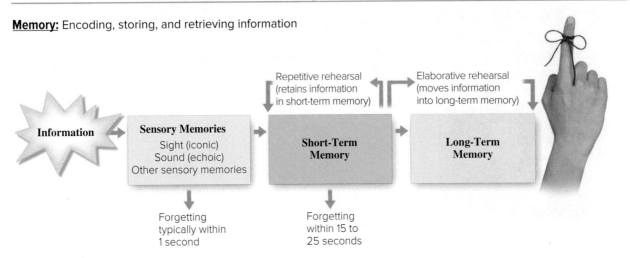

Repetitive rehearsal (retains information in short-term memory)

Elaborative rehearsal (moves information into long-term memory)

Information → Sensory Memories — Sight (iconic), Sound (echoic), Other sensory memories → Short-Term Memory → Long-Term Memory

Forgetting typically within 1 second

Forgetting within 15 to 25 seconds

MODULE 19 Recall and Forgetting

Retrieval Cues: Stimuli that allow recall of information stored in long-term memory

- Recall: Remembering specific information
- Recognition: Knowing whether one has been previously exposed to given information

Levels of Processing Theory: Recall depends on how much the information was processed when it was first encountered

Explicit Memories: Conscious recall of information

Implicit Memories: Memories of which people are not consciously aware

Flashbulb Memories: Memories of a specific, important, or surprising emotionally significant event that are recalled easily and with vivid imagery

Constructive Processes: Processes in which memories are influenced by the meaning we give to events
- Schemas: Organized bodies of stored information that bias the way we interpret, store, and recall new information

Autobiographical memory: Our recollections of our own life experiences

Decay: Loss of information through nonuse

Cue-dependent forgetting: Forgetting that occurs when insufficient retrieval cues are available

Interference: Information in memory disrupts the recall of other information

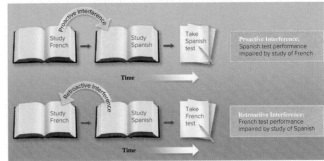

Proactive Interference

Study French → Study Spanish → Take Spanish test

Time

Proactive Interference: Spanish test performance impaired by study of French

Retroactive Interference

Study French → Study Spanish → Take French test

Time

Retroactive Interference: French test performance impaired by study of Spanish

MODULE 20 Thinking, Reasoning, and Problem Solving

Thinking: Brain activity in which people mentally manipulate information, including words, visual images, sounds, or other data

- • Mental images: Representations in the mind of an object or event
- • Concepts: Categorizations of objects, events, or people that share common properties
  - • Prototypes: Typical examples of a concept

Reasoning: Drawing a conclusion from a set of assumptions

- • Algorithms: Rules that may guarantee a correct solution
- • Heuristics: Cognitive shortcuts that may lead to a solutionn

Problem Solving: Well-defined and ill-defined problems

- • Impediments to problem solving

- • Functional fixedness

- • Mental set

MODULE 21 Language

Language Development: Acquiring language

- • Babbling: Speechlike sounds that are meaningless
- • Telegraphic speech: Sentences in which only essential words are used
- • Overgeneralization: The phenomenon in which children over-apply a language rule, thereby making a linguistic error
- • Approaches to learning language
  - • Learning-theory approach
  - • Nativist approach
  - • Interactionist approach

Linguistic-Relativity Hypothesis: The hypothesis that language shapes and may determine the way people perceive and understand the world

© Blend Images-Peathegee Inc/Getty Images RF

CHAPTER 7

CHAPTER OUTLINE

How Far She's Come

Don't tell Tessa Leen that something's impossible. The Minnesota woman and mother has lost 141 pounds (about half her body weight) over the past three years.

What motivated Tessa? She recalls seeing pictures of herself and realizing something had to change. Immediately. Her approach included a healthier diet, exercise, and a positive outlook. But it wasn't always easy. Tessa suffered two miscarriages along the way. She says the tragedies stiffened her resolve to achieve her healthy goals. She took up Zumba, and has since become a certified instructor of the popular Latin-inspired cardio dance workout.

Tessa says her success has given her confidence to tackle all her goals. Her advice? Don't be discouraged by how far you have to go; feel inspired by how far you've come (Killam, 2015).

MOTIVATION
AND EMOTION

Looking Ahead

What explains Tessa Leen's success at losing half her body weight? Is she driven mainly by concern for her health? Is she motivated by the desire to have a more attractive appearance? And what about her determination to focus on how far she's come rather than the distance ahead—has her attitude been the true determining factor? These questions and many others are addressed by psychologists who study the topics of motivation and emotion. Psychologists who study motivation seek to discover the particular desired goals—the motives—that underlie behavior. Behaviors as basic as drinking to satisfy thirst and as inconsequential as taking a stroll to get exercise exemplify motives. Psychologists specializing in the study of motivation assume that such underlying motives steer our choices of activities.

While motivation concerns the forces that direct future behavior, emotion pertains to the feelings we experience throughout our lives. The study of emotions focuses on our internal experiences at any given moment. All of us feel a variety of emotions: happiness at succeeding at a difficult task, sadness over the death of a loved one, anger at being treated unfairly. Because emotions not only play a role in motivating our behavior but also act as a reflection of our underlying motivation, they play an important role in our lives.

We begin this set of modules by focusing on the major conceptions of motivation, discussing how different motives and needs jointly affect behavior. We consider motives that are biologically based and universal in the animal kingdom, such as hunger, as well as motives that are unique to humans, such as the need for achievement.

We then turn to emotions. We consider the roles and functions that emotions play in people's lives and discuss several approaches that explain how people understand their emotions. Finally, we look at how nonverbal behavior communicates emotions.

Explaining Motivation

Learning Outcomes  **Prepare**

>> **LO22.1** Explain instinct approaches to motivation.

>> **LO22.2** Explain drive-reduction approaches to motivation.

>> **LO22.3** Explain arousal approaches to motivation.

>> **LO22.4** Explain incentive approaches to motivation.

>> **LO22.5** Explain cognitive approaches to motivation.

>> **LO22.6** Apply Maslow's hierarchy of needs to motivation.

>> **LO22.7** Apply the different approaches to motivation.

 Work

MODULE OUTLINE  **Organize**

Instinct Approaches: Born to Be Motivated

Drive-Reduction Approaches: Satisfying Our Needs

Arousal Approaches: Beyond Drive Reduction

Try It! Do You Seek Out Sensation?

Incentive Approaches: Motivation's Pull

Cognitive Approaches: The Thoughts Behind Motivation

Maslow's Hierarchy: Ordering Motivational Needs

Applying the Different Approaches to Motivation

In just a moment, 27-year-old Aron Ralston's life changed. An 800-pound boulder dislodged in a narrow canyon where Ralston was hiking in an isolated Utah canyon, pinning his lower arm to the ground.

For the next five days, Ralston lay trapped, unable to escape. An experienced climber who had search-and-rescue training, he had ample time to consider his options. He tried unsuccessfully to chip away at the rock, and he rigged up ropes and pulleys around the boulder in a vain effort to move it.

Finally, out of water and nearly dehydrated, Ralston reasoned there was only one option left short of dying. In acts of incredible bravery, Ralston broke two bones in his wrist, applied a tourniquet, and used a dull pen knife to amputate his arm beneath the elbow.

Freed from his entrapment, Ralston climbed out from where he had been pinned, and then hiked five miles to safety (Ralston, 2005; Stevenson, 2010).

What factors lay behind Ralston's resolve?

To answer such questions, psychologists employ the concept of **motivation,** the factors that direct and energize the behavior of humans and other organisms. Motivation has biological, cognitive, and social aspects; and the complexity of the concept has led psychologists to develop a variety of approaches. All seek to explain the energy that guides people's behavior in specific directions.

motivation The factors that direct and energize the behavior of humans and other organisms

» LO22.1 Instinct Approaches: Born to Be Motivated

When psychologists first tried to explain motivation, they turned to **instincts,** inborn patterns of behavior that are biologically determined rather than learned. According to **instinct approaches to motivation,** people and animals are born preprogrammed with sets of behaviors essential to their survival. Those instincts provide the energy that channels behavior in appropriate directions. Hence, sexual behavior may be a response to an instinct to reproduce, and exploratory behavior may be motivated by an instinct to examine one's territory.

This conception presents several difficulties, however. For one thing, psychologists do not agree on what, or even how many, primary instincts exist. Furthermore, instinct approaches are unable to explain why certain patterns of behavior, and not others, have appeared in a given species. In addition, although it is clear that a great deal of animal behavior is based on instincts, much of the variety and complexity of human behavior is learned, and thus cannot be seen as instinctual. As a result of these shortcomings, newer explanations have replaced most conceptions of motivation based on instincts.

instincts Inborn patterns of behavior that are biologically determined rather than learned

instinct approaches to motivation The view that people and animals are born preprogrammed with sets of behaviors essential to their survival

drive-reduction approaches to motivation Theories suggesting that a lack of a basic biological requirement such as water produces a drive to obtain that requirement (in this case, the thirst drive)

drive Motivational tension, or arousal, that energizes behavior to fulfill a need

» LO22.2 Drive-Reduction Approaches: Satisfying Our Needs

After rejecting instinct theory, psychologists first proposed simple drive-reduction theories of motivation to take its place (Hull, 1943). **Drive-reduction approaches to motivation** suggest that a lack of some basic biological requirement such as water produces a drive to obtain that requirement (in this case, the thirst drive).

To understand this approach, we need to understand the concept of drive. A **drive** is motivational tension, or arousal, that energizes behavior to fulfill a need. Many basic drives, such as hunger, thirst, sleep, and sex, are related to biological needs of the body or of the species as a whole. These are called *primary drives.* Primary drives contrast with secondary drives, in which behavior fulfills no obvious biological need. In *secondary drives,* prior experience and learning bring about needs. For instance, some people have strong needs to achieve academically and professionally. We can say that their achievement need is reflected in a secondary drive that motivates their behavior (Seli, 2007; Johnson, Stewart, & Bachman, 2015).

We usually try to satisfy a primary drive by reducing the need underlying it. For example, we become hungry after not eating for a few hours and may raid the refrigerator, especially if the next scheduled meal is not imminent. If the weather turns cold, we put on extra clothing or raise the setting on the thermostat to keep warm. If our bodies need liquids to function properly, we experience thirst and seek out water.

Understanding what motivates people can have a huge impact on how we interact. How would knowing what motivates this man help his physical therapist aid him in his recovery? © imageBROKER/Superstock

While some drives are fairly obvious as primary or secondary, others can be more complicated. How would you classify the needs pictured here? (first) ©Jon Feingersh/Blend Images LLC RF; (second) © tomazl/Getty Images RF; (third) © Fuse/Jupiter Images RF

Homeostasis

homeostasis The body's tendency to maintain a steady internal state

arousal approaches to motivation The belief that we try to maintain certain levels of stimulation and activity, increasing or reducing them as necessary

Homeostasis, the body's tendency to maintain a steady internal state, underlies primary drives. Using feedback loops, homeostasis brings deviations in body functioning back to an optimal state, similar to the way a thermostat and a furnace work in a home heating system to maintain a steady temperature. Receptor cells throughout the body constantly monitor factors such as temperature and nutrient levels. When deviations from the ideal state occur, the body adjusts in an effort to return to an optimal state. Many fundamental needs, including the needs for food, water, stable body temperature, and sleep, operate via homeostasis (Porkka-Heiskanen & Kalinchuk, 2011; Porkka-Heiskanen, 2013; Betley et al., 2015).

Although drive-reduction theories provide a good explanation of how primary drives motivate behavior, they cannot fully explain a behavior in which the goal is not to reduce a drive, but rather to maintain or even increase the level of excitement or arousal. For instance, some behaviors seem to be motivated by nothing more than curiosity, such as rushing to check e-mail messages. Similarly, many people pursue thrilling activities such as riding a roller coaster or steering a raft down the rapids of a river. Such behaviors certainly don't suggest that people seek to reduce all drives, as drive-reduction approaches would indicate (Rosenbloom & Wolf, 2002; Freeman & Beer, 2010; Studer, Scheibehenne, & Clark, 2016).

Both curiosity and thrill-seeking behavior, then, shed doubt on drive-reduction approaches as a complete explanation for motivation. In both cases, rather than seeking to reduce an underlying drive, people and animals appear to be motivated to increase their overall level of stimulation and activity. To explain this phenomenon, psychologists have devised an alternative: arousal approaches to motivation.

» LO22.3 Arousal Approaches: Beyond Drive Reduction

According to **arousal approaches to motivation,** people try to maintain a steady level of stimulation and activity. People vary widely in the optimal level of arousal they seek out, with some people looking for especially high levels of arousal. For example, people who participate in daredevil sports, high-stakes gamblers, and criminals who pull off high-risk robberies may be exhibiting a particularly high need for arousal (Roets & Van Hiel, 2011; Lang & Bradley, 2013; Stevens et al., 2015). (To get a sense of your own level of stimulation, complete the accompanying Try It!)

Try It!

Do You Seek Out Sensation?

How much stimulation do you crave in your everyday life? You will have an idea after you complete the following questionnaire, which lists some items from a scale designed to assess your sensation-seeking tendencies. Circle either A or B in each pair of statements.

1. A. I would like a job that requires a lot of traveling.
    B. I would prefer a job in one location.
2. A. I am invigorated by a brisk, cold day.
    B. I can't wait to get indoors on a cold day.
3. A. I get bored seeing the same old faces.
    B. I like the comfortable familiarity of everyday friends.
4. A. I would prefer living in an ideal society in which everyone was safe, secure, and happy.
    B. I would have preferred living in the unsettled days of our history.
5. A. I sometimes like to do things that are a little frightening.
    B. A sensible person avoids activities that are dangerous.
6. A. I would not like to be hypnotized.
    B. I would like to have the experience of being hypnotized.
7. A. The most important goal of life is to live it to the fullest and to experience as much as possible.
    B. The most important goal of life is to find peace and happiness.
8. A. I would like to try parachute jumping.
    B. I would never want to try jumping out of a plane, with or without a parachute.
9. A. I enter cold water gradually, giving myself time to get used to it.
    B. I like to dive or jump right into the ocean or a cold pool.
10. A. When I go on a vacation, I prefer the comfort of a good room and bed.
    B. When I go on a vacation, I prefer the change of camping out.
11. A. I prefer people who are emotionally expressive, even if they are a bit unstable.
    B. I prefer people who are calm and even-tempered.
12. A. A good painting should shock or jolt the senses.
    B. A good painting should give one a feeling of peace and security.
13. A. People who ride motorcycles must have some kind of unconscious need to hurt themselves.
    B. I would like to drive or ride a motorcycle.

(continued)

Scoring

Give yourself one point for each of the following responses: 1A, 2A, 3A, 4B, 5A, 6B, 7A, 8A, 9B, 10B, 11A, 12A, 13B. Find your total score by adding up the number of points and then use the following scoring key:

0–2 = Very low sensation seeking

3–5 = Low

6–9 = Average

10–11 = High

12–13 = Very high

Keep in mind that this questionnaire provides only a rough estimate of your sensation-seeking tendencies. Moreover, as people get older, their sensation-seeking scores tend to decrease. Still, the questionnaire will at least give you an indication of how your sensation-seeking tendencies compare with those of others.

Source: Based on Zuckerman, M. 1978.

» LO22.4 Incentive Approaches: Motivation's Pull

When a luscious dessert appears on the table after a filling meal, its appeal has little or nothing to do with internal drives or the maintenance of arousal. Rather, if we choose to eat the dessert, such behavior is motivated by the external stimulus of the dessert itself, which acts as an anticipated reward. This reward, in motivational terms, is an *incentive*.

Incentive approaches to motivation suggest that motivation stems from the desire to obtain valued external goals, or incentives. In this view, the desirable properties of external stimuli—whether grades, money, affection, food, or sex—account for a person's motivation (Festinger et al., 2009).

Although the theory explains why we may succumb to an incentive (such as a mouthwatering dessert) even though we lack internal cues (such as hunger), it does not provide a complete explanation of motivation, because organisms sometimes seek to fulfill needs even when incentives are not apparent. Consequently, many psychologists believe that the internal drives proposed by drive-reduction theory work in tandem with the external incentives of incentive theory to "push" and "pull" behavior, respectively. Thus, at the same time that we seek to satisfy our underlying hunger needs (the push of drive-reduction theory), we are drawn to food that appears very appetizing (the pull of incentive theory). Rather than contradicting each other, then, drives and incentives may work together in motivating behavior (Berridge, 2004; Jeffrey & Adomdza, 2011; Covell et al., 2016).

» LO22.5 Cognitive Approaches: The Thoughts Behind Motivation

Cognitive approaches to motivation suggest that motivation is a product of people's thoughts, expectations, and goals—their cognitions. For instance, the degree to which people are motivated to study for a test is based on their expectation of how well studying will pay off in terms of a good grade.

incentive approaches to motivation Theories suggesting that motivation stems from the desire to obtain valued external goals, or incentives

cognitive approaches to motivation Theories suggesting that motivation is a product of people's thoughts and expectations—their cognitions

Cognitive theories of motivation draw a key distinction between intrinsic and extrinsic motivation. *Intrinsic motivation* causes us to participate in an activity for our own enjoyment rather than for any concrete, tangible reward that it will bring us. In contrast, *extrinsic motivation* causes us to do something for money, a grade, or some other concrete, tangible reward. For example, when a physician works long hours because she loves medicine, intrinsic motivation is prompting her; if she works hard to make a lot of money, extrinsic motivation underlies her efforts (Lepper, Corpus, & Iyengar, 2005; Shaikholeslami & Khayyer, 2006; Lee et al., 2010).

We are more apt to persevere, work harder, and produce work of higher quality when motivation for a task is intrinsic rather than extrinsic. In fact, in some cases providing rewards for desirable behavior (thereby increasing extrinsic motivation) actually may decrease intrinsic motivation (Grant, 2008; Bolkan, 2015; Reyes & Simon-Gunn, 2016).

» LO22.6 Maslow's Hierarchy: Ordering Motivational Needs

What do Eleanor Roosevelt, Abraham Lincoln, and Albert Einstein have in common? The common thread, according to a model of motivation devised by psychologist Abraham Maslow, is that each of them fulfilled the highest levels of motivational needs underlying human behavior.

Maslow's model places motivational needs in a hierarchy and suggests that before more sophisticated, higher-order needs can be met, certain primary needs must be satisfied (Maslow, 1970, 1987). A pyramid can represent the model, with the more basic needs at the bottom and the higher-level needs at the top (see Figure 1). To activate a specific higher-order need, thereby guiding behavior, a person must first fulfill the more basic needs in the hierarchy.

The basic needs are primary drives: needs for water, food, sleep, sex, and the like. To move up the hierarchy, a person must first meet these basic physiological needs. Safety needs come next in the hierarchy; Maslow suggests that people need a safe, secure environment in order to function effectively. Physiological and safety needs compose the lower-order needs.

Only after meeting the basic lower-order needs can a person consider fulfilling higher-order needs, such as the needs for love and a sense of belonging, esteem, and self-actualization. Love and belongingness needs include the needs to obtain and give affection and to be a contributing member of some group or society. After fulfilling

Intrinsic and extrinsic motivations are not always separate things. Miley Cyrus is well known for her genuine love of performing and outrageous behavior (intrinsic motivation). However, she is also well compensated for performing (extrinsic motivation). How do you identify your own motivations? © Jeff Kravitz/FilmMagic/Getty Images

Only after meeting the basic lower-order needs can a person consider fulfilling higher-order needs, such as the needs for love and a sense of belonging, esteem, and self-actualization.

Figure 1 Maslow's hierarchy shows how our motivation progresses up the pyramid from the broadest, most fundamental biological needs to higher-order ones. (After Maslow, 1971.) Do you agree that lower-order needs must be satisfied before higher-order needs? Do hermits and monks who attempt to fulfill spiritual needs while denying basic physical needs contradict Maslow's hierarchy? Photos: (top left) © Brand X Pictures/Getty Images RF; (top right) © BananaStock/age fotostock RF: (bottom left) © RubberBall Selects/Alamy Stock Photo; (bottom right) © Stockbyte/Getty Images RF

these needs, a person strives for esteem. In Maslow's thinking, esteem is the result of understanding that others recognize and value one's competence.

Once these four sets of needs are fulfilled—no easy task—a person is able to strive for the highest-level need, self-actualization. **Self-actualization** is a state of self-fulfillment in which people realize their highest potentials, in their own unique way. The important thing is that people feel at ease with themselves and satisfied that they are using their talents to the fullest. In a sense, achieving self-actualization reduces the striving and yearning for greater fulfillment that mark most people's lives and instead provides a sense of satisfaction with the current state of affairs (Laas, 2006; Peterson & Park, 2010; Ivtzan et al., 2013).

Maslow's hierarchy of needs has also spawned other approaches to motivation. For example, Richard Ryan and Edward Deci have considered human needs in terms of psychological well-being. They suggest in their *self-determination theory* that people have the three basic needs of competence, autonomy, and relatedness. Competence is the need to produce desired outcomes, while autonomy is the perception that we have control over our own lives. Finally, relatedness is the

self-actualization A state of self-fulfillment in which people realize their highest potential, each in his or her own unique way

need to be involved in close, warm relationships with others. In the view of self-determination theory, these three psychological needs are innate and universal across cultures, and they are essential as basic biological needs (Jang et al., 2009; Ryan & Deci, 2011).

» LO22.7 Applying the Different Approaches to Motivation

The various theories of motivation offer several different perspectives. Which provides the fullest account of motivation? Actually, many of the approaches are complementary, rather than contradictory (see Figure 2). In fact, employing more than one approach can help us understand motivation in a particular instance.

Consider, for example, Aron Ralston's accident while hiking (described earlier). His interest in climbing in an isolated and potentially dangerous area may be explained by arousal approaches to motivation. From the perspective of instinct approaches, we realize that Aron had an overwhelming instinct to preserve his life at all costs. From a cognitive perspective, we see his careful consideration of various strategies to extricate himself from the boulder.

Figure 2   The major approaches to motivation. Photos: (top left) © Digital Vision/PunchStock RF; (top middle) © Digital Vision/Getty Images RF; (top right) © BananaStock/JupiterImages RF; (bottom left) © LCPL Casey N. Thurston, USMC/DoD Media; (bottom right) © Corbis RF

Instinct	Drive reduction	Arousal	Incentive	Cognitive	Hierarchy of needs
People and animals are born with preprogrammed sets of behaviors essential to their survival.	When some basic biological requirement is lacking, a drive is produced.	People seek an optimal level of stimulation. If the level of stimulation is too high, they act to reduce it; if it is too low, they act to increase it.	External rewards direct and energize behavior.	Thoughts, beliefs, expectations, and goals direct motivation.	Needs form a hierarchy; before higher-order needs are met, lower-order needs must be fulfilled.

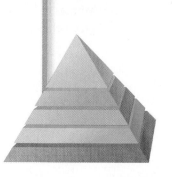

In short, applying multiple approaches to motivation in a given situation provides a broader understanding than we might obtain by employing only a single approach. We'll see this again when we consider specific motives—such as the needs for food, achievement, affiliation, and power—and draw on several of the theories for the fullest account of what motivates our behavior.

From the perspective of . . .

A Marketing Specialist How might you increase sales of a new snack food by appealing to multiple motivations for its consumption?

RECAP

Explain instinct approaches to motivation.

■ Motivation relates to the factors that direct and energize behavior.

Explain drive-reduction approaches to motivation.

■ Drive is the motivational tension that energizes behavior to fulfill a need.

■ Homeostasis, the maintenance of a steady internal state, often underlies motivational drives.

Explain arousal approaches to motivation.

■ Arousal approaches suggest that we try to maintain a particular level of stimulation and activity.

Explain incentive approaches to motivation.

■ Incentive approaches focus on the positive aspects of the environment that direct and energize behavior.

Explain cognitive approaches to motivation.

■ Cognitive approaches focus on the role of thoughts, expectations, and understanding of the world in producing motivation.

Apply Maslow's hierarchy of needs to motivation.

■ Maslow's hierarchy suggests that there are five basic needs: physiological, safety, love and belongingness, esteem, and self-actualization. Only after the more basic needs are fulfilled can a person move toward meeting higher-order needs.

Apply the different approaches to motivation.

■ Taken together, the different approaches to motivation provide a broad understanding of behavior.

[EVALUATE

1. _____ are forces that guide a person's behavior in a certain direction.

2. Biologically determined, inborn patterns of behavior are known as _____.

3. Your psychology professor tells you, "Explaining behavior is easy! When we lack something, we are motivated to get it." Which approach to motivation does your professor subscribe to?

4. I help an elderly person cross the street because doing a good deed makes me feel good. What type of motivation is at work here? What type of motivation would be at work if I were to help an elderly man across the street because he paid me $20?

5. According to Maslow, a person with no job, no home, and no friends can become self-actualized. True or false?

[RETHINK R Rethink]

Which approaches to motivation are more commonly used in the workplace? How might each approach be used to design employment policies that can sustain or increase motivation?

Answers to Evaluate Questions 1. motives; 2. instincts; 3. drive reduction; 4. intrinsic, extrinsic; 5. false; lower-order needs must be fulfilled before self-actualization can occur.

KEY TERMS

Motivation LO22.1

Instincts LO22.1

Instinct approaches to motivation LO22.1

Drive-reduction approaches to motivation LO22.2

Drive LO22.2

Homeostasis LO22.2

Arousal approaches to motivation LO22.3

Incentive approaches to motivation LO22.4

Cognitive approaches to motivation LO22.4

Self-actualization LO22.6

Human Needs and Motivation
Eat, Drink, and Be Daring

Learning Outcomes  **P Prepare**

>> **LO23.1** Describe the biological and social factors that underlie hunger.

>> **LO23.2** Summarize the varieties of sexual behavior.

>> **LO23.3** Explain how needs related to achievement, affiliation, and power are exhibited.

 W Work

As a sophomore at the University of California, Santa Cruz, Lisa Arndt followed a menu of her own making: for breakfast she ate cereal or fruit, with 10 diet pills and 50 chocolate-flavored laxatives. Lunch was a salad or sandwich; dinner: chicken and rice. But it was the feast that followed that Arndt relished most. Almost every night at about 9 p.m., she would retreat to her room and eat an entire small pizza and a whole batch of cookies. Then she'd wait for the day's laxatives to take effect. "It was extremely painful," says Arndt of those days. . . . "But I was that desperate to make up for my bingeing. I was terrified of fat the way other people are afraid of lions or guns." (Hubbard, O'Neill, & Cheakalos, 1999, p. 59)

Lisa was 1 of the 10 million women (and 1 million men) who are estimated to suffer from an eating disorder. These disorders, which usually appear during adolescence, can bring about extraordinary weight loss and other forms of physical deterioration. Extremely dangerous, they sometimes result in death.

Why are Lisa and others like her subject to such disordered eating, which revolves around the motivation to avoid weight gain at all costs? And why do so many other people engage in overeating, which leads to obesity?

>> LO23.1 The Motivation Behind Hunger and Eating

Two hundred million people in the United States—some two-thirds of the population—are overweight. More than one-third of the U.S. population is so heavy that they have **obesity,** body weight that is more than 20 percent above the average weight for a person of a particular height. And the rest of the world is not far behind: a billion people around the globe are overweight or obese. The World Health Organization has said that worldwide obesity has reached epidemic proportions, producing increases in heart disease, diabetes, cancer, and premature deaths. Projections are that by 2030, all 50 states will have obesity rates above 44 percent, and rates will exceed 60 percent in 13 states (Shugart, 2011; Sharpe, 2013; Ogden et al., 2014).

The most widely used measure of obesity is *body mass index (BMI),* which is based on a ratio of weight to height. People with a BMI greater than 30 are considered obese, whereas those with a BMI between 25 and 30 are overweight. (Use the formulas in the Try It! to determine your own BMI.)

Biological Factors in the Regulation of Hunger

Although the brain's *hypothalamus* has an important role in regulating food intake, the exact way this organ operates is still unclear. One hypothesis suggests that injury to the hypothalamus affects the **weight set point,** or the particular level of weight that the body strives to maintain, which in turn regulates food intake. Acting as a kind of internal weight thermostat, the hypothalamus calls for either greater or less food intake (Capaldi, 1996; Woods et al., 2000; Berthoud, 2002).

> **obesity** Body weight that is more than 20 percent above the average weight for a person of a particular height
>
> **weight set point** The particular level of weight that the body strives to maintain

Try It!
Find Your Body Mass Index

Use this procedure to find your body mass index (BMI).
1. Indicate your weight in pounds: _____ pounds
2. Indicate your height in inches: _____ inches
3. Divide your weight (item 1) by your height (item 2), and write the outcome here: _____
4. Divide the result above (item 3) by your height (item 2), and write the outcome here: _____
5. Multiply the number above by 703, and write the product here: _____
This is your body mass index.

Example:

For a person who weighs 210 pounds and who is 6 feet tall, divide 210 pounds by 72 inches, which equals 2.917. Then divide 2,917 by 72 inches (item 3), which yields .041. Multiplying .041 (from item 4) by 703 yields a BMI of 28.8.

Interpretation:

- Underweight = less than 18.5
- Normal weight = 18.5 – 24.9
- Overweight = 25 – 29.9
- Obesity = BMI of 30 or greater

Keep in mind that a BMI greater than 25 may or may not be due to excess body fat. For example, professional athletes may have little fat but weigh more than the average person because they have greater muscle mass.

> **Even people who are not deliberately monitoring their weight show only minor weight fluctuations in spite of substantial day-to-day variations in how much they eat and exercise.**

In most cases, the hypothalamus does a good job. Even people who are not deliberately monitoring their weight show only minor weight fluctuations in spite of substantial day-to-day variations in how much they eat and exercise. However, injury to the hypothalamus can alter the weight set point, and a person then struggles to meet the internal goal by increasing or decreasing food consumption. Even temporary exposure to certain drugs can alter the weight set point (Sternson, Betley, & Cao, 2013; Palmiter, 2015; Ornellas et al., 2016).

metabolism The rate at which food is converted to energy and expended by the body

Genetic factors determine the weight set point, at least in part. People seem destined, through heredity, to have a particular **metabolism,** the rate at which food is converted to energy and expended by the body. People with a high metabolic rate can eat virtually as much as they want without gaining weight, whereas others, with low metabolism, may eat literally half as much yet gain weight readily (Jequier, 2002; Westerterp, 2006; Lazzer et al., 2010).

Social Factors in Eating

© Ingram Publishing /Alamy Stock Photo RF

You've just finished a full meal and feel completely stuffed. Suddenly your host announces with great fanfare that he will be serving his "house specialty" dessert, bananas flambé, and that he has spent the better part of the afternoon preparing it. Even though you are full and don't even like bananas, you accept a serving of his dessert and eat it all.

Clearly, internal biological factors do not fully explain our eating behavior. External social factors, based on societal rules and on what we have learned about appropriate eating behavior, also play an important role. Take, for example, the simple fact that people customarily eat breakfast, lunch, and dinner at approximately the same times every day. Because we tend to eat on schedule every day, we feel hungry as the usual hour approaches, sometimes quite independently of what our internal cues are telling us.

Similarly, we put roughly the same amount of food on our plates every day, even though the amount of exercise we may have had, and consequently our need for energy replenishment, varies from day to day. We also tend to prefer particular foods over others. Rats and dogs may be a delicacy in certain Asian cultures, but few people in Western cultures find them appealing despite their potentially high nutritional value. Even the amount of food we eat varies according to cultural norms. For instance, people in the United States eat bigger portions than people in France. In sum, cultural influences and our individual habits play important roles in determining when, what, and how much we eat (Rozin et al., 2003; Robinson et al., 2016).

The Roots of Obesity

Given that both biological and social factors influence eating behavior, determining the causes of obesity has proved to be a challenging task. Researchers have followed several paths.

Some psychologists suggest that oversensitivity to external eating cues based on social factors, coupled with insensitivity to internal hunger cues, produces obesity. Others argue that overweight people have higher weight set points than other people do. Because their set points are unusually high, their attempts to lose weight by eating less may make them especially sensitive to external, food-related cues and therefore more apt to overeat and perpetuate their obesity (Lantz et al., 2010; Cooper, 2011; Macht & Simons, 2011).

Another biologically based explanation for obesity relates to fat cells in the body. Starting at birth, the body stores fat either by increasing the number of fat cells or by increasing the size of existing fat cells. Furthermore, any loss of weight past infancy does not decrease the number of fat cells; it only affects their size. Consequently, people are stuck with the number of fat cells they inherit from an early age, and the rate of weight gain during the first four months of life is related to being overweight during later childhood (Stettler et al., 2005; Yanovski & Yanovski, 2011).

According to the weight-set-point hypothesis, the presence of too many fat cells from earlier weight gain may result in the set point's becoming "stuck" at a higher level than is desirable. In such circumstances, losing weight becomes a difficult proposition, because one is constantly at odds with one's own internal set point when dieting (Müller, Bosy-Wesphal, & Heymsfield, 2010).

Eating Disorders

Eating disorders are among the 10 most frequent causes of disability in young women. One devastating weight-related disorder is **anorexia nervosa.** In this severe eating disorder, people may refuse to eat while denying that their behavior and appearance—which can become skeleton-like—are unusual. Some 10 percent of people with anorexia literally starve themselves to death (Striegel-Moore & Bulik, 2007; Clausen et al., 2011).

Anorexia nervosa mainly afflicts females between the ages of 12 and 40, although both men and women of any age may develop it. People with the disorder typically come from stable homes, and they are often successful, attractive, and relatively affluent. The disorder often occurs after serious dieting, which somehow gets out of control. Life begins to revolve around food: although people with the disorder eat little, they may cook for others, go shopping for food frequently, or collect cookbooks (Polivy, Herman, & Boivin, 2005; Myers, 2007; Jacobs et al., 2009).

A related problem, **bulimia,** from which Lisa Arndt (described earlier) suffered, is a disorder in which people binge on large quantities of food. For instance, they may consume an entire gallon of ice cream and a whole pie in a single sitting. After such a binge, sufferers feel guilt and depression and often induce vomiting or take laxatives to rid themselves of the food—behavior known as purging. Constant bingeing-and-purging cycles and the use of drugs to induce vomiting or diarrhea can lead to heart failure. Often, though, the weight of a person with bulimia remains normal (Mora-Giral et al., 2004; Couturier & Lock, 2006; Pohjolainen et al., 2010).

What are the causes of anorexia nervosa and bulimia? Some researchers suspect a biological cause such as a chemical imbalance in the hypothalamus or pituitary gland, perhaps brought on by genetic factors. Furthermore, scans of the brains of people with eating disorders show that they process information about food and other aspects of their environments differently from healthy individuals (Klump & Culbert, 2007; Ogden, 2010; Mohr & Messina, 2015; see Figure 1).

Others believe that the cause has roots in society's valuation of slenderness and the parallel notion that obesity is undesirable. These researchers maintain that people with anorexia nervosa and bulimia become preoccupied with their

anorexia nervosa A severe eating disorder in which people may refuse to eat while denying that their behavior and appearance—which can become skeleton-like—are unusual

bulimia A disorder in which a person binges on large quantities of food, followed by efforts to purge the food through vomiting or other means

Despite looking skeleton-like to others, people with the weight disorder anorexia nervosa see themselves as overweight. © Sally and Richard Greenhill/Alamy Stock Photo

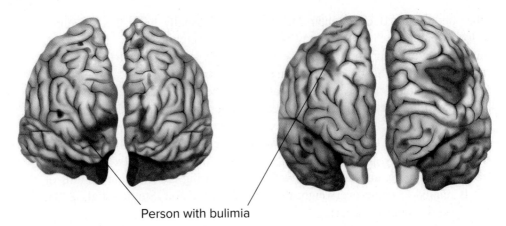

Person with bulimia

Figure 1 Research suggests that individuals with eating disorders not only show differences in behavior, but also in the brain. For example, in these images above, those with bulimia show differences in many areas of the brain that likely relate to how those with bulimia process their environment. Although researchers are not sure if these differences are the cause or the result of disordered eating, understanding these differences may help us better address it. In particular, these images show areas in which people with bulimia differ in the shape of their brains (red/yellow being areas that are larger and blue/purple being smaller) as compared to those who do not have the disorder. Source: Adapted from Marsh et al., 2015.

weight and take to heart the cliché that one can never be too thin. This may explain why eating disorders increase as countries become more developed and Westernized and dieting becomes more popular. Finally, some psychologists suggest that the disorders result from overly demanding parents or other family problems (Couturier & Lock, 2006; Kluck, 2008; Cook-Cottone & Smith, 2013).

The complete explanations for anorexia nervosa and bulimia remain elusive. These disorders most likely stem from both biological and social causes, and successful treatment probably encompasses several strategies, including therapy and dietary changes (O'Brien & LeBow, 2007; Cooper & Shafran, 2008; Mintle, 2011).

If you or a family member needs advice or help with an eating problem, contact the American Anorexia Bulimia Association at www.aabainc.org or call 212-575-6200. You can get more information at www.nlm.nih.gov/medlineplus/eatingdisorders.html.

becoming an informed consumer
of psychology

Dieting and Losing Weight Successfully

Although 60 percent of the people in the United States say they want to lose weight, it's a losing battle for most of them. Most people who diet eventually regain the weight they have lost, and so they try again and get caught in a seemingly endless cycle of weight loss and gain (Newport & Carroll, 2002; Parker-Pope, 2003; Cachelin & Regan, 2006).

You should keep several things in mind when trying to lose weight (Gathchel & Oordt, 2003; Heshka et al., 2003; Freedman & Waldrop, 2011):

■ *There is no easy route to weight control.* You will have to make permanent changes in your life to lose weight without gaining it back. The most obvious strategy—cutting down on the amount of food you eat—is just the first step toward a lifetime commitment to changing your eating habits.

- *Keep track of what you eat and what you weigh.* Unless you keep careful records, you won't really know how much you are eating and whether any diet is working.

- *Eat "big" foods.* Eat fiber and foods that are bulky and heavy but low in calories, such as grapes and soup. Such foods trick your body into thinking you've eaten more and thus decrease hunger.

- *Cut out television.* One reason for the epidemic of obesity is the number of hours people in the United States spend viewing television. Not only does watching television preclude other activities that burn calories (even walking around the house is helpful), people often gorge on junk food while watching TV (Hu et al., 2003).

- *Exercise.* Exercise at least 30 consecutive minutes three times each week. When you exercise, you use up fat stored in your body as fuel for muscles, which is measured in calories. As you use up this fat, you will probably lose weight. Almost any activity helps burn calories.

- *Decrease the influence of external, social stimuli on your eating behavior.* Serve yourself smaller portions of food, and leave the table before you see what is being served for dessert. Don't even buy snack foods such as nachos and potato chips; if they're not readily available in the kitchen cupboard, you're not apt to eat them. Wrap refrigerated foods in aluminum foil so that you cannot see the contents and be tempted every time you open the refrigerator.

- *Avoid fad diets.* No matter how popular they are at a particular time, extreme diets, including liquid diets, usually don't work in the long run and can be dangerous to your health.

- *Avoid taking any of the numerous diet pills advertised on television that promise quick and easy results.*

- *Maintain good eating habits.* When you have reached your desired weight, maintain the new habits you learned while dieting to avoid gaining back the weight you have lost.

- *Set reasonable goals.* Know how much weight you want to lose before you start to diet. Don't try to lose too much weight too quickly or you may doom yourself to failure. Even small changes in behavior—such as walking 15 minutes a day or eating a few less bites at each meal—can prevent weight gain (Kirk et al., 2003; Freedman & Waldrop, 2011).

≫ LO23.2 Sexual Motivation

Anyone who has seen two dogs mating knows that sexual behavior has a biological basis. Their sexual behavior appears to occur naturally, without much prompting on the part of others. A number of genetically controlled factors influence the sexual behavior of nonhuman animals. For instance, animal behavior is affected by the presence of certain hormones in the blood. Moreover, female animals are receptive to sexual advances only during certain relatively limited periods of the year.

Human sexual behavior, by comparison, is more complicated, although the underlying biology is not all that different from that of related species. In males, for example, the *testes* begin to secrete **androgens,** male sex hormones, at puberty. (See Figure 2 for the basic anatomy of the male and female **genitals,** or sex organs.) Not only do androgens produce secondary sex characteristics, such as the growth of body hair and a deepening of the voice, they also increase the sex drive. Because the level of androgen production by the testes is fairly constant, men are capable of (and interested in) sexual activities without any regard to biological cycles. Given the proper stimuli leading to arousal, male sexual behavior can occur at any time (Goldstein, 2000).

Women show a different pattern. When they reach maturity at puberty, the two *ovaries* begin to produce **estrogens** and **progesterone,** female sex hormones. However, those hormones are not produced consistently; instead, their production follows a cyclical pattern. The greatest output occurs during **ovulation,** when an egg is released from the ovaries, making the chances of fertilization by a sperm cell highest. Whereas in nonhumans the period around ovulation is the only time the female is receptive to sex, people are different. Although there are variations in reported sex drive, women are receptive to sex throughout their cycles (Lieblum & Chivers, 2007).

In addition, some evidence suggests that males have a stronger sex drive than females, although the difference may be the result of society's discouragement of

androgens Male sex hormones secreted by the testes

genitals The male and female sex organs

estrogens Class of female sex hormones

progesterone A female sex hormone secreted by the ovaries

ovulation The point at which an egg is released from the ovaries

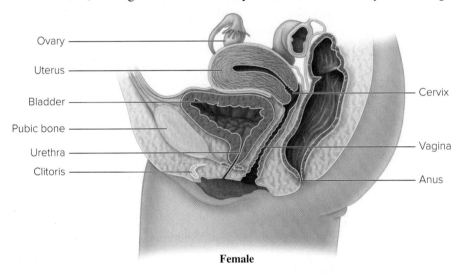

Female

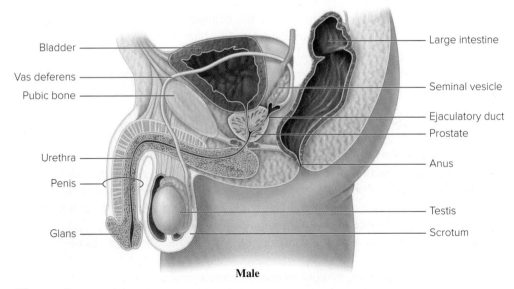

Male

Figure 2   Cutaway side views of the female and male sex organs.

female sexuality rather than of innate differences between men and women. It is clear that men think about sex more than women: 54 percent of men report thinking about sex every day, but only 19 percent of women report thinking about it on a daily basis (Gangestad et al., 2004; Baumeister & Stillman, 2006; Carvalho & Nobre, 2010).

Though biological factors "prime" people for sex, it takes more than hormones to motivate and produce sexual behavior. In animals the presence of a partner who provides arousing stimuli leads to sexual activity. Humans are considerably more versatile; not only other people but nearly any object, sight, smell, sound, or other stimulus can lead to sexual excitement. Sexual fantasies also play an important role in producing sexual arousal. Not only do people have fantasies of a sexual nature during their everyday activities, but about 60 percent of all people have fantasies during sexual intercourse. In fact, such fantasies often include having sex with someone other than one's partner of the moment (Hicks & Leitenberg, 2001; Trudel, 2002; Critelli & Bivona, 2008).

Masturbation: Solitary Sex

If you listened to physicians 75 years ago, you would have been told that **masturbation,** sexual self-stimulation, often using the hand to rub the genitals, would lead to a wide variety of physical and mental disorders, ranging from hairy palms to insanity. If those physicians had been correct, however, most of us would be wearing gloves to hide the sight of our hair-covered palms—for masturbation is one of the most frequently practiced sexual activities. Almost all men and the majority of females have masturbated to orgasm at least once, and among college students, the frequency ranges from never to several times a day (Polonsky, 2006; Herbenick et al., 2009).

Men and women typically begin to masturbate for the first time at different ages. Furthermore, men masturbate considerably more often than women, although there are differences in frequency according to age. Male masturbation is most common in the early teens and then declines, whereas females both begin and reach a maximum frequency later. There are also some racial differences: African American men and women masturbate less than whites do (Oliver & Hyde, 1993; Pinkerton et al., 2002; Das, Parish, & Laumann, 2009).

masturbation Sexual self-stimulation

heterosexuality Sexual attraction and behavior directed to the other sex

double standard The view that premarital sex is permissible for males but not for females

Heterosexuality

People often believe that the first time they have sexual intercourse they have achieved one of life's major milestones. However, **heterosexuality,** sexual attraction and behavior directed to the other sex, consists of far more than male-female intercourse. Kissing, petting, caressing, massaging, and other forms of sex play are all components of heterosexual behavior. Still, the focus of sex researchers has been on the act of intercourse, especially in terms of its first occurrence and its frequency.

Premarital Sex

At one time, premarital sexual intercourse, at least for women, was considered one of the major taboos in our society. Traditionally, women have been warned by society that "nice girls don't do it"; men have been told that premarital sex is okay for them, but they should marry virgins. This view that premarital sex is permissible for males but not for females is called the **double standard** (Liang, 2007; Lyons et al., 2011).

As recently as the 1970s, the majority of adult Americans believed that premarital sex was always wrong. But there has been a dramatic change in public opinion since then. The percentage of people who believe that premarital sex is "not wrong at all" has increased from just over 25 percent in the early 1970s

extramarital sex Sexual activity between a married person and someone who is not his or her spouse

homosexuals Persons who are sexually attracted to members of their own sex

bisexuals Persons who are sexually attracted to people of the same sex and the other sex

to more than 55 percent in 2012. More than half say that living together before marriage is morally acceptable (Thornton & Young-DeMarco, 2001; Harding & Jencks, 2003; Smith & Son, 2013).

Marital Sex

To judge by the number of articles about sex in heterosexual marriages, one would think that sexual behavior was the number one standard by which marital bliss is measured. Married couples are often concerned that they are having too little sex, too much sex, or the wrong kind of sex (Harvey, Wenzel, & Sprecher, 2005).

Although there are many different dimensions along which sex in marriage is measured, one is certainly the frequency of sexual intercourse. What is typical?

As with most other types of sexual activities, there is no easy answer to the question, because there are such wide variations in patterns between individuals. We do know that 43 percent of heterosexual married couples have sexual intercourse a few times a month and 36 percent of couples have it two or three times a week. With increasing age and length of marriage, the frequency of intercourse declines. Still, sex continues into late adulthood, with almost half of people reporting that they engage in sexual activity at least once a month and that its quality is high (Michael et al., 1994; Powell, 2006).

Although early research found **extramarital sex** to be widespread, the current reality appears to be otherwise. According to surveys, 85 percent of married women and more than 75 percent of married men are faithful to their spouses. Furthermore, the median number of sex partners, inside and outside of marriage, since the age of 18 for men was six, and for women two. Accompanying these numbers is a high, consistent degree of disapproval of extramarital sex, with 9 of 10 people saying that it is "always" or "almost always" wrong (Michael et al., 1994; Daines, 2006; Whisman & Snyder, 2007; DeMaris, 2013).

Homosexuality and Bisexuality

Homosexuals are sexually attracted to members of their own sex, whereas **bisexuals** are sexually attracted to people of the same sex and the other sex. Many male homosexuals prefer the term *gay* and female homosexuals the label *lesbian,* because they refer to a broader array of attitudes and lifestyles than the term *homosexual,* which focuses on the sexual act.

Extensive research has found that bisexuals and homosexuals enjoy the same overall degree of mental and physical health as heterosexuals.
© Image Source/Veer RF

The number of people who choose same-sex sexual partners at one time or another is considerable. Estimates suggest that around 20 to 25 percent of males and about 15 percent of females have had at least one gay or lesbian experience during adulthood. The exact number of people who identify themselves as exclusively homosexual has proved difficult to gauge, with some estimates as low as 1.1 percent and some as high as 10 percent. Most experts suggest that between 5 and 10 percent of both men and women are exclusively gay or lesbian during extended periods of their lives (Hunt, 1974; Sells, 1994; Firestein, 1996).

Although people often view homosexuality and heterosexuality as two completely distinct sexual orientations, the issue is not that simple.

Although people often view homosexuality and heterosexuality as two completely distinct sexual orientations, the issue is not that simple. Pioneering sex researcher Alfred Kinsey acknowledged this when he considered sexual orientation along a scale or continuum, with "exclusively homosexual" at one end and "exclusively heterosexual" at the other. In the middle were people who showed both homosexual and heterosexual behavior. Kinsey's approach suggests that sexual orientation is dependent on a person's sexual feelings and behaviors and romantic feelings (Weinberg, Williams, & Pryor, 1991; Jeffery, 2015).

What determines whether people become homosexual or heterosexual? Although there are a number of theories, none has proved completely satisfactory.

Some explanations for sexual orientation are biological, suggesting that there are genetic causes. Evidence for a genetic origin of sexual orientation comes from studies of identical twins. The studies have found that when one twin identified himself or herself as homosexual, the occurrence of homosexuality in the other twin was higher than it was in the general population. Such results occur even for twins who have been separated early in life and who therefore are not necessarily raised in similar social environments. Furthermore, some research suggests there is an area on the X chromosome associated with homosexuality (Gooren, 2006; LeVay, 2011; Servick, 2014).

Hormones also may play a role in determining sexual orientation. For example, research shows that women exposed to DES, or diethylstilbestrol, before birth (their mothers took the drug to avoid miscarriage) were more likely to be homosexual or bisexual (Meyer-Bahlburg, 1997).

Some evidence suggests that differences in brain structures may be related to sexual orientation. For instance, the structure of the anterior hypothalamus, an area of the brain that governs sexual behavior, differs in male homosexuals and heterosexuals. Similarly, other research shows that, compared with heterosexual men or women, gay men have a larger anterior commissure, which is a bundle of neurons connecting the right and left hemispheres of the brain (Witelson et al., 2008; Hines, 2010; Rahman & Yusuf, 2015).

However, research suggesting that biological causes are at the root of homosexuality is not conclusive. Still, it seems likely that some inherited or biological factor exists that predisposes people toward homosexuality (Teodorov et al., 2002; Rahman, Kumari, & Wilson, 2003; Burri, Spector, & Qazi, 2015).

Little evidence suggests that sexual orientation is brought about by child-rearing practices or family dynamics. Although proponents of psychoanalytic theories once argued that the nature of the parent-child relationship can produce homosexuality (e.g., Freud, 1922/1959), research evidence does not support such explanations (Isay, 1994; Roughton, 2002).

Because of the difficulty in finding a consistent explanation, we can't definitively answer the question of what determines sexual orientation. It does seem unlikely that any single factor orients a person toward homosexuality or heterosexuality (Hyde, Mezulis, & Abramson, 2008).

Although we don't know exactly why people develop a certain sexual orientation, one thing is clear: despite increasingly positive attitudes toward homosexuality many gays and lesbians still face antigay attitudes and discrimination, and it can take a toll. Lesbians and gays have higher rates of depression and suicide than their straight counterparts. There

"Frankly, I've repressed my sexuality so long I've actually forgotten what my orientation is."

are even physical health disparities due to prejudice that gays and lesbians may experience. Because of this, the American Psychological Association and other major mental health organizations have endorsed efforts to eliminate discrimination against gays and lesbians (Ashley, 2013; Lick, Durso, & Johnson, 2013; Kwon, 2013).

Transgenderism

An increasing number of individuals consider themselves transgender. **Transgender** is a broad term encompassing people whose gender identity, gender expression, or behavior does not conform to the sex to which they were assigned at birth.

Transgender people may have male bodies but view their gender identity as female, or may have female bodies and have a male gender identity. In other cases, transgender individuals may view themselves as a third gender (neither male nor female). They also may wish to be referred to not as "she" or "he," but rather some other, more neutral pronoun, such as "ze" or "they" (Prince, 2005; Hyde, Mezulis, & Abramson, 2008; Scelfo, 2015).

In some cases, transgender individuals may seek sex-change operations in which their existing genitals are surgically removed and the genitals of the desired sex are fashioned. Several steps, including intensive counseling, hormone injections, and living as a member of the desired sex for several years, precede surgery, which is, not surprisingly, highly complicated. The outcome, though, can be quite positive (Lobato, Koff, & Manenti, 2006; Richards, 2011).

Transgender issues have become increasingly prominent in recent years. For instance, college campuses have struggled with how to best provide restrooms that address the needs of the transgender community. Do individuals who have the genitals of a male, yet who identify as females, use traditional men's rooms or women's rooms? One solution has been the establishment of unisex or all-gender restrooms (Steinmetz, 2015).

Whereas transgenderism centers on gender identity concerns, some people are born having physical issues involving their genitals. An *intersex person* has an atypical combination of sexual organs or chromosomal or gene patterns. In some cases, they are born with both male and female sexual organs, or the organs are ambiguous. It is an extremely rare condition found in one in 4,500 births. Intersexism involves a complex mix of physiological and psychological issues (Lehrman, 2007; Diamond, 2009).

» LO23.3 The Needs for Achievement, Affiliation, and Power

Although hunger may be one of the more potent primary drives in our day-to-day lives, powerful secondary drives that have no clear biological basis also motivate us. Among the more prominent of these is the need for achievement.

The Need for Achievement: Striving for Excellence

The **need for achievement** is a stable, learned characteristic in which a person obtains satisfaction by striving for and attaining a level of excellence (McClelland et al., 1953). People with a high need for achievement seek out situations in which they can compete against some standard—such as grades, money, or winning a game—and prove themselves successful. But they are not indiscriminate when it comes to picking their challenges: they tend to avoid

---

transgender An umbrella term for persons whose gender identity, gender expression, or behavior does not conform to that typically associated with the sex to which they were assigned at birth

need for achievement A stable, learned characteristic in which a person obtains satisfaction by striving for and attaining a level of excellence

STUDY ALERT

The determinants of sexual orientation have proven difficult to pinpoint. It is important to know the variety of explanations that have been put forward.

situations in which success will come too easily (which would be unchallenging) and situations in which success is unlikely. Instead, people high in achievement motivation generally choose tasks that are of intermediate difficulty (Speirs Neumeister & Finch, 2006; Mills, 2011).

In contrast, people with low achievement motivation tend to be motivated primarily by a desire to avoid failure. As a result, they seek out easy tasks, being sure to avoid failure, or they seek out very difficult tasks for which failure has no negative implications, because almost anyone would fail at them. People with a high fear of failure will stay away from tasks of intermediate difficulty, because they may fail where others have been successful (Martin & Marsh, 2002; Puca, 2005; Morrone & Pintrich, 2006).

Measuring Achievement Motivation

How can we measure a person's need for achievement? The measuring instrument used most frequently is the **Thematic Apperception Test (TAT).** In the TAT, an examiner shows a series of ambiguous pictures. The examiner tells participants to write a story that describes what is happening, who the people are, what led to the situation, what the people are thinking or wanting, and what will happen next. Researchers then use a standard scoring system to determine the amount of achievement imagery in people's stories. For example, someone who writes a story in which the main character strives to beat an opponent, studies in order to do well at some task, or works hard in order to get a promotion shows clear signs of an achievement orientation. The inclusion of such achievement-related imagery in the participants' stories is assumed to indicate an unusually high degree of concern with—and therefore a relatively strong need for—achievement (Tuerlinckx, De Boeck, & Lens, 2002; Teglasi, 2010).

The Need for Affiliation: Striving for Friendship

Few of us choose to lead our lives as hermits. Why?

One main reason is that most people have a **need for affiliation,** an interest in establishing and maintaining relationships with other people. Individuals with a high need for affiliation write TAT stories that emphasize the desire to maintain or reinstate friendships and show concern over being rejected by friends.

People who have higher affiliation needs are particularly sensitive to relationships with others. They desire to be with their friends more of the time, and alone less often, compared with people who are lower in the need for affiliation. However, gender is a greater determinant of how much time is actually spent with friends: regardless of their affiliative orientation, female students spend significantly more time with their friends and less time alone than male students do (Cantwell & Andrews, 2002; Johnson, 2004; Semykina & Linz, 2007).

The Need for Power: Striving for Impact on Others

If your fantasies include becoming president of the United States or running Microsoft, your dreams may reflect a high need for power. The **need for power,** a tendency to seek impact, control, or influence over others and to be seen as a powerful individual, is an additional type of motivation (Lee-Chai & Bargh, 2001; Winter, 2007; Zians, 2007).

As you might expect, people with strong needs for power are more apt to belong to organizations and seek office than are those low in the need for power. They also tend to work in professions in which their power needs may be fulfilled, such as business management and—you may or may not be surprised—teaching (Jenkins, 1994). In addition, they seek to display the trappings of

© Mike Flippo/Shutterstock.com

Thematic Apperception Test (TAT) A test consisting of a series of pictures about which a person is asked to write a story

need for affiliation An interest in establishing and maintaining relationships with other people

need for power A tendency to seek impact, control, or influence over others, and to be seen as a powerful individual

power. Even in college, they are more likely to collect prestigious possessions, such as electronic equipment and sports cars.

Some significant gender differences exist in the display of need for power. Men with high power needs tend to show unusually high levels of aggression, drink heavily, act in a sexually exploitative manner, and participate more frequently in competitive sports—behaviors that collectively represent somewhat extravagant, flamboyant behavior. In contrast, women display their power needs with more restraint; this is in line with traditional societal constraints on women's behavior. Women with high power needs are more apt than men to channel those needs in a socially responsible manner, such as by showing concern for others or displaying highly nurturing behavior (Schubert & Koole, 2009; Schultheiss & Schiepe-Tiska, 2013; Sibunruang, Capezio, & Restubog, 2015).

From the perspective of . . .

A New Supervisor How might you use characteristics such as need for achievement, need for power, and need for affiliation to select workers for jobs? What additional criteria would you have to consider?

RECAP

Describe the biological and social factors that underlie hunger.

- Eating behavior is subject to homeostasis, as most people's weight stays within a relatively stable range. The hypothalamus in the brain is central to the regulation of food intake.

- Social factors, such as mealtimes, cultural food preferences, and other learned habits, also play a role in the regulation of eating, determining when, what, and how much one eats. An oversensitivity to social cues and an insensitivity to internal cues may also be related to obesity. In addition, obesity may be caused by an unusually high weight set point—the weight the body attempts to maintain—and genetic factors.

Summarize the varieties of sexual behavior.

- Although biological factors, such as the presence of androgens (male sex hormones) and estrogens and progesterone (female sex hormones), prime people for sex, almost any kind of stimulus can produce sexual arousal, depending on a person's prior experience.

- The frequency of masturbation is high, particularly for males. Although increasingly liberal, attitudes toward masturbation have traditionally been negative even though no negative consequences have been detected.

- Heterosexuality, or sexual attraction to members of the other sex, is the most common sexual orientation.

- Homosexuals are sexually attracted to members of their own sex; bisexuals are sexually attracted to people of the same sex and the other sex. No explanation for why people become homosexual has been confirmed; among the possibilities are genetic or biological factors and childhood and family influences. However, no relationship exists between sexual orientation and psychological adjustment.

Explain how needs related to achievement, affiliation, and power are exhibited.

- Need for achievement refers to the stable, learned characteristic in which a person strives to attain a level of excellence. Need for achievement is usually measured through the Thematic

Apperception Test (TAT), a series of pictures about which a person writes a story.

- The need for affiliation is a concern with establishing and maintaining relationships with

others, whereas the need for power is a tendency to seek to exert an impact on others.

- The need for power is a tendency to seek to exert an impact on others.

[EVALUATE [E] Evaluate]

1. The _____ is responsible for regulating food intake.
2. The _____ _____ _____ is the specific level of weight the body strives to maintain.
3. _____ is the rate at which energy is produced and expended by the body.
4. Although the incidence of masturbation among young adults is high, once men and women become involved in intimate relationships, they typically cease masturbating. True or false?
5. The increase in premarital sex in recent years has been greater for women than for men. True or false?
6. Julio is the type of person who constantly strives for excellence. He feels intense satisfaction when he is able to master a new task. Julio most likely has a high need for _____.
7. Debbie's Thematic Apperception Test (TAT) story depicts a young girl who is rejected by one of her peers and seeks to regain her friendship. What major type of motivation is Debbie displaying in her story?

    a. Need for achievement
    b. Need for motivation
    c. Need for affiliation
    d. Need for power

[RETHINK [R] Rethink]

In what ways do societal expectations, expressed by television shows and commercials, contribute to both obesity and excessive concern about weight loss? How could television contribute to better eating habits and attitudes toward weight? Should it be required to do so?

Answers to Evaluate Questions 1. hypothalamus; 2. weight set point; 3. metabolism; 4. false; 5. true; 6. achievement; 7. c.

KEY TERMS

Obesity LO23.1

Weight set point LO23.1

Metabolism LO23.1

Anorexia nervosa LO23.1

Bulimia LO23.1

Androgens LO23.2

Genitals LO23.2

Estrogens LO23.2

Progesterone LO23.2

Ovulation LO23.2

Masturbation LO23.2

Heterosexuality LO23.2

Double standard LO23.2

Extramarital sex LO23.2

Homosexuals LO23.2

Bisexuals LO23.2

Transgender LO23.2

Need for achievement LO23.3

Thematic Apperception Test LO23.3

Need for affiliation LO23.3

Need for power LO23.3

module 24

Understanding Emotional Experiences

Learning Outcomes Prepare

» **LO24.1** Define the range of emotions.

» **LO24.2** Explain the roots of emotions.

MODULE OUTLINE · Organize

Determining the Range of Emotions: Labeling Our Feelings

The Roots of Emotions

Exploring Diversity: Do People in All Cultures Express Emotion Similarly?

W Work

emotions Feelings that generally have both physiological and cognitive elements and that influence behavior

At one time or another, all of us have experienced the strong feelings that accompany both very pleasant and very negative experiences. Perhaps we have felt the thrill of getting a sought-after job, the joy of being in love, the sorrow over someone's death, or the anguish of inadvertently hurting someone. Moreover, we experience such reactions on a less intense level throughout our daily lives: the pleasure of a friendship, the enjoyment of a movie, and the embarrassment of breaking a borrowed item.

Despite the varied nature of these feelings, they all represent emotions. Although everyone has an idea of what an emotion is, formally defining the concept has proved to be an elusive task. Here, we'll use a general definition: **emotions** are feelings that generally have both physiological and cognitive elements and that influence behavior.

Think, for example, about how it feels to be happy. First, we obviously experience a feeling that we can differentiate from other emotions. It is likely that we also experience some identifiable physical changes in our bodies: perhaps the heart rate increases, or we find ourselves "jumping for joy." Finally, the emotion probably encompasses cognitive elements: our understanding and evaluation of the meaning of what is happening prompts our feelings of happiness.

Emotions are difficult to define or place. Even though it is a happy day, many people cry at weddings. Why do you think this is? © William Ju/Alamy Stock Photo RF

It is also possible, however, to experience an emotion without the presence of cognitive elements. For instance, we may react with fear to an unusual or novel situation (such as coming into contact with an erratic, unpredictable individual), or we may experience pleasure over sexual excitation without having cognitive awareness or understanding of just what makes the situation exciting (Kappas, 2011).

» LO24.1 Determining the Range of Emotions: Labeling Our Feelings

If we were to list the words in the English language that have been used to describe emotions, we would end up with at least 500 examples (Averill, 1975). The list would range from such obvious emotions as *happiness* and *fear* to less common ones, such as *adventurousness* and *pensiveness*.

One challenge for psychologists has been to sort through this list to identify the most important, fundamental emotions. Theorists have hotly contested the issue of cataloging emotions and have come up with different lists, depending on how they define the concept of emotion. In fact, some reject the question entirely, saying that no set of emotions should be singled out as most basic, and that emotions are best understood by breaking them down into their component parts. Other researchers argue for looking at emotions in terms of a hierarchy, dividing them into positive and negative categories, and then organizing them into increasingly narrower subcategories (see Figure 1; Manstead, Frijda, & Fischer, 2003; Dillard & Shen, 2007).

> One challenge for psychologists has been to sort through this list to identify the most important, fundamental emotions.

Still, most researchers suggest that a list of basic emotions would include, at a minimum, happiness, anger, fear, sadness, and disgust. Other lists are broader, including emotions such as surprise, contempt, guilt, and joy (Ekman, 1994a; Tracy & Robins, 2004; Greenberg, 2015).

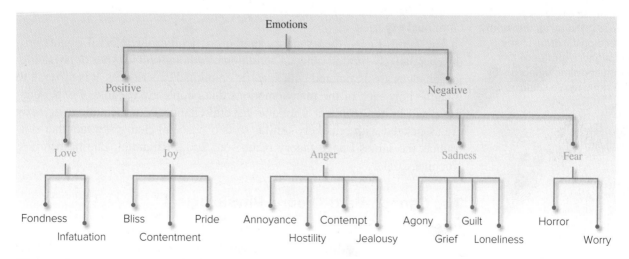

Figure 1 One approach to organizing emotions is to use a hierarchy, which divides emotions into increasingly narrow subcategories.

The Roots of Emotions

Although it is easy to describe the general physical reactions that accompany emotions, defining the specific role that those physiological responses play in the experience of emotions has proved to be a major puzzle for psychologists. As we shall see, some theorists suggest that specific bodily reactions cause us to experience a particular emotion—we experience fear, for instance, because the heart is pounding and we are breathing deeply. In contrast, other theorists suggest that the physiological reaction results from the experience of an emotion. In this view, we experience fear, and as a result the heart pounds and our breathing deepens.

The James-Lange Theory: Do Gut Reactions Equal Emotions?

To William James and Carl Lange, who were among the first researchers to explore the nature of emotions, emotional experience is, very simply, a reaction to instinctive bodily events that occur as a response to some situation or event in the environment. This view is summarized in James's statement, "we feel sorry because we cry, angry because we strike, afraid because we tremble" (James, 1890).

James and Lange took the view that the instinctive response of crying at a loss leads us to feel sorrow, that striking out at someone who frustrates us results in our feeling anger, that trembling at a menacing threat causes us to feel fear. They suggested that for every major emotion there is an accompanying physiological or "gut" reaction of internal organs—called a *visceral experience*. It is this specific pattern of visceral response that leads us to label the emotional experience.

In sum, James and Lange proposed that we experience emotions as a result of physiological changes that produce specific sensations. The brain interprets these sensations as specific kinds of emotional experiences (see the first part of Figure 2). This view has come to be called the **James-Lange theory of emotion** (Cobos et al., 2002; Stolorow & Stolorow, 2013).

The James-Lange theory has some serious drawbacks, however. For the theory to be valid, visceral changes would have to occur rapidly, because we experience some emotions—such as fear upon hearing a stranger rapidly approaching on a dark night—almost instantaneously. Yet some visceral changes occur slowly. Therefore, it's hard to see how they could be the source of immediate emotional experience.

The James-Lange theory poses another difficulty: our internal organs produce a relatively limited range of sensations. Although some types of physiological changes are associated with specific emotional experiences, it is difficult to imagine how each of the many emotions that people are capable of experiencing could be the result of a unique visceral change. Many emotions actually are associated with relatively similar sorts of visceral changes, a fact that contradicts the James-Lange theory (Cameron, 2002; Rinaman, Banihashemi, & Koehnle, 2011).

The Cannon-Bard Theory: Physiological Reactions as the Result of Emotions

In response to the difficulties inherent in the James-Lange theory, Walter Cannon, and later Philip Bard, suggested an alternative view. In what has come to be known as the **Cannon-Bard theory of emotion,** they proposed the model

James-Lange theory of emotion The belief that emotional experience is a reaction to bodily events occurring as a result of an external situation ("I feel sad because I am crying")

Cannon-Bard theory of emotion The belief that both physiological arousal and emotional experience are produced simultaneously by the same nerve stimulus

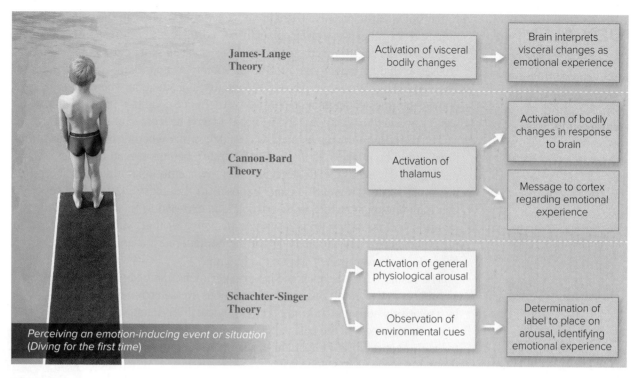

Figure 2 A comparison of three models of emotion. Photo: © Tomas Rodriguez/Getty Images

illustrated in the second part of Figure 2 (Cannon, 1929). This theory rejects the view that physiological arousal alone leads to the perception of emotion. Instead, the theory assumes that both physiological arousal *and* the emotional experience are produced simultaneously by the same nerve stimulus, which Cannon and Bard suggested emanates from the thalamus in the brain.

The theory states that after we perceive an emotion-producing stimulus, the thalamus is the initial site of the emotional response. Next, the thalamus sends a signal to the autonomic nervous system, thereby producing a visceral response. At the same time, the thalamus also communicates a message to the cerebral cortex regarding the nature of the emotion being experienced. Hence, it is not necessary for different emotions to have unique physiological patterns associated with them—as long as the message sent to the cerebral cortex differs according to the specific emotion.

The Cannon-Bard theory seems to have been accurate in rejecting the view that physiological arousal alone accounts for emotions. However, more recent research has led to some important modifications of the theory. For one thing, we now understand that the hypothalamus and the limbic system, not the thalamus, play a major role in emotional experience. In addition, the simultaneous occurrence of the physiological and emotional responses, which is a fundamental assumption of the Cannon-Bard theory, has yet to be demonstrated conclusively. This ambiguity has allowed room for yet another theory of emotions: the Schachter-Singer theory.

The Schachter-Singer Theory: Emotions as Labels

According to an explanation that focuses on the role of cognition, the **Schachter-Singer theory of emotion,** we identify the emotion we are experiencing by observing our environment and comparing ourselves with others (Schachter & Singer, 1962). Schachter and Singer's classic experiment found evidence for this hypothesis.

Schachter-Singer theory of emotion The belief that emotions are determined jointly by a nonspecific kind of physiological arousal and its interpretation, based on environmental cues

STUDY ALERT

Use Figure 2 to distinguish the three classic theories of emotion (James-Lange, Cannon-Bard, and Schachter-Singer).

In the study, participants were told that they would receive an injection of a vitamin. In reality, they were given epinephrine, a drug that causes responses that typically occur during strong emotional reactions, such as an increase in physiological arousal, including higher heart and respiration rates and a reddening of the face. The participants were then placed individually in a situation where a confederate of the experimenter acted in one of two ways. In one condition he acted angry and hostile, and in the other condition he behaved as if he were exuberantly happy.

The purpose of the experiment was to determine whether participants' emotions would be influenced by the confederate's behavior. And they were: when participants were asked to describe their own emotional state at the end of the experiment, those participants exposed to the angry confederate reported that they felt angry, while those participants exposed to the happy confederate reported feeling happy. In sum, the results suggest that participants turned to the environment and the behavior of the confederate for an explanation of the physiological arousal they were experiencing.

The results of the Schachter-Singer experiment, then, supported a cognitive view of emotions, in which emotions are determined jointly by a relatively nonspecific kind of physiological arousal and the labeling of that arousal on the basis of cues from the environment (refer to the third part of Figure 2). Later research has found that arousal is not as nonspecific as Schachter and Singer assumed. When the source of physiological arousal is unclear, however, we may look to our surroundings to determine just what we are experiencing.

From the perspective of . . .

An Advertising Assistant How might you use the findings by Schachter and Singer on the labeling of arousal to create interest in a product? Can you think of other examples whereby people's arousal could be manipulated, which would lead to different emotional responses?

© Yuri Arcurs/Getty Images RF

Contemporary Perspectives on the Neuroscience of Emotions

When Schachter and Singer carried out their groundbreaking experiment in the early 1960s, the ways in which they could evaluate the physiological changes that accompany emotion were relatively limited. However, advances in the measurement of the nervous system and other parts of the body have allowed researchers to examine more closely the biological responses involved in emotion. As a result, contemporary research on emotion points to a revision of earlier views that physiological responses associated with emotions are undifferentiated. Instead, evidence is growing that specific patterns of biological arousal are associated with individual emotions (Woodson, 2006; Stifter, Dollar, & Cipriano, 2011; Hildebrandt et al., 2016).

For instance, researchers have found that specific emotions produce activation of very different portions of the brain. In one study, participants undergoing positron emission tomography (PET) brain scans were asked to recall events, such as deaths and funerals, that made them feel sad, or events that made them feel happy, such as weddings and births. They also looked at photos of faces that appeared to be happy or sad. The results of the PET scans were clear: happiness was related to a decrease in activity in certain areas of the cerebral cortex, whereas sadness was associated with increases in activity in particular portions of the cortex (Hamann et al., 2002; Prohovnik et al., 2004; Johnston & Olson, 2015).

In addition, the *amygdala,* in the brain's temporal lobe, is important in the experience of emotions, for it provides a link between the perception of an emotion-producing stimulus and the recall of that stimulus later. For example, if we've once been attacked by a vicious pit bull, the amygdala processes that information and leads us to react with fear when we see a pit bull later—an example of a classically conditioned fear response (Miller et al., 2005; Berntson et al., 2007).

Because neural pathways connect the amygdala, the visual cortex, and the *hippocampus* (which plays an important role in the consolidation of memories), some scientists speculate that emotion-related stimuli can be processed and responded to almost instantaneously in specific areas of the brain (see Figure 3). This immediate response occurs so rapidly that higher-order, more rational thinking, which takes more time, seems not to be involved initially. In a slower, but more thoughtful, response to emotion-evoking stimuli, emotion-related sensory information is first evaluated and then sent on to the amygdala. It appears that the quicker system offers an immediate response to emotion-evoking stimuli, whereas the slower system helps confirm a threat and prepare a more thoughtful response (Dolan, 2002).

Making Sense of the Multiple Perspectives on Emotion

As new approaches to emotion continue to develop, it is reasonable to ask why so many theories of emotion exist and, perhaps more important, which one provides the most complete explanation. Actually, we have only scratched the surface. There are almost as many explanatory theories of emotion as there are individual emotions (e.g., Frijda, 2005; Prinz, 2007; Herzberg, 2009).

Why are theories of emotion so plentiful? For one thing, emotions are not a simple phenomenon but are intertwined closely with motivation, cognition, neuroscience, and a host of related branches of psychology. For example, evidence from brain-imaging studies shows that even when people come to supposedly rational, nonemotional decisions—such as making moral or philosophical judgments—emotions come into play (Greene et al., 2001).

Furthermore, contradictory evidence of one sort or another challenges each approach. Consequently, no theory has proved invariably accurate in its predictions.

This abundance of perspectives on emotion is not a cause for despair—or unhappiness, fear, or any other negative emotion. It simply reflects the fact that psychology is an evolving, developing science. As we gather more evidence, specific answers to questions about the nature of emotions will become clearer.

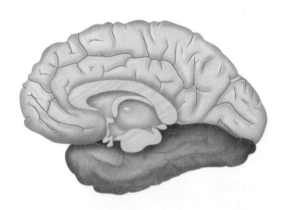

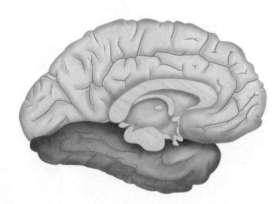

Figure 3 Experiencing different emotions activates particular areas of the brain, as these illustrations of scans show. Source: Adapted from George et al., 1995

EXPLORING diversity

Do People in All Cultures Express Emotion Similarly?

Consider, for a moment, the six photos displayed in Figure 4. Can you identify the emotions being expressed by the person in each of the photos?

If you are a good judge of facial expressions, you will conclude that these expressions display six of the basic emotions: happiness, anger, sadness, surprise, disgust, and fear. Hundreds of studies of nonverbal behavior show that these emotions are consistently distinct and identifiable, even by untrained observers (Ekman & O'Sullivan, 1991; Leu, Wang, & Koo, 2011).

Interestingly, these six emotions are not unique to members of Western cultures; rather, they constitute the basic emotions expressed universally by members of the human race, regardless of where individuals have been raised and what learning experiences they have had. Psychologist Paul Ekman convincingly demonstrated this point when he studied the members of an isolated New Guinea jungle tribe who had had almost no contact with Westerners (Ekman, 1972). The people of the tribe did not speak or understand English, had never seen a movie, and had had very limited experience with Caucasians before Ekman's arrival. Yet their nonverbal responses to emotion-evoking stories, as well as their ability to identify basic emotions, were quite similar to those of Westerners.

Being so isolated, the New Guineans could not have learned from Westerners to recognize or produce similar facial expressions. Instead, their similar abilities and manner of responding emotionally appear to have been present innately. Although one could argue that similar experiences in both cultures led the members of each one to learn similar types of nonverbal behavior, this appears unlikely, because the two cultures are so very different. The expression of basic

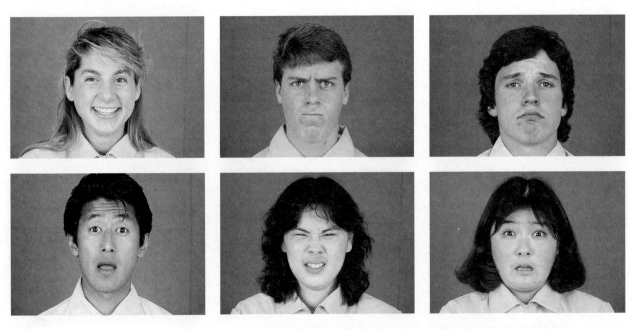

Figure 4 These photos demonstrate six of the primary emotions: happiness, anger, sadness, surprise, disgust, and fear. (all photos) © Matsumoto Photos 1988

emotions, then, seems to be universal (Ekman, 1994b; Izard, 1994; Matsumoto, 2002).

Why do people across cultures express emotions similarly? A hypothesis known as the **facial-affect program** gives one explanation. The facial-affect program—which is assumed to be universally present at birth—is analogous to a computer program that is turned on when a particular emotion is experienced. When set in motion, the "program" activates a set of nerve impulses that make the face display an appropriate expression. Each primary emotion produces a unique set of muscular movements, forming the kinds of expressions shown in Figure 4. For example, the emotion of happiness is universally displayed by movement of the zygomatic major, a muscle that raises the corners of the mouth—forming what we would call a smile (Ekman, 2003; Kim, Kim, & Kim, 2007; Kendler et al., 2008).

"And just exactly what is that expression intended to convey?"

The importance of facial expressions is illustrated by an intriguing notion known as the **facial-feedback hypothesis.** According to this hypothesis, facial expressions not only *reflect* emotional experience, they also help *determine* how people experience and label emotions (Izard, 1990). Basically put, "wearing" an emotional expression provides muscular feedback to the brain that helps produce an emotion congruent with that expression (Davis, Senghas, & Ochsner, 2009; Balconi, Bortolotti, & Crivelli, 2013).

For instance, the muscles activated when we smile may send a message to the brain indicating the experience of happiness—even if there is nothing in the environment that would produce that particular emotion. Some theoreticians have gone further, suggesting that facial expressions are *necessary* for an emotion to be experienced (Rinn, 1984, 1991). According to this view, if no facial expression is present, the emotion cannot be felt.

Support for the facial-feedback hypothesis comes from a classic experiment carried out by Paul Ekman and colleagues (Ekman, Levenson, & Friesen, 1983). In the study, professional actors were asked to follow very explicit instructions regarding the movements of muscles in their faces. You might try this example yourself:

- Raise your brows and pull them together.
- Raise your upper eyelids.
- Now stretch your lips horizontally back toward your ears.

After carrying out these directions—which, as you may have guessed, are meant to produce an expression of fear—the actors' heart rates rose and their body temperatures declined, physiological reactions that characterize fear. Overall, facial expressions representing the primary emotions produced physiological effects similar to those accompanying the genuine emotions in other circumstances (Keillor et al., 2002; Soussignan, 2002).

facial-affect program Activation of a set of nerve impulses that make the face display the appropriate expression

facial-feedback hypothesis The hypothesis that facial expressions not only reflect emotional experience but also help determine how people experience and label emotions

RECAP

Define the range of emotions.

- Emotions are broadly defined as feelings that may affect behavior and generally have both a physiological component and a cognitive component.

Explain the roots of emotions.

- Several theories explain emotions. The James-Lange theory suggests that emotional experience is a reaction to bodily, or visceral, changes that occur as a response to an environmental event and are interpreted as an emotional response.

- In contrast, the Cannon-Bard theory contends that both physiological arousal and an emotional experience are produced simultaneously by the same nerve stimulus and that the visceral experience does not necessarily differ among differing emotions.

- The Schachter-Singer theory suggests that emotions are determined jointly by a relatively nonspecific physiological arousal and the subsequent labeling of that arousal, using cues from the environment to determine how others are behaving in the same situation.

- The most recent approaches to emotions focus on their biological origins. For instance, it now seems that specific patterns of biological arousal are associated with individual emotions. Furthermore, new scanning techniques have identified the specific parts of the brain that are activated during the experience of particular emotions.

- A person's facial expressions can reveal emotions. In fact, members of different cultures understand the emotional expressions of others in similar ways. One explanation for this similarity is that an innate facial-affect program activates a set of muscle movements representing the emotion being experienced.

- The facial-feedback hypothesis suggests that facial expressions not only reflect, but also produce, emotional experiences.

[EVALUATE E Evaluate]

1. Emotions are always accompanied by a cognitive response. True or false?
2. The _____ _____ theory of emotions states that emotions are a response to instinctive bodily events.
3. According to the _____ _____ theory of emotion, both an emotional response and physiological arousal are produced simultaneously by the same nerve stimulus.
4. Your friend—a psychology major—tells you, "I was at a party last night. During the course of the evening, my general level of arousal increased. Since I was at a party where people were enjoying themselves, I assume I must have felt happy." What theory of emotion does your friend subscribe to?
5. What are the six primary emotions that can be identified from facial expressions?

[RETHINK R Rethink]

If researchers learned how to control emotional responses so that targeted emotions could be caused or prevented, what ethical concerns might arise? Under what circumstances, if any, should such techniques be used?

Answers to Evaluate Questions 1. false; emotions may occur without a cognitive response; 2. James-Lange; 3. Cannon-Bard; 4. Schachter-Singer; 5. surprise, sadness, happiness, anger, disgust, and fear

KEY TERMS

Emotions LO24.1

James-Lange theory of emotion LO24.2

Cannon-Bard theory of emotion LO24.2

Schachter-Singer theory of emotion LO24.2

Facial-affect program LO24.2

Facial-feedback hypothesis LO24.2

Psychology on the Web

1. Find two different websites that deal with nonverbal behavior. One site should present a fairly "academic" discussion of the topic, and the other should be more informal. (Hint: The terms *nonverbal behavior* and *nonverbal communication* may lead you to more formal discussions of the topic, whereas *body language* may lead you to less formal discussions.) Compare and contrast your findings from the two sites.

2. Use the Web to find instances where politicians have displayed emotions publicly. Discuss how attitudes toward emotional displays such as crying by both male and female politicians is interpreted differently.

the case of . . .

MARIA TOKARSKI, THE HAPPIEST LOSER

Maria Tokarski had been a normal weight for her height throughout much of her life, but after her first child was born she found that she just couldn't lose the extra weight she had gained during her pregnancy. Caring for an infant took a lot of her time and energy, and she wasn't as focused on her health and appearance as she once had been. Rather than returning to her normal weight, Maria slowly gained more until she was almost twice her prepregnancy weight.

Maria's weight gain affected her mood, her social life, and even her marriage. But when her physician delivered the news that it was affecting her health, Maria found the determination to make a change. It took almost two years of regular exercise, careful monitoring of her diet, and regular support group meetings, but Maria eventually returned to her former slim figure. On her son's fifth birthday, Maria pulled out her favorite pair of jeans that had been in storage since just before her maternity days and was overjoyed to find that they finally fit her once again!

1. What may have been some of the motivational and environmental factors contributing to Maria's weight gain after childbirth?

2. If you were Maria's physician, how would you explain to her the weight-set-point hypothesis?

3. Which approaches to motivation might help to explain Maria's unflagging determination to lose all the weight she had gained, and why?

4. If Maria were your friend and she asked your advice on weight-loss strategies, what would you tell her?

5. In what ways do you think emotion was tied in to Maria's weight gain and her subsequent weight loss?

profiles of **SUCCESS**

Courtesy of Stephanie C. Lewis

NAME:	Stephanie C. Lewis
SCHOOL:	Bryant & Stratton Career College
DEGREE PROGRAM:	AAS, Medical Assisting

Older students returning to school face unique challenges, and for Stephanie Lewis some of those challenges included dealing with personal family issues.

"When I began the path to obtain my degree I was going through a painful separation with my husband, and was also caring for my mother who had serious health issues," Lewis said. "If those challenges weren't enough, I had no income at the time and three children to care for."

Having committed herself to pursing a degree and furthering her education, Lewis set firm goals for herself that helped her focus on her studies.

"I learned very early on that in order to do well I had to be serious about my studies, and for me that meant sacrifice," she noted. "While many of my peers were busy 'enjoying life,' I had my nose in my books, often reading and re-reading important information in order to absorb and fully understand the meaning behind it."

Being a mother, caregiver, full-time student, and part-time employee, Lewis had to tackle time management, a major challenge for her.

"I had my hands full to say the least. Learning to put my priorities in order and to recognize my limitations went a long way in helping to balance my life," she said. "Since my education was definitely at the top of my priority list, I made sure to do my assignments as early as I was able, and stayed ahead of my reading so I didn't fall behind."

Through her college experience Lewis learned that she could be strong, intelligent, and successful, and no longer felt she had to be invisible to make others feel comfortable about themselves.

"I would definitely tell other students, no matter your circumstances, this is your future," she said. "Develop a strong routine and stick to it no matter what, and utilize all of the resources available to you. Get determined and stay determined to succeed, because you can do it no matter the odds."

[RETHINK R Rethink]

Using her knowledge of the motives that underlie behavior, how might Lewis advise another person embarking on a new course in life?

In reading Lewis's story, how does she keep herself motivated to achieve her goals?

visual summary 7
MOTIVATION AND EMOTION

MODULE 22 Explaining Motivation

Motivation: The factors that direct and energize the behavior of humans and other organisms

└─ • The major approaches to motivation

Instinct
People and animals are born with preprogrammed sets of behaviors essential to their survival.

Drive reduction
When some basic biological requirement is lacking, a drive is produced.

Arousal
People seek an optimal level of stimulation. If the level of stimulation is too high, they act to reduce it; if it is too low, they act to increase it.

Incentive
External rewards direct and energize behavior.

Cognitive
Thoughts, beliefs, expectations, and goals direct motivation.

Hierarchy of needs
Needs form a hierarchy; before higher-order needs are met, lower-order needs must be fulfilled.

MODULE 23 Human Needs and Motivation

Motivation Behind Hunger and Eating: Obesity has reached epidemic proportions

├─ • Factors that affect eating
│   ├─ • Biological factors
│   └─ • Social factors and learned eating behaviors
└─ • Eating disorders
    ├─ • Anorexia nervosa
    └─ • Bulimia

Sexual Motivation

├─ • Men and women differ in hormone production
├─ • Masturbation: high incidence
├─ • Heterosexuality: sexual attraction to the other sex
├─ • Marital sex
├─ • Homosexuality: sexual attraction to one's own sex
├─ • Bisexuality: sexual attraction to both sexes
└─ • Transgenderism: persons whose gender identity, gender expression, or behavior does not conform to that associated with the sex to which they were assigned at birth

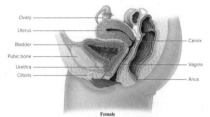

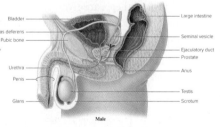

Needs for Achievement, Affiliation, and Power:
Striving for excellence Maintaining relationships

Basic Emotions

- Happiness
- Anger
- Fear
- Sadness
- Surprise
- Disgust

Theories of Emotions

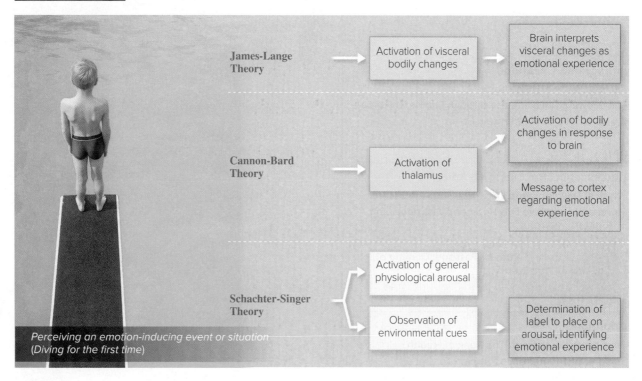

James-Lange Theory → Activation of visceral bodily changes → Brain interprets visceral changes as emotional experience

Cannon-Bard Theory → Activation of thalamus → Activation of bodily changes in response to brain / Message to cortex regarding emotional experience

Schachter-Singer Theory → Activation of general physiological arousal / Observation of environmental cues → Determination of label to place on arousal, identifying emotional experience

Perceiving an emotion-inducing event or situation (Diving for the first time)

(MODULE 22) © Digital Vision/PunchStock RF; © Digital Vision/Getty Images RF; © BananaStock/JupiterImages RF; © LCPL Casey N. Thurston, USMC/DoD Media; © Corbis; (MODULE 24) © Tomas Rodriguez/Getty Images

© Jose Luis Pelaez Inc/Getty Images RF

Still Dashing at 100

Don Pellman broke 27 seconds in the 100-meter dash at the San Diego Senior Olympics—a record for his age group. Not bad for a man who has lived 100 years. He also broke records in shot-put, discus, the long jump, and the high jump. His only disappointment came when he failed to break the pole vault record after three tries. His conclusion? He needs more practice.

Although Pellman wears a hearing aid, he shows very little bone or muscle degeneration—certainly far less than most of his peer group. A gymnast and high jumper in college, Pellman cut short his athletic career to take a job during the Depression. When he retired in 1970, one of his children suggested he enter a masters track meet. He's been running ever since (Crouse, 2015).

DEVELOPMENT

Looking Ahead

Many people dread growing older. They imagine themselves slowing down and losing their strength. They fear their health will deteriorate and they will no longer be independent. But as Don Pellman proves, later adulthood can be filled with new activities and challenges—and although hair thins and grays, regularly exercising the body can sustain and enhance one's genetic inheritance.

Pellman's continual striving to improve his performance and set new records gets to the heart of one of the broadest and most important areas of psychology: *developmental psychology.*

Developmental psychology is the branch of psychology that studies the patterns of growth and change that occur throughout life. It deals with issues ranging from new ways of conceiving children, to learning how to raise children most sensibly, to understanding the milestones of life that we all face.

Developmental psychologists study the interaction between the unfolding of biologically predetermined patterns of behavior and a constantly changing, dynamic environment. They ask how our genetic background affects our behavior throughout our lives and whether heredity limits our potential. Similarly, they seek to understand the way in which the environment works with—or against—our genetic capabilities, how the world we live in affects our development, and how we can be encouraged to reach our full potential.

We begin by examining the approaches developmental psychologists use to study the environmental and genetic factors: the nature–nurture issue. Then we consider the very start of development, beginning with conception and the nine months of life before birth. We look at both genetic and environmental influences on the unborn individual and the way they can affect behavior throughout the remainder of the life cycle.

Next, we examine development that occurs after birth: the enormous and rapid growth that takes place during the early stages of life and the physical, social, and cognitive change throughout infancy, toddlerhood, and middle childhood. We then move on to development from adolescence through adulthood. We end with a discussion of the ways in which people prepare themselves for death.

Nature, Nurture, and Prenatal Development

Learning Outcomes  Prepare

>> **LO25.1** Compare and contrast the influence of nature versus nurture.

>> **LO25.2** Describe developmental research techniques.

>> **LO25.3** Discuss prenatal development.

MODULE OUTLINE  Organize

Determining the Relative Influence of Nature and Nurture

Developmental Research Techniques

Prenatal Development: Conception to Birth

W Work

developmental psychology The branch of psychology that studies the patterns of growth and change that occur throughout life

How many bald, six-foot-six, 250-pound volunteer firefighters in New Jersey wear droopy mustaches, aviator-style eyeglasses, and a key ring on the right side of the belt?

The answer is two: Gerald Levey and Mark Newman. They are twins who were separated at birth. Each twin did not even know the other existed until they were reunited—in a fire station—by a fellow firefighter. . . .

The lives of the twins, although separate, took remarkably similar paths. Levey went to college, studying forestry; Newman planned to study forestry in college but instead took a job trimming trees. . . . Both men are unmarried and find the same kind of woman attractive: "tall, slender, long hair." They share similar hobbies, enjoying hunting, fishing, going to the beach, and watching old John Wayne movies and professional wrestling. Both like Chinese food and drink the same brand of beer.

The remarkable range of similarities we see in many pairs of identical twins raises one of the fundamental questions posed by **developmental psychology,** the study of the patterns of growth and change that occur throughout life. The question is this: How can we distinguish between the *environmental* causes of behavior (the influence of parents, siblings, family, friends, schooling, nutrition, and all the other experiences to which a child is exposed) and *hereditary* causes (those based on an individual's genetic makeup that influence growth

Gerald Levey and Mark Newman. © Thomas Wanstall/The Image Works

and development throughout life)? This question embodies the **nature–nurture issue.** In this context, nature refers to hereditary factors, and nurture to environmental influences.

Although the question was first posed as a nature-*versus*-nurture issue, developmental psychologists today agree that *both* nature and nurture interact to produce specific developmental patterns and outcomes. Consequently, the question has evolved into: *How and to what degree* do environment and heredity both produce their effects? No one develops free of environmental influences, or without being affected by his or her inherited *genetic makeup.* However, the debate over the comparative influence of the two factors remains active, with different approaches and different theories of development emphasizing the environment or heredity to a greater or lesser degree (Perovic & Radenovic, 2011; Gruber, 2013; Limberg, 2015).

For example, some developmental theories rely on basic psychological principles of learning and stress the role learning plays in producing changes in a developing child's behavior. Such theories emphasize the role of the environment in development. In contrast, other developmental theories emphasize the influence of one's physiological makeup and functioning on development. Such theories stress the role of heredity and *maturation*—the unfolding of biologically predetermined patterns of behavior—in producing developmental change. Maturation can be seen, for instance, in the development of sex characteristics (such as breasts and body hair) that occurs at the start of adolescence.

Despite their differences over theory, developmental psychologists concur on some points. They agree that genetic factors not only provide the potential for specific behaviors or traits to emerge, but also place limitations on the emergence of such behavior or traits. For instance, heredity defines people's general level of intelligence, setting an upper limit that—regardless of the quality of the environment—people cannot exceed. Heredity also places limits on physical abilities; humans simply cannot run at a speed of 60 miles an hour, nor will they grow as tall as 10 feet, no matter what the quality of their environment (Dodge, 2004; Pinker, 2004; Loehlin et al., 2015).

Figure 1 lists some of the characteristics most affected by heredity. As you consider these items, it is important to keep in mind that these characteristics are not *entirely* determined by heredity, for environmental factors also play a role.

STUDY ALERT

The nature–nurture issue is a key question that is pervasive throughout the field of psychology, asking how and to what degree environment and heredity produce their joint effects.

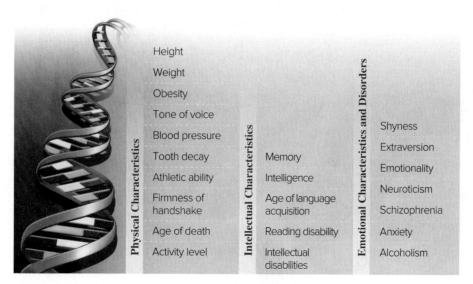

Figure 1 Characteristics influenced significantly by genetic factors. Although these characteristics have strong genetic components, they are also affected by environmental factors.

Developmental psychologists also agree that in most instances environmental factors play a critical role in enabling people to reach the potential capabilities that their genetic background makes possible. If Albert Einstein had received no intellectual stimulation as a child and had not been sent to school, it is unlikely that he would have reached his genetic potential. Similarly, a great athlete such as baseball star Derek Jeter would have been unlikely to display much physical skill if he had not been raised in an environment that nurtured his innate talent and gave him the opportunity to train and perfect his natural abilities.

Clearly, the relationship between heredity and environment is far from simple. As a consequence, developmental psychologists typically take an *interactionist* position on the nature–nurture issue by suggesting that a combination of hereditary and environmental factors influences development. Developmental psychologists face the challenge of identifying the relative strength of each of these influences on the individual, as well as that of identifying the specific changes that occur over the course of development (McGregor & Capone, 2004; Moffitt, Caspi, & Rutter, 2006; Kashima, 2016).

© Cade Martin/Getty Images RF

From the perspective of . . .

A Child-Care Provider Consider what factors might determine why a child is not learning to walk at the same pace as his peers. What kinds of environmental influences might be involved? What kinds of genetic influences might be involved? What recommendations might you make to the child's parents about the situation?

» LO25.1 Determining the Relative Influence of Nature and Nurture

Developmental psychologists use several approaches to determine the relative influence of genetic and environmental factors on behavior. In one approach, researchers can experimentally control the genetic makeup of laboratory animals by carefully breeding them for specific traits. For instance, by observing animals with identical genetic backgrounds placed in varied environments, researchers can learn the effects of specific kinds of environmental stimulation. Although researchers must be careful when generalizing the findings of nonhuman research to a human population, findings from animal research provide important information that cannot be obtained, for ethical reasons, by using human participants.

identical twins Twins who are exactly the same genetically

© Hero/Corbis/Glow Images RF

Human twins serve as another important source of information about the relative effects of genetic and environmental factors. If **identical twins** (those who are genetically identical) display different patterns of development, those differences have to be attributed to variations in the environment in which the twins were raised. The most useful data come from identical twins who are adopted at birth by different sets of adoptive parents and raised apart in differing environments. Studies of nontwin siblings who are raised in totally different environments also shed some light on the issue. Because they have relatively similar genetic backgrounds, siblings who show similarities as adults provide strong evidence for the importance of heredity (Sternberg, 2002a; Vitaro, Brendgen, & Arseneault, 2009).

Researchers can also take the opposite tack. Instead of concentrating on people with similar genetic backgrounds who are raised in different environments, they may consider people raised in similar environments who have totally dissimilar genetic backgrounds. For example, if they find similar courses of development in two adopted children who have different genetic backgrounds and have been raised in the same family, they have evidence for the importance of environmental influences on development (Greven, Rijsdijk, & Plomin, 2011; Farnsworth, 2015).

» LO25.2 Developmental Research Techniques

Because of the demands of measuring behavioral change across different ages, developmental researchers use several unique methods. The most frequently used, **cross-sectional research,** compares people of different ages at the same point in time. Cross-sectional studies provide information about differences in development between different age groups (Creasey, 2005; Huijie, 2006).

Suppose, for instance, we were interested in the development of intellectual ability in adulthood. To carry out a cross-sectional study, we might compare a sample of 25-, 45-, and 65-year-olds who all take the same IQ test. We then can determine whether average IQ test scores differ in each age group.

Cross-sectional research has limitations, however. For instance, we cannot be sure that the differences in IQ scores we might find in our example are due to age differences alone. Instead, the scores may reflect differences in the educational attainment of the cohorts represented. A *cohort* is a group of people who grow up at similar times, in similar places, and in similar conditions. In the case of IQ differences, any age differences we find in a cross-sectional study may reflect educational differences among the cohorts studied: people in the older age group may belong to a cohort that was less likely to attend college than were the people in the younger groups.

A longitudinal study, the second major research strategy developmental psychologists use, provides one way around this problem. **Longitudinal research** traces the behavior of one or more participants as the participants age. Longitudinal studies assess *change* in behavior over time, whereas cross-sectional studies assess *differences* among groups of people.

For instance, consider how we might investigate intellectual development during adulthood by using a longitudinal research strategy. First, we might give an IQ test to a group of 25-year-olds. We'd then come back to the same people 20 years later and retest them at age 45. Finally, we'd return to them once more when they were 65 years old and test them again.

By examining changes at several points in time, we can clearly see how individuals develop. Unfortunately, longitudinal research requires an enormous expenditure of time (as the researcher waits for the participants to get older. Participants who begin a study at an early age may drop out, move away, or even die as the research continues. Moreover, participants who take the same test at several points in time may become "test-wise" and perform better each time they take it because they have become more familiar with the test.

cross-sectional research A research method that compares people of different ages at the same point in time

longitudinal research A research method that investigates behavior as participants age

STUDY ALERT

Be able to distinguish the three different types of developmental research—cross-sectional (comparing people of different ages at the same time); longitudinal (studying participants as they age); and sequential (a combination of cross-sectional and longitudinal).

sequential research A research method that combines cross-sectional and longitudinal research by considering a number of different age groups and examining them at several points in time

chromosomes Rod-shaped structures that contain all basic hereditary information

genes The parts of the chromosomes through which genetic information is transmitted

To make up for the limitations in both cross-sectional and longitudinal research, investigators have devised an alternative strategy. Known as **sequential research,** it combines cross-sectional and longitudinal approaches by examining a number of different age groups at several points in time. For example, investigators might examine a group of 3-, 5-, and 7-year-olds every six months for a period of several years. This technique allows a developmental psychologist to tease out the specific effects of age changes from other possibly influential factors.

≫ LO25.3 Prenatal Development: Conception to Birth

Our increasing understanding of the first stirrings of life spent inside a mother's womb has permitted significant medical advances in prenatal care and childbirth. Yet our increasing knowledge of the biology of *conception*—when a male's sperm cell penetrates a female's egg cell—and its aftermath make the start of life no less of a miracle. Let's consider how an individual is created by looking first at the genetic endowment that a child receives at the moment of conception.

The Basics of Genetics

The one-cell entity established at conception contains 23 pairs of **chromosomes,** rod-shaped structures that contain all basic hereditary information. One member of each pair is from the mother, and the other is from the father.

Each chromosome contains thousands of **genes**—smaller units through which genetic information is transmitted. Either individually or in combination, genes produce each person's unique characteristics. Composed of sequences of *DNA (deoxyribonucleic acid)* molecules, genes are the biological equivalent of "software" that programs the future development of all parts of the body's hardware. Humans have 20,000 to 25,000 different genes (see Figure 2).

Some genes control the development of systems common to all members of the human species—the heart, circulatory system, brain, lungs, and so forth;

STUDY ALERT

It's important to understand the basic building blocks of genetics: chromosomes, which contain genes, which in turn are composed of sequences of DNA.

(A) Conception   (B) 23 pairs of chromosomes   (C) DNA sequence   (D) Genes

Figure 2   Every individual's characteristics are determined by the individual's specific genetic information. At the moment of conception (A), humans receive 23 pairs of chromosomes (B), half from the mother and half from the father. These chromosomes are made up of coils of DNA (C). Each chromosome contains thousands of genes (D) that "program" the future development of the body. (A) © Don W. Fawcett/Science Source; (B) © L. Willatt/East Anglian Regional Genetics Service/Science Source; (C) © Kenneth Eward/BioGrafx/Science Source; (D) © Biophoto Associates/Science Source

others shape the characteristics that make each human unique, such as facial configuration, height, and eye color. The child's sex is also determined by a particular combination of genes. Specifically, a child inherits an X chromosome from its mother and either an X or a Y chromosome from its father. When it receives an XX combination, it is a female; with an XY combination, it develops as a male. Male development is triggered by a single gene on the Y chromosome, and without the presence of that specific gene, the individual will develop as a female.

As behavioral geneticists have discovered, genes are also at least partially responsible for a wide variety of personal characteristics, including cognitive abilities, personality traits, and psychological disorders. Of course, few of these characteristics are determined by a single gene. Instead, most traits result from a combination of multiple genes that operate together with environmental influences (Ramus, 2006; Armbruster et al., 2011; Kazantseva et al., 2015).

> As behavioral geneticists have discovered, genes are also at least partially responsible for a wide variety of personal characteristics, including cognitive abilities, personality traits, and psychological disorders.

The Earliest Development

When an egg becomes fertilized by the sperm, the resulting one-celled entity, called a **zygote,** immediately begins to develop. The zygote starts out as a microscopic speck. Three days after fertilization, though, the zygote increases to around 32 cells, and within a week it has grown to 100–150 cells. These first two weeks are known as the *germinal period.*

Two weeks after conception, the developing individual enters the *embryonic period,* which lasts from week 2 through week 8, and he or she is now called an **embryo.** As an embryo develops through an intricate, preprogrammed process of cell division, it grows 10,000 times larger by 4 weeks of age and attains a length of about one-fifth of an inch. At this point it has developed a rudimentary beating heart, a brain, an intestinal tract, and a number of other organs. Although all these organs are at a primitive stage of development, they are clearly recognizable. Moreover, by week 8, the embryo is about an inch long, and has discernible arms, legs, and a face.

From week 8 and continuing until birth, the developing individual enters the *fetal period* and is called a **fetus.** At the start of this period, it begins to respond to touch; it bends its fingers when touched on the hand. At 16 to 18 weeks, its movements become strong enough for the mother to sense them. At the same time, hair may begin to grow on its head, and the facial features become similar to those the child will display at birth. The major organs begin functioning, although the fetus could not be kept alive outside the mother. In addition, a lifetime's worth of brain neurons are produced—although it is unclear whether the brain is capable of thinking at this early stage.

Within the womb the fetus continues to develop before birth. It begins to grow fatty deposits under the skin, and it gains weight. The fetus reaches the **age of viability,** the point at which it can survive if born prematurely, at about prenatal age 22 weeks. By week 24, a fetus has many of the characteristics it will display as a newborn. In fact, when an infant is born prematurely at this age, it can open and close its eyes; suck; cry; look up, down, and around; and even grasp objects placed in its hands.

Before birth, a fetus passes through several *sensitive periods* (also referred to as *critical periods*). A sensitive period is the time when organisms are particularly susceptible to certain kinds of stimuli. For example, fetuses are especially affected

zygote The new cell formed by the union of an egg and sperm

embryo A developed zygote that has a primitive heart, a brain, and other organs

fetus A developing individual, from eight weeks after conception until birth

age of viability The point at which a fetus can survive if born prematurely

by their mothers' use of drugs during certain sensitive periods before birth. If they are exposed to a particular drug before or after the sensitive period, it may have relatively little impact, but if exposure comes during a critical period, the impact will be significant (Uylings, 2006; Chaudhury et al., 2010; Sandman, 2015).

Sensitive periods can also occur after birth. Some language specialists suggest, for instance, that there is a period in which children are particularly receptive to developing language. If children are not exposed to appropriate linguistic stimuli, their language development may be impaired (Sohr-Preston & Scaramella, 2006; Innocenti, 2007; Gilley et al., 2010).

In the final weeks of pregnancy, the fetus continues to gain weight and grow. At the end of the normal 38 weeks of pregnancy, a fetus typically weighs around 7 pounds and is about 20 inches in length. However, the story is different for *preterm infants,* who are born before week 38. Because they have not been able to develop fully, they are at higher risk for illness, future problems, and even death. For infants who have been in the womb for more than 30 weeks, the prospects are relatively good. However, for those born before week 30, the story is often less positive. Such newborns, who may weigh as little as 2 pounds at birth, are in grave danger because they have immature organs; they have less than a 50-50 chance of survival. If they do survive—and it takes extraordinarily heroic (and expensive) medical intervention to assure this—they may later experience significant developmental delays.

Genetic Influences on the Fetus

The process of fetal growth that we have just described reflects normal development, which occurs in 95 to 98 percent of all pregnancies. Some individuals are less fortunate, for in the remaining 2 to 5 percent of cases, children are born with serious birth defects. A major cause of such defects is faulty genes or chromosomes. Here are some of the more common genetic and chromosomal difficulties.

- *Phenylketonuria (PKU).* A child born with the inherited disease phenylketonuria cannot produce an enzyme that is required for normal development. This deficiency results in an accumulation of poisons that eventually cause profound intellectual disabilities. The disease is treatable, however, if it is caught early. Most infants today are routinely tested for PKU, and children with the disorder can be placed on a special diet that allows them to develop normally (Widaman, 2009; Waisbren, 2011; Diesen, 2016).

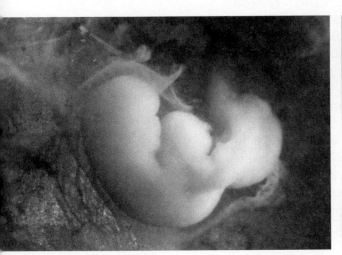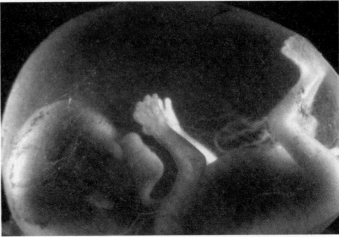

These remarkable photos of live fetuses display the degree of physical development at prenatal ages 4 and 15 weeks. (first) © Petit Format/Science Source; (second) © Claude Edelmann/Science Source

- *Sickle-cell anemia.* About 10 percent of the African American population has the possibility of passing on sickle-cell anemia, a disease that gets its name from the abnormally shaped red blood cells it causes. Children with the disease may have episodes of pain, yellowish eyes, stunted growth, and vision problems (Selove, 2007; Puffer, Schatz & Roberts, 2010; Wills, 2013).

- *Tay-Sachs disease.* Children born with Tay-Sachs disease, a disorder most often found in Jews of Eastern European ancestry, usually die by age 3 or 4 because of the body's inability to break down fat. If both parents carry the genetic defect that produces the fatal illness, their child has a 1 in 4 chance of being born with the disease (McPartland, 2016).

- *Down syndrome.* Down syndrome, one of the causes of severe mental disabilities, occurs when the zygote receives an extra chromosome at the moment of conception. Down syndrome is often related to the mother's age; mothers over 35 and younger than 18 stand a higher risk than other women of having a child with the syndrome (Roizen & Patterson, 2003; Sherman et al., 2007).

Prenatal Environmental Influences

Genetic factors are not the only causes of difficulties in fetal development. Environmental influences—the *nurture* part of the nature–nurture equation—also affect the fetus. Some of the more profound consequences are brought about by **teratogens,** environmental agents such as a drug, chemical, virus, or other factor that produce a birth defect. Among the major prenatal environmental influences on the fetus are the following:

> **Genetic factors are not the only causes of difficulties in fetal development.**

teratogens Environmental agents such as a drug, chemical, virus, or other factor that produce a birth defect

- *Mother's nutrition.* What a mother eats during her pregnancy can have important implications for the health of her baby. Seriously undernourished mothers cannot provide adequate nutrition to a growing fetus, and they are likely to give birth to underweight babies. Poorly nourished babies are also more susceptible to disease (Najman et al., 2004; Everette, 2008).

- *Mother's illness.* Several diseases can have devastating consequences for a developing fetus if they are contracted during the early part of a pregnancy. For example, rubella (German measles), syphilis, diabetes, and high blood pressure may each produce a permanent effect on the fetus (Nesheim et al., 2004; Magoni et al., 2005; Nyaradi et al., 2013).

- *Alcohol.* Alcohol is extremely dangerous to fetal development. For example, as many as 1.5 out of every 1,000 infants is born with *fetal alcohol syndrome disorder (FASD),* a condition resulting in below-average intelligence, growth delays, and facial deformities. FASD is now the primary preventable cause of intellectual disability. Even mothers who use small amounts of alcohol during pregnancy place their child at risk (Niccols, 2007; Murthy et al., 2009; Lewis et al., 2015).

- *Nicotine use.* Pregnant mothers who smoke put their children at considerable risk. Smoking while pregnant can lead to miscarriage and infant death. For children who do survive, the negative consequences of mother's tobacco use can last a lifetime (Shea & Steiner, 2008; Rogers, 2009; Magee et al., 2013).

Several other environmental factors have an impact on the child before and during birth (see Figure 3). Keep in mind that although we have been discussing

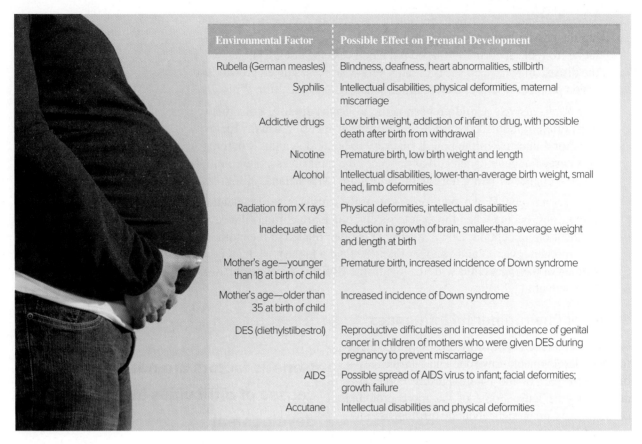

Environmental Factor	Possible Effect on Prenatal Development
Rubella (German measles)	Blindness, deafness, heart abnormalities, stillbirth
Syphilis	Intellectual disabilities, physical deformities, maternal miscarriage
Addictive drugs	Low birth weight, addiction of infant to drug, with possible death after birth from withdrawal
Nicotine	Premature birth, low birth weight and length
Alcohol	Intellectual disabilities, lower-than-average birth weight, small head, limb deformities
Radiation from X rays	Physical deformities, intellectual disabilities
Inadequate diet	Reduction in growth of brain, smaller-than-average weight and length at birth
Mother's age—younger than 18 at birth of child	Premature birth, increased incidence of Down syndrome
Mother's age—older than 35 at birth of child	Increased incidence of Down syndrome
DES (diethylstilbestrol)	Reproductive difficulties and increased incidence of genital cancer in children of mothers who were given DES during pregnancy to prevent miscarriage
AIDS	Possible spread of AIDS virus to infant; facial deformities; growth failure
Accutane	Intellectual disabilities and physical deformities

Figure 3   A variety of environmental factors can play a role in prenatal development. Photo: © Dougal Waters/Getty Images

the influences of genetics and environment separately, neither factor works alone. Furthermore, despite the emphasis here on some of the ways in which development can go wrong, the vast majority of births occur without difficulty. And in most instances, subsequent development also proceeds normally.

RECAP

Compare and contrast the influence of nature versus nurture.

- Developmental psychology studies growth and change throughout life.
- One fundamental question is how much developmental change is due to heredity and how much is due to environment—the nature–nurture issue.
- Heredity defines the upper limits of our growth and change, whereas the environment affects the degree to which the upper limits are reached.

Describe developmental research techniques.

- Cross-sectional research compares people of different ages with one another at the same point in time.

- Longitudinal research traces the behavior of one or more participants as the participants become older.
- Sequential research combines the two methods by taking several different age groups and examining them at several points in time.

Discuss prenatal development.

- At the moment of conception, a male's sperm cell and a female's egg cell unite, with each contributing to the new individual's genetic makeup.
- Each chromosome contains genes, through which genetic information is transmitted.
- The union of sperm and egg produces a zygote, which contains 23 pairs of chromosomes—with one member of each pair coming from the father and the other coming from the mother.

- After two weeks the zygote becomes an embryo. By week 8, the embryo is called a fetus and is responsive to touch and other stimulation. At week 22 it reaches the age of viability, which means it may survive if born prematurely.

- A fetus is normally born after 38 weeks of pregnancy, weighing around 7 pounds and measuring about 20 inches.

- Genes affect not only physical attributes but also a wide array of personal characteristics such as cognitive abilities, personality traits, and psychological disorders.

- Genetic abnormalities produce birth defects such as phenylketonuria (PKU) and Down syndrome.

- Among the environmental influences on fetal growth are the mother's nutrition, illnesses, and alcohol and nicotine intake.

[EVALUATE E Evaluate]

1. Developmental psychologists are interested in the effects of both _____ and _____ on development.

2. Environment and heredity both influence development, with genetic potentials generally establishing limits on environmental influences. True or false?

3. By observing genetically similar animals in differing environments, we can increase our understanding of the influences of hereditary and environmental factors in humans. True or false?

4. _____ research studies the same individuals over a period of time, whereas _____ research studies people of different ages at the same time.

5. Match each of the following terms with its definition:
   1. Zygote
   2. Gene
   3. Chromosome

   a. Smallest unit through which genetic information is passed
   b. Fertilized egg
   c. Rod-shaped structure containing genetic information

6. Specific kinds of growth must take place during a _____ period if the embryo is to develop normally.

[RETHINK R Rethink]

When researchers find similarities in development between very different cultures, what implications might such findings have for the nature–nurture issue?

Answers to Evaluate Questions 1. heredity (or nature), environment (or nurture); 2. true; 3. true; 4. longitudinal, cross-sectional; 5. 1-b, 2-a, 3-c; 6. sensitive (or critical)

KEY TERMS

Developmental psychology   LO25.1

Nature–nurture issue   LO25.1

Identical twins   LO25.1

Cross-sectional research   LO25.2

Longitudinal research   LO25.2

Sequential research   LO25.2

Chromosomes   LO25.3

Genes   LO25.3

Zygote   LO25.3

Embryo   LO25.3

Fetus   LO25.3

Age of viability   LO25.3

Teratogens   LO25.3

module 26

Infancy and Childhood

Learning Outcomes  Prepare

≫ **LO26.1** Describe the major competencies of newborns.

≫ **LO26.2** Explain the milestones of physical, social, and cognitive development during childhood.

MODULE OUTLINE  Organize

The Extraordinary Newborn

The Growing Child: Infancy through Middle Childhood

Try It! What's Your Parenting Style?

His head was molded into a long melon shape and came to a point at the back . . . He was covered with a thick greasy white material known as "vernix," which made him slippery to hold, and also allowed him to slip easily through the birth canal. In addition to a shock of black hair on his head, his body was covered with dark, fine hair known as "lanugo." His ears, his back, his shoulders, and even his cheeks were furry . . . His skin was wrinkled and quite loose, ready to scale in creased places such as his feet and hands . . . His ears were pressed to his head in unusual positions—one ear was matted firmly forward on his cheek. His nose was flattened and pushed to one side by the squeeze as he came through the pelvis. (Brazelton, 1969, p. 3)

What kind of creature is this? Although the description hardly fits that of the adorable babies seen in advertisements for baby food, we are in fact talking about a normal, completely developed child just after the moment of birth. Called a **neonate,** a newborn arrives in the world in a form that hardly meets the standards of beauty against which we typically measure babies. Yet ask any parents: nothing is more beautiful or exciting than the first glimpse of their newborn.

> **W** Work

neonate A newborn child

≫ LO26.1 The Extraordinary Newborn

Several factors cause a neonate's strange appearance. The trip through the mother's birth canal may have squeezed the incompletely formed bones of the skull together and squashed the nose into the head. The skin secretes *vernix,* a white, greasy covering, for protection before birth, and the baby may have *lanugo,* a soft fuzz, over the entire body for a similar purpose. The infant's eyelids may be puffy with an accumulation of fluids because of the upside-down position during birth.

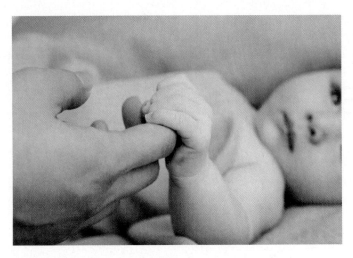

Many of the reflexes that a neonate is born with are critical to survival and unfold naturally as part of an infant's ongoing maturation. Do you think humans have more or fewer reflexes than animals? © Emma Kim/Getty Images RF

reflex An automatic, involuntary response to an incoming stimulus

All these features change during the first two weeks of life as the neonate takes on a more familiar appearance. Even more impressive are the capabilities a neonate begins to display from the moment of birth—capabilities that grow at an astounding rate over the ensuing months.

Reflexes

A neonate is born with a number of **reflexes**—unlearned, involuntary responses that occur automatically in the presence of certain stimuli. Critical for survival, many of those reflexes unfold naturally as part of an infant's ongoing maturation. The *rooting reflex,* for instance, causes neonates to turn their heads toward things that touch their cheeks—such as the mother's nipple or a bottle. Similarly, a *sucking reflex* prompts infants to suck at things that touch their lips. Among other reflexes are a *gag reflex* (to clear the throat), the *startle reflex* (a series of movements in which an infant flings out the arms, fans the fingers, and arches the back in response to a sudden noise), and the *Babinski reflex* (a baby's toes fan out when the outer edge of the sole of the foot is stroked).

Infants lose these primitive reflexes after the first few months of life and replace them with more complex and organized behaviors. Although at birth a neonate is capable of only jerky, limited voluntary movements, the ability to move independently grows enormously during the first year of life. The typical baby rolls over by the age of about 3 months, sits without support at about 6 months, stands alone at about 11 months, and walks at just over a year old. Not only does the ability to make large-scale movements improve during this time, but fine-muscle movements also become increasingly sophisticated (see Figure 1).

> **Infants lose these primitive reflexes after the first few months of life and replace them with more complex and organized behaviors.**

Development of the Senses: Taking in the World

When proud parents peer into the eyes of their neonate, is the child able to return their gaze? Although it was thought for some time that newborns can see only a hazy blur, most current findings indicate that the capabilities of neonates are far more impressive. Although their eyes have a limited capacity to focus on objects that are not within a seven- to eight-inch distance from the face, neonates can follow objects moving within their field of vision. They also show the rudiments of depth perception, as they react by raising their hands when an object appears to be moving rapidly toward the face (Maurer et al., 1999; Soska, Adolph, & Johnson, 2010; Kaufman & Needham, 2011).

Neonates can also discriminate facial expressions—and even imitate them. As you can see in Figure 2, newborns who see an adult with a happy, sad, or surprised facial expression can produce a good imitation of the adult's expression. Even very young infants, then, can respond to the emotions and moods that their caregivers' facial expressions reveal. This capability provides the foundation for social interaction skills in children (Meltzoff, 1996; Nakato et al., 2011; Bahrick, Lickliter, & Castellanos, 2013).

STUDY ALERT

The basic reflexes—unlearned, involuntary responses—include the rooting reflex, the sucking reflex, the gag reflex, the startle reflex, and the Babinski reflex.

3.2 months: Rolling over	3.3 months: Grasping rattle	5.9 months: Sitting without support	7.2 months: Standing while holding on	8.2 months: Grasping with thumb and finger
11.5 months: Standing alone well	12.3 months: Walking well	14.8 months: Building tower of two cubes	16.6 months: Walking up steps	23.8 months: Jumping in place

Figure 1 Although at birth a neonate can make only jerky, limited voluntary movements, during the first year of life the ability to move independently grows enormously. The ages indicate the time when 50 percent of children are able to perform each skill (Frankenburg et al., 1992). Remember, however, that the time when each skill appears can vary considerably. For example, 25 percent of children are able to walk well at age 11 months, and by 15 months 90 percent of children are walking well.

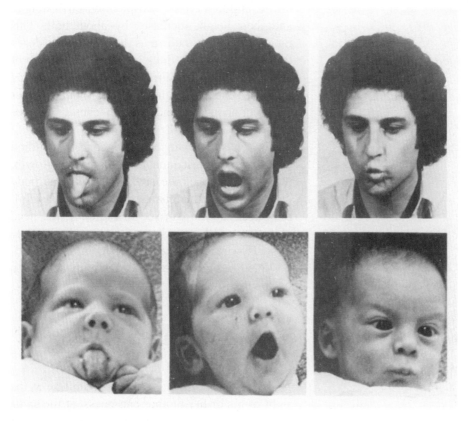

Figure 2 This newborn infant is clearly imitating the expressions of the adult model in these amazing photos. How does this ability contribute to social development? From: A.N. Meltzoff & M.K. Moore, "Imitation of facial and manual gestures by human neonates," *Science, 198,* 75–78. Copyright © 1977 Andrew Meltzoff.

In addition to vision, infants display other impressive sensory capabilities. Newborns can distinguish different sounds to the point of being able to recognize their own mothers' voices at the age of 3 days. They can also make the subtle perceptual distinctions that underlie language abilities. For example, at 2 days of age, infants can distinguish between their native tongue and foreign languages, and they can discriminate between such closely related sounds as *ba* and *pa* when they are 4 days old. By 6 months of age, they can discriminate virtually any difference in sound that is relevant to the production of language. Moreover, they can recognize different tastes and smells at a very early age. There even seems to be something of a built-in sweet tooth: neonates prefer liquids that have been sweetened with sugar over their unsweetened counterparts (Rivera-Gaxiola et al., 2005; Faith, 2010; Purdy et al., 2013).

» LO26.2 The Growing Child: Infancy through Middle Childhood

Throughout the remainder of childhood, moving from infancy into middle childhood and the start of adolescence around age 11 or 12, children develop physically, socially, and cognitively in extraordinary ways. In the remainder of this module, we'll consider this development.

Physical Development

Children's physical growth provides the most obvious sign of development. During the first year of life, children typically triple their birth weight, and their height increases by about half. This rapid growth slows down as the child gets older—think how gigantic adults would be if that rate of growth was constant. From age 3 to the beginning of adolescence at around age 13, growth averages a gain of about 5 pounds and 3 inches a year (see Figure 3).

The physical changes that occur as children develop are not just a matter of increasing growth; the relationship of the size of the various body parts to one another changes dramatically as children age. As you can see in Figure 4, the head of a fetus (and a newborn) is disproportionately large. However, the head soon becomes more proportional in size to the rest of the body as growth occurs mainly in the trunk and legs.

Development of Social Behavior: Forming Social Bonds and Attachment

As anyone who has seen an infant smiling at the sight of his or her mother can guess, at the same time that infants grow physically and hone their perceptual abilities, they also develop socially. The nature of a child's early social development provides the foundation for social relationships that will last a lifetime.

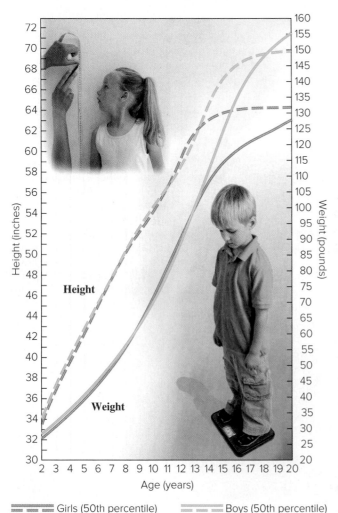

Figure 3 The average heights and weights of males and females in the United States from birth through age 20. At what ages are girls typically heavier and taller than boys? Source: National Center for Health Statistics, 2000. Photos: (first) © Image Source/Getty Images RF; (second) © McGraw-Hill Education

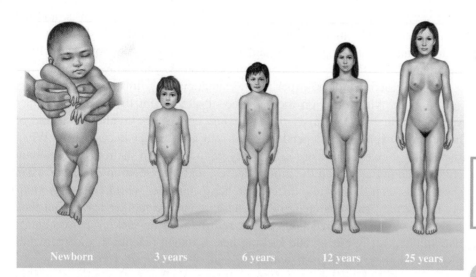

Figure 4 As development progresses, the size of the head relative to the rest of the body decreases until the individual reaches adulthood. Why do you think the head starts out so large?

Newborn   3 years   6 years   12 years   25 years

attachment The positive emotional bond that develops between a child and a particular individual

STUDY ALERT

Attachment—the positive emotional bond that develops between a child and a particular individual—is a key concept in understanding the social development of children.

Attachment, the positive emotional bond that develops between a child and a particular individual, is the most important form of social development that occurs during infancy. Our understanding of attachment progressed when psychologist Harry Harlow, in a classic study, gave infant monkeys the choice of cuddling a wire "monkey" that provided milk or a soft, terry-cloth "monkey" that was warm but did not provide milk. Their choice was clear: they spent most of their time clinging to the warm cloth "monkey," although they made occasional forays to the wire monkey to nurse. Obviously, the cloth monkey provided greater comfort to the infants; milk alone was insufficient to create attachment (Harlow & Zimmerman, 1959; Blum, 2002; Whipple, Bernier, & Mageau, 2011; see Figure 5).

Building on this pioneering work, developmental psychologists have suggested that human attachment grows through the responsiveness of infants' caregivers to the signals, such as crying, smiling, reaching, and clinging. The more that caregivers respond to the child's signals, the more likely it is that the child will become securely attached to the caregiver. Full attachment eventually develops as a result of the complex series of interactions between caregiver and child. In the course of these interactions, the infant plays as critical and active role as the caregiver in the formation of the bond between them. Infants who respond positively to a caregiver produce more positive behavior on the caregiver's part, which in turn produces an even stronger degree of attachment in the child.

Assessing Attachment

Developmental psychologists have devised a quick and direct way to measure attachment. Developed by Mary Ainsworth, the *Ainsworth strange situation* consists of a sequence of events involving a child and (typically) his or her mother. Initially, the mother and baby enter an unfamiliar room, and the mother permits the baby to explore while she sits down. Once an

Figure 5 Although the wire "mother" dispensed milk to the hungry infant monkey, the infant preferred the soft, terry-cloth "mother." Do you think human babies would react the same way? What does this experiment tell us about attachment? © Nina Leen/Getty Images

adult stranger enters the room, the mother leaves. The mother returns, and the stranger leaves. The mother once again leaves the baby alone, and the stranger returns. Finally, the stranger leaves, and the mother returns (Ainsworth et al., 1978; Bergman et al., 2010; Van Rosmalen, Van Der Veer, & Van Der Horst, 2015).

Babies' reactions to the experimental situation vary drastically, depending, according to Ainsworth, on their degree of attachment to the mother. One-year-old children who are *securely attached* employ the mother as a kind of home base, exploring independently but returning to her occasionally. When she leaves, they exhibit distress, and they go to her when she returns. Avoidant children do not cry when the mother leaves, and they seem to avoid her when she returns, as if they were indifferent to her. Ambivalent children display anxiety before they are separated and are upset when the mother leaves, but they may show ambivalent reactions to her return, such as seeking close contact but simultaneously hitting and kicking her. A fourth reaction is disorganized-disoriented; these children show inconsistent, often contradictory behavior.

The Father's Role

Although early developmental research focused largely on the mother-child relationship, more recent research has highlighted the father's role in parenting, and with good reason: the number of fathers who are primary caregivers for their children has grown significantly, and fathers play an increasingly important role in their children's lives. For example, in almost 13 percent of families with children, the father is the parent who stays at home to care for pre-schoolers (Halford, 2006; Baradon, 2010; Kulik & Sadeh, 2015).

When fathers interact with their children, their play often differs from that of mothers. Fathers engage in more physical, rough-and-tumble sorts of activities, whereas mothers play more verbal and traditional games, such as peekaboo. Despite such behavioral differences, the nature of attachment between fathers and children compared with that between mothers and children can be similar. In fact, children can form multiple attachments simultaneously (Pellis & Pellis, 2007; Diener et al., 2008; Martin & Redshaw, 2010).

Social Relationships with Peers

By the time they are 2 years old, children become less dependent on their parents and more self-reliant, increasingly preferring to play with friends. Initially, play is relatively independent: even though they may be sitting side by side, 2-year-olds pay more attention to toys than to one another when playing. Later, however, children actively interact, modifying one another's behavior and later exchanging roles during play (Lindsey & Colwell, 2003; Colwell & Lindsey, 2005; Whitney & Green, 2011).

As children reach school age, their social interactions begin to follow set patterns and become more frequent. They may engage in elaborate games involving teams and rigid rules. This play serves purposes other than mere enjoyment. It allows children to become increasingly competent in their social interactions with others. Through play they learn to take the perspective of other people and to infer others' thoughts and feelings, even when those thoughts and feelings are not directly expressed (Royzman, Cassidy, & Baron, 2003; Luby & Tandon, 2010; Ward, 2016).

In short, social interaction helps children interpret the meaning of others' behavior and develop the capacity to respond appropriately. Furthermore, children learn physical and emotional self-control: they learn to avoid hitting a playmate who beats them at a game, be polite, and control their emotional displays and facial expressions (e.g., smiling even when receiving a disappointing gift). Situations that provide children with opportunities for social interaction, then, may enhance their social development (Lengua & Long, 2002; Talukdar & Shastri, 2006; Whitebread et al., 2009).

The Consequences of Child Care Outside the Home

Research on the importance of social interaction is corroborated by work that examines the benefits of child care outside of the home, which is an important part of an increasing number of children's lives. For instance, almost 30 percent of preschool children whose mothers work outside the home spend their days in child-care centers. By the age of 6 months, almost two-thirds of infants are cared for by people other than their mothers for part of the day. Most of these infants begin child care before the age of 4 months and are cared for by people other than their mothers for almost 30 hours per week (NICHD Early Child Care Research Network, 2006; see Figure 6).

Do child-care arrangements outside the home benefit children's development? If the programs are of high quality, they can. According to the results of a large study supported by the U.S. National Institute of Child Health and Development (NICHD), children who attend high-quality child-care centers may not only do as well as children who stay at home with their parents, but in some respects may actually do better. Children in child care are generally more considerate and sociable than other children are, and they interact more positively with teachers. They may also be more compliant and regulate their own behavior more effectively, and their mothers show increased sensitivity to their children (NICHD Early Child Care Research Network, 1999, 2001; Weis & Toolis, 2010).

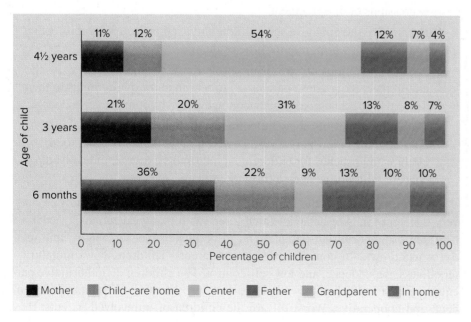

Figure 6 As they get older, children are increasingly likely to spend time in some kind of child care outside the home or family. Source: Based on National Institute of Child Health and Human Development (NICHD) Early Child Care Research Network, 2006.

In addition, especially for children from poor or disadvantaged homes, child care in specially enriched environments—those with many toys, books, a variety of children, and high-quality care providers—often proves to be more intellectually stimulating than the home environment. Such child care can lead to increased intellectual achievement, demonstrated in higher IQ scores and better language development. In fact, children in care centers sometimes are found to score higher on tests of cognitive abilities than those who are cared for by their mothers or by sitters or home day-care providers—effects lasting into adulthood (Wilgoren, 1999; Burchinal, Roberts, & Riggins, 2000; Dearing, McCartney, & Taylor, 2009).

However, child care outside the home does not have universally positive outcomes. Children may feel insecure after placement in low-quality child care or in multiple child-care settings. Furthermore, some research suggests that infants who are involved in outside care more than 20 hours a week in the first year show less secure attachment to their mothers than do those who have not been in outside-the-home child care. Finally, children who spent long hours in child care as infants and preschoolers may have a reduced ability to work independently and to manage their time effectively when they reach elementary school (NICHD Early Child Care Research Network, 2001; Vandell et al., 2005; Pluess & Belsky, 2009).

The key to the success of nonparental child care is its quality. High-quality child care produces benefits; low-quality child care provides little or no gain and may even hinder children's development. In short, significant benefits result from the social interaction and intellectual stimulation provided by high-quality child-care centers—especially for children from impoverished environments (National Association for the Education of Young Children, 2005; Zaslow, Halle, & Martin, 2006; Landry et al., 2013).

Parenting Styles and Social Development

Parents' child-rearing practices are critical in shaping their children's social competence, and—according to classic research by developmental psychologist Diana Baumrind—four main categories describe different parenting styles (Baumrind, 2005; Keller et al., 2010; Carlo et al., 2011; see Figure 7).

authoritarian parents Parents who are rigid and punitive and value unquestioning obedience from their children

permissive parents Parents who give their children relaxed or inconsistent direction and, although warm, require little of them

authoritative parents Parents who are firm, set clear limits, reason with their children, and explain things to them

uninvolved parents Parents who show little interest in their children and are emotionally detached

- **Authoritarian parents** are rigid and punitive, and value unquestioning obedience from their children. They have strict standards and discourage expressions of disagreement.

- **Permissive parents** give their children relaxed or inconsistent direction and, although warm, require little of them.

- **Authoritative parents** are firm, setting limits for their children. As the children get older, these parents try to reason and explain things to them. They also set clear goals and encourage their children's independence.

- **Uninvolved parents** show little interest in their children. Emotionally detached, they view parenting as nothing more than providing food, clothing, and shelter for children. At their most extreme, uninvolved parents are guilty of neglect, a form of child abuse.

As you might expect, the four kinds of child-rearing styles seem to produce very different kinds of behavior in children (with many exceptions, of course). Children of authoritarian parents tend to be unsociable, unfriendly, and relatively withdrawn. In contrast, permissive parents' children show immaturity, moodiness, dependence, and low self-control. The children of authoritative parents fare best: with high social skills, they are likable, self-reliant, independent, and cooperative. Worst off are the children of uninvolved parents; they

Parenting Style	Parent Behavior	Type of Behavior Produced in Child
Authoritarian	Rigid, punitive, strict standards (example: "If you don't clean your room, I'm going to take away your iPhone for good and ground you.")	Unsociable, unfriendly, withdrawn
Permissive	Lax, inconsistent, undemanding (example: "It might be good to clean your room, but I guess it can wait.")	Immature, moody, dependent, low self-control
Authoritative	Firm, sets limits and goals, uses reasoning, encourages independence (example: "You'll need to clean your room before we can go out to the restaurant. As soon as you finish, we'll leave.")	Good social skills, likable, self-reliant, independent
Uninvolved	Detached emotionally, sees role only as providing food, clothing, and shelter (example: "I couldn't care less if your room is a pigsty.")	Indifferent, rejecting behavior

Figure 7 According to developmental psychologist Diana Baumrind (1971), four main parenting styles characterize child rearing. © Gary John Norman/Getty Images RF

feel unloved and emotionally detached, and their physical and cognitive development are impeded. Children with low social skills face peer rejection that can have lasting results (Saarni, 1999; Berk, 2005; Snyder, Cramer, & Afrank, 2005). (To get a sense of your own parenting style, complete the Try It!)

Try It!

What's Your Parenting Style?

Answer whether you agree or disagree with each of the following questions:

1. Children do best when they follow their parents' wishes without questioning them. Agree or Disagree?
2. Making children follow too many rules breaks their natural spirit. Agree or Disagree?
3. Parents should encourage independence in their children. Agree or Disagree?
4. Parents don't need to set limits. Agree or Disagree?
5. Parents should always be in charge, making sure their children follow the rules. Agree or Disagree?
6. It's important to let children make their own mistakes. Agree or Disagree?
7. Parents should explain the reasons for their rules to their children. Agree or Disagree?
8. It doesn't matter much if parents are emotionally supportive of their children. Agree or Disagree?
9. There are few areas where children can question their parents. Agree or Disagree?
10. Parents shouldn't expect specific behavior from their children. Agree or Disagree?
11. If a child makes a mistake, explain to them why they were wrong. Agree or Disagree?

(continued)

12. If parents provide food, clothing, and shelter, they are doing their job. Agree or Disagree?

13. Parents have all the rights, while children have few or none. Agree or Disagree?

14. Parents should not feel guilty if they can't spend a lot of time overseeing their children. Agree or Disagree?

15. Parents should play the role of teacher to their children. Agree or Disagree?

16. It's understandable that parents sometimes have to neglect their children. Agree or Disagree?

17. Children thrive with strict parents. Agree or Disagree?

18. Parents should not micromanage their children. Agree or Disagree?

19. Children ought to have clear rules, but occasionally need to be cut some slack. Agree or Disagree?

20. Children need to figure things out on their own. Agree or Disagree?

To get a general sense of the parenting style that you agree with most, score the questionnaire as follows:

Add the number of statements you agreed with for items 1, 5, 9, 13, and 17 and write the number here: _____ These items reflect an authoritarian parenting style.

Add the number of statements you agreed with for items 2, 6, 10, 14, and 18 and write the number here: _____ These items reflect a permissive parenting style

Add the number of statements you agreed with for items 3, 7, 11, 15, and 19 and write the number here: _____ These items reflect an authoritative parenting style.

Add up the number of statements you agreed with for items 4, 8, 12, 16, and 20 and write the number here: _____. These items reflect an uninvolved parent style.

STUDY ALERT

Know the four major types of child-rearing practices—authoritarian, permissive, authoritative, and uninvolved—and their effects.

temperament The basic, innate disposition that emerges early in life

With which of the four parenting styles do you agree most, according to this questionnaire? Do you think it is an accurate assessment of your parenting style?

Remember, this questionnaire only provides a rough measure; your actual parenting style reflects many additional factors than those tapped in this questionnaire.

Before we congratulate authoritative parents and condemn authoritarian, permissive, and uninvolved ones, it is important to note that in many cases nonauthoritative parents also produce perfectly well-adjusted children. Moreover, children are born with a particular **temperament**—a basic, innate disposition. Some children are naturally easygoing and cheerful, whereas others are irritable and fussy, or pensive and quiet. The kind of temperament a baby is born with may in part bring about specific kinds of parental child-rearing styles (Miner & Clarke-Stewart, 2008; Coplan, Reichel, & Rowan, 2009; Ullsperger, Nigg & Nikolas, 2016).

In sum, a child's upbringing results from the child-rearing philosophy parents hold, the specific practices they use, and the nature of their own and their child's personalities. As is the case with other aspects of development, then, behavior is a function of a complex interaction of environmental and genetic factors.

Erikson's Theory of Psychosocial Development

In tracing the course of social development, some theorists have considered how the challenges of society and culture change as an individual matures. Following this path, psychoanalyst Erik Erikson developed one of the more comprehensive theories of social development. Erikson (1963) viewed the developmental changes occurring throughout life as a series of eight stages of psychosocial development, of which four occur during childhood.

"Please, Jason. Don't you want to grow up to be an autonomous person?"

Lee Lorenz/The New Yorker Collection/The Cartoon Bank

Psychosocial development involves changes in our interactions and understanding of one another as well as in our knowledge and understanding of ourselves as members of society.

Erikson suggests that passage through each of the stages necessitates the resolution of a crisis or conflict. Accordingly, Erikson represents each stage as a pairing of the most positive and most negative aspects of the crisis of that period. Although each crisis is never resolved entirely—life becomes increasingly complicated as we grow older—it has to be resolved sufficiently to equip us to deal with demands made during the following stage of development.

In the first stage of psychosocial development, the **trust-versus-mistrust stage** (ages birth to 1½ years), infants develop feelings of trust if their physical requirements and psychological needs for attachment are consistently met and their interactions with the world are generally positive. In contrast, inconsistent care and unpleasant interactions with others can lead to mistrust and leave an infant unable to meet the challenges required in the next stage of development.

In the second stage, the **autonomy-versus-shame-and-doubt stage** (ages 1½ to 3 years), toddlers develop independence and autonomy if exploration and freedom are encouraged, or they experience shame, self-doubt, and unhappiness if they are overly restricted and protected. According to Erikson, the key to the development of a sense of independence during this period is for the child's caregivers to provide a reasonable amount of control. If parents are overly controlling, children cannot assert themselves and develop their own sense of control over their world; if parents provide too little control, children can become demanding and dictatorial.

Next, children face the crises of the **initiative-versus-guilt stage** (ages 3 to 6). In this stage, children's desire to act independently conflicts with the guilt that comes from the unintended and unexpected consequences of such behavior. Children in this period come to understand that they are persons in their own right, and they begin to make decisions about their behavior. If parents react positively to children's attempts at independence, their children will develop skills in accomplishing tasks and overcoming challenges.

The fourth and last stage of childhood is the **industry-versus-inferiority stage** (ages 6 to 12). During this period, increasing competency in all areas, whether social interactions or academic skills, characterizes successful psychosocial development. In contrast, difficulties in this stage lead to feelings of failure and inadequacy.

Erikson's theory suggests that psychosocial development continues throughout life, and he proposes four more crises that are faced after childhood (described in the module about adolescence). Although his theory has been criticized on several grounds—such as the imprecision of the concepts he employs and his greater emphasis on male development than female development—it remains influential and is one of the few theories that encompass the entire life span.

Cognitive Development: Children's Thinking About the World

Suppose you had two drinking glasses of different shapes—one short and broad and one tall and thin. Now imagine that you filled the short, broad one with soda about halfway and then poured the liquid from that glass into the tall one. The soda would appear to fill about three-quarters of the second glass. If someone

psychosocial development Development of individuals' interactions and understanding of each other and of their knowledge and understanding of themselves as members of society

trust-versus-mistrust stage According to Erik Erikson, the first stage of psychosocial development, occurring from birth to age 1½ years, during which time infants develop feelings of trust or lack of trust

autonomy-versus-shame-and-doubt stage The period which, according to Erik Erikson, toddlers (ages 1½ to 3 years) develop independence and autonomy if exploration and freedom are encouraged, or shame and self-doubt if they are restricted and overprotected

initiative-versus-guilt stage According to Erik Erikson, the period during which children ages 3 to 6 years experience conflict between independence of action and the sometimes negative results of that action

industry-versus-inferiority stage According to Erik Erikson, the last stage of childhood, during which children ages 6 to 12 years may develop positive social interactions with others or may feel inadequate and become less sociable

asked you whether there was more soda in the second glass than there had been in the first, what would you say?

You might think that such a simple question hardly deserves an answer; of course there is no difference in the amount of soda in the two glasses. However, most 4-year-olds would be likely to say that there is more soda in the second glass. If you then poured the soda back into the short glass, they would say there is now less soda than there was in the taller glass.

> **Anyone who has observed preschoolers must be impressed by how far they have progressed from the early stages of development.**

Why are young children confused by this problem? The reason is not immediately obvious. Anyone who has observed preschoolers must be impressed by how far they have progressed from the early stages of development. They speak with ease, know the alphabet, count, play complex games, use computers, tell stories, and communicate ably. Yet despite this seeming sophistication, there are deep gaps in children's understanding of the world. Some theorists have suggested that children cannot understand certain ideas and concepts until they reach a particular stage of **cognitive development**—the process by which a child's understanding of the world changes as a function of age and experience. In contrast to the theories of physical and social development discussed earlier (such as those of Erikson), theories of cognitive development seek to explain the quantitative and qualitative intellectual advances that occur during development.

Piaget's Theory of Cognitive Development

No theory of cognitive development has had more impact than that of Swiss psychologist Jean Piaget. Piaget (1970) suggested that children around the world proceed through a series of four stages in a fixed order. He maintained that these stages differ not only in the *quantity* of information acquired at each stage but in the *quality* of knowledge and understanding as well. Taking an interactionist point of view, he suggested that movement from one stage to the next occurs when a child reaches an appropriate level of maturation *and* is exposed to relevant types of experiences. Piaget assumed that, without having such experiences, children cannot reach their highest level of cognitive growth.

Piaget proposed four stages: the sensorimotor, preoperational, concrete operational, and formal operational (see Figure 8). Let's examine each of them and the approximate ages that they span.

Cognitive Stage	Approximate Age Range	Major Characteristics
Sensorimotor	Birth–2 years	Development of object permanence, development of motor skills, little or no capacity for symbolic representation
Preoperational	2–7 years	Development of language and symbolic thinking, egocentric thinking
Concrete operational mastery	7–12 years	Development of conservation, of concept of reversibility
Formal operational	12 years–adulthood	Development of logical and abstract thinking

Figure 8 According to Piaget, all children pass through four stages of cognitive development. Photos: (baby) © Purestock/SuperStock RF; (boy with puzzle) © JGI/Getty Images RF; (two girls) © ERproductions/Getty Images RF; (boy) © Photodisc/Getty Images RF

Sensorimotor Stage: Birth to 2 Years. During the **sensorimotor stage,** children base their understanding of the world primarily on touching, sucking, chewing, shaking, and manipulating objects. In the initial part of the stage, children have relatively little competence in representing the environment by using images, language, or other kinds of symbols. Consequently, infants lack what Piaget calls **object permanence,** the awareness that objects—and people—continue to exist even if they are out of sight.

How can we know that children lack object permanence? Although we cannot ask infants, we can observe their reactions when a toy they are playing with is hidden under a blanket. Until the age of about 9 months, children will make no attempt to locate the hidden toy. However, soon after that age they will begin an active search for the missing object, indicating that they have developed a mental representation of the toy. Object permanence, then, is a critical development during the sensorimotor stage.

Preoperational Stage: 2 to 7 Years. During the **preoperational stage** children develop the use of language. The internal representational systems they develop allow them to describe people, events, and feelings. They even use symbols in play, pretending, for example, that a book pushed across the floor is a car.

Although children use more advanced thinking in this stage than they did in the earlier sensorimotor stage, their thinking is still qualitatively inferior to that of adults. We see this when we observe a preoperational child using **egocentric thought,** a way of thinking in which the child views the world entirely from his or her own perspective. Preoperational children think that everyone shares their perspective and knowledge.

In addition, preoperational children have not yet developed the ability to comprehend the **principle of conservation,** which is the understanding that quantity is unrelated to the arrangement and physical appearance of objects. Children who can use the principle of conservation have awareness that important attributes of objects (such as amount or volume) do not change despite superficial changes. In contrast, children who have not mastered conservation do not understand that the overall amount or volume of an object does not change when its shape or configuration changes.

The question about the two glasses—one short and broad, and the other tall and thin—with which we began our discussion of cognitive development illustrates this point clearly. Children who do not understand the principle of conservation believe that the amount of liquid changes as it is poured back and forth between glasses of different sizes. They simply are unable to comprehend that a change in appearance does not mean there is a change in amount. Instead, they truly believe that quantity changes as appearance changes.

Concrete Operational Stage: 7 to 12 Years. Mastery of the principle of conservation marks the beginning of the **concrete operational stage.** However, children do not fully understand some aspects of conservation—such as conservation of weight and volume—for a number of years.

During the concrete operational stage, children develop the ability to think in a more logical manner, and they begin to overcome some of the egocentrism characteristic of the preoperational period. However, their thinking still displays one major limitation: they are largely bound to the concrete, physical reality of the world. For the most part, they have difficulty understanding questions of an abstract or hypothetical nature.

Formal Operational Stage: 12 Years to Adulthood. The **formal operational stage** produces a new kind of thinking that is abstract, formal, and

---

sensorimotor stage According to Jean Piaget, the stage from birth to 2 years, during which a child has little competence in representing the environment by using images, language, or other symbols

object permanence The awareness that objects—and people—continue to exist even if they are out of sight

preoperational stage According to Jean Piaget, the period from 2 to 7 years of age that is characterized by language development

egocentric thought A way of thinking in which a child views the world entirely from his or her own perspective

principle of conservation The knowledge that quantity is unrelated to the arrangement and physical appearance of objects

concrete operational stage According to Jean Piaget, the period from 7 to 12 years of age that is characterized by logical thought and a loss of egocentrism

formal operational stage According to Jean Piaget, the period from age 12 to adulthood that is characterized by abstract thought

logical. Thinking is no longer tied to events that individuals observe in the environment but makes use of logical techniques to resolve problems.

The way in which children approach the "pendulum problem" devised by Piaget (Piaget & Inhelder, 1958) illustrates the emergence of formal operational thinking. The problem solver is asked to figure out what determines how fast a pendulum swings. Is it the length of the string, the weight of the pendulum, or the force with which the pendulum is pushed? (For the record, the answer is the length of the string.)

Children in the concrete operational stage approach the problem haphazardly, without a logical or rational plan of action. For example, they may simultaneously change the length of the string, the weight on the string, and the force with which they push the pendulum. Because they are varying all the factors at once, they cannot tell which factor is the critical one. In contrast, people in the formal operational stage approach the problem systematically. Acting as if they were scientists conducting an experiment, they examine the effects of changes in one variable at a time. This ability to rule out competing possibilities characterizes formal operational thought.

Although formal operational thought emerges during the teenage years, some individuals use this type of thinking only infrequently. Moreover, it appears that many individuals never reach this stage at all; most studies show that only 40 to 60 percent of college students and adults fully reach it, with some estimates running as low as 25 percent of the general population. In addition, in certain cultures—particularly those that are less technologically oriented than Western societies—almost no one reaches the formal operational stage (Keating & Clark, 1980; Genovese, 2006).

Information-Processing Approaches: Charting Children's Thinking

If cognitive development does not proceed as a series of stages as Piaget suggested, what does underlie the enormous growth in children's cognitive abilities that even the most untutored eye can observe? To many developmental psychologists, changes in **information processing,** the way in which people take in, use, and store information, account for cognitive development (Dwyer et al., 2010; Casasola, 2011; Lillard & Woolley, 2015).

According to this approach, quantitative changes occur in children's ability to organize and manipulate information. From this perspective, children become increasingly adept at information processing, much as a computer program may become more sophisticated as a programmer modifies it on the basis of experience. Information-processing approaches consider the kinds of "mental programs" that children invoke when approaching problems.

Several significant changes occur in children's information-processing capabilities. For one thing, speed of processing increases with age, as some abilities become more automatic. The speed at which children can scan, recognize, and compare stimuli increases with age. As they grow older, children can pay attention to stimuli longer and discriminate between different stimuli more readily, and they are less easily distracted (Myerson et al., 2003; Van den Wildenberg & Van der Molen, 2004).

Memory also improves dramatically with age. Preschoolers can hold only two or three chunks of information in short-term memory, 5-year-olds can hold four, and 7-year-olds can hold five. (Adults are able to keep seven, plus or minus two, chunks in short-term memory.) The size of chunks also grows with age, as does the sophistication and organization of knowledge stored in memory

information processing The way in which people take in, use, and store information (see Figure 9). Still, memory capabilities are impressive at a very early age: even before they can speak, infants can remember for months events in which they actively participated (Bayliss et al., 2005a; Slusarczyk & Niedzwienska, 2013).

Finally, improvement in information processing relates to advances in **metacognition,** an awareness and understanding of one's own cognitive processes. Metacognition involves the planning, monitoring, and revising of cognitive strategies. Younger children, who lack an awareness of their own cognitive processes, often do not realize their incapabilities. Thus, when they misunderstand others, they may fail to recognize their own errors. It is only later, when metacognitive abilities become more sophisticated, that children are able to know when they don't understand. Such increasing sophistication reflects a change in children's theory of mind, their knowledge and beliefs about the way the mind operates (Bernstein, Loftus, & Meltzoff, 2005; Matthews & Funke, 2006; Lockl & Schneider, 2007).

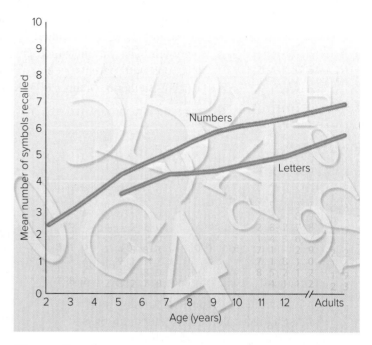

Figure 9 Memory span increases with age for both numbers and letters. Source: Adapted from Dempster, 1981.

Vygotsky's View of Cognitive Development: Considering Culture

According to Russian developmental psychologist Lev Vygotsky, the culture in which we are raised significantly affects our cognitive development. In an increasingly influential view, Vygotsky suggests that the focus on individual performance of both Piagetian and information-processing approaches is misplaced. Instead, he holds that we cannot understand cognitive development without taking into account the social aspects of learning (Vygotsky, 1926/1997; Rieber & Robinson, 2006; Fernyhough, 2010).

Vygotsky argues that cognitive development occurs as a consequence of social interactions in which children work with others to jointly solve problems. Through such interactions, children's cognitive skills increase, and they gain the ability to function intellectually on their own. More specifically, he suggests that children's cognitive abilities increase when they encounter information that falls within their zone of proximal development. The **zone of proximal development (ZPD),** is the level at which a child can almost, but not fully, comprehend or perform a task on his or her own. When children receive information that falls within the ZPD, they can increase their understanding or master a new task. In contrast, if the information lies outside children's ZPD, they will not be able to master it (Warford, 2011).

In short, cognitive development occurs when parents, teachers, or skilled peers assist a child by presenting information that is both new and within the ZPD. This type of assistance, called *scaffolding,* provides support for learning and problem solving that encourages independence and growth. Vygotsky claims that scaffolding not only promotes the solution of specific problems, but also aids in the development of overall cognitive abilities (Schaller & Crandall, 2004; Coulson & Harvey, 2013).

metacognition An awareness and understanding of one's own cognitive processes

zone of proximal development (ZPD) According to Lev Vygotsky, the level at which a child can almost, but not fully, comprehend or perform a task on his or her own

More than other approaches to cognitive development, Vygotsky's theory considers how an individual's cultural and social background affect intellectual growth. The way in which children understand the world grows out of interactions with parents, peers, and other members of their own specific culture (John-Steiner & Mahn, 2003; Kozulin et al., 2003).

RECAP

Describe the major competencies of newborns.

- Newborns, or neonates, have reflexes, unlearned, involuntary responses that occur automatically in the presence of certain stimuli.

- Sensory abilities also develop rapidly; infants can distinguish color, depth, sound, tastes, and smells relatively soon after birth.

- After birth, physical development is rapid; children typically triple their birth weight in a year.

Explain the milestones of physical, social, and cognitive development during childhood.

- Attachment—the positive emotional bond between a child and a particular individual—marks social development in infancy.

- As children become older, the nature of their social interactions with peers changes. Initially play occurs relatively independently, but it becomes increasingly cooperative.

- The different child-rearing styles include authoritarian, permissive, authoritative, and uninvolved.

- According to Erikson, eight stages of psychosocial development involve people's changing interactions and understanding of themselves and others. During childhood, the four stages are trust-versus-mistrust (birth to 1½ years), autonomy-versus-shame-and-doubt (1½ to 3 years), initiative-versus-guilt (3 to 6 years), and industry-versus-inferiority (6 to 12 years).

- Piaget's theory suggests that cognitive development proceeds through four stages in which qualitative changes occur in thinking: the sensorimotor stage (birth to 2 years), the preoperational stage (2 to 7 years), the concrete operational stage (7 to 12 years), and the formal operational stage (12 years to adulthood).

- Information-processing approaches suggest that quantitative changes occur in children's ability to organize and manipulate information about the world, such as significant increases in speed of processing, attention span, and memory. In addition, children advance in metacognition, the awareness and understanding of one's own cognitive processes.

- Vygotsky argued that children's cognitive development occurs as a consequence of social interactions in which children and others work together to solve problems.

[EVALUATE E Evaluate]

1. The emotional bond that develops between a child and his or her caregiver is known as _____.

2. Match the parenting style with its definition:

   a. Rigid; highly punitive; demanding obedience
   b. Gives little direction; lax on obedience
   c. Firm but fair; tries to explain parental decisions
   d. Emotionally detached and unloving

   1. Permissive
   2. Authoritative
   3. Authoritarian
   4. Uninvolved

3. Erikson's theory of _____ development involves a series of eight stages, each of which must be resolved for a person to develop optimally.

4. Match the stage of development with the thinking style characteristic of that stage:

   a. Sensorimotor   1. Egocentric thought
   b. Formal operational   2. Object permanence
   c. Preoperational   3. Abstract reasoning
   d. Concrete operational   4. Conservation; reversibility

5. _____ _____ theories of development suggest that the way in which a child handles information is critical to his or her development.

[RETHINK R Rethink]

Do you think the widespread use of IQ testing in the United States contributes to parents' views that their children's academic success is due largely to the children's innate intelligence? Why? Would it be possible (or desirable) to change this view?

Answers to Evaluate Questions 1. attachment; 2. b-1, c-2, a-3, d-4; 3. psychosocial; 4. c-1, a-2, b-3, d-4; 5. information-processing

KEY TERMS

Neonate   LO26.1

Reflexes   LO26.1

Attachment   LO26.2

Authoritarian parents   LO26.2

Permissive parents   LO26.2

Authoritative parents   LO26.2

Uninvolved parents   LO26.2

Temperament   LO26.2

Psychosocial development   LO26.2

Trust-versus-mistrust stage   LO26.2

Autonomy-versus-shame-and-doubt stage   LO26.2

Initiative-versus-guilt stage   LO26.2

Industry-versus-inferiority stage   LO26.2

Cognitive development   LO26.2

Sensorimotor stage   LO26.2

Object permanence   LO26.2

Preoperational stage   LO26.2

Egocentric thought   LO26.2

Principle of conservation   LO26.2

Concrete operational stage   LO26.2

Formal operational stage   LO26.2

Information processing   LO26.2

Metacognition   LO26.2

Zone of proximal development (ZPD)   LO26.2

Adolescence
Becoming an Adult

Learning Outcomes  Prepare

>> **LO27.1** Summarize the major physical transitions that characterize adolescence.

>> **LO27.2** Explain moral and cognitive development in adolescents.

>> **LO27.3** Discuss social development in adolescents.

MODULE OUTLINE  Organize

Physical Development: The Changing Adolescent

Moral and Cognitive Development: Distinguishing Right from Wrong

Social Development: Finding Oneself in a Social World

Exploring Diversity: Rites of Passage: Coming of Age around the World

 W Work

Marco Colson, Age 15: "Stay Out" says the sign on Marco's door. Inside, the floor is cluttered with dirty clothes, candy wrappers, and other debris. What color is the carpet on the floor? "I don't think I remember," says Marco with a smile.

Like other adolescents, Marco Colson has characteristics that are common to adolescence—concerns about friends, parents, appearance, independence, and his future. **Adolescence,** the developmental stage between childhood and adulthood, is a crucial period. It is a time of profound changes and, occasionally, turmoil. Considerable biological change occurs as adolescents attain sexual and physical maturity. At the same time, and rivaling these physiological changes, important social, emotional, and cognitive changes occur as adolescents strive for independence and move toward adulthood.

adolescence The developmental stage between childhood and adulthood

Because many years of schooling precede most people's entry into the workforce in Western societies, the stage of adolescence is fairly long—it begins just before the teenage years and ends just after. Adolescents are no longer children, yet society doesn't quite consider them adults. They face a period of rapid physical, cognitive, and social change that affects them for the rest of their lives.

>> LO27.1 Physical Development: The Changing Adolescent

If you think back to the start of your own adolescence, the most dramatic changes you probably remember are physical. A spurt in height, the growth of breasts in girls, deepening voices in boys, the development of body hair,

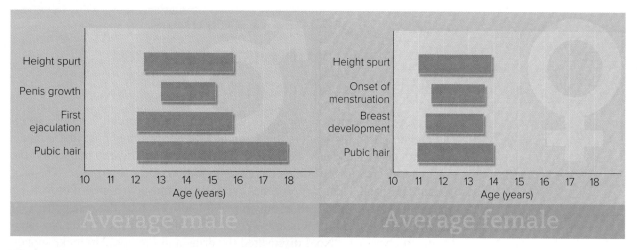

Figure 1   The range of ages during which major sexual changes occur during adolescence is shown by the colored bars. Source: Based on Tanner, 1978.

and intense sexual feelings cause curiosity, interest, and sometimes embarrassment for individuals entering adolescence.

The physical changes that occur at the start of adolescence result largely from the secretion of various hormones, and they affect virtually every aspect of an adolescent's life. Not since infancy has development been so dramatic. Weight and height increase rapidly because of a growth spurt that typically begins around age 10 for girls and age 12 for boys. Adolescents may grow as much as five inches in one year.

Puberty, the period at which maturation of the sexual organs occurs, begins at about age 11 or 12 for girls, when menstruation starts. However, there are wide variations (see Figure 1). For example, some girls begin to menstruate as early as age 8 or 9 or as late as age 16. Furthermore, in Western cultures, the average age at which adolescents reach sexual maturity has been steadily decreasing over the last century, most likely as a result of improved nutrition and medical care. Sexual *attraction* to others begins even before the maturation of the sexual organs, at around age 10 (Tanner, 1990; Herdt, 2010; Shanahan et al., 2013).

For boys, the onset of puberty is marked by their first ejaculation, known as *spermarche.* Spermarche usually occurs around the age of 13 (see Figure 1). At first, relatively few sperm are produced during an ejaculation, but the amount increases significantly within a few years.

Clearly, the rate at which physical changes occur during adolescence can affect the way in which people are viewed by others and the way they view themselves. Just as important as physical changes, however, are the psychological and social changes that unfold during adolescence.

> The physical changes that occur at the start of adolescence result largely from the secretion of various hormones, and they affect virtually every aspect of an adolescent's life.

puberty The period at which maturation of the sexual organs occurs, beginning at about age 11 or 12 for girls and 13 or 14 for boys

Although puberty begins around age 11 or 12 for girls and 13 or 14 for boys, there are wide variations. What are some advantages and disadvantages of early puberty? © Hill Creek Pictures/Purestock RF

» LO27.2 Moral and Cognitive Development: Distinguishing Right from Wrong

In a European country, a woman is near death from a special kind of cancer. The one drug that the doctors think might save her is a medicine that a medical researcher has recently discovered. The drug is expensive to make, and the researcher is charging 10 times the cost, or $5,000, for a small dose. The sick woman's husband, Henry, approaches everyone he knows in hopes of borrowing money, but he can get together only about $2,500. He tells the researcher that his wife is dying and asks him to lower the price of the drug or let him pay later. The researcher says, "No, I discovered the drug, and I'm going to make money from it." Henry is desperate and considers stealing the drug for his wife.

What would you tell Henry to do?

Kohlberg's Theory of Moral Development

In the view of psychologist Lawrence Kohlberg, the advice you give Henry in the preceding scenario reflects your level of moral development. According to Kohlberg, people pass through a series of levels in the evolution of their sense of justice and in the kind of reasoning they use to make moral judgments (Kohlberg, 1984).

Specifically, Kohlberg suggests that the changes in moral reasoning can be understood best as a three-level sequence (see Figure 2). Because of their cognitive limitations, preadolescent children who reason at Level 1 morality tend to think in terms of concrete, unvarying rules ("It is always wrong to steal" or "I'll be punished if I steal"). At Level 2 morality, older children tend to focus on the rules of society ("Good people don't steal" or "What if everyone stole?").

Adolescents, however, can reason on a higher plane and potentially have the ability to reason at Level 3. Because they are able to comprehend broad moral principles, they can understand that morality is not always black and white and that conflict can exist between two sets of socially accepted standards.

Kohlberg's theory assumes that people move through the levels in a fixed order, and that they cannot reach the highest level until about age 13—primarily because of limitations in cognitive development before that age. However, many people never reach the highest level of moral reasoning. In fact, Kohlberg found that only a relatively small percentage of adults rise above the second level of his model (Kohlberg & Ryncarz, 1990; Brugman, 2010; Vera-Estay, Dooley, & Beauchamp, 2015).

Moral Development in Women

One glaring shortcoming of Kohlberg's research is that he primarily used male participants. Furthermore, psychologist Carol Gilligan (1996) argues that because of men's and women's distinctive socialization experiences, a fundamental difference exists in the way each gender views moral behavior. According to Gilligan, men view morality primarily in terms of broad principles, such as justice and fairness. In contrast, women see it in terms of responsibility toward individuals and willingness to make sacrifices to help a specific individual within the context of a particular relationship. Compassion for individuals is a more salient factor in moral behavior for women than it is for men.

Because Kohlberg's model defines moral behavior largely in terms of abstract principles such as justice, Gilligan finds that it inadequately describes the moral

STUDY ALERT

The difference between the Kohlberg and the Gilligan approach to moral development is significant, with Kohlberg's theory focusing on stages and Gilligan's resting on gender differences.

Level	Sample Moral Reasoning of Subjects	
	In Favor of Stealing the Drug	Against Stealing the Drug
Level 1 Preconventional morality: At this level, the concrete interests of the individual are considered in terms of rewards and punishments.	"If you let your wife die, you will get in trouble. You'll be blamed for not spending the money to save her, and there'll be an investigation of you and the druggist for your wife's death."	"You shouldn't steal the drug because you'll be caught and sent to jail if you do. If you do get away, your conscience will bother you thinking how the police will catch up with you at any minute."
Level 2 Conventional morality: At this level, people approach moral problems as members of society. They are interested in pleasing others by acting as good members of society.	"If you let your wife die, you'll never be able to look anybody in the face again."	"After you steal the drug, you'll feel bad thinking how you've brought dishonor on your family and yourself; you won't be able to face anyone again."
Level 3 Postconventional morality: People accept that there are certain broad principles of morality that should govern our actions. These principles are more critical than the particular laws in a society.	"If you don't steal the drug, and if you let your wife die, you'll always condemn yourself for it afterward. You won't be blamed and you'll have lived up to the outside rule of the law, but you won't have lived up to your own conscience and standards of honesty."	"If you steal the drug, you won't be blamed by other people, but you'll condemn yourself because you won't have lived up to your own conscience and standards of honesty."

Figure 2 Developmental psychologist Lawrence Kohlberg theorized that people move through a three-level sequence of moral reasoning in a fixed order. However, he contended that few people ever reach the highest level of moral reasoning. Photo: © Steve Broulis/Purestock RF

development of females. She suggests that women's morality centers on individual well-being and social relationships—a morality of *caring*. In her view, compassionate concern for the welfare of others represents the highest level of morality.

The fact that Gilligan's conception of morality differs greatly from Kohlberg's suggests that gender plays an important role in determining what a person sees as moral. Although the research evidence is not definitive, it seems plausible that their differing conceptions of what constitutes moral behavior may lead men and women to regard the morality of a specific behavior in different ways (Sherblom, 2008; Walker & Frimer, 2009; Moshman, 2011).

» LO27.3 Social Development: Finding Oneself in a Social World

"Who am I?" "How do I fit into the world?" "What is life all about?"

Questions such as these assume special significance during the teenage years, as adolescents seek to find their place in the broader social world. As we will see, this quest takes adolescents along several routes.

Erikson's Theory of Psychosocial Development: The Search for Identity

Erikson's theory of psychosocial development emphasizes the search for identity during the adolescent years. As was noted earlier, psychosocial development encompasses the way people's understanding of themselves, one another, and the world around them changes during the course of development (Erikson, 1963).

The fifth stage of Erikson's theory (summarized, with the other stages, in Figure 3), the **identity-versus-role-confusion stage,** encompasses adolescence. During this stage, a time of major testing, people try to determine what is unique about themselves. They attempt to discover who they are, what their strengths are, and what kinds of roles they are best suited to play for the rest of their lives—in short, their **identity.** A person confused about the most appropriate role to play in life may lack a stable identity, adopt an unacceptable role such as that of a social deviant, or have difficulty maintaining close personal relationships later in life (Updegraff et al., 2004; Vleioras & Bosma, 2005; Goldstein, 2006).

During the identity-versus-role-confusion period, an adolescent feels pressure to identify what to do with his or her life. Because these pressures come at a time of major physical changes as well as important changes in what society expects of them, adolescents can find the period an especially difficult one. The identity-versus-role-confusion stage has another important characteristic: declining reliance on adults for information, with a shift toward using the peer group as a source of social judgments. The peer group becomes increasingly important, enabling adolescents to form close, adult-like relationships and helping them clarify their personal identities. According to Erikson, the identity-versus-role-confusion stage marks a pivotal point in psychosocial development, paving the way for continued growth and the future development of personal relationships.

identity-versus-role-confusion stage According to Erik Erikson, a time in adolescence of major testing to determine one's unique qualities

identity The distinguishing character of the individual: who each of us is, what our roles are, and what we are capable of

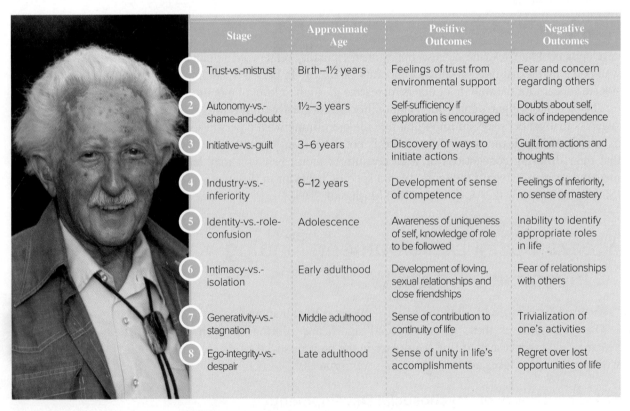

Stage	Approximate Age	Positive Outcomes	Negative Outcomes
1 Trust-vs.-mistrust	Birth–1½ years	Feelings of trust from environmental support	Fear and concern regarding others
2 Autonomy-vs.-shame-and-doubt	1½–3 years	Self-sufficiency if exploration is encouraged	Doubts about self, lack of independence
3 Initiative-vs.-guilt	3–6 years	Discovery of ways to initiate actions	Guilt from actions and thoughts
4 Industry-vs.-inferiority	6–12 years	Development of sense of competence	Feelings of inferiority, no sense of mastery
5 Identity-vs.-role-confusion	Adolescence	Awareness of uniqueness of self, knowledge of role to be followed	Inability to identify appropriate roles in life
6 Intimacy-vs.-isolation	Early adulthood	Development of loving, sexual relationships and close friendships	Fear of relationships with others
7 Generativity-vs.-stagnation	Middle adulthood	Sense of contribution to continuity of life	Trivialization of one's activities
8 Ego-integrity-vs.-despair	Late adulthood	Sense of unity in life's accomplishments	Regret over lost opportunities of life

Figure 3 Erikson's stages of psychosocial development. According to Erikson, people proceed through eight stages of psychosocial development across their lives. He suggested that each stage requires the resolution of a crisis or conflict and may produce both positive and negative outcomes. Photo: © Jon Erikson/Science Source

During early adulthood, people enter the **intimacy-versus-isolation stage.** Spanning the period of early adulthood (from post adolescence to the early thirties), this stage focuses on developing close relationships with others. Difficulties during this stage result in feelings of loneliness and a fear of such relationships, whereas successful resolution of the crises of this stage results in the possibility of forming relationships that are intimate on a physical, intellectual, and emotional level.

Development continues during middle adulthood as people enter the **generativity-versus-stagnation stage.** Generativity is the ability to contribute to one's family, community, work, and society and to assist the development of the younger generation. Success in this stage results in a person's feeling positive and optimistic about the continuity of life and their contribution to humanity. On the other hand, difficulties in this stage lead people to feel that their activities are trivial and unimportant and that their lives are stagnant. They may feel they have made poor choices.

Finally, the last stage of psychosocial development, the **ego-integrity-versus-despair stage,** spans later adulthood and continues until death. People in this stage ask themselves if they have lived a meaningful life. If they see their lives positively, they feel a sense of accomplishment; if not, they feel regret over a misspent life.

intimacy-versus-isolation stage According to Erik Erikson, a period during early adulthood that focuses on developing close relationships

generativity-versus-stagnation stage According to Erik Erikson, a period in middle adulthood during which we take stock of our contributions to family and society

ego-integrity-versus-despair stage According to Erik Erikson, a period from late adulthood until death during which we review life's accomplishments and failures

© Design Pics/Getty Images RF

From the perspective of . . .

A Retail Manager   How might the needs of adolescent employees differ from the needs of adult employees? Would you use different strategies to motivate and reward adolescent and adult workers?

Stormy Adolescence: Myth or Reality?

Does puberty invariably foreshadow a stormy, rebellious period of adolescence?

At one time, psychologists thought that most children entering adolescence were beginning a period fraught with stress and unhappiness. However, research now shows that this characterization is largely a myth, that most young people pass through adolescence without appreciable turmoil in their lives, and that parents speak easily—and fairly often—with their children about a variety of topics (van Wel, Linssen, & Abma, 2000; Granic, Hollenstein, & Dishion, 2003).

Not that adolescence is completely calm! In most families with adolescents, the amount of arguing and bickering clearly rises. Most young teenagers, as part of their search for identity, experience tension between their attempts to become independent from their parents and their actual dependence on them. They may experiment with a range of behaviors, flirting with a

THE WORLD'S FIRST GENETICALLY ENGINEERED HUMAN HITS ADOLESCENCE

We buy you the best genes in the world—FOR THIS?

So, I got my nose pierced. So what, man.

I remember checking "genius" on the order form—AND NOW LOOK!

Roz Chast/The New Yorker Collection/The Cartoon Bank

Based on your own experiences, do you believe adolescence to be stormy? © Robert A. Pears/ Getty Images RF

variety of activities that their parents, and even society as a whole, find objectionable. Happily, though, for most families such tensions stabilize during middle adolescence—around age 15 or 16—and eventually decline around age 18 (Smetana, Daddis, & Chuang, 2003; Smetana, 2005; Nicoli, 2016).

Adolescent Suicide

Although the vast majority of teenagers pass through adolescence without major psychological difficulties, some experience unusually severe psychological problems. Sometimes those problems become so extreme that adolescents take their own lives. Suicide is the third-leading cause of death for adolescents (after accidents and homicide) in the United States. More teenagers and young adults die from suicide than from cancer, heart disease, AIDS, birth defects, stroke, pneumonia and influenza, and chronic lung disease combined (Centers for Disease Control [CDC], 2004).

A teenager commits suicide every 90 minutes. Furthermore, the reported rate of suicide may actually be understated because medical personnel hesitate to report suicide as a cause of death. Instead, they frequently label a death as an accident in an effort to protect the survivors. Overall, as many as 200 adolescents may attempt suicide for every one who actually takes his or her own life (CDC, 2000; Brausch & Gutierrez, 2009).

Male adolescents are five times more likely to commit suicide than females, although females *attempt* suicide more often than males. The rate of adolescent suicide is significantly greater among whites than among nonwhites. On the other hand, Native Americans have the highest suicide rate of any ethnic group in the United States, and Asian Americans have the lowest rate (CDC, 2004; Gutierrez et al., 2005; Boden, Fergusson, & Horwood, 2007).

Although the question of why adolescent suicide rates are so high remains unanswered, several factors put

These students are mourning the death of a classmate who committed suicide. The rate of suicide among teenagers has risen significantly over the last few decades. Can you think of reasons for this phenomenon? © Design Pics/Don Hammond RF

adolescents at risk. One factor is depression, characterized by unhappiness, extreme fatigue, and—a variable that seems especially important—a profound sense of hopelessness. In other cases, adolescents who commit suicide are perfectionists, inhibited socially and prone to extreme anxiety when they face any social or academic challenge (see Figure 4; Richardson et al., 2005; Caelian, 2006; Barzilay et al., 2015).

Family background and adjustment difficulties are also related to suicide. A long-standing history of conflicts between parents and children may lead to adolescent behavior problems, such as delinquency, dropping out of school, and aggressive tendencies. In addition, teenage alcoholics and abusers of other drugs have a relatively high rate of suicide (Bagge & Sher, 2008; Hardt et al., 2008; Bidwell, 2011).

Several warning signs indicate when a teenager's problems may be severe enough to warrant concern about the possibility of a suicide attempt. They include the following:

- School problems, such as missing classes, truancy, and a sudden change in grades
- Frequent incidents of self-destructive behavior, such as careless accidents
- Loss of appetite or excessive eating
- Withdrawal from friends and peers

Figure 4 According to a review of phone calls to one telephone help line, adolescents who were considering suicide most often mentioned family, peer relationships, and self-esteem problems. Source: Adapted from Boehm & Campbell, 1995. Photo: © Myrleen Pearson/PhotoEdit

- Sleeping problems

- Signs of depression, tearfulness, or overt indications of psychological difficulties, such as hallucinations

- A preoccupation with death, an afterlife, or what would happen "if I died"

- Putting affairs in order, such as giving away prized possessions or making arrangements for the care of a pet

- An explicit announcement of thoughts of suicide

If you know someone who shows signs that he or she is considering suicide, urge that person to seek professional help. You may need to take assertive action, such as enlisting the assistance of family members or friends. Talk of suicide is a serious signal for help and not a confidence to be kept.

For immediate help with a suicide-related problem, call 1-800-273-8255, a national hotline staffed with trained counselors, or visit the Web at www.suicidepreventionlifeline.org.

EXPLORING diversity

Rites of Passage: Coming of Age around the World

It is not easy for male members of the Awa tribe in New Guinea to make the transition from childhood to adulthood. First come whippings with sticks and prickly branches, both for the boys' own past misdeeds and in honor of those tribesmen who were killed in warfare. In the next phase of the ritual, adults jab sharpened sticks into the boys' nostrils. Then they force a five-foot length of vine into the boys' throats, until they gag and vomit. Finally, tribesmen cut the boys' genitals, causing severe bleeding.

Although the rites that mark the coming of age of boys in the Awa tribe sound horrifying to Westerners, they are comparable to those in other cultures. In some, youths must kneel on hot coals without displaying pain. In others, girls must toss wads of burning cotton from hand to hand and allow themselves to be bitten by hundreds of ants (Selsky, 1997).

Other cultures have less fearsome, although no less important, ceremonies that mark the passage from childhood to adulthood. For instance, when a girl first menstruates in traditional Apache tribes, the event is marked by dawn-to-dusk chanting. Western religions, too, have several types of celebrations, including bar mitzvahs and bat mitzvahs at age 13 for Jewish boys and girls and confirmation ceremonies for children in many Christian denominations (Magida, 2006).

In most societies, males, but not females, are the focus of coming-of-age ceremonies. The renowned anthropologist Margaret Mead remarked, only partly in jest, that the preponderance of male ceremonies might reflect the fact that "the worry that boys will not grow up to be men is much more widespread than that girls will not grow up to be women" (1949, p. 195). Said another way, it may be that in most cultures men traditionally have higher status than women, and therefore those cultures regard boys' transition into adulthood as more important.

However, another fact may explain why most cultures place greater emphasis on male rather than female rites. For females, the transition from childhood is marked by a definite, biological event: menstruation. For males, in contrast, no single event can be used to pinpoint entry into adulthood. Thus, men are forced to rely on culturally determined rituals to acknowledge their arrival into adulthood.

RECAP

Summarize the major physical transitions that characterize adolescence.

■ Adolescence, the developmental stage between childhood and adulthood, is marked by the onset of puberty, the point at which sexual maturity occurs. The age at which puberty begins has implications for the way people view themselves and the way others see them.

Explain moral and cognitive development in adolescents.

■ Moral judgments during adolescence increase in sophistication, according to Kohlberg's three-level model. Although Kohlberg's levels provide an adequate description of males' moral judgments, Gilligan suggests that women view morality in terms of caring for individuals rather than in terms of broad, general principles of justice.

Describe social development in adolescents.

■ According to Erikson's model of psychosocial development, adolescence may be accompanied by an identity crisis. Adolescence is followed by three more stages of psychosocial development that cover the remainder of the life span.

■ Suicide is the third-leading cause of death in adolescents.

[EVALUATE E Evaluate]

1. _____ is the period during which the sexual organs begin to mature.
2. _____ proposed a set of three levels of moral development ranging from reasoning based on rewards and punishments to abstract thinking involving concepts of justice.
3. Gilligan's theory of moral development focuses on the morality of caring, in which concern for others represents the highest level of morality. True or false?
4. Erikson believed that during adolescence, people must search for _____, whereas during early adulthood, the major task is _____.

[RETHINK R Rethink]

What implications does the fact that puberty is starting earlier have for the nature of schooling? In what ways do school cultures help or hurt students who are going through adolescence?

Answers to Evaluate Questions 1. puberty; 2. Kohlberg; 3. true; 4. identity, intimacy

KEY TERMS

Adolescence LO27.1

Puberty LO27.1

Identity-versus-role-confusion stage LO27.3

Identity LO27.3

Intimacy-versus-isolation stage LO27.3

Generativity-versus-stagnation stage LO27.3

Ego-integrity-versus-despair stage LO27.3

module 28

Adulthood

Learning Outcomes  Prepare

>> **LO28.1** Explain physical development in adulthood.

>> **LO28.2** Discuss social development in adulthood.

>> **LO28.3** State the impact of marriage, children, and divorce on families.

>> **LO28.4** Discuss the later years of adulthood.

>> **LO28.5** Explain the physical changes that occur in late adulthood.

>> **LO28.6** Identify the cognitive changes that occur in late adulthood.

>> **LO28.7** Discuss the social aspects of late adulthood.

>> **LO28.8** Describe how people can adjust to death.

W Work

Psychologists generally agree that early adulthood begins around age 20 and lasts until about age 40 to 45 when middle adulthood begins and continues until around age 65. Despite the enormous importance of these periods of life in terms of both the accomplishments that occur in them and their overall length (together they span some 45 years), they have been studied less than has any other stage. For one reason, the physical changes that occur during these periods are less apparent and more gradual than are those at other times during the life span. In addition, the diverse social changes that arise during this period defy simple categorization. However, developmental psychologists have recently begun to focus on the period, particularly on the social changes in the family and women's careers.

The variety of changes that occur in early adulthood have led many developmental psychologists to view the start of the period as a transitional phase, called emerging adulthood. **Emerging adulthood** is the period beginning in the late teenage years and extending into the mid-20s. During emerging adulthood, people are no longer adolescents, but they haven't fully taken on the responsibilities of adulthood. Instead, they are still engaged in determining who they are and what their life and career paths should be. It is a time of uncertainty and instability, as well as self-discovery (Bukobza, 2009; Lamborn & Groh, 2009; Schwartz et al., 2013).

The view that adulthood is preceded by an extended period of emerging adulthood reflects the reality of the economies of industrialized countries. These economies have shifted away from manufacturing to a focus on technology

emerging adulthood The period beginning in the late teenage years and extending into the mid-twenties

and information, thus requiring increasing time spent in educational training. Furthermore, the age at which most people marry and have children has risen significantly (Arnett, 2007, 2011).

There's also an increasing ambivalence about reaching adulthood. When people in their late teens and early 20s are asked if they feel they have reached adulthood, most say "yes and no." In short, emerging adulthood is an age of identity exploration in which individuals are more self-focused and uncertain than they will be later in early adulthood (Arnett, 2000, 2006).

As we discuss the changes that occur through emerging adulthood, early adulthood, middle adulthood, and ultimately late adulthood, keep in mind the demarcations between the periods are fuzzy. However, the changes are certainly no less profound than they were in earlier periods of development.

» LO28.1 Physical Development: The Peak of Health

For most people, early adulthood marks the peak of physical health. From about 18 to 25 years of age, people's strength is greatest, their reflexes are quickest, and their chances of dying from disease are quite slim. Moreover, reproductive capabilities are at their highest level.

menopause The period during which women stop menstruating and are no longer fertile

Around age 25, the body becomes slightly less efficient and more susceptible to disease. Overall, however, ill health remains the exception; most people stay remarkably healthy during early adulthood. (Can you think of any machine other than the body that can operate without pause for so long a period?)

During middle adulthood people gradually become aware of changes in their bodies. People often experience weight gain (although they can avoid such increases through diet and exercise). Furthermore, the sense organs gradually become less sensitive, and reactions to stimuli are slower. But generally, the physical declines that occur during middle adulthood are minor and often unnoticeable (DiGiovanna, 1994; Whitbourne, 2007).

The major biological change that does occur during middle adulthood pertains to reproductive capabilities. On average, during their late forties or early fifties, women begin **menopause,** during which they stop menstruating and are no longer fertile. Because menopause is accompanied by a significant reduction in the production of estrogen, a female hormone, women sometimes experience symptoms such as hot flashes, sudden sensations of heat. Many symptoms can be treated through *hormone therapy (HT),* in which menopausal women take the hormones estrogen and progesterone.

However, hormone therapy poses several dangers, such as an increase in the risk of breast cancer, blood clots, and coronary heart disease. These uncertainties make the routine use of HT controversial. Currently, the medical consensus seems to be that younger women with severe menopausal symptoms ought to consider HT on a short-term basis. On the other hand, HT is less appropriate for older women after menopause (Rossouw et al., 2007; MacLennan, 2009; McCarrey & Resnick, 2015).

Women's reactions to menopause vary significantly across cultures, and according to one study the more a society values old age, the less difficulty its women have during menopause. Why do you think this would be the case? © Ronnie Kaufman/Blend Images LLC RF

For men, the aging process during middle adulthood is somewhat subtler. There are no physiological signals of increasing age equivalent to the end of menstruation in women; that is, no male menopause exists. In fact, men remain fertile and capable of fathering children until well into late adulthood. However, some gradual physical decline occurs: sperm production decreases, and the frequency of orgasm tends to decline. Once again, though, any psychological difficulties associated with these changes are usually brought about by an aging individual's ability to meet the exaggerated standards of youthfulness and not by the person's physical deterioration.

» LO28.2 Social Development: Working at Life

Whereas physical changes during adulthood reflect development of a quantitative nature, social developmental transitions are qualitative and more profound. During this period, people typically launch themselves into careers, marriage, and families.

The entry into early adulthood is usually marked by leaving one's childhood home and entering the world of work. People envision life goals and make career choices. Their lives often center on their careers, which form an important part of their identity (Vaillant & Vaillant, 1990; Levinson, 1990, 1992).

In their early forties, however, people may begin to question their lives as they enter a period called the *midlife transition*. The idea that life will end at some point becomes increasingly influential in their thinking, and they may question their past accomplishments (Gould, 1978; Boylan & Ryff, 2015).

Although some psychologists—and popular opinion—suggest that physical aging and dissatisfaction with one's life mark a so-called "midlife crisis," there is little evidence for such a "crisis." In fact, the passage into middle age is relatively calm for most people. Most 40-year-olds view their lives and accomplishments positively enough to proceed relatively smoothly through midlife, and the 40s and 50s are often a particularly rewarding period. Rather than looking to the future, people concentrate on the present; their involvement with their families, friends, and other social groups takes on new importance. A major developmental thrust of this period is coming to terms with one's circumstances (Whitbourne, 2000, 2010; Wakamoto, 2010; Dare, 2011).

Finally, during the last stages of adulthood, people become more accepting of others and of their own lives and are less concerned about issues or problems that once bothered them. They come to accept the fact that death is inevitable, and they try to understand their accomplishments in terms of the broader meaning of life. Although people may begin, for the first time, to label themselves as "old," many also develop a sense of wisdom and feel freer to enjoy life (Miner-Rubino, Winter, & Stewart, 2004; Ward-Baker, 2007; Galambos et al., 2015).

» LO28.3 Marriage, Children, and Divorce: Family Ties

In the typical fairy tale, a dashing young man and a beautiful young woman marry, have children, and live happily ever after. However, that scenario does not match the realities of love and marriage in the twenty-first century. Today, it is just as likely that the man and woman would first live together, then get married and have children, but ultimately get divorced.

The percentage of U.S. households made up of unmarried couples has increased dramatically over the last two decades. At the same time, the average age at which marriage takes place is higher than at any time since the turn of the last century. These changes have been dramatic, and they suggest that the institution of marriage has changed considerably from earlier historical periods.

When people do marry, the probability of divorce is high, especially for younger couples. Even though divorce rates have been declining since they peaked in 1981, about half of all first marriages end in divorce. Before they are 18 years old, two-fifths of children will experience the breakup of their parents' marriages. Moreover, the rise in divorce is not just a U.S. phenomenon: the divorce rate has accelerated over the last several decades in most industrialized countries. In some countries, the increase has been enormous. In South Korea, for example, the divorce rate quadrupled from 11 percent to 47 percent in the 12-year period ending in 2002 (Lankov, 2004; Olson & DeFrain, 2005; Park & Raymo, 2013).

Changes in marriage and divorce trends have doubled the number of single-parent households in the United States over the last two decades. Almost 25 percent of all family households are now headed by one parent, compared with 13 percent in 1970. If present trends continue, almost three-fourths of American children will spend some portion of their lives in a single-parent family before they turn 18. For children in minority households, the numbers are even higher. Almost 60 percent of all black children and more than a third of Hispanic children live in homes with only one parent. Furthermore, in most single-parent families, the children live with the mother rather than the father—a phenomenon that is consistent across racial and ethnic groups throughout the industrialized world (U.S. Bureau of the Census, 2000; Sarsour et al., 2011).

Changing Roles of Men and Women: The Time of Their Lives

One of the major changes in family life in the last two decades has been the evolution of men's and women's roles. More women than ever before act simultaneously as wives, mothers, and wage earners—in contrast to women in traditional marriages, in which the husband is the sole wage earner and the wife assumes primary responsibility for care of the home and children.

Almost three-fourths of all women with children under the age of 18 are employed outside the home, and 65 percent of mothers with children under age 6 are working. In the mid-1960s, only 17 percent of mothers of 1-year-olds worked full-time; now, more than half are in the labor force (Bureau of Labor Statistics, 2013).

> One of the major changes in family life in the last two decades has been the evolution of men's and women's roles.

© Jack Hollingsworth/Getty Images RF

From the perspective of . . .

A New Employee How would an understanding of human development enable you to work more effectively with co-workers who are younger than you? Older than you?

© Scott Hortop/Getty Images RF

Women's "Second Shift"

The number of hours put in by working mothers can be staggering. One survey, for instance, found that if we add the number of hours worked on the job and in the home, employed mothers of children under 3 years of age put in an average of 90 hours per week! The additional work women perform is sometimes called the "second shift." National surveys show women who are both employed and mothers put in an extra month of 24-hour days during the course of a year. Researchers see similar patterns in many developing societies throughout the world, with women working at full-time jobs and also having primary responsibilities for child care (Hochschild, 2001; Jacobs & Gerson, 2004; U.S. Bureau of Labor Statistics, 2007).

Consequently, rather than careers being a substitute for what women do at home, they are often in addition to the role of homemaker. It is not surprising that some wives feel resentment toward husbands who spend less time on child care and housework than the wives had expected before the birth of their children (Stier & Lewin-Epstein, 2000; Kiecolt, 2003; Gerstel, 2005; Fagan & Press, 2008).

≫ LO28.4 The Later Years of Life: Growing Old

By focusing on the period of life that starts at around age 65, *gerontologists,* specialists who study aging, are making important contributions to clarifying the capabilities of older adults. Their work is demonstrating that significant developmental processes continue even during old age. And as life expectancy increases, the number of people who reach older adulthood will continue to grow substantially. Consequently, developing an understanding of late adulthood has become a critical priority for psychologists (Birren, 1996; Moody, 2000; Schaie, 2005).

How might an understanding of the physical and mental changes in older adults help you treat an elderly patient, particularly in a high-stress emergency situation? U.S. Air Force photo by Master Sgt. Jack Braden

» LO28.5 Physical Changes in Late Adulthood: The Aging Body

Many physical changes are brought about by the aging process. The most obvious are those of appearance—hair thinning and turning gray, skin wrinkling and folding, and sometimes a slight loss of height as the thickness of the disks between vertebrae in the spine decreases—but subtler changes also occur in the body's biological functioning. For example, sensory capabilities decrease as a result of aging: vision, hearing, smell, and taste become less sensitive. Reaction time slows, and physical stamina changes (Schieber, 2006; Madden, 2007; Schilling & Diehl, 2015).

> **Many physical changes are brought about by the aging process.**

What are the reasons for these physical declines? **Genetic preprogramming theories of aging** suggest that human cells have a built-in time limit to their reproduction. These theories suggest that after a certain time cells stop dividing or become harmful to the body—as if a kind of automatic self-destruct button had been pushed. In contrast, **wear-and-tear theories of aging** suggest that the mechanical functions of the body simply work less efficiently as people age. Waste by-products of energy production eventually accumulate, and mistakes are made when cells divide. Eventually the body, in effect, wears out, like an old automobile (Miquel, 2006; Hayflick, 2007; Schaie & Willis, 2011).

genetic preprogramming theories of aging Theories that suggest that human cells have a built-in time limit to their reproduction, and that after a certain time they are no longer able to divide

wear-and-tear theories of aging Theories that suggest that the mechanical functions of the body simply stop working efficiently

» LO28.6 Cognitive Changes: Thinking About—and During—Late Adulthood

At one time, many gerontologists would have agreed with the popular view that older adults are forgetful and confused. Today, however, most research indicates that this assessment is far from an accurate one of older people's capabilities. One reason for the change in view is that more sophisticated research techniques exist for studying the cognitive changes that occur in late adulthood.

Still, some declines in intellectual functioning during late adulthood do occur, although the pattern of age differences is not uniform for different types of cognitive abilities (see Figure 1). In general, skills relating to *fluid intelligence* (which involves information-processing skills such as memory, calculations, and analogy solving) show declines in late adulthood. In contrast, skills relating to *crystallized intelligence* (intelligence based on the accumulation of information, skills, and strategies learned through experience) remain steady and in some cases actually improve (van Hooren, Valentijn, & Bosma, 2007; Kaufman, Johnson, & Liu, 2008; Drag & Bieliauskas, 2010; Dixon et al., 2013).

Even when changes in intellectual functioning occur during late adulthood, people often are able to compensate for any decline. They can still learn what they want to; it may just take more time. Furthermore, teaching older adults strategies for dealing with new problems can prevent declines in performance. There is even research evidence that playing video games during late adulthood can produce benefits in intellectual functioning (Saczynski, Willis, & Schaie, 2002; Basak et al., 2008; Westerberg et al., 2008).

STUDY ALERT

Two major theories of aging—the genetic preprogramming and the wear-and-tear views—explain some of the physical changes that take place in older adults.

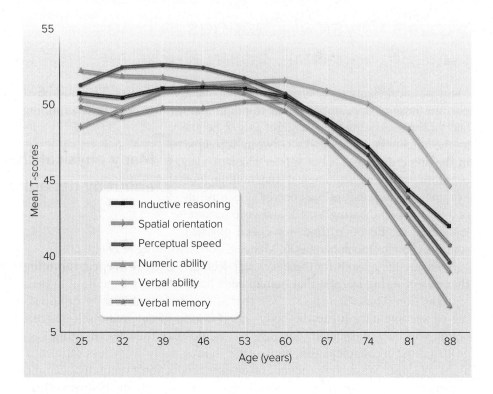

Figure 1 Age-related changes in intellectual skills vary according to the specific cognitive ability in question. Source: Adapted from Schaie, 2005.

(Legend)
- Inductive reasoning
- Spatial orientation
- Perceptual speed
- Numeric ability
- Verbal ability
- Verbal memory

(Y-axis: Mean T-scores, 5 to 55)
(X-axis: Age (years), 25 32 39 46 53 60 67 74 81 88)

Memory Changes in Late Adulthood: Are Older Adults Forgetful?

One of the characteristics most frequently attributed to late adulthood is forgetfulness. How accurate is this assumption?

Most evidence suggests that memory change is not an inevitable part of the aging process. Even when people show memory declines during late adulthood, their deficits are limited to certain types of memory. For instance, losses tend to be limited to episodic memories, which relate to specific experiences in people's lives. Other types of memories, such as semantic memories (that refer to general knowledge and facts) and implicit memories (memories of which we are not consciously aware), are largely unaffected by age (Fleischman et al., 2004; Mitchell & Schmitt, 2006; St. Jacques & Levine, 2007; Pinal, Zurrón, & Díaz, 2015).

For example, rather than use senility to describe memory loss in general, gerontologists now recognize **Alzheimer's disease** as a progressive brain disorder that leads to a gradual and irreversible decline in cognitive abilities. More than 5.3 million Americans have the disease, and 1 in 9 people age 65 and older are afflicted. Unless a cure is found, some 14 million people will experience Alzheimer's by 2050 (Rogers, 2007; Alzheimer's Association, 2013).

Alzheimer's disease A progressive brain disorder that leads to a gradual and irreversible decline in cognitive abilities.

From the perspective of . . .

A Medical Assistant How would you handle someone who believed that getting older had only negative consequences?

© Comstock/Getty Images RF

Alzheimer's occurs when production of the *beta amyloid precursor protein* goes awry, producing large clumps of cells that trigger inflammation and deterioration of nerve cells. The brain shrinks, neurons die, and several areas of the hippocampus and frontal and temporal lobes deteriorate. So far, there is no effective treatment (Medeiros et al., 2007; Behrens, Lendon, & Roe, 2009; Clement et al., 2016).

In sum, declines in cognitive functioning in late adulthood are, for the most part, not inevitable. The key to maintaining cognitive skills may lie in intellectual stimulation. Like the rest of us, older adults need a stimulating environment in order to hone and maintain their skills (Bosma et al., 2003; Glisky, 2007; Hertzog et al., 2008).

STUDY ALERT

It's important to be able to describe the nature of intellectual changes during late adulthood.

» LO28.7 The Social World of Late Adulthood: Old but Not Alone

Just as the view that old age predictably means mental decline has proved to be wrong, so has the view that late adulthood inevitably brings loneliness. People in late adulthood most often see themselves as functioning members of society, with only a small number of them reporting that loneliness is a serious problem (Berkman, Ertel, & Glymour, 2011; Luong, Rauers & Fingerman, 2015).

disengagement theory of aging A theory that suggests that aging produces a gradual withdrawal from the world on physical, psychological, and social levels

activity theory of aging A theory that suggests that the elderly who are more successful while aging are those who maintain the interests and activities they had during middle age

Certainly, late adulthood brings significant challenges. People who have spent their adult lives working enter retirement, bringing about a major shift in the role they play. Moreover, many people must face the death of their spouse. Especially if the marriage has been a long and good one, the death of a partner means the loss of a companion, confidante, and lover. It can also bring about changes in economic well-being.

There is no single way to age successfully. According to one early and influential point of view, the **disengagement theory of aging,** aging produces a gradual withdrawal from the world on physical, psychological, and social levels. Such disengagement was seen as serving an important purpose, providing an opportunity for increased reflectiveness and decreased emotional investment in others at a time of life when social relationships will inevitably be ended by death (Adams, 2004; Wrosch, Bauer, & Scheier, 2005).

However, it turned out that little research supported disengagement theory, and consequently an alternative theory emerged. According to the **activity theory of aging,** people who age most successfully are those who maintain the interests, activities, and level of social interaction they experienced during middle adulthood. Activity theory argues that late adulthood should reflect a continuation, as much as possible, of the activities in which people participated during the earlier part of their lives (Crosnoe & Elder, 2002; Nimrod & Kleiber, 2007).

Although most research is supportive of activity theory, not all people in late adulthood need a life filled with activities and social interaction to be happy; as in every stage of life, some older adults are just as satisfied leading a relatively inactive, solitary existence. What may be more

Although there are declines in fluid intelligence in late adulthood, skills relating to crystallized intelligence remain steady and may actually improve. © Deborah Davis/PhotoEdit

important is how people view the aging process: evidence shows that positive self-perceptions of aging are associated with increased longevity (Levy et al., 2002; Levy & Myers, 2004).

life review The process by which people examine and evaluate their lives

Regardless of whether people become disengaged or maintain their activities from earlier stages of life, most are involved in a process of **life review,** in which they examine and evaluate their lives. Remembering and reconsidering what has occurred in the past, people in late adulthood often come to a better understanding of themselves, sometimes resolving lingering problems and conflicts, and facing their lives with greater wisdom and serenity.

Clearly, people in late adulthood are not just marking time until death. Rather, old age is a time of continued growth and development, as important as any other period of life.

» LO28.8 Adjusting to Death

becoming an informed consumer of psychology

Adjusting to Death

At some time in our lives, we all face death—certainly our own, as well as the deaths of friends, loved ones, and even strangers. Although there is nothing more inevitable in life, death remains a frightening, emotion-laden topic. Certainly, little is more stressful than the death of a loved one or the contemplation of our own imminent death, and preparing for death is one of our most crucial developmental tasks (see the Try It! box to assess your own attitudes toward death).

Try It!
How Do You Feel About Death?

To assess your feelings about death, complete the following questionnaire. For statements 1 through 11, use these scale labels:

   1 = Never; 2 = Rarely; 3 = Sometimes; and 4 = Often

1. I think about my own death._____

2. I think about the death of loved ones._____

3. I think about dying young._____

4. I think about the possibility of my being killed on a busy road._____

5. I have fantasies of my own death._____

6. I think about death just before I go to sleep._____

7. I think of how I would act if I knew I were to die within a given period of time._____

8. I think of how my relatives would act and feel upon my death._____

9. When I am sick, I think about death._____

10. When I am outside during a lightning storm, I think about the possibility of being struck by lightning. _____

11. When I am in a car, I think about the high incidence of traffic fatalities._____

For statements 12 through 30, use these scale labels:

   1 = I strongly disagree; 2 = I disagree; 3 = I agree; 4 = I strongly agree

12. I think people should first become concerned about death when they are old._____

13. I am much more concerned about death than those around me._____

14. Death hardly concerns me._____

15. My general outlook just doesn't allow for morbid thoughts._____

16. The prospect of my own death arouses anxiety in me._____

17. The prospect of my own death depresses me._____

18. The prospect of the death of my loved ones arouses anxiety in me._____

19. The knowledge that I will surely die does not in any way affect the conduct of my life._____

20. I envisage my own death as a painful, nightmarish experience._____

21. I am afraid of dying._____

22. I am afraid of being dead._____

23. Many people become disturbed at the sight of a new grave, but it does not bother me._____

24. I am disturbed when I think about the shortness of life._____

25. Thinking about death is a waste of time._____

26. Death should not be regarded as a tragedy if it occurs after a productive life._____

27. The inevitable death of humanity poses a serious challenge to the meaningfulness of human existence._____

(continued)

28. The death of the individual is ultimately beneficial because it facilitates change in society._____

29. I have a desire to live on after death._____

30. The question of whether or not there is a future life worries me considerably._____

Scoring

If you rated any of these items—12, 14, 15, 19, 23, 25, 26, and 28—as 1, change these ratings to 4; those you rated as 2, change to 3; those you rated as 3, change to 2; and those you rated as 4, change to 1. Add up your ratings.

Average scores on the scale typically range from about 68 to 80. If you scored about 85, death is something that seems to produce some degree of anxiety. Scores lower than 68 suggest that you experience little fear of death.

Source: Adapted from Dickstein, 1972.

A generation ago, talk of death was taboo. The topic was never mentioned to dying people, and gerontologists had little to say about it. That changed, however, with the pioneering work of Elisabeth Kübler-Ross, who brought the subject of death into the open with her observation that those facing impending death tend to move through five broad stages (Kübler-Ross & Kessler, 2005):

- *Denial.* In this stage, people resist the idea that they are dying. Even if told that their chances for survival are small, they refuse to admit that they are facing death.

- *Anger.* After moving beyond the denial stage, dying people become angry—angry at people around them who are in good health, angry at medical professionals for being ineffective, angry at God.

- *Bargaining.* Anger leads to bargaining, in which the dying try to think of ways to postpone death. They may decide to dedicate their lives to religion if God saves them; they may say, "If only I can live to see my son married, I will accept death then."

- *Depression.* When dying people come to feel that bargaining is of no use, they move to the next stage: depression. They realize that their lives really are coming to an end, leading to what Kübler-Ross calls "preparatory grief" for their own deaths.

- *Acceptance.* In this stage, people accept impending death. Usually they are unemotional and uncommunicative; it is as if they have made peace with themselves and are expecting death with no bitterness.

Although Kübler-Ross believed that all people went through the stages in a similar fashion, research shows that not everyone experiences each of the stages in the same way. In fact, Kübler-Ross's stages are applicable only to people who are fully aware that they are dying and have the time to evaluate their impending death. Furthermore, vast differences occur in the way individuals react to impending death. The specific cause and duration of dying, as well as the person's sex, age, and personality and the type of support received from family and friends, all have an impact on how people respond to death (Carver & Scheier, 2002; Coyle, 2006).

Few of us enjoy the contemplation of death. Yet awareness of its psychological aspects and consequences can make its inevitable arrival less anxiety-producing and perhaps more understandable.

RECAP

Explain physical development in adulthood.

- Early adulthood marks the peak of physical health. Physical changes occur relatively gradually in men and women during adulthood.

- One major physical change occurs at the end of middle adulthood for women: they begin menopause, after which they are no longer fertile.

Discuss social development in adulthood.

- During middle adulthood, people typically experience a midlife transition in which the notion that life is not unending becomes more important. In some cases, this may lead to a midlife crisis, although the passage into middle age is typically relatively calm.

- As aging continues during middle adulthood, people realize in their fifties that their lives and accomplishments are fairly well set, and they try to come to terms with them.

State the impact of marriage, children, and divorce on families.

- Among the important developmental milestones during adulthood are marriage, family changes, and divorce. Another important determinant of adult development is work.

Discuss the later years of adulthood.

- Gerontologists, specialists who study aging, are making important contributions to clarifying the capabilities of older adults.

Explain the physical changes that occur in late adulthood.

- Old age may bring marked physical declines caused by genetic preprogramming or physical wear and tear.

- Although the activities of people in late adulthood are not all that different from those of younger people, older adults experience declines in reaction time, sensory abilities, and physical stamina.

Identify the cognitive changes that occur in late adulthood.

- Intellectual declines are not an inevitable part of aging.

- Fluid intelligence does decline with age, and long-term memory abilities are sometimes impaired.

- Crystallized intelligence shows slight increases with age, and short-term memory remains at about the same level.

Discuss the social aspects of late adulthood.

- Although disengagement theory sees successful aging as a process of gradual withdrawal from the physical, psychological, and social worlds, there is little research supporting this view. Instead, activity theory, which suggests that the maintenance of interests and activities from earlier years leads to successful aging, is a more accurate explanation.

Describe how people can adjust to death.

- According to Kübler-Ross, dying people move through five stages as they face death: denial, anger, bargaining, depression, and acceptance.

1. Rob recently turned 40 and surveyed his goals and accomplishments to date. Although he has accomplished a lot, he realized that many of his goals will not be met in his lifetime. This stage is called a _____ _____.

2. _____ _____ theories suggest that there is a maximum time span in which cells are able to reproduce. This time limit explains the eventual breakdown of the body during old age.

3. Lower IQ test scores during late adulthood do not necessarily mean a decrease in intelligence. True or false?

4. During old age, a person's _____ intelligence continues to increase, whereas _____ intelligence may decline.

5. In Kübler-Ross's _____ stage, people resist the idea of death. In the _____ stage, they attempt to make deals to avoid death, and in the _____ stage, they passively await death.

RETHINK

Is the possibility that life may be extended for several decades a mixed blessing? What societal consequences might an extended life span bring about?

Answers to Evaluate Questions 1. midlife transition; 2. genetic preprogramming; 3. true; 4. crystallized, fluid; 5. denial, bargaining, acceptance

KEY TERMS

Emerging adulthood   LO28.1

Menopause   LO28.1

Genetic preprogramming theories of aging   LO28.5

Wear-and-tear theories of aging   LO28.5

Alzheimer's disease   LO28.6

Disengagement theory of aging   LO28.7

Activity theory of aging   LO28.7

Life review   LO28.8

« « Looking Back

Psychology on the Web

1. Find information on the Web about gene therapy. What recent advances in gene therapy have been made by researchers? What developments appear to be on the horizon? What ethical issues have been raised regarding the use of gene therapy to produce children with characteristics specified by their parents?

2. Find different answers to the question "Why do people die?" Search the Web for scientific, philosophical, and spiritual/religious answers. Write a summary in which you compare the different approaches to this question. How does the thinking in any one realm influence the thinking in the others?

the case of . . .
JEAN SWEETLAND, THE WOMAN WITH TOO MANY HATS

Jean Sweetland never expected that she would one day have so many different hats to wear. But now, in her early forties, when Jean comes home from her full-time job as a nurse and takes off her nurse's cap, it seems as though her day has barely started. With two teenage children living at home, Jean next must put on her mother's hat and enforce household rules, dispense advice, help with homework, or just provide a shoulder to cry on. Before her husband comes home from his own job, Jean has to pop on her chef's hat and get dinner started; the maid's cap will come out later, when Jean does the family's laundry and cleans the bathrooms. As if all this weren't enough, the responsibility has fallen to Jean for looking after her aging mother as well. Two or three evenings a week Jean slips on her daughter's hat and makes the trip across town to her mother's house, where she spends an hour or so paying bills, restocking the cupboards, and helping with other household chores.

Jean loves her family and she tries very hard to be the mother, wife, and daughter that they all need her to be—but the conflicting demands on her time are stressful and often tiresome. In recent months Jean has increasingly found herself wondering what became of her own wants and needs, and she has begun asking herself hard questions about the direction her life is headed.

1. How typical is the Sweetland family structure? In what ways is Jean's situation typical of women her age?

2. What would be your best guess as to Jean Sweetland's parenting style, and why do you think so?

3. Describe the stage of social development that Jean Sweetland's adolescent children are most likely experiencing. In what ways might their own development be influencing Jean's?

4. If you were Jean's physician, how would you explain to her the changes that might be occurring in her aging mother?

5. Describe how Jean might react if her mother were to die? What stages of grief might she pass through?

profiles of **SUCCESS**

Courtesy of Bryce Burtosky

NAME:	**Bryce Burtosky**
SCHOOL:	**Pittsburgh Technical Institute**
DEGREE PROGRAM:	**Graphic Design**

"Set goals, conquer them, repeat."

These words form the basis of Bryce Burtosky's drive to educate himself and pursue a new vocation and profession in the field of graphic design.

"I work a full-time job as a cook while doing school full-time and having a social life," Burtosky explains. "Realize that school is your main priority, not work, and let your boss or supervisor know that you are very adamant about completing your school work.

"To balance my schedule I set out what I plan on completing during the day the night before so I know as what to expect. If I have an opportunity to go into school early before class and work on a project, I don't hesitate to take that time out of my day," he added.

Burtosky also tries to focus on what is successful instead of dwelling on what fails.

"I learned not to be afraid of failure. Taking chances on healthy risks opens the doorway for opportunities you would have never thought imaginable," he said. "Thomas Edison was asked why didn't he quit after failing 10,000 times inventing the lightbulb. He replied, 'I have not failed. I just found 10,000 ways that won't work.'"

Setting priorities as part of developing study habits is important, according to Burtosky. He also stresses that not doing what you truly love can make you lose track of your ultimate goals, and can affect grades, career, and attitude. By following his own advice Burtosky has become a better student.

"College has taught me that just because you fail does not mean that you HAVE failed. It means that you have the experience and knowledge to know not to make the same mistakes as before," he added.

While hands-on courses teaching graphic design are crucial to Burtosky's professional pursuits, the psychology course has also provided him with important skills.

"From what I learned in psychology I can better understand why people think the way they do. As a graphic designer you have to deal with customers and clients on a daily basis," he said. "Understanding the way they think will give me a head start on designs and understanding of their own position. A better understanding of your client gives you a better understanding of what they want to project within their design."

[RETHINK R Rethink]

Consider Burtosky's winding course to pursue his dream of graphic design. How does it fit with Erikson's theory of psychosocial development?

Burtosky talks about understanding how clients think. How will understanding social development throughout the life span help him in his career?

visual summary 8
DEVELOPMENT

MODULE 25 Nature, Nurture, and Prenatal Development

Developmental Research Techniques
- Cross-sectional, longitudinal, sequential

Basics of Genetics: Chromosomes and genes

Earliest Development
- Zygote: a fertilized egg
- Embryo: between 2 and 8 weeks old after conception
- Fetus: between 8 weeks and birth
- Age of viability: about 22 weeks from conception

Nature and Nurture
- Nature: Refers to hereditary factors
- Nurture: Refers to environmental influences

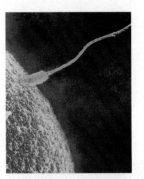

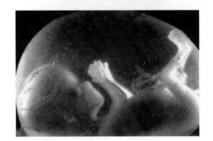

MODULE 26 Infancy and Childhood

The Extraordinary Newborn
- Reflexes: Rooting, sucking, gag, Babinski
- Development of the senses

Infancy through Middle Childhood, about age 12
- Physical development: rapid growth
- Social development: Attachment
    - Child care outside the home
    - Four parenting styles
    - Erikson's theory of psychosocial development
- Cognitive development
    - Piaget's theory of cognitive development
    - Information processing approaches

Cognitive Stage	Approximate Age Range	Major Characteristics
Sensorimotor	Birth–2 years	Development of object permanence, development of motor skills, little or no capacity for symbolic representation
Preoperational	2–7 years	Development of language and symbolic thinking, egocentric thinking
Concrete operational mastery	7–12 years	Development of conservation, of concept of reversibility
Formal operational	12 years–adulthood	Development of logical and abstract thinking

MODULE 27 Adolescence

Physical Development: Rapid weight and height gains; onset of puberty

Cognitive and Moral Development: Changes in moral reasoning

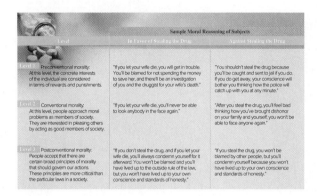

Social Development: Erikson's theory of psychosocial development

Stage	Approximate Age	Positive Outcomes	Negative Outcomes
1 Trust-vs-mistrust	Birth–1½ years	Feelings of trust from environmental support	Fear and concern regarding others
2 Autonomy-vs-shame-and-doubt	1½–3 years	Self-sufficiency if exploration is encouraged	Doubts about self, lack of independence
3 Initiative-vs-guilt	3–6 years	Discovery of ways to initiate actions	Guilt from actions and thoughts
4 Industry-vs-inferiority	6–12 years	Development of sense of competence	Feelings of inferiority, no sense of mastery
5 Identity-vs-role-confusion	Adolescence	Awareness of uniqueness of self, knowledge of role to be followed	Inability to identify appropriate roles in life
6 Intimacy-vs-isolation	Early adulthood	Development of loving, sexual relationships and close friendships	Fear of relationships with others
7 Generativity-vs-stagnation	Middle adulthood	Sense of contribution to continuity of life	Trivialization of one's activities
8 Ego-integrity-vs-despair	Late adulthood	Sense of unity in life's accomplishments	Regret over lost opportunities of life

Sample Moral Reasoning of Subjects

Level	In Favor of Stealing the Drug	Against Stealing the Drug
Level 1 Preconventional morality: At this level, the concrete interests of the individual are considered in terms of rewards and punishments.	"If you let your wife die, you will get in trouble. You'll be blamed for not spending the money to save her, and there'll be an investigation of you and the druggist for your wife's death."	"You shouldn't steal the drug because you'll be caught and sent to jail if you do. If you do get away, your conscience will bother you thinking how the police will catch up with you at any minute."
Level 2 Conventional morality: At this level, people approach moral problems as members of society. They are interested in pleasing others by acting as good members of society.	"If you let your wife die, you'll never be able to look anybody in the face again."	"After you steal the drug, you'll feel bad thinking how you've brought dishonor on your family and yourself; you won't be able to face anyone again."
Level 3 Postconventional morality: People accept that there are certain broad principles of morality that should govern our actions. These principles are more critical than the particular laws in a society.	"If you don't steal the drug, and if you let your wife die, you'll always condemn yourself for it afterward. You won't be blamed and you'll have lived up to the outside rule of the law, but you won't have lived up to your own conscience and standards of honesty."	"If you steal the drug, you won't be blamed by other people, but you'll condemn yourself because you won't have lived up to your own conscience and standards of honesty."

MODULE 28 Adulthood

Physical Development
- Early adulthood: peak of health
- Middle adulthood: menopause for women

Social Development
- Early adulthood: Focus on career, marriage, family
- Midlife transition: Relatively calm, come to terms with one's circumstances
- Late adulthood: Acceptance of others and one's circumstances

Marriage, Children, and Divorce
- People marry later in life than ever before; about half of all first marriages end in divorce
- Many single-parent households

Growing Old: Late adulthood
- Physical changes
  - Genetic preprogramming aging theory
  - Wear-and-tear aging theory
- Cognitive changes
  - Fluid intelligence declines; crystallized intelligence remains steady
  - Memory change not inevitable
  - Alzheimer's disease: Gradual, irreversible brain disorder that leads to a decline in cognitive abilities
- Social world
  - Disengagement theory of aging
  - Activity theory of aging

CHAPTER 9

© Peathegee Inc/Getty Images

CHAPTER OUTLINE

Good Guy or Good Fella?

The 60-something man called himself "Tom," and his girlfriend, "Helen." He said they were from New York, and they would spend months at a time visiting the Louisiana resort town of Grand Isle.

During his visits, Tom would drive around Grand Isle, offering biscuits to stray dogs. He wept when a dying puppy had to be shot to end its suffering. When he went fishing, he would toss back the small fish. He told a family he befriended how bad it was to permit children to watch violence on television. He bought eyeglasses for a child whose vision required correction, as well as buying a needy family a refrigerator and stove.

But to criminal investigators at the FBI, he was not so lovable. They said he was Whitey Bulger, a mobster who had run a crime empire that included drug sales and gambling. He was a reputed murderer and bank robber, a man who had held a knife to a banker's throat while extorting $50,000. To the FBI, his pleasant personality was just a front, motivated only by self-interest (Stern, 2015).

PERSONALITY
AND INDIVIDUAL
DIFFERENCES

Looking Ahead

Was Tom a soft-hearted do-gooder, or, as the FBI contends, the ruthless, greedy mobster Whitey Bulger, willing to do anything to get ahead?

Many people, like Tom, have different sides to their personalities, appearing one way to some people and quite differently to others. At the same time, you probably know people whose behavior is so consistent that you can easily predict how they are going to behave, no matter what the situation. Determining who a person truly is falls to a branch of psychology that seeks to understand the characteristic ways people behave—personality psychology.

Personality is the pattern of enduring characteristics that produce consistency and individuality in a given person. Personality encompasses the behaviors that make each of us unique and that differentiate us from others. It is also personality that leads us to act consistently in different situations and over extended periods of time.

> **personality** The pattern of enduring characteristics that produce consistency and individuality in a given person

We will consider a number of approaches to personality and the individual differences that distinguish one person from another. We begin with psychodynamic theories of personality, which emphasize the importance of the unconscious. Next, we consider approaches that concentrate on identifying the most fundamental personality traits; theories that view personality as a set of learned behaviors; biological and evolutionary perspectives on personality; and approaches, known as humanistic theories, that highlight the uniquely human aspects of personality. We then focus on how personality is measured and how personality tests can be used. Finally, we will end our discussion by looking more closely at one central individual difference: intelligence.

Psychodynamic Approaches to Personality

Learning Outcomes

>> **LO29.1** Explain Freud's psychoanalytic theory.

>> **LO29.2** Discuss Neo-Freudian psychoanalysts.

 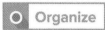

The college student was intent on making a good first impression on an attractive woman he had spotted across a crowded room at a party. As he walked toward her, he mulled over a line he had heard in an old movie the night before: "I don't believe we've been properly introduced yet." To his horror, what came out was a bit different. After threading his way through the crowded room, he finally reached the woman and blurted out, "I don't believe we've been properly seduced yet."

Although this student's error may seem to be merely an embarrassing slip of the tongue, according to some personality theorists such a mistake is not an error at all. Instead, *psychodynamic personality theorists* might argue that the error illustrates one way in which behavior is triggered by inner forces that are beyond our awareness. These hidden drives, shaped by childhood experiences, play an important role in energizing and directing everyday behavior.

psychodynamic approaches to personality Approaches that assume that personality is motivated by inner forces and conflicts about which people have little awareness and over which they have no control

psychoanalytic theory Sigmund Freud's theory that unconscious forces act as determinants of personality

Psychodynamic approaches to personality are based on the idea that personality is motivated by inner forces and conflicts about which people have little awareness and over which they have no control. The most important pioneer of the psychodynamic approach was Sigmund Freud. A number of Freud's followers, including Carl Jung, Karen Horney, and Alfred Adler, refined Freud's theory and developed their own psychodynamic approaches.

>> LO29.1 Freud's Psychoanalytic Theory: Mapping the Unconscious Mind

Sigmund Freud, an Austrian physician, developed **psychoanalytic theory** in the early 1900s. According to Freud's theory, conscious experience is only a small part of our psychological makeup and experience. He argued that much of our behavior is motivated by the **unconscious,** a part of the personality that contains the memories, knowledge, beliefs, feelings, urges, drives, and instincts of which the individual is not aware.

Like the unseen mass of a floating iceberg, the contents of the unconscious far surpass in quantity the information in our conscious awareness. Freud maintained that to understand personality, it is necessary to expose what is in the unconscious. But because the unconscious disguises the meaning of the material it holds, the content of the unconscious cannot be observed directly. It is therefore necessary to interpret clues to the unconscious—slips of the tongue, fantasies, and dreams—to understand the unconscious processes that direct behavior. A slip of the tongue such as the one quoted earlier (sometimes termed a *Freudian slip*) may be interpreted as revealing the speaker's unconscious sexual desires.

> Freud maintained that to understand personality, it is necessary to expose what is in the unconscious.

To Freud, much of our personality is determined by our unconscious. Some of the unconscious is made up of the *preconscious,* which contains material that is not threatening and is easily brought to mind, such as the knowledge that $2 + 2 = 4$. But deeper in the unconscious are instinctual drives—the wishes, desires, demands, and needs that are hidden from conscious awareness because of the conflicts and pain they would cause if they were part of our everyday lives. The unconscious provides a "safe haven" for our recollections of threatening events.

Structuring Personality: Id, Ego, and Superego

To describe the structure of personality, Freud developed a comprehensive theory that held that personality consists of three separate but interacting components: the id, the ego, and the superego. Freud suggested that the three structures can be diagrammed to show how they relate to the conscious and the unconscious (see Figure 1).

Although the three components of personality described by Freud may appear to be actual physical structures in the nervous system, they are not. Instead, they represent abstract conceptions of a general *model* of personality that describes the interaction of forces that motivate behavior.

If personality consisted only of primitive, instinctual cravings and longings, it would have just one component: the id. The **id** is the instinctual and unorganized part of personality. From the time of birth, the id attempts to reduce tension created by primitive drives related to hunger, sex, aggression, and irrational impulses. Those drives are fueled by "psychic energy," which we can think of as a limitless energy source constantly putting pressure on the various parts of the personality.

The id operates according to the *pleasure principle,* in which the goal is the immediate reduction of tension and the maximization of satisfaction. However, in most cases reality prevents the fulfillment of the demands of the pleasure principle: we cannot always eat when we are hungry, and we can discharge our sexual drives only when the time and place are appropriate. To account for this fact of life, Freud suggested a second component of personality, which he called the ego.

The **ego** is the part of personality that attempts to balance the desires of the id and the realities of the objective, outside world. It starts to develop soon after birth.

unconscious A part of the personality that contains the memories, knowledge, beliefs, feelings, urges, drives, and instincts of which the individual is not aware

id The instinctual and unorganized part of personality whose sole purpose is to reduce tension created by primitive drives related to hunger, sex, aggression, and irrational impulses

ego The part of personality that attempts to balance the desires of the id and the realities of the objective, outside world

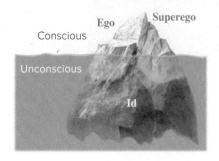

Figure 1 In Freud's model of personality, there are three major components: the id, the ego, and the superego. As the iceberg analogy shows, only a small portion of personality is conscious. Why do you think that only the ego and superego have conscious components?

superego The part of personality that harshly judges the morality of our behavior

psychosexual stages Developmental periods that children pass through during which they encounter conflicts between the demands of society and their own sexual urges

fixations Conflicts or concerns that persist beyond the developmental period in which they first occur

oral stage According to Sigmund Freud, a stage from birth to age 12 to 18 months, in which an infant's center of pleasure is the mouth

In contrast to the pleasure-seeking id, the ego operates according to the *reality principle* in which instinctual energy is restrained to maintain the individual's safety and to help integrate the person into society. In a sense, then, the ego is the "executive" of personality: it makes decisions, controls actions, and allows thinking and problem solving of a higher order than the id's capabilities permit.

The superego is the final personality structure to develop in childhood. According to Freud, the **superego** is the part of personality that harshly judges the morality of our behavior. It represents the rights and wrong of society as taught and modeled by a person's parents, teachers, and other significant individuals.

The superego includes the *conscience,* which prevents us from behaving in a morally improper way by making us feel guilty if we do wrong. The superego helps us control impulses coming from the id, making our behavior less selfish and more virtuous.

Neither the id nor superego are realistic or practical in that they do not consider the realities imposed by society. The superego, if left to operate without restraint, would create perfectionists unable to make the compromises that life requires. An unrestrained id would create a primitive, pleasure-seeking, thoughtless individual seeking to fulfill every desire without delay. As a result, the ego must negotiate between the demands of the superego and the demands of the id.

Developing Personality: Psychosexual Stages

Freud also provided us with a view of how personality develops. He suggests personality development proceeds through a series of five **psychosexual stages,** during which children encounter conflicts between the demands of society and their own sexual urges (in which sexuality is more about experiencing pleasure and less about lust). According to Freud, failure to resolve the conflicts at a particular stage can result in **fixations,** conflicts or concerns that persist beyond the developmental period in which they first occur. Such conflicts may be due to having needs ignored or (conversely) being overindulged during the earlier period.

The sequence Freud proposed is noteworthy because it explains how experiences and difficulties during a particular childhood stage may predict specific characteristics in the adult personality. This theory is also unique in associating each stage with a major biological function, which Freud assumed to be the focus of pleasure in a given period. See Figure 2 for a summary of the stages.

In the first psychosexual stage of development, called the **oral stage,** the baby's mouth is the focal point of pleasure. During the first 12 to 18 months of life, children suck, eat, mouth, and bite anything that they can put into their mouths. To Freud, this behavior suggested that the mouth is the primary site of a kind of sexual pleasure, and that weaning (withdrawing the breast or bottle) represents the main conflict during the oral stage. If infants are either overindulged (perhaps by being fed every time they cry) or frustrated in their search for oral gratification, they may become fixated at this stage. For example, fixation might occur if an infant's oral needs were constantly gratified immediately at the first sign of hunger, rather than if the infant learned that feeding takes place on a schedule because eating whenever an infant wants to eat is not always realistic. Fixation at the oral stage might produce an adult who was unusually interested in oral activities—eating,

Freud suggests that the superego, the part of personality that represents the rights and wrongs of society, develops from direct teaching from our parents, teachers, and other significant individuals. © David R. Frazier Photolibrary, Inc RF

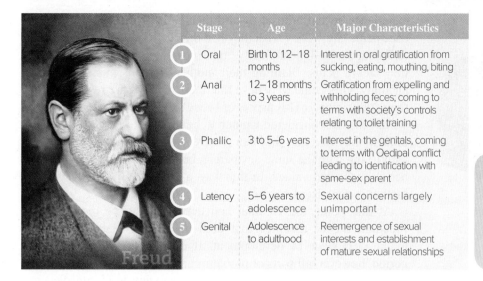

Stage	Age	Major Characteristics
1 Oral	Birth to 12–18 months	Interest in oral gratification from sucking, eating, mouthing, biting
2 Anal	12–18 months to 3 years	Gratification from expelling and withholding feces; coming to terms with society's controls relating to toilet training
3 Phallic	3 to 5–6 years	Interest in the genitals, coming to terms with Oedipal conflict leading to identification with same-sex parent
4 Latency	5–6 years to adolescence	Sexual concerns largely unimportant
5 Genital	Adolescence to adulthood	Reemergence of sexual interests and establishment of mature sexual relationships

Figure 2 Freud's theory of personality development suggests that there are several distinct stages.
Photo: © Hulton Archive/Getty Images

STUDY ALERT

The five psychosexual stages of personality development in Freud's theory—oral, anal, phallic, latency, and genital—indicate how personality develops as people age.

talking, smoking—or who showed symbolic sorts of oral interests such as being "bitingly" sarcastic or very gullible ("swallowing" anything).

From around age 12 to 18 months until 3 years of age—a period when the emphasis in Western cultures is on toilet training—a child enters the **anal stage.** At this point, the major source of pleasure changes from the mouth to the anal region, and children obtain considerable pleasure from both retention and expulsion of feces. If toilet training is particularly demanding, fixation might occur. Fixation during the anal stage might result in unusual rigidity, orderliness, punctuality—or extreme disorderliness or sloppiness—in adulthood.

At about age 3, the **phallic stage** begins. At this point, there is another major shift in the child's primary source of pleasure. Now interest focuses on the genitals and the pleasures derived from fondling them. During this stage, the child must also negotiate one of the most important hurdles of personality development: the **Oedipal conflict.** According to Freudian theory, as children focus attention on their genitals, the differences between male and female anatomy become more apparent. Furthermore, according to Freud, at this time the male unconsciously begins to develop a sexual interest in his mother, starts to see his father as a rival, and harbors a wish to kill his father—as Oedipus did in the ancient Greek tragedy. But because he views his father as too powerful, he develops a fear that his father may retaliate drastically by removing the source of the threat: the son's penis. The fear of losing one's penis leads to *castration anxiety,* which ultimately becomes so powerful that the child represses his desires for his mother and identifies with his father. **Identification** is the process of wanting to be like another person as much as possible, imitating that person's behavior and adopting similar beliefs and values. By identifying with his father, a son seeks to obtain a woman like his unattainable mother.

For girls, the process is different. Freud argued that girls begin to

anal stage According to Sigmund Freud, a stage from age 12 to 18 months to 3 years of age, in which a child's pleasure is centered on the anus

phallic stage According to Sigmund Freud, a period beginning around age 3 during which a child's pleasure focuses on the genitals

Oedipal conflict A child's sexual interest in his or her opposite-sex parent, typically resolved through identification with the same-sex parent

identification The process of wanting to be like another person as much as possible, imitating that person's behavior and adopting (taking on) similar beliefs and values

According to Freud, a child goes through the anal stage from 12 to 18 months until 3 years of age. Toilet training is a crucial event at this stage, one that psychoanalytical theory claims directly influences the formation of an individual's personality.
© Margaret Miller/Science Source

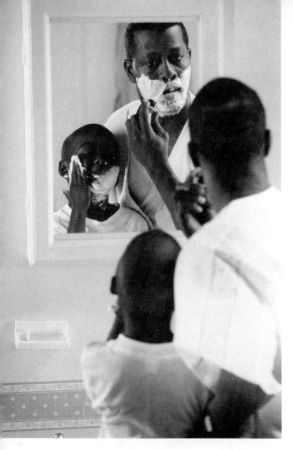

Imitating a person's behavior and adopting similar beliefs and values is part of Freud's concept of identification. How can this concept be applied to the definition of gender roles? Is identification similar in all cultures? © Andy Sacks/Getty Images

experience sexual arousal toward their fathers and begin to experience penis envy. They wish they had the anatomical part that, at least to Freud, seemed most clearly "missing"—i.e., girls come to realize they lack a penis. Blaming their mothers for this missing piece of anatomy, girls come to believe that their mothers are responsible for their "castration." (This aspect of Freud's theory later provoked accusations that he considered women to be inferior to men.) Like males, though, they find that they can resolve such unacceptable feelings by identifying with the same-sex parent, behaving like her and adopting her attitudes and values. In this way, a girl's identification with her mother is completed.

At this point, the Oedipal conflict is said to be resolved, and Freudian theory assumes that both males and females move on to the next stage of development. If difficulties arise during this period, however, all sorts of problems are thought to occur, including improper sex-role behavior and the failure to develop a conscience.

After the resolution of the Oedipal conflict, typically around age 5 or 6, children move into the **latency period,** which lasts until puberty. During this period, sexual interests become dormant, even in the unconscious. Then, during adolescence, sexual feelings reemerge, which marks the start of the final period, the **genital stage,** which extends until death. The focus during the genital stage is on mature, adult sexuality, which Freud defined as sexual intercourse.

Defense Mechanisms

Freud's efforts to describe and theorize about the underlying dynamics of personality and its development were motivated by very practical problems that his patients faced in dealing with *anxiety,* an intense, negative emotional experience. According to Freud, anxiety is a danger signal to the ego. Although anxiety can arise from realistic fears—such as seeing a poisonous snake about to strike—it can also occur in the form of *neurotic anxiety,* in which irrational impulses emanating from the id threaten to burst through and become uncontrollable.

Because anxiety is obviously unpleasant, Freud believed that people develop a range of ways to deal with it, which he called defense mechanisms. **Defense mechanisms** are unconscious strategies that people use to reduce anxiety by concealing its source from themselves and others.

The primary defense mechanism is **repression,** in which unacceptable or unpleasant id impulses are pushed back into the unconscious. Repression is the most direct method of dealing with anxiety; instead of handling an anxiety-producing impulse on a conscious level, we simply ignore it. For example, a college student who feels hatred for her mother may repress those personally and socially unacceptable feelings. The feelings remain lodged within the unconscious, because acknowledging them would provoke anxiety. Similarly, memories of childhood abuse may be repressed.

If repression is ineffective in keeping anxiety at bay, we might use other defense mechanisms. Freud and later his daughter Anna Freud (who became a well-known psychoanalyst) formulated an extensive list of potential defense mechanisms. The major defense mechanisms are summarized in Figure 3 (Perry, Presniak, & Olson, 2013; Boag, 2015; Ziegler, 2016).

All of us employ defense mechanisms to some degree, according to Freudian theory, and they can serve a useful purpose by protecting us from

latency period According to Sigmund Freud, the period between the phallic stage and puberty during which children's sexual concerns are temporarily put aside

genital stage According to Sigmund Freud, the period from puberty until death, marked by mature sexual behavior

defense mechanisms In Freudian theory, unconscious strategies that people use to reduce anxiety by concealing the source of the anxiety from themselves and others

repression The primary defense mechanism in which unacceptable or unpleasant id impulses are pushed back into the unconscious

Freud's Defense Mechanisms

Defense Mechanism	Explanation	Example
Repression	Unacceptable or unpleasant impulses are pushed back into the unconscious	A woman is unable to recall that she was raped
Regression	People behave as if they were at an earlier stage of development	A boss has a temper tantrum when an employee makes a mistake
Displacement	The expression of an unwanted feeling or thought is redirected from a more threatening powerful person to a weaker one	A brother yells at his younger sister after a teacher gives him a bad grade
Rationalization	People provide self-justifying explanations in place of the actual, but threatening, reason for their behavior	A student who goes out drinking the night before a big test rationalizes his behavior by saying the test isn't all that important
Denial	People refuse to accept or acknowledge an anxiety-producing piece of information	A student refuses to believe that he has flunked a course
Projection	People attribute unwanted impulses and feelings to someone else	A man who is angry at his father acts lovingly to his father but complains that his father is angry with him
Sublimation	People divert unwanted impulses into socially approved thoughts, feelings, or behaviors	A person with strong feelings of aggression becomes a soldier
Reaction formation	Unconscious impulses are expressed as their opposite in consciousness	A mother who unconsciously resents her child acts in an overly loving way toward the child

Figure 3   According to Freud, people are able to use a wide range of defense mechanisms to cope with anxieties.

unpleasant information. Yet some people fall prey to them to such an extent that they must constantly direct a large amount of psychic energy toward hiding and rechanneling unacceptable impulses. When this occurs, everyday living becomes difficult. In such cases, the result is a mental disorder produced by anxiety—what Freud called "neurosis" (psychologists rarely use this term today, although it endures in everyday conversation).

Evaluating Freud's Legacy

Freud's theory has had a significant impact on the field of psychology—and even more broadly on Western philosophy and literature. The ideas of the unconscious, defense mechanisms, and childhood roots of adult psychological difficulties are widely accepted.

However, contemporary personality psychologists have leveled significant criticisms against psychoanalytic theory. Among the most important is the lack of compelling scientific data to support it. Although individual case studies seem supportive, we lack conclusive evidence that shows the personality is structured and operates along the lines Freud laid out. The lack of evidence is due, in part, to the fact that Freud's conception of personality is built on unobservable abstract concepts. Moreover, it is not clear that the stages of personality that Freud laid out provide an accurate description of personality development. We also know now that important changes in personality can occur in adolescence and adulthood—something that Freud did not believe happened. Instead, he argued that personality largely is set by adolescence.

The vague nature of Freud's theory also makes it difficult to predict how certain developmental difficulties will be displayed in an adult. For instance, if a person is fixated at the anal stage, according to Freud, he or she may be unusually messy—or unusually neat. Freud's theory offers no way to predict how the difficulty will be exhibited. Furthermore, Freud can be faulted for seeming to view women as inferior to men, because he argued that women have weaker superegos than men do and in some ways unconsciously yearn to be men (the concept of penis envy).

Finally, Freud made his observations and derived his theory from a limited population. His theory was based almost entirely on upper-class Austrian women living in the strict, puritanical era of the early 1900s who had come to him seeking treatment for psychological and physical problems. How far one can generalize beyond this population is a matter of considerable debate.

Still, Freud generated an important method of treating psychological disturbances, called *psychoanalysis.* As we will see when we discuss treatment approaches to psychological disorders, psychoanalysis remains in use today (Frosch, 2011; Altman & Stile, 2015; Grünbaum, 2015).

Moreover, Freud's emphasis on the unconscious has been partially supported by current research on dreams and implicit memory. As first noted when we discussed dreaming, advances in neuroscience are consistent with some of Freud's arguments. Furthermore, cognitive and social psychologists have found evidence that unconscious processes help us think about and evaluate our world, set goals, and choose a course of action. Unconscious processes also help determine how we form attitudes toward others (Litowitz, 2007; Bargh, 2014).

» LO29.2 The Neo-Freudian Psychoanalysts: Building on Freud

Freud laid the foundation for important work done by a series of successors who were trained in traditional Freudian theory but later rejected some of its major points. These theorists are known as **neo-Freudian psychoanalysts.**

The neo-Freudians placed greater emphasis than Freud on the functions of the ego, suggesting that it has more control than the id over day-to-day activities. They focused more on the social environment and minimized the importance of sex as a driving force in people's lives. They also paid greater attention to the effects of society and culture on personality development.

Jung's Collective Unconscious

One of the most influential neo-Freudians, Carl Jung (pronounced "yoong"), rejected Freud's view of the primary importance of unconscious sexual urges. Instead, he looked at the primitive urges of the unconscious more positively, arguing that they represented a more general, and positive, life force that encompasses an inborn drive motivating creativity and more positive resolution of conflict (Cassells, 2007; Stein & Jones, 2010; Finn, 2011).

Jung suggested that we have a universal **collective unconscious,** a common set of ideas, feelings, images, and symbols that we inherit from our relatives, the whole human race, and even nonhuman animal ancestors from the distant past. This collective unconscious is shared by everyone and is displayed in behavior that is common across diverse cultures—such as love of mother, belief in a supreme being, and even behavior as specific as fear of snakes (Oehman & Mineka, 2003; Drob, 2005; Hauke, 2006).

neo-Freudian psychoanalysts Psychoanalysts who were trained in traditional Freudian theory but who later rejected some of its major points

collective unconscious According to Carl Jung, a common set of ideas, feelings, images, and symbols that we inherit from our ancestors, the whole human race, and even nonhuman ancestors from the distant past

Jung went on to propose that the collective unconscious contains **archetypes,** universal symbolic representations of a particular person, object, or experience. For instance, a mother archetype, which contains reflections of our ancestors' relationships with mother figures, is suggested by the prevalence of mothers in art, religion, literature, and mythology. (Think of the Virgin Mary, Earth Mother, wicked stepmothers in fairy tales, Mother's Day, and so forth!) (Jung, 1961; Smetana, 2007; Potash, 2015).

> **archetypes** According to Carl Jung, universal symbolic representations of a particular person, object, or experience

From the perspective of . . .

A Fashion Design Professional How might you use Jung's concept of archetypes in designing your products? Which of the archetypes would you use?

To Jung, archetypes play an important role in determining our day-to-day reactions, attitudes, and values. For example, Jung might explain the popularity of the *Hunger Games* movies as being due to their use of broad archetypes of good (Katniss Everdeen) and evil (Coriolanus Snow).

Although no reliable research evidence confirms the existence of the collective unconscious—and even Jung acknowledged that such evidence would be difficult to produce—Jung's theory has had significant influence in areas beyond psychology. For example, personality types derived from Jung's personality approach form the basis for the Myers-Briggs personality test, which is widely used in business and industry (Furnham & Crump, 2005; Wilde, 2011; Mills, 2013; Applebaum, 2016).

Horney's Neo-Freudian Perspective

Karen Horney (pronounced "HORN-eye") was one of the earliest psychologists to champion women's issues and is sometimes called the first feminist psychologist. Horney suggested that personality develops in the context of social relationships and depends particularly on the relationship between parents and child and how well the child's needs are met. She rejected Freud's suggestion that women have penis envy, asserting that what women envy most in men is not their anatomy but the independence, success, and freedom that women often are denied (Horney, 1937; Smith, 2007; Paul, 2010).

Horney was also one of the first to stress the importance of cultural factors in the determination of personality. For example, she suggested that society's rigid gender roles for women lead them to experience ambivalence about success, fearing that they will lose their friends. Her conceptualizations, developed in the 1930s

In the *Hunger Games* movies, Coriolanus Snow may represent the archetype of evil. Which character represents the archetype of evil in the *Star Wars* movies? © Color Force/Liongate/Studio Babelsberg/Close, Murray/Album/Album Photo Press/Newscom

Karen Horney was one of the earliest proponents of women's issues.
© Bettmann/Getty Images

and 1940s, laid the groundwork for many of the central ideas of feminism that emerged decades later (Eckardt, 2005; Jones, 2006).

Adler and the Other Neo-Freudians

Alfred Adler, another important neo-Freudian psychoanalyst, also considered Freudian theory's emphasis on sexual needs misplaced. Instead, Adler proposed that the primary human motivation is a striving for superiority, not in terms of superiority over others but in a quest for self-improvement and perfection.

Adler used the term **inferiority complex** to describe situations in which adults have not been able to overcome the feelings of inferiority they developed as children, when they were small and limited in their knowledge about the world. Early social relationships with parents have an important effect on children's ability to outgrow feelings of personal inferiority and instead to orient themselves toward attaining more socially useful goals, such as improving society.

Other neo-Freudians include Erik Erikson, whose theory of psychosocial development we discussed in other modules, and Freud's daughter, Anna Freud. Like Adler and Horney, they focused less than Freud on inborn sexual and aggressive drives and more on the social and cultural factors behind personality.

inferiority complex According to Alfred Adler, a problem affecting adults who have not been able to overcome the feelings of inferiority that they developed as children, when they were small and limited in their knowledge about the world

RECAP

Explain Freud's psychoanalytic theory.

- Personality is the pattern of enduring characteristics that produce consistency and individuality in a given person.

- According to psychodynamic explanations of personality, much behavior is caused by parts of personality that are found in the unconscious and of which we are unaware.

- Freud's psychoanalytic theory, one of the psychodynamic approaches, suggests that personality is composed of the id, the ego, and the superego. The id is the unorganized, inborn part of personality whose purpose is to immediately reduce tensions relating to hunger, sex, aggression, and other primitive impulses. The ego restrains instinctual energy to maintain the safety of the individual and to help the person be a member of society. The superego

represents the rights and wrongs of society and includes the conscience.

- Freud's psychoanalytic theory suggests that personality develops through a series of psychosexual stages (oral, anal, phallic, latency, and genital), each of which is associated with a primary biological function.

- Defense mechanisms, according to Freudian theory, are unconscious strategies with which people reduce anxieties relating to impulses from the id.

- Freud's psychoanalytic theory has provoked a number of criticisms, including a lack of supportive scientific data, the theory's inadequacy in making predictions, and its reliance on a highly restricted population. On the other hand, recent neuroscience research has offered some support for the concept of the unconscious.

Discuss Neo-Freudian psychoanalysts.

- Neo-Freudian psychoanalytic theorists built on Freud's work, although they placed greater emphasis on the role of the ego and paid more attention to the role of social factors in determining behavior.

[EVALUATE E Evaluate]

1. _____ approaches state that behavior is motivated primarily by unconscious forces.

2. Match each section of the personality (according to Freud) with its description:

   1. Ego
   2. Id
   3. Superego

   a. Determines right from wrong on the basis of cultural standards.
   b. Operates according to the "reality principle"; energy is redirected to integrate the person into society.
   c. Seeks to reduce tension brought on by primitive drives.

3. Which of the following represents the proper order of personality development, according to Freud?

   a. Oral, phallic, latency, anal, genital
   b. Anal, oral, phallic, genital, latency
   c. Oral, anal, phallic, latency, genital
   d. Latency, phallic, anal, genital, oral

4. _____ _____ is the term Freud used to describe unconscious strategies used to reduce anxiety.

[RETHINK R Rethink]

Can you think of ways in which Freud's theories of unconscious motivations are commonly used in popular culture? How accurately do you think such popular uses of Freudian theories reflect Freud's ideas?

Answers to Evaluate Questions 1. psychodynamic; 2. 1-b, 2-c, 3-a; 3. c; 4. defense mechanism

KEY TERMS

Personality   LO29.1

Psychodynamic approaches to personality   LO29.1

Psychoanalytic theory   LO29.1

Unconscious   LO29.1

Id   LO29.1

Ego   LO29.1

Superego   LO29.1

Psychosexual stages   LO29.1

Fixations   LO29.1

Oral stage   LO29.1

Anal stage   LO29.1

Phallic stage   LO29.1

Oedipal conflict   LO29.1

Identification   LO29.1

Latency period   LO29.1

Genital stage   LO29.1

Defense mechanisms   LO29.1

Repression   LO29.1

Neo-Freudian psychoanalysts   LO29.2

Collective unconscious   LO29.2

Archetypes   LO29.2

Inferiority complex   LO29.2

Trait, Learning, Biological and Evolutionary, and Humanistic Approaches to Personality

Learning Outcomes  Prepare

>> **LO30.1** Explain trait approaches to personality.

>> **LO30.2** Explain learning approaches to personality.

>> **LO30.3** Explain biological and evolutionary approaches to personality.

>> **LO30.4** Explain humanistic approaches to personality.

>> **LO30.5** Compare and contrast approaches to personality.

MODULE OUTLINE  Organize

Trait Approaches: Placing Labels on Personality

Learning Approaches: We Are What We've Learned

Biological and Evolutionary Approaches: Are We Born with Personality?

Humanistic Approaches: The Uniqueness of You

Try It! Assessing Your Real and Ideal Self-Concepts

Comparing Approaches to Personality

W Work

"Tell me about Nelson," said Johnetta.

"Oh, he's just terrific. He's the friendliest guy I know—goes out of his way to be nice to everyone. He hardly ever gets mad. He's just so even-tempered, no matter what's happening. And he's really smart, too. About the only thing I don't like is that he's always in such a hurry to get things done. He seems to have boundless energy, much more than I have."

"He sounds great to me, especially in comparison to Rico," replied Johnetta. "He is so self-centered and arrogant that it drives me crazy. I sometimes wonder why I ever started going out with him."

Friendly. Even-tempered. Smart. Energetic. Self-centered. Arrogant.

The preceding exchange is made up of a series of trait characterizations of the speakers' friends. In fact, much of our own understanding of others' behavior is based on the premise that people possess certain traits that are consistent across different situations. For example, we generally assume that if someone is outgoing and sociable in one situation, he or she is outgoing and sociable in other situations (Gilbert, Miller, & Ross, 1998; Mischel, 2004; Leising et al., 2014).

Dissatisfaction with the emphasis in psychoanalytic theory on unconscious—and difficult to demonstrate—processes in explaining a person's behavior led to the development of alternative approaches to personality, including a number of trait-based approaches. Other theories reflect established psychological perspectives, such as learning theory, biological and evolutionary approaches, and the humanistic approach.

» LO30.1 Trait Approaches: Placing Labels on Personality

If someone asked you to characterize another person, like Johnetta and her friend, you probably would come up with a list of traits. **Traits** are consistent, habitual personality characteristics and behaviors that are displayed across different situations.

Trait theory is the personality approach that seeks to identify the basic traits necessary to describe personality. Trait theorists do not assume that some people have a particular trait while others do not. Instead, they propose that all people possess a set of traits, but the degree to which a particular trait applies to a specific person varies and can be quantified.

For instance, they might assume that all people have the trait of "friendliness," but in different degrees. You may be relatively friendly, whereas I may be relatively unfriendly. But we both have a "friendliness" trait, although your degree of "friendliness" is higher than mine.

The major challenge for trait theorists taking this approach has been to identify the specific basic traits necessary to describe personality. As we shall see, different theorists have come up with surprisingly different sets of traits.

Eysenck's Approach: The Factors of Personality

Attempts to identify primary personality traits have centered on a statistical technique known as factor analysis. *Factor analysis* is a statistical method of identifying associations among a large number of variables to reveal more general patterns. For example, a personality researcher might administer a questionnaire to many participants that asks them to describe themselves by referring to an extensive list of traits. By statistically combining responses and computing which traits are associated with one another in the same person, a researcher can identify the most fundamental patterns or combinations of traits—called *factors*—that underlie participants' responses.

Using factor analysis, personality psychologist Raymond Cattell (1965) suggested that 16 pairs of *source traits* represent the basic dimensions of personality. Using those source traits, he developed the Sixteen Personality Factor Questionnaire, or 16 PF, a measure that provides scores for each of the source traits (Cattell, Cattell & Cattell, 2000; Djapo et al., 2011).

Another trait theorist, psychologist Hans Eysenck (1995), used factor analysis to identify patterns of traits and found that personality could best be described in terms of just three major dimensions: *extraversion, neuroticism,* and *psychoticism.* The extraversion dimension relates to the degree of sociability, whereas the neurotic dimension encompasses emotional stability. Finally, psychoticism refers to the degree to which reality is distorted. By evaluating people along these three dimensions, Eysenck was able to predict behavior accurately in a variety of situations. Figure 1 lists specific traits associated with each of the dimensions.

traits Consistent, habitual personality characteristics and behaviors that are displayed across different situations

trait theory A model of personality that seeks to identify the basic traits necessary to describe personality

STUDY ALERT

All trait theories explain personality in terms of traits (consistent personality characteristics and behaviors), but they differ in terms of which and how many traits are seen as fundamental.

Figure 1 According to Eysenck, personality could best be described in terms of just three major dimensions: extraversion, neuroticism, and psychoticism. Eysenck was able to predict behavior accurately in a variety of types of situations by evaluating people along these three dimensions. How do you think an airline pilot would score on Eysenck's scale? Source: Adapted from Eysenck, H. J., 1990.

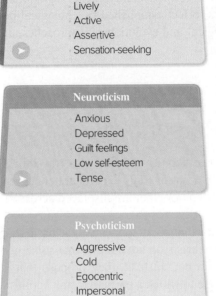

Extraversion
- Sociable
- Lively
- Active
- Assertive
- Sensation-seeking

Neuroticism
- Anxious
- Depressed
- Guilt feelings
- Low self-esteem
- Tense

Psychoticism
- Aggressive
- Cold
- Egocentric
- Impersonal
- Impulsive

The Big Five Personality Traits

The most influential trait approach contends that five traits or factors—called the "Big Five"—lie at the core of personality. Using modern factor analytic statistical techniques, a consistent body of research has identified a similar set of five factors that underlie personality. The specific five factors are *openness to experience, conscientiousness, extraversion, agreeableness,* and *neuroticism* (emotional stability). They are described in Figure 2.

The Big Five emerge consistently with different kinds of measures, in different populations of individuals, and across different cultures. In short, a growing consensus exists that the Big Five represent the best description of personality traits we have today. Still, the debate over the specific number and kinds of traits—and even the usefulness of trait approaches in general—remains a lively one (Joshanloo & Afshari, 2011; Saucier & Srivastava, 2015; Contractor et al., 2016).

Evaluating Trait Approaches to Personality

Trait approaches have several virtues. They provide a clear, straightforward explanation of people's behavioral consistencies. Furthermore, traits allow us

Figure 2 Five broad trait factors, referred to as the "Big Five," are considered to be the core of personality. Source: Adapted from Pervin, 1990, Chapter 3, and McCrae & Costa, 1986, p. 1002.

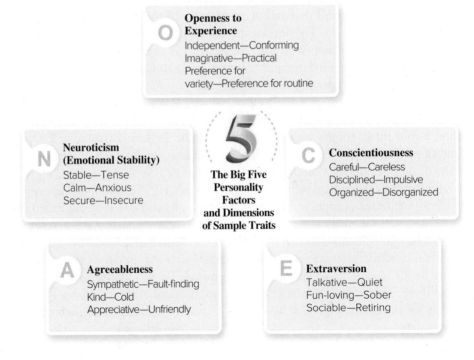

O — **Openness to Experience**
Independent—Conforming
Imaginative—Practical
Preference for variety—Preference for routine

N — **Neuroticism (Emotional Stability)**
Stable—Tense
Calm—Anxious
Secure—Insecure

C — **Conscientiousness**
Careful—Careless
Disciplined—Impulsive
Organized—Disorganized

5
The Big Five Personality Factors and Dimensions of Sample Traits

A — **Agreeableness**
Sympathetic—Fault-finding
Kind—Cold
Appreciative—Unfriendly

E — **Extraversion**
Talkative—Quiet
Fun-loving—Sober
Sociable—Retiring

to readily compare one person with another. Because of these advantages, trait approaches to personality have had an important influence on the development of several useful personality measures (Wiggins, 2003; Larsen & Buss, 2006; Cook, 2013).

However, trait approaches also have some drawbacks. For example, we have seen that various trait theories describing personality come to very different conclusions about which traits are the most fundamental and descriptive. Moreover, even if we are able to identify a set of primary traits, all that we have done is provide a set of labels for personality—but not an explanation of behavior. If we say that someone who donates money to charity has the trait of generosity, we still do not know why that person became generous in the first place or the reasons for displaying generosity in a specific situation. In the view of some critics, then, traits do not provide explanations for behavior; they merely label it.

» LO30.2 Learning Approaches: We Are What We've Learned

The psychodynamic and trait approaches we've discussed concentrate on the "inner" person—the fury of a powerful id or a critical set of traits. In contrast, learning approaches to personality focus on the "outer" person. To a strict learning theorist, personality is simply the sum of learned responses to the external environment. Internal events such as thoughts, feelings, and motivations are ignored. Although the existence of personality is not denied, learning theorists say that it is best understood by looking at features of a person's environment.

Skinner's Behaviorist Approach

According to the most influential learning theorist, B. F. Skinner (who carried out pioneering work on operant conditioning), personality is a collection of learned behavior patterns (Skinner, 1975). Similarities in responses across different situations are caused by similar patterns of reinforcement that have been received in such situations in the past. If I am sociable both at parties and at meetings, it is because I have been reinforced for displaying social behaviors—not because I am fulfilling an unconscious wish based on experiences during my childhood or because I have an internal trait of sociability.

How would a basic understanding of personality help this nurse's assistant deal with a high-maintenance patient? © Ariel Skelley/Blend Images LLC RF

Strict learning theorists such as Skinner are less interested in the consistencies in behavior across situations than in ways of modifying behavior. Their view is that humans are infinitely changeable through the process of learning new behavior patterns. If we are able to control and modify the patterns of reinforcers in a situation, behavior that other theorists would view as stable and unyielding can be changed and ultimately improved. Learning theorists are optimistic in their attitudes about the potential for resolving personal and societal problems through treatment strategies based on learning theory.

Social Cognitive Approaches to Personality

Not all learning theories of personality take such a strict view in rejecting the importance of what is "inside" a person by focusing solely on the "outside." Unlike other learning approaches to personality, **social cognitive approaches to personality** emphasize the influence of cognition—thoughts, feelings, expectations, and values—as well as observation of others' behavior, on personality. According to Albert Bandura, one of the main proponents of this point of view, people can foresee the possible outcomes of certain behaviors in a specific setting without actually having to carry them out. This understanding comes primarily through *observational learning*—viewing the actions of others and observing the consequences (Bandura, 1986, 1999).

For instance, children who view a model behaving in, say, an aggressive manner tend to copy the behavior if the consequences of the model's behavior are seen as positive. If, in contrast, the model's aggressive behavior has resulted in no consequences or negative consequences, children are considerably less likely to act aggressively. According to social cognitive approaches, then, personality develops through repeated observation of the behavior of others.

Self-Efficacy Psychologist Albert Bandura (1986, 1999), places particular emphasis on the role played by **self-efficacy,** belief in one's personal capabilities. Self-efficacy underlies people's faith in their ability to carry out a specific behavior or produce a desired outcome. People with high self-efficacy have higher aspirations and greater persistence in working to attain goals and ultimately achieve greater success than do those with lower self-efficacy (Bandura & Locke, 2003; Reuter et al., 2010; Sezgin & Erdogan, 2015; Srivastava & Singh, 2016).

How do we develop self-efficacy? One way is by paying close attention to our prior successes and failures. If we try snowboarding and experience little success, we'll be less likely to try it again. However, if our initial efforts appear promising, we'll be more likely to attempt it again. Direct reinforcement and encouragement from others also play a role in developing self-efficacy (Devonport & Lane, 2006; Buchanan & Selmon, 2008; Murray & Tenenbaum, 2010).

Compared with other learning theories of personality, social cognitive approaches are distinctive in their emphasis on the reciprocity between individuals and their environment. Not only is the environment assumed to affect personality, but people's behavior and personalities are also assumed to "feed back" and modify the environment (Bandura, 1999, 2000).

Is Personality Consistent?

Another social cognitive theorist, Walter Mischel, takes a different approach to personality from that of Albert Bandura. He rejects the view that personality consists of broad traits that lead to substantial consistencies in behavior across

social cognitive approaches to personality Theories that emphasize the influence of a person's cognitions—thoughts, feelings, expectations, and values—as well as observation of others' behavior, in determining personality

self-efficacy Belief in one's personal capabilities. Self-efficacy underlies people's faith in their ability to carry out a particular behavior or produce a desired outcome

Self-efficacy, the belief in one's own capabilities, leads to higher aspirations and greater persistence. How did self-efficacy factor into your decision to seek further education?
© Comstock Images/JupiterImages RF

different situations. Instead, he sees personality as considerably more variable from one situation to another (Mischel, 2009).

In this view, particular situations give rise to particular kinds of behavior. Some situations are especially influential (think of a movie theater, where everyone displays pretty much the same behavior by sitting quietly and watching the film). Other situations permit considerable variability in behavior (think of a party, for example, where some people may be dancing, others are eating and drinking, and some people may be seated quietly, listening to music).

From the perspective of . . .

A Health Care Provider How might a patient's self-efficacy influence her willingness to engage in health-enhancing behaviors or her ability to follow a prescribed treatment regimen?

From this perspective, personality cannot be considered without taking the particular context of the situation into account—a view known as *situationism*. In his *cognitive-affective processing system (CAPS)* theory, Mischel argues that people's thoughts and emotions about themselves and the world determine how they view, and then react, in particular situations. Personality is thus seen as a reflection of how people's prior experiences in different situations affect their behavior (Mischel & Shoda, 2008; McCrae et al., 2011; Huprich & Nelson, 2015).

Self-Esteem Our behavior also reflects the view we have of ourselves and the way we value the various parts of our personalities. **Self-esteem** is the component of personality that encompasses our positive and negative self-evaluations. Unlike self-efficacy, which focuses on our views of whether we are able to carry out a task, self-esteem relates to how we feel about ourselves.

Although people have a general level of self-esteem, it is not unidimensional. We may see ourselves positively in one domain but negatively in others. For example, a good student may have high self-esteem in academic domains but lower self-esteem in sports (Salmela-Aro & Nurmi, 2007; Gentile et al., 2009; vanDellen et al., 2011).

self-esteem The component of personality that encompasses our positive and negative self-evaluations

Evaluating Learning Approaches to Personality

Because they ignore the internal processes that are uniquely human, traditional learning theorists such as Skinner have been accused of oversimplifying personality to such an extent that the concept becomes meaningless. The critics think that reducing behavior to a series of stimuli and responses, and excluding thoughts and feelings from the realm of personality, leaves behaviorists practicing an unrealistic and inadequate form of science.

Nonetheless, learning approaches have had a major impact on the study of personality. For one thing, they have helped make personality psychology an objective, scientific venture by focusing on observable behaviors and their environment. In addition, they have produced important, successful means of treating a variety of psychological disorders. The degree of success of these treatments is a testimony to the merits of learning theory approaches to personality.

» LO30.3 Biological and Evolutionary Approaches: Are We Born with Personality?

Approaching the question of what determines personality from a different direction, **biological and evolutionary approaches to personality** suggest that important components of personality are inherited. Building on the work of behavioral geneticists, researchers using biological and evolutionary approaches argue that personality is determined at least in part by our genes, in much the same way that our height is largely a result of genetic contributions from our ancestors (see Figure 3). The evolutionary perspective assumes that personality traits that led to survival and reproductive success of our ancestors are more likely to be preserved and passed on to subsequent generations (Buss, A. H., 2011 and Buss, D. M. 2001, 2009; Yarkoni, 2015).

It is increasingly clear that the roots of adult personality emerge in the earliest periods of life. Infants are born with a specific **temperament,** an innate disposition. Temperament encompasses several dimensions, including general activity level and mood. For instance, some individuals are quite active, whereas others are relatively calm. Similarly, some are relatively easygoing, but others are irritable, easily upset, and difficult to soothe. Temperament is quite consistent, with significant stability from infancy well into adolescence (Evans

Personality characteristic	Percentage	Description
Social potency	61%	Is masterful; a forceful leader who likes to be the center of attention
Traditionalism	60%	Follows rules and authority; endorses high moral standards and strict discipline
Stress reaction	55%	Feels vulnerable and sensitive; is given to worrying and easily upset
Absorption	55%	Has a vivid imagination readily captured by rich experience; relinquishes sense of reality
Alienation	55%	Feels mistreated and used, that "the world is out to get me"
Well-being	54%	Has a cheerful disposition; feels confident and optimistic
Harm avoidance	51%	Shuns the excitement of risk and danger; prefers the safe route even if it is tedious
Aggression	48%	Is physically aggressive and vindictive; has taste for violence; is "out to get the world"
Achievement	46%	Works hard; strives for mastery; puts work and accomplishment ahead of other things
Control	43%	Is cautious and plodding; is rational and sensible; likes carefully planned events
Social closeness	33%	Prefers emotional intimacy and close ties; turns to others for comfort and help

Figure 3 The inherited roots of personality. The percentages indicate the degree to which 11 personality characteristics reflect the influence of heredity. Source: Adapted from Tellegen et al., 1988. Photos: (first) © Image Source RF; (second) © fStop/Getty Images RF; (third) © Purestock/Getty Images RF; (fourth) © Stockbyte/Getty Images RF

& Rothbart, 2007, 2009; Hori et al., 2011; Bates & Pettit, 2015).

Although an increasing number of personality theorists are taking biological and evolutionary factors into account, no comprehensive, unified theory that considers biological and evolutionary factors is widely accepted. Still, it is clear that certain personality traits have substantial genetic components, and that heredity and environment interact to determine personality (Bouchard, 2004; South & Krueger, 2008; O'Donnell, 2010). Biological and evolutionary approaches to personality seek to explain the consistencies in personality that are found in some families.

Biological and evolutionary approaches to personality seek to explain the consistencies in personality that are found in some families. © Cade Martin/CDC RF

» LO30.4 Humanistic Approaches: The Uniqueness of You

In all the approaches to personality that we have discussed, where is the explanation for the saintliness of a Mother Teresa, the creativity of a Michelangelo, and the brilliance and perseverance of an Einstein? An understanding of such unique individuals—as well as more ordinary sorts of people who have some of the same attributes—comes from humanistic theory. **Humanistic approaches to personality** emphasize people's inherent goodness and their tendency to move toward higher levels of functioning. It is this conscious, self-motivated ability to change and improve, along with people's unique creative impulses, that humanistic theorists argue make up the core of personality.

humanistic approaches to personality Theories that emphasize people's innate goodness and desire to achieve higher levels of functioning

Self-actualization A state of self-fulfillment in which people realize their highest potential, each in his or her own unique way

Rogers and the Need for Self-Actualization

The major proponent of the humanistic point of view is Carl Rogers (1971). Along with other humanistic theorists, such as Abraham Maslow, Rogers maintains that all people have a fundamental need for **self-actualization,** a state of self-fulfillment in which people realize their highest potential, each in a unique way. He further suggests that people develop a need for positive regard that reflects the desire to be loved and respected. Because others provide this positive regard, we grow dependent on them. We begin to see and judge ourselves through the eyes of other people, relying on their values and being preoccupied with what they think of us.

According to Rogers, one outgrowth of placing importance on the opinions of others is that a conflict may grow between people's experiences and their *self-concepts,* the set of beliefs they hold about what they are like as individuals. If the discrepancies are minor, so are the consequences. But if the discrepancies are great, they will lead to psychological disturbances in daily functioning, such as the experience of frequent anxiety. (Also see the Try It!.)

> **We begin to see and judge ourselves through the eyes of other people, relying on their values and being preoccupied with what they think of us.**

Assessing Your Real and Ideal Self-Concepts

How well do you know yourself? To get an idea of how well your real self-concept and ideal self-concept match up, try the following exercise. First, quickly place a check mark next to each item that describes you. (Use the first column for your check marks.) Be honest!

1. Anxious
2. Artistic
3. Brave
4. Capable
5. Careless
6. Charming
7. Clear-headed
8. Clever
9. Confused
10. Dissatisfied
11. Easy-going
12. Energetic
13. Entrepreneurial
14. Excitable
15. Forgetful
16. Funny
17. Good-looking
18. Good thinker
19. Hard-working
20. High-strung
21. Imaginative
22. Impulsive
23. Industrious
24. Inventive

(continued)

25. Irritable _____ _____

26. Nervous _____ _____

27. Optimistic _____ _____

28. Sluggish _____ _____

29. Stubborn _____ _____

30. Wise _____ _____

Next, go back through the list and place a check beside each item, this time in the second column, that describes your ideal self—the kind of person you would like to be. Once again, work through the list quickly.

Now make three lists. In the first, list the terms that are characteristic of your real, but not your ideal, self. In the second, list characteristics of your ideal, but not your real, self. Finally, make a list of the characteristics that apply both to your ideal self and your real self.

The first list will tell you things about yourself that are inconsistent with what you would like to be like. The second list gives you a sense of the way you would like to be. Finally, the third list shows you the traits on which you already match your ideal.

How well do your ideal and real self-concepts match up?

Source: Adapted from Byrne, D. and Kelly, L., 1981.

Rogers suggests that one way of overcoming the discrepancy between experience and self-concept is through the receipt of unconditional positive regard from another person—a friend, a spouse, or a therapist. **Unconditional positive regard** refers to an attitude of acceptance and respect on the part of an observer, no matter what a person says or does. This acceptance, says Rogers, gives people the opportunity to evolve and grow both cognitively and emotionally and to develop more realistic self-concepts. You may have experienced the power of unconditional positive regard when you confided in someone, revealing embarrassing secrets because you knew the listener would still love and respect you, even after hearing the worst about you (Marshall, 2007; Truscott, 2010; Patterson & Joseph, 2013).

> **unconditional positive regard** An attitude of acceptance and respect on the part of an observer, no matter what a person says or does

In contrast, *conditional positive regard* depends on your behavior. In such cases, others withdraw their love and acceptance if you do something of which they don't approve. The result is a discrepancy between your true self and what others wish you would be, which leads to anxiety and frustration.

Evaluating Humanistic Approaches

Although humanistic theories suggest the value of providing unconditional positive regard toward people, unconditional positive regard toward humanistic theories has been less forthcoming. The criticisms have centered on the difficulty of verifying the basic assumptions of the approach, as well as on the question of whether unconditional positive regard does, in fact, lead to greater personality adjustment.

"So, while extortion, racketeering, and murder may be bad acts, they don't make you a bad person."

Robert Mankoff/The New Yorker Collection/The Cartoon Bank

Humanistic approaches have also been criticized for making the assumption that people are basically "good"—a notion that is unverifiable—and, equally important, for using nonscientific values to build supposedly scientific theories. Still, humanistic theories have been important in highlighting the uniqueness of human beings and guiding the development of a significant form of therapy designed to alleviate psychological difficulties (Elkins, 2009; Kogstad, Ekeland, & Hummelvoll, 2011; Hounkpatin et al., 2015).

» LO30.5 Comparing Approaches to Personality

In light of the multiple approaches we have discussed, you may be wondering which of the theories provides the most accurate description of personality. That is a question that cannot be answered precisely. Each theory is built on different assumptions and focuses on somewhat different aspects of personality (see Figure 4). Furthermore, there is no clear way to scientifically test the various approaches and their assumptions against one another. Given the complexity of every individual, it seems reasonable that personality can be viewed from a number of perspectives simultaneously (Pervin, 2003).

Theoretical Approach and Major Theorists	Conscious versus Unconscious Determinants of Personality	Nature (Hereditary Factors) versus Nurture (Environmental Factors)	Free Will versus Determinism	Stability versus Modifiability
Psychodynamic (Freud, Jung, Horney, Adler)	Emphasizes the unconscious	Stresses innate, inherited structure of personality while emphasizing importance of childhood experience	Stresses determinism, the view that behavior is directed and caused by factors outside one's control	Emphasizes the stability of characteristics throughout a person's life
Trait (Cattell, Eysenck)	Disregards both conscious and unconscious	Approaches vary	Stresses determinism, the view that behavior is directed and caused by factors outside one's control	Emphasizes the stability of characteristics throughout a person's life
Learning (Skinner, Bandura)	Disregards both conscious and unconscious	Focuses on the environment	Stresses determinism, the view that behavior is directed and caused by factors outside one's control	Stresses that personality remains flexible and resilient throughout one's life
Biological and evolutionary (Tellegen)	Disregards both conscious and unconscious	Stresses the innate, inherited determinants of personality	Stresses determinism, the view that behavior is directed and caused by factors outside one's control	Emphasizes the stability of characteristics throughout a person's life
Humanistic (Rogers, Maslow)	Stresses the conscious more than unconscious	Stresses the interaction between both nature and nurture	Stresses the freedom of individuals to make their own choices	Stresses that personality remains flexible and resilient throughout one's life

Figure 4   The multiple perspectives of personality.

RECAP

Explain trait approaches to personality.

- Trait approaches have been used to identify relatively enduring dimensions along which people differ from one another—dimensions known as traits.

Explain learning approaches to personality.

- Learning approaches to personality concentrate on observable behavior. To a strict learning theorist, personality is the sum of learned responses to the external environment.

- Social cognitive approaches concentrate on the role of cognitions in determining personality. Those approaches pay particular attention to self-efficacy and self-esteem in determining behavior.

Explain biological and evolutionary approaches to personality.

- Biological and evolutionary approaches to personality focus on the way in which personality characteristics are inherited.

Explain humanistic approaches to personality.

- Humanistic approaches emphasize the inherent goodness of people. They consider the core of personality in terms of a person's ability to change and improve.

Compare and contrast approaches to personality.

- The major personality approaches differ substantially from one another; the differences may reflect both their focus on different aspects of personality and the overall complexity of personality.

[EVALUATE E Evaluate]

1. A person who enjoys activities such as parties and hang gliding might be described by Eysenck as high on what trait?

2. Proponents of which approach to personality would be most likely to agree with the statement "Personality can be thought of as learned responses to a person's upbringing and environment"?
   a. Humanistic
   b. Biological and evolutionary
   c. Learning
   d. Trait

3. A person who would make the statement "I know I can't do it" would be rated by Bandura as low on _____ _____.

4. Which approach to personality emphasizes the innate goodness of people and their desire to grow?
   a. Humanistic
   b. Psychodynamic
   c. Learning
   d. Biological and evolutionary

[RETHINK R Rethink]

If personality traits are merely descriptive and not explanatory, of what use are they? Can assigning a trait to a person be harmful—or helpful? Why or why not?

Answers to Evaluate Questions 1. extraversion; 2. c; 3. self-efficacy; 4. a

KEY TERMS

Traits LO30.1

Trait theory LO30.1

Social cognitive approaches to personality LO30.2

Self-efficacy LO30.2

Self-esteem LO30.2

Biological and evolutionary approaches to personality LO30.3

Temperament LO30.3

Humanistic approaches to personality LO30.4

Self-actualization LO30.4

Unconditional positive regard LO30.4

module 31

Assessing Personality
Determining What Makes Us Distinctive

You have a need for other people to like and admire you.

You have a tendency to be critical of yourself.

You have a great deal of unused potential that you have not turned to your advantage.

Although you have some personality weaknesses, you generally are able to compensate for them.

Although you appear to be disciplined and self-controlled to others, you tend to be anxious and insecure inside.

At times you have serious doubts about whether you have made the right decision or done the right thing.

You do not accept others' statements without satisfactory proof.

You have found it unwise to be too frank in revealing yourself to others.

If you think these statements provide a surprisingly accurate account of your personality, you are not alone: most people think that these descriptions are tailored just to them. In fact, the statements were designed intentionally to be so vague that they apply to just about anyone (Forer, 1949; Russo, 1981).

The ease with which we can agree with such imprecise statements underscores the difficulty in coming up with accurate and meaningful assessments of people's personalities. Psychologists interested in assessing personality must be able to define the most meaningful ways of discriminating between one person's personality and another's. To do this, they use **psychological tests,** standard measures devised to assess behavior objectively. With the results of such tests, psychologists can help people better understand themselves and make decisions about their lives. Psychological tests are also employed by researchers interested in the causes and consequences of personality (Hambleton, 2006; Baker & Mason, 2010; Hambleton & Zenisky, 2013).

psychological tests Standard measures devised to assess behavior objectively; used by psychologists to help people make decisions about their lives and understand more about themselves

Like the assessments that seek to measure intelligence, all psychological tests must have reliability and validity. *Reliability* refers to the measurement consistency of a test. If a test is reliable, it yields the same result each time it is administered to a specific person or group. In contrast, unreliable tests give different results each time they are administered.

For meaningful conclusions to be drawn, tests also must be valid. Tests have *validity* when they actually measure what they are designed to measure. If a test is constructed to measure sociability, for instance, we need to know that it actually measures sociability, and not some other trait.

Finally, psychological tests are based on norms, standards of test performance that permit the comparison of one person's score on a test with the scores of others who have taken the same test. For example, a norm permits test-takers who have received a certain score on a test to know that they have scored in the top 10 percent of all those who have taken the test.

Norms are established by administering a specific test to a large number of people and determining the typical scores. It is then possible to compare a single person's score with the scores of the group, providing a comparative measure of test performance against the performance of others who have taken the test.

The establishment of appropriate norms is not a simple endeavor. For instance, the specific group that is employed to determine norms for a test has a profound effect on the way an individual's performance is evaluated.

STUDY ALERT

The distinction between reliability and validity is important. For instance, a test that measures trustfulness is reliable if it yields the same results each time it is administered, and it would be valid if it measures trustfulness accurately.

≫ LO31.1 Self-Report Measures of Personality

self-report measures A method of gathering data about people by asking them questions about a sample of their behavior

Minnesota Multiphasic Personality Inventory-2 (MMPI-2) A widely used self-report test that identifies people with psychological difficulties and is employed to predict some everyday behaviors

Just as physicians draw only a small sample of your blood to test it, psychologists can utilize **self-report measures** that ask people about a small sample of their behavior; these are then used to infer the presence of particular personality characteristics. For example, a researcher who was interested in assessing a person's orientation to life might administer the questionnaire shown in the Try It! feature. Although the questionnaire consists of only a few questions, the answers can be used to generalize about personality characteristics.

One of the best examples of a self-report measure, and one of the most frequently used personality tests, is the **Minnesota Multiphasic Personality Inventory-2 (MMPI-2).** Although the original purpose of this measure was to identify people with specific sorts of psychological difficulties, it has been found to predict a variety of other behaviors. For instance, MMPI scores have been shown to be good predictors of whether college students will marry within 10 years and will get an advanced degree. Police departments use the test to measure whether police officers are likely to use their weapons (Sellbom, Fischler, & Ben-Porath, 2007; Williams & Butcher, 2011; Martino et al., 2016).

The test consists of a series of 567 items to which a person responds "true," "false," or "cannot say." The questions cover a variety of issues, ranging from mood ("I feel useless at times") to opinions ("People should try to understand their dreams") to

By using the Minnesota Multiphasic Personality Inventory-2 (MMPI-2), police departments acknowledge how important personality is to law enforcement. What are some other careers into which personality plays a key role? © Blend Images/ Alamy Stock Photo RF

Try It!

The Life Orientation Test

Use the following scale to answer the items below:

0 = Strongly disagree; 1 = Disagree; 2 = Neutral; 3 = Agree; 4 = Strongly agree

1. In uncertain times, I usually expect the best. _____
2. It's easy for me to relax. _____
3. If something can go wrong for me, it will. _____
4. I'm always optimistic about my future. _____
5. I enjoy my friends a lot. _____
6. It's important for me to keep busy. _____
7. I hardly ever expect things to go my way. _____
8. I don't get upset too easily. _____
9. I rarely count on good things happening to me. _____
10. Overall, I expect more good things to happen to me than bad. _____

Scoring

First, reverse your answers to questions 3, 7, and 9. Do this by changing a 0 to a 4, a 1 to a 3, a 3 to a 1, and a 4 to a 0 (answers of 2 stay as 2). Then sum the reversed scores, and add them to the scores you gave to questions 1, 4, and 10. (Ignore questions 2, 5, 6, and 8, which are filler items.)

The total score you get is a measure of a particular orientation to life: your degree of optimism. The higher your scores, the more positive and hopeful you generally are about life. For comparison purposes, the average score for college students is 14.3 (Scheier, Carver, & Bridges, 1994). People with a higher degree of optimism generally deal with stress better than do those with lower scores.

physical and psychological health ("I am bothered by an upset stomach several times a week" and "I have strange and peculiar thoughts").

There are no right or wrong answers. Instead, interpretation of the results rests on the pattern of responses. The test yields scores on 10 separate scales, plus 3 scales meant to measure the validity of the respondent's answers. For example, there is a "lie scale" that indicates when people are falsifying their responses in order to present themselves more favorably (through items such as "I can't remember ever having a bad night's sleep") (Stein & Graham, 2005; Bacchiochi, 2006; Anderson et al., 2015).

How did the authors of the MMPI determine what specific patterns of responses indicate? The procedure they used is typical of personality test construction—a process known as **test standardization.** To create the test, the test authors asked groups of psychiatric patients with a specific diagnosis, such as depression or schizophrenia, to complete a large number of items. They then determined which items best differentiated members of those groups from a comparison group of normal participants and included those specific items in the final version of the test. By systematically carrying out this procedure on groups with different diagnoses, the test authors were able to devise a number of subscales that identified different forms of abnormal behavior (see Figure 1).

> **test standardization** A technique used to validate questions in personality tests by studying the responses of people with known diagnoses

Figure 1 A profile on the MMPI-2 of a person who suffers from obsessional anxiety, social withdrawal, and delusional thinking. Source: Based on data from Halgin & Whitbourne, 1994, p. 72, and Minnesota Multiphasic Personality Inventory-2.

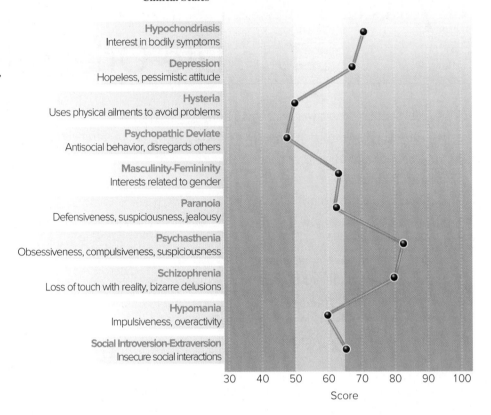

Clinical Scales

When the MMPI is used for the purpose for which it was devised—identification of personality disorders—it does a good job. However, like other personality tests, it presents an opportunity for abuse. For instance, employers who use it as a screening tool for job applicants may interpret the results improperly, relying too heavily on the results of individual scales instead of taking into account the overall patterns of results, which require skilled interpretation. Although the MMPI remains the most widely used personality test and has been translated into more than 100 different languages, it must be used with caution (Forbey & Ben-Porath, 2007; Ben-Porath & Archer, 2008; Rosenfeld et al., 2010).

≫ LO31.2 Projective Methods

If you were shown the shape presented in Figure 2 and asked what it represented to you, you might not think that your impressions would mean very much. But to a psychodynamic theoretician, your responses to such an ambiguous figure would provide valuable clues to the state of your unconscious, and ultimately to your general personality characteristics.

The shape in the figure is representative of inkblots used in **projective personality tests,** in which a person is shown an ambiguous stimulus and asked to describe it or tell a story about it. The responses are considered to be "projections" of the individual's personality.

The best-known projective test is the **Rorschach test.** Devised by Swiss psychiatrist Hermann Rorschach (1924), the test involves showing a series of symmetrical stimuli, similar to the one in Figure 2, to people who are then asked what the figures represent to them. Their responses are recorded, and people are

projective personality tests Tests in which a person is shown an ambiguous stimulus and asked to describe it or tell a story about it

Rorschach test A test that involves showing a series of symmetrical visual stimuli to people who then are asked what the figures represent to them

classified by their personality type through a complex set of clinical judgments on the part of the examiner. For instance, respondents who see a bear in one inkblot are thought to have a strong degree of emotional control, according to the scoring guidelines developed by Rorschach (Weiner, 2004b; Sultan, 2010; Pineda et al., 2011).

The **Thematic Apperception Test (TAT)** is another well-known projective test. The TAT consists of a series of pictures about which a person is asked to write a story. The stories are then used to draw inferences about the writer's personality characteristics (Weiner, 2004a; Langan-Fox & Grant, 2006).

Tests with stimuli as ambiguous as those used in the Rorschach and TAT require particular skill and care in their interpretation—too much, in many critics' estimation. The Rorschach in particular has been criticized for requiring that examiners make too many inferences, and attempts to standardize scoring of it have frequently failed.

Despite such problems, both the Rorschach and the TAT are widely used, especially in clinical settings. Their proponents suggest that their reliability and validity are great enough to provide useful inferences about personality (Society for Personality Assessment, 2005; Campos, 2011; Husain, 2015).

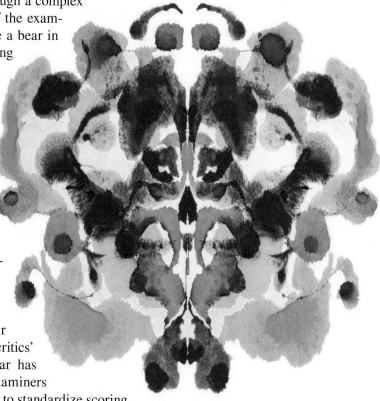

Figure 2 This inkblot is similar to the type used in the Rorschach personality test. What do you see in it? (Source: Alloy, Jacobson, & Acocella, 1999.)

Thematic Apperception Test (TAT) A test consisting of a series of pictures about which a person is asked to write a story

STUDY ALERT

In projective tests such as the Rorschach, researchers present an ambiguous stimulus and ask a person to describe or tell a story about it, and use the responses to make inferences about personality.

"Rorschach! What's to become of you?"

cartoonstock.com

» LO31.3 Behavioral Assessment

behavioral assessment Direct measures of an individual's behavior used to describe personality characteristics

If you were a psychologist subscribing to a learning approach to personality, you would be likely to object to the indirect nature of projective tests. Instead, you would be more apt to use **behavioral assessment**—direct measures of an individual's behavior designed to describe characteristics indicative of personality. As with observational research, behavioral assessment may be carried out naturalistically by observing people in their own settings: in the workplace, at home, or in school. In other cases, behavioral assessment occurs in the laboratory, under controlled conditions in which a psychologist sets up a situation and observes an individual's behavior (Ramsay, Reynolds, & Kamphaus, 2002; Gladwell, 2004; Miller & Leffard, 2007).

> As with observational research, behavioral assessment may be carried out naturalistically by observing people in their own settings: in the workplace, at home, or in school.

Regardless of the setting in which behavior is observed, an effort is made to ensure that behavioral assessment is carried out objectively, quantifying behavior as much as possible. For example, an observer may record the number of social contacts a person initiates, the number of questions asked, or the number of aggressive acts. Another method is to measure the duration of events: the duration of a temper tantrum in a child, the length of a conversation, the amount of time spent working, or the time spent in cooperative behavior.

© Jack Hollingsworth/Getty Images RF

From the perspective of . . .

A New Employee How might placing labels on others' personality at your new place of work help or harm your chances of making smart decisions? What aspects of your own personality would you like to showcase at your place of employment?

Behavioral assessment is particularly appropriate for observing—and eventually remedying—specific behavioral difficulties, such as shyness in children. It provides a means of assessing the specific nature and incidence of a problem and subsequently allows psychologists to determine whether intervention techniques have been successful.

becoming an informed consumer
of psychology

Assessing Personality Assessments

Many companies, ranging from General Motors to Microsoft, employ personality tests to help determine who gets hired. In fact, workplace personality testing has become a big business, with companies spending $500 million a year to help identify the best employees (Weber & Dwoskin, 2014).

What kinds of questions are potential workers asked? In one example, potential Microsoft employees have been asked brainteasers like, "If you had to remove one of the 50 U.S. states, which would it be?" (Hint: First define "remove." If you mean the death of everyone in the state, suggest a low-population state. If you mean quitting the country, then go for an outlying state like Alaska or Hawaii.) Other employers ask questions that are even more vague ("Describe November"). With such questions, it's not always clear that the tests are reliable or valid (McGinn, 2003).

Before relying too heavily on the results of such personality testing in the role of potential employee, employer, or consumer of testing services, you should keep several points in mind:

- *Understand what the test claims to measure.* Standard personality measures are accompanied by information that discusses how the test was developed, to whom it is most applicable, and how the results should be interpreted. Read any explanations of the test; they will help you understand the results.

- *Do not base a decision only on the results of any one test.* Test results should be interpreted in the context of other information, such as academic records, social interests, and home and community activities.

- *Remember that test results are not always accurate.* The results may be in error; the test may be unreliable or invalid. For example, you may have had a "bad day" when you took the test, or the person scoring and interpreting the test may have made a mistake. You should not place too much significance on the results of a single administration of any test.

In sum, it is important to keep in mind the complexity of human behavior—particularly your own. No single test can provide an understanding of the intricacies of someone's personality without considering a good deal more information than can be provided in a single testing session (Gladwell, 2004; Paul, 2004; Hogan, Davies, & Hogan, 2007).

RECAP

Discuss self-report measures of personality.

- Psychological tests such as the MMPI are standard assessment tools that measure behavior objectively. They must be reliable (measuring what they are trying to measure consistently) and valid (measuring what they are supposed to measure).

- Self-report measures ask people about a sample range of their behaviors. These reports are used to infer the presence of particular personality characteristics.

Define projective methods.

- Projective personality tests (such as the Rorschach and the Thematic Apperception Test) present an ambiguous stimulus; the test administrator infers information about the test-taker from his or her responses.

Explain behavioral assessment.

- Behavioral assessment is based on the principles of learning theory. It employs direct measurement of an individual's behavior to determine characteristics related to personality.

1. _____ is the consistency of a personality test; _____ is the ability of a test to actually measure what it is designed to measure.

2. _____ are standards used to compare scores of different people taking the same test.

3. Tests such as the MMPI-2, in which a small sample of behavior is assessed to determine larger patterns, are examples of
   a. Cross-sectional tests
   b. Projective tests
   c. Achievement tests
   d. Self-report tests

4. A person shown a picture and asked to make up a story about it would be taking a _____ personality test.

[RETHINK R Rethink]

Should personality tests be used for personnel decisions? Should they be used for other social purposes, such as identifying individuals at risk for certain types of personality disorders?

Answers to Evaluate Questions 1. reliability, validity; 2. norms; 3. d; 4. projective

KEY TERMS

Psychological tests   LO31.1

Self-report measures   LO31.1

Minnesota Multiphasic Personality Inventory-2 (MMPI-2)   LO31.1

Test standardization   LO31.1

Projective personality tests   LO31.2

Rorschach test   LO31.2

Thematic Apperception Test (TAT)   LO31.2

Behavioral assessment   LO31.3

module 32

Intelligence

Learning Outcomes Prepare

>> **LO32.1** Summarize the theories of intelligence.

>> **LO32.2** Compare and contrast practical and emotional intelligences.

>> **LO32.3** Explain approaches to assessing intelligence.

>> **LO32.4** Identify variations in intellectual ability.

MODULE OUTLINE  Organize

Theories of Intelligence: Are There Different Kinds of Intelligence?

Practical Intelligence and Emotional Intelligence: Toward a More Intelligent View of Intelligence

Assessing Intelligence

Variations in Intellectual Ability

Exploring Diversity: The Relative Influence of Genetics and Environment: Nature, Nurture, and IQ

Intelligence can take on many different meanings. If, for instance, you lived in a remote part of the Australian outback, the way you would differentiate between more intelligent and less intelligent people might have to do with successfully mastering hunting skills, whereas to someone living in the heart of urban Miami, intelligence might be exemplified by being "street wise" or by achieving success in business.

Each of these conceptions of intelligence is reasonable. Each represents an instance in which more intelligent people are better able to use the resources of their environment than are less intelligent people, a distinction that is presumably basic to any definition of intelligence. Yet it is also clear that these conceptions represent very different views of intelligence.

To psychologists, **intelligence** is the capacity to understand the world, think rationally, and use resources effectively when faced with challenges. This definition does not lay to rest a key question asked by psychologists: Is intelligence a unitary attribute, or are there different kinds of intelligence? We turn now to various theories of intelligence that address the issue.

> **W** Work

> **intelligence** The capacity to understand the world, think rationally, and use resources effectively when faced with challenges

>> LO32.1 Theories of Intelligence: Are There Different Kinds of Intelligence?

Perhaps you see yourself as a good writer but as someone who lacks ability in math. Or maybe you view yourself as a "science" person who easily masters physics but has few strengths in interpreting literature. Perhaps you view yourself as generally fairly smart, with intelligence that permits you to excel across domains.

The different ways in which people view their own talents mirrors a question that psychologists have grappled with: Is intelligence a single, general ability, or is it multifaceted and related to specific abilities? Early psychologists interested in intelligence assumed that there was a single, general factor for mental ability, which they called **g** or the **g-factor.** This general intelligence factor was thought to underlie performance in every aspect of intelligence, and it was the g-factor that was presumably being measured on tests of intelligence (Haier et al., 2009; Castejon, Perez, & Gilar, 2010; Das, 2015).

More recent theories see intelligence in a different light. Rather than viewing intelligence as a unitary entity, they consider it to be a multidimensional concept that includes different types of intelligence (Stankov, 2003; Sternberg & Pretz, 2005; Tutwiler, Lin, & Chang, 2013).

Fluid and Crystallized Intelligence

Some psychologists suggest that there are two different kinds of intelligence: fluid intelligence and crystallized intelligence. **Fluid intelligence** is the ability to think logically, reason abstractly, and solve novel problems, relatively independent of past specific knowledge. Fluid intelligence underlies the ability of a police detective to solve a crime by using a set of clues to figure out who committed a crime (Saggino, Perfetti, & Spitoni, 2006; DiFabio & Palazzeschi, 2009; Euler et al, 2015).

In contrast, **crystallized intelligence** is the accumulation of information, skills, and strategies that people have learned through experience and that they can apply in problem-solving situations. It reflects our ability to call up specific facts and information from long-term memory. For example, remembering the definition of a word or how to add and subtract is a reflection of crystallized intelligence (Buehner, Krumm, & Ziegler, 2006; Tranter & Koutstaal, 2008; Ackerman, 2011).

Gardner's Multiple Intelligences: The Many Ways of Showing Intelligence

Psychologist Howard Gardner has taken an approach very different from traditional thinking about intelligence. Gardner argues that rather than asking "How smart are you?" we should be asking a different question: "How are you smart?" In answering the latter question, Gardner has developed a **theory of multiple intelligences** that has become quite influential (Gardner, 2000; Kaufman, Kaufman & Plucker, 2013).

Gardner argues that we have at a minimum eight different forms of intelligence, each relatively independent of the others: musical, bodily kinesthetic, logical-mathematical, linguistic, spatial, interpersonal, intrapersonal, and naturalist. (Figure 1 describes the eight types of intelligence, with some of Gardner's examples of people who excel in each type.) In Gardner's view, each of the multiple intelligences is linked to an independent system in the brain.

Although Gardner illustrates his conception of the specific types of intelligence with descriptions of well-known people, each person has the same eight kinds of intelligence—in different degrees. Moreover, although the eight basic types of intelligence are presented individually, Gardner suggests that these separate intelligences do not operate in isolation. Normally, any activity encompasses several kinds of intelligence working together.

g or g- factor The single, general factor for mental ability assumed to underlie intelligence in some early theories of intelligence

fluid intelligence Intelligence that reflects the ability to think logically, reason abstractly, and solve problems

crystallized intelligence The accumulation of information, skills, and strategies that are learned through experience and can be applied in problem-solving situations

theory of multiple intelligences Howard Gardner's theory that proposes that there are eight distinct spheres of intelligence

In a busy pharmacy, a pharmacy technician will often rely on both fluid and crystallized intelligence. Which do you think will be most important in your chosen career? © Janine Wiedel Photolibrary/Alamy Stock Photo

Musical Intelligence (skills in tasks involving music). Case example:

When he was 3, Yehudi Menuhin was smuggled into San Francisco Orchestra concerts by his parents. By the time he was 10 years old, Menuhin was an international performer.

Bodily Kinesthetic Intelligence (skills in using the whole body or various portions of it in the solution of problems or in the construction of products or displays, exemplified by dancers, athletes, actors, and surgeons). Case example:

Fifteen-year old Babe Ruth played third base. During one game, his team's pitcher was doing very poorly and Babe loudly criticized him from third base. Brother Matthias, the coach, called out, "Ruth, if you know so much about it, **you** pitch!" Ruth said later that at the very moment he took the pitcher's mound, he knew he was supposed to be a pitcher.

Logical-Mathematical Intelligence (skills in problem solving and scientific thinking). Case example:

Barbara McClintock, who won the Nobel Prize in medicine, describes one of her breakthroughs, which came after thinking about a problem for half an hour. . . : "Suddenly I jumped and ran back to the (corn) field. At the top of the field (the others were still at the bottom) I shouted, 'Eureka, I have it!' "

Linguistic Intelligence (skills involved in the production and use of language). Case example:

At the age of 10, T. S. Eliot created a magazine called **Fireside**, to which he was the sole contributor.

Spatial Intelligence (skills involving spatial configurations, such as those used by artists and architects). Case example:

Natives of the Truk Islands navigate at sea without instruments. During the actual trip, the navigator must envision mentally a reference island as it passes under a particular star and from that he computes the number of segments completed, the proportion of the trip remaining, and any corrections in heading.

Interpersonal Intelligence (skills in interacting with others, such as sensitivity to the moods, temperaments, motivations, and intentions of others). Case example:

When Anne Sullivan began instructing the deaf and blind Helen Keller, her task was one that had eluded others for years. Yet, just two weeks after beginning her work with Keller, Sullivan achieved great success.

Intrapersonal Intelligence (knowledge of the internal aspects of oneself; access to one's own feelings and emotions). Case example:

In her essay "A Sketch of the Past," Virginia Woolf displays deep insight into her own inner life through these lines, describing her reaction to several specific memories from her childhood that still, in adulthood, shock her: "Though I still have the peculiarity that I receive these sudden shocks, they are now always welcome; after the first surprise, I always feel instantly that they are particularly valuable. And so I go on to suppose that the shock-receiving capacity is what makes me a writer."

Naturalist Intelligence (ability to identify and classify patterns in nature). Case example:

During prehistoric times, hunter/gatherers would rely on naturalist intelligence to identify what flora and fauna were edible. People who are adept at distinguishing nuances between large numbers of similar objects may be expressing naturalist intelligence abilities.

Figure 1 According to Howard Gardner, there are eight major kinds of intelligences, corresponding to abilities in different domains. In what area does your greatest intelligence reside, and why do you think you have particular strengths in that area? Source: Adapted from Gardner, 2000. Photos: (1) © Harold Holt/Getty Images; (2) © Bettmann/Getty Images; (3) © National Library of Medicine/Science Source; (4) © Bettmann/Getty Images; (5) © Danita Delimont/Ga LO Images/Getty Images; (6) © Bettmann/Getty Images; (7) © George C. Beresford/Getty Images; (8) © Corbis RF

"To be perfectly frank, I'm not nearly as smart as you seem to think I am."

The concept of multiple intelligences has led to the development of intelligence tests that include questions in which more than one answer can be correct; these provide an opportunity for test-takers to demonstrate creative thinking. In addition, many educators, embracing the concept of multiple intelligences, have designed classroom curricula that are meant to draw on different aspects of intelligence (Kelly & Tangney, 2006; Douglas, Burton, & Reese-Durham, 2008; Tirri & Nokelainen, 2008).

Is Information Processing Intelligence?

One of the newer contributions to understanding intelligence comes from the work of cognitive psychologists who take an *information-processing approach.* They assert that the way people store material in memory and use that material to solve intellectual tasks provides the most accurate measure of intelligence. Consequently, rather than focusing on the structure of intelligence or its underlying content or dimensions, information-processing approaches examine the processes involved in producing intelligent behavior (Hunt, 2005; Pressley & Harris, 2006; Sternberg, 2015).

For example, research shows that people with high scores on tests of intelligence spend more time on the initial encoding stages of problems, identifying the parts of a problem and retrieving relevant information from long-term memory, than do people with lower scores. This initial emphasis on recalling relevant information pays off in the end; those who use this approach are more successful in finding solutions than are those who spend relatively less time on the initial stages (Deary & Der, 2005; Hunt, 2005).

Other information-processing approaches examine the sheer speed of processing. For example, research shows that the speed with which people are able to retrieve information from memory is related to verbal intelligence. In general, people with high scores on measures of intelligence react more quickly on a variety of information-processing tasks, ranging from reactions to flashing lights to distinguishing between letters. The speed of information processing, then, may underlie differences in intelligence (Gontkovsky & Beatty, 2006; Helmbold, Troche, & Rammsayer, 2007; Sheppard & Vernon, 2008).

STUDY ALERT

Remember that Gardner's theory suggests that each individual has every kind of intelligence, but in different degrees.

» LO32.2 Practical Intelligence and Emotional Intelligence: Toward a More Intelligent View of Intelligence

Consider the following situation:

An employee who reports to one of your subordinates has asked to talk with you about waste, poor management practices, and possible violations of both company policy and the law on the part of your subordinate. You have been in your present position only a year, but in that time you have had no indications of trouble about the subordinate in question. Neither you nor your company has an "open door" policy, so it is expected that employees should take their concerns to their immediate supervisors before bringing a matter to the attention of anyone else. The employee who wishes to meet with you has not discussed this matter with her supervisors because of its delicate nature. (Sternberg, 1998, p. 17)

Your response to the preceding situation has a lot to do with your future success in a business career, according to psychologist Robert Sternberg. The question is one of a series designed to help give an indication of your intelligence. However, it is not traditional intelligence that the question is designed to tap, but rather intelligence of a specific kind: practical intelligence. **Practical intelligence** is intelligence related to overall success in living (Sternberg & Hedlund, 2002; Wagner, 2002; Lievens & Chan, 2010).

Noting that traditional tests were designed to relate to academic success, Sternberg points to evidence showing that most traditional measures of intelligence do not relate especially well to *career* success (McClelland, 1993). Specifically, although successful business executives usually score at least moderately well on intelligence tests, the rate at which they advance and their ultimate business achievements are only minimally associated with traditional measures of their intelligence.

Sternberg argues that career success requires a very different type of intelligence from that required for academic success. Whereas academic success is based on knowledge of a specific information base obtained from reading and listening, practical intelligence is learned mainly through observation of others' behavior. People who are high in practical intelligence are able to learn general norms and principles and apply them appropriately. Consequently, practical intelligence tests, like the one shown in Figure 2, measure the ability to employ broad principles in solving everyday problems (Stemler & Sternberg, 2006; Stemler et al., 2009).

Some psychologists broaden the concept of intelligence even further beyond the intellectual realm to include emotions. **Emotional intelligence** is the set of skills that underlie the accurate assessment, evaluation, expression, and regulation of emotions (Mayer, Salovey, & Caruso, 2004, 2008; Humphrey, Curran, & Morris, 2007).

Emotional intelligence underlies the ability to get along well with others. It provides us with an understanding of what other people are feeling and experiencing and permits us to respond appropriately to others' needs. Emotional intelligence is the basis of empathy for others, self-awareness, and social skills.

Abilities in emotional intelligence may help explain why people with only modest scores on traditional intelligence tests can be quite successful, despite their lack of traditional intelligence. High emotional intelligence may enable an individual to tune into others' feelings, permitting a high degree of responsiveness to others.

practical intelligence According to Robert Sternberg, intelligence related to overall success in living

emotional intelligence The set of skills that underlie the accurate assessment, evaluation, expression, and regulation of emotions

> Whereas academic success is based on knowledge of a specific information base obtained from reading and listening, practical intelligence is learned mainly through observation of others' behavior.

As a paralegal, how might high practical intelligence help you in your career? Would high practical intelligence help or hurt you if you suspected unethical work being done at your firm? © Artiga Photo/Getty Images

Figure 2 Most standard tests of intelligence primarily measure analytical skills; more comprehensive tests measure creative and practical abilities as well. Source: Adapted from Sternberg, 2000, p. 389.

You are given a map of an entertainment park.
You walk from the lemonade stand to the computer games arcade.
Your friend walks from the shooting gallery to the roller coaster.
Which of these are you BOTH most likely to pass?

Ⓐ the merry-go-round   Ⓑ the music hall

Ⓒ the pizza stand   Ⓓ the dog show

Entrance

STUDY ALERT

Traditional intelligence relates to academic performance; practical intelligence relates to success in life; and emotional intelligence relates to emotional skills.

The notion of emotional intelligence reminds us that there are many ways to demonstrate intelligent behavior—just as there are multiple views of the nature of intelligence (Fox & Spector, 2000; Barrett & Salovey, 2002; Parke, Seo & Sherf, 2015). Figure 3 presents a summary of the different approaches used by psychologists.

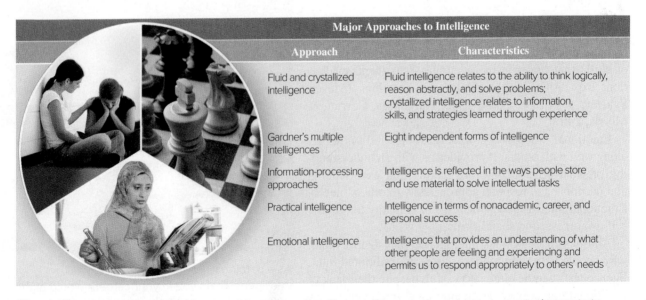

Major Approaches to Intelligence	
Approach	**Characteristics**
Fluid and crystallized intelligence	Fluid intelligence relates to the ability to think logically, reason abstractly, and solve problems; crystallized intelligence relates to information, skills, and strategies learned through experience
Gardner's multiple intelligences	Eight independent forms of intelligence
Information-processing approaches	Intelligence is reflected in the ways people store and use material to solve intellectual tasks
Practical intelligence	Intelligence in terms of nonacademic, career, and personal success
Emotional intelligence	Intelligence that provides an understanding of what other people are feeling and experiencing and permits us to respond appropriately to others' needs

Figure 3 Just as there are many views of the nature of intelligence, there are also numerous ways to demonstrate intelligent behavior. This summary provides an overview of the various approaches used by psychologists. Photos: (two girls) © Stockbyte/Thinkstock/Getty Images RF; (chess pieces) © Russell Illig/Getty Images RF; (woman cooking) © Insy Shah/Getty Images RF

» LO32.3 Assessing Intelligence

Given the variety of approaches to the components of intelligence, it is not surprising that measuring intelligence has proved challenging. Psychologists who study intelligence have focused much of their attention on the development of **intelligence tests** and have relied on such tests to quantify a person's level of intelligence. These tests have proved to be of great benefit in identifying students in need of special attention in school, diagnosing cognitive difficulties, and helping people make optimal educational and vocational choices. At the same time, their use has proved controversial, raising important social and educational issues.

Alfred Binet. © Albert Harlingue/Roger-Viollet/The Image Works.

Binet and the Development of IQ Tests

The first real intelligence tests were developed by the French psychologist Alfred Binet (1857–1911). His tests followed from a simple premise: if performance on certain tasks or test items improved with *chronological,* or physical, age, performance could be used to distinguish more intelligent people from less intelligent ones within a particular age group. On the basis of this principle, Binet devised the first formal intelligence test, which was designed to identify the "dullest" students in the Paris school system in order to provide them with remedial aid.

Binet began by presenting tasks to same-age students who had been labeled "bright" or "dull" by their teachers. If a task could be completed by the bright students but not by the dull ones, he retained that task as a proper test item; otherwise it was discarded. In the end he came up with a test that distinguished between the bright and dull groups, and—with further work—one that distinguished among children in different age groups (Binet & Simon, 1916; Sternberg & Jarvin, 2003).

On the basis of the Binet test, children were assigned a score relating to their **mental age,** the age for which a given level of performance is average or typical. For example, if the average 8-year-old answered, say, 45 items correctly on a test, anyone who answered 45 items correctly would be assigned a mental age of 8 years. Consequently, whether the person taking the test was 20 years old or 5 years old, he or she would have the same mental age of 8 years (Cornell, 2006).

Assigning a mental age to students provided an indication of their general level of performance. However, it did not allow for adequate comparisons among people of different chronological ages. By using mental age alone, for instance, we might assume that a 20-year-old responding at an 18-year-old's level would be as bright as a 5-year-old answering at a 3-year-old's level, when actually the 5-year-old would be displaying a much greater *relative* degree of slowness.

> **Assigning a mental age to students provided an indication of their general level of performance.**

A solution to the problem came in the form of the **intelligence quotient** or **IQ,** a score that takes into account an individual's mental and chronological ages. Historically, the first IQ scores employed the following formula, in which MA stands for mental age and CA for chronological age:

$$\text{IQ score} = \frac{MA}{CA} \times 100$$

Using this formula, we can return to the earlier example of a 20-year-old performing at a mental age of 18 and calculate an IQ score of $(18/20) \times 100 = 90$.

intelligence tests Tests devised to quantify a person's level of intelligence

mental age The average age of individuals who achieve a particular level of performance on a test

intelligence quotient (IQ) A score that takes into account an individual's mental and chronological ages

In contrast, the 5-year-old performing at a mental age of 3 comes out with a considerably lower IQ score: $(3/5) \times 100 = 60$.

As a bit of trial and error with the formula will show you, anyone who has a mental age equal to his or her chronological age will have an IQ equal to 100. Moreover, people with a mental age that is greater than their chronological age will have IQs that exceed 100.

Although the basic principles behind the calculation of an IQ score still hold, today IQ scores are figured in a different manner and are known as *deviation IQ scores.* First, the average test score for everyone of the same age who takes the test is determined, and that average score is assigned an IQ of 100. Then, with the aid of statistical techniques that calculate the differences (or "deviations") between each score and the average, IQ scores are assigned.

As you can see in Figure 4, when IQ scores from large numbers of people are plotted on a graph, they form a *bell-shaped distribution* (called "bell-shaped" because it looks like a bell when plotted). Approximately two-thirds of all individuals fall within 15 IQ points of the average score of 100. As scores increase or fall beyond that range, the percentage of people in a category falls considerably.

Contemporary IQ Tests: Gauging Intelligence

Remnants of Binet's original intelligence test are still with us, although the test has been revised in significant ways. Now in its fifth edition and called the *Stanford-Binet Intelligence Scale,* the test consists of a series of items that vary in nature according to the age of the person being tested (Roid, Nellis, & McLellan, 2003). For example, young children are asked to copy figures or answer questions about everyday activities. Older people are asked to solve analogies, explain proverbs, and describe similarities that underlie sets of words.

STUDY ALERT

It's important to know the traditional formula for IQ scores in which IQ is the ratio of mental age divided by chronological age, multiplied by 100. Remember, though, that the actual calculation of IQ scores today is done in a more sophisticated manner.

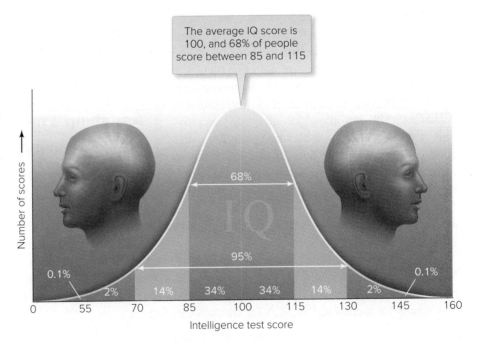

Figure 4 The average and most common IQ score is 100, and 68 percent of all people are within a 30-point range centered on 100. Some 95 percent of the population have scores that are within 30 points above or below 100, and 99.8 percent have scores that are between 55 and 145.

The average IQ score is 100, and 68% of people score between 85 and 115

The IQ test most frequently used in the United States was devised by psychologist David Wechsler and is known as the *Wechsler Adult Intelligence Scale–IV,* or, more commonly, the *WAIS-IV.* There is also a children's version, the *Wechsler Intelligence Scale for Children–V,* or *WISC-V.* Both the WAIS-IV and the WISC-V have two major parts: a verbal scale and a performance (or nonverbal) scale. As you can see from the sample questions in Figure 5, the verbal and performance scales include questions of very different types. Verbal tasks consist of more traditional kinds of problems, including vocabulary definition and comprehension of various concepts. In contrast, the performance (nonverbal) part involves the timed assembly of small objects and the arrangement of pictures in a logical order.

Because the Stanford-Binet, WAIS-IV, and WISC-V all require individualized, one-on-one administration, it is relatively difficult and time-consuming to administer and score them on a large-scale basis. Consequently, there are now a number of IQ tests that allow group administration. Rather than having one examiner ask one person at a time to respond to individual items, group IQ tests are strictly paper-and-pencil tests. The primary advantage of group tests is their ease of administration (Anastasi & Urbina, 1997).

Adaptive Testing: Computer-Administered Tests

Ensuring that tests are reliable, valid, and based on appropriate norms has become more critical with computer-administered testing. In computerized versions of tests, not only are test questions viewed and answered on a computer, but the test itself is individualized.

With *adaptive testing,* every test-taker does not receive identical sets of test questions. Instead, the computer first presents a randomly selected question of moderate difficulty. If the test-taker answers it correctly, the computer then presents a randomly chosen item of slightly greater difficulty. If the test-taker answers it incorrectly, the computer presents a slightly easier item. Each question becomes slightly harder or easier than the question preceding it, depending on whether the previous response is correct. Ultimately, the greater the number of difficult questions answered correctly, the higher the score (Marszalek, 2007; Belov & Armstrong, 2009; Deng, Ansley, & Chang, 2010; Liu, Ying, & Zhang, 2015).

Because computerized adaptive testing pinpoints a test-taker's level of proficiency fairly quickly, the total time spent taking the exam is shorter than it is with a traditional exam. Test-takers are not forced to spend a great deal of time answering questions that are either much easier or much harder than they can handle.

Critics of adaptive testing suggest that it may discriminate against test-takers who have less access to computers and thus may have less practice with them or may be more intimidated by the testing medium. In other cases, high-ability test-takers who make an early mistake and find the items getting easier may begin to feel such anxiety that their performance suffers, leading to a downward spiral in their performance. Still, most research suggests that adaptive testing provides scores equivalent to those of traditional paper-and-pencil measures for most types of testing (Passos, Berger, & Tan, 2007; Rulison & Loken, 2009).

WAIS IV (for adults) Name	Goal of Item	Example
Verbal Scale		
Information	Assess general information	Who wrote *The Adventures of Tom Sawyer*?
Comprehension	Assess understanding and evaluation of social norms and past experience	Why is copper often used for electrical wires?
Arithmetic	Assess math reasoning through verbal problems	Three women divided eighteen golf balls equally among themselves. How many golf balls did each person receive?
Similarities	Test understanding of how objects or concepts are alike, tapping abstract reasoning	In what way are a circle and a triangle alike?
Performance Scale		
Figure weights	Test perceptual reasoning	Problems require test-taker to determine which possibility balances the final scale. 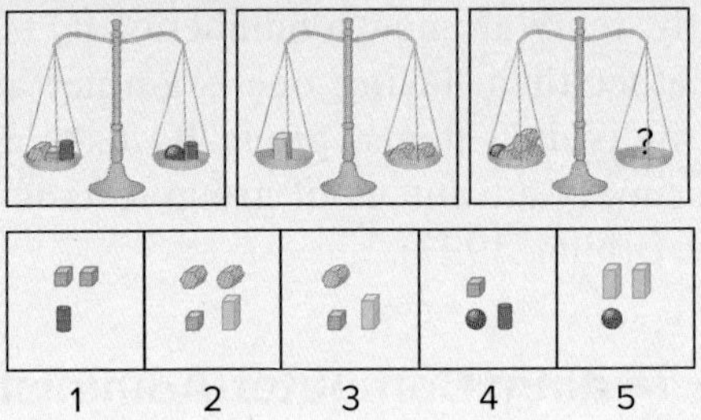
Matrix reasoning	Test spatial reasoning	Test taker must decide which of the five possibilities replaces the question mark and completes the sequence. 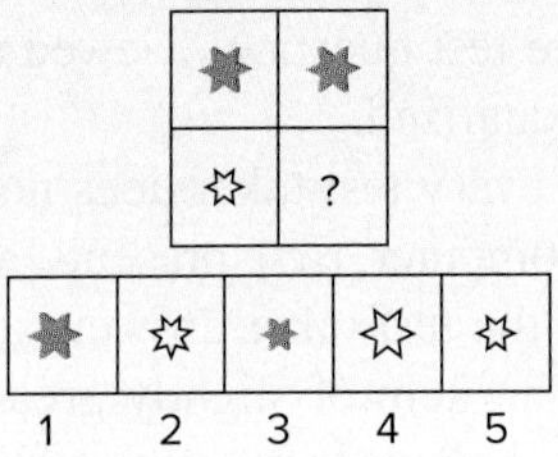
Block design item	Test understanding of relationship of parts to whole	Problems require test takers to reproduce a design in fixed amount of time. 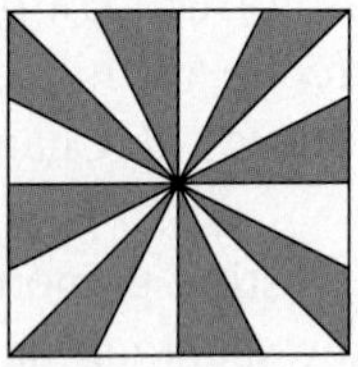

Figure 5 Typical kinds of items similar to those found on the Wechsler Adult Intelligence Scales (WAIS-IV). (Simulated items similar to those in the Wechsler Adult Intelligence Scale, Fourth Edition (WAIS-IV). Source: Adapted from Wechsler Adult Intelligence Scale, 2008.

» LO32.4 Variations in Intellectual Ability

More than 7 million people in the United States, including around 11 per 1,000 children, have been identified as far enough below average in intelligence that they can be regarded as having a serious deficit. Individuals with low IQs (people with intellectual disabilities) as well as those with unusually high IQs (the intellectually gifted) require special attention if they are to reach their full potential.

Intellectual Disabilities

Although sometimes thought of as a rare phenomenon, intellectual disability (formerly known as *mental retardation*) occurs in 1 to 3 percent of the population. There is wide variation among those with intellectual disabilities, in large part because of the inclusiveness of the definition. **Intellectual disability** is a disability characterized by significant limitations in both intellectual functioning and in adaptive behavior, which covers many everyday social and practical skills, and originates before the age of 18 (American Association of Intellectual and Developmental Disabilities, 2015).

Although below-average intellectual functioning can be measured in a relatively straightforward manner—using standard IQ tests—it is more difficult to determine how to gauge limitations in adaptive behavior. Consequently, there is a lack of uniformity in how experts apply the term *intellectual disabilities*. People labeled intellectually disabled vary from those who can be taught to work and function with little special attention to those who cannot be trained and are institutionalized throughout their lives (Detterman, Gabriel, & Ruthsatz, 2000; Greenspan, 2006; American Association of Intellectual and Developmental Disabilities, 2015).

Most people with intellectual disabilities have relatively minor deficits and are classified as having *mild intellectual disability*. These individuals, who have IQ scores ranging from 55 to 69, constitute some 90 percent of all people with intellectual disabilities. Although their development is typically slower than that of their peers, they can function quite independently by adulthood and are able to hold jobs and have families of their own (Bates et al., 2001; Smith, 2006).

With greater degrees of intellectual deficit, the difficulties are more pronounced. For people with *moderate intellectual disability* (IQs of 40 to 54), deficits are obvious early, with language and motor skills lagging behind those of peers. Although these individuals can hold simple jobs, they need to have some degree of supervision throughout their lives. Individuals with *severe intellectual disability* (IQs of 25 to 39) and *profound intellectual disability* (IQs below 25) are generally unable to function independently and typically require care for their entire lives (Garwick, 2007).

intellectual disability A disability characterized by significant limitations in both intellectual functioning and in adaptive behavior, which covers many everyday social and practical skills

STUDY ALERT

Remember that in most cases of intellectual disabilities, there is no biological deficiency, but a history of intellectual disabilities exists in the family.

Children with intellectual disabilities benefit from a stimulating environment.
© Realistic Reflections RF

Identifying the Roots of Intellectual Disabilities

What are the causes of intellectual disabilities? In nearly one-third of the cases there is an identifiable biological origin. The most common biological cause is **fetal alcohol syndrome,** caused by a mother's use of alcohol while pregnant. Increasing evidence shows that even small amounts of alcohol intake can produce intellectual deficits. One in every 750 infants is born with fetal alcohol syndrome in the United States (West & Blake, 2005; Manning & Hoyme, 2007; Murthy et al., 2009; Lewis et al., 2015).

Down syndrome represents another major biological cause of intellectual disabilities. *Down syndrome* results from the presence of an extra chromosome. In other cases of intellectual disabilities, an abnormality occurs in the structure of a chromosome. Birth complications, such as a temporary lack of oxygen, may also cause intellectual disability. In some cases, intellectual disabilities occur after birth, following a head injury, a stroke, or infections such as meningitis (Plomin & Kovas, 2005; Bittles, Bower, & Hussain, 2007; Rezazadeh & Shaw, 2010).

However, the majority of cases of intellectual disabilities are classified as **familial intellectual disability,** in which no apparent biological defect exists but there is a history of intellectual disability in the family. Whether the family background of intellectual disability is caused by environmental factors—such as extreme continuous poverty leading to malnutrition—or by some underlying genetic factor is usually impossible to determine (Zigler et al., 2002).

The Intellectually Gifted

Another group of people—the intellectually gifted—differ from those with average intelligence as much as do individuals with intellectual disabilities, although in a different manner. Accounting for 2 to 4 percent of the population, the **intellectually gifted** have IQ scores greater than 130.

Although the stereotype associated with the gifted suggests that they are awkward, shy social misfits who are unable to get along well with peers, most research indicates that just the opposite is true. The intellectually gifted are most often outgoing, well-adjusted, healthy, popular people who are able to do most things better than the average person can (Lubinski et al., 2006; Guldemond et al., 2007; Mueller, 2009; Strenze, 2015).

For example, in a famous study by psychologist Lewis Terman that started in the early 1920s, 1,500 children who had IQ scores above 140 were followed for the rest of their lives. From the start, the members of this group were more physically, academically, and socially capable than their nongifted peers. In addition to doing better in school, they also showed better social adjustment than average. All these advantages paid off in terms of career success: as a group, the gifted received more awards and distinctions, earned higher incomes, and made more contributions in art and literature than typical individuals. Perhaps most important, they reported greater satisfaction in life than the nongifted (Hegarty, 2007; Kern & Friedman, 2010).

Of course, not every member of the group Terman studied was successful. Furthermore, high intelligence is not a homogeneous quality; a person with a high overall IQ is not necessarily gifted in every academic subject, but may excel in just one or two. A high IQ is not a universal guarantee of success (Shurkin, 1992; Winner, 2003; Clemons, 2006).

fetal alcohol syndrome The most common cause of intellectual disability in newborns, occurring when the mother uses alcohol during pregnancy

familial intellectual disability Intellectual disability in which no apparent biological defect exists, but there is a history of intellectual disability in the family

intellectually gifted The 2 to 4 percent of the population who have IQ scores greater than 130

EXPLORING diversity

The Relative Influence of Genetics and Environment: Nature, Nurture, and IQ

In an attempt to produce a **culture-fair IQ test,** one that does not discriminate against the members of any minority group, psychologists have tried to devise test items that assess experiences common to all cultures or emphasize questions that do not require language usage. However, test makers have found this difficult to do, because past experiences, attitudes, and values almost always have an impact on respondents' answers (Fagan & Holland, 2009).

For example, children raised in Western cultures group things on the basis of what they *are* (such as putting *dog* and *fish* into the category of *animal*). In contrast, members of the Kpelle tribe in Africa see intelligence demonstrated by grouping things according to what they *do* (grouping *fish* with *swim*). Similarly, children in the United States asked to memorize the position of objects on a chessboard perform better than do African children living in remote villages if household objects familiar to the U.S. children are used. But if rocks are used instead of household objects, the African children do better. In short, it is difficult to produce a truly culture-fair test (Sandoval et al., 1998; Serpell, 2000; Valencia & Suzuki, 2003).

The efforts of psychologists to produce culture-fair measures of intelligence relate to a lingering controversy over differences in intelligence between members of minority and majority groups. In attempting to identify whether there are differences between such groups, psychologists have had to confront the broader issue of determining the relative contribution to intelligence of genetic factors (heredity) and experience (environment)—the nature-nurture issue that is one of the basic issues of psychology.

Richard Herrnstein, a psychologist, and Charles Murray, a sociologist, fanned the flames of the debate with the publication of their book *The Bell Curve* in the mid-1990s (Herrnstein & Murray, 1994). They argued that an analysis of IQ differences between whites and blacks demonstrated that although environmental factors played a role, there were also basic genetic differences between the two races. They based their argument on a number of findings. For instance, on average, whites score 15 points higher than do blacks on traditional IQ tests even when socioeconomic status (SES) is taken into account. According to Herrnstein and Murray, middle- and upper-SES blacks score lower than do middle- and upper-SES whites, just as lower-SES blacks score lower on average than do lower-SES whites. Intelligence differences between blacks and whites, they concluded, could not be attributed to environmental differences alone.

Moreover, intelligence in general shows a high degree of **heritability,** a measure of the degree to which a characteristic can be attributed to genetic, inherited factors (e.g., Petrill, 2005; Miller & Penke, 2007; Plomin, 2009). As can be seen in Figure 6, the closer the genetic link between two related people, the greater the correspondence of IQ scores. Using data such as these, Herrnstein and Murray argued that differences between races in IQ scores were largely caused by genetically based differences in intelligence.

culture-fair IQ test A test that does not discriminate against the members of any minority group

heritability A measure of the degree to which a characteristic is related to genetic, inherited factors

Relationship	Genetic Overlap	Rearing	Correlation
Monozygotic (identical) twins	100%	Together	.86
Dizygotic (fraternal) twins	50%	Together	.62
Siblings	50%	Together	.41
Siblings	50%	Apart	.24
Parent-child	50%	Together	.35
Parent-child	50%	Apart	.31
Adoptive parent-child	0%	Together	.16
Unrelated children	0%	Together	.25
Spouses	0%	Apart	.29

The difference between these two correlations shows the impact of the environment

The relatively low correlation for unrelated children raised together shows the importance of genetic factors

Figure 6 The relationship between IQ and closeness of genetic relationship. In general, the more similar the genetic and environmental background of two people, the greater the correlation. Note, for example, that the correlation for spouses, who are genetically unrelated and have been reared apart, is relatively low, whereas the correlation for identical twins reared together is substantial. Source: Adapted from Henderson, 1982.

However, many psychologists reacted strongly against the arguments laid out in *The Bell Curve,* refuting several of the book's basic arguments. One criticism is that even within similar socioeconomic groups, wide variations in IQ remain among individual households. Furthermore, the living conditions of blacks and whites are likely different even when their socioeconomic status is similar. In addition, there is reason to believe that traditional IQ tests may discriminate against lower-SES urban blacks by asking for information pertaining to experiences they are unlikely to have had (Hall, 2002; Horn, 2002; Nisbett, 2007).

Moreover, blacks who are raised in economically enriched environments have similar IQ scores to whites in comparable environments. For example, a study by Sandra Scarr and Richard Weinberg (1976) examined black children who had been adopted at an early age by white middle-class families of above-average intelligence. The IQ scores of those children averaged 106—about 15 points above the average IQ scores of unadopted black children in the study. Other research shows that the racial gap in IQ narrows considerably after a college education, and cross-cultural data demonstrate that when racial gaps exist in other cultures, it is the economically disadvantaged groups that typically have lower scores. In short, the evidence that genetic factors play the major role in determining racial differences in IQ is not compelling (Sternberg, Grigorenko, & Kidd, 2005; Fagan & Holland, 2007; Nisbett, 2009; Strenze, 2015).

Furthermore, drawing comparisons between different races on any dimension, including IQ scores, is an imprecise, potentially misleading, and often fruitless venture. By far, the greatest discrepancies in IQ scores occur when comparing *individuals,* not when comparing mean IQ scores of different *groups.* There are blacks who score high on IQ tests and whites who score low, just as there are whites who score high and blacks who score low. For the concept of intelligence to aid in

STUDY ALERT

Remember that the differences in IQ scores are much greater when comparing individuals than when comparing groups.

Other research shows that the racial gap in IQ narrows considerably after a college education, and cross-cultural data demonstrate that when racial gaps exist in other cultures, it is the economically disadvantaged groups that typically have lower scores.

the betterment of society, we must examine how *individuals* perform, not the groups to which they belong (Angoff, 1988; Fagan & Holland, 2002, 2007).

The more critical question to ask is not whether hereditary or environmental factors primarily underlie intelligence, but whether there is anything we can do to maximize the intellectual development of each individual. If we can find ways to do this, we will be able to make changes in the environment—which may take the form of enriched home and school environments—that can lead each person to reach his or her potential.

RECAP

Summarize the theories of intelligence.

- Because intelligence can take many forms, defining it is challenging. One commonly accepted view is that intelligence is the capacity to understand the world, think rationally, and use resources effectively when faced with challenges.

- The earliest psychologists assumed that there is a general factor for mental ability called *g*. However, later psychologists disputed the view that intelligence is unidimensional.

- Some researchers suggest that intelligence can be broken down into fluid intelligence and crystallized intelligence. Gardner's theory of multiple intelligences proposes that there are eight spheres of intelligence.

- Information-processing approaches examine the processes underlying intelligent behavior rather than focusing on the structure of intelligence.

Compare and contrast practical and emotional intelligences.

- Practical intelligence is intelligence related to overall success in living; emotional intelligence is the set of skills that underlie the accurate assessment, evaluation, expression, and regulation of emotions.

Explain approaches to assessing intelligence.

- Intelligence tests have traditionally compared a person's mental age and chronological age to yield an IQ, or intelligence quotient, score.

- Specific tests of intelligence include the Stanford-Binet test, the Wechsler Adult Intelligence Scale–IV (WAIS-IV), and the Wechsler Intelligence Scale for Children–V (WISC-V).

Identify variations in intellectual ability.

- The levels of intellectual disabilities include mild, moderate, severe, and profound intellectual disability.

- About one-third of the cases of intellectual disabilities have a known biological cause; fetal alcohol syndrome is the most common. Most cases, however, are classified as familial intellectual disability, for which there is no known biological cause.

- The intellectually gifted are people with IQ scores greater than 130. Intellectually gifted people tend to be healthier and more successful than are the nongifted.

- Traditional intelligence tests have frequently been criticized for being biased in favor of the white middle-class population. This controversy has led to attempts to devise culture-fair tests, IQ measures that avoid questions that depend on a particular cultural background.

[EVALUATE E Evaluate]

1. _____ is a measure of intelligence that takes into account a person's chronological and mental ages.

2. _____ tests predict a person's ability in a specific area; _____ tests determine the specific level of knowledge in an area.

3. _____ _____ _____ is the most common biological cause of intellectual disabilities.

4. People with high intelligence are generally shy and socially withdrawn. True or false?

5. A(n) _____ _____ test tries to use only questions appropriate to all the people taking the test.

[RETHINK R Rethink]

What is the role of emotional intelligence in the classroom? How might emotional intelligence be tested? Should emotional intelligence be a factor in determining academic promotion to the next grade?

KEY TERMS

Intelligence   LO32.1

g or g-factor   LO32.1

Fluid intelligence   LO32.1

Crystallized intelligence   LO32.1

Theory of multiple intelligences   LO32.1

Practical intelligence   LO32.2

Emotional intelligence   LO32.2

Intelligence tests   LO32.3

Mental age   LO32.3

Intelligence quotient (IQ)   LO32.3

Intellectual disability   LO32.4

Fetal alcohol syndrome   LO32.4

Familial intellectual disability   LO32.4

Intellectually gifted   LO32.4

Culture-fair IQ test   LO32.4

Heritability   LO32.4

« « Looking Back

Psychology on the Web

1. Sigmund Freud is one of the towering figures in psychology. His influence extends far beyond his psychoanalytic work. Find information about Freud on the Web. Pick one aspect of his work or influence (e.g., on therapy, medicine, literature, film, or culture and society) and summarize in writing what you have found, including your attitude toward your findings.

2. Find a website that links to personality tests and take one or two tests—remembering to take them with skepticism. For each test, summarize in writing the aspects of personality that were tested, the theoretical approach the test appeared to be based on, and your assessment of the trustworthiness of the results.

the case of . . .
MIKE AND MARTY SCANLON, THE UNLIKELY TWINS

People often have difficulty believing that Mike and Marty Scanlon are brothers, let alone twins. The two men bear a resemblance, but the similarity ends there.

Marty Scanlon was always a quiet, well-behaved child. He excelled in all his academic subjects throughout his school years, although he was shy and had few friends. Marty would always be polite to people, but he generally preferred to keep to himself. After college, Marty became a successful network administrator for a large financial company and married his longtime girlfriend. A dedicated family man, Marty spends most of his free time doing home improvement projects and looking after his two children.

Mike Scanlon, on the other hand, could never be described as shy. He was the student that teachers dreaded having in their classroom: boisterous, unruly, and indifferent to authority. Mike had many brushes with the law throughout his high school years, for crimes ranging from vandalism to public drunkenness. Mike dropped out of high school to take a job as an oil-change technician at a local garage; he spends most of his free time and money at local bars—at least the ones that haven't banned him for starting fights. Mike's current legal trouble surrounds two of his ex-girlfriends, who are independently taking him to court for child support. Mike is unfazed, however; he laughs with his friends that they'll never get a dime from him.

1. How would Freud explain the personality differences between Mike and Marty Scanlon?

2. How would you rate Mike and Marty Scanlon on the Big Five personality traits?

3. Given that Mike and Marty Scanlon are twins and share some of their genetic makeup, how would you explain the pronounced differences in their personalities? What role, if any, does temperament seem to be playing?

4. Which of the two brothers seems more likely to be achieving self-actualization, and why do you think so?

5. Do Mike and Marty Scanlon appear to have different levels of intelligence, or do they show intelligence in different ways? Why do you think so?

profiles of **SUCCESS**

Courtesy of Dominique Edgerton

NAME:	**Dominique Edgerton**
SCHOOL:	**Stratford University**
DEGREE PROGRAM:	**AD in Business Administration**

Dominique Edgerton realized that if she wanted to be successful in the field of retail, she would need to return to school. Fortunately, Stratford University provided her the right opportunity.

"It was definitely a hard decision," she explained. "But Stratford University offered me the opportunity to continue my education in a supportive, flexible environment.

"Being a single mother with a full-time job, it was very important to know that there were people around me that could support me through the journey," she added.

Having found an academic environment that suited her needs, Edgerton was then confronted with a number of challenges, the biggest being balancing school, work, and family.

"Making the decision to attend school was harder than actually jumping in and going. Getting used to homework and tests was a bit of a task of its own, and figuring out how to fit in study time was a bit tricky."

As a manager for a national retail store, Edgerton discovered the importance of scheduling her schoolwork, especially during busy holiday seasons.

"You don't get much down time during certain times of the year, like the Christmas season, to do anything, but I found that making a schedule seemed to be the best way to go about it," she noted. "Once on track with the schedule, things just started to fall in to place. I had every minute mapped out, and for the most part it was a life saver for me."

Finding ways to better utilize her time and organize herself were important for Edgerton, but the biggest challenge she confronted was personal.

"Throughout this journey there were plenty of personal and professional challenges. But one of the biggest I had to deal with was learning how to accept criticism from others," she said. "It was hard to sit back and hear the pros and cons about something I'd worked hard to accomplish. Once I got a better understanding of what positive and negative criticism really was it became easier to deal with.

"Going to Stratford University has helped me better myself personally and professionally. Now in a new chapter in my life I can honestly say attending school showed me that I decide where my life is going," Edgerton said.

[RETHINK **R Rethink**]

What kind of personality traits might allow people to accept criticism from others and react positively to it?

What do you think Edgerton meant when she said that attending college allowed her to understand that *she* determined where her life was going?

visual summary 9
PERSONALITY AND INDIVIDUAL DIFFERENCES

MODULE 29 Psychodynamic Approaches to Personality

Freud's Psychoanalytic Theory

- Conscious experience
- Unconscious
- Structure of personality
  - Id
  - Ego
  - Superego
- Psychosexual stages
- Defense mechanisms: Unconscious strategies people use to reduce anxiety

Neo-Freudian Psychoanalysts:
Emphasize the ego more than Freud: Carl Jung, Karen Horney, Alfred Adler

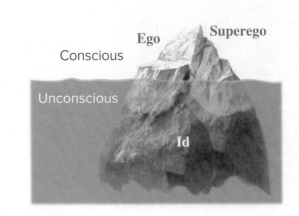

	Stage	Age	Major Characteristics
1	Oral	Birth to 12–18 months	Interest in oral gratification from sucking, eating, mouthing, biting
2	Anal	12–18 months to 3 years	Gratification from expelling and withholding feces; coming to terms with society's controls relating to toilet training
3	Phallic	3 to 5–6 years	Interest in the genitals, coming to terms with Oedipal conflict leading to identification with same-sex parent
4	Latency	5–6 years to adolescence	Sexual concerns largely unimportant
5	Genital	Adolescence to adulthood	Reemergence of sexual interests and establishment of mature sexual relationships

Freud

MODULE 30 Trait, Learning, Biological and Evolutionary, and Humanistic Approaches to Personality

Summary of the Multiple Approaches to Personality

Theoretical Approach and Major Theorists	Conscious versus Unconscious Determinants of Personality	Nature (Hereditary Factors) versus Nurture (Environmental Factors)	Free Will versus Determinism	Stability versus Modifiability
Psychodynamic (Freud, Jung, Horney, Adler)	Emphasizes the unconscious	Stresses innate, inherited structure of personality while emphasizing importance of childhood experience	Stresses determinism, the view that behavior is directed and caused by factors outside one's control	Emphasizes the stability of characteristics throughout a person's life
Trait (Cattell, Eysenck)	Disregards both conscious and unconscious	Approaches vary	Stresses determinism, the view that behavior is directed and caused by factors outside one's control	Emphasizes the stability of characteristics throughout a person's life
Learning (Skinner, Bandura)	Disregards both conscious and unconscious	Focuses on the environment	Stresses determinism, the view that behavior is directed and caused by factors outside one's control	Stresses that personality remains flexible and resilient throughout one's life
Biological and evolutionary (Tellegen)	Disregards both conscious and unconscious	Stresses the innate, inherited determinants of personality	Stresses determinism, the view that behavior is directed and caused by factors outside one's control	Emphasizes the stability of characteristics throughout a person's life
Humanistic (Rogers, Maslow)	Stresses the conscious more than unconscious	Stresses the interaction between both nature and nurture	Stresses the freedom of individuals to make their own choices	Stresses that personality remains flexible and resilient throughout one's life

MODULE 31 Assessing Personality

Psychological Tests: Standard measures that assess behavior objectively

- • Reliability
- • Validity
- • Norms

Self-report Measures: A method of gathering data by asking people questions about their own behavior and traits

Projective Methods: People are shown an ambiguous stimulus and asked to describe it or tell a story about it

- • Rorschach test
- • Thematic Apperception Test (TAT)

Behavioral Assessment: Measures of a person's behavior designed to describe characteristics indicative of personality

MODULE 32 Intelligence

Theories of Intelligence

- • *g*-factor
- • Fluid intelligence
- • Crystallized intelligence
- • Gardner's multiple intelligences
- • Practical intelligence
- • Emotional intelligence

Assessing Intelligence: Intelligence tests

- • Binet developed IQ tests
  - • Mental age
  - • IQ
- • Contemporary IQ tests
  - • Wechsler Adult Intelligence Scale–IV
  - • Wechsler Intelligence Scale for Children–V

Variations in Intellectual Ability

- • Intellectual Disability
- • Intellectually Gifted

The average IQ score is 100, and 68% of people score between 85 and 115

Number of scores

0.1%   2%   14%   34%   34%   14%   2%   0.1%

0   55   70   85   100   115   130   145   160

Intelligence test score

(MODULE 29) © Hulton Archive/Getty Images; (MODULE 31) Source: Alloy, Jacobson, & Acocella, 1999

PSYCHOLOGICAL DISORDERS

Coping with Schizophrenia

It was in the wee hours of the morning that Chris Coles first heard the voice. He was not alarmed. The voice was calm, even soothing. It directed him to go to the beach cove immediately and apologize to his friend for planning to date the man's girlfriend.

Though he had never thought about deceiving his friend in such a way, Coles followed the instructions. The beach was deserted when he arrived, and he put the whole episode down to a sort of half dream between waking and sleeping. But he continued to hear voices, and he began having visions, as well. Sometimes, he spotted an incandescent, golden Buddha in the dunes near his beach house. Other times, he saw dolphins and whales swim right onto the sand.

He began to think he could work magic—control nature. "Delusions of grandeur," Coles calls the feelings that made him believe he could direct the waves and the dolphins and the whales (Begley, 2013).

 **Looking** Ahead

Chris Coles was losing his grip on reality. It turned out that he was suffering from schizophrenia, one of the more severe psychological disorders. Although drug treatments eventually stilled the voices that ran through his head, his experience raises many questions. What caused his disorder? Were genetic factors involved, or were stressors in his life primarily responsible? Were there signs that family and friends should have noticed earlier? Could his schizophrenia have been prevented? And, more generally, how do we distinguish normal from abnormal behavior, and how can Chris's behavior be categorized and classified in such a way as to pinpoint the specific nature of his problem?

We address the issues raised by Chris's case in this set of modules. We begin by discussing the difference between normal and abnormal behavior, which can be surprisingly indistinct. We then turn to a consideration of the most significant kinds of psychological disorders. Finally, we'll consider ways of evaluating behavior—one's own and that of others—to determine whether seeking help from a mental health professional is warranted.

Normal versus Abnormal
Making the Distinction

Learning Outcomes Prepare

>> **LO33.1** Define abnormality.

>> **LO33.2** Discuss perspectives on abnormality.

>> **LO33.3** Classify abnormal behavior.

MODULE OUTLINE  Organize

Defining Abnormality

Perspectives on Abnormality: From Superstition to Science

Classifying Abnormal Behavior: The ABCs of *DSM*

 Work

Universally that person's acumen is esteemed very little perceptive concerning whatsoever matters are being held as most profitable by mortals with sapience endowed to be studied who is ignorant of that which the most in doctrine erudite and certainly by reason of that in them high mind's ornament deserving of veneration constantly maintain when by general consent they affirm that other circumstances being equal by no exterior splendour is the prosperity of a nation . . .

It would be easy to conclude that these words are the musings of a madman. To most people, the passage does not seem to make any sense at all. But literary scholars would disagree. Actually, this passage is from James Joyce's classic *Ulysses,* hailed as one of the major works of twentieth-century literature (Joyce, 1934, p. 377).

As this example illustrates, casually examining a person's writing is insufficient to determine the degree to which that person is "normal." But even when we consider more extensive samples of a person's behavior, we will see that there may be only a fine line between behavior that is considered normal and behavior that is considered abnormal.

> **Because of the difficulty in distinguishing normal from abnormal behavior, psychologists have struggled to devise a precise, scientific definition of "abnormal behavior."**

>> LO33.1 Defining Abnormality

Because of the difficulty in distinguishing normal from abnormal behavior, psychologists have struggled to devise a precise, scientific definition of "abnormal behavior." For instance, consider the following definitions, each of which has advantages and disadvantages.

- *Abnormality as deviation from the average.* According to this definition, behaviors that are unusual or rare in a society or culture are considered abnormal. It is basically a statistical definition: if most people behave in a certain way, it is viewed as normal; if only a few people do it, it is considered abnormal.

  The difficulty with this definition is that some statistically unusual behaviors hardly seem abnormal. If most people eat meat, but you are a vegetarian, this deviation from the average hardly makes your behavior abnormal. Similarly, such a concept of abnormality would unreasonably label a person who has an unusually high IQ as abnormal simply because a high IQ is statistically rare. In short, a definition of abnormality that rests on deviation from the average is insufficient.

- *Abnormality as deviation from the ideal.* An alternative definition of abnormality considers behavior in relation to some kind of ideal or morally appropriate standard toward which most people are striving. This sort of definition considers behavior abnormal if it deviates enough from some kind of ideal or cultural standard. However, society has few standards on which people universally agree. Furthermore, standards that do arise change over time and vary across cultures. Thus, the deviation-from-the-ideal approach is also inadequate.

- *Abnormality as a sense of personal discomfort.* A more useful definition concentrates on the psychological consequences of the behavior for the individual. In this approach, behavior is considered abnormal if it produces a sense of personal distress, anxiety, or guilt in an individual—or if it is harmful to others in some way.

  However, even a definition that relies on personal discomfort has drawbacks. For example, in some especially severe forms of mental disturbance, people report feeling wonderful, even though their behavior seems bizarre to others. In such cases, a person feels fine, although most people would consider the behavior abnormal. Similarly, most of us would think that a woman who says she hears uplifting messages from Martians would be displaying abnormal behavior even though she may say that the messages make her feel happy.

- *Abnormality as the inability to function effectively.* Most people are able to feed themselves, hold a job, get along with others, and in general live as productive members of society. Yet there are those who are unable to adjust to the demands of society or function effectively.

  According to this view of abnormality, people who are unable to function effectively and to adapt to the demands of society are considered abnormal.

- *Abnormality as a legal concept.* To the judicial system, the distinction between normal and abnormal behavior rests on the definition of insanity, which is a legal, but not a psychological, term. The definition of insanity varies from one jurisdiction to another. In some states, insanity simply means that defendants cannot understand the difference between right and wrong at the time they commit a criminal act. Other states consider whether defendants are substantially incapable of understanding the criminality of their behavior or unable to control themselves. And in some jurisdictions pleas of insanity are not allowed at all (Sokolove, 2003; Ferguson & Ogloff, 2011; Reisner, Piel, & Makey, 2013).

Clearly, none of the previous definitions is broad enough to cover all instances of abnormal behavior. Consequently, the distinction between normal and abnormal behavior often remains ambiguous even to trained professionals.

In a famous case, Andrea Yates was judged sane when she drowned her five children in a bathtub, according to the first jury that heard the case. At a later trial, however, she was found not guilty by reason of insanity. © Brett Coomer, Pool/AP Images

Furthermore, to a large extent, cultural expectations for "normal" behavior in a particular society influence the understanding of "abnormal behavior" (Sanderson, 2007).

Given the difficulties in precisely defining the construct, psychologists typically define **abnormal behavior** broadly as behavior that causes people to experience distress and prevents them from functioning in their daily lives (Nolen-Hoeksema, 2007; Bassett & Baker, 2015). Because of the imprecision of this definition, it's best to view abnormal behavior and normal behavior as marking two ends of a continuum rather than as absolute states. Behavior should be evaluated in terms of gradations that range from fully normal functioning to extremely abnormal behavior. Behavior typically falls somewhere between those extremes.

abnormal behavior Behavior that causes people to experience distress and prevents them from functioning in their daily lives

» LO33.2 Perspectives on Abnormality: From Superstition to Science

Throughout much of human history, people linked abnormal behavior to superstition and witchcraft. Individuals who displayed abnormal behavior were accused of being possessed by the devil or some sort of demonic god (Berrios, 1996).

Contemporary approaches take a more enlightened view. Today, six major perspectives are used to understand psychological disorders. These perspectives suggest not only different causes of abnormal behavior but different treatment approaches as well. Furthermore, some perspectives are more applicable to specific disorders than are others. Figure 1 summarizes the perspectives and the ways in which they can be applied to the experience of Chris, described in the opening of the chapter.

STUDY ALERT

Use Figure 1 to review the six major perspectives on abnormality and consider how they relate to the major perspectives on the field of psychology.

Figure 1 In considering the case of Chris Coles, discussed in the chapter opening, we can employ each of the different perspectives on abnormal behavior. Note, however, that because of the nature of his psychological disorder, some of the perspectives are more applicable than others.

Perspectives on Psychological Disorders		
Perspective	**Description**	**Possible Application of Perspective to Chris's Case**
Medical perspective	Assumes that physiological causes are at the root of psychological disorders	Examine Chris for medical problems, such as brain tumor, chemical imbalance in the brain, or disease
Psychoanalytic perspective	Argues that psychological disorders stem from childhood conflicts	Seek out information about Chris's past, considering possible childhood conflicts
Behavioral perspective	Assumes that abnormal behaviors are learned responses	Concentrate on rewards and punishments for Chris's behavior, and identify environmental stimuli that reinforce his behavior
Cognitive perspective	Assumes that cognitions (people's thoughts and beliefs) are central to psychological disorders	Focus on Chris's perceptions of himself and his environment
Humanistic perspective	Emphasizes people's responsibility for their own behavior and the need to self-actualize	Consider Chris's behavior in terms of his choices and efforts to reach his potential
Sociocultural perspective	Assumes that behavior is shaped by family, society, and culture	Focus on how societal demands contributed to Chris's disorder

Medical Perspective

When people display the symptoms of tuberculosis, medical professionals can generally find tubercular bacteria in their body tissue. Similarly, the **medical perspective** suggests that when an individual displays symptoms of a psychological disorder, the fundamental cause will be found through a physical examination of the individual, which may reveal a hormonal imbalance, a chemical deficiency, or a brain injury.

Because many psychological disorders have been linked to biological causes, the medical perspective is a reasonable approach, yet serious criticisms have been leveled against it. For one thing, no biological cause has been identified for many forms of psychological disorders. Still, recent advances in our understanding of the biological bases of behavior underscore the importance of considering physiological factors in abnormal behavior.

> Because many psychological disorders have been linked to biological causes, the medical perspective is a reasonable approach, yet serious criticisms have been leveled against it.

Psychoanalytic Perspective

Whereas the medical perspective suggests that biological causes are at the root of abnormal behavior, the **psychoanalytic perspective** holds that abnormal behavior stems from childhood conflicts over opposing wishes regarding sex and aggression. According to Freud, children pass through a series of stages in which sexual and aggressive impulses take different forms and produce conflicts that require resolution. If these childhood conflicts are not dealt with successfully, they remain unresolved in the unconscious and eventually bring about abnormal behavior during adulthood.

To uncover the roots of people's disordered behavior, the psychoanalytic perspective scrutinizes their early life history. However, because there is no conclusive way to link people's childhood experiences with the abnormal behaviors they display as adults, we can never be sure that the causes suggested by psychoanalytic theory are accurate.

On the other hand, the contributions of psychoanalytic theory have been significant. More than any other approach to abnormal behavior, this perspective highlights the fact that people can have a rich, involved inner life. Furthermore, it underscores that prior experiences can have a profound effect on current psychological functioning (Bornstein, 2003; Rangell, 2007; Lombardi, 2010; Tummala-Narra, 2016).

Behavioral Perspective

Both the medical and psychoanalytic perspectives look at abnormal behaviors as *symptoms* of an underlying problem. In contrast, the **behavioral perspective** views the behavior itself as the problem. Using the basic principles of learning, behavioral theorists see both normal and abnormal behaviors as responses to various stimuli, responses that have been learned through past experience and are guided in the present by stimuli in the individual's environment. To explain why abnormal behavior occurs, we must analyze how an individual has learned and observe the circumstances in which it is displayed.

The emphasis on observable behavior represents both the greatest strength and the greatest weakness of the behavioral approach to abnormal behavior. This perspective provides the most precise and objective approach for examining

medical perspective The view that suggests that when an individual displays symptoms of a psychological disorder, the root cause will be found in a physical problem, deficiency, or brain injury

psychoanalytic perspective The view that suggests that abnormal behavior stems from childhood conflicts over opposing wishes regarding sex and aggression

behavioral perspective The view that looks at the behavior itself as the problem

Abnormal behavior is always of concern. Can you think of how abnormal behavior in a co-worker is of particular concern when your job involves life and death decisions, like for a police officer? © Scott Olson/ Getty Images

behavioral symptoms of specific disorders such as attention-deficit hyperactivity disorder (ADHD). At the same time, though, critics charge that the perspective ignores the rich inner world of thoughts, attitudes, and emotions that may contribute to abnormal behavior.

Cognitive Perspective

The medical, psychoanalytic, and behavioral perspectives view people's behavior as the result of factors largely beyond their control. To many critics of these views, however, people's thoughts cannot be ignored.

In response to such concerns, some psychologists employ a **cognitive perspective.** Rather than considering only external behavior, as in traditional behavioral approaches, the cognitive approach assumes that *cognitions* (people's thoughts and beliefs) are central to a person's abnormal behavior. A primary goal of treatment using the cognitive perspective is to explicitly teach new, more adaptive ways of thinking.

The cognitive perspective also has its critics. For example, it is possible that instead of maladaptive cognitions being the *cause* of a psychological disorder, they are just another *symptom* of the disorder. Furthermore, there are circumstances in which negative beliefs may not be irrational at all but simply reflect accurately the unpleasant circumstances in people's lives. Still, cognitive theorists would argue that there are adaptive ways of framing beliefs even in the most negative circumstances.

cognitive perspective The view that suggests that people's thoughts and beliefs are a central component of abnormal behavior

humanistic perspective The approach that suggests that all individuals naturally strive to grow, develop, and be in control of their lives and behavior

Humanistic Perspective

Psychologists who subscribe to the **humanistic perspective** emphasize the responsibility people have for their own behavior, even when their behavior is considered abnormal. The humanistic perspective concentrates on what is uniquely human—that is, a view of people as basically rational, oriented toward a social world, and motivated to seek self-actualization (Rogers, 1995). Rather than assuming that individuals require a "cure," the humanistic perspective suggests that they can, by and large, set their own limits of

> Rather than assuming that individuals require a "cure," the humanistic perspective suggests that they can, by and large, set their own limits of what is acceptable behavior.

what is acceptable behavior. As long as they are not hurting others and do not feel personal distress, people should be free to choose the behaviors in which they engage.

Although the humanistic perspective has been criticized for its reliance on unscientific, unverifiable information and its vague, almost philosophical formulations, it offers a distinctive view of abnormal behavior. It stresses the unique aspects of being human and provides a number of important suggestions for helping those with psychological problems.

Sociocultural Perspective

The **sociocultural perspective** assumes that people's behavior—both normal and abnormal—is shaped by the kind of family group, society, and culture in which they live. According to this view, the nature of one's relationships with others may support abnormal behaviors and even cause them. Consequently, the kinds of stresses and conflicts people experience in their daily interactions with others can promote and maintain abnormal behavior.

> **sociocultural perspective** The view that assumes that people's behavior—both normal and abnormal—is shaped by the kind of family group, society, and culture in which they live

This perspective is supported by research showing that some kinds of psychological disorders are far more prevalent among particular social classes, races, and ethnicities, than they are in others. For instance, diagnoses of schizophrenia tend to be higher among members of lower socioeconomic groups than among members of more affluent groups. Proportionally more African-American individuals are hospitalized involuntarily for psychological disorders than are whites. Furthermore, poor economic times seem to be linked to general declines in psychological functioning, and social problems such as homelessness are associated with psychological disorders (Greenberg & Rosenheck, 2008; Goldman-Mellor, Saxton & Catalano, 2010; López & Guarnaccia, 2016).

On the other hand, there are many alternative explanations for the association between abnormal behavior and social factors. For example, people from lower socioeconomic levels may be less likely than those from higher levels to seek help, gradually reaching a point where their symptoms become severe and warrant a serious diagnosis (Paniagua, 2000).

» LO33.3 Classifying Abnormal Behavior: The ABCs of *DSM*

Providing appropriate and specific names and classifications for abnormal behavior has presented a major challenge to

From the perspective of . . .

An Employer Imagine that a well-paid employee was arrested for shoplifting a $15 sweater. What sort of explanation for this behavior would be provided by the proponents of each perspective on abnormality: the medical perspective, the psychoanalytic perspective, the behavioral perspective, the cognitive perspective, the humanistic perspective, and the sociocultural perspective? Based on the potential causes of the shoplifting, would you fire the employee? Why or why not?

© Andresr/Getty Images RF

"First off, you're not a nut. You're a legume."

psychologists. It is not hard to understand why, given the difficulties discussed earlier in simply distinguishing normal from abnormal behavior. Yet psychologists and other care providers need to classify abnormal behavior in order to diagnose it and, ultimately, treat it.

DSM-5: Determining Diagnostic Distinctions

The ***Diagnostic and Statistical Manual of Mental Disorders, Fifth Edition (DSM-5),*** is the most widely used system to classify and define psychological disorders (American Psychiatric Association, 2013).

The *DSM-5,* most recently revised in 2013, provides comprehensive and relatively precise definitions for more than 200 disorders. By following the criteria presented in the *DSM-5* classification system, diagnosticians use clients' reported symptoms to identify the specific problem an individual is experiencing. (Figure 2 provides a brief outline of the major diagnostic categories; American Psychiatric Association, 2013.)

The manual takes an *atheoretical* approach to identifying psychological disorders, meaning it does not rely on any particular theoretical perspective. However, practitioners have argued that this diagnostic approach is too heavily based on a medical model. The authors of the newest update of *DSM* suggest that the manual should be viewed as the "*DSM-5.0.*" The "5.0" name emphasizes that the *DSM-5* is a work in progress, subject to revision based on users' feedback. (The next revision will be called *DSM-5.1.*)

In many other respects, the *DSM* remains unchanged in the newest revision. Like its predecessors, *DSM-5* is primarily descriptive and avoids suggesting an underlying cause for an individual's behavior and problems. Instead, it paints

Diagnostic and Statistical Manual of Mental Disorders, Fifth Edition (DSM-5) A system, devised by the American Psychiatric Association, used by most professionals to classify and define psychological disorders

How might an understanding of the *DSM-5* benefit you when dealing with patients as a medical office manager?
© Image Source/Getty Images RF

Disorder	Subcategories
Anxiety (problems in which anxiety impedes daily functioning)	Generalized anxiety disorder, panic disorder, phobic disorder, obsessive-compulsive disorder, posttraumatic stress disorder
Somatoform (psychological difficulties displayed through physical problems)	Hypochondriasis, conversion disorder
Dissociative (the splitting apart of crucial parts of personality that are usually integrated)	Dissociative identity disorder (multiple personality), dissociative amnesia, dissociative fugue
Mood (emotions of depression or euphoria that are so strong they intrude on everyday living)	Major depression, bipolar disorder
Schizophrenia (declines in functioning, thought and language disturbances, perception disorders, emotional disturbances, and withdrawal from others)	Disorganized, paranoid, catatonic, undifferentiated, residual
Personality (problems that create little personal distress but that lead to an inability to function as a normal member of society)	Antisocial (sociopathic) personality disorder, narcissistic personality disorder
Sexual (problems related to sexual arousal from unusual objects or problems related to functioning)	Paraphilia, sexual dysfunction
Substance-related (problems related to drug dependence and abuse)	Alcohol, cocaine, hallucinogens, marijuana
Delirium, dementia, amnesia, and other cognitive disorders	

Figure 2   This list of disorders represents the major categories from the *DSM-5*. It is only a partial list of the dozens of disorders included there. Photos: (bookshelf) ©luoman/Getty Images RF; (DSM-5) © H.S. Photos/Alamy Stock Photo

a picture of the behavior that is being displayed. Why should this approach be important? For one thing, it allows communication between mental health professionals of diverse backgrounds and theoretical approaches. In addition, precise classification enables researchers to explore the causes of a problem. Without reliable descriptions of abnormal behavior, researchers would be hard-pressed to find ways to investigate the disorder. Finally, *DSM-5* provides a kind of conceptual shorthand through which professionals can describe the behaviors that tend to occur together in an individual (First, Frances, & Pincus, 2002; Miller et al., 2010; *DSM-5* classification, 2016).

> **DSM-5 is designed to be primarily descriptive and avoids suggesting an underlying cause for an individual's behavior and problems.**

Although the *DSM-5* was developed to provide more accurate and consistent diagnoses of psychological disorders, it isn't always successful. For instance, critics charge that it relies too much on the medical perspective. Because it was drawn up by psychiatrists—who are physicians—some condemn it for viewing psychological disorders primarily in terms of the symptoms of an underlying physiological disorder. Moreover, critics suggest that the *DSM-5* compartmentalizes people into inflexible, all-or-none categories, rather than considering the degree to which a person displays psychologically disordered behavior (Samuel & Widiger, 2006; Wakefield, Schmitz & Baer, 2010; Frances, 2013; Lasalvia, 2015).

Still, despite the drawbacks inherent in any labeling system, the *DSM* has had an important influence on the way in which mental health professionals view psychological disorders. It has increased both the reliability and the validity of diagnostic categorization. In addition, it offers a logical way to organize examination of the major types of mental disturbance.

RECAP

Define abnormality.

- Definitions of abnormality include deviation from the average, deviation from the ideal, a sense of personal discomfort, the inability to function effectively, and legal conceptions.

Discuss perspectives on abnormality.

- Although no single definition is adequate, abnormal behavior can be considered to be behavior that causes people to experience distress and prevents them from functioning in their daily lives. Most psychologists believe that abnormal and normal behavior should be considered in terms of a continuum.

- The medical perspective views abnormality as a symptom of an underlying disease.

- Psychoanalytic perspectives suggest that abnormal behavior stems from childhood conflicts in the unconscious.

- Behavioral approaches view abnormal behavior not as a symptom of an underlying problem, but as the problem itself.

- The cognitive approach suggests that abnormal behavior is the result of faulty cognitions (thoughts and beliefs). In this view, abnormal behavior can be remedied by changing one's flawed thoughts and beliefs.

- Humanistic approaches emphasize the responsibility people have for their own behavior, even when such behavior is seen as abnormal.

- Sociocultural approaches view abnormal behavior in terms of difficulties arising from family and other social relationships.

Classify abnormal behavior.

- The most widely used system for classifying psychological disorders is the *DSM-5—Diagnostic and Statistical Manual of Mental Disorders, Fifth Edition.*

[EVALUATE E Evaluate]

1. One problem in defining abnormal behavior is that
   a. Statistically rare behavior may not be abnormal.
   b. Not all abnormalities are accompanied by feelings of discomfort.
   c. Cultural standards are too general to use as a measuring tool.
   d. All of the above.

2. If abnormality is defined as behavior that causes personal discomfort or harms others, which of the following people is most likely to need treatment?
   a. An executive is afraid to accept a promotion because it would require moving from his ground-floor office to the top floor of a tall office building.
   b. A woman decides to quit her job and chooses to live on the street in order to live a "simpler life."
   c. A man believes that friendly spacemen visit his house every Thursday.
   d. A photographer lives with 19 cats in a small apartment, lovingly caring for them.

3. Virginia's mother thinks that her daughter's behavior is clearly abnormal because, despite being offered admission to medical school, Virginia decides to become a waitress. What approach is Virginia's mother using to define abnormal behavior?

4. Which of the following is a strong argument against the medical perspective on abnormality?

   a. Physiological abnormalities are almost always impossible to identify.

   b. There is no conclusive way to link past experience and behavior.

   c. The medical perspective rests too heavily on the effects of nutrition.

   d. Assigning behavior to a physical problem takes responsibility away from the individual for changing his or her behavior.

5. Cheryl is painfully shy. According to the behavioral perspective, the best way to deal with her "abnormal" behavior is to

   a. Treat the underlying physical problem.

   b. Use the principles of learning theory to modify her shy behavior.

   c. Express a great deal of caring.

   d. Uncover her negative past experiences through hypnosis.

[RETHINK R Rethink]

Do you agree or disagree that *DSM* should be updated every several years? Why? What makes abnormal behavior so variable?

Answers to Evaluate Questions 1. d; 2. a; 3. deviation from the ideal; 4. d; 5. b

KEY TERMS

Abnormal behavior   LO33.1

Medical perspective   LO33.2

Psychoanalytic perspective   LO33.2

Behavioral perspective   LO33.2

Cognitive perspective   LO33.2

Humanistic perspective   LO33.2

Sociocultural perspective   LO33.2

Diagnostic and Statistical Manual of Mental Disorders, Fifth Edition (DSM-5)   LO33.3

module 34

The Major Psychological Disorders

Learning Outcomes  Prepare

>> **LO34.1** Discuss anxiety disorders.

>> **LO34.2** Discuss somatic symptom disorders.

>> **LO34.3** Discuss dissociative disorders.

>> **LO34.4** Discuss mood disorders.

>> **LO34.5** Explain schizophrenia.

>> **LO34.6** Discuss personality disorders.

>> **LO34.7** Discuss childhood disorders.

>> **LO34.8** List other disorders.

MODULE OUTLINE Organize

Anxiety Disorders

Try It! How Anxious Are You?

Somatic Symptom Disorders

Dissociative Disorders

Mood Disorders

Try It! A Test for Depression

Schizophrenia

Personality Disorders

Childhood Disorders

Other Disorders

 Work

Sally's first panic attack was a surprise. Visiting her parents after college, she suddenly felt dizzy, broke into a cold sweat, and began hyperventilating. Her father clocked her pulse at 180 and rushed her to the hospital, where all symptoms vanished. She laughed it off and returned to her apartment.

But the panic attacks continued. At the gym, at work, in restaurants and movie theaters, Sally was never safe from them. Not just frightening, they were downright embarrassing. She quit her job to work at home. She avoided crowds and turned down dinners, parties, and movies. The only way to escape humiliation was to wall herself inside her apartment with a blanket and a pillow.

Sally suffered from panic disorder, one of the specific psychological disorders we'll consider in this module. Keep in mind that although we'll be discussing these disorders objectively, each represents a very human set of difficulties that influence, and in some cases considerably disrupt, people's lives.

>> LO34.1 Anxiety Disorders

All of us, at one time or another, experience anxiety, a feeling of apprehension or tension, in reaction to stressful situations. There is nothing "wrong" with such anxiety. It is a normal reaction to stress that often helps, rather than hinders, our daily functioning. Without some anxiety, for instance, most of us probably would not have much motivation to study hard, undergo physical exams, or spend long hours at our jobs.

But some people experience anxiety in situations in which there is no external reason or cause for such distress. When anxiety occurs without external justification and begins to affect people's daily functioning, mental health professionals consider it a psychological problem known as **anxiety disorder.** We'll discuss three major types of anxiety disorders: phobic disorder, panic disorder, and generalized anxiety disorder. (Before continuing, get a sense of your own level of anxiety by completing the accompanying Try It!)

anxiety disorder The occurrence of anxiety without an obvious external cause, affecting daily functioning

> When anxiety occurs without external justification and begins to affect people's daily functioning, mental health professionals consider it a psychological problem known as anxiety disorder.

Try It!

How Anxious Are You?

To assess the degree of anxiety you typically experience, complete the following questionnaire by writing T (for true) or F (for false) preceding each of the statements:

_____ 1. I usually have enough energy.

_____ 2. I easily feel nauseousness.

_____ 3. I'm not more nervous than most people.

_____ 4. I don't have many headaches.

_____ 5. There's a lot of stress in my life.

_____ 6. I can't concentrate very well.

_____ 7. I have concerns about money.

_____ 8. My hands sometimes shake when I'm under stress.

_____ 9. I don't blush much.

_____ 10. My stomach is often upset.

_____ 11. I worry about the future a lot.

_____ 12. My face almost never gets red from embarrassment.

_____ 13. I am frightened that I will blush at the wrong time.

_____ 14. I have many nightmares.

_____ 15. My hands don't often get cold.

_____ 16. I sweat a lot.

_____ 17. I get annoyed when I sweat a lot.

_____ 18. My heart doesn't pound much.

_____ 19. I experience hunger a lot.

_____ 20. Constipation is rarely a problem.

(continued)

_____ 21. My stomach is often upset.
_____ 22. I often worry so much I can't sleep.
_____ 23. I don't sleep well.
_____ 24. I have a lot of embarrassing dreams
_____ 25. I am easily embarrassed.
_____ 26. I am an unusually sensitive person.
_____ 27. I worry a lot.
_____ 28. I would like to be a happier person.
_____ 29. I don't get upset easily.
_____ 30. I cry a lot.
_____ 31. I am an unusually anxious person.
_____ 32. Most of the time, I am happy.
_____ 33. I get nervous if I'm waiting for things to happen.
_____ 34. I find it hard to sit still.
_____ 35. I find it hard to fall asleep.
_____ 36. I have trouble coping.
_____ 37. I worry too much.
_____ 38. I don't have a lot of worries.
_____ 39. I have many fears, some without rational cause.
_____ 40. Sometimes I feel useless.
_____ 41. I find it hard to concentrate on what I need to do.
_____ 42. I am unusually self-conscious.
_____ 43. I don't react well to failure.
_____ 44. I am an emotional person.
_____ 45. I find life difficult a lot of the time.
_____ 46. I have low self-esteem.
_____ 47. I often lack self-confidence.
_____ 48. I sometimes feel that I am going to break down emotionally.
_____ 49. I try to avoid conflict.
_____ 50. I am a very self-confident person.

Scoring

Give yourself one point for each statement that corresponds to the following key: 1.F; 2.T; 3.F; 4.F; 5.T; 6.T; 7.T; 8.T; 9.F; 10.T; 11.T; 12.F; 13.T; 14.T; 15.F; 16.T; 17.T; 18.F; 19.T; 20.F; 21.T; 22.T; 23.T; 24.T; 25.T; 26.T; 27.T; 28.T; 29.F; 30.T; 31.T; 32.T; 33.T; 34.T; 35.T; 36.T; 37.T; 38.F; 39.T; 40.T; 41.T; 42.T; 43.T; 44.T; 45.T; 46.T; 47.T; 48.T; 49.T; 50.F. The higher your score, the greater amount of anxiety you experience. Note that if you have a high score, it doesn't mean that you are disordered in any way; it simply means that you have anxiety in your life.

Source: From Taylor, 1953.

Phobic Disorder

It's not easy moving through the world when you're terrified of electricity. "Donna," 45, a writer, knows that better than most. Get her in the vicinity of an appliance or a light switch or—all but unthinkable—a thunderstorm, and she is overcome by a terror so blinding she can think of nothing but

At first glance it might somehow seem more reasonable to fear heights than flowers, but the reality of phobias is that virtually anything can create paralyzing fear in those suffering from them. What are some coping strategies for phobias? (first) © Europics/Newscom; (second) © Lawrence Lawry/Getty Images RF

fleeing. That, of course, is not always possible, so over time, Donna has come up with other answers. When she opens the refrigerator door, rubber-sole shoes are a must. If a light bulb blows, she will tolerate the dark until someone else changes it for her. (Kluger, 2001, p. 51)

Donna suffers from a **specific phobia,** an intense, irrational fear of a specific object or situation (see Figure 1). For example, claustrophobia is a fear of enclosed places, acrophobia is a fear of high places, xenophobia is a fear of

specific phobia An intense, irrational fear of specific objects or situations

Figure 1 Phobic disorders differ from generalized anxiety and panic disorders because a specific stimulus can be identified. Listed here are a number of types of phobias and their triggers. Source: Adapted from Nolen-Hoeksema, 2007. Photos: (man at window) © Ingram Publishing/Fotosearch RF; (spider) © GK Hart/Vikki Hart/Photodisc/Getty Images RF; (needle) © Stockbyte/Punchstock RF; (claustrophobic woman) © Nick Gregory/Alamy Stock Photo

Phobic Disorder	Description	Example
Agoraphobia	Fear of places where help might not be available in case of emergency	Person becomes housebound because anyplace other than the person's home arouses extreme anxiety symptoms
Specific phobias	Fear of specific objects, places, or situations	
Animal type	Specific animals or insects	Person has extreme fear of dogs, cats, or spiders
Natural environment type	Event or situations in the natural environment	Person has extreme fear of storms, heights, or water
Situational type	Public transportation, tunnels, bridges, elevators, flying, driving	Person becomes extremely claustrophobic in enclosed spaces
Blood-injection-injury type	Blood, injury, injections	Person panics when viewing a child's scraped knee
Social phobia	Fear of being judged or embarrassed by others	Person avoids all social situations and becomes a recluse for fear of encountering others' judgment

> ## Unlike phobias, which are stimulated by specific objects or situations, panic disorders do not have any identifiable stimuli.

strangers, social phobia is the fear of being judged or embarrassed by others, and—as in Donna's case—electrophobia is a fear of electricity.

The objective danger posed by an anxiety-producing stimulus (which can be just about anything) is typically small or nonexistent. However, to someone suffering from the phobia, the danger is great, and a full-blown panic attack may follow exposure to the stimulus.

Panic Disorder

panic disorder Anxiety disorder that takes the form of panic attacks lasting from a few seconds to as long as several hours

generalized anxiety disorder The experience of long-term, persistent anxiety and worry

In another type of anxiety disorder, **panic disorder,** *panic attacks* occur that last from a few seconds to several hours. Unlike phobias, which are triggered by specific objects or situations, panic disorders do not have any identifiable, specific triggers. Instead, during an attack, such as the ones experienced by Sally in the case described earlier, anxiety suddenly—and often without warning—rises, and an individual feels a sense of impending, unavoidable doom. Although the physical symptoms of a panic attack differ from person to person, they may include heart palpitations, shortness of breath, unusual amounts of sweating, faintness and dizziness, gastric sensations, and sometimes a sense of imminent death. After such an attack, it is no wonder that people tend to feel exhausted (Laederach-Hofmann & Messerli-Buergy, 2007; Batelaan et al., 2010; Lueken et al., 2011).

Panic attacks seemingly come out of nowhere and are unconnected to any specific stimulus (Figure 2). Because they don't know what triggers their feelings of panic, victims of panic attacks may become fearful of going places. In fact, some people with panic disorder develop a complication called *agoraphobia,* the fear of being in a situation in which escape is difficult and in which help for a possible panic attack would not be available. In extreme cases, people with agoraphobia never leave their homes (Chambless, 2010; Reinecke et al., 2011; Liebscher et al., 2016).

Generalized Anxiety Disorder

People with **generalized anxiety disorder** experience long-term, persistent anxiety and uncontrollable worry. Sometimes their concerns are about identifiable issues involving family, money, work, or health. In other cases, though, people with the disorder feel that something dreadful is about to happen but can't identify the reason and thus experience "free-floating" anxiety.

Because of persistent anxiety, people with generalized anxiety disorder cannot concentrate or set their worry and fears aside; their lives become centered on their worry. Figure 3 shows the most common symptoms of generalized anxiety disorder.

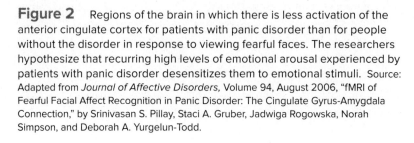

Figure 2 Regions of the brain in which there is less activation of the anterior cingulate cortex for patients with panic disorder than for people without the disorder in response to viewing fearful faces. The researchers hypothesize that recurring high levels of emotional arousal experienced by patients with panic disorder desensitizes them to emotional stimuli. Source: Adapted from *Journal of Affective Disorders,* Volume 94, August 2006, "fMRI of Fearful Facial Affect Recognition in Panic Disorder: The Cingulate Gyrus-Amygdala Connection," by Srinivasan S. Pillay, Staci A. Gruber, Jadwiga Rogowska, Norah Simpson, and Deborah A. Yurgelun-Todd.

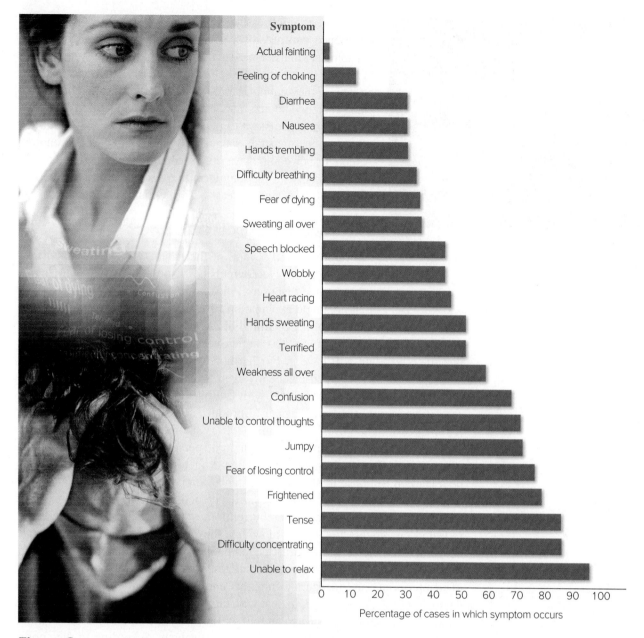

Figure 3 Frequency of symptoms in cases of generalized anxiety disorder. Photos: (top) © Stockbyte/Getty Images RF; (bottom) © Paul Thomas/Getty Images

Obsessive-Compulsive Disorder

In **obsessive-compulsive disorder (OCD),** people are plagued by unwanted thoughts, called obsessions, or feel that they must carry out actions, termed compulsions, that they feel driven to perform.

An **obsession** is a persistent, unwanted thought or idea that keeps recurring. For example, a man may go on vacation and wonder the whole time whether he locked his house or a woman may hear the same tune running through her head over and over. In each case, the thought or idea is unwanted and difficult to put out of mind. Of course, many people suffer from mild obsessions from time to time, but usually such thoughts persist only for a short period. For people with serious obsessions, however, the thoughts persist for days or months and may consist of bizarre, troubling images (Lee et al., 2005; Rassin & Muris, 2007; Hollander et al., 2011).

obsessive-compulsive disorder (OCD) A disorder characterized by obsessions or compulsions

obsession A persistent unwanted thought or idea that keeps recurring

On the television show *The Big Bang Theory,* the character Sheldon Cooper (played by Jim Parsons) appears to suffer from obsessive-compulsive disorder (OCD). © Sonja Flemming/CBS Photo Archive/Getty Images

As part of an obsessive-compulsive disorder, people may also experience **compulsions,** irresistible urges to repeatedly carry out some act that seems strange and unreasonable, even to them. Whatever the compulsive behavior is, people experience extreme anxiety if they cannot carry it out, even if it is something they want to stop. The acts may be relatively trivial, such as repeatedly checking the stove to make sure all the burners are turned off, or more unusual, such as continuously washing oneself. Although such compulsive rituals lead to some immediate reduction of anxiety, in the long term the anxiety returns (Moretz & McKay, 2009; Katerberg et al., 2010; Gillan & Sahakian, 2015).

The Causes of Anxiety Disorders

We've considered several of the major types of anxiety disorders and obsessive-compulsive disorder, but there are many other related disorders. The variety of anxiety disorders means that no single explanation fits all cases. Genetic factors clearly are part of the picture. For example, if one member of a pair of identical twins has panic disorder, there is a 30 percent chance that the other twin will have it. Furthermore, a person's characteristic level of anxiety is related to a specific gene involved in the production of the neurotransmitter serotonin. This is consistent with findings indicating that certain chemical deficiencies in the brain appear to produce some kinds of anxiety disorder (Holmes et al., 2003; Beidel & Turner, 2007; Chamberlain et al., 2008).

Psychologists who employ the behavioral perspective have taken a different approach that emphasizes environmental factors. They consider anxiety to be a learned response to stress. For instance, suppose a dog bites a young girl. When the girl next sees a dog, she is frightened and runs away—a behavior that relieves her anxiety and thereby reinforces her avoidance behavior. After repeated encounters with dogs in which she is reinforced for her avoidance behavior, she may develop a full-fledged phobia regarding dogs.

Finally, the cognitive perspective suggests that anxiety disorders grow out of inappropriate and inaccurate thoughts and beliefs about circumstances in a person's world. For example, people with anxiety disorders may view a friendly puppy as a ferocious and savage pit bull, or they may see an air disaster looming every moment they are in the vicinity of an airplane. According to the cognitive perspective, people's maladaptive thoughts about the world are at the root of an anxiety disorder (Frost & Steketee, 2002; Wang & Clark, 2002; Ouimet, Gawronski, & Dozois, 2009).

compulsion An irresistible urge to repeatedly carry out some act that seems strange or unreasonable

somatic symptom disorders Psychological difficulties that take on a physical (somatic) form, but for which there is no medical cause

illness anxiety disorder A psychological disorder in which people have a constant fear of illness and a preoccupation with their health

» LO34.2 Somatic Symptom Disorders

Somatic symptom disorders are psychological difficulties that take on a physical (somatic) form, but for which there is no medical cause. Even though an individual with a somatoform disorder reports physical symptoms, no biological cause exists, or if there is a medical problem, the person's reaction is greatly exaggerated.

Illness Anxiety Disorder

One type of somatic symptom disorder is **illness anxiety disorder,** in which people have a constant fear of illness and a preoccupation with their health. These individuals believe that everyday aches and pains are symptoms of a dreaded disease.

The "symptoms" are not faked; rather, they are misinterpreted as evidence of some serious illness—often in the face of inarguable medical evidence to the contrary (Olatunji, 2008; Longley et al., 2010; Schreiber et al., 2016).

Conversion Disorders

Another somatic symptom disorder is conversion disorder. Unlike illness anxiety disorder, in which there is no physical problem, a **conversion disorder** involves an actual physical disturbance, such as the inability to see or hear or to move an arm or leg.

> Even though an individual with a somatic symptom disorder reports physical symptoms, no biological cause exists, or if there is a medical problem, the person's reaction is greatly exaggerated.

However, *the cause* of the physical disturbance is purely psychological; there is no biological reason for the problem. Some of Freud's classic cases involved conversion disorders.

» LO34.3 Dissociative Disorders

The classic movie *The Three Faces of Eve* (about a woman with three wildly different personalities) and the book *Sybil* (about a girl who allegedly had 16 personalities) represent a highly dramatic, rare, and controversial class of disorders: dissociative disorders. **Dissociative disorders** are characterized by the separation (or dissociation) of different facets of a person's personality that are normally integrated and work together. By dissociating key parts of who they are, people are able to keep disturbing memories or perceptions from reaching conscious awareness and thereby reduce their anxiety (Maldonado & Spiegel, 2003; Houghtalen & Talbot, 2007).

Dissociative Identity Disorder

Several dissociative disorders exist, although all of them are rare. A person with a **dissociative identity disorder (DID)** (once called *multiple personality disorder*) displays characteristics of two or more distinct personalities, identities, or personality fragments. Individual personalities often have a unique set of likes and dislikes and their own reactions to situations. Some people with multiple personalities even carry several pairs of glasses because their vision changes with each personality. Moreover, each individual personality can be well adjusted when considered on its own (Stickley & Nickeas, 2006; Ross & Ness, 2010; Howell, 2011).

The diagnosis of dissociative identity disorder is controversial. It was rarely diagnosed before 1980, when it was added as a category in the third edition of DSM for the first time. At that point, the number of cases increased significantly. Some clinicians suggest the increase was due to more precise identification of the disorder, while others suggest the increase was due to an overreadiness to use the classification. In addition, widespread publicity about cases of DID may have influenced patients to report symptoms of more common personality disorders in ways that made it more likely they would receive a diagnosis of DID. There are also significant cross-cultural differences in the incidence of DID (Kihlstrom, 2005a; Xiao et al., 2006; Ross, 2015).

Dissociative Amnesia

Dissociative amnesia is another dissociative disorder in which a significant, selective memory loss occurs. Dissociative amnesia is unlike simple amnesia, which involves an actual loss of information from memory, typically resulting

conversion disorder A major somatoform disorder that involves an actual physical disturbance, such as the inability to use a sensory organ or the complete or partial inability to move an arm or a leg

dissociative disorders Psychological dysfunctions characterized by the separation of different facets of a person's personality that are normally integrated, allowing stress avoidance through escape

dissociative identity disorder (DID) A disorder in which a person displays characteristics (features) of two or more distinct personalities; once called *multiple personality disorder*

dissociative amnesia A disorder in which a significant, selective memory loss occurs

from a physiological cause. In contrast, in cases of dissociative amnesia, the "forgotten" material is still present in memory—it simply cannot be recalled. The term *repressed memories* is sometimes used to describe the lost memories of people with dissociative amnesia.

In the most severe form of dissociative amnesia, individuals cannot recall their names, are unable to recognize parents and other relatives, and do not know their addresses. In other respects, though, they may appear quite normal. Apart from an inability to remember certain facts about themselves, they may be able to recall skills and abilities that they developed earlier. For instance, even though a chef may not remember where he grew up and received training, he may still be able to prepare gourmet meals.

Dissociative Fugue

dissociative fugue A form of amnesia in which the individual leaves home and sometimes assumes a new identity

mood disorders Emotional disturbances that are strong enough to intrude on everyday living

A more unusual form of amnesia is a condition known as **dissociative fugue.** In this state, people take sudden, impulsive trips, and sometimes assume a new identity. After a period of time—days, months, or sometimes even years—they suddenly realize that they are in a strange place and completely forget the time they have spent wandering. Their last memories are those from the time just before they entered the fugue state (Hennig-Fast et al., 2008; Comparelli et al., 2010).

» LO34.4 Mood Disorders

From the time I woke up in the morning until the time I went to bed at night, I was unbearably miserable and seemingly incapable of any kind of joy or enthusiasm. Everything—every thought, word, movement—was an effort. Everything that once was sparkling now was flat. I seemed to myself to be dull, boring, inadequate, thick brained, unlit, unresponsive, chill skinned, bloodless, and sparrow drab. I doubted, completely, my ability to do anything well. It seemed as though my mind had slowed down and burned out to the point of being virtually useless. (Jamison, 1995, p. 110)

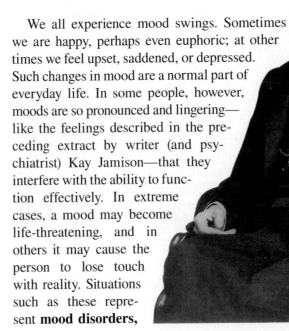

We all experience mood swings. Sometimes we are happy, perhaps even euphoric; at other times we feel upset, saddened, or depressed. Such changes in mood are a normal part of everyday life. In some people, however, moods are so pronounced and lingering—like the feelings described in the preceding extract by writer (and psychiatrist) Kay Jamison—that they interfere with the ability to function effectively. In extreme cases, a mood may become life-threatening, and in others it may cause the person to lose touch with reality. Situations such as these represent **mood disorders,**

disturbances in emotional experience that are strong enough to intrude on everyday living.

Major Depressive Disorder

President Abraham Lincoln. Queen Victoria. Author J.K. Rowling.

The common link among these people? Each suffered from periodic attacks of **major depressive disorder,** a severe form of depression that interferes with concentration, decision making, and sociability. Major depression is one of the more common forms of mood disorders. Some 15 million people in the United States suffer from major depression, and at any one time, 6 to 10 percent of the U.S. population is clinically depressed. Almost one in five people in the United States experiences major depression at some point in life, and 15 percent of college students have received a diagnosis of depression. The cost of depression is more than $44 billion a year in lost productivity (Scelfo, 2007; Simon et al., 2008; Edoka, Petrou, & Ramchandani, 2011; also see the Try It! below).

Women are twice as likely to experience major depression as men, with one-fourth of all females apt to encounter it at some point during their lives.

> **major depressive disorder** a severe form of depression that interferes with concentration, decision making, and sociability

Try It!

A Test for Depression

To complete the questionnaire, count the number of statements with which you agree.

1. I feel sad, anxious, or empty.

2. I feel hopeless or pessimistic.

3. I feel guilty, worthless, or helpless.

4. I feel irritable or restless.

5. I have lost interest in activities or hobbies that were once pleasurable, including sex.

6. I feel tired and have decreased energy.

7. I have difficulty concentrating, remembering details, and making decisions.

8. I have insomnia, early-morning wakefulness, or sleep too much.

9. I overeat or have appetite loss.

10. I have thoughts of suicide or have attempted suicide.

11. I have aches or pains, headaches, cramps, or digestive problems that do not ease even with treatment.

Scoring: If you agree with at least five of the statements, including either number 1 or 2, and if you have had these symptoms for at least two weeks, help from a professional is strongly recommended. If you answer *yes* to number 10, seek immediate help. And remember: These are only general guidelines. If you feel you may need help, seek it.

This test is based on the list of signs and symptoms of depression found on the National Institute of Mental Health website at http://www.nimh.nih.gov/health/publications/depression/what-are-the-signs-and-symptoms-of-depression.shtml

> **When psychologists speak of major depression, they do not mean the sadness that comes from experiencing one of life's disappointments, something that we all have experienced.**

Furthermore, although no one is sure why, the rate of depression is going up throughout the world. Results of in-depth interviews conducted in the United States, Puerto Rico, Taiwan, Lebanon, Canada, Italy, Germany, and France indicate that the incidence of depression has increased significantly over previous rates in every area (Kendler, Gatz, & Gardner, 2006; Ayuso-Mateos et al., 2010; Sado et al., 2011).

When psychologists speak of major depression, they do not mean the sadness that comes from experiencing one of life's disappointments, something that we all have experienced. Some depression is normal after the breakup of a long-term relationship, the death of a loved one, or the loss of a job. It is normal even after less serious problems, such as doing badly on a test or having a romantic partner forget one's birthday.

People who suffer from major depression experience similar sorts of feelings, but the severity tends to be considerably greater. They may feel useless, worthless, and lonely and may think the future is hopeless and that no one can help them. They may lose their appetite and have no energy. Moreover, they may experience such feelings for months or even years. They may cry uncontrollably, have sleep disturbances, and be at risk for suicide. The depth and duration of such behavior are the hallmarks of major depression.

Mania and Bipolar Disorder

mania An extended state of intense, wild elation

bipolar disorder A disorder in which a person alternates between periods of euphoric feelings of mania and periods of depression

While depression leads to the depths of despair, mania leads to emotional heights. **Mania** is an extended state of intense, wild elation. People experiencing mania feel intense happiness, power, invulnerability, and energy. Believing they will succeed at anything they attempt, they may become involved in wild schemes.

Some people sequentially experience periods of mania and depression. This alternation of mania and depression is called **bipolar disorder** (a condition previously known as manic-depressive disorder). The swings between highs and lows may occur a few days apart or may alternate over a period of years. In addition, in bipolar disorder, periods of depression are usually longer than periods of mania (Nivoli et al., 2011).

Causes of Mood Disorders

Because they represent a major mental health problem, mood disorders—and, in particular, depression—have received a good deal of study. Several approaches have been used to explain the disorders.

Genetic and biological factors. Some mood disorders clearly have genetic and biochemical roots. In fact, most evidence suggests that bipolar disorders are caused primarily by biological factors. For instance, bipolar disorder (and some forms of major depression) clearly run in some families. Furthermore, researchers have found that several neurotransmitters play a role in depression. For example, alterations in

How might knowing that almost twice as many women suffer from depression impact how you view yourself and the women in your life? © Ryan McVay/Getty Images RF

the functioning of serotonin and norepinephrine in the brain are related to the disorder (Plomin & McGuffin, 2003; Kato, 2007; Popa et al., 2008).

Psychological forces as a cause of depression. Other explanations for depression have focused on psychological issues. For instance, supporters of psychoanalytic perspectives see depression as the result of feelings of loss (real or potential) or of anger directed inwardly at oneself. One psychoanalytic approach, for example, suggests that depression is produced by the loss or threatened loss of a parent early in life (Vanheule et al., 2006; Sa, 2015).

Environmental factors. Some explanations of depression take a behavioral approach, looking to influences outside the person. For example, behavioral theories of depression argue that the stresses of life produce a reduction in positive reinforcers. As a result, people begin to withdraw, which only serves to reduce positive reinforcers further. In addition, people receive attention for their depressive behavior, which further reinforces the depression (Lewinsohn et al., 2003; Liu & Alloy, 2010; Domschke, 2013).

Cognitive and emotional factors. Some explanations for mood disorders attribute them to cognitive factors. For example, psychologist Martin Seligman suggests that depression is largely a response to learned helplessness. *Learned helplessness* is a learned expectation that events in one's life are uncontrollable and that one cannot escape from the situation. As a consequence, people simply give up fighting aversive events and submit to them, thereby producing depression. Other theorists go a step further, suggesting that depression results from hopelessness, a combination of learned helplessness and an expectation that negative outcomes in one's life are inevitable (Kwon & Laurenceau, 2002; Bjornstad, 2006; Li et al., 2011).

Clinical psychologist Aaron Beck has proposed that faulty cognitions underlie people's depressed feelings. Specifically, his cognitive theory of depression suggests that depressed individuals typically view themselves as life's losers, and blame themselves whenever anything goes wrong. By focusing on the negative side of situations, they feel inept and unable to act constructively to change their environment. In sum, their negative cognitions lead to feelings of depression (Newman et al., 2002).

Brain imaging studies suggest that people with depression experience a general blunting of emotional reactions. For example, one study found that the brains of people with depression showed significantly less activation when they viewed photos of human faces displaying strong emotions than those without the disorder (see Figure 4; Gotlib et al., 2004).

> **Why does depression occur in approximately twice as many women as men—a pattern that is similar across a variety of cultures?**

The various theories of depression have not provided a complete answer to an elusive question that has dogged researchers: Why does depression occur in approximately twice as many women as men—a pattern that is similar across a variety of cultures?

One explanation suggests that the stress women experience may be greater than the stress men experience at certain points in their lives—such as when a woman must simultaneously earn a living and be the primary caregiver for her children. In addition, women have a higher risk for physical and sexual abuse, typically earn lower wages than men, report greater unhappiness with their marriages, and generally experience chronic negative circumstances. Furthermore, women and men may respond to stress with different coping mechanisms. For instance, men may abuse drugs, whereas women respond with depression (Nolen-Hoeksema, 2007; Hyde, Mezulis, & Abramson, 2008; Komarovskaya et al., 2011).

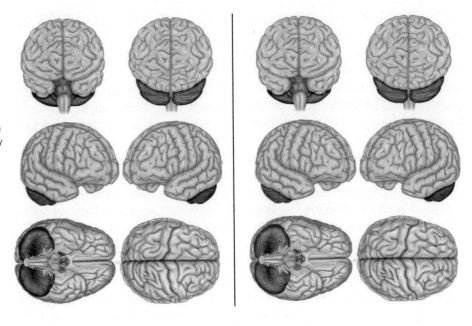

Figure 4 The brains of those with depression (left) show significantly less activation in response to photos of sad, angry, and fearful faces than those of people without the disorder (right). Source: Adapted from Ian Gotlib, Stanford Mood and Anxiety Disorders Laboratory, 2005.

Biological factors may also explain some women's depression. For example, because the rate of female depression begins to rise during puberty, some psychologists believe that hormones make women more vulnerable to the disorder. In addition, 25 to 50 percent of women who take oral contraceptives report symptoms of depression, and depression that occurs after the birth of a child is linked to hormonal changes. Finally, structural differences in men's and women's brains that we discussed in the neuroscience and behavior chapter may be related to gender differences in depression (Graham, Bancroft, & Doll, 2007; Solomon & Herman, 2009; Silverstein et al., 2013).

Ultimately it is clear that researchers have discovered no definitive solutions to the puzzle of depression, and there are many alternative explanations. Most likely, a complex interaction of several factors causes mood disorders.

» LO34.5 Schizophrenia

Things that relate, the town of Antelope, Oregon, Jonestown, Charlie Manson, the Hillside Strangler, the Zodiac Killer, Watergate, King's trial in L.A., and many more. In the last 7 years alone, over 23 Star Wars scientists committed suicide for no apparent reason. The AIDS cover-up, the conference in South America in 87 had over 1,000 doctors claim that insects can transmit it. To be able to read one's thoughts and place thoughts in one's mind without the person knowing it's being done. Realization is a reality of bioelectromagnetic control, which is thought transfer and emotional control, recording individual brainwave frequencies of thought, sensation, and emotions. (Nolen-Hoeksema, 2007, pp. 385–386)

This excerpt illustrates the efforts of a woman with schizophrenia, one of the more severe forms of mental disturbance, to hold a conversation with a clinician. People with schizophrenia account for by far the largest percentage of those hospitalized for mental disorders. They are also in many respects the least likely to recover from their psychological difficulties (Keller, Fischer, & Carpenter, 2011).

Schizophrenia refers to a class of disorders in which severe distortion of reality occurs. Thinking, perception, and emotion may deteriorate; the individual may withdraw from social interaction; and the person may display bizarre behavior. The symptoms displayed by persons with schizophrenia may vary considerably over time. Nonetheless, a number of characteristics reliably distinguish schizophrenia from other disorders. They include the following.

schizophrenia A class of disorders in which severe distortion of reality occurs

- *Decline from a previous level of functioning.* An individual can no longer carry out activities he or she was once able to do.

- *Disturbances of thought and language.* People with schizophrenia use logic and language in a peculiar way. Their thinking often does not make sense, and their information processing is frequently faulty, something referred to as a *formal thought disorder.* They also do not follow conventional linguistic rules (Penn et al., 1997). Consider, for example, the following response to the question "Why do you think people believe in God?"

    Uh, let's, I don't know why, let's see, balloon travel. He holds it up for you, the balloon. He don't let you fall out, your little legs sticking down through the clouds. He's down to the smokestack, looking through the smoke trying to get the balloon gassed up you know. Way they're flying on top that way, legs sticking out. I don't know, looking down on the ground, heck, that'd make you so dizzy you just stay and sleep you know, hold down and sleep there. I used to be sleep outdoors, you know, sleep outdoors instead of going home. (Chapman & Chapman, 1973, p. 3)

    As this selection illustrates, although the basic grammatical structure may be intact, the substance of thinking characteristic of schizophrenia is often illogical, garbled, and lacking in meaningful content (Holden, 2003; Heinrichs, 2005).

- *Delusions.* People with schizophrenia often have delusions, firmly held, unshakable beliefs with no basis in reality. Among the common delusions people with schizophrenia experience are the beliefs that they are being controlled by someone else, they are being persecuted by others, and their thoughts are being broadcast so that others know what they are thinking (Coltheart, Langdon, & McKay, 2007; Startup, Bucci, & Langdon, 2009).

- *Hallucinations and perceptual disorders.* People with schizophrenia sometimes do not perceive the world as most other people do. For example, they may have *hallucinations,* the experience of perceiving things that do not actually exist. Furthermore, they may see, hear, or smell things differently from others (see Figure 5). In fact, they may not even have a sense of their bodies in the way that others do, having difficulty determining where their bodies stop and the rest of the world begins (Thomas et al., 2007; Moritz & Laroi, 2008; Bauer, Schwab, & McAdams, 2011).

- *Inappropriate emotional displays.* People with schizophrenia sometimes show a lack of emotion in which even the most dramatic events produce little or no emotional response. Alternately, they may display strong bursts of emotion that are inappropriate to a situation. For example, a person with schizophrenia may laugh uproariously at a funeral or react with anger when being helped by someone.

■ *Withdrawal.* People with schizophrenia tend to have little interest in others. They tend not to socialize or hold real conversations with others, although they may talk at another person. In the most extreme cases they do not even acknowledge the presence of other people, appearing to be in their own isolated world.

DSM-5 classifies the symptoms of schizophrenia into two types. *Positive-symptom schizophrenia* is indicated by the presence of disordered behavior such as hallucinations, delusions, and emotional extremes. Those with positive-symptom schizophrenia clearly lose touch with reality. In contrast, those with *negative-symptom schizophrenia* show disruptions to normal emotions and behaviors. For example, there may be an absence or loss of normal functioning, such as social withdrawal or blunted emotions (Levine & Rabinowitz, 2007; Tandon et al., 2013; Lauriello & Rahman, 2015).

The distinction between positive and negative symptoms of schizophrenia is important because it suggests that two different kinds of causes might trigger schizophrenia. Furthermore, it has implications for predicting treatment outcomes.

Solving the Puzzle of Schizophrenia: Biological Causes

Although schizophrenic behavior clearly departs radically from normal behavior, its causes are less apparent. It does appear, however, that schizophrenia has both biological and environmental origins (Sawa & Snyder, 2002; Pavão, Tort, & Amaral, 2015).

Let's first consider the evidence pointing to a biological cause. Because schizophrenia is more common in some families than in others, genetic factors seem to be involved in producing at least a susceptibility to or readiness for developing schizophrenia. For example, the closer the genetic link between a person with schizophrenia and another individual, the greater the likelihood that the other person will experience the disorder (see Figure 6; Plomin & McGuffin, 2003; Gottesman & Hanson, 2005; Nicodemus et al., 2010).

However, if genetics alone were responsible for schizophrenia, the chance of both of two identical twins having schizophrenia would be 100 percent instead of just under 50 percent, because identical twins have the same genetic makeup. Moreover, attempts to find a link between schizophrenia and a particular gene have been only partly successful. Apparently, genetic factors alone do not produce schizophrenia (Franzek & Beckmann, 1996; Lenzenweger & Dworkin, 1998).

One intriguing biological hypothesis to explain schizophrenia is that the brains of people with the disorder may harbor either a biochemical imbalance or a structural abnormality. For example, the *dopamine hypothesis* suggests that schizophrenia occurs when there is excess activity in the areas of the brain that use dopamine as a neurotransmitter. This hypothesis came to light after the discovery that drugs that block dopamine action in brain pathways can be highly effective in reducing the symptoms of schizophrenia. Other research suggests that glutamate, another neurotransmitter, may be a major contributor to the disorder (Ohara, 2007; Stone, Morrison, & Pilowsky, 2007; Howes & Kapur, 2009).

Some biological explanations propose that structural abnormalities exist in the brains of people with schizophrenia, perhaps as a result of exposure to a virus during prenatal development. For example, some research shows

> **Because schizophrenia is more common in some families than in others, genetic factors seem to be involved in producing at least a susceptibility to or readiness for developing schizophrenia.**

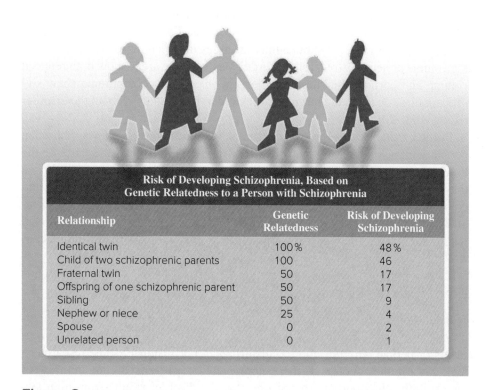

Risk of Developing Schizophrenia, Based on Genetic Relatedness to a Person with Schizophrenia

Relationship	Genetic Relatedness	Risk of Developing Schizophrenia
Identical twin	100%	48%
Child of two schizophrenic parents	100	46
Fraternal twin	50	17
Offspring of one schizophrenic parent	50	17
Sibling	50	9
Nephew or niece	25	4
Spouse	0	2
Unrelated person	0	1

Figure 6 The closer the genetic links between two people, the greater the likelihood that if one experiences schizophrenia, so will the other some time during his or her lifetime. However, genetics is not the full story, because if it were, the risk of identical twins having schizophrenia would be 100 percent, not the 48 percent shown in this figure. Source: Gottesman, 1991.

Figure 7 People with schizophrenia show differences in brain functioning from those without the disorder. Adapted from Kong et al., 2015.

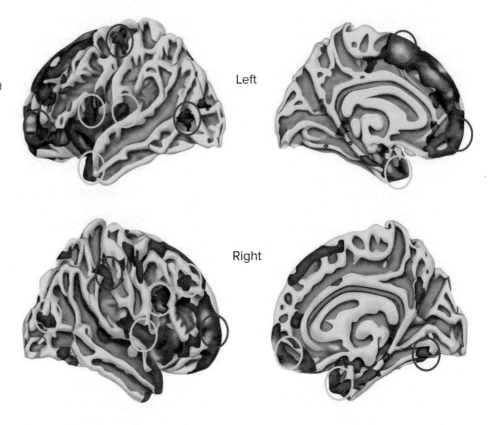

Left

Right

abnormalities in the neural circuits of the cortex and limbic systems of individuals with schizophrenia.

Consistent with such research, people with schizophrenia show differences in brain functioning from those without the disorder. For example, the representational images in Figure 7 show numerous areas in which there are decreases in the volume of neurons (red/yellow). Additionally, these areas show both reduced volume and cortical thickness. In short, people with schizophrenia show significant differences in the brain as compared to individuals without the disorder (Kong et al., 2015).

Further evidence for the importance of biological factors shows that when people with schizophrenia hear voices during hallucinations, the parts of the brain responsible for hearing and language processing become active. When they have visual hallucinations, the parts of the brain involved in movement and color are active. At the same time, people with schizophrenia often have unusually low activity in the brain's frontal lobes—the parts of the brain involved with emotional regulation, insight, and the evaluation of sensory stimuli (Stern & Silbersweig, 2001; Lavigne et al., 2015).

Environmental Perspectives on Schizophrenia

Although biological factors provide important pieces of the puzzle of schizophrenia, we still need to consider past and current experiences in the environments of people who develop the disturbance. For instance, some researchers look toward the emotional and communication patterns of the families of people with schizophrenia, suggesting that the disorder results from high levels of expressed emotion. *Expressed emotion* is an interaction style characterized by criticism, hostility, and emotional intrusiveness by family members. Other researchers suggest that faulty communication patterns lie at the heart of schizophrenia (Lobban, Barrowclough, & Jones, 2006; Nader et al., 2013).

The Multiple Causes of Schizophrenia

Most scientists now believe that schizophrenia is caused by both biological and situational factors. Specifically, the *predisposition model of schizophrenia* suggests that individuals may inherit a predisposition or an inborn sensitivity to develop schizophrenia. This genetic predisposition makes them particularly vulnerable to stress in their lives, such as social rejection or dysfunctional family communication patterns. The stressors may vary, but if they are strong enough and are coupled with a genetic predisposition, the result will be the onset of schizophrenia. Similarly, a strong genetic predisposition may lead to the onset of schizophrenia even when the environmental stressors are relatively weak.

In short, the models used today associate schizophrenia with several kinds of biological and environmental factors. It is increasingly clear, then, that no single factor, but a combination of interrelated variables, produces schizophrenia (Meltzer, 2000; McDonald & Murray, 2004; Opler et al., 2008).

» LO34.6 Personality Disorders

I had always wanted lots of things; as a child I can remember wanting a bullet that a friend of mine had brought in to show the class. I took it and put it into my school bag and when my friend noticed it was missing, I was the one who stayed after school with him and searched the room, and I was the one who sat with him and bitched about the other kids and how one of them took his bullet. I even went home with him to help him break the news to his uncle, who had brought it home from the war for him. But that was petty compared with the stuff I did later. I wanted a PhD very badly, but I didn't want to work very hard—just enough to get by. I never did the experiments I reported; hell, I was smart enough to make up the results. I knew enough about statistics to make anything look plausible. I got my master's degree without even spending one hour in a laboratory. I mean, the professors believed anything. I'd stay out all night drinking and being with my friends, and the next day I'd get in just before them and tell 'em I'd been in the lab all night. They'd actually feel sorry for me. (Source: Duke & Nowicki, 1979, pp. 309–310)

This excerpt provides a graphic first-person account of a person with a personality disorder. A **personality disorder** is characterized by a set of inflexible, maladaptive behavior patterns that keep a person from functioning appropriately in society. Personality disorders differ from the other problems we have discussed because those affected by them often have little sense of personal distress associated with the psychological maladjustment. In fact, people with personality disorders frequently lead seemingly normal lives. However, just below the surface lies a set of inflexible, maladaptive personality traits that do not permit these individuals to function as members of society (Clarkin & Lenzenweger, 2004; Friedman, Oltmanns, & Turkheimer, 2007; Anderson et al., 2015).

The best-known type of personality disorder, illustrated by the case above, is the **antisocial personality disorder** (sometimes referred to as a sociopathic personality). Individuals with this disturbance show no regard for the moral and ethical rules of society or the rights of others. Although they can appear quite intelligent and likable (at least at first), upon closer examination they turn out to be manipulative and deceptive. Moreover, they lack any guilt or anxiety about their wrongdoing. When those with antisocial personality disorder behave in a way that injures someone else, they understand intellectually that they have

personality disorder A disorder characterized by a set of inflexible, maladaptive behavior patterns that keep a person from functioning appropriately in society

antisocial personality disorder A disorder in which individuals show no regard for the moral and ethical rules of society or the rights of others

> **People with antisocial personality disorder are often impulsive and lack the ability to withstand frustration.**

caused harm but feel no remorse (Goodwin & Hamilton, 2003; Hilarski, 2007; Chang, Davies, & Gavin, 2010).

People with antisocial personality disorder are often impulsive and lack the ability to withstand frustration. They can be extremely manipulative. They also may have excellent social skills; they can be charming, engaging, and highly persuasive. Some of the best con artists have antisocial personalities.

What causes such an unusual constellation of problem behaviors? A variety of factors have been suggested, ranging from an inability to experience emotions appropriately to problems in family relationships. For example, in many cases of antisocial behavior, the individual has come from a home in which a parent has died or left, or one in which there is a lack of affection, a lack of consistency in discipline, or outright rejection. Other explanations concentrate on sociocultural factors, because an unusually high proportion of people with antisocial personalities come from lower socioeconomic groups. Still, no one has been able to pinpoint the specific causes of antisocial personalities, and it is likely that some combination of factors is responsible (Rosenstein & Horowitz, 1996; Costa & Widiger, 2002; Chen et al., 2011).

From the perspective of . . .

A Medical Assistant   Personality disorders are often not apparent to others, and many people with these problems seem to live basically normal lives and are not a threat to others. Because these people often appear from the outside to function well in society, why should they be considered psychologically disordered? What are the benefits of you having an understanding of the major psychological disorders in your career?

© Comstock/Getty Images RF

borderline personality disorder A disorder in which individuals have difficulty developing a secure sense of who they are

narcissistic personality disorder A personality disturbance characterized by an exaggerated sense of self-importance

People with **borderline personality disorder** have difficulty developing a secure sense of who they are. As a consequence, they tend to rely on relationships with others to define their identity. The problem with this strategy is that rejections are devastating. Furthermore, people with this disorder distrust others and have difficulty controlling their anger. Their emotional volatility leads to impulsive and self-destructive behavior. Individuals with borderline personality disorder often feel empty and alone. They may form intense, sudden, one-sided relationships, demanding the attention of another person and then feeling angry when they don't receive it. One reason for this behavior is that they may have a background in which others discounted or criticized their emotional reactions, and they may not have learned to regulate their emotions effectively (King-Casas et al., 2008; Hopwood et al., 2009; Samuel et al., 2013).

Another example of a personality disturbance is the **narcissistic personality disorder,** which is characterized by an exaggerated sense of self-importance. Those with the disorder expect special treatment from others, while at the same time disregarding others' feelings. In some ways, in fact, the main attribute of the narcissistic personality is an inability to experience empathy for other people.

There are several other categories of personality disorder that range in severity from individuals who may simply be regarded by others as eccentric, obnoxious, or difficult, to people who act in a manner that is criminal and dangerous to others. Although they are not out of touch with reality in the way that people with schizophrenia are, people with personality disorders lead lives that put them on the fringes of society (Millon, Davis, & Millon, 2000; Trull & Widiger, 2003).

≫ LO34.7 Childhood Disorders

We typically view childhood as a time of innocence and relative freedom from stress. In reality, though, almost 20 percent of children and 40 percent of adolescents experience significant emotional or behavioral disorders (Romano et al., 2001; Broidy, Nagan, & Tremblay, 2003; Nolen-Hoeksema, 2007).

For example, although major depression is more prevalent in adults, around 2.5 percent of children and more than 8 percent of adolescents suffer from the disorder. In fact, by the time they reach age 20, between 15 and 20 percent of children and adolescents will experience an episode of major depression. Ten percent of adolescents will have had an episode of major depression in the last year (Garber & Horowitz, 2002; Substance Abuse and Mental Health Services Administration, 2014).

Children do not always display depression in the same way adults do. Rather than showing profound sadness or hopelessness, childhood depression may produce the expression of exaggerated fears, clinginess, or avoidance of everyday activities. In older children, the symptoms may be sulking, school problems, and even acts of delinquency (Koplewicz, 2002; Seroczynski, Jacquez, & Cole, 2003).

A considerably more common childhood disorder is **attention-deficit hyperactivity disorder (ADHD),** a disorder marked by inattention, impulsiveness, a low tolerance for frustration, and generally a great deal of inappropriate activity. Although all children show such behavior some of the time, it is so common in children diagnosed with ADHD that it interferes with their everyday functioning (Barkley, 2005; Smith, Barkley, & Shapiro, 2006; Barkley, Knouse, & Murphy, 2011).

ADHD is surprisingly widespread, with estimates ranging between 3 and 5 percent of the school-age population—or some 3.5 million children under the age of 18 in the United States. Children diagnosed with the disorder are often exhausting to parents and teachers, and even their peers find them difficult to deal with.

The cause of ADHD is not known, although most experts feel that it is produced by dysfunctions in the nervous system. For example, one theory suggests that unusually low levels of arousal in the central nervous system cause ADHD. To compensate, children with ADHD seek out stimulation to increase arousal. Still, such theories are speculative. Furthermore, because many children occasionally show behaviors characteristic of ADHD, it often is misdiagnosed or, in some cases, overdiagnosed. Only the frequency and persistence of the symptoms of ADHD allow for a correct diagnosis, which only

attention-deficit hyperactivity disorder (ADHD) A disorder marked by inattention, impulsiveness, a low tolerance for frustration, and a great deal of inappropriate activity

In the most severe cases of autism spectrum disorder, children display self-injurious behavior and must wear protective head gear. © Tony Freeman/PhotoEdit

autism spectrum disorder A severe developmental disability that impairs one's ability to communicate and relate to others

a trained professional can perform (Barkley, 2000; Vloet et al., 2010; Ketisch & Jones, 2013).

Autism spectrum disorder, a severe developmental disability that impairs one's ability to communicate and relate to others, is another disorder that usually appears in the first three years and typically continues throughout life. Children with autism have difficulties in both verbal and nonverbal communication, and they may avoid social contact.

About one in 88 children are thought to have the disorder, and its prevalence has risen significantly in the last decade. Whether the increase is the result of an actual rise in the incidence of autism or is due to better reporting is a question of intense debate among researchers (Rice, 2009; Neal, Matson, & Belva, 2013).

> **Children with autism spectrum disorder have difficulties in both verbal and nonverbal communication, and they may avoid social contact.**

» LO34.8 Other Disorders

It's important to keep in mind that the various forms of psychological disorders described in *DSM-5* cover much more ground than we have been able to discuss in this module. Some relate to topics previously considered in other chapters; there are other disorders that we have not mentioned at all. Moreover, each of the classes we have discussed can be divided into several subcategories (Pratt et al., 2003; Reijonen et al., 2003; Røysamb et al., 2011).

For example, some common disorders include:

- *Psychoactive substance use disorder*
- *Alcohol use disorder*
- *Eating disorders,* including *anorexia nervosa, bulimia,* and *binge-eating disorder*
- *Sexual disorders,* including *paraphilias (atypical sexual activities that may include nonhuman objects or nonconsenting partners)*
- *Organic mental disorders* (such as *Alzheimer's disease*)

RECAP

Discuss anxiety disorders.

- Anxiety disorders are present when a person experiences so much anxiety that it affects daily functioning. Specific types of anxiety disorders include phobic disorder, panic disorder, and generalized anxiety disorder. In obsessive-compulsive disorder (OCD), people experience persistent, unwanted thoughts or ideas that keep recurring (obsessions) or feel driven to carry out particular actions (compulsions).

Discuss somatic symptom disorders.

- Somatic symptom disorders are psychological difficulties that take on a physical (somatic) form, but for which there is no medical cause. Examples are illness anxiety disorder and conversion disorders.

Discuss dissociative disorders.

- Dissociative disorders are marked by the separation, or dissociation, of different facets of a person's personality that are usually integrated. Major kinds of dissociative disorders include dissociative identity disorder, dissociative amnesia, and dissociative fugue.

Discuss mood disorders.

■ Mood disorders are characterized by emotional states of depression or euphoria so strong that they intrude on everyday living. They include major depressive disorder and bipolar disorder.

Explain schizophrenia.

■ Schizophrenia is one of the more severe forms of mental illness. Symptoms of schizophrenia include declines in functioning, thought and language disturbances, perceptual disorders, emotional disturbance, and withdrawal from others.

■ Strong evidence links schizophrenia to genetic, biochemical, and environmental factors. According to the predisposition model, an interaction among various factors produces the disorder.

Discuss personality disorders.

■ People with personality disorders experience little or no personal distress, but they do suffer from an inability to function as normal members of society. These disorders include antisocial personality disorder, borderline personality disorder, and narcissistic personality disorder.

Discuss childhood disorders.

■ Childhood disorders include major depression, attention-deficit hyperactivity disorder (ADHD), and autism spectrum disorder.

[EVALUATE E Evaluate]

1. Kathy is terrified of elevators. She could be suffering from a(n)
   a. Obsessive-compulsive disorder.
   b. Phobic disorder.
   c. Panic disorder.
   d. Generalized anxiety disorder.
2. Carmen described an incident in which her anxiety suddenly rose to a peak and she felt a sense of impending doom. Carmen experienced a(n) _____ _____.
3. Troubling thoughts that persist for weeks or months are known as
   a. Obsessions.
   b. Compulsions.
   c. Rituals.
   d. Panic attacks.
4. An overpowering urge to carry out a strange ritual is called a(n) _____.
5. The separation of the personality, providing escape from stressful situations, is the key factor in _____ disorders.
6. States of extreme euphoria and energy paired with severe depression characterize _____ disorder.
7. The _____ _____ states that schizophrenia may be caused by an excess of certain neurotransmitters in the brain.

What cultural factors might contribute to the rate of anxiety disorders found in a culture? How might the experience of anxiety differ among people of different cultures?

KEY TERMS

Anxiety disorder   LO34.1

Phobia   LO34.1

Panic disorder   LO34.1

Generalized anxiety disorder   LO34.1

Obsessive-compulsive disorder   LO34.1

Obsession   LO34.1

Compulsion   LO34.1

Somatic symptom disorders   LO34.2

Illness anxiety disorder   LO34.2

Conversion disorder   LO34.2

Dissociative disorder   LO34.3

Dissociative identity disorder (DID)   LO34.3

Dissociative amnesia   LO34.3

Dissociative fugue   LO34.3

Mood disorder   LO34.4

Major depressive disorder   LO34.4

Mania   LO34.4

Bipolar disorder   LO34.4

Schizophrenia   LO34.5

Personality disorder   LO34.6

Antisocial personality disorder   LO34.6

Borderline personality disorder   LO34.6

Narcissistic personality disorder   LO34.6

Attention-deficit hyperactivity disorder (ADHD)   LO34.7

Autism spectrum disorder   LO34.7

module 35

Psychological Disorders in Perspective

How common are the kinds of psychological disorders we've been discussing? Here's one answer: every second person you meet in the United States is likely to suffer, at some point during his or her life, from a psychological disorder.

W Work

» LO35.1 Prevalence of Psychological Disorders: The Mental State of the Union

The preceding sentence represents the conclusion drawn from a massive study on the prevalence of psychological disorders. In that study, researchers conducted face-to-face interviews with more than 8,000 men and women between the ages of 15 and 54. The sample was designed to be representative of the population of the United States. According to results of the study, 48 percent of those interviewed had experienced a disorder at some point in their lives. In addition, 30 percent experienced a disorder in any particular year, and the number of people who experienced simultaneous multiple disorders (known as *comorbidity*) was significant (Merikangas et al., 2007; Kessler & Wang, 2008; Merikangas et al., 2010).

The most common disorder reported in the study was depression, with 17 percent of those surveyed reporting at least one major episode. Ten percent had suffered from depression during the current year. The next most common disorder was alcohol dependence, which occurred at a lifetime incidence rate of 14 percent. In addition, 7 percent of those interviewed had experienced alcohol dependence in the last year. Other frequently occurring psychological disorders were drug dependence, disorders involving panic (such as an overwhelming fear of talking to strangers and terror of heights), and posttraumatic stress disorder.

The significant level of psychological disorders is a problem not only in the United States; according to the World Health Organization, mental health difficulties are also a global concern. Throughout the world, psychological disorders are

STUDY ALERT

Remember that the incidence of various types of psychological disorders in the general population is surprisingly high.

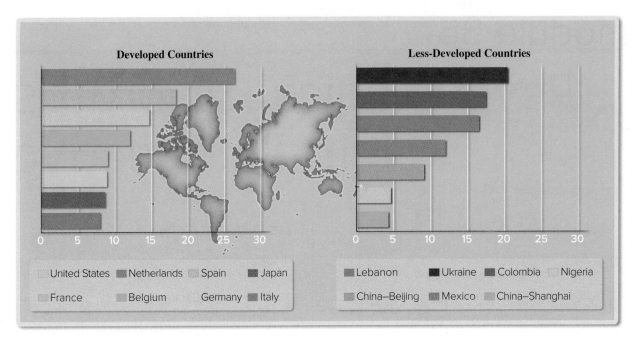

Figure 1 According to a global survey conducted by the World Health Organization, the prevalence of psychological disorders is widespread. These figures show the prevalence of any psychological disorder within the last 12 months.
Source: Adapted from The WHO World Mental Health Survey Consortium, 2004, Table 3. From World Health Organization, World Mental Health Survey Consortium, 2004.

widespread. Furthermore, there are economic disparities in treatment, such that more affluent people with mild disorders receive more and better treatment than poor people who have more severe disorders. In fact, psychological disorders make up 14 percent of global illness, and 90 percent of people in developing countries receive no care at all for their disorders (see Figure 1; The WHO World Mental Health Survey Consortium, 2004; Wang et al., 2007; Hsu, 2016).

> **Throughout the world, psychological disorders are widespread.**

» LO35.2 The Social and Cultural Context of Psychological Disorders

In considering the nature of the psychological disorders described in *DSM-5,* it's important to keep in mind that the specific disorders reflect Western cultures at the turn of the twenty-first century. The classification system provides a snapshot of how its authors viewed mental disorder when it was published. In fact, the development of the most recent version of *DSM* was a source of great debate, in part reflecting issues that divide society.

One specific newly classified disorder that has been added to *DSM-5* and that has caused controversy is known as *disruptive mood dysregulation disorder.* This particular diagnosis is characterized by temperamental outbursts grossly out of proportion to the situation, both verbally and physically, in children between the ages of 6 and 18. Some practitioners argue these symptoms simply define a child having a temper tantrum rather than a disorder (Dobbs, 2012; Marchand & Phillips, 2012; Frances, 2013).

Similarly, someone who overeats 12 times in three months can be considered to be suffering from the new classification of *binge eating disorder,* which seems

STUDY ALERT

It is important to understand that the *DSM* is a living document that presents a view of disorders that reflects the culture and historical context of its authors.

to some critics to be overly inclusive. Finally, *hoarding behavior* is now placed in its own category of psychological disorder. Some critics suggest this change is more a reflection of the rise of reality shows focusing on hoarding rather than reflecting a distinct category of psychological disturbance (Hudson et al., 2012).

Such controversies underline the fact that our understanding of abnormal behavior reflects the society and culture in which we live. Future revisions of *DSM* may include a different catalog of disorders. Even now, other cultures might include a list of disorders that looks very different from the list that appears in the current *DSM,* as we discuss next.

EXPLORING diversity

DSM and Culture—and the Culture of *DSM*

In most people's estimation, a person who hears voices of the recently deceased is probably a victim of a psychological disturbance. Yet some Plains Indians routinely hear the voices of the dead calling to them from the afterlife, and in their culture, that's considered perfectly normal.

This is only one example of the role of culture in determining whether behavior should be labeled as "abnormal." In fact, among all the major adult disorders included in the *DSM* categorization, a minority are found across all cultures of the world. Most others are prevalent primarily in North America and Western Europe (Kleinman, 1996; López & Guarnaccia, 2000; Jacob, 2014).

Take, for instance, anorexia nervosa, the disorder in which people develop inaccurate views of their body appearance, become obsessed with their weight, and refuse to eat, sometimes starving to death in the process. This disorder occurs only in cultures that hold the societal standard that slender female bodies are the most desirable. In most of the world, where such a standard does not exist, anorexia nervosa is rare. Until recently, there was little anorexia nervosa in Asia with some exceptions, such as the upper and upper-middle classes of Japan and Hong Kong, where Western influence is greatest (Watters, 2010). In fact, anorexia nervosa developed fairly recently even in Western cultures. In the 1600s and 1700s, it did not occur because the ideal female body in Western cultures at that time was a full-figured one.

Furthermore, even though disorders such as schizophrenia are found throughout the world, cultural factors influence the specific symptoms of the disorder. Hence, catatonic schizophrenia, in which unmoving patients appear to be frozen in the same position, sometimes for days, is rare in North America and Western Europe. In contrast, in India, 80 percent of those with schizophrenia are catatonic.

From the perspective of . . .

A Health Care Provider What indicators might be most important in determining whether a client is experiencing a psychological disorder? How might your responses change if the client were from a different culture (e.g., an African society)?

Other cultures have disorders that do not appear in the West. For example, in Malaysia, a behavior called *amok* is characterized by a wild outburst in which a person, usually quiet and withdrawn, kills or severely injures another. Koro is a condition found in Southeast Asian males who develop an intense panic that the penis is about to withdraw into the abdomen. Finally, *ataque de nervios* is a disorder found most often among Latinos from the Caribbean. It is characterized by trembling, crying, uncontrollable screams, and verbal or physical aggression (Cohen, Slomkowski, & Robins, 1999; Adams & Dzokoto, 2007; Ebigbo, Lekwas, & Chukwunenyem, 2015).

In sum, we should not assume that the *DSM* provides the final word on psychological disorders. The disorders it includes are very much a creation and function of Western cultures at a particular moment in time, and its categories should not be seen as universally applicable (Tseng, 2003).

becoming an informed consumer
of psychology

Deciding When You Need Help

Keep in mind that from time to time we all experience a wide range of emotions, and it is not unusual to feel deeply unhappy, fantasize about bizarre situations, or feel anxiety about life's circumstances. On the other hand, many people do have problems that merit concern, and in such cases, it is important to consider the possibility that professional help is warranted. The following list of symptoms can serve as a guideline to help you determine whether outside intervention might be useful.

- Long-term feelings of distress that interfere with your sense of well-being, competence, and ability to function effectively in daily activities
- Occasions in which you experience overwhelmingly high stress, accompanied by feelings of inability to cope with the situation
- Prolonged depression or feelings of hopelessness, especially when they do not have any clear cause (such as the death of someone close)
- Withdrawal from other people
- Thoughts of inflicting harm on oneself or suicide
- A chronic physical problem for which no physical cause can be determined
- A fear or phobia that prevents you from engaging in everyday activities
- Inability to interact effectively with others, preventing the development of friendships and loving relationships

This list offers a rough set of guidelines for determining when the normal problems of everyday living have escalated beyond your ability to deal with them by yourself. In such situations, the *least* reasonable approach would be to pore over the psychological disorders we have discussed in an attempt at self-diagnosis. A more reasonable strategy is to consider seeking professional help.

RECAP

Discuss the prevalence of psychological disorders.

- About half the people in the United States are likely to experience a psychological disorder at some point in their lives: 30 percent experience a disorder in any specific year.

Discuss the societal and cultural context for psychological disorders.

- The signals that indicate a need for professional help include long-term feelings of psychological distress, feelings of inability to cope with stress, withdrawal from other people, thoughts of inflicting harm on oneself or suicide, prolonged feelings of hopelessness, chronic physical problems with no apparent causes, phobias and compulsions, paranoia, and an inability to interact with others.

[EVALUATE ]

1. The latest version of *DSM* is considered to be the definitive guide to defining psychological disorders. True or false?

2. Match the disorder with the culture in which it is most common:

   1. amok   a. India
   2. anorexia nervosa   b. Malaysia
   3. catatonic schizophrenia   c. United States

[RETHINK R Rethink]

Why is inclusion in the *DSM-5* of disorders such as hoarding behavior so controversial and political? What disadvantages does inclusion bring? Does inclusion bring any benefits?

Answers to Evaluate Questions 1. false; the development of the latest version of DSM was a source of great controversy, in part reflecting issues that divide society; 2. 1-b, 2-c, 3-a

« « Looking Back

Psychology on the Web

1. On the Web, research the insanity defense as it is used in U.S. courts of law, consulting at least two sources. Summarize your findings, evaluating them against the perspectives on psychological disorders. Are there differences between legal and psychological interpretations of "sanity"? If so, what are they? Do you think such differences are appropriate?

2. Find information on the Web about the controversy surrounding dissociative identity (or multiple personality) disorder. Summarize both sides of the controversy. Using your knowledge of psychology, state your opinion on the matter.

the case of . . .

NANCY CHRISTOPHER, THE "CRAZY CAT LADY"

Although none of Nancy Christopher's neighbors knew her, they all knew of her. They usually referred to her as the "crazy cat lady" because of the dozen or more cats she had living on her property and in her home. No one was quite sure what Nancy did for a living, if anything. She lived alone and would only be seen leaving her house on Saturday afternoons, when she would push a shopping cart into town to shop for groceries and supplies. Nancy often appeared disheveled, with uncombed hair, smeared lipstick, and a dirty winter coat that she had owned for years and always wore outdoors, even when the weather was warm.

Nancy was not unfriendly to people—in fact, quite the contrary. On her trips into town, she would talk to almost anybody she encountered, sometimes at great length. Her chatter was always pleasant, though people would still feel uncomfortable with her inappropriately intimate disclosures and her habit of talking almost incessantly with frequent and seemingly random changes in topic. All in all, most people considered her harmless and generally left her alone.

1. Do Nancy Christopher's peculiar habits make her abnormal? Why or why not?

2. What more would you need to know about Nancy Christopher to determine whether she likely has a mental disorder or is just eccentric?

3. Imagine that you're Nancy's physician and her daughter has expressed concern that her behavior may indicate the presence of schizophrenia. How would you assure Nancy's daughter that Nancy's behavior may be odd but does not suggest the presence of schizophrenia?

4. Continue to imagine that you're Nancy's physician, and that you suspect Nancy may have an anxiety disorder of some kind. What kinds of symptoms might you check for to confirm your suspicion?

5. If Nancy's behaviors do not fit any *DSM-5* criteria for diagnosis as a mental disorder, does that mean that she is definitely normal? Why or why not?

profiles of SUCCESS

Courtesy of Bethany L. Potter

NAME: Bethany L. Potter, CMA, CPT, CEKG

SCHOOL: ECPI/MCI University

DEGREE PROGRAM: Specialized AD, Medical Assisting

Returning to school as an older student is not easy. But returning to school as a wife and mother offers its own unique set of challenges, as Bethany Potter discovered.

"The most difficult step for me was taking the initiative to go back to school," Potter said. "It was frightening! It meant stepping out of my comfort zone of being a wife and a mom and becoming a student again.

"I had to remember to stay involved with my family, and had to make the time for classes, while still helping the kids with their homework, cook dinner, make lunches, clean, do laundry, and have a bit of fun with them," she added.

Having strong support from her family was important for Potter, who maintained close communication with her husband on how each day would be planned. In addition, she developed a strong set of management skills.

"One of the approaches that I took was getting a routine down. I had to manage my family life and my school life," Potter said. "Learning time management and setting goals each day was a huge help in obtaining my success. I also designated an area just for my school supplies, backpack, and for study time. That was helpful in keeping myself organized."

Potter said she was able to adapt to her new life challenges, and going back to school gave her a renewed sense of pride and accomplishment that allowed her to expand her horizons. Her goal is to purse a bachelor's degree and to teach others to become medical assistants.

Her advice to other students:

"Take it one day at a time. Make goals for each day, each week, and each class schedule. Stay organized and with each day just breathe and try to enjoy every minute," she explained. "It was hard keeping a positive attitude. But at this point in my life, I wanted to succeed, and I was prepared to be a better person and improve my skills to help further my education and obtain a lifelong goal."

[RETHINK R Rethink]

How will Potter's understanding of psychological disorders make her a better medical assistant?

How can the support of family help a student be successful? Are there some ways in which family can also hinder a student's success?

visual summary 10
PSYCHOLOGICAL DISORDERS

MODULE 33 Normal versus Abnormal: Making the Distinction

Defining Abnormality

- Deviation from the average
- Deviation from the ideal
- Sense of personal discomfort
- Inability to function effectively
- Legal concept

Classifying Abnormal Behavior: *DSM-5* attempts to provide comprehensive and relatively precise definitions for more than 200 disorders

Perspectives on Abnormality

Perspectives on Psychological Disorders		
Perspective	Description	Possible Application of Perspective to Chris's Case
Medical perspective	Assumes that physiological causes are at the root of psychological disorders	Examine Chris for medical problems, such as brain tumor, chemical imbalance in the brain, or disease
Psychoanalytic perspective	Argues that psychological disorders stem from childhood conflicts	Seek out information about Chris's past, considering possible childhood conflicts
Behavioral perspective	Assumes that abnormal behaviors are learned responses	Concentrate on rewards and punishments for Chris's behavior, and identify environmental stimuli that reinforce his behavior
Cognitive perspective	Assumes that cognitions (people's thoughts and beliefs) are central to psychological disorders	Focus on Chris's perceptions of himself and his environment
Humanistic perspective	Emphasizes people's responsibility for their own behavior and the need to self-actualize	Consider Chris's behavior in terms of his choices and efforts to reach his potential
Sociocultural perspective	Assumes that behavior is shaped by family, society, and culture	Focus on how societal demands contributed to Chris's disorder

MODULE 34 The Major Psychological Disorders

Anxiety Disorders: Anxiety without external justification

- Specific phobia disorder
- Panic disorder
- Generalized anxiety disorder
- Causes of anxiety disorders

Somatic Symptom Disorders: Psychological difficulties that take on a physical form with no medical cause

Dissociative Disorders: Separation of different facets of a person's personality that normally work together

Mood Disorders: Disturbances in emotional experience

- Major depressive disorder
- Mania and bipolar disorder
- Causes of mood disorders
  - Genetics
  - Psychological: feelings of loss or anger
  - Behavioral: stress
  - Cognitive: learned helplessness and no hope

Schizophrenia: A class of disorders in which distortion of reality occurs

- Decline from a previous level of functioning
- Disturbances of thought and language
- Delusions
- Hallucinations and perceptual disorders
- Emotional disturbances

Personality Disorders: A set of inflexible, maladaptive behavior patterns

- Antisocial personality disorder
- Borderline personality disorder
- Narcissistic personality disorder

Childhood Disorders: Start during childhood or adolescence

- Attention-deficit hyperactivity disorder
- Autism spectrum disorder

MODULE 35 Psychological Disorders in Perspective

Social and Cultural Context: Our understanding of abnormal behavior reflects the society and culture in which we live

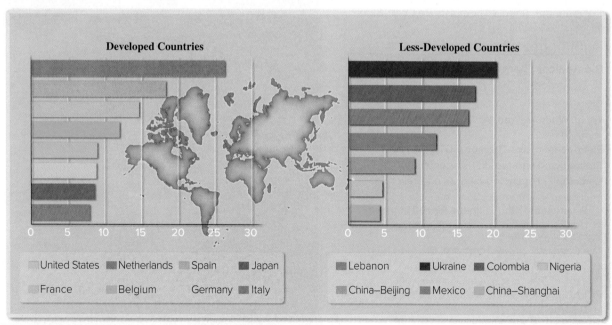

(MODULE 33) © H.S. Photos/Alamy; (MODULE 34) © GK Hart/Vikki Hart/Photodisc/Getty Images RF; (MODULE 35) Source: Adapted from The WHO World Mental Health Survey Consortium, 2004, Table 3.

CHAPTER 11

© David Harry Stewart/The Image Bank/Getty Images

A Change of Mind

Marjorie Stowe suffered decades of depression before her gynecologist suggested an experimental treatment called deep brain stimulation (DBS), a special type of brain surgery for depression that resisted traditional treatments. Marjorie didn't know if DBS would work—her long-time therapist had seemed to blame her for her continuing depression, insisting that she was *choosing* not to be healed—but she had a new baby and she was desperate for a cure.

During the DBS surgery, Marjorie was awake as tiny electrodes were implanted at the midline of her brain, their thin wires connected to a battery-powered pulse generator under her collarbone. The electrodes deliver a small amount of electrical current to the specific area of the brain that is overactive in people with depression.

Within days, Marjorie's mood brightened noticeably. She began to enjoy life, to laugh with her family (Wrobel, 2015).

TREATMENT OF PSYCHOLOGICAL DISORDERS

Looking Ahead

The transition from a life of dark, often suicidal thoughts to one of joy and engagement was something of a shock for Marjorie, but with the ongoing treatment the DBS team provides (including a psychiatrist and a behavioral therapist), she has adjusted to her newfound happiness.

Deep brain stimulation surgery is just one way in which people suffering from psychological disorders—in this instance, severe depression—can be treated. The variety of treatments available to relieve psychological pain share a common objective: to enable individuals to achieve richer, more meaningful, and more fulfilling lives.

Despite their diversity, approaches to treating psychological disorders fall into two main categories: psychologically based and biologically based therapies. Psychologically based therapy, or **psychotherapy,** is treatment in which a trained professional—a therapist—uses psychological techniques to help someone overcome psychological difficulties and disorders, resolve problems in living, or bring about personal growth. In psychotherapy, the goal is to produce psychological change in a person (called a "client" or "patient") through discussions and interactions with the therapist. In contrast, **biomedical therapy** relies on drugs and medical procedures to improve psychological functioning.

As we describe the various approaches to therapy, keep in mind that although the distinctions may seem clear-cut, the classifications and procedures overlap a good deal. In fact, many therapists today use a variety of methods with an individual patient, taking an *eclectic approach to therapy.* Assuming that both psychological and biological processes often produce psychological disorders, eclectic therapists may draw from several perspectives simultaneously to address both the psychological and the biological aspects of a person's problems (Goin, 2005; Berman, Jobes, & Silverman, 2006).

psychotherapy Treatment in which a trained professional—a therapist—uses psychological techniques to help a person overcome psychological difficulties and disorders, resolve problems in living, or bring about personal growth

biomedical therapy Therapy that relies on drugs and other medical procedures to improve psychological functioning

Psychotherapy
Psychodynamic, Behavioral, and Cognitive Approaches to Treatment

Learning Outcomes  Prepare

>> **LO36.1** Explain psychodynamic approaches to therapy.

>> **LO36.2** Explain behavioral approaches to therapy.

>> **LO36.3** Explain cognitive approaches to therapy.

MODULE OUTLINE  Organize

Psychodynamic Approaches to Therapy

Behavioral Approaches to Therapy

Cognitive Approaches to Therapy

Try It! What Do You Believe?

W Work

STUDY ALERT

To better understand how psychodynamic therapy works, review Freud's psychoanalytic theory, discussed in the chapter on personality.

Therapists use some 400 different varieties of psychotherapy, the approaches to therapy that focus on psychological factors. Although diverse in many respects, all psychological approaches see treatment as a way of solving psychological problems by modifying people's behavior and helping them gain a better understanding of themselves and their past, present, and future.

In light of the variety of psychological approaches, people who provide therapy vary considerably in educational background and training. Consequently, those seeking treatment utilize therapists based on the therapist's expertise with the type of problem an individual is experiencing (see Figure 1). For example, a person who is suffering from a severe disturbance and who has lost touch with reality will typically require some sort of biologically based drug therapy. In that case, a *psychiatrist*—who is a physician—might be the professional of choice.

In contrast, those suffering from milder disorders, such as difficulty adjusting to the death of a family member, have a broader choice that might include any of the professionals listed in Figure 1. The decision can be made easier by initial consultations with professionals in mental health facilities in communities, colleges, and health organizations, who can provide guidance in selecting an appropriate therapist.

Regardless of their specific training, almost all psychotherapists employ one of four major approaches to therapy: psychodynamic, behavioral, cognitive, and humanistic treatment approaches. These approaches grow out of the perspectives of personality and psychological disorders developed by psychologists. Here we'll consider the psychodynamic, behavioral, and cognitive approaches in turn. In the next module, we'll explore the humanistic approach, as well as interpersonal psychotherapy and group therapy, and evaluate the effectiveness of psychotherapy.

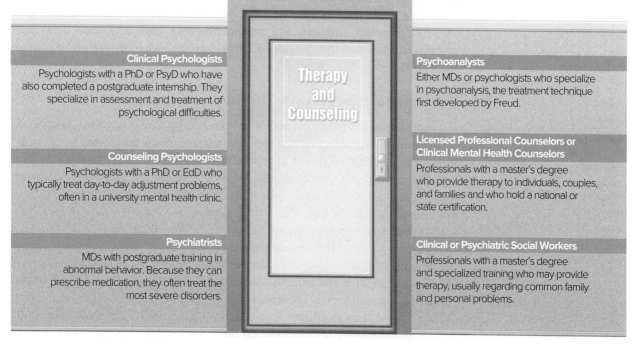

Clinical Psychologists
Psychologists with a PhD or PsyD who have also completed a postgraduate internship. They specialize in assessment and treatment of psychological difficulties.

Counseling Psychologists
Psychologists with a PhD or EdD who typically treat day-to-day adjustment problems, often in a university mental health clinic.

Psychiatrists
MDs with postgraduate training in abnormal behavior. Because they can prescribe medication, they often treat the most severe disorders.

Psychoanalysts
Either MDs or psychologists who specialize in psychoanalysis, the treatment technique first developed by Freud.

Licensed Professional Counselors or Clinical Mental Health Counselors
Professionals with a master's degree who provide therapy to individuals, couples, and families and who hold a national or state certification.

Clinical or Psychiatric Social Workers
Professionals with a master's degree and specialized training who may provide therapy, usually regarding common family and personal problems.

Figure 1 A variety of professionals provide therapy and counseling.

» LO36.1 Psychodynamic Approaches to Therapy

Psychodynamic therapy seeks to bring unresolved past conflicts and unacceptable impulses from the unconscious into the conscious, where patients may deal with the problems more effectively. Psychodynamic approaches are based on Freud's psychoanalytic approach to personality, which holds that individuals employ *defense mechanisms,* psychological strategies to protect themselves from unacceptable unconscious impulses.

The most common defense mechanism is repression, which pushes threatening conflicts and impulses back into the unconscious. However, since unacceptable conflicts and impulses can never be completely buried, some of the anxiety associated with them can produce abnormal behavior in the form of what Freud called *neurotic symptoms.*

How do we rid ourselves of the anxiety produced by unconscious, unwanted impulses and drives? To Freud, the answer was to confront the conflicts and impulses by bringing them out of the unconscious part of the mind and into the conscious part. Freud assumed that this technique would reduce anxiety stemming from past conflicts and that the patient could then participate in his or her daily life more effectively.

A psychodynamic therapist, then, faces the challenge of finding a way to assist patients' attempts to explore and understand the unconscious. The technique that has evolved has a

> **psychodynamic therapy** Therapy that seeks to bring unresolved past conflicts and unacceptable impulses from the unconscious into the conscious, where patients may deal with the problems more effectively

"Look, call it denial if you like, but I think what goes on in my personal life is none of my own damn business."

Robert Mankoff/The New Yorker Collection/ The Cartoon Bank

number of components, but basically it consists of guiding patients to consider and discuss their past experiences, in explicit detail, from the time of their first memories. This process assumes that patients will eventually stumble upon long-hidden crises, traumas, and conflicts that are producing anxiety in their adult lives. They will then be able to "work through"—understand and rectify—those difficulties.

Psychoanalysis: Freud's Therapy

psychoanalysis Freud's psychotherapy in which the goal is to release hidden thoughts and feelings from the unconscious part of our minds in order to reduce their power in controlling behavior

transference The transfer of feelings to a psychoanalyst of love or anger that had been originally directed to a patient's parents or other authority figures

Psychoanalysis is Freud's version of psychotherapy. The goal of psychoanalysis is to release hidden thoughts and feelings from the unconscious part of our mind in order to reduce their power in controlling behavior.

In psychoanalysis, which tends to be a lengthy and expensive process, patients may meet with a therapist with considerable frequency, sometimes as much as 50 minutes a day, 4 to 5 days a week, for several years. In their sessions, they often use a technique developed by Freud called *free association*. Psychoanalysts using this technique tell patients to say aloud whatever comes to mind, regardless of its apparent irrelevance or senselessness, and the analysts attempt to recognize and label the connections between what a patient says and the patient's unconscious. Therapists also use *dream interpretation*, examining dreams to find clues to unconscious conflicts and problems. Moving beyond the surface description of a dream (called the *manifest content*), therapists seek its underlying meaning (the *latent content*), thereby revealing the true unconscious meaning of the dream (Colman, 2010; Cabaniss et al., 2011; Hill et al., 2013).

The processes of free association and dream interpretation do not always move forward easily. The same unconscious forces that initially produced repression may keep past difficulties out of the conscious mind, producing resistance. *Resistance* is an inability or unwillingness to discuss or reveal particular memories, thoughts, or motivations.

Because of the close, almost intimate interaction between patient and psychoanalyst, the relationship between the two often becomes emotionally charged and takes on a complexity unlike most other relationships. Patients may eventually think of the analyst as a symbol of a significant other in their past, perhaps a parent or a lover, and apply some of their feelings for that person to the analyst—a phenomenon known as transference. **Transference** is the transfer to a psychoanalyst feelings of love or anger that had been originally directed to a patient's parents or other authority figures (Evans, 2007; Steiner, 2008; Böhmer, 2010; Turri, 2015).

Freud's psychoanalytic therapy is an intensive, lengthy process that includes techniques such as free association and dream interpretation. What are some advantages and disadvantages of psychoanalysis compared with other approaches? © KatarzynaBialasiewicz/Getty Images RF

Contemporary Psychodynamic Approaches

Few people have the time, money, or patience to participate in years of traditional psychoanalysis. Moreover, no conclusive evidence shows that psychoanalysis, as originally conceived by Freud in the nineteenth century, works better than other, more recent forms of psychodynamic therapy.

Today, psychodynamic therapy tends to be of shorter duration and usually lasts no longer than three months or 20 sessions. The therapist takes a more active role than Freud would have liked, controlling the course of therapy, prodding and advising the patient with considerable directness. Finally, contemporary psychodynamic therapists put less emphasis on a patient's past history and childhood.

Instead, they concentrate instead on an individual's current relationships and specific concerns (Wolitzky, 2006; Summers & Barber, 2010; Fisher et al., 2016).

Evaluating Psychodynamic Therapy

Even with its current modifications, psychodynamic therapy has its critics. In its longer versions, it can be time-consuming and expensive, especially in comparison with other forms of psychotherapy, such as behavioral and cognitive approaches. Furthermore, less articulate patients may not do as well as more verbal ones do.

Ultimately, the most important concern about psychodynamic treatment is whether it actually works, and there is no simple answer to this question. Psychodynamic treatment techniques have been controversial since Freud introduced them. Part of the problem is the difficulty in establishing whether patients have improved after psychodynamic therapy. Determining effectiveness depends on reports from the therapist or the patients themselves, reports that are obviously open to bias and subjective interpretation.

Despite the criticism, though, the psychodynamic treatment approach has remained viable. For some people, it provides solutions to difficult psychological issues, provides effective treatment for psychological disturbance, and also permits the potential development of an unusual degree of insight into one's life (Bond, 2006; Anestis, Anestis, & Lilienfeld, 2011; Thase, 2013).

"And when did you first realize you weren't like other precipitation?"

behavioral treatment approaches Treatment approaches that build on the basic processes of learning, such as reinforcement and extinction, and assume that normal and abnormal behavior are both learned

» LO36.2 Behavioral Approaches to Therapy

Perhaps, when you were a child, your parents rewarded you with an ice cream cone when you were especially good . . . or sent you to your room if you misbehaved. Sound principles back up such a child-rearing strategy: good behavior is maintained by reinforcement, and unwanted behavior can be eliminated by punishment.

These principles represent the basic underpinnings of **behavioral treatment approaches.** Building on the basic processes of learning, behavioral treatment approaches make this fundamental assumption: both abnormal behavior and normal behavior are learned. People who act abnormally either have failed to learn the skills they need to cope with the problems of everyday living or have acquired faulty skills and patterns that are being maintained through some form of reinforcement. To modify abnormal behavior, then, proponents of behavioral approaches propose that people must learn new behavior to replace the faulty skills they have developed and unlearn their maladaptive behavior patterns (Norton & Price, 2007; Kowalik et al., 2011; Kivlighan et al., 2015). In this view, then, there is no problem other than the

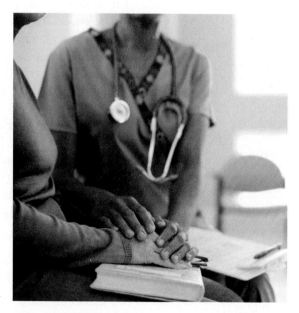

How might understanding aversive conditioning help you help a patient who has had a horrible experience with a previous doctor? © Fuse/Corbis/ Getty Images RF

maladaptive behavior itself, and if you can change that behavior, treatment is successful.

Classical Conditioning Treatments

Suppose you bite into your favorite candy bar and find that not only is it infested with ants but you've also swallowed a bunch of them. You immediately become sick to your stomach and throw up. Your long-term reaction? You never eat that kind of candy bar again, and it may be months before you eat any type of candy. You have learned, through the basic process of classical conditioning, to avoid candy so that you will not get sick and throw up.

Aversive Conditioning. This simple example illustrates how a person can be classically conditioned to modify behavior. Behavior therapists use this principle when they employ **aversive conditioning,** a form of therapy that reduces the frequency of undesired behavior by pairing an aversive, unpleasant stimulus with undesired behavior.

> **Although aversion therapy works reasonably well in inhibiting substance-abuse problems such as alcoholism and certain kinds of sexual disorders, critics question its long-term effectiveness.**

Although aversion therapy works reasonably well in inhibiting substance-abuse problems such as alcoholism and certain kinds of sexual disorders, critics question its long-term effectiveness. Clearly, though, aversion therapy offers an important procedure for eliminating maladaptive responses for some period of time—a respite that provides, even if only temporarily, an opportunity to encourage more adaptive behavior patterns (Delgado, Labouliere, & Phelps, 2006; Raes et al., 2010; Twining et al., 2015).

aversive conditioning A form of therapy that reduces the frequency of undesired behavior by pairing an aversive, unpleasant stimulus with undesired behavior

systematic desensitization A behavioral technique in which gradual exposure to an anxiety-producing stimulus is paired with relaxation to extinguish the response of anxiety

Systematic Desensitization. Another treatment that grew out of classical conditioning is systematic desensitization. In **systematic desensitization,** gradual exposure to an anxiety-producing stimulus is paired with relaxation to extinguish the response of anxiety (Choy, Fyer, & Lipsitz, 2007; Dowling, Jackson, & Thomas, 2008; Eagleson et al., 2016).

Suppose, for instance, you were extremely afraid of flying. The very thought of being in an airplane would make you begin to sweat and shake, and you couldn't get yourself near enough to an airport to know how you'd react if you actually had to fly somewhere. Using systematic desensitization to treat your problem, you would first be trained in relaxation techniques by a behavior therapist and learn to relax your body fully—a highly pleasant state, as you might imagine (see Figure 2).

The next step would involve constructing a hierarchy of fears—a list, in order of increasing severity, of the things you associate with your fears. For instance, your hierarchy might resemble this one:

1. Watching a plane fly overhead
2. Going to an airport
3. Buying a ticket
4. Stepping into the plane
5. Seeing the plane door close
6. Having the plane taxi down the runway
7. Taking off
8. Being in the air

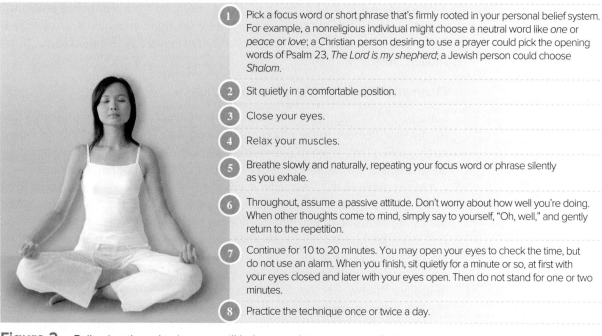

1. Pick a focus word or short phrase that's firmly rooted in your personal belief system. For example, a nonreligious individual might choose a neutral word like *one* or *peace* or *love*; a Christian person desiring to use a prayer could pick the opening words of Psalm 23, *The Lord is my shepherd*; a Jewish person could choose *Shalom*.

2. Sit quietly in a comfortable position.

3. Close your eyes.

4. Relax your muscles.

5. Breathe slowly and naturally, repeating your focus word or phrase silently as you exhale.

6. Throughout, assume a passive attitude. Don't worry about how well you're doing. When other thoughts come to mind, simply say to yourself, "Oh, well," and gently return to the repetition.

7. Continue for 10 to 20 minutes. You may open your eyes to check the time, but do not use an alarm. When you finish, sit quietly for a minute or so, at first with your eyes closed and later with your eyes open. Then do not stand for one or two minutes.

8. Practice the technique once or twice a day.

Figure 2 Following these basic steps will help you achieve a sense of calmness by employing the relaxation response. Photo: © Alex Mares-Manton/Getty Images

Once you had developed this hierarchy and had learned relaxation techniques, you would learn to associate the two sets of responses. To do this, your therapist might ask you to put yourself into a relaxed state and then imagine yourself in the first situation identified in your hierarchy. Once you could consider that first step while remaining relaxed, you would move on to the next situation. Eventually you would move up the hierarchy in gradual stages until you could imagine yourself being in the air without experiencing anxiety. Ultimately, you would be asked to make a visit to an airport and later to take a flight.

From the perspective of . . .

A Paralegal How might you use systematic desensitization to help overcome your fear of speaking in public? Meeting new people?

Flooding Treatments. Although systematic desensitization has proven to be a successful treatment, today it is often replaced with a less-complicated form of therapy called flooding. **Flooding** is a behavioral treatment for anxiety in which people are suddenly confronted with a stimulus that they fear. However, unlike systematic desensitization, relaxation training is not included. The goal behind flooding is to allow the maladaptive response of anxiety or avoidance to become extinct (Havermans et al., 2007; Hofmann, 2007; Bush, 2008).

For example, a patient who has a deep fear of germs may be made to soil her hands in dirt and to keep them dirty for hours. For a person with a fear of germs, initially this is a highly anxiety-producing situation. After a few hours, however, the anxiety will decline, leading to extinction of the anxiety.

flooding A behavioral treatment for anxiety in which people are confronted, either suddenly or gradually, with a stimulus that they fear

Flooding has proved to be an effective treatment for a number of problems, including phobias, anxiety disorders, and even impotence and fear of sexual contact. (Franklin, March, & Garcia, 2007; Powers & Emmelkamp, 2008; Hunter, 2010).

Operant Conditioning Techniques

Some behavioral approaches make use of the operant conditioning principles that we discussed earlier in the chapter about learning. These approaches are based on the notion that we should reward people for carrying out desirable behavior and extinguish undesirable behavior by either ignoring it or punishing it.

One example of the systematic application of operant conditioning principles is the *token system,* which rewards a person for desired behavior with a token such as a poker chip or play money that can later be exchanged for something the person wants. In a variant of the token system, called *contingency contracting,* the therapist and client (or teacher and student, or parent and child) draw up a written agreement. The contract states a series of behavioral goals the client hopes to achieve. It also specifies the positive consequences for the client if the client reaches goals—usually an explicit reward such as money or additional privileges.

Behavior therapists also use *observational learning,* the process in which the behavior of other people is modeled, to systematically teach people new skills and ways of handling their fears and anxieties. For example, modeling helps when therapists are teaching basic social skills such as maintaining eye contact during conversation and acting assertively. Similarly, children with dog phobias have been able to overcome their fears by watching another child—called the "Fearless Peer"—repeatedly walk up to a dog, touch it, pet it, and finally play with it. Modeling, then, can play an effective role in resolving some kinds of behavior difficulties, especially if the model receives a reward for his or her behavior (Bandura, Grusec, & Menlove, 1967; Goubert et al., 2011; Helsen, Goubert, & Vlaeyen, 2013).

Evaluating Behavior Therapy

Behavior therapy works especially well for eliminating anxiety disorders, treating phobias and compulsions, establishing control over impulses, and learning complex social skills to replace maladaptive behavior. More than any of the other therapeutic techniques, it provides methods that nonprofessionals can use to change their own behavior. Moreover, it is efficient, because it focuses on solving carefully defined problems (Barlow, 2007; Lueken et al., 2011; Kertz et al., 2015).

Critics of behavior therapy believe that because it emphasizes changing external behavior, people do not necessarily gain insight into thoughts and expectations that may be fostering their maladaptive behavior. On the other hand, neuroscientific evidence shows that behavioral treatments can produce actual changes in brain functioning, suggesting that behavioral treatments can produce changes beyond external behavior.

» LO36.3 Cognitive Approaches to Therapy

cognitive treatment approaches Treatment approaches that teach people to think in more adaptive ways by changing their dysfunctional cognitions about the world and themselves

If you assumed that illogical thoughts and beliefs lie at the heart of psychological disorders, wouldn't the most direct treatment route be to teach people new, more adaptive modes of thinking? The answer is yes, according to psychologists who take a cognitive approach to treatment.

Cognitive treatment approaches teach people to think in more adaptive ways by changing their dysfunctional cognitions about the world and themselves.

Unlike behavior therapists, who focus on modifying external behavior, cognitive therapists attempt to change the way people think as well as their behavior. Because they often use basic principles of learning, the methods they employ are sometimes referred to as the **cognitive-behavioral approach** (Beck & Rector, 2005; Friedberg, 2006; Kalodner, 2011).

Although cognitive treatment approaches take many forms, they all share the assumption that anxiety, depression, and negative emotions develop from maladaptive thinking. Accordingly, cognitive treatments seek to change the thought patterns that lead to getting "stuck" in dysfunctional ways of thinking. Therapists systematically teach clients to challenge their assumptions and adopt new approaches to old problems.

Cognitive therapy is relatively short term, usually lasting a maximum of 20 sessions. Therapy tends to be highly structured and focused on concrete problems. Therapists often begin by teaching the theory behind the approach and then continue to take an active role throughout the course of therapy, acting as a combination of teacher, coach, and partner.

> Unlike behavior therapists, who focus on modifying external behavior, cognitive therapists attempt to change the way people think as well as their behavior.

cognitive-behavioral approach A treatment approach that incorporates basic principles of learning to change the way people think

Rational-Emotive Behavior Therapy

One good example of cognitive therapy is rational-emotive behavior therapy. **Rational-emotive behavior therapy** attempts to restructure a person's belief system into a more realistic, rational, and logical set of views. By adopting more accurate thought patterns, it is assumed that people will lead more psychologically healthy lives.

Building on these views, psychologist Albert Ellis (2002, 2004) suggests that many people lead unhappy lives and suffer from psychological disorders because they harbor irrational, unrealistic ideas such as these:

rational-emotive behavior therapy A form of therapy that attempts to restructure a person's belief system into a more realistic, rational, and logical set of views by challenging dysfunctional beliefs that maintain irrational behavior

- We need the love or approval of virtually every significant other person for everything we do.

- We should be thoroughly competent, adequate, and successful in all possible respects in order to consider ourselves worthwhile.

- It is horrible when things don't turn out the way we want them to.

Such irrational beliefs trigger negative emotions, which in turn support the irrational beliefs, and lead to a self-defeating cycle. (To get a sense of whether you hold such beliefs, complete the Try It!.)

Rational-emotive behavior therapy aims to help clients eliminate maladaptive thoughts and beliefs and adopt more effective thinking. To accomplish this goal, therapists take an active, directive role during therapy, openly challenging patterns of thought that appear to be dysfunctional. Consider this example:

Martha: The basic problem is that I'm worried about my family. I'm worried about money. And I never seem to be able to relax.

Therapist: Why are you worried about your family? . . . What's to be concerned about? They have certain demands that you don't want to adhere to.

Martha: I was brought up to think that I mustn't be selfish.

Therapist: Oh, we'll have to knock that out of your head! . . .

What Do You Believe?

Rate the degree to which you agree with each of the statements below using the following five-point scale:

Totally Disagree   0   1   2   3   4   Totally Agree

1. I cannot tolerate not doing well at important tasks and it is unbearable to fail _____
2. I feel like I'm a completely stupid person when I don't do as well as my friends _____
3. I can't finish anything _____
4. Nobody cares what happens to me _____
5. I wish I were perfect _____
6. I'm a total loser _____
7. When things don't turn out like I want, I feel it's a disaster _____
8. I'll never do as well as other people _____
9. I will never overcome my failures _____
10. I can't do anything right _____

Scoring

Add up the ratings. The higher your score, the more irrational your beliefs about yourself are, because each of these statements is so extreme that it is unlikely that they are accurate. If you score high on the questionnaire, how do you think you might try to change your beliefs to make them more rational?

Source: Bridges, K. R., & Harnish, R. J., 2010.

Martha: I think it's a feeling I was brought up with that you always have to give of yourself. If you think of yourself, you're wrong.

Therapist: That's a belief. Why do you have to keep believing that—at your age? You believed a lot of superstitions when you were younger. Why do you have to retain them? Your parents indoctrinated you with this nonsense, because that's their belief. . . . Who needs that philosophy? All it's gotten you, so far, is guilt. (Ellis, 1974, pp. 223–286)

By poking holes in Martha's reasoning, the therapist is attempting to help her adopt a more realistic view of herself and her circumstances (Ellis, 2002; Dryden & David, 2008).

Cognitive Therapy

Another influential form of therapy that builds on a cognitive perspective is that of Aaron Beck (Beck, 2004; Beck, Davis & Freeman, 2015). Like rational-emotive behavior therapy, Beck's *cognitive therapy* aims to change people's illogical thoughts about themselves and the world.

However, cognitive therapy is considerably less confrontational and challenging than rational-emotive behavior therapy. Instead of the therapist's actively arguing with clients about their dysfunctional cognitions, cognitive therapists more often play the role of teacher. Therapists urge clients to obtain information on their own that will lead them to discard their inaccurate thinking through a process of cognitive appraisal. In *cognitive appraisal,* clients are asked to evaluate situations, themselves, and others in terms of their memories, values, beliefs, thoughts, and expectations. During the course of treatment, therapists help clients discover ways of thinking more appropriately about themselves and others (Beck, Freeman, & Davis, 2004; Moorey, 2007; Harvey et al., 2010).

Evaluating Cognitive Approaches to Therapy

Cognitive approaches to therapy have proved successful in dealing with a broad range of disorders, including anxiety disorders, depression, substance abuse, and eating disorders. Furthermore, the willingness of cognitive therapists to incorporate additional treatment approaches (e.g., combining cognitive and behavioral techniques in cognitive-behavioral therapy) has made this approach a particularly effective form of treatment (Mitte, 2005; Ishikawa et al., 2007; Bhar et al., 2008).

At the same time, critics have pointed out that the focus on helping people to think more rationally ignores the fact that life is, in reality, sometimes irrational. Changing one's assumptions to make them more reasonable and logical thus may not always be helpful—even assuming it is possible to bring about true cognitive change. Still, the success of cognitive approaches has made it one of the most frequently employed therapies (Beck, 2007).

RECAP

Explain psychodynamic approaches to therapy.

- Psychotherapy (psychologically based therapy) and biomedical therapy (biologically based therapy) share the goal of resolving psychological problems by modifying people's thoughts, feelings, expectations, evaluations, and ultimately behavior.

- Psychoanalytic approaches seek to bring unresolved past conflicts and unacceptable impulses from the unconscious into the conscious, where patients may deal with the problems more effectively. To do this, therapists use techniques such as free association and dream interpretation.

Explain behavioral approaches to therapy.

- Behavioral approaches to treatment view abnormal behavior as the problem, rather than

viewing that behavior as a symptom of some underlying cause. To bring about a "cure," this view suggests that the outward behavior must be changed by using methods such as aversive conditioning, systematic desensitization, observational learning, token systems, and contingency contracting.

Explain cognitive approaches to therapy.

- Cognitive approaches to treatment consider the goal of therapy to be to help a person restructure his or her faulty belief system into a more realistic, rational, and logical view of the world. Two examples of cognitive treatments are rational-emotive behavior therapy and cognitive therapy.

[EVALUATE

1. Match the following mental health practitioners with the appropriate description.

   1. Psychiatrist
   2. Clinical psychologist
   3. Counseling psychologist
   4. Psychoanalyst

   a. PhD specializing in the treatment of psychological disorders
   b. Professional specializing in Freudian therapy techniques
   c. MD trained in abnormal behavior
   d. PhD specializing in the adjustment of day-to-day problems

2. According to Freud, people use _____ _____ as a means of preventing unwanted impulses from intruding on conscious thought.

3. In dream interpretation, a psychoanalyst must learn to distinguish between the _____ content of a dream, which is what appears on the surface, and the _____ content, its underlying meaning.

4. Which of the following treatments deals with phobias by gradual exposure to the item producing the fear?

   a. Systematic desensitization
   b. Partial reinforcement
   c. Behavioral self-management
   d. Aversion therapy

[RETHINK R Rethink]

In what ways are psychoanalysis and cognitive therapy similar, and how do they differ? How would you choose between the two to get treatment for a psychological problem you may be experiencing?

Answers to Evaluate Questions 1. 1-c, 2-a, 3-d, 4-b; 2. defense mechanisms; 3. manifest, latent; 4. a

KEY TERMS

Psychotherapy   LO36.1

Biomedical therapy   LO36.1

Psychodynamic therapy   LO36.1

Psychoanalysis   LO36.1

Transference   LO36.1

Behavioral treatment approaches   LO36.2

Aversive conditioning   LO36.2

Systematic desensitization   LO36.2

Flooding   LO36.2

Cognitive treatment approaches   LO36.3

Cognitive-behavioral approach   LO36.3

Rational-emotive behavior therapy   LO36.3

Psychotherapy
Humanistic, Interpersonal, and Group Approaches to Treatment

Learning Outcomes  Prepare

》 **LO37.1** Discuss the humanistic approaches to therapy.

》 **LO37.2** Illustrate interpersonal therapy.

》 **LO37.3** Explain group therapy, family therapy, and self-help groups.

》 **LO37.4** Assess the effectiveness of psychotherapy.

MODULE OUTLINE  Organize

Humanistic Therapy

Interpersonal Therapy

Group Therapy, Family Therapy, and Self-Help Groups

Evaluating Psychotherapy: Does Therapy Work?

Exploring Diversity: Racial and Ethnic Factors in Treatment: Should Therapists Be Color-Blind?

 Work

》 LO37.1 Humanistic Therapy

As you know from your own experience, a student cannot master the material covered in a course without some hard work, no matter how good the teacher and the textbook are. *You* must take the time to study, memorize the vocabulary, and learn the concepts. Nobody else can do it for you. If you choose to put in the effort, you'll succeed; if you don't, you'll fail. The responsibility is primarily yours.

Humanistic therapy draws on this philosophical perspective of self-responsibility in developing treatment techniques. The many different types of therapy that fit into this category have a similar rationale: we have control of our own behavior, we can make choices about the kinds of lives we want to live, and it is up to us to solve the difficulties we encounter in our daily lives.

Humanistic therapists believe that people naturally are motivated to strive for self-actualization. As we discussed in the chapter on motivation, *self-actualization* is the term that clinical psychologist Abraham Maslow used to describe the state of self-fulfillment in which people realize their highest potentials, each in their own unique way.

> **humanistic therapy** Therapy in which the underlying rationale is that people have control of their behavior, can make choices about their lives, and are essentially responsible for solving their own problems

Instead of acting in the more directive manner of some psychodynamic and behavioral approaches, humanistic therapists view themselves as guides or facilitators. Therapists using humanistic techniques seek to help people understand themselves and find ways to come closer to the ideal they hold for themselves. In this view, psychological disorders result from the inability to find meaning in life, from the feelings of loneliness, and from a lack of connection to others (Cain, 2002; Schneider & Krug, 2010; Lewis & Umbreit, 2015).

> **Therapists using humanistic techniques seek to help people understand themselves and find ways to come closer to the ideal they hold for themselves.**

Person-Centered Therapy

Person-centered therapy (also called *client-centered therapy*) aims to enable people to reach their potential for self-actualization. By providing a warm and accepting environment, therapists hope to motivate clients to air their problems and feelings. In turn, this enables clients to make realistic and constructive choices and decisions about the things that bother them in their current lives (Bozarth, Zimring, & Tausch, 2002; Kirschenbaum, 2004; Bohart, 2006).

Instead of directing the choices clients make, therapists provide what Carl Rogers calls *unconditional positive regard*—expressing acceptance and understanding, regardless of the feelings and attitudes the client expresses. By doing this, therapists hope to create an atmosphere that enables clients to come to decisions that can improve their lives (Kirschenbaum & Jourdan, 2005; Vieira & Freire, 2006; Cain, 2010).

Furnishing unconditional positive regard does not mean that therapists must approve of everything their clients say or do. Rather, therapists need to communicate that they are caring, nonjudgmental, and *empathetic*—understanding of a client's emotional experiences (Fearing & Clark, 2000).

Evaluating Humanistic Approaches to Therapy

The notion that psychological disorders result from restricted growth potential appeals philosophically to many people. Furthermore, when humanistic therapists acknowledge that the freedom we possess can lead to psychological difficulties, clients find an unusually supportive environment for therapy. In turn, this atmosphere can help clients discover solutions to difficult psychological problems.

However, humanistic treatments lack specificity, a problem that has troubled their critics. Humanistic approaches are not very precise and are probably the least scientifically and theoretically developed type of treatment. Moreover, this form of treatment works best for the same type of highly verbal client who profits most from psychoanalytic treatment.

person-centered therapy Therapy in which the goal is to reach one's potential for self-actualization

interpersonal therapy (IPT) Short-term therapy designed to help patients control their moods and emotions by focusing on the context of their current social relationships

> **STUDY ALERT**
>
> To better remember the concept of unconditional positive regard, try offering it to a friend during a conversation by showing your support, acceptance, and understanding no matter what thought or attitude is being offered.

» LO37.2 Interpersonal Therapy

Interpersonal therapy (IPT) is short-term therapy designed to help patients control their moods and emotions by focusing on the context of their current social relationships. Although its roots stem from psychodynamic approaches, IPT concentrates more on the here and now with the goal of improving a client's current relationships. It typically focuses on interpersonal issues such as conflicts with others, social skills issues, role transitions (such as divorce), or grief (Safran, Eubanks-Carter, & Muran, 2010; Braaten, 2011; Tao & Banh, 2016).

Interpersonal therapy is more active and directive than traditional psychodynamic approaches, and sessions are more structured. The approach makes no assumptions about the underlying causes of psychological disorders, but focuses on the interpersonal context in which a disorder is developed and maintained. It also tends to be shorter than traditional psychodynamic approaches and typically lasts only 12 to 16 weeks. During those sessions, therapists make concrete suggestions on improving relations with others, offering recommendations and advice.

Interpersonal Therapy (IPT) is a form of short-term therapy that helps patients control their moods and emotions in the context of their social relationships. © sturti/ Getty Images RF

Because IPT is short and structured, researchers have been able to demonstrate its effectiveness more readily than longer-term types of therapy. Evaluations of the approach have shown that IPT is especially effective in dealing with depression, anxiety, addictions, and eating disorders (Grigoriadis & Ravitz, 2007; Miller et al., 2008; Bohn et al., 2013).

» LO37.3 Group Therapy, Family Therapy, and Self-Help Groups

group therapy Therapy in which people meet with a therapist to discuss problems with a group

Although most treatment takes place between a single individual and a therapist, some forms of therapy involve groups of people seeking treatment. In **group therapy,** several unrelated people meet with a therapist to discuss some aspect of their psychological functioning.

People typically discuss with the group their problems, which often center on a common difficulty, such as alcoholism or a lack of social skills. The other members of the group provide emotional support and dispense advice on ways in which they have coped effectively with similar problems (Alonso, Alonso, & Piper, 2003; Scaturo, 2004; Rigby & Waite, 2007).

Groups vary greatly in terms of the particular model they employ; there are psychoanalytic groups, humanistic groups, and groups corresponding to the other therapeutic approaches. Furthermore, groups also differ with regard to the degree of guidance the therapist provides. In some, the therapist is quite directive, whereas in others, the members of the group set their own agenda and determine how the group will proceed (Stockton, Morran, & Krieger, 2004; Watanabe et al., 2010; Uliaszek et al., 2016).

Because several people are treated simultaneously in group therapy, it is a much more economical means of treatment than individual psychotherapy. On the other hand, critics argue that group settings lack the individual attention inherent in one-to-one therapy, and that especially shy and withdrawn individuals may not receive the attention they need in a group setting.

Tom Cheney/The New Yorker Collection/The Cartoon Bank

"So, would anyone in the group care to respond to what Clifford has just shared with us?"

Family therapy is often viewed as a good way for families to reopen lines of communication. Is this something you think would work in every family? Why or why not? © Bruce Ayres/Getty Images

Family Therapy

One specialized form of group therapy is family therapy. As the name implies, **family therapy** involves two or more family members, one (or more) of whose problems led to treatment. But rather than focusing simply on the members of the family who present the initial problem, family therapists consider the family as a unit, to which each member contributes. By meeting with the entire family simultaneously, family therapists try to understand how the family members interact with one another (Cooklin, 2000; Strong & Tomm, 2007; Lebow & Slesinge, 2016).

Family therapists view the family as a "system," and they assume that individuals in the family cannot improve without understanding the conflicts found in interactions among family members. Thus, the therapist expects each member to contribute to the resolution of the problem being addressed.

family therapy An approach that focuses on the family and its dynamics

spontaneous remission Recovery without treatment

Self-Help Therapy

In many cases, group therapy does not involve a professional therapist. Instead, people with similar problems get together to discuss their shared feelings and experiences. For example, people who have recently experienced the death of a spouse might meet in a *bereavement support group,* or college students may get together to discuss their adjustment to college.

One of the best-known self-help groups is Alcoholics Anonymous (AA), designed to help members deal with alcohol-related problems. AA prescribes 12 steps that alcoholics must pass through on their road to recovery, beginning with an admission that they are alcoholics and powerless over alcohol. AA provides more treatment for alcoholics than any other therapy, and it and other 12-step programs (such as Narcotics Anonymous) can be as successful in treating alcohol and other substance-abuse problems (Galanter, 2007; Gossop, Stewart, & Marsden, 2008; Pagano et al., 2013).

» LO37.4 Evaluating Psychotherapy: Does Therapy Work?

The question of whether therapy is effective is complex. In fact, identifying the single most appropriate form of treatment is a difficult, and still unresolved, task for psychologists specializing in psychological disorders. In fact, even before considering whether one form of therapy works better than another, we need to determine whether therapy in any form effectively alleviates psychological disturbances.

Most psychologists agree: therapy does work. Several comprehensive reviews indicate that therapy brings about greater improvement than does no treatment at all, with the rate of **spontaneous remission** (recovery without treatment) being fairly low. In most cases, then, the symptoms of abnormal behavior do not go away by themselves if left untreated—although the issue continues to be hotly debated (Westen, Novotny, & Thompson-Brenner, 2004; Lutz et al., 2006).

Although most psychologists feel confident that psychotherapeutic treatment *in general* is more effective than no treatment at all, the question of whether any specific form of treatment is superior to any other has not been answered definitively (Westen, Novotny, & Thompson-Brenner, 2004; Abboud, 2005; Tyrer et al., 2015).

For instance, one classic study comparing the effectiveness of various approaches found that although success rates vary somewhat by treatment form, most treatments show fairly equal success rates. As Figure 1 indicates, the rates ranged from about 70 to 85 percent greater success for treated compared with

STUDY ALERT

Pay special attention to the discussion of (1) whether therapy is effective in general and (2) what specific types of therapy are effective, because it is a key issue for therapists.

Figure 1 Estimates of the effectiveness of different types of treatment, in comparison to control groups of untreated people (adapted from Smith, Glass, & Miller, 1980). The percentile score shows how much more effective a particular type of treatment is for the average patient than is no treatment. For example, people given psychodynamic treatment score, on average, more positively on outcome measures than about three-quarters of untreated people.

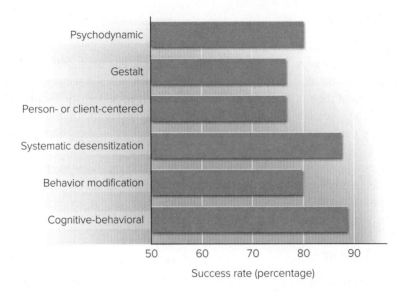

Success rate (percentage)

untreated individuals. Behavioral and cognitive approaches tended to be slightly more successful, but that result may have been due to differences in the severity of the cases treated (Smith, Glass, & Miller, 1980; Orwin & Condray, 1984).

Other research, which relies on *meta-analysis,* in which data from a large number of studies are statistically combined, yields similar general conclusions. Furthermore, a large survey of 186,000 individuals found that respondents felt they had benefited substantially from psychotherapy. However, there was little difference in "consumer satisfaction" on the basis of the specific type of treatment they had received (Seligman, 1995; Malouff, Thorsteinsson, & Schutte, 2007; Cuijpers et al., 2008).

In short, converging evidence allows us to draw several conclusions about the effectiveness of psychotherapy (Strupp & Binder, 1992; Seligman, 1996; Goldfried & Pachankis, 2007):

- *For most people, psychotherapy is effective.* This conclusion holds over different lengths of treatment, specific kinds of psychological disorders, and various types of treatment. Thus, the question "Does psychotherapy work?" appears to have been answered convincingly: it does (Westen et al., 2004; Olfson & Marcus, 2008; Gaudiano & Miller, 2013).

- *On the other hand, psychotherapy doesn't work for everyone.* As many as 10 percent of people treated show no improvement or actually deteriorate (Pretzer & Beck, 2005; Coffman et al., 2007; Lilienfeld, 2007).

- *No single form of therapy works best for every problem, and certain specific types of treatment are better, although not invariably, for specific types of problems.* For example, cognitive therapy works especially well for panic disorders, and flooding therapy relieves specific phobias effectively. However, there are exceptions to these generalizations, and often the differences in success rates for different types of treatment are not substantial (Miller & Magruder, 1999; Westen, Novotny, & Thompson-Brenner, 2004; Reinecke et al., 2011).

- *Most therapies share several basic similar elements.* Despite the fact that the specific methods used in different therapies are very different from one another, there are several common themes that lead them to be effective. These elements include the opportunity for a client to develop a positive relationship with a therapist, an explanation or interpretation of a client's symptoms, and confrontation of negative emotions. The fact that these common elements exist in most therapies makes it difficult to compare one treatment against another (Norcross, 2002; Norcross, Beutler, & Levant, 2006).

Consequently, there is no single, definitive answer to the broad question "Which therapy works best?" because of the complexity in sorting out the various factors that enter into successful therapy. Recently, however, clinicians and researchers have reframed the question by focusing on evidence-based psychotherapy practice. *Evidence-based psychotherapy practice* seeks to use the research literature to determine the best practices for treating a specific disorder. To determine best practices, researchers use clinical interviews, client self-reports of improvement in quality of life, reductions in symptoms, observations of behavior, and other outcomes to compare different therapies. By using objective research findings, clinicians are increasingly able to determine the most effective treatment for a specific disorder (APA Presidential Task Force, 2006; Brownlee, 2007; Kazdin, 2008).

Because no single type of psychotherapy is invariably effective for every individual, some therapists use an eclectic approach to therapy. In an *eclectic approach to therapy,* therapists use a variety of techniques, integrating several perspectives, to treat a person's problems. By employing more than one approach, therapists can choose the appropriate mix of evidence-based treatments to match the individual's specific needs. Furthermore, therapists with certain personal characteristics may work better with particular individuals and types of treatments, and—as we consider next—even racial and ethnic factors may be related to the success of treatment (Chambless et al., 2006; Hays, 2008; Kertz et al., 2015).

EXPLORING diversity

Racial and Ethnic Factors in Treatment: Should Therapists Be Color-Blind?

Consider the following case report, written by a school counselor about Jimmy Jones, a 12-year-old student who was referred to a counselor because of his lack of interest in schoolwork:

> Jimmy does not pay attention, daydreams often, and frequently falls asleep during class. There is a strong possibility that Jimmy is harboring repressed rage that needs to be ventilated and dealt with. His inability to directly express his anger had led him to adopt passive aggressive means of expressing hostility, i.e., inattentiveness, daydreaming, falling asleep. It is recommended that Jimmy be seen for intensive counseling to discover the basis of the anger. (Sue & Sue, 1990)

The counselor was wrong, however. Rather than suffering from "repressed rage," Jimmy lived in a poverty-stricken and disorganized home. Because of overcrowding at his house, he did not get enough sleep and consequently was tired the next day. Frequently, he was also hungry. In short, the stresses arising from his environment and not any deep-seated psychological disturbances caused his problems.

This incident underscores the importance of taking people's environmental and cultural backgrounds into account during treatment for psychological disorders. In particular, members of racial and ethnic minority groups, especially those who are also poor, may behave in ways that help them deal with a society that discriminates against them. As a consequence, behavior that may signal psychological disorder in middle-class and upper-class whites may simply be adaptive in people from other racial and socioeconomic groups. For instance, characteristically suspicious and distrustful people may be displaying a survival strategy to protect themselves from psychological and physical injury, rather than suffering from a psychological disturbance (Paniagua, 2000; Tseng, 2003; Pottick et al., 2007).

In fact, therapists must question some basic assumptions of psychotherapy when dealing with racial, ethnic, and cultural minority-group members. For example, compared with the dominant culture, Asian and Latino cultures typically place much greater emphasis on the group, family, and society. When an Asian or Latino faces a critical decision, the family helps make it—a cultural practice suggesting that family members should also play a role in psychological treatment. Similarly, the traditional Chinese recommendation for dealing with depression or anxiety is to urge people who experience such problems to avoid thinking about whatever is upsetting them. Consider how this advice contrasts with treatment approaches that emphasize the value of insight (Ponterotto, Gretchen, & Chauhan, 2001; McCarthy, 2005; Leitner, 2007).

Clearly, therapists cannot be "color-blind." Instead, they must take into account the racial, ethnic, cultural, and social class backgrounds of their clients in determining the nature of a psychological disorder and the course of treatment (Pedersen et al., 2002; Hays, 2008; Moodley, Gielen, & Wu, 2013).

RECAP

Discuss the humanistic approaches to therapy.

- Humanistic therapy is based on the premise that people have control of their behavior, that they can make choices about their lives, and that it is up to them to solve their own problems. Humanistic therapies, which take a nondirective approach, include person-centered therapy.

Illustrate interpersonal therapy.

- Interpersonal therapy considers therapy in the context of social relationships.
- It concentrates on improving a client's current relationships.

Explain group therapy, family therapy, and self-help groups.

- In group therapy, several unrelated people meet with a therapist to discuss some aspect of their psychological functioning, often centering on a common problem.

Assess the effectiveness of psychotherapy.

- Most research suggests that, in general, therapy is more effective than no therapy, although how much more effective is not known.
- The more difficult question of which therapy works best is harder to answer, but it is clear particular kinds of therapy are more appropriate for some problems than for others.
- Because no single type of psychotherapy is invariably effective, eclectic approaches, in which a therapist uses a variety of techniques, integrating several perspectives, are sometimes used.

1. Match each of the following treatment strategies with the statement you might expect to hear from a therapist using that strategy.

   1. Group therapy
   2. Unconditional positive regard
   3. Behavioral therapy
   4. Nondirective counseling

   a. "In other words, you don't get along with your mother because she hates your girlfriend, is that right?"

   b. "I want you all to take turns talking about why you decided to come and what you hope to gain from therapy."

   c. "I can understand why you wanted to wreck your friend's car after she hurt your feelings. Now tell me more about the accident."

   d. "That's not appropriate behavior. Let's work on replacing it with something else."

2. _____ therapies assume that people should take responsibility for their lives and the decisions they make.

3. One of the major criticisms of humanistic therapies is that

   a. They are too imprecise and unstructured.

   b. They treat only the symptom of the problem.

   c. The therapist dominates the patient-therapist interaction.

   d. They work well only on clients of lower socioeconomic status.

4. In a controversial study, Eysenck found that some people go into _____ _____, or recovery without treatment, if they are simply left alone instead of treated.

RETHINK R Rethink

How can people be successfully treated in group therapy when individuals with the "same" problem are so different? What advantages might group therapy offer over individual therapy?

Answers to Evaluate Questions 1. 1-b, 2-c, 3-d, 4-a; 2. humanistic; 3. a; 4. spontaneous remission

KEY TERMS

Humanistic therapy   LO37.1

Person-centered therapy   LO37.1

Interpersonal therapy (IPT)   LO37.2

Group therapy   LO37.3

Family therapy   LO37.3

Spontaneous remission   LO37.4

Biomedical Therapy
Biological Approaches to Treatment

Learning Outcomes  Prepare

》 **LO38.1** Discuss options for drug therapy.

》 **LO38.2** Explain electroconvulsive therapy.

》 **LO38.3** Offer perspective on biomedical therapies.

》 **LO38.4** Discuss the community psychology movement.

MODULE OUTLINE  Organize

Drug Therapy

Try It! What Are Your Attitudes Toward Patient Rights?

Electroconvulsive Therapy (ECT)

Biomedical Therapies in Perspective

Community Psychology: Focus on Prevention

Becoming an Informed Consumer of Psychology: Choosing the Right Therapist

 Work

If you get a kidney infection, your doctor gives you an antibiotic and with luck, about a week later, your kidney should be as good as new. If your appendix becomes inflamed, a surgeon removes it and your body functions normally once more. Could a comparable approach, focusing on the body's physiology, be effective for psychological disturbances?

According to biological approaches to treatment, the answer is yes. Therapists routinely use biomedical therapies that rely on drugs and medical procedures to improve psychological functioning.

The biomedical approach avoids focusing on a patient's psychological conflicts, past traumas, or other factors in a patient's environment that may produce psychological disorder. Instead, it focuses treatment directly on altering brain chemistry or other neurological factors. To do this, therapists can provide treatment with drugs, electric shock, or surgery, as we will discuss.

drug therapy Treatment of psychological disorders through the use of drugs

antipsychotic drugs Drugs that temporarily reduce psychotic symptoms such as agitation, hallucinations, and delusions

》 LO38.1 Drug Therapy

Drug therapy is the treatment of psychological disorders using drugs. Drug therapy works by altering the operation of neurons and neurotransmitters in the brain.

Some drugs operate by inhibiting neurotransmitters or receptor neurons, which reduces activity at particular synapses. (Remember that synapses are the gaps where nerve impulses travel from one neuron to another.) Thus, particular neurons are inhibited from firing.

Other drugs do just the opposite: they increase the activity of certain neurotransmitters or neurons, allowing particular neurons to fire more frequently (see Figure 1).

Antipsychotic Drugs

Probably no greater change has occurred in mental hospitals than the successful introduction in the mid-1950s of **antipsychotic drugs**—drugs used to reduce

STUDY ALERT

To organize your study of the different drugs, review Figure 1, which classifies them in the categories of antipsychotic, antidepressant, mood-stabilizing, and antianxiety drugs.

Drug Treatments			
Class of Drug	**Effects of Drug**	**Primary Action of Drug**	**Examples**
Antipsychotic drugs	Reduction in loss of touch with reality, agitation	Block dopamine receptors	Chlorpromazine (Thorazine®), clozapine (Clozaril®), haloperidol (Haldol®)
Antidepressant drugs			
Tricyclic	Reduction in depression	Permit rise in neurotransmitters such as norepinepherine	Trazodone (Desyrel), amitriptyline (Elavil), desipramine (Norpramin®)
MAO inhibitors	Reduction in depression	Prevent MAO from breaking down neurotransmitters	Phenelzine (Nardil®), tranylcypromine (Parnate®)
Selective serotonin reuptake inhibitors (SSRIs)	Reduction in depression	Inhibit reuptake of serotonin	Fluoxetine (Prozac®), Luvox, Paxil®, Celexa®, Zoloft® nefazodone (Serzone)
Mood stabilizers			
Lithium	Mood stabilization	Can alter transmission of impulses within neurons	Lithium (Lithonate), Depakote®, Tegretol®
Antianxiety drugs	Reduction in anxiety	Increase activity of neurotransmitter GABA	Benzodiazepines (Valium®, Xanax®)

Figure 1   The major classes of drugs used to treat psychological disorders have different effects on the brain and nervous system. © Stockdisc/PunchStock RF

severe symptoms of disturbance, such as loss of touch with reality and agitation. Previously, the typical mental hospital wasn't very different from the stereotypical nineteenth-century insane asylum, giving mainly custodial care to screaming, moaning, clawing patients who displayed bizarre behaviors. Suddenly, in just a matter of days after hospital staff members administered antipsychotic drugs, the wards became considerably calmer environments in which professionals could do more than just try to get patients through the day without causing serious harm to themselves or others.

This dramatic change came about through the introduction of the drug *chlorpromazine.* Along with other similar drugs, chlorpromazine rapidly became the most popular and successful treatment for schizophrenia. Today drug therapy is the preferred treatment for most cases of severely abnormal behavior and, as such, is used for most patients hospitalized with psychological disorders. The newest generation of antipsychotics, referred to as *atypical antipsychotics,* have fewer side effects (Savas, Yumru, & Kaya, 2007; Nasrallah et al., 2008; Selva-Vera et al., 2010).

How do antipsychotic drugs work? Most block dopamine receptors at the brain's synapses. Atypical antipsychotics affect both serotonin and dopamine levels in the brain, particularly those related to planning and goal-directed activity (Sawa & Snyder, 2002; Advokat, 2005; Mizrahi et al., 2011).

Despite the effectiveness of antipsychotic drugs, most of the time the symptoms reappear when the drug is withdrawn. Furthermore, such drugs can have long-term side effects, such as dryness of the mouth and throat, that may continue after drug treatments are stopped (Voruganti et al., 2007; Pijnenborg et al., 2015).

Antidepressant Drugs

As their name suggests, **antidepressant drugs** are a class of medications used in cases of severe depression to improve the patient's mood and feeling of well-being. They are also sometimes used for other disorders, such as anxiety disorders and bulimia (Walsh et al., 2006; Hedges et al., 2007).

As a surgical technician or surgical LPN, the need to have patients off their medications prior to surgery can become an issue when withdrawal can trigger psychological symptoms. © PhotoLink/Getty Images RF

antidepressant drugs Medications that improve a severely depressed patient's mood and feeling of well-being

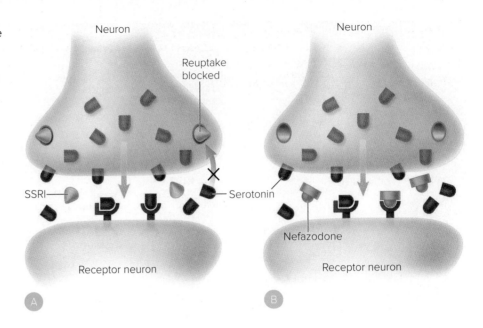

Figure 2 In (A), selective serotonin reuptake inhibitors (SSRIs) reduce depression by permitting the neurotransmitter serotonin to remain in the synapse. In (B), a newer antidepressant, nefazodone (Serzone), operates more selectively to block serotonin at some sites but not others, helping to reduce the side effects of the drug. Source: Based on Mischoulon, 2000.

Neuron

Neuron

Reuptake blocked

SSRI

Serotonin

Nefazodone

Receptor neuron

Receptor neuron

A

B

Most antidepressant drugs work by changing the concentration of specific neurotransmitters in the brain. For example, *tricyclic drugs* increase the availability of norepinephrine at the synapses of neurons, whereas *MAO inhibitors* prevent the enzyme monoamine oxidase (MAO) from breaking down neurotransmitters. Newer antidepressants—such as escitalopram (Lexapro)—are *selective serotonin reuptake inhibitors* (SSRIs). SSRIs target the neurotransmitter serotonin and permit it to linger at the synapse. Some antidepressants produce a combination of effects. For instance, nefazodone (Serzone) blocks serotonin at some receptor sites but not others, while bupropion (Wellbutrin and Zyban) affects the norepinephrine and dopamine systems (see Figure 2; Lucki & O'Leary, 2004; Robinson, 2007; Dhillon, Yang, & Curran, 2008).

Finally, there are some newer drugs on the horizon. For instance, scientists have found that the anesthetic *ketamine* blocks the neural receptor NMDA, which affects the neurotransmitter *glutamate*. Glutamate plays an important role in mood regulation and the ability to experience pleasure, and researchers believe that ketamine blockers may prove to be useful in the treatment of depression (Schwartzmant, Alexander, & Grothusen, 2011; Li et al., 2016).

The overall success of antidepressant drugs are good. In fact, antidepressants can produce lasting, long-term recovery from depression. In many cases, even after patients stop taking the drugs, their depression does not return. On the other hand, antidepressant drugs may produce side effects such as drowsiness and faintness, and there is evidence that SSRI antidepressants can increase the risk of suicide in children and adolescents (Olfson & Marcus, 2008; Daray, Thommi, & Ghaemi, 2010; Prus et al., 2015).

Another drug that has received a great deal of publicity is *St. John's wort,* an herb that some have called a "natural" antidepressant. Although it is widely used in Europe for the treatment of depression, the U.S. Food and Drug Administration considers it a dietary supplement, and therefore the substance is available here without a prescription.

Despite the popularity of St. John's wort, some clinical tests have found that the herb is ineffective in the treatment of depression. However, because other research shows that the herb successfully reduces certain

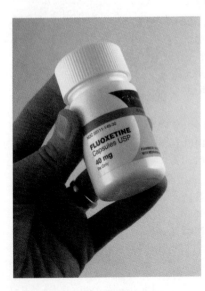

Fluoxetine, also known as Prozac®, is a widely prescribed—but still controversial—antidepressant. © McGraw-Hill Education/Jill Braaten

symptoms of depression, some proponents argue that using it is reasonable. Clearly, people should not use St. John's wort to medicate themselves without consulting a mental health care professional (Shelton et al., 2002; Thachil, Mohan, & Bhugra, 2007; Mannel et al., 2010).

Mood Stabilizers

Mood stabilizers are used to treat mood disorders. For example, the drug lithium, a form of mineral salts, has been used very successfully in patients with bipolar disorders. Although no one knows definitely why, lithium and other mood stabilizers such as divalproex sodium (Depakote®) and carbamazepine (Tegretol®) effectively reduce manic episodes. However, they do not effectively treat depressive phases of bipolar disorder, so antidepressants are usually prescribed during those phases (Smith et al., 2007; Salvi et al., 2008; Nivoli et al., 2011).

Lithium and similar drugs have a quality that sets them apart from other drug treatments: they can be a *preventive* treatment that blocks future episodes of manic depression. Often, people who have had episodes of bipolar disorder can take a daily dose of lithium to prevent a recurrence of their symptoms. Most other drugs are useful only when symptoms of psychological disturbance occur.

mood stabilizers Drugs used to treat mood disorders that prevent manic episodes of bipolar disorder

antianxiety drugs Drugs that reduce the level of anxiety a person experiences, essentially by reducing excitability and increasing feelings of well-being

Antianxiety Drugs

As the name implies, **antianxiety drugs** reduce the level of anxiety a person experiences and increase feelings of well-being. They are prescribed not only to reduce general tension in people who are experiencing temporary difficulties but also to aid in the treatment of more serious anxiety disorders (Zito, 1993).

Antianxiety drugs such as Xanax® and Valium are among the medications physicians most frequently prescribe. In fact, more than half of all U.S. families have someone who has taken such a drug at one time or another.

Although the popularity of antianxiety drugs suggests that they hold few risks, they can produce a number of potentially serious side effects. For instance, they can cause fatigue, and long-term use can lead to dependence. Moreover, when taken in combination with alcohol, some antianxiety drugs can be lethal. But a more important issue concerns their use to suppress anxiety. Almost every therapeutic approach to psychological disturbance views continuing anxiety as a signal of some other sort of problem. Thus, drugs that mask anxiety may simply be hiding other difficulties. Consequently, rather than confronting their underlying problems, people may be hiding from them through the use of antianxiety drugs.

© Comstock/Getty Images RF

From the perspective of . . .

A Legal Assistant Imagine that you're working in a high-stress office and you're having difficulty managing your anxiety. A colleague suggests that you see the staff nurse to get a prescription for an antianxiety drug. Would this action be advisable? Why or why not?

(To get a sense of your attitudes toward the use of drugs in the treatment of psychological disorders and how much control you think patients should have over their treatment, complete the accompanying Try It! questionnaire to explore your feelings about patients' rights.)

Try It!

What Are Your Attitudes Toward Patient Rights?

Check off whether you Agree or Disagree with each of the following statements:

1. Patients should have the right to refuse psychotropic medications. Agree or Disagree?
2. Staff at mental hospitals should give patients medications, even if the patient doesn't want to take the medication. Agree or Disagree?
3. There are circumstances under which psychologists and other mental health specialists have the right to confine a patient to a mental institution against the patient's will. Agree or Disagree?
4. Patients should be active partners in planning the goals for treatment and choosing particular kinds of treatments. Agree or Disagree?
5. Patients should have the right to stop or refuse psychotherapy. Agree or Disagree?
6. Therapists should have the right to force patients to participate in certain kinds of activities. Agree or Disagree?
7. Therapists should have the right to force hospitalization against an individual's wishes if they pose a threat to themselves or to others. Agree or Disagree?
8. A therapist should be allowed to give information about a patient's mental state to a spouse or other loved one, even if the patient does not wish for that information to be divulged, if the therapist feels it is in the patient's best interests. Agree or Disagree?
9. Patients should be told about the drugs or other treatments that they are being given, even if they do not fully understand what they are being told. Agree or Disagree?
10. There are circumstances under which patients in mental institutions should be prevented from having visitors. Agree or Disagree?
11. Patients should have the right to demand the specific treatment that they want and be allowed to refuse specific treatments. Agree or Disagree?

Scoring

For questions 1, 4, 5, 9, and 11, if you agreed with four or five of these, you tend to believe that patients have the right to participate in decisions regarding their own treatment, and the right to choose the treatments that they believe are best. If you agreed with four or more of questions 2, 3, 6, 7, 8, and 10, you tend to consider health care providers' opinions to hold more weight than a patient's wishes, and therefore the providers' views should be followed even over a patient's objections.

Keep in mind that you may have a mix of answers, or you may have found some of the questions difficult to answer with a clear yes or no. Doctors, caregivers, and patients struggle with these same questions in the quest to balance the rights of patients with the need to ensure safety.

Source: Adapted from Roe et al., 2002.

First introduced in the 1930s, **electroconvulsive therapy (ECT)** is a procedure used in the treatment of severe depression. In the procedure, an electric current of 70 to 150 volts is briefly administered to a patient's head and causes a loss of consciousness and causes seizures. Typically, health care professionals sedate patients and give them muscle relaxants before administering the current, and such preparations help reduce the intensity of muscle contractions produced during ECT. The typical patient receives about 10 such treatments in the course of a month, but some patients continue with maintenance treatments for months afterward (Stevens & Harper, 2007; Heijnen et al., 2010; Freudenreich & Goff, 2011).

ECT is a controversial technique. Apart from the obvious distastefulness of a treatment that evokes images of electrocution, side effects occur frequently. For instance, after treatment patients often experience disorientation, confusion, and sometimes memory loss that may remain for months. Furthermore, ECT often does not produce long-term improvement; one study found that without follow-up medication, depression returned in most patients who had undergone ECT treatments. Finally, even when ECT does work, we do not know why, and some critics believe it may cause permanent brain damage (Gardner & O'Connor, 2008; Kato, 2009; Weiner & Falcone, 2011).

In light of the drawbacks to ECT, why do therapists use it at all? Basically, they use it because, in many severe cases of depression, it offers the only quickly effective treatment. For instance, it may prevent depressed, suicidal individuals from committing suicide, and it can act more quickly than antidepressive medications.

The use of ECT has risen in the last decade with more than 100,000 people undergoing it each year. Still, ECT tends to be used only when other treatments have proved ineffective, and researchers continue to search for alternative treatments (Eranti & McLoughlin, 2003; Pandya, Pozuelo, & Malone, 2007; Tokutsu et al., 2013).

One new and promising alternative to ECT is **transcranial magnetic stimulation (TMS)**. TMS creates a precise magnetic pulse in a specific area of the brain. By activating particular neurons, TMS has been effective in relieving the symptoms of depression in a number of controlled experiments. However, the therapy can produce side effects, such as seizures and convulsions, and it is still considered experimental by the government (Leo & Latif, 2007; Kim, Pesiridou, & O'Reardon, 2009; Croarkin et al., 2010).

Another promising therapy, still in the early stages of development, is the use of implants placed deep inside the brain to provide a short jolt of electrical stimulation, a method called *deep brain stimulation (DBS)*. (DBS was the treatment Marjorie Stowe received, as discussed in the chapter.)

Unlike ECT, which involves the entire brain, DBS pinpoints specific, tiny regions of the brain to receive a short burst of electrical stimulation to provide relief from major depression. Deep-brain stimulation is not yet ready for routine use as a treatment for depression. But it does offer tremendous new hope as a potential treatment, not only for depression, but potentially for other mental disorders, including bipolar disorder and Alzheimer's disease (Sankar, Lipsman, & Lozano, 2014; Lozano & Mayberg, 2015; Sun et al., 2015).

Psychosurgery

If ECT strikes you as a questionable procedure, the use of **psychosurgery**—brain surgery in which the object is to reduce symptoms of mental disorder—probably

electroconvulsive therapy (ECT) A procedure used in the treatment of severe depression in which an electric current of 70 to 150 volts is briefly administered to a patient's head

transcranial magnetic stimulation (TMS) A depression treatment in which a precise magnetic pulse is directed to a specific area of the brain

psychosurgery Brain surgery once used to reduce the symptoms of mental disorder but rarely used today

appears even more dubious. A technique used only rarely today, psychosurgery was introduced as a "treatment of last resort" in the 1930s.

The initial form of psychosurgery, a *prefrontal lobotomy,* consisted of surgically destroying or removing parts of a patient's frontal lobes, which surgeons thought controlled emotionality. In the 1930s and 1940s, surgeons performed the procedure on thousands of patients often with little precision. For example, in one common technique, a surgeon would jab an ice pick under a patient's eyeball and swivel it back and forth (Ogren & Sandlund, 2007; Phillips, 2013; Chodakiewitz et al., 2015).

Psychosurgery often did improve a patient's behavior—but not without drastic side effects. Along with remission of the symptoms of the mental disorder, patients sometimes experienced personality changes and became bland, colorless, and unemotional. In other cases, patients became aggressive and unable to control their impulses. In the worst cases, treatment resulted in the patient's death.

With the introduction of effective drug treatments—and the obvious ethical questions regarding the appropriateness of forever altering someone's personality—psychosurgery became nearly obsolete. However, it is still used in very rare cases when all other procedures have failed and the patient's behavior presents a high risk to the patient and others.

For example, surgeons sometimes use a more precise form of psychosurgery called a *cingulotomy* in rare cases of obsessive-compulsive disorder in which they destroy tissue in the *anterior cingulate* area of the brain. In another technique, *gamma knife surgery,* beams of radiation are used to destroy areas of the brain. Finally, on rare occasions, dying patients with severe, uncontrollable pain also receive psychosurgery. Still, even these cases raise important ethical issues, and psychosurgery remains a highly controversial treatment (Lopes et al, 2009; Wilkinson, 2009; Eljamel, 2015).

> In some respects, no greater revolution has occurred in the field of mental health than biological approaches to treatment.

If you had a loved one suffering from major depressive disorder, how would you feel about him or her undergoing ECT or TMS treatments? © Hans Neleman/Getty Images

LO38.3 Biomedical Therapies in Perspective

In some respects, no greater revolution has occurred in the field of mental health than biological approaches to treatment. As previously violent, uncontrollable patients have been calmed by the use of drugs, mental hospitals have been able to concentrate more on actually helping patients and less on custodial functions. Similarly, patients whose lives have been disrupted by depression or bipolar episodes have been able to function normally, and other forms of drug therapy have also shown remarkable results.

Furthermore, new forms of biomedical therapy are promising. For example, the newest treatment possibility—which remains experimental at this point—is gene therapy. As we discussed when considering behavioral genetics, specific genes may be introduced to particular regions of the brain. These genes then have the potential to reverse or even prevent biochemical events that give rise to psychological disorders (Sapolsky, 2003; Lymberis et al., 2004; Tuszynski, 2007).

Despite their current usefulness and future promise, biomedical therapies do not represent a cure-all for psychological disorders. For one thing, critics charge that such therapies merely provide relief of the *symptoms* of mental disorder; as soon as the drugs are withdrawn, the symptoms return. Although it is considered a major step in the right direction, biomedical treatment may not solve the underlying problems that led a patient to therapy in the first place. Biomedical therapies also can produce side effects, ranging from minor to serious physical reactions to the development of *new* symptoms of abnormal behavior. Finally, an overreliance on biomedical therapies may lead therapists to overlook alternative forms of treatment that may be helpful.

Still, biomedical therapies—sometimes alone and more often in conjunction with psychotherapy—have permitted millions of people to function more effectively. Furthermore, although biomedical therapy and psychotherapy appear distinct, research shows that biomedical therapies ultimately may not be as different from talk therapies as one might imagine, at least in terms of their consequences.

community psychology A branch of psychology that focuses on the prevention and minimization of psychological disorders in the community

deinstitutionalization The transfer of former mental patients from institutions to the community

» LO38.4 Community Psychology: Focus on Prevention

Each of the treatments we have reviewed has a common element: It is a "restorative" treatment, aimed at alleviating psychological difficulties that already exist. However, an approach known as **community psychology** has a different aim: to prevent or minimize the incidence of psychological disorders.

Community psychology came of age in the 1960s, when mental health professionals developed plans for a nationwide network of community mental health centers. The hope was that those centers would provide low-cost mental health services, including short-term therapy and community educational programs. In another development, the population of mental hospitals has plunged as drug treatments made physical restraint of patients unnecessary (Schruijer & Stephenson, 2010; Perry et al., 2011).

This transfer of former mental patients out of institutions and into the community—a process known as **deinstitutionalization**—was encouraged by the growth of the community psychology movement (see Figure 3). Proponents of deinstitutionalization wanted to ensure not only that deinstitutionalized patients received proper treatment but also that their civil rights were maintained (St. Dennis et al., 2006; Henckes, 2011; Pow et al., 2015).

Unfortunately, the promise of deinstitutionalization has not been met, largely because insufficient resources are

Although deinstitutionalization has had many successes, it has also contributed to the release of mental patients into the community with little or no support. As a result, many have become homeless. © McGraw-Hill Education/ Gary He

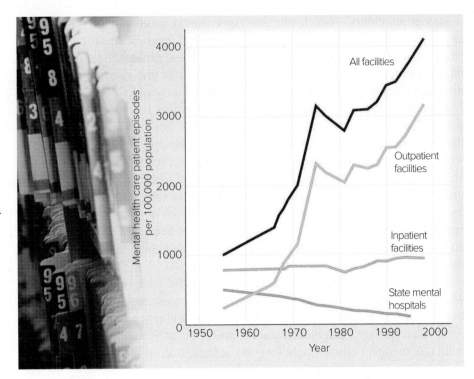

Figure 3 As deinstitutionalization has become more prevalent over the last 50 years, the number of patients being treated in state mental hospitals has declined significantly, while the number of outpatient facilities has increased. Source: National Mental Health Information Center, U.S. Department of Health and Human Services, reprinted in *Scientific American,* December, 2002, p. 38. Photo: © Steven Peters/Getty Images.

provided to deinstitutionalized patients. What started as a worthy attempt to move people out of mental institutions and into the community ended, in many cases, with former patients being dumped into the community without any real support. Many became homeless—between a third and a half of all homeless adults are thought to have a major psychological disorder—and some became involved in illegal acts caused by their disorders. In short, many people who need treatment do not get it, and in some cases care for people with psychological disorders has simply shifted from one type of treatment site to another (Dumont & Dumont, 2008; Nielson, Staub & Price, 2009; Searight, 2013).

On the other hand, the community psychology movement has had some positive outcomes. Telephone "hotlines" are now common. At any time of the day or night, people experiencing acute stress can call a trained, sympathetic listener who can provide immediate—although obviously limited—treatment (Paukert, Stagner, & Hope, 2004; Cauce, 2007; Jarrett, 2015).

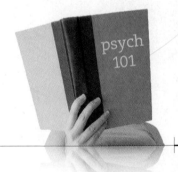

becoming an informed consumer
of psychology

Choosing the Right Therapist

If you decide to seek therapy, you're faced with a daunting task. Choosing a therapist is not a simple matter. One place to begin the process of identifying a therapist is at the "Help Center" of the American Psychological Association at www.apa.org/helpcenter. And, if you start therapy, several general guidelines can help you determine whether you've made the right choice:

You and your therapist should agree on the goals for treatment.

- *You and your therapist should agree on the goals for treatment.* They should be clear, specific, and attainable.

- *You should feel comfortable with your therapist.* You should not be intimidated by, or in awe of, a therapist. Instead, you should trust the therapist and feel free to discuss the most personal issues without fearing a negative reaction. In sum, the "personal chemistry" should be right.

- *Therapists should have appropriate training and credentials and should be licensed by appropriate state and local agencies.* Check therapists' membership in national and state professional associations. In addition, the cost of therapy, billing practices, and other business matters should be clear. It is not a breach of etiquette to put these matters on the table during an initial consultation.

- *You should feel that you are making progress after therapy has begun, despite occasional setbacks.* If you have no sense of improvement after repeated visits, you and your therapist should discuss this issue frankly. Although there is no set timetable, the most obvious changes resulting from therapy tend to occur relatively early in the course of treatment. For instance, half of patients in psychotherapy improve by the eighth session, and three-fourths by the 26th session (see Figure 4).

Be aware that you will have to put in a great deal of effort in therapy. Although our culture promises quick cures for any problem, in reality, solving difficult problems is not easy. You must be committed to making therapy work and should know that it is you, not the therapist, who must do most of the work to resolve your problems. The effort has the potential to pay off handsomely—as you experience a more positive, fulfilling, and meaningful life.

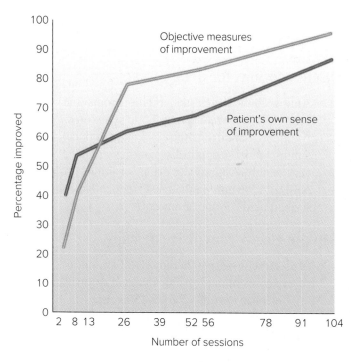

Figure 4 For most clients, improvements in psychological functioning occur relatively soon after therapy has begun. Source: Howard et al., 1986.

"Looking good!"

Gahan Wilson/The New Yorker Collection/The Cartoon Bank

RECAP

Discuss options for drug therapy.

- Antipsychotic drugs such as chlorpromazine very effectively reduce psychotic symptoms. Antidepressant drugs such as Prozac reduce depression so successfully that they are used very widely. Antianxiety drugs, or minor tranquilizers, are among the most frequently prescribed medications of any sort.

Explain electroconvulsive therapy.

- In electroconvulsive therapy (ECT), used in severe cases of depression, a patient receives a brief electric current of 70 to 150 volts.

Offer perspective on biomedical therapies.

- Biomedical treatment approaches suggest that therapy should focus on the physiological causes of abnormal behavior, rather than considering psychological factors. Drug therapy, the best example of biomedical treatments, has brought about dramatic reductions in the symptoms of mental disturbance.

Discuss the community psychology movement.

- The community psychology approach encouraged deinstitutionalization, in which previously hospitalized mental patients were released into the community.

[EVALUATE

1. Antipsychotic drugs have provided effective, long-term, and complete cures for schizophrenia. True or false?

2. One highly effective biomedical treatment for a psychological disorder, used mainly to treat bipolar disorder, is

    a. Chlorpromazine

    b. Lithium

    c. Librium

    d. Valium

3. The trend toward releasing more patients from mental hospitals and into the community is known as _____.

[RETHINK R Rethink

One of the main criticisms of biological therapies is that they treat the symptoms of mental disorder without uncovering and treating the underlying problems from which people are suffering. Do you agree with this criticism? Why?

Answers to Evaluate Questions 1. false; schizophrenia can be controlled, but not cured, by medication; 2. b; 3. deinstitutionalization

KEY TERMS

Drug therapy   LO38.1

Antipsychotic drugs   LO38.1

Antidepressant drugs   LO38.1

Mood stabilizers   LO38.1

Antianxiety drugs   LO38.1

Electroconvulsive therapy (ECT)   LO38.2

Transcranial magnetic stimulation (TMS)   LO38.2

Psychosurgery   LO38.2

Community psychology   LO38.4

Deinstitutionalization   LO38.4

Psychology on the Web

1. Investigate computer-assisted psychotherapy on the Web. Locate (a) a computerized therapy program, such as ELIZA, which offers "therapy" over the Internet, and (b) a report on "cybertherapy," in which therapists use the Web to interact with patients. Compare the two approaches, describing how each one works and relating it to the therapeutic approaches you have studied.

2. Find more information on the Web about deinstitutionalization. Try to find pro and con arguments about it and summarize the arguments, including your judgment of the effectiveness and advisability of deinstitutionalization as an approach to dealing with mental illness.

the case of . . .
TONY SCARPETTA, THE MAN WHO COULDN'T RELAX

Tony Scarpetta worked for over a decade as a freelance Web developer. He had a knack for putting his clients at ease and learning exactly what their needs were and delivering creative output to meet those needs. But Tony had a dark secret: Despite acting calm and in control around his clients, Tony often felt as if he were falling to pieces inside. His friendly banter masked a whirlwind of panicky thoughts ranging from "this new advertising director hates my work and I'm going to lose his company's business" to "what if my clients abandon me for a competitor and I can't attract any new business?"

Tony had been dealing with this kind of anxiety for years. Often it was helpful, as when it motivated him to push his creative boundaries and to work hard to please his customers. But in other ways it was a great hindrance, especially when irrational fears would distract him from his work or keep him up at night, leaving him feeling drained the next day. Tony would like to do something to relieve his anxiety, but he's not sure where to begin.

1. If you were Tony's friend, what advice would you give him for seeking out professional help with his anxiety? Where should he begin his search?

2. What kinds of therapies should Tony consider, and why? Are there any kinds of therapy that he should probably not consider?

3. What would be the benefits to Tony of seeing his family physician for a prescription for an antianxiety drug? What might be some disadvantages to taking that approach?

4. What could Tony expect if he visits a psychodynamically oriented therapist about his anxiety? What about if he sees a humanistic therapist?

5. What would a rational-emotive behavior therapist be likely to say to Tony during a therapy session?

profiles of SUCCESS

Courtesy of William Jess Greiner

NAME:	William Jess Greiner
SCHOOL:	Pima Medical Institute
DEGREE PROGRAMS:	AAS Fire Science, Central Community College of New Mexico; BS Emergency Management, University of New Mexico; AAS, Physical Therapy Assisting, Pima Medical Institute

All of us face transitions in life, but for William Jess Greiner, the transition he faced couldn't have been greater, or more challenging.

As a firefighter, which included activities such as parachuting from planes to reach fires, Greiner led a very active life. However, it all came to an abrupt end one day as the result of a serious accident. Although it left him wheelchair-bound for almost four years, it also led to a new future.

"Following my accident, I decided I wanted to start a new career," he explained. "I narrowed my choices down to the two occupations that had saved my life—nursing and physical therapy."

He settled on pursuing a career as a physical therapy assistant. He describes himself as "100 percent handi-capable" and is now a working disabled individual. But pursuing his new career demanded commitment and hard work.

"I had to re-learn how to be a student, learning a new language of sorts," he said, "and I needed to transition back to school."

According to Greiner, he found his physical challenges difficult to deal with and sought counseling for depression. While in counseling, he realized he felt challenged by those who felt his physical disabilities would impede his ability to be a physical therapist assistant. This realization only made him work harder to prove he could. And, at the same time, he drew on what he had learned from his past psychology courses.

"Studying psychology helped me understand depression," he explained. "Working with patients, I can understand the depressive side of having an injury and how the little things like not being able to pick up a glass, or button a shirt, can take an emotional toll."

Even while studying full time, Greiner endured lengthy physical therapy sessions and long commutes to and from school. It was a difficult time, but the fighter in him pushed on.

"If people tell me I can't do something, I'm intent on proving them wrong," he stated.

He added, "Don't give up if you really want something. You can obtain your goal as long as you work and study hard. You can become anything you want. Just never give up and never surrender."

[RETHINK R Rethink]

Greiner believes that his personal understanding of depression and what he learned in psychology courses gave him insight into the disorder. What symptoms of depression might he look for in patients as he assists them?

Based on what you've read in this chapter, what advice about finding the appropriate treatment provider might Greiner suggest to a patient experiencing depression?

visual summary 11
TREATMENT OF PSYCHOLOGICAL DISORDERS

MODULE 36 Psychotherapy: Psychodynamic, Behavioral, and Cognitive Approaches

Psychodynamic Therapy

- Psychoanalysis
  - Free association: say aloud whatever comes to mind
  - Dream interpretation: looking for clues to unconscious conflicts and problems in dreams
  - Frequent sessions for a long time
- Contemporary psychodynamic approaches
  - Sessions are of shorter duration
  - Therapist takes more active role: focus is more in the present

Cognitive Approaches: Teach people to think in adaptive ways
- Rational-emotive behavior therapy

Behavioral Treatment Approaches: Help modify behavior rather than find underlying causes

- Classical conditioning treatments
  - Aversive conditioning
  - Systematic desensitization
  - Flooding
- Operant conditioning techniques
  - Token system
  - Contingency contracting
  - Observational learning

MODULE 37 Psychotherapy: Humanistic, Interpersonal, and Group Approaches to Treatment

Humanistic Therapy: Focuses on self-responsibility in treatment techniques

- Person-centered therapy: helps people to reach their potential for self-actualization using unconditional positive regard

Group Therapy: Several people meet with a therapist to discuss psychological functioning

- Family therapy
- Self-help therapy

Interpersonal Therapy: Focuses on interpersonal relationships and improvement through short-term therapy

Does Psychotherapy Work?

- More effective than no treatment for most people
- Certain types of therapy work better for particular problems
- Most therapy approaches share basic elements

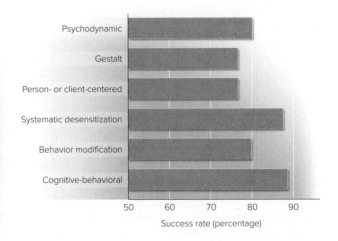

(Chart: Success rate (percentage) by therapy type)

- Psychodynamic
- Gestalt
- Person- or client-centered
- Systematic desensitization
- Behavior modification
- Cognitive-behavioral

Success rate (percentage): 50, 60, 70, 80, 90

Drug Therapy: Controlling psychological disorders with drugs

Drug Treatments			
Class of Drug	**Effects of Drug**	**Primary Action of Drug**	**Examples**
Antipsychotic drugs	Reduction in loss of touch with reality, agitation	Block dopamine receptors	Chlorpromazine (Thorazine®), clozapine (Clozaril®), haloperidol (Haldol®)
Antidepressant drugs			
Tricyclic	Reduction in depression	Permit rise in neuro-transmitters such as norepinepherine	Trazodone (Desyrel), amitriptyline (Elavil), desipramine (Norpramin®)
MAO inhibitors	Reduction in depression	Prevent MAO from breaking down neurotransmitters	Phenelzine (Nardil®), tranylcypromine (Parnate®)
Selective serotonin reuptake inhibitors (SSRIs)	Reduction in depression	Inhibit reuptake of serotonin	Fluoxetine (Prozac®), Luvox, Paxil®, Celexa®, Zoloft® nefazodone (Serzone)
Mood stabilizers			
Lithium	Mood stabilization	Can alter transmission of impulses within neurons	Lithium (Lithonate), Depakote®, Tegretol®
Antianxiety drugs	Reduction in anxiety	Increase activity of neurotransmitter GABA	Benzodiazepines (Valium®, Xanax®)

Electroconvulsive Therapy: Used as the only quickly effective treatment for severe depression

Psychosurgery: Brain surgery to reduce symptoms of mental disorders

Community Psychology: Prevention of the incidence of psychological disorders

- Deinstitutionalization: transfer of mental patients into the community where they may not receive necessary treatment

CHAPTER 12

Suspicious Minds

Ahmed Mohamed, 14, is a member of his school's robotics club and dreams of going to MIT to study engineering. But when the Irving, Texas, boy proudly showed his teacher an alarm clock he had made, she panicked and called in the principal. The school had Ahmed arrested for building a fake bomb. After an extensive interview with the teen (in which neither his parents nor an attorney was present), police released him, calling the clock a "homework experiment." No apologies were made, and his school refused to lift his three-day suspension (Fantz, Almasy, & Stapleton, 2015).

The public response to Ahmed's arrest was immediate. Many Americans expressed anger, saying that the Muslim boy had been the victim of profiling. President Obama invited him to the White House, and Facebook founder Mark Zuckerberg sent a message of support. But not all Americans were convinced. Those who view the country's 2.8 million Muslims as potential terrorists spearhead a growing wave of Islamophobia, fueled by terrorist attacks and some U.S. politicians promoting anti-Muslim policies (Reid, 2015).

SOCIAL PSYCHOLOGY

Looking Ahead

What, in general, drives some people to hate and distrust others of a different religion, race, or ethnicity—and conversely, why do other people celebrate human diversity? More broadly, how can we improve social attitudes so that people can live together in harmony?

We can fully answer these questions only by taking into account findings from the field of social psychology, the branch of psychology that focuses on the aspects of human behavior that unite—and separate—us from one another. **Social psychology** is the scientific study of how people's thoughts, feelings, and actions are affected by others. Social psychologists consider the kinds and causes of the individual's behavior in social situations. They examine how the nature of situations in which we find ourselves influences our behavior in important ways.

> **social psychology** The scientific study of how people's thoughts, feelings, and actions are affected by others

The broad scope of social psychology is conveyed by the kinds of questions social psychologists ask, such as: How can we convince people to change their attitudes or adopt new ideas and values? In what ways do we come to understand what others are like? How are we influenced by what others do and think? Why do some people display so much violence, aggression, and cruelty toward others that people throughout the world live in fear of annihilation at their hands? And why, in comparison, do some people place their own lives at risk to help others?

We begin with a look at how our attitudes shape our behavior and how we form judgments about others. We discuss how we are influenced by others, and we consider prejudice and discrimination, focusing on their roots and the ways in which we can reduce them. After examining what social psychologists have learned about how people form friendships and relationships, we look at the determinants of aggression and helping—two opposing sides of human behavior. Finally, we conclude by addressing stress and the ways that we can cope with it.

Attitudes and Social Cognition

Learning Outcomes  Prepare

>> **LO39.1** Define persuasion.

>> **LO39.2** Explain social cognition.

MODULE OUTLINE

Persuasion: Changing Attitudes

Social Cognition: Understanding Others

Exploring Diversity: Attributions in a
Cultural Context: How Fundamental Is the
Fundamental Attribution Error?

W Work

What do Rachael Ray and Tom Brady have in common?

Each has appeared in advertisements designed to mold or change our attitudes. Such commercials are part of the barrage of messages we receive each day from sources as varied as politicians, sales staff in stores, and celebrities, all of which are meant to influence us.

>> LO39.1 Persuasion: Changing Attitudes

attitudes Evaluations of a particular person, behavior, belief, or concept

Persuasion is the process of changing attitudes, one of the central concepts of social psychology. **Attitudes** are evaluations of a particular person, behavior, belief, or concept. For example, you probably hold attitudes toward the U.S. president (a person), abortion (a behavior), affirmative action (a belief), or architecture (a concept) (Hegarty & Massey, 2007; Simon & Hoyt, 2008).

The ease with which we can change our attitudes depends on a number of factors, including:

■ *Message source.* The characteristics of a person who delivers a persuasive message, known as an *attitude communicator,* have a major impact on the effectiveness of that message. Moreover, the communicator's expertise and trustworthiness are related to the impact of a message—except in situations in which the audience believes the communicator has an ulterior motive (McClure, Sutton, & Sibley, 2007; Messner, Reinhard, & Sporer, 2008; Porter, Rheinschmidt-Same, & Richeson, 2016).

■ *Characteristics of the message.* It is not just *who* delivers a message but what the message is like that affects attitudes. Generally, two-sided messages—which include both the communicator's position and the one he or she is arguing against—are more effective than one-sided messages, given the assumption that the arguments for the other side can be effectively refuted and the audience is knowledgeable about the topic (Keer et al., 2013).

- *Characteristics of the target.* Once a communicator has delivered a message, characteristics of the *target* of the message may determine whether the message will be accepted. For example, intelligent people are more resistant to persuasion than are those who are less intelligent.

Routes to Persuasion

Recipients' receptiveness to persuasive messages relates to the type of information processing they use. Social psychologists have discovered two primary information-processing routes to persuasion: central route and peripheral route processing. **Central route processing** occurs when the recipient thoughtfully considers the issues and arguments involved in persuasion. In central route processing, people are swayed in their judgments by the logic, merit, and strength of arguments.

In contrast, **peripheral route processing** occurs when people are persuaded on the basis of factors unrelated to the nature or quality of the content of a persuasive message. Instead, factors that are irrelevant or extraneous to the issue, such as who is providing the message, how long the arguments are, or the emotional appeal of the arguments, influence them (Warden, Wu, & Tsai, 2006; Kumkale, Albarracín, & Seignourel, 2010; Xie & Johnson, 2015).

In general, people who are highly involved and motivated use central route processing to comprehend a message. However, if a person is uninvolved, unmotivated, bored, or distracted, the nature of the message becomes less important, and peripheral factors become more critical (see Figure 1). Although both central route and peripheral route processing lead to attitude change, central route processing generally leads to stronger, more lasting attitude change.

Companies use celebrities such as Oprah Winfrey to persuade consumers to buy their products. Can celebrities really affect purchasing habits of consumers? How? © Mark Von Holden/AP Images

central route processing Message interpretation characterized by thoughtful consideration of the issues and arguments used to persuade

peripheral route processing Message interpretation characterized by consideration of the source and related general information rather than of the message itself

The Link between Attitudes and Behavior

Not surprisingly, attitudes influence behavior. The strength of the link between particular attitudes and behavior varies, of course, but generally people strive for consistency between their attitudes and their behavior. Furthermore, people hold fairly consistent attitudes. For instance, you would probably not hold the attitude that eating meat is immoral and still have a positive attitude toward hamburgers (Levi, Chan, & Pence, 2006; Buckley, Chapman, & Sheehan, 2010; Elen et al., 2013).

STUDY ALERT

Central route processing involves the **c**ontent of the message; **p**eripheral route processing involves how the message is **p**rovided.

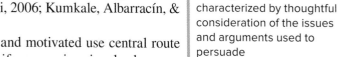

From the perspective of …

A Graphic Designer Suppose you were assigned to develop an advertisement for a product for the local newspaper and a store front. How might theories of persuasion guide you to suit the different audiences who will see the ad?

© Fuse/Getty Images RF

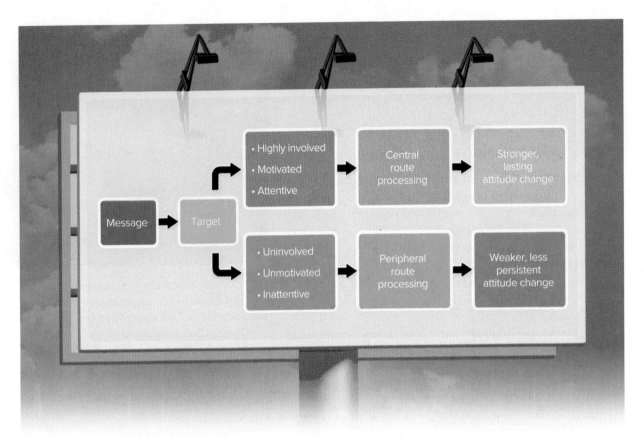

Figure 1 Routes to persuasion. Targets who are highly involved, motivated, and attentive use central route processing when they consider a persuasive message, which leads to a more lasting attitude change. In contrast, uninvolved, unmotivated, and inattentive targets are more likely to use peripheral route processing, and attitude change is likely to be less enduring. Can you think of specific advertisements that try to produce central route processing?

cognitive dissonance The conflict that occurs when a person holds two contradictory attitudes or thoughts (referred to as *cognitions*)

Ironically, the consistency that leads attitudes to influence behavior sometimes works the other way around, for in some cases our behavior shapes our attitudes. According to social psychologist Leon Festinger (1957), **cognitive dissonance** is the psychological tension that occurs when a person holds two contradictory attitudes or thoughts (referred to as *cognitions*).

Cognitive dissonance explains many everyday events involving attitudes and behavior. For example, smokers who know that smoking leads to lung cancer hold contradictory cognitions: (1) I smoke, and (2) smoking leads to lung cancer. The theory predicts that these two thoughts will lead to a state of cognitive dissonance. More important, it predicts that smokers will be motivated to reduce their dissonance.

There are four ways to reduce the dissonance in this case:

- modifying one or both of the cognitions (e.g., "I really don't smoke that much,"
- changing the perceived importance of one cognition ("the link between cancer and smoking is weak"),
- adding cognitions ("I exercise so much that I'm really a healthy person"), or
- denying that the two cognitions are related to each other ("there's no compelling evidence linking smoking and cancer").

Whichever strategy the smoker uses results in reduced dissonance (see Figure 2).

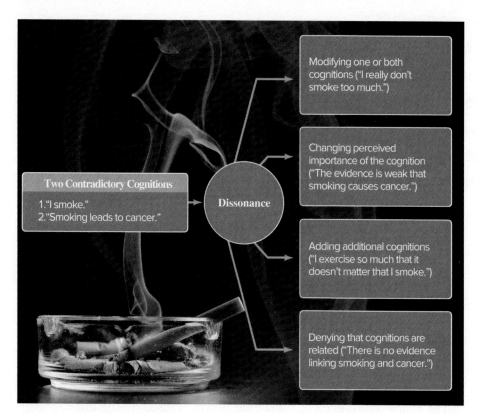

Figure 2 Cognitive dissonance. The simultaneous presence of two contradictory cognitions ("I smoke" and "Smoking leads to cancer") produces dissonance, which can be reduced through several methods. What are additional ways in which dissonance can be reduced? Photo: © Christian Zachariasen/Getty Images RF

(Within figure:)

Two Contradictory Cognitions
1. "I smoke."
2. "Smoking leads to cancer."

Dissonance

Modifying one or both cognitions ("I really don't smoke too much.")

Changing perceived importance of the cognition ("The evidence is weak that smoking causes cancer.")

Adding additional cognitions ("I exercise so much that it doesn't matter that I smoke.")

Denying that cognitions are related ("There is no evidence linking smoking and cancer.")

» LO39.2 Social Cognition: Understanding Others

One of the dominant areas in social psychology during the last few years has focused on learning how we come to understand what others are like and how we explain the reasons underlying others' behavior.

Understanding What Others Are Like

Consider for a moment the enormous amount of information about other people to which we are exposed. How can we decide what is important and what is not and make judgments about the characteristics of others? Social psychologists interested in this question study **social cognition**— the way people understand and make sense of others and themselves. Those psychologists have learned that individuals have highly developed **schemas,** sets of cognitions about people and social experiences. Those schemas organize information stored in memory, represent in our minds the way the social world operates, and give us a framework to recognize, categorize, and recall information relating to social stimuli such as people and groups (Landau, Meier, & Keefer, 2010; Mancuso et al., 2011; Leahy, 2015).

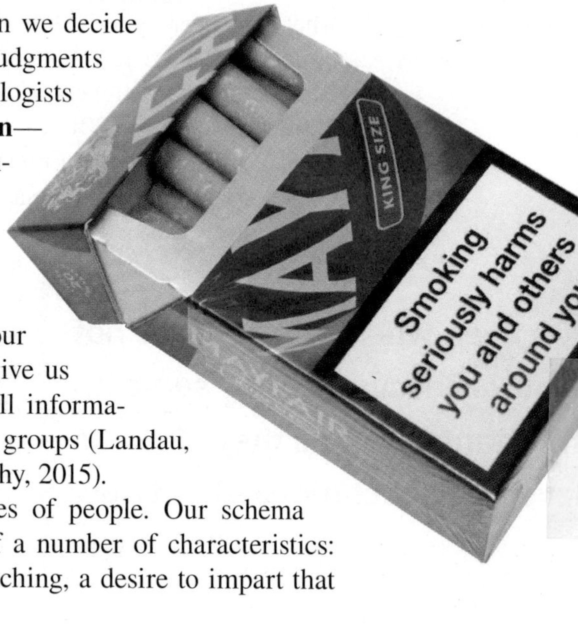

We typically hold schemas for specific types of people. Our schema for "teacher," for instance, generally consists of a number of characteristics: knowledge of the subject matter he or she is teaching, a desire to impart that

social cognition The cognitive processes by which people understand and make sense of others and themselves

schemas Organized bodies of information stored in memory that bias the way new information is interpreted, stored, and recalled; sets of cognitions about people and social experiences

© David J. Green-studio/Alamy Stock Photo

(On cigarette pack:) Smoking seriously harms you and others around you

> **Consider for a moment the enormous amount of information about other people to which we are exposed. How can we decide what is important and what is not and make judgments about the characteristics of others?**

knowledge, and an awareness of the student's need to understand what is being said. Or we may hold a schema for "mother" that includes the characteristics of warmth, nurturance, and caring. Regardless of their accuracy, schemas are important because they organize the way in which we recall, recognize, and categorize information about others. Moreover, they help us predict what others are like on the basis of relatively little information (Ruscher, Fiske, & Schnake, 2000; Yamada & Itsukushima, 2013).

Impression Formation

How do we decide that Sayreeta is a hard worker, Jacob is obnoxious, or Hector is a really nice guy? The earliest work on social cognition examined *impression formation,* the process by which an individual organizes information about another person to form an overall impression of that person. In a classic study, for instance, students learned that they were about to hear a guest lecturer (Kelley, 1950). Researchers told one group of students that the lecturer was "a rather warm person, industrious, critical, practical, and determined" and told a second group that he was "a rather cold person, industrious, critical, practical, and determined."

The simple substitution of "cold" for "warm" caused drastic differences in the way the students in each group perceived the lecturer, even though he gave the same talk in the same style in each condition. Students who had been told he was "warm" rated him considerably more positively than students who had been told he was "cold."

The findings from this experiment led to additional research on impression formation that focused on the way in which people pay particular attention to certain unusually important traits—known as **central traits**—to help them form an overall impression of others. The presence of a central trait alters the meaning of other traits. Hence, the description of the lecturer as "industrious" meant something different when it was associated with the central trait "warm" than it meant when it was associated with "cold" (Widmeyer & Loy, 1988; Glicksohn & Nahari, 2007; Oosten, Magnhagen, & Hemelrijk, 2010).

central traits The major traits considered in forming impressions of others

We make such impressions remarkably quickly. In just a few seconds, using what have been called "thin slices of behavior," we are able to make judgments of people that are accurate and that match those of people who make judgments based on longer snippets of behavior (Pavitt, 2007; Holleran, Mehl, & Levitt, 2009; Pretsch et al., 2013).

Of course, as we gain more experience with people and see them exhibiting behavior in a variety of situations, our impressions of them become more complex. However, because our knowledge of others usually has gaps, we still tend to fit individuals into personality schemas that represent particular "types" of people. For instance, we may hold a "gregarious person" schema, made up of the traits of friendliness, aggressiveness, and openness. The presence of just one or two of those traits may be sufficient to make us assign a person to a particular schema.

> **Even when schemas are not entirely accurate, they serve an important function: they allow us to develop expectations about how others will behave.**

Even when schemas are not entirely accurate, they serve an important function: they allow us to develop expectations about how others will behave.

Those expectations permit us to plan our interactions with others more easily and serve to simplify a complex social world.

Attribution Processes: Understanding the Causes of Behavior

When Barbara Washington, a new employee at the Ablex Computer Company, completed a major staffing project two weeks early, her boss, Yolanda, was delighted. At the next staff meeting, she announced how pleased she was with Barbara and explained that this was an example of the kind of performance she was looking for in her staff. The other staff members looked on resentfully, trying to figure out why Barbara had worked night and day to finish the project not just on time but two weeks early. She must be an awfully compulsive person, they decided.

At one time or another, most of us have puzzled over the reasons behind someone's behavior. In contrast to theories of social cognition, which describe how people develop an overall impression of others' personality traits, **attribution theory** seeks to explain how we decide, on the basis of samples of an individual's behavior, what the specific causes of that person's behavior are.

In seeking an explanation for behavior, we must answer one central question: Is the cause situational or dispositional? **Situational causes** are those brought about by something in the environment. For instance, someone who knocks over a quart of milk and then cleans it up probably does the cleaning not because he or she is necessarily a neat person but because the *situation* requires it. In contrast, a person who spends hours shining the kitchen floor probably does so because he or she is a neat person. Hence, the behavior has a **dispositional cause,** prompted by the person's disposition (his or her internal traits or personality characteristics).

In our example involving Barbara Washington, her fellow employees attributed her behavior to her disposition rather than to the situation. But from a logical standpoint, it is equally plausible that something about the situation caused the behavior. If asked, Barbara might attribute her accomplishment to situational factors and explain that she had so much other work to do she just had to get the project out of the way, or the project was not all that difficult and was easy to complete ahead of schedule. To her, then, the reason for her behavior might not be dispositional at all; it could be situational.

Attribution Biases: To Err Is Human

If we always processed information in the rational manner that attribution theory suggests, the world might run a lot more smoothly. Unfortunately, although attribution theory generally makes accurate predictions, people do not always process information about others as logically as the theory seems to suggest. In fact, research reveals consistent biases in the ways people make attributions. Typical biases include the following:

■ *The halo effect.* Harry is intelligent, kind, and loving. Is he also conscientious? If you were to guess, your most likely response probably would be yes. Your guess reflects the **halo effect,** a phenomenon in which an initial understanding that a person has positive traits is used to infer other uniformly positive characteristics. The opposite would also hold true. Learning that Harry was unsociable and argumentative would probably lead you to assume that he was lazy as well. However, because few people have either uniformly positive or uniformly negative traits, the halo effect

attribution theory The theory of personality that seeks to explain how we decide, on the basis of samples of an individual's behavior, what the specific causes of that person's behavior are

situational causes (of behavior) Perceived causes of behavior that are based on environmental factors

dispositional causes (of behavior) Perceived causes of behavior that are based on internal traits or personality factors

halo effect A phenomenon in which an initial understanding that a person has positive traits is used to infer other uniformly positive characteristics

STUDY ALERT

The central question in making an attribution is whether the cause of behavior is due to situational or dispositional factors.

assumed-similarity bias The tendency to think of people as being similar to oneself, even when meeting them for the first time

self-serving bias The tendency to attribute personal success to personal factors and to attribute failure to factors outside oneself

fundamental attribution error A tendency to overattribute others' behavior to dispositional causes and the corresponding minimization of the importance of situational causes

leads to misperceptions of others (Dennis, 2007; Srivastava, Guglielmo, & Beer, 2010; Gräf & Unkelbach, 2016).

■ *Assumed-similarity bias.* How similar to you—in terms of attitudes, opinions, likes and dislikes—are your friends and acquaintances? Most people believe that their friends and acquaintances are fairly similar to themselves. But this feeling goes beyond just people we know to a general tendency—known as the **assumed-similarity bias**—to think of people as being similar to oneself, even when meeting them for the first time. Given the range of people in the world, this assumption often reduces the accuracy of our judgments (Lemay, Clark & Feeney, 2007; Lemay & Clark, 2008; West & Kenny, 2011).

■ *The self-serving bias.* When their teams win, coaches usually feel that the success is due to their coaching. But when teams lose, coaches may think it's due to their players' poor skills. Similarly, if you get an A on a test, you may think it's due to your hard work, but if you get a poor grade, it's due to the professor's inadequacies. The reason is the **self-serving bias,** the tendency to attribute success to personal factors (skill, ability, or effort) and attribute failure to factors outside oneself (Krusemark, Campbell, & Clementz, 2008; Shepperd, Malone, & Sweeny, 2008; Ferring, Tournier & Mancini, 2015).

■ *The fundamental attribution error.* One of the more common attribution biases is the tendency to overattribute others' behavior to dispositional causes and the corresponding failure to recognize the importance of situational causes. Known as the **fundamental attribution error,** this tendency is prevalent in Western cultures. We tend to exaggerate the importance of personality characteristics (dispositional causes) in producing others' behavior, minimizing the influence of the environment (situational factors). For example, we are more likely to jump to the conclusion that someone who is often late to work is too lazy to take an earlier bus (a dispositional cause) than to assume that the lateness is due to situational factors, such as the bus always running behind schedule.

> The culture in which we are raised clearly plays a role in the way we attribute others' behavior.

Social psychologists' awareness of attribution biases has led, in part, to the development of a new branch of economics called behavioral economics. *Behavioral economics* is concerned with how individuals' biases irrationally affect economic decisions. Rather than viewing people as rational, thoughtful decision makers who are impartially weighing choices to draw conclusions, behavioral economists focus on the irrationality of judgments (Ariely & Norton, 2009).

Despite the importance of the fundamental attribution error in shaping the perceptions of members of Western cultures, it turns out that it's not so fundamental when we look at non-Western cultures, as we discuss next.

EXPLORING diversity

Attributions in a Cultural Context: How Fundamental Is the Fundamental Attribution Error?

Attribution biases do not affect all of us in the same way. The culture in which we are raised clearly plays a role in the way we attribute others' behavior.

Take, for example, the fundamental attribution error, the tendency to overestimate the importance of personal, dispositional factors and underattribute situational factors in determining the causes of others' behavior. The error is pervasive in Western cultures and not in Eastern societies. For instance, adults in India were more likely to use situational attributions than dispositional ones in explaining events. These findings are the opposite of those for the United States, and they contradict the fundamental attribution error (Miller, 1984; Lien et al., 2006).

Cultural differences in attributions may have profound implications. For example, parents in Asia tend to attribute good academic performance to effort and hard work (situational factors). In contrast, parents in Western cultures tend to de-emphasize the role of effort and attribute school success to innate ability (a dispositional factor). As a result, Asian students in general may strive harder to achieve and ultimately outperform U.S. students in school (Stevenson, Lee, & Mu, 2000; Lien et al., 2006).

The difference in thinking between people in Asian and Western cultures is a reflection of a broader difference in the way the world is perceived. Asian societies generally have a *collectivistic orientation,* a worldview that promotes the notion of interdependence. People with a collectivistic orientation generally see themselves as parts of a larger, interconnected social network and as responsible to others. In contrast, people in Western cultures are more likely to hold an *individualist orientation,* which emphasizes personal identity and the uniqueness of the individual. They focus more on what sets them apart from others and what makes them special (Markus, 2007; Haugen, Lund, & Ommundsen, 2008; Russell et al., 2010).

Students in Asian societies may perform exceptionally well in school because the culture emphasizes academic success and perseverance. © Tanya Constantine/Blend Images LLC

RECAP

Define persuasion.

- Social psychology is the scientific study of the ways in which people's thoughts, feelings, and actions are affected by others and the nature and causes of individual behavior in social situations.

- Attitudes are evaluations of a particular person, behavior, belief, or concept.

- Cognitive dissonance occurs when an individual simultaneously holds two cognitions—attitudes or thoughts—that contradict each other. To resolve the contradiction, the person may modify one cognition, change its importance, add a cognition, or deny a link between the two cognitions, thereby bringing about a reduction in dissonance.

Explain social cognition.

- Social cognition involves the way people understand and make sense of others and themselves. People develop schemas that organize information about people and social experiences in memory and allow them to interpret and categorize information about others.

- People form impressions of others in part through the use of central traits, personality characteristics that receive unusually heavy emphasis when we form an impression.

- Information-processing approaches have found that we tend to average together sets of traits to form an overall impression.

- Attribution theory tries to explain how we understand the causes of behavior, particularly with respect to situational or dispositional factors.

- Even though logical processes are involved, attribution is prone to error. For instance, people are susceptible to the halo effect, assumed-similarity bias, self-serving bias, and fundamental attribution error (the tendency to overattribute others' behavior to dispositional causes and the corresponding failure to recognize the importance of situational causes).

[EVALUATE E Evaluate]

1. An evaluation of a particular person, behavior, belief, or concept is called a(n) _____.

2. One brand of peanut butter advertises its product by describing its taste and nutritional value. It is hoping to persuade customers through _____ route processing. In ads for a competing brand, a popular actor happily eats the product—but does not describe it. This approach hopes to persuade customers through _____ route processing.

3. Cognitive dissonance theory suggests that we commonly change our behavior to keep it consistent with our attitudes. True or false?

4. Sopan was happy to lend his textbook to a fellow student who seemed bright and friendly. He was surprised when his classmate did not return it. His assumption that the bright and friendly student would also be responsible reflects the _____ effect.

[RETHINK R Rethink]

Joan sees Annette, a new co-worker, act in a way that seems abrupt and curt. Joan concludes that Annette is unkind and unsociable. The next day Joan sees Annette acting kindly toward another worker. Is Joan likely to change her impression of Annette? Why or why not? Finally, Joan sees several friends of hers laughing and joking with Annette, treating her in a very friendly fashion. Is Joan likely to change her impression of Annette? Why or why not?

Answers to Evaluate Questions 1. attitude; 2. central, peripheral; 3. false: we typically change our attitudes, not our behavior, to reduce cognitive dissonance; 4. halo

KEY TERMS

Social psychology LO39.1

Attitudes LO39.1

Central route processing LO39.1

Peripheral route processing LO39.1

Cognitive dissonance LO39.1

Social cognition LO39.2

Schemas LO39.2

Central traits LO39.2

Attribution theory LO39.2

Situational causes (of behavior) LO39.2

Dispositional causes (of behavior) LO39.2

Halo effect LO39.2

Assumed-similarity bias LO39.2

Self-serving bias LO39.2

Fundamental attribution error LO39.2

module 40

Social Influence and Groups

Learning Outcomes

>> **LO40.1** Define conformity.

>> **LO40.2** Explain compliance.

>> **LO40.3** Discuss obedience.

MODULE OUTLINE

Conformity: Following What Others Do

Compliance: Submitting to Direct Social Pressure

Obedience: Following Direct Orders

Social influence is the process by which the actions of an individual or group affect the behavior of others. As you undoubtedly know from your own experience, pressures to conform can be painfully strong and can bring about changes in behavior that otherwise never would have occurred.

Why can conformity pressures in groups be so strong? For one reason, groups, and other people generally, play a central role in our lives. Groups develop and hold *norms,* expectations regarding behavior appropriate to the group. Furthermore, we understand that not adhering to group norms can result in retaliation from other group members, ranging from being ignored to being overtly derided or even being rejected or excluded by the group. Thus, people conform to meet the expectations of the group (Jetten, Hornsey, & Adarves-Yorno, 2006; Hogg, 2010; Bentley, Ormerod, & Batty, 2011).

Groups exert considerable social influence over individuals, ranging from the mundane, such as the decision to wear a certain kind of jeans, to the extreme cases such as the cruelty of guards at the Abu Ghraib prison in Iraq. We'll consider three types of social pressure: conformity, compliance, and obedience.

>> LO40.1 Conformity: Following What Others Do

Conformity is a change in behavior or attitudes brought about by a desire to follow the beliefs or standards of other people. Subtle or even unspoken social pressure results in conformity.

The classic demonstration of pressure to conform comes from a series of studies carried out in the 1950s by Solomon Asch (Asch, 1951). In the experiments, the participants thought they were taking part in a test of perceptual skills with six other people. The experimenter showed the participants one card with three lines of varying length and a second card that had a fourth line that matched one of the first three (see Figure 1). The task was seemingly straightforward: each of the participants had to announce aloud which of the first three lines was identical in length to the "standard" line on the second card. Because the correct answer was always obvious, the task seemed easy to the participants.

> **STUDY ALERT**
>
> The distinction between the three types of social pressure—conformity, compliance, and obedience—depends on the nature and strength of the social pressure brought to bear on a person.

> **social influence** The process by which the actions of an individual or group affect the behavior of others
>
> **conformity** A change in behavior or attitudes brought about by a desire to follow the beliefs or standards of other people

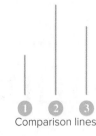

Standard line   Comparison lines

Figure 1   Which of the three comparison lines is the same length as the "standard" line?

Indeed, because the participants all agreed on the first few trials, the procedure appeared to be simple. But then something odd began to happen. From the perspective of the participant in the group who answered last on each trial, all the answers of the first six participants seemed to be wrong—in fact, unanimously wrong. And this pattern persisted. Over and over again, the first six participants provided answers that contradicted what the last participant believed to be correct. The last participant faced the dilemma of whether to follow his or her own perceptions or follow the group by repeating the answer everyone else was giving.

As you might have guessed, this experiment was more contrived than it appeared. The first six participants were actually confederates (paid employees of the experimenter) who had been instructed to give unanimously erroneous answers in many of the trials. And the study had nothing to do with perceptual skills. Instead, the issue under investigation was conformity.

> In some cases, though, social roles influence us so profoundly that we engage in behavior in entirely atypical—and damaging—ways.

Asch found that in about one-third of the trials, the participants conformed to the unanimous but erroneous group answer, with about 75 percent of all participants conforming at least once. However, he found strong individual differences. Some participants conformed nearly all the time, whereas others never did. Subsequent research further shows that conformity is considerably higher when people must respond publicly than it is when they can do so privately. Also, having just one person present who shares the minority point of view is sufficient to reduce conformity pressures (Prislin, Brewer, & Wilson, 2002; Goodwin, Costa, & Adonu, 2004; Levine & Moreland, 2006).

Conformity to Social Roles

Conformity also influences behavior through social roles. *Social roles* are the behaviors that are associated with people in a given position, such as a restaurant waiter or a schoolteacher. In some cases, though, social roles influence us so profoundly that we engage in behavior in entirely atypical—and

It is easy to think of conformity in the context of teenagers and their desire to fit in. However, conformity is equally as pervasive in adults. Can you think of a time that you conformed to the group norm? (first) © BananaStock/PunchStock RF; (second) © Paul Bradbury/Getty Images RF

damaging—ways. This fact was brought home in an influential experiment conducted by Philip Zimbardo and colleagues. In the study, the researchers set up a mock prison, complete with cells, solitary confinement cubicles, and a small recreation area. The researchers then advertised for participants who were willing to spend 2 weeks in a study of prison life. Once they identified the study participants, a flip of a coin designated who would be a prisoner and who would be a prison guard. Neither prisoners nor guards were told how to fulfill their roles (Zimbardo, Maslach, & Haney, 2000; Zimbardo, 1973, 2007).

After just a few days in this mock prison, the students assigned to be guards became abusive to the prisoners, waking them at odd hours and subjecting them to arbitrary punishment. They withheld food from the prisoners and forced them into hard labor. On the other hand, the students assigned to the prisoner role soon became docile and submissive to the guards. They became extremely demoralized, and one slipped into a depression so severe he was released after just a few days. In fact, after only 6 days of captivity, the remaining prisoners' reactions became so extreme that the study was ended.

The experiment (which, it's important to note, drew criticism on both methodological and ethical grounds) provided a clear lesson: conforming to a social role can have a powerful consequence on the behavior of even normal, well-adjusted people, inducing them to change their behavior in sometimes undesirable ways (Zimbardo, 2007; Haney & Zimbardo, 2009; Coultas & van Leeuwen, 2015).

» LO40.2 Compliance: Submitting to Direct Social Pressure

When we refer to conformity, we usually mean a phenomenon in which the social pressure is subtle or indirect. But in some situations social pressure is much more obvious, with direct, explicit pressure to endorse a particular point of view or behave in a certain way. Social psychologists call the type of behavior that occurs in response to direct social pressure **compliance.**

Several specific techniques represent attempts to gain compliance. Those frequently employed include the following:

compliance Behavior that occurs in response to direct social pressure

- *Foot-in-the-door technique.* The use of the *foot-in-the-door technique* begins when a person first makes a small, trivial request. Because the request is easy to comply with, the likelihood that the target of the request will comply is high. Later, though, the target is asked to comply with a significantly larger request. It turns out that compliance with the second request increases substantially when the target has first agreed to the initial, smaller request.

  Why does the foot-in-the-door technique work? For one reason, involvement with the small request leads to an interest in an issue; taking an action—any action—makes the individual more committed to the issue, thereby increasing the likelihood of future compliance. Another explanation revolves around people's self-perceptions. By complying with the initial request, individuals may come to see themselves as people who provide help when asked. Then, when confronted with the larger request, they agree in order to maintain the kind of consistency in attitudes and behavior that we described earlier. Although we don't know which of these two explanations is more accurate, it is clear that the foot-in-the-door strategy is effective (Bloom, McBride, & Pollak, 2006; Guéguen et al., 2008).

- *Door-in-the-face technique.* A fund-raiser asks for a $500 contribution. You laughingly refuse and tell her that the amount is way out of your league. She then asks for a $10 contribution. What do you do? If you are like most people, you'll probably be a lot more compliant than you would be if she hadn't asked for the huge contribution first. In this tactic, called the *door-in-the-face technique,* someone makes a large request, expecting it to be refused, and follows it with a smaller one. This strategy, which is the opposite of the foot-in-the-door approach, has also proved to be effective (Pascual & Guéguen, 2005, 2006; Turner et al., 2007; Ebster & Neumayr, 2008).

- *That's-not-all technique.* In this technique, a salesperson offers you a deal at an inflated price. But immediately after the initial offer, the salesperson offers an incentive, discount, or bonus to clinch the deal. Although it sounds transparent, this practice can be quite effective. In one study, the experimenters set up a booth and sold cupcakes for 75 cents each. In one condition, the experimenters directly told customers that the price was 75 cents. But in another condition, they told customers that the price was originally $1 but had been reduced to 75 cents. As we might predict, more people bought cupcakes at the "reduced" price—even though it was identical to the price in the other experimental condition (Burger, Reed, & DeCesare, 1999; Pratkanis, 2007).

- *Not-so-free sample.* The *norm of reciprocity* is the social standard that we should treat other people as they treat us. (It's a variant of the "Golden Rule" we learn as kids: "Do unto others as they will do unto you.") It's a strong cultural standard: when someone does something nice for us, we tend to feel obligated to return the favor. In the case of the *not-so-free sample,* receiving a free sample activates the norm of reciprocity and makes us feel that we should return the favor—in the form of a purchase (Cialdini, 2006; Park & Antonioni, 2007; Burger, 2009).

industrial-organizational (I/O) psychology The branch of psychology focusing on work- and job-related issues, including worker motivation, satisfaction, safety, and productivity

Companies seeking to sell their products to consumers often use the techniques identified by social psychologists for promoting compliance.

Companies seeking to sell their products to consumers often use the techniques identified by social psychologists for promoting compliance. But employers also use them to bring about compliance and raise the productivity of employees in the workplace. In fact, **industrial-organizational (I/O) psychology,** a close cousin to social psychology, considers issues such as worker motivation, satisfaction, safety, and productivity. I/O psychologists also focus on the operation and design of organizations, asking

From the perspective of …

A Salesperson   Imagine that you have been trained to use the various compliance techniques described in this section. Because these compliance techniques are so powerful, should the use of certain of these techniques be banned? Should consumers be taught defenses against such techniques? Is the use of such techniques ethically and morally defensible? Why?

© Design Pics/Getty Images RF

questions such as how decision making can be improved in large organizations and how the fit between workers and their jobs can be maximized.

» LO40.3 Obedience: Following Direct Orders

Compliance techniques are used to gently lead people toward agreement with a request. In some cases, however, requests aim to produce **obedience,** a change in behavior in response to the commands of others. Although obedience is considerably less common than conformity and compliance, it does occur in several specific kinds of relationships. For example, we may show obedience to our bosses, teachers, or parents merely because of the power they hold to reward or punish us.

obedience A change in behavior in response to the commands of others

To acquire an understanding of obedience, consider for a moment how you might respond if a stranger said to you:

> I've devised a new way of improving memory. All I need is for you to teach people a list of words and then give them a test. The test procedure requires only that you give learners a shock each time they make a mistake on the test. To administer the shocks you will use a "shock generator" that gives shocks ranging from 15 to 450 volts. You can see that the switches are labeled from "slight shock" through "danger: severe shock" at the top level, where there are three red X's. But don't worry; although the shocks may be painful, they will cause no permanent damage.

Presented with this situation, you would be likely to think that neither you nor anyone else would go along with the stranger's unusual request. Clearly, it lies outside the bounds of what we consider good sense.

Or does it? Suppose the stranger asking for your help were a psychologist conducting an experiment. Or suppose the request came from your teacher, your employer, or your military commander—all people in authority with a seemingly legitimate reason for the request.

If you still believe it's unlikely that you would comply—think again. In a classic experiment conducted by social psychologist Stanley Milgram in the 1960s, an experimenter told participants to give increasingly stronger shocks to another person as part of a study on learning (see Figure 2). In reality, the

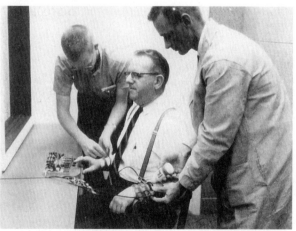

Figure 2   This fearsome-looking "shock generator" led participants to believe they were administering electric shocks to another person, who was connected to the generator by electrodes that were attached to the skin. From the film OBEDIENCE © 1968 by Stanley Milgram, © renewed 1993 by Alexandra Milgram. Permission granted by Alexandra Milgram.

STUDY ALERT

Because of its graphic demonstration of obedience to authority, the Milgram experiment is one of the most famous and influential studies in social psychology.

experiment had nothing to do with learning; the real issue under consideration was the degree to which participants would obey the experimenter's requests. In fact, the "learner" supposedly receiving the shocks was a confederate who never really received any punishment (Milgram, 2005; Baumrind & Milgram, 2010; Maher, 2015).

Most people who hear a description of Milgram's experiment feel it is unlikely that *any* participant would give the maximum level of shock—or, for that matter, any shock at all. Even a group of psychiatrists to whom the situation was described predicted that fewer than 2 percent of the participants would fully comply and administer the strongest shocks. However, the actual results contradicted both experts' and nonexperts' predictions. Some 65 percent of the participants eventually used the highest setting on the shock generator—450 volts—to shock the learner. This obedience occurred even though the learner, who had mentioned at the start of the experiment that he had a heart condition, demanded to be released, screaming, "Let me out of here! Let me out of here! My heart's bothering me. Let me out of here!" Despite the learner's pleas, most participants continued to administer the shocks.

Why did so many individuals comply with the experimenter's demands? The participants, who were extensively interviewed after the experiment, said they obeyed primarily because they believed that the experimenter would be responsible for any potential ill effects that befell the learner. The participants accepted the experimenter's orders, then, because they thought that they personally could not be held accountable for their actions—they could always blame the experimenter (Blass, 1996, 2004).

We need only consider actual instances of obedience to authority to witness some frightening real-life parallels. For instance, after World War II, the major defense that Nazi officers gave to excuse their participation in atrocities during the war was that they were "only following orders." Milgram's experiment, which was motivated in part by his desire to explain the behavior of everyday Germans during World War II, forces us to ask ourselves this question: Would we be able to withstand the intense power of authority?

> **We need only consider actual instances of obedience to authority to witness some frightening real-life parallels.**

Despite possible ethical concerns about the methods used, Milgram's research remains the strongest laboratory demonstration of obedience. And partial replications of Milgram's work, conducted in an ethically defensible way, find similar results, which add believability to the original work (Blass, 2009; Burger, 2009).

RECAP

Define conformity.

- Social influence is the area of social psychology concerned with situations in which the actions of an individual or group affect the behavior of others.

- Conformity refers to changes in behavior or attitudes that result from a desire to follow the beliefs or standards of others.

Explain compliance.

- Compliance is behavior that results from direct social pressure. Among the ways of eliciting compliance are the foot-in-the-door, door-in-the-face, that's-not-all, and not-so-free-sample techniques.

Discuss obedience.

- Obedience is a change in behavior in response to the commands of others.

[EVALUATE E Evaluate]

1. A _____ _____, or a person who agrees with the dissenting viewpoint, is likely to reduce conformity.

2. Which of the following techniques asks a person to comply with a small initial request to enhance the likelihood that the person will later comply with a larger request?
   a. Door-in-the-face
   b. Foot-in-the-door
   c. That's-not-all
   d. Not-so-free sample

3. The _____ _____ _____ _____ technique begins with an outrageous request that makes a subsequent, smaller request seem reasonable.

4. _____ is a change in behavior that is due to another person's orders.

[RETHINK R Rethink]

Why do you think the Milgram experiment is so controversial? What sorts of effects might the experiment have had on participants? Do you think the experiment would have had similar results if it had been conducted not in a laboratory setting, but among members of a social group (such as a fraternity or sorority) with strong pressures to conform?

Answers to Evaluate Questions 1. social supporter; 2. b; 3. door-in-the-face; 4. obedience

KEY TERMS

Social influence LO40.1

Conformity LO40.1

Compliance LO40.2

Industrial-organizational (I/O) psychology LO40.2

Obedience LO40.3

Prejudice and Discrimination

Learning Outcomes

>> **LO41.1** Identify the foundations of prejudice.

>> **LO41.2** Distinguish measuring practices for prejudice and discrimination.

>> **LO41.3** Assess ways to reduce prejudice and discrimination.

MODULE OUTLINE

The Foundations of Prejudice

Measuring Prejudice and Discrimination: The Implicit Personality Test

Reducing Prejudice and Discrimination

stereotype A set of generalized beliefs and expectations about a particular group and its members

prejudice A negative (or positive) evaluation of a particular group and its members

discrimination Behavior directed toward individuals on the basis of their membership in a particular group

What do you think when someone says, "He's African American," "She's Chinese," or "That's a woman driver"?

If you're like most people, you'll probably automatically form some sort of impression of what each person is like. Most likely your impression is based on a **stereotype,** a set of generalized beliefs and expectations about a specific group and its members. Stereotypes, which may be negative or positive, grow out of our tendency to categorize and organize the vast amount of information we encounter in our everyday lives. All stereotypes share the common feature of oversimplifying the world: we view individuals not in terms of their unique, personal characteristics, but also in terms of characteristics we attribute to all the members of a particular group.

Stereotypes can lead to **prejudice,** a negative (or positive) evaluation of a group and its members. For instance, racial prejudice occurs when a member of a racial group is evaluated in terms of race and not because of his or her own characteristics or abilities.

Common stereotypes and forms of prejudice involve racial, religious, and ethnic groups. Over the years, various groups have been called "lazy" or "shrewd" or "cruel" with varying degrees of regularity by those who are not members of that group. Even people who on the surface appear to be unprejudiced may harbor hidden prejudice. For example, when white participants in experiments are shown faces on a computer screen so rapidly that they cannot consciously perceive the faces, they react more negatively to black than to white faces—an example of what has been called *modern racism* (Liu & Mills, 2006; Pearson, Dovidio, & Pratto, 2007; Henry & Pratto, 2010; Jackson, 2011; Blanton, Jaccard, & Burrows, 2015).

Although usually backed by little or no evidence, stereotypes can have harmful consequences. Acting on negative stereotypes results in **discrimination**— behavior directed toward individuals on the basis of their membership in a particular group. Discrimination can lead to exclusion from jobs, neighborhoods, and educational opportunities, and it may result in lower salaries and benefits for members of specific groups. Discrimination can also result in more favorable treatment to favored groups—for example, when an employer hires a job applicant of his or her own racial group because of the applicant's race (Avery, McKay, & Wilson, 2008; Pager & Shepherd, 2008; Leskinen, Rabelo, & Cortina, 2015).

Stereotyping not only leads to overt discrimination, but also can cause members of stereotyped groups to behave in ways that reflect the stereotype through a phenomenon known as the *self-fulfilling prophecy.* Self-fulfilling prophecies are expectations about the occurrence of a future event or behavior that act to increase the likelihood the event or behavior will occur. For example, if people think that members of a specific group lack ambition, they may treat them in a way that actually brings about a lack of ambition.

> **Although usually backed by little or no evidence, stereotypes can have harmful consequences.**

» LO41.1 The Foundations of Prejudice

No one has ever been born disliking a specific racial, religious, or ethnic group. People learn to hate, in much the same way that they learn the alphabet.

According to *observational learning approaches* to stereotyping and prejudice, the behavior of parents, other adults, and peers shapes children's feelings about members of various groups. For instance, bigoted parents may commend their children for expressing prejudiced attitudes. Likewise, young children learn prejudice by imitating the behavior of adult models. Such learning starts at an early age: children as young as 3 years of age begin to show preferences for members of their own race (Dovidio & Gaertner, 2006; Bronson & Merryman, 2009; Forscher & Devine, 2016).

The mass media also provide information about stereotypes, not just for children but for adults as well. Even today, some television shows and movies portray Italians as Mafia-like mobsters, Jews as greedy bankers, and African Americans as promiscuous or lazy. When such inaccurate portrayals are the primary source of information about minority groups, they can lead to the development and maintenance of unfavorable stereotypes (Ward, 2004; Do, 2006; Scharrer & Ramasubramanian, 2015).

Other explanations of prejudice and discrimination focus on how being a member of a specific group helps to magnify one's sense of self-esteem. According to *social identity theory,* we use group membership as a source of pride and self-worth. Social identity theory suggests that people tend to be *ethnocentric,* viewing the world from their own perspective and judging others in terms of their group membership. Slogans such as "gay pride" and "black is beautiful" illustrate that the groups to which we belong give us a sense of self-respect (Tajfel & Turner, 2004; Hogg, 2006; Spears et al., 2010).

Like father, like son: social learning approaches to stereotyping and prejudice suggest that attitudes and behaviors toward members of minority groups are learned through the observation of parents and other individuals. How can this cycle be broken? © Barbara Burnes/Science Source

However, the use of group membership to provide social respect produces an unfortunate outcome. In an effort to maximize our sense of self-esteem, we may come to think that our own group (our *ingroup*) is better than groups to which we don't belong (our *outgroups*). Consequently, we inflate the positive aspects of our ingroup—and, at the same time, devalue outgroups. Ultimately, we come to view members of outgroups as inferior to members of our ingroup. The end result is prejudice toward members of groups of which we are not a part (Tajfel & Turner, 2004).

Neither the observational learning approach nor the social identity approach provides a full explanation for stereotyping and prejudice. For instance, some psychologists argue that prejudice results when there is perceived competition for scarce societal resources. Thus, when competition exists for jobs or housing, members of majority groups may believe (however unjustly or inaccurately) that minority group members are hindering their efforts to attain their goals, and this belief can lead to prejudice. In addition, other explanations for prejudice emphasize human cognitive limitations that lead us to categorize people on the basis of visually conspicuous physical features such as race, sex, and ethnic group. Such categorization can lead to the development of stereotypes and, ultimately, to discriminatory behavior (Weeks & Lupfer, 2004; Hugenberg & Sacco, 2008; Yoo & Pituc, 2013).

» LO41.2 Measuring Prejudice and Discrimination: The Implicit Personality Test

Could you be prejudiced and not even know it? The answer, according to the researchers who developed the *Implicit Association Test,* is probably yes. People often fool themselves, and they are very careful about revealing their true attitudes about members of various groups, not only to others but to themselves. However, even though they may truly believe that they are unprejudiced, the reality is that they actually routinely differentiate between people on the basis of race, ethnicity, and sexual orientation.

The Implicit Association Test, or IAT, is an ingenious measure of prejudice that permits a more accurate assessment of people's discrimination between members of different groups. It was developed, in part, as a reaction to the difficulty in finding a questionnaire that would reveal prejudice. Direct questions such as, "Would you prefer interacting with a member of Group X rather than Group Y?" typically identify only the most blatant prejudices, because people try to censor their responses (Rudman & Ashmore, 2007; Schnabel, Asendorpf, & Greenwald, 2008; Greenwald et al., 2009).

In contrast, the IAT makes use of the fact that people's automatic reactions often provide the most valid indicator of what they actually believe. The test asks people a series of questions on a computerized survey that assess the degree to which people associate members of target groups (say, African Americans versus whites) with positive stimuli (such as a puppy) versus negative stimuli (such as a funeral). The test is based on the fact that growing up in a particular culture teaches us to unconsciously associate members of particular groups with positive or negative qualities, and we tend to absorb associations about those groups that reflect the culture without even being aware of it (Lane et al., 2007; Blanton, Jaccard, & Burrows, 2015).

STUDY ALERT

Remember that the Implicit Association Test (IAT) allows measurement of attitudes about which people might not be consciously aware, as well as attitudes they wish to keep hidden from others.

The results of the IAT show that almost 90 percent of test takers have a pro-white implicit bias, and more than two-thirds of non-Arab, non-Muslim volunteers display implicit biases against Arab Muslims. Moreover, more than 80 percent of heterosexuals display an implicit bias against gays and lesbians (Wittenbrink & Schwarz, 2007).

Of course, having an implicit bias does not mean that people will overtly discriminate, which is a criticism that has been made of the test. Yet it does mean that the cultural lessons to which we are exposed have a considerable unconscious influence on us. (Interested in how you would perform on the IAT? Go to this website to take the test: https://implicit.harvard.edu/implicit).

» LO41.3 Reducing Prejudice and Discrimination

How can we diminish the effects of prejudice and discrimination? Psychologists have developed several strategies that have proved effective, including the following:

- *Increasing contact between the target of stereotyping and the holder of the stereotype.* Research consistently has shown that increasing the amount of interaction between people can reduce negative stereotyping. But only certain kinds of contact are likely to reduce prejudice and discrimination. Situations in which contact is relatively intimate, the individuals are of equal status, or participants must cooperate with one another or are dependent on one another are more likely to reduce stereotyping. On the other hand, even virtual contact via social media may be sufficient to improve intergroup relations (Tropp & Pettigrew, 2005; Pettigrew & Tropp, 2006; Ruggs, Martinez, & Hebl, 2011; White, Harvey, & Abu-Rayya, 2015).

From the perspective of …

A Criminal Justice Worker How might overt forms of prejudice and discrimination toward disadvantaged groups (such as African Americans) be reduced in a state or federal prison?

- *Making values and norms against prejudice more conspicuous.* Sometimes just reminding people about the values they already hold regarding equality and fair treatment of others is enough to reduce discrimination. Similarly, people who hear others making strong, vehement antiracist statements are subsequently more likely to strongly condemn racism (Ponterotto, Utsey, & Pedersen, 2006; Tropp & Bianchi, 2006; Rutland & Killen, 2015).

- *Providing information about the targets of stereotyping.* Probably the most direct means of changing stereotypical and discriminatory attitudes is education: teaching people to be more aware of the positive

characteristics of targets of stereotyping. For instance, when the meaning of puzzling behavior is explained to people who hold stereotypes, they may come to appreciate the actual significance of the behavior (Isbell & Tyler, 2003; Banks, 2006; Nagda, Tropp, & Paluck, 2006).

■ *Reducing stereotype threat.* Social psychologist Claude Steele suggests that many African Americans suffer from *stereotype vulnerability,* obstacles to performance that stem from their awareness of society's stereotypes regarding minority group members. He argues that African-American students too often receive instruction from teachers who doubt their students' abilities and who set up remedial programs to assist their students. As a result of their teachers' (as well as society's) low expectations for their performance, African-American students may come to accept society's stereotypes and come to believe that they are likely to fail (Aronson & Steele, 2005; Nussbaum & Steele, 2007; Aronson & Dee, 2012).

Such beliefs can have devastating effects. When confronted with an academic task, African-American students may fear that their performance will simply confirm society's negative stereotypes. The immediate consequence of this fear is anxiety that hampers performance. But the long-term consequences may be even worse: doubting their ability to perform successfully in academic environments, African Americans may decide that the risks of failure are so great it is not worth the effort even to attempt to do well. Ultimately, they may "disidentify" with academic success by minimizing the importance of academic endeavors (Steele, 1997; Stone, 2002).

However, Steele's analysis suggests that African Americans may be able to overcome their predicament. Specifically, schools can design intervention programs to train minority group members about their vulnerability to stereotypes and provide them with self-affirmation that reinforces their confidence in their abilities and thereby inoculates them against the fear and doubt triggered by negative stereotypes (Cohen et al., 2006; Wilson, 2006; Shnabel et al., 2013).

■ *Increasing the sense of social belonging of ethnic minority students.* Although almost every college student faces feelings of inadequacy and uncertainty about belonging at the start of college, such feelings are especially strong for members of groups who are underrepresented and have been the targets of prejudice and discrimination. However, research shows that a simple intervention in which members of minority groups are made to understand that feelings of inadequacy are not unique to them—and that such feelings usually diminish with time—can help minority students increase their sense of social belonging (Walton & Cohen, 2011).

RECAP

Identify the foundations of prejudice.

- Stereotypes are generalized beliefs and expectations about a specific group and its members. Stereotyping can lead to prejudice and self-fulfilling prophecies.

- Prejudice is the negative (or positive) evaluation of a particular group and its members.

- According to observational learning approaches, children learn stereotyping and prejudice by observing the behavior of parents, other adults, and peers. Social identity theory suggests that group membership is used as a source of pride and self-worth, and this may lead people to think of their own group as better than others.

Distinguish measuring practices for prejudice and discrimination.

- Stereotyping and prejudice can lead to discrimination, behavior directed toward individuals on the basis of their membership in a particular group.

Assess ways to reduce prejudice and discrimination.

- Among the ways of reducing prejudice and discrimination are increasing contact, demonstrating positive values against prejudice, and education.

[EVALUATE] E Evaluate

1. Any expectation—positive or negative—about an individual solely on the basis of that person's membership in a group can be a stereotype. True or false?

2. The negative (or positive) evaluation of a group and its members is called

   a. Stereotyping.

   b. Prejudice.

   c. Self-fulfilling prophecy.

   d. Discrimination.

3. Paul is a store manager who does not expect women to succeed in business. He therefore offers important, high-profile responsibilities only to men. If the female employees fail to move up in the company, it could be an example of a _____ _____ prophecy.

[RETHINK] R Rethink

Do you think it matters that some people have implicit biases against certain groups if those people never express their biases explicitly? Why or why not?

Answers to Evaluate Questions 1. true; 2. b; 3. self-fulfilling

KEY TERMS

Stereotype   LO41.1

Prejudice   LO41.1

Discrimination   LO41.1

Positive and Negative Social Behavior

Learning Outcomes

>> **LO42.1** Compare and contrast the concepts of "like" and love.

>> **LO42.2** Explain aggression and prosocial behavior.

MODULE OUTLINE

Liking and Loving: Interpersonal Attraction and the Development of Relationships

Try It! Understand Your Relationship Style

Aggression and Prosocial Behavior: Hurting and Helping Others

W **Work**

Are people basically good or bad?

Like philosophers and theologians, social psychologists have pondered the basic nature of humanity. Is it represented mainly by the violence and cruelty we see throughout the world, or does something special about human nature permit loving, considerate, unselfish, and even noble behavior as well?

We turn to two routes that social psychologists have followed in seeking answers to these questions. We first consider what they have learned about the sources of our attraction to others, and end with a look at two opposite sides of human behavior: aggression and helping.

>> LO42.1 Liking and Loving: Interpersonal Attraction and the Development of Relationships

Nothing is more important in most people's lives than their feelings for others. Consequently, it is not surprising that liking and loving have become a major focus of interest for social psychologists. Known more formally as the study of **interpersonal attraction** or **close relationships,** this area addresses the factors that lead to positive feelings for others.

interpersonal attraction (or close relationship) Positive feelings for others; liking and loving

How Do I Like Thee? Let Me Count the Ways

Research has given us a good deal of knowledge about the factors that initially attract two people to each other. The important factors considered by social psychologists are the following:

- *Proximity.* Consider the friends you made when you first moved to a new neighborhood. Chances are that you became friendliest with those who lived geographically closest to you. In fact, this is one of the more firmly established findings in the literature on interpersonal attraction: proximity leads to liking (Burgoon et al., 2002; Smith & Weber, 2005; Semin & Garrido, 2013).

- *Mere exposure.* Repeated exposure to a person is often sufficient to produce attraction. Interestingly, repeated exposure to *any* stimulus—a person, picture, compact disc, or virtually anything— usually makes us like the stimulus more. In cases of strongly negative initial interactions, though, repeated exposure may instead intensify our initial dislike (Zajonc, 2001; Butler & Berry, 2004).

- *Similarity.* Discovering that others have similar attitudes, values, or traits makes us like them more. Furthermore, the more similar others are, the more we like them. One reason similarity increases the likelihood of interpersonal attraction is that we assume that people with similar attitudes will evaluate us positively. Because we experience a strong *reciprocity-of-liking effect* (a tendency to like those who like us), knowing that someone evaluates us positively promotes our attraction to that person (Umphress, Smith-Crowe, & Brief, 2007; Montoya & Insko, 2008; Heffernan & Fraley, 2015).

"I'm attracted to you, but then I'm attracted to me, too."

- *Physical attractiveness.* For most people, the equation *beautiful = good* is literally true. As a result, physically attractive people are more popular than physically unattractive ones, if all other factors are equal. This finding, which contradicts the values that most people say they hold, is apparent even in childhood—with nursery-school-age children rating their peers' popularity on the basis of attractiveness—and continues into adulthood (Little, Burt, & Perrett, 2006; Luo & Zhang, 2009; Fales et al., 2016).

Friendship and Social Networking. The newest forms of friendship are found on social network sites. One out of 10 people *worldwide* belongs to Facebook, and the concentration of college students using the social network site is more than 90 percent.

For college students, the primary motivation in using social network sites is to keep in touch with their friends. In addition, younger college students use Facebook to explore their developing identities. Because users can control how they present themselves to the world on a social network profile, it is easy for college students to "try on" an identity by posting selected photos of themselves, revealing specific tastes and interests, or otherwise presenting themselves in new and different ways. The feedback they get from others may help them decide which identities and forms of self-presentation suit them best (Subrahmanyam et al., 2008; Pempek, Yermolayeva, & Calvert, 2009; Yang & Bradford Brown, 2016).

But how do social network sites affect users' nonvirtual social lives? Maintaining social connections that might otherwise have withered and died seems like a good thing, but it may be detrimental if someone spends so much time maintaining online distant or superficial friendships that they sacrifice time spent on intimate, face-to-face interactions with close friends (Steinfeld, Ellison, & Lampe, 2008).

It turns out, though, that intensity of Facebook use is positively related to college students' life satisfaction, social trust, and civic engagement. In short, research suggests that users of social network sites are not disengaged from the real world, and that the benefits of social networking may outweigh the costs to real-world social lives (Valenzuela, Park, & Kee, 2009; Brandtzæg, Lüders, & Skjetne, 2010).

How Do I Love Thee? Let Me Count the Ways

As a first step to investigating love, researchers tried to identify the characteristics that distinguish between mere liking and full-blown love. They discovered that love is not simply a greater quantity of liking, but a qualitatively different psychological state. For instance, at least in its early stages, love includes relatively intense physiological arousal, an all-encompassing interest in another individual, fantasizing about the other, and relatively rapid swings of emotion. Similarly, love, unlike liking, includes elements of passion, closeness, fascination, exclusiveness, sexual desire, and intense caring. We idealize partners by exaggerating their good qualities and minimizing their imperfections (Murray, Holmes, & Griffin, 2004; Tamini, Bojhd, & Yazdani, 2011).

Other researchers have theorized that there are two main types of love: passionate love and companionate love. **Passionate** (or **romantic**) **love** represents a state of intense absorption in someone. It includes intense physiological arousal, psychological interest, and caring for the needs of another. In contrast, **companionate love** is the strong affection we have for those with whom our lives are deeply involved. The love we feel for our parents, other family members, and even some close friends falls into the category of companionate love (Masuda, 2003; Regan, 2006; Loving, Crockett, & Paxson, 2009).

Psychologist Robert Sternberg makes an even finer differentiation between types of love. He proposes that love consists of three parts:

- *Decision/commitment,* the initial thoughts that one loves someone and the longer-term feelings of commitment to maintain love.

passionate (or romantic) love A state of intense absorption in someone that includes intense physiological arousal, psychological interest, and caring for the needs of another

companionate love The strong affection we have for those with whom our lives are deeply involved

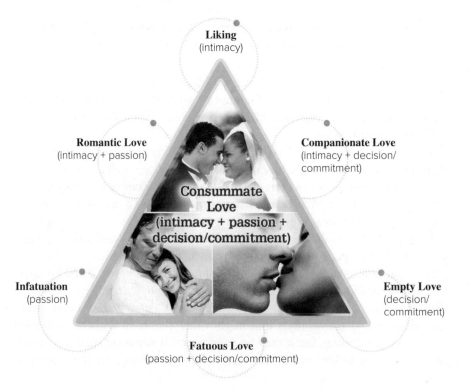

Figure 1 According to Sternberg, love has three main components: intimacy, passion, and decision/commitment. Different combinations of these components can create other types of love. Nonlove contains none of the three components. Photos: (wedding couple) © Brand X Pictures/PunchStock RF; (hugging couple) © BananaStock/Getty Images RF; (kissing couple) © Digital Vision/Getty Images RF

Rank Ordering of Desired Characteristics in a Mate							
	United States		China		South Africa Zulu		
	Females	Males	Females	Males	Females	Males
Mutual attraction—love	1	1	8	4	5	10
Emotional stability and maturity	2	2	1	5	2	1
Dependable character	3	3	7	6	1	3
Pleasing disposition	4	4	16	13	3	4
Education and intelligence	5	5	4	8	6	6
Good health	9	6	3	1	4	5
Good looks	13	7	15	11	16	14
Sociability	8	8	9	12	8	11
Desire for home and children	7	9	2	2	9	9
Refinement, neatness	12	10	10	7	10	7
Ambition and industriousness	6	11	5	10	7	8
Similar education	10	12	12	15	12	12
Good cook and houskeeper	16	13	11	9	15	2
Favorable social status or rating	14	14	13	14	14	17
Similar religious background	15	15	18	18	11	16
Good financial prospect	11	16	14	16	13	18
Chastity (no prior sexual intercourse)	18	17	6	3	18	13
Similar political background	17	18	17	17	17	15

Figure 2 Although love may be an important factor in choosing a marriage partner if you live in the United States, other cultures place less importance on it. Source: Based on Buss, Abbott, & Angleitner, 1990.

- *Intimacy component,* feelings of closeness and connectedness.
- *Passion component,* the motivational drives relating to sex, physical closeness, and romance.

According to Sternberg, these three components combine to produce the different types of love (see Figure 1). He suggests that different combinations of the three components vary over the course of relationships. For example, in strong, loving relationships the level of commitment peaks and then remains stable. Passion, on the other hand, peaks quickly, and then declines and levels off relatively early in most relationships. In addition, relationships are happiest in which the strength of the various components are similar between the two partners (Sternberg, Hojjat, & Barnes, 2001; Sternberg, 2004, 2006).

Is love a necessary ingredient in a good marriage? Yes, if you live in the United States. But it's considerably less important in other cultures. Although mutual attraction and love are the two most important characteristics men and women in the United States desire in a mate, men in China rated good health as most important, and women there rated emotional stability and maturity as most important. Among the Zulu in South Africa, men rated emotional stability first and women rated dependable character first (Buss, Abbott, & Angleitner, 1990; see Figure 2). (To consider how you approach relationships, complete the Try It!.)

> Is love a necessary ingredient in a good marriage? Yes, if you live in the United States. But it's considerably less important in other cultures.

How we meet our romantic partners and spouses has changed drastically over the years. In the 1940s, heterosexual Americans met their future family members

Understand Your Relationship Style

Each of us has a general manner in which we approach close relationships with others. Read the three statements below, and determine which best describes you.

1. I find it relatively easy to get close to others and am comfortable depending on them and having them depend on me. I don't often worry about being abandoned or about someone getting too close to me.

2. I am somewhat uncomfortable being close to others; I find it difficult to trust them completely and to allow myself to depend on them. I am nervous when anyone gets too close, and often love partners want me to be more intimate than I feel comfortable being.

3. I find that others are reluctant to get as close as I would like. I often worry that my partner doesn't really love me or won't want to stay with me. I want to merge completely with another person, and this desire sometimes scares people away.

The choice you make suggests the general style of emotional bonds that you develop with others.

If you thought the first statement described you best, it is probably easy for you to develop close ties with others. Around 55 percent of people describe themselves in this way.

If statement 2 describes you best, you probably have a more difficult time getting close to others, and you may have to work harder to develop close ties with other people. About 25 percent of people place themselves in this category.

Finally, if statement 3 describes you best, you, along with the 20 percent of people who describe themselves in this way, aggressively seek out close relationships. However, they probably present a source of concern to you.

Keep in mind that this is an inexact assessment and presents only a very rough estimate of your general approach to close relationships. But your response can be helpful in answering these questions: Are you generally satisfied with your relationships? Would you like to change them in some way?

most often through family. Now friends and the Internet are much more frequent matchmakers (see Figure 3). The likelihood of meeting online is even greater for same-sex couples today; some 70 percent of gay couples report meeting online (Rosenfeld & Thomas, 2012).

Liking and loving clearly show a positive side of human social behavior. Now we turn to behaviors that are just as much a part of social behavior: aggression and helping behavior.

» LO42.2 Aggression and Prosocial Behavior: Hurting and Helping Others

Drive-by shootings, carjackings, and abductions are just a few examples of the violence that seems all too common today. But also common are the simple kindnesses of life: lending a valued compact disc, stopping to help a child who has fallen off her bicycle, or merely sharing a candy bar with a friend. Such instances of helping are no less characteristic of human behavior than the distasteful examples of aggression.

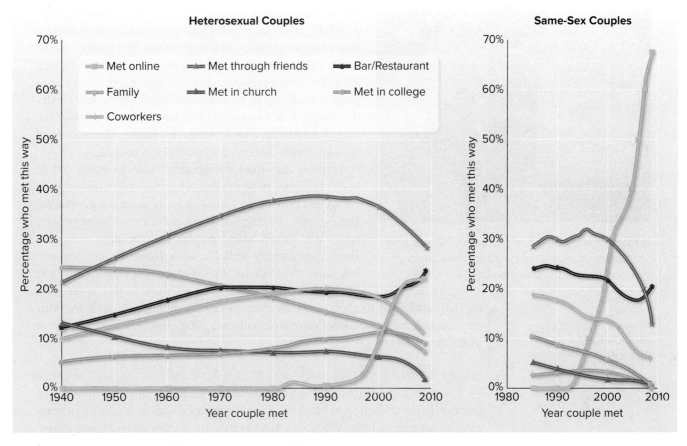

Figure 3 Couples are considerably more likely to meet online today than for couples in earlier generations, a change that holds true both for heterosexual and gay couples. Source: Rosenfeld, M.J., & Thomas, R.J. (2012). Searching for a mate: The rise of the Internet as a social intermediary. *American Sociological Review, 77,* 523-547.

Hurting Others: Aggression

We need look no further than the daily paper or the nightly news to be bombarded with examples of **aggression,** the intentional injury of, or harm to, another person, both on a societal level (war, invasion, assassination) and on an individual level (crime, child abuse, and the many petty cruelties humans are capable of inflicting on one another). Is such aggression an inevitable part of the human condition? Or is aggression primarily a product of particular circumstances that, if changed, could lead to its reduction?

It is also clear that the everyday aggression we encounter in our daily lives can take many forms. Not only do we hurt others through direct physical or verbal attacks, but we can hurt people indirectly by doing such things as spreading rumors or by purposely ignoring someone. In fact, psychologists have found that *microaggressions*—small, daily slights, put downs, and insults, often perpetrated against members of marginalized groups based on race, gender, and sexual orientation—may be more harmful in the long run than highly visible acts of aggression (Sue, 2010; South Richardson, 2014).

Instinct Approaches: Aggression as a Release. Instinct theories, noting the prevalence of aggression not only in humans but in animals as well, propose that aggression is primarily the outcome of innate—or inborn—urges.

Sigmund Freud was one of the first to suggest, as part of his theory of personality, that aggression is a primary instinctual drive. Konrad Lorenz, an ethologist (a scientist who studies animal behavior), expanded Freud's notions by arguing

> **aggression** The intentional injury of, or harm to, another person

Is road rage the result of frustration? According to frustration-aggression approaches, frustration is a likely cause. © Chris Ryan/AGE Fotostock RF

that humans, along with members of other species, have a fighting instinct, which in earlier times ensured protection of food supplies and weeded out the weaker of the species (Lorenz, 1966, 1974). Lorenz's instinct approach led to the controversial notion that aggressive energy constantly builds up in an individual until the person finally discharges it in a process called **catharsis.** The longer the energy builds up, says Lorenz, the greater the amount of the aggression displayed when it is discharged.

Probably the most controversial idea to come out of instinct theories of aggression is Lorenz's proposal that society should provide acceptable ways of permitting catharsis. For example, he suggested that participation in aggressive sports and games would prevent the discharge of aggression in less socially desirable ways. However, little research has found evidence for the existence of a pent-up reservoir of aggression that needs to be released. In fact, some studies flatly contradict the notion of catharsis, leading psychologists to look for other explanations for aggression (Verona & Sullivan, 2008; Potegal, 2010; Shaver & Mikulincer, 2011).

catharsis The process of discharging built-up aggressive energy

Frustration-Aggression Approaches: Aggression as a Reaction to Frustration. Frustration-aggression theory suggests that *frustration* (the reaction to the thwarting or blocking of goals) produces anger, leading to a readiness to act aggressively. Whether actual aggression occurs depends on the presence of aggressive cues, stimuli that have been associated in the past with actual aggression or violence and that will trigger aggression again (Berkowitz, 2001).

What kinds of stimuli act as aggressive cues? They can range from the most explicit, such as the presence of weapons, to more subtle cues, such as the mere mention of the name of an individual who behaved violently in the past (Berkowitz, 2001; Jovanović, Stanojević, & Stanojević, 2011; Wang & Zhong, 2015).

Observational Learning Approaches: Learning to Hurt Others. Do we learn to be aggressive? The observational learning (sometimes called social learning) approach to aggression says that we do. Taking an almost opposite view from instinct theories, which focus on innate explanations of aggression, observational learning theory emphasizes that social and environmental conditions can teach individuals to be aggressive. The theory sees aggression not as inevitable, but rather as a learned response that can be understood in terms of rewards and punishments.

What kinds of stimuli act as aggressive cues? They can range from the most explicit, such as the presence of weapons, to more subtle cues, such as the mere mention of the name of an individual who behaved violently in the past.

Observational learning theory pays particular attention not only to direct rewards and punishments that individuals themselves receive, but also to the rewards and punishments that models—individuals who provide a guide to appropriate behavior—receive for their aggressive behavior. According to observational learning theory, people observe the behavior of models and the subsequent consequences of that behavior. If the consequences are positive, the behavior is likely to be imitated when observers find themselves in a similar situation.

Suppose, for instance, a girl hits her younger brother when he damages one of her new toys.

Whereas instinct theory would suggest that the aggression had been pent up and was now being discharged and frustration-aggression theory would examine the girl's frustration at no longer being able to use her new toy, observational learning theory would look to previous situations in which the girl had viewed others being rewarded for their aggression. For example, perhaps she had watched a friend get to play with a toy after he painfully twisted it out of the hand of another child.

Observational learning theory has received wide research support. For example, nursery-school-age children who have watched an adult model behave aggressively and then receive reinforcement for it later display similar behavior themselves if they have been angered, insulted, or frustrated after exposure. Furthermore, a significant amount of research links watching television shows containing violence with subsequent viewer aggression (Winerman, 2005; Greer, Dudek-Singer, & Gautreaux, 2006; Carnagey, Anderson, & Bartholow, 2007).

STUDY ALERT

Understand the distinction between the instinctual, frustration-aggression, and observational learning approaches to aggression.

From the perspective of . . .

A Criminal Justice Worker How would the aggression of Eric Rudolph, who was convicted of exploding a bomb during the 1996 Summer Olympics in Atlanta and later attacking several women's clinics, be interpreted by proponents of the three main approaches to the study of aggression: instinct approaches, frustration-aggression approaches, and observational learning approaches? Do you think any of these approaches fits the Rudolph case more closely than the others?

Helping Others: The Brighter Side of Human Nature

Turning away from aggression, we move now to the opposite—and brighter—side of human nature: helping behavior. Helping behavior, or **prosocial behavior** as it is more formally known, has been considered under many different conditions. However, the question that psychologists have looked at most closely relates to bystander intervention in emergency situations. What are the factors that lead someone to help a person in need?

One critical factor is the number of others present. When more than one person witnesses an emergency situation, a sense of **diffusion of responsibility** can arise among the bystanders. Diffusion of responsibility is the tendency for people to feel that responsibility for acting is shared, or diffused, among those present. The more people who are present in an emergency, the less personally responsible each individual feels—and therefore the less help he or she provides (Gray, 2006; Li et al., 2010; Martin & North, 2015).

For example, think back to the classic case of Kitty Genovese that we described when discussing the topic of research. Genovese was stabbed multiple times, and—according to some accounts of the event—no one offered help, despite the fact that allegedly close to 40 people who lived in nearby apartments heard her screams for help. The lack of help has been attributed to diffusion of responsibility:

prosocial behavior Helping behavior

diffusion of responsibility The tendency for people to feel that responsibility for acting is shared, or diffused, among those present

Altruism is often the only bright side of a natural disaster. Library of Congress Prints and Photographs Division [LC-DIG-ppmsca-01814]

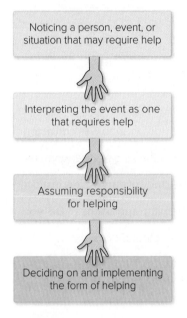

Figure 4 The basic steps of helping. Source: Based on Latané & Darley, 1970.

altruism Helping behavior that is beneficial to others but clearly requires self-sacrifice

the fact that there were so many potential helpers led each individual to feel diminished personal responsibility (Fischer et al., 2011; Gallo, 2015; Griggs, 2015).

Although most research on helping behavior supports the diffusion-of-responsibility explanation, other factors are clearly involved in helping behavior. The decision to give aid involves four basic steps (Latané & Darley, 1970; Garcia et al., 2002; see Figure 4):

- *Noticing a person, event, or situation that may require help.* If we are to provide help, we first have to perceive that a situation is one that potentially requires our help and intervention.

- *Interpreting the event as one that requires help.* Even if we notice an event, it may be sufficiently ambiguous for us to interpret it as a nonemergency situation that requires no help. Thus, we make an interpretation as to whether or not the event requires help.

- *Assuming responsibility for helping.* It is at this key point that diffusion of responsibility is likely to occur if others are present.

- *Deciding on and implementing the form of helping.* After we assume responsibility for helping, we must decide how to provide assistance. Helping can range from very indirect forms of intervention, such as calling the police, to more direct forms, such as giving first aid or taking the victim to a hospital. Most social psychologists use a rewards-costs approach for helping to predict the nature of the assistance a bystander will choose to provide. The general notion is that the bystander's perceived rewards for helping must outweigh the costs if helping is to occur, and most research tends to support this notion (Bartlett & DeSteno, 2006; Lin & Lin, 2007; Levine & Cassidy, 2010).

After determining the nature of the assistance needed, the actual help must be implemented. A rewards-costs analysis suggests that we are most likely to use the least costly form of implementation. However, this is not always the case: in some situations, people behave altruistically. **Altruism** is helping behavior that is beneficial to others but clearly requires self-sacrifice. For example, people who put themselves at mortal risk to help strangers escape from the burning World Trade Center towers during the 9/11 terrorist attack would be considered altruistic (Krueger, Hicks, & McGue, 2001; Batson & Powell, 2003; Manor & Gailliot, 2007; Marshall, 2011).

People who intervene in emergency situations tend to possess certain personality characteristics that differentiate them from nonhelpers. For example, helpers are more self-assured, sympathetic, and emotionally understanding, and they have greater *empathy* (a personality trait in which someone observing another person experiences the emotions of that person) than nonhelpers (Graziano et al., 2007; Walker & Frimer, 2007; Stocks, Lishner, & Decker, 2009).

Still, most social psychologists agree that no single set of attributes differentiates helpers from nonhelpers. For the most part, temporary situational factors (such as the mood we're in) determine whether we will intervene in a situation requiring aid (Eisenberg, Guthrie, & Cumberland, 2002; Dovidio & Gaertner, 2006).

RECAP

Compare and contrast the concepts of "like" and love.

- The primary determinants of liking include proximity, exposure, similarity, and physical attractiveness.

- Loving is distinguished from liking by the presence of intense physiological arousal, an all-encompassing interest in another, fantasies about the other, rapid swings of emotion, fascination, sexual desire, exclusiveness, and strong feelings of caring.

- Love can be categorized as passionate or companionate. In addition, love has several components: intimacy, passion, and decision/commitment.

Explain aggression and prosocial behavior.

- Aggression is intentional injury of, or harm to, another person.
- Explanations of aggression include instinct approaches, frustration-aggression theory, and observational learning.

- Helping behavior in emergencies is determined in part by the phenomenon of diffusion of responsibility, which results in a lower likelihood of helping when more people are present.
- Deciding to help is the outcome of a four-stage process consisting of noticing a possible need for help, interpreting the situation as requiring aid, assuming responsibility for taking action, and deciding on and implementing a form of assistance.

[EVALUATE E Evaluate]

1. We tend to like people who are similar to us. True or false?
2. Which of the following sets are the three components of love proposed by Sternberg?
   a. Passion, closeness, sexuality
   b. Attraction, desire, complementarity
   c. Passion, intimacy, decision/commitment
   d. Commitment, caring, sexuality
3. Based on research evidence, which of the following might be the best way to reduce the amount of fighting a young boy does?
   a. Take him to the gym and let him work out on the boxing equipment.
   b. Make him repeatedly watch violent scenes from the film *The Matrix Reloaded* in the hope that it will provide catharsis.
   c. Reward him if he doesn't fight during a certain period.
   d. Ignore it and let it die out naturally.
4. If a person in a crowd does not help in an apparent emergency situation because many other people are present, that person is falling victim to the phenomenon of _____ _____ _____.

[RETHINK R Rethink]

Can love be studied scientifically? Is there an elusive quality to love that makes it at least partially unknowable? How would you define "falling in love"? How would you study it?

Answers to Evaluate Questions 1. true; 2. c; 3. c; 4. diffusion of responsibility

KEY TERMS

Interpersonal attraction (or close relationship) LO42.1

Passionate (or romantic) love LO42.1

Companionate love LO42.1

Aggression LO42.2

Catharsis LO42.2

Prosocial behavior LO42.2

Diffusion of responsibility LO42.2

Altruism LO42.2

Stress and Coping

Learning Outcomes

>> **LO43.1** Define stress and discuss how it affects us.

>> **LO43.2** Explain the nature of stressors.

>> **LO43.3** Describe how people cope with stress.

MODULE OUTLINE

Stress: Reacting to Threat and Challenge

The Nature of Stressors: My Stress Is Your Pleasure

Coping with Stress

Try It! How Resilient Are You?

Becoming an Informed Consumer of Psychology: Effective Coping Strategies

Sheila Gray remembers the worst moment of her life: the day she heard about the mass shootings at Sandy Hook Elementary School in 2012 in Connecticut. Though Gray lives in Michigan, she immediately jumped in the car and drove to her 7-year-old daughter's school. She brought the girl home. "My heart was pounding. I started crying and I just couldn't stop," Gray says. Then and there, she decided that her daughter, Merilee, would never return to her school. She began homeschooling the girl. Friends could come over, but Gray found she couldn't let Merilee out of her sight. "So much can happen when you walk away from your child," Gray says. "I was terrified by that loss of control."

>> LO43.1 Stress: Reacting to Threat and Challenge

stress A person's response to events that are threatening or challenging

Most of us need little introduction to the phenomenon of **stress,** people's response to events that threaten or challenge them. Whether it is a family problem or even the ongoing threat of a terrorist attack, life is full of circumstances and events, known as *stressors,* that produce threats to our well-being. Even pleasant events—such as planning a party or beginning a sought-after job—can produce stress, although negative events result in greater detrimental consequences than positive ones.

All of us face stress in our lives. Some psychologists believe that daily life actually involves a series of repeated sequences of perceiving a threat, considering ways to cope with it, and ultimately adapting to the threat, with greater or lesser success. Although adaptation is often minor and occurs without our awareness, adaptation requires a major effort when stress is more severe or longer lasting. Ultimately, our attempts to overcome stress may produce biological and psychological responses that result in health problems (Dolbier, Smith, & Steinhardt, 2007; Clements & Bailey, 2010; Finan, Zautra, & Wershba, 2011).

STUDY ALERT

Remember the distinction between stressors and stress, which can be tricky: stressors (like an exam) cause stress (the physiological and psychological reaction that comes from the exam).

» LO43.2 The Nature of Stressors: My Stress Is Your Pleasure

Stress is a very personal thing. Although certain kinds of events, such as the death of a loved one or participation in military combat, are universally stressful, other situations may or may not be stressful to a specific person.

Consider, for instance, bungee jumping. Some people would find jumping off a bridge while attached to a slender rubber tether extremely stressful. However, there are individuals who see such an activity as challenging and fun-filled. Whether bungee jumping is stressful depends in part, then, on a person's perception of the activity.

For people to consider an event stressful, they must perceive it as threatening or challenging and must lack all the resources to deal with it effectively. Consequently, the same event may at some times be stressful and at other times provoke no stressful reaction at all. A young man may experience stress when he is turned down for a date—if he attributes the refusal to his unattractiveness or unworthiness. But if he attributes it to some factor unrelated to his self-esteem, such as a previous commitment by the woman he asked, the experience of being refused may create no stress at all. Hence, a person's interpretation of events plays an important role in the determination of what is stressful (Giacobbi et al., 2004; MacKinnon & Luecken, 2008; Tuckey et al., 2015).

> For people to consider an event stressful, they must perceive it as threatening or challenging and must lack all the resources to deal with it effectively.

Categorizing Stressors

What kinds of events tend to be seen as stressful? There are three general types of stressors: cataclysmic events, personal stressors, and background stressors.

Cataclysmic events are strong stressors that occur suddenly and typically affect many people simultaneously. Disasters such as tornadoes and plane crashes, as well as terrorist attacks, are examples of cataclysmic events that can affect hundreds or thousands of people simultaneously.

Although it might seem that cataclysmic events would produce potent, lingering stress, in many cases they do not. In fact, cataclysmic events involving natural disasters may produce less stress in the long run than events that initially are not as devastating. One reason is that natural disasters have a clear resolution. Once they are over, people can look to the future knowing that the worst is behind them. Moreover, others who also experienced the disaster share the stress induced by cataclysmic events. Such sharing permits people to offer one another social support and a firsthand understanding of the difficulties others are going through (Yesilyaprak, Kisac, & Sanlier, 2007; Schwarzer & Luszczynska, 2013).

The second major category of stressor is the personal stressor. **Personal stressors** include major life events such as the death of a parent or spouse,

cataclysmic events Strong stressors that occur suddenly, affecting many people at once (e.g., natural disasters)

personal stressors Major life events, such as the death of a family member, that have immediate consequences that generally fade with time

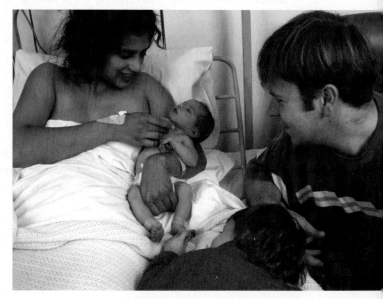

Even positive events can produce significant stress.
© Jennie Hart/Alamy Stock Photo

the loss of one's job, a major personal failure, or even something positive such as getting married. Typically, personal stressors produce an immediate major reaction that soon tapers off. For example, stress arising from the death of a loved one tends to be greatest just after the time of death, but people begin to feel less stress and are better able to cope with the loss after the passage of time.

Some victims of major catastrophes and severe personal stressors experience **posttraumatic stress disorder (PTSD),** in which a person has experienced a significantly stressful event that has long-lasting effects that may include reexperiencing the event in vivid flashbacks or dreams. An episode of PTSD may be triggered by an otherwise innocent stimulus, such as the sound of a honking horn that leads a person to reexperience a past event that produced considerable stress.

Symptoms of posttraumatic stress disorder also include emotional numbing, sleep difficulties, interpersonal problems, alcohol and drug abuse, and in some cases suicide. For instance, the suicide rate for military veterans, many of whom participated in the Iraq and Afghanistan wars, is twice as high as for nonveterans (Pole, 2007; Kaplan et al., 2007; Magruder & Yeager, 2009).

Between 10 to 18 percent of soldiers returning from Iraq and Afghanistan show symptoms of PTSD, and the United States spends $3 billion a year on treating the disorder in military veterans. Furthermore, those who have experienced child abuse or rape, rescue workers facing overwhelming situations, and victims of sudden natural disasters or accidents that produce feelings of helplessness and shock may suffer from the same disorder. Even witnessing aggression between two people may trigger PTSD (Horesh et al., 2011; Huang & Kashubeck-West, 2015; Thompson, 2015).

Background stressors, or more informally, *daily hassles,* are the third major category of stressors. Exemplified by standing in a long line at a bank and getting stuck in a traffic jam, daily hassles are the minor irritations of life that we all face time and time again. Another type of background stressor is a long-term, chronic problem, such as experiencing dissatisfaction with school or a job, being in an unhappy relationship, or living in crowded quarters without privacy (Weinstein et al., 2004; McIntyre, Korn, & Matsuo, 2008; Barke, 2011).

By themselves, daily hassles do not require much coping or even a response on the part of the individual, although they certainly produce unpleasant emotions and moods. Yet daily hassles add up—and ultimately they may take as great of a toll as a single, more stressful incident. In fact, the *number* of daily hassles people face is associated with psychological symptoms and health problems such as flu, sore throat, and backaches.

The flip side of hassles is *uplifts,* the minor positive events that make us feel good—even if only temporarily. As indicated in Figure 1, uplifts range from relating well to a companion to finding one's surroundings pleasing. What is especially intriguing about uplifts is that they are associated with people's psychological health in just the opposite way that hassles are: the greater the number of uplifts we experience, the fewer the psychological symptoms we report later (Chamberlain & Zika, 1990; Jain, Mills, & Von Känel, 2007; Hurley & Kwon, 2013).

The High Cost of Stress

Stress can produce both biological and psychological consequences. Often the most immediate reaction to stress is biological. Specifically, exposure

posttraumatic stress disorder (PTSD) A phenomenon in which victims of major catastrophes or strong personal stressors feel long-lasting effects that may include reexperiencing the event in vivid flashbacks or dreams

background stressors ("daily hassles") Everyday annoyances, such as being stuck in traffic, that cause minor irritations and may have long-term ill effects if they continue or are compounded by other stressful events

> **Exemplified by standing in a long line at a bank and getting stuck in a traffic jam, daily hassles are the minor irritations of life that we all face time and time again.**

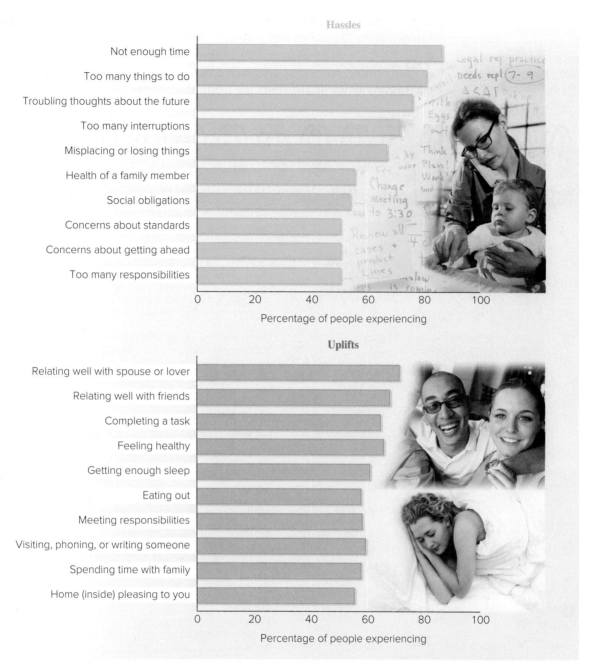

Figure 1 The most common everyday hassles and uplifts. How many of these are part of your life, and how do you cope with them? Source: Hassles adapted from Chamberlain, K. and S. Zika, 1990; Uplifts adapted from Kanner et al., 1981. Photos: (first) © Purestock/PunchStock RF; (second) © Purestock/Getty Images RF; (third) © Royalty-Free/CORBIS RF

to stressors generates a rise in hormone secretions by the adrenal glands, an increase in heart rate and blood pressure, and changes in how well the skin conducts electrical impulses. On a short-term basis, these responses may be adaptive because they produce an "emergency reaction" in which the body prepares to defend itself through activation of the sympathetic nervous system. Those responses may allow more effective coping with the stressful situation (Akil & Morano, 1996; McEwen, 1998; de Rooij et al., 2010; Vliegenthart et al., 2016).

However, continued exposure to stress results in a decline in the body's overall level of biological functioning because of the constant secretion of stress-related hormones. Over time, stressful reactions can promote deterioration of

psychophysiological disorders Medical problems influenced by an interaction of psychological, emotional, and physical difficulties

body tissues such as blood vessels and the heart. Ultimately, we become more susceptible to disease as our ability to fight off infection is lowered (Brydon et al., 2004; Dean-Borenstein, 2007; Ellins et al., 2008).

Furthermore, stress can produce or worsen physical problems. Specifically, **psychophysiological disorders** are medical problems that are influenced by an

---

Q How Stressful Is Your Life?

Test your level of stress by answering these questions, and adding the score from each box. Questions apply to the last month only. A key below will help you determine the extent of your stress.

1 How often have you been upset because of something that happened unexpectedly?

☐ 0 = never, 1 = almost never, 2 = sometimes, 3 = fairly often, 4 = very often

2 How often have you felt that you were unable to control the important things in your life?

☐ 0 = never, 1 = almost never, 2 = sometimes, 3 = fairly often, 4 = very often

3 How often have you felt nervous and "stressed"?

☐ 0 = never, 1 = almost never, 2 = sometimes, 3 = fairly often, 4 = very often

4 How often have you felt confident about your ability to handle your personal problems?

☐ 4 = never, 3 = almost never, 2 = sometimes, 1 = fairly often, 0 = very often

5 How often have you felt that things were going your way?

☐ 4 = never, 3 = almost never, 2 = sometimes, 1 = fairly often, 0 = very often

6 How often have you been able to control irritations in your life?

☐ 4 = never, 3 = almost never, 2 = sometimes, 1 = fairly often, 0 = very often

7 How often have you found that you could not cope with all the things that you had to do?

☐ 0 = never, 1 = almost never, 2 = sometimes, 3 = fairly often, 4 = very often

8 How often have you felt that you were on top of things?

☐ 4 = never, 3 = almost never, 2 = sometimes, 1 = fairly often, 0 = very often

9 How often have you been angered because of things that were outside your control?

☐ 0 = never, 1 = almost never, 2 = sometimes, 3 = fairly often, 4 = very often

10 How often have you felt difficulties were piling up so high that you could not overcome them?

☐ 0 = never, 1 = almost never, 2 = sometimes, 3 = fairly often, 4 = very often

How You Measure Up

Stress levels vary among individuals—compare your total score to the averages below:

AGE		GENDER	
18–29	14.2	Men	12.1
30–44	13.0	Women	13.7
45–54	12.6		
55–64	11.9		
65 & over	12.0		

MARITAL STATUS

Widowed	12.6
Married or living with a partner	12.4
Single or never wed	14.1
Divorced	14.7
Separated	16.6

Figure 2 To get a sense of the level of stress in your life, complete this questionnaire. Source: Adapted from Cohen, 1999.

interaction of psychological, emotional, and physical difficulties. Common psychophysiological disorders include high blood pressure, headaches, backaches, skin rashes, indigestion, fatigue, and constipation. Stress has even been linked to the common cold (Andrasik, 2006; Gupta, 2013; Gianaros & Wager, 2015).

In short, stress affects us in multiple ways. It may increase the risk that we will become ill, it may directly cause illness, it may make us less able to recover from a disease, and it may reduce our ability to cope with future stress. (See Figure 2 to get a measure of your own level of stress.)

The General Adaptation Syndrome Model: The Course of Stress

The effects of long-term stress are illustrated in a series of stages proposed by Hans Selye (pronounced "sell-yay"), a pioneering stress theorist (Selye, 1976, 1993). This model, the **general adaptation syndrome (GAS),** suggests that the physiological response to stress follows the same set pattern regardless of the cause of stress.

As shown in Figure 3, the GAS has three phases. The first stage—*alarm and mobilization*—occurs when people become aware of the presence of a stressor. On a biological level, the sympathetic nervous system becomes energized, with levels of the hormone cortisol rising. This helps a person cope initially with the stressor.

However, if the stressor persists, people move into the second response stage: *resistance*. During this stage, the body prepares to fight the stressor. During resistance,

Everyone confronts daily hassles, or background stressors, at some point. At what point do daily hassles become more than mere irritants? © Digital Vision/ PunchStock RF

general adaptation syndrome (GAS) A theory developed by Hans Selye that suggests that a person's response to a stressor consists of three stages: alarm and mobilization, resistance, and exhaustion

© Andresr/Getty Images RF

From the perspective of . . .

A Supervisor How would you help people deal with and avoid stress in their everyday lives? How might you encourage people to create social support networks?

Figure 3 The general adaptation syndrome (GAS) suggests that there are three major stages to stress responses. Source: Adapted from Selye, 1976.

people use a variety of means to cope with the stressor—sometimes successfully but at a cost of some degree of physical or psychological well-being. For example, a worker who faces the stress of impending layoffs might spend long hours working overtime, seeking to cope with the stress.

If resistance is inadequate, people enter the last stage of the GAS: *exhaustion*. During the exhaustion stage, a person's ability to adapt to the stressor declines to the point where negative consequences of stress appear: physical illness and psychological symptoms in the form of an inability to concentrate, heightened irritability, or, in severe cases, disorientation and a loss of touch with reality. In a sense, people wear out, and their physical reserves are used up.

How do people move out of the third stage after they have entered it? In some cases, exhaustion allows people to avoid a stressor. For example, people who become ill from overwork may be excused from their duties for a time, giving them a temporary respite from their responsibilities. At least for a time, then, the immediate stress is reduced.

Psychoneuroimmunology and Stress

psychoneuroimmunology (PNI) The study of the relationship among psychological factors, the immune system, and the brain

coping The efforts to control, reduce, or learn to tolerate the threats that lead to stress

Psychologists specializing in **psychoneuroimmunology (PNI),** the study of the relationship among psychological factors, the immune system, and the brain, have taken a broader approach to stress. Focusing on the outcomes of stress, they have identified three main consequences (see Figure 4).

First, stress has direct physiological results, including an increase in blood pressure, an increase in hormonal activity, and an overall decline in the functioning of the immune system. Second, stress leads people to engage in behaviors that are harmful to their health, including increased nicotine, drug, and alcohol use; poor eating habits; and decreased sleep. Finally, stress produces indirect consequences that result in declines in health: a reduction in the likelihood of obtaining health care and decreased compliance with medical advice when it is sought (Broman, 2005; Lindblad, Lindahl, & Theorell, 2006; Stowell, Robles, & Kane, 2013).

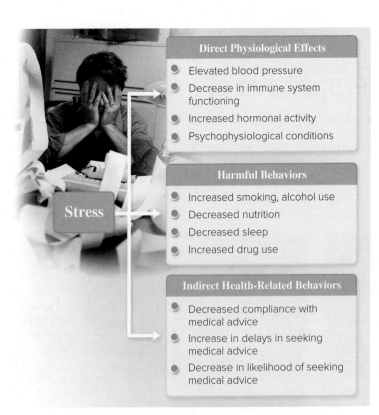

Figure 4 Three major types of consequences result from stress: direct physiological effects, harmful behaviors, and indirect health-related behaviors. Source: Adapted from Baum, 1994. Photo: © Russell Monk/ Getty Images

» LO43.3 Coping with Stress

Stress is a normal part of life—and not necessarily a completely bad part. For example, without stress, we might not be sufficiently motivated to complete the activities we need to accomplish. However, it is also clear that too much stress can take a toll on physical and psychological health. How do people deal with stress? Is there a way to reduce its negative effects?

Efforts to control, reduce, or learn to tolerate the threats that lead to stress are known as **coping.** We habitually use certain coping responses to deal with stress. Most of the time, we're not aware of these responses—just as we may be unaware of the minor stressors of life until they build up to harmful levels (Wrzesniewski & Chylinska, 2007; Collins, Onwuegbuzie, & Jiao, 2010).

We also have other, more direct, and potentially more positive ways of coping with stress, which fall into two main categories (Folkman & Moskowitz, 2000, 2004; Baker & Berenbaum, 2007):

- *Emotion-focused coping.* In emotion-focused coping, people try to manage their emotions in the face of stress, seeking to change the way they feel about or perceive a problem. Examples of emotion-focused coping include strategies such as accepting sympathy from others and looking at the bright side of a situation.

- *Problem-focused coping.* Problem-focused coping attempts to modify the stressful problem or source of stress. Problem-focused strategies lead to changes in behavior or to the development of a plan of action to deal with stress. Getting your resume ready when impending layoffs are announced is an example of problem-focused coping.

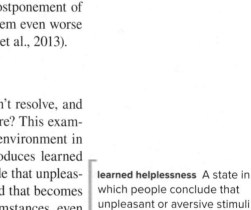

The ability to fight off disease is related to psychological factors. Here, a cell from the body's immune system engulfs and destroys disease-producing bacteria. © Science Source

People often employ both emotion-focused and problem-solving coping strategies to deal with stress. In other cases, the type of strategy differs according to the situation. For example, they tend to use emotion-focused strategies more frequently when they perceive circumstances as being unchangeable, and they use problem-focused strategies more often in situations they see as relatively modifiable (Penley, Tomaka, & Wiebe, 2002).

Some forms of coping are less successful. One of the least effective forms of coping is avoidant coping. In *avoidant coping,* a person may use wishful thinking to reduce stress or use more direct escape routes, such as drug use, alcohol use, and overeating. Avoidant coping usually results in a postponement of dealing with a stressful situation, and this often makes the problem even worse (Hutchinson, Baldwin, & Oh, 2006; Glass et al., 2009; Sikkema et al., 2013).

Learned Helplessness

Have you ever faced an intolerable situation that you just couldn't resolve, and you finally simply gave up and accepted things the way they were? This example illustrates one of the possible consequences of being in an environment in which control over a situation is not possible—a state that produces learned helplessness. **Learned helplessness** occurs when people conclude that unpleasant or aversive stimuli cannot be controlled—a view of the world that becomes so ingrained that they cease trying to remedy the aversive circumstances, even if they actually can exert some influence on the situation (Aujoulat, Luminet, & Deccache, 2007; Seligman, 2007; Filippello et al., 2015).

Victims of learned helplessness have concluded that there is no link between the responses they make and the outcomes that occur. People experience more physical symptoms and depression when they perceive that they have little or no control than they do when they feel a sense of control over a situation (Chou, 2005; Bjornstad, 2006).

learned helplessness A state in which people conclude that unpleasant or aversive stimuli cannot be controlled—a view of the world that becomes so ingrained that they cease trying to remedy the aversive circumstances, even if they actually can exert some influence

Resilience

For those who confront the most profound difficulties, such as the death of a loved one or a permanent injury such as paralysis after an accident, a key ingredient in their psychological recovery is their degree of resilience. *Resilience* is the ability to withstand, overcome, and actually thrive after profound adversity (Bonanno, 2004; Norlander, Von Schedvin, & Archer, 2005; Jackson, 2006). (To get a sense of your own resilience, complete the Try It!.)

Resilient people are generally easygoing and good-natured and have good social skills. They are usually independent, and they have a sense of control over their own destiny—even if fate has dealt them a devastating blow. In short, they work with what they have and make the best of whatever situation they find themselves in (Deshields et al., 2006; Friborg et al., 2005; Sinclair et al., 2013).

Try It!

How Resilient Are You?

Rate how much each of the following applies to you on a scale from 1 to 5, with 1 = Very little and 5 = Very much.

1 2 3 4 5   Curious, ask questions, want to know how things work, experiment.

1 2 3 4 5   Constantly learn from your experience and the experiences of others.

1 2 3 4 5   Need and expect to have things work well for yourself and others. Take good care of yourself.

1 2 3 4 5   Play with new developments, find the humor, laugh at self, chuckle.

1 2 3 4 5   Highly flexible, adapt quickly to change.

1 2 3 4 5   Feel comfortable with paradoxical qualities.

1 2 3 4 5   Anticipate problems and avoid difficulties.

1 2 3 4 5   Develop better self-esteem and self-confidence with the passage of time. Develop a conscious self-concept of professionalism.

1 2 3 4 5   Listen well. Read others, including difficult people, with empathy.

1 2 3 4 5   Think up creative solutions to challenges, invent ways to solve problems. Trust intuition and hunches.

1 2 3 4 5   Manage the emotional side of recovery from trauma; let go of the past.

1 2 3 4 5   Expect tough situations to work out well, keep on going. Help others, bring stability to times of uncertainty and turmoil.

1 2 3 4 5   Find the good in accidents and bad experiences.

1 2 3 4 5   Convert misfortune into good fortune.

Scoring

Add up the numbers you circled, and use the following scale as a rough guide to your level of resilience:

60–70: Highly resilient

50–60: Above average resiliency

40–50: Average resiliency

30–40: Below average resiliency

Below 30: Unusually low resiliency

Source: Adapted from Siebert, 1998.

Social Support: Turning to Others

Our relationships with others also help us cope with stress. Researchers have found that **social support,** the knowledge that we are part of a mutual network of caring, interested others, enables us to experience lower levels of stress and better cope with the stress we do undergo (Cohen, 2004; Bolger & Amarel, 2007; Jimmieson et al., 2010; García-Herrero et al., 2013).

The social and emotional support people provide each other helps in dealing with stress in several ways. For instance, such support demonstrates that a person is an important and valued member of a social network. Similarly, other people can provide information and advice about appropriate ways of dealing with stress (Day & Livingstone, 2003; Lindorff, 2005; Li et al., 2015).

Finally, people who are part of a social support network can provide actual goods and services to help others in stressful situations. For instance, they can supply temporary living quarters to a person whose house has burned down, or they can offer babysitting to a parent who is experiencing stress because of the serious illness of a spouse (Natvig, Albrektsen, & Ovarnstrom, 2003; Takizawa, Kondo, & Sakihara, 2007).

social support A mutual network of caring, interested others

> The social and emotional support people provide each other helps in dealing with stress in several ways.

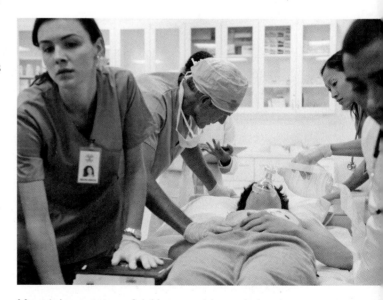

becoming an informed consumer of psychology

Effective Coping Strategies

How can we deal with the stress in our lives? Although there is no universal solution, because effective coping depends on the nature of the stressor and the degree to which it can be controlled, here are some general guidelines (Aspinwall & Taylor, 1997; Folkman & Moskowitz, 2000):

- *Turn a threat into a challenge.* When a stressful situation might be controllable, the best coping strategy is to treat the situation as a challenge and focus on ways to control it. For instance, if you experience stress because your car is always breaking down, you might take a course in auto mechanics and learn to deal directly with the car's problems.

- *Make a threatening situation less threatening.* When a stressful situation seems to be uncontrollable, you need to take a different approach. It is possible to change your appraisal of the situation, view it in a different light, and modify your attitude toward it. Research supports the old truism "Look for the silver lining in every cloud" (Smith & Lazarus, 2001; Cheng & Cheung, 2005).

- *Change your goals.* If you are faced with an uncontrollable situation, a reasonable strategy is to adopt new goals that are practical in view

Most jobs are stressful. How would good stress coping techniques help you in this situation? © Ariel Skelley/Blend Images LLC RF

of the particular situation. For example, a dancer who has been in an automobile accident and has lost full use of her legs may no longer aspire to a career in dance but might modify her goals and try to become a choreographer.

■ *Take physical action.* Exercise can be effective in reducing stress.

■ *Prepare for stress before it happens.* A final strategy for coping with stress is *proactive coping,* anticipating and preparing for stress *before* it is encountered (Aspinwall & Taylor, 1997; Bode et al., 2007).

RECAP

Define stress and discuss how it affects us.

■ Stress is a response to threatening or challenging environmental conditions. People encounter stressors—the circumstances that produce stress—of both a positive and a negative nature.

Explain the nature of stressors.

■ The way an environmental circumstance is interpreted affects whether it will be considered stressful. Still, there are general classes of events that provoke stress: cataclysmic events, personal stressors, and background stressors (daily hassles).

■ Stress produces immediate physiological reactions. In the short term those reactions may be adaptive, but in the long term they may have negative consequences, including the development of psychophysiological disorders.

■ The consequences of stress can be explained in part by Selye's general adaptation syndrome (GAS), which suggests that there are three stages in stress responses: alarm and mobilization, resistance, and exhaustion.

Describe how people cope with stress.

■ Stress can be reduced by developing a sense of control over one's circumstances. In some cases, however, people develop a state of learned helplessness.

■ Coping with stress can take a number of forms, including the use of emotion-focused or problem-focused coping strategies.

[EVALUATE E Evaluate]

1. _____ is defined as a response to challenging or threatening events.

2. Match each portion of the GAS with its definition:

   1. Alarm and mobilization   a. Ability to adapt to stress diminishes; symptoms appear.

   2. Exhaustion   b. Activation of sympathetic nervous system.

   3. Resistance   c. Various strategies are used to cope with a stressor.

3. Stressors that affect a single person and produce an immediate major reaction are known as

   a. Personal stressors.

   b. Transpersonal stressors.

   c. Cataclysmic stressors.

   d. Daily stressors.

[RETHINK R Rethink]

Why are cataclysmic stressors less stressful in the long run than are other types of stressors? Does the reason relate to the coping phenomenon known as social support? How?

KEY TERMS

Stress   LO43.1

Cataclysmic events   LO43.2

Personal stressors   LO43.2

Posttraumatic stress disorder (PTSD)   LO43.2

Background stressors ("daily hassles")   LO43.2

Psychophysiological disorders   LO43.2

General adaptation syndrome (GAS)   LO43.2

Psychoneuroimmunology (PNI)   LO43.2

Coping   LO43.3

Learned helplessness   LO43.3

Social support   LO43.3

 Looking **Back**

Psychology on the Web

1. Find examples on the Web of advertisements or other persuasive messages that use central route processing and peripheral route processing. What type of persuasion appears to be more prevalent on the Web? For what type of persuasion does the Web appear to be better suited? Is there a difference between Web-based advertising and other forms of advertising?

2. Is "hate crimes legislation" a good idea? Use the Web to find at least two discussions of hate crimes legislation—one in favor and one opposed—and summarize in writing the main issues and arguments presented. Using your knowledge of prejudice and aggression, evaluate the arguments for and against hate crimes legislation. State your opinion about whether this type of legislation is advisable.

the case of . . .

JOHN BUCKINGHAM, THE NEW GUY ON THE JOB

When John Buckingham moved across the country to take a new job, he didn't expect to run into much difficulty. He would be doing the same kind of work he was used to doing, just for a new company. But when he arrived on his first day, he realized there was more for him to adjust to than he had realized.

Clearly, John had moved to a region where the culture was much more laid back and casual than he was used to. He showed up for his first day in his usual business suit only to find that almost all the other employees wore jeans, Western shirts, and cowboy boots. Many of them merely stared awkwardly when they first saw John, and then hurriedly tried to look busy while avoiding eye contact.

John got the message. On his second day at work John also wore jeans and a casual shirt, although he didn't yet own a pair of cowboy boots. He found that people seemed more relaxed around him, but that they continued to treat him warily. It would be several weeks—after he'd gone out and bought boots and started wearing them to work—before certain people warmed up to John enough to even talk to him.

1. What does the behavior of John's co-workers toward John suggest about their attributions for his initial manner of dress?

2. Describe the kinds of biases that might have affected John's co-workers as they formed impressions of him on his first day. Could they have been using a faulty schema to understand him? Is there evidence of the halo effect?

3. Explain why John changed his manner of dress so soon after starting his new job. What processes were likely involved in his decision to do so?

4. John's co-workers seemed very hesitant to "warm up" to John. How would you explain to John their initial reluctance to like him very much?

5. If you were the human resources director for this company, what strategies could you employ to prevent experiences like John's? How would you justify the implementation of these strategies to the company president?

profiles of SUCCESS

Courtesy of Samantha Moore

NAME: **Samantha C. Moore**

SCHOOL: **Beckfield College**

DEGREE PROGRAM: **BA, Criminal Justice**

Sometimes it's not so much what one specifically learns in college that adds to one's character, but rather facing those unexpected experiences while pursuing a degree. For Samantha Moore, it was a sudden flurry of family issues that created major challenges.

"About nine months from completing my bachelor's degree my brother passed away," she said. "A few days following his funeral my father was diagnosed with cancer."

Because her mother needed to care for her father, bringing him to treatments on a regular basis, the task of caring for nephews left in the custody of her parents required Moore to become more involved.

"It was very new to me to have to care for young children, and this made it very difficult to keep up with my studies and work," Moore said. "I had to take leave from my job and every week find a sitter to watch my nephews while I went to class. I had to do my homework and write papers late at night while my boys were in bed. Then, I was up early the next day to get them off to school."

Not too long after, her father passed away as well, and Moore felt the pressures almost too much to overcome and wanted to quit. But with the guidance and help of a dean at Beckfield she decided to hang on and pursue her degree.

"With everything I dealt with and still being able to earn my degree, I learned that I am a lot stronger than I thought, and I can overcome anything," Moore noted. "I also learned that if I put my mind to it, I can accomplish it."

Her advice to other students facing adversity is borne of experience:

"Don't give up," she stresses. "Sometimes you may have to take some time off or cut down on how many classes you take, but you can make it. It may take longer than you want it to, but it is worth it. You always have to remind yourself what you are working toward and how it will make your life better."

[RETHINK R Rethink]

How do the concepts of helping and altruism, discussed in this chapter, figure into Moore's description of the challenges she faced?

How do you balance work-school-family issues in your own life?

visual summary 12
SOCIAL PSYCHOLOGY

MODULE 39 Attitudes and Social Cognition

Persuasion: Attitudes: Evaluations of a particular person, behavior, belief, or concept

Social Cognition: How people understand what others and themselves are like
- Forming impressions of others
- Attribution theory

MODULE 40 Social Influence and Groups

Conformity: A desire to follow the beliefs or standards of other people

Compliance: Social pressure to behave in a certain way

Obedience: Behavior change in response to the commands of others

MODULE 41 Prejudice and Discrimination

Prejudice: A negative or positive evaluation of a group

Discrimination: Behavior directed toward individuals on the basis of their membership in a particular group

Stereotype: Generalized beliefs and expectations about a specific group that arise when we categorize information

Reducing Prejudice and Discrimination
- Increase contact
- Make values and norms against prejudice more conspicuous
- Provide information about the targets of stereotyping
- Reduce stereotype threat
- Increase a sense of belonging

MODULE 42 Positive and Negative Social Behavior

Liking and Loving

- Determinants of liking
  - Proximity
  - Mere exposure
  - Similarity
  - Physical attractiveness
- What is love?
  - Qualitatively different from liking
  - Three components of love

Aggression: Intentional injury of or harm to another person

- Instinct approaches
- Frustration-aggression approach
- Observational learning approaches

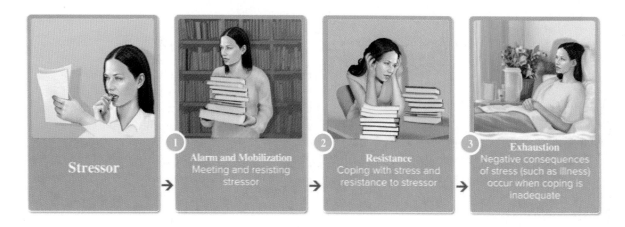

Liking
(intimacy)

Romantic Love
(intimacy + passion)

Companionate Love
(intimacy + decision/
commitment)

Consummate
Love
(intimacy + passion +
decision/commitment)

Infatuation
(passion)

Empty Love
(decision/
commitment)

Fatuous Love
(passion + decision/commitment)

Helping (Prosocial) Behavior: Actions intended to provide aid to others

MODULE 43 Stress and Coping

Stress: People's response to events that threaten or challenge them

- Interpretation of events is important in determining what is stressful
- Posttraumatic Stress Disorder (PTSD)

The Cost of Stress

- Psychophysiological disorders: An interaction of psychological, emotional, and physical difficulties
- General Adaptation Syndrome (GAS) Model: The physiological response to stress follows the same pattern regardless of the cause of stress
- Psychoneuroimmunology: Relationship among psychological factors, the immune system, and the brain

Stressor

1 **Alarm and Mobilization**
Meeting and resisting stressor

2 **Resistance**
Coping with stress and resistance to stressor

3 **Exhaustion**
Negative consequences of stress (such as illness) occur when coping is inadequate

Coping with Stress: Emotion-focused or problem-focused coping

GLOSSARY

abnormal behavior Behavior that causes people to experience distress and prevents them from functioning in their daily lives

absolute threshold The smallest intensity of a stimulus that must be present for the stimulus to be detected

action potential An electric nerve impulse that travels through a neuron when it is set off by a "trigger," changing the neuron's charge from negative to positive

activation-synthesis theory J. Allan Hobson's theory that the brain produces random electrical energy during REM (rapid eye movement) sleep that stimulates memories stored in the brain

activity theory of aging A theory that suggests that the elderly who are more successful while aging are those who maintain the interests and activities they had during middle age

adaptation An adjustment in sensory capacity after prolonged exposure to unchanging stimuli

addictive drugs Drugs that produce a biological or psychological dependence in the user so that withdrawal from them leads to a craving for the drug that, in some cases, may be nearly irresistible

adolescence The developmental stage between childhood and adulthood

age of viability The point at which a fetus can survive if born prematurely

aggression The intentional injury of, or harm to, another person

algorithm A rule that, if applied appropriately, guarantees a solution to a problem

all-or-none law The rule that neurons are either on or off

altruism Helping behavior that is beneficial to others but clearly requires self-sacrifice

Alzheimer's disease A progressive brain disorder that leads to a gradual and irreversible decline in cognitive abilities

anal stage According to Sigmund Freud, a stage from age 12 to 18 months to 3 years of age, in which a child's pleasure is centered on the anus

androgens Male sex hormones secreted by the testes

anorexia nervosa A severe eating disorder in which people may refuse to eat while denying that their behavior and appearance—which can become skeleton-like—are unusual

antianxiety drugs Drugs that reduce the level of anxiety a person experiences, essentially by reducing excitability and increasing feelings of well-being

antidepressant drugs Medications that improve a severely depressed patient's mood and feeling of well-being

antipsychotic drugs Drugs that temporarily reduce psychotic symptoms such as agitation, hallucinations, and delusions

antisocial personality disorder A disorder in which individuals show no regard for the moral and ethical rules of society or the rights of others

anxiety disorder The occurrence of anxiety without an obvious external cause, affecting daily functioning

archetypes According to Carl Jung, universal symbolic representations of a particular person, object, or experience

archival research Research in which existing data, such as census documents, college records, and newspaper clippings, are examined to test a hypothesis

arousal approaches to motivation The belief that we try to maintain certain levels of stimulation and activity, increasing or reducing them as necessary

association areas One of the major regions of the cerebral cortex; the site of the higher mental processes, such as thought, language, memory, and speech

assumed-similarity bias The tendency to think of people as being similar to oneself, even when meeting them for the first time

attachment The positive emotional bond that develops between a child and a particular individual

attention-deficit hyperactivity disorder (ADHD) A disorder marked by inattention, impulsiveness, a low tolerance for frustration, and a great deal of inappropriate activity

attitudes Evaluations of a particular person, behavior, belief, or concept

attribution theory The theory of personality that seeks to explain how we decide, on the basis of samples of an individual's behavior, what the specific causes of that person's behavior are

authoritarian parents Parents who are rigid and punitive and value unquestioning obedience from their children

authoritative parents Parents who are firm, set clear limits, reason with their children, and explain things to them

autism spectrum disorder A severe developmental disability that impairs one's ability to communicate and relate to others

autobiographical memories Our recollections of circumstances and episodes from our own lives

autonomic division The part of the peripheral nervous system that controls involuntary movement of the heart, glands, lungs, and other organs

autonomy-versus-shame-and-doubt stage The period which, according to Erik Erikson, toddlers (ages 1½ to 3 years) develop independence and autonomy if exploration and freedom are encouraged, or shame and self-doubt if they are restricted and overprotected

aversive conditioning A form of therapy that reduces the frequency of undesired behavior by pairing an aversive, unpleasant stimulus with undesired behavior

axon The part of the neuron that carries messages destined for other neurons

babble Meaningless speechlike sounds made by children from around the age of 3 months through 1 year

background stressors ("daily hassles") Everyday annoyances, such as being stuck in traffic, that cause minor irritations and may have long-term ill effects if they continue or are compounded by other stressful events

behavior modification A formalized technique for promoting the frequency of desirable behaviors and decreasing the incidence of unwanted ones

behavioral assessment Direct measures of an individual's behavior used to describe personality characteristics

behavioral genetics The study of the effects of heredity on behavior

behavioral neuroscientists (or biopsychologists) Psychologists who specialize in considering the ways in which the biological structures and functions of the body affect behavior

behavioral perspective The perspective that looks at the behavior itself as the problem (regarding psychological disorders)

behavioral treatment approaches Treatment approaches that build on the basic processes of learning, such as reinforcement and extinction, and assume that normal and abnormal behavior are both learned

biofeedback A procedure in which a person learns to control through conscious thought internal physiological processes such as blood pressure, heart and respiration rate, skin temperature, sweating, and the constriction of particular muscles

biological and evolutionary approaches to personality Theories that suggest that important components of personality are inherited

biomedical therapy Therapy that relies on drugs and other medical procedures to improve psychological functioning

bipolar disorder A disorder in which a person alternates between periods of euphoric feelings of mania and periods of depression

bisexuals Persons who are sexually attracted to people of the same sex and the other sex

borderline personality disorder A disorder in which individuals have difficulty developing a secure sense of who they are

bottom-up processing Perception that consists of the progression of recognizing and processing information from individual components of a stimuli and moving to the perception of the whole

bulimia A disorder in which a person binges on large quantities of food, followed by efforts to purge the food through vomiting or other means

Cannon-Bard theory of emotion The belief that both physiological arousal and emotional experience are produced simultaneously by the same nerve stimulus

case study An in-depth, intensive investigation of an individual or small group of people

cataclysmic events Strong stressors that occur suddenly, affecting many people at once (e.g., natural disasters)

catharsis The process of discharging built-up aggressive energy

central core The "old brain," which controls basic functions such as eating and sleeping and is common to all vertebrates

central nervous system (CNS) The part of the nervous system that includes the brain and spinal cord

central route processing Message interpretation characterized by thoughtful consideration of the issues and arguments used to persuade

central traits The major traits considered in forming impressions of others

cerebellum The part of the brain that controls bodily balance

cerebral cortex The "new brain," responsible for the most sophisticated information processing in the brain; contains four lobes

chromosomes Rod-shaped structures that contain all basic hereditary information

chunk A meaningful grouping of stimuli that can be stored as a unit in short-term memory

circadian rhythms Biological processes that occur regularly on approximately a 24-hour cycle

classical conditioning A type of learning in which a neutral stimulus comes to bring about a response after it is paired with a stimulus that naturally brings about that response

cognitive approaches to motivation Theories suggesting that motivation is a product of people's thoughts and expectations—their cognitions

cognitive development The process by which a child's understanding of the world changes as a function of age and experience

cognitive dissonance The conflict that occurs when a person holds two contradictory attitudes or thoughts (referred to as *cognitions*)

cognitive learning theory An approach to the study of learning that focuses on the thought processes that underlie learning

cognitive perspective The perspective that suggests that people's thoughts and beliefs are a central component of abnormal behavior

cognitive psychology The branch of psychology that focuses on the study of higher mental processes, including thinking, language, memory, problem solving, knowing, reasoning, judging, and decision making

cognitive treatment approaches Treatment approaches that teach people to think in more adaptive ways by changing their dysfunctional cognitions about the world and themselves

cognitive-behavioral approach A treatment approach that incorporates basic principles of learning to change the way people think

collective unconscious According to Carl Jung, a common set of ideas, feelings, images, and symbols that we inherit from our ancestors, the whole human race, and even nonhuman ancestors from the distant past

community psychology A branch of psychology that focuses on the prevention and minimization of psychological disorders in the community

companionate love The strong affection we have for those with whom our lives are deeply involved

compliance Behavior that occurs in response to direct social pressure

compulsion An irresistible urge to repeatedly carry out some act that seems strange or unreasonable

concepts Mental groupings of similar objects, events, or people

concrete operational stage According to Jean Piaget, the period from 7 to 12 years of age that is characterized by logical (rational) thought and a loss of egocentrism

conditioned response (CR) A response that, after conditioning, follows a previously neutral stimulus (e.g., salivation at the ringing of a bell)

conditioned stimulus (CS) A once-neutral stimulus that has been paired with an unconditioned stimulus to bring about a response formerly caused only by the unconditioned stimulus

cones Cone-shaped, light-sensitive receptor cells in the retina that are responsible for sharp focus and color perception, particularly in bright light

conformity A change in behavior or attitudes brought about by a desire to follow the beliefs or standards of other people

consciousness The awareness of sensations, thoughts, and feelings being experienced at a given moment

constructive processes Processes in which memories are influenced by the meaning we give to events

continuous reinforcement schedule Reinforcement of a behavior every time it occurs

control group A group participating in an experiment that receives no treatment

conversion disorder A major somatoform disorder that involves an actual physical disturbance, such as the inability to use a sensory organ or the complete or partial inability to move an arm or a leg

coping The efforts to control, reduce, or learn to tolerate the threats that lead to stress

correlational research Research in which the relationship between two sets of variables is examined to determine whether they are associated, or "correlated"

cross-sectional research A research method that compares people of different ages at the same point in time

crystallized intelligence The accumulation of information, skills, and strategies that are learned through experience and can be applied in problem-solving situations

cue-dependent forgetting Forgetting that occurs when there are insufficient retrieval cues to rekindle information that is in memory

culture-fair IQ test A test that does not discriminate against the members of any minority group

D

decay The loss of information in memory through its nonuse

declarative memory Memory for factual information: names, faces, dates, and the like

defense mechanisms In Freudian theory, unconscious strategies that people use to reduce anxiety by concealing the source of the anxiety from themselves and others

deinstitutionalization The transfer of former mental patients from institutions to the community

dendrite A cluster of fibers at one end of a neuron that receive messages from other neurons

dependent variable The variable that is measured and is expected to change as a result of changes caused by the experimenter's manipulation of the independent variable

depressants Drugs that slow down the nervous system

depth perception The ability to view the world in three dimensions and to perceive distance

descriptive research An approach to research designed to systematically investigate a person, group, or patterns of behavior

determinism The idea that people's behavior is produced primarily by factors outside of their willful control

developmental psychology The branch of psychology that studies the patterns of growth and change that occur throughout life

Diagnostic and Statistical Manual of Mental Disorders, Fifth Edition (DSM-5) A system, devised by the American Psychiatric Association, used by most professionals to classify and define psychological disorders

difference threshold (just noticeable difference) The smallest level of added or reduced stimulation required to sense that a change in stimulation has occurred

diffusion of responsibility The tendency for people to feel that responsibility for acting is shared, or diffused, among those present

discrimination Behavior directed toward individuals on the basis of their membership in a particular group

disengagement theory of aging A theory that suggests that aging produces a gradual withdrawal from the world on physical, psychological, and social levels

dispositional causes (of behavior) Perceived causes of behavior that are based on internal traits or personality factors

dissociative amnesia A disorder in which a significant, selective memory loss occurs

dissociative disorders Psychological dysfunctions characterized by the separation of different facets of a person's personality that are normally integrated, allowing stress avoidance through escape

dissociative fugue A form of amnesia in which the individual leaves home and sometimes assumes a new identity

dissociative identity disorder (DID) A disorder in which a person displays characteristics of two or more distinct personalities; once called *multiple personality disorder*

double standard The view that premarital sex is permissible for males but not for females

dreams-for-survival theory The theory suggesting that dreams permit information that is critical for our daily survival to be reconsidered and reprocessed during sleep

drive Motivational tension, or arousal, that energizes behavior to fulfill a need

drive-reduction approaches to motivation Theories suggesting that a lack of a basic biological requirement such as water produces a drive to obtain that requirement (in this case, the thirst drive)

drug therapy Treatment of psychological disorders through the use of drugs

eardrum The part of the ear that vibrates when sound hits it

ego The part of personality that attempts to balance the desires of the id and the realities of the objective, outside world

ego-integrity-versus-despair stage According to Erik Erikson, a period from late adulthood until death during which we review life's accomplishments and failures

egocentric thought A way of thinking in which a child views the world entirely from his or her own perspective

electroconvulsive therapy (ECT) A procedure used in the treatment of severe depression in which an electric current of 70 to 150 volts is briefly administered to a patient's head

embryo A developed zygote that has a primitive heart, a brain, and other organs

emerging adulthood The period beginning in the late teenage years and extending into the mid-twenties

emotional intelligence The set of skills that underlie the accurate assessment, evaluation, expression, and regulation of emotions

emotions Feelings that generally have both physiological and cognitive elements and that influence behavior

endocrine system A chemical communication network that sends messages throughout the body via the bloodstream

episodic memory Memory for events that occur in a particular time, place, or context

estrogens Class of female sex hormones

excitatory messages Chemical messages that make it more likely that a receiving neuron will fire and an action potential will travel down its axon

experiment The investigation of the relationship between two (or more) variables by deliberately producing a change in one variable in a situation and observing the effects of that change on other aspects of the situation

experimental bias Factors that distort how the independent variable affects the dependent variable in an experiment

experimental group Any group participating in an experiment that receives a treatment

experimental manipulation The change that an experimenter deliberately produces in a situation

explicit memory Intentional or conscious recollection of information

flooding A behavioral treatment for anxiety in which people are confronted, either suddenly or gradually, with a stimulus that they fear

extinction A basic phenomenon of learning that occurs when a previously conditioned response decreases in frequency and eventually disappears

extramarital sex Sexual activity between a married person and someone who is not his or her spouse

facial-affect program Activation of a set of nerve impulses that make the face display the appropriate expression

facial-feedback hypothesis The hypothesis that facial expressions not only reflect emotional experience but also help determine how people experience and label emotions

familial intellectual disability Intellectual disability in which no apparent biological defect exists, but there is a history of intellectual disability in the family

family therapy An approach that focuses on the family and its dynamics

feature detection The activation of neurons in the cortex by visual stimuli of specific shapes or patterns

fetal alcohol syndrome The most common cause of intellectual disability in newborns, occurring when the mother uses alcohol during pregnancy

fetus A developing individual, from eight weeks after conception until birth

fixations Conflicts or concerns that persist beyond the developmental period in which they first occur

fixed-interval schedule A schedule that provides reinforcement for a response only if a fixed time period has elapsed, making overall rates of response relatively low

fixed-ratio schedule A schedule by which reinforcement is given only after a specific number of responses are made

flashbulb memories Memories centered on a specific, important, or surprising event that are so vivid it is as if they represented a snapshot of the event

flooding A behavioral treatment for anxiety in which people are confronted, either suddenly or gradually, with a stimulus that they fear

fluid intelligence Intelligence that reflects the ability to think logically, reason abstractly, and solve problems

formal operational stage According to Jean Piaget, the period from age 12 to adulthood that is characterized by abstract thought

free will The idea that behavior is caused primarily by choices that are made freely by the individual

functional fixedness The tendency to think of an object only in terms of its typical use

functionalism An early approach to psychology that concentrated on what the mind does—the functions of mental activity—and the role of behavior in allowing people to adapt to their environments

fundamental attribution error A tendency to overattribute others' behavior to dispositional causes and the corresponding minimization of the importance of situational causes

g or g- factor The single, general factor for mental ability assumed to underlie intelligence in some early theories of intelligence

gate-control theory of pain The theory that particular nerve receptors lead to specific areas of the brain related to pain

general adaptation syndrome (GAS) A theory developed by Hans Selye that suggests that a person's response to a stressor consists of three stages: alarm and mobilization, resistance, and exhaustion

generalized anxiety disorder The experience of long-term, persistent anxiety

generativity-versus-stagnation stage According to Erik Erikson, a period in middle adulthood during which we take stock of our contributions to family and society

genes The parts of the chromosomes through which genetic information is transmitted

genetic preprogramming theories of aging Theories that suggest that human cells have a built-in time limit to their reproduction, and that after a certain time they are no longer able to divide

genital stage According to Sigmund Freud, the period from puberty until death, marked by mature sexual behavior

genitals The male and female sex organs

Gestalt laws of organization The principles of organization of perception

Gestalt psychology An approach that focuses on the organization of perception through a series of principles describing how we organize bits and pieces of information into meaningful wholes

group therapy Therapy in which people meet with a therapist to discuss problems with a group

hallucinogen A drug that is capable of producing hallucinations, or changes in the perceptual process

halo effect A phenomenon in which an initial understanding that a person has positive traits is used to infer other uniformly positive characteristics

hemispheres Symmetrical left and right halves of the brain that control the side of the body opposite to their location

heritability A measure of the degree to which a characteristic is related to genetic, inherited factors

heterosexuality Sexual attraction and behavior directed to the other sex

heuristic A thinking strategy that may lead us to a solution to a problem or decision, but—unlike algorithms—may sometimes lead to errors

homeostasis The body's tendency to maintain a steady internal state

homosexuals Persons who are sexually attracted to members of their own sex

hormones Chemicals that circulate through the blood and regulate the functioning or growth of the body

humanistic approaches to personality Theories that emphasize people's innate goodness and desire to achieve higher levels of functioning

humanistic perspective The approach that suggests that all individuals naturally strive to grow, develop, and be in control of their lives and behavior

humanistic therapy Therapy in which the underlying rationale is that people have control of their behavior, can make choices about their lives, and are essentially responsible for solving their own problems

hypnosis A trancelike state of heightened susceptibility to the suggestions of others

hypothalamus A tiny part of the brain, located below the thalamus, that maintains homeostasis and produces and regulates vital behavior, such as eating, drinking, and sexual behavior

hypothesis A prediction, stemming from a theory, stated in way that allows it to be tested

id The instinctual and unorganized part of personality whose sole purpose is to reduce tension created by primitive drives related to hunger, sex, aggression, and irrational impulses

identical twins Twins who are exactly the same genetically

identification The process of wanting to be like another person as much as possible, imitating that person's behavior and adopting similar beliefs and values

identity The distinguishing character of the individual: who each of us is, what our roles are, and what we are capable of

identity-versus-role-confusion stage According to Erik Erikson, a time in adolescence of major testing to determine one's unique qualities

illness anxiety disorder A psychological disorder in which people have a constant fear of illness and a preoccupation with their health

implicit memory Memories of which people are not consciously aware, but which can affect subsequent performance and behavior

incentive approaches to motivation Theories suggesting that motivation stems from the desire to obtain valued external goals, or incentives

independent variable The variable that is manipulated by an experimenter

industrial-organizational (I/O) psychology The branch of psychology focusing on work- and job-related issues, including worker motivation, satisfaction, safety, and productivity

industry-versus-inferiority stage According to Erik Erikson, the last stage of childhood, during which children ages 6 to 12 years may develop positive social interactions with others or may feel inadequate and become less sociable

inferiority complex According to Alfred Adler, a problem affecting adults who have not been able to overcome the feelings of inferiority that they developed as children, when they were small and limited in their knowledge about the world

information processing The way in which people take in, use, and store information

informed consent A document signed by participants affirming that they have been told the basic outlines of the study and are aware of what their participation will involve

inhibitory messages Chemical messages that prevent or decrease the likelihood that a receiving neuron will fire

initiative-versus-guilt stage According to Erik Erikson, the period during which children ages 3 to 6 years experience conflict between independence of action and the sometimes negative results of that action

instinct approaches to motivation The view that people and animals are born preprogrammed with sets of behaviors essential to their survival

instincts Inborn patterns of behavior that are biologically determined rather than learned

intellectual disability A disability characterized by significant limitations in both intellectual functioning and in adaptive behavior, which covers many everyday social and practical skills

intellectually gifted The 2 to 4 percent of the population who have IQ scores greater than 130

intelligence The capacity to understand the world, think rationally, and use resources effectively when faced with challenges

intelligence quotient (IQ) A score that takes into account an individual's mental and chronological ages

intelligence tests Tests devised to quantify a person's level of intelligence

interactionist approach to language development The view that language development is produced through a combination of genetically determined predispositions and environmental circumstances that help teach language

interference The phenomenon by which information in memory disrupts the recall of other information

interneurons Neurons that connect sensory and motor neurons, carrying messages between the two

interpersonal attraction (or close relationship) Positive feelings for others; liking and loving

interpersonal therapy (IPT) Short-term therapy designed to help patients control their moods and emotions by focusing on the context of their current social relationships

intimacy-versus-isolation stage According to Erik Erikson, a period during early adulthood that focuses on developing close relationships

introspection A procedure used to study the structure of the mind in which subjects are asked to describe in detail what they are experiencing when they are exposed to a stimulus

James-Lange theory of emotion The belief that emotional experience is a reaction to bodily events occurring as a result of an external situation ("I feel sad because I am crying")

language The communication of information through symbols arranged according to systematic rules

language-acquisition device A neural system of the brain hypothesized by Noam Chomsky to permit understanding of language

latency period According to Sigmund Freud, the period between the phallic stage and puberty during which children's sexual concerns are temporarily put aside

latent content of dreams According to Sigmund Freud, the "disguised" meaning of dreams, hidden by more obvious subjects

latent learning Learning in which a new behavior is acquired but is not demonstrated until some incentive is provided for displaying it

lateralization The dominance of one hemisphere of the brain in specific functions, such as language

learned helplessness A state in which people conclude that unpleasant or aversive stimuli cannot be controlled—a view of the world that becomes so ingrained that they cease trying to remedy the aversive circumstances, even if they actually can exert some influence

learning A relatively permanent change in behavior brought about by experience

learning-theory approach to language development The theory suggesting that language acquisition follows the principles of reinforcement and conditioning

levels-of-processing theory The theory of memory that emphasizes the degree to which new material is mentally analyzed

life review The process by which people examine and evaluate their lives

limbic system The part of the brain that includes the amygdala and hippocampus, and controls eating, aggression, and reproduction

linguistic-relativity hypothesis The notion that language shapes and may determine the way people in a particular culture perceive and understand the world

lobes The four major sections of the cerebral cortex: frontal, parietal, temporal, and occipital

long-term memory Memory that stores information on a relatively permanent basis, although it may be difficult to retrieve

longitudinal research A research method that investigates behavior as participants age

major depressive disorder a severe form of depression that interferes with concentration, decision making, and sociability

mania An extended state of intense, wild elation

manifest content of dreams According to Sigmund Freud, the apparent story line of dreams

masturbation Sexual self-stimulation

means-ends analysis Problem solving which involves repeated tests for differences between the desired outcome and what currently exists

medical perspective The view that suggests that when an individual displays symptoms of a psychological disorder, the root cause will be found in a physical problem, deficiency, or brain injury

meditation A learned technique for refocusing attention that brings about an altered state of consciousness

memory The process by which we encode, store, and retrieve information

menopause The period during which women stop menstruating and are no longer fertile

mental age The average age of individuals who achieve a particular level of performance on a test

mental images Representations in the mind that resemble the object or event being represented

mental set A framework for thinking about a problem based on our prior experience with similar problems

metabolism The rate at which food is converted to energy and expended by the body

metacognition An awareness and understanding of one's own cognitive processes

Minnesota Multiphasic Personality Inventory-2 (MMPI-2) A widely used self-report test that identifies people with psychological difficulties and is employed to predict some everyday behaviors

mirror neurons Specialized neurons that fire not only when a person enacts a particular behavior, but also when a person simply observes *another* individual carrying out the same behavior

mood disorders Emotional disturbances that are strong enough to intrude on everyday living

mood stabilizers Drugs used to treat mood disorders that prevent manic episodes of bipolar disorder

motivation The factors that direct and energize the behavior of humans and other organisms

motor (efferent) neurons Neurons that communicate information from the nervous system to muscles and glands

motor area The part of the cortex that is largely responsible for the body's voluntary movement

myelin sheath A protective coat of fat and protein that wraps around the neuron

narcissistic personality disorder A personality disturbance characterized by an exaggerated sense of self-importance

narcotics Drugs that increase relaxation and relieve pain and anxiety

nativist approach to language development The theory that a genetically determined, innate mechanism directs language development

naturalistic observation Research in which an investigator simply observes some naturally occurring behavior and does not make a change in the situation

nature-nurture issue The issue of the degree to which environment and heredity influence behavior

need for achievement A stable, learned characteristic in which a person obtains satisfaction by striving for and attaining a level of excellence

need for affiliation An interest in establishing and maintaining relationships with other people

need for power A tendency to seek impact, control, or influence over others, and to be seen as a powerful individual

negative reinforcer An unpleasant stimulus whose removal leads to an increase in the probability that a preceding response will be repeated in the future

neo-Freudian psychoanalysts Psychoanalysts who were trained in traditional Freudian theory but who later rejected some of its major points

neonate A newborn child

neurons Nerve cells, the basic elements of the nervous system

neuroplasticity Changes in the brain that occur throughout the life span relating to the addition of new neurons, new interconnections between neurons, and the reorganization of information-processing areas

neuroscience perspective The approach that views behavior from the perspective of the brain, the nervous system, and other biological functions

neurotransmitters Chemicals that carry messages across the synapse to the dendrite (and sometimes the cell body) of a receiver neuron

neutral stimulus A stimulus that, before conditioning, does not naturally bring about the response of interest

obedience A change in behavior in response to the commands of others

obesity Body weight that is more than 20 percent above the average weight for a person of a particular height

object permanence The awareness that objects—and people—continue to exist even if they are out of sight

observational learning Learning by observing the behavior of another person, or model

obsession A persistent, unwanted thought or idea that keeps recurring

obsessive-compulsive disorder (OCD) A disorder characterized by obsessions or compulsions

Oedipal conflict A child's sexual interest in his or her opposite-sex parent, typically resolved through identification with the same-sex parent

operant conditioning Learning in which a voluntary response is strengthened or weakened, depending on its favorable or unfavorable consequences

operational definition The translation of a hypothesis into specific, testable procedures that can be measured and observed

opponent-process theory of color vision The theory that receptor cells for color are linked in pairs, working in opposition to each other

optic nerve A bundle of ganglion axons that carry visual information to the brain

oral stage According to Sigmund Freud, a stage from birth to age 12 to 18 months, in which an infant's center of pleasure is the mouth

overgeneralization The phenomenon by which children apply language rules even when the application results in an error

ovulation The point at which an egg is released from the ovaries

panic disorder Anxiety disorder that takes the form of panic attacks lasting from a few seconds to as long as several hours

parasympathetic division The part of the autonomic division of the nervous system that acts to calm the body after an emergency or a stressful situation has ended

partial (or intermittent) reinforcement schedule Reinforcing of a behavior some but not all of the time

passionate (or romantic) love A state of intense absorption in someone that includes intense physiological arousal, psychological interest, and caring for the needs of another

perception The sorting out, interpretation, analysis, and integration of stimuli by the sense organs and brain

peripheral nervous system The part of the nervous system that includes the autonomic and somatic subdivisions; made up of neurons with long axons and dendrites, it branches out from the spinal cord and brain and reaches the extremities of the body

peripheral route processing Message interpretation characterized by consideration of the source and related general information rather than of the message itself

permissive parents Parents who give their children relaxed or inconsistent direction and, although warm, require little of them

person-centered therapy Therapy in which the goal is to reach one's potential for self-actualization

personal stressors Major life events, such as the death of a family member, that have immediate consequences that generally fade with time

personality The pattern of enduring characteristics that produce consistency and individuality in a given person

personality disorder A disorder characterized by a set of inflexible, maladaptive behavior patterns that keep a person from functioning appropriately in society

phallic stage According to Sigmund Freud, a period beginning around age 3 during which a child's pleasure focuses on the genitals

pituitary gland The major component of the endocrine system, or "master gland," which secretes hormones that control growth and other parts of the endocrine system

placebo A false treatment, such as a pill, "drug," or other substance, without any significant chemical properties or active ingredient

positive reinforcer A stimulus added to the environment that brings about an increase in a preceding response

posttraumatic stress disorder (PTSD) A phenomenon in which victims of major catastrophes or strong personal stressors feel long-lasting effects that may include reexperiencing the event in vivid flashbacks or dreams

practical intelligence According to Robert Sternberg, intelligence related to overall success in living

prejudice A negative (or positive) evaluation of a particular group and its members

preoperational stage According to Jean Piaget, the period from 2 to 7 years of age that is characterized by language development

principle of conservation The knowledge that quantity is unrelated to the arrangement and physical appearance of objects

proactive interference Interference in which information learned earlier disrupts the recall of newer information

procedural memory Memory for skills and habits, such as riding a bike or hitting a baseball, sometimes referred to as *nondeclarative memory*

progesterone A female sex hormone secreted by the ovaries

projective personality tests Tests in which a person is shown an ambiguous stimulus and asked to describe it or tell a story about it

prosocial behavior Helping behavior

prototypes Typical, highly representative samples of a concept

psychoactive drugs Drugs that influence a person's emotions, perceptions, and behavior

psychoanalysis Freud's psychotherapy in which the goal is to release hidden thoughts and feelings from the unconscious part of our minds in order to reduce their power in controlling behavior

psychoanalytic perspective The view that suggests that abnormal behavior stems from childhood conflicts over opposing wishes regarding sex and aggression

psychoanalytic theory Sigmund Freud's theory that unconscious forces act as determinants of personality

psychodynamic approaches to personality Approaches that assume that personality is motivated by inner forces and conflicts about which people have little awareness and over which they have no control

psychodynamic perspective The approach based on the view that behavior is motivated by unconscious inner forces over which the individual has little control

psychodynamic therapy Therapy that seeks to bring unresolved past conflicts and unacceptable impulses from the unconscious into the conscious, where patients may deal with the problems more effectively

psychological tests Standard measures devised to assess behavior objectively; used by psychologists to help people make decisions about their lives and understand more about themselves

psychology The scientific study of behavior and mental processes

psychoneuroimmunology (PNI) The study of the relationship among psychological factors, the immune system, and the brain

psychophysics The study of the relationship between the physical aspects of stimuli and our psychological experience of them

psychophysiological disorders Medical problems influenced by an interaction of psychological, emotional, and physical difficulties

psychosexual stages Developmental periods that children pass through during which they encounter conflicts between the demands of society and their own sexual urges

psychosocial development Development of individuals' interactions and understanding of each other and of their knowledge and understanding of themselves as members of society

psychosurgery Brain surgery once used to reduce the symptoms of mental disorder but rarely used today

psychotherapy Treatment in which a trained professional—a therapist—uses psychological techniques to help a person overcome psychological difficulties and disorders, resolve problems in living, or bring about personal growth

puberty The period at which maturation of the sexual organs occurs, beginning at about age 11 or 12 for girls and 13 or 14 for boys

punishment A stimulus that decreases the probability that a previous behavior will occur again

random assignment to condition A procedure in which participants are assigned to different experimental groups or "conditions" on the basis of chance and chance alone

rapid eye movement (REM) sleep Sleep occupying 20 percent of an adult's sleeping time, characterized by increased heart rate, blood pressure, and breathing rate; erections (in males); eye movements; and the experience of dreaming

rational-emotive behavior therapy A form of therapy that attempts to restructure a person's belief system into a more realistic, rational, and logical set of views by challenging dysfunctional beliefs that maintain irrational behavior

recall Memory task in which specific information must be retrieved

recognition Memory task in which individuals are presented with a stimulus and asked whether they have been exposed to it in the past or to identify it from a list of alternatives

reflex An automatic, involuntary response to an incoming stimulus

rehearsal The repetition of information that has entered short-term memory

reinforcement The process by which a stimulus increases the probability that a preceding behavior will be repeated

reinforcer Any stimulus that increases the probability that a preceding behavior will occur again

replication Research that is repeated, sometimes using other procedures, settings, and groups of participants, to increase confidence in prior findings

repression The primary defense mechanism in which unacceptable or unpleasant id impulses are pushed back into the unconscious

resting state The state in which there is a negative electrical charge of about –70 millivolts within a neuron

reticular formation The part of the brain extending from the medulla through the pons and made up of groups of nerve cells that can immediately activate other parts of the brain to produce general bodily arousal

retina The part of the eye that converts the electromagnetic energy of light to electrical impulses for transmission to the brain

retroactive interference Interference in which there is difficulty in the recall of information learned earlier because of later exposure to different material

reuptake The reabsorption of neurotransmitters by a terminal button

rods Thin, cylindrical receptor cells in the retina that are highly sensitive to light

Rorschach test A test that involves showing a series of symmetrical visual stimuli to people who then are asked what the figures represent to them

Schachter-Singer theory of emotion The belief that emotions are determined jointly by a nonspecific kind of physiological arousal and its interpretation, based on environmental cues

schedules of reinforcement Different patterns of frequency and timing of reinforcement following desired behavior

schemas Organized bodies of information stored in memory that bias the way new information is interpreted, stored, and recalled; sets of cognitions about people and social experiences

schizophrenia A class of disorders in which severe distortion of reality occurs

scientific method The approach through which psychologists systematically acquire knowledge and understanding about behavior and other phenomena of interest

self-actualization A state of self-fulfillment in which people realize their highest potential, each in his or her own unique way

self-efficacy Belief in one's personal capabilities. Self-efficacy underlies people's faith in their ability to carry out a particular behavior or produce a desired outcome

self-esteem The component of personality that encompasses our positive and negative self-evaluations

self-report measures A method of gathering data about people by asking them questions about a sample of their behavior

self-serving bias The tendency to attribute personal success to personal factors and to attribute failure to factors outside oneself

semantic memory Memory for general knowledge and facts about the world, as well as memory for the rules of logic that are used to deduce other facts

semicircular canals Three tubelike structures of the inner ear containing fluid that sloshes through them when the head moves, signaling rotational or angular movement to the brain

sensation The activation of the sense organs by a source of physical energy

sensorimotor stage According to Jean Piaget, the stage from birth to 2 years, during which a child has little competence in representing the environment by using images, language, or other symbols

sensory (afferent) neurons Neurons that transmit information from the perimeter of the body to the central nervous system

sensory area The site in the brain of the tissue that corresponds to each of the senses, with the degree of sensitivity related to the amount of the tissue allocated to that sense

sensory memory The initial, momentary storage of information, lasting only an instant

sequential research A research method that combines cross-sectional and longitudinal research by considering a number of different age groups and examining them at several points in time

shaping The process of teaching a complex behavior by rewarding closer and closer approximations of the desired behavior

short-term memory Memory that holds information for 15 to 25 seconds

situational causes (of behavior) Perceived causes of behavior that are based on environmental factors

skin senses The senses of touch, pressure, temperature, and pain

social cognition The cognitive processes by which people understand and make sense of others and themselves

social cognitive approaches to personality Theories that emphasize the influence of a person's cognitions—thoughts, feelings, expectations, and values—as well as observation of others' behavior, in determining personality

social influence The process by which the actions of an individual or group affect the behavior of others

social psychology The scientific study of how people's thoughts, feelings, and actions are affected by others

social support A mutual network of caring, interested others

sociocultural perspective The view that assumes that people's behavior—both normal and abnormal—is shaped by the kind of family group, society, and culture in which they live

somatic division The part of the peripheral nervous system that specializes in the control of voluntary movements and the communication of information to and from the sense organs

somatic symptom disorders Psychological difficulties that take on a physical (somatic) form, but for which there is no medical cause

sound The movement of air molecules brought about by a source of vibration

specific phobia An intense, irrational fear of specific objects or situations

spinal cord A bundle of neurons that leaves the brain and runs down the length of the back and is the main means for transmitting messages between the brain and the body

spontaneous recovery The reemergence of an extinguished conditioned response after a period of rest and with no further conditioning

spontaneous remission Recovery without treatment

stage 1 sleep The state of transition between wakefulness and sleep, characterized by relatively rapid, low-amplitude brain waves

stage 2 sleep A sleep deeper than that of stage 1, characterized by a slower, more regular wave pattern, along with momentary interruptions of sleep spindles

stage 3 sleep A sleep characterized by slow brain waves, with greater peaks and valleys in the wave pattern than in stage 2 sleep

stage 4 sleep The deepest stage of sleep, during which we are least responsive to outside stimulation

stereotype A set of generalized beliefs and expectations about a particular group and its members

stimulants Drugs that have an arousal effect on the central nervous system, causing a rise in heart rate, blood pressure, and muscular tension

stimulus Physical energy that produces a response in a sense organ

stimulus discrimination The process that occurs if two stimuli are sufficiently distinct from each other that one evokes a conditioned response but the other does not; the ability to differentiate between stimuli

stimulus generalization A process in which, after a stimulus has been conditioned to produce a particular response, stimuli that are similar to the original stimulus produce the same response

stress A person's response to events that are threatening or challenging

structuralism Wilhelm Wundt's approach, which focuses on uncovering the fundamental mental components (parts) of consciousness, thinking, and other kinds of mental states and activities

superego The part of personality that harshly judges the morality of our behavior

survey research Research in which people chosen to represent a larger population are asked a series of questions about their behavior, thoughts, or attitudes

sympathetic division The part of the autonomic division of the nervous system that acts to prepare the body for action in stressful situations, engaging all the organism's resources to respond to a threat

synapse The space between two neurons where the axon of a sending neuron communicates with the dendrites of a receiving neuron by using chemical messages

systematic desensitization A behavioral technique in which gradual exposure to an anxiety-producing stimulus is paired with relaxation to extinguish the response of anxiety

telegraphic speech Sentences in which words not critical to the message are left out

temperament The basic, innate disposition that emerges early in life

teratogens Environmental agents such as a drug, chemical, virus, or other factor that produce a birth defect

terminal buttons Small bulges at the end of axons that send messages to other neurons

test standardization A technique used to validate questions in personality tests by studying the responses of people with known diagnoses

thalamus The part of the brain located in the middle of the central core that acts primarily to relay information about the senses

Thematic Apperception Test (TAT) A test consisting of a series of pictures about which a person is asked to write a story

theories Broad explanations and predictions concerning phenomena of interest

theory of multiple intelligences Howard Gardner's theory that proposes that there are eight distinct spheres of intelligence

thinking Brain activity in which people mentally manipulate information, including words, visual images, sounds, or other data

tip-of-the-tongue phenomenon The inability to recall information that one realizes one knows—a result of the difficulty of retrieving information from long-term memory

top-down processing Perception that is guided by higher-level knowledge, experience, expectations, and motivations

trait theory A model of personality that seeks to identify the basic traits necessary to describe personality

traits Consistent, habitual personality characteristics and behaviors that are displayed across different situations

transcranial magnetic stimulation (TMS) A depression treatment in which a precise magnetic pulse is directed to a specific area of the brain

transference The transfer of feelings to a psychoanalyst of love or anger that had been originally directed to a patient's parents or other authority figures

transgender An umbrella term for persons whose gender identity, gender expression, or behavior does not conform to that typically associated with the sex to which they were assigned at birth

treatment The manipulation implemented by the experimenter

trichromatic theory of color vision The theory that there are three kinds of cones in the retina, each of which responds primarily to a specific range of wavelengths

trust-versus-mistrust stage According to Erik Erikson, the first stage of psychosocial development, occurring from birth to age 1½ years, during which time infants develop feelings of trust or lack of trust

unconditional positive regard An attitude of acceptance and respect on the part of an observer, no matter what a person says or does

unconditioned response (UCR) A response that is natural and needs no training (e.g., salivation at the smell of food)

unconditioned stimulus (UCS) A stimulus that naturally brings about a particular response without having been learned

unconscious A part of the personality that contains the memories, knowledge, beliefs, feelings, urges, drives, and instincts of which the individual is not aware

unconscious wish fulfillment theory Sigmund Freud's theory that dreams represent unconscious wishes that dreamers desire to see fulfilled

uninvolved parents Parents who show little interest in their children and are emotionally detached

universal grammar Noam Chomsky's theory that all the world's languages share a common underlying structure

variable-interval schedule A schedule by which the time between reinforcements varies around some average rather than being fixed

variable-ratio schedule A schedule by which reinforcement occurs after a varying number of responses rather than a fixed number

variables Behaviors, events, or other characteristics that can change, or vary, in some way

visual illusions Physical stimuli that consistently produce errors in perception

wear-and-tear theories of aging Theories that suggest that the mechanical functions of the body simply stop working efficiently

Weber's law A basic law of psychophysics stating that a just noticeable difference is in constant proportion to the intensity of an initial stimulus

weight set point The particular level of weight that the body strives to maintain

zone of proximal development (ZPD) According to Lev Vygotsky, the level at which a child can almost, but not fully, comprehend or perform a task on his or her own

zygote The new cell formed by the union of an egg and sperm

REFERENCES

Aazh, H., & Moore, B. C. J. (2007). Dead regions in the cochlea at 4 kHz in elderly adults: Relation to absolute threshold, steepness of audiogram, and pure-tone average. *Journal of the American Academy of Audiology, 18,* 97–106.

Abboud, L. (2005, July 27). The next phase in psychiatry. *The Wall Street Journal,* pp. D1, D5.

Accardi, M., & Milling, L. (2009, August). The effectiveness of hypnosis for reducing procedure-related pain in children and adolescents: A comprehensive methodological review. *Journal of Behavioral Medicine, 32,* 328–339.

Ackerman, P. L. (2011). Intelligence and expertise. In R. J. Sternberg & S. Kaufman (Eds.), *The Cambridge handbook of intelligence.* New York: Cambridge University Press.

Acuna, D. E., Berniker, M., Fernandes, H. L., & Kording, K. P. (2015). Using psychophysics to ask if the brain samples or maximizes. *Journal of Vision, 15,* 7–18.

Adachi, P. C., & Willoughby, T. (2011). The effect of violent video games on aggression: Is it more than just the violence? *Aggression and Violent Behavior, 16,* 55–62.

Adams, G., & Dzokoto, V. A. (2007). Genital shrinking panic in Ghana: A cultural psychological analysis. *Culture & Psychology, 13,* 83–104.

Adams, M., Zuniga, X., Hackman, H. W., Castaneda, C. R., & Blumenfeld, W. J. (2000). *Readings for diversity and social justice: An anthology on racism, sexism, anti-Semitism, heterosexism, classism, and ableism.* New York: Routledge.

Addus, A. A., Chen, D., & Khan, A. S. (2007). Academic performance and advisement of university students: A case study. *College Student Journal, 41,* 316–326.

Advokat, C. (2005). Differential effects of clozapine versus other antipsychotics on clinical outcome and dopamine release in the brain. *Essential Psychopharmacology, 6,* 73–90.

Aftanas, L., & Golosheykin, S. (2005). Impact of regular meditation practice on EEG activity at rest and during evoked negative emotions. *International Journal of Neuroscience, 115,* 893–909.

Ainsworth, M. D. S., Blehar, M. C., Waters, E., & Wall, S. (1978). *Patterns of attachment: A psychological study of the strange situation.* Hillsdale, NJ: Erlbaum.

Airuehia, E., Walker, L. Y., & Nittler, J. (2015). A review of "bath salts": Evolving designer drugs of abuse. *Journal of Child & Adolescent Substance Abuse, 24,* 186–190.

Akil, H., & Morano, M. I. (1996). The biology of stress: From periphery to brain. In S. J. Watson (Ed.), *Biology of schizophrenia and affective disease.* Washington, DC: American Psychiatric Press.

Albala, I., Doyle, M., & Appelbaum, P. (2010). The evolution of consent forms for research: A quarter century of changes. *IRB: Ethics & Human Research, 32,* 7–11.

Albanese, M., & Case, S. M. (2015). Progress testing: Critical analysis and suggested practices. *Advances in Health Sciences Education.* Retrieved from http://www.ncbi.nlm.nih.gov/pubmed/25662873

Albuquerque, L., Martins, M., Coelho, M., Guedes, L., Ferreira, J. J., Rosa, M., & Martins, I. P. (2016). Advanced Parkinson disease patients have impairment in prosody processing. *Journal of Clinical & Experimental Neuropsychology, 38* (2), 208–216.

Aleksander, I. (2013, June 23). Molly: Pure, but not so simple. *The New York Times,* p. ST1.

Alfaro, A., Bernabeu, Á., Agulló, C., Parra, J., & Fernández, E. (2015). Hearing colors: An example of brain plasticity. *Frontiers in Systems Neuroscience, 9,* 42–50.

Alix, J. P., & de Jesus Domingues, A. M. (2011). White matter synapses: Form, function, and dysfunction. *Neurology, 76,* 397–404.

Alloy, L. B., Jacobson, N. S., & Acocella, J. (1999). *Abnormal psychology* (8th ed.). New York: McGraw-Hill.

Ally, B. A., Hussey, E. P., & Donahue, M. J. (2013). A case of hyperthymesia: Rethinking the role of the amygdala in autobiographical memory. *Neuroscience, 19,* 166–181.

Alonso, A., Alonso, S., & Piper, W. (2003). Group psychotherapy. In G. Stricker & T. A. Widiger, et al. (Eds.), *Handbook of psychology: Clinical psychology* (Vol. 8). New York: Wiley.

Altman, N., & Stile, J. (2015). Staying alive: Freud for a new generation. *PsycCRITIQUES, 60,* 25–32.

Alzheimer's Association. (2013). *2013 Alzheimer's Disease: Facts and Figures.* Chicago, IL: Alzheimer's Association.

American Association of Intellectual and Developmental Disabilities. (2015). *Frequently Asked Questions on Intellectual Disability and the AAIDD Definition.* Retrieved from http://aaidd.org/docs/default-source/sis-docs/aaiddfaqonid_template.pdf?sfvrsn=2

American Psychiatric Association. (2013). *Diagnostic and Statistical Manual of Mental Disorders, Fifth Edition (DSM-5).* Washington, DC: Author.

American Psychological Association (2009). *Psychology, careers for the twenty-first century.* Washington, DC: American Psychological Association.

American Psychological Association (2015). *Demographics of the U.S. psychology workforce: Findings from the American Community Survey.* Washington, DC: Author.

American Psychological Association (APA). (2002, August 21). *APA Ethics Code, 2002.* Washington, DC: American Psychological Association.

Anastasi, A., & Urbina, S. (1997). *Psychological testing* (7th ed.). Englewood Cliffs, NJ: Prentice Hall.

Anderson, C. A., & Carnagey, N. L. (2009). Causal effects of violent sports video games on aggression: Is it competitiveness or violent content? *Journal of Experimental Social Psychology, 45,* 731–739.

Anderson, C. A., Carnagey, N. L., Flanagan, M., Benjamin, A. J., Jr., Eubanks, J., & Valentine, J. C. (2004). Violent video games: Specific effects of violent content on aggressive thoughts and behavior. In M. P. Zanna (Ed.), *Advances in experimental social psychology* (Vol. 36). San Diego, CA: Elsevier Academic Press.

Anderson, C., & Home, J. A. (2006). Sleepiness enhances distraction during a monotonous task. *Sleep: Journal of Sleep and Sleep Disorders Research, 29,* 573–576.

Anderson, C., Shibuya, A., Ihori, N., Swing, E., Bushman, B., Sakamoto, A., et al. (2010). Violent video game effects on aggression, empathy, and prosocial behavior in Eastern and Western countries: A meta-analytic review. *Psychological Bulletin, 136,* 151–173.

Anderson, J. A., & Adams, M. (1992). Acknowledging the learning styles of diverse student populations: Implications for instructional design. *New Directions for Teaching and Learning, 49,* 19–33.

Anderson, J. L., Sellbom, M., Pymont, C., Smid, W., De Saeger, H., & Kamphuis, J. H. (2015). Measurement of DSM-5 section II personality disorder constructs using the MMPI-2-RF in clinical and forensic samples. *Psychological Assessment, 27,* 786–800.

Andrasik, F. (2006). Psychophysiological disorders: Headache as a case in point. In F. Andrasik, *Comprehensive handbook of personality and psychopathology, Vol. 2: Adult psycho-pathology.* Hoboken, NJ: John Wiley & Sons.

Andrasik, F. (2007). What does the evidence show? Efficacy of behavioural treatments for recurrent headaches in adults. *Neurological Science, 28, Supplement,* S70–S77.

Anestis, M. D., Anestis, J. C., & Lilienfeld, S. O. (2011). When it comes to evaluating psychodynamic therapy, the devil is in the details. *American Psychologist, 66,* 149–151.

Angoff, W. H. (1988). The nature-nurture debate, aptitudes, and group differences. *American Psychologist, 43,* 713–720.

Antonini, A., & Barone, P. (2008, December). Dopamine agonist-based strategies in the treatment of Parkinson's disease. *Neurological Sciences, 29,* S371–SS374.

APA Presidential Task Force on Evidence-Based Practice. (2006). *Evidence-Based Practice in Psychology, 61,* 271–285.

Applebaum, E. (2016). *Unfolding the unconscious psyche: Pathways to the arts.* New York: Routledge/Taylor & Francis Group.

Ariely, D., & Norton, M. I. (2009). Conceptual consumption. *Annual Review of Psychology, 60,* 475–499.

Arimoto, M., Shiomi, T., Sasanabe, R., Inagawa, S., Ueda, H., & Inafuku, S. (2011). A sheet-type device for home-monitoring sleep apneas in children. *Sleep and Biological Rhythms, 9,* 103–111.

Armbruster, D., Mueller, A., Strobel, A., Lesch, K., Kirschbaum, C., & Brocke, B. (2011). Variation in genes involved in dopamine clearance influence the startle response in older adults. *Journal of Neural Transmission, 118,* 1281–1292.

Arnett, J. (2008). The neglected 95%: Why American psychology needs to become less American. *American Psychologist, 63,* 602–614.

Arnett, J. (2011). Emerging adulthood(s): The cultural psychology of a new life stage. In L. Jensen (Ed.), *Bridging cultural and developmental approaches to psychology: New syntheses in theory, research, and policy.* New York: Oxford University Press.

Arnett, J. J. (2000). Emerging adulthood. *American Psychologist, 55,* 469–480.

Arnett, J. J. (2006). *Emerging adulthood: The winding road from the late teens through the twenties.* New York: Oxford University Press.

Arnett, J. J. (2007). Afterword: Aging out of care—Toward realizing the possibilities of emerging adulthood. *New Directions for Youth Development, 113,* 151–161.

Aronson J., & Dee T. (2012). Stereotype threat in the real world. In M. Inzlicht & T. Schmader (Eds.), *Stereotype Threat: Theory, Processes, and Application.* New York: Oxford.

Aronson, J., & Steele, Claude M. (2005). Stereotypes and the fragility of academic competence, motivation, and self-concept. In A. J. Elliot & C. S. Dweck (Eds.), *Handbook of competence and motivation.* New York, NY: Guilford Publications.

Arshamian, A., Iannilli, E., Gerber, J. C., Willander, J., Persson, J., Seo, H., Hummel, T., & Larsson, M. (2013). The functional neuroanatomy of odor evoked auto-biographical memories cued by odors and words. *Neuropsychologia, 51,* 123–131.

Asch, S. E. (1951). Effects of group pressure upon the modification and distortion of judgments. In H. Guetzkow (Ed.), *Groups, leadership, and men.* Pittsburgh: Carnegie Press.

Ashley, K. B. (2013). The science on sexual orientation: A review of the recent literature. *Journal of Gay & Lesbian Mental Health, 17,* 175–182.

Aspinwall, L. G., & Taylor, S. E. (1997). A stitch in time: Self-regulation and proactive coping. *Psychological Bulletin, 121,* 417–436.

Atkinson, R. C., & Shiffrin, R. M. (1968). Human memory: A proposed system and its control processes. In K. W. Spence & J. T. Spence (Eds.), *The psychology of learning and motivation: Advances in research and theory* (Vol. 2, pp. 80–195). New York: Academic Press.

Atkinson, R. C., & Shiffrin, R. M. (1971). The control of short-term memory. *Scientific American, 225,* 82–90.

Auer, J. A., Goodship, A., Arnoczky, S., Pearce, S., Price, J., Claes, L., von Rechenberg, B., Hofmann-Amtenbrinck, M., Schneider, E., Muller-Terpitz, R., Thiele, F., Rippe, K. P., & Grainger, D. W. (2007). Refining animal models in fracture research: Seeking consensus for changing the agenda in optimising both animal welfare and scientific validity for appropriate biomedical use. *BMC Musculoskeletal Disorders, 8,* 72.

Aujoulat, I., Luminet, O., & Deccache, A. (2007). The perspective of patients on their experience of powerlessness. *Quality Health Research, 17,* 772–785.

Avenanti, A., & Urgesi, C. (2011). Understanding 'what' others do: Mirror mechanisms play a crucial role in action perception. *Social Cognitive and Affective Neuroscience, 6,* 257–259.

Averill, J. R. (1975). A semantic atlas of emotional concepts. *Catalog of Selected Documents in Psychology, 5,* 330.

Avery, D., McKay, P., & Wilson, D. (2008). What are the odds? How demographic similarity affects the prevalence of perceived employment discrimination. *Journal of Applied Psychology, 93,* 235–249.

Ayuso-Mateos, J., Nuevo, R., Verdes, E., Naidoo, N., & Chatterji, S. (2010). From depressive symptoms to depressive disorders: The relevance of thresholds. *British Journal of Psychiatry, 196,* 365–371.

Baars, B., & Seth, A. K. (2009). Consciousness: Theories and models. In W. Banks (Ed.), *Encyclopedia of consciousness.* New York: Elsevier.

Bacchiochi, J. R. (2006). Development and validation of the Malingering Discriminant Function Index (M-DFI) for the Minnesota Multiphasic Personality Inventory—2 (MMPI-2). *Dissertation Abstracts International: Section B: The Sciences and Engineering, 66*(10-B), 5673.

Bærentsen, K., Størkilde-Jørgensen, H., Sommerlund, B., Hartmann, T., Damsgaard-Madsen, J., Fosnæs, M., et al. (2010). An investigation of brain processes supporting meditation. *Cognitive Processing, 11,* 57–84.

Bagattini, C., Mele, S., Brignani, D., & Savazzi, S. (2015). No causal effect of left hemisphere hyperactivity in the genesis of neglect-like behavior. *Neuropsychologia, 72,* 12–21.

Bagge, C., & Sher, K. (2008). Adolescent alcohol involvement and suicide attempts: Toward the development of a conceptual framework. *Clinical Psychology Review, 28,* 1283–1296.

Bagnall, D. (2010). The use of spinal cord stimulation and intrathecal drug delivery in the treatment of low back-related pain. *Physical Medicine & Rehabilitation Clinics of North America, 21,* 851–858.

Bahrick, L. E., Lickliter, R., & Castellanos, I. (2013). The development of face perception in infancy: Intersensory interference and unimodal visual facilitation. *Developmental Psychology, 49,* 1919–1930.

Baker, J., & Berenbaum, H. (2007). Emotional approach and problem-focused coping: A comparison of potentially adaptive strategies. *Cognition and Emotion, 21,* 95–118.

Baker, N., & Mason, J. (2010). Gender issues in psychological testing of personality and abilities. *Handbook of gender research in psychology, Vol 2: Gender research in social and applied psychology.* New York: Springer Publishing.

Baker, S. C., & Serdikoff, S. L. (2013). Addressing the role of animal research in psychology. In D. S. Dunn, R. R. Gurung, K. Z. Naufel, & J. H. Wilson (Eds.), *Controversy in the psychology classroom: Using hot topics to foster critical thinking.* Washington, DC: American Psychological Association.

Balconi, M., Bortolotti, A., & Crivelli, D. (2013). Self-report measures, facial feedback, and personality differences (BEES) in cooperative vs. noncooperative situations: Contribution of the mimic system to the sense of empathy. *International Journal of Psychology, 48,* 631–640.

Baluch, F., & Itti, L. (2011). Mechanisms of top-down attention. *Trends in Neurosciences, 34,* 210–224.

Bandura, A. (1977). *Social learning theory.* Englewood Cliffs, NJ: Prentice Hall.

Bandura, A. (1986). *Social foundations of thought and action: A social cognitive theory.* Englewood Cliffs, NJ: Prentice Hall.

Bandura, A. (1994). Social cognitive theory of mass communication. In J. Bryant & D. Zillmann (Eds.), *Media effects: Advances in theory and research: LEA's communication series.* Hillsdale, NJ: Erlbaum.

Bandura, A. (1999). Social cognitive theory of personality. In D. Cervone & Y. Shod (Eds.), *The coherence of personality.* New York: Guilford.

Bandura, A. (2000). Self-efficacy: The foundation of agency. In W. J. Perrig & A. Grob (Eds.), *Control of human behavior, mental processes, and consciousness: Essays in honor of the 60th birthday of August Flammer.* Mahwah, NJ: Erlbaum.

Bandura, A. (2004). Swimming against the mainstream: The early years from chilly tributary to transformative mainstream. *Behaviour Research and Therapy, 42,* 613–630.

Bandura, A., & Locke, E. A. (2003). Negative self-efficacy and goal effects revisited. *Journal of Applied Psychology, 88,* 87–99.

Bandura, A., Grusec, J. E., & Menlove, F. L. (1967). Vicarious extinction of avoidance behavior. *Journal of Personality and Social Psychology, 5,* 16–23.

Bandura, A., Ross, D., & Ross, S. (1963a). Imitation of film-mediated aggressive models. *Journal of Abnormal and Social Psychology, 66,* 3–11.

Bandura, A., Ross, D., & Ross, S. (1963b). Vicarious reinforcement and imitative learning. *Journal of Abnormal and Social Psychology, 67,* 601–607.

Banks, J. A. (2006). Improving race relations in schools: From theory and research to practice. *Journal of Social Issues, 62,* 607–614.

Baradon, T. (2010). *Relational trauma in infancy.* New York: Routledge.

Barcott, B., & Scherer, M. (2015, May 25). The great pot experiment. *Time,* pp. 38–44.

Bargh, J. A. (2014, January). Our unconscious mind. *Scientific American,* pp. 30–37.

Barke, D. B. (2011). Self-selection for stressful experiences. *Stress and Health: Journal of the International Society for the Investigation of Stress, 27,* 194–205.

Barkley, R. (2000). *Taking charge of ADHD* (rev. ed.). New York: Guilford Press.

Barkley, R. (2005). *ADHD and the nature of self-control.* New York: Guildford Press.

Barkley, R. A., Knouse, L. E., & Murphy, K. R. (2011). Correspondence and disparity in the self- and other ratings of current and childhood ADHD symptoms and impairment in adults with ADHD. *Psychological Assessment, 23,* 437–446.

Barlow, D. H. (2007). *Clinical handbook of psychological disorders: A step-by-step treatment manual* (4th ed.). New York: Guilford Press.

Barnett, J. E., Wise, E. H., & Johnson-Greene, D. (2007). Informed consent: Too much of a good thing or not enough? *Professional Psychology: Research and Practice, 38,* 179–186.

Barrett, L. F., & Salovey, P. (Eds.). (2002). *The wisdom in feeling: Psychological processes in emotional intelligence.* New York: Guilford Press.

Bartholow, B. D., Bushman, B. J., & Sestir, M. A. (2006). Chronic violent video game exposure and desensitization to violence: Behavioral and event-related brain potential data. *Journal of Experimental Social Psychology, 42,* 532–539.

Bartlett, F. (1932). *Remembering: A study in experimental and social psychology.* Cambridge, England: Cambridge University Press.

Bartlett, M. Y., & DeSteno, D. (2006). Gratitude and prosocial behavior: Helping when it costs you. *Psychological Science, 17,* 319–325.

Bartocci, G. (2004). Transcendence techniques and psychobiological mechanisms underlying religious experience. *Mental Health, Religion and Culture, 7,* 171–181.

Bartoshuk, L., & Lucchina, L. (1997, January 13). Are you a supertaster? *U.S. News & World Report,* pp. 58–59.

Baruss, I. (2003). *Alterations of consciousness: An empirical analysis for social scientists.* Washington, DC: American Psychological Association.

Barzilay, S., Feldman, D., Snir, A., Apter, A., Carli, V., Hoven, C. W., & . . . Wasserman, D. (2015). The interpersonal theory of suicide and adolescent suicidal behavior. *Journal of Affective Disorders, 183,* 68–74.

Basak, C., Boot, W., Voss, M., & Kramer, A. (2008). Can training in a real-time strategy video game attenuate cognitive decline in older adults? *Psychology and Aging, 23,* 765–777.

Bassett, A. M., & Baker, C. (2015). Normal or abnormal? "Normative uncertainty" in psychiatric practice. *Journal of Medical Humanities, 36,* 89–111.

Bastian, B., Jetten, J, Hornsey, M. J., & Leknes, S. (2014). The positive consequences of pain: A biopsychosocial approach. *Personality and Social Psychology Review, 18,* 256–279.

Batelaan, N., de Graaf, R., Spijker, J., Smit, J., van Balkom, A., Vollebergh, W., et al. (2010). The course of panic attacks in individuals with panic disorder and subthreshold panic disorder: A population-based study. *Journal of Affective Disorders, 121,* 30–38.

Bates, E. (2005). Plasticity, localization, and language development. In S. T. Parker and J. Langer (Eds.), *Biology and knowledge revisited: From neurogenesis to psychogenesis.* Mahwah, NJ: Erlbaum.

Bates, J. E., & Pettit, G. S. (2015). Temperament, parenting, and social development. In J. E. Grusec & P. D. Hastings (Eds.), *Handbook of socialization: Theory and research* (2nd ed.). New York: Guilford Press.

Bates, P. E., Cuvo, T., Miner, C. A., & Korabek, C. A. (2001). Simulated and community-based instruction involving persons with mild and moderate mental retardation. *Research in Developmental Disabilities, 22,* 95–115.

Batson, C. D., & Powell, A. A. (2003). Altruism and prosocial behavior. In T. Millon & M. J. Lerner (Eds.), *Handbook of psychology: Personality and social psychology* (Vol. 5). New York: Wiley.

Bauer, J. J., Schwab, J. R., & McAdams, D. P. (2011). Self-actualizing: Where ego development finally feels good? *The Humanistic Psychologist, 39,* 121–136.

Baum, A. (1994). Behavioral, biological, and environmental interactions in disease processes. In S. Blumenthal, K. Matthews, & S. Weiss (Eds.), *New research frontiers in behavioral medicine: Proceedings of the National Conference.* Washington, DC: NIH Publications.

Baumeister, R. F., & Stillman, T. (2006). Erotic plasticity: Nature, culture, gender, and sexuality. In R. D. McAnulty & M. M. Burnette, *Sex and sexuality, Vol 1: Sexuality today: Trends and controversies.* Westport, CT: Praeger Publishers/Greenwood Publishing.

Baumrind, D. (1971). Current patterns of parental authority. *Developmental Psychology Monographs, 4* (1, pt. 2).

Baumrind, D. (2005). Patterns of parental authority and adolescent autonomy. *New Directions for Child and Adolescent Development, 108,* 61–69.

Baumrind, D., & Milgram, S. (2010). Classic dialogue: Was Stanley Milgram's study of obedience unethical? In B. Slife (Ed.), *Clashing views on psychological issues* (16th ed.). New York: McGraw-Hill.

Baumrucker, S., Mingle, P., Harrington, D., Stolick, M., Carter, G. T., & Oertli, K. A. (2011). Medical marijuana and organ transplantation: Drug of abuse, or medical necessity? *American Journal of Hospice & Palliative Medicine, 28,* 130–134.

Bayliss, D. M., Jarrold, C., Baddeley, A. D., & Gunn, D. M. (2005a). The relationship between short-term memory and working memory: Complex span made simple? *Memory, 13,* 414–421.

Bazalakova, M. H., Wright, J., Schneble, E. J., McDonald, M. P., Heilman, C. J., Levey, A. I., & Blakely, R. D. (2007). Deficits in acetylcholine homeostasis, receptors and behaviors in choline transporter heterozygous mice. *Genes, Brain & Behavior, 6,* 411–424.

Beaudry, J. L., Lindsay, R. C. L., Leach, A., Mansour, J. K., Bertrand, M. I., & Kalmet, N. (2015). The effect of evidence type, identification accuracy, line-up presentation, and line-up administration on observers' perceptions of eyewitnesses. *Legal and Criminological Psychology, 20,* 343–364.

Beck, A. T. (2004). Cognitive therapy, behavior therapy, psychoanalysis, and pharmacotherapy: A cognitive continuum. In A. Freeman, M. J. Mahoney, P. Devito, & D. Martin (Eds.), *Cognition and psychotherapy* (2nd ed.). New York: Springer.

Beck, A. T. (2007). *Cognitive therapy in clinical practice.* J. Scott., J. Williams., G. Mark, & A. T. Beck (Eds.). New York: Taylor & Francis.

Beck, A. T., & Rector, N. A. (2005). Cognitive approaches to schizophrenia: Theory and therapy. *Annual Review of Clinical Psychology, 1,* 577–606.

Beck, A. T., Davis, D. D., & Freeman, A. (2015). *Cognitive therapy of personality disorders* (3rd ed.). New York: Guilford Press.

Beck, A. T., Freeman, A., & Davis, D. D. (2004). *Cognitive therapy of personality disorders* (2nd ed.). New York: Guilford Press.

Beck, H. P., Levinson, S., & Irons, G. (2009). Finding Little Albert: A journey to John B. Watson's infant laboratory. *American Psychologist, 64,* 605–614.

Begley, S. (2013, June 5). *The schizophrenic mind.* Retrieved from http://www.sharonlbegley.com/the-schizophrenic-mind

Behrens, M., Lendon, C., & Roe, C. (2009). A common biological mechanism in cancer and Alzheimer's disease? *Current Alzheimer Research, 6,* 196–204.

Beidel, D. C., & Turner, S. M. (2007). Etiology of social anxiety disorder. In D. C. Beidel & S. M. Turner, *Shy children, phobic adults: Nature and treatment of social anxiety disorders* (2nd ed.). Washington, DC: American Psychological Association.

Belov, D. I., & Armstrong, R. D. (2009). Direct and inverse problems of item pool design for computerized adaptive testing. *Edcational and Psychological Measurement, 69,* 533–547.

Ben-Porath, Y., & Archer, R. (2008). The MMPI-2 and MMPI-A. *Personality assessment.* New York: Routledge/Taylor & Francis Group.

Benca, R. M. (2005). Diagnosis and treatment of chronic insomnia: A review. *Psychiatric Services, 56,* 332–343.

Benet-Martínez, V., Lee, F., & Leu, J. (2006). Biculturalism and cognitive complexity: Expertise in cultural representations. *Journal of Cross-Cultural Psychology, 37,* 386–407.

Benham, G., Woody, E. Z., & Wilson, K. S. (2006). Expect the unexpected: Ability, attitude, and responsiveness to hypnosis. *Journal of Personality and Social Psychology, 91,* 342–350.

Bensing, J., & Verheul, W. (2010). The silent healer: The role of communication in placebo effects. *Patient Education and Counseling, 80,* 293–299.

Bentley, R., Ormerod, P., & Batty, M. (2011). Evolving social influence in large populations. *Behavioral Ecology and Sociobiology, 65,* 537–546.

Bergman, K., Sarkar, P., Glover, V., & O'Connor, T. (2010). Maternal prenatal cortisol and infant cognitive development: Moderation by infant–mother attachment. *Biological Psychiatry, 67,* 1026–1032.

Berk, L. E. (2005). Why parenting matters. In S. Olfman (Ed.), *Childhood lost: How American culture is failing our kids* (pp. 19–53). Westport, CT: Praeger Publishers/Greenwood Publishing Group.

Berkman, L. F., Ertel, K. A., & Glymour, M. M. (2011). Aging and social intervention: Life course perspectives. In R. H. Binstock & L. K. George (Eds.), *Handbook of aging and the social sciences* (7th ed.). San Diego, CA: Elsevier Academic Press.

Berkowitz, L. (2001). On the formation and regulation of anger and aggression: A cognitive-neoassociationistic analysis. In W. G. Parrott (Ed.), *Emotions in social psychology: Essential readings.* New York: Psychology Press.

Berman, A. L., Jobes, D. A., & Silverman, M. M. (2006). An integrative-eclectic approach to treatment. In A. L. Berman, D. A. Jobes, & M. M. Silverman, *Adolescent suicide: Assessment and intervention* (2nd ed.). Washington, DC: American Psychological Association.

Bernstein, D. M., Loftus, G. R., & Meltzoff, A. N. (2005). Object identification in preschool children and adults. *Developmental Science, 8,* 151–161.

Berntsen, D., & Rubin, D. C. (2004). Cultural life scripts structure recall from autobiographical memory. *Memory and Cognition, 32,* 427–442.

Berntson, G., Bechara, A., & Damasio, H., Tranel, D., & Cacioppo, J. (2007). Amygdala contribution to selective dimensions of emotion. *Social Cognitive and Affective Neuroscience, 2,* 123–129.

Berridge, K. C. (2004). Motivation concepts in behavioral neuroscience. *Physiology and Behavior, 81,* 179–209.

Berrios, G. E. (1996). *The history of mental symptoms: Descriptive psychopathology since the nineteenth century.* Cambridge, England: Cambridge University Press.

Berthoud, H. R. (2002). Multiple neural systems controlling food intake and body weight. *Neuroscience and Biobehavioral Reviews, 26,* 393–428.

Betley, J. N., Xu, S., Cao, Z. H., Gong, R., Magnus, C. J., Yu, Y., & Sternson, S. M. (2015). Neurons for hunger and thirst transmit a negative-valence teaching signal. *Nature, 521,* 180–185.

Bhar, S., Gelfand, L., Schmid, S., Gallop, R., DeRubeis, R., Hollon, S., et al. (2008). Sequence of improvement in depressive symptoms across cognitive therapy and pharmacotherapy. *Journal of Affective Disorders, 110,* 161–166.

Bialystok, E., Barac, R., Blaye, A., & Poulin-Dubois, D. (2010). Word mapping and executive functioning in young monolingual and bilingual children. *Journal of Cognition and Development, 11,* 485–508.

Bidwell, D. R. (2011). Wanting to die: How to prevent suicide. In C. Franklin, R. Fong, C. Franklin, R. Fong (Eds.), *The church leader's counseling resource book: A guide to mental health and social problems.* New York: Oxford University Press.

Bieberstein, A., & Roosen, J. (2015). Gender differences in the meanings associated with food hazards: A means-end chain analysis. *Food Quality and Preference, 42,* 165–176.

Binder, A., & Baron, R. (2010). Utility of transcutaneous electrical nerve stimulation in neurologic pain disorders. *Neurology, 74,* 104–105.

Binet, A., & Simon, T. (1916). *The development of intelligence in children (The Binet-Simon Scale).* Baltimore: Williams & Wilkins.

Birren, J. E. (Ed.). (1996). *Encyclopedia of gerontology: Age, aging and the aged.* San Diego, CA: Academic Press.

Bitterman, M. E. (2006). Classical conditioning since Pavlov. *Review of General Psychology, 10,* 365–376.

Bittles, A. H., Bower, C., & Hussain, R. (2007). The four ages of Down syndrome. *European Journal of Public Health, 17,* 121–225.

Bizley, J., Walker, K., Silverman, B., King, A., & Schnupp, J. (2009, February). Interdependent encoding of pitch, timbre, and spatial location in auditory cortex. *Journal of Neuroscience, 29,* 2064–2075.

Bjornsdottir, E., Keenan, B. T., Eysteinsdottir, B., Arnardottir, E. S., Janson, C., Gislason, T., & . . . Benediktsdottir, B. (2015). Quality of life among untreated sleep apnea patients compared with the general population and changes after treatment with positive airway pressure. *Journal of Sleep Research, 24,* 328–338.

Bjornstad, R. (2006). Learned helplessness, discouraged workers, and multiple unemployment equilibria. *The Journal of Socio-Economics, 35,* 458–475.

Blakeslee, S. (1992, August 11). Finding a new messenger for the brain's signals to the body. *The New York Times,* p. C3.

Blanton, H., Jaccard, J., & Burrows, C. N. (2015). Implications of the Implicit Association Test D-transformation for psychological assessment. *Assessment, 22,* 429–440.

Blasi, C., & Causey, K. (2010). Evolutionary psychology and evolutionary developmental psychology: Understanding the evolution of human behavior and development. *Psicothema, 22,* 1–3.

Blass, T. (1996). Attribution of responsibility and trust in the Milgram obedience experiment. *Journal of Applied Social Psychology, 26,* 1529–1535.

Blass, T. (2004). *The man who shocked the world: The life and legacy of Stanley Milgram.* New York: Basic Books.

Blass, T. (2009). From New Haven to Santa Clara: A historical perspective on the Milgram obedience experiments. *American Psychologist, 64,* 37–45.

Blatter, K., & Cajochen, C., (2007). Circadian rhythms in cognitive performance: Methodological constraints, protocols, theoretical underpinnings. *Physiology & Behavior, 90,* 196–208.

Bloom, P. N., McBride, C. M., & Pollak, K. I. (2006). Recruiting teen smokers in shopping malls to a smoking-cessation program using the foot-in-the-door technique. *Journal of Applied Social Psychology, 36,* 1129–1144.

Blum, D. (2002). *Love at Goon Park: Harry Harlow and the science of affection.* Cambridge, MA: Perseus.

Boag, S. (2015). Repression, defence, and the psychology of science. In S. Boag, L. W. Brakel, & V. Talvitie (Eds.), *Philosophy, science, and psychoanalysis: A critical meeting.* London: Karnac Books.

Boahen, K. (2005, May). Neuromorphic microchips. *Scientific American,* pp. 56–64.

Boahen, K. (2005, May). Neuromorphic microchips. *Scientific American,* pp. 56–64.

Boake, C. (2008, April). Clinical neuropsychology. *Professional Psychology: Research and Practice, 39,* 234–239.

Bode, C., de Ridder, D. T., Kuijer, R. G., & Bensing, J. M. (2007). Effects of an intervention promoting proactive coping competencies in middle and late adulthood. *Gerontologist, 47,* 42–51.

Boden, J. M., Fergusson, D. M., & Horwood, L. J. (2007). Anxiety disorders and suicidal behaviours in adolescence and young adulthood: Findings from a longitudinal study. *Psychological Medicine, 37,* 431–440.

Boehm, K. E., & Campbell, N. B. (1995). Suicide: A review of calls to an adolescent peer listening phone service. *Child Psychiatry and Human Development, 26,* 61–66

Bohart, A. C. (2006). Understanding person-centered therapy: A review of Paul Wilkins' person-centered therapy in focus. *Person-Centered and Experiential Psychotherapies, 5,* 138–143.

Böhmer, M. W. (2010). "Communication by impact" and other forms of non-verbal communication: A review of transference, counter-transference and projective identification. *African Journal of Psychiatry, 13,* 179–183.

Bohn, A., & Berntsen, D. (2007). Pleasantness bias in flashbulb memories: Positive and negative flashbulb memories of the fall of the Berlin Wall among East and West Germans. *Memory and Cognition, 35,* 565–577.

Bohn, C., Aderka, I. M., Schreiber, F., Stangier, U., & Hofmann, S. G. (2013). Sudden gains in cognitive therapy and interpersonal therapy for social anxiety disorder. *Journal of Consulting and Clinical Psychology, 81,* 177–182.

Boles, D. B. (2005). A large-sample study of sex differences in functional cerebral lateralization. *Journal of Clinical and Experimental Neuropsychology, 27,* 759–768.

Bolger, N., & Amarel, D. (2007). Effects of social support visibility on adjustment to stress: Experimental evidence. *Journal of Personality and Social Psychology, 92,* 458–475.

Bolkan, S. (2015). Intellectually stimulating students' intrinsic motivation: The mediating influence of affective learning and student engagement. *Communication Reports, 28,* 80–91.

Bonanno, G.A. (2004). Loss, trauma, and human resilience: Have we underestimated the human capacity to thrive after extremely aversive events? *American Psychologist, 59,* 20–28.

Bond, M. (2006). Psychodynamic psychotherapy in the treatment of mood disorders. *Current Opinion in Psychiatry, 19*(1), 40–43.

Bonezzi, A., Brendl, C., & De Angelis, M. (2011). Stuck in the middle: The psychophysics of goal pursuit. *Psychological Science, 22,* 607–612.

Bonnardel, V. (2006). Color naming and categorization in inherited color vision deficiencies. *Visual Neuroscience, 23,* 637–643.

Borbély, Alexander. *Secrets of Sleep* (1986). Basic Books, a member of the Perseus Books Group.

Bornstein, R. F. (2003). Psychodynamic models of personality. In T. Millon & M. J. Lerner (Eds.), *Handbook of psychology: Personality and social psychology* (Vol. 5). New York: Wiley.

Bosma, H., van Boxtel, M. P. J., Ponds, R. W. H. M., Houx, P. J. H., & Jolles, J. (2003). Education and age-related cognitive decline: The contribution of mental workload. *Educational Gerontology, 29,* 165–173.

Bosse, T., Gerritsen, C., & Treur, J. (2011). Combining rational and biological factors in virtual agent decision making. *Applied Intelligence, 34,* 87–101.

Böttche, M., Kuwert, P., Pietrzak, R. H., & Knaevelsrud, C. (2016). Predictors of outcome of an Internet-based cognitive-behavioural therapy for post-traumatic stress disorder in older adults. *Psychology and Psychotherapy: Theory, Research and Practice, 89,* 82–96.

Bouchard, T. J., Jr. (2004). Genetic influence on human psychological traits: A survey. *Current Directions in Psychological Science, 13,* 148–151.

Bouton, M. E., Todd, T. P., Vurbic, D., & Winterbauer, N. E. (2011). Renewal after the extinction of free operant behavior. *Learning & Behavior, 39,* 57–67.

Boxer, P., Huesmann, L., Bushman, B., O'Brien, M., & Moceri, D. (2009). The role of violent media preference in cumulative developmental risk for violence and general aggression. *Journal of Youth and Adolescence, 38,* 417–428.

Boylan, J. M., & Ryff, C. D. (2015). Psychological well-being and metabolic syndrome: Findings from the Midlife in the United States national sample. *Psychosomatic Medicine, 77,* 548–558.

Boyraz, G., Waits, J. B., Felix, V. A., & Wynes, D. D. (2016). Posttraumatic stress and physical health among adults: The role of coping mechanisms. *Journal of Loss and Trauma, 21*(1), 47–61.

Bozarth, J. D., Zimring, F. M., & Tausch, R. (2002). Client-centered therapy: The evolution of a revolution. In D. J. Cain (Ed.), *Humanistic psychotherapies: Handbook of research and practice* (pp. 147–188). Washington, DC: American Psychological Association.

Braaten, E. B. (2011). Psychotherapy: Interpersonal and insight-oriented approaches. In E. B. Braaten (Ed.) , *How to find mental health care for your child.* Washington, DC: American Psychological Association.

Brandon, M., & Saffran, J. R. (2011). Apparent motion enhances visual rhythm discrimination in infancy. *Attention, Perception, & Psychophysics, 73,* 1016–1020.

Brandtzæg, P., Lüders, M., & Skjetne, J. (2010). Too many Facebook "friends"? Content sharing and sociability versus the need for privacy in social network sites. *International Journal of Human-Computer Interaction, 26,* 1006–1030.

Brausch, A. M., & Gutierrez, P. M. (2009). Differences in non-suicidal self-injury and suicide attempts in adolescents. *Journal of Youth and Adolescence, 21,* 46–51.

Brazelton, T. B. (1969). *Infants and mothers: Differences in development*. New York: Dell.

Bridges, K. R., & Harnish, R. J. (2010). Role of irrational beliefs in depression and anxiety: A review. *Health, 2,* 862–877.

Broidy, L. M., Nagin, D. S., & Tremblay, R. E. (2003). Developmental trajectories of childhood disruptive behaviors and adolescent delinquency: A six-site, cross-national study. *Developmental Psychology, 39,* 222–245.

Broman, C. L. (2005). Stress, race and substance use in college. *College Student Journal, 39,* 340–352.

Bronson, P., & Merryman, A. (2009). *NurtureShock*. New York: Twelve.

Brooker, R. J., Widmaier, E. P., Graham, L., & Stiling, P. (2008). *Biology*. New York: McGraw-Hill.

Brown, B. (1982). *Stress and the art of biofeedback*. New York: Bantam Books.

Brown, P. K., & Wald, G. (1964). Visual pigments in single rod and cones of the human retina. *Science, 144,* 45–52.

Brownlee, K. (2007). What works for whom? A critical review of psychotherapy research (2nd ed.). *Psychiatric Rehabilitation Journal, 30,* 239–240.

Brucker, B., Ehlis, A., Häußinger, F. B., Fallgatter, A. J., & Gerjets, P. (2015). Watching corresponding gestures facilitates learning with animations by activating human mirror-neurons: An fNIRS study. *Learning And Instruction, 36,* 27–37.

Bruggeman, H., Yonas, A., & Konczak, J. (2007). The processing of linear perspective and binocular information for action and perception. *Neuropsychologia, 45,* 1420–1426.

Brugman, D. (2010). Moral reasoning competence and the moral judgment-action discrepancy in young adolescents. *The development and structure of conscience*. New York: Psychology Press.

Brydon, L., Edwards, S., Mohamed-Ali, V., & Steptoe, A. (2004). Socioeconomic status and stress-induced increases in interleukin-6. *Brain, Behavior, and Immunity, 18,* 281–290.

Buchanan, J. J., & Wright, D. L. (2011). Generalization of action knowledge following observational learning. *Acta Psychologica, 136,* 167–178.

Buchanan, T., & Selmon, N. (2008). Race and gender differences in self-efficacy: Assessing the role of gender role attitudes and family background. *Sex Roles, 58,* 822–836.

Buchert, R., Thomasius, R., Wilke, F., Petersen, K., Nebeling, B., Obrocki, J., Schulze, O., Schmidt, U., & Clausen, M. (2004). A voxel-based PET investigation of the long-term effects of "ecstasy" consumption on brain serotonin transporters. *American Journal of Psychiatry, 161,* 1181–1189.

Buckley, L., Chapman, R., & Sheehan, M. (2010). Protective behaviour in adolescent friendships: The influence of attitudes towards the consequences, friendship norms and perceived control. *Journal of Youth Studies, 13,* 661–679.

Buckner, J. D., & Shah, S. M. (2015). Fitting in and feeling fine: Conformity and coping motives differentially mediate the relationship between social anxiety and drinking problems for men and women. *Addiction Research & Theory, 23,* 231–237.

Buehner, M., Krumm, S., & Ziegler, M. (2006). Cognitive abilities and their interplay: Reasoning, crystallized intelligence, working memory components, and sustained attention. *Journal of Individual Differences, 27,* 57–72.

Bukobza, G. (2009). Relations between rebelliousness, risk-taking behavior, and identity status during emerging adulthood. *Identity, 9,* 159–177.

Bunce, J. A. (2015). Incorporating ecology and social system into formal hypotheses to guide field studies of color vision in primates. *American Journal of Primatology, 77,* 516-526.

Bunting, M. (2006). Proactive interference and item similarity in working memory. *Journal of Experimental Psychology: Learning, Memory, and Cognition, 32,* 183–196.

Burchinal, M. R., Roberts, J. E., & Riggins, R., Jr. (2000). Relating quality of center-based child care to early cognitive and language development longitudinally. *Child Development, 71,* 338–357.

Bureau of Labor Statistics. (2013, April 26). Employment characteristics of families—2012. Washington, DC: Bureau of Labor Statistics.

Burger, J. M. (2009). Replicating Milgram: Would people still obey today? *American Psychologist, 64,* 1–11.

Burger, J. M., Reed, M., & DeCesare, K. (1999). The effects of initial request size on compliance: More about the that's-not-all technique. *Basic and Applied Social Psychology, 21,* 243–249.

Burgoon, J. K., Bonito, J. A., Ramirez, A. J. R., Dunbar, N. E., Kam, K., & Fischer, J. (2002). Testing the interactivity principle: Effects of mediation, propinquity, and verbal and nonverbal modalities in interpersonal interaction [Special issue: Research on the relationship between verbal and nonverbal communication: Emerging integrations]. *Journal of Communication, 52,* 657–677.

Burns, N. R., Bryan, J., & Nettlebeck, T. (2006). Ginkgo biloba: No robust effect on cognitive abilities or mood in healthy young or older adults. *Human Psychopharmacology: Clinical and Experimental, 21,* 27–37.

Burri, A., Spector, T., & Qazi, R. (2015). Common genetic factors among sexual orientation, gender nonconformity, and number of sex partners in female twins: Implications for the evolution of homosexuality. *Journal of Sexual Medicine, 12,* 1004–1011.

Busey, T. A., & Loftus, G. R. (2007). Cognitive science and the law. *Trends in Cognitive Science, 11,* 111–117.

Bush, J. (2008). Viability of virtual reality exposure therapy as a treatment alternative. *Computers in Human Behavior, 24,* 1032–1040.

Bushman, B. J., & Anderson, C. A. (2001). Media violence and the American public: Scientific facts versus media misinformation. *American Psychologist, 56,* 477–489.

Bushman, B., Chandler, J., & Huesmann, L. (2010). Do violent media numb our consciences?. *The development and structure of conscience*. New York: Psychology Press.

Buss, A. H. (2011). *Pathways to individuality: Evolution and development of personality traits*. Washington, DC: American Psychological Association.

Buss, D. (2009). How can evolutionary psychology successfully explain personality and individual differences? *Perspectives on Psychological Science, 4,* 359–366.

Buss, D. M. (2001). Human nature and culture: An evolutionary psychological perspective. *Journal of Personality, 69,* 955–978.

Buss, D. M., Abbott, M., & Angleitner, A. (1990). International preferences in selecting mates: A study of 37 cultures. *Journal of Cross-Cultural Psychology, 21,* 5–47.

Butler, L. T., & Berry, D. C. (2004). Understanding the relationship between repetition priming and mere exposure. *British Journal of Psychology, 95,* 467–487.

Byrne, D., & Kelley, L. (1981). *An introduction to personality* (3rd ed.). Pearson Education.

Cabaniss, D. L., Cherry, S., Douglas, C. J., & Schwartz, A. R. (2011). *Psychodynamic psychotherapy: A clinical manual*. New York: Wiley-Blackwell.

Cachelin, F. M., & Regan, P. C. (2006). Prevalence and correlates of chronic dieting in a multi-ethnic U.S. community sample. *Eating and Weight Disorders, 11,* 91–99.

Caelian, C. F. (2006). The role of perfectionism and stress in the suicidal behaviour of depressed adolescents. *Dissertation Abstracts International: Section B: The Sciences and Engineering, 66* (12-B), 6915.

Cain, D. J. (2010). Evaluation. In D. J. Cain (Ed.), *Person-centered psychotherapies*. Washington, DC: American Psychological Association.

Cain, D. J. (Ed.). (2002). *Humanistic psychotherapies: Handbook of research and practice*. Washington, DC: American Psychological Association.

Cameron, O. G. (2002). *Visceral sensory neuroscience: Interoception*. London: Oxford University Press.

Campos, R. C. (2011). 'It might be what I am': Looking at the use of Rorschach in psychological assessment. *Journal of Projective Psychology & Mental Health, 18,* 28–38.

Cannon, W. B. (1929). Organization for physiological homeostatics. *Physiological Review, 9,* 280–289.

Cantwell, R. H., & Andrews, B. (2002). Cognitive and psychological factors underlying secondary school students' feelings towards group work. *Educational Psychology, 22,* 75–91.

Capafons, A., Mendoza, M. E., Begona, E., Green, J. P., Lopes-Pires, C., et al. (2008). Attitudes and beliefs about hypnosis: A multicultural study. *Contemporary Hypnosis, 25,* 141–155.

Capaldi, E. D. (Ed.). (1996). *Why we eat what we eat: The psychology of eating.* Washington, DC: American Psychological Association.

Cardini, F. (2010). Evidence against Whorfian effects in motion conceptualisation. *Journal of Pragmatics, 42,* 1442–1459.

Carhart-Harris, R., (2007). Speed > Ecstasy > Ritalin: The science of amphetamines. *Journal of Psychopharmacology, 21,* 225.

Carlo, G., Mestre, M., Samper, P., Tur, A., & Armenta, B. E. (2011). The longitudinal relations among dimensions of parenting styles, sympathy, prosocial moral reasoning, and prosocial behaviors. *International Journal of Behavioral Development, 35,* 116–124.

Carnagey, N. L., Anderson, C. A., & Bushman, B. J. (2007). The effect of video game violence on physiological desensitization to real-life violence. *Journal of Experimental Social Psychology, 43,* 489–496.

Carnagey, N., Anderson, C. A., & Bushman, B. J. (2007). The effect of video game violence on physiological desensitization to real-life violence. *Journal of Experimental Social Psychology, 43,* 489–496.

Carpenter, S. (2002, April). What can resolve the paradox of mental health disparities? *APA Monitor, 33,* 18.

Carter, L. (2010). Night terrors: A Titanic experience considered from science, art and psychology. *Sacral revolutions: Reflecting on the work of Andrew Samuels—Cutting edges in psychoanalysis and Jungian analysis.* New York: Routledge/Taylor & Francis.

Carter, R. T. (2003). Becoming racially and culturally competent: The racial-cultural counseling laboratory. *Journal of Multicultural Counseling and Development, 31,* 20–30.

Cartwright, R.(2006). A neuroscientist looks at how the brain makes up our minds. *PsycCRITIQUES, 51,* 35–41.

Carvalho, J., & Nobre, P. (2010). Gender issues and sexual desire: The role of emotional and relationship variables. *Journal of Sexual Medicine, 7,* 2469–2478.

Carver, C., & Scheier, M. (2002). Coping processes and adjustment to chronic illness. In A. Christensen & M. Antoni (Eds.), *Chronic physical disorders: Behavioral medicine's perspective.* Malden: Blackwell Publishers.

Casasanto, D. (2008). Who's afraid of the big bad whorf? Cross-linguistic differences in temporal language and thought. *Language Learning, 58,* 63–79.

Casasola, M. (2011). Infant spatial categorization from an information processing approach. In L. M. Oakes, C. H. Cashon, M. Casasola, & D. H. Rakison (Eds.), *Infant perception and cognition: Recent advances, emerging theories, and future directions.* New York: Oxford University Press.

Casey, S. D., Cooper-Brown, L. J., & Wacher, D. P. (2006). The use of descriptive analysis to identify and manipulate schedules of reinforcement in the treatment of food refusal. *Journal of Behavioral Education, 15,* 41–52.

Cassells, J. V. S. (2007). The virtuous roles of truth and justice in integral dialogue: Research, theory, and model practice of the evolution of collective consciousness. *Dissertation Abstracts International Section A: Humanities and Social Sciences, 67* (10-A), 4005.

Castejon, J., Perez, A., & Gilar, R. (2010). Confirmatory factor analysis of project spectrum activities. A second-order g factor or multiple intelligences? *Intelligence, 38,* 481–496.

Cattell, R. B. (1965). Factor analysis: An introduction to essentials. *Biometrics, 21,* 190–215.

Cattell, R. B., Cattell, A. K., & Cattell, H. E. P. (2000). *The sixteen personality factor*[TM] *(16PF®) questionnaire.* Champaign, IL: Institute for Personality and Ability Testing.

Cauce, A. M. (2007). Bringing community psychology home: The leadership, community and values initiative. *American Journal of Community Psychology, 39,* 1–11.

Center for Science in the Public Interest. (2007). *Caffeine Content of Food & Drugs.* Washington, DC: Center for Science in the Public Interest.

Centers for Disease Control and Prevention (CDC). (2000). *Suicide prevention fact sheet.* Atlanta: National Center for Injury Prevention and Control.

Centers for Disease Control and Prevention (CDC). (2004). *Suicide prevention fact sheet.* Atlanta: National Center for Injury Prevention and Control.

Chamberlain, K., & Zika, S. (1990). The minor events approach to stress: Support for the use of daily hassles. *British Journal of Psychology, 81,* 469–481.

Chamberlain, S. R., Menzies, L., Hampshire, A., Suckling, J., Fineberg, N. A., del Campo, N., et al. (2008, July 18). Orbitofrontal dysfunction in patients with obsessive-compulsive disorder and their unaffected relatives. *Science, 321,* 421–422.

Chambless, D. (2010). Interpersonal aspects of panic disorder and agoraphobia. *Interpersonal processes in the anxiety disorders: Implications for understanding psychopathology and treatment.* Washington, DC: American Psychological Association.

Chambless, D. L., Crits-Christoph, P., Wampold, B. E., Norcross, J. C., Lambert, M. J., Bohart, A. C., Beutler, L. E., & Johannsen, B. E. (2006). What should be validated? In J. C. Norcross, L. E. Beutler, & R. F. Levant (Eds.), *Evidence-based practices in mental health: Debate and dialogue on the fundamental questions.* Washington, DC: American Psychological Association.

Chandler, D. R. (2011). Proactively addressing the shortage of Blacks in psychology: Highlighting the school psychology subfield. *Journal of Black Psychology, 37,* 99–127.

Chandran, S., & Menon, G. (2004). When a day means more than a year: Effects of temporal framing on judgments of health risk. *Journal of Consumer Research, 31,* 375–389.

Chang, W., Davies, P., & Gavin, W. (2010). Individual differences in error monitoring in healthy adults: Psychological symptoms and antisocial personality characteristics. *European Journal of Neuroscience, 32,* 1388–1396.

Chapkis, W., & Webb, R. (2008). *Dying to get high: Marijuana as medicine.* New York: New York University Press.

Chapman, L. J., & Chapman, J. P. (1973). *Disordered thought in schizophrenia.* New York: Appleton-Century-Crofts.

Chapman, S. C., & Wu, L. (2015). Epidemiology and demography of illicit drug use and drug use disorders among adults aged 50 and older. In I. Crome, L. Wu, & P. Crome (Eds.), *Substance use and older people.* New York: Wiley-Blackwell.

Charlton, S. (2009, January). Driving while conversing: Cell phones that distract and passengers who react. *Accident Analysis & Prevention, 41,* 160–173.

Chaudhury, R., Jones, H., Wechsberg, W., O'Grady, K., Tuten, M., & Chisolm, M. (2010). Addiction severity index composite scores as predictors for sexual-risk behaviors and drug-use behaviors in drug-using pregnant patients. *The American Journal of Drug and Alcohol Abuse, 36,* 25–30.

Chelune, G. J. (2010). Evidence-based research and practice in clinical neuropsychology. *The Clinical Neuropsychologist, 24,* 454–467.

Chen, Z., Fu, L., Peng, Y., Cai, R., & Zhou, S. (2011). The relationship among childhood

(references as above)

abuse, parenting styles, and antisocial personality disorder tendency. *Chinese Journal of Clinical Psychology, 19,* 212–214.

Cheng, C., & Cheung, M. L. (2005). Cognitive processes underlying coping flexibility: Differentiation and integration. *Journal of Personality, 73,* 859–886.

Cho, S. H., Shin, H. K., Kwon, Y. H., Lee, M. Y., Lee, Y. H., Lee, C. H., Yang, D. S., & Jang, S. H. (2007). Cortical activation changes induced by visual biofeedback tracking training in chronic stroke patients. *Neurorehabilitation and Neural Repair, 22,* 77–84.

Chodakiewitz, Y., Williams, J., Chodakiewitz, J., & Cosgrove, G. R. (2015). Ablative surgery for neuropsychiatric disorders: Past, present, future. In B. Sun & A. De Salles (Eds.), *Neurosurgical treatments for psychiatric disorders.* New York: Springer Science + Business Media.

Chomsky, N. (1978). On the biological basis of language capacities. In G. A. Miller & E. Lennenberg (Eds.), *Psychology and biology of language and thought.* New York: Academic Press.

Chomsky, N. (1991). Linguistics and cognitive science: Problems and mysteries. In A. Kasher (Ed.), *The Chomskyan turn.* Cambridge, MA: Blackwell.

Chou, K. (2005). Everyday competence and depressive symptoms: Social support and sense of control as mediators or moderators? *Aging and Mental Health, 9,* 177–183.

Choy, Y., Fyer, A. J., & Lipsitz, J. D. (2007). Treatment of specific phobia in adults. *Clinical Psychology Review, 27*(3), 266–286.

Christoffels, I. K., de Haan, A. M., Steenbergen, L., van den Wildenberg, W. M., & Colzato, L. S. (2015). Two is better than one: Bilingual education promotes the flexible mind. *Psychological Research, 79,* 371–379.

Chrysikou, E. G. (2006). When a shoe becomes a hammer: Problem solving as goal-derived, ad hoc categorization. *Dissertation Abstracts International: Section B: The Sciences and Engineering, 67* (1-B), 569.

Cialdini, R. B. (2006). *Influence: The psychology of persuasion.* New York: Collins.

Clarkin, J. F., & Lenzenweger, M. F. (Eds.). (2004). *Major theories of personality disorders* (2nd ed.). New York: Guilford.

Clausen, L., Rosenvinge, J. H., Friborg, O., & Rokkedal, K. (2011). Validating the Eating Disorder Inventory-3 (EDI-3): A comparison between 561 female eating disorders patients and 878 females from the general population. *Journal of Psychopathology and Behavioral Assessment, 33,* 101–110.

Claydon, L. S., Chesterton, L. S., Barlas, P. & Sim, J. (2008). Effects of simultaneous dual-site TENS stimulation on experimental pain. *European Journal of Pain, 12*(6), 696–704.

Clement, C., Hill, J. M., Dua, P., Culicchia, F., & Lukiw, W. J. (2016). Analysis of RNA from Alzheimer's disease post-mortem brain tissues. *Molecular Neurobiology, 53,* 1322–1328.

Clements, A. D., & Bailey, B. A. (2010). The relationship between temperament and anxiety: Phase I in the development of a risk screening model to predict stress-related health problems. *Journal of Health Psychology, 15,* 515–525.

Clements, A. M., Rimrodt, S. L., & Abel, J. R. (2006). Sex differences in cerebral laterality of language and visuospatial processing. *Brain and Language, 98,* 150–158.

Clemons, T. L. (2006). Underachieving gifted students: A social cognitive model. *Dissertation Abstracts International Section A: Humanities and Social Sciences, 66*(9-A), 3208.

Cobos, P., Sanchez, M., Garcia, C., Vera, M. N., & Vila, J. (2002). Revisiting the James versus Cannon debate on emotion: Startle and autonomic modulation in patients with spinal cord injuries. *Biological Psychology, 61,* 251–269.

Coffman, S. J., Martell, C. R., Dimidjian, S., Gallop, R., & Holon, S. D. (2007). Extreme nonresponse in cognitive therapy: Can behavioral activation succeed where cognitive therapy fails? *Journal of Consulting Clinical Psychology, 75,* 531–545.

Cohen, G. L., Garcia, J., Apfel, N., & Master, A. (2006). Reducing the racial achievement gap: A social-psychological intervention. *Science, 313,* 1307–1310.

Cohen, P. (2009). Medical marijuana: The conflict between scientific evidence and political ideology. Part one of two. *Journal of Pain & Palliative Care Pharmacotherapy, 23,* 4–25.

Cohen, P., Slomkowski, C., & Robins, L. N. (Eds.). (1999). *Historical and geographical influences on psychopathology.* Mahwah, NJ: Erlbaum.

Cohen, S. (2004, November). Social relationships and health. *American Psychologist, 59*(8), 676–684.

Collins, K., Onwuegbuzie, A., & Jiao, Q. (Eds.). (2010). *Toward a broader understanding of stress and coping: Mixed methods approaches.* Greenwich, CT: IAP Information Age Publishing.

Colman, W. (2010). Dream interpretation and the creation of symbolic meaning. In M. Stein (Ed.), *Jungian psychoanalysis: Working in the spirit of C. G. Jung.* Chicago: Open Court Publishing.

Coltheart, M., Langdon, R., & McKay, R. (2007). Schizophrenia and monothematic delusions. *Schizophrenia Bulletin, 33,* 642–647.

Colwell, M. J., & Lindsey, E. W. (2005). Preschool children's pretend and physical play and sex of play partner: Connections to peer competence. *Sex Roles, 52,* 497–509.

Comparelli, A., De Carolis, A., Kotzalidis, G., Masillo, A., Ferracuti, S., & Tatarelli, R. (2010). A woman lost in the cemetery: A case of time-limited amnesia. *Neurocase, 16,* 23-30.

Connolly, A. C. (2007). Concepts and their features: Can cognitive science make good on the promises of concept empiricism? *Dissertation Abstracts International: Section B: The Sciences and Engineering, 67*(7-B), 4125.

Contractor, A. A., Armour, C., Shea, M. T., Mota, N., & Pietrzak, R. H. (2016). Latent profiles of DSM-5 PTSD symptoms and the "Big Five" personality traits. *Journal of Anxiety Disorders, 37,* 10–20.

Conway, M. A. (Ed). (2002). *Levels of processing 30 years on special issue of memory.* Hove, UK: Psychology Press.

Cook, L. (2015, August 19). The heroin epidemic in 9 graphs. *US News & World Report.* Retrieved from http://www.usnews.com/news/blogs/data-mine/2015/08/19/the-heroin-epidemic-in-9-graphs

Cook, M. (2013). *Levels of personality* (3rd ed.). New York: Cambridge University Press.

Cook-Cottone, C., & Smith, A. (2013). Eating disorders. In C. A. Noggle & R. S. Dean (Eds.), *The neuropsychology of psychopathology.* New York: Springer Publishing Co.

Cooklin, A. (2000). Therapy, the family and others. In H. Maxwell (Ed.), *Clinical psychotherapy for health professionals.* Philadelphia: Whurr Publishers, Ltd.

Cooper, C. (2011). Review of 'Fat: A cultural history of obesity.' *Sociology, 45,* 181–183.

Cooper, Z., & Shafran, R. (2008). Cognitive behaviour therapy for eating disorders. *Behavioural and Cognitive Psychotherapy, 36,* 713–722.

Coplan, R., Reichel, M., & Rowan, K. (2009). Exploring the associations between maternal personality, child temperament, and parenting: A focus on emotions. *Personality and Individual Differences, 46,* 241–246.

Coren, S., & Ward, L. M. (1989). *Sensation and perception* (3rd ed.). San Diego, CA: Harcourt Brace Jovanovich.

Cornell, C. B. (2006). A graduated scale for determining mental age. *Dissertation Abstracts International: Section B: The Sciences and Engineering, 66* (9-B), 5121.

Costa, P. T., Jr., & Widiger, T. A. (Eds.). (2002). *Personality disorders and the five-factor model of personality* (2nd ed.). Washington, DC: American Psychological Association.

Cottencin, O., Rolland, B., & Karila, L. (2013). New designer drugs (synthetic cannabinoids and synthetic cathinones): Review of literature. *Current Pharmaceutical Design.* Retrieved from http://www.ncbi.nlm.nih.gov/pubmed/24001292

Coulson, D., & Harvey, M. (2013). Scaffolding student reflection for experience-based learning: A framework. *Teaching in Higher Education, 18,* 401–413.

Coultas, J. C., & van Leeuwen, E. C. (2015). Conformity: Definitions, types, and evolutionary grounding. In V. Zeigler-Hill, L. M. Welling, & T. K. Shackelford (Eds.), *Evolutionary perspectives on social psychology.* Cham, Switzerland: Springer International Publishing.

Couturier, J., & Lock, J. (2006). Eating disorders: Anorexia nervosa, bulimia nervosa, and binge eating disorder. In T. G. Plante, *Mental disorders of the new millennium: Biology and function* (Vol. 3). Westport, CT: Praeger Publishers/Greenwood Publishing.

Covell, N. H., Margolies, P. J., Myers, R. W., Sederer, L., Ruderman, D., Bramer, J. V., & . . . Dixon, L. B. (2016). Using incentives for training participation. *Psychiatric Rehabilitation Journal, 39,* 81–83.

Coyle, N. (2006). The hard work of living in the face of death. *Journal of Pain and Symptom Management, 32,* 266–274.

Craik, F., & Lockhart, R. (2008). Levels of processing and Zinchenko's approach to memory research. *Journal of Russian & East European Psychology, 46,* 52–60.

Crano, W. D., Brewer, M. B., & Lac, A. (2015). *Principles and methods of social research* (3rd ed.). New York: Routledge/Taylor & Francis Group.

Creasey, G. L. (2005). *Research methods in lifespan development* (6th ed.). Boston: Allyn & Bacon.

Critchley, H. D., & Nagai, Y. (2016). Comment: What does left–right autonomic asymmetry signify? *Emotion Review, 8,* 76–77.

Critelli, J., & Bivona, J. (2008). Women's erotic rape fantasies: An evaluation of theory and research. *Journal of Sex Research, 45,* 57–70.

Croarkin, P. E., Wall, C. A., McClintock, S. M., Kozel, F., Husain, M. M., & Sampson, S. M. (2010). The emerging role for repetitive transcranial magnetic stimulation in optimizing the treatment of adolescent depression. *The Journal of ECT, 26,* 323–329.

Crosnoe, R., & Elder, G. H., Jr. (2002). Successful adaptation in the later years: A life course approach to aging. *Social Psychology Quarterly, 65,* 309–328.

Crouse, K. (2015, September 21). 100 years old. 5 world records. *New York Times* Retrieved from http://www.nytimes.com/2015/09/22/sports/a-bolt-from-the-past-don-pellmann-at-100-is-still-breaking-records.html?_r=1

Crum, A. J., & Langer, E. J. (2007). Mind-set matters: Exercise and the placebo effect. *Psychological Science, 18,* 165–171.

Cuijpers, P., van Straten, A., Andersson, G., & van Oppen, P. (2008). Psychotherapy for depression in adults: A meta-analysis of comparative outcome studies. *Journal of Consulting and Clinical Psychology, 76,* 909–922.

Cullinane, C. A., Chu, D. Z. J., & Mamelak, A. N. (2002). Current surgical options in the control of cancer pain. *Cancer Practice, 10,* s21–s26.

Cupertino, R. B., Kappel, D. B., Bandeira, C. E., Schuch, J. B., da Silva, B. S., Müller, D., & . . . Mota, N. R. (2016). Snare complex in developmental psychiatry: Neurotransmitter exocytosis and beyond. *Journal of Neural Transmission.* Accessed online 2.17.16; http://link.springer.com/article/10.1007%2Fs00702-016-1514-9

Díaz, E., & De la Casa, L. G. (2011). Extinction, spontaneous recovery and renewal of flavor preferences based on taste–taste learning. *Learning and Motivation, 42,* 64–75.

Daftary, F., & Meri, J. W. (2002). *Culture and memory in medieval Islam.* London: I. B. Tauris.

Daines, B. (2006). Violations of agreed and implicit sexual and emotional boundaries in couple relationships—Some thoughts arising from Levine's "A clinical perspective on couple infidelity." *Sexual and Relationship Therapy, 21,* 45–53.

Dale, J. W., & von Schantz, M. (2007). *From genes to genomes: Concepts and applications of DNA technology.* New York: John Wiley & Sons.

Damasio, A. (1999). *The feeling of what happens: Body and emotion in the making of consciousness.* New York: Harcourt Brace.

Dang-Vu, T. T., Schabus, M., Desseilles, M., Sterpenich, V., Bonjean, M., & Maquet, P. (2010). Functional neuroimaging insights into the physiology of human sleep. *Sleep, 22,* 1589–1603.

Daray, F. M., Thommi, S. B., & Ghaemi, S. (2010). The pharmacogenetics of antidepressant-induced mania: A systematic review and meta-analysis. *Bipolar Disorders, 12,* 702–706.

Dare, J. S. (2011). Transitions in midlife women's lives: Contemporary experiences. *Health Care for Women International, 32,* 111–133.

Das, A., Parish, W., & Laumann, E. (2009). Masturbation in urban China. *Archives of Sexual Behavior, 38,* 108–120.

Das, J. P. (2015). Search for intelligence by PASSing g. *Canadian Psychology/Psychologie Canadienne, 56,* 39–45.

Davern, M. (2013). Nonresponse rates are a problematic indicator of nonresponse bias in survey research. *Health Services Research, 48,* 905–912.

Davis, J., Senghas, A., & Ochsner, K. (2009). How does facial feedback modulate emotional experience? *Journal of Research in Personality, 43,* 822–829.

Davis, O., Haworth, C., & Plomin, R. (2009, January). Learning abilities and disabilities: Generalist genes in early adolescence. *Cognitive Neuropsychiatry, 14,* 312–331.

Day, A. L., & Livingstone, H. A. (2003). Gender differences in perceptions of stressors and utilization of social support among university students. *Canadian Journal of Behavioural Science, 35,* 73–83.

De Beni, R., Pazzaglia, F., & Gardini, S. (2007). The generation and maintenance of visual mental images: Evidence from image type and aging. *Brain and Cognition, 63,* 271–278.

De Lucia, M., Clarke, S., & Murray, M. (2010). A temporal hierarchy for conspecific vocalization discrimination in humans. *The Journal of Neuroscience, 30,* 11210–11221.

de Rooij, S. R., Schene, A. H., Phillips, D. I., & Roseboom, T. J. (2010). Depression and anxiety: Associations with biological and perceived stress reactivity to a psychological stress protocol in a middle-aged population. *Psychoneuroendocrinology, 35,* 866–877.

Dean-Borenstein, M. T. (2007). The long-term psychosocial effects of trauma on survivors of human-caused extreme stress situations. *Dissertation Abstracts International: Section B: The Sciences and Engineering, 67*(11-B), 6733.

DeAngelis, D., & Monahan, J. (2008). Professional credentials and professional regulations: Social work professional development. In B. W. White, K. M. Sowers, & C. N. Dulmus, (Eds.), *Comprehensive handbook of social work and social welfare, Vol. 1: The profession of social work.* Hoboken, NJ: John Wiley & Sons.

Dearing, E., McCartney, K., & Taylor, B. (2009). Does higher quality early child care promote low-income children's math and reading achievement in middle childhood? *Child Development, 80,* 1329–1349.

Deary, I. J., & Der, G. (2005). Reaction time, age, and cognitive ability: Longitudinal findings from age 16 to 63 years in representative population samples. *Aging, Neuropsychology, & Cognition, 12,* 187–215.

Del Arco, A., Segovia, G., de Blas, M., Garrido, P., Acuña-Castroviejo, D., Pamplona, R., & Mora, F., et al. (2010). Prefrontal cortex, caloric restriction and stress during aging: Studies on dopamine and acetylcholine release, BDNF and working memory. *Behavioural Brain Research, 216,* 136–145.

Delgado, M. R., Labouliere, C. D., & Phelps, E. A. (2006). Fear of losing money? Aversive conditioning with secondary reinforcers [Special issue: Genetic, comparative and cognitive studies of social behavior]. *Social Cognitive and Affective Neuroscience, 1,* 250–259.

Della Sala, S. (2011). A daguerreotype of Phineas Gage? *Cortex: A Journal Devoted to the Study of the Nervous System and Behavior, 47,* 83–90.

DeMaris, A. (2013). Burning the candle at both ends: Extramarital sex as a precursor of marital disruption. *Journal of Family Issues, 34,* 1474–1499.

Dempster, F. N. (1981). Memory span: Sources for individual and developmental differences. *Psychological Bulletin, 89,* 63–100.

Deng, H., Ansley, T., & Chang, H. (2010). Stratified and maximum information item selection procedures in computer adaptive testing. *Journal of Educational Measurement, 47,* 202–226.

Dennis, I. (2007). Halo effects in grading student projects. *Journal of Applied Psychology, 92,* 1169–1176.

Deregowski, J. B. (1973). Illusion and culture. In R. L. Gregory & G. H. Combrich (Eds.), *Illusion in nature and art* (pp. 161–192). New York: Scribner.

Deshields, T., Tibbs, T., Fan, M. Y., & Taylor, M. (2006). Differences in patterns of depression after treatment for breast cancer [Electronic article published August 12, 2005]. *Psycho-Oncology, 15(5),* 398–406.

Detterman, D. K., Gabriel, L. T., & Ruthsatz, J. M. (2000). Intelligence and mental retardation. In R. J. Sternberg (Ed.), *Handbook of intelligence.* New York: Cambridge University Press.

Devonport, J. J., & Lane, A. M. (2006). Relationships between self-efficacy, coping and student retention. *Social Behavior and Personality, 34,* 127–138.

Devonport, T. (2016). Understanding stress coping among competitive athletes in sport: Applying psychological theory and research. In A. M. Lane (Ed.), *Sport and exercise psychology* (2nd ed.). New York: Routledge/Taylor & Francis Group.

Dhillon, S., Yang, L., & Curran, M. (2008). Spotlight on bupropion in major depressive disorder. *CNS Drugs, 22,* 613–617.

Di Fabio, A., & Palazzeschi, L. (2009). An in-depth look at scholastic success: Fluid intelligence, personality traits or emotional intelligence? *Personality and Individual Differences, 46,* 581–585.

Diamond, M. (2009). Human intersexuality: Difference or disorder? *Archives of Sexual Behavior, 38,* 172.

Dickstein, L. S. (1972). Death concern: Measurement and correlates. *Psychological Reports, 30(2),* 563–571.

Diener, M., Isabella, R., Behunin, M., & Wong, M. (2008). Attachment to mothers and fathers during middle childhood: Associations with child gender, grade, and competence. *Social Development, 17,* 84–101.

Diesen, P. S. (2016). "I feel lucky"—Gratitude among young adults with phenylketonuria (pku). *Journal of Genetic Counseling.*

Retrieved from http://www.ncbi.nlm.nih.gov/pubmed/26888542

DiGiovanna, A. G. (1994). *Human aging: Biological perspectives.* New York: McGraw-Hill.

Dillard, J. P., & Shen, L. (2007). Self-report measures of discrete emotions. In R. A. Reynolds, R. Woods, & J. D. Baker, *Handbook of research on electronic surveys and measurements.* Hershey, PA: Idea Group Reference/IGI Global.

Dixon, R. A., McFall, G., Whitehead, B. P., & Dolcos, S. (2013). Cognitive development in adulthood and aging. In R. M. Lerner, M. Easterbrooks, J. Mistry, & I. B. Weiner (Eds.), *Handbook of psychology, Vol. 6: Developmental psychology* (2nd ed.). Hoboken, NJ: John Wiley & Sons Inc.

Djapo, N., Kolenovic-Djapo, J., Djokic, R., & Fako, I. (2011). Relationship between Cattell's 16PF and fluid and crystallized intelligence. *Personality and Individual Differences, 51,* 63–67.

Do, V. T. (2006). Asian American men and the media: The relationship between ethnic identity, self-esteem, and the endorsement of stereotypes. *Dissertation Abstracts International: Section B: The Sciences and Engineering, 67* (6-B), 3446.

Dobbs, D. (2012). The new temper tantrum disorder. Posted Friday, Dec. 7, 2012 in *Slate.* Retrieved from http://www.slate.com/articles/double_x/doublex/2012/12/disruptive_mood_dysregulation_disorder_in_dsm_5_criticism_of_a_new_diagnosis.html

Dodge, K. A. (2004). The nature-nurture debate and public policy. *Merrill-Palmer Quarterly, 50,* 418–427.

Dolan, R. J. (2002, November 8). Emotion, cognition, and behavior. *Science, 298,* 1191–1194.

Dolbier, C. L., Smith, S. E., & Steinhardt, M. A. (2007). Relationships of protective factors to stress and symptoms of illness. *American Journal of Health Behavior, 31,* 423–433.

Domhoff, G. W., & Schneider, A. (1999). Much ado about very little: The small effect sizes when home and laboratory collected dreams are compared. *Dreaming, 9,* 139–151.

Domschke, K. (2013). Clinical and molecular genetics of psychotic depression. *Schizophrenia Bulletin, 39,* 766–775.

Dortch, S. (1996, October). Our aching heads. *American Demographics,* pp. 4–8.

Doty, R. (2010). *The great pheromone myth.* Baltimore, MD: Johns Hopkins University Press.

Doty, R. L., Green, P. A., Ram, C., & Yankell, S. L. (1982). Communication of gender from human breath odors: Relationship to perceived intensity and pleasantness. *Hormones and Behavior, 16,* 13–22.

Douglas, O., Burton, K. S., & Reese-Durham, N. (2008). The effects of the multiple intelligence teaching strategy on the

academic achievement of eighth grade math students. *Journal of Instructional Psychology, 35,* 182–187.

Dovidio, J. F., & Gaertner, S. L. (2006). A multilevel perspective on prejudice: Crossing disciplinary boundaries. In P. A. M. Van Lange, *Bridging social psychology: Benefits of transdisciplinary approaches.* Mahwah, NJ: Erlbaum.

Dowling, N., Jackson, A., & Thomas, S. (2008). Behavioral interventions in the treatment of pathological gambling: A review of activity scheduling and desensitization. *International Journal of Behavioral Consultation and Therapy, 4,* 172–187.

Drag, L., & Bieliauskas, L. (2010). Contemporary review 2009: Cognitive aging. *Journal of Geriatric Psychiatry and Neurology, 23,* 75–93.

Drews, F., Pasupathi, M., & Strayer, D. (2008, December). Passenger and cell phone conversations in simulated driving. *Journal of Experimental Psychology: Applied, 14,* 392–400.

Drob, S. (2005). The mystical symbol: Some comments on Ankor, Giegerich, Scholem, and Jung. *Journal of Jungian Theory & Practice, 7,* 25–29.

Dryden, W., & David, D. (2008). Rational emotive behavior therapy: Current status. *Journal of Cognitive Psychotherapy, 22,* 195–209.

DSM-5 classification. (2016). Arlington, VA: American Psychiatric Publishing, Inc.

Duesbury, E. M. (2011). *The counselor's guide for facilitating the interpretation of dreams: Family and other relationship systems perspectives.* New York: Routledge/Taylor & Francis Group.

Duke, M., & Nowicki, S., Jr. (1979). *Abnormal psychology: Perspectives on being different.* Monterey, CA: Brooks/Cole.

Dulebohn, J. H., Davison, R. B., Lee, S. A., Conlon, D. E., McNamara, G., & Sarinopoulos, I. C. (2016). Gender differences in justice evaluations: Evidence from fMRI. *Journal of Applied Psychology, 101,* 151–170.

Dumont, M., & Dumont, D. (2008). Deinstitutionalization in the United States and Italy: A historical survey. *International Journal of Mental Health, 37,* 61–70.

Duncker, K. (1945). On problem solving. *Psychological Monographs, 58*(5, whole no. 270).

Dwyer, K., Fredstrom, B., Rubin, K., Booth-LaForce, C., Rose-Krasnor, L., & Burgess, K. (2010). Attachment, social information processing, and friendship quality of early adolescent girls and boys. *Journal of Social and Personal Relationships, 27,* 91–116.

Eagleson, C., Hayes, S., Mathews, A., Perman, G., & Hirsch, C. R. (2016). The power of positive thinking: Pathological worry is reduced by thought replacement in

Generalized Anxiety Disorder. *Behaviour Research And Therapy, 78,* 13–18.

Ebbinghaus, H. (1885/1913). *Memory: A contribution to experimental psychology* (H. A. Roger & C. E. Bussenius, Trans.). New York: Columbia University Press.

Ebigbo, P. O., Lekwas, E. C., & Chukwunenyem, N. F. (2015). Brain fag: New perspectives from case observations. *Transcultural Psychiatry, 52,* 311–330.

Ebster, C., & Neumayr, B. (2008). Applying the door-in-the-face compliance technique to retailing. *The International Review of Retail, Distribution and Consumer Research, 18,* 121–128.

Eckardt, M. H. (2005). Karen Horney: A portrait: The 120th anniversary, Karen Horney, September 16, 1885. *American Journal of Psychoanalysis, 65,* 95–101.

Ecker, U. H., Tay, J., & Brown, G. A. (2015). Effects of prestudy and poststudy rest on memory: Support for temporal interference accounts of forgetting. *Psychonomic Bulletin & Review, 22,* 772–778.

Edoka, I. P., Petrou, S., & Ramchandani, P. G. (2011). Healthcare costs of paternal depression in the postnatal period. *Journal of Affective Disorders, 133,* 356–360.

Ehde, D. M., Dillworth, T. M., & Turner, J. A. (2014). Cognitive-behavioral therapy for individuals with chronic pain: Efficacy, innovations, and directions for research. *American Psychologist, 69, 153–177.*

Eidelman, P., Talbot, L., Ivers, H., Bélanger, L., Morin, C. M., & Harvey, A. G. (2016). Change in dysfunctional beliefs about sleep in behavior therapy, cognitive therapy, and cognitive-behavioral therapy for insomnia. *Behavior Therapy, 47,* 102–115.

Eisenberg, N., Guthrie, I. K., & Cumberland, A. (2002). Prosocial development in early adulthood: A longitudinal study. *Journal of Personality and Social Psychology, 82,* 993–1006.

Eizenberg, M. M., & Zaslavsky, O. (2004). Students' verification strategies for combinatorial problems. *Mathematical Thinking and Learning, 6,* 15–36.

Ekman, P. (1972). Universals and cultural differences in facial expressions of emotion. In J. Cole (Ed.), *Darwin and facial expression: A century of research in review* (pp. 169–222). New York: Academic Press.

Ekman, P. (1994a). All emotions are basic. In P. Ekman & R. J. Davidson (Eds.), *The nature of emotion: Fundamental questions.* New York: Oxford University Press.

Ekman, P. (1994b). Strong evidence for universals in facial expressions: A reply to Russell's mistaken critique. *Psychological Bulletin, 115,* 268–287.

Ekman, P. (2003). *Emotions revealed: Recognizing faces and feelings to improve communication and emotional life.* New York: Times Books.

Ekman, P., & O'Sullivan, M. (1991). Facial expression: Methods, means, and moues. In R. S. Feldman & B. Rimé (Eds.), *Fundamentals of nonverbal behavior.* Cambridge, England: Cambridge University Press.

Ekman, P., Levenson, R. W., & Friesen, W. V. (1983, September 16). Autonomic nervous system activity distinguishes among emotions. *Science, 223,* 1208–1210.

Ekonomou, A., Savva, G. M., Brayne, C., Forster, G., Francis, P. T., Johnson, M., Perry, E. K., Attems, J., Somani, A., Minger, S. L., & Ballard, C. G. (2015). Stage-specific changes in neurogenic and glial markers in Alzheimer's disease. *Biological Psychiatry, 77,* 711–719.

El-Mallakh, R. S., & Abraham, H. D. (2007). MDMA (Ecstasy). *Annals of Clinical Psychiatry, 19,* 45–52.

Elen, M., D'Heer, E., Geuens, M., & Vermeir, I. (2013). The influence of mood on attitude–behavior consistency. *Journal of Business Research, 66,* 917–923.

Elias, M. (2009, January 28). MRIs reveal possible source of woman's super-memory. Retrieved from http://usatoday30.usatoday.com/news/health/2009-01-27-mri-super-memory_N.htm

Eljamel, S. (2015). Ablative surgery for depression. In B. Sun & A. De Salles (Eds.), *Neurosurgical treatments for psychiatric disorders.* New York: Springer Science + Business Media.

Elkins, D. (2009). Why humanistic psychology lost its power and influence in American psychology: Implications for advancing humanistic psychology. *Journal of Humanistic Psychology, 49,* 267–291.

Ellins, E., Halcox, J., Donald, A., Field, B., Brydon, L., Deanfield, J., et al. (2008). Arterial stiffness and inflammatory response to psychophysiological stress. *Brain, Behavior, and Immunity, 22,* 941–948.

Ellis, A. (1974). *Growth through reason.* Hollywood, CA: Wilshire Books.

Ellis, A. (2002). *Overcoming resistance: A rational emotive behavior therapy integrated approach* (2nd ed.). New York: Springer.

Ellis, A. (2004). *Expanding the ABCs of rational emotive behavior therapy.* In A. Freeman, M. J. Mahoney, P. Devito, & D. Martin (Eds.), *Cognition and psychotherapy* (2nd ed.). New York: Springer Publishing Co.

Enge, L. R., Lupo, A. K., & Zárate, M. A. (2015). Neurocognitive mechanisms of prejudice formation: The role of time-dependent memory consolidation. *Psychological Science, 26,* 964–971.

Engel, U., Jann, B., Lynn, P., Scherpenzeel, A., & Sturgis, P. (2015). *Improving survey methods: Lessons from recent research.* NY: Routledge/Taylor & Francis Group.

Eranti, S. V., & McLoughlin, D. M. (2003). Electroconvulsive therapy: State of the art. *British Journal of Psychiatry, 182,* 8–9.

Erb, J., Henry, M. J., Eisner, F., & Obleser, J. (2013). The brain dynamics of rapid perceptual adaptation to adverse listening conditions. *The Journal of Neuroscience, 33,* 10688–10697.

Erdle, S., & Rushton, J. (2010). The general factor of personality, BIS–BAS, expectancies of reward and punishment, self-esteem, and positive and negative affect. *Personality and Individual Differences, 48,* 762–766.

Erikson, E. H. (1963). *Childhood and society* (2nd ed.). New York: Norton.

Ervik, S., Abdelnoor, M., & Heier, M. S. (2006). Health-related quality of life in narcolepsy. *Acta Neurologica Scandinavica, 114,* 198–204.

Etienne, J. (2013). Thoughts on how to regulate behaviours: An overview of the current debate. *British Journal of Guidance & Counselling, 41,* 36–45.

Euler, M. J., Weisend, M. P., Jung, R. E., Thoma, R. J., & Yeo, R. A. (2015). Reliable activation to novel stimuli predicts higher fluid intelligence. *Neuroimage, 114,* 311–319.

Evans, A. M. (2007). Transference in the nurse-patient relationship. *Journal of Psychiatric and Mental Health Nursing, 14,* 189–195.

Evans, D., & Rothbart, M. (2007). Developing a model for adult temperament. *Journal of Research in Personality, 41,* 868–888.

Evans, D., & Rothbart, M. (2009). A two-factor model of temperament. *Personality and Individual Differences, 47,* 565–570.

Evcik, D., Kavuncu, V., Cakir, T., Subasi, V., & Yaman, M. (2007). Laser therapy in the treatment of carpal tunnel syndrome: A randomized controlled trial. *Photomedical Laser Surgery, 25,* 34–39.

Everette, M. (2008). Gestational weight and dietary intake during pregnancy: Perspectives of African American women. *Maternal & Child Health Journal, 12,* 718–724.

Everitt, B. J. (2014). Neural and psychological mechanisms underlying compulsive drug seeking habits and drug memories—Indications for novel treatments of addiction. *European Journal of Neuroscience, 40,* 2163-2182.

Eysenck, H. J. (1990). Biological dimensions of personality. In L. A. Pervin (Ed.), *Handbook of personality: Theory and research* (p. 246). New York: Guilford Press.

Eysenck, H. J. (1995). *Eysenck on extraversion.* New York: Wiley.

Fagan, J. F., & Holland, C. R. (2002). Equal opportunity and racial differences in IQ. *Intelligence, 30,* 361–387.

Fagan, J. F., & Holland, C. R. (2007). Racial equality in intelligence: Predictions from a theory of intelligence as processing. *Intelligence, 35,* 319–334.

Fagan, J. F., & Holland, C. R. (2009). Culture-fair prediction of academic achievement. *Intelligence, 37,* 62–67.

Fagan, J., & Press, J. (2008). Father influences on employed mothers' work-family balance. *Journal of Family Issues, 29,* 1136–1160.

Faith, M. (2010). Development of child taste and food preferences: The role of exposure. *The Oxford handbook of eating disorders.* New York: Oxford University Press.

Falasca, N. W., D'Ascenzo, S., Di Domenico, A., Onofrj, M., Tommasi, L., Laeng, B., & Franciotti, R. (2015). Hemispheric lateralization in top-down attention during spatial relation processing: A Granger causal model approach. *European Journal of Neuroscience, 41,* 912–922.

Fales, M. R., Frederick, D. A., Garcia, J. R., Gildersleeve, K. A., Haselton, M. G., & Fisher, H. E. (2016). Mating markets and bargaining hands: Mate preferences for attractiveness and resources in two national U.S. studies. *Personality and Individual Differences, 88,* 78–87.

Fallon, A. (2006). Informed consent in the practice of group psychotherapy. *International Journal of Group Psychotherapy, 56,* 431–453.

Fantz, A., Almasy, S., and Stapleton, A. (2015, September 16). Muslim teen Ahmed Mohamed creates clock, shows teachers, gets arrested. *CNN.* Retrieved from http://www.cnn.com/2015/09/16/us/texas-student-ahmed-muslim-clock-bomb/

Farnsworth, D. L. (2015). Identical twins raised apart. *Teaching Statistics, 37,* 1–6.

Fearing, V. G., & Clark, J. (Eds.). (2000). *Individuals in context: A practical guide to client-centered practice.* Chicago: Slack Publishing.

Feldman, R. S. (2016). *P.O.W.E.R. learning: Strategies for success in college and life* (8th ed). New York: McGraw-Hill.

Fergenbaum, J., Bruce, S., Lou, W., Hanley, A., Greenwood, C., & Young, T. (2010). Window to the brain: Can retinopathy be used to assess cognitive function. *Brain Injury, 24,* 1448–1454.

Ferguson, C. J. (2010). Blazing angels or resident evil? Can violent video games be a force for good? *Review of General Psychology, 14,* 68–81.

Ferguson, C. J. (2011). Video games and youth violence: A prospective analysis in adolescents. *Journal of Youth and Adolescence, 40,* 377–391.

Ferguson, C. J. (2015). Does media violence predict societal violence? It depends on what you look at and when. *Journal of Communication, 65,* E1–E22.

Ferguson, C. J. (2015). Do angry birds make for angry children? A meta-analysis of video game influences on children's and adolescents' aggression, mental health, prosocial behavior, and academic performance. *Psychological Science, 26,* 1–22.

Ferguson, M., & Ogloff, J. P. (2011). Criminal responsibility evaluations: Role of psychologists in assessment. *Psychiatry, Psychology and Law, 18,* 79–94.

Fernald, R. D. (2015). Social behaviour: Can it change the brain? *Animal Behaviour, 103,* 259–265.

Fernyhough, C. (2010). Vygotsky, Luria, and the social brain. *Self and social regulation: Social interaction and the development of social understanding and executive functions.* New York: Oxford University Press.

Ferring, D., Tournier, I., & Mancini, D. (2015). "The closer you get …": Age, attitudes and self-serving evaluations about older drivers. *European Journal of Ageing.* Retrieved from http://link.springer.com/article/10.1007%2Fs10433-015-0337-0

Festinger, D., Marlowe, D., Croft, J., Dugosh, K., Arabia, P., & Benasutti, K. (2009). Monetary incentives improve recall of research consent information: It pays to remember. *Experimental and Clinical Psychopharmacology, 17,* 99–104.

Festinger, L. (1957). *A theory of cognitive dissonance.* Stanford, CA: Stanford University Press.

Filippello, P., Sorrenti, L., Buzzai, C., & Costa, S. (2015). Perceived parental psychological control and learned helplessness: The role of school self-efficacy. *School Mental Health.* Retrieved from http://link.springer.com/article/10.1007%2Fs12310-015-9151-2#page-1

Fillingim, R. B. (2011). Review of 'Functional pain syndromes'. *The Clinical Journal of Pain, 27,* 82–84.

Finan, P. H., Zautra, A. J., & Wershba, R. (2011). The dynamics of emotion in adaptation to stress. In R. J. Contrada, A. Baum, R. J. Contrada, & A. Baum (Eds.), *The handbook of stress science: Biology, psychology, and health.* New York: Springer Publishing Co.

Finkler, K. (2004). Traditional healers in Mexico: The effectiveness of spiritual practices. In U. P. Gielen, J. M. Fish, & J. G. Draguns (Eds.), *Handbook of culture, therapy, and healing.* Mahwah, NJ: Erlbaum.

Finley, C. L., & Cowley, B. J. (2005). The effects of a consistent sleep schedule on time taken to achieve sleep. *Clinical Case Studies, 4,* 304–311.

Finn, A. (2011). Jungian analytical theory. In D. Capuzzi, D. R. Gross, D. Capuzzi, D. R. Gross (Eds.), *Counseling and psychotherapy* (5th ed.). Alexandria, VA: American Counseling Association.

Firestein, B. A. (Ed.). (1996). *Bisexuality: The psychology and politics of an invisible minority.* Thousand Oaks, CA: Sage.

First, M. B., Frances, A., & Pincus, H. A. (2002). *DSM-IV-TR handbook of differential diagnosis.* Washington, DC: American Psychiatric Publishing.

Fischer, P., Krueger, J. I., Greitemeyer, T., Vogrincic, C., Kastenmüller, A., Frey, D., & Kainbacher, M. (2011). The bystander-effect: A meta-analytic review on bystander intervention in dangerous and non-dangerous emergencies. *Psychological Bulletin, 137,* 517–537.

Fischmann, T. (2016). Dreams, unconscious fantasies and epigenetics. In S. Weigel, G. Scharbert, S. Weigel, G. Scharbert (Eds.), *A neuro-psychoanalytical dialogue for bridging Freud and the neurosciences.* Cham, Switzerland: Springer International Publishing.

Fishbach, A., Dhar, R., & Zhang, Y. (2006). Subgoals as substitutes or complements: The role of goal accessibility. *Journal of Personality and Social Psychology, 91,* 232–242.

Fisher, C. B. (2003). *Decoding the ethics code: A practical guide for psychologists.* Thousand Oaks, CA: Sage.

Fisher, G. G., & Barnes-Farrell, J. L. (2013). Use of archival data in occupational health psychology research. In R. R. Sinclair, M. Wang, & L. E. Tetrick (Eds.), *Research methods in occupational health psychology: Measurement, design, and data analysis.* New York: Routledge/Taylor & Francis Group.

Fisher, H., Atzil-Slonim, D., Bar-Kalifa, E., Rafaeli, E., & Peri, T. (2016). Emotional experience and alliance contribute to therapeutic change in psychodynamic therapy. *Psychotherapy, 53,* 105–116.

Fitzgibbons, P. J., & Gordon-Salant, S. (2010). Age-related differences in discrimination of temporal intervals in accented tone sequences. *Hearing Research, 264,* 41–47.

Flavell, S. W., Cowan, C. W., Kim, T., Greer, P. L., Lin, Y., Paradis, S., Griffith, E. C., Hu, L. S., Chen, C., & Greenberg, M. E. (2006, February 17). Activity-dependent regulation of MEF2 transcription factors suppresses excitatory synapse number. *Science, 311,* 1008–1010.

Fleischman, D. A., Wilson, R. S., Gabrieli, J. D. E., Bienias, J. L., & Bennett, D. A. (2004). A longitudinal study of implicit and explicit memory in old persons. *Psychology and Aging, 19,* 617–625.

Foell, J., Bekrater-Bodmann, R., Diers, M., & Flor, H. (2014). Mirror therapy for phantom limb pain: Brain changes and the role of body representation. *European Journal of Pain, 18,* 729–739.

Folkman, S., & Moskowitz, J. T. (2000). Stress, positive emotion, and coping. *Current Directions in Psychological Science, 9,* 115–118.

Folkman, S., & Moskowitz, J. T. (2004). Coping: Pitfalls and promise. *Annual Review of Psychology, 55,* 745–774.

Forbey, J., & Ben-Porath, Y. (2007). Computerized adaptive personality testing: A review and illustration with the MMPI-2 computerized adaptive version. *Psychological Assessment, 19,* 14–24.

Forer, B. (1949). The fallacy of personal validation: A classroom demonstration of gullibility. *Journal of Abnormal and Social Psychology, 44,* 118–123.

Forscher, P. S., & Devine, P. G. (2016). The role of intentions in conceptions of prejudice: An historical perspective. In T. D. Nelson (Ed.), *Handbook of prejudice, stereotyping, and discrimination* (2nd ed.). New York: Psychology Press.

Fosshage, J. L. (2011). How do we "know" what we "know?" And change what we "know?" *Psychoanalytic Dialogues, 21,* 55–74.

Fost, J. (2015). Are there psychological species? *Review of Philosophy and Psychology, 6,* 293–315.

Foster, K. M. (2005). Introduction: John Uzo Ogbu (1939–2003): How do you ensure the fair consideration of a complex ancestor? Multiple approaches to assessing the work and legacy of John Uzo Ogbu. *International Journal of Qualitative Studies in Education, 18,* 559–564.

Foster, R., Fantoni, C., Caudek, C., & Domini, F. (2011). Integration of disparity and velocity information for haptic and perceptual judgments of object depth. *Acta Psychologica, 136,* 300–310.

Fox, J., Fairhall, A., & Daniel, T. (2010). Encoding properties of haltere neurons enable motion feature detection in a biological gyroscope. *PNAS Proceedings of the National Academy of Sciences of the United States of America, 107,* 3840–3845.

Fox, S., & Spector, P. E. (2000). Relations of emotional intelligence, practical intelligence, general intelligence, and trait affectivity with interview outcomes: It's not all just "G." *Journal of Organizational Behavior, 21,* 203–220.

Frances, A. (2013). *Saving normal: An insider's revolt against out-of-control psychiatric diagnosis, DSM-5, Big Pharma, and the medicalization of ordinary life.* New York: Morrow.

Frankenburg, W. K., et al. (1992). *Denver II training manual.* Denver: Denver Developmental Materials.

Franklin, M. E., March, J. S., & Garcia, A. (2007). Treating obsessive-compulsive disorder in children and adolescents. In C. Purdon, M. M. Antony, & L. J. Summerfeldt (Eds.), *Psychological treatment of obsessive-compulsive disorder: Fundamentals and beyond.* Washington, DC: American Psychological Association.

Franzek, E., & Beckmann, H. (1996). Gene-environment interaction in schizophrenia: Season-of-birth effect reveals etiologically different subgroups. *Psychopathology, 29,* 14–26.

Freedman, M. R., & Waldrop, J. (2011). Freshman orientation sessions can teach incoming students about healthful lifestyles. *Journal of Nutrition Education and Behavior, 43,* 69–70.

Freeman, D. (2012, March 20). Face blindness: '60 Minutes' spotlights mysterious condition of prosopagnosia. *Huffington Post.* Retrieved from http://www.huffingtonpost.com/2012/03/19/face-blindness-60-minutes-cbs-news_n_1362295.html

Freeman, H., & Beer, J. (2010). Frontal lobe activation mediates the relation between sensation seeking and cortisol increases. *Journal of Personality, 78,* 1497–1528.

Freud, S. (1900). *The interpretation of dreams.* New York: Basic Books.

Freud, S. (1922/1959). *Group psychology and the analysis of the ego.* London: Hogarth.

Freudenreich, O., & Goff, D. C. (2011). Treatment of psychotic disorders. In D. A. Ciraulo, R. Shader, D. A. Ciraulo, & R. Shader (Eds.), *Pharmacotherapy of depression* (2nd ed.). New York: Springer Science + Business Media.

Friborg, O., Barlaug, D., Martinussen, M., Rosenvinge, J. H., & Hjemdal, O. (2005). Resilience in relation to personality and intelligence. *International Journal of Methods in Psychiatric Research, 14,* 29–42.

Friedberg, R. D. (2006). A cognitive-behavioral approach to family therapy. *Journal of Contemporary Psychotherapy, 36,* 159–165.

Friedman, J. N. W., Oltmanns, T. F., & Turkheimer, E. (2007). Interpersonal perception and personality disorders: Utilization of a thin slice approach. *Journal of Research in Personality, 41,* 667–688.

Frijda, N. H. (2005). Emotion experience. *Cognition and Emotion, 19,* 473–497.

Frings, L., Wagner, K., Unterrainer, J., Spreer, J., Halsband, U., & Schulze-Bonhage, A. (2006). Gender-related differences in lateralization of hippocampal activation and cognitive strategy. *Neuroreport, 17,* 417–421.

Frosch, A. (2011). The effect of frequency and duration on psychoanalytic outcome: A moment in time. *Psychoanalytic Review, 98,* 11–38.

Frost, R. O., & Steketee, G. (Eds.). (2002). *Cognitive approaches to obsessions and compulsions: Theory, assessment, and treatment.* New York: Pergamon Press.

Furnham, A., & Crump, J. (2005). Personality traits, types, and disorders: An examination of the relationship between three self-report measures. *European Journal of Personality, 19,* 167–184.

Furumoto, L., & Scarborough, E. (2002). Placing women in the history of psychology: The first American women psychologists. In W. E. Pickren (Ed.), *Evolving perspectives on the history of psychology* (pp. 527–543). Washington, DC: American Psychological Association.

Fusari, A., & Ballesteros, S. (2008, August). Identification of odors of edible and nonedible stimuli as affected by age and gender. *Behavior Research Methods, 40,* 752–759.

Gadzichowski, K. M., Kapalka, K., & Pasnak, R. (2016). Response to stimulus relations by a dog (canis lupus familiaris). *Learning & Behavior.* Retrieved from http://www.ncbi.nlm.nih.gov/pubmed/26850761

Galambos, N. L., Fang, S., Krahn, H. J., Johnson, M. D., & Lachman, M. E. (2015). Up, not down: The age curve in happiness from early adulthood to midlife in two longitudinal studies. *Developmental Psychology.* Retrieved from http://www.ncbi.nlm.nih.gov/pubmed/26347986

Galanter, E. (1962). Contemporary psychophysics. In R. Brown, E. Galanter, E. Hess, & G. Maroler (Eds.), *New directions in psychology* (pp. 87–157). New York: Holt.

Galanter, M. (2007). Spirituality and recovery in 12-step programs: An empirical model. *Journal of Substance Abuse Treatment, 33,* 265–272.

Galdi, G. (2015). Celebrating the 75th anniversary of the American Journal of Psychoanalysis. *The American Journal of Psychoanalysis, 75,* 1–2.

Gallo, M. M. (2015). *"No one helped": Kitty Genovese, New York City, and the myth of urban apathy.* New York: Cornell University Press.

Gangestad, S. (2010). Evolutionary biology looks at behavior genetics. *Personality and Individual Differences, 49,* 289–295.

Gangestad, S. W., Simpson, J. A., Cousins, A. J., Garver-Apgar, C. E., & Christensen, P. N. (2004). Women's preferences for male behavioral displays change across the menstrual cycle. *Psychological Science, 15,* 203–207.

Ganio, M. S., Johnson, E. C., Lopez, R. M., Stearns, R. L., Emmanuel, H., Anderson, J. M., & Armstrong, L. E. (2011). Caffeine lowers muscle pain during exercise in hot but not cool environments. *Physiology & Behavior, 102,* 429–435.

Garber, J., & Horowitz, J. L. (2002). Depression in children. In I. H. Gotlib & C. L. Hammen (Eds.), *Handbook of depression.* New York: Guilford Press.

Garcia, S. M., Weaver, K., Moskowitz, G. B., & Darley, J. M. (2002). Crowded minds: The implicit bystander effect. *Journal of Personality and Social Psychology, 83,* 843–853.

García-Herrero, S., Mariscal, M. A., Gutiérrez, J. M., & Ritzel, D. O. (2013). Using Bayesian networks to analyze occupational stress caused by work demands: Preventing stress through social support. *Accident Analysis and Prevention, 57,* 114–123.

Gardini, S., Cornoldi, C., De Beni, R., & Venneri, A. (2009). Cognitive and neuronal processes involved in sequential generation of general and specific mental images. *Psychological Research/Psychologische Forschung, 73,* 633–643.

Gardner, B., & O'Connor, D. (2008). A review of the cognitive effects of electroconvulsive therapy in older adults. *The Journal of ECT, 24,* 68–80.

Gardner, E. P., & Kandel, E. R. (2000). Touch. In E. R. Kandel, J. H. Schwartz, & T. M. Jessell (Eds.), *Principles of neural science* (4th ed.). New York: McGraw-Hill.

Gardner, H. (2000). *Intelligence reframed: Multiple intelligences for the 21st century.* New York: Basic Books.

Garwick, G. B. (2007). Intelligence-related terms in mental retardation, learning disability, and gifted/talented professional usage, 1983–2001: The 1992 mental retardation redefinition as natural experiment. *Dissertation Abstracts International Section A: Humanities and Social Sciences, 67*(9-A), 3296.

Gatchel, R. J., & Oordt, M. S. (2003). Obesity. In R. J. Gatchel & M. S. Oordt, *Clinical health psychology and primary care: Practical advice and clinical guidance for successful collaboration* (pp. 149–167). Washington, DC: American Psychological Association.

Gatchel, R. J., & Weisberg, J. N. (2000). *Personality characteristics of patients with pain.* Washington, DC: APA Books.

Gaudiano, B. A., & Miller, I. W. (2013). The evidence-based practice of psychotherapy. *Clinical Psychology Review, 33,* 813–824.

Gazzaniga, M. S., Ivry, R. B., & Mangun, G. R. (2002). *Cognitive neuroscience: The biology of the mind* (2nd ed.). New York: W. W. Norton.

Gejman, P., Sanders, A., & Duan, J. (2010). The role of genetics in the etiology of schizophrenia. *Psychiatric Clinics of North America, 33,* 35–66.

Genovese, J. E. C. (2006). Piaget, pedagogy, and evolutionary psychology. *Evolutionary Psychology, 4,* 2127–2137.

Gentile, B., Grabe, S., Dolan-Pascoe, B., Twenge, J., Wells, B., & Maitino, A. (2009). Gender differences in domain-specific self-esteem: A meta-analysis. *Review of General Psychology, 13,* 34–45.

George, M. S., Wassermann, E. M., Williams, W. A., Callahan, A., et al. (1995). Daily repetitive transcranial magnetic stimulations (rTMS) improves mood in depression. *Neuroreport: An International Journal for the Rapid Communication of Research in Neuroscience, 6,* 1853–1856.

George, S., & Moselhy, H. (2005). Cocaine-induced trichotillomania. *Addiction, 100,* 255–256.

Gershkoff-Stowe, L., Connell, B., & Smith, L. (2006). Priming overgeneralizations in two- and four-year-old children. *Journal of Child Language, 33,* 461–486.

Gerstel, N. (2005, April 8). In search of time. *Science, 308,* 204–205.

Ghose, T. (2015, January 27). What Facebook addiction looks like in the brain. *LiveScience.* Retrieved from http://www.livescience.com/49585-facebook-addiction-viewed-brain.html

Giacobbi, P. R. Jr., Lynn, T. K. Wetherington, J. M., Jenkins, J., Bodendorf, M., & Langley, B. (2004). Stress and coping during the transition to university for first-year female athletes. *Sports Psychologist, 18,* 1–20.

Gianaros, P. J., & Wager, T. D. (2015). Brain-body pathways linking psychological stress and physical health. *Current Directions in Psychological Science, 24,* 313–321.

Gilbert, D. T., Miller, A. G., & Ross, L. (1998). Speeding with Ned: A personal view of the correspondence bias. In J. M. Darley & J. Cooper (Eds.), *Attribution and social interaction: The legacy of Edward E. Jones.* Washington, DC: American Psychological Association.

Gillan, C. M., & Sahakian, B. J. (2015). Which is the driver, the obsessions or the compulsions, in OCD? *Neuropsychopharmacology, 40,* 247–248.

Gilley, P., Sharma, A., Mitchell, T., & Dorman, M. (2010). The influence of a sensitive period for auditory-visual integration in children with cochlear implants. *Restorative Neurology and Neuroscience, 28,* 207–218.

Gilligan, C. (1996). The centrality of relationships in psychological development: A puzzle, some evidence, and a theory. In G. G. Noam & K. W. Fischer (Eds.), *Development and vulnerability in close relationships.* Hillsdale, NJ: Erlbaum.

Gizer, I. R., Ehlers, C. L., Vieten, C., Seaton-Smith, K. L., Feiler, H. S., Lee, J. V., & . . . Wilhelmsen, K. C. (2011). Linkage scan of alcohol dependence in the UCSF Family Alcoholism Study. *Drug and Alcohol Dependence, 113,* 125–132.

Gladwell, M. (2004, September 20). Annals of psychology: Personality, plus how corporations figure out who you are. *The New Yorker,* pp. 42–45.

Glass, K., Flory, K., Hankin, B., Kloos, B., & Turecki, G. (2009). Are coping strategies, social support, and hope associated with psychological distress among Hurricane Katrina survivors? *Journal of Social and Clinical Psychology, 28,* 779–795.

Glicksohn, J., & Nahari, G. (2007). Interacting personality traits? Smoking as a test case. *European Journal of Personality, 21,* 225–234.

Glisky, E. L. (2007). Changes in cognitive function in human aging. In D. R. Riddle, *Brain aging: Models, methods, and mechanisms.* Boca Raton, FL: CRC Press.

Goin, M. K. (2005). A current perspective on the psychotherapies. *Psychiatric Services, 56,* 255–257.

Goldfried, M. R., & Pachankis, J. E. (2007). On the next generation of process research. *Clinical Psychological Review, 27,* 760–768.

Goldman-Mellor, S., Saxton, K., & Catalano, R. (2010). Economic contraction and mental health: A review of the evidence, 1990–2009. *International Journal of Mental Health, 39,* 6–31.

Goldstein, I. (2000). Female sexual arousal disorder: New insights. *International Journal of Impotence Research, 12* (Suppl. 4), S152–S157.

Goldstein, S. N. (2006). The exploration of spirituality and identity status in adolescence. *Dissertation Abstracts International: Section B: The Sciences and Engineering, 67*(6-B), 3481.

Golimbet, V. E., Alfimova, M. V., Gritsenko, I. K., & Ebstein, R. P. (2007). Relationship between dopamine system genes and extraversion and novelty seeking. *Neuroscience Behavior and Physiology, 37,* 601–606.

Gómez-Ortiz, O., Romera, E. M., & Ortega-Ruiz, R. (2015). Parenting styles and bullying. The mediating role of parental psychological aggression and physical punishment. *Child Abuse & Neglect.* Retrieved from http://www.ncbi.nlm.nih.gov/pubmed/26598076

Gontier, N. (2008). Genes, brains, and language: An epistemological examination of how genes can underlie human cognitive behavior. *Review of General Psychology, 12,* 170–180.

Gontkovsky, S. T., & Beatty, W. W. (2006). Practical methods for the clinical assessment of information processing speed. *International Journal of Neuroscience, 116,* 1317–1325.

Goode, E. (1999, April 13). If things taste bad, "phantoms" may be at work. *The New York Times,* pp. D1–D2.

Goodwin, C. J. (2010). *Annotated readings in the history of modern psychology.* Hoboken, NJ: John Wiley & Sons Inc.

Goodwin, R. D., & Hamilton, S. P. (2003). Lifetime comorbidity of antisocial personality disorder and anxiety disorders among adults in the community. *Psychiatry Research, 117,* 159–166.

Goodwin, R., Costa, P., & Adonu, J. (2004). Social support and its consequences: "Positive" and "deficiency" values and their implications for support and self-esteem. *British Journal of Social Psychology, 43,* 465–474.

Gooren, L. (2006). The biology of human psychosexual differentiation. *Hormones and Behavior, 50,* 589–601.

Gossop, M., Stewart, D., & Marsden, J. (2008). Attendance at Narcotics Anonymous and Alcoholics Anonymous meetings, frequency of attendance and substance use outcomes after residential treatment for drug dependence: A 5-year follow-up study. *Addiction, 103,* 119–125.

Gotlib, I. H., Krasnoperova, E., Yue, D. N., & Joorman, J. (2004). Attentional biases for negative interpersonal stimuli in clinical depression. *Journal of Abnormal Psychology, 113,* 127–135.

Goto, T., Ishibashi, Y., Kajimura, S., Oka, R., & Kusumi, T. (2015). Development of free will and determinism scale in Japanese. *Japanese Journal of Psychology, 86,* 32–41.

Gottesman, I. I. (1991). *Schizophrenia genesis: The origins of madness.* New York: Freeman.

Gottesman, I. I., & Hanson, D. R. (2005). Human development: Biological and genetic processes. *Annual Review of Psychology, 56,* 263–286.

Gotts, S. J., Jo, H., Wallace, G. L., Saad, Z. S., Cox, R. W., & Martin, A. (2013). Two distinct forms of functional lateralization in the human brain. *PNAS Proceedings of the National Academy of Sciences of the United States of America, 110,* E3435–E3444.

Goubert, L., Vlaeyen, J. S., Crombez, G., & Craig, K. D. (2011). Learning about pain from others: An observational learning account. *The Journal of Pain, 12,* 167–174.

Gould, R. L. (1978). *Transformations.* New York: Simon & Schuster.

Gräf, M., & Unkelbach, C. (2016). Halo effects in trait assessment depend on information valence: Why being honest makes you industrious, but lying does not make you lazy. *Personality and Social Psychology Bulletin, 42,*290– 310.

Grünbaum, A. (2015). Critique of psychoanalysis. In S. Boag, L. W. Brakel, & V. Talvitie (Eds.), *Philosophy, science, and psychoanalysis: A critical meeting.* London: Karnac Books.

Grünert, U., Jusuf, P. R., Lee, S. S., & Nguyen, D. (2011). Bipolar input to melanopsin containing ganglion cells in primate retina. *Visual Neuroscience, 28,* 39–50.

Gradinaru, V., Mogri, M., Thompson, K. R., Henderson, J. M., & Deisseroth, K. (2009). Optical deconstruction of Parkinsonian neural circuitry. *Science, 324,* 354–359.

Grady, C. L., St-Laurent, M., & Burianová, H. (2015). Age differences in brain activity related to unsuccessful declarative memory retrieval. *Brain Research, 161,* 230–247.

Graham, C. A., Bancroft, J., & Doll, H. A. (2007). Does oral contraceptive-induced reduction in free testosterone adversely affect the sexuality or mood of women? *Psychoneuroendocrinology, 32,* 246–255.

Granic, I., Hollenstein, T., & Dishion, T. (2003). Longitudinal analysis of flexibility and reorganization in early adolescence: A dynamic systems study of family interactions. *Developmental Psychology, 39,* 606–617.

Grann, J. D. (2007). Confidence in knowledge past: An empirical basis for a differential decay theory of very long-term memory monitoring. *Dissertation Abstracts International Section A: Humanities and Social Sciences, 67,* 2462.

Grant, A. (2008). Does intrinsic motivation fuel the prosocial fire? Motivational synergy in predicting persistence, performance, and productivity. *Journal of Applied Psychology, 93,* 48–58.

Grant, D. M., & Wingate, L. R. (2011). Cognitive-behavioral therapy. In C. Silverstein (Ed.), *The initial psychotherapy interview: A gay man seeks treatment.* Amsterdam Netherlands: Elsevier.

Gray, G. C. (2006). The regulation of corporate violations: Punishment, compliance, and the blurring of responsibility. *British Journal of Criminology, 46,* 875–892.

Graziano, W. G., Habashi, M. M., Sheese, B. E., & Tobin, R. M. (2007). Agreeableness, empathy, and helping: A person situation perspective. *Journal of Personality and Social Psychology, 93,* 583–599.

Greenberg, G., & Rosenheck, R. (2008). Jail incarceration, homelessness, and mental health: A national study. *Psychiatric Services, 59,* 170–177.

Greenberg, L. S. (2015). Working with primary emotions. In *Emotion-focused therapy: Coaching clients to work through their feelings,* (2nd ed.). Washington, DC: American Psychological Association.

Greene, J. D., Sommerville, R. B., Nystrom, L. E., Darley, J. M., & Cohen, J. D. (2001, September 14). An fMRI investigation of emotional engagement in moral judgment. *Science, 293,* 2105–2108.

Greenspan, S. (2006). Functional concepts in mental retardation: Finding the natural essence of an artificial category. *Exceptionality, 14,* 205–224.

Greenwald, A., Poehlman, T., Uhlmann, E., & Banaji, M. (2009). Understanding and using the Implicit Association Test: III. Meta-analysis of predictive validity. *Journal of Personality and Social Psychology, 97,* 17–41.

Greer, R. D., Dudek-Singer, J., & Gautreaux, G. (2006). Observational learning. *International Journal of Psychology, 41,* 486–499.

Gregor, M. A., & O'Brien, K. M. (2015). The changing face of psychology: Leadership aspirations of female doctoral students. *The Counseling Psychologist, 43*(8), 1090–1113.

Gregory, R. L. (1978). *The psychology of seeing* (3rd ed.). New York: McGraw-Hill.

Gregory, R. L. (2008). Emmert's Law and the moon illusion. *Spatial Vision, 21,* 407–720.

Grenfell-Essam, R., Ward, G., & Tan, L. (2013). The role of rehearsal on the output order of immediate free recall of short and long lists. *Journal of Experimental Psychology: Learning, Memory, and Cognition, 39,* 317–347.

Greven, C. U., Rijsdijk, F. V., & Plomin, R. (2011). A twin study of ADHD symptoms in early adolescence: Hyperactivity-impulsivity and inattentiveness show substantial genetic overlap but also genetic specificity. *Journal of Abnormal Child Psychology: An official publication of the International Society for Research in Child and Adolescent Psychopathology, 39,* 265–275.

Griggs, R. A. (2015). Psychology's lost boy: Will the real Little Albert please stand up? *Teaching of Psychology, 42,* 14–18.

Grigorenko, E. (2009). Speaking genes or genes for speaking? Deciphering the genetics of speech and language. *Journal of Child Psychology and Psychiatry, 50,* 116–125.

Grigoriadis, S., & Ravitz, P. (2007). An approach to interpersonal psychotherapy for postpartum depression: Focusing on interpersonal changes. *Canadian Family Physician, 53,* 1469–1475.

Gronholm, P., Rinne, J. O., Vorobyev, V., & Laine, M. (2005). Naming of newly learned objects: A PET activation study. *Brain Research and Cognitive Brain Research, 14,* 22–28.

Gruber, T. R. (2013). Nature, nurture, and knowledge acquisition. *International Journal of Human-Computer Studies, 71,* 191–194.

Grundy, D. (2015). Principles and standards for reporting animal experiments in the *Journal of Physiology and Experimental Physiology. The Journal of Physiology, 593,* 2547–2549.

Guéguen, N., Marchand, M., Pascual, A., & Lourel, M. (2008). Foot-in-the-door technique using a courtship request: A field experiment. *Psychological Reports, 103,* 529–534.

Guilleminault, C., Kirisoglu, C., Bao, G., Arias, V., Chan, A., & Li, K. K. (2005). Adult chronic sleepwalking and its treatment based on polysomnography. *Brain, 128*(Pt. 5), 1062–1069.

Guldemond, H., Bosker, R., Kuyper, H., & van der Werf, G. (2007). Do highly gifted students really have problems? [Special issue: Current research on giftedness: International perspectives]. *Educational Research and Evaluation, 13,* 555–568.

Gupta, M. A. (2013). Review of somatic symptoms in post-traumatic stress disorder. *International Review of Psychiatry, 25,* 86–99.

Gutierrez, P. M., Muehlenkamp, J. L., Konick, L. C., & Osman, A. (2005). What role does race play in adolescent suicidal ideation? *Archives of Suicide Research, 9,* 177–192.

Haas, H. S., Fuerst, M. P., Tönz, P., & Gubser-Ernst, J. (2015). Analyzing the psychological and social contents of evidence—Experimental comparison between guessing, naturalistic observation, and systematic analysis. *Journal of Forensic Sciences, 60,* 659–668.

Haberstick, B. C., Timberlake, D., & Ehringer, M. A. (2007). Genes, time to first cigarette and nicotine dependence in a general population sample of young adults. *Addiction, 102,* 655–665.

Haier, R. J., Colom, R., Schroeder, D. H., Condon, C. A., Tang, C., Eaves, E., et al. (2009). Gray matter and intelligence factors: Is there a neuro-g? *Intelligence, 37,* 136–144.

Halford, S. (2006). Collapsing the boundaries? Fatherhood, organization and home-working. *Gender, Work & Organization, 13,* 383–402.

Halgin, R. P. & Whitbourne, S. K. (1994). *Abnormal Psychology*. New York: William C. Brown Publishing.

Hall, R. E. (2002). *The Bell Curve:* Implications for the performance of black/white athletes. *Social Science Journal, 39,* 113–118.

Hamann, S. B., Ely, T. D., Hoffman, J. M., & Kilts, C. D. (2002). Ecstasy and agony: Activation of human amygdala in positive and negative emotion. *Psychological Science, 13,* 135–141.

Hambleton, R. K. (2006). Psychometric models, test designs and item types for the next generation of educational and psychological tests. In D. Bartram & R. K. Hambleton, *Computer-based testing and the Internet: Issues and advances.* New York: Wiley.

Hambleton, R. K., & Zenisky, A. L. (2013). Reporting test scores in more meaningful ways: A research-based approach to score report design. In K. F. Geisinger, B. A. Bracken, J. F. Carlson, J. C. Hansen, N. R. Kuncel, S. P. Reise, & M. C. Rodriguez (Eds.), *APA handbook of testing and assessment in psychology, Vol. 3: Testing and assessment in school psychology and education.* Washington, DC: American Psychological Association.

Hamilton, A. C., & Martin, R. C. (2007). Semantic short-term memory deficits and resolution of interference: A case for inhibition? In D. S. Gorfein & C. M. MacLeod, *Inhibition in cognition.* Washington, DC: American Psychological Association.

Hamilton, L. K., Joppé, S. E., Cochard, L. M., & Fernandes, K. L. (2013). Aging and neurogenesis in the adult forebrain: What we have learned and where we should go from here. *European Journal of Neuroscience, 37,* 1978–1986.

Haney, C., & Zimbardo, P. (2009). Persistent dispositionalism in interactionist clothing: Fundamental attribution error in explaining prison abuse. *Personality and Social Psychology Bulletin, 35,* 807–814.

Hangya, B., Tihanyi, B. T., Entz, L., Fabo, D., Erőss, L., Wittner, L., & . . . Ulbert, I. (2011). Complex propagation patterns characterize human cortical activity during slow-wave sleep. *The Journal of Neuroscience, 31,* 8770–8779.

Harding, D. J., & Jencks, C. (2003). Changing attitudes toward premarital sex: Cohort, period, and aging effects. *The Public Opinion Quarterly, 67,* 211–226.

Hardt, J., Sidor, A., Nickel, R., Kappis, B., Petrak, P., & Egle, U. (2008). Childhood adversities and suicide attempts: A retrospective study. *Journal of Family Violence, 23,* 713–718.

Harlow, H. F., & Zimmerman, R. R. (1959). Affectional responses in the infant monkey. *Science, 130,* 421–432.

Harlow, J. M. (1869). Recovery from the passage of an iron bar through the head. *Massachusetts Medical Society Publication, 2,* 329–347.

Hartmann, E. (1967). *The biology of dreaming.* Springfield, IL: Charles C Thomas.

Harvey, A., Nathens, A. B., Bandiera, G., & LeBlanc, V. R. (2010). Threat and challenge: Cognitive appraisal and stress responses in simulated trauma resuscitations. *Medical Education, 44,* 587–594.

Harvey, J. H., Wenzel, A., & Sprecher, S. (Eds.). (2005) *Handbook of sexuality in close relationships.* Mahwah, NJ: Erlbaum.

Hauer, P. (2010). Systemic affects of methamphetamine use. *South Dakota Medicine, 63,* 285–287.

Haugen, R., Lund, T. & Ommundsen, Y. (2008). Personality dispositions, expectancy and context in attributional thinking. *Scandinavian Journal of Educational Research, 52*(2), 171–185.

Hauke, C. (2006). The unconscious: Personal and collective. In R. K. Papadopoulos, *The handbook of Jungian psychology: Theory, practice and applications.* New York: Routledge.

Haviland-Jones, J., & Chen, D. (1999, April 17). *Human olfactory perception.* Paper presented at the Association for Chemoreception Sciences, Sarasota, Florida.

Hawkes, Christopher H., & Doty, R. L. (2009). *The neurology of olfaction.* Cambridge, UK: Cambridge University Press.

Hayes, S. C. (2015). Humanistic psychology and contextual behavioral perspectives. In K. J. Schneider, J. F. Pierson, & J. T. Bugental (Eds.), *The handbook of humanistic psychology: Theory, research, and practice* (2nd ed.). Thousand Oaks, CA: Sage Publications, Inc.

Hayflick, L. (2007). Biological aging is no longer an unsolved problem. *Annals of the New York Academy of Sciences, 1100,* 1–13.

Hays, P. A. (2008). *Addressing cultural complexities in practice: Assessment, diagnosis, and therapy* (2nd ed.). Washington, DC: American Psychological Association.

Hedges, D. W., Brown, B. L., Shwalk, D. A., Godfrey, K., & Larcher, A. M. (2007). The efficacy of selective serotonin reuptake inhibitors in adult social anxiety disorder: A meta-analysis of double-blind, placebo-controlled trials. *Journal of Psychopharmacology, 21,* 102–111.

Heffernan, M. E., & Fraley, R. C. (2015). How early experiences shape attraction, partner preferences, and attachment dynamics. In V. Zayas & C. Hazan (Eds.), *Bases of adult attachment: Linking brain, mind and behavior.* New York: Springer Science + Business Media.

Hegarty, P. (2007). From genius inverts to gendered intelligence: Lewis Terman and the power of the norm [Special issue: Power matters: Knowledge politics in the history of psychology]. *History of Psychology, 10,* 132–155.

Hegarty, P., & Massey, S. (2007). Anti-homosexual prejudice … as opposed to what? Queer theory and the social psychology of anti-homosexual attitudes. *Journal of Homosexuality, 52,* 47–71.

Heijnen, W. T., Birkenhäger, T. K., Wierdsma, A. I., & van den Broek, W. W. (2010). Antidepressant pharmacotherapy failure and response to subsequent electroconvulsive therapy: A meta-analysis. *Journal of Clinical Psychopharmacology, 30,* 616–619.

Heinrichs, R. W. (2005). The primacy of cognition in schizophrenia. *American Psychologist, 60,* 229–242.

Helfand, S. J. (2011). Managing disruptive offenders: A behavioral perspective. In T. J. Fagan, R. K. Ax, T. J. Fagan, & R. K. Ax (Eds.), *Correctional mental health: From theory to best practice.* Thousand Oaks, CA: Sage Publications, Inc.

Helmbold, N., Troche, S., & Rammsayer, T. (2007). Processing of temporal and nontemporal information as predictors of psychometric intelligence: A structural-equation-modeling approach. *Journal of Personality, 75,* 985–1006.

Helmuth, L. (2000, August 25). Synapses shout to overcome distance. *Science, 289,* 1273.

Helsen, K., Goubert, L., & Vlaeyen, J. S. (2013). Observational learning and pain-related fear: Exploring contingency learning in an experimental study using colored warm water immersions. *The Journal of Pain, 14,* 676–688.

Henckes, N. (2011). Reforming psychiatric institutions in the mid-twentieth century: A framework for analysis. *History of Psychiatry, 22,* 164–181.

Henderson, N. D. (1982). Correlations in IQ for pairs of people with varying degrees of genetic relatedness and shared environment. *Annual Review of Psychology, 33,* 219–243.

Hennig-Fast, K., Meister, F., Frodl, T., Beraldi, A., Padberg, F., Engel, R., et al. (2008). The case of persistent retrograde amnesia following a dissociative fugue: Neuropsychological and neurofunctional underpinnings of loss of autobiographical memory and self-awareness. *Neuropsychologia, 46*(12), 2993–3005.

Henrich, J., Heine, S., & Norenzayan, A. (2010). The weirdest people in the world? *Behavioral and Brain Sciences, 33,* 61–83.

Henry, D., McClellan, D., Rosenthal, L., Dedrick, D., & Gosdin, M. (2008, February). Is sleep really for sissies? Understanding the role of work in insomnia in the US. *Social Science & Medicine, 66,* 715–726.

Henry, P. J., & Pratto, F. (2010). Power and racism. In A. Guinote, T. K. Vescio, A. Guinote, & T. K. Vescio (Eds.), *The social psychology of power.* New York: Guilford Press.

Herbenick, D., Reece, M., Sanders, S., Dodge, B., Ghassemi, A., & Fortenberry, J. (2009). Prevalence and characteristics of vibrator use by women in the

United States: Results from a nationally representative study. *Journal of Sexual Medicine, 6,* 1857–1866.

Havermans, R. C., Mulkens, S., Nederkoorn, C., & Jansen, A. (2007). The efficacy of cue exposure with response prevention in extinguishing drug and alcohol cue reactivity. *Behavioral Interventions, 22,* 121–135.

Herdt, G. (2010). Sex/gender, culture, and development: Issues in the emergence of puberty and attraction. *Formative experiences: The interaction of caregiving, culture, and developmental psychobiology.* New York: Cambridge University Press.

Herlin, B., Leu-Semenescu, S., Chaumereuil, C., & Arnulf, I. (2015). Evidence that non-dreamers do dream: A REM sleep behaviour disorder model. *Journal of Sleep Research, 24,* 602–609.

Herrington, D. M., & Howard, T. D. (2003). From presumed benefit to potential harm— Hormone therapy and heart disease. *New England Journal of Medicine, 349,* 519–521.

Herrnstein, R. J., & Murray, D. (1994). *The bell curve.* New York: Free Press.

Hertzog, C., Kramer, A., Wilson, R., & Lindenberger, U. (2008). Enrichment effects on adult cognitive development: Can the functional capacity of older adults be preserved and enhanced? *Psychological Science in the Public Interest, 9,* 1–65.

Herz, R. (2010). The emotional, cognitive, and biological basics of olfaction: Implications and considerations for scent marketing. *Sensory marketing: Research on the sensuality of products.* New York: Routledge/Taylor & Francis Group.

Herzberg, L. (2009). Direction, causation, and appraisal theories of emotion. *Philosophical Psychology, 22,* 167–186.

Heshka, S., Anderson, J. W., Atkinson, R. L., Greenway, F. L., Hill, J. O., Phinney, S. D., Kolotkin, R. L., Miller-Kovach, K., & Pi-Sunyer, F. X. (2003). Weight loss with self-help compared with a structured commercial program: A randomized trial. *Journal of the American Medical Association, 289,* 1792–1798.

Hess, M. J., Houg, S., & Tammaro, E. (2007). The experience of four individuals with paraplegia enrolled in an outpatient interdisciplinary sexuality program. *Sexuality and Disability, 25,* 189–195.

Hiby, E. F., Rooney, N. J., & Bradshaw, J. W. S. (2004). Dog training methods: Their use, effectiveness and interaction with behaviour and welfare. *Animal Welfare, 13,* 63–69.

Hickok, G. (2010). The role of mirror neurons in speech perception and action word semantics. *Language and Cognitive Processes, 25,* 749–776.

Hicks, T. V., & Leitenberg, H. (2001). Sexual fantasies about one's partner versus someone else: Gender differences in incidence and frequency. *Journal of Sex Research, 38,* 43–50.

Hilarski, C. (2007). Antisocial personality disorder. In B. A. Thyer, & J. S. Wodarski, *Social work in mental health: An evidence-based approach.* Hoboken, NJ: Wiley.

Hildebrandt, L. K., McCall, C., Engen, H. G., & Singer, T. (2016). Cognitive flexibility, heart rate variability, and resilience predict fine-grained regulation of arousal during prolonged threat. *Psychophysiology,* Retrieved from http://www.ncbi.nlm.nih.gov/pubmed/26899260

Hill, B. D., Foster, J. D., Elliott, E. M., Shelton, J., McCain, J., & Gouvier, W. (2013). Need for cognition is related to higher general intelligence, fluid intelligence, and crystallized intelligence, but not working memory. *Journal of Research in Personality, 47,* 22–25.

Hines, M. (2004) *Brain gender.* New York: Oxford University Press.

Hines, M. (2010). Sex-related variation in human behavior and the brain. *Trends in Cognitive Sciences, 14,* 448–456.

Hinterberger, T., Schöner, J., & Halsband, U. (2011). Analysis of electrophysiological state patterns and changes during hypnosis induction. *International Journal of Clinical and Experimental Hypnosis, 59,* 165–179.

Hirschler, B. (2007, May 1). Doctors test gene therapy to treat blindness. *Reuters,* p. 9.

Hobson, J. (2007). States of consciousness: Normal and abnormal variation. In P. D. Zelazo, M. Moscovitch & E. Thompson (Eds.), *The Cambridge handbook of consciousness* (pp. 435–444). New York, NY: Cambridge University Press.

Hobson, J. A. (2005). In bed with Mark Solms? What a nightmare! A reply to Domhoff (2005). *Dreaming, 15,* 21–29.

Hobson, J. A. *The dreaming brain* (1989). Basic Books, a member of the Perseus Books Group.

Hochschild, A. (2001, February). A generation without public passion. *Atlantic Monthly,* pp. 33–42.

Hoff, E. (2008). *Language development.* New York: Wadsworth.

Hofmann, S. G. (2007). Enhancing exposure-based therapy from a translational research perspective. *Behaviour Research and Therapy, 45,* 1987–2001.

Hofmann, W., Gschwendner, T., Castelli, L., & Schmitt, M. (2008). Implicit and explicit attitudes and interracial interaction: The moderating role of situationally available control resources. *Group Processes & Intergroup Relations, 11,* 69–87.

Hogan, J., Davies, S., & Hogan, R. (2007). Generalizing personality-based validity evidence. In S. M. McPhail, *Alternative validation strategies: Developing new and leveraging existing validity evidence.* Hoboken, NJ: Wiley.

Hogg, M. A. (2006). Social identity theory. In P. J. Burke, *Contemporary social psychological theories.* Stanford, CA: Stanford University Press.

Hogg, M. A. (2010). Influence and leadership. In S. T. Fiske, D. T. Gilbert, & G. Lindzey (Eds.), *Handbook of social psychology* (Vol. 2, 5th ed.). Hoboken, NJ: John Wiley & Sons.

Holbrook, A., & Krosnick, J. (2010). Social desirability bias in voter turnout reports: Tests using the item count technique. *Public Opinion Quarterly, 74,* 37–67.

Holden, C. (2003, January 17). Deconstructing schizophrenia. *Science, 299,* 333–335.

Hollander, E. (Ed.), Zohar, J. (Ed.), Sirovatka, P. (Ed.), & Regier, D. (Ed.). (2011). *Obsessive-compulsive spectrum disorders: Refining the research agenda for DSM-V.* Washington, DC: American Psychiatric Association.

Holleran, S., Mehl, M., & Levitt, S. (2009). Eavesdropping on social life: The accuracy of stranger ratings of daily behavior from thin slices of natural conversations. *Journal of Research in Personality, 43,* 660–672.

Hollingworth, H. L. (1943/1990). *Leta Stetter Hollingworth: A biography.* Boston: Anker.

Holloway, L. (2000, December 16). Chief of New York City schools plans to revamp bilingual study. *The New York Times,* p. A1.

Holmes, A., Yang, R. J., Lesch, K. P., Crawley, J. N., & Murphy, D. L. (2003). Mice lacking the serotonin transporter exhibit 5-HT-sub(1A) receptor-mediated abnormalities in tests for anxiety-like behavior. *Neuropsychopharmacology, 28,* 2077–2088.

Holt, M., & Jahn, R. (2004, March, 26). Synaptic vesicles in the fast lane. *Science, 303,* 1986–1987.

Holtyn, A. F., & Lattal, K. A. (2013). Briefly delayed reinforcement effects on variable "ratio and yoked" interval schedule performance. *Journal of the Experimental Analysis of Behavior, 100,* 198–210.

Holtzheimer, P., McDonald, W., Mufti, M., Kelley, M., Quinn, S., Corso, G., et al. (2010). Accelerated repetitive transcranial magnetic stimulation for treatment-resistant depression. *Depression and Anxiety, 27,* 960–963.

Hongchun, W., & Ming, L. (2006). About the research on suggestibility and false memory. *Psychological Science (China), 29,* 905–908.

Hopkins, W., & Cantalupo, C. (2008, June). Theoretical speculations on the evolutionary origins of hemispheric specialization. *Current Directions in Psychological Science, 17,* 233–237.

Hopwood, C., Newman, D., Donnellan, M., Markowitz, J., Grilo, C., Sanislow, C., et al. (2009). The stability of personality traits in individuals with borderline personality disorder. *Journal of Abnormal Psychology, 118,* 806–815.

Horesh, D., Solomon, Z. Z., Zerach, G. G., & Ein-Dor, T. T. (2011). Delayed-onset PTSD among war veterans: The role of life events throughout the life cycle. *Social Psychiatry and Psychiatric Epidemiology, 46,* 863–870.

Hori, H., Teraishi, T., Sasayama, D., Matsuo, J., Kawamoto, Y., Kinoshita, Y., & Kunugi, H. (2011). Relationships between season of birth, schizotypy, temperament, character and neurocognition in a non-clinical population. *Psychiatry Research, 189,* 388–397.

Horiguchi, H., Winawer, J., Dougherty, R. F., & Wandell, B. A. (2013). Human trichromacy revisted. *Proceedings of the National Academy of Sciences, 110,* 199–106.

Horn, J. L. (2002). Selections of evidence, misleading assumptions, and over-simplifications: The political message of *The Bell Curve.* In J. M. Fish (Ed.), *Race and intelligence: Separating science from myth* (pp. 297–325). Mahwah, NJ: Erlbaum.

Horney, K. (1937). *Neurotic personality of our times.* New York: Norton.

Horton, C. L. (2011). Recall and recognition of dreams and waking events: A diary paradigm. *International Journal of Dream Research, 4,* 8–16.

Houghtalen, R. P., & Talbot, N. (2007). Dissociative disorders and cognitive disorders. In O. J. Z. Sahler & J. E. Carr, *The behavioral sciences and health care* (2nd rev. and updated ed.). Ashland, OH: Hogrefe & Huber Publishers.

Hounkpatin, H. O., Wood, A. M., Boyce, C. J., & Dunn, G. (2015). An existential-humanistic view of personality change: Co-occurring changes with psychological well-being in a 10 year cohort study. *Social Indicators Research, 121,* 455–470.

Howard, A., Pion, G. M., Gottfredson, G. D., Flattau, P. E., Oskamp, S., Pfaffin, S. M., et al. (1986). The changing face of American psychology: A report from the Committee on Employment and Human Resources. *American Psychologist, 41*(12), 1311–1327.

Howe, C. J. (2002). The countering of overgeneralization. *Journal of Child Language, 29,* 875–895.

Howell, E. F. (2011). *Understanding and treating dissociative identity disorder: A relational approach.* New York: Routledge/Taylor & Francis Group.

Howes, O., & Kapur, S. (2009). The dopamine hypothesis of schizophrenia: Version III—The final common pathway. *Schizophrenia Bulletin, 35,* 549–562.

Hsu, S. (2016). Psychological disorders. In C. Tien-Lun Sun, C. Tien-Lun Sun (Eds.), *Psychology in Asia: An introduction.* Boston: Cengage Learning.

Hu, F. B., Li, T. Y., Colditz, G. A., Willett, W. C., & Manson, J. E. (2003). Television watching and other sedentary behaviors in relation to risk of obesity and type 2 diabetes mellitus in women. *Journal of the American Medical Association, 289,* 1785–1791.

Huang, C. (2010). Internet use and psychological well-being: A meta-analysis.

Cyberpsychology, Behavior, and Social Networking, 13, 241–249.

Huang, H., & Kashubeck-West, S. (2015). Exposure, agency, perceived threat, and guilt as predictors of posttraumatic stress disorder in veterans. *Journal of Counseling & Development, 93,* 3–13.

Hubbard, K., O'Neill, A., & Cheakalos, C. (1999, April 12). Out of control. *People,* pp. 52–72.

Hudson, J. I., Coit, C. E., Lalonde, J. K., & Pope, H. G. (2012). By how much will the proposed new DSM-5 criteria increase the prevalence of binge eating disorder? *International Journal of Eating Disorders, 45,* 139–141.

Hudson, W. (1960). Pictorial depth perception in subcultural groups in Africa. *Journal of Social Psychology, 52,* 183–208.

Huesmann, L., Dubow, E. F., & Boxer, P. (2011). The transmission of aggressiveness across generations: Biological, contextual, and social learning processes. In P. R. Shaver & M. Mikulincer (Eds.), *Human aggression and violence: Causes, manifestations, and consequences.* Washington, DC: American Psychological Association.

Hugenberg, K., & Sacco, D. (2008). Social categorization and stereotyping: How social categorization biases person perception and face memory. *Social and Personality Psychology Compass, 2,* 1052–1072.

Huijie, T. (2006). The measurement and assessment of mental health: A longitudinal and cross-sectional research on undergraduates, adults and patients. *Psychological Science (China), 29,* 419–422.

Hull, C. L. (1943). *Principles of behavior.* New York: Appleton-Century-Crofts.

Hummer, T. A., & McClintock, M. K. (2009). Putative human pheromone and rostadienone attunes the mind specifically to emotional information. *Hormones and Behavior, 55,* 548–559.

Humphrey, N., Curran, A., & Morris, E. (2007). Emotional intelligence and education: A critical review. *Educational Psychology, 27,* 235–254.

Hunt, E. (2005). Information processing and intelligence: Where we are and where we are going. In R. J. Sternberg & J. E. Pretz, *Cognition and intelligence: Identifying the mechanisms of the mind.* New York: Cambridge University Press.

Hunt, M. (1974). *Sexual behaviors in the 1970s.* New York: Dell.

Hunter, C. (2011). *Mastering the power of self-hypnosis: A practical guide to self-empowerment* (2nd ed.). Norwalk, CT: Crown House Publishing Limited.

Hunter, J. A. (2010). Prolonged exposure treatment of chronic PTSD in juvenile sex offenders: Promising results from two case studies. *Child & Youth Care Forum, 39,* 367–384.

Huprich, S. K., & Nelson, S. M. (2015). Advancing the assessment of personality pathology with the Cognitive-Affective

Processing System. *Journal of Personality Assessment, 97,* 467–477.

Hurley, D. B., & Kwon, P. (2013). Savoring helps most when you have little: Interaction between savoring the moment and uplifts on positive affect and satisfaction with life. *Journal of Happiness Studies, 14,* 1261–1271.

Husain, O. (2015). From persecution to depression: A case of chronic depression—Associating the Rorschach, the TAT, and Winnicott. *Journal of Personality Assessment, 97,* 230–240.

Huston, J. P., Silva, M., Komorowski, M., Schulz, D., & Topic, B. (2013). Animal models of extinction-induced depression: Loss of reward and its consequences. *Neuroscience and Biobehavioral Reviews.* Retrieved from http://www.ncbi.nlm.nih.gov/pubmed/23466533

Hutchinson, S. L., Baldwin, C. K., & Oh, S-S. (2006). Adolescent coping: Exploring adolescents' leisure-based responses to stress. *Leisure Sciences, 28,* 115–131.

Hyde, J., Mezulis, A. H., & Abramson, L. Y. (2008). The ABCs of depression: Integrating affective, biological, and cognitive models to explain the emergence of the gender difference in depression. *Psychological Review, 115,* 291–313.

Iaria, G., Fox, C., Scheel, M., Stowe, R., & Barton, J. (2010). A case of persistent visual hallucinations of faces following LSD abuse: A functional magnetic resonance imaging study. *Neurocase, 16,* 106–118.

Iaria, G., Palermo, L., Committeri, G., & Barton, J. (2009). Age differences in the formation and use of cognitive maps. *Behavioural Brain Research, 196,* 187–191.

If you don't have a penny handy, the correct answer is "A."

Igo, S. E. (2006). Review of a telescope on society: Survey research and social science at the University of Michigan and beyond. *Journal of the History of the Behavioral Sciences, 42,* 95–96.

Imtiaz, A., Maqsood, A., Rehman, A. U., Morell, R. J., Holt, J. R., Friedman, T. B., & Naz, S. (2016). Recessive mutations of tmc1 associated with moderate to severe hearing loss. *Neurogenetics.* Retrieved from http://link.springer.com/article/10.1007%2Fs10048-016-0477-1

Innocenti, G. M. (2007). Subcortical regulation of cortical development: Some effects of early, selective deprivations. *Progressive Brain Research, 164,* 23–37.

Internetwriter62. (2011, November 26). Remembering it all, living with hyperthymestic syndrome. Retrieved from http://internetwriter62.hubpages.com/hub/Remembering-It-All-Living-with-Hyperthymestic-Syndrome

Irwin, R. R. (2006). Spiritual development in adulthood: Key concepts and models. In C. Hoare (Ed.), *Handbook of adult development and learning.* New York: Oxford University Press.

Isacson, O., & Kordower, J. (2008). Future of cell and gene therapies for Parkinson's disease. *Annals of Neurology, 64,* S122–SS138.

Isay, R. A. (1994). *Being homosexual: Gay men and their development.* Lanham, MD: Jason Aronson.

Isbell, L. M., & Tyler, J. M. (2003). Teaching students about in-group favoritism and the minimal groups paradigm. *Teaching of Psychology, 30,* 127–130.

Ishikawa, S., Okajima, I., Matsuoka, H., & Sakano, Y. (2007). Cognitive behavioural therapy for anxiety disorders in children and adolescents: A meta-analysis. *Child and Adolescent Mental Health, 12*(4), 164–172.

Iversen, L. L. (2000). *The science of marijuana.* Oxford, England: Oxford University Press.

Iverson, S. D, & Iversen, L. L. (2007). Dopamine: 50 years in perspective. *Trends in Neurosciences, 30,* 188–191.

Ivtzan, I., Gardner, H. E., Bernard, I., Sekhon, M., & Hart, R. (2013). Well-being through self-fulfilment: Examining developmental aspects of self-actualization. *The Humanistic Psychologist, 41,* 119–132.

Izard, C. E. (1990). Facial expressions and the regulation of emotions. *Journal of Personality and Social Psychology, 58,* 487–498.

Izard, C. E. (1994). Innate and universal facial expressions: Evidence from developmental and cross-cultural research. *Psychological Bulletin, 115,* 288–299.

Jackson, J. D. (2006). Trauma, attachment, and coping: Pathways to resilience. *Dissertation Abstracts International: Section B: The Sciences and Engineering, 67*(1-B), 547.

Jackson, L. M. (2011). *The psychology of prejudice: From attitudes to social action.* Washington, DC: American Psychological Association.

Jackson, M. L., Gunzelmann, G., Whitney, P., Hinson, J. M., Belenky, G., Rabat, A., & Van Dongen, H. A. (2013). Deconstructing and reconstructing cognitive performance in sleep deprivation. *Sleep Medicine Reviews, 17,* 215–225.

Jacob, K.S. (2014). DSM-5 and culture: The need to move towards a shared model of care within a more equal patient-physican partnership. *Asian Journal of Psychiatry, 7,* 89–91.

Jacobs, J. A., & Gerson, K. (2004). *The time divide: Work, family, and gender inequality.* Cambridge, MA: Harvard University Press.

Jacobs, M., Roesch, S., Wonderlich, S., Crosby, R., Thornton, L., Wilfley, D., et al. (2009). Anorexia nervosa trios: Behavioral profiles of individuals with anorexia nervosa and their parents. *Psychological Medicine, 39,* 451–461.

Jacoby, L. L., Bishara, A. J., & Hessels, S. (2007). Probabilistic retroactive interference: The role of accessibility bias in interference effects. *Journal of Experimental Psychology: General, 136,* 200–216.

Jain, S., Mills, P. J., & Von Känel, R. (2007). Effects of perceived stress and uplifts on inflammation and coagulability. *Psychophysiology, 44,* 154–160.

James, R. C. (1966). Photo of dog. In J. Thurston & R. G. Carraher (Eds.), *Optical illusions and the visual arts.* New York: Von Nostrand Reinhold.

James, W. (1890). *The principles of psychology.* New York: Holt.

Jamieson, G. A. (2007). *Hypnosis and conscious states: The cognitive neuroscience perspective.* New York: Oxford University Press.

Jamison, K. R. (1995). *An unquiet mind: A memoir of moods and madness.* New York: Knopf.

Jang, H., Reeve, J., Ryan, R. M., & Kim, A. (2009, August). Can self-determination theory explain what underlies the productive, satisfying learning experiences of collectivistically oriented Korean students? *Journal of Educational Psychology, 101,* 644–661.

Jarlais, D. C. D., Arasteh, K., & Perlis, T. (2007). The transition from injection to non-injection drug use: Long-term outcomes among heroin and cocaine users in New York City. *Addiction, 102,* 778–785.

Jarrett, S. (2015). The meaning of 'community' in the lives of people with intellectual disabilities: An historical perspective. *International Journal of Developmental Disabilities, 61,* 107–112.

Jarrold, C., & Tam, H. (2011). Rehearsal and the development of working memory. In P. Barrouillet & V. Gaillard (Eds.), *Cognitive development and working memory: A dialogue between neo-Piagetian theories and cognitive approaches.* New York: Psychology Press.

Jefferson, D. J. (2005, August 8). American's most dangerous drug. *Newsweek,* pp. 41–47.

Jeffery, A. J. (2015). Two behavioral hypotheses for the evolution of male homosexuality in humans. In T. K. Shackelford & R. D. Hansen (Eds.), *The evolution of sexuality.* Cham, Switzerland: Springer International Publishing.

Jeffrey, S. A., & Adomdza, G. K. (2011). Incentive salience and improved performance. *Human Performance, 24,* 47–59.

Jenkins, S. R. (1994). Need for power and women's careers over 14 years: Structural power, job satisfaction, and motive change. *Journal of Personality and Social Psychology, 66,* 155–165.

Jennings, D. J., Alonso, E., Mondragón, E., Franssen, M., & Bonardi, C. (2013). The effect of stimulus distribution form on the acquisition and rate of conditioned responding: Implications for theory. *Journal of Experimental Psychology: Animal Behavior Processes, 39,* 233–248.

Jensen, M. P., & Patterson, D. R. (2014). Hypnotic approaches for chronic pain management: Clinical implications of recent research findings. *American Psychologist, 69,* 167–177.

Jensen, M. P., & Turk, D. C. (2014). Contributions of psychology to the understanding and treatment of people with chronic pain: Why it matters to ALL psychologists. *American Psychologist, 69,* 105–118.

Jequier, E. (2002). Pathways to obesity. *International Journal of Obesity and Related Metabolic Disorders, 26,* S12–S17.

Jetten, J., Hornsey, M. J., & Adarves-Yorno, I. (2006). When group members admit to being conformist: The role of relative intragroup status in conformity self-reports. *Personality and Social Psychology Bulletin, 32,* 162–173.

Jia, C., & Hegg, C. C. (2015). Effect of IP3R3 and NPY on age-related declines in olfactory stem cell proliferation. *Neurobiology of Aging, 36,* 1045–1056.

Jimmieson, N. L., McKimmie, B. M., Hannam, R. L., & Gallagher, J. (2010). An investigation of the stress-buffering effects of social support in the occupational stress process as a function of team identification. *Group Dynamics: Theory, Research, and Practice, 14,* 350–367.

Joe, G. W., Flynn, P. M., & Broome, K. M. (2007). Patterns of drug use and expectations in methadone patients. *Addictive Behaviors, 32,* 1640–1656.

Johnson, G. B. (2000). *The living world* (p. 600). Boston: McGraw-Hill.

Johnson, H. D. (2004). Gender, grade and relationship differences in emotional closeness within adolescent friendships. *Adolescence, 39,* 243–255.

Johnson, J. G., Cohen, P., Smailes, E. M., Kasen, S., & Brook, J. S. (2002, March 29). Television viewing and aggressive behavior during adolescence and adulthood. *Science, 295,* 2468–2471.

Johnson, R., Stewart, C., & Bachman, C. (2015). What drives students to complete online courses? What drives faculty to teach online? Validating a measure of motivation orientation in university students and faculty. *Interactive Learning Environments, 23,* 528–543.

John-Steiner, V., & Mahn, H. (2003). Sociocultural contexts for teaching and learning. In W. M. Reynolds & G. E. Miller (Eds.), *Handbook of psychology: Educational psychology* (Vol. 7, pp. 125–151). New York: Wiley.

Johnston, E., & Olson, L. (2015). *The feeling brain: The biology and psychology of emotions.* New York: W. W. Norton & Co.

Johnston, L. D., O'Malley, P. M., Bachman, J. G., & Schulenberg, J. E. (2014). *Monitoring the Future Study.* Ann

Arbor, MI: University of Michigan News Service. Retrieved from http://www.monitoringthefuture.org

Jones, A. L. (2006). The contemporary psychoanalyst: Karen Horney's theory applied in today's culture. *PsycCRITIQUES, 51,* 127–134.

Jones, D. (2010). A WEIRD view of human nature skews psychologists' studies. *Science, 328,* 1627.

Jones, K., Callen, F., Blagrove, M., & Parrott, A. (2008). Sleep, energy and self rated cognition across 7 nights following recreational ecstasy/MDMA use. *Sleep and Hypnosis, 10,* 2–38.

Jordan, G., Deeb, S., Bosten, J., & Mollon, J. (2010). The dimensionality of color vision in carriers of anomalous trichromacy. *Journal of Vision, 10,* 37–60.

Joshanloo, M., & Afshari, S. (2011). Big Five personality traits and self-esteem as predictors of life satisfaction in Iranian Muslim university students. *Journal of Happiness Studies, 12,* 105–113.

Jovanović, D., Stanojević, P., & Stanojević, D. (2011). Motives for, and attitudes about, driving-related anger and aggressive driving. *Social Behavior and Personality, 39,* 755–764.

Joyce, J. (1934). *Ulysses.* New York: Random House.

Julien, R. M (2001). *A primer of drug action* (9th ed.). New York: Freeman.

Jung, C. G. (1961). *Freud and psychoanalysis.* New York: Pantheon.

Jung, J. (2002). *Psychology of alcohol and other drugs: A research perspective.* Thousand Oaks, CA: Sage.

Kalarchian, M. A., Levine, M. D., Klem, M. L., Burke, L. E., Soulakova, J. N., & Marcus, M. D. (2011). Impact of addressing reasons for weight loss on behavioral weight-control outcome. *American Journal of Preventive Medicine, 40,* 18–24.

Kalb, C. (2003, May 19). Taking a new look at pain. *Newsweek,* pp. 51–52.

Kaller, C. P., Unterrainer, J. M., Rahm, B., & Halsband, U. (2004). The impact of problem structure on planning: Insights from the Tower of London task. *Cognitive Brain Research, 20,* 462–472.

Kalodner, C. R. (2011). Cognitive-behavioral theories. In D. Capuzzi & D. R. Gross (Eds.), *Counseling and psychotherapy* (5th ed.). Alexandria, VA: American Counseling Association.

Kamimori, G. H., McLellan, T. M., Tate, C. M., Voss, D. M., Niro, P., & Lieberman, H. R. (2015). Caffeine improves reaction time, vigilance and logical reasoning during extended periods with restricted opportunities for sleep. *Psychopharmacology, 232,* 2031–2042.

Kandell, E. R., Schwartz, J. H., & Jessell, T. M. (Eds.). (2000). *Principles of neural science* (4th ed.). New York: McGraw-Hill.

Kanner, A. D., Coyne, J. C., Schaefer, C., & Lazarus, R. (1981). Comparison of two modes of stress measurement: Daily hassles and uplifts versus major life events. *Journal of Behavioral Medicine, 4,* 14.

Kaplan, J. R., & Manuck, S. B. (1989). The effect of propranolol on behavioral interactions among adult male cynomolgus monkeys (Macaca fascicularis) housed in disrupted social groupings. *Psychosomatic Medicine, 51,* 449–462.

Kaplan, M. S., Huguer, N., McFarland, B. H., & Newsom, J. T. (2007). Suicide among male veterans: A prospective population-based study. *Journal of Epidemiological Community Health, 61,* 619–624.

Kappas, A. (2011). Emotion and regulation are one! *Emotion Review, 3,* 17–25.

Kara, P., & Boyd, J. (2009, April). A micro-architecture for binocular disparity and ocular dominance in visual cortex. *Nature, 458*(7238), 627–631.

Karatsoreos, I. N., Bhagat, S., Bloss, E. B., Morrison, J. H., & McEwen, B. S. (2011). Disruption of circadian clocks has ramifications for metabolism, brain, and behavior. *PNAS Proceedings of the National Academy of Sciences of the United States of America, 108,* 1657–1662.

Karlson, C. W., Gallagher, M. W., Olson, C. A., & Hamilton, N. A. (2013). Insomnia symptoms and well-being: Longitudinal follow-up. *Health Psychology, 32,* 311–319.

Kashima, Y. (2016). Culture and psychology in the 21st century: Conceptions of culture and person for psychology revisited. *Journal of Cross-Cultural Psychology, 47,* 4–20.

Katerberg, H., Delucchi, K., Stewart, S., Lochner, C., Denys, D., Stack, D., et al. (2010). Symptom dimensions in OCD: Item-level factor analysis and heritability estimates. *Behavior Genetics, 40,* 505–517.

Kato, N. (2009). Neurophysiological mechanisms of electroconvulsive therapy for depression. *Neuroscience Research, 64,* 3–11.

Kato, T. (2007). Molecular genetics of bipolar disorder and depression. *Psychiatry and Clinical Neurosciences, 61,* 3–19.

Kaufman, A., Johnson, C., & Liu, X. (2008). A CHC theory-based analysis of age differences on cognitive abilities and academic skills at ages 22 to 90 years. *Journal of Psychoeducational Assessment, 26,* 350–381.

Kaufman, J. C., Kaufman, S., & Plucker, J. A. (2013). Contemporary theories of intelligence. In D. Reisberg (Ed.), *The Oxford handbook of cognitive psychology.* New York: Oxford University Press.

Kazantseva, A., Gaysina, D., Kutlumbetova, Y., Kanzafarova, R., Malykh, S., Lobaskova, M., & Khusnutdinova, E. (2015). Brain derived neurotrophic factor gene (BDNF) and personality traits: The modifying effect of season of birth and sex. *Progress in Neuro-Psychopharmacology & Biological Psychiatry, 56,* 58–65.

Kazdin, A. (2008). Evidence-based treatment and practice: New opportunities to bridge clinical research and practice, enhance the knowledge base, and improve patient care. *American Psychologist, 63,* 146–159.

Keating, D. P., & Clark, L. V. (1980). Development of physical and social reasoning in adolescence. *Developmental Psychology, 16,* 23–30.

Keer, M., van den Putte, B., Neijens, P., & de Wit, J. (2013). The influence of affective and cognitive arguments on message judgement and attitude change: The moderating effects of meta-bases and structural bases. *Psychology & Health, 28,* 895–908.

Keillor, J. M., Barrett, A. M., Crucian, G. P., Kortenkamp, S., & Heilman, K. M. (2002). Emotional experience and perception in the absence of facial feedback. *Journal of the International Neuropsychological Society, 8,* 130–135.

Keller, H., Borke, J., Chaudhary, N., Lamm, B., & Kleis, A. (2010). Continuity in parenting strategies: A cross-cultural comparison. *Journal of Cross-Cultural Psychology, 41,* 391–409.

Keller, W. R., Fischer, B. A., & Carpenter, W. R. (2011). Revisiting the diagnosis of schizophrenia: Where have we been and where are we going? *CNS Neuroscience & Therapeutics, 17,* 83–88.

Kelley, H. (1950). The warm-cold variable in first impressions of persons. *Journal of Personality and Social Psychology, 18,* 431–439.

Kelly, D., & Tangney, B. (2006). Adapting to intelligence profile in an adaptive educational system. *Interacting with Computers, 18*(3), 385–409.

Kempermann, G. (2011). Seven principles in the regulation of adult neurogenesis. *European Journal of Neuroscience, 33,* 1018–1024.

Kendall-Tackett, K. (2010). *The psychoneuroimmunology of chronic disease: Exploring the links between inflammation, stress, and illness.* Washington, DC: American Psychological Association.

Kendler, K. S., Gatz, M., & Gardner, C. O. (2006). Personality and major depression. *Archives of General Psychiatry, 63,* 1113–1120.

Kendler, K., Halberstadt, L., Butera, F., Myers, J., Bouchard, T., & Ekman, P. (2008). The similarity of facial expressions in response to emotion-inducing films in reared-apart twins. *Psychological Medicine, 38*(10), 1475–1483.

Kennedy, C. E., Moore, P. J., Peterson, R. A., Katzman, M. A., Vermani, M., & Charmak, W. D. (2011). What makes people anxious about pain? How personality and perception combine to determine pain anxiety responses in clinical and non-clinical populations.

Anxiety, Stress & Coping: An International Journal, 24, 179–200.

Kennedy, D. O., & Haskell, C. F. (2011). Cerebral blood flow and behavioural effects of caffeine in habitual and non-habitual consumers of caffeine: A near infrared spectroscopy study. *Biological Psychology, 86,* 296–305.

Kennison, S. M., & Bowers, J. (2011). Illustrating brain lateralisation in a naturalistic observation of cell-phone use. *Psychology Learning & Teaching, 10,* 46–51.

Kenshalo, D. R. (1968). *The skin senses.* Charles C. Thomas Publisher.

Kern, M., & Friedman, H. (2010). Why do some people thrive while others succumb to disease and stagnation? Personality, social relations, and resilience. *New frontiers in resilient aging: Life-strengths and well-being in late life.* New York: Cambridge University Press.

Kertz, S. J., Koran, J., Stevens, K. T., & Björgvinsson, T. (2015). Repetitive negative thinking predicts depression and anxiety symptom improvement during brief cognitive behavioral therapy. *Behaviour Research and Therapy, 68,* 54–63.

Kessler, R. C., & Wang, P. S. (2008). The descriptive epidemiology of commonly occurring mental disorders in the United States. *Annual Review of Public Health, 29,* 115–129.

Ketisch, T., & Jones, R. A. (2013). Review of 'ADHD diagnosis & management'. *American Journal of Family Therapy, 41,* 272–274.

Khalil, E. L. (2011). The mirror neuron paradox: How far is understanding from mimicking? *Journal of Economic Behavior & Organization, 77,* 86–96.

Kidd, E., & Lum, J. (2008). Sex differences in past tense overregularization. *Developmental Science, 11,* 882–889.

Kiecolt, J. K. (2003). Satisfaction with work and family life: No evidence of a cultural reversal. *Journal of Marriage and Family, 65,* 23–35.

Kihlstrom, J. F. (2005a). Dissociative disorders. *Annual Review of Clinical Psychology, 1,* 227–253.

Kihlstrom, J. F. (2005b). Is hypnosis an altered state of consciousness or what? Comment. *Contemporary Hypnosis, 22,* 34–38.

Killam, A. (2015, August 18). Kasson woman loses nearly half her body weight, becomes inspiration for thousands. *KTTC* Retrieved from http://www.kttc.com/story/29808617/2015/08/18/kasson-woman-loses-nearly-half-her-body-weight-becomes-inspiration-for-thousands

Kim, D. R., Pesiridou, A., & O'Reardon, J. P. (2009). Transcranial magnetic stimulation in the treatment of psychiatric disorders. *Current Psychiatry Reports, 11,* 447–452.

Kim, J., & Grunig, J. E. (2011). Problem solving and communicative action: A situational theory of problem solving. *Journal of Communication, 61,* 120–149.

Kim, N. (2008). The moon illusion and the size-distance paradox. In Cummins-Sebree, S., Riley, M. A., & Shockley, K. (Eds). *Studies in perception and action IX: Fourteenth International Conference on Perception and Action.* Mahwah, NJ: Lawrence Erlbaum Associates.

Kim, S-E., Kim, J-W., & Kim, J-J. (2007). The neural mechanism of imagining facial affective expression. *Brain Research, 1145,* 128–137.

King-Casas, B., Sharp, C., Lomax-Bream, L., Lohrenz, T., Fonagy, P., & Montague, P. R. (2008, August, 8). The rupture and repair of cooperation in borderline personality disorder. *Science, 321,* 806–810.

Kingstone, A. (2010). Mike's attentional network. *The cognitive neuroscience of mind: A tribute to Michael S. Gazzaniga.* Cambridge, MA: MIT Press.

Kirk, E. P., Jacobsen, D. J., Gibson, C., Hill, J. O., & Donnelly, J. E. (2003). Time course for changes in aerobic capacity and body composition in overweight men and women in response to long-term exercise: The Midwest exercise trial (MET). *International Journal of Obesity, 27,* 912–919.

Kirschenbaum, H. (2004). Carl Rogers's life and work: An assessment on the 100th anniversary of his birth. *Journal of Counseling and Development, 82,* 116–124.

Kirschenbaum, H., & Jourdan, A. (2005). The current status of Carl Rogers and the person-centered approach. *Psychotherapy: Theory, Research, Practice, Training, 42,* 37–51.

Kish, S., Fitzmaurice, P., Boileau, I., Schmunk, G., Ang, L., Furukawa, Y., et al. (2009). Brain serotonin transporter in human methamphetamine users. *Psychopharmacology, 202,* 649–661.

Kivlighan, D. M., Goldberg, S. B., Abbas, M., Pace, B. T., Yulish, N. E., Thomas, J. G., & . . . Wampold, B. E. (2015). The enduring effects of psychodynamic treatments vis-à-vis alternative treatments: A multilevel longitudinal meta-analysis. *Clinical Psychology Review, 40,* 1–14.

Kleinman, A. (1996). How is culture important for DSM-IV? In J. E Mezzich, A. Kleinman, H. Fabrega, Jr., & D. L. Parron (Eds.), *Culture and psychiatric diagnosis: A DSM-IV perspective.* Washington, DC: American Psychiatric Press.

Kluck, A. (2008). Family factors in the development of disordered eating: Integrating dynamic and behavioral explanations. *Eating Behaviors, 9,* 471–483.

Kluger, J. (2001, April 2). Fear not! *Time,* pp. 51–62.

Kluger, J. (2013, July 29). The power of the bilingual brain. *Time,* 42–47.

Klump, K., & Culbert, K. (2007). Molecular genetic studies of eating disorders: Current status and future directions. *Current Directions in Psychological Science, 16,* 37–41.

Knoblich, G., & Sebanz, N. (2006). The social nature of perception and action. *Current Directions in Psychological Science, 15,* 99–111.

Koçak, O., Özpolat, A., Atbaşoğlu, C., & Çiçek, M. (2011). Cognitive control of a simple mental image in patients with obsessive–compulsive disorder. *Brain and Cognition, 76,* 390–399.

Kogstad, R. E., Ekeland, T. J., & Hummelvoll, J. K. (2011). In defence of a humanistic approach to mental health care: Recovery processes investigated with the help of clients' narratives on turning points and processes of gradual change. *Journal of Psychiatric and Mental Health Nursing, 18,* 479–486.

Kohlberg, L. (1984). *The psychology of moral development: Essays on moral development* (Vol. 2). San Francisco: Harper & Row.

Kohlberg, L., & Ryncarz, R. A. (1990). Beyond justice reasoning: Moral development and consideration of a seventh stage. In C. N. Alexander & E. J. Langer (Eds.), *Higher stages of human development: Perspectives on adult growth.* New York: Oxford University Press.

Komarovskaya, I., Loper, A., Warren, J., & Jackson, S. (2011). Exploring gender differences in trauma exposure and the emergence of symptoms of PTSD among incarcerated men and women. *Journal of Forensic Psychiatry & Psychology, 22,* 395–410.

Kong, D., Soon, C., & Chee, M. L. (2011). Reduced visual processing capacity in sleep deprived persons. *NeuroImage, 55,* 629–634.

Kong, L., Herold, C. J., Zöllner, F., Salat, D. H., Lässer, M. M., Schmid, L. A., Fellhauer, I., Thomann, P.A., Essig, M., Schad, L. R., Erickson, K. I., & Schröder, J. (2015). Comparison of grey matter volume and thickness for analysing cortical changes in chronic schizophrenia: A matter of surface area, grey/white matter intensity contrast, and curvature. *Psychiatry Research: Neuroimaging, 231*(2), 176–183.

Kookoolis, A., Pace-Schott, E., & McNamara, P. (2010). Dream content and memory processing: Dream lag effects within a single night and across several nights: A pilot study. *Dreaming, 20,* 211–217.

Koplewicz, H. (2002). *More than moody: Recognizing and treating adolescent depression.* New York: Putnam.

Kosinski, M., Matz, S. C., Gosling, S. D., Popov, V., & Stillwell, D. (2015). Facebook as a research tool for the social sciences. *American Psychologist, 70,* 543–556.

Kouimtsidis, C., & Drummond, C. (2010). Cognitive behaviour therapy for opiate misusers in methadone maintenance treatment. *Responding to drug misuse: Research and policy priorities in health and social care*. New York: Routledge/Taylor & Francis Group.

Kovacs, A. M., & Mehler, J. (2009, July 31). Flexible learning of multiple speech structures in bilingual infants. *Science, 325,* 611–612.

Kowalik, J., Weller, J., Venter, J., & Drachman, D. (2011). Cognitive behavioral therapy for the treatment of pediatric posttraumatic stress disorder: A review and meta-analysis. *Journal of Behavior Therapy and Experimental Psychiatry, 42,* 405–413.

Kozulin, A., Gindis, B., Ageyev, V. S., & Miller, S. M. (2003). *Vygotsky's educational theory in cultural context*. New York: Cambridge University Press.

Kremen, W. S., & Lyons, M. J. (2011). Behavioral genetics of aging. In K. Schaie & S. L. Willis (Eds.), *Handbook of the psychology of aging* (7th ed.). San Diego, CA: Elsevier Academic Press.

Kreppner, J., Rutter, M., Marvin, R., O'Connor, T., & Sonuga-Barke, E. (2011). Assessing the concept of the 'insecure-other' category in the Cassidy–Marvin scheme: Changes between 4 and 6 years in the English and Romanian adoptee study. *Social Development, 20,* 1–16.

Krishman, S., Cairns, R., & Howard, R. (2009). Cannabinoids for the treatment of dementia. *Cochrane Database of Systematic Reviews*. Retrieved from http://www.ncbi.nlm.nih.gov/pubmed/19370677

Krueger, K., & Dayan, P. (2009). Flexible shaping: How learning in small steps helps. *Cognition, 110,* 380–394.

Krueger, R. G., Hicks, B. M., & McGue, M. (2001). Altruism and antisocial behavior: Independent tendencies, unique personality correlates, distinct etiologies. *Psychological Science, 12,* 397–402.

Krusemark, E., Campbell, W., & Clementz, B. (2008). Attributions, deception, and event related potentials: An investigation of the self-serving bias. *Psychophysiology, 45,* 511–515.

Kübler-Ross, E., & Kessler, D. (2005). *On grief and grieving*. Simon & Schuster.

Kubanek, J., Snyder, L. H., & Abrams, R. A. (2015). Reward and punishment act as distinct factors in guiding behavior. *Cognition, 139,* 154–167.

Kulik, L., & Sadeh, I. (2015). Explaining fathers' involvement in childcare: An ecological approach. *Community, Work & Family, 18,* 19–40.

Kumkale, G., Albarracín, D., & Seignourel, P. J. (2010). The effects of source credibility in the presence or absence of prior attitudes: Implications for the design of persuasive communication campaigns. *Journal of Applied Social Psychology, 40,* 1325–1356.

Kuo, L.-J. (2007). Effects of bilingualism on development of facets of phonological competence (China). *Dissertation Abstracts International Section A: Humanities and Social Sciences, 67*(11-A), 4095.

Kurdziel, L., Duclos, K., & Spencer, R. M. C. (2013). Sleep spindles in midday naps enhance learning in preschool children. *PNAS Early Edition,* 1–6.

Kuriyama, K., Stickgold, R., & Walker, M. P. (2004). Sleep-dependent learning and motor-skill complexity. *Learning and Memory, 11,* 705–713.

Kwon, P. (2013). Resilience in lesbian, gay, and bisexual individuals. *Personality and Social Psychology Review, 17,* 371–383.

Kwon, P., & Laurenceau, J. P. (2002). A longitudinal study of the hopelessness theory of depression: Testing the diathesis-stress model within a differential reactivity and exposure framework [Special issue: Reprioritizing the role of science in a realistic version of the scientist-practitioner model]. *Journal of Clinical Psychology, 50,* 1305–1321.

Kyriacou, C., & Hastings, M. (2010). Circadian clocks: Genes, sleep, and cognition. *Trends in Cognitive Sciences, 14,* 259–267.

Laas, I. (2006). Self-actualization and society: A new application for an old theory. *Journal of Humanistic Psychology, 46,* 77–91.

Labrecque, N., & Cermakian, N. (2015). Circadian clocks in the immune system. *Journal of Biological Rhythms, 30,* 277–290.

Laederach-Hofmann, K., & Messerli-Buergy, N. (2007). Chest pain, angina pectoris, panic disorder, and Syndrome X. In J. Jordan, B. Barde, & A. M. Zeiher (Eds.), *Contributions toward evidence-based psychocardiology: A systematic review of the literature*. Washington, DC: American Psychological Association.

Lagro-Janssen, A., Knufing, M., Schreurs, L., & van Weel, C. (2010). Significant fall in hormone replacement therapy prescription in general practice. *Family Practice, 27,* 424–429.

Lai, Y., Chen, S., & Chien, N. (2007). Video-assisted thoracoscopic neurectomy of intercostal nerves in a patient with intractable cancer pain. *American Journal of Hospice & Palliative Medicine, 23*(6), 475–478.

Lakhan, S., & Vieira, K. (2009, May 15). Schizophrenia pathophysiology: Are we any closer to a complete model? *Annals of General Psychiatry, 8.*

Lal, S. (2002). Giving children security: Mamie Phipps Clark and the racialization of child psychology. *American Psychologist, 57,* 20–28.

LaLumiere, R. (2010). A new technique for controlling the brain: Optogenetics and its potential for use in research and the clinic. *Brain Stimulation, 8,* 45–51.

Lamal, P. A. (1979). College students' common beliefs about psychology. *Teaching of Psychology, 6,* 155–158.

Lamborn, S. D., & Groh, K. (2009). A four-part model of autonomy during emerging adulthood: Associations with adjustment. *International Journal of Behavioral Development, 33,* 393–401.

Lancy, D. F. (2015). *The anthropology of childhood: Cherubs, chattel, changelings* (2nd ed.). New York, NY, US: Cambridge University Press.

Landau, M. J., Meier, B. P., & Keefer, L. A. (2010). A metaphor-enriched social cognition. *Psychological Bulletin, 136,* 1045–1067.

Landry, S. H., Zucker, T. A., Taylor, H. B., Swank, P. R., Williams, J. M., Assel, M., & . . . Klein, A. (2013). Enhancing Early Child Care Quality and Learning for Toddlers at Risk: The Responsive Early Childhood Program. *Developmental Psychology*. Retrieved from http://www.ncbi.nlm.nih.gov/pubmed/23772822

Lane, K. A., Banaji, M. R., Nosek, B. A., & Greenwald, A. G. (Eds.). (2007). Understanding and using the implicit association test: iv: What we know (so far) about the method. In B. Wittenbrink, & N. Schwarz, *Implicit measures of attitudes*. New York: Guilford Press.

Lang, P. J., & Bradley, M. M. (2013). Appetitive and defensive motivation: Goal-directed or goal-determined? *Emotion Review, 5,* 230–234.

Langan-Fox, J., & Grant, S. (2006). The Thematic Apperception Test: Toward a standard measure of the big three motives. *Journal of Personality Assessment, 87,* 277–291.

Lankov, A. (2004). The dawn of modern Korea: Changes for better or worse. *The Korea Times,* p. A1.

Lantz, P., Golberstein, E., House, J., & Morenoff, J. (2010). Socioeconomic and behavioral risk factors for mortality in a national 19-year prospective study of U.S. adults. *Social Science & Medicine, 70,* 1558–1566.

LaPointe, L. L. (2013). *Paul Broca and the origins of language in the brain*. San Diego, CA: Plural Publishing.

Larsen, R. J., & Buss, D. M. (2006). *Personality psychology: Domains of knowledge about human nature with PowerWeb* (2nd ed.). New York: McGraw-Hill.

Lasalvia, A. (2015). DSM-5 two years later: Facts, myths and some key open issues. *Epidemiology and Psychiatric Sciences, 24,* 185–187.

Latané, B., & Darley, J. M. (1970). *The unresponsive bystander: Why doesn't he help?* New York: Appleton-Century-Crofts.

Lauriello, J., & Rahman, T. (2015). Schizophrenia spectrum and other psychotic disorders. In L. W. Roberts & A. K. Louie (Eds.), *Study Guide to DSM-5®*.

Arlington, VA: American Psychiatric Publishing, Inc.

Lavigne, K. M., Rapin, L. A., Metzak, P. D., Whitman, J. C., Jung, K., Dohen, M., & . . . Woodward, T. S. (2015). Left-dominant temporal-frontal hypercoupling in schizophrenia patients with hallucinations during speech perception. *Schizophrenia Bulletin, 41,* 259–267.

Lazzer, S., Bedogni, G., Lafortuna, C., Marazzi, N., Busti, C., Galli, R., et al. (2010). Relationship between basal metabolic rate, gender, age, and body composition in 8,780 white obese subjects. *Obesity, 18,* 71–78.

León-Carrión, J., & Chacartegui-Ramos, F. (2010). Brain injuries and violent crime. *Violent crime: Clinical and social implications.* Thousand Oaks, CA: Sage Publications.

Leahy, R. L. (2015). Emotional schema therapy. In N. C. Thoma & D. McKay (Eds.), *Working with emotion in cognitive-behavioral therapy: Techniques for clinical practice.* New York: Guilford Press.

Lebow, J., & Slesinge, N. (2016). Family therapy with families in intractable conflicts about child custody and visitation. In M. L. Goldstein (Ed.), *Handbook of child custody.* Cham, Switzerland: Springer International Publishing.

Leclair-Visonneau, L., Oudiette, D., Gaymard, B., Leu-Semenescu, S., & Arnulf, I. (2010). Do the eyes scan dream images during rapid eye movement sleep? Evidence from the rapid eye movement sleep behaviour disorder model. *Brain: A Journal of Neurology, 133,* 1737–1746.

Lee, D., Kleinman, J., & Kleinman, A. (2007). Rethinking depression: An ethnographic study of the experiences of depression among Chinese. *Harvard Review of Psychiatry, 15,* 1–8.

Lee, F. H., & Raja, S. N. (2011). Complementary and alternative medicine in chronic pain. *Pain, 152,* 28–30.

Lee, H. J., Kwon, S. M., Kwon, J. S., & Telch, M. J. (2005). Testing the autogenous-reactive model of obsessions. *Depression and Anxiety, 21,* 118–129.

Lee, J., McInerney, D., Liem, G., & Ortiga, Y. (2010). The relationship between future goals and achievement goal orientations: An intrinsic–extrinsic motivation perspective. *Contemporary Educational Psychology, 35,* 264–279.

Lee, M. J., Hust, S., Zhang, L., & Zhang, Y. (2011). Effects of violence against women in popular crime dramas on viewers' attitudes related to sexual violence. Mass *Communication & Society, 14,* 25–44.

Lee-Chai, A. Y., & Bargh, J. A. (Eds.). (2001). *The use and abuse of power: Multiple perspectives on the causes of corruption.* Philadelphia, PA: Psychology Press.

Lee-Chiong, T. Part VI: Parasomnias. (2006). In T. L. Lee-Chiong (Ed.), *Sleep: A comprehensive handbook.* New York: Wiley-Liss.

Lehrman, S. (2007). Going beyond X and Y. *Scientific American,* pp. 40–41.

Leising, D., Scharloth, J., Lohse, O., & Wood, D. (2014). What types of terms do people use when describing an individual's personality? *Psychological Science, 25,* 1787–1794.

Leitner, L. M. (2007). Diversity issues, postmodernism, and psychodynamic therapy. *PsycCRITIQUES, 52,* No pagination specified.

Lemay, E. P., Jr., Clark, M. S., & Feeney, B. C. (2007). Projection of responsiveness to needs and the construction of satisfying communal relationships. *Journal of Personality and Social Psychology, 92,* 834–853.

Lemay, E., & Clark, M. (2008). How the head liberates the heart: Projection of communal responsiveness guides relationship promotion. *Journal of Personality and Social Psychology, 94,* 647–671.

Lengua, L. J., & Long, A. C. (2002). The role of emotionality and self-regulation in the appraisal-coping process: Tests of direct and moderating effects. *Journal of Applied Developmental Psychology, 23,* 471–493.

Lenzenweger, M. F., & Dworkin, R. H. (Eds.). (1998). *The origins and development of schizophrenia: Advances in experimental psychopathology.* Washington, DC: American Psychological Association.

Leo, R. J., & Latif, T. (2007). Repetitive transcranial magnetic stimulation (rTMS) in experimentally induced and chronic neuropathic pain: A review. *The Journal of Pain, 8,* 453–459.

Lepper, M. R., Corpus, J. H., & Iyengar, S. S. (2005). Intrinsic and extrinsic motivational orientations in the classroom: Age differences and academic correlates. *Journal of Educational Psychology, 97,* 184–196.

Leskinen, E. A., Rabelo, V. C., & Cortina, L. M. (2015). Gender stereotyping and harassment: A "catch-22" for women in the workplace. *Psychology, Public Policy, And Law, 21,* 192–204.

Leu, J., Wang, J., & Koo, K. (2011). Are positive emotions just as "positive" across cultures? *Emotion,* Retrieved from www.ncbi.nlm.nih.gov/pubmed/21443338

LeVay, S. (2011). *Gay, straight, and the reason why: The science of sexual orientation.* New York: Oxford University Press.

Levi, A., Chan, K. K., & Pence, D. (2006). Real men do not read labels: The effects of masculinity and involvement on college students' food decisions. *Journal of American College Health, 55,* 91–98.

Levine, J. M., & Moreland, R. L. (2006). Small groups: An overview. In J. M. Levine & R. L. Moreland, *Small groups.* New York: Psychology Press.

Levine, M., & Cassidy, C. (2010). Groups, identities, and bystander behavior: How group processes can be used to promote helping. In S. Stürmer & M. Snyder (Eds.), *The psychology of prosocial behavior: Group processes, intergroup relations, and helping.* Wiley-Blackwell.

Levine, S. Z., & Rabinowitz, J. (2007). Revisiting the 5 dimensions of the Positive and Negative Syndrome Scale. *Journal of Clinical Psychopharmacology, 27,* 431–436.

Levinson, D. (1992). *The seasons of a woman's life.* New York: Knopf.

Levinson, D. J. (1990). A theory of life structure development in adulthood. In C. N. Alexander & E. J. Langer (Eds.), *Higher stages of human development: Perspectives on adult growth.* New York: Oxford University Press.

Levy, B. R., & Myers, L. M. (2004). Preventive health behaviors influenced by self-perceptions of aging. *Preventive Medicine: An International Journal Devoted to Practice and Theory, 39,* 625–629.

Levy, B. R., Slade, M. D., Kunkel, S. R., & Kasl, S. V. (2002). Longevity increased by positive self-perceptions of aging. *Journal of Personality & Social Psychology, 83,* 261–270.

Lewinsohn, P. M., Petit, J. W., Joiner, T. E., Jr., & Seeley, J. R. (2003). The symptomatic expression of major depressive disorder in adolescents and young adults. *Journal of Abnormal Psychology, 112,* 244–252.

Lewis, C. E., Thomas, K. F., Dodge, N. C., Molteno, C. D., Meintjes, E. M., Jacobson, J. L., & Jacobson, S. W. (2015). Verbal learning and memory impairment in children with fetal alcohol spectrum disorders. *Alcoholism: Clinical and Experimental Research, 39,* 724–732.

Lewis, T., & Umbreit, M. (2015). A humanistic approach to mediation and dialogue: An evolving transformative practice. *Conflict Resolution Quarterly.* Retrieved from http://onlinelibrary.wiley.com/doi/10.1002/crq.21130/abstract

Li, B., Piriz, J., Mirrione, M., Chung, C., Proulx, C. D., Schulz, D., & . . . Malinow, R. (2011). Synaptic potentiation onto habenula neurons in learned helplessness model of depression. *Nature, 470,* 535–539.

Li, C., Chen, M., Lin, W., Hong, C., Yang, B., Liu, R., & . . . Su, T. (2016). The effects of low-dose ketamine on the prefrontal cortex and amygdala in treatment-resistant depression: A randomized controlled study. *Human Brain Mapping, 37,* 1080–1090.

Li, J. (2011). Cultural frames of children's learning beliefs. In L. Jensen (Ed.), *Bridging cultural and developmental approaches to psychology: New syntheses in theory, research, and policy.* New York: Oxford University Press.

Li, P., Jia, S., Feng, T., Liu, Q., Suo, T., & Li, H. (2010). The influence of the diffusion of responsibility effect on outcome evaluations: Electrophysiological evidence from an ERP study. *NeuroImage, 52,* 1727–1733.

Li, T-K., Volkow, N. D., & Baler, R. D. (2007). The biological bases of nicotine and alcohol co-addiction. *Biological Psychiatry, 61,* 1–3.

Li, Y., Hofstetter, C. R., Wahlgren, D., Irvin, V., Chhay, D., & Hovell, M. F. (2015). Social networks and immigration stress among first-generation mandarin-speaking Chinese immigrants in Los Angeles. *International Journal of Social Welfare, 24,* 170–181.

Liang, K. A. (2007). Acculturation, ambivalent sexism, and attitudes toward women who engage in premarital sex among Chinese American young adults. *Dissertation Abstracts International: Section B: The Sciences and Engineering, 67*(10-B), 6065.

Lick, D. J., Durso, L. E., & Johnson, K. L. (2013). Minority stress and physical health among sexual minorities. *Perspectives on Psychological Science, 8,* 521–548.

Liddle, E. B., Price, D., Palaniyappan, L., Brookes, M. J., Robson, S. E., Hall, E. L., Morris, P. G., & Liddle, P. F. (2016). Abnormal salience signaling in schizophrenia: The role of integrative beta oscillations. *Human Brain Mapping.* Retrieved from http://www.ncbi.nlm.nih.gov/pubmed/26853904

Lidz, J., & Gleitman, L. R. (2004). Argument structure and the child's contribution to language learning. *Trends in Cognitive Sciences, 8,* 157–161.

Lieberman, P. (2015). A tangled tale of circuits, evolution, and language. *Psyccritiques, 60,* 88–97.

Lieblum, S. R., & Chivers, M. L. (2007). Normal and persistent genital arousal in women: New perspectives. *Journal of Sex & Marital Therapy, 33,* 357–373.

Liebscher, C., Wittmann, A., Gechter, J., Schlagenhauf, F., Lueken, U., Plag, J., & . . . Ströhle, A. (2016). Facing the fear—clinical and neural effects of cognitive behavioural and pharmacotherapy in panic disorder with agoraphobia. *European Neuropsychopharmacology.* Retrieved from http://www.ncbi.nlm.nih.gov/pubmed/26837851

Liedl, A., Müller, J., Morina, N., Karl, A., Denke, C., & Knaevelsrud, C. (2011). Physical activity within a CBT intervention improves coping with pain in traumatized refugees: Results of a randomized controlled design. *Pain Medicine, 12,* 138–145.

Lien, Y-W., Chu, R-L., Jen, C-H., & Wu, C-H. (2006). Do Chinese commit neither fundamental attribution error nor ultimate attribution error? *Chinese Journal of Psychology, 48,* 163–181.

Lievens, F., & Chan, D. (2010). Practical intelligence, emotional intelligence, and social intelligence. *Handbook of employee selection.* New York: Routledge/Taylor & Francis Group.

Lilienfeld, S. O. (2007). Psychological treatments that cause harm. *Perspectives on Psychological Science, 2,* 53–58.

Lillard, A. S., & Woolley, J. D. (2015). Grounded in reality: How children make sense of the unreal. *Cognitive Development, 34,* 111–114.

Limberg, B. (2015). Nature vs. nurture . . . again: Examining the interplay between genetics and the environment. *Psyccritiques, 60,* 88–98.

Lin, C-H. & Lin, H-M. (2007). What price do you ask for the "extra one"? A social value orientation perspective. *Social Behavior and Personality, 35,* 9–18.

Lin, Y., Li, K., Sung, W., Ko, H., Tzeng, O. L., Hung, D. L., & Juan, C. (2011). The relationship between development of attention and learning in children: A cognitive neuroscience approach. *Bulletin of Educational Psychology, 42,* 517–542.

Lindblad, F., Lindahl, M., & Theorell, T. (2006). Physiological stress reactions in 6th and 9th graders during test performance. *Stress and Health: Journal of the International Society for the Investigation of Stress, 22,* 189–195.

Lindemann, O., & Bekkering, H. (2009). Object manipulation and motion perception: Evidence of an influence of action planning on visual processing. *Journal of Experimental Psychology: Human Perception and Performance, 35,* 1062–1071.

Lindín, M., & Díaz, F. (2010). Event-related potentials in face naming and tip-of-the-tongue state: Further results. *International Journal of Psychophysiology, 77,* 53–58.

Lindley, L. D. (2006). The paradox of self-efficacy: Research with diverse populations. *Journal of Career Assessment, 14,* 143–160.

Lindorff, M. (2005). Determinants of received social support: Who gives what to managers? *Journal of Social and Personal Relationships, 22,* 323–337.

Lindsey, E., & Colwell, M. (2003). Preschoolers' emotional competence: Links to pretend and physical play. *Child Study Journal, 33,* 39–52.

Linley, P. (2013). Human strengths and well-being: Finding the best within us at the intersection of eudaimonic philosophy, humanistic psychology, and positive psychology. In A. S. Waterman (Ed.), *The best within us: Positive psychology perspectives on eudaimonia.* Washington, DC: American Psychological Association.

Lins, B. R., & Howland, J. G. (2016). Effects of the metabotropic glutamate receptor 5 positive allosteric modulator CDPPB on rats tested with the paired associates learning task in touchscreen-equipped operant conditioning chambers. *Behavioural Brain Research, 301,* 152–160.

Litowitz, B. E. (2007). Unconscious fantasy: A once and future concept. *Journal of the American Psychoanalytic Association, 55,* 199–228.

Little, A., Burt, D. M., & Perrett, D. I. (2006). What is good is beautiful: Face preference reflects desired personality. *Personality and Individual Differences, 41,* 1107–1118.

Little, K., Ramssen, E., Welchko, R., Volberg, V., Roland, C., & Cassin, B. (2009). Decreased brain dopamine cell numbers in human cocaine users. *Psychiatry Research, 168,* 173–180.

Liu, J. H., & Mills, D. (2006). Modern racism and neo-liberal globalization: The discourses of plausible deniability and their multiple functions. *Journal of Community & Applied Social Psychology, 16,* 83–99.

Liu, J., Ying, Z., & Zhang, S. (2015). A rate function approach to computerized adaptive testing for cognitive diagnosis. *Psychometrika, 80,* 468–490.

Liu, R., & Alloy, L. (2010). Stress generation in depression: A systematic review of the empirical literature and recommendations for future study. *Clinical Psychology Review, 30,* 582–593.

Lobato, M. I., Koff, W. J., & Manenti, C. (2006). Follow-up of sex reassignment surgery in transsexuals: A Brazilian cohort. *Archives of Sexual Behavior, 35,* 711–715.

Lobban, F., Barrowclough, C., & Jones, S. (2006). Does expressed emotion need to be understood within a more systemic framework? An examination of discrepancies in appraisals between patients diagnosed with schizophrenia and their relatives. *Social Psychiatry and Psychiatric Epidemiology, 41,* 50–55.

Lockl, K., & Schneider, W. (2007). Knowledge about the mind: Links between theory of mind and later metamemory. *Child Development, 78,* 148–167.

Loehlin, J. (2010). Environment and the behavior genetics of personality: Let me count the ways. *Personality and Individual Differences, 49,* 302–305.

Loehlin, J. C., Bartels, M., Boomsma, D. I., Bratko, D., Martin, N. G., Nichols, R. C., & Wright, M. J. (2015). Is there a genetic correlation between general factors of intelligence and personality? *Twin Research and Human Genetics, 18,* 234–242.

Lofthouse, N., McBurnett, K., Arnold, L., & Hurt, E. (2011). Biofeedback and neurofeedback treatment for ADHD. *Psychiatric Annals, 41,* 42–48.

Lombardi, R. (2010). Flexibility of the psychoanalytic approach in the treatment of a suicidal patient: Stubborn silences as "playing dead." *Psychoanalytic Dialogues, 20,* 269–284.

Longley, S., Broman-Fulks, J., Calamari, J., Noyes, R., Wade, M., & Orlando, C. (2010). A taxometric study of hypochondriasis symptoms. *Behavior Therapy, 41,* 505–514.

Longo, M. R., Trippier, S., Vagnoni, E., & Lourenco, S. F. (2015). Right hemisphere control of visuospatial attention in near space. *Neuropsychologia, 70,* 350–357.

Lopes, A. C., Greenberg, B. D., Noren, G., Canteras, M. M., Busatto, G. F. de Mathis, et al. (2009). Treatment of resistant obsessive-compulsive disorder with ventral capsular/ventral striatal gamma capsulotomy: A pilot prospective study. *The Journal of Neuropsychiatry and Clinical Neurosciences, 21,* 381–392.

López, S. R., & Guarnaccia, P. J. (2000). Cultural psychopathology: Uncovering the social world of mental illness. *Annual Review of Psychology, 51,* 571–598.

López, S. R., & Guarnaccia, P. J. (2016). Cultural dimensions of psychopathology: The social world's impact on mental disorders. In J. E. Maddux, B. A. Winstead, J. E. Maddux, & B. A. Winstead (Eds.), *Psychopathology: Foundations for a contemporary understanding* (4th ed.). New York: Routledge/Taylor & Francis Group.

Lorenz, K. (1966). *On aggression.* New York: Harcourt Brace Jovanovich.

Lorenz, K. (1974). *Civilized man's eight deadly sins.* New York: Harcourt Brace Jovanovich.

Lotze, M., Heymans, U., Birbaumer, N., Veit, R., Erb, M., Flor, H., & Halsband, U. (2006). Differential cerebral activation during observation of expressive gestures and motor acts. *Neuropsychologia, 44,* 1787–1795.

Loving, T., Crockett, E., & Paxson, A. (2009). Passionate love and relationship thinkers: Experimental evidence for acute cortisol elevations in women. *Psychoneuroendocrinology, 34,* 939–946.

Lowe, P., Humphreys, C., & Williams, S. J. (2007). Night terrors: Women's experiences of (not) sleeping where there is domestic violence. *Violence Against Women, 13,* 549–561.

Lozano, A.M., & Mayberg, H.S. (2015, February). Treating depression at the source: Electrical stimulation deep within the brain may alleviate devastating mood disorders. *Scientific American,* pp. 68–73.

Lozito, J., & Mulligan, N. (2010). Exploring the role of attention during implicit memory retrieval. *Journal of Memory and Language, 63,* 387–399.

Lubinski, D., Benbow, C. P., Webb, R. M., & Bleske-Rechek, A. (2006). Tracking exceptional human capital over two decades. *Psychological Science, 17,* 194–199.

Luby, J., & Tandon, M. (2010). Assessing the preschool-age child. *Dulcan's textbook of child and adolescent psychiatry.* Arlington, VA: American Psychiatric Publishing, Inc.

Lucidi, A., Langerock, N., Hoareau, V., Lemaire, B., Camos, V., & Barrouillet, P. (2016). Working memory still needs verbal rehearsal. *Memory & Cognition, 44,* 197–206.

Lucki, I., & O'Leary, O. F. (2004). Distinguishing roles for norepinephrine and serotonin in the behavioral effects of antidepressant drugs. *Journal of Clinical Psychiatry, 65,* 11–24.

Luckiesh, M. (1921). Visual illusions in the arts. *Scientific American Monthly, 3,* 497–501.

Luders, E., Narr, K. L., Zaidel, E., Thompson, P. M., & Toga, A. W. (2006). Gender effects on callosal thickness in scaled and unscaled space. *Neuroreport, 17,* 1103–1106.

Lueken, U., Kruschwitz, J., Muehlhan, M., Siegert, J., Hoyer, J., & Wittchen, H. (2011). How specific is specific phobia? Different neural response patterns in two subtypes of specific phobia. *NeuroImage, 56,* 363–72.

Lueken, U., Muehlhan, M., Wittchen, H., Kellermann, T., Reinhardt, I., Konrad, C., & . . . Kircher, T. (2011). (Don't) panic in the scanner! How panic patients with agoraphobia experience a functional magnetic resonance imaging session. *European Neuropsychopharmacology, 21,* 516–525.

Luo, S., & Zhang, G. (2009). What leads to romantic attraction: Similarity, reciprocity, security, or beauty? Evidence from a speed-dating study. *Journal of Personality, 77,* 933–964.

Luong, G., Rauers, A., & Fingerman, K. L. (2015). The multifaceted nature of late-life socialization: Older adults as agents and targets of socialization. In J. E. Grusec & P. D. Hastings (Eds.), *Handbook of socialization: Theory and research* (2nd ed.). New York: Guilford Press.

Lutz, C.K. & Novak, M. A. (2005). Environmental enrichment for nonhuman primates: Theory and application. *ILAR Journal, 46,* 178–191.

Lutz, W., Lambert, M. J., Harmon, S. C., Tschitsaz, A., Schurch, E., & Stulz, N. (2006). The probability of treatment success, failure and duration—what can be learned from empirical data to support decision making in clinical practice? *Clinical Psychology & Psychotherapy, 13,* 223–232.

Lymberis, S. C., Parhar, P. K., Katsoulakis, E., & Formenti, S. C. (2004). Pharmacogenomics and breast cancer. *Pharmacogenomics, 5,* 31–55.

Lynn, S. J., Kirsch, I., Barabasz, A., Cardena, E., & Patterson, D. (2000). Hypnosis as an empirically supported clinical intervention: The state of the evidence and a look to the future. *International Journal of Clinical and Experimental Hypnosis, 48,* 23–259.

Lynn, S. J., Laurence, J., & Kirsch, I. (2015). Hypnosis, suggestion, and suggestibility: An integrative model. *American Journal of Clinical Hypnosis, 57,* 314–329.

Lynn, S., Stamplis, T., Barrington, W., Weida, N., & Hudak, C. (2010). Food, stress, and reproduction: Short-term fasting alters endocrine physiology and reproductive behavior in the zebra finch. *Hormones and Behavior, 58,* 214–222.

Lyons, H., Giordano, P. C., Manning, W. D., & Longmore, M. A. (2011). Identity, peer relationships, and adolescent girls' sexual behavior: An exploration of the contemporary double standard. *Journal of Sex Research, 48,* 437–449.

Macht, M., & Simons, G. (2011). Emotional eating. In I. Nyklíček, A. Vingerhoets, M. Zeelenberg, I. Nyklíček, A. Vingerhoets, M. Zeelenberg (Eds.), *Emotion regulation and well-being.* New York: Springer Science + Business Media.

Mack, J. (2003). *The museum of the mind.* London: British Museum Publications.

Mackey, A. P., Finn, A. S., Leonard, J. A., Jacoby-Senghor, D. S., West, M. R., Gabrieli, C. F. O., & Gabrieli, J. D. E. (2015). Neuroanatomical correlates of the income-achievement gap. *Psychological Science, 1–9.*

MacKinnon, D. P., & Luecken, L. J. (2008). How and for whom? Mediation and moderation in health psychology. *Health Psychology, 27*(Suppl. 2), S99–S100.

MacLean, L., Edwards, N., Garrard, M., Sims-Jones, N., Clinton, K., & Ashley, L. (2009, March). Obesity, stigma and public health planning. *Health Promotion International, 24,* 88–93.

MacLennan, A. (2009). Evidence-based review of therapies at the menopause. *International Journal of Evidence-Based Healthcare, 7,* 112–123.

MacNeilage, P. F., Rogers, L. J., & Vallortigara, G. (2009, July). Origins of the left & right brain. *Scientific American,* pp. 60–67.

Madden, D. J. (2007). Aging and visual attention. *Current Directions in Psychological Science, 16,* 70–74.

Mader, S. S. (2000). *Biology.* Boston: McGraw-Hill.

Magee, S. R., Bublitz, M. H., Orazine, C., Brush, B., Salisbury, A., Niaura, R., & Stroud, L. R. (2013). The relationship between maternal–fetal attachment and cigarette smoking over pregnancy. *Maternal and Child Health Journal.* Retrieved from http://www.ncbi.nlm.nih.gov/pubmed/23892790

Magida, A. J. (2006). *Opening the doors of wonder: Reflections on religious rites of passage.* Berkeley, CA: University of California Press.

Magoni, M., Bassani, L., Okong, P., Kituuka, P., Germinario, E. P., Giuliano, M., & Vella, S. (2005). Mode of infant feeding and HIV infection in children in a program for prevention of mother-to-child transmission in Uganda. *AIDS, 19,* 433–437.

Magoon, M., & Critchfield, T. (2008). Concurrent schedules of positive and negative reinforcement: Differential-impact and differential-outcomes hypotheses. *Journal of the Experimental Analysis of Behavior, 90,* 1–22.

Magruder, K., & Yeager, D. (2009). The prevalence of PTSD across war eras and the effect of deployment on PTSD: A systematic review and meta-analysis. *Psychiatric Annals, 39,* 778–788.

Maher, B. (2015). The anatomy of obedience. *Nature, 523,* 408–409.

Majorano, M., & D'Odorico, L. (2011). The transition into ambient language: A longitudinal study of babbling and first word production of Italian children. *First Language, 31,* 47–66.

Maldonado, J. R., & Spiegel, D. (2003). Dissociative disorders. In R. E. Hales & S. C. Yudofsky (Eds.), *The American Psychiatric Publishing textbook of clinical psychiatry* (4th ed.). Washington, DC: American Psychiatric Publishing.

Malin, D. H., Schaar, K. L., Izygon, J. J., Nghiem, D. M., Jabitta, S. Y., Henceroth, M. M., & . . . Ward, C. P. (2015). Validation and scopolamine-reversal of latent learning in the water maze utilizing a revised direct platform placement procedure. *Pharmacology, Biochemistry and Behavior, 13,* 590–596.

Mallery, R., Olomu, O., Uchanski, R., Militchin, V., & Hullar, T. (2010). Human discrimination of rotational velocities. *Experimental Brain Research, 204,* 11–20.

Malouff, J. M., & Rooke, S. E. (2013). Expert-recommended warnings for medical marijuana. *Substance Abuse, 34,* 92–93.

Malouff, J. M., Thorsteinsson, E. B., & Schutte, N. S. (2007). The efficacy of problem solving therapy in reducing mental and physical health problems: A meta-analysis. *Clinical Psychology Review, 27,* 46–57.

Mancinelli, R., Binetti, R., & Ceccanti, M. (2007). Woman, alcohol and environment: Emerging risks for health. *Neuroscience & Biobehavioral Reviews, 31,* 246–253.

Mancuso, F., Horan, W. P., Kern, R. S., & Green, M. F. (2011). Social cognition in psychosis: Multidimensional structure, clinical correlates, and relationship with functional outcome. *Schizophrenia Research, 125,* 143–151.

Mann, K., Ackermann, K., Croissant, B., Mundle, G., Nakovics, H., & Diehl, A. (2005). Neuroimaging of gender differences in alcohol dependence: Are women more vulnerable? *Alcoholism: Clinical & Experimental Research, 29,* 896–901.

Mannel, M., Kuhn, U., Schmidt, U., Ploch, M., & Murck, H. (2010). St. John's wort extract LI160 for the treatment of depression with atypical features—A double-blind, randomized, and placebo-controlled trial. *Journal of Psychiatric Research, 44,* 760–767.

Manni, R., & Terzaghi, M. (2013). Dreaming and enacting dreams in nonrapid eye movement and rapid eye movement parasomnia: A step toward a unifying view within distinct patterns? *Sleep Medicine, 14,* 387–388.

Manning, M. A., & Hoyme, E. H. (2007). Fetal alcohol spectrum disorders: A practical clinical approach to diagnosis. *Neuroscience & Biobehavioral Reviews, 31,* 230–238.

Manor, J. K., & Gailliot, M. T. (2007). Altruism and egoism: Prosocial motivations for helping depend on relationship context. *European Journal of Social Psychology, 37,* 347–358.

Manstead, A. S. R., Frijda, N., & Fischer, A. H. (Eds.). (2003). *Feelings and emotions: The Amsterdam Symposium.* Cambridge, England: Cambridge University Press.

Manzo, L., Gómez, M. J., Callejas-Aguilera, J. E., Fernández-Teruel, A., Papini, M. R., & Torres, C. (2015). Partial reinforcement reduces vulnerability to anti-anxiety self-medication during appetitive extinction. *International Journal of Comparative Psychology, 28,* 22–30.

Marchand, S., & Phillips, G. E., (2012). Hoarding's place in the DSM-5: Another symptom, or a newly listed disorder? *Issues in Mental Health Nursing, 33,* 591–597.

Markus, H. R. (2007). Sociocultural psychology: The dynamic interdependence among self systems and social systems. In S. Kitayama & D. Cohen (Eds.), *Handbook of cultural psychology.* New York: Guilford Press.

Marsh, R., Stefan, M., Bansal, R., Hao, X., Walsh, B. T., & Peterson, B. S. (2015). Anatomical characteristics of the cerebral surface in bulimia nervosa. *Biological Psychiatry, 77*(7), 616–623.

Marshall, J. R. (2011). Ultimate causes and the evolution of altruism. *Behavioral Ecology and Sociobiology, 65,* 503–512.

Marshall, M. K. (2007). The critical factors of coaching practice leading to successful coaching outcomes. *Dissertation Abstracts International: Section B: The Sciences and Engineering, 67*(7-B), 4092.

Marszalek, J. (2007). Computerized adaptive testing and the experience of flow in examinees. *Dissertation Abstracts International Section A: Humanities and Social Sciences, 67*(7-A), 2465.

Martelle, S., Hanley, C., & K. Yoshino (2003, January 28). "Sopranos" scenario in slaying? *Los Angeles Times,* p. B1.

Martin, A. J., & Marsh, H. W. (2002). Fear of failure: Friend or foe? *Australian Psychologist, 38,* 31–38.

Martin, C., & Redshaw, M. (2010). Fathers in the twenty-first century: Essential role or accessory? *Journal of Reproductive and Infant Psychology, 28,* 113–115.

Martin, K. K., & North, A. C. (2015). Diffusion of responsibility on social networking sites. *Computers in Human Behavior, 44,* 124–131.

Martin, L., & Pullum, G. K. (1991). *The great Eskimo vocabulary hoax.* Chicago: University of Chicago Press.

Martino, V., Grattagliano, I., Bosco, A., Massaro, Y., Lisi, A., Campobasso, F., & . . . Catanesi, R. (2016). A new index for the MMPI-2 test for detecting dissimulation in forensic evaluations: A pilot study. *Journal of Forensic Sciences, 61,* 249–253.

Maslow, A. H. (1970). *Motivation and personality.* New York: Harper & Row.

Maslow, A. H. (1971). *The farther reaches of human nature.* New York: Viking Press.

Maslow, A. H. (1987). *Motivation and personality* (3rd ed.). New York: Harper & Row.

Masuda, M. (2003). Meta-analyses of love scales: Do various love scales measure the same psychological constructs? *Japanese Psychological Research, 45,* 25–37.

Matsumoto, D. (2002). Methodological requirements to test a possible in-group advantage in judging emotions across cultures: Comment on Elfenbein and Ambady (2002) and evidence. *Psychological Bulletin, 128,* 236–242.

Matthen, M. (2010). How things look (and what things look that way). In B. Nanay (Ed.), *Perceiving the world.* New York: Oxford University Press.

Matthews, G., & Funke, G. J. (2006). Worry and information-processing. In G. C. L. Davey & A. Wells, *Worry and its psychological disorders: Theory, assessment and treatment.* Hoboken, NJ: Wiley.

Maturana, M. J., Pudell, C., Targa, A. S., Rodrigues, L. S., Noseda, A. D., Fortes, M. H., & . . . Lima, M. S. (2015). REM sleep deprivation reverses neurochemical and other depressive-like alterations induced by olfactory bulbectomy. *Molecular Neurobiology, 51,* 349–360.

Maurer, D., Lewis, T. L., Brent, H. P., & Levin, A. V. (1999, October 1). Rapid improvement in the acuity of infants after visual input. *Science, 286,* 108–110.

Maxson, S. C. (2013). Behavioral genetics. In R. J. Nelson, S. Y. Mizumori, & I. B. Weiner (Eds.), *Handbook of psychology, Vol. 3: Behavioral neuroscience* (2nd ed.). New York: John Wiley & Sons Inc.

Mayer, J. D., Salovey, P., & Caruso, D. R. (2004). Emotional intelligence: Theory, findings, and implications. *Psychological Inquiry, 15,* 197–215.

Mayer, J. D., Salovey, P., & Caruso, D. R. (2008). Emotional intelligence: New ability or eclectic traits? *American Psychologist, 63,* 503–517.

Mayer, R. E. (2013). Problem solving. In D. Reisberg (Ed.), *The Oxford handbook of cognitive psychology.* New York: Oxford University Press.

McCarrey, A. C., & Resnick, S. M. (2015). Postmenopausal hormone therapy and cognition. *Hormones and Behavior.* Retrieved from http://www.sciencedirect.com/science/article/pii/S0018506X15000690

McCarthy, D., Curtin, J., Piper, M., & Baker, T. (2010). Negative reinforcement: Possible clinical implications of an integrative model. *Substance abuse and emotion.* Washington, DC: American Psychological Association.

McCarthy, J. (2005). Individualism and collectivism: What do they have to do with counseling? *Journal of Multicultural Counseling and Development, 33,* 108–117.

McClelland, D. C. (1993). Intelligence is not the best predictor of job performance. *Current Directions in Psychological Research, 2,* 5–8.

McClelland, D. C., Atkinson, J. W., Clark, R. A., & Lowell, E. L. (1953). *The achievement motive.* New York: Appleton-Century-Crofts.

McClure, J., Sutton, R. M., & Sibley, C. G. (2007). Listening to reporters or engineers? How instance-based messages about building design affect earthquake fatalism. *Journal of Applied Social Sciences, 37,* 1956–1973.

McCrae, R. R., & Costa, P. T., Jr. (1986). A five-factor theory of personality. In L. A. Pervin & O. P. John (Eds.), *Handbook of personality: Theory and research* (2nd ed.). New York: Guilford.

McCrae, R. R., Kurtz, J. E., Yamagata, S., & Terracciano, A. (2011). Internal consistency, retest reliability, and their implications for personality scale validity. *Personality and Social Psychology Review, 15,* 28–50.

McDaniel, M. A., Maier, S. F., & Einstein, G. O. (2002). "Brain specific" nutrients: A memory cure? *Psychological Science in the Public Interest, 3,* 12–18.

McDonald, C., & Murray, R. M. (2004). Can structural magnetic resonance imaging provide an alternative phenotype for genetic studies of schizophrenia? In M. S. Keshavan, J. L. Kennedy, & R. M. Murray (Eds.), *Neurodevelopment and schizophrenia.* New York: Cambridge University Press.

McDonald, H. E., & Hirt, E. R. (1997). When expectancy meets desire: Motivational effects in reconstructive memory. *Journal of Personality and Social Psychology, 72,* 5–23.

McDougle, S. (2010, June 6). The country of the face-blind. *The Beautiful Brain.* Retrieved from http://thebeautifulbrain.com/2010/06/the-country-of-the-face-blind/

McElreath, R., Wallin, A., & Fasolo, B. (2013). The evolutionary rationality of social learning. In R. Hertwig & U. Hoffrage (Eds.), *Simple heuristics in a social world.* New York: Oxford University Press.

McEwen, B. S. (1998, January 15). Protective and damaging effects of stress mediators [Review article]. *New England Journal of Medicine, 338,* 171–179.

McGaugh, J. L., & LePort, A. (2014, February.) Remembrance of all things past. *Scientific American, 310,* 41–45.

McGilvray, J. (Ed.). (2004). *The Cambridge companion to Chomsky.* Oxford, England: Cambridge University Press.

McGinn, D. (2003, June 9). Testing, testing: The new job search. *Time,* pp. 36–38.

McGregor, K. K., & Capone, N. C. (2004). Genetic and environmental interactions in determining the early lexicon: Evidence from a set of tri-zygotic quadruplets. *Journal of Child Language, 31,* 311–337.

McIntyre, K., Korn, J., & Matsuo, H. (2008). Sweating the small stuff: How different types of hassles result in the experience of stress. *Stress and Health: Journal of the International Society for the Investigation of Stress, 24,* 383–392.

McMurtray, A. M., Licht, E., Yeo, T., Krisztal, E., Saul, R. E., & Mendez, M. F. (2007). Positron emission tomography facilitates diagnosis of early-onset Alzheimer's disease. *European Neurology, 59,* 31–37.

McNamara, P. (2004). *An evolutionary psychology of sleep and dreams.* Westport, CT: Praeger Publishers/Greenwood Publishing Group.

McNamara, T. P. (2013). Semantic memory and priming. In A. F. Healy, R. W. Proctor, & I. B. Weiner (Eds.), *Handbook of psychology, Vol. 4: Experimental psychology* (2nd ed.). Hoboken, NJ: John Wiley & Sons Inc.

McPartland, R. (2016). *Tay-Sachs Disease.* New York: Cavendish Square.

Mead, M. (1949). *Male and female.* New York: Morrow.

Medeiros, R., Prediger, R. D. S., Passos, G. F., Pandolfo, P., Duarte, F. S., Franco, J. L., et al. (2007). Connecting TNF-α signaling pathways to iNOS expression in a mouse model of Alzheimer's disease: Relevance for the behavioral and synaptic deficits induced by amyloid β protein. *Journal of Neuroscience, 27*(20), 5394–5404.

Mel, B. W. (2002, March 8). What the synapse tells the neuron. *Science, 295,* 1845–1846.

Meltzer, H. Y. (2000). Genetics and etiology of schizophrenia and bipolar disorder. *Biological Psychiatry, 47,* 171–173.

Meltzoff, A. N. (1996). The human infant as imitative generalist: A 20-year progress report on infant imitation with implications for comparative psychology. In C. M. Heyes & B. G. Galef, Jr. (Eds.), *Social learning in animals: The roots of culture.* San Diego, CA: Academic Press.

Meltzoff, A. N. & Moore, M. K. (1977). "Imitation of facial and manual gestures by human neonates", *Science, 198,* 75–78.

Melzack, R., & Katz, J. (2004). *The gate control theory: Reaching for the brain.* Mahwah, NJ: Erlbaum.

Merikangas, K. R., Ames, M., Cui, L., Stang, P. E., Ustun, T. B., VonKorff, M., & Kessler, R. C. (2007). The impact of comorbidity of mental and physical conditions on role disability in the U.S. adult household population. *Archives of General Psychiatry, 64,* 1180–1188.

Merikangas, K., He, J., Burstein, M., Swanson, S., Avenevoli, S., Cui, L., et al. (2010). Lifetime prevalence of mental disorders in U.S. adolescents: Results from the National Comorbidity Survey Replication-Adolescent Supplement (NCS-A). *Journal of the American Academy of Child & Adolescent Psychiatry, 49,* 980–989.

Messner, M., Reinhard, M., & Sporer, S. (2008). Compliance through direct persuasive appeals: The moderating role of communicator's attractiveness in interpersonal persuasion. *Social Influence, 3,* 67–83.

Meyer-Bahlburg, H. (1997). The role of prenatal estrogens in sexual orientation. In L. Ellis & L. Ebertz (Eds.), *Sexual orientation: Toward biological understanding.* Westport, CT: Praeger.

Michael, R. T., Gagnon, J. H., Laumann, E. O., & Kolata, G. (1994). *Sex in America: A definitive survey.* Boston: Little, Brown.

Midanik, L. T., Tam, T. W., & Weisner, C. (2007). Concurrent and simultaneous drug and alcohol use: Results of the 2000 national alcohol survey. *Drug and Alcohol Dependence, 90,* 72–80.

Miesenbock, G. (2008, October). Lighting up the brain. *Scientific American,* pp. 52–59.

Milgram, S. (2005). *Obedience to authority.* Pinter & Martin: New York.

Miller, G. F., & Penke, L. (2007). The evolution of human intelligence and the coefficient of additive genetic variance in human brain size. *Intelligence, 35,* 97–114.

Miller, J. A., & Leffard, S. A. (2007). Behavioral assessment. In S. R. Smith & L. Handler, *The clinical assessment of children and adolescents: A practitioner's handbook.* Mahwah, NJ: Erlbaum.

Miller, J. G. (1984). Culture and the development of everyday social explanation. *Journal of Personality and Social Psychology, 46,* 961–978.

Miller, J., Maples, J., Few, L., Morse, J., Yaggi, K., & Pilkonis, P. (2010). Using clinician-rated five-factor model data to score the DSM-IV personality disorders. *Journal of Personality Assessment, 92,* 296–305.

Miller, L. A., Taber, K. H., Gabbard, G. O., & Hurley, R. A. (2005). Neural underpinnings of fear and its modulation: Implications for anxiety disorders. *Journal of Neuropsychiatry and Clinical Neurosciences, 17,* 1–6.

Miller, L., Gur, M., Shanok, A., & Weissman, M. (2008). Interpersonal psychotherapy with pregnant adolescents: Two pilot studies. *Journal of Child Psychology and Psychiatry, 49,* 733–742.

Miller, N. E., & Magruder, K. M. (Eds.). (1999). *Cost-effectiveness of psychotherapy: A guide for practitioners, researchers, and policymakers.* New York: Oxford University Press.

Miller-Perrin, C., Perrin, R., & Kocur, J. (2009). Parental physical and psychological aggression: Psychological symptoms in young adults. *Child Abuse & Neglect, 33,* 1–11.

Millon, T., Davis, R., & Millon, C. (2000). *Personality disorders in modern life.* New York: Wiley.

Mills, J. (2013). Jung's metaphysics. *International Journal of Jungian Studies, 5,* 19–43.

Mills, M. J. (2011). Associations among achievement measures and their collective prediction of work involvement. *Personality and Individual Differences, 50,* 360–364.

Miner, J., & Clarke-Stewart, K. (2008). Trajectories of externalizing behavior from age 2 to age 9: Relations with gender, temperament, ethnicity, parenting, and rater. *Developmental Psychology, 44,* 771–786.

Miner-Rubino, K., Winter, D. G., & Stewart, A. J. (2004). Gender, social class, and the subjective experience of aging: Self-perceived personality change from early adulthood to late midlife. *Personality and Social Psychology Bulletin, 30,* 1599–1610.

Mintle, L. (2011). To eat or not to eat: Eating disorders. In C. Franklin, R. Fong, C. Franklin, & R. Fong (Eds.), *The church leader's counseling resource book: A guide to mental health and social problems.* New York: Oxford University Press.

Mintz, A., & Brule, D. (2009). Methodological issues in studying suicide terrorism. *Political Psychology, 30,* 361–367.

Miquel, J., (2006). Integración de teorías del envejecimiento (parte I). [Integration of theories of ageing.] *Revista Espanola de Geriatria y Gerontologia, 41,* 55–63.

Mischel, W. (2004). Toward an integrative science of the person. *Annual Review of Psychology, 55,* 1–22.

Mischel, W. (2009). From Personality and Assessment (1968) to Personality Science, 2009. *Journal of Research in Personality, 43,* 282–290.

Mischel, W., & Shoda, Y. (2008). Toward a unified theory of personality: Integrating dispositions and processing dynamics within the cognitive-affective processing system. In O. P. Oliver, R. W. Robins, & L. A. Pervin (Eds.) *Handbook of personality psychology: Theory and research* (3rd ed.) New York: Guilford Press.

Mischoulon, D. (2000, June). Anti-depressants: Choices and controversy. *HealthNews,* p. 4.

Mitchell, D. B., & Schmitt, F. A. (2006). Short- and long-term implicit memory in aging and Alzheimer's disease. *Neuropsychological Development and Cognition, B, Aging and Neuropsychological Cognition, 13,* 611–635.

Mitte, K. (2005). Meta-analysis of cognitive-behavioral treatments for generalized anxiety disorder: A comparison with pharmacotherapy. *Psychological Bulletin, 131,* 785–795.

Mizrahi, R., Agid, O., Borlido, C., Suridjan, I., Rusjan, P., Houle, S., & … Kapur, S. (2011). Effects of antipsychotics on D3 receptors: A clinical PET study in first episode antipsychotic naive patients with schizophrenia using [11C]-(+)-PHNO. *Schizophrenia Research, 131,* 63–68.

MLA. (2010). MLA Language Map; all languages other than English combined. Retrieved from http://www.mla.org/census_map&source= county (based on 2000 U.S. Census Bureau figures).

Moffitt, T. E., Caspi, A., & Rutter, M. (2006). Measured gene-environment interactions in psychopathology: Concepts, research strategies, and implications for research, intervention, and public understanding of genetics. *Perspectives on Psychological Science, 1,* 5–27.

Mograss, M., Guillem, F., Brazzini-Poisson, V., & Godbout, R. (2009, May). The effects of total sleep deprivation on recognition memory processes: A study of event-related potential. *Neurobiology of Learning and Memory, 91,* 343–352.

Moher, C., Gould, D., Hegg, E., & Mahoney, A. (2008). Non-generalized and generalized conditioned reinforcers: Establishment and validation. *Behavioral Interventions, 23,* 13–38.

Mohr, C., & Messina, S. (2015). Brain dysfunctions, psychopathologies, and body image distortions: Propositions for a possible common cause. *European Psychologist, 20,* 72–81.

Montgomery, C., Fisk, J. E., Newcombe, R., Wareing, M., & Murphy, P. N. (2005). Syllogistic reasoning performance in MDMA (Ecstasy) users. *Experimental and Clinical Psychopharmacology, 13,* 137–145.

Montoya, R., & Insko, C. (2008). Toward a more complete understanding of the reciprocity of liking effect. *European Journal of Social Psychology, 38,* 477–498.

Moodley, R., Gielen, U. P., & Wu, R. (2013). *Handbook of counseling and psychotherapy in an international context.* New York: Routledge/Taylor & Francis Group.

Moody, H. R. (2000). *Aging: Concepts and controversies.* Thousand Oaks, CA: Sage.

Moore, J. (2010). What do mental terms mean? *The Psychological Record, 60,* 699–714.

Moorey, S. (2007) Cognitive therapy. In W. Dryden, *Dryden's handbook of individual therapy* (5th ed.). Thousand Oaks, CA: Sage.

Mora-Giral, M., Raich-Escursell, R. M., Segues, C. V., Torras-Clarasó, J., & Huon, G. (2004). Bulimia symptoms and risk factors in university students. *Eating and Weight Disorders, 9,* 163–169.

Morad, Y., Barkana, Y., Zadok, D., Hartstein, M., Pras, E., & Bar-Dayan, Y. (2009, July). Ocular parameters as an objective tool for the assessment of truck drivers fatigue. *Accident Analysis and Prevention, 41,* 856–860.

Moran, A. (2009). Cognitive psychology in sport: Progress and prospects. *Psychology of Sport and Exercise, 10,* 420–426.

Moretz, M., & McKay, D. (2009). The role of perfectionism in obsessive-compulsive symptoms: "Not just right" experiences and checking compulsions. *Journal of Anxiety Disorders, 23,* 640–644.

Moritz, S., & Laroi, F. (2008). Differences and similarities in the sensory and cognitive signatures of voice-hearing, intrusions and thoughts. *Schizophrenia Research, 102*(1–3), 96–107.

Morone, N. E., & Greco, C. M. (2007). Mind-body interventions for chronic pain in older adults: A structured review. *Pain Medicine, 8,* 359–375.

Morrone, A. S., & Pintrich, P. R. (2006). Achievement motivation. In G. G. Bear & K. M. Minke (Eds.), *Children's needs III: Development, prevention, and intervention.* Washington, DC: National Association of School Psychologists.

Morrow, J., & Wolff, R. (1991, May). Wired for a miracle. *Health,* pp. 64–84.

Morton, B. E. (2003). Asymmetry questionnaire outcomes correlate with several hemisphericity measures. *Brain and Cognition, 51,* 372–374.

Moscoso, S. C., Chaves, S. S., & Argilaga, M. T. A. (2013). Reporting a program evaluation: Needs, program plan, intervention, and decisions. *International Journal of Clinical and Health Psychology, 13,* 58–66.

Moshman, D. (2011). *Adolescent rationality and development: Cognition, morality, and identity* (3rd ed.). New York: Psychology Press.

Mueller, C. E. (2009). Protective factors as barriers to depression in gifted and nongifted adolescents. *Gifted Child Quarterly, 53,* 3–14.

Mullen, K. T., Beaudot, W. H. A. & Ivanov, I. V. (2011). Evidence that global processing does not limit thresholds for RF shape discrimination. *Journal of Vision, 11,* 1–21.

Müller, M., Bosy-Wesphal, A., & Heymsfield, S.B. (2010). Is there evidence for a set point that regulates human body weight? *Medicine Reports* (doi:10.3410/M2-59).

Mungan, E., Peynircioğlu, Z. F., & Halpern, A. R. (2011). Levels-of-processing effects on 'remember' responses in recognition for familiar and unfamiliar tunes. *The American Journal of Psychology, 124,* 37–48.

Murphy, G. L. (2005). The study of concepts inside and outside the laboratory: Medin versus Medin. In W. Ahn, R. L. Goldstone, B. C. Love, A. B. Markman, & P. Wolff (Eds.), *Categorization inside and outside the laboratory: Essays in honor of Douglas L. Medin.* Washington, DC: American Psychological Association.

Murray, M., & Tenenbaum, G. (2010). Computerized pedagogical agents as an educational means for developing physical self-efficacy and encouraging activity in youth. *Journal of Educational Computing Research, 42,* 267–283.

Murray, S. L., Holmes, J. G., & Griffin, D. W. (2004). The benefits of positive illusions: Idealization and the construction of satisfaction in close relationships. In H. T. Reis & C. E. Rusbult (Eds.), *Close relationships: Key readings.* Philadelphia, PA: Taylor & Francis.

Murthy, P., Kudlur, S., George, S., & Mathew, G. (2009). A clinical overview of fetal alcohol syndrome. *Addictive Disorders & Their Treatment, 8,* 1–12.

Myers, L. L. (2007). Anorexia nervosa, bulimia nervosa, and binge eating disorder. In B. A. Thyer & J. S. Wodarski (Eds.), *Social work in mental health: An evidence-based approach.* Hoboken, NJ: Wiley.

Myerson, J., Adams, D. R., Hale, S., & Jenkins, L. (2003). Analysis of group differences in processing speed: Brinley plots, Q-Q plots, and other conspiracies. *Psychonomic Bulletin and Review, 10,* 224–237.

Nader, E. G., Kleinman, A., Gomes, B., Bruscagin, C., Santos, B., Nicoletti, M., & Caetano, S. C. (2013). Negative expressed emotion best discriminates families with bipolar disorder children. *Journal of Affective Disorders, 148,* 418–423.

Nagai, Y., Goldstein, L. H., Fenwick, P. B. C., & Trimble, M. R. (2004). Clinical efficacy of galvanic skin response biofeedback training in reducing seizures in adult epilepsy: A preliminary randomized controlled study. *Epilepsy and Behavior, 5,* 216–223.

Nagda, B. A., Tropp, L. R., & Paluck, E. L. (2006). Looking back as we look ahead: Integrating research, theory, and practice on intergroup relations. *Journal of Social Research, 62,* 439–451.

Nagy, T. F. (2011). *Essential ethics for psychologists: A primer for understanding and mastering core issues.* Washington, DC: American Psychological Association.

Naimi, T., Nelson, D., & Brewer, R. (2010). The intensity of binge alcohol consumption among U.S. adults. *American Journal of Preventive Medicine, 38,* 201–207.

Najman, J. M., Aird, R., Bor, W., O'Callaghan, M., Williams, G. M., & Shuttlewood, G. J. (2004). The generational transmission of socioeconomic inequalities in child cognitive development and emotional health. *Social Science and Medicine, 58,* 1147–1158.

Nakato, E., Otsuka, Y., Kanazawa, S., Yamaguchi, M. K., & Kakigi, R. (2011). Distinct differences in the pattern of hemodynamic response to happy and angry facial expressions in infants—A near-infrared spectroscopic study. *NeuroImage, 54,* 1600–1606.

Namdar, G., Ganel, T., & Algom, D. (2016). The extreme relativity of perception: A new contextual effect modulates human resolving power. *Journal of Experimental Psychology: General.* Retrieved from http://www.ncbi.nlm.nih.gov/pubmed/26854497

Nasrallah, H., Black, D., Goldberg, J., Muzina, D., & Pariser, S. (2008). Issues associated with the use of atypical antipsychotic medications. *Annals of Clinical Psychiatry, 20,* S24–S29.

National Association for the Education of Young Children. (2005). *Position statements of the NAEYC.* Retrieved from www.naeyc.org/about/positions.asp#where

National Center for Health Statistics. (2000). 2000 CDC Growth Charts: United States. 28 pp. (PHS) 2000–1250. Washington, DC.

National Institute of Child Health and Human Development (NICHD) Early Child Care Research Network. (2001). Child-care and family predictors of preschool attachment and stability from infancy. *Development Psychology, 37,* 847–862.

National Institute of Child Health and Human Development (NICHD) Early Child Care Research Network. (2006). Child-care effect sizes for the NICHD study of early child care and youth development. *American Psychologist, 61,* 99–116.

National Institute on Drug Abuse. (2000). *Principles of drug addiction treatment: A research-based guide.* Washington, DC: National Institute on Drug Abuse.

Natvig, G. K., Albrektsen, G., & Ovarnstrom, U. (2003). Methods of teaching and class participation in relation to perceived social support and stress: Modifiable factors for improving health and well-being among students. *Educational Psychology, 23,* 261–274.

Navarrete, E., Pastore, M., Valentini, R., & Peressotti, F. (2015). First learned words are not forgotten: Age-of-acquisition effects in the tip-of-the-tongue experience. *Memory & Cognition, 43,* 1085–1103.

Neal, D., Matson, J. L., & Belva, B. C. (2013). An examination of the reliability of a new observation measure for Autism spectrum disorders: The autism spectrum disorder observation for children. *Research in Autism Spectrum Disorders, 7,* 29–34.

Nesheim, S., Henderson, S., Lindsay, M., Zuberi, J., Grimes, V., Buehler, J., Lindegren, M. L., & Bulterys, M. (2004). *Prenatal HIV testing and antiretroviral prophylaxis at an urban hospital—Atlanta, Georgia, 1997–2000.* Atlanta, GA: Centers for Disease Control.

Nestoriuc, Y., Martin, A., Rief, W., & Andrasik, F. (2008, September). Biofeedback treatment for headache disorders: A comprehensive efficacy review. *Applied Psychophysiology and Biofeedback, 33,* 125–140.

Neumark-Sztainer, D. (2009, March). Preventing obesity and eating disorders in adolescents: What can health care providers do? *Journal of Adolescent Health, 44,* 206–213.

Newby-Clark, I. R., & Ross, M. (2003). Conceiving the past and future. *Personality and Social Psychology Bulletin, 29,* 807–818.

Newman, C. F., Leahy, R. L., Beck, A. T., Reilly-Harrington, N. A., & Gyulai, L. (2002). *Bipolar disorder: A cognitive therapy approach.* Washington, DC: American Psychological Association.

Newman, S. D., Willoughby, G., & Pruce, B. (2011). The effect of problem structure on problem-solving: An fMRI study of word versus number problems. *Brain Research, 30,* 88–96.

Newport, F., & Carroll, J. (2002, November 27). Battle of the bulge: Majority of Americans want to lose weight. *Gallup News Service,* pp. 1–9.

Niccols, A. (2007). Fetal alcohol syndrome and the developing socio-emotional brain. *Brain Cognition, 65,* 135–142.

NICHD Early Child Care Research Network. (1999). Child care and mother-child interaction in the first three years of life. (1999). *Developmental Psychology, 35,* 1399–1413.

NICHD Early Child Care Research Network. (2001). Child-care and family predictors of preschool attachment and stability from infancy. Preview. *Developmental Psychology, 37,* 847–862.

Nichols, S. (2011, March 18). Experimental philosophy and the problem of free will. *Science, 331,* 1401–1403.

Nickerson, R. S., & Adams, M. J. (1979). *Cognitive Psychology, 11,* 297.

Nicodemus, K., Law, A., Radulescu, E., Luna, A., Kolachana, B., Vakkalanka, R., et al. (2010). Biological validation of increased schizophrenia risk with NRG1, ERBB4, and AKT1 epistasis via functional neuroimaging in healthy controls. *Archives of General Psychiatry, 67,* 991–1001.

Nicoli, L. (2016). I play doh: The art of plasticine in the process of adolescent subjectivation. *The International Journal of Psychoanalysis.* Retrieved from http://www.ncbi.nlm.nih.gov/pubmed/26895608

Nielsen, C., Staud, R., & Price, D. (2009, March). Individual differences in pain sensitivity: Measurement, causation, and consequences. *The Journal of Pain, 10,* 231–237.

Nielsen, T., O'Reilly, C., Carr, M., Dumel, G., Godin, I., Solomonova, E., Lara-Carrasco, J., Blanchette-Carrière ,C. & Paquette, T. (2015). Overnight improvements in two REM sleep-sensitive tasks are associated with both REM and NREM sleep changes, sleep spindle features, and awakenings for dream recall. *Neurobiology of Learning and Memory, 122,* 88–97.

Nimrod, G., & Kleiber, D. A. (2007). Reconsidering change and continuity in later life: Toward an innovation theory of successful aging. *International Journal of Human Development, 65,* 1–22.

Nisbett, R. E. (2007, December 9). All brains are the same color. *The New York Times*, p. E11.

Nisbett, R. E. (2009, February). All brains are the same color. *Association for Psychological Science Observer, 22*(3), 20–21.

Nittrouer, S., Lowenstein, J. H. (2007). Children's weighting strategies for word-final stop voicing are not explained by auditory sensitivities. *Journal of Speech, Language, and Hearing Research, 50*, 58–73.

Nivoli, A. A., Colom, F., Murru, A., Pacchiarotti, I., Castro-Loli, P., González-Pinto, A., & . . . Vieta, E. (2011). New treatment guidelines for acute bipolar depression: A systematic review. *Journal of Affective Disorders, 129*, 14–26.

Nolen-Hoeksema, S. (2007). *Abnormal psychology*. Boston: McGraw-Hill

Norcross, J. C. (2002). Empirically supported therapy relationships. In J. C. Norcross (Ed.), *Psychotherapy relationships that work: Therapist contributions and responsiveness to patients*. New York: Oxford University Press.

Norcross, J. C., Beutler, L. E., & Levant, R. F. (2006). *Evidence-based practices in mental health: Debate and dialogue on the fundamental questions*. Washington, DC: American Psychological Association.

Norlander, T., Von Schedvin, H., & Archer, T. (2005). Thriving as a function of affective personality: Relation to personality factors, coping strategies and stress. *Anxiety, Stress & Coping: An International Journal, 18*, 105–116.

Norman, P. (2011). The theory of planned behavior and binge drinking among undergraduate students: Assessing the impact of habit strength. *Addictive Behaviors, 36*, 107–116.

Norton, P. J., & Price, E. C. (2007). A meta-analytic review of adult cognitive-behavioral treatment outcome across the anxiety disorders. *Journal of Nervous and Mental Disease, 195*, 521–531.

Nosek, C. L., Kerr, C. W., Woodworth, J., Wright, S. T., Grant, P. C., Kuszczak, S. M., & . . . Depner, R. M. (2015). End-of-life dreams and visions: A qualitative perspective from hospice patients. *American Journal of Hospice & Palliative Medicine, 32*, 269–274.

Nourouzpour, N., Salomonczyk, D., Cressman, E. K., & Henriques, D. Y. (2015). Retention of proprioceptive recalibration following visuomotor adaptation. *Experimental Brain Research, 233*, 1019–1029.

Nurnberger, J. I., Jr., & Bierut, L. J. (2007, April). Seeking the connections: Alcoholism and our genes. *Scientific American*, 46–53.

Nussbaum, A. D., & Steele, C. M. (2007). Situational disengagement and persistence in the face of adversity. *Journal of Experimental Social Psychology, 43*, 127–134.

Nyaradi, A., Li, J., Hickling, S., Foster, J., & Oddy, W. H. (2013). The role of nutrition in children's neurocognitive development, from pregnancy through childhood. *Frontiers in Human Neuroscience*. Retrieved from http://www.ncbi.nlm.nih.gov/pubmed/23532379

O'Brien, K. M., & LeBow, M. D. (2007). Reducing maladaptive weight management practices: Developing a psychoeducational intervention program. *Eating Behaviors, 8*, 195–210.

O'Donnell, S. (2010). Understanding human development. *PsycCRITIQUES, 55*, 25–32.

O'Neill, S., McBride, C., Alford, S., & Kaphingst, K. (2010). Preferences for genetic and behavioral health information: The impact of risk factors and disease attributions. *Annals of Behavioral Medicine, 40*, 127–137.

Oberauer, K. (2010). Declarative and procedural working memory: Common principles, common capacity limits? *Psychologica Belgica, 50*, 277–308.

Odom, G., Banks, G., Schultz, B., Gregorevic, P., & Chamberlain, J. (2010). Preclinical studies for gene therapy of Duchenne muscular dystrophy. *Journal of Child Neurology, 25*, 1149–1157.

Oehman, A., & Mineka, S. (2003). The malicious serpent: Snakes as a prototypical stimulus for an evolved module of fear. *Current Directions in Psychological Science, 12*, 5–9.

Offer, D., Kaiz, M., Howard, K. I., & Bennett, E. S. (2000). The altering of reported experiences. *Journal of the American Academy of Child & Adolescent Psychiatry, 39*, 735–742.

Ogbu, J. (1992). Understanding cultural diversity and learning. *Educational Researcher, 21*, 5–14.

Ogbu, J. U. (2003). *Black American students in an affluent suburb*. Mahwah, NJ: Erlbaum.

Ogden, C. L., Carroll, M. D., Kit, B. K., & Flegal, K. M. (2014). Prevalence of childhood and adult obesity in the United States, 2011–2012. *Journal of the American Medical Association, 311*, 806–814.

Ogden, J. (2010). *The psychology of eating: From healthy to disordered behavior* (2nd ed.). New York: Wiley-Blackwell.

Ogren, K., & Sandlund, M. (2007). Lobotomy at a state mental hospital in Sweden. A survey of patients operated on during the period 1947–1958. *Nordic Journal of Psychiatry, 61*, 355–362.

Ohara, K. (2007). The n-3 polyunsaturated fatty acid/dopamine hypothesis of schizophrenia. *Progress in Neuro-Psychopharmacology & Biological Psychiatry, 31*, 469–474.

Okouchi, H. (2010). An exploration of remote history effects in humans: II. The effects under fixed-interval, variable-interval, and fixed-ratio schedules. *The Psychological Record, 60*, 27–42.

Olatunji, B. (2008). New directions in research on health anxiety and hypochondriasis: Commentary on a timely special series. *Journal of Cognitive Psychotherapy, 22*, 183–190.

Olfson, M., & Marcus, S. (2008). A case-control study of antidepressants and attempted suicide during early phase treatment of major depressive episodes. *Journal of Clinical Psychiatry, 69*, 425–432.

Oliver, M. B., & Hyde, J. S. (1993). Gender differences in sexuality: A meta-analysis. *Psychological Bulletin, 114*, 29–51.

Olson, D. H., & DeFrain, J. (2005). *Marriages and families: Intimacy, diversity, and strengths with PowerWeb*. New York: McGraw-Hill.

Oosten, J. E., Magnhagen, C., & Hemelrijk, C. K. (2010). Boldness by habituation and social interactions: A model. *Behavioral Ecology and Sociobiology, 64*, 793–802.

Opler, M., Perrin, M., Kleinhaus, K., & Malaspina, D. (2008). Factors in the etiology of schizophrenia: Genes, parental age, and environment. *Primary Psychiatry, 15*, 37–45.

Ornat, S. L., & Gallo, P. (2004). Acquisition, learning, or development of language? Skinner's "Verbal behavior" revisited. *Spanish Journal of Psychology, 7*, 161–170.

Ornellas, F., Souza-Mello, V., Mandarim-de-Lacerda, C. A., & Aguila, M. B. (2016). Combined parental obesity augments single-parent obesity effects on hypothalamus inflammation, leptin signaling (JAK/STAT), hyperphagia, and obesity in the adult mice offspring. *Physiology & Behavior, 153*, 47–55.

Orwin, R. G., & Condray, D. S. (1984). Smith and Glass' psychotherapy conclusions need further probing: On Landman and Dawes' re-analysis. *American Psychologist, 39*, 71–72.

Ouimet, A., Gawronski, B., & Dozois, D. (2009). Cognitive vulnerability to anxiety: A review and an integrative model. *Clinical Psychology Review, 29*, 459–470.

Oviedo-Joekes, E., et al. (2009). Diacetylmorphine versus methadone for the treatment of opioid addiction. *The New England Journal of Medicine, 361*, 777–786.

Pagani, C., Robustelli, F., & Ascione, F. (2010). Investigating animal abuse: Some theoretical and methodological issues. *Anthrozoös, 23*, 259–276.

Pagano, M. E., White, W. L., Kelly, J. F., Stout, R. L., & Tonigan, J. S. (2013). The 10-year course of Alcoholics Anonymous participation and long-term outcomes: A follow-up study of outpatient subjects in Project MATCH. *Substance Abuse, 34*, 51–59.

Pager, D., & Shepherd, H. (2008). The sociology of discrimination: Racial discrimination in employment, housing, credit, and consumer markets. *Annual Review of Sociology, 34,* 181–209.

Palmer, S., & Schloss, K. (2010). An ecological valence theory of human color preference. *PNAS Proceedings of the National Academy of Sciences of the United States of America, 107,* 8877–8882.

Palmiter, R. (2015). Hunger logic. *Nature Neuroscience, 18,* 789–791.

Palomar-García, M-Á., Bueicheků, E., Ávila, C., Sanjuán, A., Strijkers, K., Ventura-Campos, N., & Costa, A. (2015). Do bilinguals show neural differences with monolinguals when processing their native language? *Brain and Language, 142,* 36–44.

Pandya, M., Pozuelo, L., & Malone, D. (2007). Electroconvulsive therapy: What the internist needs to know. *Cleveland Clinic Journal of Medicine, 74,* 679–685.

Paniagua, F. A. (2000). *Diagnosis in a multicultural context: A casebook for mental health professionals.* Thousand Oaks, CA: Sage.

Pardini, D., White, H. R., Xiong, S., Bechtold, J., Chung, T., Loeber, R., & Hipwell, A. (2015). Unfazed or dazed and confused: Does early adolescent marijuana use cause sustained impairments in attention and academic functioning? *Journal of Abnormal Child Psychology.* Retrieved from http://www.ncbi.nlm.nih.gov/pubmed/25862212

Park, A. (2011, March 7). Healing the hurt. *Time,* 64–71.

Park, H., & Antonioni, D. (2007). Personality, reciprocity, and strength of conflict resolution strategy. *Journal of Research in Personality, 41,* 110–125.

Park, H., & Raymo, J. M. (2013). Divorce in Korea: Trends and educational differentials. *Journal of Marriage and Family, 75,* 110–126.

Parke, M. R., Seo, M., & Sherf, E. N. (2015). Regulating and facilitating: The role of emotional intelligence in maintaining and using positive affect for creativity. *Journal of Applied Psychology, 100,* 917–934.

Parker-Pope, T. (2003, April 22). The diet that works. *The Wall Street Journal,* pp. R1, R5.

Pascual, A., & Guéguen, N. (2005). Foot-in-the-door and door-in-the-face: A comparative meta-analytic study. *Psychological Reports, 96,* 122–128.

Pascual, A., & Guéguen, N. (2006). Door-in-the-face technique and monetary solicitation: An evaluation in a field setting. *Perceptual and Motor Skills, 103,* 974–978.

Passer, M. W., & Smith, R. E. (2001). *Psychology.* New York: McGraw-Hill.

Passos, V. L., Berger, M. P. F., & Tan, F. E. (2007). Test design optimization in CAT early stage with the nominal response model. *Applied Psychological Measurement, 31,* 213–232.

Pastukhov, A. (2016). Perception and the strongest sensory memory trace of multi-stable displays both form shortly after the stimulus onset. *Attention, Perception, & Psychophysics, 78,* 674–678.

Patterson, T. G., & Joseph, S. (2013). Unconditional positive self-regard. In M. E. Bernard (Ed.), *The strength of self-acceptance: Theory, practice and research.* New York: Springer Science + Business Media.

Paukert, A., Stagner, B., & Hope, K. (2004). The assessment of active listening skills in helpline volunteers. *Stress, Trauma, and Crisis: An International Journal, 7,* 61–76.

Paul, A. M. (2004). *Cult of personality: How personality tests are leading us to miseducate our children, mismanage our companies and misunderstand ourselves.* New York: Free Press.

Paul, H. (2010). The Karen Horney Clinic and the legacy of Horney. *The American Journal of Psychoanalysis, 70,* 63–64.

Paulmann, S., & Pell, M. (2010). Dynamic emotion processing in Parkinson's disease as a function of channel availability. *Journal of Clinical and Experimental Neuropsychology, 32,* 822–835.

Paulozzi, L. J. (2006). Opioid analgesic involvement in drug abuse deaths in American metropolitan areas. *American Journal of Public Health, 96,* 1755–1757.

Pavão, R., Tort, A. L., & Amaral, O. B. (2015). Multifactoriality in psychiatric disorders: A computational study of schizophrenia. *Schizophrenia Bulletin, 41,* 980–988.

Pavitt, C. (2007). Impression formation. In B. B. Whaley & W. Samter, *Explaining communication: Contemporary theories and exemplars.* Mahwah, NJ: Erlbaum.

Pearson, A. R., Dovidio, J. F., & Pratto, F. (2007). Racial prejudice, intergroup hate, and blatant and subtle bias of whites toward blacks in legal decision making in the United States. *International Journal of Psychology & Psychological Therapy, 7,* 125–134.

Pedersen, P. B., Draguns, J. G., Lonner, W. J., & Trimble, J. E. (Eds.). (2002). *Counseling across cultures* (5th ed.). Thousand Oaks, CA: Sage.

Pellis, S. M., & Pellis, V. C. (2007). Rough-and-tumble play and the development of the social brain. *Current Directions in Psychological Science, 16,* 95–97.

Pempek, T., Yermolayeva, Y., & Calvert, S. (2009). College students' social networking experiences on Facebook. *Journal of Applied Developmental Psychology, 30,* 227–238.

Penley, J. A., Tomaka, J., & Wiebe, J. S. (2002). The association of coping to physical and psychological health outcomes: A meta-analytic review. *Journal of Behavioral Medicine, 25,* 551–603.

Penn, D. L., Corrigan, P. W., Bentall, R. P., Racenstein, J. M., & Newman, L. (1997). Social cognition in schizophrenia. *Psychological Bulletin, 121,* 114–132.

Penney, J. B., Jr., (2000). Neurochemistry. In B. S. Fogel, R. B. Schiffer, et al. (Eds.), *Synopsis of neuropsychiatry.* New York: Lippincott Williams & Wilkins.

Pérez-Leroux, A. T., Pirvulescu, M., & Roberge, Y. (2011). Topicalization and object omission in child language. *First Language, 31,* 280–299.

Perovic, S., & Radenovic, L. (2011). Fine-tuning nativism: The 'nurtured nature' and innate cognitive structures. *Phenomenology and the Cognitive Sciences, 10,* 399–417.

Perry, J., Felce, D., Allen, D., & Meek, A. (2011). Resettlement outcomes for people with severe challenging behaviour moving from institutional to community living. *Journal of Applied Research in Intellectual Disabilities, 24,* 1–17.

Perry, J., Presniak, M. D., & Olson, T. R. (2013). Defense mechanisms in schizotypal, borderline, antisocial, and narcissistic personality disorders. *Psychiatry: Interpersonal and Biological Processes, 76,* 32–52.

Pervin, L. A. (1990). *Handbook of personality: Theory and research.* New York: Guilford Press.

Pervin, L. A. (2003). *The science of personality* (2nd ed.). London: Oxford University Press.

Pesmen, C. (2006). Health and wealth techniques to help keep chronic pain from taking over. *Money Builder, 35,* 48.

Peterson, C., & Park, N. (2010). What happened to self-actualization? Commentary on Kenrick et al. (2010). *Perspectives on Psychological Science, 5,* 320–322.

Peterson, R. A., & Brown, S. P. (2005). On the use of beta coefficients in meta-analysis. *Journal of Applied Psychology, 90,* 175–181.

Petersson, K. M., Silva, C., Castro-Caldas, A., Ingvar, M., & Reis, A. (2007). Literacy: A cultural influence on functional left-right differences in the inferior parietal cortex. *European Journal of Neuroscience, 26,* 791–799.

Petrill, S. A. (2005). Introduction to this special issue: Genes, environment, and the development of reading skills. *Scientific Studies of Reading, 9,* 189–196.

Pettigrew, T. F., & Tropp, L. R. (2006). A meta-analytic test of intergroup contact theory. *Journal of Personality and Social Psychology, 90,* 751–783.

Pettito, L. A. (1993). On the ontogenetic requirements for early language acquisition. In B. de Boysson-Bardies, S. de Schonen, P. W. Jusczyk, P. McNeilage, & J. Morton (Eds.), *Developmental neurocognition: Speech and face processing in the first year of life. NATO ASI series D: Behavioural and social sciences* (Vol. 69). Dordrecht, Netherlands: Kluwer Academic.

Phillips, M. (2013, December 12). The Lobotomy Files. *Wall Street Journal,* p. A1.

Piaget, J. (1970). Piaget's theory. In P. H. Mussen (Ed.), *Carmichael's manual of child psychology* (3rd ed., Vol. I). New York: Wiley.

Piaget, J., & Inhelder, B. (1958). *The growth of logical thinking from childhood to adolescence* (A. Parsons & S. Seagrin, Trans.). New York: Basic Books.

Pickering, G. J., & Gordon, R. (2006). Perception of mouthfeel sensations elicited by red wine are associated with sensitivity to 6-N-propylthiouracil. *Journal of Sensory Studies, 21,* 249–265.

Pickersgill, M. (2011). 'Promising' therapies: Neuroscience, clinical practice, and the treatment of psychopathy. *Sociology of Health & Illness, 33,* 448–464.

Pijnenborg, G. M., Timmerman, M. E., Derks, E. M., Fleischhacker, W. W., Kahn, R. S., & Aleman, A. (2015). Differential effects of antipsychotic drugs on insight in first episode schizophrenia: Data from the European First-Episode Schizophrenia Trial (EUFEST). *European Neuropsychopharmacology, 25,* 808–816.

Pinal, D., Zurrón, M., & Díaz, F. (2015). Age-related changes in brain activity are specific for high order cognitive processes during successful encoding of information in working memory. *Frontiers in Aging Neuroscience, 7,* 88– 97.

Pincus, T., & Morley, S. (2001). Cognitive-processing bias in chronic pain: A review and integration. *Psychological Bulletin, 127,* 599–617.

Pineda, J. A., Giromini, L., Porcelli, P., Parolin, L., & Viglione, D. J. (2011). Mu suppression and human movement responses to the Rorschach test. *NeuroReport: For Rapid Communication of Neuroscience Research, 22,* 223–226.

Pinker, S. (1994). *The language instinct.* New York: William Morrow.

Pinker, S. (2004). *How the mind works.* New York: Gardner Books.

Pinker, S., & Jackendoff, R. (2005). The faculty of language: What's special about it? *Cognition, 96,* 201–236.

Pinkerton, S. D., Bogart, L. M., Cecil, H., & Abramson, P. R. (2002). Factors associated with masturbation in a collegiate sample. *Journal of Psychology and Human Sexuality, 14,* 103–121.

Platek, S., & Kemp, S. (2009, February). Is family special to the brain? An event-related fMRI study of familiar, familial, and self-face recognition. *Neuropsychologia, 47,* 849–858.

Plomin, R., & Davis, O. (2009, January). The future of genetics in psychology and psychiatry: Microarrays, genome-wide association, and non-coding RNA. *Journal of Child Psychology and Psychiatry, 50,* 63–71.

Plomin, R., & Kovas, Y. (2005). Generalist genes and learning disabilities. *Psychological Bulletin, 131,* 592–617.

Plomin, R., & McGuffin, P. (2003). Psychopathology in the postgenomic era. *Annual Review of Psychology, 54,* 205–228.

Pluess, M., & Belsky, J. (2009). Differential susceptibility to rearing experience: The case of childcare. *Journal of Child Psychology and Psychiatry, 50,* 396–404.

Pohjolainen, V., Räsänen, P., Roine, R., Sintonen, H., Wahlbeck, K., & Karlsson, H. (2010). Cost-utility of treatment of bulimia nervosa. *International Journal of Eating Disorders, 43,* 596–602.

Pole, N. (2007). The psychophysiology of post-traumatic stress disorder: A meta-analysis. *Psychological Bulletin, 133,* 34–45.

Polivy, J., Herman, C. P., & Boivin, M. (2005). Eating disorders. In J. E. Maddux and B. A. Winstead, *Psychopathology: Foundations for a contemporary understanding* (pp. 229–254). Mahwah, NJ: Erlbaum.

Polonsky, D. C. (2006). Review of the big book of masturbation: From angst to zeal. *Journal of Sex & Marital Therapy, 32,* 75–78.

Ponterotto, J. G., Gretchen, D., & Chauhan, R. V. (2001). Cultural identity and multicultural assessment: Quantitative and qualitative tools for the clinician. In L. A. Suzuki, & J. G. Ponterotto (Eds.), *Handbook of multicultural assessment: Clinical, psychological, and educational applications* (2nd ed.). San Francisco: Jossey-Bass/Pfeiffer.

Ponterotto, J. G., Utsey, S. O., & Pedersen, P. B. (2006). *Preventing prejudice: A guide for counselors, educators, and parents.* Thousand Oaks, CA: Sage Publications.

Poo, C., & Isaacson, J. S. (2007). An early critical period for long-term plasticity and structural modification of sensory synapses in olfactory cortex. *Journal of Neuroscience, 27,* 7553–7558.

Popa, D., Léna, C., Alexandre, C., & Adrien, J. (2008). Lasting syndrome of depression produced by reduction in serotonin uptake during postnatal development: Evidence from sleep, stress, and behavior. *The Journal of Neuroscience, 28,* 88–97.

Porkka-Heiskanen, T. (2013). Sleep homeostasis. *Current Opinion in Neurobiology, 23,* 799–805.

Porkka-Heiskanen, T., & Kalinchuk, A. V. (2011). Adenosine, energy metabolism and sleep homeostasis. *Sleep Medicine Reviews, 15,* 123–135.

Porter, S. C., Rheinschmidt-Same, M., & Richeson, J. A. (2016). Inferring identity from language: Linguistic intergroup bias informs social categorization. *Psychological Science, 27,* 94–102.

Porto, R. R. (2011). The placebo effect: Its importance in treatment. *Sexologies: European Journal of Sexology and Sexual Health/Revue européenne de sexologie et de santé sexuelle, 20,* 15–19.

Post, J. M. (2015). Terrorism and right-wing extremism: The changing face of terrorism and political violence in the 21st century: The virtual community of hatred. *International Journal of Group Psychotherapy,* Special Issue: Violence in America: Part II. pp. 243–271.

Post, J., Ali, F., Henderson, S., Shanfield, S., Victoroff, J., & Weine, S. (2009, Spring). The psychology of suicide terrorism. *Psychiatry: Interpersonal and Biological Processes, 72,* 13–31.

Potash, J. S. (2015). Archetypal aesthetics: Viewing art through states of consciousness. *International Journal of Jungian Studies, 7,* 139–153.

Potegal, M. (2010). The temporal dynamics of anger: Phenomena, processes, and perplexities. In M. Potegal, G. Stemmler, & C. Spielberger (Eds.) *International handbook of anger: Constituent and concomitant biological, psychological, and social processes.* New York: Springer Science + Business Media.

Pottick, K. J., Kirk, S. A., Hsieh, D. K., & Tian, X. (2007). Judging mental disorder in youths: Effects of client, clinician, and contextual differences. *Journal of Consulting Clinical Psychology, 75,* 1–8.

Pow, J. L., Baumeister, A. A., Hawkins, M. F., Cohen, A. S., & Garand, J. C. (2015). Deinstitutionalization of American public hospitals for the mentally ill before and after the introduction of antipsychotic medications. *Harvard Review of Psychiatry, 23,* 176–187.

Powell, L. H. (2006). Review of marital and sexual lifestyles in the United States: attitudes, behaviors, and relationships in social context. *Family Relations, 55,* 149.

Powell, R. A., Digdon, N., Harris, B., & Smithson, C. (2014). Correcting the record on Watson, Rayner, and Little Albert: Albert Barger as "Psychology's Lost Boy." *American Psychologist, 69,* 600–611.

Powers, M., & Emmelkamp, P. (2008). Virtual reality exposure therapy for anxiety disorders: A meta-analysis. *Journal of Anxiety Disorders, 22,* 561–569.

Prasser, J., Schecklmann, M., Poeppl, T. B., Frank, E., Kreuzer, P. M., Hajak, G., Rupprecht, R., Landgrebe, M. & Langguth, B. (2015). Bilateral prefrontal rTMS and theta burst TMS as an add-on treatment for depression: A randomized placebo controlled trial. *The World Journal of Biological Psychiatry, 16,* 57–65.

Pratkanis, A. R. (2007). Social influence analysis: An index of tactics. In A. R. Pratkanis, *The science of social influence: Advances and future progress.* New York: Psychology Press.

Pratt, H. D., Phillips, E. L., Greydanus, D. E., & Patel, D. R. (2003). Eating disorders in the adolescent population: Future directions [Special issue: Eating disorders in adolescents]. *Journal of Adolescent Research, 18,* 297–317.

Pressley, M. P., & Harris., K. R. (2006). Cognitive strategies instruction: From basic research to classroom instruction. In P. A. Alexander & P. H. Winne, *Handbook of educational psychology.* Mahwah, NJ: Erlbaum.

Pretsch, J., Heckmann, N., Flunger, B., & Schmitt, M. (2013). Agree or disagree? Influences on consensus in personality judgments. *European Journal of Psychological Assessment.* Retrieved from http://psycnet.apa.org/psycinfo/2013-30588-001/

Pretzer, J. L., & Beck, A. T. (2005). A cognitive theory of personality disorders. In M. F. Lenzenweger & J. F. Clarkin (Eds.), *Major theories of personality disorder* (2nd ed.). New York: Guilford Press.

Price, J. (2013). Meet the real Jill Price. http://www.jillprice.com/. Downloaded October 15, 2013.

Prime, D., & Jolicoeur, P. (2010). Mental rotation requires visual short-term memory: Evidence from human electric cortical activity. *Journal of Cognitive Neuroscience, 22,* 2437–2446.

Prince, C. V. (2005). Homosexuality, transvestism and transsexuality: Reflections on their etymology and differentiation. *International Journal of Transgenderism, 8,* 15–18.

Prinz, J. J. (2007). Emotion: Competing theories and philosophical issues. In P. Thagard, *Philosophy of psychology and cognitive science.* Amsterdam, Netherlands: North Holland/Elsevier.

Prislin, R., Brewer, M., & Wilson, D. J. (2002). Changing majority and minority positions within a group versus an aggregate. *Personality and Social Psychology Bulletin, 28,* 650–647.

Proffitt, D. R. (2006). Distance perception. *Current Directions in Psychological Science, 15,* 131–139.

Prohovnik, I., Skudlarski, P., Fulbright, R. K., Gore, J. C., & Wexler, B. E. (2004). Functional MRI changes before and after onset of reported emotions. *Psychiatry Research: Neuroimaging, 132,* 239–250.

Proudfoot, D. (2009). Meaning and mind: Wittgenstein's relevance for the 'does language shape thought?' debate. *New Ideas in Psychology, 27,* 163–183.

Proyer, R. T., Gander, F., Wellenzohn, S., & Ruch, W. (2013). What good are character strengths beyond subjective well-being? The contribution of the good character on self-reported health-oriented behavior, physical fitness, and the subjective health status. *The Journal of Positive Psychology, 8,* 222–232.

Prus, A. J., Mooney-Leber, S. M., Berquist, M. I., Pehrson, A. L., Porter, N. P., & Porter, J. H. (2015). The antidepressant drugs fluoxetine and duloxetine produce anxiolytic-like effects in a schedule-induced polydipsia paradigm in rats: Enhancement of fluoxetine's effects by the α_2 adrenoceptor antagonist yohimbine. *Behavioural Pharmacology, 26,* 489–494.

Puca, R. M. (2005). The influence of the achievement motive on probability estimates in pre- and post-decisional action phases. *Journal of Research in Personality, 39,* 245–262.

Puffer, E., Schatz, J., & Roberts, C. (2010). Relationships between somatic growth and cognitive functioning in young children with sickle cell disease. *Journal of Pediatric Psychology, 35,* 892–904.

Puhl, R. M. & Liu, S. (2015). A national survey of public views about the classification of obesity as a disease. *Obesity, 23,* 1288–1295.

Puller, C., & Haverkamp, S. (2011). Bipolar cell pathways for color vision in non-primate dichromats. *Visual Neuroscience, 28,* 51–60.

Purdy, S. C., Sharma, M. M., Munro, K. J., & Morgan, C. A. (2013). Stimulus level effects on speech-evoked obligatory cortical auditory evoked potentials in infants with normal hearing. *Clinical Neurophysiology, 124,* 474–480.

Qin, S., Ge, S., Yin, H., Xia, J., & Heynderickx, I. (2010). Just noticeable difference in black level, white level and chroma for natural images measured in two different countries. *Displays, 31,* 25–34.

Qu, C., Zhang, A., & Chen, Q. (2013). Monetary effects on fear conditioning. *Psychological Reports, 112,* 353–364.

Rabin, J. (2004). Quantification of color vision with cone contrast sensitivity. *Visual Neuroscience, 21,* 483–485.

Radvansky, G. A., Pettijohn, K. A., & Kim, J. (2015). Walking through doorways causes forgetting: Younger and older adults. *Psychology and Aging, 30,* 259–265.

Radvansky, G.A. (2010). *Human memory.* N.Y.: Psychology Press.

Raes, A. K., Koster, E. W., Van Damme, S., Fias, W., & De Raedt, R. (2010). Aversive conditioning under conditions of restricted awareness: Effects on spatial cueing. *The Quarterly Journal of Experimental Psychology, 63,* 2336–2358.

Rahman, Q., & Yusuf, S. (2015). Lateralization for processing facial emotions in gay men, heterosexual men, and heterosexual women. *Archives Of Sexual Behavior, 44,* 1405–1413.

Rahman, Q., Kumari, V., & Wilson, G. D. (2003). Sexual orientation-related differences in prepulse inhibition of the human startle response. *Behavioral Neuroscience, 117,* 1096–1102.

Rajagopal, S. (2006). The placebo effect. *Psychiatric Bulletin, 30,* 185–188.

Ralston, A. (2005). *Between a rock and a hard place.* NY: Atria.

Ramsay, M. C., Reynolds, C. R., & Kamphaus, R. W. (2002). *Essentials of behavioral assessment.* New York: Wiley.

Ramus, F. (2006). Genes, brain, and cognition: A roadmap for the cognitive scientist. *Cognition, 101,* 247–269.

Rangell, L. (2007). *The road to unity in psychoanalytic theory.* Lanham, MD: Jason Aronson.

Rapport, R. L. (2005). *Nerve endings: The discovery of the synapse.* New York: W. W. Norton.

Rassin, E., & Muris, P. (2007). Abnormal and normal obsessions: A reconsideration. *Behaviour Research and Therapy, 45,* 1065–1070.

Rastad, C., Ulfberg, J., & Lindberg, P. (2008). Light room therapy effective in mild forms of seasonal affective disorder—A randomised controlled study. *Journal of Affective Disorders, 108*(3), 291–296.

Ray, R., et al. (2008). Neuroimaging, genetics and the treatment of nicotine addiction. *Behavioural Brain Research, 193,* 159–169.

Raz, A. (2007). Suggestibility and hypnotizability: Mind the gap. *American Journal of Clinical Hypnosis, 49,* 205–210.

Reddy, S. (2013, September 3). A field guide to the perfect nap. *Wall Street Journal,* pp. D1–D2.

Redish, A. D. (2004). Addiction as a computational process gone awry. *Science, 306,* 1944–1947.

Reed, P. (2007). Response rate and sensitivity to the molar feedback function relating response and reinforcement rate on VI + schedules of reinforcement. *Journal of Experimental Psychology: Animal Behavior Processes, 33,* 428–439.

Reed, P., & Morgan, T. (2008). Effect on subsequent fixed-interval schedule performance of prior exposure to ratio and interval schedules of reinforcement. *Learning & Behavior, 36,* 82–91.

Rees, P., & Seaton, N. (2011). Psychologists' response to crises: International perspectives. *School Psychology International, 32,* 73–94.

Refinetti, R. (2005). Time for sex: Nycthemeral distribution of human sexual behavior. *Journal of Circadian Rhythms, 3,* 1–4.

Regan, P. C. (2006). Love. In R. D. McAnulty, & M. M. Burnette, *Sex and sexuality, Vol 2: Sexual function and dysfunction.* Westport, CT: Praeger Publishers/Greenwood Publishing.

Reid, J. R., MacLeod, J., & Robertson, J. R. (2010). Cannabis and the lung. *Journal of the Royal College of Physicians, 40,* 328–334.

Reid, T. (2015, September 21). American Muslims fear a new wave of Islamophobia. *Reuters.* Retrieved from http://www.reuters.com/article/2015/09/22/us-usa-election-muslims-idUSKCN0RL2HU20150922

Reijonen, J. H., Pratt, H. D., Patel, D. R., & Greydanus, D. E. (2003). Eating disorders in the adolescent population: An overview [Special issue: Eating disorders in adolescents]. *Journal of Adolescent Research, 18,* 209–222.

Reinecke, A., Cooper, M., Favaron, E., Massey-Chase, R., & Harmer, C. (2011). Attentional bias in untreated panic disorder. *Psychiatry Research, 185,* 387–393.

Reiner, R. (2008, March). Integrating a portable biofeedback device into clinical practice for patients with anxiety disorders: Results of a pilot study. *Applied Psychophysiology and Biofeedback, 33,* 55–61.

Reisberg, D. (2009). *Cognition: Exploring the science of the mind.* New York: Norton.

Reisner, A. D., Piel, J., & Makey, M. R. (2013). Competency to stand trial and defendants who lack insight into their mental illness. *Journal of the American Academy of Psychiatry and the Law, 41,* 85–91.

Renken, L. (2015, August 1). Treatment offers hope to Princeton woman fighting rare neurological disease. *Princeton Journal Star.* Retrieved from http://www.pjstar.com/article/20150801/NEWS/150809986

Repp, B. H., & Knoblich, G. (2007). Action can affect auditory perception. *Psychological Science, 18,* 6–7.

Reuter, T., Ziegelmann, J., Wiedemann, A., Geiser, C., Lippke, S., Schüz, B., et al. (2010). Changes in intentions, planning, and self-efficacy predict changes in behaviors: An application of latent true change modeling. *Journal of Health Psychology, 15,* 935–947.

Reyes, R., & Simon-Gunn, J. (2016). Motivation. In R. Bargdill & R. Broomé (Eds.), *Humanistic contributions for psychology 101: Growth, choice, and responsibility.* New York: University Professors Press.

Rezazadeh, S., & Shaw, S. (2010). Rare chromosomal disorders. *Genetic and acquired disorders.* Thousand Oaks, CA/Washington, DC: Corwin Press.

Reznikova, T. N., Seliverstova, N. A., Kataeva, G. V., Aroev, R. A., Ilves, A. G., Kuznetsova, A. K., & Makeeva, E. (2015). Functional activity of brain structures and predisposition to aggression in patients with lingering diseases of the CNS. *Human Physiology, 41,* 27–33.

Rice, C. (2009, December 18). Prevalence of Autism Spectrum Disorders—Autism and Developmental Disabilities Monitoring Network, United States, 2006. *MMWR, 58*(SS10), 1–20.

Rice, E., Milburn, N. G., & Monro, W. (2011). Social networking technology, social network composition, and reductions in substance use among homeless adolescents. *Prevention Science, 12,* 80–88.

Rice, M. L., Tomblin, J. B., Hoffman, L., Richman, W. A., & Marquis, J. (2004). Grammatical tense deficits in children with SLI and nonspecific language impairment: Relationships with non-verbal IQ over time. *Journal of Speech, Language, and Hearing Research, 47,* 816–834.

Richards, C. (2011). Transsexualism and existentialism. *Existential Analysis, 22*(2), 272–279.

Richards, G. (2010). *Putting psychology in its place: Critical historical perspectives* (3rd ed.). New York: Routledge/Taylor & Francis Group.

Richardson, A. S., Bergen, H. A., Martin, G., Roeger, L., & Allison, S. (2005). Perceived academic performance as an indicator of risk of attempted suicide in young adolescents. *Archives of Suicide Research, 9,* 163–176.

Richardson, J. E. (2011). The academic engagement of White and ethnic minority students in distance education. *Educational Psychology, 31,* 123–139.

Rieber, R. W., & Robinson, D. K. (2006). Review of the essential Vygotsky. *Journal of the History of the Behavioral Sciences, 42,* 178–180.

Rigby, L., & Waite, S. (2007). Group therapy for self-esteem, using creative approaches and metaphor as clinical tools. *Behavioural and Cognitive Psychotherapy, 35,* 361–364.

Rimmele, J. M., Sussman, E., & Poeppel, D. (2015). The role of temporal structure in the investigation of sensory memory, auditory scene analysis, and speech perception: A healthy-aging perspective. *International Journal of Psychophysiology, 95,* 175–183.

Rinaman, L., Banihashemi, L., & Koehnle, T. J. (2011). Early life experience shapes the functional organization of stress-responsive visceral circuits. *Physiology & Behavior, 104,* 632–640.

Rindone, H. G. (2015). Methamphetamine addiction. In R. L. Smith (Ed.), *Treatment strategies for substance and process addictions.* Alexandria, VA: American Counseling Association.

Rinn, W. E. (1984). The neuropsychology of facial expression: A review of neurological and psychological mechanisms for producing facial expressions. *Psychological Bulletin, 95,* 52–77.

Rinn, W. E. (1991). Neuropsychology of facial expression. In R. S. Feldman & B. Rimé (Eds.), *Fundamentals of nonverbal behavior.* Cambridge, England: Cambridge University Press.

Rivera-García, A., Ramírez-Salado, I., Corsi-Cabrera, M., & Calvo, J. (2011). Facial muscle activation during sleep and its relation to the rapid eye movements of REM sleep. *Journal of Sleep Research, 20,* 82–91.

Rivera-Gaxiola, M., Klarman, L., Garcia-Sierra, A., & Kuhl, P. K. (2005). Neural patterns to speech and vocabulary growth in American infants. *Neuroreport: For Rapid Communication of Neuroscience Research, 16,* 495–498.

Robinson-Papp, J., George, M. C., Dorfman, D., & Simpson, D. M. (2015). Barriers to chronic pain measurement: A qualitative study of patient perspectives. *Pain Medicine, 16,* 1256–1264.

Robinson, D. N. (2007). Theoretical psychology: What is it and who needs it? *Theory & Psychology, 17,* 187–198.

Robinson, E., Oldham, M., Cuckson, I., Brunstrom, J. M., Rogers, P. J., & Hardman, C. A. (2016). Visual exposure to large and small portion sizes and perceptions of portion size normality: Three experimental studies. *Appetite, 98,* 28–34.

Roe, D., Weishut, D. J. N., Jaglom, M. & Rabinowitz, J. (2002). Patients' and staff members' attitudes about the rights of hospitalized psychiatric patients. *Psychiatric Services, 53*(1), 87–91.

Roehm, M. L. (2016). An exploration of flashbulb memory. *Journal of Consumer Psychology, 26,* 1–16.

Roets, A., & Van Hiel, A. (2011). An integrative process approach on judgment and decision making: The impact of arousal, affect, motivation, and cognitive ability. *The Psychological Record, 61,* 497–520.

Roffman, R. A. (2013). Legalization of marijuana: Unraveling quandaries for the addiction professional. *Frontiers in Psychiatry, 4,* 88–93.

Rogers, B., & Naumenko, O. (2015). The new moon illusion and the role of perspective in the perception of straight and parallel lines. *Attention, Perception, & Psychophysics, 77,* 249–257.

Rogers, C. R. (1971). A theory of personality. In S. Maddi (Ed.), *Perspectives on personality.* Boston: Little, Brown.

Rogers, C. R. (1995). *A way of being.* Boston: Houghton Mifflin.

Rogers, J. M. (2009). Tobacco and pregnancy: Overview of exposures and effects. *Birth Defects Res. C. Embryo Today, 84,* 152–160.

Rogers, L. J. (2011). Review of "The master and his emissary: The divided brain and the making of the western world." *Laterality: Asymmetries of Body, Brain and Cognition, 16,* 125–128.

Rogers, S. (2007). The underlying mechanisms of semantic memory loss in Alzheimer's disease and semantic dementia. *Dissertation Abstracts International: Section B: The Sciences and Engineering, 67*(10-B), 5591.

Roid, G., Nellis, L. & McLellan, M. (2003). Assessment with the Leiter International Performance Scale—Revised and the S-BIT. In R. S. McCallum & R. Steve (Eds.), *Handbook of nonverbal assessment.* New York, NY: Kluwer Academic/Plenum Publishers.

Roizen, N. J., & Patterson, D. (2003). Down's syndrome. *Lancet, 361,* 1281–1289.

Romano, E., Tremblay, R. E, Vitaro, E., Zoccolillo, M., & Pagani, L. (2001.) Prevalence of psychiatric diagnoses and the role of perceived impairment: Findings from an adolescent community sample. *Journal of Child Psychology and Psychiatry and Allied Disciplines, 42,* 451–461.

Romero-Guevara, R., Cencetti, F., Donati, C., & Bruni, P. (2015). Sphingosine 1-phosphate signaling pathway in inner ear biology. New therapeutic strategies for hearing loss? *Frontiers in Aging Neuroscience, 7,* 101–111.

Rorschach, H. (1924). *Psychodiagnosis: A diagnostic test based on perception.* New York: Grune & Stratton.

Rosch, E., & Mervis, C. B. (1975). Family resemblances: Studies in the internal structure of categories. *Cognitive-Psychology, 7,* 573–605.

Rosellini, A. J., Stein, M. B., Colpe, L. J., Heeringa, S. G., Petukhova, M. V., Sampson, N. A., & . . . Kessler, R. C. (2015). Approximating a DSM-5 diagnosis of PTSD using DSM-IV criteria. *Depression and Anxiety, 32,* 493–501.

Rosenbloom, T., & Wolf, Y. (2002). Sensation seeking and detection of risky road signals: A developmental perspective. *Accident Analysis and Prevention, 34,* 569–580.

Rosenfeld, B., Green, D., Pivovarova, E., Dole, T., & Zapf, P. (2010). What to do with contradictory data? Approaches to the integration of multiple malingering measures. *The International Journal of Forensic Mental Health, 9,* 63–73.

Rosenfeld, M. J., & Thomas, R. J. (2102). Searching for a mate: The rise of the internet as a social intermediary. *American Sociological Review, 77,* 523–547.

Rosenstein, D. S., & Horowitz, H. A. (1996). Adolescent attachment and psychopathology. *Journal of Consulting and Clinical Psychology, 64,* 244–253.

Rosenthal, R. (2002). Covert communication in classrooms, clinics, courtrooms and cubicles. *American Psychologist, 57,* 838–849.

Rosenthal, R. (2003). Covert communication in laboratories, classrooms, and the truly real world. *Current Directions in Psychological Science, 12,* 151–154.

Ross, C. A. (2015). When to suspect and how to diagnose dissociative identity disorder. *Journal of EMDR Practice And Research, 9,* 114–120.

Ross, C., & Ness, L. (2010). Symptom patterns in dissociative identity disorder patients and the general population. *Journal of Trauma & Dissociation, 11,* 458–468.

Ross, J. (2006). Sleep on a problem. . . . It works like a dream. *The Psychologist, 19,* 738–740.

Rossato, M., Pagano, C., & Vettor, R. (2008). The cannabinoid system and male reproductive functions. *Journal of Neuroendocrinology, 20,* 90–93.

Rossell, S. L., Bullmore, E. T., Williams, S. C. R., & David, A. S. (2002). Sex differences in functional brain activation during a lexical visual field task. *Brain and Language, 80,* 97–105.

Rossouw, J. E., Prentice, R. L., Manson, J. E., Wu, L., Barad, D., Barnabei, V. M., Ko, M., LaCroix, A. Z., Margolis, K. L., & Stefanick, M. L. (2007). Postmenopausal hormone therapy and risk of cardiovascular disease by age and years since menopause. *Journal of the American Medical Association, 297,* 1465–1477.

Roughton, R. E. (2002). Rethinking homosexuality: What it teaches us about psychoanalysis. *Journal of the American Psychoanalytic Association, 50,* 733–763.

Rowe, J. B., Toni, I., Josephs, O., Frackowiak, R. S. J., & Passingham, R. E. (2000, June 2). The prefrontal cortex: Response selection or maintenance within working memory? *Science, 288,* 1656–1660.

Røysamb, E., Kendler, K. S., Tambs, K., Ørstavik, R. E., Neale, M. C., Aggen, S. H., & … Reichborn-Kjennerud, T. (2011). The joint structure of DSM-IV Axis I and Axis II disorders. *Journal of Abnormal Psychology, 120,* 198–209.

Royzman, E. B., Cassidy, K. W., & Baron, J. (2003). "I know, you know": Epistemic egocentrism in children and adults. *Review of General Psychology, 7,* 38–65.

Rozin, P., Kabnick, K., Pete, E., Fischler, C., & Shields, C. (2003). The ecology of eating: Smaller portion sizes in France than in the United States help explain the French paradox. *Psychological Science, 14,* 450–454.

Rubichi, S., Ricci, F., Padovani, R., & Scaglietti, L. (2005). Hypnotic susceptibility, baseline attentional functioning, and the Stroop task. *Consciousness and Cognition: An International Journal, 14,* 296–303.

Rubin, D. C. (1985, September). The subtle deceiver: Recalling our past. *Psychology Today,* pp. 39–46.

Rubin, D. C., Schrauf, R. W., Gulgoz, S., & Naka, M. (2007). Cross-cultural variability of component processes in autobiographical remembering: Japan, Turkey, and the USA. *Memory, 15,* 536–547.

Rudman, L. A., & Ashmore, R. D. (2007). Discrimination and the Implicit Association Test. *Group Processes & Intergroup Relations, 10,* 359–372.

Rueckemann, J. W., DiMauro, A. J., Rangel, L. M., Han, X., Boyden, E. S., & Eichenbaum, H. (2016). Transient optogenetic inactivation of the medial entorhinal cortex biases the active population of hippocampal neurons. *Hippocampus, 26,* 246–260.

Ruggs, E. N., Martinez, L. R., & Hebl, M. R. (2011). How individuals and organizations can reduce interpersonal discrimination. *Social and Personality Psychology Compass, 5,* 29–42.

Ruiz, M. R. (2015). Behaviourisms: Radical behaviourism and critical inquiry. In I. Parker (Ed.), *Handbook of critical psychology.* NY: Routledge/Taylor & Francis Group.

Rulison, K. L., & Loken, E. (2009). I've fallen and I can't get up: Can high-ability students recover from early mistakes in CAT? *Applied Psychological Measurement, 33,* 83–101.

Ruscher, J. B., Fiske, S. T., & Schnake, S. B. (2000). The motivated tactician's juggling act: Compatible vs. incompatible impression goals. *British Journal of Social Psychology, 39,* 241–256.

Russell, S. T., Chu, J. Y., Crockett, L. J., & Lee, S. (2010). Interdependent independence: The meanings of autonomy among Chinese American and Filipino American adolescents. In S. T. Russell, L. J. Crockett, & R. K. Chao (Eds.), *Asian American parenting and parent–adolescent relationships.* New York: Springer Science + Business Media.

Russo, N. (1981). Women in psychology. In L. T. Benjamin, Jr., & K. D. Lowman (Eds.), *Activities handbook for the teaching of psychology.* Washington, DC: American Psychological Association.

Rutherford, B., Rose, S., Sneed, J., & Roose, S. (2009, April). Study design affects participant expectations: A survey. *Journal of Clinical Psychopharmacology, 29,* 179–181.

Rutland, A., & Killen, M. (2015). A developmental science approach to reducing prejudice and social exclusion: Intergroup processes, social-cognitive development, and moral reasoning. *Social Issues and Policy Review, 9,* 121–154.

Ryan, R. M., & Deci, E. L. (2011). A self-determination theory perspective on social, institutional, cultural, and economic supports for autonomy and their importance for well-being. In V. I. Chirkov, R. M. Ryan, & K. M. Sheldon (Eds.), *Human autonomy in cross-cultural context: Perspectives on the psychology of agency, freedom, and well-being.* New York: Springer Science + Business Media.

Sa, M. (2015). Mood and personality disorders. In G. M. Kapalka (Ed.), *Treating disruptive disorders: A guide to psychological, pharmacological, and combined therapies.* New York: Routledge/Taylor & Francis Group.

Saarni, C. (1999). *Developing emotional competence.* New York: Guilford Press.

Saczynski, J., Willis, S., & Schaie, K. (2002). Strategy use in reasoning training with older adults. *Aging, Neuropsychology, & Cognition, 9,* 48–60.

Sado, M., Yamauchi, K., Kawakami, N., Ono, Y., Furukawa, T. A., Tsuchiya, M., & . . . Kashima, H. (2011). Cost of depression among adults in Japan in 2005. *Psychiatry and Clinical Neurosciences, 65,* 442–450.

Safran, J. D., Eubanks-Carter, C., & Muran, J. (2010). Emotion-focused/interpersonal cognitive therapy. In N. Kazantzis, M. A. Reinecke, & A. Freeman (Eds.), *Cognitive and behavioral theories in clinical practice.* New York: Guilford Press.

Saggino, A., Perfetti, B., & Spitoni, G. (2006). Fluid intelligence and executive functions: New perspectives. In L. V. Wesley, *Intelligence: New research.* Hauppauge, NY: Nova Science Publishers.

Salazar, L. F., Crosby, R. A., & DiClemente, R. J. (2015). Experimental research designs. In L. F. Salazar, R. A. Crosby, & R. J. DiClemente (Eds.), *Research methods in health promotion* (2nd ed.). San Francisco: Jossey-Bass.

Salmela-Aro, K., & Nurmi, J-E. (2007). Self-esteem during university studies predicts career characteristics 10 years later. *Journal of Vocational Behavior, 70,* 463–477.

Salvi, V., Fagiolini, A., Swartz, H., Maina, G., & Frank, E. (2008). The use of antidepressants in bipolar disorder. *Journal of Clinical Psychiatry, 69,* 1307–1318.

Samoilov, V., & Zayas, V. (2007). Ivan Petrovich Pavlov (1849–1936). *Journal of the History of the Neurosciences, 16,* 74–89.

Samuel, D. B., & Widiger, T. A. (2006). Differentiating normal and abnormal personality from the perspective of the DSM. In S. Strack, *Differentiating normal and abnormal personality* (2nd ed.). New York: Springer Publishing.

Samuel, D. B., Carroll, K. M., Rounsaville, B. J., & Ball, S. A. (2013). Personality disorders as maladaptive, extreme variants of normal personality: Borderline personality disorder and neuroticism in a substance using sample. *Journal of Personality Disorders, 27,* 625–635.

Sanderson, M. (2007). Assessment of manic symptoms in different cultures. *British Journal of Psychiatry, 190,* 178.

Sandman, C. A. (2015). Mysteries of the human fetus revealed. *Monographs of the Society for Research in Child Development, 80,* 124–137.

Sandomir, R. (2007, July 17). W. W. E.'s testing is examined after Benoit murder-suicide. *The New York Times,* p. S3.

Sandoval, J., Frisby, C. L., Geisinger, K. F., Scheuneman, J. D., & Grenier, J. R. (Eds.). (1998). *Test interpretation and diversity: Achieving equity in assessment.* Washington, DC: American Psychological Association.

Sanes, J. R., & Masland, R. H. (2015). The types of retinal ganglion cells: Current status and implications for neuronal classification. *Annual Review of Neuroscience, 38,* 221–246.

Sankar, T., Lipsman, N., & Lozano, A. M. (2014). Deep brain stimulation for disorders of memory and cognition. *Neurotherapeutics, 11*(3), 527-534.

Sapolsky, R. M. (2003). Gene therapy for psychiatric disorders. *American Journal of Psychiatry, 160,* 208–220.

Sarsour, K., Sheridan, M., Jutte, D., Nuru-Jeter, A., Hinshaw, S., & Boyce, W. (2011). Family socioeconomic status and child executive functions: The roles of language, home environment, and single parenthood. *Journal of the International Neuropsychological Society, 17,* 120–132.

Sass, E. (2015, January 2). Over half of teens feel they are addicted to social media. *Social Media & Marketing Daily: The Social Graf.* Retrieved from http://www.mediapost.com/publications/ article/241024/over-half-of-teens-feel-they-are-addicted-to-socia.html

Saucier, G., & Srivastava, S. (2015). What makes a good structural model of personality? Evaluating the big five and alternatives. In M. Mikulincer, P. R. Shaver, M. L. Cooper, & R. J. Larsen (Eds.), *APA handbook of personality and social psychology, Volume 4: Personality processes and individual differences.* Washington, DC: American Psychological Association.

Savage, J., & Yancey, C. (2008). The effects of media violence exposure on criminal aggression: A meta-analysis. *Criminal Justice and Behavior, 35,* 772–791.

Savas, H. A., Yumru, M., & Kaya, M. C. (2007). Atypical antipsychotics as "mood stabilizers": A retrospective chart review. *Progress in Neuro-Psychopharmacology & Biological Psychiatry, 31,* 1064–1067.

Savazzi, S., Fabri, M., Rubboli, G., Paggi, A., Tassinari, C. A., & Marzi, C. A. (2007). Interhemispheric transfer following callosotomy in humans: Role of the superior colliculus, *Neuropsychologia, 45,* 2417–2427.

Saville, B. (2009). Performance under competitive and self-competitive fixed-interval schedules of reinforcement. *The Psychological Record, 59,* 21–38.

Sawa, A., & Snyder, S. H. (2002, April 26). Schizophrenia: Diverse approaches to a complex disease. *Science, 296,* 692–695.

Sayette, M. A. (1993). An appraisal disruption model of alcohol's effects on stress responses in social drinkers. *Psychological Bulletin, 114,* 459–476.

Scarr, S., & Weinberg, R. A. (1976). I.Q. test performance of black children adopted by white families. *American Psychologist, 31,* 726–739.

Scaturo, D. J. (2004). Fundamental clinical dilemmas in contemporary group psychotherapy. *Group Analysis, 37,* 201–217.

Scelfo, J. (2007, February 26). Men & depression: Facing darkness. *Newsweek,* 43–50.

Scelfo, J. (2015, February 8). They. *New York Times,* p. ED18.

Schachter, S., & Singer, J. E. (1962). Cognitive, social, and physiological determinants of emotional state. *Psychological Review, 69,* 379–399.

Schaie, K. (Ed.), & Willis, S. (Ed.). (2011). *Handbook of the psychology of aging* (7th ed.). San Diego, CA: Elsevier Academic Press.

Schaie, K. W. (2005). *Developmental influences on adult intelligence: The Seattle Longitudinal Study.* New York: Oxford University Press.

Schaller, M., & Crandall, C. S. (Eds.). (2004). *The psychological foundations of culture.* Mahwah, NJ: Erlbaum.

Scharrer, E., & Ramasubramanian, S. (2015). Intervening in the media's influence on stereotypes of race and ethnicity: The role of media literacy education. *Journal of Social Issues, 71,* 171–185.

Scheier, M. F., Carver, C. S., & Bridges, M. W. (1994). Distinguishing optimism from neuroticism (and trait anxiety, self-mastery, and self-esteem): A revision of the Life Orientation Test. *Journal of Personality and Social Psychology, 67,* 1063–1078.

Schermer, V. (2010). Mirror neurons: Their implications for group psychotherapy. *International Journal of Group Psychotherapy, 60,* 487–513.

Schieber, F. (2006). Vision and aging. In J. E. Birren & K. W. Schaire, *Handbook of the psychology of aging* (6th ed.). Amsterdam, Netherlands: Elsevier.

Schilling, O. K., & Diehl, M. (2015). Psychological vulnerability to daily stressors in old age: Results of short-term longitudinal studies. *Zeitschrift Für Gerontologie Und Geriatrie, 48,* 517–523.

Schindler, A., & Bartels, A. (2016). Motion parallax links visual motion areas and scene regions. *Neuroimage, 125,* 803–812.

Schlinger, H. D. (2015). Behavior analysis and behavioral neuroscience. *Frontiers in Human Neuroscience, 9,* 98–105

Schlinger, H. R. (2011). Skinner as missionary and prophet: A review of Burrhus F. Skinner: Shaper of behaviour. *Journal of Applied Behavior Analysis, 44,* 217–225.

Schmidt, J. P. (2006). The discovery of neurotransmitters: A fascinating story and a scientific object lesson. *PsycCRITIQUES, 61,* 101–115.

Schmitt, M., Dehay, B., Bezard, E., & Garcia-Ladona, F. J. (2016). Harnessing the trophic and modulatory potential of statins in a dopaminergic cell line. *Synapse, 70,* 71–86.

Schnabel, K., Asendorpf, J., & Greenwald, A. (2008). Assessment of individual differences in implicit cognition: A review of IAT measures. *European Journal of Psychological Assessment, 24,* 210–217.

Schneider, K. J., & Krug, O. T. (2010). *Existential–humanistic therapy.* Washington, DC US: American Psychological Association.

Schredl, M., & Piel, E. (2005). Gender differences in dreaming: Are they stable over time? *Personality and Individual Differences, 39,* 309–316.

Schreiber, F., Witthöft, M., Neng, J. M., & Weck, F. (2016). Changes in negative implicit evaluations in patients of hypochondriasis after treatment with cognitive therapy or exposure therapy. *Journal of Behavior Therapy and Experimental Psychiatry, 50,* 139–146.

Schreurs, B. G., Smith-Bell, C. A., & Burhans, L. B. (2011). Classical conditioning and conditioning-specific reflex modification of rabbit heart rate as a function of unconditioned stimulus location. *Behavioral Neuroscience, 125,* 604–612.

Schruijer, S. L., & Stephenson, G. M. (2010). Trends and developments in community and applied social psychology: JCASP 1991–2010. *Journal of Community & Applied Social Psychology, 20,* 437–444.

Schubert, T., & Koole, S. (2009). The embodied self: Making a fist enhances men's power-related self-conceptions. *Journal of Experimental Social Psychology, 45,* 828–834.

Schultheiss, O. C., & Schiepe-Tiska, A. (2013). The role of the dorsoanterior striatum in implicit motivation: The case of the need for power. *Frontiers in Human Neuroscience, 7,* Retrieved from http://www.ncbi.nlm.nih.gov/pubmed/23626531

Schwartz, B. (2008). Working memory load differentially affects tip-of-the-tongue states and feeling-of-knowing judgments. *Memory & Cognition, 36,* 9–19.

Schwartz, B. L. (2001). The relation of tip-of-the-tongue states and retrieval time. *Memory & Cognition, 29,* 117–126.

Schwartz, B. L. (2002). The phenomenology of naturally-occurring tip of-the-tongue states: A diary study. In S. P. Shohov (Ed.), *Advances in psychology research* (Vol. 8, pp. 73–84). Huntington, NY: Nova.

Schwartz, M. & Andrasik, F. (2005). *Biofeedback: A practitioner's guide* (3rd ed.). New York: The Guilford Press.

Schwartz, S. J., Donnellan, M., Ravert, R. D., Luyckx, K., & Zamboanga, B. L. (2013). Identity development, personality, and well-being in adolescence and emerging adulthood: Theory, research, and recent advances. In R. M. Lerner, M. Easterbrooks, J. Mistry, & I. B. Weiner (Eds.), *Handbook of psychology, Vol. 6: Developmental psychology* (2nd ed.). Hoboken, NJ: John Wiley & Sons Inc.

Schwartzmant, R. J., Alexander, G. M., & Grothusen, J. R. (2011). The use of ketamine in complex regional pain syndrome: Possible mechanisms. *Expert Review of Neurotherapeutics, 11,* 719–734.

Schwarzer, R., & Luszczynska, A. (2013). Stressful life events. In A. M. Nezu, C. Nezu, P. A. Geller, & I. B. Weiner (Eds.), *Handbook of psychology, Vol. 9: Health psychology* (2nd ed.). Hoboken, NJ: John Wiley & Sons Inc.

Schwenkreis, P., El Tom, S., Ragert, P., Pleger, B., Tegenthoff, M., & Dinse, H. (2007, December). Assessment of sensorimotor cortical representation asymmetries and motor skills in violin players. *European Journal of Neuroscience, 26,* 3291–3302.

Seamon, M. J., Fass, J. A., Maniscalco-Feichtl, M., & Abu-Shraie, N. A. (2007). Medical marijuana and the developing role of the pharmacist. *American Journal of Health System Pharmacy, 64,* 1037–1044.

Searight, H. (2013). Deinstitutionalization of people with mental illness: A failed policy that could have succeeded. *PsycCRITIQUES, 58,* 88–94.

Sebel, P. S., Bonke, B., & Winograd, E. (Eds.). (1993). *Memory and awareness in anesthesia.* Englewood Cliffs, NJ: Prentice Hall.

Seeley, R., Stephens, T., & Tate, P. (2000). *Anatomy & Physiology,* 5th ed., p. 384. Boston: McGraw-Hill.

Seeman, P. (2011). All roads to schizophrenia lead to dopamine supersensitivity and elevated dopamine D2[sup]High[/sup] receptors. *CNS Neuroscience & Therapeutics, 17,* 118–132.

Sefcek, J. A., Brumbach, B. H., & Vasquez, G. (2007). The evolutionary psychology of human mate choice: How ecology, genes, fertility, and fashion influence mating strategies. *Journal of Psychology & Human Sexuality, 18,* 125–182.

Segall, M. H., Campbell, D. T., & Herskovits, M. J. (1966). *The influence of culture on visual perception.* New York: Bobbs-Merrill.

Seger, D. (2010). Neuroadaptations and drugs of abuse. *Toxicology Letters, 196,* S15.

Seli, H. (2007). "Self" in self-worth protection: The relationship of possible selves to achievement motives and self-worth protective strategies. *Dissertation Abstracts International Section A: Humanities and Social Sciences, 67*(9-A), 3302.

Seligman, M. E. (2007). *What you can change . . . and what you can't: The complete guide to successful self-improvement.* New York: Vintage.

Seligman, M. E. P. (1995, December). The effectiveness of psychotherapy: The *Consumer Reports* study. *American Psychologist, 50,* 965–974.

Seligman, M. E. P. (1996, October). Science as an ally of practice. *American Psychologist, 51,* 1072–1079.

Sellbom, M., Fischler, G., & Ben-Porath, Y. (2007). Identifying MMPI-2 Predictors of police officer integrity and misconduct. *Criminal Justice and Behavior, 34,* 985–1004.

Sells, R. (1994, August). *Homosexuality study.* Paper presented at the annual meeting of the American Statistical Association, Toronto.

Selove, R. (2007). The glass is half full: Current knowledge about pediatric cancer and sickle cell anemia. *PsycCRITIQUES, 52,* 88–99.

Selsky, A. (1997, February 16). African males face circumcision rite. *The Boston Globe,* p. C7.

Selva-Vera, G., Balanzá-Martínez, V., Salazar-Fraile, J., Sánchez-Moreno, J., Martinez-Aran, A., Correa, P., & Tabarés-Seisdedos, R. (2010). The switch from conventional to atypical antipsychotic treatment should not be based exclusively on the presence of cognitive deficits. A pilot study in individuals with schizophrenia. *BMC Psychiatry, 10,* 10–18.

Selye, H. (1976). *The stress of life.* New York: McGraw-Hill.

Selye, H. (1993). History of the stress concept. In L. Goldberger & S. Breznitz (Eds.), *Handbook of stress: Theoretical and clinical aspects* (2nd ed.). New York: Free Press.

Semin, G. R., & Garrido, M. V. (2013). A systemic approach to impression formation: From verbal to multimodal processes. In J. P. Forgas, K. Fiedler, & C. Sedikides (Eds.), *Social thinking and interpersonal behavior.* New York: Psychology Press.

Semykina, A., & Linz, S. J. (2007). Gender differences in personality and earnings: Evidence from Russia. *Journal of Economic Psychology, 28,* 387–410.

Seroczynski, A. D., Jacquez, F. M., & Cole, D. A. (2003). Depression and suicide during adolescence. In G. R. Adams & M. D. Berzonsky (Eds.), *Blackwell handbook of adolescence.* Malden, MA: Blackwell Publishers.

Serpell, R. (2000). Intelligence and culture. In R. Sternberg (Ed.), *Handbook of intelligence.* Cambridge, England: Cambridge University Press.

Servick, K. (2014, November 21). New support for 'gay gene.' *Science, 346,* 900.

Sezgin, F., & Erdogan, O. (2015). Academic optimism, hope and zest for work as predictors of teacher self-efficacy and perceived success. *Kuram Ve Uygulamada Eğitim Bilimleri, 15,* 7–19.

Shafer, V. L., & Garrido-Nag, K. (2007). The neurodevelopmental bases of language. In E. Hoff & M. Shatz, *Blackwell handbook of language development* (pp. 21–45). Malden, MA: Blackwell Publishing.

Shah, A.S., Young, J., & Vieira, K. (2014). Long-term Suboxone treatment and its benefit on long-term remission for opiate dependence. *African Journal of Psychiatry, 17,* 1-4.

Shahan, T. (2010). Conditioned reinforcement and response strength. *Journal of the Experimental Analysis of Behavior, 93,* 269–289.

Shaikholeslami, R., & Khayyer, M. (2006). Intrinsic motivation, extrinsic motivation, and learning English as a foreign language. *Psychological Reports, 99,* 813–818.

Shanahan, L., Copeland, W. E., Worthman, C. M., Erkanli, A., Angold, A., & Costello, E. (2013). Sex-differentiated changes in C-reactive protein from ages 9 to 21: The contributions of BMI and physical/ sexual maturation. *Psychoneuroendocrinology, 38,* 2209–2217.

Shankar, G., & Simmons, A. (2009, January). Understanding ethics guidelines using an internet-based expert system. *Journal of Medical Ethics, 35,* 65–68.

Sharpe, Lindsey. (2013, November 1). U.S. obesity rate climbing in 2013. *Gallup Poll.*

Shaver, P. (Ed.), & Mikulincer, M. (Ed.). (2011). *Human aggression and violence: Causes, manifestations, and consequences.* Washington, DC: American Psychological Association.

Shea, A., & Steiner, M. (2008). Cigarette smoking during pregnancy. *Nicotine & Tobacco Research, 10,* 267–278.

Shehata-Dieler, W., Ehrmann-Mueller, D., Wermke, P., Voit, V., Cebulla, M., &

Wermke, K. (2013). Pre-speech diagnosis in hearing-impaired infants: How auditory experience affects early vocal development. *Speech, Language and Hearing, 16,* 99–106.

Shelton, R. C., Keller, M. B., Gelenberg, A., Dunner, D. L., Hirschfeld, R. M. A., Thase, M. E., Russell, J., Lydiard, R. B., Crits-Cristoph, P., Gallop, R., Todd, L., Hellerstein, D., Goodnick, P., Keitner, G., Stahl, S. M., & Halbreich, R. U. (2002). The effectiveness of St. John's wort in major depression: A multi-center, randomized placebo-controlled trial. *Journal of the American Medical Association, 285,* 1978–1986.

Sheppard, L. D., & Vernon, P. A. (2008). Intelligence and speed of information-processing: A review of 50 years of research. *Personality and Individual Differences, 44,* 535–551.

Shepperd, J., Malone, W., & Sweeny, K. (2008). Exploring causes of the self-serving bias. *Social and Personality Psychology Compass, 2,* 895–908.

Sherblom, S. (2008). The legacy of the 'care challenge': Re-envisioning the outcome of the justice-care debate. *Journal of Moral Education, 37,* 81–98.

Sherman, S. L., Allen, E. G., Bean, L. H., & Freeman, S. B. (2007). Epidemiology of Down syndrome [Special issue: Down syndrome]. *Mental Retardation and Developmental Disabilities Research Reviews, 13,* 221–227.

Shier, D., Butler, J., & Lewis, R. (2000). *Hole's essentials of human anatomy and physiology* (7th ed., p. 283). Boston: McGraw-Hill.

Shimono, K., & Wade, N. J. (2002). Monocular alignment in different depth planes. *Vision Research, 42,* 1127–1135.

Shin, Hyon B., & Kominski, R. A. 2010. *Language Use in the United States: 2007.* American Community Survey Reports, ACS-12. U.S. Census Bureau, Washington, DC.

Shnabel, N. Purdie-Vaughns, V. Cook, J.E., Garcia, J., & Cohen, G.L. (2013). Demystifying values-affirmation interventions writing about social belonging is a key to buffering against identity threat. *Personality and Social Psychology Bulletin, 39,* 663–676.

Shors, T. J. (2009, March). Saving new brain cells. *Scientific American,* pp. 47–54.

Shugart, H. A. (2011). Shifting the balance: The contemporary narrative of obesity. *Health Communication, 26,* 37–47.

Shurkin, J. N. (1992). *Terman's kids: The groundbreaking study of how the gifted grow up.* Boston: Little, Brown.

Sibunruang, H., Capezio, A., & Restubog, S. D. (2015). In pursuit of success: The differential moderating effects of political skill on the relationships among career-related psychological needs and ingratiation. *Journal of Career Assessment, 23,* 336–348.

Sidman, M. (2006). The distinction between positive and negative reinforcement: Some additional considerations. *Behavior Analyst, 29,* 135–139.

Siebert, Al. (1998). *The resiliency advantage.* New York: Berrett-Koehler

Siegel, A. (2010). Dream interpretation in clinical practice: A century after Freud. *Sleep Medicine Clinics, 5,* 299–313.

Sikkema, K. J., Ranby, K. W., Meade, C. S., Hansen, N. B., Wilson, P. A., & Kochman, A. (2013). Reductions in traumatic stress following a coping intervention were mediated by decreases in avoidant coping for people living with HIV/AIDS and childhood sexual abuse. *Journal of Consulting and Clinical Psychology, 81,* 274–283.

Silverstein, B. B., Edwards, T. T., Gamma, A. A., Ajdacic-Gross, V. V., Rossler, W. W., & Angst, J. J. (2013). The role played by depression associated with somatic symptomatology in accounting for the gender difference in the prevalence of depression. *Social Psychiatry and Psychiatric Epidemiology, 48,* 257–263.

Simon, G., Ludman, E., Unützer, J., Operskalski, B., & Bauer, M. (2008). Severity of mood symptoms and work productivity in people treated for bipolar disorder. *Bipolar Disorders, 10,* 718–725.

Simon, S., & Hoyt, C. (2008). Exploring the gender gap in support for a woman for president. *Analyses of Social Issues and Public Policy (ASAP), 8,* 157–181.

Sinclair, R. R., Waitsman, M. C., Oliver, C. M., & Deese, M. (2013). Personality and psychological resilience in military personnel. In R. R. Sinclair & T. W. Britt (Eds.), *Building psychological resilience in military personnel: Theory and practice.* Washington, DC: American Psychological Association.

Sininger, Y. S., & Cone-Wesson, B. (2004, September 10). Asymmetric cochlear processing mimics hemispheric specialization. *Science, 305,* 1581.

Sininger, Y. S., & Cone-Wesson, B. (2006). Lateral asymmetry in the ABR of neonates: Evidence and mechanisms. *Hearing Research, 212,* 203–211.

Skinner, B. F. (1957). *Verbal behavior.* New York: Appleton-Century-Crofts.

Ślusarczyk, E., & Niedzwienska, A. (2013). A naturalistic study of prospective memory in preschoolers: The role of task interruption and motivation. *Cognitive Development, 28,* 179–192.

Smetana, J. B. (2007). Strategies for understanding archetypes and the collective unconscious of an organization. *Dissertation Abstracts International Section A: Humanities and Social Sciences, 67*(12-A), 4714.

Smetana, J. G. (2005). Adolescent-parent conflict: Resistance and subversion as developmental process. In L. Nucci (Ed.), *Conflict, contradiction, and contrarian elements in moral development and education* (pp. 69–91). Mahwah, NJ: Erlbaum.

Smetana, J., Daddis, C., & Chuang, S. (2003). "Clean your room!" A longitudinal investigation of adolescent-parent conflict and conflict resolution in middle-class African American families. *Journal of Adolescent Research, 18,* 631–650.

Smith, B. H., Barkley, R. A., & Shapiro, C. J. (2006). Attention-deficit/hyperactivity disorder. In E. J. Mash & R. A. Barkley, *Treatment of childhood disorders* (3rd ed.). New York: Guilford Press.

Smith, C. (2006). Symposium V—Sleep and learning: New developments [Special issue: Methods and learning in functional MRI.] *Brain and Cognition, 60,* 331–332.

Smith, C. A., & Lazarus, R. S. (2001). Appraisal components, core relational themes, and the emotions. In W. G. Parrott (Ed.), *Emotions in social psychology: Essential readings* (pp. 94–114). Philadelphia: Psychology Press.

Smith, C. D., Chebrolu, J., Wekstein, D. R., Schmitt, F. A., & Markesbery, W. R. (2007). Age and gender effects on human brain anatomy: A voxel-based morphometric study in healthy elderly. *Neurobiology of Aging, 28,* 1057–1087.

Smith, D. (October 2001). Can't get your 40 winks? Here's what the sleep experts advise. *Monitor on Psychology, 37.*

Smith, D. B. (2007). Can you live with the voices in your head? *The New York Times Magazine,* p. 50.

Smith, D. E., Springer, C. M., & Barrett, S. (2011). Physical discipline and socioemotional adjustment among Jamaican adolescents. *Journal of Family Violence, 26,* 51–61.

Smith, E. S., Geissler, S. A., Schallert, T., & Lee, H. J. (2013). The role of central amygdala dopamine in disengagement behavior. *Behavioral Neuroscience, 127,* 164–174.

Smith, M. B. (2003). Moral foundations in research with human participants. In A. E. Kazdin (Ed.), *Methodological issues & strategies in clinical research* (3rd ed.). Washington, DC: American Psychological Association.

Smith, M. L., Glass, G. V., & Miller, T. J. (1980). *The benefits of psychotherapy.* Baltimore: Johns Hopkins University Press.

Smith, R. A., & Weber, A. L. (2005). Applying social psychology in everyday life. In F. W. Schneider, J. A. Gruman, & L. M. Coutts, *Applied social psychology: Understanding and addressing social and practical problems.* Thousand Oaks, CA: Sage.

Smith, T. W., & Son, J. (2013). *Trends in public attitudes about sexual morality.* Chicago: NORC at the University of Chicago.

Snyder, D. J., Fast, K., & Bartoshuk, L. M. (2004). Valid comparisons of suprathreshold sensations. *Journal of Consciousness Studies, 11,* 96–112.

Snyder, J., Cramer, A., & Afrank, J. (2005). The contributions of ineffective discipline and parental hostile attributions of child misbehavior to the development of conduct problems at home and school. *Developmental Psychology, 41,* 30–41.

Society for Personality Assessment. (2005). The status of Rorschach in clinical and forensic practice: An official statement by the board of trustees of the Society for Personality Assessment. *Journal of Personality Assessment, 85,* 219–237.

Sohr-Preston, S. L. & Scaramella, L.V. (2006). Implications of timing of maternal depressive symptoms for early cognitive and language development. *Clinical Child and Family Psychology Review, 9*(1), 65–83.

Sokolove, M. (2003, November 16). Should John Hinckley go free? *The New York Times Magazine,* pp. 52–54, 92.

Solesio-Jofre, E., Lorenzo-López, L., Gutiérrez, R., López-Frutos, J., Ruiz-Vargas, J., & Maestú, F. (2011). Age effects on retroactive interference during working memory maintenance. *Biological Psychology, 88,* 72–82.

Solomon, M., & Herman, J. (2009). Sex differences in psychopathology: Of gonads, adrenals and mental illness. *Physiology & Behavior, 97,* 250–258.

Soska, K., Adolph, K., & Johnson, S. (2010). Systems in development: Motor skill acquisition facilitates three-dimensional object completion. *Developmental Psychology, 46,* 129–138.

Soussignan, R. (2002). Duchenne smile, emotional experience, and automatic reactivity: A test of the facial feedback hypothesis. *Emotion, 2,* 52–74.

South Richardson, D. (2014). Everyday aggression takes many forms. *Current Directions in Psychological Science, 23,* 220–224.

South, S., & Krueger, R. (2008). An interactionist perspective on genetic and environmental contributions to personality. *Social and Personality Psychology Compass, 2,* 929–948.

Spadoni, A. D., Kosheleva, E., Buchsbaum, M. S., & Simmons, A. N. (2015). Neural correlates of malingering in mild traumatic brain injury: A positron emission tomography study. *Psychiatry Research: Neuroimaging, 233,* 367–372.

Spataro, P., Mulligan, N. W., & Rossi-Arnaud, C. (2011). Attention and implicit memory: The role of the activation of multiple representations. *Experimental Psychology, 58,* 110–116.

Spaulding, S. (2013). Mirror neurons and social cognition. *Mind & Language, 28,* 233–257.

Spears, R., Greenwood, R., Lemus, S., & Sweetman, J. (2010). Legitimacy, social identity, and power. In A. Guinote & T. K. Vescio (Eds.), *The social psychology of power.* New York: Guilford Press.

Speirs Neumeister, K. L., & Finch, H. (2006). Perfectionism in high-ability students: Relational precursors and influences on achievement motivation. *Gifted Child Quarterly, 50,* 238–251.

Spence, C., Auvray, M., & Smith, B. (2015). Confusing tastes with flavours. In D. Stokes, M. Matthen, & S. Biggs (Eds.), *Perception and its modalities.* New York: Oxford University Press.

Sperry, R. (1982). Some effects of disconnecting the cerebral hemispheres. *Science, 217,* 1223–1226.

Springen, K. (2004, August 9). Sweet, elusive sleep. *Newsweek,* p. 47.

Srivastava, S., & Singh, P. (2016). The mediating role of self-efficacy between perceived stigma and self-esteem. *Journal of the Indian Academy of Applied Psychology, 42,* 124–132.

Srivastava, S., Guglielmo, S., & Beer, J. S. (2010). Perceiving others' personalities: Examining the dimensionality, assumed similarity to the self, and stability of perceiver effects. *Journal of Personality and Social Psychology, 98,* 520–534.

St. Dennis, C., Hendryx, M., Henriksen, A. L., Setter, S. M., & Singer, B. (2006). Postdischarge treatment costs following closure of a state geropsychiatric ward: Comparison of 2 levels of community care. *Primary Care Companion Journal of Clinical Psychiatry, 8,* 279–284.

St. Jacques, P. L., & Levine, B. (2007). Ageing and autobiographical memory for emotional and neutral events. *Memory, 15,* 129–144.

Stankov, L. (2003). Complexity in human intelligence. In R. J. Sternberg, J. Lautrey, et al. (Eds.), *Models of intelligence: International perspectives* (pp. 27–42). Washington, DC: American Psychological Association.

Startup, M., Bucci, S., & Langdon, R. (2009). Delusions of reference: A new theoretical model. *Cognitive Neuropsychiatry, 14,* 110–126.

Staub, A. (2011). Word recognition and syntactic attachment in reading: Evidence for a staged architecture. *Journal of Experimental Psychology: General, 140,* 407–433.

Stedenfeld, K. A., Clinton, S. M., Kerman, I. A., Akil, H., Watson, S. J., & Sved, A. F. (2011). Novelty-seeking behavior predicts vulnerability in a rodent model of depression. *Physiology & Behavior, 24,* 127–133.

Steele, C. M., & Josephs, R. A. (1990). Alcohol myopia: Its prized and dangerous effects. *American Psychologist, 45,* 921–933.

Steele, J. D., Christmas, D., Eljamel, M. S., & Matthews, K. (2007). Anterior cingulotomy for major depression: Clinical outcome and relationship to lesion characteristics. *Biological Psychiatry, 12,* 127–134.

Steiger, A. (2007). Neurochemical regulation of sleep. *Journal of Psychiatric Research, 41,* 537–552.

Stein, L. A. R., & Graham, J. R. (2005). Ability of substance abusers to escape detection on the Minnesota Multiphasic Personality Inventory-Adolescent (MMPI-A) in a juvenile correctional facility. *Assessment, 12,* 28–39.

Stein, M., & Jones, R. (2010). *Cultures and identities in transition: Jungian perspectives.* New York: Routledge/Taylor & Francis Group.

Steiner, J. (2008). Transference to the analyst as an excluded observer. *The International Journal of Psychoanalysis, 89,* 39–54.

Steinfeld, C., Ellison, N., & Lampe, C. (2008). Social capital, self-esteem, and use of online social network sites: A longitudinal analysis. *Journal of Applied Developmental Psychology, 29,* 434–445.

Steinhubl, S. R., Wineinger, N. E., Patel, S., Boeldt, D. L., Mackellar, G., Porter, V., & . . . Topol, E. J. (2015). Cardiovascular and nervous system changes during meditation. *Frontiers in Human Neuroscience, 9,* 88–97.

Steinmetz, Katy. (2015, March 6). States battle over bathroom access for transgender people. *Time.* Retrieved from http://time.com/3734714/transgender-bathroom-bills-lgbtdiscrimination/

Stemler, S. E., & Sternberg, R. J. (2006). Using situational judgment tests to measure practical intelligence. In J. A. Weekley & R. E. Ployhart (Eds.), *Situational judgment tests: Theory, measurement, and application.* Mahwah, NJ: Erlbaum.

Stemler, S. E., Sternberg, R. J., Grigorenko, E. L., Jarvin, L., & Sharpes, K. (2009). Using the theory of successful intelligence as a framework for developing assessments in AP physics. *Contemporary Educational Psychology, 34,* 195–209.

Stenbacka, L., & Vanni, S. (2007). fMRI of peripheral visual field representation. *Clinical Neurophysiology, 108,* 1303–1314.

Stern, E., & Silbersweig, D. A. (2001). Advances in functional neuroimaging methodology for the study of brain systems underlying human neuropsychological function and dysfunction. In D. A. Silbersweig & E. Stern (Eds.), *Neuropsychology and functional neuro-imaging: Convergence, advances and new directions.* Amsterdam, Netherlands: Swets and Zeitlinger.

Stern, M. (2015). Whitey Bulger's enforcer slams "Black Mass": "The movie is pure fiction." Retrieved from http://www.thedailybeast.com/articles/2015/09/20/whitey-bulger-s-enforcer-slams-black-mass-the-movie-is-pure-fiction.html

Sternberg, R. J. (1998). *Successful intelligence: How practical and creative intelligence determine success in life.* New York: Plume.

Sternberg, R. J. (2000). Intelligence and wisdom. In R. J. Sternberg (Ed.), *Handbook of intelligence*. New York: Cambridge University Press.

Sternberg, R. J. (2002a). Individual differences in cognitive development. In U. Goswami (Ed.), *Blackwell handbook of childhood cognitive development. Blackwell handbooks of developmental psychology* (pp. 600–619). Malden, MA: Blackwell.

Sternberg, R. J. (2004). A triangular theory of love. In H. T. Reis & C. E. Rusbult (Eds.), *Close relationships: Key readings*. Philadelphia, PA: Taylor & Francis.

Sternberg, R. J. (2006). A duplex theory of love. In R. J. Sternberg (Ed.), *The new psychology of love*. New Haven, CT: Yale University Press.

Sternberg, R. J. (2015). Multiple intelligences in the new age of thinking. In S. Goldstein, D. Princiotta, & J. A. Naglieri (Eds.), *Handbook of intelligence: Evolutionary theory, historical perspective, and current concepts*. New York: Springer Science + Business Media.

Sternberg, R. J., & Beall, A. E. (1991). How can we know what love is? An epistemological analysis. In G. J. O. Fletcher & F. D. Fincham (Eds.), *Cognition in close relationships*. Hillsdale, NJ: Erlbaum.

Sternberg, R. J., & Hedlund, J. (2002). Practical intelligence, "g," and work psychology. *Human Performance, 15,* 143–160.

Sternberg, R. J., & Jarvin, L. (2003). Alfred Binet's contributions as a paradigm for impact in psychology. In R. J. Sternberg (Ed.), *The anatomy of impact: What makes the great works of psychology great* (pp. 89–107). Washington, DC: American Psychological Association.

Sternberg, R. J., & Pretz, J. E. (2005). *Cognition and intelligence: Identifying the mechanisms of the mind*. New York: Cambridge University Press, 2005.

Sternberg, R. J., Grigorenko, E. L., & Kidd, K. K. (2005). Intelligence, race, and genetics. *American Psychologist, 60,* 46–59.

Sternberg, R. J., Hojjat, M., & Barnes, M. L. (2001). Empirical aspects of a theory of love as a story. *European Journal of Personality, 15,* 1–20.

Sternson, S. M., Betley, J., & Cao, Z. (2013). Neural circuits and motivational processes for hunger. *Current Opinion in Neurobiology, 23,* 353–360.

Stettler, N., Stallings, V. A., Troxel, A. B., Zhao, J., Z., Schinnar, R., Nelson, S. E., Ziegler, E. E., & Strom, B. L. (2005). Weight gain in the first week of life and overweight in adulthood. *Circulation, 111,* 1897–1903.

Stevens, G. (2015). Black psychology: Resistance, reclamation, and redefinition. In I. Parker (Ed.), *Handbook of critical psychology* (pp. 182–190). New York: Routledge/Taylor & Francis Group.

Stevens, G., & Gardner, S. (1982). *The women of psychology: Pioneers and innovators* (Vol. 1). Cambridge, MA: Schenkman.

Stevens, M. J., & Gielen, U.P. (Eds.). (2007). *Toward a global psychology: Theory, research, intervention, and pedagogy*. Mahwah, NJ: Lawrence Erlbaum.

Stevens, P. & Harper, D. J. (2007). Professional accounts of electroconvulsive therapy: A discourse analysis. *Social Science & Medicine, 64,* 1475–1486.

Stevens, T., Brevers, D., Chambers, C. D., Lavric, A., McLaren, I. L., Mertens, M., & . . . Verbruggen, F. (2015). How does response inhibition influence decision making when gambling? *Journal of Experimental Psychology: Applied, 21,* 15–36.

Stevenson, H. W., Lee, S., & Mu, X. (2000). Successful achievement in mathematics: China and the United States. In C. F. M. van Lieshout & P. G. Heymans (Eds.), *Developing talent across the life span*. New York: Psychology Press.

Stevenson, J. (2010, November 26). Joy amid tears for Ralston. *Winnipeg Sun* (Manitoba), 34.

Stickgold, R., Hobson, J. A., Fosse, R., & Fosse, M. (2001, November 2). Sleep, learning, and dreams: Off-line memory reprocessing. *Science, 294,* 1052–1057.

Stickley, T., & Nickeas, R. (2006). Becoming one person: Living with dissociative identity disorder. *Journal of Psychiatric and Mental Health Nursing, 13,* 180–187.

Stier, H., & Lewin-Epstein, N. (2000). Women's part-time employment and gender inequality in the family. *Journal of Family Issues, 21,* 390–410.

Stifter, C. A., Dollar, J. M., & Cipriano, E. A. (2011). Temperament and emotion regulation: The role of autonomic nervous system reactivity. *Developmental Psychobiology, 53,* 266–279.

Stocks, E., Lishner, D., & Decker, S. (2009). Altruism or psychological escape: Why does empathy promote prosocial behavior? *European Journal of Social Psychology, 39,* 649–665.

Stockton, R., Morran, D. K., & Krieger, K. M. (2004). An overview of current research and best practices for training beginning group leaders. In D. A. Gerrity, C. R. Kalodner, & M. T. Riva (Eds.), *Handbook of group counseling and psychotherapy*. Thousand Oaks, CA: Sage.

Stolorow, R. D., & Stolorow, B. A. (2013). Blues and emotional trauma. *Clinical Social Work Journal, 41,* 5–10.

Stone, J. (2002). Battling doubt by avoiding practice: The effects of stereotype threat on self-handicapping in white athletes. *Personality and Social Psychology Bulletin, 28,* 1667–1678.

Stone, J., Morrison, P., & Pilowsky, L. (2007). Glutamate and dopamine dysregulation in schizophrenia—A synthesis and selective review. *Journal of Psychopharmacology, 21,* 440–452.

Stowell, J. R., Robles, T. F., & Kane, H. S. (2013). Psychoneuroimmunology: Mechanisms, individual differences, and interventions. In A. M. Nezu, C. Nezu, P. A. Geller, & I. B. Weiner (Eds.), *Handbook of psychology, Vol. 9: Health psychology* (2nd ed.). Hoboken, NJ: John Wiley & Sons Inc.

Strathern, A., & Stewart, P. J. (2003). *Landscape, memory and history: Anthropological perspectives*. London: Pluto Press.

Strauss, E. (1998, May 8). Writing, speech separated in split brain. *Science, 280,* 287.

Strayer, D. L., Drews, F. A., Crouch, D. J., & Johnston, W. A. (2005). Why do cell phone conversations interfere with driving? In W. R. Walker & D. Herrmann (Eds.), *Cognitive technology: Transforming thought and society*. Jefferson, NC: McFarland & Company.

Strenze, T. (2015). Intelligence and success. In S. Goldstein, D. Princiotta, & J. A. Naglieri (Eds.), *Handbook of intelligence: Evolutionary theory, historical perspective, and current concepts* (pp. 405–413). New York: Springer Science + Business Media.

Striegel-Moore, R., & Bulik, C. M. (2007). Risk factors for eating disorders. *American Psychologist, 62,* 181–198.

Strong, T., & Tomm, K. (2007). Family therapy as re-coordinating and moving on together. *Journal of Systemic Therapies, 26,* 42–54.

Strupp, H. H., & Binder, J. L. (1992). Current developments in psychotherapy. *The Independent Practitioner, 12,* 119–124.

Studer, B., Scheibehenne, B., & Clark, L. (2016). Psychophysiological arousal and inter- and intraindividual differences in risk-sensitive decision making. *Psychophysiology*. Retrieved from http://onlinelibrary.wiley.com/doi/10.1111/psyp.12627/abstract

Subrahmanyam, K., Reich, S., Waechter, N., & Espinoza, G. (2008). Online and offline social networks: Use of social networking sites by emerging adults. *Journal of Applied Developmental Psychology, 29,* 420–433.

Substance Abuse and Mental Health Services Administration, Results from the 2013 National Survey on Drug Use and Health: Mental Health Findings, NSDUH Series H-49, HHS Publication No. (SMA) 14-4887. Rockville, MD: Substance Abuse and Mental Health Services Administration, 2014.

Sue, D. W. (2010). Racial microaggressions in everyday life. *Psychology Today*. Retrieved from https://www.psychologytoday.com/blog/microaggressions-in-everyday-life/201010/racial-microaggressions-in-everyday-life

Sue, D. W., & Sue, D. (1990). *Counseling the culturally different: Theory and practice* (2nd ed.). Oxford, England: John Wiley & Sons.

Sultan, S. (2010). Special section: Rorschach and health psychology: Translational research experiences in health psychology with the Rorschach. *Rorschachiana, 31,* 113–116.

Summers, R. F., & Barber, J. P. (2010). *Psychodynamic therapy: A guide to evidence-based practice.* New York: Guilford Press.

Sumner, J. A., Griffith, J. W., & Mineka, S. (2011). Examining the mechanisms of overgeneral autobiographical memory: Capture and rumination, and impaired executive control. *Memory, 19,* 169–183.

Sun, Y., Giacobbe, P., Tang, C. W., Barr, M. S., Rajji, T., Kennedy, S. H., Fitzgerald, P. B., Lozano, A. M., Wong, W., & Daskalakis, Z. J. (2015, June 26). Deep brain stimulation modulates gamma oscillations and theta-gamma coupling in treatment resistant depression. *Brain Stimulation, 6,* 1033–1042.

Sundqvist, A., Nordqvist, E., Koch, F., & Heimann, M. (2016). Early declarative memory predicts productive language: A longitudinal study of deferred imitation and communication at 9 and 16months. *Journal of Experimental Child Psychology.* Retrieved from http://www.ncbi.nlm.nih.gov/pubmed/26925719

Surette, R. (2002). Self-reported copycat crime among a population of serious and violent juvenile offenders. *Crime & Delinquency, 48,* 46–69.

Sutin, A. R., & Robins, R. W. (2007). Phenomenology of autobiographical memories: The Memory Experiences Questionnaire. *Memory, 15,* 390–411.

Suto, N., Ecke, L., You, Z., & Wise, R. (2010). Extracellular fluctuations of dopamine and glutamate in the nucleus accumbens core and shell associated with lever-pressing during cocaine self-administration, extinction, and yoked cocaine administration. *Psychopharmacology, 211,* 267–275.

Swing, E., & Anderson, C. A. (2007). The unintended negative consequences of exposure to violent games. *International Journal of Cognitive Technology, 12,* 3–13.

Tadmor, C. T. (2007). Biculturalism: The plus side of leaving home? The effects of second-culture exposure on integrative complexity and its consequences for overseas performance. *Dissertation Abstracts International Section A: Humanities and Social Sciences, 67*(8-A), 3068.

Taggi, F., Crenca, A., Cedri, C., Giustini, M., Dosi, G., & Marturano, P. (2007). Road safety and the tsunami of cell phones. *Anali di igiene: Medicina preventiva e di comunità, 19,* 269–274.

Tajfel, H., & Turner, J. C. (2004). The social identity theory of intergroup behavior. In J. T. Jost & J. Sidanius (Eds.), *Political psychology: Key readings.* New York: Psychology Press.

Taki, Y., Thyreau, B., Kinomura, S., Sato, K., Goto, R., Wu, K., Kawashima, R., & Fukuda, H. (2013). A longitudinal study

of age and gender related annual rate of volume changes in regional gray matter in healthy adults. *Human Brain Mapping, 34,* 2292–2301.

Takizawa, T., Kondo, T., & Sakihara, S. (2007). "Stress buffering effects of social support on depressive symptoms in middle age: Reciprocity and community mental health": Corrigendum. *Psychiatry and Clinical Neurosciences, 61,* 336–337.

Talarico, J. (2009). Freshman flashbulbs: Memories of unique and first-time events in starting college. *Memory, 17,* 256–265.

Talukdar, S., & Shastri, J. (2006). Contributory and adverse factors in social development of young children. *Psychological Studies, 51,* 294–303.

Tamini, B., Bojhd, F., & Yazdani, S. (2011). Love types, psychological well-being and self-concept. *Journal of the Indian Academy of Applied Psychology, 37,* 169–178.

Tan, L., Chan, A., Kay, P., Khong, P., Yip, L., & Luke, K. (2008). Language affects patterns of brain activation associated with perceptual decision. *PNAS Proceedings of the National Academy of Sciences of the United States of America, 105*(10), 4004–4009.

Tandon, R., Gaebel, W., Barch, D. M., Bustillo, J., Gur, R. E., Heckers, S., & … Carpenter, W. (2013). Definition and description of schizophrenia in the *DSM-5. Schizophrenia Research.* Retrieved from http://ccpweb.wustl.edu/pdfs/2013_defdes.pdf

Tanner, J. M. (1978). *Education and physical growth* (2nd ed.). New York: International Universities Press.

Tanner, J. M. (1990). *Foetus into man: Physical growth from conception to maturity* (Rev. ed.). Cambridge, MA: Harvard University Press.

Tao, R., & Banh, M. K. (2016). Dialectical behavioral therapy and interpersonal therapy. In A. Breland-Noble, C. S. Al-Mateen, & N. N. Singh (Eds.), *Handbook of mental health in African American youth.* Cham, Switzerland: Springer International Publishing.

Tateo, L., & Valsiner, J. (2015). Time breath of psychological theories: A meta-theoretical focus. *Review of General Psychology, 19,* 357–364.

Taylor, F., & Bryant, R. A. (2007). The tendency to suppress, inhibiting thoughts, and dream rebound. *Behaviour Research and Therapy, 45,* 163–168.

Taylor, J. A. (1953). A personality scale of manifest anxiety. *The Journal of Abnormal and Social Psychology, 48* (2), 285–290.

Teglasi, H. (2010). *Essentials of TAT and other storytelling assessments* (2nd ed.). Hoboken, NJ: John Wiley & Sons Inc.

Teitelbaum, S. (2010). *Athletes who indulge their dark side: Sex, drugs, and cover-ups.* Santa Barbara, CA: Praeger/ABC-CLIO.

Tellegen, A., Lykken, D. T., Bouchard, T. J., Jr., Wilcox, K. J., Segal, N. L., & Rich,

S. (1988). Personality similarity in twins reared apart and together. *Journal of Personality and Social Psychology, 54,* 1031–1039.

Tenenbaum, H. R., & Ruck, M. D. (2007). Are teachers' expectations different for racial minority than for European American students? A meta-analysis. *Journal of Educational Psychology, 99,* 253–273.

Teodorov, E., Salzgerber, S. A., Felicio, L. F., Varolli, F. M. F., & Bernardi, M. M. (2002). Effects of perinatal picrotoxin and sexual experience on heterosexual and homosexual behavior in male rats. *Neurotoxicology and Teratology, 24,* 235–245.

Thachil, A. F., Mohan, R., & Bhugra, D. (2007). The evidence base of complementary and alternative therapies in depression. *Journal of Affective Disorders, 97,* 23–35.

Tharp, R. G. (1989). Psychocultural variables and constants: Effects on teaching and learning in schools [Special issue: Children and their development: Knowledge base, research agenda, and social policy application]. *American Psychologist, 44,* 349–359.

Thase, M. E. (2013). Comparative effectiveness of psychodynamic psychotherapy and cognitive-behavioral therapy: It's about time, and what's next? *The American Journal of Psychiatry, 170,* 953–956.

Thatcher, D. L., & Clark, D. B. (2006). Adolescent alcohol abuse and dependence: Development, diagnosis, treatment and outcomes. *Current Psychiatry Reviews, 2,* 159–177.

Thimm, J. (2010). Personality and early maladaptive schemas: A five-factor model perspective. *Journal of Behavior Therapy and Experimental Psychiatry, 41,* 373–380.

Thomas, P., Mathur, P., Gottesman, I. I., Nagpal, R., Nimgaonkar, V. L., & Deshpande, S. N. (2007). Correlates of hallucinations in schizophrenia: A cross-cultural evaluation. *Schizophrenia Research, 92,* 41–49.

Thompson, M. (2015, April 6.) Unlocking the secrets of PTSD. *Time,* pp. 41–43.

Thompson, R. D., Goldsmith, A. A., & Tran, G. Q. (2011). Alcohol and drug use in socially anxious young adults. In C. A. Alfano & D. C. Beidel (Eds.), *Social anxiety in adolescents and young adults: Translating developmental science into practice.* Washington, DC: American Psychological Association.

Thompson, W. L., Hsiao, Y., & Kosslyn, S. M. (2011). Dissociation between visual attention and visual mental imagery. *Journal of Cognitive Psychology, 23,* 256–263.

Thorkildsen, T. A. (2006). An empirical exploration of language and thought. *PsycCRITIQUES, 51,* No pagination specified.

Thornton, A., & Young-DeMarco, L. (2001). Four decades of trends in attitudes toward family issues in the United States: The 1960s through the 1990s. *Journal of Marriage and the Family, 63,* 1009–1017.

Tian, F. F., Tu, S. S., Qiu, J. J., Lv, J. Y., Wei, D. T., Su, Y. H., & Zhang, Q. L. (2011). Neural correlates of mental preparation for successful insight problem solving. *Behavioural Brain Research, 216,* 626–630.

Tian, F., Tu, S., Qiu, J., Lv, J., Wei, D., Su, Y., et al. (2010). Neural correlates of mental preparation for successful insight problem solving. *Behavioural Brain Research, 216,* 626–630.

Tippin, J., Sparks, J., & Rizzo, M. (2009, August). Visual vigilance in drivers with obstructive sleep apnea. *Journal of Psychosomatic Research, 67,* 143–151.

Tirri, K., & Nokelainen, P. (2008). Identification of multiple intelligences with the Multiple Intelligence Profiling Questionnaire III [Special issue: High-ability assessment]. *Psychology Science, 50,* 206–221.

Tokutsu, Y., Umene-Nakano, W., Shinkai, T., Yoshimura, R., Okamoto, T., Katsuki, A., & . . . Nakamura, J. (2013). Follow-up study on electroconvulsive therapy in treatment-resistant depressed patients after remission: A chart review. *Clinical Psychopharmacology and Neuroscience, 11,* 34–38.

Tolman, E. C., & Honzik, C. H. (1930). Introduction and removal of reward and maze performance in rats. *University of California Publications in Psychology, 4,* 257–275.

Toma, C. L., & Choi, M. (2015). The couple who Facebooks together, stays together: Facebook self-presentation and relationship longevity among college-aged dating couples. *Cyberpsychology, Behavior, and Social Networking, 18,* 367–372.

Tommasi, L. (2009). Mechanisms and functions of brain and behavioural asymmetries. *Philosophical Transactions of the Royal Society B, 364,* 855–859.

Tononi, G., & Cirelli, C. (2013, August). Perchance to prune. *Scientific American,* pp. 34–39.

Tracy, J. L., & Robins, R. W. (2004). Show your pride: Evidence for a discrete emotion expression. *Psychological Science, 15,* 194–197.

Tranter, L. J., & Koutstaal, W. (2008). Age and flexible thinking: An experimental demonstration of the beneficial effects of increased cognitively stimulating activity on fluid intelligence in healthy older adults. *Neuropsychology and Cognition, 15,* 184–207.

Travis, F. (2006). From I to I: Concepts of self on an object-referral/self-referral continuum. In A. P. Prescott, *The concept of self in psychology.* Hauppauge, NY: Nova Science Publishers.

Travis, F., et al. (2009, February). Effects of transcendental meditation practice on

brain functioning and stress reactivity in college students. *International Journal of Psychophysiology, 71,* 170–176.

Tritsch, N., & Bergles, D. (2010). Developmental regulation of spontaneous activity in the mammalian cochlea. *The Journal of Neuroscience, 30,* 1539–1550.

Tropp, L. R., & Bianchi, R. A. (2006). Valuing diversity and interest in intergroup contact. *Journal of Social Issues, 62,* 533–551.

Tropp, L. R., & Pettigrew, T. F. (2005). Differential relationships between intergroup contact and affective and cognitive dimensions of prejudice. *Personality and Social Psychology Bulletin, 31,* 1145–1158.

Trudel, G. (2002). Sexuality and marital life: Results of a survey. *Journal of Sex and Marital Therapy, 28,* 229–249.

Trull, T. J., Stepp, S. D., & Durrett, C. A. (2003). Research on borderline personality disorder: An update. *Current Opinion in Psychiatry, 16,* 77–82.

Truscott, D. (2010). Person-centered. *Becoming an effective psychotherapist: Adopting a theory of psychotherapy that's right for you and your client.* Washington, DC: American Psychological Association.

Tseng, W. S. (2003). *Clinician's guide to cultural psychiatry.* San Diego, CA: Elsevier Publishing.

Tsuchida, K., Ueno, K., & Shimada, S. (2015). Motor area activity for action-related and nonaction-related sounds in a three-dimensional sound field reproduction system. *Neuroreport: For Rapid Communication of Neuroscience Research, 26,* 291–295.

Tuckey, M. R., Searle, B. J., Boyd, C. M., Winefield, A. H., & Winefield, H. R. (2015). Hindrances are not threats: Advancing the multidimensionality of work stress. *Journal of Occupational Health Psychology, 20,* 131–147.

Tuerlinckx, F., De Boeck, P., & Lens, W. (2002). Measuring needs with the Thematic Apperception Test: A psychometric study. *Journal of Personality and Social Psychology, 82,* 448–461.

Tugay, N., Akbayrak, T., Demirturk, F., Karakaya, I. C., Kocaacar, O., Tugay, U., Karakay, M. G., & Demirturk, F. (2007). Effectiveness of transcutaneous electrical nerve stimulation and interferential current in primary dysmenorrhea. *Pain Medicine, 8,* 295–300.

Tulving, E. (2002). Episodic memory and common sense: How far apart? In A. Baddeley & J. P. Aggleton (Eds.), *Episodic memory: New directions in research* (pp. 269–287). London: Oxford University Press.

Tummala-Narra, P. (2016). Implications of a culturally informed psychoanalytic perspective: Some thoughts on future directions. In P. Tummala-Narra, *Psychoanalytic theory and cultural competence in psychotherapy.*

Washington, DC: American Psychological Association.

Tunstall, B. J., Verendeev, A., & Kearns, D. N. (2013). Outcome specificity in deepened extinction may limit treatment feasibility: Co-presentation of a food cue interferes with extinction of cue-elicited cocaine seeking. *Drug and Alcohol Dependence.* Retrieved from http://www.ncbi.nlm.nih.gov/pubmed/24071568

Turk, D. C. (1994). Perspectives on chronic pain: The role of psychological factors. *Current Directions in Psychological Science, 3,* 45–49.

Turner, M., Tamborini, R., Limon, M., & Zuckerman-Hyman, C. (2007). The moderators and mediators of door-in-the-face requests: Is it a negotiation or a helping experience? *Communication Monographs, 74,* 333–356.

Turri, M. G. (2015). Transference and katharsis, Freud to Aristotle. *The International Journal of Psychoanalysis, 96,* 369–387.

Tuszynski, M. H. (2007). Nerve growth factor gene therapy in Alzheimer's disease. *Alzheimer's Disease and Associated Disorders, 21,* 179–1898.

Tutwiler, S., Lin, M., & Chang, C. (2013). The use of a gesture-based system for teaching multiple intelligences: A pilot study. *British Journal of Educational Technology, 44,* E133–E138.

Tversky, A., & Kahneman, D. (1987). Rational choice and the framing of decisions. In R. Hogarth & M. Reder (Eds.), *Rational choice: The contrast between economics and psychology.* Chicago: University of Chicago Press.

Twining, R. C., Wheeler, D. S., Ebben, A. L., Jacobsen, A. J., Robble, M. A., Mantsch, J. R., & Wheeler, R. A. (2015). Aversive stimuli drive drug seeking in a state of low dopamine tone. *Biological Psychiatry, 77,* 895–902.

Tyrer, H., Tyrer, P., Lisseman-Stones, Y., McAllister, S., Cooper, S., Salkovskis, P., & . . . Wang, D. (2015). Therapist differences in a randomised trial of the outcome of cognitive behaviour therapy for health anxiety in medical patients. *International Journal of Nursing Studies, 52,* 686–694.

U.S. Bureau of Labor Statistics. (2007). *American time use survey.* Washington, DC: Bureau of Labor Statistics.

U.S. Bureau of the Census. (2000). *Census 2000.* Retrieved from American Fact Finder. http://factfinder.census.gov/servlet/BasicFactsServlet.

Ubell, E. (1993, January 10). Could you use more sleep? *Parade,* pp. 16–18.

Ugbolue, U. C., & Nicol, A. C. (2010). A comparison of two interventions designed to promote neutral wrist postures during simple computer operations. *Work: A Journal of Prevention, Assessment and Rehabilitation, 37,* 413–424.

Uliaszek, A. A., Rashid, T., Williams, G. E., & Gulamani, T. (2016). Group therapy for university students: A randomized control trial of dialectical behavior therapy and positive psychotherapy. *Behaviour Research and Therapy, 77*,78–85.

Ullsperger, J. M., Nigg, J. T., & Nikolas, M. A. (2016). Does child temperament play a role in the association between parenting practices and child attention deficit/hyperactivity disorder? *Journal of Abnormal Child Psychology, 44*(1), 167–178.

Umphress, E. E., Smith-Crowe, K., & Brief, A. P. (2007). When birds of a feather flock together and when they do not: Status composition, social dominance orientation, and organizational attractiveness. *Journal of Applied Psychology, 92*, 396–409.

Updegraff, K. A., Helms, H. M., McHale, S. M., Crouter, A. C., Thayer, S. M., & Sales, L. H. (2004). Who's the boss? Patterns of perceived control in adolescents' friendships. *Journal of Youth & Adolescence, 33*, 403–420.

Uylings, H. B. M. (2006). Development of the human cortex and the concept of 'critical' or 'sensitive' periods. *Language Learning, 56*, 59–90.

Vaillant, G. E., & Vaillant, C. O. (1990). Natural history of male psychological health: XII. A 46-year study of predictors of successful aging at age 65. *American Journal of Psychiatry, 147*, 31–37.

Valencia, R. R., & Suzuki, L. A. (2003). *Intelligence testing and minority students: Foundations, performance factors, and assessment issues.* Thousand Oaks, CA: Sage.

Valenzuela, S., Park, N., & Kee, K. F. (2009). Is there social capital in a social network site? *Facebook* use and college students' life satisfaction, trust, and participation. *Journal of Computer-Mediated Communications, 14*, 875–901.

Valkenburg, P. M., Peter, J., & Walther, J. B. (2016). Media effects: Theory and research. *Annual Review of Psychology, 67*, 315–338.

Valsecchi, M., Caziot, B., Backus, B. T., & Gegenfurtner, K. R. (2013). The role of binocular disparity in rapid scene and pattern recognition. *I-Perception, 4*(2), 254–262.

Van De Graaff, K. (2000). *Human anatomy* (5th ed.). Boston: McGraw-Hill.

Van den Wildenberg, W. P. M., & Van der Molen, M. W. (2004). Developmental trends in simple and selective inhibition of compatible and incompatible responses. *Journal of Experimental Child Psychology, 87*, 201–220.

Van der Zee, E. A., Platt, B. B., & Riedel, G. G. (2011). Acetylcholine: Future research and perspectives. *Behavioural Brain Research, 221*, 583–586.

van Hooren, S. A. H., Valentijn, A. M., & Bosma, H. (2007). Cognitive functioning in healthy older adults aged 64–81: A cohort study into the effects of age, sex, and education. *Aging, Neuropsychology, and Cognition, 14*, 40–54.

Van Rosmalen, L., Van Der Veer, R., & Van Der Horst, F. (2015). Ainsworth's strange situation procedure: The origin of an instrument. *Journal of the History of the Behavioral Sciences, 51*, 261–284.

van Wel, F., Linssen, H., & Abma, R. (2000). The parental bond and the well-being of adolescents and young adults. *Journal of Youth & Adolescence, 29*, 307–318.

Vandell, D. L., Burchinal, M. R., Belsky, J., Owen, M. T., Friedman, S. L., Clarke-Stewart, A., McCartney, K., & Weinraub, M. (2005). *Early child care and children's development in the primary grades: Follow-up results from the NICHD Study of Early Child Care.* Paper presented at the biennial meeting of the Society for Research in Child Development, Atlanta, GA.

vanDellen, M. R., Hoy, M. B., Fernandez, K., & Hoyle, R. H. (2011). Academic-contingent self-worth and the social monitoring system. *Personality and Individual Differences, 50*, 59–63.

Vandervert, L. R., Schimpf, P. H., & Liu, H. (2007). How working memory and the cerebellum collaborate to produce creativity and innovation. *Creativity Research Journal, 19*, 1–18.

Vanheule, S., Desmet, M., Rosseel, Y., & Meganck, R. (2006). Core transference themes in depression. *Journal of Affective Disorders, 91*, 71–75

Varma, S., (2007). A computational model of Tower of Hanoi problem solving. *Dissertation Abstracts International: Section B: The Sciences and Engineering, 67*(8-B*)*, 4736.

Vasudeva, K., Vodovotz, Y., Azhar, N., Barclay, D., Janjic, J. M., & Pollock, J. A. (2015). In vivo and systems biology studies implicate IL-18 as a central mediator in chronic pain. *Journal of Neuroimmunology, 28*, 343–349.

Velentzas, K., Heinen, T., & Schack, T. (2011). Routine integration strategies and their effects on volleyball serve performance and players' movement mental representation. *Journal of Applied Sport Psychology, 23*, 209–222.

Vera-Estay, E., Dooley, J. J., & Beauchamp, M. H. (2015). Cognitive underpinnings of moral reasoning in adolescence: The contribution of executive functions. *Journal of Moral Education, 44*, 17–33.

Verdejo, A., Toribio, I., & Orozco, C. (2005). Neuropsychological functioning in methadone maintenance patients versus abstinent heroin abusers. *Drug and Alcohol Dependence, 78*, 283–288.

Vernon, P., Villani, V., Vickers, L., & Harris, J. (2008, January). A behavioral genetic investigation of the Dark Triad and the Big 5. *Personality and Individual Differences, 44*, 445–452.

Verona, E., & Sullivan, E. (2008). Emotional catharsis and aggression revisited: Heart rate reduction following aggressive responding. *Emotion, 8*, 331–340.

Vieira, E. M., & Freire, J. C. (2006). Alteridade e Psicologia Humanista: Uma leitura ética da abordagem centrada na pessoa. [Alterity and humanistic psychology: An ethical reading of the Person-Centered Approach.] *Estudos de Psicologia, 23*, 425–432.

Vignatelli, L., Plazzi, G., Peschechera, F., Delaj, L., & D'Alessandro, R. (2011). A 5-year prospective cohort study on health-related quality of life in patients with narcolepsy. *Sleep Medicine, 12*, 19–23.

Vitaro, F., Brendgen, M., & Arseneault, L. (2009). Methods and measures: The discordant MZ-twin method: One step closer to the holy grail of causality. *International Journal of Behavioral Development, 33*, 376–382.

Vitello, P. (2006, June 12). A ring tone meant to fall on deaf ears. *The New York Times*, D1.

Vitiello, A. L., Bonello, R. P., & Pollard, H. P. (2007). The effectiveness of ENAR(R) for the treatment of chronic neck pain in Australian adults: A preliminary single-blind, randomised controlled trial. *Chiropractic Osteopathology, 9*, 9.

Vlassova, A., & Pearson, J. (2013). Look before you leap: Sensory memory improves decision making. *Psychological Science, 24*, 1635–1643.

Vleioras, G., & Bosma, H. A. (2005). Are identity styles important for psychological well-being? *Journal of Adolescence, 28*, 397–409.

Vliegenthart, J., Noppe, G., van Rossum, E. C., Koper, J. W., Raat, H., & van den Akker, E. T. (2016). Socioeconomic status in children is associated with hair cortisol levels as a biological measure of chronic stress. *Psychoneuroendocrinology, 6*, 59–14.

Vloet, T., Konrad, K., Herpertz-Dahlmann, B., Polier, G., & Günther, T. (2010). Impact of anxiety disorders on attentional functions in children with ADHD. *Journal of Affective Disorders, 124*, 283–290.

Volterra, V., Caselli, M. C., Capirci, O., Tonucci, F., & Vicari, S. (2003). Early linguistic abilities of Italian children with Williams syndrome [Special issue: Williams syndrome]. *Developmental Neuropsychology, 23*, 33–58.

Vonasch, A. J., & Baumeister, R. F. (2013). Implications of free will beliefs for basic theory and societal benefit: Critique and implications for social psychology. *British Journal of Social Psychology, 52*, 219–227.

Voruganti, L. P., Awad, A. G., Parker, B., Forrest, C., Usmani, Y., Fernando, M. L. D., & Senthilal, S. (2007). Cognition, functioning and quality of life in schizophrenia treatment: Results of a one-year randomized controlled trial of olanzapine and quetiapine. *Schizophrenia Research, 96*, 146–155.

Voss, J., & Paller, K. (2008). Brain substrates of implicit and explicit memory: The importance of concurrently acquired neural signals of both memory types. *Neuropsychologia, 46*(13), 3021–3029.

Vukasović, T., & Bratko, D. (2015). Heritability of personality: A meta-analysis of behavior genetic studies. *Psychological Bulletin, 141,* 769–785.

Vygotsky, L. S. (1926/1997). *Educational psychology.* Delray Beach, FL: St. Lucie Press.

Waddell, J., & Shors, T.J. (2008). Neurogenesis, learning and associative strength. *European Journal of Neurosciences, 27,* 3020–3028.

Wagemans, J., Elder, J. H., Kubovy, M., Palmer, S. E., Peterson, M. A., Singh, M., & von der Heydt, R. (2012). A century of Gestalt psychology in visual perception: I. Perceptual grouping and figure–ground organization. *Psychological Bulletin, 138,* 1172–1217.

Wagner, H. J., Bollard, C. M., Vigouroux, S., Huls, M. H., Anderson, R., Prentice, H. G., Brenner, M. K., Heslop, H. E., & Rooney, C. M. (2004). A strategy for treatment of Epstein Barr virus-positive Hodgkin's disease by targeting interleukin 12 to the tumor environment using tumor antigen-specific T cells. *Cancer Gene Therapy, 2,* 81–91.

Wagner, R. K. (2002). Smart people doing dumb things: The case of managerial incompetence. In R. J. Sternberg (Ed.), *Why smart people can be so stupid* (pp. 42–63). New Haven, CT: Yale University Press.

Wagstaff, G. (2009, January) Is there a future for investigative hypnosis? *Journal of Investigative and Offender Profiling, 6,* 43–57.

Waisbren, S. E. (2011). Phenylketonuria. In S. Goldstein, C. R. Reynolds, S. Goldstein, C. R. Reynolds (Eds.), *Handbook of neurodevelopmental and genetic disorders in children* (2nd ed.). New York: Guilford Press.

Wakamoto, J. (2010). Differences in awareness of and coping with aging in midlife in relation to activation of domain-specific concern/interest. *Japanese Journal of Educational Psychology, 58,* 151–162.

Wakefield, J., Schmitz, M., & Baer, J. (2010). Does the DSM-IV clinical significance criterion for major depression reduce false positives? Evidence from the National Comorbidity Survey Replication. *The American Journal of Psychiatry, 167,* 298–304.

Waleed. (2014, January 14). Jill Price (AJ): A woman who remembers minute detail of her entire. Retrieved from http://hyperthymesia.net/jill-price-aj-woman-remembers-minute-detail-entire/.

Walker, L. J., & Frimer, J. A. (2007). Moral personality of brave and caring exemplars. *Journal of Personality and Social Psychology, 93,* 845–860.

Walker, L., & Frimer, J. (2009). The song remains the same: Rebuttal to Sherblom's re-envisioning of the legacy of the care challenge. *Journal of Moral Education, 38,* 53–68.

Walsh, B. T., Kaplan, A. S., Attia, E., Olmstead, M., Parides, M., Carter, J. C., Pike, K. M., Devlin, M. J., Woodside, B., Robert, C. A., & Rockert, W. (2006). Fluoxetine after weight restoration in anorexia nervosa: A randomized controlled trial. *Journal of the American Medical Association, 295,* 2605–2612.

Walsh, R., & Shapiro, S. L. (2006). The meeting of meditative disciplines and western psychology. *American Psychologist, 61,* 227–239.

Walton, G. M., & Cohen, G. L. (2011, March 18). A brief social-belonging intervention improves academic and health outcomes of minority students. *Science, 331,* 1447–1451.

Wang, A., & Clark, D. A. (2002). Haunting thoughts: The problem of obsessive mental intrusions [Special issue: Intrusions in cognitive behavioral therapy]. *Journal of Cognitive Psychotherapy, 16,* 193–208.

Wang, M. T., & Kenny, S. (2013). Longitudinal links between fathers' and mothers' harsh verbal discipline and adolescents' conduct problems and depressive symptoms. *Child Development.* Retrieved from http://onlinelibrary.wiley.com/doi/10.1111/cdev.12143/abstract

Wang, P. S., Aguilar-Gaxiola, S., Alonso, J., Angermeyer, M. C., Borges, G., Bromet, E. J., Bruffaerts, R., deGirolamo, G., deGraaf, R., Gureje, O., Haro, J. M., Karam, E. G., Kessler, R. C., Kovess, V., Lane, M. C., Lee, S., Levinson, D., Ono, Y., Petukhova, M., Posada-Villa, J., Seedat, S., & Wells, J. E. (2007, September 8). Use of mental health services for anxiety, mood, and substance disorders in 17 countries in the WHO world mental health surveys. *Lancet, 370,* 841–850.

Wang, Q., & Conway, M. A. (2006). Autobiographical memory, self, and culture. In L-G. Nilsson & N. Ohta (Eds.), *Memory and society: Psychological perspectives.* New York: Psychology Press.

Wang, Y., & Zhong, Z. (2015). Effects of frustration situation and resilience on implicit aggression. *Chinese Journal of Clinical Psychology, 23,* 209–212.

Ward, K. (2016). The natural world as content for interconnection and divergence of pretense and storytelling in children's play. In S. Douglas & L. Stirling (Eds.), *Children's play, pretense, and story: Studies in culture, context, and autism spectrum disorder.* New York: Routledge/Taylor & Francis Group.

Ward, L. M. (2004). Wading through the stereotypes: Positive and negative associations between media use and black adolescents' conceptions of self. *Developmental Psychology, 40,* 284–294.

Ward-Baker, P. D. (2007). The remarkable oldest old: A new vision of aging. *Dissertation Abstracts International Section A: Humanities and Social Sciences, 67*(8-A), 3115.

Warden, C. A., Wu, W-Y., & Tsai, D. (2006). Online shopping interface components: Relative importance as peripheral and central cues. *CyberPsychology & Behavior, 9,* 285–296.

Warford, M. K. (2011). The zone of proximal teacher development. *Teaching and Teacher Education, 27,* 252–258.

Wark, B., Lundstrom, B., & Fairhall, A. (2007, August). Sensory adaptation. *Current Opinion in Neurobiology, 17,* 423–429.

Watanabe, N., Furukawa, T., Chen, J., Kinoshita, Y., Nakano, Y., Ogawa, S., & Noda, Y. (2010). Change in quality of life and their predictors in the long-term follow-up after group cognitive behavioral therapy for social anxiety disorder: A prospective cohort study. *BMC Psychiatry, 10,* 133–140.

Watters, E. (2010, January 10). The Americanization of mental illness. *The New York Times,* p. C2.

Waxman, S. (2009). Learning from infants' first verbs. *Monographs of the Society for Research in Child Development, 74,* 127–132.

Weber, L., & Dwoskin, E. (2014, September 30). As personality tests multiply, employers are split. *Wall Street Journal,* pp. A1, A12.

Weber, R., Ritterfeld, U., & Kostygina, A. (2006). Aggression and violence as effects of playing violent video games? In P. Vorderer & J. Bryant, *Playing video games: Motives, responses, and consequences.* Mahwah, NJ: Erlbaum.

Wechsler Adult Intelligence Scale-Fourth Edition (WAIS-IV). (2008). Pearson Education, Inc.

Weeks, M., & Lupfer, M. B. (2004). Complicating race: The relationship between prejudice, race, and social class categorizations. *Personality and Social Psychology Bulletin, 30,* 972–984.

Weinberg, M. S., Williams, C. J., & Pryor, D. W. (1991, February 27). *Personal communication.* Indiana University, Bloomington.

Weiner, I. B. (2004a). Monitoring psychotherapy with performance-based measures of personality functioning. *Journal of Personality Assessment, 83,* 323–331.

Weiner, I. B. (2004b). Rorschach Inkblot method. In M. E. Maruish (Ed.), *Use of psychological testing for treatment planning and outcomes assessment, Vol. 3: Instruments for adults* (3rd ed.). Mahwah, NJ: Lawrence Erlbaum Associates.

Weiner, R. D., & Falcone, G. (2011). Electroconvulsive therapy: How effective is it? *Journal of the American Psychiatric Nurses Association, 17,* 217–218.

Weinstein, M., Glei, D. A., Yamazaki, A., & Ming-Cheng, C. (2004). The role of intergenerational relations in the association between life stressors and depressive symptoms. *Research on Aging, 26*, 511–530.

Weis, R., & Toolis, E. (2010). Parenting across cultural contexts in the USA: Assessing parenting behaviour in an ethnically and socioeconomically diverse sample. *Early Child Development and Care, 180*, 849–867.

Weller, P. D., Anderson, M. C., Gomez-Ariza, C. J., & Bajo, M. T. (2013). On the status of cue independence as a criterion for memory inhibition. *Journal of Experimental Psychology: Learning, Memory, and Cognition, 39*, 1232–1245.

Wells, R., Phillips, R. S., & McCarthy, E. P. (2011). Patterns of mind-body therapies in adults with common neurological conditions. *Neuroepidemiology, 36*, 46–51.

Wenzel, A., Zetocha, K., & Ferraro, R. F. (2007). Depth of processing and recall of threat material in fearful and nonfearful individuals. *Anxiety, Stress & Coping: An International Journal, 20*, 223–237.

Wertheimer, M. (1923). Untersuchungen zur Lehre von der Gestalt. II. *Psychol. Forsch., 5*, 301–350. In R. Beardsley and M. Wertheimer (Eds.) (1958), *Readings in perception*. New York: Van Nostrand.

West, J. R., & Blake, C. A. (2005). Fetal alcohol syndrome: An assessment of the field. *Experimental Biological Medicine, 6*, 354–356.

West, T. V., & Kenny, D. A. (2011). The truth and bias model of judgment. *Psychological Review, 118*, 357–378.

Westen, D., Novotny, C. M., & Thompson-Brenner, H. (2004). The empirical status of empirically supported psychotherapies: Assumptions, findings, and reporting in controlled clinical trials. *Psychological Bulletin, 130*, 631–663.

Westerberg, H., Brehmer, Y., D'Hondt, N., Söderman, D., & Bäckman, L. (2008, April). *Computerized training of working memory: A controlled, randomized trial.* Paper presented at the 2008 annual meeting of the Cognitive Neuroscience Society.

Westerhausen, R., Moosmann, M., Alho, K., Medvedev, S., Hämäläinen, H., & Hugdahl, K. (2009, January). Top-down and bottom-up interaction: Manipulating the dichotic listening ear advantage. *Brain Research, 1250*, 183–189.

Westerterp, K. R. (2006). Perception, passive overfeeding and energy metabolism. *Physiology & Behavior, 89*, 62–65.

Whipple, N., Bernier, A., & Mageau, G. A. (2011). Broadening the study of infant security of attachment: Maternal autonomy-support in the context of infant exploration. *Social Development, 20*, 17–32.

Whisman, M., & Snyder, D. (2007). Sexual infidelity in a national survey of American women: Differences in prevalence and correlates as a function of method of assessment. *Journal of Family Psychology, 21*, 14–154.

Whitbourne, S. (2007). *Adult development and aging. Biopsychosocial perspectives.* New York: Wiley.

Whitbourne, S. (2010). *The search for fulfillment.* New York: Ballantine.

Whitbourne, S. K. (2000). The normal aging process. In S. K. Whitbourne & S. Krauss (Eds.), *Adult development and aging.* New York: Wiley.

White, F. A., Harvey, L. J., & Abu-Rayya, H. M. (2015). Improving intergroup relations in the Internet Age: A critical review. *Review of General Psychology, 19*, 129–139.

White, L. (2007). Linguistic theory, universal grammar, and second language acquisition. In B. Van Patten & J. Williams (Eds.), *Theories in second language acquisition: An introduction.* Mahwah, NJ: Erlbaum.

Whitebread, D., Coltman, P., Jameson, H., & Lander, R. (2009). Play, cognition and self-regulation: What exactly are children learning when they learn through play? *Educational and Child Psychology, 26*, 40–52.

Whitney, P. G., & Green, J. A. (2011). Changes in infants' affect related to the onset of independent locomotion. *Infant Behavior & Development, 34*, 459–466.

WHO World Mental Health Survey Consortium. (2004). Prevalence, severity, and unmet need for treatment of mental disorders in the World Health Organization World Mental Health Surveys. *Journal of the American Medical Association, 291*, 2581–2590.

Whorf, B. L. (1956). *Language, thought, and reality.* New York: Wiley.

Widaman, K. (2009). Phenylketonuria in children and mothers: Genes, environments, behavior. *Current Directions in Psychological Science, 18*, 48–52.

Widmeyer, W. N., & Loy, J. W. (1988). When you're hot, you're hot! Warm-cold effects in first impressions of persons and teaching effectiveness. *Journal of Educational Psychology, 80*, 118–121.

Wiggins, J. S. (2003). *Paradigms of personality assessment.* New York: Guilford Press.

Wildavsky, B. (2000, September 4). A blow to bilingual education. *U.S. News & World Report,* pp. 22–28.

Wilde, D. J. (2011). *Jung's personality theory quantified.* New York: Springer-Verlag Publishing.

Wilgoren, J. (1999, October 22). Quality day care, early, is tied to achievements as an adult. *The New York Times,* p. A16.

Wilkinson, H. A. (2009). Cingulotomy. *Journal of Neurosurgery, 110*, 607–611.

Wilkinson, L., & Olliver-Gray, Y. (2006). The significance of silence: Differences in meaning, learning styles, and teaching strategies in cross-cultural settings. *Psychologia: An International Journal of Psychology in the Orient, 49, Special issue: Child language*, 74–88.

Willert, V., & Eggert, J. (2011). Modeling short-term adaptation processes of visual motion detectors. *Neurocomputing: An International Journal, 74*, 1329–1339.

Williams, C. L., & Butcher, J. N. (2011). History and development of the MMPI-A. In C. L. Williams, J. N. Butcher (Eds.), *A beginner's guide to the MMPI—A.* Washington, DC: American Psychological Association.

Willis, G. (2008, June). Intraocular microinjections repair experimental Parkinson's disease. *Brain Research, 1217*, 119-131.

Wills, K. E. (2013). Sickle cell disease. In I. Baron & C. Rey-Casserly (Eds.), *Pediatric neuropsychology: Medical advances and lifespan outcomes.* New York, NY: Oxford University Press.

Willyard, C. (2011). Men: A growing minority? Women earning doctoral degrees in psychology outnumber men three to one. What does this mean for the future of the field? *GradPsych, 40.* Retrieved from http://www.apa.org/gradpsych/2011/01/cover-men.aspx

Wilson, T. D. (2006, September 1). The power of social psychological interventions. *Science, 22*, 37–43.

Winerman, L. (2005, June). ACTing up. *Monitor on Psychology,* pp. 44–45.

Winner, E. (2003). Creativity and talent. In M. H. Bornstein & L. Davidson (Eds.), *Well-being: Positive development across the life course* (pp. 371–380). Mahwah, NJ: Erlbaum.

Winter, D. G. (2007). The role of motivation, responsibility, and integrative complexity in crisis escalation: Comparative studies of war and peace crises. *Journal of Personality and Social Psychology, 92*, 920–937.

Witelson, S., Kigar, D., Scamvougeras, A., Kideckel, D., Buck, B., Stanchev, P., et al. (2008). Corpus callosum anatomy in right-handed homosexual and heterosexual men. *Archives of Sexual Behavior, 37*, 857–863.

Wittenbrink, B., & Schwarz, N. (2007). *Implicit measures of attitudes.* New York: Guilford Press.

Wixted, J. T, Mickes, L., Clark, S. E., Gronlund, S. D., & Roediger, H. L. III. (2015). Initial eyewitness confidence reliably predicts eyewitness identification accuracy. *American Psychologist, 70*, 515–526.

Wixted, J. T., & Carpenter, S. K. (2007). The Wickelgren Power Law and the Ebbinghaus Savings Function. *Psychological Science, 18*, 133–134.

Wolitzky, D. L. (2006). Psychodynamic theories. In J. C. Thomas, D. L. Segal, & M. Hersen, *Comprehensive handbook of personality and psychopathology, Vol.*

1: Personality and everyday functioning. Hoboken, NJ: Wiley.

Woods, S. C., Schwartz, M. W., Baskin, D. G., & Seeley, R. J. (2000). Food intake and the regulation of body weight. *Annual Review of Psychology, 51,* 255–277.

Woodson, S. R. J. (2006). Relationships between sleepiness and emotion experience: An experimental investigation of the role of subjective sleepiness in the generation of positive and negative emotions. *Dissertation Abstracts International: Section B: The Sciences and Engineering, 67*(5-B), 2849.

Wrobel, S. (2015, April 27). Targeting depression with deep brain stimulation. *Emory News Center.* Retrieved from http://news.emory.edu/stories/2015/04/hspub_brain_hacking_depression/campus.html

Wrosch, C., Bauer, I., & Scheier, M. F. (2005). Regret and quality of life across the adult life span: The influence of disengagement and available future goals. *Psychology and Aging, 20*(4), 657–670.

Wrzesniewski, K., & Chylinska, J. (2007). Assessment of coping styles and strategies with school-related stress. *School Psychology International, 28,* 179–194.

Wu, L-T., Schlenger, W. E., & Galvin, D. M. (2006). Concurrent use of methamphetamine, MDMA, LSD, ketamine, GHB, and flunitrazepam among American youths. *Drug and Alcohol Dependence, 84,* 102–113.

Wu, Y. (2013). An empirical study of narrative imagery in implicit and explicit contexts. *Computers in Human Behavior, 29,* 1580–1589.

Wurtz, R. H., & Kandel, E. R. (2000). Central visual pathways. In E. R. Kandel, J. H. Schwartz, & T. M. Jessell (Eds.), *Principles of neural science* (4th ed.). New York: McGraw-Hill.

Wyra, M., Lawson, M. J., & Hungi, N. (2007). The mnemonic keyword method: The effects of bidirectional retrieval training and of ability to image on foreign language vocabulary recall. *Learning and Instruction, 17*(3) 360–371.

Xiao, Z., Yan, H., Wang, Z., Zou, Z., Xu, Y., Chen, J., et al. (2006). Trauma and dissociation in China. *American Journal of Psychiatry, 163,* 1388–1391.

Xie, G., & Johnson, J. Q. (2015). Examining the third-person effect of baseline omission in numerical comparison: The role of consumer persuasion knowledge. *Psychology & Marketing, 32,* 438–449.

Yamada, R., & Itsukushima, Y. (2013). The schema provokes a disparity of false recollection between actions and objects in an everyday scene. *Scandinavian Journal of Psychology, 54,* 276–282.

Yang, C., & Bradford Brown, B. (2016). Online self-presentation on Facebook and self development during the college transition. *Journal of Youth and Adolescence, 45,* 402–416.

Yanovski, S. Z., & Yanovski, J. A. (2011). Obesity prevalence in the United States—Up, down, or sideways? *The New England Journal of Medicine, 364,* 987–989.

Yardley, L., & Moss-Morris, R. (2009, January). Current issues and new directions in psychology and health: Increasing the quantity and quality of health psychology research. *Psychology & Health, 24,* 1–4.

Yarkoni, T. (2015). Neurobiological substrates of personality: A critical overview. In M. Mikulincer, P. R. Shaver, M. L. Cooper, & R. J. Larsen (Eds.), *APA handbook of personality and social psychology, Volume 4: Personality processes and individual differences.* Washington, DC: American Psychological Association.

Yeomans, M. R., Tepper, B. J., & Reitzschel, J. (2007). Human hedonic responses to sweetness: Role of taste genetics and anatomy. *Physiology & Behavior, 91,* 264–273.

Yesilyaprak, B., Kisac, I., & Sanlier, N. (2007). Stress symptoms and nutritional status among survivors of the Marmara region earthquakes in Turkey. *Journal of Loss & Trauma, 12,* 1–8.

Yim, D., & Rudoy, J. (2013). Implicit statistical learning and language skills in bilingual children. *Journal of Speech, Language, and Hearing Research, 56,* 310–322.

Yoder, R. M., Goebel, E. A., Köppen, J. R., Blankenship, P. A., Blackwell, A. A., & Wallace, D. G. (2015). Otolithic information is required for homing in the mouse. *Hippocampus, 25,* 890–899.

Yoo, H., & Pituc, S. T. (2013). Assessments of perceived racial stereotypes, discrimination, and racism. In K. F. Geisinger, B. A. Bracken, J. F. Carlson, J. C. Hansen, N. R. Kuncel, S. P. Reise, & M. C. Rodriguez (Eds.), *APA handbook of testing and assessment in psychology, Vol. 2: Testing and assessment in clinical and counseling psychology.* Washington, DC: American Psychological Association.

Young, M. W. (2000, March). The tick-tock of the biological clock. *Scientific American,* pp. 64–71.

Yu, Y., Burton, S. D., Tripathy, S. J., & Urban, N. N. (2015). Postnatal development attunes olfactory bulb mitral cells to high-frequency signaling. *Journal of Neurophysiology, 114,* 2830–2842.

Zajonc, R. B. (2001). Mere exposure: A gateway to the subliminal. *Current Directions in Psychological Science, 10,* 224–228.

Zale, E. L., Maisto, S. A., & Ditre, J. W. (2016). Anxiety and depression in bidirectional relations between pain and smoking: Implications for smoking cessation. *Behavior Modification, 40,* 7–28.

Zamarian, L., Högl, B., Delazer, M., Hingerl, K., Gabelia, D., Mitterling, T., & . . . Frauscher, B. (2015). Subjective deficits of attention, cognition and depression in patients with narcolepsy. *Sleep Medicine, 16,* 45–51.

Zaslow, M., Halle, T., & Martin, L. (2006). Child outcome measures in the study of child care quality. *Evaluation Review, 30,* 577–610.

Zeigler, D. W., Wang, C. C., Yoast, R. A., Dickinson, B. D., McCaffree, M. A., Robinowitz, C. B., & Sterling, M. L. (2005). The neurocognitive effects of alcohol on adolescents and college students. *Preventive Medicine: An International Journal Devoted to Practice and Theory, 40,* 23–32.

Zhuang, X., & Shevell, S. K. (2015). Monocular and binocular mechanisms mediating flicker adaptation. *Vision Research, 11,* 741–48.

Zians, J. (2007). A comparison of trait anger and depression on several variables: Attribution style, dominance, submissiveness, "need for power," efficacy and dependency. *Dissertation Abstracts International: Section B: The Sciences and Engineering, 67*(7-B), 4124.

Ziegler, D. J. (2016). Defense mechanisms in rational emotive cognitive behavior therapy personality theory. *Journal of Rational-Emotive & Cognitive-Behavior Therapy.* Retrieved from http://link.springer.com/article/10.1007%2Fs10942-016-0234-2

Zigler, E., Bennett-Gates, D., Hodapp, R., & Henrich, C. (2002). Assessing personality traits of individuals with mental retardation. *American Journal on Mental Retardation, 107,* 181–193.

Zimbardo, P. G. (1973). On the ethics of intervention in human psychological research: With special reference to the Stanford Prison Experiment. *Cognition, 2,* 243–256.

Zimbardo, P. G. (2007). *The Lucifer effect: Understanding how good people turn evil.* New York: Random House.

Zimbardo, P. G., Maslach, C., & Haney, C. (2000). Reflections on the Stanford Prison Experiment: Genesis, transformations, consequences. In T. Blass (Ed.), *Obedience to authority: Current perspectives on the Milgram paradigm.* Mahwah, NJ: Erlbaum.

Zito, J. M. (1993). *Psychotherapeutic drug manual* (3rd ed., rev.). New York: Wiley.

Zou, Z., & Buck, L. B. (2006, March 10). Combinatorial effects of odorant mixes in olfactory cortex. *Science,* 1477–1481.

Zuckerman, M. (1978). The search for high sensation. *Psychology Today,* pp. 30–46.

NAME INDEX

Buss, A. H., 366
Buss, D. M., 363, 366, 511, 511f
Butcher, J. N., 374
Butler, J., 94f
Butler, L. T., 509
Butlik, C. M., 265
Byrne, D., 369

Cabaniss, D. L., 450
Cachelin, F. M., 266
Caelian, C. F., 327
Cain, D. J., 460, 461
Cairns, R., 158
Cajochen, C., 138
Calkins, M., 14f, 15
Calvert, S., 509
Cameron, O. G., 278
Campbell, D. T., 118
Campbell, N. B., 327f
Campbell, W., 492
Campos, R. C., 376
Cannon, W. B., 278–279
Cantalupo, C., 72
Cantwell, R. H., 273
Cao, Z., 264
Capafons, A., 143
Capaldi, E. D., 263
Capezio, A., 274
Capone, N. C., 294
Cardini, F., 241
Carlo, G., 310
Carnagey, N. L., 194, 515
Carpenter, S., 37
Carpenter, S. K., 221
Carpenter, W. R., 426f
Carroll, J., 266
Carter, R. T., 242
Cartwright, R., 47
Caruso, D. R., 385
Carvalho, J., 269
Carver, C. S., 340, 375
Casasanto, D., 240
Casasola, M., 316
Case, S. M., 215
Casey, S. D., 181
Caspi, A., 294
Cassells, J. V. S., 356
Cassidy, C., 516
Cassidy, K. W., 309
Castejon, J., 382
Castellanos, I., 304
Catalano, R., 409
Cattell, A. K., 361
Cattell, H. E. P., 361
Cattell, R. B., 361, 370f
Cauce, A. M., 476
Causey, K., 8
CDC (Centers for Disease Control and
    Prevention), 153, 326
Ceccanti, M., 153
Center for Science in the Public Interest,
    149f, 164

Centers for Disease Control and
    Prevention (CDC), 153, 326
Cermakian, N., 138
Chacartegui-Ramos, F., 68
Chamberlain, K., 520, 521f
Chamberlain, S. R., 420
Chambless, D. L., 418, 465
Chan, D., 385
Chan, K. K., 487
Chandler, D. R., 9
Chandler, J., 194
Chandran, S., 231
Chang, H., 389
Chang, W., 432
Chapkis, W., 158
Chapman, J. P., 427
Chapman, L. J., 427
Chapman, R., 487
Chapman, S. C., 149
Chara, Z., 19
Charlton, S., 19
Chaudhury, R., 298
Chauhan, R. V., 466
Chaves, S. S., 9
Cheakalos, C., 262
Chee, M. L., 132
Chelune, G. J., 8
Chen, D., 27, 103
Chen, Q., 177
Chen, S., 108
Chen, Z., 432
Cheng, C., 527
Cheung, M. L., 527
Chien, N., 108
Chivers, M. L., 268
Cho, S. H., 76
Chodakiewitz, Y., 474
Choi, M., 18
Chomsky, N., 239, 240, 241
Chou, K., 525
Choy, Y., 452
Christoffels, I. K., 242
Chrysikou, E. G., 232
Chu, D. Z. J., 108
Chuang, S., 326
Chukwunenyem, N. F., 440
Chylinska, J., 525
Cialdini, R. B., 498
Cipriano, E. A., 280
Cirelli, C., 132
Clark, D. A., 420
Clark, D. B., 153
Clark, I., 254
Clark, J., 461
Clark, L. V., 316
Clark, M. P., 15
Clark, M. S., 492
Clarke, S., 101
Clarke-Stewart, K., 312
Clarkin, J. F., 431
Clausen, L., 265
Claydon, L. S., 107

Clement, C., 337
Clements, A. D., 518
Clements, A. M., 74
Clementz, B., 492
Clemons, T. L., 392
Close, C., 85
Cobos, P., 278
Coffman, S. J., 464
Cohen, G. L., 506
Cohen, P., 158, 440
Cohen, S., 527
Cole, D. A., 433
Coles, C., 403, 405, 405f
Collins, K., 525
Colman, W., 450
Colson, M., 320
Coltheart, M., 427
Colwell, M. J., 308
Comparelli, A., 422
Condray, D. S., 464
Cone-Wesson, B., 102
Connell, B., 239
Connolly, A. C., 227
Contractor, A. A., 362
Conway, M. A., 215, 218
Cook, L., 156
Cook, M., 363
Cook-Cottone, C., 266
Cooklin, A., 463
Cooper, C., 265
Cooper, Z., 266
Cooper-Brown, L. J., 181
Coplan, R., 312
Coren, S., 113f, 117, 125
Cornell, C. B., 387
Corpus, J. H., 257
Cortina, L. M., 503
Costa, P., 496
Costa, P. T. Jr., 362f, 432
Cottencin, O., 151
Coulson, D., 317
Coultas, J. C., 497
Couturier, J., 265, 266
Covell, N. H., 256
Cowley, B. J., 138
Coyle, N., 340
Coyne, J. C., 521f
Craik, F., 214
Cramer, A., 311
Crandall, C. S., 317
Crano, W. D., 36
Creasey, G. L., 295
Critchfield, T., 178
Critchley, H. D., 72
Critelli, J., 269
Crivelli, D., 283
Croarkin, P. E., 473
Crockett, E., 510
Crosby, R. A., 30
Crosnoe, R., 337
Crouse, K., 291
Crum, A. J., 39

Fallon, A., 37
Fantz, A., 485
Farnsworth, D. L., 295
Fasolo, B., 192
Fast, K., 104
Fearing, V. G., 461
Feeney, B. C., 492
Feldman, R. S., 223
Fergenbaum, J., 70
Ferguson, C. J., 194
Ferguson, M., 405
Fergusson, D. M., 326
Fernald, R. D., 192
Fernyhough, C., 317
Ferraro, R. F., 215
Ferring, D., 492
Festinger, D., 256
Festinger, L., 14f, 488
Filippello, P., 525
Fillingim, R. B., 106
Finan, P. H., 518
Finch, H., 273
Fingerman, K. L., 337
Finkler, K., 146
Finley, C. L., 138
Finn, A., 356
Firestein, B. A., 270
First, M. B., 411
Fischer, A. H., 277
Fischer, B. A., 426f
Fischer, P., 516
Fischler, G., 374
Fischmann, T., 135
Fishbach, A., 232
Fisher, C. B., 36
Fisher, G. G., 26
Fisher, H., 451
Fiske, S. T., 490
Fitzgibbons, P. J., 102
Flavell, S. W., 52
Fleischman, D. A., 336
Flynn, P. M., 156
Foell, J., 108
Folkman, S., 525, 527
Forbey, J., 376
Forer, B., 373
Forscher, P. S., 503
Fosshage, J. L., 210
Fost, J., 8
Foster, K. M., 198
Foster, R., 114
Fowler, R., 102
Fox, J., 95
Fox, M. J., 53, 54
Fox, S., 386
Fraley, R. C., 509
Frances, A., 411, 438
Frankenburg, W. K., 305f
Franklin, M. E., 454
Franzek, E., 429
Freedman, M. R., 266, 267
Freeman, A., 456, 457

Freeman, D., 85
Freeman, H., 254
Freire, J. C., 461
Freud, A., 15, 354, 358
Freud, S., 14f, 16, 28, 133, 134f, 135, 271, 350–356, 351f, 353f, 355f, 370f, 407, 421, 449, 450, 451, 513
Freudenreich, O., 473
Friborg, O., 526
Friedberg, R. D., 455
Friedman, H., 392
Friedman, J. N. W., 431
Friesen, W. V., 283
Frijda, N. H., 277, 281
Frimer, J. A., 323, 516
Frings, L., 74
Frosch, A., 356
Frost, R. O., 420
Funke, G. J., 317
Furnham, A., 357
Furumoto, L., 15
Fusari, A., 103
Fyer, A. J., 452

Gabriel, L. T., 391
Gadzichowski, K. M., 182
Gaertner, S. L., 503
Gage, P., 70–71
Gailliot, M. T., 516
Galambos, N. L., 332
Galanter, E., 87
Galanter, M., 463
Galdi, G., 15
Gall, F. J., 12, 14f
Gallo, M. M., 516
Gallo, P., 239
Galvin, D. M., 158
Ganel, T., 88
Gangestad, S. W., 47, 269
Ganio, M. S., 150
Garber, J., 433
Garcia, A., 454
Garcia, S. M., 516
García-Herrero, S., 527
Gardini, S., 227
Gardner, B., 473
Gardner, C. O., 424
Gardner, E. P., 105
Gardner, H., 382, 383f
Gardner, S., 15
Garrido, M. V., 509
Garrido-Nag, K., 238
Garwick, G. B., 391
Gatchel, R. J., 107, 266
Gatz, M., 424
Gaudiano, B. A., 464
Gautreaux, G., 515
Gavin, W., 432
Gawronski, B., 420
Gazzaniga, M. S., 47
Gejman, P., 59
Genovese, J. E. C., 316

Genovese, K., 515–516
Gentile, B., 365
George, M. S., 281f
George, S., 151
Gerritsen, C., 232
Gershkoff-Stowe, L., 239
Gerson, K., 334
Gerstel, N., 334
Ghaemi, S., 470
Ghose, T., 167
Giacobbi, P. R. Jr., 519
Gianaros, P. J., 523
Gielen, U. P., 9, 466
Gilar, R., 382
Gilbert, D. T., 360
Gillan, C. M., 420
Gilley, P., 298
Gilligan, C., 322–323
Gizer, I. R., 154
Gladwell, M., 378, 379
Glass, G. V., 464, 464f, 482
Glass, K., 525
Gleitman, L. R., 239
Glicksohn, J., 490
Glisky, E. L., 337
Glymour, M. M., 337
Goff, D. C., 473
Goin, M. K., 447
Goldfried, M. R., 464
Goldman-Mellor, S., 409
Goldsmith, A. A., 149
Goldstein, L., 268
Goldstein, S. N., 324
Goleman, D., 440
Golimbet, V. E., 60
Golosheykin, S., 145
Gómez-Ortiz, O., 180
Gontier, N., 240
Gontkovsky, S. T., 384
Goode, E., 102
Goodwin, C. J., 15, 169
Goodwin, R., 496
Goodwin, R. D., 432
Gooren, L., 271
Gordon, R., 104
Gordon-Salant, S., 102
Gossop, M., 463
Gotlib, I. H., 425, 426f
Goto, T., 21
Gottesman, I. I., 428, 429f
Gotts, S. J., 72
Goubert, L., 454
Gould, R. L., 332
Gräf, M., 492
Graham, C. A., 426f
Graham, J. R., 375
Granic, I., 325
Grann, J. D., 221
Grant, A., 257
Grant, D. M., 169

Grant, S., 376
Gray, G. C., 515
Gray, S., 518
Graziano, W. G., 516
Greco, C. M., 76
Green, J. A., 308
Greenberg, G., 409
Greenberg, L. S., 277
Greene, J. D., 281
Greenspan, S., 391
Greenwald, A., 504
Greer, R. D., 515
Gregor, M. A., 9
Gregory, R. L., 114, 118
Grenfell-Essam, R., 209
Gretchen, D., 466
Greven, C. U., 295
Griffin, D. W., 510
Griffith, J. W., 218
Griggs, R. A., 171, 516
Grigorenko, E. L., 240, 394
Grigoriadis, S., 462
Groh, K., 330
Gronholm, P., 65
Grothusen, J. R., 470
Gruber, S. A., 418f
Gruber, T. R., 293
Grünbaum, A., 356
Grundy, D., 38
Grünert, U., 95
Grunig, J. E., 230
Grusec, J. E., 192, 454
Guarnaccia, P. J., 409, 439
Guéguen, N., 497, 498
Guglielmo, S., 492
Guilleminault, C., 137
Guldemond, H., 392
Gupta, M. A., 523
Guthrie, I. K., 516
Gutierrez, P. M., 326

Haas, H. S., 26
Haberstick, B. C., 150
Haier, R. J., 382
Halford, S., 308
Halgin, R. P., 376f
Hall, R. E., 394
Halle, T., 310
Halpern, A. R., 214
Halsband, U., 143
Hamann, S. B., 281
Hambleton, R. K., 373
Hamilton, A. C., 208
Hamilton, L. K., 72
Hamilton, S. P., 432
Haney, C., 497
Hangya, B., 135
Hanley, C., 193
Hanson, D. R., 428
Harding, D. J., 270
Hardt, J., 327
Harlow, H. F., 307

Harlow, J. M., 71
Harnish, R. J., 456
Harper, D. J., 473
Harris, K. R., 384
Hartmann, E., 130f
Harvey, A., 457
Harvey, J. H., 270
Harvey, L. J., 505
Harvey, M., 317
Haskell, C. F., 150
Hastings, M., 138
Hauer, P., 151
Haugen, R., 493
Hauke, C., 356
Haverkamp, S., 98
Haviland-Jones, J., 103
Hawkes, C. H., 103
Haworth, C., 59
Hayflick, L., 335
Hays, P. A., 465, 466
Hays, S. C., 18
Hebl, M. R., 505
Hedges, D. W., 469
Hedlund, J., 385
Heffernan, M. E., 509
Hegarty, P., 392, 486
Hegg, C. C., 103
Heier, M. S., 137
Heijnen, W. T., 473
Heine, S., 37
Heinen, T., 227
Heinrichs, R. W., 427
Helfand, S. J., 17
Helmbold, N., 384
Helmuth, L., 52
Helsen, K., 454
Hemelrijk, C. K., 490
Henckes, N., 475
Henderson, N. D., 394f
Hennig-Fast, K., 422
Henrich, J., 37
Henry, D., 136
Henry, P. J., 502
Herbenick, D., 269
Herdt, G., 321
Herlin, B., 131
Herman, C. P., 265
Herman, J., 426f
Herrington, D. M., 61
Herrnstein, R., 393
Herskovits, M. J., 118
Hertzog, C., 337
Herz, R., 103
Herzberg, L., 281
Heshka, S., 266
Hess, M. J., 76
Hessels, S., 222
Heymsfield, S. B., 265
Hiby, E. F., 180
Hickok, G., 51
Hicks, B. M., 516
Hicks, T. V., 269

Hilarski, C., 432
Hildebrandt, L. K., 280
Hill, B. D., 450
Hines, M., 72, 271
Hinterberger, T., 143
Hippocrates, 14f
Hirschler, B., 60
Hirt, E. R., 217
Hobson, J. A., 130f, 135, 164
Hochschild, A., 334
Hoff, E., 237, 240
Hofmann, W., 215
Hogan, J., 379
Hogan, R., 379
Hogg, M. A., 495, 503
Hojjat, M., 511
Holbrook, A., 27
Holden, C., 427
Holland, C. R., 393, 394, 395
Hollander, E., 419
Hollenstein, T., 325
Holleran, S., 490
Hollingworth, H. L., 15
Hollingworth, L. S., 14f, 15
Holloway, L., 241
Holmes, A., 420
Holmes, J. G., 510
Holt, M., 52
Holtyn, A. F., 181
Holtzheimer, P., 66
Home, J. A., 132
Hongchun, W., 143
Honzik, C. H., 190
Hope, K., 476
Hopkins, W., 72
Hopwood, C., 432
Horesh, D., 520
Hori, H., 366
Horiguchi, H., 98
Horn, J. L., 394
Horney, K., 15, 350, 357, 358, 370f
Hornsey, M. J., 495
Horowitz, H. A., 432
Horowitz, J. L., 433
Horton, C. L., 135
Horwood, L. J., 326
Houg, S., 76
Houghtalen, R. P., 421
Hounkpatin, H. O., 370
Howard, A., 477f
Howard, R., 158
Howard, T. D., 61
Howe, C. J., 239
Howell, E. F., 421
Howes, O., 54, 429
Howland, J. G., 177
Hoyme, E. H., 392
Hoyt, C., 486
Hsiao, Y., 227
Hsu, S., 438
Hu, F. B., 267
Huang, C., 32

Weber, L., 378
Weber, R., 194
Wechsler, D., 389
Wechsler Adult Intelligence Scale (WAIS-IV), 390f
Weeks, M., 504
Weinberg, M. S., 271
Weinberg, R. A., 394
Weiner, I. B., 376
Weiner, R. D., 473
Weinstein, M., 520
Weis, R., 309
Weisberg, J. N., 107
Weisner, C., 153
Weller, P. D., 222
Wells, R., 127
Wenzel, A., 215, 270
Wershba, R., 518
Wertheimer, M., 111
West, J. R., 392
West, T. V., 492
Westen, D., 463, 464
Westerberg, H., 335
Westerhausen, R., 113
Westerterp, K. R., 264
Whipple, N., 307
Whisman, M., 270
Whitbourne, S. K., 331, 332, 376f
White, F. A., 505
White, L., 239
Whitebread, D., 309
Whitney, P. G., 308
Whorf, B. L., 240
WHO World Mental Health Survey Consortium, 438, 438f, 444
Widaman, K., 298
Widiger, T. A., 411, 432, 433
Widmeyer, W. N., 490
Wiebe, J. S., 525
Wiesel, T., 14f
Wiggins, J. S., 363
Wildavsky, B., 242
Wilde, D. J., 357
Wilgoren, J., 310
Wilkinson, H. A., 474
Wilkinson, L., 195
Willert, V., 89
Williams, B., 205
Williams, C. J., 271
Williams, C. L., 374
Willis, G., 5
Willis, S., 335

Willoughby, G., 230
Willoughby, T., 194
Wills, K. E., 299
Willyard, C., 9
Wilson, D., 503
Wilson, D. J., 496
Wilson, G. D., 271
Wilson, K. S., 143
Wilson, T. D., 506
Winerman, L., 515
Winfrey, O., 487
Wingate, L. R., 169
Winner, E., 392
Winograd, E., 215
Winter, D. G., 273, 332
Wise, E. H., 37
Witelson, S., 271
Wittenbrink, B., 505
Wixted, J. T., 19, 221
Wolf, Y., 254
Wolff, R., 76
Wolitzky, D. L., 451
Woods, S. C., 263
Woodson, S. R. J., 280
Woody, E. Z., 143
Woolf, V., 383f
Woolley, J. D., 316
Wright, D. L., 192
Wrobel, S., 447
Wrosch, C., 337
Wrzesniewski, K., 525
Wu, I., 149
Wu, L-T., 158
Wu, R., 466
Wu, W-Y., 487
Wu, Y., 215
Wundt, W., 13, 14f
Wurtz, R. H., 70
Wyra, M., 223

Xiao, Z., 421
Xie, G., 487

Yamada, R., 490
Yancy, C., 194
Yang, C., 509
Yang, L., 470
Yanovski, J. A., 265
Yanovski, S. C., 265
Yardley, L., 7
Yarkoni, T., 366

Yates, A., 405
Yazdani, S., 510
Yeager, D., 520
Yeomans, M. R., 104
Yermolayeva, Y., 509
Yesilyaprak, B., 519
Yim, D., 242
Ying, Z., 389
Yoder, R., 102
Yonas, A., 116
Yoo, H., 504
Yoshino, K., 193
Young, J., 156
Young, M. W., 138f
Young-DeMarco, L., 270
Yu, Y., 103
Yumru, M., 469
Yurgelun-Todd, D. A., 418f
Yusuf, S., 271

Zajonc, R. B., 509
Zale, E. L., 185
Zamarian, I., 137
Zárate, M. A., 215
Zaslavsky, O., 232
Zaslow, M., 310
Zatorre, R., 70
Zautra, A. J., 518
Zayas, V., 169
Zeigler, D. W., 153
Zenisky, A. L., 373
Zetocha, K., 215
Zhang, A., 177
Zhang, G., 509
Zhang, S., 389
Zhang, Y., 232
Zhong, Z., 514
Zhuang, X., 89
Zians, J., 273
Ziegler, D. J., 354
Ziegler, M., 382
Zigler, E., 392
Zika, S., 520, 521f
Zimbardo, P., 497
Zimbardo, P. G., 497
Zimmerman, R. R., 307
Zimring, F. M., 461
Zito, J. M., 471
Zou, Z., 103
Zuckerberg, M., 485
Zuckerman, M., 256
Zurrón, M., 336

SUBJECT INDEX

Assumed-similarity bias, 492
Ataque de nervios, 440
Attachment
   assessment of, 307–308
   development of, in infancy, 307, 307f
   effects of child care on, 310
Attention, research on, 19
Attention-deficit hyperactivity disorder
   (ADHD), 407–408, 433–434
Attitude(s), 486–488, 532
   link to behavior, 487–488, 489f
   prejudice. *See* Prejudice
   toward death, survey of, 339–340
Attitude communicator, 486
Attribution biases, 491–492
Attribution processes, 491
Attributions, 492–493
Attribution theory, 491
Atypical antipsychotic drugs, 469
Auditory area, 69f, 70
Auditory canal, 101, 101f
Auditory cortex, 101–102
Authoritarian parents, 310, 311f
Authoritative parents, 310, 311f
Authority, obedience to, 499f, 499–500
Autism spectrum disorder, 434
Autobiographical memory, 217–218
Autonomic division, 57f, 58, 59f
Autonomy needs, 258, 259
Autonomy-versus-shame-and-doubt
   stage, 313, 324f
Aversive conditioning, 452
Avoidant children, 308
Avoidant coping, 525
Axon, 49, 49f, 50f

Babble, 237
Babinski reflex, 304
Background stressors, 520, 521f
Balance, 101f, 102
Barbiturates, 152f, 154
Bargaining stage of dying, 340
Basilar membrane, 101
"Bath salts" (cathinone), 151, 152f
Behavior(s)
   aggressive, causes of, 29f, 180, 192
   attribution theory of, 491
   biological foundations of, 4–5
   classical conditioning of, 171–172
   complex, shaping, 183–184
   conscious versus unconscious,
      20f, 20–21
   discrimination. *See* Discrimination
   expectations regarding, 490–491
   genetic influences on, 292–293, 293f
   hoarding behavior, 439
   link to attitudes, 487–488, 489f
   nonverbal, emotion and, 282, 282f
   observational learning of, 192
   role of limbic system in, 68
   social. *See* Social behavior
   thrill seeking, 254

Behavioral assessment, 378
Behavioral economics, 492
Behavioral genetics, 6f, 8, 58–61
Behavioral neuroscience, 4–5, 6f
Behavioral neuroscientists, 47, 127
Behavioral perspective, 16f, 17, 20f, 21
   on abnormal behavior, 406f,
      407–408
   on anxiety disorders, 420
   on mood disorders, 425
   on personality, 363–364
Behavioral treatment approaches,
   451–454, 483
   classical conditioning, 452–453
   evaluation of, 454
   learning and, 451–452
   operant techniques, 454
   rational-emotive therapy, 455–456
Behavior analysis, 184–185
Behavior analysts, 184–185
Behavior modification, 185–186, 464f
Beliefs, irrational, 455–456
The Bell Curve (Herrnstein & Murray),
   393–394
Bell-shaped distribution, 388, 388f
Benzedrine, 150, 152f
Bereavement support groups, 463
Beta amyloid precursor protein, 337
Biculturalism, 242
"Big Five" personality traits, 362, 362f
Bilingual education, 241–242, 242f, 243f
Binge drinking, 153, 153f
Binge eating disorder (bulimia),
   265–266, 266f, 438–439
Binocular disparity, 114
Biofeedback, 76, 77, 108
Biological approaches to personality,
   366f, 366–367, 370f, 400
Biological changes during hypnosis,
   144, 145f
Biological factors
   consequences of stress, 520–523
   in depression, 426
   in emotion, 280–281, 281f
   importance of, 47
   in mood disorders, 424–425
   in obesity, 264–265
   in psychological disorders, 407
   regulation of hunger, 263–264
   in schizophrenia, 428–430, 429f, 430f
   in sexual behavior, 267–269, 268f
   in sexual orientation, 271
Biology
   behavior based on, 4–5
   in neuroscience perspective, 15–16,
      16f, 20f
Biomedical therapy, 447, 468–477, 484
   deep brain stimulation (DBS), 447, 473
   drug therapy. *See* Drug therapy
   electroconvulsive therapy (ECT), 473
   perspectives on, 474–475
   psychosurgery, 473–474

Biopsychologists, 47
Bipolar disorder, 424, 471
Birth defects, 298–299
Bisexuality, 270–272
Blind spot, 92f, 93–94
BMI (body mass index), 263
Bodily kinesthetic intelligence, 383f
Body mass index (BMI), 263
Borderline personality disorder, 432
Bottom-up processing, 113
Brain, 56, 57f–59f, 64–76, 83
   Alzheimer's disease, 53, 72, 336–337
   auditory cortex of, 101–102
   central core of ("old brain"), 66f,
      66–67, 67f
   cerebral cortex ("new brain"), 67f,
      68–71, 69f, 96f
   deep brain stimulation, 447, 473
   in depression, 425, 426, 426f
   ECT and, 473
   effects of multiple languages on, 242
   electrical activity during hypnosis,
      143, 144f
   electrical activity during sleep,
      128, 130f, 135
   hemispheres of, 72–76
   injury to, 70–71, 80
   integration of visual information,
      95–96
   limbic system, 68, 68f
   lobes of, 68f, 69, 69f
   neuroplasticity and, 71–72
   in panic disorder, 418, 418f
   role in eating disorders, 265, 266f
   role in emotion, 280–281, 281f
   in schizophrenia, 430, 430f
   sexual orientation and, 271
Brain imaging, 205
   bilingualism and, 242, 243f
   in depression, 425, 426f
   fMRI, 65, 65f, 74, 145f, 193f
   techniques, 64–66, 65f
Bulimia (binge eating disorder),
   265–266, 266f, 438–439

Caffeine, 139, 149f, 149–150
Candle problem, 232–233, 233f, 234f
Cannon-Bard theory of emotion,
   278–279, 279f
CAPS (cognitive-affective processing
   system) theory, 365
Career success, intelligence and, 385
Caregivers, attachment to, 307
Case study, 27–28, 33f
Castration anxiety, 353
Cataclysmic events, 519
Catatonic schizophrenia, 439
Catharsis, 514
Cathinone ("bath salts"), 151, 152f
Causal relationships, 28–29, 30
Central core ("old brain"), 66f,
   66–67, 67f

FASD (fetal alcohol syndrome disorder), 299, 392
Fathers, 308, 310–312, 311f
Fear(s)
  fear response, 171, 174, 281
  hierarchy of, 452–453
"Fearless Peer" model, 454
Feature detection, 95
Feedback loops, 254
Females (women)
  changing roles of, 333
  depression in, 423, 425–426
  "double standard" and, 269–270
  drinking by, 153
  eating disorders in, 265
  menopause, 331
  moral development in, 322–323
  Oedipal conflict in, 353–354
  power needs in, 274
  as psychologists, 9
  psychology of, 6f
  puberty in, 321, 321f
  "second shift," 334
  sexual behavior in, 268f, 268–269
Feminist psychologists, 357–358
Fetal alcohol syndrome disorder (FASD), 299, 392
Fetal period, 297
Fetus, 297, 298–299
Figure and ground, 110f, 110–111
Fixations, 352, 356
Fixed-interval reinforcement schedule, 182f, 183
Fixed-ratio reinforcement schedule, 181, 182f
Flashbacks, in PTSD, 520
Flashbulb memories, 215–216, 217f
Flooding treatments, 453
Fluid intelligence, 335, 336f, 382, 386f
fMRI (functional magnetic resonance imaging), 65, 65f, 74, 145f, 193f
Foot-in-the-door technique, 497
Forebrain, 67
Forensic psychology, 6f, 7
Forgetting, 248. See also Memory; Recall
  in late adulthood, 336–337
  reasons for, 221f, 221–222
  research on, 220f, 220–221
Formal operational stage, 314f, 315–316
Formal thought disorder, 427
Fovea, 92f, 93, 94f
Free association, 450
Free will, 18, 21
Free will-determinism issue, 20f, 21
Freudian slip, 350, 351
Friendships, 509–510
Frontal lobes, 68f, 69, 69f, 430
Frustration, 514
Frustration-aggression approaches, 514
Fugue state, 422

Functional fixedness, 232–233, 233f, 234f
Functionalism, 13
Functional magnetic resonance imaging (fMRI), 65, 65f, 74, 145f, 193f
Fundamental attribution error, 492

GABA (gamma-amino-butyric acid), 53f
Gag reflex, 304
Gamma-amino-butyric acid (GABA), 53f
Gamma knife surgery, 474
GAS (general adaptation syndrome), 523f, 523–524
Gate-control theory of pain, 107
Gender differences
  in brain lateralization, 73, 74–75
  in learning styles, 198
  in needs, 273, 274
  in pain sensation, 106
Gender identity, 272
General adaptation syndrome (GAS), 523f, 523–524
General intelligence factor (g), 381–382
Generalized anxiety disorder, 418, 419f
Generativity-versus-stagnation stage, 324f, 325
Genes, 60, 296f, 296–297
Gene therapy, 60, 474–475
Genetic counseling, 60–61
Genetic factors. See also Nature-nurture issue
  in anxiety disorders, 420
  in behavior, 292–293, 293f
  in mood disorders, 424–425
  in personality, 366f, 366–367
  in prenatal development, 298–299
  in schizophrenia, 428–429
Genetic preprogramming theories of aging, 335
Genetics
  basic principles, 296f, 296–297
  behavioral genetics, 6f, 8
  in language development, 239–240
  optogenetics, 66
Genitals, 268, 268f
Genital stage, 353f, 354
Genome, 60
Germinal period, 297
Gerontologists, 334, 335
Gestalt laws of organization, 111f, 111–112, 112f
Gestalt psychology, 13–15, 112
g-factor, 381–382
Giftedness, intellectual, 392
Glutamate, 53f, 470
Goals, in coping, 527–528
Grammar, 239
Ground, figure and, 110f, 110–111
Group(s)
  ethnocentrism in, 503
  peer groups, 324

racial. See Race and ethnicity
  in research, 30
  social influence of, 495–500, 532
  as source of self-worth, 503–504
  support groups, 324, 463
Group therapy, 462, 483
Gustation (taste), 102–105, 125, 306

Habituation, 168
Hair cells, 101
Hallucinations, 427, 430
Hallucinogens, 152f, 157–158, 165
  marijuana, 152f, 157f, 157–158
  MDMA and LSD, 152f, 158
Halo effect, 491–492
Handedness, 72–73
Health psychology, 6f, 7
Hearing, 100–108, 125
  balance and, 101f, 102
  in neonates, 305
  sensing sound, 100–102, 101f
Helping (prosocial) behavior, 512, 515–516
Hemispheres of brain
  effects of gender and culture, 74–75
  lateralization of, 72–76
  research on, 75f, 75–76
Heredity. See Genetic factors; Nature-nurture issue
Heritability of intelligence, 392, 393, 394, 394f
Heroin, 152f, 156
Heterosexuality, 269, 512, 513f
Heuristics, in reasoning, 229
Hierarchy(ies)
  of emotions, 277, 277f
  of fears, 452–453
  of needs, 257–259, 258f
Hindbrain, 66, 67f
Hippocampus, 68, 68f, 281
Hoarding behavior, 439
Homelessness, 476
Homeostasis, 67, 254
Homosexuality, 270–272, 512, 513f
Hormone(s), 61
  sex hormones, 268
  sexual orientation and, 271
  stress-related, 520–521
Hormone replacement therapy (HRT), 61
Hormone therapy (HT), 331
Human development, 290–347
  in adolescence. See Adolescence
  adulthood. See Adulthood; Older adults
  case study of, 344
  in childhood. See Childhood development
  developmental psychology, 292–294
  nature versus nurture and, 294–295
  newborns. See Neonates
  prenatal. See Prenatal development
  research techniques in, 295–296

Reaction formation, 355f
Reality principle, 352
Reasoning, 228–229, 249
Rebound effect, 131
Recall, 213–218, 248. *See also*
    Forgetting; Memory
    of autobiographical memory, 217–218
    case study, 246
    constructive processes and, 216–218
    of explicit and implicit memory, 215
    of flashbulb memories, 215–216, 217f
    intelligence testing and, 384
    levels-of-processing theory, 214–215
    retrieval cues in, 213–214, 214f
Receptive learning style, 195, 196–197
Receptor cells, 51f, 89, 105
Receptor sites, 51f, 52
Reciprocity-of-liking effect, 509
Recognition, 213–214, 214f
Reflexes
    neonatal development of, 304, 305f
    spinal cord and, 57
Reflex sympathetic dystrophy syndrome
    (RSDS), 104
Regression, 355f
Rehearsal, memory and, 208–209
Reinforcement, 177–179, 179f
    in behavior modification, 185, 363
    in developing self-efficacy, 364
    effectiveness of, 179–180
    in language development, 239
    positive versus negative, 178–179, 179f
    schedules of, 180–183
Reinforcers, 177, 178–179, 179f, 363
Relatedness needs, 258–259
Relational learning style, 195, 195f
Relationship(s)
    close. *See* Interpersonal attraction
    friendships, 509–510
    peer relationships, 308–309
Relationship styles, 512
Relative size cue, 115
Relaxation techniques, 108, 452, 453f
Reliability of test, 374
REM (rapid eye movement) sleep, 129,
    130f, 131, 135
Repetition, memory and, 223
Replication of findings, 32
Repressed memories, 354, 422
Repression, 354–355, 355f, 449
Research, 24–33, 45
    Ainsworth strange situation, 307–308
    animals as subjects in. *See* Animals as
        research subjects
    in attachment, 307, 307f
    avoiding bias, 38–39
    in conformity, 495–496, 496f
    correlational, 28–29, 29f
    critical evaluation of, 39–40
    cross-cultural, 117
    cross-sectional, 295
    descriptive. *See* Descriptive research

developmental, techniques in, 295–296
ethics of. *See* Ethics of research
experimental. *See* Experimental
    research
in forgetting, 220f, 220–221
on hemispheric lateralization,
    75f, 75–76
in impression formation, 490
longitudinal, 295
observational, 26–27, 33f, 378
participants in. *See* Participant(s)
scientific method, 24–26, 25f
sequential, 296
as systematic inquiry, 26
Research findings, 32, 40
Resilience, 525–526
Resistance, 450
Resistance phase of GAS, 523f, 523–524
Responses
    conditioned (CR), 170, 170f
    fear response, 171, 174, 281
    reinforcement of, 177
    unconditioned (UCR), 169, 170f
    voluntary, 176
Resting state of neurons, 49
Reticular formation, 67, 67f
Retina, 92f, 93, 94f
    depth perception and, 114, 116
    trichromatic processes in, 97, 98
Retrieval, 206, 207f
Retrieval cues, in recall, 213–214, 214f
Retroactive interference, 222, 222f
Reuptake, 52
Rewards-costs approach to helping, 516
Rites of passage, 328
Rods, 93, 94f
Rohypnol, 152f, 155
Romantic (passionate) love, 510
Rooting reflex, 304
Rorschach test, 376–377, 377f
Rote memorization, 215
RSDS (reflex sympathetic dystrophy
    syndrome), 104

S

Safety needs, 257, 258f
Sample, in research, 27
Scaffolding, 317
Schachter-Singer theory of emotion,
    279f, 279–280
Schedules of reinforcement, 180–183
    fixed- and variable-interval, 182f,
        182–183
    fixed- and variable-ratio, 181–182, 182f
Schemas
    constructive processes, 216–217
    in social cognition, 489–490
Schizophrenia, 411f, 426–431, 428f, 445
    biological causes of, 428–430, 429f,
        430f
    cultural factors in, 439
    dopamine and, 54, 429
    drug therapy for, 403, 469

DSM-5 classification of, 428
environmental influences on, 430
example of, 403, 406, 406f
predisposition model of, 431
race and, 409
symptoms of, 426–428, 428f
School psychology, 6f
Scientific method, 24–26, 25f, 45
    hypotheses in, 25–26
    theories in, 24–25
Seconal, 152f, 154
Secondary drives, 253
Secondary reinforcers, 177
"Second shift," 334
Secure attachment, 308
Seizure disorders, treatment of, 74
Selective serotonin reuptake inhibitors
    (SSRIs), 469f, 470, 470f
Self-actualization, 258, 258f, 367,
    369, 460
Self-concepts, 367–369
Self-determination theory, 258–259
Self-efficacy, 364
Self-esteem, 365
Self-fulfilling prophecy, 503
Self-help therapy, 463
Self-report measures of personality,
    374–376, 376f
Self-serving bias, 492
Self-worth, 503–504
Semantic memory, 210, 211f, 336
Semicircular canals, 102
Sensation, 86–89, 124
    absolute thresholds, 87–88
    difference thresholds, 88–89
    effects of marijuana and, 157
    hearing. *See* Hearing
    in late adulthood, 335
    sensory adaptation, 89
    skin senses, 104–107, 106f
    smell, 102–103
    taste, 102–105, 125, 306
    vision. *See* Vision
Sensitive (critical) periods, 297–298
Sensorimotor stage, 314f, 315
Sensory adaptation, 89
Sensory area of cortex, 70, 70f
Sensory development, neonatal, 304–
    306, 305f
Sensory memory, 207, 207f, 208
Sensory (afferent) neurons, 57
Sequential research, 296
Serotonin, 53f, 158
Severe intellectual disability, 391
Sexual behavior
    biological bases of, 267–269, 268f
    in females, 268f, 268–269
    heterosexuality, 269, 512, 513f
    homosexuality, 270–272, 512, 513f
    as instinctive, 253
    in males, 267–268, 268f, 269
    marital and extramarital sex, 270